J.K. LASSER'S™ YOUR INCOME TAX 2007

Prepared by the
J.K. LASSER INSTITUTE™

John Wiley & Sons, Inc.

New York • Chichester • Weinheim • Brisbane • Singapore • Toronto

Staff for This Book

J.K. Lasser Editorial

Elliott Eiss, Member of the New York Bar, Senior Editor
Donna LeValley, Member of the New York Bar, Contributing Editor
Barbara Weltman, Consulting Editor
Angelo C. Jack, Senior Production Editor
Sixto Rodriguez-Mancini, Production Assistant
Bill Hamill, Production Assistant
Carolyn Francis, Copyediting and Proofreading
Helen Chin, Indexing

John Wiley & Sons, Inc.

John Wiley & Sons, Inc.
111 River Street
Hoboken, NJ 07030

Published by John Wiley & Sons, Inc., Hoboken, New Jersey
Published simultaneously in Canada

ISBN-10 0-471-78670-5
ISBN-13 978-0471-78670-2

ISBN-10 0-13-205686-0

Printed in the United States of America

10 9 8 7 6 5 4 3 2 1

Seventieth Edition

How To Use *Your Income Tax 2007*

Tax alert symbols. Throughout the text of *Your Income Tax*, these special symbols alert you to advisory tips about filing your federal tax return and tax planning opportunities:

Filing Tip or Filing Instruction............A **Filing Tip** or **Filing Instruction** helps you prepare your 2006 return.

Planning Reminder............A **Planning Reminder** highlights year-end tax strategies for 2006 or planning opportunities for 2007 and later years.

Caution............A **Caution** points out potential pitfalls to avoid and areas where IRS opposition may be expected.

Law Alert............A **Law Alert** indicates recent changes in the tax law and pending legislation before Congress.

Court Decision............A **Court Decision** highlights key rulings from the Tax Court and other federal courts.

IRS Alert............An **IRS Alert** highlights key rulings and announcements from the IRS.

The federal income tax law, despite efforts at simplification, remains a maze of statutes, regulations, rulings, and court decisions written in technical language covering thousands and thousands of pages. For over 69 years, J.K. Lasser's™ *Your Income Tax* has aided and guided millions of taxpayers through this complex law. Every effort has been made to provide a direct and easy-to-understand explanation that shows how to comply with the law and at the same time take advantage of tax-saving options and plans.

The 2007 edition of *Your Income Tax*—our 70th edition—continues this tradition. To make maximum use of this tax guide, we suggest that you use these aids:

Contents Chapter by Chapter. The contents, on pages ***vii–xxii,*** lists the chapters in *Your Income Tax*. References direct you to sections within a particular chapter. Thus a reference to *21.1* directs you to Chapter 21 and then to section 1 within that chapter. Section and page references are provided in the index at the back of the book.

What's New for 2006. Pages ***xxv-xxvii*** alert you to tax developments that may affect your 2006 tax return.

Key Tax Numbers for 2006. Pages ***xxviii-xxix.***

Looking Ahead to Tax Changes for Years After 2006. Pages ***xxx–xxxi*** provide an overview of the tax law changes for years after 2006.

Filing tax basics. Pages 1–7 alert you to filing requirements, filing addresses shown on a map of IRS Service Centers, and a calendar with 2007 filing deadlines.

Download FREE *e-Supplement*

You can download a free *e-Supplement* to *Your Income Tax 2007* at www.jklasser.com. The *e-Supplement* will provide an update on tax developments and links to IRS and state tax forms.

Form 1040 with references to *Your Income Tax 2007*

Form **1040** Department of the Treasury—Internal Revenue Service
U.S. Individual Income Tax Return 2006 (99) IRS Use Only—Do not write or staple in this space.

For the year Jan. 1–Dec. 31, 2006, or other tax year beginning , 2006, ending , 20 OMB No. 1545-0074

Label (See instructions on page 16.) **Use the IRS label.** Otherwise, please print or type.

LABEL HERE

Your first name and initial	Last name		**Your social security number**
If a joint return, spouse's first name and initial	Last name		**Spouse's social security number**
Home address (number and street). If you have a P.O. box, see page 16.		Apt. no.	▲ You **must** enter your SSN(s) above. ▲
City, town or post office, state, and ZIP code. If you have a foreign address, see page 16.			Checking a box below will not change your tax or refund.

Presidential Election Campaign ▶ Check here if you, or your spouse if filing jointly, want $3 to go to this fund (see page 16) ▶ ☐ **You** ☐ **Spouse**

Filing Status

Check only one box.

1 ☐ Single
2 ☐ Married filing jointly (even if only one had income)
3 ☐ Married filing separately. Enter spouse's SSN above and full name here. ▶
4 ☐ Head of household (with qualifying person). (See page 17.) If the qualifying person is a child but not your dependent, enter this child's name here. ▶ **Chapter 1**
5 ☐ Qualifying widow(er) with dependent child (see page 17)

Exemptions

6a ☐ **Yourself.** If someone can claim you as a dependent, **do not** check box 6a
b ☐ **Spouse**

Boxes checked on 6a and 6b **21.1**

c **Dependents:**

(1) First name Last name	(2) Dependent's social security number	(3) Dependent's relationship to you	(4) ✓ if qualifying child for child tax credit (see page 19)
			☐
			☐
			☐
			☐

If more than four dependents, see page 19.

No. of children on 6c who:
- lived with you **21.1**
- did not live with you due to divorce or separation (see page 20) **21.7**

Dependents on 6c not entered above

d Total number of exemptions claimed

Add numbers on lines above ▶

Income

Attach Form(s) W-2 here. Also attach Forms W-2G and 1099-R if tax was withheld.

If you did not get a W-2, see page 22.

Enclose, but do not attach, any payment. Also, please use **Form 1040-V.**

Line	Description	Sub-line	Sub-amount	Line	Reference
7	Wages, salaries, tips, etc. Attach Form(s) W-2			7	2.1
8a	**Taxable** interest. Attach Schedule B if required			8a	4.12
b	**Tax-exempt** interest. **Do not** include on line 8a	8b	4.24 / 4.26		
9a	Ordinary dividends. Attach Schedule B if required			9a	4.1
b	Qualified dividends (see page 23)	9b	4.2		
10	Taxable refunds, credits, or offsets of state and local income taxes (see page 23)			10	11.5 / 11.6
11	Alimony received			11	37.1
12	Business income or (loss). Attach Schedule C or C-EZ			12	40.3 / 40.6
13	Capital gain or (loss). Attach Schedule D if required. If not required, check here ▶ ☐			13	5.3 / 32.8
14	Other gains or (losses). Attach Form 4797			14	5.3 / 44.8
15a	IRA distributions	15a	8.8 - 8.14	15b	8.8 - 8.14
	b Taxable amount (see page 25)				
16a	Pensions and annuities	16a	7.1 / 7.26	16b	7.23 / 7.26
	b Taxable amount (see page 25)				
17	Rental real estate, royalties, partnerships, S corporations, trusts, etc. Attach Schedule E			17	9.1
18	Farm income or (loss). Attach Schedule F			18	---------
19	Unemployment compensation			19	2.5
20a	Social security benefits	20a	34.2	20b	34.3
	b Taxable amount (see page 27)				
21	Other income. List type and amount (see page 29)			21	Chapter 11
22	Add the amounts in the far right column for lines 7 through 21. This is your **total income** ▶			22	---------

Adjusted Gross Income

Line	Description	Sub-line	Sub-amount	Line	Reference
23	Archer MSA deduction. Attach Form 8853	23	12.2		
24	Certain business expenses of reservists, performing artists, and fee-basis government officials. Attach Form 2106 or 2106-EZ	24	12.2		
25	Health savings account deduction. Attach Form 8889	25	12.2 / 12.10		
26	Moving expenses. Attach Form 3903	26	12.7		
27	One-half of self-employment tax. Attach Schedule SE	27	12.2 / 45.3		
28	Self-employed SEP, SIMPLE, and qualified plans	28	12.2 / Ch. 41		
29	Self-employed health insurance deduction (see page 30)	29	12.2 / 17.5		
30	Penalty on early withdrawal of savings	30	7.15 / 8.12		
31a	Alimony paid b Recipient's SSN ▶	31a	37.1		
32	IRA deduction (see page 31)	32	8.4 / 12.2		
33	Student loan interest deduction (see page 33)	33	12.2 / 33.14		
34	Jury duty pay you gave to your employer	34	12.2		
35	Domestic production activities deduction. Attach Form 8903	35	12.2 / 40.23		
36	Add lines 23 through 31a and 32 through 35			36	---------
37	Subtract line 36 from line 22. This is your **adjusted gross income** ▶			37	Chapter 12

For Disclosure, Privacy Act, and Paperwork Reduction Act Notice, see page 78. Cat. No. 11320B Form **1040** (2006)

When this book went to press, Congress had not yet extended to 2006 the deduction for educator expenses or the deduction for tuition and fees *(12.2)*. If legislation allows the deductions, as expected, they may be restored to their former positions on Lines 23 and 34, or the IRS may require them to be claimed as "write-ins" on Line 36. See the final version of Form 1040 and the instructions, and the ***e-Supplement*** for a legislation update.

Form 1040 with references to *Your Income Tax 2007*

Form 1040 (2006) Page **2**

Tax and Credits

Standard Deduction for—
- People who checked any box on line 39a or 39b **or** who can be claimed as a dependent, see page 36.
- All others:

Single or Married filing separately, $5,150

Married filing jointly or Qualifying widow(er), $10,300

Head of household, $7,550

Line	Description		Amount	Line	Reference
38	Amount from line 37 (adjusted gross income)			38	----------
39a	Check if: ☐ **You** were born before January 2, 1942, ☐ Blind. ☐ **Spouse** was born before January 2, 1942, ☐ Blind. **Total boxes checked ▶ 39a** ☐				
b	If your spouse itemizes on a separate return or you were a dual-status alien, see page 35 and check here ▶39b ☐				
40	**Itemized deductions** (from Schedule A) **or** your **standard deduction** (see left margin)			40	13.2 - 13.3
41	Subtract line 40 from line 38			41	----------
42	If line 38 is over $112,875, or you provided housing to a person displaced by Hurricane Katrina, see page 37. Otherwise, multiply $3,300 by the total number of exemptions claimed on line 6d			42	21.12
43	**Taxable income.** Subtract line 42 from line 41. If line 42 is more than line 41, enter -0-			43	----------
44	**Tax** (see page 37). Check if any tax is from: **a** ☐ Form(s) 8814 **b** ☐ Form 4972			44	22.1/24.4/7.4
45	**Alternative minimum tax** (see page 39). Attach Form 6251			45	Chapter 23
46	Add lines 44 and 45 ▶			46	----------
47	Foreign tax credit. Attach Form 1116 if required	47	36.14		
48	Credit for child and dependent care expenses. Attach Form 2441	48	25.4		
49	Credit for the elderly or the disabled. Attach Schedule R	49	34.7		
50	Education credits. Attach Form 8863	50	33.7		
51	Retirement savings contributions credit. Attach Form 8880	51	25.16		
52	Residential energy credits. Attach Form 5695	52	25.20 - 25.21		
53	Child tax credit (see page XX). Attach Form 8901 if required	53	25.2 - 25.3		
54	Credits from: **a** ☐ Form 8396 **b** ☐ Form 8839 **c** ☐ Form 8859	54	25.18 - 25.19		
55	Other credits: **a** ☐ Form 3800 **b** ☐ Form 8801 **c** ☐ Form_____	55	23.6/25.21		
56	Add lines 47 through 55. These are your **total credits**			56	
57	Subtract line 56 from line 46. If line 56 is more than line 46, enter -0- ▶			57	

Other Taxes

Line	Description		Amount	Line	Reference
58	Self-employment tax. Attach Schedule SE			58	45.3
59	Social security and Medicare tax on tip income not reported to employer. Attach Form 4137			59	26.7
60	Additional tax on IRAs, other qualified retirement plans, etc. Attach Form 5329 if required			60	7.15 / 8.12
61	Advance earned income credit payments from Form(s) W-2, box 9			61	25.13
62	Household employment taxes. Attach Schedule H			62	38.3
63	Add lines 57 through 62. This is your **total tax** ▶			63	Chapter 22

Payments

If you have a qualifying child, attach Schedule EIC.

Line	Description		Amount	Line	Reference
64	Federal income tax withheld from Forms W-2 and 1099	64	26.1/26.11		
65	2006 estimated tax payments and amount applied from 2005 return	65	27.2		
66a	**Earned income credit (EIC)**	66a	25.10		
b	Nontaxable combat pay election ▶ 66b 25.11				
67	Excess social security and tier 1 RRTA tax withheld (see page 59)	67	26.10		
68	Additional child tax credit. Attach Form 8812	68	25.3		
69	Amount paid with request for extension to file (see page 59)	69	46.3		
70	Payments from: **a** ☐ Form 2439 **b** ☐ Form 4136 **c** ☐ Form 8885	70	32.8/25.17		
71	Credit for federal telephone excise tax paid. Attach Form 8913 if required	71			
72	Add lines 64, 65, 66a, and 67 through 71. These are your **total payments** ▶			72	

Refund

Direct deposit? See page 59 and fill in 74b, 74c, and 74d, or Form 8888.

Line	Description		Amount	Line	Reference
73	If line 72 is more than line 63, subtract line 63 from line 72. This is the amount you **overpaid**			73	46.4
74a	Amount of line 73 you want **refunded to you.** If Form 8888 is attached, check here ▶ ☐			74a	46.4
▶ b	Routing number ▶ **c** Type: ☐ Checking ☐ Savings				
▶ d	Account number				
75	Amount of line 73 you want **applied to your 2007 estimated tax** ▶	75			

Amount You Owe

Line	Description		Amount	Line	Reference
76	**Amount you owe.** Subtract line 72 from line 63. For details on how to pay, see page 60 ▶			76	46.4
77	Estimated tax penalty (see page 60)	77			

Third Party Designee

Do you want to allow another person to discuss this return with the IRS (see page 61)? ☐ **Yes.** Complete the following. ☐ **No**

Designee's name ▶ Phone no. ▶ ( ) Personal identification number (PIN) ▶

Sign Here

Joint return? See page 17. Keep a copy for your records.

Under penalties of perjury, I declare that I have examined this return and accompanying schedules and statements, and to the best of my knowledge and belief, they are true, correct, and complete. Declaration of preparer (other than taxpayer) is based on all information of which preparer has any knowledge.

Your signature	Date	Your occupation	Daytime phone number ( )
Spouse's signature. If a joint return, **both** must sign.	Date	Spouse's occupation	

Paid Preparer's Use Only

Preparer's signature	Date	Check if self-employed ☐	Preparer's SSN or PTIN
Firm's name (or yours if self-employed), address, and ZIP code		EIN	
		Phone no.	( )

Form **1040** (2006)

Contents Chapter by Chapter

12 Deductions Allowed in Figuring Adjusted Gross Income 283

13 Claiming the Standard Deduction or Itemized Deductions 294

14 Charitable Contribution Deductions 302

15 Itemized Deduction for Interest Expenses 323

What's New for 2006

For an update on tax developments and a free download of the *e-Supplement* to this book, visit us online at www.jklasser.com.

Tax News for 2006

Item—	*Highlight—*
Extension pending for these deductions: tuition and fees deduction, state and local general sales tax deduction, and the educator expense deduction	When this book went to press, Congress had not yet extended to 2006 the laws authorizing the above-the-line deduction for higher education tuition and fees *(33.13)*, the above-the-line deduction of up to $250 of educator expenses *(12.2)*, and the option to deduct state and local general sales taxes *(16.3)* in lieu of state and local income taxes as an itemized deduction. Without an extension, these deductions will not be available on 2006 returns. An extension is expected. *See* the *e-Supplement* for an update.
Tax rates	The tax rate brackets for 2006, reflecting an inflation adjustment, are shown in *1.2*.
AMT exemption increased	The AMT exemption amounts for 2006 are $62,550 for joint filers, $42,500 for single filers and heads of household, and $31,275 for married/separate filers, up from $58,000, $40,250, and $29,000, respectively. The increase is for 2006 only, assuming no law change.
Tax credit for residential energy improvements	Energy improvements installed in or on a principal residence in the United States qualify for a limited tax credit on Form 5695. The total credit for both 2006 and 2007 is limited to $500, of which no more than $200 can be for exterior windows. There is also a limit of $50 for any advanced main air circulating fan, $150 for a qualified furnace or hot water boiler, or $300 for any qualified central air conditioner, heat pump, or water heater. *See 25.20* for additional information.
Tax credit for residential solar and fuel cell equipment	For property placed in service in 2006 and 2007, a credit is allowed for 30% of the cost of qualifying photovoltaic (electricity-generating) solar panels up to $2,000 per year, and a similar 30%/$2,000 credit limit for qualifying solar water heaters. The credits do not apply to equipment used to heat swimming pools or hot tubs. In addition, a 30% credit is allowed for fuel cell property, up to $500 for each half-kilowatt of capacity installed per year. *See 25.20.*
Tax credit for hybrid vehicles	For 2006 a tax credit replaces the prior law deduction for hybrid vehicles. The full credit is available only for a limited time. The certified credit amount is phased out for all hybrid vehicles of a particular manufacturer once the combined total of qualifying vehicles (regardless of model) sold after 2005 by the manufacturer for use in the United States exceeds 60,000. *See 25.21.*
Exemption phaseout and itemized deduction reduction	The reduction to itemized deductions and the personal exemption phaseout for high-income taxpayers are being gradually eliminated between 2006 and 2010. The reduction/phaseout for 2006 is $^{2}/_{3}$ of the "full" amount required under pre-2006 rules; one-third of the previously disallowed amount is allowed. *See 13.7* and *21.12*.
IRS mileage rates	The business mileage rate for 2006 is 44.5 cents per mile; *see 43.1.* For charitable volunteers *(14.4)*, the deductible mileage rate is generally 14 cents per mile but the rate is 32 cents per mile for Katrina-related volunteer activity. The rate for figuring deductible medical *(17.9)* and moving *(12.3)* expenses is 18 cents per mile. ***Note:*** When this book went to press, there was a possibility that the IRS might raise the business mileage rate for the latter part of the year; any increase will be reported in the *e-Supplement*.
Kiddie tax extended to children under age 18	The age limit for applying the "kiddie tax" has been raised to include children under 18. For a child who was under age 18 on January 1, 2007, the kiddie tax generally applies to the child's 2006 investment income exceeding $1,700. *See 24.2.*
Early distribution penalty exceptions for reservists and public safety officers	The 10% early distribution penalty does not apply to reservists called to active duty for more than 179 days after September 11, 2001, and before December 31, 2007. The exception applies to distributions from an IRA or distributions attributable to elective 401(k) or 403(b) plan deferrals. *See 35.8.* A penalty exception also applies to distributions after August 17, 2006, from state or local defined benefit pension plans to public safety officers who separate from service after age 50. *See 7.15.*
IRA based on tax-free combat pay	Members of the military serving in a combat zone may base a contribution to a traditional IRA or Roth IRA on their tax-free combat pay. Contributions for 2004 or 2005 can be made until May 28, 2009. *See 8.2* and *8.20.*

Optional Roth 401(k) or 403(b	If your plan permits, starting in 2006 you may treat elective deferrals as after-tax Roth contributions to be held in a separate account. As under Roth IRA rules, tax-free distributions would be allowed after a five-year waiting period if you are at least age 59½.
Deduction for clothing and household items limited	A donation after August 17, 2006, of used clothing or household items is deductible only if the property is in good used condition or better. *See 14.7.*
Recapture for donation of appreciated tangible personal property	For donations after September 1, 2006, of appreciated tangible personal property, a deduction may be limited or recaptured if the charity disposes of it within three years of the donation. *See 14.6.*
Increased deduction ceiling for qualified conservation contributions	For qualified conservation contributions made in 2006 and 2007, the charitable deduction ceiling is raised and a special carry forward is allowed for excess contributions. *See 14.17.*
Exclusion for direct donations from IRAs	For 2006 and also 2007, taxpayers age 70½ and older may avoid tax on up to $100,000 of otherwise taxable IRA distributions (traditional or Roth) if the funds are transferred directly from the IRA to a 50% limit charitable organization. Excludable transfers are treated as required minimum distributions and are not deductible as charitable contributions. *See 8.8* and *14.17.*
Recapture of deduction for donation of fractional interest	Donations after August 17, 2006, of fractional interests in art or other tangible personal property must be completed within 10 years of the initial contribution or by the death of the donor, whichever is first. Otherwise, all prior charitable deductions will be recaptured, plus interest and a 10 percent penalty. *See 14.9.*
Restrictions on façade easement donations	Façade easements donated after July 25, 2006, for buildings in registered historic districts must preserve the entire exterior and are subject to additional restrictions. *See 14.10.*
Foreign income exclusion increased	The foreign earned income exclusion for 2006 has been increased by an inflation adjustment to $82,400 (from $80,000); *see 36.1.*
Exclusion for foreign housing cost limited	Beginning in 2006, the definition of the base housing amount is changed and the amount of housing costs that can be taken into account is limited when figuring the housing cost exclusion; *see 36.4.*
Expenses qualifying for dependent care credit	IRS proposed regulations clarify that eligible expenses include costs of specialty day camps, and transportation by the care provider to a care center, day camp, or after-school program. *See 25.8.*
Child tax credit	For 2006 the credit for each qualifying child is $1,000 and the refundable portion is 15% of earned income exceeding $11,300. *See 25.2* and *25.3.* Tax-free combat pay is treated as earned income when figuring the refundable credit.
Depreciation limits for autos	The first-year depreciation limit for an auto placed in service in 2006 is $2,960 and for a truck/van the limit is $3,260. *See 43.4* for exceptions and further details.
Traditional IRA deduction phaseout	The 2006 IRA deduction limit begins to phase out for active plan participants with MAGI exceeding $50,000 if single or head of household, or $75,000 if married filing jointly; *see 8.4.*
Elective deferrals	The 2006 deferral limit for 401(k), 403(b), and 457 plans, and salary-reduction SEPs is $15,000. The deferral limit for SIMPLE plans is $10,000. For those age 50 and over the plan could allow an additional deferral of up to $5,000 to a 401(k), 403(b), SEP, or governmental Section 457 plan. For a SIMPLE plan the additional deferral limit is $2,500; *see 7.17.*
Health savings accounts (HSAs)	For 2006, eligible individuals covered by a high deductible health plan can make deductible contributions to an HSA up to the lesser of the plan deductible or $2,700 for self-only coverage or $5,450 for family coverage; *see 12.10.*
FICA and self-employment tax base	For 2006, wages and self-employment earnings of up to $94,200 (up from $90,000) are subject to the 6.2% Social Security tax; *see 26.10* and *45.4.*
First-year expensing (Section 179) deduction	For 2006, the limit on the first-year expensing deduction for business equipment is $108,000. The limit is reduced if the cost of qualifying property placed in service during the year exceeds $430,000; *see 42.3.*
Gift tax annual exclusion	The annual exclusion increases to $12,000 for gifts made in 2006 (up from $11,000); *see 39.2.*
Earned income credit (EIC)	The increased credit and phaseout limits for 2006 are at *25.10–25.11.* An election may be made to treat tax-free combat pay as earned income when figuring the credit for 2006.
Loan to continuing care facility	For 2006 through 2010, loans in the form of refundable entrance fees to qualified continuing care facilities are completely exempt from the imputed interest rules. *See 34.11.*

Hurricane Tax Relief

Item—	Highlight—
Retirement plan withdrawals	Qualified hurricane (Katrina, Rita, Wilma) distributions in 2005 and 2006 up to an overall two-year limit of $100,000 from all plans are exempt from the penalty for pre-age-59½ withdrawals, can be reported as income over three years, and can be recontributed within three years to a rollover-eligible plan. Form 8915 is used to report qualified distributions and repayments. *See 7.30* for employer plan distributions and *8.25* for IRA distributions.
Loans from qualified employer plans	The tax-free limit for loans before 2007 is increased for employees who lived in the Hurricane Katrina, Rita, or Wilma disaster areas and suffered economic loss due to the hurricane. Up to 100% of the nonforfeitable accrued balance may be borrowed, but no more than $100,000. Loan repayments due before 2007 are suspended for one year. *See 7.30* and *7.31*.
Suspension of $100/10% AGI floors for personal casualty losses	An otherwise allowable casualty and theft loss arising within the Hurricane Katrina, Rita, or Wilma disaster area and attributable to the hurricane is deductible on Form 4684 without regard to the generally applicable floors for personal losses. The regular $100 per casualty/theft floor does not apply to the hurricane loss and neither does the 10% of adjusted gross income (AGI) floor. *See 18.12*.
Extended replacement period for nonrecognition of gain	The replacement period for deferring gain is extended to five years for property located in the Hurricane Katrina disaster area that was compulsorily or involuntarily converted due to the hurricane, but only if substantially all of the use of the replacement property is in the Hurricane Katrina disaster area. *See 18.22*.
Discharged non-business debt	The discharge of a non-business debt by a commercial lender or certain government agencies after 8/24/05 and before 1/1/07 generally is excluded from the income of an individual whose principal residence was within the Katrina disaster area on 8/25/05. *See 11.8* for further details.
Charitable volunteers	Volunteers who use their vehicles in donating services to a charity related to Hurricane Katrina relief during 2006 may claim a charitable mileage rate of 32 cents per mile rather than the regular mileage rate of 14 cents per mile. *See 14.4*. Charitable volunteers who are reimbursed in 2006 for using their passenger automobiles in donating services to a charity related to Hurricane Katrina relief are not taxed on reimbursements up to 44.5 cents per mile. *See 14.4*.
Extra exemption for housing displaced person	If you provide free housing in your principal residence for at least 60 consecutive days to a person (other than your spouse or dependent) displaced by Hurricane Katrina, you may claim on Form 8914 an additional exemption of $500 for up to four displaced persons. The overall limit of $2,000 ($1,000 if married separately) applies to both 2005 and 2006 so any amount claimed for 2005 reduces the amount available for 2006. *See 21.1*.

Key Tax Numbers for 2006

Exemptions	
Each allowable exemption *(21.1)*	$3,300
Phaseout starts/ends *(21.12)*	
Joint return/Qualifying widow(er)	$225,750 / $348,250
Head of Household	$188,150 / $310,650
Single	$150,500 / $273,000
Married filing separately	$112,875 / $174,125
Standard Deduction *(13.1)*	
Joint return/Qualifying widow(er)	$10,300
Head of Household	$7,550
Single	$5,150
Married filing separately	$5,150
Dependents-minimum deduction	$850
Additional deduction if age 65 or older, or blind *(13.5)*	
Married-per spouse, filing jointly or separately	$1,000 ($2,000 for age and blindness)
Qualifying widow(er)	$1,000 ($2,000 for age and blindness)
Single or head of household	$1,250 ($2,500 for age and blindness
AMT Exemption *(23.1)*	
Joint return/Qualifying widow(er)	$62,550
Single or Head of Household	$42,500
Married filing separately	$31,275
Long-term Care Premiums *(17.15)*	
Limit on premium allowed as medical expense	
Age 40 or under	$280
Over 40 but not over 50	$530
Over 50 but not over 60	$1,060
Over 60 but not over 70	$2,830
Over 70	$3,530
Overall Limit on Itemized Deductions *(13.7)*	
Reduction starts	
Married filing separately	$75,250
All others	$150,500
IRA Contributions	
Traditional IRA contribution limit *(8.2)*	$4,000
Additional contribution if age 50 or older	$1,000
Deduction phaseout for active plan participant *(8.4)*	
Single or head of household	$50,000–$60,000
Married filing jointly, two participants	$75,000–$85,000
Married filing jointly, one participant	
Participant spouse	$75,000–$85,000
Non-participant spouse	$150,000–$160,000
Married filing separately, live together, either participates	$0–$10,000
Married filing separately, live apart all year	
Participant spouse	$50,000–$60,000
Non-participant spouse	no phaseout
Roth IRA contribution limit *(8.20)*	$4,000
Additional contribution if age 50 or older	$1,000
Contribution limit phaseout range	
Single, head of household	$95,000–$110,000

Married filing separately, live apart all year	$95,000–$110,000
Married filing jointly, or qualifying widow(er)	$150,000–$160,000
Married filing separately, live together at any time	$0–$10,000

Elective deferral limits

401(k), 403(b), 457 plans *(7.18)*	$15,000
Salary-reduction SEP *(8.16)*	$15,000
SIMPLE plan *(8.17)*	$10,000
Additional contribution if age 50 or older	
401(k), 403(b), governmental 457 and SEP plans *(7.18, 8.16)*	$5,000
SIMPLE plan *(8.17)*	$2,500

Education

Hope credit limit *(33.8)*	$1,650
Lifetime learning credit limit *(33.9)*	$2,000
Phaseout of credits *(33.10)*	
Married filing jointly	$90,000–$110,000
Single, head of household, or qualifying widow(er)	$45,000–$55,000
Student loan interest deduction limit *(33.14)*	$2,500
Phaseout of deduction limit	
Married filing jointly	$105,000–$135,000
Single, head of household, or qualifying widow(er)	$50,000–$65,000
Coverdell ESA limit *(33.11)*	$2,000
Phaseout of limit	
Married filing jointly	$190,000–$220,000
All others	$95,000–$110,000
Tuition and fees deduction—(assuming deduction is extended by Congress—*see 33.13*)	
Tuition and fees deduction-tier 1 limit	$4,000
Income cut-off	
• Married filing jointly	$130,000
• Single, head of household, or qualifying widow(er)	$65,000
Tuition and fees deduction limit-tier 2 limit	$2,000
Income cut-off	
• Married filing jointly	$160,000
• Single, head of household, or qualifying widow(er)	$80,000

Capital gain rates-assets held over one year *(5.3)*

Top bracket of 10% or 15%	5%
Top bracket over 15%	15%
All collectibles gain	28%
All unrecaptured Section 1250 gain on depreciated real estate	25%

Qualified dividends tax rate *(4.1)*

Top bracket of 10% or 15%	5%
Top bracket over 15%	15%

IRS mileage rates

Business *(43.1)*	44.5 cents
Charitable volunteers *(14.4)*	
Non-Katrina related volunteer activity	14 cents
Katrina-related volunteer activity	32 cents
Medical *(17.9)* and moving *(12.3)* expenses	18 cents

Exclusion for employer provided transportation *(3.8)*

Transit passes and commuter vehicle transport	$105/month
Qualified parking	$205/month

Looking Ahead to Tax Changes for Years After 2006

See the *e-Supplement* (www.jklasser.com) for further updates.

Item	*Highlight*
AMT exemption	Unless new legislation is enacted, the AMT exemption will fall in 2007 to pre-2001 amounts of $45,000 for joint return filers or qualified widow(ers), $33,750 for single or head of household filers, or $22,500 for married persons filing separately.
Nonrefundable personal tax credits	The law allowing nonrefundable personal credits to offset regular tax and AMT liability will not apply after 2006 unless the law is extended. If it is not extended, the aggregate amount of nonrefundable personal credits other than the child tax credit, adoption credit, and retirement savings credit will be allowed in 2007 only to the extent that regular tax liability exceeds tentative AMT (disregarding AMT foreign tax credit).
All charitable cash contributions must be substantiated	Beginning in 2007, all charitable cash contributions, regardless of amount, must be substantiated by a cancelled check, bank record, or detailed receipt from the charity.
Retirement saver's credit extended and indexed for inflation	The retirement saver's credit has been permanently extended beyond 2006. Starting in 2007, the income ranges for the three credit rates are subject to inflation indexing.
Inflation indexing for deductible IRA and Roth IRA phaseout thresholds	For 2007 and later years, the IRA deduction phaseout thresholds are subject to inflation indexing. The phaseout thresholds for Roth IRA contributions will also be indexed for inflation.
Rollover by non-spouse beneficiary	A distribution after 2006 from a qualified employer plan, 403 (b) plan, or governmental 457 plan can be rolled over by a non-spouse beneficiary in a trustee-to-trustee transfer to an IRA, provided the IRA is treated as an inherited IRA subject to the required minimum distribution rules for non-spouse beneficiaries.
Foreign earned income exclusion indexed for inflation	The foreign earned income exclusion ($82,400 for 2006) will be subject to an inflation adjustment for 2007 and for later years.
Tax-free government pension distributions to pay health insurance premiums of retired public safety officers	Starting in 2007, up to $3,000 of otherwise taxable distributions from a government pension plan may be excluded from income by a retired public safety officer who elects to have the amount withheld from the distribution and paid directly to a health insurance company to pay premiums for accident or health insurance coverage, or qualifying long-term care insurance. Premiums may be for the retired public safety officer, his or her spouse, or dependents.
Direct rollover from retirement plans to ROTH IRAs	A distribution after 2007 from a qualified retirement plan, 403 (b) plan or governmental 457 plan may be directly rolled into a ROTH IRA, subject to the Roth conversion rules. Thus, for years before 2010, the direct rollover is allowed only if the employee's modified adjusted gross income is $100,000 or less. A rollover is taxable except to the extent it is attributable to after-tax contributions, but the 10% penalty for withdrawals before age 59½ does not apply.
Child tax credit	The maximum credit per qualifying child will remain $1,000 through 2010.
First-year expensing	The first-year expensing limit ($108,000 for 2006) and the phaseout threshold ($430,000 for 2006) will continue to be indexed for inflation for property placed in service in 2007 through 2009. Without further legislation, the expensing limit will drop to $25,000 and the phaseout threshold to $200,000 in 2010.

Domestic production activities deduction	The deductible percentage increases from 3% to 6% for 2007–2009 and to 9% in 2010.
Contribution limits for traditional and Roth IRAs	For individuals under age 50, the annual contribution limit will stay at $4,000 for 2007 and increase to $5,000 for 2008, with inflation indexing thereafter. These limits will be $1,000 higher for individuals age 50 and over; the $1,000 additional contribution amount is not scheduled for an increase.
Elective deferrals	The $15,000 deferral limit that applied in 2006 for 401(k), 403(b), SEP, and 457 plans is subject to inflation indexing for 2007 and later years. If the plan allows additional contributions for individuals age 50 or older, the 2006 limit of $5,000 is also subject to inflation indexing for 2007 and later years. The 2006 SIMPLE IRA deferral limit of $10,000, and additional SIMPLE contribution limit of $2,500 for individuals age 50 or older are subject to inflation adjustments for 2007 and later years.
Exemption phaseout and itemized deduction reduction	The gradual elimination of the reduction to itemized deductions and the phaseout of personal exemptions which began in 2006 continues until 2010. The reduction/phaseout for 2007 will remain (as in 2006) at $^2/_3$ of the "full" amount required under pre-2006 rules. In 2008–2009, only $^1/_3$ of the full reduction/phaseout will apply, and in 2010 these deduction restrictions will be repealed.
Capital gain rates	The favorable capital rates, which had been scheduled to apply through 2008, have been extended for two years. For taxpayers with a top bracket over 15%, the 15% rate will apply to net capital gains realized and to qualified dividends received before 2011. For those with a top bracket of 10% or 15%, the rate will be 5% for net gains and qualified dividends received before 2008 and in 2008–2010, there will be no tax; the rate will be "zero".
Roth IRA conversions encouraged after 2009	Beginning in 2010, the $100,000 adjusted gross income (AGI) limit will be lifted, allowing individuals at all income levels to convert a traditional IRA to a Roth IRA. For conversions made in 2010, the taxable income from the conversion can be spread ratably over 2011 and 2012. The two-year spread applies only to conversions in 2010.
Estate tax rates and exclusion amounts	The future of the estate tax was unclear when this book went to press, as Congressional Democrats and Republicans could not agree on a plan to reform the estate tax for years after 2009. In the absence of new legislation, the rules at *39.11* will apply. Legislative developments will be covered in the *e-Supplement*.

Part 1

Filing Basics

In this part, you will learn these income tax basics:

- Whether you must file a return
- When and where to file your return
- Which tax form to file
- What filing status you qualify for
- When filing separately is an advantage for married persons
- How to qualify as head of household
- How filing rules for resident aliens and nonresident aliens differ
- How to claim personal exemption deductions for yourself, your spouse, and your dependents.

Do You Have To File a 2006 Tax Return?	
If you are—	**You must file if gross income is at least—**
Single	
Under age 65	$8,450
Age 65 or older on or before January 1, 2007	9,700
Married and living together at the end of 2006	
Filing a joint return—both spouses under age 65	16,900
Filing a joint return—one spouse age 65 or older	17,900
Filing a joint return—both spouses age 65 or older	18,900
Filing a separate return (any age)	3,300
Married and living apart at the end of 2006	
Filing a joint or separate return	3,300
Head of a household maintained for a child or other relative *(see 1.12)*	
Under age 65	10,850
Age 65 or older on or before January 1, 2007	12,100
Widowed in 2005 or 2004 and have a dependent child *(see 1.11)*	
Under age 65	13,600
Age 65 or older on or before January 1, 2007	14,600

Marital status. For federal tax purposes, only a man and woman in a legal union as husband and wife are considered married. For 2006 returns, marital status is generally determined as of December 31, 2006. Thus, if you were divorced or legally separated during 2006, you are not considered married for 2006 tax purposes, and you must use the filing threshold for single persons unless you qualify as a head of household *(1.12)*, or you remarried in 2006 and are filing a joint return with your new spouse.

If your spouse died in 2006 and you were living together on the date of death, use the filing threshold shown for married persons living together at the end of 2006. If you were not living together on the date of death, the $3,300 filing threshold applies, unless you remarried during 2006 and are filing jointly with your new spouse.

Age 65. Whether you are age 65 or older is generally determined as of the end of the year, but if your 65th birthday is on January 1, 2007, you are treated as being age 65 at the end of 2006.

Gross income. Gross income is generally all the income that you received in 2006, except for items specifically exempt from tax.

Include wages and tips (Chapter 2), self-employment income (Chapter 45), taxable scholarships (Chapter 33), taxable interest and dividends (Chapter 4), capital gains (Chapter 5), taxable pensions and annuities (Chapter 7), rents (Chapter 9), and trust distributions (Chapter 11). Home sale proceeds that are tax free (Chapter 29) and tax-free foreign earned income (Chapter 36) *are* considered gross income for purposes of the filing test.

Exclude tax-exempt interest (Chapter 4), tax-free fringe benefits (Chapter 3), qualifying scholarships (Chapter 33), and life insurance (Chapter 11). Also exclude Social Security benefits *unless* you are married filing separately and you lived with your spouse at any time during 2006.

Other situations when you must file. Even if you are not required to file under the gross income tests, you must file a 2006 return if:

- You are self-employed and you owe self-employment tax because your net self-employment earnings for 2006 are $400 or more (Chapter 45), *or*
- You are entitled to a refund of taxes withheld from your wages (Chapter 26) or a refund based on the earned income credit for working families (Chapter 25), *or*
- You received any earned income credit payments in advance from your employer (Chapter 25), *or*
- You owe any special tax such as alternative minimum tax (Chapter 23), IRA penalty (Chapter 8), and FICA on tips (Chapter 26), *or*
- You are a nonresident alien with a U.S. business or have tax liability not covered by withholding; *see* Form 1040NR.

Filing tests for dependents. If you can be claimed as a dependent by your parent, or by any other taxpayer, *see* the rules on the next page to determine if you must file a return.

Filing Tests for Dependents: 2006 Returns

The income threshold for filing a tax return is generally lower for an individual who may be claimed as a dependent than for a nondependent. You are a "dependent" if you are the qualifying child or qualifying relative of another taxpayer, and the other tests for dependents at *21.1* are met.

If, under the tests at *21.1*, you may be claimed as a dependent by someone else, use the chart on this page to determine if you must file a 2006 return. Include as unearned income taxable interest and dividends, capital gains, pensions, annuities, unemployment compensation, and distributions of unearned income from a trust. Earned income includes wages, tips, self-employment income, and taxable scholarships or fellowships *(Chapter 33)*. Gross income is the total of unearned and earned income.

For married dependents, the filing requirements in the chart assume that the dependent is filing a separate return and not a joint return *(Chapter 1)*. Generally, a married person who files a joint return may not be claimed as a dependent by a third party who provides support.

If you are the parent of a dependent child who was under age 18 on January 1, 2007, and who had only investment income, you may elect to report the child's income on your own return instead of filing a separate return for the child; *see 24.5* for the election rules.

For purposes of the following chart, a person is treated as being age 65 (or older) if his or her 65th birthday is on or before January 1, 2007. Blindness is determined as of December 31, 2006.

Filing Instruction

File for Refund of Withholdings

Even if you are not required to file a return under the income tests on this page, you should file to obtain a refund of federal tax withholdings. Also *see* page 3 for other situations when you must file.

File a Return for 2006 If You Are a—

Single dependent. Were you **either** age 65 or older **or** blind?

☐ **No.** You must file a return if **any** of the following apply:

- Your **unearned income** was over $850.
- Your **earned income** was over $5,150.
- Your **gross income** was more than the **larger** of—
  - $850 **or**
  - Your earned income (up to $4,850) plus $300.

☐ **Yes.** You must file a return if **any** of the following apply:

- Your unearned income was over $2,100 ($3,350 if 65 or older **and** blind).
- Your earned income was over $6,400 ($7,650 if 65 or older **and** blind).
- Your gross income was more than—

The larger of:	Plus	This amount:
• $850 **or** • Your earned income (up to $4,850) plus $300	}	$1,250 ($2,500 if 65 or older **and** blind)

Married dependent. Were you **either** age 65 or older **or** blind?

☐ **No.** You must file a return if **any** of the following apply:

- Your unearned income was over $850.
- Your earned income was over $5,150.
- Your gross income was at least $5 and your spouse files a separate return and itemizes deductions.
- Your gross income was more than the **larger** of—
  - $850 **or**
  - Your earned income (up to $4,850) plus $300.

☐ **Yes.** You must file a return if **any** of the following apply:

- Your unearned income was over $1,850 ($2,850 if 65 or older **and** blind).
- Your earned income was over $6,150 ($7,150 if 65 or older **and** blind).
- Your gross income was at least $5 and your spouse files a separate return and itemizes deductions.
- Your gross income was more than—

The larger of:	Plus	This amount:
• $850 **or** • Your earned income (up to $4,850) plus $300	}	$1,000 ($2,000 if 65 or older **and** blind)

Where To File

If you are filing—	File with the Internal Revenue Service Center—
Form 1040, 1040A, or 1040EZ	For your place of legal residence. If you received an IRS packet of forms with a pre-addressed envelope, use it unless you have moved. If you do not have an envelope, mail your return to the Service Center shown on the map below for your residence.
A partnership (Form 1065) or S corporation (Form 1120S) return	For the location of your principal place of business; follow the Form 1065 or 1120S instructions.
As a U.S. citizen working abroad	File Form 1040, 1040A, or 1040EZ at Austin, TX 73301-0215 USA.
As a service member in the Armed Forces	For the place you are stationed. If you are overseas and have an APO or FPO address, file Form 1040, 1040A, or 1040EZ with the Service Center at Austin, TX 73301-0215 USA.

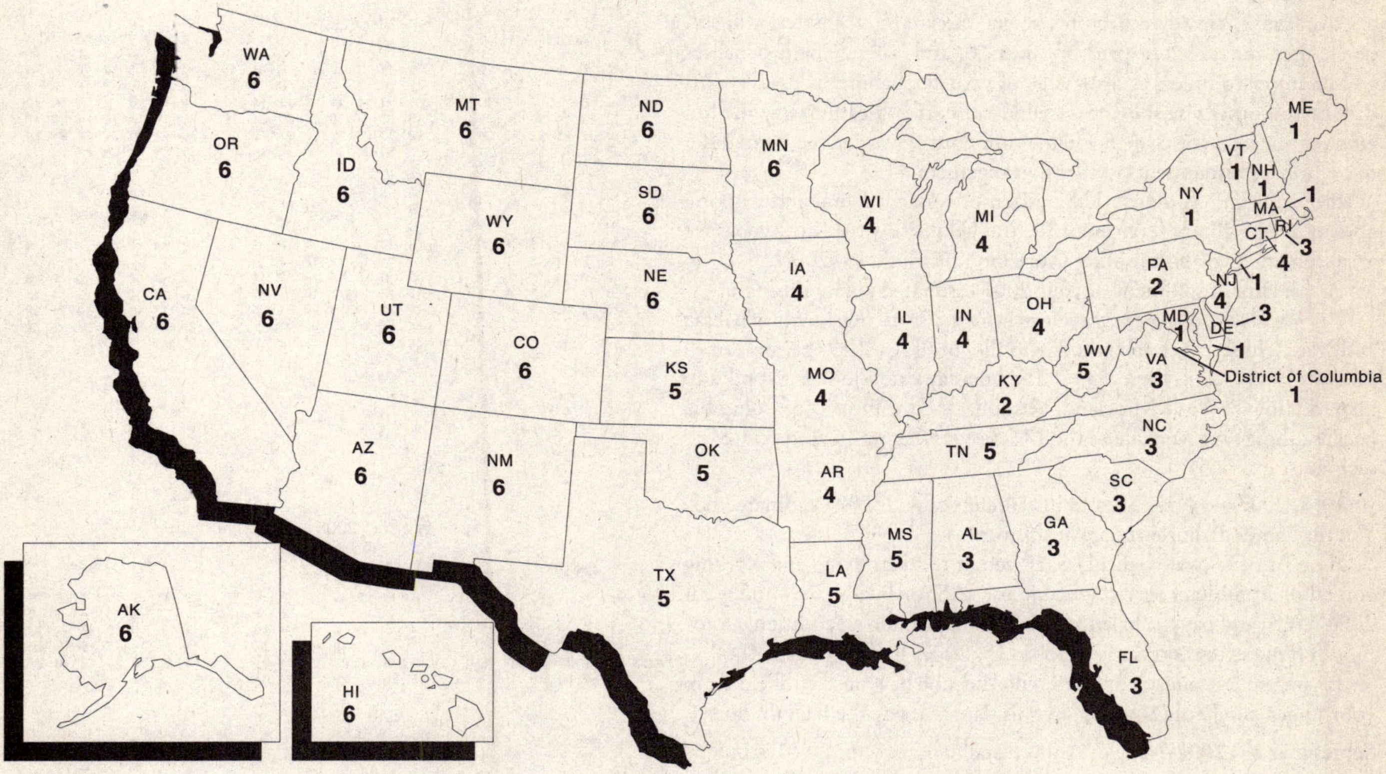

Key to Service Center Map

Key	Form 1040 Mailing Address—*
1.	Internal Revenue Service, Andover, Massachusetts 05501-0102 if making a payment; otherwise 05501-0002. Residents of the District of Columbia file here.
2.	Internal Revenue Service, Philadelphia, Pennsylvania 19255-0102 if making a payment; otherwise 19255-0002. ***Note:*** After June 30, 2007, residents of Kentucky and Pennsylvania will send their tax information to Kansas City, MO; *see* Key 4 on the right.
3.	Internal Revenue Service, Atlanta, Georgia 39901-0102 if making a payment; otherwise 39901-0002.
4.	Internal Revenue Service, Kansas City, Missouri 64999-0102 if making a payment; otherwise 64999-0002.
5.	Internal Revenue Service, Austin, Texas 73301-0102 if making a payment; otherwise 73301-0002.
6.	Internal Revenue Service, Fresno, California 93888-0102 if making a payment; otherwise 93888-0002.

* ***Filing Form 1040A or 1040EZ:*** *If you are filing Form 1040A, the last four digits of the zip codes for the IRS Service Centers are 0015 (no payment) or 0115 (payment). For Form 1040EZ the last four digits are 0014 (no payment) or 0114 (payment). Check your tax form instructions and the e-Supplement for any late changes to the addresses or zip codes on this page.*

Filing Deadlines (on or Before)

January 16, 2007—Pay the balance of your 2006 estimated tax. If you do not meet this date, you may avoid an estimated tax penalty for the last quarter by filing your 2006 return and paying the balance due by January 31, 2007.

Farmers and fishermen: File your single 2006 estimated tax payment by this date. If you do not, you may still avoid an estimated tax penalty by filing a final tax return and paying the full tax by March 1, 2007.

January 31, 2007—Make sure you have received a Form W-2 from each employer for whom you worked in 2006.

April 16, 2007—File your 2006 tax return and pay the balance of your tax. If you cannot meet the April 16 deadline, you may obtain an automatic six-month filing extension by filing Form 4868 (on paper or electronically). However, even if you get an extension, interest will still be charged for taxes not paid by April 16, and late payment penalties will be imposed unless at least 90% of your tax liability is paid by this date or you otherwise show reasonable cause. If you cannot pay the full amount of tax you owe when you file your return, you can file Form 9465 to request an installment payment arrangement.

If on this date you are a U.S. citizen or resident living and working abroad or in military service outside the U.S. or Puerto Rico, you have an automatic two-month filing extension until June 15, 2007.

Pay the first installment of your 2007 estimated tax by this date.

Patriots Day gives some taxpayers an extra day to file: Residents of Maine and Massachusetts get an extra day to file, until April 17, because April 16 is Patriots Day in these states. The one-day extension also applies to taxpayers in New York, Maryland, Vermont, and the District of Columbia because these taxpayers file at the IRS Service Center in Andover, Massachusetts (*see* p. 5).

June 15, 2007—Pay the second installment of your 2007 estimated tax. You may amend your estimate at this time.

If on April 16 you were a U.S. citizen or resident living and working abroad or in military service outside the U.S. or Puerto Rico, file your 2006 return and pay the balance due. You may obtain an additional four-month filing extension until October 15, 2007, by filing Form 4868.

If you are a nonresident alien who did not have tax withheld from your wages, file Form 1040NR by this date and pay the balance due.

September 17, 2007—Pay the third installment of your 2007 estimated tax. You may amend your estimate at this time.

October 15, 2007—File your 2006 return if you received an automatic six-month filing extension using Form 4868. Also file your 2006 return and pay the balance due if on April 16 you were a U.S. citizen or resident living and working abroad or in military service outside the U.S. or Puerto Rico, and by June 15 you qualified for an additional four-month extension by filing Form 4868.

December 31, 2007—If self-employed, this is the last day to set up a Keogh plan for 2007.

January 15, 2008—Pay the balance of your 2007 estimated tax.

April 15, 2008—File your 2007 return and pay the balance of your tax. Pay the first installment of your 2008 estimated tax by this date.

15th day of the 4th month after the fiscal year ends—File your fiscal year return and pay the balance of the tax due. If you cannot meet the filing deadline, apply for an automatic four-month filing extension on Form 4868.

2007

JANUARY

S	M	T	W	T	F	S
	1	2	3	4	5	6
7	8	9	10	11	12	13
14	15	16	17	18	19	20
21	22	23	24	25	26	27
28	29	30	31			

FEBRUARY

S	M	T	W	T	F	S
				1	2	3
4	5	6	7	8	9	10
11	12	13	14	15	16	17
18	19	20	21	22	23	24
25	26	27	28			

MARCH

S	M	T	W	T	F	S
				1	2	3
4	5	6	7	8	9	10
11	12	13	14	15	16	17
18	19	20	21	22	23	24
25	26	27	28	29	30	31

APRIL

S	M	T	W	T	F	S
1	2	3	4	5	6	7
8	9	10	11	12	13	14
15	16	17	18	19	20	21
22	23	24	25	26	27	28
29	30					

MAY

S	M	T	W	T	F	S
		1	2	3	4	5
6	7	8	9	10	11	12
13	14	15	16	17	18	19
20	21	22	23	24	25	26
27	28	29	30	31		

JUNE

S	M	T	W	T	F	S
					1	2
3	4	5	6	7	8	9
10	11	12	13	14	15	16
17	18	19	20	21	22	23
24	25	26	27	28	29	30

JULY

S	M	T	W	T	F	S
1	2	3	4	5	6	7
8	9	10	11	12	13	14
15	16	17	18	19	20	21
22	23	24	25	26	27	28
29	30	31				

AUGUST

S	M	T	W	T	F	S
			1	2	3	4
5	6	7	8	9	10	11
12	13	14	15	16	17	18
19	20	21	22	23	24	25
26	27	28	29	30	31	

SEPTEMBER

S	M	T	W	T	F	S
						1
2	3	4	5	6	7	8
9	10	11	12	13	14	15
16	17	18	19	20	21	22
23	24	25	26	27	28	29
30						

OCTOBER

S	M	T	W	T	F	S
	1	2	3	4	5	6
7	8	9	10	11	12	13
14	15	16	17	18	19	20
21	22	23	24	25	26	27
28	29	30	31			

NOVEMBER

S	M	T	W	T	F	S
				1	2	3
4	5	6	7	8	9	10
11	12	13	14	15	16	17
18	19	20	21	22	23	24
25	26	27	28	29	30	

DECEMBER

S	M	T	W	T	F	S
						1
2	3	4	5	6	7	8
9	10	11	12	13	14	15
16	17	18	19	20	21	22
23	24	25	26	27	28	29
30	31					

2008

JANUARY

S	M	T	W	T	F	S
		1	2	3	4	5
6	7	8	9	10	11	12
13	14	15	16	17	18	19
20	21	22	23	24	25	26
27	28	29	30	31		

FEBRUARY

S	M	T	W	T	F	S
					1	2
3	4	5	6	7	8	9
10	11	12	13	14	15	16
17	18	19	20	21	22	23
24	25	26	27	28	29	

MARCH

S	M	T	W	T	F	S
						1
2	3	4	5	6	7	8
9	10	11	12	13	14	15
16	17	18	19	20	21	22
23	24	25	26	27	28	29
30	31					

APRIL

S	M	T	W	T	F	S
		1	2	3	4	5
6	7	8	9	10	11	12
13	14	15	16	17	18	19
20	21	22	23	24	25	26
27	28	29	30			

MAY

S	M	T	W	T	F	S
				1	2	3
4	5	6	7	8	9	10
11	12	13	14	15	16	17
18	19	20	21	22	23	24
25	26	27	28	29	30	31

JUNE

S	M	T	W	T	F	S
1	2	3	4	5	6	7
8	9	10	11	12	13	14
15	16	17	18	19	20	21
22	23	24	25	26	27	28
29	30					

JULY

S	M	T	W	T	F	S
		1	2	3	4	5
6	7	8	9	10	11	12
13	14	15	16	17	18	19
20	21	22	23	24	25	26
27	28	29	30	31		

AUGUST

S	M	T	W	T	F	S
					1	2
3	4	5	6	7	8	9
10	11	12	13	14	15	16
17	18	19	20	21	22	23
24	25	26	27	28	29	30
31						

SEPTEMBER

S	M	T	W	T	F	S
	1	2	3	4	5	6
7	8	9	10	11	12	13
14	15	16	17	18	19	20
21	22	23	24	25	26	27
28	29	30				

OCTOBER

S	M	T	W	T	F	S
			1	2	3	4
5	6	7	8	9	10	11
12	13	14	15	16	17	18
19	20	21	22	23	24	25
26	27	28	29	30	31	

NOVEMBER

S	M	T	W	T	F	S
						1
2	3	4	5	6	7	8
9	10	11	12	13	14	15
16	17	18	19	20	21	22
23	24	25	26	27	28	29
30						

DECEMBER

S	M	T	W	T	F	S
	1	2	3	4	5	6
7	8	9	10	11	12	13
14	15	16	17	18	19	20
21	22	23	24	25	26	27
28	29	30	31			

Choosing Which Tax Form to File

There are three individual tax forms: Form 1040, Form 1040A, and Form 1040EZ. Use the simplified Form 1040EZ or Form 1040A only if you find the return will save you time and not cause you to give up tax-saving deductions or credits that are only available if you file Form 1040. To help you make your selection, fill in the following chart.

By checking the box that indicates your tax status, income, expenses, and credit items, you will be guided in choosing which form to use.

Item—	Form 1040EZ—	Form 1040A—	Form 1040—
Single	X[1, 2]	X[1]	X
Head of household		X[1]	X
Married filing jointly	X[1, 2]	X[1]	X
Married filing separately		X[1]	X
Widow or widower		X[1]	X
Exemption for dependents		X	X
Wages, salary	X	X	X
Interest	X[3]	X	X
Ordinary dividends		X	X
Qualified dividends taxed as long-term capital gains		X[5]	X
Unemployment compensation	X	X	X
Self-employment income			X
Pension-annuity		X	X
IRA distributions		X	X
Rents and royalties			X
Gains and losses from property sales			X
Capital gain distributions from mutual funds		X[5]	X
Alimony			X
State tax refunds			X
Social Security benefits		X	X
IRA deduction		X	X
Alimony paid			X
Student loan interest		X	X
Tuition and fees deduction, if extended; *see 33.13*		X	X
Educator expenses, if extended; *see 12.2*		X	X
Moving expenses			X
Self-employed health insurance			X
50% of self-employment tax			X
Archer MSA deduction			X
Penalty for early withdrawal of savings			X
Deduction for Keogh, SEP, and SIMPLE plans			X
Employee business expenses			X
State and local taxes			X
Real estate taxes			X
Home mortgage interest, investment and business interest			X
Charitable contributions			X
Medical and dental expenses			X
Casualty and theft losses			X
Miscellaneous deductions (investment expenses, tax preparation)			X
Credit for child and dependent care		X	X
Earned income credit	X[4]	X	X
Credit for elderly and totally disabled		X	X
Child tax credit or additional child tax credit		X	X
Adoption credit		X	X
Retirement savings contributions credit		X	X
Education credits		X	X
All other credits			X
Estimated tax payments and estimated tax penalty		X	X
Advance earned income credit (EIC) payments		X	X
Self-employment tax			X
Roth conversion IRA			X
Penalty tax on an IRA			X
Alternative minimum tax			X
Social Security tax on tips not reported to your employer			X
Uncollected Social Security tax on tips shown on your Form W-2			X
"Kiddie" tax on child's return		X	X
"Kiddie" tax on parent's return			X
Household employee taxes			X
All other taxes or penalties			X

[1] *Taxable income less than $100,000.*
[2] *Under age 65 and not blind on January 1, 2007.*
[3] *Up to $1,500.*
[4] *If you did not receive any advance earned income credit payments.*
[5] *If you do not need Schedule D of Form 1040 for any other transaction.*

Chapter 1

Filing Status

The filing status you use when you file your return determines the tax rates that will apply to your taxable income; *see 1.2.* Filing status also determines the standard deduction you may claim if you do not itemize deductions *(see 13.1)* and your ability to claim certain other deductions, credits, and exclusions.

This chapter explains the five different filing statuses: single, married filing jointly, married filing separately, head of household, and qualifying widow(er). If you are married, filing a joint return is generally advantageous, but there are exceptions discussed in *1.3.* If you are unmarried and are supporting a child who lives with you, you may qualify as a head of household *(see 1.12)*, which will enable you to use more favorable tax rates than those allowed for single taxpayers. If you were widowed in either 2005 or 2004 and in 2006 a dependent child lived with you, you may be able to file as a qualifying widow(er) for 2006, which allows you to use joint return rates *(see 1.11)*.

Special filing situations, such as for children, nonresident aliens, and deceased individuals, are also discussed in this chapter.

Your personal or family status also determines the number of personal exemptions you may claim on your return. For 2006, each personal exemption you claim is the equivalent of a $3,300 deduction. Exemptions for children, parents, and other dependents are allowed if the tests in Chapter 21 are met.

Importance of Filing Status

1.1 Which Filing Status Should You Use?

Your filing status generally depends on whether you are married at the end of the year, and, if unmarried, whether you maintain a household for a qualifying dependent. The five filing statuses are: single, married filing jointly, married filing separately, head of household, and qualifying widow or widower.

If you are *married at the end of the year*, you may file jointly *(1.4)* or separately *(1.3)*. If you lived apart from your spouse for the last half of 2006 and your child lived with you, you may qualify as an "unmarried" head of household *(see 1.12)*, which allows you to apply more favorable tax rates than you could as a married person filing separately.

If you are *unmarried at the end of the year*, your filing status is single unless you meet the tests for a head of household or qualifying widow(er). Generally, you are a head of household if you pay more than 50% of the household costs for a dependent child or relative who lives with you, or a dependent parent, whether or not he or she lives with you; *see 1.12*. You generally are a qualifying widow(er) if you were widowed in 2004 or 2005 and in 2006 you pay more than 50% of the household costs for you and your dependent child; *see 1.11*. The tax rates for heads of households and for qualifying widow(er)s are more favorable than those for single taxpayers; *see 1.2*.

The filing status you use determines the tax rates that apply to your taxable income, as shown in *1.2*, as well as the standard deduction you may claim *(see 13.1)* if you do not itemize deductions. Certain other deductions, credits, or exclusions are also affected by filing status. For example, if you are married, certain tax benefits are only allowed if you file jointly, but more deductions overall may be allowed in certain cases if you file separately; *see 1.3*. The deduction for personal exemptions is phased out for high income taxpayers at levels based upon filing status; *see 21.12*.

Planning Reminder

Getting Married Can Raise Your Taxes

The so-called marriage penalty is faced by couples whose joint return tax liability exceeds the combined tax they would pay if single. This is generally the case where each spouse earns a substantial share of the total income. On the other hand, if one spouse has little or no income, there generally is a marriage bonus or singles penalty, as the couple's tax on a joint return is less than the sum of the tax liabilities that would be owed if they were single.

Tax legislation has reduced the marriage penalty by increasing the standard deduction for married couples filing jointly to double the amount allowed to a single person, and also making the 15% bracket *(see 1.2)* twice as wide.

Marital status determined at the end of the year. For federal tax purposes, a marriage means only a legal union between a man and a woman as husband and wife.

If you are divorced during the year under a final decree of divorce or separate maintenance, you are treated as unmarried for that whole year, assuming you have not remarried before the end of the year. For the year of the divorce, file as a single person unless you care for a child and qualify as a head of household under the rules at 1.12.

If at the end of the year you are living apart from your spouse, or you are separated under a provisional decree that has not yet been finalized, you are not considered divorced. If you care for a child and meet the other tests at *1.12*, you may file as an unmarried head of household. Otherwise, you must file a joint return or as a married person filing separately.

If at the end of the year you live together in a common law marriage that is recognized by the law of the state in which you live or the state where the marriage began, you are treated as married.

If your spouse dies during the year, you are treated as married for that entire year and may file a joint return for you and your deceased spouse, assuming you have not remarried before year's end; *see 1.10*.

1.2 Tax Rates Based on Filing Status

The most favorable tax brackets apply to married persons filing jointly and qualifying widow(er)s *(see 1.11)*, who also use the joint return rates. The least favorable brackets are those for married persons filing separately, but filing separately is still advisable for married couples in certain situations, as discussed in *1.3*. Table 1-1 on the next page compares 2006 tax rate brackets.

If you have children and are unmarried at the end of the year, do not assume that your filing status is single. If your child lives with you in a home you maintain, you generally may file as a head of household *(see 1.12)*, which allows you to use more favorable tax rates than a single person. If you were widowed in either of the two prior years and maintain a household for your dependent child, you generally may file as a qualified widow(er), which allows you to use favorable joint return rates; *see 1.11*.

If you are married at the end of the year but for the second half of the year you lived with your child apart from your spouse, and you and your spouse agree not to file jointly, you may use head of household tax rates, which are more favorable than those for married persons filing separately.

What is your top tax bracket? Your top marginal tax rate is 10%, 15%, 25%, 28%, 33%, or 35%, depending on your taxable income, as shown in Table 1-1. If your top bracket is 25%, for example, this means that each additional dollar of *ordinary* income (such as salary or interest income) will be taxed at 25% for regular income tax purposes.

The tax rate on qualified dividends and net capital gains *(5.3)* is generally lower than your top bracket rate on ordinary income. Qualified dividends are subject to a rate of 5% or 15%, depending on your top bracket, and net capital gains are also generally subject to a rate of 5% or 15% (depending on your top bracket), but the rate can be higher if you have 28% rate gains or unrecaptured Section1250 gains, as discussed in *5.3*.

To actually compute your 2006 regular income tax, you will either look up your tax in the Tax Table, use the Tax Computation Worksheet, or, if you have net capital gains or qualified dividends, use the Qualified Dividends and Capital Gain Tax Worksheet or Schedule D Tax Worksheet. Chapter 22 explains these alternatives.

AMT. In determining if you are subject to alternative minimum tax (AMT) on Form 6251, you generally apply either a 26% or 28% rate to your AMT taxable income (as reduced by the applicable AMT exemption), but the favorable regular tax rates for net capital gains and qualified dividends also apply for AMT purposes; *see 23.1*.

Table 1-1 Taxable Income Brackets for 2006

	10% bracket ends at—	*15% bracket ends at—*	*25% bracket ends at—*	*28% bracket ends at—*	*33% bracket ends at—*	*35% bracket applies to—*
Married filing separately	$ 7,550	$ 30,650	$ 61,850	$ 94,225	$ 168,275	over $ 168,275
Single	7,550	30,650	74,200	154,800	336,550	over 336,550
Head of household	10,750	41,050	106,000	171,650	336,550	over 336,550
Married filing jointly or Qualifying widow(er)	15,100	61,300	123,700	188,450	336,550	over 336,550

Married Taxpayers

1.3 Filing Separately Instead of Jointly

Filing a joint return saves taxes for a married couple where one spouse earns all, or substantially all, of the taxable income. If both you and your spouse earn taxable income, you should figure your tax on joint and separate returns to determine which method provides the lower tax.

Although your tax rate *(1.2)* will generally be higher on a separate return, filing separately may provide an overall tax savings (for both of you together) where filing separately allows you to claim more deductions. On separate returns, larger amounts of medical expenses, casualty losses, or miscellaneous deductions may be deductible because lower adjusted gross income floors apply. Unless one spouse earns substantially more than the other, separate and joint tax rates are likely to be the same, regardless of the type of returns filed. The Example on page 12 illustrates how filing separately can save you taxes.

Suspicious of your spouse's tax reporting? If you suspect that your spouse is evading taxes and may be liable on a joint return, you may want to file a separate return. By filing separately, you avoid liability for unpaid taxes due on a joint return, plus interest and penalties.

If you do file jointly and the IRS tries to collect tax due on the joint return from you personally, you may be able to avoid liability under the innocent spouse rules *(see 1.7)*. If you are no longer married to or are separated from the person with whom you jointly filed, you may be able to elect separate liability treatment *(see 1.8)*.

Standard deduction restriction on separate returns. Keep in mind that if you and your spouse file separately, both must either itemize or claim the standard deduction, which is $5,150 in 2006 for married persons filing separately *(13.3)*. Thus, if one spouse itemizes, the other spouse must also itemize even if he or she would get a larger deduction by taking the $5,150 standard deduction.

Planning Reminder

Switching From Separate to Joint Return

If you and your spouse file separate returns, you have three years from the due date (without extensions) to change to a joint return. If a joint return is filed, you may not change to separate returns once the due date has passed. The filing of separate or joint estimated tax installments (Chapter 27) does not commit you to a similar tax return.

Filing Tip

Can Filing Separately Avoid Exemption Phaseout or Itemized Deduction Reduction?

Filing separately will sometimes allow either you or your spouse to avoid part of the personal exemption phaseout *(21.12)* or the reduction to specified itemized deductions *(13.7)*. If you file jointly and have total 2006 adjusted gross income (AGI) exceeding $225,750, the exemption phaseout applies. If you file separately, the phaseout does not apply to the spouse reporting separate AGI of $112,875 or less. On the other hand, where your joint AGI is $225,750 or less, a spouse reporting AGI over $112,875 on a separate return will be subject to the phaseout although no phaseout would apply on a joint return.

If for 2006 you itemize deductions, the deductions for taxes, mortgage interest, charitable donations, and miscellaneous deductions are reduced if AGI exceeds $150,500 on a joint return, or exceeds $75,250 on a separate return. If you file separately, the reduction does not apply on a separate return showing AGI of $75,250 or less. Where joint AGI is $150,500 or less, a spouse filing separately with separate AGI over $75,250 is subject to the reduction although no reduction would apply on a joint return.

EXAMPLE

Mike Palmer's 2007 adjusted gross income (AGI) is $77,650, and Fran, his wife, has AGI of $60,000. Neither of them has dependents. Mike has unreimbursed medical expenses of $7,450 *(17.2)* before taking into account the 7.5% of AGI floor *(17.1)*; Fran's unreimbursed expenses are $1,000. A tornado damaged property owned by Mike in his own name, and he has a casualty loss of $19,265 prior to taking into account the 10% of AGI floor *(18.13)*. Mike has unreimbursed miscellaneous expenses of $2,853 and Fran has $500 prior to taking into account the 2% of AGI floor *(19.1)*. Mike has deductible mortgage interest expenses of $5,000 and Fran has $2,000. Mike's deductible state and local taxes are $2,499; Fran's are $1,000. If they file separately and Mike itemizes deductions, Fran must also itemize even if the standard deduction would give her a larger deduction; *see 13.3.*

As the example worksheet below shows, filing separate returns saves Mike and Fran an overall $2,063, because they can deduct more on separate returns. If they filed jointly, their deductible casualty loss would be substantially lower and they would receive no deduction for medical expenses because it would be eliminated by the adjusted gross income floor. If they file separately, the reduction of itemized deductions *(13.7)* applies to Mike but not Fran because only Mike's AGI exceeds the $75,250 threshold. If they file jointly, the reduction does not apply because their AGI is below the $150,500 threshold for joint returns. The phaseout of personal exemptions *(21.12)* does not apply regardless of how they file.

Item		*Mike (Separately)*	*Fran (Separately)*	*Joint Return*
1.	**AGI**	**$ 77,650**	**$ 60,000**	**$ 137,650**
2.	Medical expenses	7,450	1,000	8,450
	Less 7½% of AGI	5,824	4,500	10,324
	Allowable medical	1,626	0	0
3.	Taxes	2,499	1,000	3,499
4.	Mortgage interest	5,000	2,000	7,000
5.	Casualty loss	19,265	0	19,265
	Less 10% of AGI	7,765		13,765
	Allowable casualty	11,500		5,500
6.	Miscellaneous expenses	2,853	500	3,353
	Less 2% of AGI	1,553	1,200	2,753
	Allowable miscellaneous	1,300	0	600
7.	**Total itemized *(Lines 2–6)***	**21,925**	**3,000**	**16,599**
	Less reduction *(see 13.7)*	48	0	0
8.	**Net itemized**	**21,877**	**3,000**	**16,599**
9.	Personal exemptions	3,300	3,300	6,600
10.	**Net itemized plus exemptions**	**25,177**	**6,300**	**23,199**
11.	**Taxable income** *(Line 1 minus Line 10)*	52,473	53,700	114,451
12.	**Tax liability**	**9,676**	**9,989**	**21,728**
	Total tax filing separately			19,665
	Savings from filing separately			***2,063***

Joint return required for certain benefits. Also be aware that certain tax benefits may be claimed by married persons only if they file jointly.

If you want to take advantage of the $25,000 rental loss allowance *(10.2)* or the credit for the elderly and disabled (Chapter 34), you must file jointly unless you live apart for the whole year. You must file jointly to claim an IRA deduction for a nonworking spouse *(8.3)*. Roth IRA contributions generally may not be made by a married person filing separately because of an extremely low phase-out range *(8.20)*. You must file jointly to convert a traditional IRA to a Roth IRA *(8.21)*. A joint return is required to claim the Hope credit or Lifetime Learning credit *(33.7)*, the tuition and fees deduction *(33.13)*, or the deduction for student loan interest *(33.14)*. You must file jointly to claim the dependent care credit or the earned income credit (Chapter 25), unless you live apart for the last six months of the year.

Other restrictions may increase your tax if you file a separate return. In figuring whether you are subject to alternative minimum tax (AMT), your exemption amount is half that allowed to a joint return filer; *see 23.1*. Furthermore, if you receive Social Security benefits, 85% of your benefits are generally subject to tax on a separate return; *see* Chapter 34.

1.4 Filing a Joint Return

If you are married at the end of the year, you may file a joint return with your spouse. For federal tax purposes, a marriage means only a legal union between a man and woman as husband and wife. Filing jointly saves taxes for many married couples, but if you and your spouse both earn taxable income, in some cases overall tax liability is reduced by filing separately; *see 1.3*.

You may not file a 2006 joint return if you were divorced under a decree of divorce or separate maintenance that is *final* by the end of the year. You may file jointly if you separated during 2006 under an interlocutory (temporary or provisional) decree or order, so long as a final divorce decree was not entered by the end of the year. If during the period that a divorce decree is interlocutory you are permitted to remarry in another state, the IRS recognizes the new marriage and allows a joint return to be filed with the new spouse. However, courts have refused to allow a joint return where a new marriage took place in Mexico during the interlocutory period in violation of California law.

Both spouses generally liable on joint return but "innocent" spouse may be relieved of liability. When you and your spouse file jointly, each of you may generally be held individually liable for the entire tax due, plus interest and any penalties. The IRS may try to collect the entire amount due from you even if your spouse earned all of the income reported on the joint return, or even if you have divorced under an agreement that holds your former spouse responsible for the taxes on the joint returns you filed together. However, there are exceptions to this joint liability rule for "innocent" spouses and for divorced or separated persons.

You may be able to obtain *innocent spouse* relief where tax on your joint return was understated without your knowledge because your spouse omitted income or claimed erroneous deductions or tax credits. In such a case, you may make an innocent spouse election within two years from the time the IRS begins a collection effort from you for taxes due on the return. *See 1.7* for details on the innocent spouse rules.

Filing Tip

Spouse in Combat Zone

If your spouse is in a combat zone or a qualified hazardous duty area *(35.4)*, you can sign a joint return for your spouse. Attach a signed explanation to the return.

Furthermore, if you are divorced, legally separated, living apart or the spouse with whom you filed jointly has died, you may be able to avoid tax on the portion of a joint return deficiency that is allocable to your ex-spouse by making an election within two years of the time the IRS begins collection efforts against you. *See 1.8* for details on this separate liability election. You may make the separate liability election even if you apply for innocent spouse relief. In some cases, it may be easier to qualify for relief under the separate liability rules than under the innocent spouse rules because innocent spouse relief may be denied if you had "reason to know" that tax was understated on the joint return, whereas the IRS must show that you had "actual knowledge" of the omitted income or erroneous deductions or credits to deny a separate liability election.

Signing the joint return. Both you and your spouse must sign the joint return. Under the following rules, if your spouse is unable to sign, you may sign for him or her.

If, because of illness, your spouse is physically unable to sign the joint return, you may, with the oral consent of your spouse, sign his or her name on the return followed by the words "By _______, Husband (or Wife)." You then sign the return again in your own right and attach a signed and dated statement with the following information: (1) the type of form being filed, (2) the tax year, (3) the reason for the inability of the sick spouse to sign, and (4) that the sick spouse has consented to your signing.

To sign for your spouse in other situations, you need authorization in the form of a power of attorney, which must be attached to the return. IRS Form 2848 may be used.

If your spouse does not file, you may be able to prove you filed a joint return even if your spouse did not sign and you did not sign as your spouse's agent where:

- You intended it to be a joint return—your spouse's income was included (or the spouse had no income).

- Your spouse agreed to have you handle tax matters and you filed a joint return.
- Your answers to the questions on the tax return indicate you intended to file a joint return.
- Your spouse's failure to sign can be explained.

EXAMPLE

The Hills generally filed joint returns. In one year, Mr. Hill claimed joint return filing status and reported his wife's income as well as his own; in place of her signature on the return, he indicated that she was out of town caring for her sick mother. She did not file a separate return. The IRS refused to treat the return as joint. The Tax Court disagreed. Since Mrs. Hill testified that she would have signed had she been available, her failure to do so does not bar joint return status. The couple intended to make a joint return at the time of filing.

1.5 Nonresident Alien Spouse

If either you or your spouse was a nonresident alien *(1.16)* during any part of the year, a joint return may be filed only if both of you make a special election to be taxed on your worldwide income. Thus, if you are a U.S. citizen and your spouse is a nonresident alien at the beginning of the year who becomes a resident during the year, the special election to file jointly must be made.

If the election is not made, you may be able to claim your nonresident alien spouse as an exemption on a return filed as married filing separately, but only if the spouse had no income and could not be claimed as a dependent by another taxpayer; *see 21.2*. If the alien spouse becomes a resident before the beginning of the next tax year, you may file jointly for that year.

A couple who make the election must keep books and records of their worldwide income and give the IRS access to such books and records. If either spouse does not provide the necessary information to the IRS, the election is terminated. Furthermore, the election is terminated if either spouse revokes it or dies; revocation before the due date of the return is effective for that return. The election automatically terminates in the year following the year of the death of either spouse. However, if the survivor is a U.S. citizen or resident and has a qualifying child, he or she may be able to use joint return rates as a qualifying widow or widower in the two years following the year of the spouse's death; *see 1.11*. The election to file jointly also terminates if the couple is legally separated under a decree of divorce or separate maintenance. Termination is effective as of the beginning of the taxable year of the legal separation. If neither spouse is a citizen or resident for any part of the taxable year, an election may not be made and an existing election is suspended. If an election is suspended it may again become effective if either spouse becomes a U.S. citizen or resident. Once the election is terminated, neither spouse may ever again make the election to file jointly.

Electing to file a joint return does not terminate the special withholding on the nonresident alien's income.

Filing Tip

Election To File a Joint Return

Where a U.S. citizen or resident is married to a nonresident alien, the couple may file a joint return if both elect to be taxed on their worldwide income. The requirement that one spouse be a U.S. citizen or resident need be met only at the close of the year. Joint returns may be filed in the year of the election and all later years until the election is terminated.

Filing Tip

Nonresident Alien Becomes Resident

Where one spouse is a U.S. citizen or resident and the other is a nonresident alien who becomes a resident during the tax year, the couple may make a special election to file a joint return for that year and be taxed on their worldwide income. Thereafter, neither spouse may make the election again even if married to a new spouse. Tests for determining status as a resident or nonresident alien are at *1.18*.

1.6 Community Property Rules

If you live in Arizona, California, Idaho, Louisiana, Nevada, New Mexico, Texas, Washington, or Wisconsin, the income and property you and your spouse acquire during the marriage is generally regarded as community property. Community property means that each of you owns half of the community income and community property, even if legal title is held by only one spouse. But note that there are some instances in which community property rules are disregarded for tax purposes; these instances are clearly highlighted in the pertinent sections of this book.

Separate property may still be owned. Property owned before marriage generally remains separate property; it does not become community property when you marry. Property received during the marriage by one spouse as a gift or an inheritance from a third party is generally separate property. In some states, if the nature of ownership cannot be fixed, the property is presumed to be community property.

In some states, income from separate property may be treated as community property income. In other states, income from separate property remains the separate property of the individual owner.

Divorce or separation. If you and your spouse divorce, your community property automatically becomes separate property. A separation agreement or a decree of legal separation or of separate maintenance may or may not end the marital community, depending on state law.

Community income rules may not apply to separated couples. If a husband and wife in a community property state file separate returns, each spouse must generally report one-half of the community income. However, a spouse may be able to avoid reporting income earned by his or her spouse if they live apart during the entire calendar year and do not file a joint return.

To qualify, one or both spouses must have earned income for the year and none of that earned income may be transferred, directly or indirectly, between the spouses during the year. One spouse's payment to the other spouse solely to support the couple's dependent children is not a disqualifying transfer. If the separated couple qualifies under these tests, community income is allocated as follows:

- Earned income (excluding business or partnership income) is taxed to the spouse who performed the personal services.
- Business income (other than partnership income) is treated as the income of the spouse carrying on the business.
- Partnership income is taxed to the spouse entitled to a distributive share of partnership profits.

Innocent spouse rules apply to community property. As discussed above, community property rules may not apply to earned income where spouses live apart for the entire year and file separate returns. In addition, a spouse who files a separate return may be relieved of tax liability on community income that is attributable to the other spouse if he or she does not know (or have reason to know) about the income and if it would be inequitable under the circumstances for him or her to be taxed on such income. Even if you fail to qualify for such relief because you knew (or had reason to know) about the income, the IRS may relieve you of liability if it would be inequitable to hold you liable.

The IRS may disregard community property rules and tax income to a spouse who treats such income as if it were solely his or hers and who fails to notify the other spouse of the income before the due date of the return (including extensions).

Relief from liability on joint return. If you file jointly, you may elect to avoid liability under the innocent spouse rules discussed at *1.7* and the separate liability rules at *1.8*. In applying those rules, items that would otherwise be allocable solely to your spouse will not be partly allocated to you merely because of the community property laws.

Death of spouse. The death of a spouse dissolves the community property relationship, but income earned and accrued from community property before death is community income.

Moving from a community property to a common law (separate property) state. Most common law states (those which do not have community property laws) recognize that both spouses have an interest in property accumulated while residing in a community property state. If the property is not sold or reinvested, it may continue to be treated as community property. If you and your spouse sell community property after moving to a common law state and reinvest the proceeds, the reinvested proceeds are generally separate property, which you may hold as joint tenants or in another form of ownership recognized by common law states.

Moving from a common law to a community property state. Separate property brought into a community property state generally retains its character as separately owned property. However, property acquired by a couple after moving to a community property state is generally owned as community property. In at least one state (California), personal property that qualifies as community property is treated as such, even though it was acquired when the couple lived in a common law state.

Supporting a dependent with separate rather than community income. Filing a Form 2120 multiple support agreement is not necessary where either parent can prove that he or she has income that is considered separate income rather than community income; that parent may be able to satisfy the more-than-50% support test. In certain community property states, the law may provide that income of a husband and wife living apart is considered separate income rather than community income.

IRS Alert

Income Splitting Barred to California Registered Domestic Partner

In a 2006 legal memorandum, the IRS concluded that the community property income-splitting rule allowed to California spouses does not apply to registered domestic partners, despite the California law (effective in 2005) that extended to registered domestic partners community property rights and virtually all other spousal rights and responsibilities. Thus, a California registered domestic partner must report all of his or her earned income from personal services. He or she cannot report on a separate federal return only one-half of the combined income of both partners, as he or she could if married. According to the IRS, domestic partners under the new California law are not married and Supreme Court precedent allowing married couples in community property states to split income applies only to husbands and wives.

Avoiding or Limiting Liability on Joint Returns

1.7 Innocent Spouse Rules

Unless you qualify for relief, you are personally liable for any tax due on a joint return you have filed, whether you are still married to the spouse with whom you filed the joint return or you have since divorced or separated.

If you are still married and living with the same spouse, the only way to avoid personal liability on the joint return is to qualify as an innocent spouse under the rules in this section, or to apply for equitable relief from the IRS, discussed at *1.9*.

If you are divorced, legally separated, living apart, or your spouse has died, you may either seek relief under the innocent spouse rules below or you may be able to elect separate liability treatment as discussed at *1.8* or seek equitable relief *(1.9)* from the IRS.

Caution

Knowledge May Bar Innocent Spouse Relief

The IRS may try to defeat your claim for innocent spouse relief on the grounds that you knew, or should have known, that tax was understated on the joint return.

Qualifying tests for innocent spouse election. You must satisfy *all* of the following conditions to qualify for innocent spouse relief:

1. The tax shown on the joint return was understated due to the omission of income by your spouse, or erroneous deductions or credits claimed by your spouse.
2. When signing the joint return, you did not know and had no reason to know that tax on the return was understated.

   According to the IRS and Tax Court, where your claim for innocent spouse relief is based on the omission of income by your spouse, knowledge of the underlying transaction that produced the omitted income (such as a retirement distribution received by your spouse or an investment held by your spouse in his own name) is enough to bar your claim, even if you did not know that the amount of taxable income reported on the joint return was incorrect. The Courts of Appeal for both the Fifth Circuit and the District of Columbia Circuit agree with the Tax Court that knowledge of the underlying transaction that produced the omitted income defeats a claim for innocent spouse relief.

   The Tax Court may also hold that knowledge of the underlying transaction bars innocent spouse relief where the request for relief is based on improper deductions or tax credits attributed to the other spouse. However, in erroneous deduction (or credit) cases arising under prior law, most appeals courts held that relief should be denied under the knowledge test only if, given all the facts and circumstances, the spouse seeking relief knew or had reason to know that the deduction would result in a tax understatement, and this depends on his or her education level and involvement in the couple's financial affairs.

   Although the "knowledge" test continues to be a significant hurdle, partial relief may be available. If you knew or had reason to know that there was "some" tax understatement on the return but were unaware of the extent of the understatement, innocent spouse relief is available for the liability attributable to the portion of the understatement that you did not know about or have reason to know about.
3. Taking all the circumstances into account, it would be inequitable to hold you liable for the tax. This test also applied under prior law. In deciding the "equity" issue, the IRS and courts consider the extent to which you benefitted from the tax underpayment, beyond receiving normal support. Thus, it is possible to be held liable for a tax understatement that you did not know about or have reason to know about, on the grounds that you benefitted from the underpayment in the form of a high standard of living. The IRS will also consider whether you later divorced or were deserted by your spouse.
4. You file an innocent spouse election with the IRS on Form 8857.

Law Alert

IRS Must Notify Non-Electing Spouse

After the filing of Form 8857, the IRS is required to notify the non-electing spouse (or former spouse) of an electing spouse's request for relief and allow the non-electing spouse an opportunity to participate in the determination. If the IRS makes a preliminary determination granting full or partial relief to the electing spouse, the non-electing spouse may file a written protest and obtain an Appeals Office conference.

Election must be filed on Form 8857 to obtain relief. You must file an election on Form 8857 to claim innocent spouse relief. You do this by attaching a statement explaining why you qualify; follow the Form 8857 instructions. The election must be made no later than two years from the date that the IRS first begins collection activity (such as IRS garnishment of your wages) against you for tax due on the joint return. If the election is not made by the end of that two-year period, you will not be granted innocent spouse relief even if you meet the above qualification tests.

Planning Reminder

Deadline for Innocent Spouse Election

You have until two years from the date that the IRS first attempts to collect tax from you on the joint return to make an innocent spouse election.

Tax Court appeal. If the IRS denies your election for innocent spouse relief, you have 90 days to petition the Tax Court for review under the rules discussed at the end of *1.8*. If you petition the Tax Court, the non-electing spouse has the right to intervene in the proceeding.

Did your spouse fail to pay the tax due on a correct return? Innocent spouse relief applies to tax understatements; that is, where the amount of tax shown on a joint return is incorrect. If the proper amount of tax liability is shown on the return but not paid, innocent spouse relief is not available. However, the IRS can provide equitable relief where innocent spouse relief is unavailable and it would be unfair to hold you liable. *See 1.9.*

1.8 Separate Liability Election for Former Spouses

If the IRS attempts to collect the taxes due on a joint return from you and you have since divorced or separated, you may be able to avoid or at least limit your liability by filing a separate liability election on Form 8857. If you qualify, you will be liable only for the part of the tax liability (plus interest and any penalties) that is allocable to you. If you make the election and a tax deficiency is entirely allocable to your former spouse under the rules discussed below, you will not have to pay any part of it. However, you may *not* avoid liability for any part of a tax deficiency allocable to the other spouse if you had actual knowledge of the income or expense item that gave rise to the tax deficiency that the IRS is trying to collect. *See* below for details of the knowledge test.

Furthermore, you may not avoid liability to the extent that certain disqualified property transfers were made between you and the other spouse. An election may be completely denied for both spouses if transfers were made as part of a fraudulent scheme.

As with innocent spouse relief *(1.7)*, the separate liability election applies only to tax understatements where the proper tax liability was *not* shown on the joint return. If the proper liability was shown but not paid, equitable relief *(1.9)* may be requested.

Are you eligible for the separate liability election? You may make the separate liability election on Form 8857 if at the time of the election:

1. You are divorced or legally separated from the spouse with whom you filed the joint return, *or*
2. You have not lived with your spouse (with whom you filed the return) at any time in the 12-month period ending on the date you file the election, *or*
3. The spouse with whom you filed the joint return has died.

If you qualify under any of the above, you may make the separate liability election on Form 8857 by attaching a statement that identifies which items giving rise to the tax understatement are allocable to you and which are allocable to the other spouse. You do not have to actually compute your separate liability, however. You may make the separate liability election in addition to the innocent spouse election *(1.7)*.

Timing of the election. The separate liability election must be filed with the IRS on Form 8857 no later than two years after the IRS begins collection activities against you.

Actual knowledge of the item allocable to the other spouse bars relief. If you elect separate liability treatment and the IRS shows that at the time you signed the joint return you had actual knowledge of an erroneous item (omitted income or improper deduction or credit) that would otherwise be allocated to the other spouse, you may not avoid liability for the portion of a deficiency attributable to that item. However, if you signed the return under duress, separate liability is not barred despite your knowledge.

Caution

Actual Knowledge Bars Relief

The separate liability election generally allows you to avoid liability for the portion of a tax deficiency that is allocable to the other spouse. Such relief is unavailable, however, to the extent that you had actual knowledge of the omitted income or deducted item that gave rise to the tax deficiency.

The actual knowledge test is intended by Congress to be more favorable to the taxpayer than the "had reason to know" test under the innocent spouse rules *(1.7)*. Congressional committee reports state that the IRS is required to prove that an electing spouse had actual knowledge of an erroneous item and may not infer such knowledge. According to the Tax Court, the IRS must prove actual knowledge by a "preponderance of the evidence." If the IRS proves actual knowledge of an erroneous item, that item is treated as allocable to both spouses, so the IRS can collect that portion of the deficiency from either spouse.

However, there is a controversy as to how to apply the actual knowledge test. Taxpayers and commentators have argued that Congress intended separate liability relief to be available to a spouse unless she or he knew that the tax return was incorrect. The IRS position is that relief is barred to a spouse who had knowledge of the income or expenditure that gave rise to the tax deficiency, even if the electing spouse did not know that the entry on the return was incorrect. The Tax Court, the Fifth Circuit, and the District of Columbia Circuit agree with the IRS in cases involving omitted income; *see* Example 1 below.

In erroneous deduction cases, the Tax Court definition of "actual knowledge" is not as clear, but it has indicated that it will look at whether the electing spouse was aware of the "factual circumstances" that made the item nondeductible. If the electing spouse knew the factual basis for denial of the deduction, separate liability relief will be denied. In cases involving limited partnership tax-shelter deductions, the IRS may be unable to prove that an electing spouse had such disqualifying knowledge, but relief may still be partially denied if the spouse received a tax benefit from the deductions; *see* Example 3 below.

EXAMPLES

1. Cheshire knew that her husband had received an early retirement distribution. She knew that the distribution had been deposited into their joint account and used to pay off a mortgage, buy a truck, pay other family expenses and provide start-up capital for the husband's business. Cheshire's husband falsely told her that a CPA had determined that most of his retirement distribution was not taxable. After they divorced, Cheshire made a separate liability election to avoid tax on the unreported income. She claimed that she was entitled to relief because she did not know that the taxable amount of the retirement distribution had been misstated on their joint return. The Tax Court held that she could not obtain relief because she knew about the retirement distribution. It is immaterial that she did not know that the reporting of the distribution on the tax return was incorrect. The Court of Appeals for the Fifth Circuit affirmed. The District of Columbia Circuit has also denied a wife's claim for relief because she had actual knowledge of her husband's retirement income.
2. You file a joint return on which you report wages of $150,000 and your husband reports $30,000 of self-employment income. The IRS examines your return and determines that your husband failed to report $20,000 of income, resulting in a $9,000 deficiency. You file a separate liability election with the IRS after obtaining a divorce.

   Assume that the IRS proves that you had actual knowledge of $5,000 of the unreported income but not the other $15,000. You are liable for 25% of the deficiency, or $2,250, allocable to the $5,000 of income that you knew about ($2,250 = $5,000 × $20,000 × $9,000). Your former spouse is liable for the entire deficiency since the unreported income was his. The IRS can collect the entire deficiency from him, or can collect $2,250 from you and the balance from him.
3. Mora's husband arranged an investment in a cattle-breeding tax shelter partnership. He put the partnership in both of their names, although Mora did not sign any of the partnership papers. On their joint returns, they claimed partnership losses which turned out to be inflated; deductions were based on overvalued cattle. After their divorce, the IRS disallowed the partnership losses and Mora elected separate liability relief. The IRS refused, claiming that she participated in making the investment so the claimed losses were allocable to her as well as her husband. The Tax Court held that Mora was not involved in making the investment and so the partnership losses are allocable to the husband unless Mora knew the factual basis for the denial of the deductions or she received a tax benefit from the deductions. She did not know about the overvaluation of the cattle, which was the factual basis for the IRS's denial of the deductions. In fact, the IRS conceded that neither spouse understood the nature of their investment or the basis of the deductions. This may often be the case where passive investors claim deductions passed through to them by a limited partnership. For this reason, the IRS argued that the "knowledge of the factual basis" test makes it too easy for limited partnership investors to obtain relief. The Tax Court responded that the law does not distinguish between passive and active investments and there is no policy reason for the courts to create a distinction. Furthermore, although the husband also lacked knowledge of the factual basis for the disallowance of the losses, he cannot avoid liability for the deficiency since the erroneous deductions would be allocable to him on a separate return.

   Despite Mora's "win" on the actual knowledge issue, she remained partially liable for the deficiency because she received a tax benefit from the erroneous deductions. Under the tax benefit rule discussed below, the deductions first offset the income that would have been reported by the husband had he filed a separate return. The balance of the deductions benefitted Mora by reducing her separate return income. If she benefitted from 25% of the deductions, she would remain liable for 25% of the deficiency.

Allocating tax liability between spouses. Generally, if you make a separate liability election, you are liable only for the portion of the tax due on the joint return that is allocable to you, determined as if you had filed a separate return. If erroneous items (omitted income or improper deductions or credits) are allocable to the other spouse but you had actual knowledge of the items as discussed above, you cannot avoid liability and the IRS remains able to collect the tax due from either of you. Where deductions are allocable to the other spouse and you are not barred from relief by the actual knowledge test, you can still be held partially liable if you received a tax benefit from the deductions; *see* the discussion of the tax benefit rule below.

In general, the allocation of a tax deficiency depends on which spouse's "items" gave rise to the deficiency. The items may be omitted income or disallowed deductions or credits. Items are generally allocated to the spouse who would have reported them on a separate return. If a deficiency is based on unreported income, the deficiency is allocated to the spouse who earned the income. Income from a jointly owned business is allocated equally unless you provide evidence that more should be allocated to the other spouse. Similarly, if a deficiency is based on the denial of personal deductions, the deficiency is allocated equally between you unless you show that a different allocation is appropriate. A deficiency based on the denial of business deductions is allocated according to your respective ownership shares in the business. If the IRS can show fraud, it can reallocate joint return items.

On Form 8857, you do *not* have to figure the portion of the deficiency for which you are liable. The IRS will figure your separate liability (and any related interest and penalties). However, you can use a worksheet in IRS Publication 971 to figure your separate liability.

EXAMPLES

1. After you obtain a divorce, the IRS examines a joint return you filed with your former husband and assesses a tax deficiency attributable to income he failed to report. If you did not know about the omitted income and timely elect separate liability treatment, you are not liable for any part of the tax deficiency, which is entirely allocable to your former husband who earned the income. You are not liable even if the IRS is unable to collect the tax from your former husband and you have substantial assets from which the tax could be paid.
2. The IRS assesses a joint return deficiency attributable to $35,000 of income that your former spouse failed to report and $15,000 of disallowed deductions that you claimed. Both of you may make the separate liability election and limit your respective liabilities.

   If you make the election, your liability will be limited to 30% of the deficiency, as your disallowed deductions of $15,000 are 30% of the $50,000 of items causing the deficiency. If your former husband makes the election, he will be liable for the remaining 70% of the deficiency (his $35,000 of unreported income is 70% of the $50,000 of items causing the deficiency).

   If either of you does not make the election, the non-electing person could be held liable for 100% of the deficiency unless innocent spouse relief is available or the IRS grants equitable relief.

Planning Reminder

Unpaid Tax on Correct Return

The separate liability election is not available where the proper amount of tax was reported on a joint return but your spouse did not pay the tax. However, equitable relief *(1.9)* may be available in this type of tax underpayment situation.

Tax benefit rule limits relief based on erroneous deductions or credits. The tax benefit limitation is an exception to the general rule that allocates items between the spouses as if separate returns had been filed. If you received a tax benefit from an erroneous deduction or credit that is allocable to the other spouse, you remain liable for the proportionate part of the deficiency. You are treated as having received a tax benefit if the disallowed deduction exceeded the income that would have been reported by the other spouse on a hypothetical separate return.

EXAMPLE

On a joint return, you report wages of $100,000 and your husband reports $15,000 of self-employment income. You divorce the following year. The IRS examines the return and disallows a $20,000 business expense deduction claimed by your former husband, resulting in a $5,600 tax deficiency. Of the $20,000 deduction, $15,000 is allocable to your former husband as that amount offset his entire income. The $5,000 balance offset your separate income and thereby gave you a tax benefit. Your former husband will be liable for 75% of the deficiency ($4,200) and you will be liable for the 25% balance ($1,400).

If your former husband had reported income of $30,000 instead of $15,000, you would not be liable for any part of the deficiency under the tax benefit rule. The deduction is attributed entirely to his income, so the entire deficiency is allocated to him.

These allocations assume that the IRS does not show that you had "actual knowledge" (*see* above) of the deductions attributable to your former husband. To the extent you had such knowledge, the deductions are allocable to both of you, so both of you remain liable for that part of the deficiency.

Transfers intended to avoid tax. You may be held liable for more than your allocable share of a deficiency if a disqualified asset transfer was made to you by your spouse with a principal purpose of avoiding tax. Transfers made to you within the one-year period preceding the date on which the IRS sends the first letter of proposed deficiency are presumed to have a tax avoidance purpose unless they are pursuant to a divorce decree or decree of separate maintenance. You may rebut the presumption by showing that tax avoidance was not the principal purpose of the transfer. If the tax avoidance presumption is not rebutted, the transfer is considered a disqualified transfer and the value of the transferred asset adds to your share of the liability as otherwise determined under the above election rules.

If the IRS proves that you and your former spouse transferred assets between you as part of a fraudulent scheme, neither of you will be allowed to make the separate liability election; both of you will remain individually liable for the entire joint return deficiency.

Appeal to Tax Court. You may petition the Tax Court if the IRS disputes your election or your allocation of liability. The petition must be filed within 90 days of the date on which the IRS mails a determination to you by registered or certified mail if the IRS mailing is within six months of the filing of the election. If an IRS notice is not mailed within the six-month period, a Tax Court petition may be filed without waiting for an IRS response or, if you do wait, you have until 90 days after the date the IRS mails the notice to file the petition.

The IRS may not take any collection action against you during the 90-day period and if the Tax Court petition is filed, the suspension lasts until a final court decision is made.

1.9 Equitable Relief

The IRS may grant equitable relief for liability on a joint return where innocent spouse relief *(1.7)* and separate liability *(1.8)* are not available. For example, the separate liability election and innocent spouse relief are not available where the proper amount of tax was reported on a joint return but your spouse failed to pay the tax owed. If you signed a correct return on which tax was owed and, without your knowledge, your spouse used the funds intended for payment of the tax for other purposes, the IRS may grant you equitable relief. A request for equitable relief is made on Form 8857. The IRS may also grant equitable relief in cases where the proper amount of tax was understated on the joint return if it would be inequitable to hold you liable.

Threshold conditions you must meet for relief. There are seven conditions, each of which must be met, before the IRS will even consider granting you equitable relief:

1. You filed a joint return for the year that relief is sought.
2. Relief is not available under the innocent spouse *(1.7)* or separate liability election *(1.8)* rules.
3. You filed the request for relief on Form 8857 no later than two years after the IRS's first collection activity after July 22, 1998.
4. No assets were transferred between you and your spouse as part of a fraudulent scheme.
5. Your spouse did not transfer assets to you for the purpose of tax avoidance. If there was such a transfer, relief can be granted only to the extent income tax liability exceeds the value of these assets.
6. You did not file or fail to file the return with fraudulent intent.
7. The income tax liability for which you are seeking relief is attributable to the other spouse (with whom the joint return was filed). There are exceptions to this requirement if community property law applies, you have nominal ownership of property subject to a deficiency, the other spouse misappropriated funds intended for payment of the tax without your knowledge, or you did not challenge the treatment of items on the joint return because of prior abuse that made you fear retaliation by the other spouse.

Safe harbor for tax liability reported on return but unpaid. The IRS will ordinarily grant you equitable relief for unpaid tax liability if when you filed for relief you were divorced, legally separated, or living apart from the other spouse for the 12-month period before your request, and both of the following tests are also met: (1) you would face economic hardship if forced to pay the tax, meaning that you would be unable to meet reasonable basic living expenses, and (2) you can show that at the time the joint return was filed, it was reasonable for you to believe that the other spouse would pay the tax liability.

Factors the IRS will consider. If the threshold conditions are satisfied and you do not qualify for relief under the safe harbor discussed in the preceding paragraph, you must convince the IRS that equitable relief is appropriate. The IRS will consider all the facts and circumstances.

The following is a nonexclusive list of factors that the IRS will take into account in determining whether to grant equitable relief: whether you are separated or divorced from the other spouse, whether you would suffer economic hardship (*i.e.*, be unable to meet basic living expenses), whether the other spouse was legally obligated to pay the outstanding liability, whether you received any significant benefit from the unpaid tax or item giving rise to the deficiency (beyond normal support), whether you have made a good faith effort to comply with the tax laws in later years. The case for relief is strengthened if there was a history of abuse by the other spouse or you were in poor health (physical or mental) at the time the return was filed.

The IRS will also consider whether you had knowledge or constructive knowledge (reason to know) that should bar relief. If the tax was properly reported but not paid, the IRS will look at whether you knew or had reason to know that it would not be paid by the other spouse. If the liability results from an IRS deficiency notice, the issue is whether you knew or had reason to know of the item (omitted income or erroneous deduction or credit) giving rise to the deficiency. Actual knowledge strongly weighs against relief, although relief may still be granted in limited cases where there are compelling grounds. If you had constructive knowledge—reason to know—of the item giving rise to the deficiency, this is considered a factor weighing against relief but it is not weighed more heavily than other factors. In determining constructive knowledge, the IRS will look at your level of education, your involvement in family finances and business matters, whether the other spouse deceived you, and whether there was an increase in lavish or unusual expenditures.

How Widows and Widowers File

1.10 Death of Your Spouse in 2006

If your spouse died in 2006, you are considered married for the whole year. If you did not remarry in 2006, you may file a 2006 joint return for you and your deceased spouse. Generally, you file a joint return with the executor or administrator. But you alone may file a joint return if you are otherwise entitled to file jointly and:

1. The deceased did not file a separate return, and
2. Someone other than yourself has not been appointed as executor or administrator before the due date for filing the return. An executor or administrator appointed after the joint return is filed may revoke the joint return within the one-year period following the due date.

If you do file jointly, you include on the return all of your income and deductions for the full year and your deceased spouse's income and deductions *up to the date of death (see 1.14)*.

For 2007 and 2008, you may be able to file as a qualifying widow(er) if a dependent child lives with you; *see 1.11*.

Filing Instruction

Reporting Income of Deceased Spouse

If your spouse died during the year and you are filing a joint return, include his or her income earned through the date of death.

Joint return barred. As a surviving spouse, you may not file a joint return for you and your deceased spouse if:

1. You remarry before the end of the year of your spouse's death. In this case you may file jointly with your new spouse. A final return for the deceased spouse must be filed by the executor or administrator using the filing status of married filing separately.
2. You or your deceased spouse has a short year because of a change in annual accounting period.
3. Either of you was a nonresident alien at any time during the tax year; but *see 1.5*.

Executor or administrator may revoke joint return. If an executor or administrator is later appointed, he or she may revoke a joint return that you alone have filed by filing a separate return for the decedent. Even if you have properly filed a joint return for you and the deceased spouse (as just discussed), the executor or administrator is given the right to revoke the joint return. But a state court held that a co-executrix could not refuse to sign a joint return where it would save the estate money.

To revoke the joint return, the executor must file a separate return within one year of the due date (including extensions). The executor's separate return is treated as a late return; interest charges and a late filing penalty apply. The joint return that you filed is deemed to be your separate return. Tax on that return is recalculated by excluding items belonging to your deceased spouse.

Planning Reminder

Possible Estate Insolvency

If you will be appointed executor or administrator and are concerned about estate insolvency, it may be advisable to hedge as follows: (1) File separate returns. If it is later seen that a joint return is preferable, you have three years to change to a joint return. (2) File jointly but postpone being appointed executor or administrator until after the due date of the joint return. In this way, the joint return may be disaffirmed if the estate cannot cover its share of the taxes.

Signing the return. A joint return reporting your deceased spouse's income should list both of your names. Where there is an executor or administrator, the return is signed by you as the surviving spouse and the executor or administrator in his or her official capacity. If you are the executor or administrator, sign once as surviving spouse and again as the executor or administrator. Where there is no executor or administrator, you sign the return, followed by the words "filing as surviving spouse."

Surviving spouse's liability. If a joint return is filed and the estate cannot pay its share of the joint income tax liability, you, as the surviving spouse, may be liable for the full amount. Once the return is filed and the filing date passes, you can no longer change the joint return election and file a separate return unless an administrator or executor is appointed after the due date of the return.

In that case, as previously discussed, the executor may disaffirm the joint return.

1.11 Qualifying Widow(er) Status If Your Spouse Died in 2005 or 2004

If your spouse died in either 2005 or 2004 and you meet the following three requirements, your 2006 filing status is *qualifying widow or widower*, which allows you to use joint return rates on an individual return.

1. You did not remarry before 2007 (if you did remarry, you may file a 2006 joint return with your new spouse).
2. You may claim as your dependent (*see* Chapter 21) in 2006 a child, stepchild, or adopted child who lived with you during 2006 and you paid over half the cost of maintaining your home. The child must live with you for the entire year, not counting temporary absences such as to attend school or take a vacation. A foster child is not considered your child for purposes of these rules.
3. You were entitled to file jointly in the year of your spouse's death, even if you did not do so.

If you meet all these tests and do not itemize deductions (Schedule A, Form 1040), use the standard deduction for married couples filing jointly *(13.1)*. Use the IRS Tax Table or Tax Computation Worksheet for qualifying widows or widowers, the same one used by married couples filing jointly; *see 1.2*.

Spouse's death before 2004. If your spouse died before 2004 and you did not remarry before 2007, you may be able to use head of household rates for 2006 if you qualify under the rules discussed in *1.12*.

Filing as Head of Household

Filing Tip

Advantages of Head of Household Status

Tax rates are lower for a head of household than for those filing as single. The standard deduction is also higher. For a married person who lived apart from his or her spouse during the last half of the year, qualifying as a head of household allows use of tax rates that are more favorable than those for married persons filing separately.

1.12 Qualifying as Head of Household

You can file as "head of household" for 2006 if you are unmarried at the end of 2006 and you maintained a household for your child, parent, or other qualifying relative. You must be a U.S. citizen or resident *(see 1.18)* for the entire year. Tax rates are lower for a head of household than for a person filing as single *(see 1.2)* and the standard deduction is higher (*see* Chapter 13). If you are married but for the last half of 2006 you lived apart from your spouse, you may be treated as unmarried and able to qualify for head of household tax rates and standard deduction, which are more favorable than those for a married person filing separately; *see* Test 1 below.

Head of household tests. You must meet both of these tests to qualify as a head of household:

1. You were unmarried at the end of the year or treated as unmarried.
2. You paid more than half of the year's maintenance costs for the home of a qualifying person. A qualifying person other than your parent must live with you in that same house for over half the year, disregarding temporary absences. A qualifying parent does not have to live with you.

Details of the tests are in the following paragraphs.

Test 1: Are you unmarried? You are "unmarried" for 2006 head of household purposes if you are any one of the following:

- *Single as of the end of 2006.*
- *A widow or widower and your spouse died before 2006.* If a dependent child lives with you, *see 1.11* to determine if you may use the even more advantageous filing status of qualifying widow(er). If your spouse died in 2006, you are treated as married for the entire year and *cannot* qualify as a 2006 head of household, but a joint return may be filed; *see 1.10*.
- *Legally separated or divorced under a final court decree as of the end of 2006.* A custody and support order does not qualify as a legal separation. A provisional decree (not final), such as a support order

pendente lite (while action is pending) or a temporary order, has no effect for tax purposes until the decree is made final.

- *Married but living apart from your spouse.* You are considered unmarried for 2006 head of household purposes if your spouse was not a member of your household during the last six months of 2006, you file separate returns, and you maintain a household for more than half the year for a dependent child, stepchild, or adopted child. You are not considered to be "living apart" if you and your spouse lived under the same roof during the last six months of the year. A foster child qualifies if he or she was placed with you by an authorized placement agency, or by a court judgment, decree, or order. You must be able to claim the child as a dependent unless your spouse (the noncustodial parent) has the right to the exemption under the rules in *21.7*.
- *Married to an individual who was a nonresident alien during any part of 2006 and you do not elect to file a joint return reporting your joint worldwide income (1.5).*

Note: Same-sex marriages are *not* recognized as marriages under the federal tax law.

Test 2: Did you maintain a home for a qualifying person? You must pay more than half the costs of maintaining a home for a qualifying person.

Qualifying person. A child or relative can be your qualifying person for head of household purposes only if he or she is a qualifying child or relative under the exemption rules for dependents at *21.1*. However, you may be eligible for head of household status even if you are unable to actually claim the person as your dependent. For example, an unmarried child who meets the definition of a qualifying child *(21.1)* but who cannot be claimed as your dependent because of one of the disqualifiers at *21.1* is nonetheless a qualifying person for head of household purposes. If, under the special rules at *21.7* for divorced or separated parents, you are the custodial parent and you waive your right to the exemption for your child in favor of the other parent, you may claim head of household status; the other parent may not.

A married child must be your dependent to be a qualifying person for head of household purposes unless the only reason you cannot claim the dependency exemption for the child is that you are the dependent of another taxpayer; *see 21.1*.

Your parent or any other qualifying relative can be your qualifying person for head of household purposes only if you can claim an exemption for him or her as your dependent under *21.1*. However, even if you can claim the exemption, you are not eligible for head of household status if the relative is your dependent only because (1) you have a multiple support agreement granting you the right to the exemption *(21.6)* or (2) he or she is your qualifying relative under the member-of-household test *(21.4)*.

Maintaining a household. For a qualifying person other than your parent, the home that you maintain must be the principal residence for both of you for more than half the year, disregarding temporary absences; *see* Example 2 below. If the qualifying person is your parent, it does not matter where he or she lives, so long as you pay more than half of the household costs.

You must pay for more than half of the rent, property taxes, mortgage interest, utilities, repairs, property insurance, domestic help, and food eaten in the home. Do not consider the rental value of the lodgings provided to the qualifying person or the cost of clothing, medical expenses, education, vacation costs, life insurance, or transportation you provide, or the value of your work around the house.

Temporary absences disregarded. In determining whether you and a qualifying person lived in the same home for more than half the year, temporary absences are ignored if the absence is due to illness, or being away at school, on a business trip, on vacation, serving in the military, or staying with a parent under a child custody agreement. The IRS requires that it be reasonable to expect your qualifying child or relative to return to your household after such a temporary absence, and that you continue to maintain the household during the temporary absence. Under this rule, you would lose the right to file as head of household if your qualifying person moved into his or her own permanent residence before the end of the year.

EXAMPLES

1. Your mother lived with your sister in your sister's apartment, which cost $12,000 to maintain in 2006. Of this amount, you contributed $7,000 and your sister $5,000. Your mother has no income and did not contribute any funds to the household. You qualify as head of household for 2006 because you paid over half the cost of maintaining the home for your mother, who qualifies as your dependent *(21.1)*. A child or dependent relative other than your parent would have to live with you to enable you to file as head of household.

Planning Reminder

Special Separate Household Rule for Parent

If your dependent parent is the qualifying person, you may claim head of household status even if he or she does not live with you. You must pay over half of your parent's household expenses, whether your parent lives alone, with someone else, or in a senior citizens' residence.

2. Doctors advised McDonald that her mentally ill son might become self-sufficient if he lived in a separate residence, but one nearby enough for her to provide supervision. She took the advice and kept up a separate home for her son that was about a mile from her own home. She frequently spent nights at his home and he at hers. The Tax Court agreed with the IRS that McDonald could not file as head of household since her principal residence was not the same as her son's.

Tax Returns for Children

Law Alert

Kiddie Tax for Children Under Age 18

Children who are under age 18 at the end of 2006 generally must use Form 8615 to figure their 2006 tax if they had more than $1,700 of investment income; *see 24.3.* On Form 8615, the investment earnings over $1,700 are taxed at the parent's top tax rate. However, in certain cases under the rules of *24.5*, parents may elect to report their children's investment income on their own return using Form 8814.

1.13 Filing for Your Child

The income of your minor child is *not* included on your return unless you make a special election to report a child's investment income under the rules of *24.5.* A minor is considered a taxpayer in his or her own right. If the child is required to file a return but is unable to do so because of age or for any other reason, the parent or guardian is responsible for filing the return.

A tax return must be filed for a dependent child who had more than $850 of investment income and no earned income (for personal services) for 2006. If your child had only earned income (for personal services) and no investment income, a tax return must be filed if the earned income exceeded $5,150. *See* page 4 for further filing threshold rules.

If the child is unable to sign the return, the parent or guardian should sign the child's name in the proper place, followed by the words, "by [signature], parent [or guardian] for minor child." A parent is liable for tax due on pay earned by the child for services, but not on investment income.

A child who is not required to file a return should still do so for a refund of taxes withheld.

Social Security numbers. A parent or guardian must obtain a Social Security number for a child before filing the child's first income tax return. The child's Social Security number must also be provided to banks, brokers, and other payers of interest and dividends to avoid penalties and backup withholding; *see 26.12.* To obtain a Social Security number, file Form SS-5 with your local Social Security office. If you have applied for a Social Security number but not yet received it by the filing due date, write "applied for" on the tax return in the space provided for the number.

Whether or not you are filing a return for a child, you must obtain and report on your return a Social Security number for a child whom you are claiming as a dependent; *see 21.11.*

Wages you pay your children. You may deduct wages paid to your children in your business. Keep records showing that their activities are of a business rather than personal nature.

Withholding for children. Children with wages are generally subject to withholding and should file Form W-4 with their employer. An exemption from withholding may be claimed only in limited cases. The child must certify on Form W-4 that he or she had no federal tax liability in the prior year and expects no liability in the current year for which the withholding exemption is sought. For example, on Form W-4 for 2006, a child with investment income exceeding $300 who expected to be claimed as another taxpayer's dependent could claim an exemption from withholding only if the expected amount of investment income plus wages was $850 or less (this amount may change annually).

Wages you pay to your own children under age 18 for working in your business are not subject to FICA taxes (Social Security and Medicare); *see 26.9.*

Filing for a Deceased or Incompetent Person

1.14 Return for Deceased

When a person dies, another tax-paying entity is created—the decedent's estate. Until the estate is fully distributed, it will generally earn income for which a return must be filed. For example, Carlos Perez dies on June 30, 2006. The wages and bank interest he earned through June 30 are reported on his final income tax return, Form 1040, which is due by April 16, 2007. Interest earned on his bank account after June 30 is attributed to the estate, or to the account beneficiary if the right to the account passes by law directly to the account beneficiary. Income received by the estate is reported on Form 1041, the income tax return for the estate, if the estate has gross income of $600 or more. If Carlos was married, his surviving spouse could file a joint return *(1.10)* for 2006 and include all of Carlos's earnings through June 30. If she jointly owned the bank account with Carlos, the interest after as well as before June 30 could be reported on their joint return.

What income tax returns must be filed on behalf of the deceased? If the individual died after the close of the taxable year but before the income tax return was filed, the following must be filed:

1. Income tax return for the prior year;
2. Final income tax return, covering earnings in the period from the beginning of the taxable year to the date of death; *and*
3. Estate income tax return, covering earnings in the period after the decedent's death.

If the individual died after filing a return for the prior tax year, then only 2 and 3 are filed.

EXAMPLE

Steven Jones died on January 31, 2007, before he could file his 2006 tax return. His 2006 income tax return must be filed by April 16, 2007, unless an extension is obtained. A final income tax return to report earnings from January 1, 2007, through January 31, 2007, will have to be filed by April 15, 2008. Jones's estate will have to file an income tax return on Form 1041 to report earnings and other income that were not earned by Jones before February 1, 2007, unless the gross income of the estate is under $600.

Who is responsible for filing? The executor, administrator, or other legal representative is responsible for filing all returns. For purposes of determining whether a final income tax return for the decedent is due, the annual gross income test at page 3 is considered in full. You do not prorate it according to the part of the year the decedent lived. A surviving spouse may assume responsibility for filing a joint return for the year of death if no executor or administrator has been appointed and other tests are met *(1.10)*. However, if a legal representative has been appointed, he or she must give the surviving spouse consent to file a joint return for the year of the decedent's death. In one case, a state court held that a co-executrix could not refuse consent and was required to sign a joint return where it would save the estate money.

How do you report the decedent's income and deductions? You follow the method used by the decedent during his or her life, either the cash method or the accrual method, to account for the income up to the date of death. The income does not have to be put on an annual basis. Each item is taxed in the same manner as it would have been taxed had the decedent lived for the entire year.

If the decedent owned U.S. Savings Bonds, *see 4.29*.

When one spouse dies in a community property state *(1.6)*, how should the income from the community property be reported during the administration of the estate? The IRS says that half the income is the estate's and the other half belongs to the surviving spouse.

Deductible expenses paid (or accrued under the accrual method) by the decedent before death are claimed on the final return.

Medical expenses of the decedent. If the estate pays the decedent's personal medical expenses (not those for the decedent's dependents) within one year of the date of death, the expenses can be deducted on the decedent's final return, subject to the regular 7.5% of adjusted gross income floor *(17.8)*. However, the expenses are not deductible for income tax purposes if they are deducted for estate tax purposes. To deduct such medical expenses on the decedent's final return, a statement must be attached to the final return affirming that no estate tax deduction has been taken and that the rights to the deduction have been waived.

Partnership income. The death of a partner closes the partnership tax year for that partner. The final return for the partner must include his or her distributive share of partnership income and deductions for the part of the partnership's tax year ending on the date of death. Thus, if a partner dies on July 26, 2006, and the partnership's taxable year ends December 31, 2006, the partner's final 2006 return must include partnership items for January 1, 2006 through July 26, 2006. Partnership items for the balance of 2006 must be reported by the partner's executor or other successor in interest on the estate's income tax return.

Filing Instruction

IRD Not Included on Decedent's Final Return

Do not report on the decedent's final return income that is received after his or her death, or accrues after or because of death if the decedent used the accrual method. This income is considered "income in respect of a decedent," or IRD *(11.16)*. IRD is taxed to the estate or beneficiary receiving the income in the year of the receipt. On the decedent's final return, only deductible expenses paid up to and including the date of death may be claimed. If the decedent reported on the accrual basis, those deductions accruable up to and including the date of death are deductible. If a check for payment of a deductible item was delivered or mailed before the date of the decedent's death, a deduction is allowable on the decedent's last return, even though the check was not cashed or deposited until after the decedent's death. If the check was not honored by the bank, the item is not deductible.

Planning Reminder

Promptly Closing the Estate

To expedite the closing of the decedent's estate, an executor or other personal representative of the decedent may file Form 4810 for a prompt assessment. Once filed, the IRS has 18 months to assess additional taxes. The request does not extend the assessment period beyond the regular limit, which is three years from the date the return was filed. Form 4810 must be filed separately from the final return.

Exemptions allowed on a final return. These are generally the same exemptions the decedent would have had if he or she had not died; *see 21.1.* You do not reduce the exemptions because of the shorter taxable year.

Estimated taxes. No estimated tax need be paid by the executor after the death of an unmarried individual; the entire tax is paid when filing the final tax return. But where the deceased and a surviving spouse paid estimated tax jointly, the rule is different. The surviving spouse is still liable for the balance of the estimated tax unless an amended estimated tax voucher is filed. Further, if the surviving spouse plans to file a joint return *(1.10)* that includes the decedent's income, estimated tax payments may be required; *see* Chapter 27.

Where the estate has gross income, estimated tax installments are not required on Form 1041-ES for the first two years after the decedent's death.

Signing the return. An executor or administrator of the estate signs the return. If it is a joint return, *see 1.10.*

When a refund is due on a final return. The decedent's final return may also be used as a claim for a refund of an overpayment of withheld or estimated taxes. Form 1310 may be used to get the refund, but the form is not required if you are a surviving spouse filing a joint return for the year your spouse died. If you are an executor or administrator of the estate and you are filing Form 1040, 1040A, or 1040EZ for the decedent, you do not need Form 1310, but you must attach to the return a copy of the court certificate showing your appointment as personal representative.

Itemized deduction for IRD subject to estate tax. Items of gross income that the decedent had a right to receive but did not receive before death (or accrue if under the accrual method) are subject to income tax when received by the estate or beneficiary. This "income in respect of a decedent," or IRD, is also included in the decedent's estate for estate tax purposes. If estate tax is paid, an individual beneficiary may claim an itemized deduction for an allocable share of the estate tax paid on IRD items; *see 11.17* for deduction details.

1.15 Return for an Incompetent Person

A legal guardian of an incompetent person files Form 1040 for an incompetent whose gross income meets the filing tests on page 3. Where a spouse becomes incompetent, the IRS says the other spouse may file a return for the incompetent without a power of attorney, if no legal guardian has been appointed. For example, during the period an individual was in a mental hospital, and before he was adjudged legally incompetent, his wife continued to operate his business. She filed an income tax return for him and signed it for him although she had no power of attorney. The IRS accepted the return as properly filed. Until a legal guardian was appointed, she was charged with the care of her husband and his property.

The IRS has accepted a joint return filed by a wife in her capacity as legal guardian for her missing husband. However, the Tax Court has held that where one spouse is mentally incompetent, a joint return may not be filed because the incompetent spouse was unable to consent to a joint return; an appeals court agreed.

How Resident and Nonresident Aliens File

1.16 How a Nonresident Alien Is Taxed

A nonresident alien is generally taxed only on income from U.S. sources. A nonresident alien's income that is effectively connected with a U.S. business and capital gains from the sale of U.S. real property interests are subject to tax at regular U.S. rates. Other capital gains are not taxed unless a nonresident alien has a U.S. business or is in the U.S. for 183 days during the year. Generally, investment income of a nonresident alien from U.S. sources that is not effectively connected with a U.S. business is subject to a 30% tax rate (or lower rate if provided by treaty).

Nonresident aliens who are required to file must do so on Form 1040NR. If you are a nonresident alien, get a copy of IRS Publication 519, U.S. Tax Guide for Aliens. It explains how nonresident aliens pay U.S. tax.

Dual status. In the year a person arrives in or departs from the U.S., both resident and nonresident status may apply.

Caution

Who Is a Resident?

An alien's mere presence in the U.S. does not make him or her a "resident." An alien is generally treated as a "resident" only if he or she is a lawful permanent resident who has a "green card" or meets a substantial presence test; *see 1.18.*

EXAMPLE

On May 1, 2006, Leon Marchand arrived on a non-immigrant visa and was present in the U.S. for the rest of the year. From January 1 to April 30, 2006, he is a nonresident; from May 1 to the end of the year, he is a resident, under the 183-day test *(1.18)*. Despite "dual status," he does not file two returns. Since he is a U.S. resident on the last day of the year, he files Form 1040 and reports income on the basis of his status for each part of the year. He writes "Dual-Status Return" across the top of the Form 1040. The income for the nonresident portion of the year should be shown on Form 1040NR (or, if eligible, Form 1040NR-EZ) and "Dual-Status Statement" marked across the top.

Certain restrictions apply to dual status taxpayers. For example, a joint return may not be filed, unless you and your spouse agree to be taxed as U.S. residents for the entire year.

For details on filing a return for a dual status year, *see* IRS Publication 519 and the instructions to Form 1040NR.

1.17 How a Resident Alien Is Taxed

A resident alien *(1.18)* is taxed on worldwide income from all sources, just like a U.S. citizen. The exclusion for foreign earned income may be claimed if the foreign physical presence test is satisfied or if the bona fide residence test is met by an individual residing in a treaty country; *see 36.5*. A resident alien may generally claim a foreign tax credit; *see 36.14*. A resident alien's pension from a foreign government is subject to regular U.S. tax. A resident alien working in the United States for a foreign government is not taxed on the wages if the foreign government allows a similar exemption to U.S. citizens.

1.18 Who Is a Resident Alien?

The following tests determine whether an alien is taxed as a U.S. resident. Intent to remain in the U.S. is not considered.

You are treated as a resident alien and taxed as a U.S. resident for 2006 tax purposes if you meet either of the following tests:

1. You have been issued a "green card," which grants you the status of lawful permanent resident. If you were outside the U.S. for part of 2006 and then became a lawful permanent resident, *see* the rules for dual tax status on page 28.
2. You meet a 183-day substantial presence test. Under this test, you are treated as a U.S. resident if you were in the U.S. for at least 31 days during the calendar year and have been in the U.S. for at least 183 days within the last three years (the current year and the two preceding calendar years). The 183-day test is complicated and there are several exceptions.

To determine if you meet the 183-day test for 2006, the following cumulative times are totaled. Each day in the U.S. during 2006 is counted as a full day. Each day in 2005 counts as $^1/_3$ of a day; each day in 2004 counts as $^1/_6$ of a day. Note that you must be physically present in the U.S. for at least 31 days in the current year. If you are not, the 183-day test does not apply.

Other exceptions to the substantial presence test are: commuting from Canada or Mexico; keeping a tax home and close contacts or connections in a foreign country; having a diplomat, teacher, trainee, or student status; being a professional athlete temporarily in the U.S. to compete in a charitable sports event; or being confined in the U.S. for certain medical reasons. These exceptions are explained in the following paragraphs.

Commute from Mexico or Canada. If you regularly commute to work in the U.S. from Mexico or Canada, commuting days do not count as days of physical presence for the 183-day test.

Tax home/closer connection exception. If you are in the United States for less than 183 days during 2006, show that you had a closer connection with a foreign country than with the U.S., and keep a tax home there for the year, you generally will not be subject to tax as a U.S. resident even if you meet the substantial presence test. Under this exception, it is possible to have a U.S. abode and a tax home in a foreign country. A tax home is usually where a person has his or her principal place of business; if there is no principal place of business, it is the place of regular abode. Proving a tax home alone is not sufficient; the closer connection relationship must also be shown.

Planning Reminder

Is 2006 Your First Year of Residency?

If you were not a resident during 2005 but in 2006 you satisfy both the lawful resident (green card) test and the 183-day presence test, your residence begins on the earlier of the first day you are in the U.S. while a lawful permanent resident and the first day of physical presence.

To claim the closer connection exception, you must file Form 8840 explaining the basis of your claim. The tax home/closer connection exception does not apply to an alien who is present for 183 days or more during a year or who has applied for a "green card." A relative's application is not considered as the alien's application.

Exempt-person exception. Days of presence in the U.S. are not counted under the 183-day test if you are considered an exempt person such as a teacher, trainee, student, foreign-government-related person, or professional athlete temporarily in the U.S. to compete in a charitable sports event.

To exclude days of presence as a teacher, trainee, student, or professional athlete, you must file Form 8843 with the IRS.

A foreign-government-related person is any individual temporarily present in the U.S. who (1) has diplomatic status or a visa that the Secretary of the Treasury (after consultation with the Secretary of State) determined represents full-time diplomatic or consular status; or (2) is a full-time employee of an international organization; or (3) is a member of the immediate family of a diplomat or international organization employee.

A teacher or trainee is any individual other than a student who is temporarily present in the U.S. under a "J" or "Q" visa and who substantially complies with the requirements for being so present.

A student is any individual who is temporarily present in the U.S. under either an "F," "J," "M," or "Q" visa and who substantially complies with the requirements for being so present.

The exception generally does not apply to a teacher or trainee who has been exempt as a teacher, trainee, or student for any part of two of the six preceding calendar years. However, if during the period you are temporarily present in the U.S. under an "F," "J," "M," or "Q" visa and all of your compensation is received from outside the U.S., you may qualify for the exception if you were exempt as a teacher, trainee, or student for less than four years in the six preceding calendar years. The exception also does not apply to a student who has been exempt as a teacher, trainee, or student for more than five calendar years, unless you show that you do not intend to reside permanently in the U.S. and that you have substantially complied with the requirements of the student visa providing for temporary presence in the U.S.

Medical exception. If you plan to leave but cannot physically leave the U.S. because of a medical condition that arose in the U.S., you may be treated as a nonresident, even if present here for more than 183 days during the year. You must file Form 8843 to claim the medical exception.

Tax treaty exceptions. The lawful permanent residence test and the substantial physical presence test do not override tax treaty definitions of residence. Thus, you may be protected by a tax treaty from being treated as a U.S. resident even if you would be treated as a resident under either test.

Dual tax status in first year of residency. If you first became a lawful permanent resident of the U.S. (received a green card) during 2006 and were not a U.S. resident during 2005, your period of U.S. residency begins with the first day in 2006 that you are present in the U.S. with the status of lawful permanent resident. Before that date, you are a nonresident alien. This means that if you become a lawful permanent resident after January 1, 2006, you have a dual status tax year. On Form 1040, you attach a separate statement showing the income for the part of the year you are a nonresident. Form 1040NR (or 1040NR-EZ) may be used as the statement. Write "Dual-Status Return" or "Dual-Status Statement" across the top, as applicable.

To figure tax for a dual status year, *see* IRS Publication 519 and the instructions to Form 1040NR.

You also may have a dual status year if you were not a U.S. resident in 2005, and in 2006 you are a U.S. resident under the 183-day presence test. Your period of U.S. residency starts on the first day in 2006 for which you were physically present; before that date you are treated as a nonresident alien. However, if you meet the 183-day presence test (but not the green card test) and also spent 10 or fewer days in the U.S. during a period in which you had a closer connection to a foreign country than to the U.S., you may disregard the 10-day period. The purpose of this exception is to allow a brief presence in the U.S. for business trips or house hunting before the U.S. residency period starts.

If you are married at the end of the year to a U.S. citizen or resident alien, you and your spouse may elect to be treated as U.S. residents for the entire year by reporting your worldwide income on a joint return. You must attach to the joint return a statement signed by both of you that you are choosing to be treated as full-year U.S. residents.

EXAMPLES

1. Manuel Riveras, who has never before been a U.S. resident, lives in Spain until May 15, 2006. He moves to the U.S. and remains in the U.S. through the end of the year, thereby satisfying the physical presence test. On May 15, he is a U.S. resident. However, for the period before May 15, he is taxed as a nonresident.
2. Same facts as in Example 1, but Riveras attends a meeting in the U.S. on February 2 through 8. On May 15, he moves to the U.S.; May 15, not February 2, is the starting date of the residency. During February, he had closer connection to Spain than to the U.S. Thus, his short stay in February is an exempt period.

First-year choice. If you do not meet either the green card test or the 183-day substantial presence test for the year of your arrival in the U.S. or for the immediately preceding year, but you do meet the substantial presence test for the year immediately following the year of your arrival, you may elect to be treated as a U.S. resident for part of the year of your arrival. To do this, you must (1) be present in the U.S. for at least 31 consecutive days in the year of your arrival; and (2) be present in the U.S. for at least 75% of the number of days beginning with the first day of the 31-consecutive-day period and ending with the last day of the year of arrival. For purposes of this 75% requirement, you may treat up to five days of absence from the U.S. as days of presence within the U.S.

Do not count as days of presence in the U.S. days for which you are an *exempt individual* as discussed earlier.

You make the first-year election to be treated as a U.S. resident by attaching a statement to Form 1040 for the year of your arrival. A first-year election, once made, may not be revoked without the consent of the IRS.

If you make the election, your residence starting date for the year of your arrival is the first day of the earliest 31-consecutive-day period of presence that you use to qualify for the choice. You are treated as a U.S. resident for the remainder of the year.

Last year of residence. You are no longer treated as a U.S. resident as of your *residency termination date*. If you do not have a green card but are a U.S. resident for the year under the 183-day presence test, and you leave the U.S. during that year, your residency termination date is the last day you are present in the U.S., provided that: (1) after leaving the U.S. you had a closer connection to a foreign country than to the U.S. and had your tax home in that foreign country for the rest of the year, and (2) you are not treated as a U.S. resident for any part of the next calendar year.

If during the year you give up your green card (lawful permanent resident status) and meet tests (1) and (2), your residency termination date is the first day that you are no longer a lawful permanent resident. If during the year you meet both the green card test and the 183-day presence test and meet tests (1) and (2), your residency termination date is the *later* of the last day of U.S. presence or the first day you are no longer a lawful permanent resident. If tests (1) and (2) are not met, the residency termination date is the last day of the calendar year. In the year of your residency termination date, the filing rules for dual status taxpayers in this section apply.

For the year you give up your residence in the United States, you must file Form 1040NR (or Form 1040NR-EZ if eligible) and write "Dual-Status Return" across the top. Attach Form 1040 (or other statement) to show the income for the part of the year you are a resident; across the top write "Dual-Status Statement." *See* the instructions to Form 1040NR and IRS Publication 519 for filing the dual status return.

1.19 When an Alien Leaves the United States

Current law generally requires an alien who leaves the U.S., regardless of how long the trip is, to obtain a "sailing" or "departure" permit, technically known as a "certificate of compliance." The permit states that you have fulfilled your income tax obligations to the U.S. Without it, unless you are excused from obtaining one, you will be required at your point of departure to file a tax return and pay any tax due or post a bond. Diplomats, employees of international organizations or foreign governments, and students are generally exempt from the permit requirement. If a permit is required, Form 1040-C or in some cases a shorter Form 2063 must be filed with the IRS. See Publication 519 for further details.

Planning Reminder

Departure Permit

An alien planning to leave the U.S. should obtain a copy of Form 1040-C from the IRS to review his or her tax reporting obligations.

1.20 Expatriation Tax

Special tax rules apply to U.S. citizens who renounce their citizenship and long-term residents who end their residency. A long-term resident is someone who was a lawful permanent resident of the United States (with a green card) in at least eight of the last 15 years ending with the last year of residency. In general, if Code Section 877 applies, a former citizen or long-term resident is no longer taxed as a citizen or resident on his worldwide income. Instead, he or she is subject to federal income tax (or AMT) on U.S. source gross income and gains for the 10 years following the relinquishment of citizenship or termination of U.S. residency.

The American Jobs Creation Act of 2004 made substantial changes to the tax and information reporting rules for citizens who expatriated and long-term residents who terminated residency after June 3, 2004. Individuals who expatriated or terminated residency on or before June 3, 2004, are subject to tax under Code Section 877 if tax avoidance was a principal purpose for leaving the U.S. The law presumed a tax-avoidance purpose if thresholds for income tax liability or net worth were exceeded, although in certain cases a private ruling could have been requested within one year of expatriation to rebut the presumption of a tax-avoidance purpose.

For expatriations and terminations of residency after June 3, 2004, Code Section 877 applies if the thresholds are exceeded unless certain limited exceptions are met. Tax motivation is irrelevant. There is no presumption or private ruling procedure. Former citizens or long-term residents are subject to tax under Code Section 877 if they: (1) had average annual net income tax liability exceeding $131,000 (to be indexed for inflation) for the five years ending before the date of expatriation or termination of residency, or (2) had net worth of $2 million or more when citizenship or residency ended, or (3) fail to certify on Form 8854 that they complied with all U.S. federal tax obligations for the five years preceding the date of expatriation or termination of residency. Certain dual citizens and minors are exempt from tax under Section 877 if they provide the required certification of prior tax compliance on Form 8854.

Form 8854 is necessary but not sufficient to establish a date for tax expatriation. Until both Form 8854 is filed and notification is given to either the Department of State (former citizens) or Department of Homeland Security (former long-term residents), an individual will continue to be taxed on his or her worldwide income, as if he or she were still a U.S. citizen or resident.

Form 8854 must be filed not only for the year of expatriation or termination of residency, but also for each year in the 10-year period that the Section 877 rules apply, even if no tax for the year is due under Section 877. The annual report must identify the country of foreign residency or citizenship, list the number of days of physical presence within the United States during the year and give details on income, assets, and liabilities. There is a $10,000 penalty for failure to file Form 8854 or omitting required information, unless the failure is due to reasonable cause.

If an individual returns to the United States for more than 30 days in any year within the 10-year period during which he or she would otherwise be subject to Section 877, he or she will not be taxed under Section 877 for that year but will instead be taxed as a U.S. citizen or resident on worldwide income. However, there is a limited exception for those providing personal services in the United States for an unrelated employer; see IRS Publication 519 and the Form 8854 instructions for details.

PART 2

Reporting Your Income

In this part, you will learn what income is taxable, what income is tax free, and how to report income on your tax return.

Pay special attention to—

- Form W-2, which shows your taxable wages and provides other important information on fringe benefits received (Chapter 2).
- Tax-free fringe benefit plans available from your employer (Chapter 3).
- Reporting rules for interest and dividend income (Chapter 4).
- Reporting gains and losses from sales of property (Chapter 5).
- Rules for tax-free exchanges of like-kind property (Chapter 6).
- Planning for retirement distributions. Lump-sum distributions from employer plans may qualify for special averaging or tax-free rollover (Chapter 7).
- IRA contributions and distributions. Penalties for distributions before age 59½ and after age 70½ may be avoided by advance planning (Chapter 8).
- Restrictions on rental losses where a rented residence is used personally by you or by family members during the year (Chapter 9).
- Passive activity restrictions. Losses from rentals or passive business operations are generally not allowed, but certain real estate professionals are exempt from the loss restrictions, and for others, a special rental loss allowance of up to $25,000 may be available (Chapter 10).
- Reporting refunds of state and local taxes. A refund of previously deducted taxes is generally taxable unless you had no benefit from the deduction (Chapter 11).
- Cancellation of debts. When your creditor cancels debts you owe, you generally have taxable income, but there are exceptions for debts discharged while you are bankrupt or insolvent (Chapter 11).
- Damages received in court proceedings. Learn when these are tax free and when taxable (Chapter 11).
- How life insurance proceeds are taxed (Chapter 11).

Chapter 2

Taxable Wages, Salary, and Other Compensation

Except for tax-free fringe benefits (*see* Chapter 3), practically everything you receive for your work or services is taxed, whether paid in cash, property, or services. Your employer will generally report your taxable compensation on Form W-2 and other information returns, such as Form 1099-R for certain retirement payments. Do not reduce the amount you report on your return by withholdings for income taxes, Social Security taxes, union dues, or U.S. Savings Bond purchases. Your Form W-2 does not include in taxable pay your qualifying salary-reduction contributions to a retirement plan, although the amount may be shown on the form.

Attach Copy B of Form W-2 to your return; do not attach Forms 1099 unless there are withholdings.

Unemployment benefits are fully taxable. The benefits are reported to the IRS on Form 1099-G. You do not have to attach your copy of Form 1099-G to your return.

Income and expenses from self-employment are discussed in Chapter 40.

Table 2-1 Understanding Your Form W-2 for 2006 Wages and Tips

Amount in—	*What You Should Know—*
Box 1	***Taxable wages and tips.*** Your taxable wages, tips, and other forms of taxable compensation *(2.1)* are listed in Box 1. Taxable fringe benefits will also be included in Box 1 and may be shown in Box 14.
Box 2	***Federal tax withholdings.*** This is the amount of federal income tax withheld from your pay. Enter the amount on Line 63 of Form 1040, Line 39 of Form 1040A, or on Line 7 of Form 1040EZ.
Boxes 3, 4, and 7	***Social Security withholdings.*** Wages subject to Social Security withholding are shown in Box 3. Tips you reported to your employer are shown separately in Box 7. The total of Boxes 3 and 7 should not exceed $94,200, the maximum Social Security wage base for 2006. Social Security taxes withheld from wages and tips are shown in Box 4 and should not exceed the maximum 2006 tax of $5,840.40 ($94,200 × 6.2% rate). If you worked for more than one employer in 2006 and total Social Security tax withholdings exceeded $5,840.40, you claim the excess as a tax payment on your tax return; *see 26.9.* Elective salary deferrals to a 401(k), SIMPLE, salary-reduction SEP, or 403(b) plan, as well as employer payments of qualified adoption expenses, are included in Box 3 even though these amounts are not includible in Box 1 taxable wages. Amounts deferred under a nonqualified plan or a 457 plan are included in Box 3 in the year that the deferred amounts are no longer subject to a substantial risk of forfeiture.
Boxes 5–6	***Medicare tax withholdings.*** Wages, tips, elective salary deferrals, and other compensation subject to Social Security tax (Boxes 3 and 7) are also subject to a 1.45% Medicare tax, except that there is no wage base limit for Medicare tax. Thus, the Medicare wages shown in Box 5 are not limited to the $94,200 maximum for Boxes 3 and 7. In Box 6, total Medicare withholdings are reported.
Box 8	***Allocated tips.*** If you worked in a restaurant employing at least 10 people, your employer will report in Box 8 your share of 8% of gross receipts unless you reported tips at least equal to that share *(26.8).* The amount shown here is not included in Boxes 1, 3, 5, or 7, but you must add it to wages on Line 7 of Form 1040; you cannot file Form 1040A or 1040EZ.
Box 9	***Advance earned income payment.*** If you filed a Form W-5 asking for a part of the credit to be added to your wages, the amount of the advance is shown in Box 9. You report the advance as a tax liability when you file Form 1040 or 1040A; *see* Chapter 25.
Box 10	***Dependent care benefits.*** Reimbursements from your employer for dependent care expenses and the value of employer-provided care services under a qualifying plan *(3.5)* are included in Box 10. Amounts in excess of $5,000 are also included as taxable wages in Boxes 1, 3, and 5. Generally, amounts up to $5,000 are tax free, but you must determine the amount of the exclusion on Form 2441 if you file Form 1040, or on Schedule 2 if you file Form 1040A. The tax-free amount reduces expenses eligible for the dependent care credit; *see* Chapter 25.
Box 11	***Nonqualified plan distributions.*** Distributions shown in Box 11 are from a nonqualified deferred compensation plan, or a nongovernmental Section 457 plan *(7.21).* Do not report these distributions separately since they have already been included as taxable wages in Box 1.
Box 12	***Elective deferrals to retirement plans.*** Elective salary deferrals to a 401(k) plan (including any excess over the annual deferral limit; *see 7.18)* are shown in Box 12 with Code D. For example, if you made elective pre-tax salary deferrals of $4,500 to a 401(k) plan, your employer would enter D 4500.00 in Box 12. Designated Roth contributions *(7.20)* to a 401(k) plan are reported in Box 12 with Code AA. Code E is used for deferrals to a 403(b) tax-sheltered annuity plan *(7.20)*, Code F for deferrals to a salary-reduction simplified employee pension *(8.16)*, Code G for deferrals (including non-elective as well as elective) to a Section 457 plan *(7.21)*, Code H for elective deferrals to a pension plan created before June 25, 1959, and funded only by employee contributions, and Code S for salary-reduction deferrals to a SIMPLE IRA *(8.18).* ***Travel allowance reimbursements.*** If you received a flat mileage allowance from your employer for business trips *(20.33)*; or a *per diem* travel allowance to cover meals, lodging, and incidentals *(20.32)*; and the allowance exceeded the IRS rate, the amount up to the IRS rate (the nontaxable portion) is shown in Box 12 using Code L. The excess is included as taxable wages in Box 1. ***Group-term life insurance over $50,000.*** The cost of taxable coverage over $50,000 is shown in Box 12 using Code C. It is also included in Box 1 wages, Box 3 Social Security wages, and Box 5 Medicare wages and tips. If you are a retiree or other former employee who received group-term coverage over $50,000, any uncollected Social Security tax is shown using Code M and uncollected Medicare tax using Code N. The uncollected amount must be reported on Line 63 of Form 1040 (total tax); write "UT" next to it. ***Nontaxable sick pay.*** If you contributed to a sick pay plan, an allocable portion of benefits received is tax free and is shown using Code J.

Table 2-1 (continued)

Box 12	***Uncollected Social Security and Medicare taxes on tips.*** If your employer could not withhold sufficient Social Security on tips, the uncollected amount is shown using Code A. For uncollected Medicare tax, Code B is used. This amount must be reported on Line 63 of Form 1040 (total tax); write "UT" next to it. ***Excess golden parachute payments.*** If you received an "excess parachute payment as wages," Code K identifies the 20% penalty tax on the excess payment that was withheld by the employer. This withheld amount is included in Box 2, but you also must add it as an additional tax on Line 63 (total tax) of Form 1040. ***Moving expense reimbursements.*** Tax-free employer reimbursements to you for deductible moving expenses *(12.8)* are shown with Code P. ***Employer contributions to health savings account (HSA) or Archer MSA.*** Total employer contributions to an HSA are shown with Code W. Total employer contributions to an MSA are shown with Code R. Contributions exceeding the excludable limit (Chapter 3) are included as taxable wages in Boxes 1, 3, and 5. ***Employer-financed adoption benefits.*** Total qualified adoption expenses paid or reimbursed by your employer *(3.6)* plus *any* pre-tax contributions you made to an adoption plan account under a cafeteria plan *(3.13)* are shown with Code T. ***Nonstatutory stock option exercised.*** If you exercised a nonstatutory stock option, Code V shows the taxable "spread" (excess of fair market value of stock over exercise price). The income should be included in Boxes 1, 3 (up to the $94,200 Social Security wage ceiling), and 5. ***Deferrals and income under Section 409A nonqualified deferred compensation plan.*** Current year deferrals plus all earnings under a 409A plan are shown with Code Y. Code Z shows amounts included as income in Box 1; this income is subject to a penalty plus interest on Form 1040; *see 2.8.*
Box 13	***Statutory employee.*** If this box is checked you report your wage income and deductible job expenses on Schedule C *(see 40.6)*. Your earnings are not subject to income tax withholding, but are subject to Social Security and Medicare taxes. ***Retirement plan.*** This box is checked if you were an active participant in an employer plan at some point during the year. As an active participant, you are subject to the phase-out rules for IRA deductions); *see 8.4.*
Box 14	***Taxable fringe benefits and miscellaneous payments.*** Your employer may use Box 14 to report fringe benefits or deductions from your pay, such as union dues, educational assistance, health insurance premiums, or voluntary after-tax contributions to profit-sharing or pension plans. If your employer included in Box 1 the lease value of a car *(3.7)* provided to you, this value must also be shown in Box 14 or on a separate statement.
Boxes 17 and 19	***State and local taxes.*** If you itemize, deduct on Schedule A state and local tax withholdings shown in Boxes 17 and 19, unless you elect to deduct state and local general sales taxes; *see 16.3.*

a Control number — OMB No. 1545-0008 — Safe, accurate, FAST! Use IRS e-file — Visit the IRS website at *www.irs.gov/efile.*

b Employer identification number (EIN) **08-X1X0X1X**

c Employer's name, address, and ZIP code
Finkle Construction Company
5532 Glasgow Plaza
City, State XX111

d Employee's social security number **0X1 - XX - 1X00**

e Employee's first name and initial — Last name — Suff.
Mary Moll
176 Garden Road
City, State 1XXX1

f Employee's address and ZIP code

Box	Amount	Box	Amount
1 Wages, tips, other compensation	57,800.00	2 Federal income tax withheld	10,000.00
3 Social security wages	63,580.00	4 Social security tax withheld	3,941.96
5 Medicare wages and tips	63,580.00	6 Medicare tax withheld	921.91
7 Social security tips		8 Allocated tips	
9 Advance EIC payment		10 Dependent care benefits	
11 Nonqualified plans		12a See instructions for box 12	5,780.00
13 Statutory employee [ ] Retirement plan [X] Third-party sick pay [ ]		12b	
14 Other		12c	
		12d	

15 State	Employer's state ID number	16 State wages, tips, etc.	17 State income tax	18 Local wages, tips, etc.	19 Local income tax	20 Locality name
State	11-X1X0X1X	57,800.00	2,980.00	57,800.00	1,734.00	City

Form **W-2** Wage and Tax Statement **2006** Department of the Treasury—Internal Revenue Service

Copy B—To Be Filed With Employee's FEDERAL Tax Return.
This information is being furnished to the Internal Revenue Service.

Reporting Compensation

Caution

Severance Pay Taxable

You must pay tax on severance pay received upon losing a job. The severance pay is taxable even if you signed a waiver releasing your former employer from potential future damage claims. The waiver does not change the nature of the payments from taxable pay to tax-free personal injury damages; *see 11.7.*

Filing Instruction

Tips

Tips you receive are taxable income. You must report tips to your employer so your employer can withhold FICA and income tax from your regular pay to cover the tips; *see 26.8.*

2.1 Salary and Wage Income

The key to reporting your pay is Form W-2, sent to you by your employer. It lists your taxable wages, which may include not only your regular pay, but also other taxable items, such as taxable fringe benefits. Table 2-1 on pages 34 and 35 explains how employee pay benefits and tax withholdings are reported on Form W-2.

Your employer reports your taxable pay under a simple rule. Unless the item is specifically exempt from tax, you are taxed on practically everything you receive for your work whether paid in cash, property, or services. Benefits that the law specifically excludes from tax are discussed in Chapter 3. The most common tax-free benefits are employer-paid premiums for health and accident plans, medical expense reimbursements, and group-term life insurance coverage up to $50,000.

Your employer will include in Box 1 of your Form W-2 the total wages, tips, and other compensation, before payroll deductions, that were paid to you during the year. Box 1 may include, in addition to regular wages and tips, the following types of taxable compensation:

- Bonuses (including signing bonuses)
- Taxable fringe benefits (*see* Chapter 3)
- *Per diem* or mileage allowances exceeding the IRS rate *(20.32–20.33)*
- Expense allowances or business expense reimbursements under a non-accountable plan *(20.34)*
- Awards or prizes not exempt under *3.11*
- Cost of group-term life insurance over $50,000 *(3.4)*
- Cost of accident and health insurance premiums paid by an S corporation for 2%-or-more shareholder-employees
- Deferred income that is currently taxable under a Section 409A nonqualified deferred compensation plan *(2.7)*

Compensation reported in Box 1 must be reported as wages on Line 7 of Form 1040 or 1040A, or Line 1 of Form 1040EZ. Other types of income must also be reported as wages on your return although they are not included in Box 1 of Form W-2, such as non-excludable dependent care *(3.5)* or adoption *(3.6)* benefits, tips not reported to your employer or allocated tips *(26.8)*, disability pension shown on Form 1099-R if you are under your employer's minimum retirement age, or excess salary deferrals to an employer retirement plan *(7.18)*.

Withholdings for retirement plans. Amounts withheld from wages as your contribution to your pension or profit-sharing account are generally taxable as compensation unless they are tax-deferred elective deferrals under the limits allowed for Section 401(k) plans (7.18), simplified employee pension plans *(8.16)*, SIMPLE IRAs *(8.18)*, or tax-sheltered annuity plans *(7.20)*. Elective deferrals are reported in Box 12 of Form W-2.

Wages withheld for compulsory forfeitable contributions to a nonqualified pension plan are not taxable if these conditions exist:

1. The contribution is forfeited if employment is terminated prior to death or retirement.
2. The plan does not provide for a refund of employee contributions and, in the administration of the plan, no refund will be made. Where only part of the contribution is subject to forfeiture, the amount of withheld contribution not subject to forfeiture is taxable income.

You should check with your employer to determine the status of your contributions.

Assigning your pay. You may not avoid tax on income you earned by assigning the right to payment to another person. For example, you must report earnings that you donate to charity, even if they are paid directly by your employer to a charity. If you claim itemized deductions, you may claim a contribution deduction for the donation; *see* Chapter 14. Assignments of income-generating intellectual property are held taxable to the assignee. However, if the assignor retained power or control of the property, the assignor could be held liable for the tax according to the 8th Circuit.

The IRS allowed an exception for doctors working in a clinic. The doctors were not taxed on fees for treating patients with limited income (teaching cases) where they were required to assign the fees to a foundation.

Gifts from employers. A payment may be called a gift but still be taxable income. Any payment made in recognition of past services or in anticipation of future services or benefits is taxable as wages even if the employer is not obligated to make the payment. Exceptions for employee achievement awards are discussed at *3.11*.

To prove a gift is tax free, you must show that the employer acted with pure and unselfish motives of affection, admiration, or charity. This is difficult to do, given the employer-employee relationship. A gift of stock by majority stockholders to key employees has been held to be taxable.

Employee leave-sharing plan. Some companies allow employees to contribute their unused leave into a "leave fund" for use by other employees who have suffered medical emergencies. If you use up your regular leave and benefit from additional leave that has been donated to the plan, the benefit is taxable and will be reported as wages on Form W-2.

"Golden parachute" payments. Golden parachute arrangements are agreements to pay key employees additional compensation upon a change in company control. If you receive such a payment, part of it may be deemed to be an "excess payment" under a complex formula in the law. You must pay a 20% penalty tax on the "excess" amount in addition to regular income tax on the total. The 20% penalty should be identified on Form W-2 with Code K in Box 12; *see* Table 2-1 at the beginning of this chapter.

If the golden parachute payment is made to a non-employee, the company will report it in Box 7 (non-employee compensation) of Form 1099-MISC. If you are self-employed, report the total compensation on Schedule C *(40.6)* and compute self-employment tax on Schedule SE *(45.3)*. Any "excess parachute payment" should be separately labeled in Box 13 of Form 1099-MISC. Multiply the Box 13 amount by 20% and report it on Line 63 (total tax) of Form 1040; label it "EPP."

Court Decision

Tax on Assigned Contingent Fee

An attorney who took a medical malpractice case on a contingent fee basis agreed to split the net fee with his ex-wife pursuant to their divorce agreement. After a favorable settlement, the attorney's take was approximately $40,000 after expenses, half of which went to his ex-wife. Each paid tax on his or her share. The attorney argued that his partial assignment of the fee could shift the tax liability because collection was contingent on the outcome of the lawsuit. However, the IRS and the Tax Court held that the attorney was liable for the tax on the entire contingent fee, and an appeals court agreed. The attorney transferred only the right to receive income. Although his fee was contingent upon the successful outcome of the case, once the fee materialized, it was indisputably compensation for his personal services.

2.2 Constructive Receipt of Year-End Paychecks

As an employee, you use the cash-basis method of accounting. This means that you report all income items in the year they are actually received and deduct expenses in the year you pay them.

You are also subject to the "constructive receipt rule," which requires you to report income not actually received but which has been credited to your account, subject to your control, or put aside for you. Thus, if you received a paycheck at the end of 2006, you must report the pay on your 2006 return, even though you do not cash or deposit it to your account until 2007. This is true even if you receive the check after banking hours on the last business day of the year and cannot cash or deposit it until the next year. The Tax Court has also ruled that receipt by an agent (e.g., an attorney) is constructive receipt by the principal. In one case, a woman argued that alimony received by her in 1991 was taxable in 1991. Because the funds were given to her attorney on December 27, 1990, the Tax Court held that she was in constructive receipt of the funds and that they were taxable in 1990.

If your employer does not have funds in the bank and asks you to hold the check before depositing it, you do not have taxable income until the check is cashed. If services rendered in 2006 are paid for by check dated for 2007, the pay is taxable in 2007.

The IRS has ruled that an employee who is not at home on December 31 to take delivery of a check sent by certified mail must still report the check in that year. However, where an employee was not at home to take certified mail delivery of a year-end check that she did not expect to receive until the next year, the Tax Court held that the funds were taxable when received in the following year.

2.3 Pay Received in Property Is Taxed

Your employer may pay you with property instead of cash. You report the fair market value of the property as wages.

EXAMPLE

For consulting services rendered, Kate Chong receives a check for $10,000 and property with a fair market value of $5,000. She reports $15,000 as wages.

If you receive your unrestricted company stock as payment for your services, you include the value of the stock as pay in the year you receive it. However, if the stock is nontransferable or subject to substantial risk of forfeiture, you do not have to include its value as pay until the restrictions no longer apply; *see 2.18*. You must report dividends on the restricted stock in the year you receive the income.

If you receive your employer's note that has a fair market value, you are taxed on the value of the note less what it would cost you to discount it. If the note bears interest, report the full face value. But do not report income if the note has no fair market value. Report income on the note only when payments are made on it.

A debt cancelled by an employer is taxable income.

Salespeople employed by a dealer have taxable income on receipt of "prize points" redeemable for merchandise from a distributor.

2.4 When Commissions Are Taxed

Earned commissions are taxable in the year they are credited to your account and subject to your drawing, whether or not you actually draw them.

On your 2006 tax return, you do not report commissions that were earned in 2006 but cannot be computed or collected until a later year.

Caution

Earned Commissions Credited to Your Account

You may not postpone tax on earned commissions credited to your account in 2006 by not drawing them until 2007 or a later year. However, where a portion of earned commissions is not withdrawn because your employer is holding it to cover future expenses, you are not taxed on the amount withheld.

EXAMPLE

Arno Jeffers earns commissions based on a percentage of the profits from realty sales. In 2006 he draws $10,000 from his account. However, at the end of 2006 the full amount of his commissions is unknown because profits for the year have not been figured. In January 2007, his 2006 commissions are computed to be $15,000, and the $5,000 balance is paid to him. The $5,000 is taxable in 2007 even though earned in 2006.

Advances against unearned commissions. Under standard insurance industry practice, an agent who sells a policy does not earn commissions until premiums are received by the insurance company. However, the company may issue a cash advance on the commissions before the premiums are received. Agents have claimed that they may defer reporting the income until the year the premiums are earned. The IRS, recognizing that in practice companies rarely demand repayment, requires that advances be included in income in the year received if the agent has full control over the advanced funds. A repayment of unearned commissions in a later year is deducted on Schedule A; *see 2.8*.

Salespeople have been taxed on commissions received on property bought for their personal use. In one case, an insurance agent was taxed on commissions paid to him on his purchase of an insurance policy. In another case, a real estate agent was taxed on commissions he received on his purchase of land. A salesman was also taxed for commissions waived on policies he sold to friends, relatives, and employees.

Kickback of commissions. An insurance agent's kickback of his or her commission is taxable where agents may not under local law give rebates or kickbacks of premiums to their clients. The commissions are income and may not be offset with a business expense deduction; illegal kickbacks may not be deducted.

However, in one case, a federal appeals court allowed an insurance broker to avoid tax when he did not charge clients the basic first-year commission. The clients paid the broker the net premium (gross premium less the commission), which he remitted to the insurance company. The IRS and Tax Court held that the commissions were taxable despite the broker's voluntary waiver of his right to them. He could not deduct them because his discount scheme violated state anti-rebate law (Oklahoma). On appeal, the broker won. The Tenth Circuit Court of Appeals held that since the broker never had any right to commissions under the terms of the contracts he structured with his clients, he was not taxed on the commissions. The court cautioned that if the broker had remitted the full premium (including commission) to the insurance company and then reimbursed the client after having received the commission from the company, the commission probably would have been taxable.

2.5 Unemployment Benefits Are Taxable

All unemployment benefits you receive in 2006 from a state agency or the federal government are treated as taxable income. You should receive Form 1099-G, showing the amount of the payments. Report the payments separately from wages on Line 19 of Form 1040, Line 13 of Form 1040A, or Line 3 of Form 1040EZ.

Supplemental unemployment benefits paid from company-financed funds are taxable as wages and not reported as unemployment compensation. Such benefits are usually paid under guaranteed annual wage plans made between unions and employers.

Unemployment benefits from a private or union fund to which you voluntarily contribute dues are taxable as "other" income on Form 1040, but only to the extent the benefits exceed your contributions to the fund. Your contributions to the fund are not deductible.

Worker's compensation payments are not taxable; *see 2.13.*

Taxable unemployment benefits include federal trade readjustment allowances (1974 Trade Act), airline deregulation benefits (1978 Airline Deregulation Act), and disaster unemployment assistance (1974 Disaster Relief Act).

Repaid supplemental unemployment benefits. If you had to repay supplemental unemployment benefits to receive trade readjustment allowances (1974 Trade Act), taxable unemployment benefits are reduced by repayments made in the same year. If you repay the benefits in a later year, the benefits are taxed in the year of receipt and a deduction may be claimed in the later year. If the repayment is $3,000 or less, the deduction is added to your other adjustments to income on Line 36 of Form 1040. If the repayment exceeds $3,000, a deduction or a credit may be claimed under the rules at *2.8*.

2.6 Strike Pay Benefits and Penalties

Strike and lockout benefits paid out of regular union dues are taxable as wages unless the payment qualifies as a gift, as discussed below. However, if you have made voluntary contributions to a strike fund, benefits you receive from the fund are tax free up to the amount of your contributions and are taxable to the extent they exceed your contributions.

Strike benefits as tax-free gifts. Here are factors indicating that benefits are gifts: Payments are based on individual need; they are paid to both union and non-union members; and no conditions are imposed on the strikers who receive benefits.

If you receive benefits under conditions by which you are to participate in the strike and the payments are tied to your scale of wages, the benefits are taxable.

EXAMPLE

A striking union pilot claimed that strike benefits were tax-free gifts because they were funded by assessments paid by other union pilots who were not on strike. The IRS and Tax Court held that the benefits were taxable. They were not gifts because they were not motivated by a "detached and disinterested generosity." The union was promoting its own self-interest by giving pilots an incentive to support the strike. The non-striking pilots contributed to the strike fund as an obligation of union membership. The strikers were eligible for benefits only if they agreed to perform any strike activities requested by the union, did not fly for airlines in dispute with the union, and did not take actions that could adversely affect the outcome of the dispute.

Caution

Law Violation Not Deductible

No deduction is allowed for a fine or penalty paid to a government for the violation of a law.

Strike pay penalties. Pay penalties charged to striking teachers are not deductible. State law may prohibit public school teachers from striking and charge a penalty equal to one day's pay for each day spent on strike. For example, when striking teachers returned to work after a one-week strike, a penalty of one week's salary was deducted from their pay. Although they did not actually receive pay for the week they worked after the strike, they earned taxable wages. Furthermore, the penalty is not deductible. No deduction is allowed for a fine or penalty paid to a government for the violation of a law.

2.7 Nonqualified Deferred Compensation

The rules for determining whether tax may be deferred under a nonqualified deferred compensation plan have been substantially revised by Code Section 409A enacted as part of the American Jobs Creation Act of 2004. Section 409A applies to amounts deferred after 2004. Amounts deferred before 2005 become subject to the new law if the plan is materially modified after October 3, 2004.

Law Alert

Penalty and Interest on Nonqualified Deferred Compensation

If deferred pay is currently taxable under the rules of Code Section 409A, you must also pay a 20% penalty and interest at a rate 1% higher than the regular underpayment rate.

If a plan subject to Section 409A does not meet requirements pertaining to plan elections and distributions at any time during a taxable year, all amounts deferred for the taxable year and all preceding years will be currently includable in a participant's gross income to the extent the amounts are not subject to a substantial risk of forfeiture and have not previously been included in gross income.

Unless an exception applies, Code Section 409A applies to all plans, including arrangements between an independent contractor and a service recipient, and a partner and partnership, under which the service provider has a legally binding right during a year to compensation that is not actually or constructively received, and which is payable in a later year. The law does ***not*** apply to qualified retirement plans (such as 401(k) plans), Section 403(b) tax-deferred annuities, SIMPLE accounts, simplified employee pensions, and Section 457 plans; these are excluded from the definition of "nonqualified deferred compensation plans." Also excluded are welfare benefit plans such as vacation, sick leave, and disability programs. The IRS has allowed exceptions for short-term deferrals, certain stock options, and certain stock appreciation rights (SARs); *see* IRS Notice 2006-4.

For plans subject to Code Section 409A, specified requirements regarding the timing of deferral elections and availability of distributions and funding techniques must be satisfied for income to be deferred. An election to defer income generally must be made prior to the beginning of the year during which the services will be performed. If compensation is contingent on performance-based criteria over a performance period of at least 12 months, a deferral election may be made as late as six months before the end of that period. The plan generally may not permit distributions earlier than:

- the participant's separation from service
- the participant's disability
- a specific date or under a fixed schedule that is spelled out in the plan on the date of the deferral
- an unforeseeable financial emergency resulting from events beyond the participant's control
- a change in the ownership of a corporation, change in a substantial portion of the corporation's assets, or change in the effective control of the corporation
- the death of the participant

Acceleration of benefits is permitted in limited situations, such as to make payments to a third party in order to satisfy the terms of a domestic relations order, or to permit a lump-sum payment of up to $10,000 to a participant who has separated from service.

Income tax, interest, and penalty if Section 409A requirements not met. If the plan does not meet the specified requirements or the plan is not operated in accordance with the requirements, all amounts deferred for that year and all preceding years become currently taxable to the participants unless the amounts were previously included in income or the amounts remain subject to a substantial risk of forfeiture. In addition, the law imposes a penalty equal to 20% of the includible compensation, plus interest at a rate that is 1% higher than the regular underpayment rate.

Section 409A plan deferrals are reported to employees in Box 12 of Form W-2 for 2006 using Code Y, and Code Z will be used to report taxable amounts where the plan fails to meet the law's requirements; *see* Table 2-1 at the beginning of this chapter. Deferrals for non-employees will be reported in Box 15a of Form 1099-MISC, and taxable amounts in Box 15b.

IRS guidelines. The IRS has issued proposed regulations (Prop. Reg. 1.409A-1 through 1.409A-6) that reflect guidance previously announced in Notice 2005-1 and also provide substantial additional guidance. Final regulations had not yet been released when this book went to press; *see* the *e-Supplement* for an update.

Financial health triggers and offshore rabbi trusts. Section 409A blocks the benefit of two funding arrangements that set aside assets to secure the payment of promised deferred compensation. If a nonqualified deferred compensation plan provides that assets will be restricted to payment of deferrals if the employer's financial condition deteriorates, the setting aside of the assets will be considered a transfer of restricted property to the participants, taxable under the Section 83 rules discussed at *2.17*. This is so even if the assets nominally remain available to satisfy the claims of the employer's general creditors.

Also, a Section 83 transfer *(2.17)* is generally deemed to occur when assets to pay nonqualified deferred compensation are set aside in an offshore rabbi trust. Section 409A treats the funding of an offshore trust as a transfer of property to the participants, taxable under the Section 83 rules at *2.17*, unless substantially all of the services relating to the deferred compensation were performed in the foreign jurisdiction where the assets are held. A Section 83 transfer is deemed to occur whether or not the offshore assets are nominally available to satisfy the claims of the employer's general creditors.

If deferrals are includible in a participant's income because of the financial health trigger or offshore trust provisions, there is an additional 20% penalty plus interest at 1% more than the regular rate.

Transitional relief. In the Gulf Opportunity Zone Act of 2005 (GOZA), Congress clarified that the effective date of the Section 409A provisions relating to financial health triggers and offshore trusts was January 1, 2005, even if the amount was set aside in an offshore trust, or financial health trigger provision was in place, before 2005. However, GOZA required the IRS to provide transition relief and in Notice 2006-33, the IRS announced that for assets set aside or restricted on or before March 21, 2006, the plan has until the end of 2007 to come into compliance with Section 409A.

Rabbi trusts. If IRS tests are met, employer contributions to a domestic "rabbi trust" are not taxed until distributions from the trust are received or made available. The trust must be irrevocable and the trust assets must be subject to the claims of the employer's creditors in the event of insolvency or bankruptcy. Employees and their beneficiaries must have no preferred claim on the trust assets.

Offshore rabbi trusts are subject to Section 409A, as discussed above.

2.8 Did You Return Wages Received in a Prior Year?

Did you return income in 2006 such as salary or commissions that you reported in a prior taxable year because it appeared you had an unrestricted right to them in the earlier year? If so, you may deduct the repayment as a miscellaneous itemized deduction. If the repayment of wages exceeds $3,000, the deduction is claimed on Line 27 of Schedule A and is *not* subject to the 2% adjusted gross income (AGI) floor *(19.1)*. However, if the repayment is $3,000 or less, the deduction must be claimed on Line 20 of Schedule A, where it *is* subject to the 2% floor.

Option of tax credit or deduction for repayments over $3,000. If your repayment of wages exceeded $3,000, you may claim the repayment as an itemized deduction, *or* you may claim a tax credit, based upon a recomputation of the prior year's tax; *see* the Filing Instruction on this page.

Repayment of supplemental unemployment benefits. Where repayment is required to qualify for trade readjustment allowances, you may deduct the repayment from gross income. Claim the deduction on Line 36 of Form 1040, and to the left of the line write "subpay TRA." The deduction is allowed even if you do not itemize. If repayment exceeds $3,000, you have the choice of a deduction or claiming a tax credit based on a recomputation of your tax for the year supplemental unemployment benefits were received, as explained in the Filing Instruction on this page.

Repayment of disallowed travel and entertainment expenses. If a "hedge" agreement between you and your company requires you to repay salary or travel and entertainment ("T & E") expenses if they are disallowed to the company by the IRS, you may claim a deduction in the year of repayment. According to the IRS, you may not recalculate your tax for the prior year and claim a tax credit under the rules of Section 1341. However, an appeals court rejected the position taken by the IRS and allowed a tax recomputation under Section 1341 to an executive who returned part of a disallowed salary under the terms of a corporate by-law.

Filing Instruction

Repayments Exceeding $3,000

If a repayment of wages in 2006 exceeds $3,000, a special law (Code Section 1341) gives this alternative: Instead of claiming an itemized deduction from 2006 income, you may recompute your tax for the prior year as if the wages had not been reported. The difference between the actual tax paid in the prior year and the recomputed tax may be claimed as a credit on your 2006 return. The credit is claimed on Line 70 of Form 1040; write next to the line "IRC 1341." If you claim the repayment as a miscellaneous itemized deduction, enter it on Line 27 of Schedule A, where it is not subject to the 2% floor. Choose either the credit or the itemized deduction, whichever gives you the larger tax reduction.

2.9 Waiver of Executor's and Trustee's Commissions

Commissions received by an executor for services performed are taxable as compensation. An executor may waive commissions without income or gift tax consequences by giving a principal legatee or devisee a formal waiver of the executor's right to commissions within six months after the initial appointment or by not claiming commissions at the time of filing the usual accountings.

The waiver may not be recognized if the executor takes any action that is inconsistent with the waiver. An example of an inconsistent action would be the claiming of an executor's fee as a deduction on an estate, inheritance, or income tax return.

A *bequest* received by an executor from an estate is tax free if it is not compensation for services.

2.10 Life Insurance Benefits

Company-financed insurance gives employees benefits at low or no tax cost.

Group life insurance. Group insurance plans may furnish not only life insurance protection but also accident and health benefits. Premium costs are low and tax deductible to the company while tax free to you unless you have nonforfeitable rights to permanent life insurance, or, in the case of group-term life insurance, your coverage exceeds $50,000; *see 3.4*. Even where your coverage exceeds $50,000, the tax incurred on your employer's premium payment is generally less than what you would have to pay privately for similar insurance.

Caution

Charitable Split-Dollar Insurance

In a charitable split-dollar insurance plan, you give money to a charity, which invests in a life insurance policy and splits the proceeds with your beneficiaries. Taxpayers have attempted to deduct the initial "donations," but the tax law was changed to disallow the deduction.

It may be possible to avoid estate tax on the group policy proceeds if you assign all of your ownership rights in the policy, including the right to convert the policy, and if the beneficiary is other than your estate. Where the policy allows assignment of the conversion right, in addition to all other rights, and state law does not bar the assignment, you are considered to have made a complete assignment of the group insurance for estate tax purposes.

The IRS has ruled that where an employee assigns a group life policy and the value of the employee's interest in the policy cannot be ascertained, there is no taxable gift. This is so where the employer could simply have stopped making payments. However, there is a gift by the employee to the assignee to the extent of premiums paid by the employer. The gift may be a present interest qualifying for the annual gift tax exclusion discussed at *39.2*.

Split-dollar insurance. Where you want more insurance than is provided by a group plan, your company may be able to help you get additional protection through a split-dollar insurance plan. Under the basic split-dollar plan, your employer purchases permanent cash value life insurance on your life and pays all or part of the annual premium. At your death, your employer is entitled to part of the proceeds equal to the premiums he or she paid. You have the right to name a beneficiary to receive the remaining proceeds which, under most policies, are substantial compared with the employer's share. Equity split-dollar arrangements allow employees to retain the right to the cash surrender value in excess of the premiums paid by the employer.

In final regulations applicable to split-dollar arrangements entered into or materially modified after September 17, 2003, the IRS has provided two sets of rules, depending on whether the employee or the employer owns the insurance policy. If the employee is the owner, the employer's premium payments will be treated as loans and the imputed interest will be taxed to the employee. If the employer owns the policy, the employee will be taxed on the value of the life insurance protection, the policy cash value that the employee has access to, and the value of any other economic benefits received from the policy.

2.11 Educational Benefits for Employees' Children

Private foundations. The IRS has published guidelines for determining whether educational grants made by a private foundation established by an employer to children of employees constitute scholarships. An objective, nondiscriminatory program must be adopted. If the guidelines are satisfied, employees are not taxed on the benefits provided to their children. Advance approval of the grant program must be obtained from the IRS.

Caution

Primary Purpose Determination

If all guidelines other than the percentage test are satisfied, the IRS will determine whether the primary purpose of the program is to educate the children. If it is, the grants will be considered scholarships or fellowships; if it is not, the grants are taxed to the parent-employees as extra compensation.

IRS guidelines require that:

- Grant recipients must be selected by a scholarship committee that is independent of the employer and the foundation. Former employees of the employer or the foundation are not considered independent.
- Eligibility for the grants may be restricted to children of employees who have been employed for a minimum of up to three years, but eligibility may not be related to the employee's position, services, or duties.
- Once awarded, a grant may not be terminated if the parent leaves his job with the employer, regardless of the reason for the termination of employment. If a one-year grant is awarded or a multi-year grant is awarded subject to renewal, a child who reapplies for a later grant may not be considered ineligible because his parent no longer works for the employer.
- Grant decisions must be based solely upon objective standards unrelated to the employer's business and the parent's employment such as prior academic performance, aptitude tests, recommendations from instructors, financial needs, and conclusions drawn from personal interviews.
- Recipients must be free to use the grants for courses that are not of particular benefit to the employer or the foundation.
- The grant program must not be used by the foundation or employer to recruit employees or induce employees to continue employment.
- There must be no requirement or suggestion that the child or parent is expected to render future employment services.
- A percentage test generally must be met. The number of grants awarded in a given year to children of employees must not exceed (1) 25% of the number of employ-

ees' children who were eligible, applied for the grants, and were considered by the selection committee in that year; or (2) 10% of the number of employees' children who were eligible during that year, whether or not they applied. Renewals of grants are not considered in determining the number of grants awarded.

If all of the above tests *other than* the percentage test are met, the educational grant program can still qualify if the facts and circumstances indicate that the primary purpose of the program is to provide educational benefits rather than to compensate the employees.

Educational benefit trusts and other plans. A medical professional corporation set up an educational benefit plan to pay college costs for the children of "key" employees. Children enrolled in a degree program within two years of graduating from high school could participate in the plan. If an eligible employee quit for reasons other than death or permanent disability, his or her children could not longer receive benefits except for expenses actually incurred before termination. The company made annual contributions to a trust administered by a bank. According to the IRS, amounts contributed to the trust were a form of pay to qualified employees, because the contributions were made on the basis of the parents' employment and earnings records, not on the children's need, merit, or motivation. However, the employees could not be taxed when the funds were deposited because the children's right to receive benefits was conditioned upon each employee's future performance of services and was subject to a substantial risk of forfeiture. Tax is not incurred until a person has a vested right to receive benefits; here, vesting did not occur until a child became a degree candidate and incurred educational expenses while his or her parent was employed by the corporation. Once the child's right to receive a distribution from the plan became vested, the parent of the child could be taxed on the amount of the distribution. The company could deduct the same amount.

The Tax Court and appeals court have upheld the IRS position in similar cases.

Disability and Workers' Compensation

2.12 Sick Pay Is Taxable

Sick pay received from an employer is generally taxable as wages unless it qualifies as workers' compensation under the rules at *2.13*. Payments received under accident or health plans are generally tax free *(3.3)*, unless they constitute excess reimbursements, as discussed at *17.4*. Payments from your employer's plan for certain serious permanent injuries are tax free; *see 3.3*.

Disability pensions are discussed at *2.14*.

Sick pay received from your employer is subject to income tax withholding as if it were wages. Sick pay from a third party such as an insurance company is not subject to withholdings unless you request it on Form W-4S.

2.13 Workers' Compensation Is Tax Free

You do not pay tax on workers' compensation payments for job-related injuries or illness. However, your employer might continue paying your regular salary but require you to turn over your workers' compensation payments. Then you are taxed on the difference between what was paid to you and what you returned.

EXAMPLE

John Wright was injured while at work and was out of work for two months. His company continues to pay his weekly salary of $775. He also receives workers' compensation of $200 a week from the state, which is tax free. He gives the $200 back to his employer. The balance of $575 a week is considered taxable wages.

To qualify as tax-free workers' compensation, the payments must be made under the authority of a *law* (or regulation having the force of a law) that provides compensation for on-the-job injury or illness. Payments made under a labor agreement do *not* qualify as tax-free workers' compensation.

A retirement pension or annuity does *not* qualify for tax-free treatment if benefits are based on age, length of service, or prior plan contributions. Such benefits are taxable even if retirement was triggered by a work-related injury or sickness.

Caution

Job-Related Injury or Illness

Not all payments for job-related illness or injury qualify as tax-free workers' compensation. Unless the statute or regulation authorizing your disability payment restricts awards to on-the-job injury or illness, your payment is taxable. Even if your payments are in fact based upon job-related injury or illness, they are taxed if other individuals can receive payments from the plan for disabilities that are not work related; *see* Example 1 on the following page.

State law may impose a penalty for unreasonable delay in paying a worker's compensation award. If the penalty is considered to have the remedial purpose of facilitating the injured employee's return to work, the IRS may treat the amount as part of the original tax-free compensation award.

EXAMPLES

1. Kane, a federal district judge, suffered from sleep apnea, a condition characterized by a cessation of breathing during sleep, which was aggravated by the stress of his judicial work. He received a retirement disability payment of $65,135.

   A federal appeals court held that the payment was taxable because it was paid under a statute which did not specifically require that the payments be for work-related injuries. Here, the federal law under which the judge received his payments provided benefits for all permanent disabilities, whether or not job related.
2. A teacher, injured while working, received full salary during a two-year sick leave. She argued that the payments, made under board of education regulations, were similar to workers' compensation and thus tax free. The IRS disagreed; the regulations were not the same as a workers' compensation statute. The Tax Court supported the teacher. The payments were made because of job-related injuries and were authorized by regulations having the force of law.
3. The IRS, relying on the court decision in Example 2, claimed that a police officer in Lynbrook, N.Y., was subject to tax on line-of-duty disability pay because the payment was under a labor agreement with the Police Benevolent Association (PBA). The Tax Court supported the police officer's claim that the payments were authorized by a specific New York State law requiring full salary for job-related police injuries. The PBA agreement did not affect the officer's rights to those state law payments. Lynbrook treated the case as a workers' compensation claim and in fact received reimbursement from the state workers' compensation board for the payments made to the officer.
4. A Los Angeles sheriff injured on the job retired on disability and, under the Los Angeles workers' compensation law, was allowed to elect sick pay in lieu of the regular workers' compensation amount because the sick pay was larger. The IRS argued that the sheriff had merely received taxable sick pay because he would have received the same amount as sick pay if his injuries had been suffered in a personal accident. However, the Tax Court allowed tax-free treatment. The sick leave was paid under a workers' compensation law that applied solely to work-related injuries. The fact that sick leave may also have been available to other employees under other laws does not mean that it may not be included as an option under a workers' compensation statute.

   The IRS announced that it does not agree with the Tax Court's decision allowing full tax-free treatment. According to the IRS, benefits up to the regular workers' compensation amount should be tax free but excess amounts should be taxed.

Court Decision

Is Sick Leave Tax-Free Workers' Compensation?

According to the Tax Court, sick leave may qualify as tax-free workers' compensation if it is paid under a specific workers' compensation statute or similar government regulation that authorizes the sick leave payment for job-related injuries or illness; *see* Examples 2, 3, and 4 in *2.13*.

Effect of workers' compensation on Social Security. In figuring whether Social Security benefits are taxable *(34.2)*, workers' compensation that reduces Social Security or equivalent Railroad Retirement benefits is treated as a Social Security (or Railroad Retirement) benefit received during the year. Thus, the workers' compensation may be indirectly subject to tax as discussed at *34.2*.

2.14 Disability Pensions

Disability pensions financed by your employer are taxable wages unless they are for severe permanent physical injuries that qualify for tax-free treatment under the rules at *3.3*, they are tax-free workers' compensation *(2.13)*, or they are tax-free government payments as discussed in this section.

Taxable disability pensions are reported as wages until you reach the minimum retirement age under the employer's plan. After reaching minimum retirement age, payments are reported as a pension under the rules of *7.25*.

If you receive little or no Social Security and your other income is below a specified threshold, you may be eligible to claim a tax credit for disability payments received while you are under the age of 65 and permanently and totally disabled; *see 34.7*.

Filing Tip

Military Disability Tax Free

Military disability benefits from the Veterans Administration are tax free.

Injury or sickness resulting from active military service. Disability pensions for personal injuries or sickness resulting from active service in the armed forces are taxable if you joined the service after September 24, 1975.

Military disability payments are tax free if before September 25, 1975, you were entitled to military disability benefits or if on that date you were a member of the armed forces (or reserve unit) of the U.S. or any other country or were under a binding written commitment to become a member. A similar tax-free rule applies to disability pensions from the following government agencies if you were entitled to the payments before September 25, 1975, or were a member of the service (or committed to joining) on that date: The Foreign Service, Public Health Service, or National Oceanic and Atmospheric Administration. The exclusion for pre–September 25, 1975, service applies to disability pensions based upon percentage of disability. However, if a disability pension was based upon years of service, you do not pay tax on the amount that would be received based upon percentage of disability.

Veterans Administration benefits. Disability pensions from the Veterans Administration (now called the Department of Veterans Affairs) are tax free. If you retire from the military and are later given a retroactive award of VA disability benefits, retirement pay during the retroactive period is tax free (other than a lump-sum readjustment payment upon retirement) to the extent of the VA benefit.

If a veteran receives a VA pension for a military service disability, and also disability benefits from the Social Security Administration, the VA benefits are tax free but the Social Security payments may be taxable; *see* below.

Pension based on combat-related injuries. Tax-free treatment applies to payments for combat-related injury or sickness that is incurred as a result of any one of the following activities: (1) as a direct result of armed conflict; (2) while engaged in extra-hazardous service, even if not directly engaged in combat; (3) under conditions simulating war, including maneuvers or training; or (4) that is caused by an instrumentality of war, such as weapons.

Social Security disability benefits. Disability benefits from the Social Security Administration (SSA) are treated as regular Social Security retirement benefits that may be taxable under the rules at *34.2*.

In one case, a veteran who received disability benefits from the SSA as well as a disability pension from the Department of Veterans Affairs (VA) for cancer caused by exposure to Agent Orange during the Vietnam War tried to exclude both benefits from income. The IRS did not dispute the exclusion for the VA payments, but it held that the SSA disability benefits were subject to tax as if they were Social Security retirement benefits. The Tax Court and the Second Circuit Court of Appeals rejected the taxpayer's argument that his SSA disability benefits were excludable as amounts received for personal injuries/sickness resulting from active military service. The Second Circuit held that the military service exclusion is not applicable for SSA disability payments because they are a wage-replacement benefit based on the number of quarters of Social Security coverage, and are payable whether or not the disability arose from military service.

Terrorist attacks or U.S. military actions. Tax-free treatment applies to disability payments received by any individual for injuries incurred as the direct result of a terrorist attack against the United States or its allies. The exclusion also applies to disability income received as a direct result of a military action involving U.S. Armed Forces in response to aggression against the United States or its allies.

Law Alert

Terrorist Attacks

Tax-free treatment applies to disability payments resulting from terrorist attacks inside as well as outside the United States.

Stock Plans and Options

2.15 Stock Appreciation Rights (SARs)

Stock appreciation rights, or SARs, enable employees to receive the benefit of an increase in value of the employer's stock between the date the SARs are granted and the date they are exercised. When the SARs are exercised, cash or stock may be delivered as payment for the post-grant appreciation. For example, when your employer's stock is worth $30 a share, you get 100 SARs exercisable within five years. Two years later, when the stock price has increased to $50 a share, you exercise the SARs and receive $2,000.

If IRS tests are satisfied, the employee is taxed when the post-grant appreciation is received. The situation has been complicated by the enactment of Code Section 409A *(see 2.7)*, which restricts deferrals of income under nonqualified deferred compensation plans. However, the IRS has provided an exception to the Section 409A rules for SARs issued with an exercise price equal to the stock's fair market value when the rights are granted and in Notice 2006-4, the IRS provides good-faith valuation standards.

Caution

Possible AMT Liability for ISO

If you exercise an incentive stock option and your rights in the acquired stock are transferrable and not subject to a substantial risk of forfeiture, you have to treat as an adjustment for alternative minimum tax purposes *(23.2)* the excess of the fair-market value of the stock when the option was exercised over the option price. Unless you sell the stock by the end of that year, you must report an AMT adjustment based on the value of the stock when the option was exercised, even if the value later declines substantially. You avoid the AMT adjustment if you sell the stock in the same year the option was exercised. If your rights in the stock are restricted in the year you exercise the option, the AMT adjustment applies for the year the restrictions are lifted. *See 23.2* for further details.

2.16 Stock Options

Employees receiving statutory stock options do not incur regular income tax liability either at the time the option is granted or when the option is exercised. However, the option spread is generally subject to AMT; *see 23.2.* Statutory options include incentive stock options (ISOs) and options under an employee stock purchase plan (ESPP). Receipt of a nonstatutory (nonqualified) stock option generally results in an immediate tax.

Incentive stock options (ISOs). A corporation may provide its employees with incentive stock options to acquire its stock (or the stock of its parent or subsidiaries). For regular income tax purposes, ISOs meeting tax law tests are not taxed when granted or exercised. Income or loss is not reported until you sell the stock acquired from exercising the ISO. The option must be exercisable within 10 years of the date it is granted and the option price must be at least equal to the fair market value of the stock when the option is granted. If the fair market value of stock for which ISOs may first be exercised in a particular year by an employee exceeds $100,000 (valued at date of grant), the excess is not considered a qualifying ISO. An ISO may be exercised by a former employee within three months of the termination of employment; if exercised after three months, income is realized under the rules for nonqualified options, discussed later in this section.

AMT consequences of exercising ISO. Although you do not realize taxable income for regular tax purposes when you exercise an ISO, you may incur a substantial liability for alternative minimum tax (AMT). *See* the Caution on this page and *23.2.*

Gain or loss on sale of ISO stock. If the stock acquired by the exercise of the ISO is held for more than one year after acquisition and more than two years after the ISO was granted, you have long-term capital gain or loss *(5.3)* on the sale, equal to the difference between the selling price of the stock and the option price you paid when you exercised the ISO.

If you sell *before* meeting the one-year and two-year holding period tests, a gain on the sale is generally treated as ordinary wage income to the extent of the option spread—the excess of the value of the stock when you exercised the ISO over the option price. Any gain in excess of the spread is reported as capital gain. In figuring the capital gain, cost basis for the stock is increased by the amount treated as wages. If the fair market value of the stock declines between the date the option was exercised and the date the stock is sold, the amount that must be treated as wages is generally reduced. The ordinary income (wages) is limited to the actual gain on the stock sale where the gain is less than the option spread at exercise. However, the reduction to ordinary income does *not* apply on a sale of the stock to a related person or if replacement shares are purchased within the wash-sale period *(30.6)* because the reduction applies only if a loss "would be" recognized if sustained (actual loss is not required for limitation to apply so long as a loss "would be" recognized).

If you have a loss on the sale of stock acquired by exercising an ISO, it is a capital loss and there is no ordinary wage income to report.

Employee stock purchase plans (ESPPs). These plans allow employees to buy their company's stock, usually at a discount. The plan must be nondiscriminatory and meet tax law tests on option terms. Options granted under qualified plans are not taxed until you sell the shares acquired from exercising the option.

If you sell the stock more than one year after exercising the option and also more than two years after the option was granted, gain on the sale is capital gain unless the option was granted at a discount. If at the time the option was granted the fair market value of the stock exceeded the option price, then when you sell the stock, gain is ordinary wage income to the extent of that discount. Any excess gain is long-term capital gain. A loss on the sale is long-term capital loss.

If you sell the acquired stock before meeting the one-year and two-year holding period tests, you must report as ordinary wage income the option spread—the excess of the value of the stock when you exercised the option over the option price. This amount must be reported as ordinary income even if it exceeds the gain on the sale (which would occur if the sale price were lower than the exercise price). Add the ordinary income amount to your cost basis for the stock. If the increased basis is less than the selling price, the difference is capital gain. You have a capital loss if the increased basis exceeds the selling price.

EXAMPLES

1. You were granted an incentive stock option (ISO) on March 5, 2004, to buy 1,000 shares of your employer company's stock at its then fair market value of $10 a share. You exercised the option on January 7, 2005, when the market price for the stock was $15 a share. You sold the stock on January 19, 2006, for $20 a share. Although you held the stock for more than one year, you did not sell more than two years after the date the option was granted. Therefore, part of your gain on the sale in 2006 is ordinary wage income. You have ordinary wage income of $5,000, equal to the option spread ($15,000 value on January 7, 2005, minus $10,000 option price) and $5,000 of long-term capital gain.

Selling price ($20 × 1,000 shares)	$20,000
Less: Cost of stock ($10 exercise price × 1,000 shares)	10,000
Gain	10,000
Less: Ordinary wage income	5,000
($15,000 value – $10,000 option price)	
Capital gain ($20,000 sales price – basis of $15,000	$5,000
($10,000 cost + $5,000 treated as wages))	

2. You are granted an option to buy 1,000 shares from your employer's ESPP for $20 a share at a time when the market price is $22 a share. You exercise the option 14 months later when the value of the stock is $23 a share. You sell the stock for $30 a share 18 months after exercising the option. You meet the one-year and two-year holding period tests but because the option was granted at a discount, part of the gain on the sale is treated as ordinary income.

Selling price ($30 × 1,000 shares)	$30,000
Less: Cost of stock ($20 × 1,000 shares)	20,000
Gain	10,000
Less: Ordinary wage income	2,000
($22,000 value at grant – $20,000 option price)	
Capital gain ($30,000 sales price – basis of $22,000	$8,000
($20,000 cost + $2,000 treated as wages))	

3. Same facts as in Example 2, except that you sold the stock only six months after you exercised the ESPP option. Since the one-year holding period test was not met, $3,000 of your $10,000 gain is taxed as ordinary wage income. The $3,000 ordinary income equals the option spread between the $23,000 value of the stock when you exercised the option and the $20,000 option price. You also have a $7,000 short-term capital gain: $30,000 sales price – $23,000 basis ($20,000 cost + $3,000 treated as wages).

Caution

Tax Due on Option Exercise

Determine the amount of cash you will need to make the purchases and meet your tax liability before you exercise a nonqualified option and receive vested stock. If you receive vested stock when you exercise the option, you will realize wage income equal to the excess of the value of the stock over the option price. In addition to the cash to buy the stock, you will need cash to pay the tax on the wage income. The tax is due even if you plan to hold onto the stock before selling.

Nonstatutory (nonqualified) stock options. A nonstatutory stock option (also called a nonqualified option) can in some cases be considered nonqualified deferred compensation subject to the requirements of Code Section 409A. Under IRS proposed regulations, the Section 409A rules apply if the exercise price can be less than the value of the underlying stock when the option is granted or the option permits any other deferral feature.

If the Section 409A rules do *not* apply, the amount of income to include and the time to include it depends on whether the option has a readily ascertainable fair market value when the option is granted. It is very rare for a nonstatutory option to be actively traded on an established securities market or to meet the other tests in IRS regulations for having a readily ascertainable fair market value.

In the usual case where there is no readily ascertainable fair market value for the option at the time it is granted, no income is realized on the receipt of the option. Income will not be realized until the year the option is exercised, assuming you are vested in the stock in the year you receive it. If the stock is *not* vested when you exercise the option, income is deferred until the vesting year, under the restricted property rules at *2.17*. In the year that you become vested in the stock, you must report as ordinary wage income the value of the stock (as of the vesting date), minus the amount you paid. If you receive vested stock when the option is exercised, you are taxed on the difference between the fair market value of the stock when you exercise the option and the option price. For example, in 2006, you exercise a nonstatutory stock option to buy 1,000 shares of your employer's stock at $10 a share when the stock has a value of $30 a share. Your rights to the stock are vested when you buy it. When you exercise the option you are treated as receiving wages of $20,000, equal to the option spread ($30,000 value – $10,000 cost). This income is subject to withholding taxes that you will have to pay out-of-pocket at the time of exercise unless the withholding can be taken from regular cash wages. The taxable spread will be reported as wages on Form W-2 and will be separately identified in Box 12, using Code V. Your cost basis for the shares is increased by the ordinary income reported for exercising the option. If you hold the shares for more than one year after exercising the option and then sell them for $35,000 ($35 a share × 1,000 shares), you will have a $5,000 long-term capital gain ($35,000 – $30,000 increased basis).

If in a rare case a nonstatutory stock option has an ascertainable fair market value, the value of the option less any amount you paid is taxable under the restricted property rules *(2.17)* as ordinary wage income in the first year that your right to the option is freely transferable or not subject to a substantial risk of forfeiture. A Section 83(b) election *(2.17)* may *not* be made for the nonstatutory option. For other details and requirements, *see* IRS Regulation Section 1.83-7.

Nonstatutory stock options may be granted in addition to or in place of incentive stock options. There are no restrictions on the amount of nonstatutory stock options that may be granted.

2.17 Restricted Stock

Planning Reminder

Electing Immediate Tax on Restricted Stock

If you expect restricted stock to appreciate, consider making an election (Section 83(b) election) to be immediately taxed on the value of the restricted stock, minus your cost. If you make the election, any appreciation in value that has accrued since the election was made will not be taxable when the stock becomes substantially vested. Tax on appreciation will not be due until the stock is sold.

If in return for performing services you buy or receive company stock (or other property) subject to restrictions, special tax rules apply. Unless you make the Section 83(b) election discussed below, you do not have to pay tax on the stock until the first year in which it is substantially vested, meaning that it is either transferable or not subject to a substantial risk of forfeiture. A risk of forfeiture exists where your rights are conditioned upon the future performance of substantial services. In the year the property becomes substantially vested, you must report as compensation (wages) the difference between the amount, if any, that you paid for the stock and its value at the time the risk of forfeiture is removed. The valuation at the time the forfeiture restrictions lapse is not reduced because of restrictions imposed on the right to sell the property. However, restrictions that will never lapse do affect valuation.

SEC restrictions on insider trading are considered a substantial risk of forfeiture, so that there is no tax on the receipt of stock subject to such restrictions. However, the SEC permits insiders to immediately resell stock acquired through exercise of an option granted at least six months earlier. As the stock acquired through such options is not subject to SEC restrictions, the executive is subject to immediate tax upon exercise of an option held for at least six months.

If the stock is subject to a restriction on transfer to comply with SEC pooling-of-interests accounting rules, the stock is considered to be subject to a substantial restriction.

Non-employees. The tax rules for restricted property are not limited to employees. They also apply to independent contractors who are compensated for services with restricted stock or other property.

Sale of property that is not substantially vested. If you sell restricted property in an arm's-length transaction before it has become substantially vested and you did not make the Section 83(b) election discussed below, gain on the sale (amount realized minus what you paid) must be reported as compensation income for the year of the sale. If the sale is to a related person or is otherwise not at arm's length, compensation must be reported not only for the year of sale but also for the year the original property becomes substantially vested, as if you still held it. In the later year, the compensation income equals the fair market value of the stock minus the total of the amount you paid for it and the compensation reported on the earlier sale.

Election to include value of restricted stock in income when received (Section 83(b) election). Although restricted stock is generally not taxable until the year in which it is substantially vested, you may elect to be taxed in the year you receive it on the unrestricted value (as of the date the stock is received), less any payment you made. This election, called a Section 83(b) election, must be made by filing a statement with the IRS no later than 30 days after the date the stock is transferred to you. The election may not be revoked without the consent of the IRS.

If you make the election, you are treated as an investor and later appreciation in value is not taxed as pay when your rights to the stock become vested. To figure capital gain or loss when you sell the stock, your cost basis for the stock is increased by the amount of income you reported as pay under the election. If you forfeit the stock after the election is made, a capital loss *(5.4)* is allowed for your cost minus any amount realized on the forfeiture.

EXAMPLES

1. In 2006, when your employer's stock has a market value of $100 a share, your employer allows you to buy 100 shares at $10 a share, or $1,000. Under the terms of your purchase, you must resell the stock to your employer at $10 a share if you leave your job within five years. Because your rights to the stock are subject to a substantial risk of forfeiture, you do not have to include any amount as income in 2006 when you buy it. Assume that in 2011, when the restrictions are lifted, the stock is selling for $200 a share. In 2011, you will have to report $19,000 as ordinary wage income ($20,000 unrestricted value – $1,000 you paid).
2. Same facts as in Example 1, except that within 30 days after you receive the stock, you file a Section 83(b) election with the IRS. With the election, you have wage income for 2006 of $9,000, the value of the stock when you received it ($10,000 for 100 shares) minus your cost ($1,000).

   A signed election statement must be filed with the IRS Service Center where you file your return no later than 30 days after the date you received the stock. The statement must include the following: your name, address, Social Security number, the year for which you are making the election, a description of the stock and the restrictions on the stock, the date you received the stock, the fair market value of the stock at receipt (ignoring restrictions unless they never lapse), your cost, if any, for the stock, and a statement that you have provided a copy of the statement to your employer.

   You will not have to report any wage income when the stock vests in 2011. If after vesting you sell the shares for $20,000, you will have a long-term capital gain of $10,000 ($20,000 – $10,000 increased basis ($1,000 cost plus $9,000 wage income from election)).

Chapter 3

Fringe Benefits

Employer-furnished fringe benefits are exempt from tax if the tests discussed in this chapter are met.

The most common tax-free benefits are accident and health plan coverage, including employer contributions to health savings accounts (HSAs), group-term life insurance plans, dependent care plans, education assistance plans, tuition reduction plans, adoption benefit plans, cafeteria plans, and plans providing employees with discounts, no-additional-cost services, or employer-subsidized meal facilities.

Highly compensated individuals may be taxed on certain benefits from such plans if nondiscrimination rules are not met.

Table 3-1 Are Your Fringe Benefits Tax Free?

Fringe benefit—	*Tax Pointer—*
Adoption benefits	Employer payments to a third party or reimbursements to you in 2006 for qualified adoption expenses are generally tax free up to a limit of $10,960. The exclusion is phased out if modified adjusted gross income is between $164,410 and $204,410; *see 3.6* for further details.
Athletic facilities	The fair market value of athletic facilities, such as gyms, swimming pools, golf courses, and tennis courts, is tax free if the facilities are on property owned or leased by the employer (not necessarily the main business premises) and substantially all of the use of the facilities is by employees, their spouses, and dependent children. Such facilities must be open to all employees on a nondiscriminatory basis in order for the company to deduct related expenses.
Child or dependent care plans	The value of day-care services provided or reimbursed by an employer under a written, nondiscriminatory plan is tax free up to a limit of $5,000, or $2,500 for married persons filing separately. Expenses are excludable if they would qualify for the dependent care credit; *see* Chapter 25. On your tax return, you must report employer-provided benefits to figure the tax-free exclusion. Tax-free employer benefits reduce eligibility for the dependent care tax credit; *see 3.5.*
De minimis *(minor)* fringe benefits	These are small benefits that are administratively impractical to tax, such as occasional supper money and taxi fares for overtime work, company parties or picnics, and occasional theater or sporting event tickets; *see 3.10.*
Discounts on company products and services	Services from your employer that are usually sold to customers are tax free if your employer does not incur additional costs in providing them to you; *see 3.16.* Merchandise discounts and other discounted services are also eligible for a tax-free exclusion; *see 3.17.*
Education plans	An up-to-$5,250 exclusion applies to employer-financed undergraduate and graduate courses; *see 3.7.*
Employee achievement awards	Achievement awards are taxable unless they qualify under special rules for length of service or safety achievement; *see 3.11.*
Group-term life insurance	Premiums paid by employers are not taxed if policy coverage is $50,000 or less; *see 3.4.*
Health and accident plans including HSAs	Premiums paid by an employer are tax free. For 2006, employer contributions to a health savings account, or HSA, on behalf of an eligible employee are generally not taxed up to $2,700 for self-only coverage or $5,450 for family coverage; *see 3.2* for details. Benefits under an employer plan are also generally tax free; *see 3.1–3.3.*
Interest-free or low-interest loans	Interest-free loans received from your employer may be taxed; *see 4.31.*
Retirement planning advice	Employer-provided retirement income planning advice and information are tax free to employees (and their spouses) so long as the employer maintains a qualified retirement plan. The exclusion does not apply to tax preparation, accounting, legal, or brokerage services.
Transportation benefits	Within limits, employer-provided parking benefits and transit passes are tax free; *see 3.8.*
Tuition reductions	Tuition reductions for courses below the graduate level are generally tax free. Graduate students who are teaching or research assistants are not taxed on tuition reduction unless the reduction is compensation for teaching services; *see 3.7.*
Working condition benefits	Benefits provided by your employer that would be deductible if you paid the expenses yourself are a tax-free working condition fringe benefit. Company cars are discussed at *3.8* and other working condition benefits at *3.9.*

Health, Accident, and Group Life Insurance Benefits

3.1 Tax-Free Health and Accident Coverage Under Employer Plans

You are not taxed on *contributions* or *insurance premiums* your employer makes to a health, hospitalization, or accident plan to cover you, your spouse, or your dependents. If you obtain coverage by making *pre-tax* salary-reduction contributions under your employer's cafeteria plan *(3.14)*, the salary reductions are treated as employer contributions that are tax free to you. If you are temporarily laid off and continue to receive health coverage, the employer's contributions during this layoff period are tax free. If you are retired, you do not pay tax on insurance paid by your former employer. Medical coverage provided to the family of a deceased employee is tax free since it is treated as a continuation of the employee's fringe-benefit package.

If your employer provides health and accident coverage to your live-in companion, the coverage is taxable to you where the companion is not recognized as a "spouse" under state law or "dependent" status is barred (even if support and household membership tests in Chapter 21 are met) because the relationship violates local law. Furthermore, under the 1996 Defense of Marriage Act, a gay or lesbian companion is not treated as a spouse for federal tax purposes.

If you are age 65 or older, Medicare premiums paid by your employer are not taxed. If you retire and have the option of receiving continued coverage under the medical plan or a lump-sum payment covering unused accumulated sick leave instead of coverage, the lump-sum amount is reported as income at the time you have the option to receive it. If you elect continued coverage, the amount reported as income may be deductible as medical insurance if you itemize deductions; *see 17.5*.

Disability coverage. If your employer pays the premiums for your disability coverage (short term or long term) and does not report the payment as compensation income on your Form W-2, or if you pay the premiums with pre-tax salary-reduction contributions, your coverage is tax free but any benefits you subsequently receive from the plan upon becoming disabled will be includible in your gross income; *see 3.3*. If you pay the premiums with after-tax contributions or your employer makes contributions that are included on your Form W-2, any disability benefits you receive from the plan will not be taxable to you.

Health Reimbursement Arrangements (HRAs). Employer contributions to health reimbursement arrangements (HRAs) are not taxed to the employees. The contributions must be paid by the employer and not provided by salary reduction. As discussed at *3.3*, HRA contributions can be used to reimburse the medical costs of employees, their spouses, and their dependents, and unused expenses may be carried forward to later years.

Long-term care coverage. An employee is not taxed on employer-provided long-term care coverage that pays benefits in the event the employee becomes *chronically ill*, as defined at *17.15*. However, the coverage is taxable if provided through a cafeteria plan *(3.14)* and reimbursements of long-term care expenses may not be made through a flexible spending arrangement *(3.15)*.

Access and Portability Rules for Group Health Plans

Generally, a group health plan may not bar eligibility to an employee and his or her dependents because of health status or medical history. A plan may exclude coverage for specified conditions or procedures, or limit such coverage, but only if there is no discrimination among similarly situated employees based on health-related factors. Employers are subject to daily penalties if they do not comply with the rules, but small employers with an average of no more than 50 employees in the preceding year are not subject to the penalties, except for those relating to the hospital-length-of-stay requirements for mothers and newborns.

Pre-existing conditions can bar coverage only in limited circumstances. Coverage may be denied for a condition that was diagnosed or treated within six months before enrollment. However, the exclusion cannot last more than 12 months, or 18 months for those who enroll late, and the 12- or 18-month period must be reduced by creditable coverage the employee had before enrollment in the new plan if there was no break in the prior coverage of more than 62 days. Coverage may not be denied to women pregnant on the enrollment date. Newborn children who are enrolled within 30 days of birth must be covered and if the parent changes jobs and enrolls in a new plan without a break in coverage of more than 62 days, the new plan may not exclude the child. A similar protective rule applies to adopted children under age 18 who are enrolled within 30 days of the adoption.

Continuing coverage for group health plans (COBRA coverage). Employers are subject to daily penalties unless they offer continuing group health and accident coverage to employees who leave the company and to spouses and dependent children who would lose coverage in the case of divorce or the death of the employee. The employer may charge the employee or beneficiary a premium of up to 102% of the regular premium imposed under the plan for the applicable (individual or family) coverage. The employer must wait at least 45 days after continuing coverage is elected to require payment of premiums.

Continuing coverage rules do not apply to small employers who in the previous calendar year had fewer than 20 employees on a typical day, or government agencies and churches. For other employers, continuing coverage must be offered in these situations:

1. An employee with coverage who voluntarily or involuntarily leaves the company—unless termination is for gross misconduct. Employees who would lose coverage because of a reduction in hours must also be offered continuing coverage. Continuing coverage must also be offered for the employee's spouse and dependent children who were covered before the employee's termination or reduction in hours. If accepted, the coverage must last for at least 18 months. Within this period, an employee who elects continuing coverage is protected against the possibility of a coverage gap if he or she joins a new company that limits group health coverage for pre-existing conditions; the old employer's continuing coverage must remain available.

   Extended coverage may apply to disabled individuals. The coverage period is extended from 18 months to 29 months for individuals who notify the plan administrator within 60 days of a determination under Title II or XVI of the Social Security Act that they are disabled. The coverage extension applies if the disability exists at any time during the first 60 days of continuing coverage. During the extended coverage period, the maximum premium that can be charged is increased from 102% to 150% of the applicable premium.
2. On the death of a covered employee, continuing coverage must be offered to the surviving spouse and dependent children who are beneficiaries under the plan on the day before the death. Coverage must be for at least 36 months.
3. If a covered employee obtains a divorce or legal separation, continuing coverage must be offered to the spouse and dependent children for at least 36 months.

   If a covered employee drops the coverage for his or her spouse in anticipation of a divorce or legal separation, the spouse must be offered continuing coverage for at least 36 months beginning with the date of divorce or separation. However, the plan does not have to make COBRA coverage available for the period between the date the spouse is dropped from the plan and the date of divorce or separation.
4. If a covered employee becomes eligible for Medicare benefits, continuing coverage under the employer's plan must be offered to the employee's spouse and dependent children for at least 36 months.
5. If a dependent child becomes ineligible under the plan upon reaching a certain age, continuing coverage must be offered for at least 36 months.
6. If an employee with health coverage takes unpaid leave under the Family and Medical Leave Act of 1993 (FMLA) upon the birth or adoption of a child or to deal with a serious family illness, and the employee does not return to work following the leave, continuing coverage must be offered as of the last day of the leave. Continuing coverage must also be offered to the employee's spouse and dependent children if they would otherwise lose coverage.

Court Decision

COBRA Required Despite Other Coverage

The Supreme Court has held that an employer may not deny continuing care coverage to a former employee who on the date of election has coverage under his or her spouse's group health plan.

Caution

Cost of Continuing Coverage

If you leave your job and elect continuing health coverage, you may be charged a premium of 102% of the regular cost of similar coverage under the plan. If the COBRA coverage period is extended because you are disabled, you may be charged 150% of the regular premium during the extended period.

Employers must provide written notice of the continuing coverage option. If one of the previously discussed qualifying events occurs, the eligible employees, spouses, and/or dependent children generally have 60 days to elect continuing coverage.

3.2 Health Savings Accounts (HSAs) and Archer MSAs

If you are covered by a qualifying high-deductible health plan (HDHP), your employer may make tax-free contributions to a health savings account (HSA) on your behalf. Earnings accumulate tax free within an HSA and distributions are tax free if used to pay your qualified medical expenses, or those of your spouse or dependents. If your employer does not make the maximum tax-free contribution to your HSA, you can make a deductible contribution, so long as the total does not exceed the annual contribution limit (*see* below).

Archer MSAs are an older type of medical savings plan that HSAs are intended to replace. The law authorizing the establishment of new Archer MSAs had not been extended beyond 2005 when this book went to press; *see* the *e-Supplement* for an update. However, if your employer set up an Archer MSA on your behalf before 2006, your employer may continue to contribute to the account. If you work for an eligible small employer with a high-deductible plan, your employer may make tax-free contributions to an Archer MSA on your behalf. A rollover can be made from an Archer MSA to a new health savings account (HSA) that accepts rollovers. If the Archer MSA is retained, withdrawals will be tax free if used to pay qualified medical expenses for you, your spouse, or your dependents.

Health Savings Account (HSA)

You may set up an HSA only if you are covered by a qualifying high-deductible health plan (HDHP, *see* details below), you are not enrolled in Medicare, and you are not the dependent of another taxpayer. Generally, you must have no coverage other than HDHP coverage, but there are exceptions. You are allowed to have separate coverage for vision, dental, or long-term care, accidents, disability, *per diem* insurance while hospitalized, insurance for a specific disease or illness, car insurance (or similar insurance for owning or using property), or insurance for workers' compensation or tort liabilities. Preventive care is also exempt from the deductible requirement. Prescription drug coverage before 2006 was also exempt; *see* below.

As an eligible employee, you, your employer, or both may contribute to your HSA. The same maximum annual contribution limit applies (*see* below) regardless of the number of contributors. Your employer may allow you to make pre-tax salary-reduction contributions to an HDHP and HSA as an option under a "cafeteria" plan; *see 3.13*.

Law Alert

Above-the-Line Deduction for HSA Contributions

If you are an eligible employee, contributions you make to your HSA are reported on Form 8889 and deducted on Line 25 of Form 1040; *see 3.2* for contribution limits. The deduction is "above the line", so it is allowed even if you claim the standard deduction.

If you are self-employed, you may claim the "above-the-line" HSA deduction subject to the same limits; *see* Chapter 12 for further details.

High-deductible health plan (HDHP). An HDHP must have a minimum annual deductible and an annual out-of-pocket maximum. For 2006 self-only coverage, an HDHP must have an annual deductible of at least \$1,050 and an annual out-of-pocket maximum of \$5,250 for co-payments, deductibles, and other payments excluding premiums. The annual deductible for 2006 family coverage must be at least \$2,100 and there is a \$10,500 limit on out-of-pocket expenses (excluding premiums). The minimum deductibles and out-of-pocket maximums may be increased for 2007 by a cost-of-living adjustment; *see* the *e-Supplement.*

In the case of family coverage, the terms of the HDHP must deny payments to all family members until the family as a unit incurs annual covered expenses in excess of the minimum annual deductible (\$2,100 for 2006). Thus, if a plan for 2006 allowed payment of an individual family member's medical expenses exceeding \$1,050 even if the family as a whole did not have expenses over \$2,100, the plan would not be a qualified HDHP.

However, the minimum annual HDHP deductible does not apply to preventive care benefits. The plan can qualify as an HDHP even if it pays for preventive care without a deductible or after a small deductible (below the regular HDHP minimum). The IRS has provided a safe harbor list of preventive care benefits, including annual physicals, routine prenatal and well-child care, immunizations, tobacco cessation and obesity programs, and screening services for a broad range of conditions including cancer (such as breast, cervical, prostate, ovarian, and colorectal cancer) and cardiovascular disease. Prescription drugs qualify for the preventive care safe harbor if taken by asymptomatic patients with risk factors for a disease, or by recovering patients to prevent the recurrence of a disease.

Caution

Exception for Prescription Drug Coverage Has Expired

An IRS transition rule allowed individuals with HDHP coverage to make contributions to an HSA in 2004 and 2005 while covered by a separate plan or rider providing prescription drug coverage with no deductible or a deductible lower than the minimum required deductible for HDHPs. However, starting in 2006, separate drug coverage, other than a plan for preventive care medications, is subject to the HDHP deductible.

By law, prescription drug coverage, other than coverage meeting the preventive care safe harbor, is not a permitted exception to the high-deductible requirement. This is a problem for employees whose employers offer separate prescription drug plans that provide first-dollar drug coverage with either a flat dollar or percentage co-payment. HSA contributions cannot be made for individuals with an HDHP and such a prescription drug plan because the prescription drug benefits are not subject to the HDHP minimum annual deductible (\$1,050 for a self-only policy or \$2,100 for a family policy in 2006). The IRS provided a transition rule for 2004 and 2005 that for months before January 1, 2006, allowed HSA contributions for individuals with both an HDHP and a separate plan or rider that provides prescription drug benefits with no deductible or a lower-than-HDHP deductible. However, the IRS did not extend this relief beyond 2005. Thus, prescription drug benefits, other than preventive care medications, are now subject to the high-deductible requirement.

Maximum annual HSA contribution for employees. The maximum annual contribution to an HSA is the sum of the monthly limits. A contribution may be made to an HSA for any month for which an eligible employee had HDHP coverage on the first day of that month.

For 2006, the maximum annual HSA contribution for an employee with self-only coverage is the lesser of the amount of the deductible under the HDHP (which must be at least $1,050) or $2,700. For an employee with family coverage, the maximum contribution for 2006 is the lesser of the deductible under the HDHP (which must be at least $2,100) or $5,450. For eligible individuals who are age 55 or older and younger than 65 in 2006, an additional "catch-up" contribution of $700 may be made. The limit must be reduced by any contributions to an Archer MSA. If HDHP coverage began after the first of the year, $^1/_{12}$ of the annual limit is allowed for each month of coverage.

All employer contributions must be reported on Form 8889, which you attach to your Form 1040. Contributions by your employer up to the above limit are tax free and are not subject to withholding for income tax or FICA (Social Security and Medicare) purposes. All employer contributions to an HSA are reported in Box 12 of Form W-2 with Code W. Contributions exceeding the excludable limit are also reported in Box 1 of Form W-2 as taxable wages. If you do not remove an excess contribution (and any net income) by the due date for your return (including extensions), the excess is subject to a 6% penalty; *see* the instructions to Forms 8889 and 5329.

If your employer contributes less than the limit, you may contribute to your HSA but the same overall limit applies to the aggregate contributions. Contributions you make are reported on Form 8889 and deductible "above the line" from gross income on Line 25 of Form 1040. You must attach Form 8889 to your Form 1040.

For years after 2006, the $2,700 and $5,450 maximum amounts will be increased by an inflation adjustment. The catch-up amount for eligible individuals who are age 55 or older (but under age 65) will be increased by statute to $800 in 2007, $900 in 2008, and $1,000 in 2009.

Archer MSAs

Archer MSAs (medical savings accounts) are in the process of being replaced by HSAs. However, an Archer MSA that is not rolled over to a new HSA may continue to be funded.

To contribute, you must have coverage under a high-deductible health plan and must work for a "small employer," one that had an average of 50 or fewer employees during either of the two preceding years. For 2006, a high-deductible health plan for self-only coverage must have a deductible of at least $1,800 and no more than $2,700. For family coverage, the deductible must be at least $3,650 and no more than $5,450. The high-deductible plan must limit out-of-pocket expenses (other than premiums) for 2006 to $3,650 for self-only coverage and $6,650 for family coverage.

Generally, you are not eligible for an Archer MSA if you have any other health insurance in addition to the high-deductible plan coverage, except for policies covering only disability, vision or dental care, long-term care, or accidental injuries, or plans that pay a flat amount during hospitalization.

Employer contribution limits. Your employer's contributions to your Archer MSA are tax free up to an annual limit of 65% of the plan deductible if you have individual coverage and 75% of the deductible for family coverage. The limit is reduced on a monthly basis if you are not covered for the entire year. For example, if for all of 2006 you were covered by a qualifying family coverage high-deductible plan with a $5,000 annual deductible, the maximum tax-free contribution is $3,750 (75% of $5,000). If you had coverage for only 10 months, the limit would be $3,125 ($^{10}/_{12} \times$ $3,750). All employer contributions to your Archer MSA are reported in Box 12 of Form W-2 (Code R). If the contributions exceed the tax-free limit, the excess is reported in Box 1 of Form W-2 as taxable wages. You must report all employer contributions on Form 8853, which you attach to your Form 1040.

If your employer makes any contributions to your account, you may not make any contributions for that year. In addition, if you and your spouse have family coverage under a high-deductible plan and your spouse's employer contributes to his or her Archer MSA, you cannot contribute to your Archer MSA. If your employer (or spouse's employer) does not contribute, you may make deductible contributions up to the above employer contribution limits. You report your contributions on Form 8853 and claim your deduction on Line 36 of Form 1040. Contributions exceeding the annual limit are subject to a 6% penalty.

3.3 Reimbursements and Other Tax-Free Payments From Employer Health and Accident Plans

Several types of payments from a health or accident plan are not taxable even if your employer paid the entire cost of your coverage:

1. Reimbursements of your medical expenses; *see* below.
2. Payments for permanent physical injuries; *see* below.
3. Distributions from a health savings account (HSA) or Archer MSA if they are used to pay for qualified medical expenses; *see* below.
4. Payments to a chronically ill individual from a qualifying long-term-care insurance contract, but if payments are made on a *per diem* or other periodic basis the exclusion may be limited. For 2006, payments of up to $250 per day are tax free regardless of actual expenses. If the payments exceed $250 per day, you are only taxed to the extent that the payments exceed your qualifying long-term-care expenses. *See 17.15* for further details.

Caution

Reimbursed Cosmetic Surgery

An employer's reimbursement of expenses for cosmetic surgery is taxable unless the employee had surgery to correct disfigurement from an accident, disease, or congenital deformity.

Payments that are not within the above tax-free categories, such as disability benefits, are not taxable to you if you paid all of the premiums with after-tax contributions. If your contributions were made on a pre-tax basis, benefits received from the plan are taxable. For example, benefits are taxable if you paid premiums paid under a cafeteria plan *(3.14)* with pre-tax contributions that were excluded from your income. If your employer paid all the premiums and you were not taxed on your employer's payment, any benefits you receive from the plan are fully taxable. If both you (with after-tax contributions) and your employer contributed to the plan, only the amount received that is attributable to your employer's payments is taxable.

Tax-Free Reimbursements for Medical Expenses

Reimbursements of medical expenses *(17.2)* that you paid for yourself, your spouse, or any dependent are tax free, provided you incurred the expenses after the plan was established. Payment does not have to come directly to you to be tax free; it may go directly to your medical care providers. Reimbursements made under a qualifying health reimbursement arrangement (HRA) qualify for tax-free treatment; *see* below.

Tax-free treatment applies only for reimbursed expenses, not amounts you would have received anyway, such as sick leave that is not dependent on actual medical expenses. If your employer reimburses you for premiums you paid, the reimbursement is tax free so long as your payment was from after-tax funds. If you paid premiums with pre-tax salary reductions, a "reimbursement" from the employer will be taxable to you because the salary reductions are treated as your employer's payment, not yours.

Reimbursements for cosmetic surgery do *not* qualify for tax-free treatment, unless the surgery is for disfigurement related to congenital deformity, disease, or accidental injury.

Reimbursements for your *dependents'* medical expenses are tax free. This exclusion applies not only to reimbursed expenses of persons claimed as dependents *(21.1)* on your return, but also to expenses of qualifying children or relatives who *cannot* be claimed as your dependents because: (1) they are claimed by the other parent under the special rules for divorced/separated parents *(21.7)*, (2) their gross income exceeds the limit for qualifying relatives ($3,300 for 2006), (3) they file a joint return with their spouse, or (4) you are the dependent of another taxpayer and thus are barred from claiming any dependents on your return.

A qualifying dependent does *not* include a live-in mate where the relationship violates local law.

If the reimbursement is for medical expenses you deducted in a previous year, the reimbursement may be taxable. *See 17.4* for the rules on reimbursements of deducted medical expenses.

If you receive payments from more than one policy and the total exceeds your actual medical expenses, the excess is taxable if your employer paid the entire premium; *see* the Examples in *17.4.*

Health Reimbursement Arrangements (HRAs). Employers can set up health reimbursement arrangements (HRAs) to reimburse out-of-pocket medical expenses of employees, their spouses, and their dependents. Former employees including retired employees, and spouses and dependents of deceased employees can be covered. Self-employed individuals are not eligible. An HRA must be funded solely by employer contributions and not by salary reductions or after-tax contributions from employees.

Employees are not taxed on HRA reimbursements for medical expenses that may be claimed as itemized deductions *(17.2)*, including premiums. For contributions and reimbursements *(see 3.1)* to be tax free, employees must not receive cash or any benefit (taxable or nontaxable) from an HRA other than reimbursement for medical expenses. If the reimbursement limit is not fully used up by the end of a coverage year, the unused limit can be carried forward to a subsequent year. Nondiscrimination rules apply to self-insured HRAs.

IRS Alert

Health Reimbursement Arrangements (HRAs)

Employer contributions to an HRA can be used to reimburse the out-of-pocket medical costs of employees, their spouses, and dependents. Contributions to and reimbursements from a qualifying HRA are not taxed to the employees. Unused amounts can be carried forward for reimbursement use in later years.

Self-employed health plan that includes spouse. If a self-employed person hires his or her spouse and provides family coverage under a health plan purchased in the name of the business, the employee-spouse may be reimbursed tax-free for medical expenses incurred by both spouses and their dependent children.

Executives taxed in discriminatory self-insured medical reimbursement plans. Although reimbursements from an employer plan for medical expenses of an employee and his or her spouse and dependents are generally tax free, this exclusion does not apply to certain highly compensated employees and stockholders if the plan is self-insured and it discriminates on their behalf. A plan is self-insured if reimbursement is not provided by an unrelated insurance company. If coverage is provided by an unrelated insurer, these discrimination rules do not apply. If a self-insured plan is deemed discriminatory, rank-and-file employees are not affected; only highly compensated employees are subject to tax.

Highly compensated participants subject to these rules include employees owning more than 10% of the employer's stock, the highest paid 25% of all employees (other than employees who do not have to be covered under the law), and the five highest paid officers.

If highly compensated employees are entitled to reimbursement for expenses not available to other plan participants, any such reimbursements are taxable to them. For example, if only the five highest paid officers are entitled to dental benefits, any dental reimbursements they receive are taxable. However, routine physical exams may be provided to highly compensated employees (but not their dependents) on a discriminatory basis. This exception does not apply to testing for, or treatment of, a specific complaint.

If highly compensated participants are entitled to a higher reimbursement limit than other participants, any excess reimbursement over the lower limit is taxable to the highly compensated participant. For example, if highly compensated employees are entitled to reimbursements up to $5,000 while all others have a $1,000 limit, a highly compensated employee who receives a $4,000 reimbursement must report $3,000 ($4,000 received minus the $1,000 lower limit) as income.

A separate nondiscrimination test applies to plan *eligibility.* The eligibility test requires that the plan benefit: (1) 70% or more of all employees or (2) 80% or more of employees eligible to participate, provided that at least 70% of all employees are eligible. A plan not meeting either test is considered discriminatory unless proven otherwise. In applying these tests, employees may be excluded if they have less than three years of service, are under age 25, do part-time or seasonal work, or are covered by a union collective bargaining agreement. A fraction of the benefits received by a highly compensated individual from a nonqualifying plan is taxable. The fraction equals the total reimbursements to highly compensated participants divided by total plan reimbursements; benefits available only to highly compensated employees are disregarded. For example, assume that a plan failing the eligibility tests pays total reimbursements of $50,000, of which $30,000 is to highly compensated participants. A highly compensated executive who is reimbursed $4,500 for medical expenses must include $2,700 in income:

$$\frac{30{,}000}{50{,}000} \times 4{,}500 = 2{,}700$$

Taxable reimbursements are reported in the year during which the applicable plan year ends. For example, in early 2007 you are reimbursed for a 2006 expense from a calendar-year plan. If under plan provisions the expenses are allocated to the 2006 plan year, the taxable amount should be reported as 2006 income. If the plan does not specify the plan year to which the reimbursement relates, the reimbursement is attributed to the plan year in which payment is made.

Tax-Free Payments for Permanent Physical Injuries

Payments from an employer plan are tax free if they are for the permanent loss of part of the body, permanent loss of use of part of the body, or for permanent disfigurement of yourself, your spouse, or a dependent. An appeals court held that severe hypertension does not involve loss of a bodily part or function and thus does not qualify for the exclusion.

To be tax free, the payments must be based on the kind of injury and have no relation to the length of time you are out of work or prior years of service. If the employer's plan does not specifically allocate benefits according to the nature of the injury, the benefits are taxable even if an employee is in fact permanently disabled.

Filing Tip

Permanent Physical Injuries

An employer's payment for permanent disfigurement or permanent loss of bodily function is tax free if the payment is based solely on the nature of the injury. Whether or not you qualify for this exclusion, you may deduct as an itemized deduction any unreimbursed medical expense you have in connection with these injuries subject to the 7.5% adjusted gross income floor; *see 17.1* for details.

EXAMPLE

After he loses a foot in an accident, Marc Jones receives $50,000 as specified in his employer's plan. The payment is tax free as it does not depend on how long Jones is out from work.

Disability payments from profit-sharing plan. The Tax Court has held that a profit-sharing plan may provide benefits that qualify for the exclusion for permanent disfigurement or permanent loss of bodily function. The plan must clearly state that its purpose is to provide qualifying tax-free benefits, and a specific payment schedule must be provided for different types of injuries. Without such provisions, payments from the plan are treated as taxable retirement distributions.

HSA or Archer MSA Payments

Tax-free distributions from a health savings account (HSA). Distributions from an HSA *(3.2)* are tax free if used to pay qualified medical expenses for you, your spouse, or your dependents. Qualified medical expenses are unreimbursed costs eligible for the itemized deduction *(17.2)* on Schedule A of Form 1040. Medical expenses are "qualified" only if incurred *after* the HSA has been established. A distribution is taxable to the extent it is not used to pay qualified medical expenses. A taxable distribution is also subject to a 10% penalty unless you are disabled or are age 65 or older. Distributions will be reported to you on Form 1099-SA and you must report them on Form 8889, which you attach to Form 1040. On Form 8889, you determine if any part of the distribution is taxable and, if it is, that amount must be included as "Other income" on Line 21 of Form 1040. The 10% penalty from Form 8889, if any, is entered on Form 1040, Line 63 (total tax). On the dotted lines next to Lines 21 and 63, enter "HSA" and the amount on the dotted line.

A non-spouse beneficiary who inherits an HSA after the death of the account owner generally must include in income the fair market value of the assets as of the date of death. However, the beneficiary is not subject to the 10% penalty for taxable distributions. If the beneficiary is the account owner's spouse, he or she becomes the owner of the HSA and will be taxed only on distributions that are not used for qualified medical expenses.

Tax-free distributions from Archer MSA. If you work for a small-business employer and have a qualifying Archer MSA *(3.2)*, earnings accumulate in the account tax free. Withdrawals are tax free if used to pay deductible medical costs for you, your spouse, or dependents. Withdrawals used for any other purpose are taxable and a taxable distribution before age 65 or becoming disabled is also subject to a 15% penalty. *See 12.12* for further details.

3.4 Group-Term Life Insurance Premiums

You are not taxed on your employer's payments of premiums on a policy of up to $50,000 on your life. You are taxed only on the cost of premiums for coverage of over $50,000 as determined by the IRS rates shown in the table below. On Form W-2 your employer should include the taxable amount as wages in Box 1 and separately label the amount in Box 12 with Code C. You may not avoid tax by assigning the policy to another person.

If two or more employers provide you with group-term insurance coverage, you get only one $50,000 exclusion. You must figure the taxable cost for coverage over $50,000 by using the IRS rates below.

Regardless of the amount of the policy, you are not taxed if, for your entire tax year, the beneficiary of the policy is a tax-exempt charitable organization or your employer.

Your payments reduce taxable amount. If you pay part of the cost of the insurance, your payment reduces dollar for dollar the amount includible as pay on Form W-2.

Retirees. If you retired before 1984 at normal retirement age or on disability and are still covered by a company group-term life insurance policy, you are not taxed on premium payments made by your employer even if coverage is over $50,000. If you retired after 1983 because of disability and remain covered by your company's plan, you are not taxed even if coverage exceeds $50,000. Furthermore, if you retired after 1983 and are not disabled, you may qualify for tax-free coverage over $50,000 if the following tests are met:

1. The insurance is provided under a plan existing on January 1, 1984, or under a comparable successor plan;
2. You were employed during 1983 by the company having the plan, or a predecessor employer; and
3. You were age 55 or over on January 1, 1984.

However, even if the three tests are met, you may be taxed under the rule below for discriminatory plans if you retired after 1986 and were a key employee.

Key employees taxed under discriminatory plans. The $50,000 exclusion is not available to key employees unless the group plan meets nondiscrimination tests for eligibility and benefits. For 2006, key employees include those who during the year were: (1) more-than-5% owners; (2) more-than-1% owners earning over $150,000; and (3) officers with compensation over $140,000. If the plan discriminates, a key employee's taxable benefit is based on the larger of (1) the actual cost of coverage or (2) the amount for coverage using the IRS rate table below.

The nondiscrimination rules also apply to former employees who were key employees when they separated from service. The discrimination tests are applied separately with respect to active and former employees.

Group-term life insurance for dependents. Employer-paid coverage for your spouse or dependents is a tax-free *de minimis* fringe benefit *(3.10)* if the policy is $2,000 or less. For coverage over $2,000, you are taxed on the excess of the cost (determined under the IRS table below) over your after-tax payments for the insurance, if any.

Filing Instruction

Uncollected Social Security and Medicare of Former Employees

If you receive coverage as a former employee, you must pay with Form 1040 (Line 63) your share of Social Security and Medicare taxes on group-term life insurance over $50,000. The taxable amounts are shown in Box 12 of Form W-2, with Codes M and N.

Table 3-2 Taxable Premiums for Group-Term Insurance Coverage Over $50,000

*Age—**	*Monthly cost for each $1,000 of coverage over $50,000—*
Under 25	$0.05
25–29	0.06
30–34	0.08
35–39	0.09
40–44	0.10
45–49	0.15
50–54	0.23
55–59	0.43
60–64	0.66
65–69	1.27
70 and over	2.06

*Age is determined at end of year.

EXAMPLE

Lynda Jackson, a 52-year-old executive, is provided $200,000 of group-term life insurance in 2006. The taxable value of the coverage is based on the $150,000 coverage in excess of the $50,000 exclusion. As shown in the rate table above, the premium used to determine the taxable coverage is $0.23 for every $1,000 of coverage over $50,000. The taxable amount for the year is $414 ($0.23 x 12 months x 150).

If Lynda had paid $120 towards the coverage, the taxable amount would be reduced to $294 ($414 – $120).

Permanent life insurance. If your employer pays premiums on your behalf for permanent nonforfeitable life insurance, you report as taxable wages the cost of the benefit, less any amount you paid. A permanent benefit is an economic value that extends beyond one year and includes paid-up insurance or cash surrender value, but does not include, for example, the right to convert or continue life insurance coverage after group coverage is terminated. Where permanent benefits are combined with term insurance, the permanent benefits are taxed under formulas found in IRS regulations.

Dependent Care, Adoption Benefits, and Educational Assistance

Caution

Figuring Tax-Free Exclusion for Employer-Provided Dependent Care

You cannot assume that your employer-provided dependent care benefit is completely tax free merely because your employer has not included any part of it in Box 1 of Form W-2 as taxable wages. Although up to $5,000 of benefits are generally tax free, the tax-free amount is reduced where you or your spouse earn less than $5,000 or where you file separately from your spouse. You must show the amount of your qualifying dependent care expenses and figure the tax-free exclusion on Form 2441 if you file Form 1040, or on Schedule 2 of Form 1040A.

3.5 Dependent Care Assistance

The value of qualifying day-care services provided by your employer under a written, nondiscriminatory plan is generally not taxable up to a limit of $5,000, or $2,500 if you are filing separately. The same tax-free limits apply if you make pre-tax salary deferrals to a flexible spending account for reimbursing dependent care expenses *(3.15)*. However, you may not exclude from income more than your earned income. If you are married and your spouse earns less than you do, your tax-free benefit is limited to his or her earned income. If your spouse does not work, all of your benefits are taxable unless he or she is a full-time student or is disabled. If a full-time student or disabled, your spouse is treated as earning $250 a month if your dependent care expenses are for one dependent, or $500 a month if the expenses are for two or more dependents.

Expenses are excludable from income only if they would qualify for the dependent care credit; *see* Chapter 25. If you are being reimbursed by your employer, the exclusion is not allowed if dependent care is provided by a relative who is your dependent (or your spouse's dependent) or by your child under the age of 19. You must give your employer a record of the care provider's name, address, and tax identification number. The identifying information also must be listed on your return.

Reporting employer benefits on your return. Your employer will show the total amount of your dependent care benefits in Box 10 of your Form W-2. Any benefits over $5,000 will also be included as taxable wages in Box 1 of Form W-2 and as Social Security wages (Box 3) and Medicare wages (Box 5).

If you file Form 1040, you must report the benefits on Part III of Form 2441. If you file Form 1040A, you report the employer benefits on Schedule 2. On these forms, you determine both the tax-free and taxable (if any) portions of the employer-provided benefits. If any part is taxable, that amount must be included on Line 7 of your return as wages and labeled "DCB."

Follow IRS instructions for identifying the care provider (employer, babysitter, etc.) on Form 2441 or on Schedule 2 of Form 1040A.

The tax-free portion of employer benefits reduces eligibility for the dependent care credit; see *Chapter 25.*

Filing Tip

Claiming Credit and Exclusion

If you paid adoption expenses in 2006 that were not reimbursed by your employer, and the adoption was final in 2006, you may be able to claim the adoption credit; *see* Chapter 25.

3.6 Adoption Benefits

If your employer pays or reimburses you in 2006 for qualifying adoption expenses under a written, nondiscriminatory plan, up to $10,960 per qualifying child may be tax free. The limit may be increased for 2007 by an inflation adjustment. Employer-provided adoption assistance may be for any child under age 18, or a person physically or mentally incapable of self-care. The exclusion applies to adoption fees, attorney fees, court costs, travel expenses, and other expenses directly related to a legal adoption. Expenses for adopting your spouse's child and the costs of a surrogate-parenting arrangement do *not* qualify. If you have other qualifying adoption expenses, you may also be able to claim a tax credit up to a separate $10,960 limit; both the exclusion and the credit may be claimed for the same adoption if they are not for the same expenses. The exclusion and the credit are subject to similar limitations, including a phaseout based on income. *See* Chapter 25 for a full discussion of the credit.

The full $10,960 exclusion limit is available for the adoption of a "special needs" child even if actual adoption expenses are less than $10,960. A "special needs" designation is made when a state determines that adoption assistance is required to place a child (U.S. citizen or resident) with adoptive parents because of special factors, such as the child's physical condition or ethnicity.

If you are adopting a child who is not a U.S. citizen or resident when the adoption effort begins, the exclusion is available only in the year the adoption becomes final. For example, if in 2006 your employer pays for expenses of adopting a foreign child but the adoption has not become final by the end of the year, you must report the employer's payment as wage income for 2006. You will claim the exclusion on Form 8839 in the year the adoption is final.

Reporting employer benefits and claiming the exclusion on your 2006 return. You must file Form 8839 to report your employer's payments and to figure the tax-free and taxable portions of the benefits. The employer's payments will be included in Box 12 of Form W-2 (Code T). This total includes pre-tax salary reduction contributions that you made to a cafeteria plan *(3.14)* to cover such expenses.

If you are married, you generally must file a joint return to exclude the benefits as income. However, if you are legally separated or if you lived apart from your spouse for the last six months of the year, the exclusion may be available on a separate return; *see* Form 8839 for details.

On 2006 tax returns, the allowable exclusion is phased out if your modified adjusted gross income (MAGI) is between $164,410 and $204,410 (including the employer's adoption assistance and adding back certain tax-free income from foreign sources). Figure the tax-free amount on Form 8839. If your modified adjusted income for 2006 is $204,410 or more, employer-paid adoption expenses are fully taxable.

3.7 Education Assistance Plans

If your employer pays for job-related courses, the payment is tax free to you provided that the courses do not satisfy the employer's minimum education standards and do not qualify you for a new profession. If these tests are met, the employer's education assistance is a tax-free working condition fringe benefit *(3.9)*.

Even if not job related, your employer's payment for courses is tax free up to $5,250, provided the assistance is under a qualifying Section 127 plan meeting nondiscriminatory tests. Graduate courses qualify for the exclusion as well as undergraduate courses. The Section 127 exclusion covers tuition, fees, books, and equipment, plus supplies that you cannot keep at the end of the course. Lodging, meals, and transportation are not covered by the exclusion. Sports or hobby-type courses qualify only if the courses are related to your business or are required as part of a degree program.

Tuition reductions. Employees and retired employees of educational institutions, their spouses, and their dependent children are not taxed on tuition reductions for *undergraduate* courses provided the reduction is not payment for teaching or other services. However, an exclusion is allowed for tuition reductions under the National Health Services Corps Scholarship Program and the Armed Forces Health Professions Scholarship Program despite the recipient's service obligation. Widows or widowers of deceased employees or of former employees also qualify. Officers and highly paid employees may claim the exclusion only if the employer plan does not discriminate on their behalf. The exclusion applies to tuition for undergraduate education at any educational institution, not only the employer's school.

Graduate students who are teaching or research assistants at an educational institution are not taxed on tuition reductions for courses at that school if the tuition reduction is in addition to regular pay for the teaching or research services or the reduction is provided under the National Health Services Corps Scholarship Program or the Armed Forces Health Professions Scholarship Program. The graduate student exclusion for tuition reductions applies only to teaching and research assistants, and not to faculty or other staff members (or their spouses and dependents) who take graduate courses and also do research for or teach at the school. However, if the graduate courses are work related, a tuition reduction for faculty and staff may qualify as a tax-free working condition fringe benefit *(3.9)*.

Planning Reminder

Graduate Courses

Your employer's payment of graduate school expenses qualifies for the up-to-$5,250 exclusion.

Company Cars, Working Condition and *De Minimis* Benefits, and Employee Achievement Awards

3.8 Company Cars, Parking, and Transit Passes

The costs of commuting to a regular job site are not deductible *(20.2)*, but employees who receive transit passes or travel to work on an employer-financed van get a tax break by not having to pay tax on some or all of such benefits. Where a company car is provided, the value of personal use is generally taxable, as discussed below.

Company cars. The use of a company car is tax free under the working condition fringe benefit rule *(3.9)*, provided you use the car for business. If you use the car for personal driving, your company has the responsibility of calculating taxable income, which generally is based on IRS tables that specify the annual lease value of various priced cars. You are also required to keep for your employer a mileage log or similar record to substantiate your business use. Your employer should tell you what type of records are required.

Planning Reminder

Year-End Benefits

Your employer may decide to treat fringe benefits provided during the last two months of the calendar year as if they were paid during the following year. For example, if your employer makes this election for a company car provided to you in November or December of 2006, only the value of personal use from January through October is taxable to you in 2006; personal use in November and December is taxable in 2007. If your employer elects this special year-end rule, you should be notified near the end of the year or when you receive Form W-2.

Regardless of personal use, you are not subject to tax for a company vehicle that the IRS considers to be of limited personal value. These are ambulances or hearses; flatbed trucks; dump, garbage, or refrigerated trucks; one-passenger delivery trucks (including trucks with folding jump seats); tractors, combines, and other farm equipment; or forklifts. Also not taxable is personal use of school buses, passenger buses (seating at least 20), and moving vans where such personal use is restricted; and police or fire vehicles, or an unmarked law enforcement vehicle, where personal use is authorized by a government agency.

Demonstration cars. The value of a demonstration car used by a full-time auto salesperson is tax free as a working condition fringe benefit if the use of the car facilitates job performance and if there are substantial personal-use restrictions, including a prohibition on use by family members and for vacation trips. Furthermore, mileage outside of normal working hours must be limited and personal driving must generally be restricted to a 75-mile radius around the dealer's sales office.

Chauffeur services. If chauffeur services are provided for both business and personal purposes, you must report as income the value of the personal services. For example, if the full value of the chauffeur services is $30,000 and 30% of the chauffeur's workday is spent driving on personal trips, then $9,000 is taxable (30% of $30,000) and $21,000 is tax free.

If an employer provides a bodyguard-chauffeur for business security reasons, the entire value of the chauffeur services is considered a tax-free working condition fringe benefit if: (1) the automobile is specially equipped for security and (2) the bodyguard is trained in evasive driving techniques and is provided as part of an overall 24-hour-a-day security program. If the value of the bodyguard-chauffeur services is tax free, the employee is still taxable on the value of using the vehicle for commuting or other personal travel.

How your employer reports taxable automobile benefits. Social Security and Medicare tax must be withheld. Income tax withholding is not required, but your employer may choose to withhold income tax. If income tax is *not* withheld, you must be notified of this fact so that you may consider the taxable benefits when determining whether to make estimated tax installments; *see* Chapter 27. Whether or not withholdings are taken, the taxable value of the benefits is entered on your Form W-2 in Box 14 or on a separate Form W-2 for fringe benefits.

A special IRS rule allows your employer to include 100% of the lease value of using the car on Form W-2, even if you used the car primarily for business. Your employer must specifically indicate on Form W-2 (Box 14) or on a separate statement if 100% of the lease value has been included as income on your Form W-2. If it has, you should compute a deduction on Form 2106 for the business-use value of the car. However, this deduction, plus any unreimbursed car operating expenses, may be claimed only as a miscellaneous itemized deduction on Schedule A subject to the 2% AGI floor; *see 19.1*.

Company planes. Under rules similar to those for company cars, employees who use a company airplane for personal trips are taxable on the value of the flights, as determined by the employer using IRS tables.

Qualified Transportation Benefits

Your employer may provide you with transportation benefits that are tax free within certain limits. There are two categories of qualified benefits: (1) transit passes and commuter transportation in a van, bus, or similar highway vehicle are considered together, and (2) parking.

Transit passes and commuter transportation are subject to a *combined* tax-free limit of $105 a month in 2006. The tax-free exclusion for qualified parking in 2006 is $205 a month. You may receive benefits from each category so long as the applicable monthly limit is not exceeded. If the benefits exceed the monthly limit, the excess is treated as wages subject to income tax, Social Security, and Medicare tax.

The benefits may be provided through a salary-reduction arrangement. An irrevocable salary-reduction election may be made prospectively for a monthly amount of transportation benefits. The salary reduction for any month may not exceed the total limit for both categories, which for 2006 was $310, $105 for transit passes and commuter vehicles, plus $205 for parking. Unused salary reductions may be carried over to later months and from year to year. However, if you leave the company before using the carryover, the unused amount is forfeited; you cannot get a refund.

Cash reimbursements of qualified transportation benefits are generally tax free if provided under a bona fide reimbursement arrangement. However, for transit passes, vouchers, not reimbursements, are the preferred method. A cash reimbursement for a transit pass is taxable if vouchers (or similar items) are readily available to the employer for distribution to employees. "Ready availability" is determined under tests in IRS regulations. Cash advances for either category of benefits are taxable.

Additional details on the two categories of qualified transportation benefits are in the following paragraphs.

Employer-provided transit passes and van pooling. For regular employees, up to $105 a month is tax free in 2006 for the combined value of employer-provided transit passes plus commuting on an employer's van or bus. For example, if in 2006 the monthly value of a transit pass was $130, $25 per month was treated as taxable wages. If the value of benefits was less than $105 in any month, the unused exclusion cannot be carried over to later months. For years after 2006, the $105 monthly exclusion limit may be increased for inflation.

Qualifying transit passes include tokens, fare cards, or vouchers for mass transit or private transportation businesses using highway vehicles seating at least six passengers.

Qualifying van or bus pool vehicles must seat at least six passengers and be used at least 80% of the time for employee commuting; on average, the number of employees must be at least half the seating capacity.

The exclusion applies only to regular employees. For partners, more than 2% S corporation shareholders, and independent contractors who are provided transit passes, the IRS allows up to $21 per month as a tax-free *de minimis* benefit. If the monthly value exceeds $21, the full value is taxable and not just the excess over $21.

Parking provided by employer. For regular employees, the value of employer-provided parking spots or subsidized parking is tax free in 2006 up to a limit of $205 per month. Parking must be on or near the employer's premises, at a mass transit facility such as a train station or car pooling center. The value of parking benefits exceeding $205 per month is taxable in 2006. For years after 2006, the $205 monthly cap may be adjusted for inflation.

According to the IRS, parking benefits are to be valued according to the regular commercial price for parking at the same or nearby locations. For example, if an employer in a rural or suburban location provides free parking for employees and there are no commercial parking lots in the area, the employee parking is tax free. Where free parking is available to both business customers and employees, the employee parking is considered to have "zero" value unless the employee has a *reserved* parking space that is closer to the business entrance than the spaces allotted to customers.

If the value of the right of access to a parking space exceeds $205 in a month, an employee will be taxed on the excess for 2006 even if he or she actually uses the space for only a few days during the month.

If the employee pays a reduced monthly price for parking in 2006, there is a taxable benefit for that month only if the price paid plus the $205 exclusion is less than the value of the parking.

Commuter parking benefits for self-employed partners, independent contractors, or more than 2% S corporation shareholders do not qualify for the $205 exclusion but may qualify as a tax-free *de minimis* benefit *(3.10)*.

Planning Reminder

Transportation Benefits

If your employer offers you the choice of receiving parking, transit pass, or van pooling benefits instead of cash salary as part of a "cafeteria" plan *(3.13)* and you elect the benefits rather than the cash, you are not taxed, provided the value does not exceed the monthly tax-free limit.

3.9 Working Condition Fringe Benefits

An employer-provided benefit that would be deductible by you if you paid for it yourself *(19.3)* is a tax-free working condition fringe benefit. Under IRS regulations, such benefits include:

Company car or plane. The value of a company car or plane is tax free to the extent that you use it for business; *see 3.8* for more on company cars.

Employer-paid business subscriptions or reimbursed membership dues in professional associations.

Product testing. This is a limited exclusion for employees who test and evaluate company manufactured goods away from company premises.

Employer-provided education assistance. Employer-paid undergraduate and graduate courses may be a tax-free working condition fringe benefit if the courses maintain or improve job skills but are not needed to meet your employer's minimum educational requirements and do not prepare you for a new profession.

Job-placement assistance. According to the IRS, job placement services are tax free so long as they are geared to helping the employees find jobs in the same line of work and the employees do not have an option to take cash instead of the benefits. The employer must also have a business purpose for providing such assistance, such as maintaining employee morale.

For tax-free treatment, there is no nondiscrimination requirement; different types of job placement assistance may be offered, or no assistance at all, in the case of discharged employees with readily transferable skills. Tax-free benefits include the value of counseling on interviewing skills and resume preparation. Executives may be given secretarial support and the use of a private office during the job search.

Job placement benefits received as part of a severance pay arrangement are taxable to the extent that cash could have been elected. An offsetting deduction can be claimed only as a miscellaneous itemized deduction subject to the 2% of adjusted gross income floor *(19.3)*.

3.10 *De Minimis* Fringe Benefits

Small benefits that would be administratively impractical to tax are considered tax-free *de minimis* (minor) fringe benefits. Examples are occasional meal money or local transportation fares given to employees working overtime, employer-provided coffee, doughnuts, or soft drinks, personal use of company copying machines, company parties, or tickets for the theater or sporting events. Other *de minimis* benefits include:

Company eating facility. The value of meals received by employees on workdays at a subsidized eating facility is a tax-free *de minimis* fringe benefit if the facility is located on or near the business premises and the annual revenue from meal charges equals or exceeds the facility's direct operating costs. Revenue is treated as equal to operating costs for meals that are tax-free to employees under the employer convenience test discussed at *3.12*.

Highly compensated employees or owners with special access to executive dining rooms may not exclude the value of their meals as a *de minimis* fringe benefit; however, the meals may be tax free under the rules in *3.12* if meals must be taken on company premises for business reasons.

Planning Reminder

Occasional Overtime Meal Money or Cab Fare

If you work overtime and occasionally receive meal money or cab fare home, the amount is tax free. The IRS has not provided a numerical standard for determining when payments are "occasional."

Commuting under unsafe circumstances. If you are asked to work outside your normal working hours and due to unsafe conditions your employer provides transportation such as taxi fare, the first $1.50 per one-way commute is taxable but the excess over $1.50 is a tax-free *de minimis* benefit. This exclusion is not available to certain highly compensated employees and officers, corporate directors, or owners of 1% or more of the company.

Even when working their regular shift, hourly employees who are not considered highly compensated are taxed on only $1.50 per one-way commute if their employer pays for car service or taxi fare because walking or taking public transportation to or from work would be unsafe. The excess value of the transportation over $1.50 is tax free. These rules can apply to day-shift employees who work overtime as well as night-shift employees working regular hours so long as transportation is provided because of unsafe conditions.

3.11 Employee Achievement Awards

Achievement awards are taxable unless they meet special rules for awards of tangible personal property (such as a watch, television, or golf clubs) given to you in recognition of length of service or safety achievement. Cash awards, gift certificates, and similar items are taxable.

As a general rule, if your employer is allowed to deduct the cost of a tangible personal property award, you are not taxed. The employer's deduction limit, and therefore the excludable limit for you, is $400 for awards from nonqualified plans and $1,600 for awards from qualified plans or from a combination of qualified and nonqualified plans. If your employer's deduction is less than the item's cost, you are taxed on the greater of: (1) the difference between the cost and your employer's deduction, but no more than the award's fair market value; or (2) the excess of the item's fair market value over your employer's deduction. Deduction tests for achievement awards are discussed at *20.25*. Your employer must tell you if the award qualifies for full or partial tax-free treatment.

An award will not be treated as a tax-free safety achievement award if employee safety achievement awards (other than those of *de minimis* value) during the year have already been granted to more than 10% of employees (not counting managers, administrators, clerical employees, or other professional employees). An award made to a manager, administrator, clerical employee, or other professional employee for safety achievement does not qualify for tax-free treatment.

Tax-free treatment also does not apply when you receive an award for length of service during the first five years of employment or when you previously received such awards during the last five years, unless the prior award qualified as a *de minimis* fringe benefit.

Caution

Underpriced Award Items

If the value of an achievement award item is disproportionately high compared to the employer's cost, the IRS may conclude that the award is disguised compensation, in which case the entire value would be taxable.

Meals and Lodging

3.12 Employer-Furnished Meals or Lodging

The value of employer-furnished *meals* is not taxable if furnished on your employer's business premises for the employer's convenience. The value of *lodging* is not taxable if, as a condition of your employment, you must accept the lodging on the employer's business premises for the employer's convenience.

Business premises test. The IRS generally defines business premises as the place of employment, such as a company cafeteria in a factory for a cook or an employer's home for a household employee. The Tax Court has a more liberal view, extending the area of business premises beyond the actual place of business in such cases as these:

- A house provided a hotel manager, although located across the street from the hotel. The IRS has agreed to the decision.
- A house provided a motel manager, two blocks from the motel. However, a court of appeals reversed the decision and held in the IRS's favor.
- A rented hotel suite that is used daily by executives for a luncheon conference.

Convenience of employer test. The employer convenience test requires proof that an employer provides the free meals or lodging for a business purpose other than providing extra pay. In the case of meals, the employer convenience test is deemed to be satisfied for *all* meals provided on employer premises if a qualifying business purpose is shown for more than 50% of the meals. If meals and lodging are described in a contract or state statute as extra pay, this does not bar tax-free treatment provided they are *also* furnished for other substantial, noncompensatory business reasons; for example, you are required to be on call 24 hours a day, or there are inadequate eating facilities near the business premises.

Meal charges. Your company may charge for meals on company premises and give you an option to accept or decline the meals. However, by law, the IRS must disregard the charge and option factors in determining whether meals that you buy are furnished for noncompensatory business reasons. If such business reasons exist, the convenience-of-employer test is satisfied. If such reasons do not exist, the value of the meals may be tax free as a *de minimis* benefit *(3.10)*; otherwise, the value of the meal subsidy provided by the employer is taxable.

Where your employer provides meals on business premises at a fixed charge that is subtracted from your pay whether you accept the meals or not, the amount of the charge is excluded from your taxable pay. If the meal is provided for the employer's convenience, as in the previous Examples, the value of the meals received is also tax free. If it is not provided for the employer's convenience, the value is taxable whether it exceeds or is less than the amount charged.

Planning Reminder

Meal Exclusion

You may be able to avoid tax on meals that you receive on your employer's premises even if your meals do not satisfy the employer convenience test. If more than half of the employees to whom meals are furnished on the employer's business premises are furnished the meals for the employer's convenience, *all* of the on-premises meals are treated as being furnished for the employer's convenience.

EXAMPLES

1. A Las Vegas casino operator provided free cafeteria meals to employees, who were required to remain on casino premises during their entire shift. A federal appeals court (Ninth Circuit) held that the casino's "stay-on-premises" requirement constituted a legitimate business reason for the meals and thus all of the employee meals were tax free under the employer convenience test. The court refused to second guess the casino's business decision that a "stay-on-premises" policy was necessary for security and logistics reasons. Once that policy was adopted, the casino employees had no choice but to eat on the premises. The IRS responded to the decision by announcing that it would not challenge "employer convenience" treatment in similar cases where employees are precluded from obtaining a meal off-premises within a normal meal period.
2. A waitress who works from 7 a.m. to 4 p.m. is furnished two meals a day without charge. Her employer encourages her to have her breakfast at the restaurant before working, but she is required to have her lunch there. The value of her breakfast and lunch is not taxable under IRS regulations because it is furnished during her work period or immediately before or after the period. But say she is also allowed to have free meals on her days off and a free supper on the days she works. The value of these meals is taxable; they are not furnished during or immediately before or after her work period.
3. A hospital maintains a cafeteria on its premises where all of its employees may eat during their working hours. No charge is made for these meals. The hospital furnishes meals to have the employees available for emergencies. The employees are not required to eat there. Since the hospital furnishes the meals in order to have employees available for emergency call during meal periods, the meals are not income to any of the hospital employees who obtain their meals at the hospital cafeteria.
4. To assure bank teller service during the busy lunch period, a bank limits tellers to 30 minutes for lunch and provides them with free meals in a cafeteria on the premises so they can eat within this time period. The value of the meals is tax free.

Court Decision

House One Block Away

Two federal courts held that a school superintendent received tax-free lodging where the home was one block away from the school and separated by a row of other houses. This met the business premises test. The IRS announced that it would continue to litigate similar cases arising outside the Eighth Circuit in which the case arose. The Eighth Circuit includes the states of Arkansas, Iowa, Minnesota, Missouri, Nebraska, and North and South Dakota.

Lodging must be condition of employment. This test requires evidence that the lodging is necessary for you to perform your job properly, as where you are required to be available for duty at all times. The IRS may question the claim that you are required to be on 24-hour duty. For example, at one college, rent-free lodgings were provided to teaching and administrative staff members, maintenance workers, dormitory parents who supervised and resided with students, and an evening nurse. The IRS ruled that only the lodgings provided to the dorm parents and the nurse met the tax-free lodging tests because for the convenience of the college, they had to be available after regular school hours to respond to emergencies.

If you are given the choice of free lodging at your place of employment or a cash allowance, the lodging is not considered to be a condition of employment, and its value is taxable.

If the lodging qualifies as tax free, so does the value of employer-paid utilities such as heat, electricity, gas, water, sewerage, and other utilities. Where these services are furnished by the employer and their value is deducted from your salary, the amount deducted is excluded from taxable wages on Form W-2. But if you pay for the utilities yourself, you may not exclude their cost from your income.

EXAMPLE

Tyrone Jones is employed at a construction project at a remote job site. His pay is $1,500 a week. Because there are no accessible places near the site for food and lodging, the employer furnishes meals and lodging for which it charges $400 a week, which is taken out of Jones's pay. Jones reports only the net amount he receives—$1,100 a week. The value of the meals and lodging is a tax-free benefit.

Groceries. An employer may furnish unprepared food, such as groceries, rather than prepared meals. Courts are divided on whether the value of the groceries is excludable from income. One court allowed an exclusion for the value of nonfood items, such as napkins and soap—as well as for groceries—furnished to a doctor who ate at his home on the hospital grounds so that he would be available for emergencies.

Cash allowances. A cash allowance for meals and lodging is taxable.

Faculty lodging. Teachers and other employees (and their spouses and dependents) of an educational institution, including a state university system or academic health center, do not have to pay tax on the value of school-provided lodging if they pay a minimal rent. The lodging must be on or near the campus. The minimal required rent is the smaller of: (1) 5% of the appraised value of the lodging; or (2) the average rental paid for comparable school housing by persons who are neither employees nor students. Appraised value must be determined by an independent appraiser and the appraisal must be reviewed annually.

For purposes of the 5% minimum rent rule, academic health centers include medical teaching hospitals and medical research organizations with regular faculties and curricula in basic and clinical medical science and research.

EXAMPLE

Carol Eng, a professor, pays annual rent of $6,000 for university housing appraised at $100,000. The average rent for comparable university housing paid by non-employees and non-students is $7,000. She does not have to pay any tax on the housing since her rental payments are at least 5% of the appraised housing value (5% of $100,000, or $5,000). If her rent was $4,000, she would have to report income of $1,000 ($5,000 minimum required rent – $4,000).

Caution

Housing as Job Requirement

If housing is provided to some employees with a certain job and not others, the IRS may hold that the lodging is not a condition of employment. For example, the IRS taxed medical residents on the value of hospital lodging where other residents lived in their own apartments.

Peace Corps and VISTA volunteers. Peace Corps volunteers working overseas may exclude subsistence allowances from income under a specific code provision. The law does not provide a similar exclusion for the small living expense allowances received by VISTA volunteers.

Table 3-3 Are Your Board and Lodging Tax Free?

Yes—	No—
Hotel executives, managers, housekeepers, and auditors who are required to live at the hotel. Domestics, farm laborers, fishermen, canners, seamen, servicemen, building superintendents, and hospital and sanitarium employees who are required to have meals and lodging on employer premises. Restaurant and other food service employees who have meals furnished during or immediately before or after working hours. Employees who must be available during meal periods for emergencies. Employees who, because of the nature of the business, must be given short meal periods. Workers who must use company-supplied facilities in remote areas. Park employees who voluntarily live in rent-free apartments provided by a park department in order to protect the park from vandalism.	Your employer gives you a cash allowance for your meals or lodgings. You have a choice of accepting cash or getting the meals or lodging. For example, under a union contract you get meals, but you may refuse to take them and get an automatic pay increase. A state hospital employee is given a choice. He or she may live at the institution rent free or live elsewhere and get extra pay each month. Whether he or she stays at the institution or lives outside, the extra pay is included in his or her income. A waitress, on her days off, is allowed to eat free meals at the restaurant where she works.

Caution

Partners Are Not Employees

The IRS does not consider partners or self-employed persons as employees and so does not allow them to exclude the value of partnership-provided meals and lodging.

3.13 Minister's Rental or Housing Allowance

A duly ordained minister pays no tax on the rental value of a home provided as part of his or her pay. If a minister is provided with an allowance rather than a home itself, the allowance is generally tax free if used to pay rent, to make a down payment to buy a house, to pay mortgage installments, or for utilities, interest, tax, and repair expenses of the house. However, the exclusion for an allowance is limited to the fair rental value of the home, including furnishings and appurtenances such as a garage, *plus* the cost of utilities. A rabbi or cantor is treated the same as a minister for purposes of the allowance or in-kind housing exclusion.

The church or local congregation must officially designate the part of the minister's compensation that is a rental or housing allowance. To qualify for tax-free treatment, the designation must be made in advance of the payments. Official action may be shown by an employment contract, minutes, a resolution, or a budget allowance.

Filing Tip

Mortgage Interest and Taxes

If you itemize deductions on Schedule A (Form 1040), deduct payments for qualifying home mortgage interest *(15.1)* and real estate taxes *(16.6)* on your home even if you use a tax-free housing allowance to finance the payments.

Who qualifies for tax-free allowance? Tax-free treatment is allowed to ordained ministers, rabbis, and cantors who receive housing allowances as part of their compensation for ministerial duties. Retired ministers qualify if their allowance is furnished in recognition of past services.

The IRS has allowed the tax-free exclusion to ministers working as teachers or administrators for a parochial school, college, or theological seminary which is an integral part of a church organization. A traveling evangelist was allowed to exclude rental allowances from out-of-town churches to maintain his permanent home. Church officers who are not ordained, such as a "minister" of music (music director) or "minister" of education (Sunday School director), do not qualify.

The IRS has generally barred an exclusion to ordained ministers working as executives of nonreligious organizations even where services or religious functions are performed as part of the job. The Tax Court has focused on the duties performed. A minister employed as a chaplain by a municipal police department under church supervision was allowed a housing exclusion, but the exclusion was denied to a minister-administrator of an old-age home that was not under the authority of a church and a rabbi who worked for a religious organization as director of inter-religious affairs.

Allowance subject to self-employment tax. Although parsonage allowances are not taxable income, they are reported by self-employed ministers, rabbis, and cantors as self-employment income for Social Security purposes; *see* Chapter 45. If you do not receive a cash allowance, report the rental value of the parsonage as self-employment income. Rental value is usually equal to what you would pay for similar quarters in your locality. Also include as self-employment income the value of house furnishings, utilities, appurtenances supplied—such as a garage—and the value of meals furnished that meet the rules at *3.12*.

Business expenses allocable to tax-free allowance are not deductible. A minister may deduct business expenses allocable to taxable compensation, but not expenses allocable to a tax-free housing allowance. If part of a minister's salary is designated as a housing allowance, and the minister also has self-employment earnings from the exercise of his ministry, a double allocation is required, first between salary income and self-employment income, and then between the taxable and tax free parts of salary.

For example, in one case a minister had self-employment income comprising 21.56% of his annual income. Of the rest, 53.85% was a tax-free housing allowance and 46.15% was taxable salary. The Tax Court agreed with the double allocation required by the IRS. Since the minister did not provide evidence as to which expenses were generated by which type of income, the Court allocated expenses on a pro rata basis, applying the ratio of salary and self-employment income to total income. Since the self-employment income was 21.56% of total income (including the allowance), 21.56% of the expenses were deductible on Schedule C. The remaining expenses were treated as job-related costs deductible, if at all, as miscellaneous itemized expenses on Schedule A. However, because 53.85% of the minister's salary was a tax-free housing allowance, 53.85% of the expenses were nondeductible. The balance (46.15% of the expenses) could be claimed on Schedule A as a miscellaneous itemized deduction subject to the 2% of adjusted gross income floor; *see 19.3*.

Cafeteria Plans and Flexible Spending Arrangements

3.14 Cafeteria Plans Provide Choice of Benefits

"Cafeteria plans" is a nickname for plans that give an employee a choice of selecting either cash or at least one qualifying nontaxable benefit. You are not taxed when you elect qualifying nontaxable benefits, although cash could have been chosen instead. A cafeteria plan may offer tax-free benefits such as group health insurance or life insurance coverage, long-term disability coverage, dependent care or adoption assistance, medical expense reimbursements, or group legal services. Long-term care insurance may *not* be offered through a cafeteria plan under current law.

Employees may be offered a premium-only plan (POP), which allows them to purchase group health insurance coverage or life insurance on a pre-tax basis using salary-reduction contributions.

Health savings accounts (HSAs) and their related high-deductible health plans (HDHPs) may be offered as options by a cafeteria plan; *see 3.2*. If so, employees may elect to have contributions made to an HSA and an HDHP on a pre-tax salary-reduction basis.

A cafeteria plan may also offer benefits that are nontaxable because they are attributable to after-tax employee contributions. For example, employees may be offered the opportunity to purchase disability benefits (short term or long term) with after-tax contributions. If a covered employee subsequently receives disability benefits that are attributable to after-tax contributions, the benefits will be tax free. On the other hand, the plan may allow employees to elect paying for disability coverage on a pre-tax basis and, in this case, any benefits from the plan attributable to the pre-tax contributions will be taxable when received.

Under a flexible spending arrangement (FSA), employees may be allowed to make tax-free salary-reduction contributions to a medical or dependent care reimbursement plan; *see 3.15*.

A qualified cafeteria plan must be written and not discriminate in favor of highly compensated employees and stockholders. If the plan provides for health benefits, a special rule applies to determine whether the plan is discriminatory. If a plan is held to be discriminatory, the highly compensated participants are taxed to the extent they could have elected cash. Furthermore, if key employees *(3.4)* receive more than 25% of the "tax-free" benefits under the plan, they are taxed on the benefits.

3.15 Flexible Spending Arrangements

A flexible spending arrangement (FSA) allows employees to get reimbursed for medical or dependent care expenses from an account they set up with pre-tax dollars. Under a typical FSA, you agree to a salary reduction that is deducted from each paycheck and deposited in a separate account. The salary-reduction contributions are not included in your taxable wages reported on Form W-2. As expenses are incurred, you are reimbursed from the account.

The tax advantage of an FSA is that your salary-reduction contributions are not subject to federal income tax or Social Security taxes, allowing your medical or dependent care expenses to be paid with pre-tax rather than after-tax income. The salary deferrals are also exempt from state and local taxes except in New Jersey and Pennsylvania; check with the administrator of your employer's plan.

In the case of a health FSA, paying medical expenses with pre-tax dollars allows you to avoid the 7.5% adjusted gross income (AGI) floor *(17.1)* that limits itemized deductions for medical costs.

However, to get these tax advantages, you must assume some risk. Under a "use-it-or-lose-it" rule, if your out-of-pocket expenses for the year are less than your contributions, the balance is generally forfeited although your employer can give you an additional 2½ months to spend the funds, as discussed below.

FSA election to contribute generally irrevocable. The IRS has imposed restrictions on FSAs that make them unattractive for many employees. An election to set up an FSA for a given year must be made before the start of that year. You elect how much you want to contribute during the coming year and that amount will be withheld from your pay in monthly installments.

Once the election for a particular year takes effect, you may not discontinue contributions to your account or increase or decrease a coverage election unless there is a change in family or work status that qualifies under IRS regulations.

Use-it-or-lose-it deadline may be extended 2½ months by employer. The use-it-or-lose-it rule in IRS regulations generally prevents employees from using salary-reduction contributions made in one year to pay expenses incurred after the end of that year. Any unused account balance as of the end of the year must be forfeited to the employer.

The use-it-or-lose-it rule was criticized for discouraging participation in FSAs and encouraging participants to incur unnecessary expenses at the end of the year to avoid forfeiture of unused contributions. In response to pressure from Congress, the IRS in 2005 relaxed the rule by permitting unused amounts from a health-care FSA or dependent care FSA to pay or reimburse expenses incurred within a 2½-month (two months and 15 days) grace period following the end of each plan year. The grace period is allowed only if the employer amends the cafeteria plan document (which includes the FSA option) to allow it.

For the grace period to apply to the current plan year, the employer must amend the plan before the end of the plan year. For example, if a calendar year plan is amended before the end of 2006, employees with unused health FSA funds at the end of 2006 may use them to reimburse qualified

Planning Reminder

2½-Month Grace Period Eases Use-It-or-Lose-It Deadline

The IRS has given employers an opportunity to relax the use-it-or-lose-it deadline for health-care and dependent care FSAs. Employers have the option of amending their plans to allow employees an additional 2½ months to use the money in their FSAs. If the grace period is adopted, FSA funds that are unused at the end of a plan year can be applied to expenses incurred within the first 2½ months of the following year.

Filing Instruction

Tax-Free Dependent Care Reimbursements

Whether all or only part of your dependent care FSA reimbursements are tax free is figured on Part III of Form 2441 if you file Form 1040. If you file Form 1040A, the calculation is made on Part III of Schedule 2.

medical expenses incurred during the grace period beginning January 1 and ending March 15, 2007. If the expenses incurred by March 15, 2007, did not cover the unused amount from 2006, the balance would be forfeited to the employer. The end-of-year balance of health FSA funds may only be applied to health expenses incurred during the grace period and not to dependent care or other expenses. Similarly, unused dependent care FSA amounts may be used only for dependent care expenses incurred during the grace period. During the grace period, unused amounts may not be cashed out or converted to any other benefit (taxable or nontaxable). The employer may allow additional time following the end of the grace period to submit reimbursement claims for qualified expenses paid during the plan year and the grace period.

Health-care FSA. Funds from a *health* FSA may be used to reimburse you for expenses that you could claim as a medical expense deduction *(17.2)* such as the annual deductible under your employer's regular health plan, co-payments you must make to physicians or for prescriptions, and any other expenses that your health plan does not cover. These may include eye examinations, eyeglasses, routine physicals, and orthodontia work for you and your dependents. The IRS ruled that a health-care FSA may also reimburse the cost of over-the-counter medications such as cold remedies, pain relievers, and allergy medications even though they are not deductible as medical expenses *(17.2)*. The IRS concluded that the definition of "medical care" is broader for FSA reimbursement purposes than for itemized deduction purposes and so such over-the-counter medications, which are taken to alleviate or treat personal injuries or sickness, can be covered by a health FSA. However, vitamins purchased without a prescription to maintain general health are not reimbursable from a health FSA.

In addition, a health FSA may *not* be used to reimburse you for premiums paid for other health plan coverage, including premiums for coverage under a plan of your spouse or dependent. Also, expenses for long-term care services *cannot* be reimbursed under a health FSA. You may *not* receive tax-free reimbursements for cosmetic surgery expenses unless the surgery is necessary to correct a deformity existing since birth or resulting from a disease or from injury caused by an accident. Nonqualifying reimbursements are taxable.

At any time during the year, you may receive reimbursements up to your designated limit, even though your payments into the FSA account up to that point may add up to less. For example, if you elect to make salary-reduction contributions of $100 per month to a health-care FSA and you incur $500 of qualifying medical expenses in January, you may get the full $500 reimbursement even though you have paid only $100 into the plan. Your employer may not require you to accelerate contributions to match reimbursement claims.

Filing Instruction

Dependent Care Reimbursements Affect Credit

Reimbursements received tax free from your dependent care FSA reduce the expense base for figuring the dependent care credit; *see* Chapter 25.

Employees on medical or family leave. Employees who take unpaid leave under the Family and Medical Leave Act (FMLA) to deal with medical emergencies or care for a newborn child may either continue or revoke their coverage during FMLA leave. If the coverage continues, the maximum reimbursement selected by such an employee must be available at all times during the leave period. If the coverage is terminated, the employee must be reinstated under the FSA after returning from the leave, but no reimbursement claims may be made for expenses incurred during the leave.

Dependent care FSA. You may contribute to a dependent care FSA if you expect to have expenses qualifying for the dependent care tax credit discussed in Chapter 25, but if you contribute to a dependent care FSA, *any tax-free reimbursement from the account reduces the expenses eligible for the credit; see 25.7.* If you are married, both you and your spouse must work in order for you to receive tax-free reimbursements from an FSA, unless your spouse is disabled or a full-time student; *see 3.5.*

The maximum tax-free reimbursement under the FSA is $5,000, but if either you or your spouse earns less than $5,000, the tax-free limit is the lesser earnings. If your spouse's employer offers a dependent care FSA, total tax-free reimbursements for both of you are limited to $5,000. Furthermore, if you are considered a highly compensated employee, your employer may have to lower your contribution ceiling below $5,000 to comply with nondiscrimination rules.

Unlike health FSAs, an employer may limit reimbursements from a dependent care FSA to your account balance. For example, if you contribute $400 a month to the FSA and in January you pay $1,500 to a day-care center for your child, your employer may reimburse you $400 a month as contributions are made to your account.

Free or Low-Cost Company Products or Services

3.16 Company Services Provided at No Additional Cost

Employees are not taxed on the receipt of services usually sold by their employer to customers where the employer does not incur additional costs in providing them to the employees. Examples are free or low-cost flights provided by an airline to its employees; free or discount lodging for employees of a hotel; and telephone service provided to employees of telephone companies. These tax-free fringes also may be provided to the employee's spouse and dependent children; retired employees, including employees retired on disability; and widows or widowers of deceased or retired employees. Tax-free treatment also applies to free or discount flights provided to parents of airline employees. Benefits provided by another company under a reciprocal arrangement, such as standby tickets on another airline, may also qualify as tax free.

The employer must have excess service capacity to provide the service and not forego potential revenue from regular customers. For example, airline employees who receive free reserved seating on company planes must pay tax on the benefit because the airline is foregoing potential revenue by reserving seating that could otherwise be sold.

Line of business limitations. If a company has two lines of business, such as an airline and a hotel, an employee of the airline may not receive tax-free benefits provided by the hotel. However, there are exceptions. An employee who provides services to both business lines may receive benefits from both business lines. Benefits from more than one line in existence before 1984 may also be available under a special election made by the company for 1985 and later years. Your employer should notify you of this tax benefit.

Caution

Highly Compensated Employees

Highly compensated employees can receive tax-free company services only if the same benefits are available to other employees on a nondiscriminatory basis. For 2006, highly compensated employees include employees owning more than a 5% interest in 2006 or 2005, and employees who in 2005 had compensation over $100,000. Employers have the option of including only the top-paid 20% in the over-$100,000 category. The $100,000 compensation threshold may be increased for 2007.

3.17 Discounts on Company Products or Services

The value of discounts on company products is a tax-free benefit if the discount does not exceed the employer's gross profit percentage. For example, if a company's profit percentage is 40%, the maximum tax-free employee discount for merchandise is 40% of the regular selling price. If you received a 50% discount, then 10% of the price charged customers would be taxable income. The employer has a choice of methods for figuring profit percentage.

Discounts on services that are not tax free under *3.16* for no-additional-cost services qualify for an exclusion, limited to 20% of the selling price charged customers. Discounts above 20% are taxable. An insurance policy is treated as a service. Thus, insurance company employees are not taxed on a discount of up to 20% of the policy's price.

Some company products do not qualify for the exclusion. Discounts on real estate and investment property such as securities, commodities, currency, or bullion are taxable. Interest-free or low-interest loans given by banks or other financial institutions to employees are not excludable. Such loans are subject to tax under the rules discussed at *4.31*.

Highly compensated employees are subject to the nondiscrimination rules discussed at *3.16* for no-additional-cost services.

Caution

Line of Business Rule

The line of business limitation discussed at *3.16* for no-additional-cost services also applies to qualified employee discounts. Thus, if a company operates an airline and a hotel, employees who work for the airline may generally not receive tax-free hotel room discounts. However, if a special election was made by the company, employees may receive tax-free benefits from any line of business in existence before 1984.

Chapter 4

Dividend and Interest Income

Dividends and interest that are paid to you in 2006 are reported by the payer to the IRS on Forms 1099.

You will receive copies of:

- Forms 1099-DIV, for dividends
- Forms 1099-INT, for interest
- Forms 1099-OID, for original issue discount

Dividends paid by most domestic corporations and many foreign corporations are subject to the same preferential tax rates (5% or 15%) as net long-term capital gains; *see 4.2*.

Report the amounts shown on the Forms 1099 on your tax return. The IRS uses the Forms 1099 to check the income you report. If you fail to report income reported on Forms 1099, you will receive a statement asking for an explanation and a bill for the tax deficiency. If you receive a Form 1099 that you believe is incorrect, contact the payer for a corrected form.

Do not attach your copies of Forms 1099 to your return. Keep them with a copy of your tax return.

Reporting Dividends

4.1 Reporting Dividends and Mutual-Fund Distributions

Dividends paid to you out of a corporation's earnings and profits are taxable as ordinary income. The corporation will report dividends on Form 1099-DIV (or equivalent statement). Mutual-fund dividends and distributions are also reported on Form 1099-DIV (or similar form). Corporate dividends and mutual-fund distributions are reported on Form 1099-DIV (or equivalent) whether you receive them in cash or they have been reinvested at your request.

Form 1099-DIV. Form 1099-DIV for 2006 gives you a breakdown of the dividends and distributions paid to you during the year. A mutual-fund or real estate investment trust (REIT) dividend paid to you in January 2007 will also be reported to you on the 2006 Form 1099-DIV if it was declared and was payable in October, November, or December of 2006. The company or fund may send a statement that is similar to Form 1099-DIV. You do not have to attach the Form 1099-DIV (or similar statement) to your tax return.

Box 1a. Ordinary dividends taxed to you are shown in Box 1. These are the most common type of distribution, payable out of a corporation's earnings and profits. Your share of a mutual fund's ordinary dividends is also shown on Form 1099-DIV; short-term capital gain distributions are included in the Box 1a total.

Box 1b. Part of the Box 1a amount may be qualified dividends. Qualified dividends reported in Box 1b are generally taxed at the same favorable rates (5% or 15%) as net capital gains. *See 4.2* for further details on qualified dividends.

Boxes 2a–2d. Capital gain distributions (long term) from a mutual fund (or real estate investment trust) are shown in Box 2a. Box 2b shows the portion of the Box 2a amount, if any, that is unrecaptured Section 1250 gain from the sale of depreciable real estate. Box 2c shows the part of Box 2a that is Section 1202 gain from small business stock eligible for a 50% exclusion. Box 2d shows the amount from Box 2a that is 28% rate gain from the sale of collectibles. If any amount is reported in Box 2b, 2c, or 2d, you must file Schedule D with Form 1040; *see 5.3.*

Box 3. Nontaxable distributions that are a return of your investment are shown in Box 3; *see* "Return of capital distributions" below.

Box 4. If you did not give your taxpayer identification number to the payer, backup withholding at a 28% rate *(26.11)* is shown in Box 4.

Box 5. Your share of expenses from a non–publicly offered mutual fund is shown in Box 5 and may be deductible as a miscellaneous itemized deduction subject to the 2% floor; *see 19.15.* This amount is included in Box 1a.

Boxes 6 and 7. The foreign tax shown in Box 6 (imposed by the country shown in Box 7) may be claimed as a tax credit on Form 1116 or as an itemized deduction on Schedule A; *see 36.14.*

Boxes 8 and 9. Cash and noncash liquidation distributions are shown in these boxes.

Nominee distribution—joint accounts. If you receive dividends on stock held as a nominee for someone else, or you receive a Form 1099-DIV that includes dividends belonging to another person, such as a joint owner of the account, you are considered to be a "nominee recipient." If the other owner is someone other than your spouse, you should file a separate Form 1099-DIV showing you as the payer and the other owner as the recipient of the allocable income. Give the owner a copy of Form 1099-DIV by January 31, 2007, so the dividends can be reported on his or her 2006 return. File the Form 1099-DIV, together with a Form 1096 ("Transmittal of Information Return"), with the IRS by February 28, 2007; the deadline is April 2, 2007, if filing electronically.

On your Schedule B (Form 1040) or Schedule I (Form 1040A), you list on Line 5 the ordinary dividends reported to you on Form 1099-DIV. Several lines above Line 6, subtract the nominee distribution (the amount allocable to the other owner) from the total dividends. Thus, the nominee distribution is not included in the taxable dividends shown on Line 6 of Schedule B or Schedule I.

Return of capital distributions. A distribution that is not paid out of earnings is a nontaxable return of capital, that is, a partial payback of your investment. The company will report the distribution in Box 3 of Form 1099-DIV as a nontaxable distribution. You must reduce the cost basis of your stock by the nontaxable distribution. If your basis is reduced to zero by a return of capital distributions, any further distributions are taxable as capital gains, which you report on Schedule D of Form 1040. Form 1040A or Form 1040EZ may not be used.

Planning Reminder

So-Called Dividends That Are Really Interest

Distributions from the following financial institutions are called "dividends," but are actually interest reported on Form 1099-INT: dividends from credit unions, cooperative banks, savings and loan associations, building and loan associations, and mutual savings banks.

Planning Reminder

Dividends on Life Insurance Policies

Dividends on a life insurance policy (other than a modified endowment contract) are actually a refund of your premiums and are not taxed until they exceed the total premiums paid.

☐ CORRECTED (if checked)

PAYER'S name, street address, city, state, ZIP code, and telephone no.	1a Total ordinary dividends	OMB No. 1545-0110	
Very Mutual Fund 155 East 38th Street City, State 010X0	$ 500	2006	Dividends and Distributions
	1b Qualified dividends $ 435	Form 1099-DIV	
	2a Total capital gain distr. $ 375	2b Unrecap. Sec. 1250 gain $	Copy B For Recipient
PAYER'S federal identification number X1-01X0110	RECIPIENT'S identification number 00X-1X-0X00		
RECIPIENT'S name Noelle Ballesteros	2c Section 1202 gain $	2d Collectibles (28%) gain $	This is important tax information and is being furnished to the Internal Revenue Service. If you are required to file a return, a negligence penalty or other sanction may be imposed on you if this income is taxable and the IRS determines that it has not been reported.
	3 Nondividend distributions $	4 Federal income tax withheld $	
Street address (including apt. no.) 21 Chauncy Street		5 Investment expenses $	
City, state, and ZIP code City, State 111X0	6 Foreign tax paid $	7 Foreign country or U.S. possession	
Account number (see instructions)	8 Cash liquidation distributions $	9 Noncash liquidation distributions $	

Form **1099-DIV** (keep for your records) Department of the Treasury - Internal Revenue Service

4.2 Qualified Corporate Dividends Taxed at Favorable Capital Gain Rates

Dividends paid out of current or accumulated earnings of a corporation are taxable; *see 4.5.* Stock dividends on common stock are generally not taxable, but other types of stock dividends are taxed; *see 4.6* and *4.8.*

The tax rate on dividends received by individuals from most domestic corporations and many foreign corporations is 15% for taxpayers whose top bracket exceeds 15%, or 5% for taxpayers whose top bracket is 10% or 15%. These are the same rates applicable to net long-term capital gains *(5.3).* To get the benefit of the reduced rates, qualified dividends generally must be reported together with net long-term capital gains on the "Qualified Dividends and Capital Gain Tax Worksheet" in the instructions for Form 1040 or Form 1040A; *see 5.8.* The reduced rates apply to qualified dividends received after 2002 and before 2011. For 2008 through 2010, taxpayers otherwise eligible for the 5% rate will owe no tax on qualified dividends; their rate for 2008–2010 will be "zero."

On Form 1099-DIV for 2006, the amount of qualified dividends eligible for the 5% or 15% rate will be shown in Box 1b. Certain dividend distributions are not eligible. The reduced rate does not apply unless the dividend is received on stock held at least 61 days during the 121-day period beginning 60 days before the ex-dividend date. The ex-dividend date is the first date following the declaration of a dividend on which the purchaser of the stock is *not entitled* to receive the dividend *(4.9).*

Generally, distributions on preferred stock instruments do not qualify for qualified dividend treatment because the instruments are hybrid securities that are treated as debt and not stock. Payments on such hybrid instruments are considered interest rather than dividends and thus are not eligible for the reduced tax rate. If the preferred instrument is treated as stock, the reduced rate does not apply to dividends attributable to periods totaling less than 367 days unless the 61-day holding period (discussed above) is met. If the dividends are attributable to periods of more than 366 days, the stock must be held at least 91 days in the 181-day period starting 90 days before the ex-dividend date.

Distributions that are called dividends but are actually interest income, such as payments from credit unions and mutual savings banks, are not eligible for the reduced dividend rate. Similarly, mutual-fund dividends that represent interest earnings are not eligible for the reduced rate, although dividends passed through by a mutual fund from corporations generally qualify and will be shown in Box 1b of Form 1099-DIV; *see 4.1* and *32.5.* Dividends paid by a real estate investment trust (REIT) generally are not eligible, but the reduced rate does apply to REIT distributions that are attributable to corporate tax at the REIT level or which represent qualified dividends received by the REIT and passed through to shareholders.

Filing Tip

Dividends Eligible for Reduced Rates

In Box 1b of Form 1099-DIV, payers of dividends will report the amount eligible for the reduced tax rate of 15% (if your top bracket exceeds 15%) or 5% (if your top bracket is 10% or 15%). You must enter the qualified dividends on the "Qualified Dividends and Capital Gain Tax Worksheet" in the IRS instructions for Form 1040 or Form 1040A to obtain the benefit of the preferential rate, unless you need the "Schedule D Tax Worksheet" to report other transactions; *see 5.3.*

Dividends from foreign corporations qualify for the reduced rate if the corporation is traded on an established U.S. securities market, incorporated in a U.S. possession, or certain treaty requirements are met.

If your broker loans out your shares as part of a short sale, substitute payments in lieu of dividends may be received on your behalf while the short sale is open. Such substitute payments are not considered dividends and should be included in Box 8 of Form 1099-MISC and reported by you as "Other income" on Line 21 of Form 1040.

Tax-deferred retirement accounts such as traditional IRAs and 401(k) plans do not benefit from the reduced dividend rate. Distributions from such retirement plans are taxable as ordinary income even if the distribution is attributable to dividends.

4.3 Dividends From a Partnership, S Corporation, Estate, or Trust

Dividends you receive as a member of a partnership, stockholder in an S corporation, or as a beneficiary of an estate or trust may be qualified dividends eligible for the reduced tax rate of 15% or 5%; *see 4.2.*

A distribution from a partnership or S corporation is reported as a dividend only if it is portfolio income derived from nonbusiness activities. Your allowable share of the dividend will be shown on the Schedule K-1 you receive from the partnership or S corporation.

4.4 Real Estate Investment Trust (REIT) Dividends

Dividends from a real estate investment trust (REIT) are shown on Form 1099-DIV. Ordinary dividends reported in Box 1a are taxable at ordinary income rates except for the portion, if any, shown in Box 1b that qualifies for the 15% or 5% capital gain rate. Dividends designated by the trust as capital gain distributions in Box 2a are reported by you as long-term capital gains regardless of how long you have held your trust shares. A loss on the sale of REIT shares held for six months or less is treated as a long-term capital loss to the extent of any capital gain distribution received before the sale plus any undistributed capital gains. However, this long-term loss rule does not apply to sales under periodic redemption plans.

4.5 Taxable Dividends of Earnings and Profits

You pay tax on dividends only when the corporation distributing the dividends has earnings and profits. Publicly held corporations will tell you whether their distributions are taxable. If you hold stock in a close corporation, you may have to determine the tax status of its distribution. You need to know earnings and profits at two different periods:

1. Current earnings and profits as of the *end of the current taxable year.* A dividend is considered to have been made from earnings most recently accumulated.
2. Accumulated earnings and profits as of the *beginning of the current year.* However, when current earnings and profits are large enough to meet the dividend, you do not have to make this computation. It is only when the dividends exceed current earnings (or there are no current earnings) that you match accumulated earnings against the dividend.

The tax term "accumulated earnings and profits" is similar in meaning to the accounting term "retained earnings." Both stand for the net profits of the company after deducting distributions to stockholders. However, "tax" earnings may differ from "retained earnings" for the following reason: Reserve accounts, the additions to which are not deductible for income tax purposes, are ordinarily included as tax earnings.

EXAMPLES

1. During 2006, Corporation A paid dividends of $25,000. At the beginning of 2006 it had accumulated earnings of $50,000. It lost $25,000 during 2006. You are taxed on your dividend income in 2006 because the corporation's net accumulated earnings and profits exceed its dividends.
2. At the end of 2005, Corporation B had a deficit of $200,000. Earnings for 2006 were $100,000. In 2006, it paid stockholders $25,000. The dividends are taxed; earnings exceeded the dividends.

Planning Reminder

Dividend Reinvestment in Company Stock

Your company may allow you either to take cash dividends or automatically reinvest the dividends in company stock. If you elect the stock plan, and pay fair market value for the stock, the full cash dividend is taxable.

If the plan lets you buy the stock at a discount, the amount of the taxable dividend is the fair market value of the stock on the dividend payment date plus any service fee charged for the acquisition. The basis of the stock is also the fair market value at the dividend payment date. The service charge may be claimed as an itemized deduction subject to the 2% adjusted gross income floor; *see 19.1.* If at the same time you also have the option to buy additional stock at a discount and you exercise the option, you have additional dividend income for the difference between the fair market value of the optional shares and the discounted amount you paid for the shares.

Filing Tip

Stock Splits Are Not Taxed

The receipt of stock under a stock split is not taxable. Stock splits resemble the receipt of stock dividends, but they are not dividends. They do not represent a distribution of surplus as in the case of stock dividends. Although you own more shares, your ownership percentage has not changed. The purpose of a stock split is generally to reduce the price of individual shares in order to increase their marketability. The basis of the old holding is divided among all the shares in order to find the basis for the new shares; *see 30.4*.

4.6 Stock Dividends on Common Stock

If you own common stock in a company and receive additional shares of the same company as a dividend, the dividend is generally not taxable; *see 30.3* and *30.4* for the method of computing cost basis of stock dividends and rights and sales of such stock.

Exceptions to tax-free rule. A stock dividend on common stock is taxable when (1) you may elect to take either stock or cash; (2) there are different classes of common stock, one class receiving cash dividends and another class receiving stock; or (3) the dividend is of convertible preferred stock; *see 4.8* for further details on taxable stock dividends.

Fractional shares. If a stock dividend is declared and you are only entitled to a fractional share, you may be given cash instead. To save the trouble and expense of issuing fractional shares, many companies directly issue cash in lieu of fractional shares or they set up a plan, with shareholder approval, for the fractional shares to be sold and the cash proceeds distributed to the shareholders. Your company should tell you how to report the cash payment. According to the IRS, you are generally treated as receiving a tax-free dividend of fractional shares, followed by a taxable redemption of the shares by the company. You report on Schedule D capital gain or loss equal to the excess of the cash over the basis of the fractional share; long- or short-term treatment depends on the holding period of the original stock. In certain cases, a cash distribution may be taxed as an ordinary dividend and not as a sale reported on Schedule D; your company should tell you if this is the case.

Stock rights. The rules that apply to stock dividends also apply to distributions of stock rights. If you, as a common stockholder, receive rights to subscribe to additional common stock, the receipt of the rights is not taxable provided the terms of the distribution do not fall within the taxable distribution rules discussed in *4.8*.

4.7 Dividends Paid in Property

A dividend may be paid in property such as securities of another corporation or merchandise. You report as income the fair market value of the property. A dividend paid in property is sometimes called a *dividend in kind*.

EXAMPLE

You receive one share of X corporation stock as a dividend from the G company of which you are a stockholder. You received the X stock when it had a market value of $25; you report $25, the value of the property received. The $25 value is also your basis for the stock.

Corporate benefit may be treated as constructive dividend. On an audit, the IRS may charge that a benefit given to a shareholder-employee should be taxed as a constructive dividend. For example, the Tax Court agreed with the IRS that a corporation's payment for a license that gave the sole shareholder the right to buy season tickets to Houston Texans football games was a constructive dividend.

4.8 Taxable Stock Dividends

The most frequent type of stock dividend is not taxable: the receipt by a common stockholder of a corporation's own common stock as a dividend; *see 4.6*.

Taxable stock dividends. The following stock dividends are taxable:

- Stock dividends paid to holders of preferred stock. However, no taxable income is realized where the conversion ratio of convertible preferred stock is increased only to take account of a stock dividend or split involving the stock into which the convertible stock is convertible.
- Stock dividends elected by a shareholder of common stock who had the choice of taking stock, property, or cash. A distribution of stock that was immediately redeemable for cash at the stockholder's option was treated as a taxable dividend.
- Stock dividends paid in a distribution where some shareholders receive property or cash and other shareholders' proportionate interests in the assets or earnings and profits of the corporation are increased.
- Distributions of preferred stock to some common shareholders and common stock to other common shareholders.

- Distributions of convertible preferred stock to holders of common stock, unless it can be shown that the distribution will not result in the creation of disproportionate stock interests.

Constructive stock dividends. You may not actually receive a stock dividend, but under certain circumstances, the IRS may treat you as having received a taxable distribution. This may happen when a company increases the ratio of convertible preferred stock.

4.9 Who Reports the Dividends

Stock held by broker in street name. If your broker holds stock for you in a street name, dividends earned on this stock are received by the broker and credited to your account. You report all dividends credited to your account in 2006. The broker is required to file an information return on Form 1099 (or similar form) showing all such dividends.

If your statement shows only a gross amount of dividends, check with your broker if any of the dividends represented nontaxable returns of capital.

Dividends on stock sold or bought between ex-dividend date and record date. Record date is the date set by a company on which you must be listed as a stockholder on its records to receive the dividend. However, in the case of publicly traded stock, an ex-dividend date, which usually precedes the record date by several business days, is fixed by the exchange to determine who is entitled to the dividend.

If you buy stock before the ex-dividend date, the dividend belongs to you and is reported by you. If you buy on or after the ex-dividend date, the dividend belongs to the seller.

If you sell stock before the ex-dividend date, you do not have a right to the dividend. If you sell on or after the ex-dividend date, you receive the dividend and report it as income.

The dividend declaration date and date of payment do not determine who receives the dividend.

Nominees or joint owners. If you receive ordinary dividends on stock held as a nominee for another person, other than your spouse, give that owner a Form 1099-DIV and file a copy of that return with the IRS, along with a Form 1096 ("Transmittal of U.S. Information Return"). The actual owner then reports the income. List the nominee dividends on Schedule B of Form 1040 (or Schedule 1, Form 1040A) along with your other dividends, and then subtract the nominee dividends from the total.

Follow the same procedure if you receive a Form 1099-DIV for an account owned jointly with someone other than your spouse. Give the other owner a Form 1099-DIV, and file a copy with the IRS, along with a Form 1096. The other owner then reports his or her share of the joint income. On your return, you list the total dividends shown on Forms 1099-DIV and avoid tax by subtracting from the total the nominee dividends reported to the other owner.

EXAMPLE

You receive Form 1099-DIV showing dividends of $960 including a $200 nominee distribution. You prepare a Form 1099-DIV for the actual owner showing the $200 distribution, and file a copy of the form with the IRS, plus Form 1096. When you file your return, report the nominee distribution along with other ordinary dividends on Schedule B of Form 1040 and then subtract it from the total.

Dividend Income	*Amount*
Mutual Fund	$ 310
Computer Inc.	450
Utility Inc.	200
Subtotal	$960
Less: Nominee distribution	(200)
Net dividends	$ 760

4.10 Year Dividends Are Reported

Dividends are generally reported on the tax return for the year in which the dividend is credited to your account or when you receive the dividend check.

Dividends received from a corporation in a year after the one in which they were declared, when you held the stock on the record date, are taxed in the year they are received; *see* Example 4 below.

Caution

Year-End Dividend From Mutual Fund

A dividend declared and made payable in October through December by a mutual fund or REIT is taxable in the year it is declared, even if it is not paid until January of the following year.

EXAMPLES

1. A corporation declares a dividend payable on December 27, 2006. It follows a practice of paying dividends by checks that are mailed so that stockholders do not receive them until January 2007. You report this dividend on your 2007 return.
2. On December 27, 2006, a dividend is declared by a mutual fund. You receive it in January 2007. The dividend is taxable in 2006, when declared, and not 2007, when received.
3. On December 27, 2006, a dividend is credited by a corporation to a stockholder's account and made immediately available. The dividend is taxable in 2006 as the crediting is considered constructive receipt in 2006, even though the dividend is not received until 2007 or a later year.
4. You own stock in a corporation. In April 2006, the corporation declared a dividend, but it provided that the dividend will be paid when it gets the cash. It finally pays the dividend in September 2007; the dividend is taxable in 2007.

4.11 Distribution Not Out of Earnings: Return of Capital

A return of capital or "nontaxable distribution" reduces the cost basis of the stock. If your shares were purchased at different times, reduce the basis of the oldest shares first. When the cost basis is reduced to zero, further returns of capital are taxed as capital gains on Schedule D. Whether the gain is short term or long term depends on the length of time you have held the stock. The company paying the dividend will usually inform you of the tax treatment of the payment.

Filing Tip

Insurance Premium Refund

Dividends on insurance policies are actually returns of premiums you previously paid. They are not subject to tax until they exceed the net premiums paid for the contract.

Life insurance dividends. Dividends on insurance policies are not true dividends. They are returns of premiums you previously paid. They reduce the cost of the policy and are not subject to tax until they exceed the net premiums paid for the contract. Interest paid or credited on dividends left with the insurance company is taxable. Dividends on VA insurance are tax free, as is interest on dividends left with the VA.

Where insurance premiums were deducted as a business expense in prior years, receipts of insurance dividends are included as business income. Dividends on capital stock of an insurance company are taxable.

Reporting Interest Income

4.12 Reporting Interest on Your Tax Return

You must report all taxable interest. Forms 1099-INT, sent by payers of interest income, give you the amount of interest to enter on your tax return. Although they are generally correct, you should check for mistakes, notify payers of any error, and request a new form marked "corrected." If tax was withheld *(26.12)*, claim this tax as a payment on your tax return. The IRS will check interest reported on your return against the Forms 1099-INT sent by banks and other payers. If you earn over $1,500 of taxable interest, you list the payers of interest on Part I of Schedule B if you file Form 1040, or on Part I of Schedule 1 if you file Form 1040A. Form 1040EZ may not be used if your taxable interest exceeds $1,500. You must also list tax-exempt interest on your return even though it is not taxable.

You must report interest that has been shown on a Form 1099-INT in your name although it may not be taxable to you. For example, you may have received interest as a nominee or as accrued interest on bonds bought between interest dates. In these cases, list the amounts reported on Form 1099 along with your other interest income on Schedule B if you file Form 1040, or Schedule 1 if you file Form 1040A. On a separate line, label the amount as "Nominee distribution," or "Accrued interest," and subtract it from the total interest shown. Accrued interest is discussed below and at *4.15*. Nominee distributions are discussed below under "Joint Accounts."

If you received interest on a frozen account *(4.13)*, include the interest from Form 1099 on Schedule B if you file Form 1040, or on Schedule 1 if you use Form 1040A. On a separate line, write "frozen deposits" and subtract the amount from the total interest reported.

You generally do not have to list the payers of interest if your interest receipts are $1,500 or less. However, complete Part I of Schedule B if you have to reduce the interest shown on Form 1099 by nontaxable amounts such as accrued interest, tax-exempt interest, nominee distributions, frozen deposit interest, amortized bond premium, or excludable interest on savings bonds used for tuition.

Filing Instruction

Tax-Exempt Interest

Tax-exempt interest, such as from municipal bonds, must be reported on your return although it is not taxable. Report it on Line 8b of Form 1040 or Form 1040A. On Part I of Schedule B of Form 1040 or Schedule 1 of Form 1040A, report the tax-exempt interest on Line 1 but then subtract it from a subtotal of the total interest so that it is not included in the amount shown on Line 2 of the schedule.

Joint accounts. Form 1099-INT will be sent to the joint owner whose name and Social Security number was reported to the bank (or other payer) on Form W-9 when the account was opened. If you receive a Form 1099-INT for interest on an account you own with someone other than your spouse, you should file a nominee Form 1099-INT with the IRS to indicate that person's share of the interest, together with Form 1096 ("Transmittal of Information Return"). Give a copy of the Form 1099-INT to the other person. When you file your own return, you report the total interest shown on Form 1099-INT and then subtract the other person's share so you are taxed only on your portion of the interest; *see* the Example below.

Do not follow this procedure if you contributed all of the funds and set up the joint account merely as a "convenience" account to allow the other person to automatically inherit the account when you die. In this case, you report all of the interest income.

EXAMPLE

Your Social Security number is listed on a bank account owned jointly with your sister. You each invested 50% of the account principal and have agreed to share the interest income. You receive a Form 1099-INT for 2006 reporting total interest of $1,700 on the account. By January 31, 2007, prepare and give to your sister another Form 1099-INT that identifies you as the payer and her as the recipient of her share, or $850 interest. Send a copy of the Form 1099-INT and a Form 1096 to the IRS no later than February 28, 2007 (April 2, if filing electronically). Your sister will report the $850 interest on her return. On your Form 1040, report the full $1,700 interest on Line 1 of Schedule B, along with your other interest income. Above Line 2, subtract the $850 belonging to your sister to avoid being taxed on that amount; label the subtraction "Nominee distribution."

Savings certificates, deferred interest. The interest element on certificates of deposit and similar plans of more than one year is treated as *deferred interest* original issue discount (OID) and is taxable on an annual basis. The bank notifies you of the taxable OID amount on Form 1099-OID. If you discontinue a savings plan before maturity, you may have a loss deduction for forfeited interest, which is listed on Form 1099-INT or Form 1099-OID; *see 4.16*.

Tax on interest can be deferred on a savings certificate with a term of one year or less. Interest is taxable in the year it is available for withdrawal without substantial penalty. Where you invest in a six-month certificate before July 1, the entire amount of interest is paid six months later and is taxable in the year of payment. However, when you invest in a six-month certificate after June 30, only interest actually paid or made available for withdrawal before the end of the year without substantial penalty is taxable in the year of issuance. The balance is taxable in the year of maturity. You can defer interest to the following year by investing in a six-month certificate after June 30, provided the payment of interest is specifically deferred to the year of maturity by the terms of the certificate. Similarly, interest may be deferred to the following year by investing in longer term certificates of up to one year, provided that the crediting of interest is specifically deferred until the year of maturity.

Accrued interest on a bond bought between interest payment dates. Interest accrued between interest payment dates is part of the purchase price of the bond. This amount is taxable to the seller as explained at *4.15*. If you purchased a bond and received a Form 1099-INT that includes accrued interest on a bond, include the interest on Line 1 of Schedule B, Form 1040, and then on a separate line above Line 2 subtract the accrued interest from the Line 1 total.

Custodian account of a minor (Uniform Transfers to Minors Act). The interest is taxable to the child if his or her name and Social Security number were provided to the payer on Form W-9. If a child was under age 18 as of January 1, 2007, and had net investment income for 2006 exceeding $1,700, the excess is subject to tax at the parent's top tax rate; *see 24.3*.

4.13 Interest on Frozen Accounts Not Taxed

If you have funds in a bankrupt or insolvent financial institution that freezes your account by limiting withdrawals, you do not pay tax on interest allocable to the frozen deposits. The interest is taxable when withdrawals are permitted. Officers and owners of at least a 1% interest in the financial institution, or their relatives, may not take advantage of this rule and must still report interest on frozen deposits.

On Part I of Schedule B of Form 1040 or on Schedule 1 of Form 1040A, report the full amount shown on Form 1099-INT, even if the interest is on a "frozen" deposit. Then, on a separate line, subtract the amount allocable to the frozen deposit from the total interest shown on the Schedule; label the subtraction "frozen deposits." Thus, the interest on the frozen deposit is not included on the line of your return showing taxable interest.

Refund opportunity. If you reported interest on a frozen deposit on a tax return for a prior year, you generally have three years to file a refund claim for the tax paid on the interest; *see 47.2.*

Filing Tip

Lost Deposits

If you lose funds because of a financial institution's bankruptcy or insolvency, and you can reasonably estimate such a loss, you may deduct the loss as a nonbusiness bad debt, as a casualty loss, or as a miscellaneous itemized deduction; *see 18.5.*

4.14 Interest Income on Debts Owed to You

You report interest earned on money that you loan to another person. If you are on the cash basis, you report interest in the year you actually receive it or when it is considered received under the "constructive receipt rule." If you are on the accrual basis, you report interest when it is earned, whether or not you have received it.

See 4.31 for minimum interest rates required for loans and *4.18* when OID rules apply.

Where partial payment is being made on a debt, or when a debt is being compromised, the parties may agree in advance which part of the payment covers interest and which covers principal. If a payment is not identified as either principal or interest, the payment is first applied against interest due and reported as interest income to the extent of the interest due.

Interest income is not realized when a debtor gives you a new note for an old note where the new note includes the interest due on the old note.

If you give away a debtor's note, you report as income the collectible interest due at the date of the gift. To avoid tax on the interest, the note must be transferred before interest becomes due.

4.15 Reporting Interest on Bonds Bought or Sold

When you buy or sell bonds between interest dates, interest is included in the price of the bonds. If you are the buyer, you do not report as income the interest that accrued before your date of purchase. The seller reports the accrued interest. Reduce the basis of the bond by the accrued interest reported by the seller. The following Examples illustrate these rules.

Filing Tip

Accrued Interest

When you buy bonds between interest payment dates and pay accrued interest to the seller, this interest is taxable to the seller. The accrued interest is included on the Form 1099-INT you receive, but you should subtract it from your taxable interest; *see* Example 1 in *4.15.*

EXAMPLES

1. *Purchase.* On April 30, you buy for $5,200 a $5,000 corporate bond bearing interest at 5% per year, payable January 1 and July 1. The purchase price of the bond included accrued interest of $88.33 for the period January 1–April 30.

Interest received on 7/1	$125.00
Less: Accrued interest	83.33
Taxable interest	$ 41.67

   Form 1099 sent to you includes the $83.33 of accrued interest. On Schedule B of Form 1040, you report the total interest of $125 received on July 1 and then on a separate line subtract the accrued interest of $83.33. Write "Accrued Interest" on the line where you show the subtraction.

   Your basis for the bond is $5,117 ($5,200 – $83.33) for purposes of figuring gain or loss on a later sale of the bond.

2. *Sale.* On April 30, you sell for $5,200 a $5,000 5% bond with interest payable January 1 and July 1. The sales price included interest of $83.33 accrued from January 1–April

30. Your cost for the bond was $5,000. On your return, you report interest of $83.33 and capital gain of $117.

You receive	$ 5,200.00
Less: Accrued interest	83.33
Sales proceeds	$ 5,116.67
Less: Your cost	5,000.00
Capital gain	$ 116.67, or $117

Redemptions, bankruptcy, reorganizations. On a redemption, interest received in excess of the amount due at that time is not treated as interest income but as capital gain.

EXAMPLE

You hold a $5,000 9% bond with interest payable January 1 and July 1. The company can call the bonds for redemption on any interest date. In May, the company announces it will redeem the bonds on July 1. But you may present the bond for redemption beginning with June 1 and it will be redeemed with interest to July 1. On June 1 you present the bond and receive $5,225 – $5,000 principal, $187.50 interest to June 1, and $37.50 extra interest to July 1. The $37.50 is treated as a capital gain; the $187.50 is interest.

Taxable interest may continue on bonds after the issuer becomes bankrupt, if a guarantor continues to pay the interest when due. The loss on the bonds will occur only when they mature and are not redeemed or when they are sold below your cost. In the meantime, the interest received from the guarantor is taxed.

Bondholders exchanging their bonds for stock, securities, or other property in a tax-free reorganization, including a reorganization in bankruptcy, have interest income to the extent the property received is attributable to accrued but unpaid interest; *see* Internal Revenue Code Section 354(a)(2)(B).

Bonds selling at a flat price. When you buy bonds with defaulted interest at a "flat" price, a later payment of the defaulted interest is not taxed. It is a tax-free return of capital that reduces your cost of the bond. This rule applies only to interest in default at the time the bond is purchased. Interest that accrues after the date of your purchase is taxed as ordinary income.

4.16 Forfeiture of Interest on Premature Withdrawals

Banks usually impose an interest penalty if you withdraw funds from a savings certificate before the specified maturity date. You may lose interest if you prematurely withdraw funds in order to switch to higher paying investments, or if you need the funds for personal use. In some cases, the penalty may exceed the interest earned so that principal is also forfeited to make up the difference.

If you are penalized, you must still report the full amount of interest credited to your account. However, on Form 1040, you may deduct the full amount of the penalty-forfeited principal as well as interest. The deductible penalty/forfeited amount is shown in Box 2 of Form 1099-INT sent to you. You may claim the deduction even if you do not itemize deductions. On Form 1040, enter the deduction on Line 30, marked "Penalty on early withdrawal of savings."

Loss on redemption before maturity of a savings certificate. If you redeem a long-term (more than one year) savings certificate for a price less than the stated redemption price at maturity, you are allowed a loss deduction for the amount of original issue discount (OID) reported as income but not received. The deductible amount is shown in Box 3 of Form 1099-OID. Claim the deduction on Line 30 of Form 1040. The basis of the obligation is reduced by the amount of the deductible loss.

Do not include in the computation any amount based on a fixed rate of simple or compound interest that is actually payable or is treated as constructively received at fixed periodic intervals of one year or less.

Caution

CD Early Withdrawal

If you are penalized for making an early withdrawal from a certificate of deposit, you may lose part of your interest or principal. You must report the full amount of interest credited to your account, but you may deduct the full amount of the penalty/forfeited principal as well as interest on Line 30 of Form 1040.

Premiums and Discounts on Bonds

4.17 Amortization of Bond Premium

Bond premium is the extra amount paid for a bond in excess of its principal or face amount when the value of the bond has increased due to falling interest rates. Investors may elect to amortize the premium on a taxable bond by deducting it over the life of the bond. Amortizing the premium annually is usually advantageous because it gives an annual deduction to offset the interest income from the bond. Basis of the bond is reduced by the amortized premium. If you claim amortization deductions and hold the bond to maturity, basis is reduced by the entire amortized premium and you have neither gain nor loss at redemption.

You may not claim a deduction for a premium paid on a *tax-exempt* bond; however, you must still decrease your basis by the premium.

Dealers in bonds may not deduct amortization but must include the premium as part of cost.

Capital loss alternative to amortizing premium. If you do not elect to amortize the premium on a taxable bond, you will realize a capital loss when the bond is redeemed at par or you sell it for less than you paid for it. For example, you bought a $1,000 corporate bond for $1,300 and did not amortize the $300 premium; you will realize a $300 capital loss when the bond is redeemed at par: $1,000 proceeds less $1,300 cost basis ($1,000 face value plus $300 premium). You could realize a capital gain if you sell the bond for more than the premium price you paid.

Determining the amortizable amount for the year. The annual amortizable premium is based on the constant yield method if the bond was issued after September 27, 1985. This method is the same as the optional constant yield method for reporting market discount discussed at *4.20*. *See* IRS Publication 1212 or consult a tax professional for making the complex computations.

For bonds issued before September 28, 1985, a monthly straight-line method or a yield method based upon IRS Revenue Ruling 82-10 could be used.

For taxable bonds subject to a call before maturity, the amortization computation is based on the earlier call date if that results in a smaller amortization deduction.

Amortization election allowed in or after the year you acquire a bond. An election to amortize premium on a taxable bond does not have to be made in the year you acquire the bond. Attach a statement to the tax return for the first year to which you want the election to apply. If the election is made after the year of acquisition, the premium allocable to the years prior to the year of election is not amortizable; the unamortized amount is included in your cost basis for the bond and will result in a capital loss when the bond is redeemed at par or sold prior to maturity for less than basis.

How to deduct amortized premium on taxable bonds acquired after 1987. The premium amortization for such bonds offsets your interest income from the bonds; *see* the Filing Tip in this section. Any excess of the allocable premium over interest income may be fully deducted as a miscellaneous deduction (not subject to the 2% floor) on Line 27 of Schedule A (Form 1040). However, the miscellaneous deduction is limited to the excess of total interest inclusions on the bonds in prior years over total bond premium deductions in the prior years.

How to deduct premium amortization on taxable bonds acquired after October 22, 1986, but before 1988. The method of claiming amortized premium on taxable bonds acquired after October 22, 1986, but before 1988 depends on whether you made an election to amortize premium for any taxable bond before 1998. If the election was first made for 1998 or a later year, the allocable premium amortization for the bonds offsets interest income on your return. If a pre-1998 election to amortize was made, you may elect to offset the allocable premium against interest income on the bond or treat it as investment interest deductible on Line 13 of Schedule A (Form 1040), subject to the deduction limits at *15.10*.

How to deduct premium amortization on taxable bonds acquired before October 23, 1986. For bonds acquired before October 23, 1986, the allocable premium is fully deductible on Line 27 of Schedule A (Form 1040) as a miscellaneous deduction not subject to the 2% floor *(19.1)*.

Effect of amortization election on other taxable bonds you acquire. If you elect to amortize the premium for one bond, you must also amortize the premium on all similar bonds owned by you at the beginning of the tax year, and also to all similar bonds acquired thereafter. An

Planning Reminder

Amortized Premium Reduces Basis

You reduce the cost basis of the bond by the amount of the premium taken as a deduction.

If you hold the bond to maturity, the entire premium is amortized and you have neither gain nor loss on redemption of the bond. If before maturity you sell the bond at a gain (selling price exceeds your basis for the bond), you realize long-term capital gain if you held the bond long term. A sale of the bond for less than its adjusted basis gives a capital loss.

Filing Tip

How To Deduct Amortized Premium

If you paid a premium on a taxable bond during 2006, you offset interest income on the bond by the amortized premium. You must file Form 1040 and show the reduction on Schedule B. Report the full interest from the bond on Line 1 of Schedule B, along with the rest of your interest income. On a separate line, subtract the amortized premium from a subtotal of the other interest. Label the subtraction "ABP Adjustment."

This interest offset rule applies to all taxable bonds acquired at a premium after 1987; *see 4.17* for bonds acquired before 1988.

election to amortize may not be revoked without IRS permission. If you file your return without claiming the deduction, you may not change your mind and make the election for that year by filing an amended return or refund claim.

Callable bonds. On taxable bonds, amortization is based either on the maturity or earlier call date, depending on which date gives a smaller yearly deduction. This rule applies regardless of the issue date of the bond. If the bond is called before maturity, you may deduct as an ordinary loss the unamortized bond premium in the year the bond is redeemed.

Convertible bonds. A premium paid for a convertible bond that is allocated to the conversion feature may not be amortized; the value of the conversion option reduces basis in the bond.

Premium on tax-exempt bonds. You may not take a deduction for the amortization of a premium paid on a tax-exempt bond. However, you must still figure the amortization for each year and reduce your basis in the bond by the amortized amount. When you dispose of the bond, you amortize the premium for the period you held the bond and reduce the basis of the bond by the amortized amount. If the bond has call dates, the IRS may require the premium to be amortized to the earliest call date.

4.18 Discount on Bonds

There are two types of bond discounts: original issue discount and market discount.

Market discount. Market discount arises when the price of a bond declines because its interest rate is less than the current interest rate. For example, a bond originally issued at its face amount of $1,000 declines in value to $900 because the interest payable on the bond is less than the current interest rate. The difference of $100 is called market discount. The tax treatment of market discount is explained in *4.20.*

Original issue discount (OID). OID arises when a bond is issued for a price less than its face or principal amount. OID is the difference between the principal amount (redemption price at maturity) and the issue price. For publicly offered obligations, the issue price is the initial offering price to the public at which a substantial amount of such obligations were sold. All obligations that pay no interest before maturity, such as zero coupon bonds, are considered to be issued at a discount. For example, a bond with a face amount of $1,000 is issued at an offering price of $900. The $100 difference is OID.

Generally, part of the OID must be reported as interest income each year you hold the bond, whether or not you receive any payment from the bond issuer. This is also true for certificates of deposit (CDs), time deposits, and similar savings arrangements with a term of more than one year, provided payment of interest is deferred until maturity. OID is reported to you by the issuer (or by your broker if you bought the obligation on a secondary market) on Form 1099-OID; *see 4.19* for reporting OID.

Exceptions to OID. OID rules do *not* apply to: (1) obligations with a term of one year or less held by *cash-basis taxpayers*; *see 4.21*; (2) tax-exempt obligations, except for certain stripped tax-exempts; *see 4.26*; (3) U.S. Savings Bonds; (4) an obligation issued by an individual before March 2, 1984; and (5) loans of $10,000 or less from individuals who are not professional money lenders, provided the loans do not have a tax avoidance motivation.

EXAMPLES

1. A 10-year bond with a face amount of $1,000 is issued at $980. One-fourth of one percent (.0025) of $1,000 times 10 is $25. As the $20 OID is less than $25, it may be ignored for tax purposes.
2. Same facts as in Example 1, except that the bond is issued at $950. As OID of $50 is more than the $25, OID must be reported under the rules explained at *4.19*.

Bond bought at premium or acquisition premium. You do not report OID as ordinary income if you buy a bond at a premium. You buy at a premium where you pay more than the total amount payable on the bond after your purchase, not including qualified stated interest. When you dispose of a bond bought at a premium, the difference between the sale or redemption price and your basis is a capital gain or loss; *see 4.17*.

Filing Tip

When OID May Be Ignored

You may disregard OID that is less than one-fourth of one percent (.0025) of the principal amount multiplied by the number of full years from the date of original issue to maturity. On most long-term bonds, the OID will exceed this amount and must be reported.

If you do not pay more than the total due at maturity, you do not have a premium, but there is "acquisition premium" if you pay more than the adjusted issue price. This is the issue price plus previously accrued OID but minus previous payments on the bond other than qualified stated interest. The acquisition premium reduces the amount of OID you must report as income. The rules for computing the reduction to OID depend on when the bond was purchased. For bonds purchased after July 18, 1984, OID is reduced by a fraction, the numerator of which is the acquisition premium; the denominator is the OID remaining after your purchase date to the maturity date. *See* IRS Publication 1212 for further details on how to make the computation.

4.19 Reporting Original Issue Discount on Your Return

The issuer of the bond (or your broker) will make the Original Issue Discount (OID) computation and report in Box 1 of Form 1099-OID the OID for the actual dates of your ownership during the calendar year. In most cases, the entire OID must be reported as interest income on your return. However, the amount shown in Box 1 of Form 1099-OID must be adjusted if you bought the bond at a premium or acquisition premium, the bond is indexed for inflation, the obligation is a stripped bond or stripped coupon (including zero coupon instruments backed by U.S. Treasury securities), or if you received Form 1099-OID as a nominee for someone else. Your basis in the bond is increased by the OID included in income.

If you did not receive a Form 1099-OID, contact the issuer or check IRS Publication 1212 for OID amounts.

Treasury inflation-indexed securities. You must report as OID any increase in the inflation-adjusted principal amount of a Treasury inflation-indexed security that occurs while you held the bond during the tax year. This amount should be reported to you in Box 6 of Form 1099-OID, but this amount must be adjusted if during the year you bought the bond after original issue or sold it. The adjusted amount of OID must be computed using the coupon bond method discussed in IRS Publication 1212.

Periodic interest (non-OID) paid to you during the year on a Treasury inflation-indexed security may be reported to you either in Box 2 of Form 1099-OID or in Box 3 of Form 1099-INT.

Premium. If you paid a premium *(see 4.18)* for a bond originally issued at discount, you do not have to report any OID as income. Report the amount shown on Form 1099-OID and then subtract it as discussed in the Filing Tip in this section.

Acquisition premium. The amount that is shown in Box 1 of Form 1099-OID is not correct if you pay an acquisition premium *(see 4.18)* because such premium reduces the amount of OID you must report as income. *See* IRS Publication 1212 to recompute OID. On your return, report the amount shown on Form 1099-OID and then reduce it, as discussed in the Filing Tip in this section.

Stripped bonds or coupons. The amount that is shown in Box 1 of Form 1099-OID may not be correct for a stripped bond or coupon; *see 4.22.* If it is incorrect, adjust it following the rules in Publication 1212 and report the proper amount, as discussed in the Filing Tip in this section.

Nominee. If you receive a Form 1099-OID for an obligation owned by someone else, other than your spouse, you must file another Form 1099-OID for that owner. The OID computation rules shown in IRS Publication 1212 should be used to compute the other owner's share of OID. You file the other owner's Form 1099-OID and a transmittal Form 1096 with the IRS, and give the other owner a copy of the Form 1099-OID. On your own tax return, report the amount shown on the Form 1099-OID you received and then reduce it, as discussed in the Filing Tip in this section.

Periodic interest reported on Form 1099-OID. If in addition to OID there is regular interest payable on the bond, such interest will be reported in Box 2 of Form 1099-OID. However, for a Treasury inflation-indexed security, the interest may be reported in Box 3 of Form 1099-INT. Report the full amount as interest income if you held the bond for the entire year. If you acquired the bond or disposed of it during the year, *see 4.15* for figuring the interest allocable to your ownership period.

REMICS. If you are a regular interest holder in a REMIC (real estate mortgage investment conduit), Box 1 of Form 1099-OID shows the amount of OID you must report on your return and Box 2 includes periodic interest other than OID. If you bought the regular interest at a premium or acquisition, the OID shown on Form 1099-OID must be adjusted as discussed above. If you are

Filing Tip

Reporting OID and Recomputed OID

If you are reporting the full amount of OID from Box 1 of Form 1099-OID include the amount as interest on your Form 1040, 1040A, or 1040EZ. However, if, as discussed in *4.19*, you are reporting less OID than the amount shown in Box 1 of Form 1099-OID, you must file Form 1040 and fill out Schedule B. Include the full amount shown in Box 1 of Form 1099-OID on Line 1 of Schedule B, along with other interest income. Make a subtotal of the Line 1 amounts and subtract from it the OID you are not required to report. Write "OID Adjustment" on the line where you show the subtraction, or "Nominee distribution," if that is the reason for the reduction. If you are reporting more OID than the amount shown in Box 1 of Form 1099-OID, add the additional amount to the subtotal of the interest on Line 1 of Schedule B, and label it "OID Adjustment."

Your basis for the obligation is increased by the taxable OID for purposes of figuring gain on a sale or redemption; *see 4.23.*

a regular interest holder in a single-class REMIC, Box 2 also includes your share of the REMIC's investment expenses. These expenses should be listed in a separate statement and are deductible on Schedule A as a miscellaneous itemized deduction subject to the 2% adjusted gross income floor; *see 19.1*.

4.20 Reporting Income on Market Discount Bonds

Market discount arises where the price of a bond declines below its face amount because it carries an interest rate that is below the current rate of interest.

When you realize a profit on the sale of a market discount bond, the portion of the profit equal to the accrued discount must be reported as ordinary interest income rather than as capital gain. Alternatively, an election may be made to report the accrued market discount annually instead of in the year of disposition.

These rules apply to taxable as well as tax-exempt *bonds bought after April 30, 1993*. However, there are these exceptions: (1) bonds with a maturity date of up to one year from date of issuance; (2) certain installment obligations; and (3) U.S. Savings Bonds. Furthermore, you may treat as zero any market discount that is less than one-fourth of one percent (.0025) of the redemption price multiplied by the number of full years after you acquire the bond to maturity. Such minimal discount will not affect capital gain on a sale.

Planning Reminder

Older Tax-Exempts

Tax-exempt bonds bought before May 1, 1993, are *not* subject to the market discount interest income rule; all the gain at disposition is capital gain.

Bonds bought before May 1, 1993. A *tax-exempt* bond bought before May 1, 1993, is not subject to the market discount rules; *see* the Planning Reminder in this section. For *taxable* bonds bought before May 1, 1993, application of the market discount rules depends on the issue date.

If you bought a *taxable* bond before May 1, 1993, the market discount interest income rule applies if the bond was issued *after* July 18, 1984. If the bond was issued before July 19, 1984, the market discount interest income rule does *not* apply. However, if you borrowed money to purchase or carry a market discount bond acquired after July 18, 1984 and before May 1, 1993, the interest deduction deferral rules discussed in the next paragraph apply, and in the year you sell the bond, gain is treated as interest income to the extent of the deferred interest that is deductible in the year of disposition.

Deferral of interest deduction and ordinary income at disposition if you borrow to buy or carry market discount bonds. If you took a loan to buy or carry a market discount bond, and your interest expense exceeds the income earned on the bond (including OID income, if any), the excess may not be currently deducted to the extent of the market discount allocated to the days you held the bond during the year. The allocation of market discount is based on either the ratable accrual method or constant yield method; *see* below.

You can avoid this interest deduction limitation if you elect to report the market discount annually as interest income; *see* below for "How to figure accrued market discount."

In the year you dispose of the bond, you may deduct the interest expenses that were disallowed in prior years because of the above limitations.

You may choose to deduct disallowed interest in a year before the year of disposition if you have net interest income from the bond. Net interest income is interest income for the year (including OID) less the interest expense incurred during the year to purchase or carry the bond. This election lets you deduct any disallowed interest expense to the extent it does not exceed the net interest income of that year. The balance of the disallowed interest expense is deductible in the year of disposition.

Filing Instruction

Discount Bonds Held to Maturity

If you do not report the discount annually and hold a bond until maturity, the discount is reported as interest income in the year of redemption; *see* Example 2 on page on the following page. However, you have the option of reporting the market discount annually instead of at sale.

EXAMPLE

In 2006, you borrowed to buy a market discount bond. During 2006, your interest expense is $1,000. Income from the bond is $900 and ratable market discount allocated to the annual holding period is $75. On Form 4952 (Investment Interest Expense Deduction), $925 of interest ($1,000 – $75) is reported as investment interest; *see 15.10*.

A similar interest deduction limitation will apply every year you hold the bond, assuming you do not elect to report the market discount annually.

In the year you dispose of the bond, interest deferred under the limitation will be deductible, subject to the investment interest limits of *15.10*. Gain on the disposition will be treated as interest income to the extent of this deferred interest deduction.

How to figure accrued market discount. Where the market discount rules apply, gain is taxed as ordinary interest income to the extent of the market discount accrued to the date of sale. There are two methods for figuring the accrued market discount. The basic method, called the *ratable accrual method*, is figured by dividing market discount by the number of days in the period from the date you bought the bond until the date of maturity. This daily amount is then multiplied by the number of days you held the bond to determine your accrued market discount; *see* Example 1 below.

Instead of using the ratable accrual method to compute accrual of market discount you may elect to figure the accrued discount for any bond under an optional *constant yield* (economic accrual) method. If you make the election, you may not change it. The constant yield method initially provides a smaller accrual of market discount than the ratable method, but it is more complicated to figure. It is generally the same as the constant yield method used in IRS Publication 1212 to compute taxable OID *(4.19)*. For accruing market discount, treat your acquisition date as the original issue date and your basis for the market discount bond (immediately after you acquire it) as the issue price when applying the formula in Publication 1212.

Reporting discount annually. Rather than report market discount in the year you sell the bond, you may elect, in the year you acquire the bond, to report market discount currently as interest income. You may use either the ratable accrual method, as in Example 3 below, or the elective constant yield method discussed earlier. Your election to report annually applies to all market discount bonds subject to the interest income rule that you later acquire. You may not revoke the election without IRS consent. If the election is made, the interest deduction deferral rule discussed earlier does not apply. Furthermore, the election could provide a tax advantage if you sell the bond at a profit and you can benefit from lower tax rates applied to net long-term capital gains.

EXAMPLES

1. You buy a taxable bond at a market discount of $200. There are 1,000 days between the date of your purchase and the maturity date. The daily accrual rate is 20 cents. You hold the bond for 600 days before selling it for a price exceeding what you paid for the bond. Under the ratable accrual method, up to $120 of your profit is market discount taxable as interest income (600 × $0.20).
2. You paid $9,100 for a $10,000 bond maturing in 2006. If you hold the bond to maturity, you will receive $10,000, giving you a gain of $900, equal to the market discount. The entire $900 market discount will be taxable as interest income in 2006 when the bond is redeemed.
3. In 2006, you buy at a $200 discount a bond that was issued after July 18, 1984. There are 1,000 days between the date of your purchase and the maturity date, so that daily accrual is 20 cents. You elect to report the market discount currently using the ratable accrual method. If you held the bond for 112 days in 2006, on your 2006 return you report $22 as interest income (112 × $0.20).

Partial principal payments on bonds acquired after October 22, 1986. If the issuer of a bond (acquired by you after October 22, 1986) makes a partial payment of the principal (face amount), you must include the payment as ordinary interest income to the extent it does not exceed the accrued market discount on the bond. *See* IRS Publication 550 for options on determining accrued market discount. A taxable partial principal payment reduces the amount of remaining accrued market discount when figuring your tax on a later sale or receipt of another partial principal payment.

Market discount on a bond originally issued at a discount. A bond issued at original issue discount may later be acquired at a market discount because of an increase in interest rates. If you acquire at market discount an OID bond issued after July 18, 1984, the market discount is the excess of: (1) the issue price of the bond plus the total original issue discount includible in the gross income of all prior holders of the bond over (2) what you paid for the bond.

Exchanging a market discount bond in corporate mergers or reorganizations. If you hold a market discount bond and exchange it for another bond as part of a merger or other reorganization, the new bond is subject to the market discount rules when you sell it. However, under an exception, market discount rules will not apply to the new bond if the old market discount bond was issued before July 19, 1984, and the terms and interest rates of both bonds are identical.

4.21 Discount on Short-Term Obligations

Short-term obligations (maturity of a year or less from date of issue) may be purchased at a discount from face value. If you are on the cash basis, you report the discount as interest income in the year the obligation is paid. The interest is reported on Form 1099-INT.

EXAMPLE

In May 2005, you paid $920 for a short-term note with a face amount of $1,000. In January 2006, you receive payment of $1,000 on the note. On your 2006 tax return, you report $80 as interest.

Discount must be currently reported by dealers and accrual-basis taxpayers. Discount allocable to the current year must be reported as income by accrual-basis taxpayers, dealers who sell short-term obligations in the course of business, banks, regulated investment companies, common trust funds, certain pass-through entities, and for obligations identified as part of a hedging transaction. Current reporting also applies to persons who separate or strip interest coupons from a bond and then retain the stripped bond or stripped coupon; the accrual rule applies to the retained obligation.

For short-term nongovernmental obligations, OID is generally taken into account instead of acquisition discount, but an election may be made to report the accrued acquisition discount. *See* IRS Publication 550 for details.

Basis in the obligation is increased by the amount of acquisition discount (or OID for nongovernmental obligations) that is currently reported as income.

Interest deduction limitation for cash-basis investors. A cash-basis investor who borrows funds to buy a short-term discount obligation may not fully deduct interest on the loan unless an election is made to report the accrued acquisition discount as income. If the election is not made, a complicated formula limits deductible interest to the excess of the interest expense for the year over the taxable interest from the bond during the year less (1) the portion of the discount allocated to the days you held the bond during the year, and (2) the portion of interest not taxable for the year under your method of accounting. Any interest expense disallowed under this limitation is deductible in the year in which the obligation is disposed.

The interest deduction limitation does *not* apply if you elect to include in income the accruable discount under the ratable accrual method or constant yield method discussed in *4.20*. The election applies to all short-term obligations acquired during the year and also in all later years.

Gain or loss on disposition of short-term obligations for cash-basis investors. If you have a gain on the sale or exchange of a discounted short-term governmental obligation (other than tax-exempt local obligations), the gain is ordinary income to the extent of the ratable share of the acquisition discount received when you bought the obligation. Follow the computation shown in *4.27* for Treasury bills to figure this ordinary income portion. Any gain over this ordinary income portion is short-term capital gain; a loss would be a short-term capital loss.

Gain on short-term *nongovernmental* obligations is treated as ordinary income up to the ratable share of OID. The formula for figuring this ordinary income portion is similar to that shown in *4.27* for short-term governmental obligations, except that the denominator of the fraction is days from original issue to maturity, rather than days from acquisition. A constant yield method may also be elected to figure the ordinary income portion. Gain above the computed ordinary income amount is short-term capital gain (*see* Chapter 5). For more information, *see* IRS Publication 550.

Filing Tip

Discount on Short-Term Government Obligations

For short-term governmental obligations (other than tax-exempts), the acquisition discount is accrued in daily installments under the ratable method, unless an election is made to use the constant yield method.

4.22 Stripped Coupon Bonds and Stock

Brokers holding coupon bonds may separate or strip the coupons from the bonds and sell the bonds or coupons to investors. Examples include zero-coupon instruments sold by brokerage houses that are backed by U.S. Treasury bonds (such as CATS and TIGRS).

The U.S. Treasury also offers its version of zero coupon instruments, with the name STRIPS, which are available from brokers and banks.

Brokers holding preferred stock may strip the dividend rights from the stock and sell the stripped stock to investors.

If you buy a stripped bond or coupon, the spread between the cost of the bond or coupon and its higher face amount is treated as original issue discount (OID). This means that you annually report a part of the spread as interest income. For a stripped bond, the amount of the original issue discount is

Caution

Recomputing Form 1099-OID Amount

Do not report the amount shown in Box 1 of Form 1099-OID for a stripped bond or coupon; that amount must be recomputed under complicated rules described in IRS Publication 1212. *See 4.19* for reporting the recomputed OID on your return.

Caution

Reporting Zero Coupon Bond Discount

Zero coupon bond discount is reported annually as interest over the life of the bond, even though interest is not received. This tax cost tends to make zero coupon bonds unattractive to investors, unless the bonds can be bought for IRA and other retirement plans that defer tax on income until distributions are made.

Zero coupon bonds also may be a means of financing a child's education. A parent buys the bond for the child. The child must report the income annually, and if the income is not subject to the parent's marginal tax bracket under the "kiddie tax" (Chapter 24), the income subject to tax may be minimal.

The value of zero coupon bonds fluctuates sharply with interest rate changes. This fact should be considered before investing in long-term zero coupon bonds. If you sell zero coupon bonds before the maturity term at a time when interest rates rise, you may lose part of your investment.

the difference between the stated redemption price of the bond at maturity and the cost of the bond. For a stripped coupon, the amount of the discount is the difference between the amount payable on the due date of the coupon and the cost of the coupon. The rules for figuring the amount of OID to be reported annually are in IRS Publication 1212. *See 4.19* for reporting OID.

If you strip a coupon bond, interest accrual and allocation rules prevent you from creating a tax loss on a sale of the bond or coupons. You are required to report interest accrued up to the date of the sale and also add the amount to the basis of the bond. If you acquired the obligation after October 22, 1986, you must also include in income any market discount that accrued before the date you sold the stripped bond or coupons. The method of accrual depends on the date you bought the obligation; *see* IRS Publication 1212. The accrued market discount is also added to the basis of the bond. You then allocate this basis between the bond and the coupons. The allocation is based on the relative fair market values of the bond and coupons at the date of sale. Gain or loss on the sale is the difference between the sales price of the stripped item (bond or coupons) and its allocated basis. Furthermore, the original issue discount rules apply to the stripped item which you keep (bond or coupon). Original issue discount for this purpose is the difference between the basis allocated to the retained item and the redemption price of the bond (if retained) or the amount payable on the coupons (if retained). You must annually report a ratable portion of the discount.

4.23 Sale or Retirement of Bonds and Notes

Gain or loss on the sale, redemption, or retirement of debt obligations issued by a government or corporation is generally capital gain or loss.

A redemption or retirement of a bond at maturity must be reported as a sale on Schedule D of Form 1040 *(5.8)* although there may be no gain or loss realized.

Corporate bonds with OID issued after 1954 and before May 28, 1969, and government bonds with OID issued after 1954 and before July 2, 1982. If the bonds were originally issued at a discount (OID), you report your ratable monthly share of the OID element as ordinary income when the bonds are sold or redeemed; any gain exceeding OID is reported as capital gain. However, if there was an intention to call before maturity, gain is ordinary income to the full extent of the OID. A loss is a capital loss.

Corporate bonds with OID issued after May 27, 1969, and government bonds with OID issued after July 1, 1982. The accrued amount of OID is reported annually as interest income *(see 4.19)* and added to basis; this includes the accrued OID for the year the bond is sold. If the bonds are sold or redeemed before maturity, you realize capital gain for the proceeds over the adjusted basis (as increased by accrued OID) of the bond, provided there was no intention to call the bond before maturity. If at the time of original issue there was an intention to call the obligation before maturity, the entire OID that has not yet been included in your income is taxable as ordinary income; the balance is capital gain. IRS Publication 1212 has examples for figuring the amount taxable as ordinary income.

Market discount on bonds is taxable under the rules at *4.20*.

Tax-exempts. *See 4.26* for discount on tax-exempt bonds.

Obligations issued by individuals. If you hold an individual's note issued after March 1, 1984, for over $10,000, accrued OID must be reported annually *(4.19)* and added to basis. Gain on your sale of the note is subject to the rules discussed above for corporate and government OID bonds.

If the note is $10,000 or less (when combined with other prior outstanding loans from the same individual), OID is not reported annually provided you are not a professional lender and tax avoidance was not a principal purpose of the loan. On a sale of the note at a gain, your ratable share of the OID is taxed as ordinary income; any balance is capital gain. A loss is a capital loss.

Tax-Free Interest on State and Local Government Obligations

4.24 State and City Interest Generally Tax Exempt

Generally, you pay no tax on interest on bonds or notes of states, cities, counties, the District of Columbia, or a possession of the United States. This includes bonds or notes of port authorities, toll road commissions, utility services activities, community redevelopment agencies, and similar bodies created for public purposes. Bonds issued after June 30, 1983, must be in registered form for the interest to be tax exempt. Interest on federally guaranteed obligations is generally taxable, but *see* exceptions at *4.25*.

Check with the issuer of the bond to verify the tax-exempt status of the interest.

Reporting on Schedule B or Schedule 1. On your 2006 return, you must list the amount of tax-exempt interest received during the year although it is not taxable. On Form 1040, you list the tax-exempt interest on Line 8b. On Form 1040A, you list the amount on Line 8b. On Form 1040EZ, you write "TEI" and then the amount of tax-exempt interest to the right of the last word on Line 2, but do not include it in the taxable interest shown on Line 2.

Private activity bonds. Interest on so-called private activity bonds is generally taxable *(see 4.25)*, but there are certain exceptions. For example, interest on the following bonds is tax exempt even if the bond may technically be in the category of private activity bonds: qualified student loan bonds; exempt facility bonds, including New York Liberty bonds and enterprise zone facility bonds; qualified small issue bonds; qualified mortgage bonds and qualified veterans' mortgage bonds; qualified redevelopment bonds; and qualified 501(c)(3) bonds issued by charitable organizations and hospitals.

However, while interest on such bonds is not subject to regular tax, interest that you receive on such bonds issued after August 7, 1986, *other than* qualified 501(c)(3) bonds, New York Liberty bonds, and qualified Gulf Opportunity Zone bonds, is considered a tax preference item that may be subject to alternative minimum tax; *see* Chapter 23.

Check with the issuer for the tax status of a private activity bond.

Law Alert

Payers Must Report to IRS

A new law requires payers of tax-exempt interest to report post-2005 payments to the IRS. Previously, taxpayers were required to report tax-exempt interest on their tax returns but payers were not required to file annual information returns.

The new law allows the IRS to match taxpayer reporting of tax-exempt interest against the information returns filed by payers. Although the interest is not subject to regular income tax, tax-exempt interest from specified private activity bonds is a tax preference for AMT purposes *(23.3)* and tax-exempt interest is included in the formula for determining whether (and how much) Social Security benefits are subject to tax *(34.3)*.

4.25 Taxable State and City Interest

Interest on certain state and city obligations is taxable. These taxable obligations include federally guaranteed obligations, mortgage subsidy bonds, private activity bonds, and arbitrage bonds.

Federally guaranteed obligations. Interest on state and local obligations issued after April 14, 1983, is generally taxable if the obligation is federally guaranteed, but there are exceptions allowing tax exemptions for obligations guaranteed by the Federal Housing Administration, Department of Veterans Affairs, Bonneville Power Authority, Federal Home Loan Mortgage Corporation, Federal National Mortgage Association, Government National Mortgage Corporation, Resolution Funding Corporation, and Student Loan Marketing Association.

Mortgage subsidy bonds. Interest on bonds issued by a state or local government after April 24, 1979, may not be tax exempt if funds raised by the bonds are used for home mortgages. There are exceptions for certain qualified mortgage bonds and veterans' bonds. Check on the tax-exempt status of mortgage bonds with the issuing authority.

Private activity bonds. Generally, a private activity bond is any bond where more than 10% of the issue's proceeds are used by a private business whose property secures the issue, or if at least 5% of the proceeds (or $5 million if less) are used for loans to parties other than governmental units. Interest on such bonds is generally taxable, but there are exceptions as discussed in *4.24*. Check on the tax status of the bonds with the issuing authority.

Caution

Arbitrage Bonds

These are state and local bonds issued after October 9, 1969, used to provide funds for reinvestment in higher yielding instruments except where the bond proceeds are part of a required reserve or replacement fund or are being invested temporarily before the purposes of a bond issue can be fulfilled. Interest on arbitrage bonds is taxable.

4.26 Tax-Exempt Bonds Bought at a Discount

Original issue discount (OID) on tax-exempt obligations is not taxable, and on a sale or redemption, gain attributed to OID is tax exempt. Gain attributed to market discount is capital gain or ordinary income depending on whether the bond was purchased before May 1, 1993, or on or after that date; *see 4.20*. Amortization of premiums is discussed at *4.17*.

Original issue discount tax-exempt bond. This arises when a bond is issued for a price less than the face amount of the bond. The discount is considered tax-exempt interest. Thus, if you are the original buyer and hold the bond to maturity, the entire amount of the discount is tax free. If before maturity you sell a bond that was issued before September 4, 1982, and acquired before March 2, 1984, your part of the OID is tax free. On a disposition of a tax-exempt bond issued after September 3, 1982, and acquired after March 1, 1984, you must add to basis accrued OID before determining gain or loss. OID must generally be accrued using a constant yield method; *see* IRS Publication 1212.

When bonds issued after June 8, 1980, are redeemed before maturity, the portion of the original issue discount earned to the date of redemption is tax-free interest; the balance is capital gain. Bonds issued with an intention to redeem before maturity are not subject to this rule; all interest is tax exempt.

Market discount tax-exempts. A market discount arises when a bond originally issued at not less than par is bought at below par because its market value has declined. If *before* May 1, 1993, you bought at a market discount a tax-exempt bond which you sell for a price exceeding your purchase price, the excess is capital gain. If the bond was held long term, the gain is long term. A redemption of the bond at a price exceeding your purchase price is similarly treated.

However, for market discount tax-exempt bonds purchased *after* April 30, 1993, the ordinary income rules discussed at *4.20* apply.

Stripped tax-exempt obligations. OID is not currently taxed on a stripped tax-exempt bond or stripped coupon from the bond if you bought it before June 11, 1987. However, for any stripped bond or coupon you bought or sold after October 22, 1986, OID must be accrued and added to basis for purposes of figuring gain or loss on a disposition. Furthermore, if you bought the stripped bond or coupon after June 10, 1987, part of the OID may be taxable; *see* Publication 1212 for figuring the tax-free portion.

Interest on Treasury Securities and U.S. Savings Bonds

4.27 Treasury Bills, Notes, and Bonds

Interest on securities issued by the federal government is fully taxable on your federal return. However, interest on federal obligations is not subject to state or local income taxes. Interest on Treasury bills, notes, and bonds is reported on Form 1099-INT.

Treasury bonds and notes. Treasury notes have maturities of two to 10 years. Treasury bonds have maturities of over 10 years. You report the fixed or coupon interest as interest income in the year the coupon becomes due and payable. Treasury bonds and notes are capital assets; gain or loss on their sale, exchange, or redemption is reported as capital gain or loss on Schedule D; *see* Chapter 5. If you purchased a federal obligation below par (at a discount) after July 1, 1982, *see 4.19* for the rules on reporting original issue discount. If you purchased a Treasury bond or note above par (at a premium), you may elect to amortize the premium; *see 4.17.* If you do not elect to amortize and you hold the bond or note to maturity, you have a capital loss.

Planning Reminder

Tax Deferral: T-Bill Maturing Next Year

If you are a cash-basis taxpayer, you may postpone the tax on Treasury bill interest by selecting a Treasury bill maturing next year. Income is not recognized until the date on which the Treasury bill is paid at maturity, unless it has been sold or otherwise disposed of earlier.

Treasury inflation-indexed bonds. These pay interest semiannually at a fixed rate on a principal amount that is adjusted to take into account inflation or deflation. The interest is taxable when received and any increase in the inflation-adjusted principal amount while you hold the bond must be reported as original issue discount (OID); *see 4.19.* Your basis in the bond is increased by the OID included in income. On a sale or redemption before maturity, any gain is generally capital gain, but if there was an intention to call before maturity, gain is ordinary income to the extent of the previously unreported OID; *see 4.23* ("Corporate bonds with OID issued after May 27, 1969, and government bonds with OID issued after July 1, 1982").

Treasury bills. These are short-term U.S. obligations with maturities of four weeks, 13 weeks, or 26 weeks. On a bill held to maturity, you report as interest income the difference between the discounted price and the amount you receive on a redemption of the bills at maturity.

Treasury bills are capital assets and a loss on a disposition before maturity is taxed as a capital loss. If you are a cash-basis taxpayer and have a gain on a sale or exchange, ordinary income is realized up to the amount of the ratable share of the discount received when you bought the obligation. This amount is treated as interest income and is figured as follows:

$$\frac{\text{Days T-bill was held}}{\text{Days from acquisition to maturity}} \times \text{Acquisition discount (redemption value at maturity } \textit{minus} \text{ your cost)}$$

Any gain over this amount is capital gain; *see* the Example below. Instead of using the above fractional computation for figuring the ordinary income portion of the gain, an election may be made to apply the constant yield method. This method follows the OID computation rules shown in IRS Publication 1212 for obligations issued after 1984, except that the acquisition cost of the Treasury bill would be treated as the issue price in applying the Publication 1212 formula.

Accrual-basis taxpayers and dealers who are required to currently report the acquisition discount element of Treasury bills using either the ratable accrual method or the constant yield method *(4.20)* do not apply the above formula on a sale before maturity. In figuring gain or loss, the discount included as income is added to basis.

EXAMPLE

You buy at original issue a 26-week $10,000 Treasury bill (182-day maturity) for $9,800. You sell it 95 days later for $9,900. Your entire $100 gain ($9,900 – $9,800) is taxed as interest income as it is less than the $104 treated as interest income under the ratable daily formula:

$$\frac{\text{95 days held}}{\text{182 days from acquisition to maturity}} \times \text{\$200 discount} = \text{\$104}$$

Interest deduction limitation. Interest incurred on loans used to buy Treasury bills is deductible by a cash-basis investor only to the extent that interest expenses exceed the following: (1) the portion of the acquisition discount allocated to the days you held the bond during the year; and (2) the portion of interest not taxable for the year under your method of accounting. The deferred interest expense is deductible in the year the bill is disposed of. If an election is made to report the acquisition discount as current income under the rules in *4.21* for governmental obligations, the interest expense may also be deducted currently. The election applies to all future acquisitions.

4.28 Interest on U.S. Savings Bonds

Savings Bond Tables: The e-Supplement *at www.jklasser.com will contain redemption tables showing the 2006 year-end values of Series E bonds, Series EE bonds, and Series I bonds.*

Series E and EE Bonds. Series EE bonds have been available since 1980; before 1980, Series E bonds were issued. Both Series E and Series EE bonds may be cashed for what you paid for them plus an increase in their value over stated periods of time. *See 30.14* for interest accrual and redemption rules for U.S. Savings Bonds.

The increase in redemption value is taxable as interest, but you do not have to report the increase in value each year on your federal return. You may defer *(4.29)* the interest income until the year in which you cash the bond or the year in which the bond finally matures, whichever is earlier. But if you want, you may report the annual increase by merely including it on your tax return. If you use the accrual method of reporting, you must include the interest each year as it accrues. Savings bond interest is not subject to state or local taxes.

If you initially choose to defer the reporting of interest and later want to switch to annual reporting, you may do so. You may also change from the annual reporting method to the deferral method. *See 4.29* for rules on changing reporting methods.

Series I bonds. "I bonds," first offered in 1998, are inflation-indexed bonds issued at face amount (see 30.15). As with EE bonds, you may defer the interest income (the increase in redemption value each year is interest) until the year in which the bond is redeemed or matures in 30 years, whichever is earlier; *see 4.29*.

Education funding. If you buy EE or I bonds to pay for educational expenses and you defer the reporting of interest *(4.29)*, you may be able to exclude the accumulated interest from income when you redeem the bonds. *See* Chapter 38.

Bonds registered in name of child. Interest on U.S. savings bonds bought for and registered in the name of a child will be taxed to the child, even if the parent paid for the bonds and is named as beneficiary. Unless an election is made to report the increases in redemption value annually, the accumulated interest will be taxable to the child in the year he or she redeems the bond, or if earlier, when the bond finally matures. However, if the interest is reported annually by a child under age 18, or the child is under age 18 in the year bonds are redeemed, the interest may be subject to tax at the parent's top rate under the "kiddie tax"; see Chapter 24. For example, if a child under age 18 has 2006 investment income over $1,700, the excess is taxed at the parent's top tax rate on the child's 2006 return; *see 24.3*. To avoid kiddie tax, savings bond interest may be deferred, as discussed in *4.29*.

Planning Reminder

Election for Children Under 18

Where the kiddie tax for children under age 18 *(24.3)* does *not* apply, making the election to report the interest annually may be advisable, such as where the child has little or no other income and the bond interest can be offset by personal deductions. For example, a dependent child is not allowed to claim a personal exemption, but he or she may claim a standard deduction for 2006 of at least $850; *see 13.5*. If the election to report the savings bond interest currently was made for 2006, up to $850 of the interest would be offset by the standard deduction, assuming the child had no other income.

Bonds must be reissued to make gift. Assume you have bought I, E or EE bonds and had them registered in joint names of yourself and your daughter. The law of your state provides that jointly owned property may be transferred to a co-owner by delivery or possession. You deliver the bonds to your daughter and tell her they now belong to her alone. According to Treasury regulations, this is not a valid gift of the bonds. The bonds must be surrendered and reissued in your daughter's name. For the year of reissue, you must include in your income all of the interest earned on the bonds other than interest you previously reported.

If you do not have the bonds reissued and you die, the bonds are taxable to your estate. Ownership of the bonds is a matter of contract between the United States and the bond purchaser. The bonds are nontransferable. A valid gift cannot be accomplished by manual delivery to a donee unless the bonds also are surrendered and registered in the donee's name in accordance with Treasury regulations.

Series HH. These bonds were available after 1979 and before September 1, 2004, in exchange for E or EE bonds, or for Freedom Shares. They were issued at face value and pay semiannual interest that is taxable when received. They mature in 20 years. August 31, 2004, was the last day that owners of E or EE bonds could exchange them for HH bonds, or owners of matured H or HH bonds could reinvest them in HH bonds.

Series H. These bonds were available before 1980. They were bought at face value and pay semiannual interest that is taxable when received. If you obtained Series H bonds in an exchange for Series E bonds, and you did not report the E bond interest annually, you do not have to report the interest due on the old E bonds until the H bonds are redeemed or mature, whichever occurs first. H bonds issued after January 1957 cease earning interest when they mature in 30 years. At maturity, or on a disposal before maturity, you must report as interest the accumulated interest from any exchanged E bonds.

4.29 Deferring U.S. Savings Bond Interest

You do not have to make a special election on your tax return in order to defer the interest on Series E, EE, or I savings bonds. You may simply postpone reporting the interest until the year you redeem the bond or the year in which it reaches final maturity, whichever is earlier. If you choose to defer the interest, you may decide in a later year to begin reporting the increase in redemption value each year as interest. You may also switch from annual reporting to the deferral method. These options are discussed in this section.

Changing from deferral to annual reporting. If you have deferred reporting of annual increases in redemption value and want to elect to report annual increases on your 2006 return, make sure you report as 2006 interest income the total of all prior and 2006 increases in value. But next year, report only the increases accruing then, plus increases accruing on bonds newly purchased. Suppose you do not include the annual increase on your 2006 return and later change your mind. If the due date of the return has passed, it is too late to make the election. You may not file an amended return reporting the increase in value for 2006. You have to wait until next year's return to make the election.

Filing Tip

Form 1099-INT When Savings Bond Is Cashed

When you cash in an E, EE, or I bond, you receive Form 1099-INT that lists as interest the difference between the amount received and the amount paid for the bond. The form may show more taxable interest than you are required to report because you have regularly reported the interest or a prior owner reported the interest. Report the full amount shown on Form 1099-INT on Schedule B if you file Form 1040, or on Part I of Schedule 1 if you file Form 1040A, along with your other interest income. Enter a subtotal of the total interest and then, on a separate line, reduce the subtotal by the savings bond interest that was previously reported and identify the reduction as "Previously Reported U.S. Savings Bond Interest." The interest is exempt from state and local taxes.

Changing from annual reporting to deferral. If you have been reporting annual increases in redemption value as interest income, you may change your method and elect to defer interest reporting until the bonds mature or are redeemed. You make the election by attaching to your federal income tax return for the year of the change a statement that meets the conditions of IRS Revenue Procedure 2002-9; *see* IRS Publication 550 for details.

Extended maturity periods. E bonds may be held for additional periods of maturity after their initial maturity dates. Bonds held for additional periods increase in value and may be cashed in at any time. If you chose to postpone paying tax on accumulated interest, you may continue to postpone the tax during the extended period. You would then report the entire accumulated interest at the final maturity date or in the year you redeem the bond, whichever occurs earlier.

Co-Owners. How to report interest on a Series E, EE, or I bond depends on how it was bought or issued:

1. You paid for the entire bond: Either you or the co-owner may redeem it. You are taxed on all the interest, even though the co-owner cashes the bond and you receive no proceeds. If the other co-owner does cash in the bond, he or she will receive a Form 1099-INT reporting the accumulated interest. However, since that interest is taxable to you, the co-owner should give you a nominee Form 1099-INT, as explained in the rules for joint accounts in *4.12*.

2. You paid for only part of the bond: Either of you may redeem it. You are taxed on that part of the interest which is in proportion to your share of the purchase price. This is so even though you do not receive the proceeds.
3. You paid for part of the bond, and then had it reissued in another's name. You pay tax only on the interest accrued while you held the bond. The new co-owner picks up his or her share of the interest accruing afterwards.
4. You and another person were named co-owners on a bond bought as a gift by a third party. You are taxed on 50% of the interest income; your co-owner is taxed on the remaining half.

Changing the form of registration. Changing the form of registration of an E or EE bond may result in tax. Assume you use your own funds to purchase a bond issued in your name, payable on your death to your son. Later, at your request, a new bond is issued in your son's name only. The increased value of the original bond up to the date it was redeemed and reissued in your son's name is taxed to you as interest income.

As shown in the Examples below, certain changes in registration do not result in an immediate tax.

EXAMPLES

1. Jones buys an EE bond and has it registered in his name and in the name of his son as co-owner. Jones has the bonds reissued solely in his own name; he is not required to report the accumulated interest at that time.
2. You and your spouse each contributed an equal amount toward the purchase of a $1,000 EE bond, which was issued to you as co-owners. You later have the bond reissued as two $500 bonds, one in your name and one in your spouse's name. Neither of you has to report the interest earned to the date of reissue. But if you bought the $1,000 bond entirely with your own funds, you report half the interest earned to the date of reissue.
3. You add another person's name as co-owner to facilitate a transfer of the bond on death. The change in registration does not result in a tax.

Transfer to a spouse. Interest on U.S. Savings Bonds transferred to a spouse in a divorce or settlement may result in tax to the transferor; *see 6.7*.

Transfer to a trust. If you transfer U.S. Savings Bonds to a trust giving up all rights of ownership, you are taxed on the accumulated interest to date of transfer. If, however, you are considered to be the owner of the trust and the interest earned before and after the transfer is taxable to you, you may continue to defer reporting the interest.

Transfer to a charity. Tax on the accumulated interest is not avoided by having the bonds reissued to a philanthropy. The IRS held that by having the bonds reissued in the philanthropy's name, the owner realized taxable income on the accumulated bond interest.

Transfer of savings bond at death. If an owner does not report the bond interest annually and dies before redeeming the bond, the income tax liability on the interest accumulated during the deceased's lifetime becomes the liability of the person who acquires the bond, unless an election is made to report the accrued interest in the decedent's final income tax return; *see 1.14*. If the election is not made on the decedent's final return, the new owner may choose to report the accumulated interest annually, or defer reporting it until the bond is redeemed or reaches final maturity, whichever is earlier. If the election is made on the decedent's final return, the new owner is taxable only on interest earned after the date of death.

Caution

When Accumulated Interest Becomes Taxable

You may not indefinitely defer the tax on E bond interest. E bonds cease earning interest once the bonds reach their final maturity date. For example, bonds issued during 1976 ceased earning interest in 2006, 30 years from the date of issuance. In the year of final maturity, all deferred interest becomes taxable. *See 30.14* for a listing of final maturity dates.

Filing Tip

Deduction for Estate Tax Paid on Interest

Where an estate tax has been paid on bond interest accrued during the owner's lifetime, the new bondholder may claim the estate tax as a miscellaneous itemized deduction in the year that he or she pays tax on the accumulated interest. The deduction is not subject to the 2% adjusted gross income floor *(11.17)*.

Minimum Interest for Loans and Seller-Financed Debt

4.30 Minimum Interest Rules

The law requires a minimum rate of interest to be charged on loan transactions unless a specific exception covers the transaction. Where minimum interest is not charged, the law imputes interest as if the parties agreed to the charge.

The rules are complicated and have been subject to several revisions. There are different minimum interest rates and reporting rules depending on the nature of the transaction. The following discussion provides the important details for understanding the rules. For specific cases and computations, we suggest that you consult IRS regulations for details not covered in this book.

There are two broad classes of transactions:

Loans. These are generally covered by Internal Revenue Code Section 7872. Below-market or low-rate interest loans are discussed at *4.31*.

Seller-financed sales of property. These are covered by either Internal Revenue Code Section 1274 or Section 483. Seller-financed sales are discussed at *4.32*. If parties fail to charge the minimum required interest rate, the same minimum rate is imputed by law.

4.31 Interest-Free or Below-Market-Interest Loans

For many years, the IRS tried to tax interest-free or below-market-interest loans. However, court decisions supported taxpayers who argued that such loans did not result in taxable income or gifts. To reverse these decisions, the IRS convinced Congress to pass a law imposing tax on interest-free or low-interest loans made by individuals and businesses. You may not make interest-free or low-interest loans to a relative who uses the loan for personal or investment purposes without adverse income tax consequences, unless the exception discussed in this section for $10,000 or $100,000 loans applies.

How the imputed interest rules work. If interest at least equal to the applicable federal rate set by the IRS is not charged, the law generally treats a below-market-interest loan as two transactions:

1. The law assumes that the lender has transferred to the borrower an amount equal to the "foregone" interest element of the loan. In the case of a loan between individuals, such as a parent and child, the lender is subject to gift tax on this element; in the case of a stockholder borrowing from a company, the element is a taxable dividend; in the case of a loan made to an employee, it is taxable pay.
   Note: For *gift tax* purposes *(39.2)*, a term loan is treated as if the lender gave the borrower the excess of the amount of the loan over the present value of payments due during the loan term. Demand loans are treated as if the lender gave the borrower annually the amount of the foregone interest.
2. The law assumes that imputed interest equal to the applicable federal rate is paid by the borrower to the lender. The borrower may be able to claim a deduction for the interest if the loan is used to buy a home and the loan is secured by the residence *(15.1)*, or the loan is used to buy investment property *(15.10)*.

In applying the imputed interest rules, all loans to or from a husband are combined with all loans to or from his wife; they are treated as one person.

With gift loans between individuals, interest computed during the borrower's taxable year is treated for both the lender and the borrower as transferred on the last day of the borrower's taxable year. Treasury regulations to Section 7872 provide rules for figuring "foregone" interest. Where a demand loan is in effect for the entire calendar year, a "blended annual rate" issued by the IRS to simplify reporting may be used to compute the imputed interest. The blended annual rate is announced by the IRS each July. For 2006, the blended rate is 4.71%. The blended rate is not available if the loan was not outstanding for the entire year or if the loan balance fluctuated; computations provided by Treasury regulations must be used.

Caution

Get Professional Advice To Draft Loan Agreement

Given the complexity of the imputed interest rules and exceptions, you and your tax advisor should carefully review regulations to the Internal Revenue Code Section 7872 when drafting a loan agreement.

Charging the applicable federal rate avoids the imputed interest rules. Gift loans qualifying for the $10,000 and $100,000 exceptions are not subject to imputed interest rules. For other loans, the rules imputing income to you as the lender may be avoided by charging interest at least equal to the applicable federal rate. Applicable federal rates are set by the IRS monthly and published in the Internal Revenue Bulletin; you can also get the rates from your local IRS office. For a term loan, the applicable rate is the one in effect as of the day on which the loan is made, computed semiannually. The short-term rate applies to loans of three years or less; the mid-term rate to loans over three and up to nine years; the long-term rate applies to loans over nine years. For a demand loan, the applicable federal rate is the short-term rate in effect at the start of each semiannual period (January and July).

Different computations for different types of loans. There are two general classes of loans: (1) Gift loans, whether term or demand, and nongift demand loans, and (2) nongift term loans.

The distinction is important for figuring and reporting imputed interest. For example, in the case of nongift term loans, the imputed interest element is treated as original issue discount; *see 4.19*.

Gift loans and nongift loans payable on demand. As a lender, you are taxable on the "foregone interest," that is, the interest that you would have received had you charged interest at the applicable federal rate over any interest actually charged. The borrower may be able to claim an interest deduction if the funds are used to buy investment property; *see 15.10.*

Nongift term loans. A term loan is any loan not payable on demand. As a lender of a nongift term loan, you are taxable on any excess of the loan principal over the present value of all payments due under the loan. The excess is treated as original issue (OID) which you report annually as interest income; *see 4.19.*

Reporting imputed interest. Imputed interest is generally treated as transferred by the lender to the borrower and retransferred by the borrower to the lender on December 31 in the calendar year of imputation and is reported under the regular accounting method of the borrower and lender.

EXAMPLE

On January 1, 2006, Jones Company makes a $200,000 interest-free demand loan to Frank, an executive. The loan remains outstanding for the entire 2006 calendar year. Jones Company has a taxable year ending September 30. Frank is a calendar year taxpayer. For 2006, the imputed compensation payment and the imputed interest payment are treated as made on December 31, 2006.

Certain Loans Are Exempt From Imputed Interest Rules

The $10,000 gift loan exception. In the case of a gift loan to an individual, no interest is imputed to any day on which the aggregate outstanding amount of all loans between the parties is not over $10,000, provided the loan is not attributed to the purchase or carrying of income-producing assets. If the exception applies, there are no income tax or gift tax consequences to the loan.

The $100,000 gift loan exception. No interest is imputed on an interest-free or low-interest loan to an individual of up to $100,000 if the borrower's net investment income is $1,000 or less; *see* the Planning Reminder in this section.

EXAMPLES

1. On January 1, 2006, you make a $100,000 interest-free loan to your son, payable on demand, which he uses for a down payment on a home. This is the only outstanding loan between you and your son. Your son's net investment income for 2006 is $650. Since the loan does not exceed $100,000, and your son's net investment income does not exceed $1,000, you do not have to report the "foregone interest" as interest income. Imputed interest is limited to the borrower's net investment income and net investment income of $1,000 or less is treated as zero.

   For gift tax purposes, the foregone interest is a taxable gift. Using the IRS blended annual rate for 2006 of 4.71%, the foregone interest of $4,710 ($100,000 × 4.71%) is a taxable gift, but if this was your only gift to your son in 2006, there would be no gift tax, and a gift tax return would not have to be filed because of the annual gift tax exclusion of $12,000 per donee; *see 39.2.*
2. Same facts as in Example 1 above except that your son's net investment income is $1,500. Since net investment income exceeds $1,000, the imputed interest is limited to the $1,500 of net investment income. Thus, although the foregone interest using the blended annual rate is $4,710, you report only $1,500 of imputed interest income.

Exceptions for compensation-related loans. For compensation-related and corporate-shareholder loans, the imputed interest rules do not apply to any day on which the total amount of outstanding loans between the parties is $10,000 or less, provided the principal purpose of the loan is not tax avoidance. Certain low-interest loans given to employees by employers to buy a new residence in a new job location are exempt from the imputed interest requirements.

Loans to continuing care facilities. Senior citizens moving into a community with a continuing care facility are required to pay a fee to the facility. The fee may be treated as a "loan" subject to the imputed interest rules but loans to qualified continuing care facilities are completely exempt; *see 34.11.*

Planning Reminder

Gift Loans up to $100,000

If you give a child or other individual an interest-free or below-market-interest loan, such as to buy a home or start a business, imputed interest is limited or completely avoided provided (1) the total outstanding loan balance owed to you by the borrower at all times during the year does not exceed $100,000, and (2) avoidance of federal tax is not a principal purpose of the interest arrangement.

If the above tests are met, imputed interest is limited to the borrower's net investment income where that income exceeds $1,000. If the borrower's net investment income is $1,000 or less, it is treated as zero, so no interest is imputed.

Filing Instruction

Tax Return Statement Requirements

A lender reporting imputed interest income or a borrower claiming an interest deduction must attach statements to their income tax returns reporting the interest, how it was calculated, and the names of the parties and their tax identification numbers.

4.32 Minimum Interest on Seller-Financed Sales

The law requires minimum interest charges for seller-financed sales. If the minimum rate is not charged, the IRS imputes interest at the minimum applicable rate requiring both buyer and seller to treat part of the purchase price as interest even though it is not called interest in the sales contract. Generally, interest at the applicable federal rate (AFR) must be charged; see the chart at the end of this section for minimum required rates. For example, investment property is sold on the installment basis for $100,000 and the parties fail to charge adequate interest. Assume the IRS imputes interest of $5,000. For tax purposes, $95,000 is allocated to the sale of the property and the principal amount of the debt; the balance is imputed interest of $5,000, taxable to the seller and deductible by the buyer if allowed under the rules of Chapter 15.

Caution

Buyer's Personal-Use Property

If adequate interest is not charged on an installment sale of personal-use property, such as a residence to be used by the buyer, imputed interest rules do not apply to the buyer. Thus, the buyer may not deduct the imputed interest. The buyer's deduction is limited to the payment of interest stated in the contract if a deduction is allowed under the home mortgage interest rules in Chapter 15.

Two statute classes. The minimum or imputed interest rules are covered by two Internal Revenue Code statutes: Sections 1274 and 483. Under both, the same minimum interest rates apply but the timing of interest reporting is different, as discussed below.

Section 483 applies to any payment due more than six months after the date of sale under a contract which calls for some or all payments more than one year after the date of sale. If the sales price cannot exceed $3,000, Section 483 does not apply. Transactions within Section 483 are sales or exchanges of: (1) principal residences; (2) any property if total payments, including interest and any other consideration to be received by the seller, cannot exceed $250,000; (3) farms if the total price is $1 million or less; and (4) sales of land between family members to the extent the aggregate sales price of all sales between the same parties in the same year is $500,000 or less.

If the selling price exceeds the respective $250,000, $1 million, or $500,000 amount listed in (2) through (4) above, the sale is subject to Section 1274 reporting rules provided some or all payments are due more than six months after the date of sale. Section 1274 also applies to all other transactions where neither the debt instrument nor the property being sold is publicly traded as long as some payments are deferred more than six months.

Timing of interest reporting. One important practical difference between the two statutes covering minimum interest involves the timing of the reporting and deducting of interest.

Under Section 483, a seller and lender use their regular reporting method for imputed interest. For a cash-basis seller, interest is taxed when received; a cash-basis buyer deducts interest when paid if a deduction is allowable. However, if too much interest is allocated to a payment period, the excess interest is treated as prepaid interest, and the deduction is postponed to the year or years interest is earned. Section 483 also describes imputed interest as unstated interest.

Under Section 1274, the interest element is generally reported by both buyer and seller according to the OID accrual rules, even if they otherwise report on the cash basis. Where the seller financing is below an annual threshold ($3,307,400 for 2006 sales), the parties can elect the cash method to report the interest regardless of the OID and accrual rules if: (1) the seller-lender is on a cash-basis method and is not a dealer of the property sold and (2) the seller and buyer jointly elect to use the cash method. The cash-basis election binds any cash-basis successor of the buyer or seller. If the lender transfers his interest to an accrual-basis taxpayer, the election no longer applies; interest is thereafter taxed under the accrual-method rules. The OID rules also do not apply to a cash-basis buyer of personal-use property; here, the cash-basis debtor deducts only payments of interest required by the contract, assuming a deduction is allowed under the home mortgage rules discussed in Chapter 15.

Figuring applicable federal rate (AFR). There is no imputed interest if the sales contract provides for interest that is at least equal to the AFR. *See* the chart below for determining the AFR.

Assumptions of loans. The imputed interest rules of Sections 1274 and 483 do not generally apply to debt instruments assumed as part of a sale or exchange, or if the property is taken subject to the debt, provided that neither the terms of the debt instrument nor the nature of the transactions are changed.

Important: *In planning deferred or installment sales, review Treasury regulations to the Internal Revenue Code Sections 483 and 1274 for further examples and details.*

Table 4-1 Minimum Interest Rate for Seller Financing

Type—	*Description—*
Applicable federal rates	The IRS determines the AFR rates which are published at the beginning of each month in the Internal Revenue Bulletin. There are three AFR rates depending on the length of the contract: *Short-term AFR*—A term of three years or less. *Mid-term AFR*—A term of over three years but not over nine years. *Long-term AFR*—A term of over nine years. The imputed interest rules do not apply if the interest rate provided for in the sales contract is at least the lesser of (1) the lowest AFR in effect during the three-month period ending with the month in which a binding written sales contract is entered into, or (2) the lowest AFR in effect during the three-month period ending with the month of sale. If insufficient interest is charged, the total unstated interest is allocated to payments under an OID computation.
9% safe harbor rate	If seller financing in 2006 is $4,630,300 or less, the minimum required interest is the lower of 9% compounded semiannually and the applicable federal rate (AFR). The amount of seller financing is the stated principal amount under the contract. If the seller-financed amount exceeds $4,630,300, the minimum interest rate is 100% of the AFR. The threshold for the 9% safe harbor is indexed for inflation. The 9% safe harbor provides a benefit only if it is less than the AFR, but in recent years the AFR has been much lower than 9%. Thus, until prevailing interest rates substantially increase, charging interest at the AFR will be sufficient to avoid application of the minimum interest rules. IRS regulations allow the parties to use an interest rate lower than the AFR if it is shown that the borrower could obtain a loan on an arm's-length basis at lower interest.
Seller-financed sale-lease-back transactions	Interest equal to 110% of AFR must be charged.
Sales of land between family members	To the extent that the sales price does not exceed $500,000 during a calendar year, the minimum required interest rate is 6%, compounded semiannually. To prevent multiple sales from being used to avoid the $500,000 limit, the $500,000 ceiling applies to all land sales between family members during the same year. To the extent that the $500,000 sales price limit is exceeded, the general 9% or 100% of AFR rules apply.

Chapter 5

Reporting Property Sales

Long-term capital gains are generally taxed at lower rates than those imposed on ordinary income. The maximum tax rate on long-term gains is generally 15% for taxpayers whose top bracket exceeds 15%, and generally 5% for taxpayers whose top bracket is 10% or 15%.

If in 2006 you sold property and will be receiving payments in a later year, you may report the sale as an installment sale on Form 6252 and spread the tax on your gain over the installment period; *see 5.21*.

Sales of business assets and depreciable rental property are reported on Form 4797. As discussed in *44.8*, most assets used in a business are considered Section 1231 assets, and capital gain or ordinary loss treatment may apply depending upon the result of a netting computation made on Form 4797 for all such assets sold during the year.

Special types of sale situations are detailed in other chapters.

See Chapter 29 for the exclusion of gain on the sale of a principal residence.

See Chapter 32 for figuring gain or loss on the sale of mutual-fund shares.

See Chapter 6 for tax-free exchanges of property.

See Chapter 30 for sales of stock dividends, stock rights, wash sales, short sales, and sales by traders in securities.

Figuring Capital Gains and Losses

5.1 Tax Pattern of Property Sales

1. Property is classified according to its nature and your purpose for holding it; *see 5.2*, the table on the next page, and holding period rules at *5.3* and *5.9–5.12*.
2. If you sell property at a gain, the applicable tax rate depends on the classification of the property (*see* the table on the next page) and, in the case of capital assets, the period you held the property before sale. Short-term capital gains are subject to regular income tax rates. Capital gain rates lower than the regular rates apply only to long-term capital gains. A capital gain is long term if you held the asset for more than one year; *see 5.3*.

   A capital gain rate is applied to long-term capital gains if the rate is less than the top regular income tax rate applied to your taxable income. For taxpayers in the 10% or 15% bracket, the capital gain rate is generally 5%. For taxpayers with a top bracket over 15%, the rate is generally 15%. However, these favorable rates do not apply to gains on sales of collectibles or to unrecaptured Section 1250 gain on sales of depreciated real estate. *See 5.3* for further details on capital gain rates.

   Sales of capital assets must generally be reported on Schedule D of Form 1040, and the lower capital gain rates are applied on the Qualified Dividends and Capital Gains Tax Worksheet in the Form 1040 instructions, where you compute your tax liability taking into account the favorable capital gain rates. If you have either 28% gain or unrecaptured Section 1250 gain, use the Schedule D Tax Worksheet in the Schedule D instructions to compute your tax liability. Filing Schedule D may not be necessary if your only capital gains are from a mutual fund or REIT; *see 32.8*.
3. Loss deductions are allowed on the sale of investment and business property but not personal assets; *see* the table on the following page. Capital loss deductions in excess of capital gains are limited to $3,000 annually, $1,500 if married filing separately; *see 5.4* and *5.5* for details on the capital loss limitations.

Caution

Loss on Personal-Use Assets

You may not deduct a capital loss on the sale of property held for personal use, such as a car or vacation home. The loss is not deductible.

Losses on the sale of property held for investment, such as stock or mutual-fund shares, are fully deductible against capital gains but any excess loss is subject to the $3,000 limit discussed at *5.4*.

5.2 How Property Sales Are Classified and Taxed

The tax treatment of gains and losses is not the same for all types of property sales. Tax reporting generally depends on your purpose in holding the property, as shown in the table on page 100.

When capital gain or loss treatment does not apply. Certain sales do not qualify for capital gain or loss treatment. Business inventory and property held for sale to customers are not capital assets. Depreciable business and rental property are not capital assets, but you may still realize capital gain after following a netting computation for Section 1231 assets discussed at *44.8*.

Although assets held for *personal* use, such as a car or home, are technically capital assets, you may not deduct a capital loss on their sale.

Certain other assets held for investment or personal use are excluded by law from the capital asset category. These include copyrights, literary or musical compositions, letters, memoranda, or similar property that: (1) you created by your personal efforts or (2) you acquired as a gift from the person who created the property or for whom the property was prepared or produced. However, musical compositions and copyrighted musical works are removed from this list for sales in tax years beginning after 2006 and before 2011. Thus, a composer's sale in 2007 of his or her musical composition will be subject to capital gain or loss treatment.

Also excluded from the capital asset category are letters, memoranda, or similar property prepared or produced for you by someone else. Finally, U.S. government publications obtained from the government for free or for less than the normal sales price do not qualify as capital assets.

Stock is generally treated as a capital asset, but losses on *Section 1244 stock* of qualifying small businesses may be claimed as ordinary losses on Form 4797, rather than on Schedule D as capital losses subject to the $3,000 deduction limit ($1,500 if married filing separately); *see 30.13*.

Traders in securities may elect to report their sales as ordinary income or loss rather than as capital gain or loss; *see 30.16*.

Small business stock deferral. As discussed in *5.7*, taxable gains from the sale of publicly traded securities may be postponed if you roll over the proceeds to stock or a partnership interest in an SSBIC (specialized small business investment company). Furthermore, gains from the sale of qualifying small business stock may be deferred by making a tax-free rollover to other small business stock.

Filing Tip

Holding Periods

The time you own a capital asset determines short-term or long-term treatment. The short-term holding period is a year or less, the long-term period more than one year; *see 5.9–5.12*.

Small business/empowerment zone business stock exclusion. Gains on the sale of qualifying small business stock held for more than five years qualify for a 50% exclusion. The exclusion is 60% for gains on the sale of qualifying empowerment zone business stock; *see 5.7.*

Like-kind exchanges of business or investment property. Exchanges of *like-kind* business or investment property are subject to special rules that allow gain to be deferred, generally until you sell the property received in the exchange; *see 6.1.* When property received in a tax-free exchange is held until death, the unrecognized gain escapes income tax forever because the basis of property in the hands of an heir is generally the fair market value of the property at the date of death; *see 5.17.* A loss on a like-kind exchange is not deductible.

Table 5-1 Capital or Ordinary Gains and Losses From Sales and Exchanges of Property

If you sell—	*Your gain is—*	*Your loss is—*	*Reported on—*
Stocks, mutual funds, bonds, land, art, gems, stamps, and coins held for investment are capital assets.	*Capital gain.* Holding period determines short-term or long-term gain treatment; *see 5.3.* Security traders may report ordinary income and loss under a mark-to-market election; *see 30.17.*	*Capital loss.* Capital losses are deductible from capital gains with only $3,000 of any excess deductible from ordinary income, $1,500 if married filing separately; *see 5.4.*	Schedule D. However, if the only amounts you have to report on Schedule D are mutual-fund capital gain distributions, then you may report the distributions directly on Form 1040A or Form 1040; *see 32.8* Form 4797 for gains and losses of a trader in securities who makes the mark-to-market election; *see 30.17.*
Business inventory held for sale to customers. Also, accounts or notes receivable acquired in the ordinary course of business or from the sale of inventory or property held for sale to customers, or acquired for services as an employee.	*Ordinary income.* Such property is excluded by law from the definition of capital assets.	*Ordinary loss.* Ordinary loss is not subject to the $3,000 deduction limit imposed on capital losses. However, passive loss restrictions, discussed in Chapter 10, may defer the time when certain ordinary losses are deductible.	Schedule C if self-employed; Schedule F if a farmer; Form 1065 for a business operated as a partnership; Form 1120 or 1120-S for an incorporated business.
Depreciable residential rental property or trucks, autos, computers, machinery, fixtures, or equipment used in your business.	*Capital gain or ordinary income.* Section 1231, as explained in *44.8,* determines whether gain is taxable as ordinary income or capital gain. Where an asset such as an auto or residence is used partly for personal purposes and partly for business or rental purposes, the asset is treated as two separate assets for purposes of figuring gain or loss; *see 44.9*	*Ordinary loss if there is a net Section 1231 loss; see 44.8.* However, if you are considered to be an investor in a passive activity, *see 10.12* and *10.13.*	Form 4797 for Section 1231 transactions.
Personal residence, car, jewelry, furniture, art objects, and coin or stamp collection held for personal use.	*Capital gain. See 5.3* for the holding period rules that determine short-term or long-term gain treatment and the preferential tax rates applied to net long-term capital gains. Where an asset such as an auto or residence is used partly for personal purposes and partly for business or rental purposes, the asset is treated as two separate assets for purposes of figuring gain or loss; *see 44.9.* Tax on all or part of a profit from a sale of a principal residence may be avoided; *see* Chapter 29.	*Not deductible.* Losses on assets held for personal use are not deductible although profits are taxable.	Schedule D

5.3 Capital Gains Rates and Holding Periods

Sales of capital assets during 2006 should be separated into short-term and long-term categories. Assets held for one year or less are in the short-term category and assets held for more than one year are in the long-term category. Follow the line-by-line computation on Schedule D (Form 1040) to report your sales and obtain the benefit of the lower rates on qualifying long-term gains.

A sample Schedule D, shown at *5.8*, illustrates the reporting of capital asset sales. The computation of tax liability using the favorable long-term capital gain rates is not made directly on Schedule D, but on worksheets in the IRS instructions. Mutual-fund and REIT investors may be able to apply the favorable rates on the "Qualified Dividends and Capital Gain Tax Worksheet" included in the Form 1040 or Form 1040A instructions, without having to file Schedule D; *see 32.8*.

Held for a year or less. Gains and losses realized on sales of capital assets held for a year or less are short term and reported in Part I of Schedule D. Short-term gains and losses are netted in this part. A net gain is subject to regular tax rates. A net short-term loss offsets a net long-term gain, if any, from Part II of Schedule D. A net short-term loss in excess of net long-term gain is deductible up to the $3,000 capital loss limit; *see 5.4*.

Held for more than a year. Gains and losses on sales of capital assets held for more than a year are long term. They are generally reported in Part II of Schedule D, where long-term gains and losses are netted. A net long-term loss offsets a net short-term gain, if any, from Part I of Schedule D. If you have a net long-term gain and also a net short-term loss from Part I of Schedule D, the short-term loss offsets the net long-term gain. If the net short-term loss exceeds the net long-term gain, the excess short-term loss is deductible up to the $3,000 capital loss limit; *see 5.4*. If you have a net long-term gain in excess of net short-term capital loss (if any), the excess is called *net capital gain* and it is this amount to which the favorable capital gain rates apply, as discussed below.

Part II of Schedule D is not used for gains and losses on collectibles, unrecaptured Section 1250 gains, gains on qualified small business stock eligible for a 50% exclusion, or gains on qualified empowerment zone business stock eligible for a 60% exclusion. As discussed below, these transactions are entered in worksheets included in the Schedule D instructions and the tax figured on the worksheets is entered on Form 1040.

Reduced rates on net capital gain

Net capital gain (net long-term capital gain in excess of net short-term capital loss) is subject to maximum tax rates that are generally lower than the rates applied to ordinary income. Qualified dividends *(4.1)* are subject to the same favorable rates as net capital gain.

If your top tax bracket is 10% or 15%, your capital gain rate is generally 5%. This means that net capital gain and qualified dividends that would otherwise be taxed at 10% or 15% after taking into account your other income are instead taxed at 5%. However, your regular rate (10% or 15%) applies to collectibles gain, unrecaptured Section 1250 gain, or qualified small business stock gain; *see* below.

If your top tax bracket is 25%, 28%, 33%, or 35%, your capital gain rate is generally 15%. As discussed below, long-term gains on the sale of collectibles and qualified small business stock are subject to a maximum 28% rate, and a 25% maximum rate applies to unrecaptured Section 1250 gain.

Tax liability must be computed on IRS worksheets to benefit from capital gain rates. If you have a net capital gain that does *not* include a 28% rate gain or unrecaptured Section 1250 gain (*see* below), you should compute your 2006 regular tax liability on the "Qualified Dividends and Capital Gain Tax Worksheet" in the IRS instructions for Line 44 of Form 1040. On the Worksheet, a copy of which is shown at the end of *5.8*, you figure the tax on your net capital gain using the maximum capital gain rates, and the tax on the rest of your taxable income using regular tax rates. The Worksheet must be used instead of the regular IRS Tax Table or Tax Computation Worksheet to benefit from the maximum capital gain rates. The tax liability from the Worksheet is entered on Line 44 of Form 1040.

If you have a net capital gain that includes either a net 28% rate gain or unrecaptured Section 1250 gain, you must compute your tax liability on the "Schedule D Tax Worksheet" in the Schedule D instructions to benefit from the maximum capital gain rates. The tax liability from the Worksheet is entered on Line 44 of Form 1040.

On both the Qualified Dividends and Capital Gain Tax Worksheet and the Schedule D Tax Worksheet, net capital gain eligible for the maximum capital gain rates is reduced by any gains

Law Alert

Favorable Rates Extended Through 2010

The Tax Increase Prevention and Reconciliation Act extends for two years the reduced rates for net capital gains that had been scheduled to expire at the end of 2008. Thus, the 15% rate currently allowed to taxpayers with a top tax bracket of over 15% will apply through 2010. For individuals in the 10% and 15% brackets, the current 5% rate will apply through 2007 and then fall to zero for 2008 through 2010, instead of being zero only for 2008 as previously scheduled.

Planning Reminder

Gift Planning Opportunity

The difference between the 5% (zero in 2008 through 2010) and 15% rates provides a gift planning opportunity. If your regular tax bracket exceeds 15% and you own appreciated property, consider making a gift of the property (*see 39.2* for the per-donee annual gift tax exclusion) to a child age 18 or older (and thus not subject to the "kiddie tax"; *see 24.1*) or other individual whose top bracket is 10% or 15%. Your donee picks up your holding period and on a sale can pay tax at only 5% before 2008, or no tax in 2008, 2009, or 2010, whereas you would pay a 15% tax on the same gain.

that you elect to treat as investment income on Form 4952 to increase your itemized deduction for investment interest; *see 15.10.*

28% rate gains from sales of collectibles and small business or empowerment zone business stock eligible for exclusion. Long-term gains on the sale of collectibles such as art, antiques, precious metals, gems, stamps, and coins are considered "28% rate gains." If you sell qualified small business stock eligible for the 50% exclusion or empowerment zone business stock eligible for the 60% exclusion (Section 1202 exclusion; *see 5.7*), the taxable 50% or 40% portion of the gain is also treated as a 28% rate gain. The 28% rate gains are reported in the "28% Rate Gain Worksheet" in the Schedule D instructions. On the Worksheet, 28% rate gains are reduced by any long-term collectibles losses and net short-term capital loss for the current year, and any long-term capital loss carryover from the previous year.

A net 28% rate gain from the 28% Rate Gain Worksheet is entered on Line 18 of Schedule D and then on the "Schedule D Tax Worksheet" in the Schedule D instructions. Your tax liability on all of your taxable income (including net capital gain and qualified dividends) is figured on the Schedule D Tax Worksheet.

If your regular top tax bracket exceeds 28%, net 28% rate gains are taxed at 28% on the "Schedule D Tax Worksheet." If your top bracket is 10% or 15%, that regular rate applies to the gains. If your regular top bracket is 25%, the 25% rate generally applies to the net 28% rate gains. However, if you also have long-term gains eligible for the 15% rate, the worksheet computation may tax all or part of the 28% rate gains at the 28% rate even though your regular top bracket is 25%.

The tax figured on the "Schedule D Tax Worksheet" is entered on Line 44 of Form 1040.

Unrecaptured Section 1250 gain on sale of real estate. Long-term gain attributable to real estate depreciation is not eligible for the favorable 15% rate if your top bracket exceeds 15%. Gain attributable to pre-1987 depreciation may be recaptured as ordinary income; *see 44.2.* To the extent of depreciation that is not recaptured, gain is considered "unrecaptured Section 1250 gain." Unrecaptured Section 1250 gain is figured on the "Unrecaptured Section 1250 Gain Worksheet" in the Schedule D instructions. The computation reduces unrecaptured Section 1250 gain by a net loss, if any, from the 28% rate group.

The net unrecaptured Section 1250 gain from the worksheet is entered on the Schedule D Tax Worksheet, where tax liability on all of your taxable income is computed. On the Schedule D Tax Worksheet, the unrecaptured Section 1250 gain is subject to a 25% tax rate if your regular top bracket exceeds 15%. If your regular top bracket is 10% or 15%, that rate applies.The tax figured on the Schedule D Tax Worksheet is entered on Line 44 of Form 1040.

Capital gain distributions from mutual funds. Your fund will report long-term capital gain distributions on Form 1099-DIV. *See* Chapter 32 for details on how to report the distributions.

Capital gain from Schedule K-1. Net capital gain or loss from a pass-through entity such as a partnership, S corporation, estate, or trust is reported to you on a Schedule K-1. Report net short-term gain or loss in Part I of Schedule D and net long-term gain or loss in Part II of Schedule D.

5.4 Capital Losses and Carryovers

Capital losses are fully deductible against capital gains on Schedule D, and if losses exceed gains, you may deduct the excess from up to $3,000 of ordinary income on Form 1040. Net losses over $3,000 are carried over to future years. On a joint return, the $3,000 limit applies to the combined losses of both spouses; *see 5.5.* The $3,000 limit is reduced to $1,500 for married persons filing separately.

Although qualified dividends *(4.1)* are subject to the same rates as net capital gains, such dividends are not reported as long-term gains on Part II of Schedule D and thus are *not* offset by capital losses in determining whether you have net capital gain or loss.

In preparing your 2006 Schedule D, remember to include any capital loss carryovers from your 2005 return. Short-term carryover losses are entered on Line 6 of Part I and long-term carryover losses are entered on Line 14, Part II. Use the carryover worksheet in the 2006 Schedule D instructions for figuring your short-term and long-term loss carryovers from 2005 to 2006.

Death of taxpayer cuts off carryover. If an individual dies and on his or her final income tax return net capital losses, including prior year carryovers, exceed the $3,000 or $1,500 limit, the excess may not be deducted by the individual's estate. If the deceased individual was married, his or her unused individual losses may not be carried over by the surviving spouse; *see 5.5.*

Filing Tip

Keep Records of Loss Carryovers

If you have capital losses for 2006 in excess of the deductible limit, keep a copy of your 2006 Form 1040 and Schedule D to figure your loss carryover when you file your 2007 Schedule D. The 2007 Schedule D instructions will have a worksheet you can use to figure your loss carryovers from 2006 to 2007.

5.5 Capital Losses of Married Couples

On a joint return, the capital asset transactions of both spouses are combined and reported on one Schedule D. A carryover loss of one spouse may offset capital gains of the other spouse on a jointly filed Schedule D. Where you and your spouse separately incur net capital losses, $3,000 is the maximum capital loss deduction that may be claimed for the combined losses on your joint return. This limitation may not be avoided by filing separate returns. If you file separately, the deduction limit for each return is $1,500. Neither of you may deduct any of the other's losses on a separate return.

EXAMPLE

In 2006, you individually incurred net long-term capital losses of $5,000 and your spouse incurred net long-term losses of $4,000. If you file separate returns, the maximum amount deductible from ordinary income on each return is $1,500. The balance must be carried forward to 2007.

If you had net losses below the $1,500 limit, you could not claim any part of your spouse's losses on your separate return.

Filing Tip

Carryovers From Joint or Separate Returns

If you or your spouse has a capital loss carryover from a year in which separate returns were filed, and you are now filing a joint return, the carryovers from the separate returns may be combined on the joint return. If you previously filed jointly and are now filing separately, any loss carryover from the joint return may be claimed only on the separate return of the spouse who originally incurred the loss; *see 5.5*.

Death of a spouse. The IRS holds that if a capital loss is incurred by a spouse on his or her own property and that spouse dies, the loss may be deducted only on the final return for the spouse (which may be a joint return). The surviving spouse may not claim any unused loss carryover on a separate return and the decedent's estate may not deduct the unused carryover.

EXAMPLE

In 2003, Alex Smith realized a substantial net long-term capital loss on separately owned property, which was reported on a 2003 joint return filed with his wife, Anne. Part of the excess loss (over the $3,000 limit) was carried over to the couple's 2004 joint return. In 2005, before the carryover loss was used up, Alex died. Anne could claim the unused carryover, up to the $3,000 limit, on a joint return filed for 2005, the year of Alex's death. However, any remaining loss carryover to 2006 or later years is lost. Although the loss was originally reported on a joint return, Anne may claim only her allocable share of the loss on her individual returns for years after 2005, the year of Alex's death. However, since the loss property was owned solely by Alex, no part of the loss is allocable to Anne.

5.6 Losses May Be Disallowed on Sales to Related Persons

A loss on a sale to certain related taxpayers may not be deductible, even though you make the sale at an arm's-length price, the sale is involuntary (for example, a member of your family forecloses a mortgage on your property), or you sell through a public stock exchange and related persons buy the equivalent property; *see* Examples 1 and 2 on the following page.

Related parties. Losses are not allowed on sales between you and your brothers or sisters (whether by the whole or half blood), parents, grandparents, great-grandparents, children, grandchildren, or great-grandchildren. Furthermore, no loss may be claimed on a sale to your spouse; the tax-free exchange rules discussed at *6.7* apply.

A loss is disallowed where the sale is made to your sister-in-law, as nominee of your brother. This sale is deemed to be between you and your brother. But you may deduct the loss on sales to your spouse's relative (for example, your brother-in-law or spouse's step-parent) even if you and your spouse file a joint return.

The Tax Court has allowed a loss on a direct sale to a son-in-law. In a private ruling, the IRS allowed a loss on a sale of a business to a son-in-law where it was shown that his wife (the seller's daughter) did not own an interest in the company. Losses have been disallowed upon withdrawal from a joint venture and from a partnership conducted by members of a family. Family members have argued that losses should be allowed where the sales were motivated by family hostility. The Tax Court ruled that family hostility may not be considered; losses between proscribed family members are disallowed in all cases.

Losses are barred on sales between an individual and a controlled partnership or controlled corporation (where that individual owns more than 50% in value of the outstanding stock or capital interests). In calculating the stock owned, not only must the stock held in your own name be taken into account, but also that owned by your family. You also add (1) the proportionate share of any stock held by a corporation, estate, trust, or partnership in which you have an interest as a shareholder, beneficiary, or partner; and (2) any other stock owned individually by your partner.

Losses may also be disallowed in sales between controlled companies, a trust and its creator, a trust and a beneficiary, a partnership and a corporation controlled by the same person (more than 50% ownership), or a tax-exempt organization and its founder. An estate and a beneficiary of that estate are also treated as related parties, except where a sale is in satisfaction of a pecuniary bequest. Check with your tax counselor whenever you plan to sell property at a loss to a buyer who may fit one of these descriptions.

Related buyer's resale at profit. Sometimes, the disallowed loss may be saved. When you sell to a related party who resells the property at a profit, he or she gets the benefit of your disallowed loss. Your purchaser's gain up to the amount of your disallowed loss is not taxed; *see* Example 4 below.

EXAMPLES

1. You sell 100 shares of A Co. stock to your brother for $1,000. They cost you $5,000. You may not deduct your $4,000 loss.
2. The stock investments of a mother and son were managed by the same investment counselor. But neither the son nor mother had any right or control over the other's securities. The counselor followed separate and independent policies for each. Without the son's or his mother's prior approval, the counselor carried out the following transactions: (1) on the same day, he sold at a loss the son's stock in four companies and bought the same stock for the mother's account; and (2) he sold at a loss the son's stock in a copper company, and 28 days later bought the same stock for his mother. The losses of the first sale were disallowed, but not the losses of the copper stock sale because of the time break of 28 days. However, the court did not say how much of a minimum time break is needed to remove a sale-purchase transaction from the rule disallowing losses between related parties.
3. You own 30% of the stock of a company. A trust in which you have a one-half beneficial interest owns 30%. Your partner owns 10% of the stock of the same company. You are deemed the owner of 55% of the stock of that company (30%, plus one-half of 30%, plus 10%) and may not deduct a loss on the sale of property to that company since your deemed ownership exceeds 50%.
4. Smith bought securities in 2001 that cost $10,000. In 2004, he sold them to his sister for $8,000. The $2,000 loss was not deductible by Smith. His sister's basis for the securities is $8,000. In 2006, she sells them for $9,000. The $1,000 gain is not taxed because it is washed out by part of the brother's disallowed loss. If she sold the securities for $11,000, then only $1,000 of the $3,000 gain would be taxed.

5.7 Deferring or Excluding Gain on Small Business Stock Investment

To encourage investments in certain "small" businesses, the tax law provides special tax benefits.

Rollover from small business stock to small business stock. Gain on the sale of qualifying small business stock (QSB stock) held for more than six months may be rolled over tax free to other QSB stock. The rollover must be made within 60 days of the sale. To qualify as QSB stock, the stock must be stock in a C corporation (not S corporation) that was originally issued after August 10, 1993. The gross assets of the corporation must have been no more than $50 million at all times after August 9, 1993, and before issuance of the stock, as well as immediately after issuance of the stock. An active business requirement must also be met. If the reinvestment in a qualifying small business is for less than the sale proceeds, your gain is taxed to the extent of the difference. Your basis in the small business stock acquired during the 60-day replacement period is reduced by the amount of the deferred gain.

To elect deferral, you must report the entire gain on Part I (short-term gain) or Part II (long-term gain) of Schedule D. Then, directly below that entry, write "Section 1045 Rollover" and report the rolled-over amount as a loss in column (f). Generally, the election to defer gain must be made by the due date or extended due date for your return. If you timely file your original return without the election, the election may be made on an amended return filed no more than six months after the original due date.

Law Alert

Exclusion for Small Business Stock Gain

You generally may claim a 50% exclusion on a profitable sale of qualifying small business stock issued after August 10, 1993, provided you held the stock for more than five years before the sale. A 60% exclusion is allowed on the sale of qualifying empowerment zone business stock. The balance of the gain is treated as a 28% rate gain; *see 5.3*. For purposes of the alternative minimum tax (Chapter 23), 7% of the excluded gain must be added back to income as a preference item.

Exclusion of gain on small business stock (Section 1202 exclusion). You only have to pay tax on 50% of a gain from the sale of qualified small business stock (QSB stock) issued after August 10, 1993, *provided* you hold the stock for more than five years before the sale. If you qualify for the exclusion, report the entire gain as a long-term gain on Line 8 of Schedule D and then, below it, enter the allowable exclusion as a loss, labelling it "Section 1202 exclusion." If you have a net capital gain (net long-term gain in excess of net short-term loss, if any), the amount of the exclusion is included on the 28% Rate Gain Worksheet in the Schedule D instructions; *see 5.3*.

The amount of the Section 1202 exclusion increases to 60% if the gain is on the sale of stock held for more than five years in a corporation that qualified as an empowerment zone business. The gain and exclusion are reported as described above for the 50% QSB exclusion.

There is a lifetime limit on the Section 1202 exclusion for QSB stock or empowerment zone business stock from any one issuer. For 2006, the amount of gain from any one issuer that is eligible for the 50% or 60% exclusion is limited to the greater of (1) 10 times your basis in the qualified stock that you disposed of during 2006, or (2) $10 million ($5 million if married filing separately) minus any gain on stock from the same issuer that you excluded in prior years.

Rollover from publicly traded securities to SSBIC. You may be able to defer taxable gain on the sale of publicly traded securities provided the sale proceeds are rolled over within 60 days into common stock or a partnership interest in a "specialized small business investment company," or SSBIC. Subject to an annual deferrable limit (*see* below), the entire gain is deferrable if the cost of your SSBIC stock or partnership interest is at least equal to the sale proceeds. If the SSBIC investment is less than the sale proceeds, your gain is taxed to the extent of the difference.

The annual deferrable limit is $50,000, or $25,000 if you are married filing separately. There is a lifetime limit of $500,000, or $250,000 if married filing separately.

To elect deferral, you must report the sale on Schedule D and attach an explanation of your SSBIC investment. After reporting the entire gain on Line 1 or Line 8 of Schedule D, immediately below that line enter the amount of the deferred gain as a loss and label it "SSBIC Rollover"; *see* IRS Publication 550 for further details. The deferred gain reduces the basis of your SSBIC stock or partnership interest.

An SSBIC is a small business (partnership or corporation) licensed by the Small Business Administration to invest in small businesses that are owned by socially or economically disadvantaged individuals.

Planning Reminder

Rollover of Gain From Sale of Empowerment Zone Assets

You may be able to defer capital gain on the sale of qualified empowerment zone assets that you acquired after December 21, 2000, and held for more than one year. You must purchase replacement assets in the same empowerment zone during the 60-day period beginning on the date of the sale. *See* IRS Publications 550 and 954 for details.

5.8 Sample Entries of Capital Asset Sales on Schedule D

You report many different types of transactions on Schedule D of Form 1040: sales of securities, redemptions of mutual-fund shares, worthless personal loans, sales of stock rights and warrants, sales of land held for investment, and sales of personal residences where part of the gain does not qualify for the home sale exclusion *(29.1)*. Although capital gain distributions from mutual funds and REITs are generally reported as long-term capital gains on Line 13 of Schedule D, investors who receive such distributions but have no other capital gains or losses to report may generally report the distributions directly on Form 1040 or 1040A without having to file Schedule D; *see 32.8* for details.

The favorable maximum capital gain rates *(5.3)* apply to net capital gain (net long-term capital gain in excess of net short-term capital loss) from Schedule D, and also to qualified dividends *(4.1)*. Although qualified dividends are subject to the same favorable maximum rates as net capital gain, they are not entered as long-term gains in Part II of Schedule D. The favorable rates are applied to qualified dividends when tax liability is computed on either the Qualified Dividends and Capital Gain Tax Worksheet or the Schedule D Tax Worksheet. The Schedule D Tax Worksheet in the Schedule D instructions is used only if you have a net 28% rate gain or unrecaptured Section 1250 gain; *see 5.3*. If you do not have a net 28% rate gain or unrecaptured Section 1250 gain, use the Qualified Dividends and Capital Gain Tax Worksheet in the Form 1040 instructions. The applicable Worksheet must be used to obtain the benefit of the favorable maximum capital gain rates for your net capital gain and qualified dividends.

Caution

Selling Price Reported to IRS

If you sold stocks, bonds, or other investment property through a broker, the sale is reported to the IRS on Form 1099-B. You are sent Copy B of Form 1099-B or a substitute statement. On your statement, the broker must indicate whether gross proceeds or gross proceeds minus commissions and option premiums were reported to the IRS. If the gross proceeds were reported, enter that amount as the sales price in column (d) of Schedule D and add any commissions or option premiums to cost basis in column (e). If only the net proceeds were reported, enter that amount as the sales price in column (d) of Schedule D and do not include commissions or option premiums in column (e).

EXAMPLE

For 2006, John and Karen Taylor report three short-term transactions in Part I of Schedule D and four long-term transactions and a long-term loss carryover in Part II of Schedule D, as shown below and on the sample Schedule D on pages 107 and 108. For each stock sale, broker's commissions and state and local transfer taxes, if any, have been added to the cost of the stock in column (e) of Schedule D.

1. ***Sale of stock (short-term gain)***—The Taylors bought 200 shares of Bio-X-Cell Research, Inc. stock on July 25, 2006, for $1,400. On October 6, 2006, they sold the 200 shares for $1,600.
2. ***Sale of stock received as a gift (short-term loss)***—Karen's father gave the Taylors a gift of 100 shares of Ajax Auto stock on November 3, 2006, which he had bought on February 15, 1990, for $4,000. The value of the stock at the time of the gift was $3,000. The couple sold the stock on November 20, 2006, for $2,000. Since the value of the stock at the time of the gift was less than the father's basis, the Taylors' basis for loss purposes is the $3,000 date-of-gift value *(5.17)* and the holding period begins on the day after the date of the gift *(5.12)*.
3. ***Sale of mutual-fund shares (short-term gain)***—The Taylors bought 200 shares of the XYZ Mutual Fund on February 7, 2006, for $4,000. On August 9, they bought another 200 shares for $6,480. They sell 200 of the shares on September 26, 2006, for $6,000. They decide to use the average basis method (single-category method) to figure the basis of the sold shares. Their average basis is $26.20 per share, the total cost basis of $10,480 divided by 400 shares. Thus, their basis for the 200 sold shares is $5,240 (200 × $26.20). In column (a) of Line 1 on Schedule D, they enter "AVGB" to indicate that they are using an average basis. *See 32.10* for further details on determining basis of mutual-fund shares.
4. ***Sale of stock (long-term gain)***—The Taylors bought 100 shares of Acme Steel stock on October 1, 1991, for $6,000. On April 24, 2006, they sold the 100 shares for $13,000.
5. ***Sale of stock (long-term loss)***—The Taylors bought 200 shares of Zero Computer Co. stock for $5,000 on July 10, 1997. On March 10, 2006, they sold the shares for $2,000.
6. ***Sale of mutual-fund shares (long-term gain)***—The Taylors bought 1,435 shares of the ABC Mutual Fund between 1996 and 2001, including reinvested dividends. On July 14, 2006, they sold 500 of the shares for $21,500. The statement from the ABC Fund shows that their average basis (single-category method) is $24.50 per share. Thus, their basis for the 500 sold shares is $12,250 (500 × $24.50). In column (a) of Line 8, Schedule D, they enter "AVGB" to indicate that they are using the average basis method; *see 32.10* for further details.
7. ***Worthless bond***—On August 10, 1998, the Taylors bought a $5,000 bond of Tech Co. at par. The bond became completely worthless during 2006; *see 5.32*.
8. ***Capital gain distributions***—The Taylors received capital gain distributions of $1,050 in December 2006 from mutual funds; *see 32.4* and *32.8*.
9. ***Long-term capital loss carryover***—The Taylors had a long-term capital loss carryover of $950 from their 2005 return.

Because the Taylors do not have a net 28% rate gain or unrecaptured Section 1250 gain, they use the Qualified Dividends and Capital Gain Tax Worksheet in the Form 1040 instructions to compute their tax liability for 2006; *see* the sample worksheet on page 109. If they did have a net 28% rate gain or unrecaptured Section 1250 gain, the Taylors would use the Schedule D Tax Worksheet in the Schedule D instructions to figure their tax.

For purposes of the tax computation on the Qualified Dividends and Capital Gain Tax Worksheet, we have assumed that John and Karen file a joint return and have taxable income of $75,000 for 2006. In addition to the long-term gains reported in Part II of Schedule D, the Taylors have $400 of qualified dividends *(4.1)* that are eligible for the maximum capital gain rates. The qualified dividends are reported on Line 2 of the Qualified Dividends and Capital Gain Tax Worksheet.

Under this set of facts, the Taylors have total tax liability of $10,991, as shown on Line 19 of the Qualified Dividends and Capital Gain Tax Worksheet. This is $880 less than the $11,871 liability that would apply (Line 18 of the Worksheet) if there were no favorable rates for net capital gain and qualified dividends. The Taylors enter their $10,991 liability from the Worksheet on Line 44 of their Form 1040. This is their regular tax for 2006.

SCHEDULE D (Form 1040)

Department of the Treasury Internal Revenue Service (99)

Capital Gains and Losses

▶ Attach to Form 1040 or Form 1040NR. ▶ See Instructions for Schedule D (Form 1040).

▶ Use Schedule D-1 to list additional transactions for lines 1 and 8.

OMB No. 1545-0074

2006

Attachment Sequence No. 12

Name(s) shown on Form 1040: John and Karen Taylor

Your social security number: X11 01 11X0

Part I Short-Term Capital Gains and Losses—Assets Held One Year or Less

	(a) Description of property (Example: 100 sh. XYZ Co.)	(b) Date acquired (Mo., day, yr.)	(c) Date sold (Mo., day, yr.)	(d) Sales price (see page D-6 of the instructions)	(e) Cost or other basis (see page D-7 of the instructions)	(f) Gain or (loss) Subtract (e) from (d)
1	200 Shares Bio-X-Cell Research, Inc.	07/25/2006	10/06/2006	1,600	1,400	200
	100 Shares Ajax Auto	11/03/2006	11/20/2006	2,000	3,000	(1,000)
	200 Shares XYZ Mutual Fund: "AVGB"	Various	09/26/2006	6,000	5,240	760

2	Enter your short-term totals, if any, from Schedule D-1, line 2	2		
3	**Total short-term sales price amounts.** Add lines 1 and 2 in column (d)	3	9,600	
4	Short-term gain from Form 6252 and short-term gain or (loss) from Forms 4684, 6781, and 8824		4	
5	Net short-term gain or (loss) from partnerships, S corporations, estates, and trusts from Schedule(s) K-1		5	
6	Short-term capital loss carryover. Enter the amount, if any, from line 10 of your **Capital Loss Carryover Worksheet** on page D-7 of the instructions		6	( )
7	**Net short-term capital gain or (loss).** Combine lines 1 through 6 in column (f)		7	(40)

Part II Long-Term Capital Gains and Losses—Assets Held More Than One Year

	(a) Description of property (Example: 100 sh. XYZ Co.)	(b) Date acquired (Mo., day, yr.)	(c) Date sold (Mo., day, yr.)	(d) Sales price (see page D-6 of the instructions)	(e) Cost or other basis (see page D-7 of the instructions)	(f) Gain or (loss) Subtract (e) from (d)
8	100 Shares Acme Steel	10/01/1991	04/24/2006	13,000	6,000	7,000
	200 Shares Zero Computer Company	07/10/1997	03/10/2006	2,000	5,000	(3,000)
	500 Shares ABC Mutual Fund "AVGB"	Various	07/14/2006	21,500	12,250	9,250
	Tech Co.	08/10/1998	Worthless	Worthless	(5,000)	(5,000)

9	Enter your long-term totals, if any, from Schedule D-1, line 9	9		
10	**Total long-term sales price amounts.** Add lines 8 and 9 in column (d)	10	36,500	
11	Gain from Form 4797, Part I; long-term gain from Forms 2439 and 6252; and long-term gain or (loss) from Forms 4684, 6781, and 8824		11	
12	Net long-term gain or (loss) from partnerships, S corporations, estates, and trusts from Schedule(s) K-1		12	
13	Capital gain distributions. See page D-1 of the instructions		13	1,050
14	Long-term capital loss carryover. Enter the amount, if any, from line 15 of your **Capital Loss Carryover Worksheet** on page D-7 of the instructions		14	(950)
15	**Net long-term capital gain or (loss).** Combine lines 8 through 14 in column (f). Then go to Part III on the back		15	8,350

For Paperwork Reduction Act Notice, see Form 1040 instructions. Cat. No. 11338H **Schedule D (Form 1040) 2006**

Part III **Summary**

16	Combine lines 7 and 15 and enter the result. If line 16 is a loss, skip lines 17 through 20, and go to line 21. If a gain, enter the gain on Form 1040, line 13, or Form 1040NR, line 14. Then go to line 17 below	16	8,310
17	Are lines 15 and 16 **both** gains? ☑ **Yes.** Go to line 18. ☐ **No.** Skip lines 18 through 21, and go to line 22.		
18	Enter the amount, if any, from line 7 of the **28% Rate Gain Worksheet** on page D-8 of the instructions ▶	18	
19	Enter the amount, if any, from line 18 of the **Unrecaptured Section 1250 Gain Worksheet** on page D-9 of the instructions ▶	19	
20	Are lines 18 and 19 **both** zero or blank? ☑ **Yes.** Complete Form 1040 through line 43, or Form 1040NR through line 40. Then complete the **Qualified Dividends and Capital Gain Tax Worksheet** on page 38 of the Instructions for Form 1040 (or in the Instructions for Form 1040NR). **Do not** complete lines 21 and 22 below. ☐ **No.** Complete Form 1040 through line 43, or Form 1040NR through line 40. Then complete the **Schedule D Tax Worksheet** on page D-10 of the instructions. **Do not** complete lines 21 and 22 below.		
21	If line 16 is a loss, enter here and on Form 1040, line 13, or Form 1040NR, line 14, the **smaller** of: • The loss on line 16 or • ($3,000), or if married filing separately, ($1,500) **Note.** When figuring which amount is smaller, treat both amounts as positive numbers.	21	( )
22	Do you have qualified dividends on Form 1040, line 9b, or Form 1040NR, line 10b? ☐ **Yes.** Complete Form 1040 through line 43, or Form 1040NR through line 40. Then complete the **Qualified Dividends and Capital Gain Tax Worksheet** on page 38 of the Instructions for Form 1040 (or in the Instructions for Form 1040NR). ☐ **No.** Complete the rest of Form 1040 or Form 1040NR.		

Schedule D (Form 1040) 2006

Sample worksheet for John and Karen Taylor (see the Example on page 106)

Qualified Dividends and Capital Gain Tax Worksheet—Line 44

Before you begin:
√ See the instructions for line 44 that begin on page 36 to see if you can use this worksheet to figure your tax.
√ If you do not have to file Schedule D and you received capital gain distributions, be sure you checked the box on line 13 of Form 1040.

1. Enter the amount from Form 1040, line 43		**1.** 75,000	
2. Enter the amount from Form 1040, line 9b	**2.** 400		
3. Are you filing Schedule D? ☒ **Yes.** Enter the **smaller** of line 15 or 16 of Schedule D. If either line 15 or line 16 is a loss, enter -0- ☐ **No.** Enter the amount from Form 1040, line 13	**3.** 8,310		
4. Add lines 2 and 3	**4.** 8,710		
5. If you are claiming investment interest expense on Form 4952, enter the amount from line 4g of that form. Otherwise, enter -0-	**5.** - 0 -		
6. Subtract line 5 from line 4. If zero or less, enter -0-		**6.** 8,710	
7. Subtract line 6 from line 1. If zero or less, enter -0-		**7.** 66,290	
8. Enter the **smaller** of: • The amount on line 1, or • $30,650 if single or married filing separately, $61,300 if married filing jointly or qualifying widow(er), $41,050 if head of household.		**8.** 61,300	
9. Is the amount on line 7 equal to or more than the amount on line 8? ☒ **Yes.** Skip lines 9 through 11; go to line 12 and check the "No" box. ☐ **No.** Enter the amount from line 7		**9.**	
10. Subtract line 9 from line 8		**10.**	
11. Multiply line 10 by 5% (.05)			**11.**
12. Are the amounts on lines 6 and 10 the same? ☐ **Yes.** Skip lines 12 through 15; go to line 16. ☒ **No.** Enter the **smaller** of line 1 or line 6		**12.** 8,710	
13. Enter the amount from line 10 (if line 10 is blank, enter -0-)		**13.** - 0 -	
14. Subtract line 13 from line 12		**14.** 8,710	
15. Multiply line 14 by 15% (.15)			**15.** 1,307
16. Figure the tax on the amount on line 7. Use the Tax Table or Tax Computation Worksheet, whichever applies			**16.** 9,684
17. Add lines 11, 15, and 16			**17.** 10,991
18. Figure the tax on the amount on line 1. Use the Tax Table or Tax Computation Worksheet, whichever applies			**18.** 11,871
19. **Tax on all taxable income.** Enter the **smaller** of line 17 or line 18. Also include this amount on Form 1040, line 44			**19.** 10,991

Holding Period for Capital Assets

5.9 Counting the Months in Your Holding Period

The period of time you own a capital asset before its sale or exchange determines whether capital gain or loss is short term or long term.

These are the rules for counting the holding period:

1. A holding period is figured in months and fractions of months.
2. The beginning date of a holding month is generally the day after the asset was acquired. The same numerical date of each following month starts a new holding month regardless of the number of days in the preceding month.
3. The last day of the holding period is the day on which the asset is sold.

As a rule of thumb, use the numerical date on which you acquired the asset as the numerical date ending a holding month in each following month. However, if you acquire an asset on the last day of a month, a holding month ends on the last day of a following calendar month, regardless of the number of days in each month.

EXAMPLES

1. On September 19, 2006, you buy stock. The holding months begin on September 20, October 20, November 20, and December 20, and end on October 19, November 19, December 19, etc. A sale on or after September 20, 2007, would result in long-term gain or loss.
2. You buy stock on November 30. A holding month ends on December 31, January 31, February 28 (or 29 in a leap year), etc.

5.10 Holding Period for Securities

Rules for counting your holding period for various securities transactions are as follows:

Stock sold on a public exchange. The holding period starts on the day after your purchase order is executed (trade date). The day your sale order is executed (trade date) is the last day of the holding period, even if delivery and payment are not made until several days after the actual sale (settlement date).

Planning Reminder

Long-Term Holding Period of More Than a Year

To obtain the benefit of favorable long-term capital gains rates *(5.3)*, you must hold an asset more than a year before selling it.

EXAMPLES

1. On June 3, you sell a stock at a profit. Your holding period ends on June 3, although proceeds are not received until June 6.
2. You sell stock at a gain on a public exchange on December 29, 2006. The gain must be reported in 2006 even though the proceeds are received in 2007. The installment sale rule does not apply; *see 5.21.*

Stock subscriptions. If you are bound by your subscription but the corporation is not, the holding period begins the day after the date on which the stock is issued. If both you and the company are bound, the date the subscription is accepted by the corporation is the date of acquisition, and your holding period begins the day after.

Tax-free stock rights. When you exercise rights to acquire corporate stock from the issuing corporation, your holding period for the stock begins on the day of exercise, not on the day after. You are deemed to exercise stock rights when you assent to the terms of the rights in the manner requested or authorized by the corporation. An option to acquire stock is not a stock right.

Stock sold from different lots. If you purchased shares of the same stock on different dates and cannot determine which shares you are selling, the shares purchased at the earliest time are considered the stock sold first; this is called the FIFO (first-in, first-out) method; *see 30.2.*

EXAMPLE

You purchased 100 shares of ABC stock on May 3, 1995, 100 shares of ABC stock on May 1, 1997, and 300 shares of ABC stock on September 2, 1998. In 2006, you sell 250 shares of ABC stock, and are unable to determine when those particular shares were bought. Using the "first-in, first-out" method, 100 shares are from May 3, 1995, 100 shares from May 1, 1997, and 50 shares are from September 2, 1998. *See also 30.2.*

Commodities. If you acquired a commodity futures contract, the holding period of a commodity accepted in satisfaction of the contract includes your holding period of the contract, unless you are a dealer in commodities.

Employee stock options. When an employee exercises a stock option, the holding period of the acquired stock begins on the day after the option is exercised. If an employee option plan allows the exercise of an option by giving notes, the terms of the plan should be reviewed to determine when ownership rights to the stock are transferred. The terms may affect the start of the holding period for the stock.

Wash sales. After a wash sale, the holding period of the new stock includes the holding period of the old stock for which a loss has been disallowed; *see 30.6.*

Other references. For the holding period of stock dividends, *see 30.3*; for short sales, *see 30.5*; and for convertible securities, *see 30.7.*

5.11 Holding Period for Real Estate

The holding period starts the day after the date of acquisition, which is the earlier of: (1) the date title passes to you or (2) the date you take possession and you assume the burdens and privileges of ownership. In disputes involving the starting and closing dates of a holding period, you may refer to the state law that applies to your sale or purchase agreement. State law determines when title to property passes.

If you convert a residence to rental property and later sell the home, the holding period includes the time you held the home for personal purposes.

Year-end sale. The date of sale is the last day of your holding period even if you do not receive the sale proceeds until the following year. For example, you sell land at a gain on December 29, 2006, receiving payment in January 2007. The holding period ends on December 29, although the sale is reported in 2007 when the proceeds are received. Note that the December 29 gain transaction can be reported in 2006 by making an election to "elect out" of installment reporting; *see 5.23*. A sale at a loss is reported in 2006.

Planning Reminder

Year-End Sales

Tax reporting for year-end sales of real estate is different from that for publicly traded securities. Gain on a sale of realty at the end of 2006 may be deferred under the installment sale rules *(5.22)* if payments will be received in 2007 or later years. Gain on a sale of publicly traded securities at the end of 2006 must be reported on your 2006 return although you receive payment in 2007.

5.12 Holding Period: Gifts, Inheritances, and Other Property

Gift property. If, in figuring a gain or loss, your basis for the property under *5.17* is the same as the donor's basis, you add the donor's holding period to the period you held the property. If you sell the property at a loss using as your basis the fair market value at the date of the gift *(5.17)*, your holding period begins on the day after the date of the gift.

Inherited property. The law gives an automatic holding period of more than one year for inherited property. Report the transaction on Line 8 of Schedule D and enter "INHERITED" in column (b) as the date of acquisition.

Where property is purchased by the executor or trustee and distributed to you, your holding period begins the day after the date on which the property was purchased.

Partnership property. When you receive property as a distribution in kind from your partnership, the period your partnership held the property is added to your holding period. But there is no adding on of holding periods if the partnership property distributed was inventory and was sold by you within five years of distribution.

Involuntary conversions. When you have an involuntary conversion and elect to defer tax on gain, the holding period for the qualified replacement property generally includes the period you held the converted property. A new holding period begins for new property if you do not make an election to defer tax.

Filing Tip

Selling Inherited Property

When you sell property that you inherited, report the sale as long-term gain or loss on Schedule D even if you actually held the property for less than one year. The law automatically treats inherited property as if it were held for more than one year.

Figuring Your Profit or Loss

5.13 Calculating Gain or Loss

In most cases, you know if you have realized an *economic* profit or loss on the sale or exchange of property. You know your cost and selling price. The difference between the two is your profit or loss. The computation of gain or loss for tax purposes is similarly figured, except that the basis adjustment rules may require you to increase or decrease your cost or selling price and the amount-realized rules may require you to increase the selling price. As a result, your gain or loss for tax purposes may differ from your initial calculation.

Worksheet 5-A Figuring Gain or Loss on Schedule D

1.	Amount realized or total selling price *(5.14)*.		$_____
2.	Cost or other unadjusted basis *(5.16)*.	$_____	
3.	*Plus:* Improvements; certain legal fees *(5.20)*.	$_____	
4.	*Minus:* Depreciation, casualty losses *(5.20)*.	$_____	
5.	Adjusted basis: 2 *plus* 3 *minus* 4 *(5.20)*.	$_____	
6.	Add selling expenses to 5. This is the total cost shown on Schedule D.	$_____	$_____
7.	Gain or loss: Subtract 6 from 1.		$_____

Planning Reminder

Records for Rental Property Improvements

Keep records of permanent improvements and legal fees for rental property. These increase your basis and lower any potential gain when you sell the property.

EXAMPLE

You sell rental property to a buyer who pays you cash of $50,000 and assumes your $35,000 mortgage. You bought the property for $55,000 and made $12,000 of permanent improvements. You deducted depreciation of $7,250. Selling expenses were $2,000. Your gain on the sale is $23,250, figured as follows:

1.	Amount realized *(5.14)*	
	Cash	$50,000
	Mortgage assumed by buyer	35,000
		$85,000
2.	Original cost	55,000
3.	*Plus* improvements	12,000
		$67,000
4.	*Minus* depreciation	7,250
5.	Adjusted basis	59,750
6.	*Plus* selling expenses*	2,000
7.	Total cost: Combined result of Lines 2–6	61,750
8.	Gain: Subtract Line 7 from Line 1	$23,250

***Selling expenses on Schedule D.** When reporting a sale on Schedule D, IRS instructions require you to include *selling expenses* (Step 6) in the column for *cost*, rather than as a reduction to the sales price. The only exception is where a broker has reported *net* sale proceeds (gross proceeds *less* selling expenses) on Form 1099-B; you would then report the net amount as the sales price. Where a broker has reported the *gross* sales price on Form 1099-B, the IRS wants you to treat sales commissions as an addition to cost (rather than a reduction to selling price) so that it can compare the gross amount shown on Form 1099-B with the sales price reported on your return.

Using the facts in the previous Example, you report the gross selling price of $85,000 in column (d) of Schedule D. In column (e), enter the adjusted basis of $59,750 *plus* the selling expenses of $2,000 for a total of $61,750. The final result, a gain of $23,250 ($85,000 – $61,750), is the same as if the selling price were reduced by the selling expenses.

5.14 Amount Realized Is the Total Selling Price

Amount realized is the tax term for the total selling price. It includes cash, the fair market value of additional property received, and any of your liabilities that the buyer agrees to pay. The buyer's note is included in the selling price at fair market value. This is generally the discounted amount that a bank or other party will pay for the note.

Caution

Mortgaged Property

When you sell mortgaged property, you must include the unpaid balance of the mortgage as part of the sales price received, in addition to any cash.

Sale of mortgaged property. The selling price includes the amount of the unpaid mortgage. This is true whether or not you are personally liable on the debt, and whether or not the buyer assumes the mortgage or merely takes the property subject to the mortgage. The full amount of the unpaid mortgage is included, even where the value of the property is less than the unpaid mortgage. *See also 31.9* for computing amount realized on foreclosure sales.

If, at the time of the sale, the buyer pays off the existing mortgage or your other liabilities, you include the payment as part of the sales proceeds.

EXAMPLES

1. You sell property subject to a mortgage of $60,000. The seller pays you cash of $30,000 and takes the property subject to the mortgage. The sales price or "amount realized" is $90,000.
2. A partnership receives a nonrecourse mortgage of $1,851,500 from a bank to build an apartment project. Several years later, the partnership sells the project for the buyer's agreement to assume the unpaid mortgage. At the time, the value of the project is $1,400,000 and the partnership basis in the project is $1,455,740. The partnership figures a loss of $55,740, the difference between

basis and the value of the project. The IRS figures a gain of $395,760, the difference between the unpaid mortgage and basis. The partnership claims the selling price is limited to the lower fair market value and is supported by an appeals court. The Supreme Court reverses, supporting the IRS position. That the value of property is less than the amount of the mortgage has no effect on the rule requiring the unpaid mortgage to be part of the selling price. A mortgagor realizes value to the extent that his or her obligation to repay is relieved by a third party's assumption of the mortgage debt.

5.15 Finding Your Cost

In figuring gain or loss, you need to know the "unadjusted basis" of the property sold. This term refers to the original cost of your property if you purchased it. The general rules for determining your unadjusted basis are in *5.16*. Basis for property received by gift or inheritance is in *5.17*; rules for surviving joint tenants are in *5.18*. Keep in mind that you have to adjust this figure for improvements to the property, depreciation, or losses; *see 5.20*.

5.16 Unadjusted Basis of Your Property

To determine your tax cost for property, first find in the following section the unadjusted basis of the property, and then increase or decrease that basis as explained at *5.20*.

Property you bought. Unadjusted basis is your cash cost plus the value of any property you gave to the seller. If you assumed a mortgage or bought property subject to a mortgage, the amount of the mortgage is part of your unadjusted basis.

Purchase expenses are included in your cost, such as commissions, title insurance, recording fees, survey costs, and transfer taxes.

When you buy real estate, you usually reimburse the seller for property taxes he or she paid that cover the period after you took title. If you bought the property before 1954, you add such payments to basis. If you bought the property after 1953, taxes paid are not added to basis because they are immediately deductible in the year paid; *see 16.6*. However, if at the closing you also paid property taxes attributable to the time the seller held the property, you add such taxes to basis.

EXAMPLE

You bought a building for $120,000 in cash and a purchase money mortgage of $60,000. The unadjusted basis of the building is $180,000.

Property obtained for services. If you paid for the property by providing services, the value of the property, which is taxable compensation, is also your adjusted basis.

Property received in taxable exchange. Technically, your unadjusted basis for the new property is the fair market value of the surrendered property at the time of exchange. In practice, however, the basis usually is equal to the fair market value of the property received. *See* below for tax-free exchanges.

EXAMPLE

You acquire real estate for $35,000. When the property has a fair market value of $40,000, you exchange it for machinery also worth $40,000. You have a gain of $5,000 and the basis of the machinery is $40,000.

Property received in a tax-free exchange. The computation of basis is made on Form 8824. If the exchange is completely tax free *(6.1)*, your basis for the new property will be your basis for the property you gave up in the exchange, plus any additional cash and exchange expenses you paid. If the exchange is partly nontaxable and partly taxable because you received "boot" *(6.3)*, your basis for the new property will be your basis for the property given up in the exchange, decreased by any cash received and by any liabilities on the property you gave up, and increased by any cash and exchange expenses you paid, liabilities on the property you received, and gain taxed to you on the exchange. Gain is taxed to the extent you receive "boot," in the form of cash or a transfer of liabilities that exceeds the liabilities assumed in the exchange; *see 6.3* for a discussion on taxable boot. *The Example at* 6.3 *illustrates the basis computation.*

Filing Tip

Basis of Mutual-Fund Shares

To figure gain or loss on the sale of mutual-fund shares where purchases are made at various times, you may use an averaging method to determine the cost basis of the shares sold; *see 32.10*.

Planning Reminder

Carryover Basis From Spouse or Ex-Spouse

If you receive a gift of property from your spouse or you receive property from a former spouse in a divorce settlement, your basis for the property is generally the same as the spouse's basis; *see 6.7*.

Property received from a spouse or former spouse. As explained at *6.7*, tax-free exchange rules apply to property transfers after July 18, 1984, to a spouse, or to a former spouse where the transfer is incident to a divorce. The spouse receiving the property takes a basis equal to that of the transferor. Certain adjustments may be required where a transfer of mortgaged property is made in trust.

If you received property before July 19, 1984, under a prenuptial agreement in exchange for your release of your dower and marital rights, your basis is the fair market value at the time you received it.

EXAMPLES

1. You exchange investment real estate, which cost you $20,000, for other investment real estate. Both properties have a fair market value of $35,000 and neither property is mortgaged. You pay no tax on the exchange. The unadjusted basis of the new property received in the exchange is $20,000.
2. Same facts as in Example 1, but you receive real estate worth $30,000 and cash of $5,000. On this transaction, you realize gain of $15,000 (amount realized of $35,000 less your basis of $20,000), but only $5,000 of the gain is taxable, equal to the cash "boot" received. Your basis for the new property is $20,000, figured this way:

Basis of old property	$20,000
Less: Cash received	5,000
	15,000
Plus: Gain recognized	5,000
Basis of new property	$20,000

New residence purchased under tax deferral rule of prior law. If you sold your old principal residence and bought a qualifying replacement under the prior law deferral rules, your basis for the new house is what you paid for it, less any gain that was not taxed on the sale of the old residence.

Property received as a trust beneficiary. Generally, you take the same basis the trust had for the property. But if the distribution is made to settle a claim you had against the trust, your basis for the property is the amount of the settled claim.

If you received a distribution in kind for your share of trust income before June 2, 1984, the basis of the distribution is generally the value of the property to the extent allocated to distributable net income. For distributions in kind after June 1, 1984, in taxable years ending after June 1, 1984, your basis is the basis of the property in the hands of the trust. If the trust elects to treat the distribution as a taxable sale, your basis is generally fair market value.

Property acquired with involuntary conversion proceeds. If you acquire replacement property with insurance proceeds from destroyed property, or a government payment for condemned property, basis is the cost of the new property decreased by deferred gain; *see 18.23* for figuring the deferred gain. If the replacement property consists of more than one piece of property, basis is allocated to each piece in proportion to its respective cost.

EXAMPLE

A building with an adjusted basis of $100,000 is destroyed by fire. The owner receives an insurance award of $200,000, realizing a gain of $100,000. He buys a building as a replacement for $150,000. Of the $100,000 gain, $50,000 is taxable, while the remaining $50,000 is deferred. Taxable gain is limited to the portion of the insurance award not used to buy replacement property ($200,000 – $150,000). The basis of the new building is $100,000:

Cost of the new building	$150,000
Less: deferred gain	50,000
Basis	$100,000

5.17 Basis of Property You Inherited or Received as a Gift

Special basis rules apply to property you received as a gift or that you inherited. Gifts from a spouse are subject to the rules discussed in *6.7.* If you are a surviving joint tenant who received full title to property upon the death of the other joint tenant, *see 5.18.*

Basis of Property Received as Gift

If the fair market value of the property *equalled or exceeded* the donor's adjusted basis *(5.20)* at the time you received the gift, your basis for figuring gain or loss when you sell it is the donor's adjusted basis plus all or part of any gift tax paid; *see* the gift tax rule below. Additional basis adjustments may be required for the period you held the property; *see 5.20.*

If on the date of the gift the fair market value was *less* than the donor's adjusted basis, your basis for purposes of figuring gain is the donor's adjusted basis, and your basis for figuring loss is the fair market value on the date of the gift. Additional basis adjustments may be required for the period you held the property; *see 5.20.*

EXAMPLE

Assume that in 1997 you received a gift of stock from your father that you sold in 2006. His adjusted basis was $1,000.

The basis you use to determine gain or loss depends on whether the fair market value of the stock on the date of the gift equalled or exceeded your father's $1,000 adjusted basis. If it did, your basis is your father's $1,000 basis and you will realize a gain if your selling price exceeds $1,000, as on Line 1 below, or a loss if the selling price is below $1,000, as on Line 4.

If the value of the stock on the date of the gift was less than $1,000 (father's basis) then you have: a gain if you sell for more than $1,000, as on Line 5; a loss if you sell for less than the date-of-gift value, as on Line 2; or neither gain nor loss if you sell for more than the date-of-gift value but no more than $1,000 (father's basis), as on Line 3.

	If value of the gift at receipt was—	*And you sold it for—*	*Your basis is—*	*Your gain is—*	*Your loss is—*
1.	$3,000	$2,000	$1,000	$1,000	none
2.	700	500	700	none	$200
3.	300	500	*	none	none
4.	1,500	500	1,000	none	500
5.	500	1,200	1,000	200	none

*On Line 3 of the Example, where you sell for more than the date-of-gift value but for no more than the donor's basis, there is neither gain nor loss. To see if you have a gain, you use the donor's $1,000 basis as your basis, but on a sale for $500, you have a loss ($500) and not a gain. To see if you have a loss, you use the $300 date-of-gift value of the stock as your basis, but on a sale for $500, you have a gain ($200) and not a loss. Thus, you have neither gain nor loss under the basis rules, which require you to use the donor's basis for determining if you have a gain and the date-of-gift value for determining if you have a loss.

Did the donor pay gift tax? If the donor paid a gift tax *(39.2)* on the gift to you, your basis for the property is increased under these rules:

Did the donor pay gift tax? If the donor paid a gift tax *(39.2)* on the gift to you, your basis for the property is increased under these rules:

1. For property received after December 31, 1976, the basis is increased for the gift tax paid by an amount that bears the same ratio to the amount of tax paid as the net appreciation in the value of the gift bears to the amount of the gift after taking into account the $12,000 annual gift tax exclusion *(39.2).* The increase may not exceed the tax paid. Net appreciation in the value of any gift is the amount by which the fair market value of the gift exceeds the donor's adjusted basis immediately before the gift. *See* Example 2 below.

Caution

Basis for Gift

The basis of gift property you receive generally depends on the donor's basis. Make sure you get this information from the donor.

Filing Tip

No Gain or Loss

When you sell property received as a gift, it is possible that you may realize neither gain nor loss. *See* Line 3 of the Example on the left for an illustration of how this can happen.

2. For property received after September 1, 1958, but before 1977, basis is increased by the gift tax paid on the property but not above the fair market value of the property at the time of the gift.
3. For property received before September 2, 1958, the gift tax paid increases the basis. But this increase may not be more than the excess of the fair market value of the property at the time of the gift over the basis of the property in the donor's hands. Ask the donor or his or her advisor for these amounts.

EXAMPLES

1. In 1975, your father gave you rental property with a fair market value of $78,000. The basis of the property in his hands was $60,000. He paid a gift tax of $15,000 on the gift. The basis of the property in your hands is $75,000 ($60,000 + $15,000).
2. In 2001, your father gave you rental property with a fair market value of $178,000. His basis in the property was $160,000. He paid a gift tax of $44,560 on a taxable gift of $168,000, after claiming the $10,000 annual exclusion. The basis of the property in your hands is your father's basis increased by the gift tax attributable to the appreciation. Gift tax attributable to the appreciation is:

$$\frac{\text{Appreciation}}{\text{Gift } \textit{minus} \text{ annual exclusion}} \times \text{Gift tax paid}$$

$$\frac{\$18{,}000}{\$168{,}000} \times \$44{,}560 = \$\,4{,}774$$

Your basis for figuring gain or loss or depreciation is $164,774 ($4,774 + $160,000 father's basis).

Filing Tip

Advantage of Leaving Appreciated Property to an Heir

Since your basis for inherited property is the value at the decedent's death or alternate valuation date, income tax is completely avoided on the appreciation in value that occurred while the decedent owned the property.

Depreciation on property received as a gift. If the property is depreciable (*see* Chapter 42), your basis for computing depreciation deductions is the donor's adjusted basis *(5.20)*, plus all or part of the gift tax paid by the donors as previously discussed.

To figure gain or loss when you sell the property, you must adjust basis for depreciation you claimed and make other adjustments required for the period you hold the property; *see 5.20.* If accelerated depreciation is claimed and you sell at a gain, you are subject to the ordinary income recapture rules discussed at *44.1.*

Basis of Inherited Property

Your basis for inherited property is generally the fair market value of the property on the date of the decedent's death, regardless of when you acquire the property. If the executor of the decedent's estate elected to use an *alternate valuation date* after the death, your basis is the alternate value at that date.

If you owned the property jointly with the deceased, *see 5.18.*

If you inherit appreciated property that you (or your spouse) gave to the deceased person within one year of his or her death, your basis is the decedent's basis immediately before death, not its fair market value.

If the inherited property is subject to a mortgage, your basis is the value of the property, and not its equity at the date of death. If the property is subject to a lease under which no income is to be received for years, the basis is the value of the property—not the equity.

You might be given the right to buy the deceased person's property under his or her will. This is not the same as inheriting that property. Your basis is what you pay—not what the property is worth on the date of the deceased's death.

If property was inherited from an individual who died after 1976 and before November 7, 1978, and the executor elected to apply a carryover basis to all estate property, your basis is figured with reference to the decedent's basis. The executor must inform you of the basis of such property.

Community property. Upon the death of a spouse in a community property state, one-half of the fair market value of the community property is generally included in the deceased spouse's estate for estate tax purposes. The surviving spouse's basis for his or her half of the property is 50% of the total fair market value. For the other half, the surviving spouse, if he/she receives the asset, or the other heirs of the deceased spouse have a basis equal to 50% of the fair market value.

5.18 Joint Tenancy Basis Rules for Surviving Tenants

If you are a surviving joint tenant, your basis for the property depends on how much of the value was includible in the deceased tenant's gross estate, and this depends on whether the joint tenant was your spouse or someone other than your spouse.

Qualified joint interest rule for survivor of spouse who died after 1981. A "qualified joint interest" rule applies to a joint tenancy with right of survivorship where the spouses are the only joint tenants, and to a tenancy by the entirety between a husband and wife. Where the surviving spouse is a U.S. citizen, one-half of the fair market value of the property is includible in the decedent's gross estate. This is true regardless of how much each spouse contributed to the purchase price. Fair market value is fixed at the date of death, or six months later if an estate tax return is filed and the optional alternate valuation date is elected.

The surviving spouse's basis equals 50% of the date-of-death fair market value (the amount included in the decedent's gross estate), plus one-half of the original cost basis for the property; *see* Example 1 below. If no estate tax return was due because the value of the estate was below the filing threshold, the surviving spouse's basis is one-half of the fair market value of the property at the date of death (alternate valuation is not available) plus one-half of the original cost basis. If depreciation deductions for the property were claimed before the date of death, the surviving spouse must reduce basis by his or her share (under local law) of the depreciation; *see* Example 2 below. ***Caution***: A surviving spouse should use these rules only if the other spouse died after 1981; *see* the following page if the spouse died before 1982. Furthermore, these rules do not apply if the surviving spouse is *not* a U.S. citizen on the due date of the estate tax return. In this case, the basis rule is generally the same as the rule discussed on the next page for unmarried joint tenants.

EXAMPLES

1. John and Jennifer Jones jointly own a house that cost them $50,000 in 1979. John paid $45,000 of the purchase price and Jennifer $5,000. In 2006, John dies when the house is worth $200,000. One-half, or $100,000, is included in his estate although he contributed 90% of the purchase price. For income tax purposes, Jennifer's basis for the house is $125,000.

One-half of cost basis	$25,000
Inherited portion	100,000
Jennifer's basis	$125,000

2. Same facts as in Example 1 except that the home was rental property for which $20,000 of depreciation deductions had been allowed before John's death. Under local law, Jennifer had a right to 50% of the income from the property and, thus, a right to 50% of the depreciation. Her basis for the property is $115,000: $125,000 as shown in Example 1, reduced by $10,000, her share of the depreciation.

3. The Gallensteins purchased farm property in 1955 as joint tenants; Mr. Gallenstein provided all the funds. When he died in 1987, Mrs. Gallenstein claimed that 100% of the property was includible in her husband's gross estate and she had a stepped-up basis for that full amount. The IRS argued that under the rules for estates of spouses dying after 1981, she received a stepped-up basis for only 50% of the date-of-death value. The federal appeals court for the Sixth Circuit (Kentucky, Michigan, Ohio, and Tennessee) agreed with Mrs. Gallenstein. The appeals court held that pre-1977 spousal joint tenancies were not affected when the law was changed to provide a 50% estate tax inclusion and 50% stepped-up basis for spousal deaths after 1981. For pre-1977 spousal joint tenancies, the prior law rule continues to apply: 100% of the date-of-death value of jointly held property is included in the estate of the first spouse to die unless it is shown that the survivor contributed towards the purchase. In this case, where Mrs. Gallenstein's deceased husband had paid the entire purchase price, her basis was 100% of the value of the property and she realized no taxable gain when she sold the property at a price equal to that stepped-up basis.

Planning Reminder

Spousal Joint Tenancies Created Before 1977

If spouses jointly own property and one spouse dies, the surviving spouse generally receives a stepped-up basis of 50% of the date-of-death value. The IRS at one time took the position that the 50% stepped-up basis rule applied to pre-1997 spousal joint tenancies. However, after the Tax Court and two federal appeals courts allowed a surviving spouse a 100% stepped-up basis if the spousal joint tenancy was created before 1977 (*see* Example 3 in the left column), the IRS decided to follow the Tax Court decision and will no longer litigate the issue.

The Tax Court and the Fourth Circuit Appeals Court (Maryland, North Carolina, South Carolina, Virginia, and West Virginia) agreed with the Sixth Circuit's approach of allowing a 100% stepped-up basis for a pre-1977 spousal joint interest where the deceased spouse had paid the entire purchase price. In October 2001, the IRS acquiesced to the Tax Court decision and will no longer litigate the issue.

If the statute of limitations has not expired, a surviving spouse who reported gain on a sale of property using the 50% basis rule should consult with his or her tax adviser about filing a refund claim based upon the 100% basis rule.

Unmarried joint tenants. If you are a surviving joint tenant who owned property with someone other than your spouse, your basis for the entire property is your basis for your share before the joint owner died plus the fair market value of the decedent's share at death (or on the alternate valuation date if the estate uses the alternate date). Even if the estate is too small to require the filing of an estate tax return, you may still include the decedent's share of the date-of-death value in your basis. However, if no estate tax return is required, you may not use the alternate valuation date basis.

Planning Reminder

Joint Property Held With Non-Spouse

If you own property with someone other than your spouse, then at the other owner's death your basis for the property equals your original contribution to the purchase plus the portion of the property's value that was includible in the gross estate of the deceased owner.

EXAMPLE

You and your sister bought a home in 1990 for $120,000. She paid $72,000, and you paid $48,000. Title to the house was held by both of you as joint tenants. In 2006, when she died, the house was worth $250,000. Since she paid 60% of the cost of the house, 60% of the value at her death, $150,000, is included in her estate tax return (or would be included if an estate tax return was due). Your basis for the house is now $198,000—the $48,000 you originally paid plus the $150,000 fair market value of your sister's 60% share at her death.

Exception for pre-1954 deaths. Where property was held in joint tenancy and one of the tenants died before January 1, 1954, no part of the interest of the surviving tenant is treated, for purposes of determining the basis of the property, as property transmitted at death. The survivor's basis is the original cost of the property.

Survivor of spouse who died before 1982. The basis rule for a surviving spouse who held property jointly (or as tenancy by the entirety) with a spouse who died before 1982 is generally the same as the above rule for unmarried joint tenants. However, special rules applied to qualified joint interests and eligible joint interests are discussed below.

EXAMPLE

A husband and wife owned rental property as tenants by the entirety that they purchased for $30,000. The husband furnished two-thirds of the purchase price ($20,000) and the wife furnished one-third ($10,000). Depreciation deductions taken before the husband's death were $12,000. On the date of his death in 1979, the property had a fair market value of $60,000. Under the law of the state in which the property is located, as tenants by the entirety, each had a half interest in the property. The wife's basis in the property at the date of her husband's death was $44,000, computed as follows:

Interest acquired with her own funds	$10,000
Interest acquired from husband (2/3 of $60,000)	40,000
	$50,000
Less: Depreciation of 1/2 interest not acquired	
by reason of death (1/2 of $12,000)	6,000
Wife's basis at date of husband's death	$44,000

If she had not contributed any part of the purchase price, her basis at the date of her husband's death would be $54,000 ($60,000 fair market value less $6,000 depreciation). This basis would be increased by any additions or improvements made to the property by the wife since the husband's death, and reduced by any depreciation; *see 5.20.*

Qualified joint interest and eligible joint interest where spouse died before 1982. Where, after 1976, a spouse dying before 1982 elected to treat realty as a "qualified joint interest" subject to gift tax, such joint property was treated as owned 50–50 by each spouse, and 50% of the value was included in the decedent's estate. Thus, for income tax purposes, the survivor's basis for the inherited 50% half of the property is the estate tax value; the basis for the other half is determined under the gift rules detailed in *5.17*. Personal property is treated as a "qualified joint interest" only if it was created or deemed to have been created after 1976 by a husband and wife and was subject to gift tax.

Where death occurred before 1982 and a surviving spouse materially participated in the operation of a farm or other business, an estate may elect to treat the farm or business property as an "eligible joint interest," which means that part of the investment in the property may be attributed to the surviving spouse's services and that part is not included in the deceased spouse's estate. Where such an election was made, the survivor's basis for income tax purposes includes the estate tax value of property included in the decedent's estate.

5.19 Allocating Cost Among Several Assets

Allocation of basis is generally required in these cases: when the property includes land and building; the land is to be divided into lots; securities or mutual-fund shares are purchased at different times; stock splits; and in the purchase of a business.

Purchase of land and building. To figure depreciation on the building, part of the purchase price must be allocated to the building. The allocation is made according to the fair market values of the building and land. The amount allocated to land is not depreciated.

Purchase of land to be divided into lots. The purchase price of the tract is allocated to each lot, so that the gain or loss from the sale of each lot may be reported in the year of its sale. Allocation is not made ratably, that is, with an equal share to each lot or parcel. It is based on the relative value of each piece of property. Comparable sales, competent appraisals, or assessed values may be used as guides.

Securities. *See 30.2* for details on methods of identifying securities bought at different dates. *See 30.3* for allocating basis of stock dividends and stock splits and *30.4* for allocating the basis of stock rights.

Mutual-fund shares. *See 32.10* for determining the basis of mutual-fund shares where purchases were made at different times.

Purchase price of a business. *See 44.9* for allocation rule.

5.20 How To Find Adjusted Basis

After determining the *unadjusted* cost basis for property under the rules at *5.16–5.19*, you may have to increase it or decrease it to find your *adjusted basis*, which is the amount used to figure your gain or loss on a sale, as shown at *5.13*.

1. **Additions to basis.** You add to unadjusted basis the cost of these items:
   - ***All permanent improvements and additions to the property and other capital costs.*** Increase basis for capital improvements such as adding a room or a fence, putting in new plumbing or wiring, and paving a driveway. Also include capital costs such as the cost of extending utility service lines, assessments for local improvements such as streets, sidewalks, or water connections, and repairing your property after a casualty (for example, repair costs after a fire or storm).
   - ***Legal fees,*** including fees incurred for defending or perfecting title, or for obtaining a reduction of an assessment levied against property to pay for local benefits.
   - ***Sale of unharvested land.*** If you sell land with unharvested crops, add the cost of producing the crops to the basis of the property sold.

2. **Decreases to basis.** You reduce cost basis for these items:
   - ***Return of capital,*** such as dividends on stock paid out of capital or out of a depletion reserve when the company has no available earnings or surplus; *see 4.11*.
   - ***Losses from casualties,*** including insurance awards and payments in settlement of damages to your property.
   - ***Depletion allowances;*** *see 9.15*.
   - ***Depreciation, first-year expensing deduction, ACRS deductions, amortization, and obsolescence on property used in business or for the production of income.*** In some years, you may have taken more or less depreciation than was allowable.

Court Decision

Improvements Covered by Note

In an unusual case, the owner of office condominiums financed substantial improvements to the units by giving promissory notes to a contracting company that he controlled. Before paying off the notes he sold the units. He included the cost of the improvements in basis to figure his gain on the sale, but the IRS, with the approval of a federal district court, held that this was improper. The court held that as a cash-basis taxpayer, he could not include the face amount of the notes in the basis of the condominiums until the notes were paid.

If you claim less than what was allowable, you must deduct from basis the allowable amount rather than what was actually claimed. You may be able to file an amended return to claim the full allowable depreciation for a year. If IRS rules do not allow the correction on an amended return, you can change your accounting method in order to claim the correct amount of depreciation; *see* Publication 946 for details.

If you took more depreciation than was allowable, you may have to make the following adjustments: If you have deducted more than what was allowable and you received a tax benefit from the deduction, you deduct from basis the full amount of the depreciation. But if the excess depreciation did not give you a tax benefit, because income was eliminated by other deductions, the excess is not deducted from basis.

- ***Amortized bond premium;*** *see 4.17.*
- ***Cancelled debt excluded from income.*** If you did not pay tax on certain cancellations of debt because of bankruptcy or insolvency, or on qualifying farm debt or business real property, you reduce basis of your property for the amount forgiven under the rules at *11.8.*
- ***Investment credit.*** Where the full investment credit was claimed in 1983 or later years, basis is reduced by one-half the credit.

EXAMPLE

Your vacation home, which cost $75,000, is damaged by fire. You deducted the uninsured loss of $10,000 and spent $11,000 to repair the property. Several years later, you sell the house for $90,000. To figure your profit, increase the original cost of the house by the $11,000 of repairs and then reduce basis by the $10,000 casualty loss to get an adjusted basis of $76,000 ($75,000 + $11,000 – $10,000). Your gain on the sale is $14,000 ($90,000 – $76,000).

Reporting an Installment Sale

5.21 Tax Advantage of Installment Sales

If you sell property at a *gain* in 2006 and you will receive one or more payments in a later year or years, you may use the installment method to defer tax unless the property is publicly traded securities or you are a dealer of the property sold. If you report the sale as an installment sale on Form 6252, your profit is taxed as installments are received. You may elect not to use the installment method if you want to report the entire profit in the year of sale; *see* Example 1 below and *5.23.*

Losses may not be deferred under the installment method.

Filing Instruction

Payments from Prior Installment Sales

If you reported a pre-2006 sale on the installment method, use Form 6252 to report any 2006 payments on the sale.

How the installment method works. For each year you receive installment payments, report your gain on Form 6252. Installment income from the sale of a capital asset is then transferred to Schedule D. If your gain in the year of sale is long-term capital gain, gain in later years is also long term; short-term treatment in the year of sale applies also to later years. Interest payments you receive on the deferred sale installments are reported with your other interest income on Form 1040, not on Form 6252.

Installment income from the sale of business or rental property is figured on Form 6252 and then entered on Form 4797. If you make an installment sale of depreciable property, any *depreciation recapture (44.1)* is reported as income in the year of disposition. The recaptured amount is first figured on Form 4797 and then entered on Form 6252. On Form 6252, recaptured income is added to basis of the property for purposes of figuring the gross profit ratio for the balance of gain to be reported, if any, over the installment period; *see also 44.6.*

Installment sales of business or rental property for over $150,000 may be subject to a special tax if deferred payments exceed $5 million; *see 5.31.*

EXAMPLES

1. In October 2006, you sell vacant land for $100,000 that you bought in 1999 for $44,000. Selling expenses were $6,000. You are to receive $20,000 in 2006, 2007, and 2008, and $40,000 in 2009, plus interest of 5% compounded semiannually. Your gross profit is

$50,000 ($100,000 contract price less $44,000 cost and $6,000 selling expenses). For installment sale purposes, your gross profit percentage, which is the percentage of each payment that you must report, is 50% ($50,000 profit ÷ $100,000 contract price). When the buyer makes the installment note payments, you report the following:

In	You report Payment of:	Income of:
2006	$20,000	$10,000
2007	20,000	10,000
2008	20,000	10,000
2009	40,000	20,000
Total	$100,000	$50,000

In 2006, you file Form 6252 to figure your gross profit and gross profit percentage. You report only $10,000 as profit on Line 11, column (f), of Schedule D; *see* the sample Schedule D at *5.8*. If you do not want to use the installment method, you make an election by reporting the entire gain of $50,000 on Schedule D; *see 5.23*.

The buyer's interest payments are separately reported as interest income on Form 1040.

2. On December 16, 2006, you sell a building for $150,000, realizing a profit of $25,000. You take a note payable in January 2007. You report the gain in 2007. Receiving a lump-sum payment in a taxable year after the year of sale is considered an installment sale.

Caution

Year-End Sales of Securities

You cannot defer to 2007 reporting of gain on a 2006 year-end sale of publicly traded securities, even if you do not receive payment until early January 2007.

Year-end sales of publicly traded stock or securities. You have no choice about when to report the gain from a sale of publicly traded stock or securities made at the end of 2006. Any gain must be reported in 2006, even if the proceeds are not received until early 2007. The sale is not considered an installment sale.

Farm property. A farmer may use the installment method to report gain from the sale of property that does not have to be inventoried under his method of accounting. This is true even though such property is held for regular sale.

Dealer sales. Generally, dealers must report gain in the year of sale for personal property regularly sold on an installment plan or real estate held for resale to customers. However, the installment method may be used by dealers of certain time shares (generally time shares of up to six weeks per year) and residential lots, but only if an election is made to pay interest on the tax deferred by using the installment method. For further details, *see* the instructions to Line 1 of Schedule C (Form 1040).

5.22 Figuring the Taxable Part of Installment Payments

On the installment method, a portion of each payment other than interest represents part of your gain and is taxable. This taxable gain amount is based on the gross profit percentage or ratio, which is figured by dividing gross profit by the selling price or the contract price. The contract price is the same as the selling price unless an adjustment is made for an existing mortgage assumed or "taken subject to" by the buyer. The term *contract price* is used in the computation to describe only payments that the seller receives or is considered to have received. Thus, it does not include the buyer's assumption of an existing mortgage; *see* below for the mortgage adjustment to contract price. By following the line-by-line instructions to Form 6252, you get the gross profit percentage. Selling price, gross profit, and contract price are explained in the following paragraphs.

Interest equal to the *lesser* of 100% of the applicable federal rate and 9% compounded semiannually must generally be charged on a deferred payment sale. Otherwise, the IRS treats part of the sale price as interest; *see 4.32*.

EXAMPLE

On December 12, 2006, you sell real estate for $100,000. The property had an adjusted basis of $56,000. Selling expenses are $4,000. You are to receive installment payments of $25,000 in 2006, 2007, 2008, and 2009, plus interest at 5%, compounded semiannually. The gross profit percentage of 40% is figured as follows:

Selling price (contract price)	$100,000
Less: Adjusted basis and selling expenses	60,000
Gross profit	$ 40,000

Gross profit / Contract price = $40,000 / $100,000 = 40% (gross profit percentage)

In 2006, you report a profit of $10,000 (40% of $25,000) on Form 6252. Interest received is separately reported as income on your Form 1040. Similarly, in each of the following three years, a profit of $10,000 is reported so that by the end of four years, the entire $40,000 profit will have been reported.

Caution

Foreclosures

If your property is foreclosed, the amount of the mortgage is treated as sales proceeds even if you do not receive anything on the sale.

Selling price. Include cash, fair market value of property received from the buyer, the buyer's notes (at face value), and any outstanding mortgage on the property that the buyer assumes or takes subject to. If, under the contract of sale, the buyer pays off an existing mortgage or assumes liability for any other liens on the property, such as taxes you owe, or pays the sales commissions, such payments are also included in the selling price.

Interest, including minimum interest imputed under the rules in *4.32*, is not included in the selling price.

Notes of a third party given to you by the buyer are valued at fair market value.

Gross profit and gross profit percentage. Gross profit is the selling price less what the IRS calls installment sale basis, which is the total of adjusted basis of the property *(5.20)*, selling expenses, such as brokers' commissions and legal fees, and recaptured depreciation income, if any *(44.1)*.

Divide the gross profit by the contract price to get the gross profit percentage. Each year, you multiply this percentage by your payments to determine the taxable amount under the installment method.

Caution

Recapture of Depreciation or First-Year Expensing Deduction

The entire recaptured amount, discussed in *44.1–44.3*, is reported in the year of sale on Form 4797, even though you report the sale on the installment basis. An installment sale does not defer the reporting of the recaptured deduction. You also add the recaptured amount to the basis of the sold asset on Line 12 of Form 6252 to compute the amount of the remaining gain to be reported on each installment. *See* the instructions to Form 6252.

Contract price where the buyer takes subject to or assumes an existing mortgage. To figure the gross profit percentage first reduce the selling price by the amount of your existing mortgages that the buyer assumes or takes the property subject to. The reduced amount is the *contract price*. You then divide your gross profit by the contract price to get the gross profit percentage.

If the mortgage exceeds your installment sale basis (total of adjusted basis of the property, selling expenses, and depreciation recapture), you are required to report the excess as a payment received in the year of sale and also increase the *contract price* by that excess amount. Where the mortgage equals or exceeds your installment sale basis, the gross profit percentage will be 100%; *see* Example 3 below.

In a wraparound mortgage transaction, the buyer does not assume the seller's mortgage or take the property subject to it, but instead makes payments that cover the seller's outstanding mortgage liability. At one time, the IRS treated a wraparound mortgage transaction as an assumption of a mortgage by the buyer and required a reduction of the selling price by the mortgage to compute the contract price. The Tax Court rejected the IRS position, and the IRS acquiesced in the decision. Currently, the IRS does not require a reduction of selling price for a wraparound mortgage in the Form 6252 instructions or in Publication 537; *see* Example 4 below.

EXAMPLES

1. You sell a building for $300,000. The building was secured by an existing mortgage of $50,000 that you pay off at the sale closing from the buyer's initial payment. The contract price is $300,000.

2. Same facts as in Example 1, but the buyer assumes the mortgage of $50,000. The contract price is $250,000 ($300,000 – $50,000).
3. You sell a building for $90,000. The buyer will pay you $10,000 annually for three years and assume an existing mortgage of $60,000. The adjusted basis of the property is $45,000. Selling expenses are $5,000. The total installment sale basis is $50,000 ($45,000 plus $5,000). The mortgage exceeds this basis by $10,000 ($60,000 – $50,000). This $10,000 excess is included in the contract price and treated as a payment made in the year of sale. The contract price is $40,000:

Selling price	$90,000
Less: Mortgage	60,000
	$30,000
Add: Excess of mortgage ($60,000) over installment sale basis ($50,000)	10,000
Contract price	$40,000
Selling price	$90,000
Less: Installment sale basis	50,000
Gross Profit	$40,000
Gross profit percentage ($40,000 gross profit ÷ $40,000 contract price)	100%

4. Abel sells real property worth $2 million, encumbered by a mortgage of $900,000. Installment sale basis (adjusted basis plus selling costs) is $700,000. The buyer pays $200,000 cash and gives an interest-bearing wraparound mortgage note for $1.8 million. Abel remains obligated to pay off the $900,000 mortgage. The gross profit ratio is 65% ($1,300,000 gross profit ÷ $2,000,000 contract price). In the year of sale, Abel reports the $200,000 cash of which 65% of $200,000, or $130,000, is taxable income.

Change of selling price. If the selling price is changed during the period payments are outstanding, the gross profit percentage is refigured on the new selling price. The adjusted profit ratio is then applied to payments received after the adjustment.

EXAMPLE

Jones sold real estate in 2003 for $100,000. His basis, including selling expenses, was $40,000, so his gross profit was $60,000. The buyer agreed to pay, starting in 2004, five annual installments of $20,000 plus 10% interest. As the gross profit percentage was 60% ($60,000 ÷ $100,000), Jones reported profit of $12,000 (60% of $20,000) on the installments received in 2004 and 2005.

In 2006, the parties renegotiated the sales price, reducing it from $100,000 to $85,000, and reducing payments for 2006, 2007, and 2008 to $15,000. Jones's original profit of $60,000 is reduced to $45,000 ($85,000 revised sales price less $40,000 basis). Of the $45,000 profit, $12,000 was reported in 2004 and an additional $12,000 in 2005. To get the revised profit percentage, Jones must divide the $21,000 of profit not yet received by the remaining sales price of $45,000 ($85,000 *less* $40,000 in total installments in 2004 and 2005). The revised profit percentage is 46.67% ($21,000 ÷ $45,000). In 2006, 2007, and 2008, Jones reports profit of $7,000 on each $15,000 installment (46.67% of $15,000).

Caution

Extension of Pledge Rule

If a loan arrangement gives you the right to repay the debt by transferring an installment obligation, you are treated as if you had directly pledged the obligation as security for the debt. As a result, the loan proceeds are treated as a payment on the installment obligation, which will increase installment income for the year of the "deemed pledge."

Payments received. Payments include cash, the fair market value of property, and payments on the buyer's notes. Payments do not include receipt of the buyer's notes or other evidence of indebtedness, unless payable on demand or readily tradable. "Readily tradable" means registered bonds, bonds with coupons attached, debentures, and other evidences of indebtedness of the buyer that are readily tradable in an established securities market. This rule is directed mainly at corporate acquisitions. A third-party guarantee (including a standby letter of credit) is not treated as a payment received on an installment obligation.

If the buyer has assumed or taken property subject to a mortgage that exceeds your installment sale basis (adjusted basis plus selling expenses plus depreciation recapture, if any), you include as a payment in the year of the sale the excess of the mortgage over the installment basis; *see* the Johnson Example below.

EXAMPLE

Johnson sells a building for $160,000, subject to a mortgage of $60,000. Installments plus interest are to be paid over five years. His adjusted basis in the building was $30,000 and his selling expenses were $10,000, so his installment sale basis is $40,000 and his gross profit is $120,000 ($160,000 – $40,000). The contract price is also $120,000, the selling price of $160,000 less $40,000, the part of the mortgage that did not exceed the installment sale basis.

The $20,000 difference between the $60,000 mortgage and the installment sale basis of $40,000 is part of the contract price and is also treated as a payment received in the year of sale. Since the mortgage exceeds Johnson's installment sale basis, he is treated as having recovered his entire basis in the year of sale, and all installment payments will be taxable, as his gross profit ratio is 100%: gross profit of $120,000 ÷ contract price of $120,000. In the year of sale, Johnson must report as taxable gain 100% of the installment payment received, plus the $20,000 difference between the mortgage and his installment sale basis.

Pledging installment obligation as security. If, as security for a loan, you pledge an installment obligation from a sale of property of more than $150,000 (excluding farm or personal-use property), the net loan proceeds must be treated as a payment on the installment obligation. The net loan proceeds are treated as received on the later of the date the loan is secured and the date you receive the loan proceeds. These pledging rules do not apply if the debt refinances a debt that was outstanding on December 17, 1987, and secured by the installment obligation until the refinancing. If the refinancing exceeds the loan principal owed immediately before the refinancing, the excess is treated as a payment on the installment obligation. *See* the Form 6252 instructions.

5.23 Electing Not To Report on the Installment Method

If any sale proceeds are to be received after the year of sale, you must file Form 6252 and use the installment method unless you "elect out" by making a timely election to report the entire gain in the year of sale. If you want to report the entire gain in the year of sale, include it on Schedule D or Form 4797 by the due date for filing your return (plus extensions) for the year of sale. Do not use Form 6252.

Filing Tip

"Electing Out" of Installment Reporting

When you have losses to offset your gain in the year of sale, installment sale reporting may not be advantageous. In such a case, you may want to report the full gain in the year of sale so the gain may be offset by the losses. However, there is a risk. If the losses are later disallowed by an IRS audit, you may not be given a second chance to use the installment method to spread the gain over the payment period. The IRS *may* not allow you to revoke your "election out" on the grounds that to do so would result in tax avoidance.

Switching from full reporting to installment method. If you do report the entire gain in the year of sale, you may change to the installment method on an amended return only with the consent of the IRS. In a private ruling, the IRS refused to allow a seller to use the installment method after inadvertently including the entire gain from the sale on his return. Although reporting of the entire gain was a mistake, this was treated as an election not to use the installment method. The IRS refused permission to revoke the election on the grounds that a second chance to apply the installment method would be tax avoidance. However, in other private rulings, permission to revoke was granted where the seller's accountant erroneously reported the entire gain.

In one case, a seller "elected out" in a year in which he planned to deduct a net operating loss carryforward from an installment sale gain. In a later year, the IRS substantially reduced the loss. The seller then asked the IRS to allow him to revoke the "election out" so he could use the installment method. The IRS refused in a private ruling, claiming that the seller asked for the revocation to avoid tax. The installment sale would defer gain to a later year, which is a tax avoidance purpose.

5.24 Restriction on Installment Sales to Relatives

The installment sale method is not allowed where you sell depreciable property to a controlled business, or to a trust in which you or your spouse is a beneficiary. All payments to be received over the installment period are considered received in the year of sale.

Further, if you sell property to a relative on the installment basis, and the relative later resells the property, you could lose the benefit of installment reporting. If the family member's resale is within two years of the original sale, the original seller is taxed on that sale under the two-year rule discussed below.

EXAMPLE

In 2006, Jones sells land to his son for $250,000, realizing a profit of $100,000. The son agrees to pay in five annual installments of $50,000 plus interest, starting in 2007. Later in 2006, the son sells the land to a third party for $260,000. Jones Sr. reports his profit of $100,000 in 2006, even though he received no payment that year. Payments other than interest received by Jones Sr. after 2006 are tax free because he reported the entire profit in 2006.

Caution

Installment Sale to Relative

If you sell property on the installment basis to a relative who later resells the property, you could lose the benefit of installment reporting.

Two-year resale rule for property. If you make an installment sale of property to a related party, you are taxed on a second sale by the related party only if it occurs within two years of the initial installment sale and before all payments from the first installment sale are made. Related parties include a spouse, child, grandchild, parent, grandparent, brother or sister, controlled corporation (50% or more direct or indirect ownership), any S corporation in which you own stock or partnership in which you are a partner, a trust in which you are a beneficiary, or a grantor trust of which you are treated as the owner. You are treated as owning stock held by your spouse, brothers, sisters, children, grandchildren, parents, and grandparents.

You must report as additional installment sale income: (1) the proceeds from the related party's sale or the contract price from the initial installment sale, whichever is less, *minus* (2) installment payments received from the related party as of the end of the year. The computation is made in Part III of Form 6252.

The two-year period is extended during any period in which the buyer's risk is lessened by a put on the property, an option by another person to acquire the property, or a short sale or other transaction lessening the risk of loss.

Exceptions to two-year rule. There are exceptions to this related-party rule. Second dispositions resulting from an involuntary conversion of the property will not be subject to the related-party rule so long as the first disposition occurred before the threat or imminence of conversion. Similarly, transfers after the death of the person making the first disposition or the death of the person acquiring the property in the first disposition are not treated as second dispositions. Also, a sale or exchange of stock to the issuing corporation is not treated as a first disposition. Finally, you may avoid tax on a related party's second sale by satisfying the IRS that neither the initial nor the second sale was made for tax avoidance purposes.

Caution

IRS Notice of Related Party Transfer

Where you transfer property to a related party, the IRS has two years from the date you notify it that there has been a second disposition to assess a deficiency with respect to your transfer.

Sales of depreciable property to related party. Installment reporting is not allowed for sales of depreciable property made to a controlled corporation or partnership (50% control by seller) and between such controlled corporations and partnerships. In figuring control of a corporation, you are considered to own stock held by your spouse, children, grandchildren, brothers or sisters, parents, and grandparents. Installment reporting is also disallowed on a sale to a trust in which you or a spouse is a beneficiary unless your interest is considered a remote contingent interest whose actuarial value is 5% or less of the trust property's value. On these related-party sales, the entire gain is reported in the year of sale, unless the seller convinces the IRS that the transfer was not motivated by tax avoidance purposes.

On a sale of depreciable property to a related party, if the amounts of payments are contingent (for example, payments are tied to profits), the seller must make a special calculation. He or she must treat as received in the year of sale all noncontingent payments plus the fair market value of the contingent payments if such value may be reasonably ascertained. If the fair market value of the contingent payments may not be reasonably calculated, the seller recovers basis ratably. The purchaser's basis for the acquired property includes only amounts that the seller has included in income under the basis recovery rule. Thus, the purchaser's basis is increased annually as the seller recovers basis.

5.25 Contingent Payment Sales

Where the final selling price or payment period of an installment sale is not fixed at the end of the taxable year of sale, you are considered to have transacted a "contingent payment sale." Special rules apply where a maximum selling price may be figured under the terms of the agreement or there is no fixed price but there is a fixed payment period, or there is neither a fixed price nor a fixed payment period.

Caution

Contingent Sales

An example of a contingent sale in which the selling price cannot be determined by the end of the year of the sale is a sale of your business where the selling price includes a percentage of future profits. You and your tax advisor should consult the technical rules in IRS regulation 15A.453-1(c) for details on reporting such sales.

Filing Tip

Installment Reporting on Escrow Allowable

If an escrow arrangement imposes a substantial restriction, the IRS may allow installment reporting. An example of a substantial restriction: Payment of the escrow is tied to the condition that the seller refrain from entering a competing business for a period of five years. If, at any time during the escrow period, he or she engages in a competing business, all rights to the amount then held in escrow would be forfeited.

Stated maximum selling price. Under IRS regulations, a stated maximum selling price may be determined by assuming that all of the contingencies contemplated under the agreement are met. When the maximum amount is later reduced, the gross profit ratio is recomputed.

EXAMPLE

Smith sells stock in Acme Co. for a down payment of $100,000 plus an amount equal to 5% of the net profits of Acme for the next nine years. The contract provides that the maximum amount payable, including the $100,000 down payment but exclusive of interest, is $2,000,000. Smith's basis for the stock is $200,000; $2,000,000 is the selling price and contract price. Gross profit is $1,800,000. The gross profit ratio is 90% ($1,800,000 ÷ $2,000,000). Thus, $90,000 of the first payment is reportable as gain and $10,000 as a recovery of basis.

Fixed period. When a stated maximum selling price is not determinable but the maximum payment period is fixed, basis—including selling expenses—is allocated equally to the taxable years in which payment may be received under the agreement. If, in any year, no payment is received or the amount of payment received is less than the basis allocated to that taxable year, no loss is allowed unless the taxable year is the final payment year or the agreement has become worthless. When no loss is allowed in a year, the basis allocated to the taxable year is carried forward to the next succeeding taxable year.

EXAMPLE

Brown sells property for 10% of the property's gross rents over a five-year period. Brown's basis is $5,000,000. The sales price is indefinite and the maximum selling price is not fixed under the terms of the contract; basis is recovered ratably over the five-year period.

Year	*Payment*	*Basis recovered*	*Gain*
First	$ 1,300,000	$ 1,000,000	$ 300,000
Second	1,500,000	1,000,000	500,000
Third	1,400,000	1,000,000	400,000
Fourth	1,800,000	1,000,000	800,000
Fifth	2,100,000	1,000,000	1,100,000

No stated maximum selling price or fixed period. If the agreement fails to specify a maximum selling price and payment period, the IRS may view the agreement as a rent or royalty income agreement. However, if the arrangement qualifies as a sale, basis (including selling expenses) is recovered in equal annual increments over a 15-year period commencing with the date of sale. If in any taxable year no payment is received or the amount of payment received (exclusive of interest) is less than basis allocated to the year, no loss is allowed unless the agreement has become worthless. Excess basis not recovered in one year is reallocated in level amounts over the balance of the 15-year term. Any basis not recovered at the end of the 15th year is carried forward to the next succeeding year, and to the extent unrecovered, carried forward from year to year until basis has been recovered or the agreement is determined to be worthless. The rule requiring initial level allocation of basis over 15 years may not apply if you prove to the IRS that a 15-year general rule will substantially and inappropriately defer recovery of basis.

In some cases, basis recovery under an income forecast type of method may also be allowed.

5.26 Using Escrow and Other Security Arrangements

You sell property and the sales proceeds are placed in escrow pending the possible occurrence of an event such as the approval of title or your performance of certain contractual conditions. The IRS may argue that installment reporting is not allowed unless there are escrow restrictions preventing immediate payment.

If the terms of the escrow involve no genuine conditions that prevent you from demanding immediate payment, there will be immediate tax. Substitution of an escrow account for unpaid notes or deeds of trust disqualifies installment reporting.

EXAMPLES

1. Anderson sold stock and mining property for almost $5 million. He agreed to place $500,000 in escrow to protect the buyer against his possible breaches of warranty and to provide security for certain liabilities. The escrow agreement called for Anderson to direct the investments of the escrow fund and receive income from the fund in excess of $500,000.

   The IRS claimed that in the year of sale Anderson was taxable on the $500,000 held in escrow on the ground that Anderson's control of the fund rendered the fund taxable immediately. Anderson argued he was only taxable as the funds were released to him, and the Tax Court agreed. The fund was not under his unqualified control. He might never get the fund if the liabilities materialized. Although Anderson had a free hand with investment of the money, he still lacked ultimate ownership.
2. Rhodes sold a tract to a buyer who was willing to pay at once the entire purchase price of $157,000. But Rhodes wanted to report the sale on the installment basis over a period of years. The buyer refused to execute a purchase money mortgage on the property to allow the installment sale election (required under prior law) because he wanted clear and unencumbered title to the tract. As a solution, Rhodes asked the buyer to turn over the purchase price to a bank, as escrow agent, which would pay the sum over a five-year period.

   The escrow arrangement failed to support an installment sale. Rhodes was fully taxable on the entire price in the year of the sale. The buyer's payment was unconditional and irrevocable. The escrow arrangement involved no genuine conditions that could defeat Rhodes's right to payment, as the buyer could not revoke, alter, or end the arrangement.
3. In January, an investor sold real estate for $100,000. He received $10,000 as a down payment and six notes, each for $15,000, secured by a deed of trust on the property. The notes, together with interest, were due annually over the next six years. In July, the buyer deposited the remainder of the purchase price with an escrow agent and got the seller to cancel the deed of trust.

   The agreement provides that the escrow agent will pay off the buyer's notes as they fall due. The buyer remains liable for the installment payments. The escrow deposit is irrevocable, and the payment schedule may not be accelerated by any party under any circumstances. According to the IRS, the sale, which initially qualified as an installment sale, is disqualified by the escrow account.

5.27 Minimum Interest on Deferred Payment Sales

The tax law requires a minimum amount of interest to be charged on deferred payment sales. The rules for imputing interest on sales are discussed at *4.32*. Imputed interest is included in the taxable income of the seller. Imputed interest is deductible by the buyer if the property is business or investment property, but not if it is used substantially all the time for personal purposes.

Caution

Charging Minimum Interest

If you do not charge a minimum interest rate, the IRS may do so. This would require you and the buyer to treat part of the purchase price as interest.

5.28 Dispositions of Installment Notes

A sale, a gift, an exchange or other transfer or cancellation of mortgage notes or other obligations received in an installment sale has tax consequences. If you sell or exchange the notes or if you accept less than face value in satisfaction of the obligation, gain or loss results to the extent of the difference between the basis of the notes and the amount realized. For example, if in satisfaction of an installment note, the buyer gives you other property worth less than the face value of the note, you have gain (or loss) to the extent your amount realized exceeds (or is less than) your *basis* in the installment note. The basis of an installment note or obligation is the face value of the note less the income that would be reported if the obligation were paid in full; *see* Example 2 below.

Gain or loss is long term if the original sale was entitled to long-term capital gain treatment. This is true even if the notes were held short term. If the original sale resulted in short-term gain or ordinary income, the sale of the notes gives short-term gain or ordinary income, regardless of the holding period of the notes.

Suppose you make an installment sale of your real estate, taking back a land contract. Later a mortgage is substituted for the unpaid balance of the land contract. The IRS has ruled that the substitution is not the same as a disposition of the unpaid installment obligations. There is no tax on the substitution.

Filing Tip

Installment Notes in Marital Transfer

A transfer of installment obligations to your spouse or a transfer to a former spouse that is incident to a divorce is treated as a tax-free exchange under the rules discussed in *6.7* unless the transfer is in trust.

EXAMPLES

1. You sell a lot for $200,000 that cost you $100,000. In the year of the sale, you received $50,000 in cash and the purchaser's notes for the remainder of the selling price, or $150,000. A year later, before the buyer makes a payment on the notes, you sell them for $130,000 cash:

Selling price of property	$200,000
Cost of property	100,000
Total profit	$100,000
Profit percentage, or proportion of each payment returnable as income, is 50% ($100,000 total profit ÷ $200,000 contract price)	
Unpaid balance of notes	$150,000
Amount of income reportable if notes were paid in full (50% of $150,000)	75,000
Adjusted basis of the notes	$75,000

Your profit on the sale is $55,000 ($130,000 – $75,000). It is capital gain if the sale of the lot was taxable as capital gain.

2. You sell a lot on the installment basis for $200,000 that cost you $120,000. In the year of sale, you received $20,000 in cash and the buyer's note for $180,000. Your gross profit percentage is 40% ($80,000 total profit ÷ $200,000 contract price).

Two years later, the buyer is facing financial difficulties and is unable to make payments on the $180,000 note. In satisfaction of the installment note, the buyer agrees to give you two other parcels of real estate, each worth $50,000. By accepting less than the $180,000 face value of the note in satisfaction of the obligation, you realize an $8,000 capital loss; the difference between the amount you realize and your basis in the installment obligation is figured as follows:

Amount realized ($50,000 for each parcel)	$100,000
Face value of note	180,000
Less: Amount of income reportable if note was paid in full given 40% profit percentage (40% of $180,000 = $72,000)	72,000
Basis in installment note	$108,000

The difference between the $100,000 amount realized and $108,000 basis gives you an $8,000 loss. Assuming your profit on the original sale was long-term capital gain, the loss would be deducted as a long-term capital loss.

Gift of installment obligation. If the installment obligations are disposed of other than by sale or exchange, such as when you make a gift of the installment obligations to someone else, gain or loss is the difference between the basis of the obligations and their fair market value at the time of the disposition. If an installment obligation is *cancelled* or otherwise becomes unenforceable, the same rule for determining gain or loss applies. However, no gain or loss is recognized on a gift to a spouse; *see 6.7.*

A gift of installment obligations to a person other than a spouse or to a charitable organization is treated as a taxable disposition. Gain or loss is the difference between the basis of the obligations and their fair market value at the time of the gift. If the notes are donated to a qualified charity, you may claim a contribution deduction for the fair market value of the obligations at the time of the gift.

Transfer at death. A transfer of installment obligations at the death of the holder of the obligation is not taxed as a disposition. As the notes are paid, the estate or beneficiaries report income in the same proportion as the decedent would have, had he or she lived. A transfer of installment obligations to a revocable trust is also not taxed. However, the estate is subject to tax if the obligation is cancelled, becomes unenforceable, or is transferred to the buyer because of the death of the obligation holder.

5.29 Repossession of Personal Property Sold on Installment

When a buyer defaults and you repossess personal property, either by a voluntary surrender or a foreclosure, you may realize gain or loss. The method of calculating gain or loss is similar to the method used for disposition of installment notes; *see 5.28.* Gain or loss is the difference between the fair market value of the repossessed property and your basis for the installment obligations satisfied by the repossession. This rule is followed whether or not title has been kept by you or transferred to the buyer. The amount realized is reduced by costs incurred during the repossession. The basis of the obligation is face value less unreported profit.

If the property repossessed is bid in at a lawful public auction or judicial sale, the fair market value of the property is presumed to be the purchase or bid price, in the absence of proof to the contrary.

Gain or loss in the repossession is reported in the year of the repossession.

EXAMPLE

In December 2005, you sell furniture for $1,500—$300 down and $100 a month plus 6% interest beginning January 2006. You reported the installment sale on your 2005 tax return. The buyer defaulted after making three monthly payments. You foreclosed and repossessed the property; the fair market value was $1,400. The legal costs of foreclosure were $100. The gain on the repossession in 2006 is computed as follows:

Fair market value of property repossessed		$ 1,400
Basis of the buyer's notes at time of repossession:		
Selling price	$ 1,500	
Less: Payments made	600	
Face value of notes at repossession	$ 900	
Less: Unrealized profit (assume gross		
profit percentage of $33^1/_3$ × $900)	$ 300	
		600
Gain on repossession		$ 800
Less: Repossession costs		100
Taxable gain on repossession		$ 700

Repossession gain or loss keeps the same character as the gain or loss realized on the original sale. If the sale originally resulted in a capital gain, the repossession gain is also a capital gain.

Your basis in the repossessed property is its fair market value at the time of repossession.

Real property. Repossessions of real property are at *31.12.*

5.30 Boot in Like-Kind Exchange Payable in Installments

An exchange of like-kind property is tax free unless boot is received. "Boot" may be cash or notes. If you transfer property subject to a mortgage and the amount of the mortgage you give up exceeds the mortgage you assume on the property received, that excess is boot; *see 6.3.* Boot is taxable, and if payable in installments, the following rules apply. Contract price is reduced by the fair market value of like-kind property received. Gross profit is reduced by gain not recognized. "Payment" does not include like-kind property.

The same treatment applies to certain tax-free reorganizations that are not treated as dividends, to exchanges of certain insurance policies, exchanges of the stock of the same corporation, and exchanges of United States obligations.

Planning Reminder

Taxable Boot Received in Exchange

If you make an exchange of like-kind property and also receive cash or other property that is payable in one or more future years, you may report the gain using the installment method.

EXAMPLE

In 2006, property with an installment sale basis (basis plus selling expenses) of $400,000 is exchanged for like-kind property worth $200,000, plus installment obligations of $800,000, of which $100,000 is payable in 2007, plus interest. The balance of $700,000 plus interest will be paid in 2008. The contract price is $800,000 ($1 million selling price less $200,000 like-kind property received). The gross profit is $600,000 ($1 million less $400,000 installment sale basis). The gross profit ratio is 75% (gross profit of $600,000 ÷ contract price of $800,000). Like-kind property is not treated as a payment received in the year of sale, so no gain is reported in 2006. In 2007, gain of $75,000 will have to be reported (75% gross profit ratio × $100,000 payment), and in 2008 there will be a gain of $525,000 (75% of $700,000 payment).

5.31 "Interest" Tax on Sales Over $150,000 Plus $5 Million Debt

If deferred payments from installment sales of over $150,000 exceed $5 million, an interest charge is imposed on the tax-deferred amount. The special tax applies to sales of business or rental property (real estate or personal property) for over $150,000.

Farm property and personal-use property, such as a residence, are exempt from the tax.

How to report interest tax. The interest charge is an additional tax. The method of computing the interest tax is complicated; the rules are in Internal Revenue Code Section 453A. In general, you compute the ratio of the face amount of outstanding installment obligations in excess of $5 million to the face amount of all outstanding installment obligations. This ratio is multiplied by the year-end unrecognized gain on the obligation, the top tax rate of 35% and also by the IRS interest rate for the last month of the year.

The interest tax is reported on Line 63 of Form 1040, the line for total tax. The tax is considered personal interest, and is not deductible; *see* Chapter 15.

Dealer sale of time shares and residential lots. The above interest tax and pledging rules do not apply to installment obligations from the sale of certain time-share rights (generally time shares of up to six weeks per year) or residential lots. However, under a separate rule, the seller must pay interest on tax deferred under the installment method; *see* the instructions to Line 1 of Schedule C (Form 1040) for reporting the interest charge as an additional tax.

Worthless Securities and Bad Debt Deductions

Filing Tip

Refund Deadline for Worthless Stock

You have seven years from the due date of your return to claim a refund based on a deduction of a bad debt or worthless security.

For example, if you have held securities that you learn became worthless in 1999, you still have until April 16, 2007, to file for a refund of 1999 taxes by claiming a deduction for the worthless securities on an amended return (Form 1040X) for 1999.

5.32 Worthless Securities

As an investor (not a securities dealer), you may deduct as a capital loss on Schedule D for 2006 the cost basis of a security (stock or bond) that became totally worthless in 2006. Capital loss treatment applies unless ordinary loss treatment is available for worthless Section 1244 stock; *see 30.13.*

A loss of worthless securities is deductible only in the year the securities become completely worthless. The loss may not be deducted in any other year. You may not claim a loss for a partially worthless security. However, if there is a market for it, sell the security and deduct the capital loss on Schedule D.

Because it is sometimes difficult to determine the year in which a security becomes completely worthless, the law allows you to file a refund claim within seven years from the due date of the return for the proper year (the year the security actually became completely worthless), or if later, within two years from the date you paid the tax for that year.

To support a deduction for 2006, you must show:

1. The security had some value in 2005. That is, you must be ready to show that the stock did not become worthless in a year prior to 2006. If you learn that the security did become worthless in a prior year, file an amended return for that year; *see* the Filing Tip on this page.
2. The security became totally worthless in 2006. You must be able to present facts fixing the time of loss during this year. For example, the company went bankrupt, stopped doing business, and is insolvent. Despite evidence of worthlessness, such as insolvency, the stock may be considered to have some value if the company continues to do business, or there are plans to reorganize the company. No deduction may be claimed for a partially worthless corporate bond.

If you are making payments on a negotiable note you used to buy the stock that became worthless and you are on the cash-basis method, your payments are deductible losses in the years the payments are made, rather than in the year the stock became worthless.

If the security is a bond, note, certificate, or other evidence of a debt incurred by a corporation, the loss is deducted as a capital loss, provided the obligation is in registered form or has attached interest coupons. A loss on a worthless corporate obligation is always deemed to have been sustained on the last day of the year, regardless of when the company failed during the year.

If the obligation is not issued with interest coupons or in registered form, or if it is issued by an individual, the loss is treated as a bad debt. If you received the obligation in a business transaction, the loss is fully deductible. You may also make a claim for a partially worthless business bad debt. If it is a nonbusiness debt, the loss is a capital loss and no claim may be made for partial worthlessness; *see 5.33*.

When to deduct worthless stock. If at the end of 2006 a company is in financial trouble but you are not sure whether its condition is hopeless, it is advisable to claim the deduction for 2006 to protect your claim. This advice was given by a court: "The taxpayer is at times in a very difficult position in determining in what year to claim a loss. The only safe practice, we think, is to claim a loss for the earliest year when it may possibly be allowed and to renew the claim in subsequent years if there is a reasonable chance of its being applicable for those years."

If you claim the deduction for 2006 and it turns out that complete worthlessness did not occur until a later year, claim the deduction for the proper year and then file an amended return for 2006 to eliminate the deduction.

Reporting long-term or short-term loss on Schedule D. If securities became worthless during 2006, they are treated as if they were sold on the last day of the year, regardless of when worthlessness actually occurred.

EXAMPLE

You bought 100 shares of Z Co. stock on July 1, 1999. On March 20, 2006, the stock is considered wholly worthless. The loss is deemed to have been incurred on December 31, 2006. The loss is deducted as a long-term capital loss; the holding period is from July 2, 1999, to December 31, 2006.

Ordinary loss on Small Business Investment Company (SBIC) stock. On Form 4797, investors may take ordinary loss deductions for losses on the worthlessness or sale of SBIC stock. The loss may also be treated as a business loss for net operating loss purposes. However, a loss realized on a short sale of SBIC stock is deductible as a capital loss. A Small Business Investment Company is a company authorized to provide small businesses with equity capital. Do not confuse investments in these companies with investments in small business stock (Section 1244 stock) discussed at Chapter 30.

S corporation stock. If an S corporation's stock becomes worthless during the taxable year, the basis in the stock is adjusted for the stockholder's share of corporate items of income, loss, and deductions before a deduction for worthlessness is claimed.

Bank deposit loss. If you lose funds in a bank that becomes insolvent, you may claim the loss as a nonbusiness bad debt *(5.33)*, a casualty loss *(18.4)*, or in some cases, an investment expense *(19.15)*.

Planning Reminder

Selling Before the Security Becomes Worthless

To claim a deduction for worthless stock or bonds, you must be able to prove that the stock became completely worthless in the year for which you are claiming the deduction. Sometimes you can avoid the problem of proving worthlessness by selling while there is still a market for the security. For example, a company is on the verge of bankruptcy, but in 2007 there is some doubt about the complete worthlessness of its securities. You might sell the securities for whatever you can get for them and claim the loss on the sale. However, if the security became worthless in a prior year, say in 2006, a sale for a nominal sum in 2007 will not give you a deduction in 2007.

5.33 Tax Consequences of Bad Debts

When you lend money or sell on credit and your debtor does not repay, you may deduct your loss. The type of deduction depends on whether the debt was incurred in a business or personal transaction. This distinction is important because business bad debts receive favored tax treatment.

Business bad debt. A business bad debt is fully deductible from gross income on Schedule C if you are self-employed, or on Schedule F if your business is farming. You may deduct partially worthless business debts; *see* IRS Publication 535 for details.

Nonbusiness bad debt. A nonbusiness bad debt is deducted as a short-term capital loss on Schedule D. This is a limited deduction. In 2006, you deduct it from capital gains, if any, and $3,000 of ordinary income. Any excess is deductible as a capital loss carryover to 2007 and later years; *see 5.4*. You may not deduct partially worthless nonbusiness bad debts. The debt must be totally worthless.

Caution

Accounts and Notes Receivable

You may claim a bad debt deduction for accounts and notes receivable on unpaid goods or services only if you have included the amount due as gross income. Thus, if a client or customer fails to pay a bill for services rendered, you do not have a deductible bad debt where you have not reported the amount as income; *see 40.6*.

Examples of nonbusiness bad debts:

- You enter into a deal for profit that is not connected with your business; for example, debts arising from investments are nonbusiness bad debts.
- You make a personal loan to a family member or friend with a reasonable hope of recovery and are not in the business of making loans.
- You are assigned a debt that arose in the assignor's business. The fact that he or she could have deducted it as a business bad debt does not make it your business debt. A business debt must arise in your business.
- You pay liens filed against your property by mechanics or suppliers who have not been paid by your builder or contractor. Your payment is considered a deductible bad debt when there is no possibility of recovering reimbursement from the contractor and a judgment obtained against him or her is uncollectible.
- You lose a deposit on a house when the contractor becomes insolvent.
- You loan money to a corporation in which you are a shareholder, and your primary motivation is to protect your investment rather than your job; *see* below.
- You had an uninsured savings account in a savings association that went into default; *see 18.5*.
- You are held secondarily liable on a mortgage debt assumed but not paid by a buyer of your home. Your payment to the bank or other holder of the mortgage is deductible as a bad debt if you cannot collect it from the buyer of the home.

Guarantor or endorsement losses as bad debts. If you guarantee a loan and must pay it off after the principal debtor defaults, your payment is deductible as a business bad debt if you had a business reason for the guarantee. For example, to protect a business relationship with a major client, you guarantee the client's loan. Your payment on the guarantee qualifies as a business bad debt. If, as a result of your payment, you have a legal right to recover the amount from the client (right of subrogation or similar right), you may not claim a bad debt deduction unless that right is partially or totally worthless.

A loss on a guarantee may be a nonbusiness bad debt if you made the guarantee to protect an investment, such as where you are a main shareholder of a corporation and guarantee a bank loan to the company. No deduction is allowed if you guaranteed the loan as a favor to a relative or friend. Bank deposit losses are discussed in *18.5*.

Loans by shareholders. It is a common practice for stockholders to make loans to their corporations or to guarantee loans made to the company by banks or other lenders. If the corporation fails and the stockholder is not repaid or has to make good on the guarantee, tax treatment of the bad debt depends on whether the stockholder is an employee who made the loan to protect his or her job. If the dominant motivation for the loan was to maintain employment, the bad debt is an employee business expense deductible only as a miscellaneous itemized deduction subject to the 2% of adjusted gross income floor; *see 19.1*. If the dominant motivation for the loan was to protect the stockholder's investment in the company and not his or her job, the bad debt is generally a nonbusiness bad debt deductible on Schedule D as a short-term capital loss.

If the stockholder is in the business of lending money and the loan was made in that capacity, the bad debt would be a business bad debt, deductible on Schedule C by a sole proprietor.

Filing Instruction

Nonbusiness Bad Debt

If a nonbusiness bad debt became totally worthless in 2006, claim it as a short-term capital loss in Part I of Schedule D. Attach a statement describing the loan, your relationship to the debtor, how you tried to collect it, and why you decided it was worthless.

5.34 Four Rules To Prove a Bad Debt Deduction

To determine whether you have a bad debt deduction in 2005, read the four rules explained below. Pay close attention to the fourth rule, which requires proof that the debt became worthless in the year the deduction is claimed. Your belief that your debt is bad, or the mere refusal of the debtor to pay, is not sufficient evidence. There must be an event, such as the debtor's bankruptcy, to fix the debt as worthless.

Rule 1. You must have a valid debt. You have no loss if your right to repayment is not fixed or depends upon some event that may not happen. Thus, advances to a corporation already insolvent are not valid debts. Nor are advances that are to be repaid only if the corporation has a profit. Voluntary payment of another's debt is also nondeductible. If usurious interest was charged on a worthless debt, and under state law the debt was void or voidable, the debt is not deductible as a bad debt. However, where the lender was in the business of lending money, a court allowed him to deduct the unpaid amounts as business losses.

If advances are made to a company that has lost outside borrowing sources and is thinly capitalized, with heavy debt-to-equity ratio, this indicates that the advances are actually capital contributions and not loans.

Rule 2. A debtor-creditor relationship must exist at the time the debt arose. You have a loss if there was a promise to repay at the time the debt was created and you had the right to enforce it. If the advance was a gift and you did not expect to be repaid, you may not take a deduction. Loans to members of your family, to a controlled corporation, or to a trust may be treated as gifts or contributions to capital.

Rule 3. The funds providing the loan or credit were previously reported as income or part of your capital. If you are on the cash basis, you may not deduct unpaid salary, rent, or fees. On the cash basis, you do not include these items in income until you are paid.

Rule 4. You must show that the debt became worthless during 2006. To prove the debt became worthless in 2006 , you must show:

First, that the debt had some value at the end of the previous year (2005), and that there was a reasonable hope and expectation of recovering something on the debt. Your personal belief unsupported by other facts is not enough.

Second, that an identifiable event occurred in 2006—such as a bankruptcy proceeding—that caused you to conclude the debt was worthless. In the case of a business debt that has become partially worthless, you need evidence that the debt has declined in value. Additionally, reasonable collection steps must have been undertaken. That you cancel a debt does not make it worthless. You must still show that the debt was worthless when you cancelled it. You do not have to go to court to try to collect the debt if you can show that a court judgment would be uncollectible.

Third, that there is no reasonable hope the debt may have some value in a later year. You are not required to prove that there is no possibility of ever receiving some payment on your debt.

Effect of statute of limitations. A debt is not deductible merely because a statute of limitations has run against the debt. Although the debtor has a legal defense against your demand for payment, he or she may still recognize the obligation to pay. A debt is deductible only in the year it becomes worthless. This event—for example, the debtor's insolvency—may have occurred even before the statute became effective. What if your debtor recognized his or her moral obligation to pay in spite of the expiration of the statute of limitations, but dies before paying? Your claim would be defeated if the executor raises the statute of limitations. You have a bad debt deduction in the year you made the claim against the estate.

Planning Reminder

Debt Worthless Before Due

You do not have to wait until the debt is due in order to deduct a bad debt. Claim the deduction for the year that you can prove worthlessness occurred.

5.35 Family Bad Debts

The IRS views loans to relatives, especially to children and parents, as gifts, so that it is rather difficult to deduct family bad debts.

To overcome the presumption of a gift when you advance money to a relative, take the same steps you would in making a business loan. Take a note, set a definite payment date, and require interest and collateral. If the relative fails to pay, make an attempt to collect. Failure to enforce collection of a family debt is viewed by the courts as evidence of a gift, despite the taking of notes and the receipt of interest.

Husband's default on child support—a basis for wife's deductible bad debt? A wife who supports her children when her husband defaults on court-ordered support payments may consider claiming her expenses as a nonbusiness bad debt deduction, arguing that her position is similar to a guarantor who pays a creditor when the principal debtor defaults. The IRS does not agree with the grounds of such a claim and will disallow the deduction; its position is supported by the Tax Court.

The federal appeals court for the Ninth Circuit left open the possibility that such a claim may have merit if a wife can show: (1) what she spent on the children; and (2) that her husband's obligation to support was worthless in the year the deduction is claimed.

The Tax Court has subsequently reiterated its position that defaulted child support payments are not a basis for a bad debt deduction. Following these Tax Court decisions, the IRS also announced its continuing opposition to the Ninth Circuit's suggestion that a deduction may be possible. The IRS holds that since the support obligation of the defaulting spouse is imposed directly by the divorce court, the other parent who pays support to make up for the arrearage has no "basis" to support a bad debt deduction.

Periodically, legislation has been proposed to allow a bad debt deduction for unpaid child support, but none of the proposals have been enacted into law.

Caution

Formalize Loan With Relative

To protect against a possible IRS claim that your loan was a gift and not a loan, put the loan in writing with repayment terms as if the debtor were a third party.

Chapter 6

Tax-Free Exchanges of Property

You may exchange property without incurring a tax in the year of exchange if you meet the rules detailed in this chapter. Gain may be taxed upon a later disposition of the property because the basis of the property received in the exchange is usually the same as the basis of the property surrendered in the exchange. Thus, if you exchange property with a tax basis of $10,000 for property worth $50,000, the basis of the property received in exchange is fixed at $10,000, even though its fair market value is $50,000. The gain of $40,000 ($50,000 – $10,000), which is not taxed, is technically called "unrecognized gain." If you later sell the property for $50,000, you will realize a taxable gain of $40,000 ($50,000 – $10,000).

Where property received in a tax-free exchange is held until death, the unrecognized gain escapes income tax forever because basis of the property in the hands of an heir is generally the value of the property at the date of death. If the exchange involves the transfer of boot, such as cash or other property, gain on the exchange is taxable to the extent of the value of boot.

You may not exchange U.S. real estate for foreign real estate tax free.

Tax-free exchanges between related parties may become taxable if either party disposes of the exchanged property within a two-year period.

6.1 Trades of Like-Kind Property

You may not have to pay tax on gain realized on the "like-kind" exchange of business or investment property. By making a qualifying exchange, you can defer the gain. On the other hand, a loss is not deductible unless you give up "unlike" property (not like-kind); *see* below. For tax-free gain treatment, you must trade property held for business use or investment for like-kind business or investment property. If the properties are not simultaneously exchanged, the time limits discussed in *6.4* must be satisfied. Gain is *completely* tax free only if you do not receive any "boot"; as discussed in *6.3*, gain is taxed to the extent of boot received. Where gain on a qualifying exchange is deferred and not immediately taxed, it may be taxable in a later year when you sell the property because your basis for the new property is generally the same as the basis for the property you traded; basis is discussed at *5.16 – 5.20*.

If you make a qualifying like-kind exchange with certain related parties, tax-free treatment may be lost unless both of you keep the exchanged properties for at least two years; *see 6.6*.

The term *like-kind* refers to the nature or character of the property, that is, whether real estate is traded for real estate. It does not refer to grade or quality, that is, whether the properties traded are new or used, improved or unimproved. In the case of real estate, land may be traded for a building, farm land for city lots, or a leasehold interest of 30 years or more for an outright ownership in realty. Trades of personal property are discussed at *6.2*.

EXAMPLES

1. Jones, a real estate investor, purchased Parcel A for investment in 1986 for $5,000. In 2004, he exchanged it for another parcel, Parcel B, which had a fair market value of $50,000. The gain of $45,000 was not taxed in 2004.
2. Same facts as above, except that in 2006 Jones sells Parcel B for $50,000. His taxable gain in 2006 is $45,000. The "tax-free" exchange rules have the effect of deferring tax on appreciation until the property received in the exchange is sold.
3. Same facts as in 1 above, but the value of Parcel B was $3,000 in 2004. Jones could not deduct the loss in 2004. The basis of the parcel is $5,000, the same as the basis of Parcel A. If Jones sells Parcel B in 2006 for $3,000, he may deduct a loss of $2,000.

Losses. If a loss is incurred on a like-kind exchange, the loss is not deductible, whether you receive only like-kind property or "unlike" property together with like-kind property. However, a deductible loss may be incurred if you give up unlike property as part of the exchange; the loss equals any excess of the adjusted basis of the unlike property over its fair market value.

Reporting an exchange. You must file Form 8824 to report an exchange of like-kind property. If you figure a recognized gain or loss on Form 8824, you also must report the exchange on Schedule D (investment property) or Form 4797 (business property).

See 6.6 for reporting an exchange with a related party.

Property not within the tax-free trade rules:

Property used for personal purposes (but exchanges of principal residences may qualify as tax free under different rules; *see* Chapter 29)
Foreign real estate
Property held for sale
Inventory or stock-in-trade
Securities
Notes
Partnership interest; *see* below

See also 31.3 for tax-free exchanges of realty and *6.12* for tax-free exchanges of insurance policies.

Exchange of partnership interests. Exchanges of partnership interests in different partnerships are not within the tax-free exchange rules. Under IRS regulations, tax-free exchange treatment is denied regardless of whether the interests are in the same or different partnerships.

If you made an election to exclude a partnership interest from the application of partnership rules, your interest is treated as interest in each partnership asset, not as an interest in the partnership.

Filing Instruction

Depreciation of Property Received in Exchange

If you make a like-kind exchange of depreciable MACRS property *(42.4)* for other MACRS property, your basis for the new property is the same as the basis of the traded property. You depreciate that basis over the remaining recovery period, and using the same rate and convention *(42.5)* as for the traded property.

If you also paid cash as part of the exchange, you have an additional basis attributable to that investment that is depreciable as new MACRS property subject to a new recovery period.

Caution

Exchanging Depreciable Realty Subject to Depreciation Recapture

Recapture provisions supersede tax-free exchange rules. Thus, if you exchange a depreciable building placed in service before 1987, depreciation recapture may apply, so check the consequences of any "recapture" element. For example, if you exchange the building for land, the recaptured amount is fully taxable as ordinary income; *see 44.2*.

Real estate or personal property in foreign countries. You may not make a tax-free exchange of U.S. real estate for foreign real estate. However, in the case of an involuntary conversion *(18.22)*, a tax-free reinvestment may be made in foreign real estate.

Similarly, you may not make tax-free exchanges of personal property used predominantly in the U.S. for personal property used predominantly outside the U.S.

6.2 Personal Property Held for Business or Investment

Gain on an exchange of depreciable tangible personal property held for productive business or investment use is not taxed if the properties meet either the general like-kind test at *6.1* or a more specific "like-class" test created by IRS regulations. The assumption of liabilities is treated as "boot"; *see 6.3*. Where each party assumes a liability of the other party, the respective liabilities are offset against each other to figure boot, if any.

Under the like-class test, there are two types of "like" classes: (1) General Asset Classes and (2) Product Classes. The like-class test is satisfied if the exchanged properties are both within the same General Asset Class or the same Product Class. A specific asset may be classified within only one class. Thus, if an asset is within an Asset Class, it is not within a Product Class. The Asset Class or Product Class is determined as of the date of the exchange. This limitation may disqualify an exchange when exchanged assets do not fit within the same Asset Class and are not allowed to qualify within the Product Class; *see* the Brown Example below.

Planning Reminder

The "Like-Class" Test

Gain on an exchange is not taxed if the exchanged properties are either "like kind" or "like class." The like-class test is satisfied if the exchanged properties are both within the same General Asset Class or the same Product Class; *see 6.2.* The Asset Class or Product Class is determined at the time of transfer.

General Asset Classes. There are 13 classes of depreciable tangible business property. Here are some of the asset classifications: office furniture, fixtures, and equipment (class 00.11); information systems: computers and peripheral equipment (class 00.12); data handling equipment, except computers (class 00.13); airplanes and helicopters, except for airplanes used to carry passengers or freight (class 00.21); automobiles and taxis (class 00.22); light trucks (class 00.241); heavy trucks (class 00.242); and over-the-road tractor units (class 00.26). For example, trades of trucks in class 00.241 would be of like class.

Even if exchanged properties are in different General Asset Classes (and thus are not of "like class"), they can be of like kind, so that gain on the exchange is not immediately taxed under the rules at *6.1*. For example, the IRS in a private ruling held that although an SUV and an automobile are in different asset classes, the differences between them are merely in grade or quality and do not rise to the level of a difference in nature or character. They are therefore of like kind and gain on the exchange is not taxed.

Product Classes. The IRS uses the North American Industry Classification System (NAICS) for determining product classes of depreciable tangible personal property. A product class is assigned a six-digit NAICS code.

EXAMPLES

1. Baker exchanges a personal computer used in his business for a printer. Both assets are productively used in business and are in the same General Asset Class of 00.12; the exchange meets the like-class test.
2. Brown exchanges an airplane (asset class 00.21) used in her business for a heavy truck (asset class 00.242).The exchanged properties are not of a like class. Furthermore, since each property is within a specific General Asset Class, the Product Class test may not be applied to qualify the exchange. Brown must report any gain realized on the exchange because the properties also do not meet the general like-kind test.

Intangible personal property and goodwill. Exchanges of intangible personal property (such as a patent or copyright) or nondepreciable personal property must meet the general like-kind test to qualify for tax-free treatment; the like-class tests do not apply. However, regulations close the door for qualifying exchanges of goodwill in an exchange of going businesses. According to the regulations, goodwill or going concern value of one business can never be of a like kind to goodwill or going concern value of another business.

Exchanges of multiple properties. Generally, exchanges of assets are considered on a one-to-one basis. Regulations provide an exception for exchanges of multiple properties, such as an exchange of businesses. Transferred assets are separated into exchange groups. An exchange group consists of all properties transferred and received in the exchange that are of a like kind or like class. All properties within the same General Asset Class or same Product Class are in the same exchange group. For example, automobiles and computers are exchanged for other automobiles and computers; two exchange groups are set up—one for the automobiles and the other for the computers. If the aggregate fair market values of the properties transferred and received in each exchange group are not equal, the regulations provide calculations for setting up a residual group for purposes of calculating taxable gain, if any.

All liabilities of which a taxpayer is relieved in the exchange are offset against all liabilities assumed by the taxpayer in the exchange, regardless of whether the liabilities are recourse, nonrecourse, or are secured by the specific property transferred or received. If excess liabilities are assumed by the taxpayer as part of the exchange, regulations provide rules for allocating the excess among the properties.

6.3 Receipt of Cash and Other Property—"Boot"

If, in addition to like-kind *(6.1)* property, you receive cash or other property (unlike kind), gain is taxable up to the amount of the cash and the fair market value of any *unlike* property received. The additional cash or unlike property is called "boot." If a loss was incurred on the exchange, the receipt of boot does not permit you to deduct the loss unless it is attributable to *unlike*-kind property you gave up in the exchange.

If you transfer mortgaged property, the amount of the mortgage is part of your boot. If both you and the other party transfer and receive mortgaged property, the party giving up the larger debt treats the excess as taxable boot. The party giving up the smaller debt does not have boot; *see also 31.3.* If you pay cash to the other party, add this to the mortgage you receive in figuring which party has given up the larger debt.

Form 8824. The computation of boot, gain (or loss), and basis of the property received is made on Form 8824. Form 8824 must be filed for the year in which you transfer like-kind property. If the other party to the exchange is related to you, Form 8824 must also be filed for each of the two years following your transfer; *see 6.6.*

EXAMPLE

Jones owns an apartment house with a fair market value of $220,000, subject to an $80,000 mortgage. His adjusted basis is $100,000. Jones exchanges his building for Smith's apartment building, which has a value of $250,000, subject to a $150,000 mortgage. Jones also receives $40,000 in cash. Smith's adjusted basis for the building he trades is $175,000. Smith and Jones each pay $5,000 in exchange expenses.

The sample Forms 8824 for Jones and Smith on page 138 show how they report the exchange. On Line 15, they show the boot received; their taxable gain is limited to this boot. For Jones, boot is the $40,000 in cash received. The $80,000 in liabilities transferred to Smith is not included because it does not exceed the $150,000 of liabilities Jones assumed.

For Smith, the Line 15 boot is $30,000:

Mortgage transferred	$150,000
Less: Mortgage assumed	(80,000)
Less: Cash paid	(40,000)
Boot received by Smith	$30,000

On Line 18, Jones and Smith increase their basis for the buildings they traded by exchange expenses and the net amounts paid to the other party. For Jones, the Line 18 total of $175,000 includes:

Adjusted basis of building traded		$100,000
Plus: Exchange expenses		5,000
Plus: Net mortgage assumed:		
Mortgage assumed	$150,000	
Less: Mortgage transferred	80,000	70,000
	70,000	$175,000

Caution

Deducting a Loss

You may deduct a loss incurred on an exchange if it is attributable to unlike property *transferred* in the exchange. The loss is recognized to the extent that the basis of the unlike property (other than cash) transferred exceeds its fair market value. However, a loss is not recognized if the unlike property is *received* together with the like-kind property in the exchange. Such a loss is *not* deductible.

Sample Form 8824 for Jones (see the Example on the preceding page)

Part III **Realized Gain or (Loss), Recognized Gain, and Basis of Like-Kind Property Received**

Caution: *If you transferred **and** received **(a)** more than one group of like-kind properties or **(b)** cash or other (not like-kind) property, see **Reporting of multi-asset exchanges** in the instructions.*

Note: *Complete lines 12 through 14 **only** if you gave up property that was not like-kind. Otherwise, go to line 15.*

Line	Description			Line	Amount
12	Fair market value (FMV) of other property given up	12			
13	Adjusted basis of other property given up	13			
14	Gain or (loss) recognized on other property given up. Subtract line 13 from line 12. Report the gain or (loss) in the same manner as if the exchange had been a sale. **Caution:** *If the property given up was used previously or partly as a home, see **Property used as home** in the instructions.*			14	
15	Cash received, FMV of other property received, plus net liabilities assumed by other party, reduced (but not below zero) by any exchange expenses you incurred (see instructions)			15	40,000
16	FMV of like-kind property you received			16	250,000
17	Add lines 15 and 16			17	290,000
18	Adjusted basis of like-kind property you gave up, net amounts paid to other party, plus any exchange expenses **not** used on line 15 (see instructions)			18	175,000
19	**Realized gain or (loss).** Subtract line 18 from line 17			19	115,000
20	Enter the smaller of line 15 or line 19, but not less than zero			20	40,000
21	Ordinary income under recapture rules. Enter here and on Form 4797, line 16 (see instructions)			21	-0-
22	Subtract line 21 from line 20. If zero or less, enter -0-. If more than zero, enter here and on Schedule D or Form 4797, unless the installment method applies (see instructions)			22	40,000
23	**Recognized gain.** Add lines 21 and 22			23	40,000
24	Deferred gain or (loss). Subtract line 23 from line 19. If a related party exchange, see instructions			24	75,000
25	**Basis of like-kind property received.** Subtract line 15 from the sum of lines 18 and 23			25	175,000

Form **8824** (2006)

Sample Form 8824 for Smith (see the Example on the preceding page)

Part III **Realized Gain or (Loss), Recognized Gain, and Basis of Like-Kind Property Received**

Caution: *If you transferred **and** received **(a)** more than one group of like-kind properties or **(b)** cash or other (not like-kind) property, see **Reporting of multi-asset exchanges** in the instructions.*

Note: *Complete lines 12 through 14 **only** if you gave up property that was not like-kind. Otherwise, go to line 15.*

Line	Description			Line	Amount
12	Fair market value (FMV) of other property given up	12			
13	Adjusted basis of other property given up	13			
14	Gain or (loss) recognized on other property given up. Subtract line 13 from line 12. Report the gain or (loss) in the same manner as if the exchange had been a sale. **Caution:** *If the property given up was used previously or partly as a home, see **Property used as home** in the instructions.*			14	
15	Cash received, FMV of other property received, plus net liabilities assumed by other party, reduced (but not below zero) by any exchange expenses you incurred (see instructions)			15	30,000
16	FMV of like-kind property you received			16	220,000
17	Add lines 15 and 16			17	250,000
18	Adjusted basis of like-kind property you gave up, net amounts paid to other party, plus any exchange expenses **not** used on line 15 (see instructions)			18	180,000
19	**Realized gain or (loss).** Subtract line 18 from line 17			19	70,000
20	Enter the smaller of line 15 or line 19, but not less than zero			20	30,000
21	Ordinary income under recapture rules. Enter here and on Form 4797, line 16 (see instructions)			21	-0-
22	Subtract line 21 from line 20. If zero or less, enter -0-. If more than zero, enter here and on Schedule D or Form 4797, unless the installment method applies (see instructions)			22	30,000
23	**Recognized gain.** Add lines 21 and 22			23	30,000
24	Deferred gain or (loss). Subtract line 23 from line 19. If a related party exchange, see instructions			24	40,000
25	**Basis of like-kind property received.** Subtract line 15 from the sum of lines 18 and 23			25	180,000

Form **8824** (2006)

For Smith, the Line 18 total of $180,000 includes:

Adjusted basis of building traded		$175,000
Plus: Exchange expenses		5,000
Plus: Net amount paid:		
Mortgage assumed	$80,000	
Plus: Cash paid	40,000	
Less: Mortgage transferred	(150,000)	0
	(30,000)	$180,000

The liabilities Smith assumed and the cash he paid are not included on Line 18 because their total does not exceed the $150,000 of liabilities he transferred to Jones.

Line 25 shows the basis of the buildings Jones and Smith received in the exchange.

6.4 Time Limits for Deferred Exchanges

Assume you own property that has appreciated in value. You want to sell it and reinvest the proceeds in other property, but you would like to avoid having to pay tax on the appreciation. You can defer the tax on the gain if you are able to arrange an exchange for like-kind *(6.1)* property.

The problem is that it may be difficult to find a buyer who has property you want in exchange, and the time for closing the exchange is restricted. If IRS tests are met, intermediaries and security arrangements may be used without running afoul of constructive receipt rules that could trigger an immediate tax.

Caution

Strict Time Limits

No extensions of time are allowed if the 45-day or 180-day statutory deadline for a deferred exchange cannot be met. If extra time is needed for finding suitable replacement property, it is advisable to delay the date of your property transfer because the transfer date starts the 45-day identification period.

Deferred exchange distinguished from a reverse exchange. A *deferred* exchange is one in which you first transfer investment or business property and then later receive like-kind investment or business property *(6.1)*. If before you receive the replacement property you actually or constructively receive money or unlike property as full payment for the property you have transferred, the transaction will be treated as a sale rather than a deferred exchange. In that case, you must recognize gain (or loss) on the transaction even if you later receive like-kind replacement property. In determining whether you have received money or unlike property, you may take advantage of certain safe harbor security arrangements that allow you to ensure that the replacement property will be provided to you without jeopardizing like-kind exchange treatment; *see* below for the safe harbor security tests.

A *reverse* exchange is one in which you acquire replacement property before you transfer the relinquished property. The like-kind exchange rules generally do not apply to reverse exchanges. However, the IRS has provided safe harbor rules that allow like-kind exchange treatment to be obtained if either the replacement property or the relinquished property is held in a *qualified exchange accommodation arrangement (QEAA)*; *see 6.5* for the QEAA tests.

Time limits for completing deferred exchanges. You generally have up to 180 days to complete an exchange, but the period may be shorter. Specifically, property will not be treated as like-kind property if received (1) more than 180 days after the date you transferred the property you are relinquishing or (2) after the due date of your return (including extensions) for the year in which you made the transfer, whichever is earlier. Furthermore, the property to be received must be identified within 45 days after the date on which you transferred property.

If the transaction involves more than one property, the 45-day identification period and the 180-day exchange period are determined by the earliest date on which any property is transferred. When the identification or exchange period ends on a Saturday, Sunday, or legal holiday, the deadline is not advanced to the next business day (as it is when the deadline for filing a tax return is on a weekend or holiday).

How to identify replacement property. You must identify replacement property in a written document signed by you and either hand delivered, mailed, telecopied, or otherwise sent before the end of the 45-day identification period to a person involved in the exchange other than yourself or a related party. The identification may also be made in a written agreement. The property must be unambiguously described by a legal description or street address.

You may identify more than one property as replacement property. However, the maximum number of replacement properties that you may identify without regard to the fair market value is three properties. You may identify any number of properties provided the aggregate fair market value at the end of the 45-day identification period does not exceed 200% of the aggregate fair market value of all the relinquished properties as of the date you transferred them. If, as of the end of the identification period, you have identified more than the allowable number of properties, you are generally treated as if no replacement property has been identified.

If property is valued at no more than 15% of the total value of a larger item of property that it is transferred with, the smaller property is considered "incidental" and does not have to be separately identified.

Receipt of security. In a deferred exchange, you want financial security for the buyer's performance and compensation for delay in receiving property. To avoid immediate tax, you must not make a security arrangement that gives you an unrestricted right to funds before the deal is closed.

EXAMPLE

You and Jones agree to enter a deferred exchange under the following terms and conditions. On May 12, 2006, you transfer to Jones real estate that has been held for investment; it is unencumbered and has a fair market value of $100,000. On or before June 26, 2006 (the end of the 45-day identification period), you must identify like-kind replacement property. On or before November 8, 2005 (the end of the 180-day exchange period), Jones is required to buy the property and transfer it to you. At any time after May 12, 2006, and before Jones has purchased the replacement property, you have the right, upon notice, to demand that he pay you $100,000 instead of acquiring and transferring the replacement property. However, you identify replacement property, and Jones purchases and transfers it to you. According to the regulations, you have an unrestricted right to demand the payment of $100,000 as of May 12, 2006. You are therefore in constructive receipt of $100,000 on that date. Thus, the transaction is treated as a taxable sale, and the transfer of the real property does not qualify as a tax-free exchange. You are treated as if you received the $100,000 for the sale of your property and then purchased replacement property.

Caution

Proposed Regulations Would Tax Escrow Earnings to Exchanging Taxpayer

Small qualified intermediary companies as well as members of Confress have asked the IRS to withdraw controversial proposed regulations that would require a taxpayer who has relinquished property to report as income *all* of the interest earned on an escrow account holding the proceeds from the sale of that property during the exchange period. Intermediary companies have typically retained some of the interest to supplement the flat fees they charge and they claim that the proposals would force them to raise their fees, putting them at a severe competitive disadvantage to banks that serve as intermediaries. Bank intermediaries can lend out the escrow funds at a higher interest rate than that paid to the taxpayers making exchanges and this internal spread would allow the banks to keep their fees lower than the fees non-bank intermediaries would have to charge were the proposals to take effect.

See the *e-Supplement* for an update on the proposed regulations.

Safe harbor tests for deferred exchange security arrangements. If one of the following safe harbors applies to your security arrangement, you are not taxed as if a sale were made and like-kind exchange treatment may be obtained.

The first two "safe harbors" cover transfers dealing directly with the buyer. The third allows the use of professional intermediaries who, for a fee, arrange the details of the deferred exchange. The fourth allows you to earn interest on an escrow account. The safe harbors generally prohibit you from receiving money or other non-like-kind property before replacement property is received. The terms of the agreement govern whether your right to receive the funds is limited as required by the safe harbor rules; possible state law complications are disregarded.

1. The transferee may give you a mortgage, deed of trust, or other security interest in property (other than cash or a cash equivalent), or a third-party guarantee. A standby letter of credit may be given if you are not allowed to draw on such standby letter except upon a default of the transferee's obligation to transfer like-kind replacement property.
2. The transferee may put cash or a cash equivalent in a qualified escrow account or a qualified trust. The escrow holder or trustee must not be related to you. Your rights to receive, pledge, borrow, or otherwise obtain the cash must be limited. For example, you may obtain the cash after all of the replacement property to which you are entitled is received. After you identify replacement property, you may obtain the cash after the later of (1) the end of the identification period and (2) the occurrence of a contingency beyond your control that you have specified in writing. You may receive the funds after the end of the identification period if within that period you do not identify replacement property. In other cases, there can be no right to the funds until the exchange period ends.
3. You may use a *qualified intermediary* if your right to receive money or other property is limited (as discussed in safe harbor rule 2, above). A qualified intermediary is an unrelated party who, for a fee, acts to facilitate a deferred exchange by entering into an agreement with you for the exchange of properties pursuant to which the intermediary acquires your property from you, acquires the replacement property, and transfers the replacement property to you. The acquisitions may be on the intermediary's own behalf or as the agent of any party to the transaction.

   The transfer of property that is facilitated by the use of a qualified intermediary may occur through a "direct deed" of legal title by the current owner of the property to you. The transferee of your property does *not* have to receive title to the property you want and then transfer it to you.

There are restrictions on who may act as an intermediary. You may not employ any person as an intermediary who is your employee or is related to you or your agent or has generally acted as your professional adviser, such as an attorney, accountant, investment broker, real estate agent, or banker, in a two-year period preceding the exchange. Related parties include family members and controlled businesses or trusts *(see 5.6)*, except that for purposes of control, a 10% interest is sufficient under the intermediary rule. The performance of routine financial, escrow, trust, or title insurance services by a financial institution or title company within the two-year period is not taken into account. State laws that may be interpreted as fixing an agency relationship between the transferor and transferee or fixing the transferor's right to security funds are ignored.

In a simultaneous exchange, the intermediary is not considered the transferor's agent.

4. You are permitted to receive interest or a "growth factor" on escrowed funds if your right to receive the amount is limited as discussed under safe harbor rule 2.

Payment of acquisition and closing costs. The use of funds from a security account to pay specific acquisition and closing costs such as commissions, prorated taxes, and recording and transfer fees will not result in constructive receipt of the remaining funds.

6.5 Qualified Exchange Accommodation Arrangements (QEAAs) for Reverse Exchanges

The like-kind exchange rules *(6.1)* generally do not apply to a so-called reverse exchange in which you acquire replacement property *before* you transfer relinquished property. However, if you use a qualified exchange accommodation arrangement (QEAA), the transfer may qualify as a like-kind exchange.

Under a QEAA, either the replacement property or the relinquished property is transferred to an exchange accommodation titleholder (EAT) who is treated as the beneficial owner of the property for federal income tax purposes. If the property is held in a QEAA, the IRS will accept the qualification of property as either replacement property or relinquished property, and the treatment of an EAT as the beneficial owner of the property for federal income tax purposes.

The QEAA rules allow taxpayers to structure "parking transactions" in which the replacement property is acquired by the EAT before the transfer of the relinquished property. However, the QEAA safe harbor does *not* apply if the taxpayer transfers property to an EAT and receives that same property back as replacement property for other property of the taxpayer. This limitation applies to transfers after July 19, 2004.

Caution

Parking Transactions

Property transferred to an exchange accommodation titleholder by a taxpayer cannot be transferred back to the taxpayer as replacement property under the QEAA rules. *See* Revenue Procedure 2004-51 for details.

The IRS has set numerous technical requirements for QEAAs. Property is held in a QEAA only if you have a written agreement with the EAT, the time limits for identifying and transferring the property are met, and the qualified indicia of ownership of property are transferred to the EAT.

The EAT must meet all the following requirements: (1) Hold qualified indicia of ownership (*see* below) at all times from the date of acquisition of the property until the property is transferred within the 180-day period (*see* below); (2) be someone other than you, your agent, or a person related to you or your agent; (3) be subject to federal income tax. If the EAT is treated as a partnership or S corporation, more than 90% of its interests or stock must be owned by partners or shareholders who are subject to federal income tax.

The IRS defines qualified indicia of ownership as either legal title to the property, other indicia of ownership of the property that are treated as beneficial ownership of the property under principles of commercial law (for example, a contract for deed), or interests in an entity that is disregarded as an entity separate from its owner for federal income tax purposes (for example, a single member limited liability company) and that holds either legal title to the property or other indicia of ownership.

There are time limits for identifying and transferring property under a QEAA. No later than 45 days after the transfer of qualified indicia of ownership of the replacement property to the EAT, you must identify the relinquished property in a manner consistent with the principles for deferred exchanges discussed at *6.4*. If qualified indicia of ownership in replacement property have been transferred to the EAT, then no later than 180 days after that transfer, the replacement property must be transferred to you either directly or indirectly through a qualified intermediary, defined earlier in *6.4*. If the EAT receives qualified indicia of ownership in the relinquished property, then no later than 180 days after that transfer, the relinquished property must be transferred to a person other than you, your agent at the time of the transaction, or a person who is related to you or your agent.

Note: For further details on the IRS's guidelines for QEAAs, *see IRS Publication 544 and* Revenue Procedure 2000-37, as modified by Revenue Procedure 2004-51 (parking transactions).

6.6 Exchanges Between Related Parties

Tax-free treatment of like-kind exchanges between related persons may be lost if either party disposes of property received in the exchange within two years after the date of the last transfer that was part of the exchange. Any gain not recognized on the original exchange is taxable as of the date of the later disposition of the original like-kind property by either party within the two-year period. If a loss was not recognized, the loss becomes deductible if allowed under the rules in *5.6*.

Indirect dispositions of the property within the two-year period, such as transfer of stock of a corporation or interests in a partnership that owns the property, may also be treated as taxable dispositions.

Related parties. Related persons falling within the two-year rule include your children, grandchildren, parent, brother, or sister, controlled corporations or partnerships (more than 50% ownership), and a trust in which you are a beneficiary. A transfer to a spouse is not subject to the two-year rule unless he or she is a nonresident alien.

Plan to avoid two-year rule. If you set up a prearranged plan under which you first transfer property to an unrelated party who within two years makes an exchange with a party related to you, the related party will not qualify for tax-free treatment on that exchange.

Exceptions. No tax will be incurred on a disposition made because of death; in an involuntary conversion provided the original exchange occurred before the threat of the conversion; or if you can prove that neither the exchange nor the later disposition was for a tax avoidance purpose.

Filing Instruction

Filing Form 8824

The IRS requires related parties who exchange property to file Form 8824 for the year of the exchange and also for the two years following the exchange. If either party disposes of the property received in the original exchange in any of these years, the deferred gain must be reported in the year of disposition as if the property had been sold.

The two-year period is suspended for a holder of exchanged property who has substantially diminished his or her risk of loss, such as by use of a put or short sale.

6.7 Property Transfers Between Spouses and Ex-Spouses

Under Section 1041, all transfers of property between spouses are treated as tax-free exchanges, *other* than transfers to a nonresident alien spouse, certain trust transfers of mortgaged property, and transfers of U.S. Savings Bonds; these exceptions are discussed below. Section 1041 applies to transfers during marriage as well as to property settlements incident to a divorce. In a Section 1041 transfer, there is no taxable gain or deductible loss to the transferor spouse. The transferee-spouse takes the transferor's basis in the property, and so appreciation in value will be taxed to the recipient on a later sale. These rules apply to all property received after July 18, 1984, under divorce or separation instruments in effect after that date.

A transfer is "incident to a divorce" if it occurs either within one year after the date the marriage ceases or, if later, is related to the cessation of the marriage, such as a transfer authorized by a divorce decree. Under temporary regulations, any transfer pursuant to a divorce or separation agreement occurring within six years of the end of the marriage is considered "incident to a divorce." Later transfers qualify only if a transfer within the six-year period was hampered by legal or business disputes such as a fight over the property value.

Planning Reminder

Recipient Spouse Bears Tax Consequences of Transferred Property

Under the tax-free exchange rules, there is no taxable gain or deductible loss on the transfer of property, even if cash is received for the property or the other spouse (or former spouse) assumes liabilities or gives up marital rights as part of a property settlement. The spouse who receives property may incur tax on a later sale because his or her basis in the property is the same as the transferor-spouse's basis; *see* the Examples in *6.7*. Because the transferee bears the tax consequences of a later sale, he or she should consider the potential tax on the appreciation in negotiating a marital settlement. In a marital settlement, the transferee spouse can lessen the tax burden by negotiating for assets that have little or no unrealized appreciation.

EXAMPLES

1. In a property settlement accompanying a divorce, a husband plans to transfer to his wife stock worth $250,000 that cost him $50,000. In deciding whether to agree to the transfer, the wife should be aware that her basis for the stock will be $50,000; if she sells the stock, she will have to pay tax on the $200,000 gain. This tax cost should be accounted for in arriving at the settlement.
2. Basis of the property in the hands of the transferee-spouse is not increased even if cash is paid as part of the transfer. For example, a husband received a house originally owned by the wife as part of a marital settlement. Her basis for the house was $32,200. He paid her $18,000 cash as part of the settlement and when he later sold the house for $64,000, he argued that his basis for purposes of computing profit was $50,200—the wife's $32,200 basis plus his $18,000 cash payment. The IRS refused to consider the cash payment as part of basis, and the Tax Court agreed that the carryover basis rule applies.

Nonresident alien. The tax-free exchange rule does not apply to transfers to a nonresident alien spouse or former spouse.

Transfers of U.S. Savings Bonds. The IRS has ruled that the tax-free exchange rules do not apply to transfers of U.S. Savings Bonds. For example, if a husband has deferred the reporting of interest on E or EE bonds and transfers the bonds to his ex-wife as part of a divorce settlement, the deferred interest is taxed to him on the transfer. The wife's basis for the bonds is the husband's basis plus the income he realizes on the transfer. When she redeems the bonds, she will be taxed on the interest accrued from the date of the transfer to the redemption date.

Payment for release of community property interest in retirement pay. The Tax Court allowed tax-free treatment for a payment made to a wife for releasing her community property claim to her husband's military retirement pay. The IRS had argued that the tax-free exchange rules discussed in this section did not apply to the release of rights to retirement pay that would otherwise be subject to ordinary income tax. The Tax Court disagreed, holding that the tax-free exchange rule applies whether the transfer is for relinquishment of marital rights, cash, or other property.

Transfers in trust. The tax-free exchange rules generally apply to transfers in trust for the benefit of a spouse or a former spouse if incident to a divorce. However, gain cannot be avoided on a trust transfer of heavily mortgaged property. If the trust property is mortgaged, the transferor spouse must report a taxable gain to the extent that the liabilities assumed by the transferee spouse plus the liabilities to which the property is subject (even if not assumed) exceed the transferor's adjusted basis for the property. If the transferor realizes a taxable gain under this rule, the transferee's basis for the property is increased by the gain.

Sole proprietorship sale to spouse. Tax-free exchange rules may apply to a sale of business property by a sole proprietor to a spouse. The buyer spouse assumes a carryover basis even if fair market value is paid. The transferor is not required to recapture previously claimed depreciation deductions or investment credits. However, the transferee is subject to the recapture rules on premature dispositions or if the property ceases to be used for business purposes.

Transfer of nonqualified options or nonqualified deferred compensation. According to the IRS, if a vested interest in nonqualified stock options or nonqualified deferred compensation is transferred to a former spouse as part of a property settlement, the transferor-spouse (the employee) does not have to report any income; the Section 1041 tax-free exchange rules apply. When the transferee-spouse later exercises the options or receives the deferred compensation, he or she will be taxed on the option spread *(2.17)* or the deferred compensation as if he or she was the employee. Income tax withholding and FICA tax withholding (Social Security and Medicare taxes) is generally required from the payments made to the transferee-spouse. Under an exception, if the parties to the divorce specifically provided in an agreement or court order before November 9, 2002, that the transferor will be taxed on the income attributable to the transferred interest, the IRS will recognize that provision. Section 1041 will not apply and the transferor rather than the transferee will be taxed. *See* Revenue Ruling 2004-60 for further details.

Divorce-related redemptions of stock in closely held corporation. When a married couple own all (or most) of the stock in a closely held corporation, the corporation may redeem the stock of one of the spouses as part of an overall divorce settlement. Does the transferring spouse avoid tax on the redemption under the Section 1041 tax-free exchange rules?

If the redemption of one of the spouses' stock is treated as a transfer to a third party *on behalf of* the other spouse, Section 1041 applies and the transferor-spouse would escape tax on the redemption. However, there has been much confusion and litigation as to the standards for determining whether a redemption is "on behalf of" the non-transferor spouse, and whether different tests should apply for determining the tax treatment of each spouse. Court decisions have generally supported tax-free treatment for a spouse whose stock is redeemed under the terms of the couple's divorce or separation instrument, or where the other (non-transferring) spouse requests or consents to the redemption. However, the courts are divided on the issue of whether the non-transferor spouse, who is left in control of the corporation, has realized a constructive dividend as a result of the redemption. *See* Example 2 below for the disputed positions taken by Tax Court judges in the *Read* case.

In response to the inconsistent standards used by the courts (*see* the Examples below), the IRS amended its regulations to provide a specific rule for determining which spouse will be taxed on the redemption. The regulation allows tax-free exchange treatment under Section 1041 to the transferor spouse (whose stock was redeemed) only if under applicable law the redemption is treated as resulting in a constructive dividend to the non-transferor spouse. If constructive dividend treatment does not apply to the non-transferor spouse, the form of the redemption transaction is followed and the transferor-spouse taxed on the redemption. The IRS regulation adopts the position of some of the dissenting judges in the *Read* case; *see* Example 2 below. The spouses are allowed to provide in

Court Decision

Interest on Marital Property Settlements

Parties may agree to pay interest on property transfers relating to divorce settlements when payments are to be made over time. The actual property transfer is generally a tax-free exchange. According to the Tax Court, the interest is separate and apart from the property transferred. The deductibility of the interest paid depends on the nature of the property transferred. Interest allocated to residential property, for instance, is deductible as residential mortgage interest; interest allocated to investment property is deductible as investment interest subject to the net investment income limit. *See* Chapter 15.

a divorce or separation agreement that the redemption will be taxable to the nontransferor spouse even if the redemption would not result in a constructive dividend to that spouse under applicable law. Alternatively, they can provide that the transferor will be taxed on the redemption although the redemption would otherwise be treated as a constructive dividend to the nontransferor spouse.

Planning Reminder

Transfers to Third Parties

If you transfer property to a third party on behalf of your spouse or former spouse where the transfer is required by a divorce or separation instrument, or if you have your spouse's or former spouse's written request or consent for the transfer, the transfer is tax free to you under Section 1041. The transfer is treated as if made to your spouse or former spouse, who then retransfers the property to the third party. A written request or consent must specifically state that the tax-free exchange rules of Code Section 1041 are intended, and you must receive it before filing the tax return for the year of the transfer. As discussed in the Examples on this page, a divorce-related stock redemption may qualify for Section 1041 treatment as a transfer "on behalf of" the other spouse.

EXAMPLES

1. A federal district court and the Ninth Circuit Court of Appeals held that, under Section 1041, a wife was not taxable on the redemption of her stock by the couple's closely held corporation where the redemption was pursuant to their divorce agreement and incorporated into the divorce decree. The Ninth Circuit viewed the transfer as if the husband had received the stock directly from the wife and then transferred it to the company.

   After the Ninth Circuit held that the redemption was not taxable to the wife, the IRS argued in a separate case against the nonredeeming husband that he received a taxable constructive dividend. However, the Tax Court disagreed, holding that there was no dividend to the husband because under state law he was merely a guarantor; he was not primarily and unconditionally obligated to buy the stock. The IRS did not appeal the Tax Court decision.

   In this unusual situation, the IRS is in the position of being unable to collect tax on the redemption proceeds from either the transferor or transferee spouse.

2. After William and Carol Read divorced, William, pursuant to their divorce decree, elected to have their controlled corporation purchase all of Carol's stock. A Tax Court majority held that her transfer was on behalf of William and qualified for Section 1041 non-recognition treatment.

   The Tax Court majority also held that William realized a constructive dividend on the corporation's redemption of Carol's stock. However, the majority relied on a concession by William and did not specify a legal standard for determining whether he should be taxed. Concurring judges suggested that constructive dividend treatment for William followed automatically from the holding that Carol's stock transfer was on his behalf and thus within Section 1041. There were four dissenting opinions, all of which held that under traditional law for constructive dividends, there is no constructive dividend unless William had a "primary and unconditional obligation" to buy the shares, an obligation the corporation satisfied by making the redemption. Most of the dissenters argued that William did not have such an obligation and should not be taxed. They further argued that if William was not obligated to buy the shares, Section 1041 does not apply and thus Carol realized capital gain on the redemption of her shares. Other dissenting judges held that a spouse can never avoid taxable gain under Section 1041 on a redemption incident to divorce.

3. The Eleventh Circuit Court of Appeals allowed tax-free treatment to a redemption of a wife's stock, following the Tax Court majority in *Read* (Example 2 above). The redemption was on behalf of her ex-husband. The redemption was required by their divorce decree and it left him in control of 98% of the corporation's stock. He had guaranteed the corporation's 10-year promissory note to her, and the terms of the note specifically said that the guarantee was in his interests.

   Furthermore, although the corporation's note did not provide for interest, interest income was not imputed to the wife. Imputed interest does not apply where the underlying transfer is not taxable under Section 1041.

Basis of property received before July 19, 1984, or under instruments in effect before that date. The tax-free exchange rules do not apply to property received before July 19, 1984, from your spouse (or former spouse if the transfer was incident to divorce). Your basis for determining gain or loss when you sell such property is its fair market value when you received it. The same fair market value basis rule applies to property received after June 18, 1984, under an instrument in effect on or before that date unless a Section 1041 election was made to have the tax-free exchange rules apply. For property subject to such an election, your basis is the same as the transferor-spouse's adjusted basis.

6.8 Tax-Free Exchanges of Stock in Same Corporation

Gain on the exchange of common stock for other common stock of the same corporation is not taxable. The same rule generally applies to an exchange of preferred stock of the same corporation, but not if "nonqualified" preferred with special redemption rights or a varying dividend rate is received. Loss realized on a qualifying exchange is not deductible. The exchange may take place between the stockholder and the company or between two stockholders.

An exchange of preferred stock for common, or common for preferred, in the same company is generally not tax free, unless the exchange is part of a tax-free recapitalization. In such exchanges, the company should inform you of the tax consequences.

Convertible securities. Conversion of securities under a conversion privilege is tax free under the rules discussed at *30.7*.

6.9 Joint Ownership Interests

The change to a tenancy in common from a joint tenancy is tax free. You may convert a joint tenancy in corporate stock to a tenancy in common without income-tax consequences. The transfer is tax free even though survivorship rights are eliminated. Similarly, a partition and issuance of separate certificates in the names of each joint tenant is also tax free.

A joint tenancy and a tenancy in common differ in this respect. On the death of a joint tenant, ownership passes to the surviving joint tenant or tenants. But on the death of a tenant holding property in common, ownership passes to his or her heirs, not to the other tenant or tenants with whom the property was held.

A tenancy by the entirety is a form of joint ownership recognized in some states and can be only between a husband and wife.

Dividing properties held in common. A division of properties held as tenants in common may qualify as tax-free exchanges.

For example, three men owned three pieces of real estate as tenants in common. Each man wanted to be the sole owner of one of the pieces of property. They disentangled themselves by exchanging interests in a three-way exchange. No money or property other than the three pieces of real estate changed hands, and none of the men assumed the others' liability. The transactions qualified as tax-free exchanges and no gain or loss was recognized.

Receipt of boot. Exchanges of jointly owned property are tax free as long as no "boot," such as cash or other property, passes between the parties; *see 6.3*.

6.10 Setting up Closely Held Corporations

Tax-free exchange rules facilitate the organization of a corporation. When you transfer property to a corporation that you control solely in exchange for corporate stock, no gain or loss is recognized on the transfer. For control, you alone or together with other transferors (such as partners, where a partnership is being incorporated) must own at least 80% of the combined voting power of the corporation and 80% of all other classes of stock immediately after the transfer to the corporation. If you receive securities in addition to stock, the securities are treated as taxable "boot." The corporation takes your basis in the property, and your basis in the stock received in the exchange is the same as your basis in the property. Gain not recognized on the organization of the corporation may be taxed when you sell your stock, or the corporation disposes of the property.

Caution

Consider Taxable Transfer

Before making a property transfer to a closely held corporation, consult an accountant or an attorney on the tax consequences. There may be instances when you have potential losses or you desire the corporation to take a stepped-up basis that would make tax-free treatment undesirable.

EXAMPLE

You transfer a building worth $100,000, which cost you $20,000, to your newly organized corporation in exchange for all of its outstanding stock. You realize an $80,000 gain ($100,000 – $20,000) that is not recognized. Your basis in the stock is $20,000; the corporation's basis in the building is $20,000. The following year, you sell all your stock to a third party for $100,000. The $80,000 gain is now recognized.

Transfer of liabilities. When assets subject to liabilities are transferred to the corporation, the liability assumed by the corporation is not treated as taxable "boot," but your stock basis is reduced by the amount of liability. The transfer of liabilities may be taxable when the transfer is part of a tax avoidance scheme, or the liabilities exceed the basis of the property transferred to the corporation.

6.11 Exchanges of Coins and Bullion

An exchange of "gold for gold" coins or "silver for silver" coins may qualify as a tax-free exchange of like-kind investment property. An exchange is tax free if both coins represent the same type of underlying investment. An exchange of bullion-type coins for bullion-type coins is a tax-free like-kind exchange. For example, the exchange of Mexican pesos for Austrian coronas has been held to be a tax-free exchange as both are bullion-type coins.

However, an exchange of silver bullion for gold bullion is not tax free. Silver and gold bullion represent different types of property. Silver is an industrial commodity, whereas gold is primarily an investment in itself. Similarly, an exchange of U.S. gold collector's coins for South African Krugerrands is taxable. Krugerrands are bullion-type coins whose value is determined solely by metal content, whereas the U.S. gold coins are numismatic coins whose value depends on age, condition, number minted, and artistic merit, as well as metal content. Although both coins appear to be similar in gold content, each represents a different type of investment.

Planning Reminder

Financially Troubled Insurer

If your annuity contract or insurance policy is with an insurance company that is in a rehabilitation, conservatorship, insolvency, or a similar state proceeding, you may surrender the policy and make a tax-free reinvestment of the proceeds in a new policy with a different insurance company. The transfer must be completed within 60 days. If a government agency does not allow you to withdraw your entire balance from the troubled insurance company, you must assign all rights to any future distributions to the issuer of the new contract or policy. *See* IRS Revenue Procedure 92-44.

6.12 Tax-Free Exchanges of Insurance Policies

These exchanges of insurance policies are considered tax free:

- Life insurance policy for another life insurance policy, endowment policy, or an annuity contract.
- Endowment policy for another endowment policy that provides for regular payments beginning no later than the date payments would have started under the old policy, or in exchange for an annuity contract.
- Annuity contract for another annuity contract with identical annuitants.

These exchanges are not tax free:

- Endowment policy for a life insurance policy, or for another endowment policy that provides for payments beginning at a date later than payments would have started under the old policy.
- Annuity contract for a life insurance or endowment policy.
- Transfers of life insurance contracts where the insured is not the same person in both contracts. The IRS held that a company could not make a tax-free exchange of a key executive policy where the company could change insured executives as they leave or join the firm.

Chapter 7

Retirement and Annuity Income

For employees, coverage in a qualified employer retirement plan is a valuable fringe benefit, as employer contributions are tax free within specified limits. Certain salary-reduction plans allow you to make elective deferrals of salary that are not subject to income tax. An advantage of all qualified retirement plans is that earnings accumulate tax free until withdrawal.

Along with tax savings opportunities come technical restrictions and pitfalls. For example, retirement plan distributions eligible for rollover are subject to a mandatory 20% withholding tax if you receive the distribution rather than asking your employer to make a direct trustee-to-trustee transfer of the distribution to an IRA or another qualified employer plan.

This chapter discusses tax treatment of annuities and employer plan distributions, including how to avoid tax penalties, such as for distributions before age 59½. IRAs are discussed in Chapter 8. Retirement plans for self-employed individuals are discussed further in Chapter 41.

A tax credit is available to low-to-moderate income taxpayers who make traditional or Roth IRA contributions, electives deferrals to a 401(k) or other employer plan, and voluntary after-tax contributions to a qualified plan. The credit is discussed in Chapter 25.

Table 7-1 Key to Tax-Favored Retirement Plans

Type—	*General Tax Considerations—*	*Tax Treatment of Distributions—*
Company qualified plan	A company qualified pension or profit-sharing plan offers these benefits: (1) You do not realize current income on your employer's contributions to the plan on your behalf. (2) Income earned on funds contributed to your account compounds tax free. (3) Your employer may allow you to make voluntary after-tax contributions. Although these contributions may not be deducted, income earned on the voluntary contributions is not taxed until withdrawn.	If you were born before January 2, 1936, and receive a lump sum, tax on employer contributions and plan earnings may be reduced by a special averaging rule; *see 7.4.* If you receive a lump-sum distribution including company securities, unrealized appreciation on those securities is not taxed until you finally sell the stock; *see 7.10.* Distributions before age 59½ are generally subject to penalties, but there are exceptions; *see 7.15.* Rather than pay an immediate tax, you may elect to roll over a lump-sum payment to an IRA account; *see 7.7.* If you collect your retirement benefits as an annuity over a period of years, *see 7.27.*
Plans for self-employed	You may set up a self-employed retirement plan called a Keogh plan if you earn self-employment income through your performance of personal services. You may deduct contributions up to limits discussed in Chapter 41; income earned on assets held by the plan is not taxed. You must include employees in your Keogh under rules explained in Chapter 41. Other retirement plan options, such as a SEP or SIMPLE plan, are also discussed in Chapter 41.	You may not withdraw Keogh plan funds until age 59½ unless you are disabled or meet other exceptions at *7.15.* Qualified distributions to self-employed persons or to beneficiaries at death may qualify for favored lump-sum treatment under the rules discussed in *7.2.* Distributions from a SEP are subject to traditional IRA rules; *see 8.8.* Distributions from a SIMPLE-IRA also are subject to traditional IRA rules, but a 25% penalty (instead of 10%) applies to pre-age-59½ distributions in the first two years; *see 8.18.*
IRA and Roth IRA	Anyone who has earned income may contribute to a traditional IRA, but the contribution is deductible only if certain requirements are met. Your status as a participant in an employer retirement plan and your income determine whether you may claim a deduction up to the annual contribution limit ($4,000 for 2006, $5,000 if age 50 or older), a partial deduction, or no deduction at all. *See* Chapter 8 for these deduction limitations. Income earned on IRA accounts is not taxed until the funds are withdrawn. This tax-free buildup of earnings also applies where you make nondeductible contributions to a Roth IRA under the rules in Chapter 8.	Traditional IRA distributions are fully taxable unless you have previously made nondeductible contributions; *see 8.9.* A taxable withdrawal before age 59½ is subject to a 10% penalty, but there are exceptions if you are disabled, have substantial medical expenses, pay medical premiums while unemployed, or receive payments in a series of substantially equal installments; *see 8.12* for details on these and other exceptions. Starting at age 70½, you must receive minimum annual distributions to avoid a 50% penalty; *see 8.13.* Distributions from a Roth IRA of contributions are tax free. Distributions of earnings are taxable unless you are over age 59½ and have held the account for at least five years; *see 8.23.*
SEP	A simplified employee pension plan set up by your employer allows the employer to contribute to an IRA more than you can under regular IRA rules; *see 8.15.* Employer contributions to your account of up to 25% of your compensation (but no more than $44,000 for 2006) are not taxable to you. Elective deferrals of salary may be made to qualifying plans set up before 1997; *see 8.16.*	Withdrawals from a SEP are taxable under the rules explained above for IRAs.
Deferred salary or 401(k) plans	If your company has a profit-sharing or stock bonus plan, the tax law allows the company to add a cash or deferred pay plan that can operate in one of two ways: (1) Your employer contributes an amount for your benefit to your trust account. You are not taxed on your employer's contribution. (2) You agree to take a salary reduction or to forego a salary increase. The reduction is placed in a trust account for your benefit. The reduction is treated as your employer's contribution. S*ee 7.18.* Income earned on the trust account accumulates tax free until it is withdrawn.	Withdrawals are penalized unless you have reached age 59½, become disabled, or meet other exceptions listed at *7.15.* If you were born before January 2, 1936, and receive a qualifying lump sum, tax on the lump sum may be computed according to the rules in *7.2.*

Distributions From Qualified Retirement Plans

7.1 Retirement Distributions on Form 1099-R

On Form 1099-R, payments from pensions, annuities, IRAs, Roth IRAs, SIMPLE IRAs, insurance contracts, profit-sharing, and other employer plans are reported to you and the IRS. Social Security benefits are reported on Form SSA-1099; *see* Chapter 34 for the special rules to apply in determining the taxable portion of Social Security benefits.

Here is a guide to the information reported on Form 1099-R. A sample form is on the next page.

Box 1. The total amount received from the payer is shown here without taking any withholdings into account. If you file Form 1040, report the Box 1 total on Line 15a if the payment is from an IRA, or on Line 16a if from a pension or an annuity. However, if the amount is a qualifying lump-sum distribution for which you are claiming averaging, use Form 4972; *see 7.4*.

If you file Form 1040A, report the Box 1 total on Line 11a if from an IRA or on Line 12a if from a pension or an annuity.

If an exchange of insurance contracts was made, the value of the contract will be shown in Box 1, but if the exchange qualified as tax free, a zero taxable amount will be shown in Box 2a and Code 6 will be entered in Box 7.

Boxes 2a and 2b. The taxable portion of distributions from employer plans and insurance contracts may be shown in Box 2a. The taxable portion does not include your after-tax contributions to an employer plan or insurance premium payments.

If the payer cannot figure the taxable portion, the first box in 2b should be checked; Box 2a should be blank. You will then have to figure the taxable amount yourself. A payment from a pension or an annuity is only partially taxed if you contributed to the cost and you did not recover your entire cost investment before 2006. *See 7.23* (commercial annuity) or *7.27* (employee annuity) for details on computing the taxable portion if you have an unrecovered investment.

The payer of a traditional IRA distribution will probably not compute the taxable portion, and in this case, the total distribution from Box 1 will be entered as the taxable portion in Box 2a. This amount is fully taxable unless you have made nondeductible contributions, in which case Form 8606 is used to figure the taxable portion of the distribution; *see 8.9*. Form 8606 is also used to figure the taxable part, if any, of a Roth IRA distribution; *see 8.23*.

If the payment is from an employer plan and the "total distribution" box has been checked in 2b, *see 7.2* for possible rollover and special averaging options. The taxable amount in Box 2a should not include net unrealized appreciation (NUA; *see 7.10*) in any employer securities included in the lump sum or the value of an annuity contract included in the distribution.

Box 3. If the payment is a lump-sum distribution, you were born before January 2, 1936, and you participated in the plan before 1974, the amount shown here may be treated as capital gain; *see 7.5*.

Box 4. Any federal income tax withheld is shown here. Do not forget to include it on Line 64 of Form 1040 or Line 38 of Form 1040A. If Box 4 shows any withholdings, attach Copy B of Form 1099-R to your return.

Box 5. If you made after-tax contributions to your employer's plan, or paid premiums for a commercial annuity or insurance contract, your contribution is shown here, less any such contributions previously distributed. IRA or SEP contributions (*see* Chapter 8) are not shown here.

Box 6. If you received a qualifying lump-sum distribution that includes securities of your employer's company, the total net unrealized appreciation (NUA) is shown here. Unless you elect to pay tax on it currently *(7.10)*, this amount is not taxed until you sell the securities. If you did not receive a qualifying lump sum, the amount shown here is the net unrealized appreciation attributable to your after-tax employee contributions, which are also not taxed until you sell the securities; *see 7.10*.

Box 7. In Box 7, the payer will indicate if the distribution is from a traditional IRA, SEP, or SIMPLE and enter codes that are used by the IRS to check whether you have reported the distribution correctly, including the penalty for distributions before age 59½.

Law Alert

Tax-Favored Withdrawals for Qualified Hurricane Distributions

See 7.30 and *7.31* for the special rules applicable to qualifying retirement plan withdrawals, repayments, and loans attributable to Hurricane Katrina, Rita, or Wilma.

Filing Instruction

Conversion of Traditional IRA to Roth IRA

If in 2006 you converted a traditional IRA to a Roth IRA, the conversion amount is included in Box 1 and in Box 2a of Form 1099-R as a taxable distribution. The entire conversion amount is taxable on your 2006 return, except for any portion allocable to nondeductible contributions; *see 8.21*.

Code 2 will be entered in Box 7 if you are under age 59½ and the payer knows that you qualify for an exception to the 10% early distribution penalty *(7.15)*, such as the exception for separation of service after age 55 for an employer-plan distribution or for a distribution that is part of a series of substantially equal payments. Code 3 will be used if the disability exception applies. Code 4 is the exception for distributions paid to beneficiaries. If Code 1 is entered, this indicates that you were under age 59½ at the time of the distribution and, as far as the payer knows, no penalty exception applies. However, although Code 1 is entered, you may not be subject to a penalty. For example, you may qualify for the medical expense exception *(7.15)* or you may have made a tax-free rollover instead of having your employer make a direct rollover under the rules at *7.7*.

If the employer did make a direct rollover, Code G will be entered.

If you are at least age 59½, Code 7 should be entered.

If you are the beneficiary of a deceased employee, Code 4 should be entered. The 10% early distribution penalty does not apply.

If you contribute to a 401(k) plan and are a highly compensated employee, your employer may have to make a corrective distribution to you of contributions (and allocable income) that exceed allowable nondiscrimination ceilings. In this case, the employer will enter Code 8 if the corrective distribution is taxable in 2006, Code P if taxable in 2005, or Code D if taxable in 2004.

If you receive a lump-sum distribution that qualifies for special averaging, Code A will be entered. *See* the sample Form 1099-R below and *7.4* for the special averaging rules.

Filing Tip

Lump-Sum Distribution

If you are paid a distribution that qualifies for lump-sum averaging, Code A will be entered in Box 7 of Form 1099-R. *See 7.4* for averaging rules.

Box 8. If the value of an annuity contract was included as part of a lump sum you received, the value of the contract is shown here. It is not taxable when you receive it and should not be included in Boxes 1 and 2a. For purposes of computing averaging on Form 4972, this amount is added to the ordinary income portion of the distribution; *see 7.4*.

Box 9. If several beneficiaries are receiving payment from an employer plan total distribution, the amount shown in Box 9a is your share of the distribution. Box 9b may show your after-tax contributions to your employer's qualified annuity plan or tax-sheltered annuity plan.

Boxes 10–15. The payer may make entries in these boxes to show state or local income tax withholdings.

See Andrew Kellogg Example in 7.4.

☐ CORRECTED (if checked)

PAYER'S name, street address, city, state, and ZIP code		1 Gross distribution / 2a Taxable amount	OMB No. 1545-0119	Distributions From Pensions, Annuities, Retirement or Profit-Sharing Plans, IRAs, Insurance Contracts, etc.
StarShine Systems, Inc. Retirement Plan **1220 Silver Lake Drive** **City, State 1X001**		1 $ **182,438** 2a $ **182,438**	**2006** Form **1099-R**	
		2b Taxable amount not determined ☐	Total distribution ☒	**Copy B**
PAYER'S federal identification number **X0-1101X01**	RECIPIENT'S identification number **010-XX-10XX**	3 Capital gain (included in box 2a) $ **8,620**	**4 Federal income tax withheld** $ **36,488**	**Report this income on your federal tax return. If this form shows federal income tax withheld in box 4, attach this copy to your return.**
RECIPIENT'S name **Andrew Kellogg**		5 Employee contributions /Designated Roth contributions or insurance premiums $	6 Net unrealized appreciation in employer's securities $	
Street address (including apt. no.) **44 Hampton Lane**		7 Distribution code(s) **7A** — IRA/SEP/SIMPLE ☐	8 Other $ %	This information is being furnished to the Internal Revenue Service.
City, state, and ZIP code **City, State 1X011**		9a Your percentage of total distribution %	9b Total employee contributions $	
	1st year of desig. Roth contrib.	10 State tax withheld $ $	11 State/Payer's state no.	12 State distribution $ $
Account number (see instructions)		13 Local tax withheld $ $	14 Name of locality	15 Local distribution $ $

Form **1099-R** Department of the Treasury — Internal Revenue Service

7.2 Lump-Sum Distributions

If you are entitled to a lump-sum distribution from a qualified company retirement plan or self-employed Keogh plan, you may avoid current tax by asking your employer to make a direct rollover of your account to an IRA or another qualified employer plan. If the distribution is made to you, 20% will be withheld, but it is still possible to make a tax-free rollover within 60 days; *see 7.7* for rollover details.

If you receive a lump sum and do *not* make a rollover, the taxable part of the distribution (shown in Box 2a of Form 1099-R) must be reported as ordinary pension income on your return unless you were born before January 2, 1936, and qualify for special averaging, as discussed below. Your after-tax contributions and any net unrealized appreciation (NUA, *7.10*) in employer securities that are included in the lump sum are recovered tax free; they are not part of the taxable distribution.

A taxable distribution before age 59½ is subject to a 10% penalty in addition to regular income tax, unless you qualify for an exception; *see 7.15.*

Lump-sum distribution defined. A lump-sum distribution is the payment within a single taxable year of a plan participant's entire balance from an employer's qualified plan. If the employer has more than one qualified plan of the same kind (profit-sharing, pension, stock bonus), you must receive the balance from all of them within the same year. A series of payments may qualify as a lump-sum distribution provided you receive them within the same tax year. The account balance does not include deductible voluntary contributions you made after 1981 and before 1987; these are not eligible for lump-sum distribution treatment.

Requirements for 10-year averaging or capital gain election. If you were born before January 2, 1936, and receive a qualified lump-sum distribution (defined above), you generally may elect to figure your tax on the distribution using the 10-year averaging method. The law technically requires that you be born before 1936, but a favorable IRS rule treats you as born before 1936 if you were born *on* January 1, 1936. If you participated in the plan before 1974, you may elect to apply a 20% rate to the pre-1974 part of the lump-sum distribution if 20% is lower than the averaging rate.

However, averaging and capital gain treatment are *not allowed* for a lump-sum distribution if any of the following are true: (1) you rolled over any part of the lump-sum distribution to an IRA or an employer qualified plan, (2) you received the distribution during the first five years that you participated in the plan, (3) you previously received a distribution from the same plan and you rolled it over tax free to an IRA or another qualified employer plan, (4) you elected 10-year or five-year averaging or capital gain treatment for any other lump-sum distribution after 1986, (5) after 2001 you rolled over to the same plan a distribution from a traditional IRA (other than a conduit IRA *(7.3)*), a 403(b) plan *(7.21)*, or a governmental 457 plan *(7.22)*, or (6) after 2001 you rolled over to the same plan a distribution that you received as a surviving spouse from the qualified plan of your deceased spouse.

See 7.4 and *7.5* for details on electing averaging and the 20% capital gain rate.

If you are the beneficiary of a deceased plan participant, the participant's age, not yours, determines your right to claim averaging, and the five-year participation rule does not apply; *see 7.6.*

Spousal consent to lump-sum distribution. If you are married, you may have to obtain your spouse's consent to elect a lump-sum distribution; *see 7.11.*

Withholding tax. An employer must withhold a 20% tax from a lump-sum distribution that is paid to you and not rolled over directly by the employer; *see 7.7* for further details.

Beneficiaries. A surviving spouse who receives a lump-sum distribution upon the death of an employee may avoid tax by making a tax-free rollover to his or her own IRA. Beneficiaries other than surviving spouses could not make a tax-free rollover before 2007, but a distribution after 2006 may be rolled over by a nonspouse beneficiary to an inherited IRA; *see 7.8.*

If the deceased employee was born before January 2, 1936, any beneficiary (not just a surviving spouse) may elect special averaging or capital gain treatment for a lump-sum distribution of the account, unless the distribution is disqualified as discussed above under "Requirements for 10-year averaging or capital gain election"; *see 7.6.*

Court ordered lump-sum distribution to a spouse or former spouse. A distribution received by a spouse or former spouse of an employee under a qualified domestic relations order (QDRO) may be eligible for tax-free rollover or, in some cases, special averaging treatment; *see 7.12.*

Caution

Prior Rollover Bars Averaging

You may not claim averaging for a lump-sum distribution if you previously received a distribution from the same plan that was rolled over tax free *(7.7)* to an IRA or to another qualified employer plan.

7.3 Lump-Sum Options If You Were Born Before January 2, 1936

Plan ahead if you expect to receive a lump-sum distribution eligible for averaging *(7.2)*. You must decide whether to pay tax currently using the averaging method (and possibly the 20% capital gain method for pre-1974 participation), or to defer tax by making a tax-free rollover *(7.7)*. If you receive more than one lump sum during the year, you must make the same choice for all of them; you may not roll over one lump sum and claim averaging for another.

If you do not instruct the payer to make a direct rollover *(7.8)*, 80% of the taxable distribution will be paid to you; a 20% tax will be withheld. If you later decide to make a rollover, you have 60 days from the time of receiving the distribution to do so; *see 7.8*. However, to avoid tax on the entire distribution, you will have to include in the rollover an amount equal to the withheld tax. Withholding is discussed further at *7.8* and *26.11*. Ordinary income tax rates apply to the amount not rolled over, unless you are eligible for averaging or the 20% capital gain method.

Planning Reminder

Once in a Lifetime Election

You are allowed to elect averaging only once as a plan participant after 1986. If before 1987 you elected 10-year averaging and were under age $59^1/_2$, you may elect averaging for a current distribution. However, if you were over age $59^1/_2$ when you made the pre-1987 election, you are barred from electing averaging again.

If you were born before January 2, 1936, have not previously elected averaging, and elect averaging for a distribution received in 2006, you will not be able to claim averaging again if you join another company and receive a lump-sum distribution from the new employer.

Even if you are barred from electing averaging for a lump sum from your own plan, you can make the election as a beneficiary of a deceased plan participant born before January 2, 1936.

Conduit IRA preserves averaging option. If you are changing jobs, a direct rollover or personal rollover may be made to a traditional IRA or a qualified plan of your new employer. However, if the distribution is rolled over to a traditional IRA, you lose the right to claim averaging for those assets unless the IRA is a "conduit IRA" that serves as a holding account until a later rollover may be made to another employer's plan. As long as the distribution and earnings on the distribution are the only assets in the conduit IRA, a rollover may later be made from the conduit IRA to a new employer's plan, from which a lump-sum distribution eligible for averaging may later be received; see the Planning Reminder on page 156. Distributions from a traditional IRA are taxable as ordinary income.

If you plan to continue working and expect to receive another lump sum in the future, you may not claim averaging for the current lump sum and also for the later distribution. Averaging may be claimed only once as a plan participant after 1986.

An IRA rollover cannot be revoked to claim averaging. If you make a rollover to an IRA, you cannot change your mind and cancel the IRA account in order to apply special averaging. The rollover election is irrevocable, according to an IRS regulation that has been upheld by the Tax Court. If an IRA rollover account is revoked, the entire distribution is taxable as ordinary income, and a 10% penalty may be imposed if the recipient is under age 59½ *(7.15)*.

Disqualification of retirement plan. If you receive a lump-sum distribution from a plan that loses its exempt status, the IRS may argue that the distribution does not qualify for lump-sum treatment. Under the IRS position, you may not roll over the distribution to an IRA or elect special averaging. The Tax Court previously took the position that if the plan qualified when contributions were made, an allocable portion of the distribution was a qualified lump sum. However, the majority of appeals courts that reviewed Tax Court decisions on this issue supported the IRS position. In response, the Tax Court reversed its position and adopted the harsher IRS approach: no part of the distribution qualifies for rollover or averaging if the plan loses its exempt status.

7.4 Averaging on Form 4972

If you were born before January 2, 1936, and the other averaging tests at *7.2* are satisfied, you may elect on Form 4972 to compute the tax on a lump-sum distribution received using a 10-year averaging method based on 1986 tax rates for single persons.

If you were born after January 1, 1936, you may not elect averaging for a lump-sum distribution of your account balance. However, you may elect averaging as the beneficiary of a deceased plan participant who was born before January 2, 1936; *see 7.6*.

Caution

Averaging Not Allowed for Those Born After January 1, 1936

If you were born after January 1, 1936, a lump-sum distribution from your plan is not eligible for averaging.

Averaging on 2006 returns. If you qualify for averaging *(7.2)*, follow IRS instructions to Form 4972 for applying the 10-year averaging method. If you received more than one qualified lump sum, you may elect averaging for one of the distributions only if you elect averaging for all.

The amount eligible for averaging is the taxable portion of the distribution shown in Box 2a of Form 1099-R. You may also elect to add to the Box 2a amount any net unrealized appreciation in employer securities (shown in Box 6) included in the lump sum. If you are receiving the distribution as a beneficiary of a plan participant who died before August 21, 1996, follow the instructions to Form 4972 for claiming a death benefit exclusion that reduces the Box 2a taxable portion.

Form **4972**

Department of the Treasury
Internal Revenue Service (99)

Tax on Lump-Sum Distributions

(From Qualified Plans of Participants Born Before January 2, 1936)

▶ Attach to Form 1040, Form 1040NR, or Form 1041.

OMB No. 1545-0193

2006

Attachment Sequence No. **28**

Name of recipient of distribution	Identifying number
Andrew Kellogg	010 - XX - 10XX

Part I Complete this part to see if you can use Form 4972

			Yes	No
1	Was this a distribution of a plan participant's entire balance (excluding deductible voluntary employee contributions and certain forfeited amounts) from all of an employer's qualified plans of one kind (pension, profit-sharing, or stock bonus)? If "No," **do not** use this form	1	✓	
2	Did you roll over any part of the distribution? If "Yes," **do not** use this form	2		✓
3	Was this distribution paid to you as a beneficiary of a plan participant who was born before January 2, 1936?	3		✓
4	Were you **(a)** a plan participant who received this distribution, **(b)** born before January 2, 1936, **and (c)** a participant in the plan for at least 5 years before the year of the distribution?	4	✓	
	If you answered "No" to both questions 3 **and** 4, **do not** use this form.			
5a	Did you use Form 4972 after 1986 for a previous distribution from your own plan? If "Yes," **do not** use this form for a 2006 distribution from your own plan	5a		✓
b	If you are receiving this distribution as a beneficiary of a plan participant who died, did you use Form 4972 for a previous distribution received for that participant after 1986? If "Yes," **do not** use the form for this distribution	5b		

Part II Complete this part to choose the 20% capital gain election (see instructions)

6	Capital gain part from Form 1099-R, box 3	6	8,620
7	Multiply line 6 by 20% (.20) ▶	7	1,724
	If you also choose to use Part III, go to line 8. Otherwise, include the amount from line 7 in the total on Form 1040, line 44, Form 1040NR, line 41, or Form 1041, Schedule G, line 1b, whichever applies.		

Part III Complete this part to choose the 10-year tax option (see instructions)

8	Ordinary income from Form 1099-R, box 2a minus box 3. If you did not complete Part II, enter the taxable amount from Form 1099-R, box 2a			8	173,818
9	Death benefit exclusion for a beneficiary of a plan participant who died before August 21, 1996			9	- 0 -
10	Total taxable amount. Subtract line 9 from line 8			10	173,818
11	Current actuarial value of annuity from Form 1099-R, box 8. If none, enter -0-			11	- 0 -
12	Adjusted total taxable amount. Add lines 10 and 11. If this amount is $70,000 or more, **skip** lines 13 through 16, enter this amount on line 17, and go to line 18			12	173,818
13	Multiply line 12 by 50% (.50), but **do not** enter more than $10,000	13			
14	Subtract $20,000 from line 12. If line 12 is $20,000 or less, enter -0-	14			
15	Multiply line 14 by 20% (.20)	15			
16	Minimum distribution allowance. Subtract line 15 from line 13			16	
17	Subtract line 16 from line 12			17	173,818
18	Federal estate tax attributable to lump-sum distribution			18	- 0 -
19	Subtract line 18 from line 17. If line 11 is zero, **skip** lines 20 through 22 and go to line 23			19	173,818
20	Divide line 11 by line 12 and enter the result as a decimal (rounded to at least three places)	20	.		
21	Multiply line 16 by the decimal on line 20	21			
22	Subtract line 21 from line 11	22			
23	Multiply line 19 by 10% (.10)			23	17,382
24	Tax on amount on line 23. Use the Tax Rate Schedule in the instructions			24	3,012
25	Multiply line 24 by ten (10). If line 11 is zero, **skip** lines 26 through 28, enter this amount on line 29, and go to line 30			25	30,120
26	Multiply line 22 by 10% (.10)	26			
27	Tax on amount on line 26. Use the Tax Rate Schedule in the instructions	27			
28	Multiply line 27 by ten (10)			28	
29	Subtract line 28 from line 25. Multiple recipients, see instructions ▶			29	30,120
30	**Tax on lump-sum distribution.** Add lines 7 and 29. Also include this amount in the total on Form 1040, line 44, Form 1040NR, line 41, or Form 1041, Schedule G, line 1b, whichever applies ▶			30	31,844

For Paperwork Reduction Act Notice, see instructions. Cat. No. 13187U Form **4972** (2006)

If the distribution includes capital gain (Box 3 of Form 1099-R) and you want to apply the special 20% capital gain rate *(7.5)*, you should subtract the capital gain in Box 3 from the taxable amount in Box 2a and apply averaging to the balance of ordinary income.

The tax computed on Form 4972 is reported on Form 1040, Line 44, as an additional tax. It is completely separate from the tax computed on your other income reported on Form 1040.

See the following Example and the Sample Form 4972 on page 153.

EXAMPLE

Andrew Kellogg was born in 1935. In 2006, he retired from StarShine Systems, Inc., and received a lump-sum distribution of $182,438, before withholdings. The Form 1099-R provided by the company (*see* page 150) shows in Box 3 the capital gain portion of $8,620, attributable to pre-1974 participation.

On Form 4972, Andrew applies the special 20% rate to the capital gain portion for a tax of $1,724. He then figures the tax on the $173,818 ordinary income part of the distribution under the 10-year averaging method. As shown on the sample Form 4972 on page 153, Andrew's total tax on the distribution is $31,844, the sum of the $30,120 tax under 10-year averaging and the $1,724 tax on the capital gain portion. In Andrew's case, the special 20% capital gains rate is advantageous because it results in a lower tax than if the capital gain were treated as ordinary income subject to the averaging computation. The tax would be $32,360 if the special capital gain rate was not elected.

Filing Tip

Pre-1974 Capital Gain Portion of Distribution

If you were born before January 2, 1936, and a portion of your lump-sum distribution is attributable to plan participation before 1974 *(7.5)*, you may treat it as ordinary income eligible for averaging, or you may elect to treat it as capital gain taxable at a flat 20% rate; choose the method on Form 4972 that gives the lower overall tax.

Community property. Only the spouse who has earned the lump sum may use averaging. Community property laws are disregarded for this purpose. If a couple files separate returns and one spouse elects averaging, the other spouse is not taxed on the amount subject to the computation.

EXAMPLE

A husband in a community property state receives a lump-sum distribution of which the ordinary income portion is $10,000. He and his wife file separate returns. If averaging is not elected, $5,000, or one-half, is taxable on the husband's return and the other $5,000 on his wife's return. However, if he elects the averaging method, only he reports the $10,000 on Form 4972.

7.5 Capital Gain Treatment for Pre-1974 Participation

The portion of a qualifying lump-sum distribution attributable to pre-1974 participation is eligible for a 20% capital gain rate if you were born before January 2, 1936, and the other tests at *7.2* are met.

On Form 1099-R, the company paying the lump-sum distribution shows the capital gain portion in Box 3. The ordinary income portion is Box 2a (taxable amount) *minus* Box 3. If you elect to treat the pre-1974 portion as capital gain subject to a flat rate of 20% on Form 4972, the tax on the balance of the distribution may be figured under the averaging method *(7.4)*. The 20% rate for the capital gain portion is fixed by law, and applies regardless of the tax rate imposed on your other capital gains. Alternatively, you may elect to treat the capital gain portion as ordinary income eligible for averaging on Form 4972. You may not elect to report any portion of the pre-1974 portion of the lump-sum distribution as long-term capital gain on Schedule D.

Under the one-time election rule, if you elect to apply the averaging and/or 20% capital gain rule for a 2006 distribution, you may not elect averaging or capital gain treatment for any later distribution.

Capital gain treatment not allowed for individuals born after January 1, 1936. If you were born after January 1, 1936, you may *not* treat any portion of a lump-sum distribution as capital gain. You may not apply the flat 20% rate to the pre-1974 portion of the lump-sum distribution on Form 4972, or include any part of it as capital gain on Schedule D.

7.6 Lump-Sum Payments Received by Beneficiary

A beneficiary of a deceased employee or self-employed plan participant may elect 10-year averaging on Form 4972 for a qualifying lump-sum distribution *(7.2)* because of the participant's death, provided the participant was born before January 2, 1936. The age of the beneficiary is irrelevant.

A beneficiary may elect averaging even though the deceased employee was in the plan for less than five years. If the participant was born before January 2, 1936, and had participated in the plan before 1974, a 20% capital gain election may be made for that portion of the distribution *(7.5)*, and the averaging method applied to the balance.

Form 4972 is used to compute tax under the averaging method or to make the 20% capital gain election *(7.5)*. Follow the Form 4972 instructions to claim the up-to-$5,000 death benefit exclusion where the plan participant died before August 21, 1996. Any federal estate tax attributable to the distribution reduces the taxable amount on Form 4972. Any election that you make as a beneficiary does not affect your right to elect lump-sum treatment for a distribution from your own plan.

A lump sum paid because of an employee's death may qualify for capital gain and averaging treatment, although the employee received annuity payments before death.

An election may be made on Form 4972 only once as the beneficiary of a particular plan participant. A beneficiary who receives more than one lump-sum distribution for the same participant in the same year must treat them all the same way. Averaging must be elected for all of the distributions on a single Form 4972 or for none of them.

Payment received by a second beneficiary (after the death of the first beneficiary) is not entitled to lump-sum treatment or the death benefit exclusion.

Beneficiaries of plan participants born after January 1, 1936. A beneficiary may *not* claim averaging or capital gain treatment for a lump-sum distribution if the plan participant was born after January 1, 1936.

Distribution to trust or estate. If a qualifying lump sum is paid to a trust or an estate, the employee, or, if deceased, his or her personal representative, may elect averaging.

EXAMPLE

Gunnison's father was covered by a company benefit plan. The father died, as did Gunnison's mother, before benefits were fully paid out. Gunnison received a substantial lump sum. He argued that he collected on account of his father's death. The IRS disagreed.

The Tax Court and an appeals court sided with the IRS. Gunnison was entitled to the payment following his mother's death, not his father's death. For special lump-sum treatment, the payout must arise solely on account of the death of the covered employee.

Filing Tip

Lump Sums to Multiple Beneficiaries

A lump-sum distribution to two or more beneficiaries may qualify for averaging and capital gain treatment, so long as the plan participant was born before January 2, 1936. Each beneficiary may separately elect the averaging method for the ordinary income portion, even though other beneficiaries do not so elect. Follow the Form 4972 instructions for multiple recipients.

7.7 Tax-Free Rollovers From Qualified Plans

A rollover allows you to make a tax-free transfer of a distribution from a qualified employer retirement plan to another qualified plan, a traditional IRA, a 403(b) plan *(7.21)*, or a state or local government 457 plan *(7.22)* that accepts rollovers. If a rollover is made to a traditional IRA, later distributions are subject to the IRA rules (8.8) and will not qualify for special averaging (7.4). Caution: If the distribution is for part of your account balance and you roll it over, a later lump-sum distribution from the same plan will not qualify for averaging even if you were born before January 2, 1936; *see 7.4*.

Eligible rollover distributions. Almost all taxable distributions received from a qualified corporate or self-employed pension, profit-sharing, stock bonus, or annuity plan are eligible for tax-free rollover. The major exceptions are substantially equal periodic payments over your lifetime or over a period of at least 10 years, hardship distributions, and minimum distributions *(7.13)* required after age 70½; *see* below for other ineligible distributions.

Rollover of after-tax contributions. After-tax contributions may be rolled over to a traditional IRA. A trustee-to-trustee transfer of after-tax contributions may also be made to a qualified defined contribution plan (qualified employer plan, 403(b) plan, or government 457 plan) that agrees to separately account for the after-tax amount.

Rollover options. If you want to make a tax-free rollover of an eligible rollover distribution, you should instruct your employer to directly roll over the funds to a traditional IRA you designate or to the plan of your new employer. You could also choose to have the distribution paid to you, and within 60 days you could make a tax-free rollover yourself. *However, to avoid the 20% mandatory withholding tax, you must elect to have the plan make a direct rollover. If an eligible rollover distribution is paid to you, the 20% withholding tax applies. Before a distribution is made, your employer must provide you with written notice concerning the rollover options and the withholding tax rules.* See 7.8 *for further details on the direct rollover and personal rollover alternatives.*

Law Alert

Direct Rollover to Roth IRA Not Allowed Before 2008

Under current law, you may *not* roll over an employer plan distribution to a Roth IRA. You may make a tax-free rollover to a traditional IRA and then make a taxable conversion to a Roth IRA if you qualify under the rules at *8.21*.

However, a new law will allow a distribution made after 2007 from a qualified employer plan, 403(b) plan, or governmental 457 plan to be directly rolled over to a Roth IRA, provided you qualify under the taxable conversion rules at *8.21*.

Rollover from employer plan to IRA after age 70½. Starting with the year you reach age 70½, you may no longer make contributions to a traditional IRA. However, if you are over age 70½ and you receive an eligible rollover distribution from your employer's plan, you may instruct your employer to make a direct rollover of the distribution to a traditional IRA, as discussed in *7.8*. If you receive the distribution from the employer, a 20% tax will be withheld. You may then make a tax-free rollover within 60 days of the distribution; *see 7.8* for the discussion of "personal rollovers." In the year of the rollover, you must receive a minimum distribution from the IRA; *see 8.13*.

Beneficiaries. *See 7.8* for the rollover options open to beneficiaries.

Distributions that may not be rolled over. Any lump-sum or partial distribution from your account is eligible for rollover *except for the following:*

- Hardship distributions from a 401(k) plan or 403(b) plan *(7.19)*.
- Payments that are part of a series of substantially equal payments made at least annually over a period of 10 years or more or over your life or life expectancy (or the joint lives or joint life and last survivor expectancies of you and your designated beneficiary).
- Minimum required distributions after attaining age 70½ or retiring *(7.13)*.
- Corrective distributions of excess 401(k) plan contributions and deferrals.
- Dividends on employer stock.
- Life insurance coverage costs.
- Loans that are deemed to be taxable distributions because they exceed the limits discussed in *7.16*.

For all of the above taxable distributions that are *ineligible* for rollover, you may elect to completely avoid withholding on Form W-4P.

7.8 Direct Rollover or Personal Rollover

If you receive an eligible rollover distribution *(7.7)* from a qualified plan, you may choose a direct rollover, or if you actually receive the distribution you may make a personal rollover. To avoid withholding, choose a direct rollover. You must receive a written explanation of your rollover rights from your employer before an eligible rollover distribution is made.

Planning Reminder

IRA Conduit Between Employer Plans

If you roll over a distribution from an employer plan to a traditional IRA, you may later roll over a distribution from the IRA to a new employer's plan. You can make the subsequent rollover from the IRA even if the funds from the first employer were mixed with regular IRA contributions and earnings.

However, if you were born before January 2, 1936, expect to join another employer's qualified plan, and want to preserve the possibility of claiming averaging for a lump-sum distribution *(7.2)* from the new employer's plan, a rollover from the first employer plan should be to a segregated "conduit IRA." A conduit IRA contains only the assets distributed from the first qualified plan plus the earnings on those assets. If you then join a company with a plan that accepts rollovers and make the rollover from the conduit IRA into that plan, a subsequent lump-sum distribution from the new employer plan will qualify for 10-year averaging (and possibly 20% capital gain treatment for pre-1974 participation), assuming the distribution otherwise qualifies under the rules at *7.2*.

Direct Rollover to Traditional IRA or Another Employer Plan

If you choose to have your employer make a direct rollover of an eligible rollover distribution to a traditional IRA or another eligible employer plan *(7.7)*, you avoid tax on the payment and no tax will be withheld. If you are changing jobs and want a direct rollover to the plan of the new employer, make sure that the plan accepts rollovers; if it does not, choose a direct rollover to a traditional IRA.

When you select the direct rollover option, your employer may transfer the funds directly by check or wire to the new plan, or you may be given a check payable to the new plan that you deliver.

In choosing a direct rollover to a traditional IRA, the terms of the payer-employer's plan will determine whether you may divide the distribution among several IRAs or whether you will be restricted to one IRA. For example, you may want to split up your distribution into several traditional IRAs, but the employer may force you to select only one. After the direct rollover is made, you may then diversify your holdings by making tax-free trustee-to-trustee transfers to other traditional IRAs.

You may elect to make a direct rollover of part of your distribution and to receive the balance. The portion paid to you will be subject to 20% withholding and is not eligible for special averaging. Withholding is generally not required on distributions of less than $200.

A direct rollover will be reported by the payer plan to the IRS and to you on Form 1099-R, although the transfer is not taxable. The direct rollover will be reported in Box 1 of Form 1099-R, but zero will be entered as the taxable amount in Box 2a. In Box 7, Code G should be entered.

Personal Rollover After Receiving a Distribution

If you do not tell your employer to make a direct rollover of an eligible rollover distribution, and you instead receive the distribution yourself, you will receive only 80% of the taxable portion (generally the entire distribution unless you made after-tax contributions); 20% will be withheld. Withholding does not apply to the portion of the distribution consisting of net unrealized appreciation from employer securities that is tax-free under the rules at *7.10*.

Although you receive only 80% of the taxable eligible rollover distribution, the full amount before withholding will be reported as the gross distribution in Box 1 of Form 1099-R. To avoid tax you must roll over the full amount within 60 days to a traditional IRA or another eligible employer plan. However, to roll over 100% of the distribution you will have to use other funds to replace the 20% withheld. If you roll over only the 80% received, the 20% balance will be taxable; *see* the John Anderson Example below. For the taxable part that is not rolled over, you may not use special averaging or capital gain treatment even if you meet the age test in *7.4*. In addition, if the distribution was made to you before you reached age 59½, the taxable amount will be subject to a 10% penalty unless you are disabled, separating from service after reaching age 55, or have substantial medical expenses; *see 7.15* for a full list of exceptions.

If a distribution includes your voluntary after-tax contributions to the qualified plan, they are tax free to you when you receive them. However, after-tax contributions may be rolled over to another qualified plan, a 403(b) plan, or a state or local government 457 plan.

A rollover *may* include salary deferral contributions that were excludable from income when made, such as qualifying deferrals to a 401(k) plan. The rollover may also include accumulated deductible employee contributions (and allocable income) made after 1981 and before 1987. Your employer's retirement plan may invest in a limited amount of life insurance which is then distributed to you as part of a lump-sum retirement distribution. You may be able to roll over the life insurance contract to the qualified plan of your new employer but not to a traditional IRA. The law bars investment of IRA funds in life insurance contracts.

You may not claim a deduction for your rollover.

Planning Reminder

Pre-Age-59$^1/_2$ Distributions

If you are under age 59$^1/_2$ and do not roll over an eligible distribution, you will generally be subject to a 10% penalty in addition to regular income tax. However, penalty exceptions apply if you separate from service and are age 55 or older, you are disabled, or you pay substantial medical expenses; *see 7.15* for a full list of penalty exceptions.

Multiple rollover accounts allowed. You may wish to diversify a distribution in different investments. There is no limit on the number of rollover accounts you may have. A lump-sum distribution from a qualified plan may be rolled over to several traditional IRAs.

EXAMPLE

In June 2007, John Anderson retires. He is due a lump-sum distribution of $100,000 from a qualified plan of his company. If he instructs his employer to make a direct rollover of the amount to a traditional IRA or eligible employer plan, there is no tax withholding, and the $100,000 is transferred tax free.

Now assume that John decides not to choose a direct rollover because he is planning to use the funds to invest in a business. The plan will pay him $80,000 and withhold a tax of $20,000 that John will apply to his tax liability when he files his 2007 return. But, say, a month later John changes his mind about the investment and now wants to roll over his benefits to a traditional IRA. He must make the rollover within 30 days because 30 days of the 60-day rollover period have already passed. Furthermore, to avoid tax on the entire distribution, he must deposit $100,000 in the traditional IRA, even though $20,000 tax has been withheld. If he does not have the $20,000, he must borrow the $20,000 and deposit it in the IRA. If he rolls over only $80,000, he must report $20,000 as a taxable distribution on his 2007 return and if John is under age 59½, the 10% penalty for early withdrawals would apply; based on these facts, John does not qualify for a penalty exception *(7.15)*.

Caution

IRA Rollover Election Is Irrevocable

A rollover from an employer plan to a traditional IRA is irrevocable, according to the IRS. At the time of the rollover, you must elect in writing to irrevocably treat the contribution as a rollover. If a qualifying lump-sum distribution is made to you and you roll it over, you may not later change your mind in order to claim averaging even though you were born before January 2, 1936, and the other tests for averaging are met *(7.4)*. Before making a rollover, figure what the current tax would be on the lump-sum distribution under the special averaging method. Compare it with an estimate of the regular tax that will be payable on a later distribution of the rolled-over account from the IRA.

Reporting a personal rollover on your return. When you receive a distribution that could have been rolled over, the payer will report on Form 1099-R the full taxable amount before withholding, although 20% has been withheld. However, if you make a rollover yourself within the 60-day period, the rollover reduces the taxable amount on your tax return. For example, if in 2006 you were entitled to a $100,000 lump-sum distribution and received $80,000 after mandatory 20% withholding and then you rolled over the full $100,000 into an IRA, report $100,000 on Line 16a of Form 1040 or Line 12a of Form 1040A, but enter zero as the taxable amount on Line 16b or Line 12b and write "Rollover" next to the line. If you roll over only part of the distribution, the amount of the lump sum *not* rolled over is entered as the taxable amount. Remember to include the 20% withholding on the line for federal income tax withheld.

IRS may waive 60-day deadline for personal rollover on equitable grounds. Generally, a personal rollover must be completed by the 60th day following the day on which you receive a distribution from the employer plan. However, the IRS has discretion to waive the 60-day deadline and permit more time for a rollover where failure to complete a timely rollover was due to events beyond your reasonable control, and failure to waive the deadline would be "against equity or good conscience."

The same waiver rule applies to rollovers from traditional IRAs. *See 8.10* for IRS guidelines on granting a waiver.

Extension of 60-day rollover period for frozen deposits. If you receive a qualifying distribution from a retirement plan and deposit the funds in a financial institution that becomes bankrupt or insolvent, you may be prevented from withdrawing the funds in time to complete a rollover within 60 days. If this happens, the 60-day period is extended while your account is "frozen." The 60-day rollover period does not include days on which your account is frozen. Further, you have a minimum of 10 days after the release of the funds to complete the rollover.

Rollover by Beneficiary

Surviving spouse. If you are your deceased spouse's beneficiary, you may roll over your interest in his or her qualified plan account. You may choose to have the plan make a direct rollover to your own traditional IRA. The advantage of choosing the direct rollover is to avoid a 20% withholding. If the distribution is paid to you, 20% will be withheld. You may make a rollover within 60 days, but to completely avoid tax, you must include in the rollover the withheld amount, as illustrated in the John Anderson Example on page 157. If you receive the distribution but do not make the rollover, you will be taxed on the distribution, but if your spouse was born before January 2, 1936, you may be able to use special averaging *(7.4)* to compute the tax. As a surviving spouse, you are *not* subject to the 10% penalty for premature distributions *(7.15)* even if you are under age 59½.

You may also roll over a distribution from your deceased spouse's account to your own qualified plan, 403(a) qualified annuity, 403(b) tax-sheltered annuity, or governmental section 457 plan. However, if you were born before January 2, 1936, and want to preserve the option of electing averaging *(7.4)* or capital gain treatment (for pre-1974 participation, *see 7.5*) for a later distribution from your employer's qualified plan, you should *not* roll over your deceased spouse's account to your employer's qualified plan. If the rollover is made to your employer's qualified plan, a lump-sum distribution from the plan will not be eligible for averaging or capital gains treatment.

Rollover of distribution received under a divorce or support proceeding. In a qualified domestic relations order (QDRO) meeting special tax law tests, a state court may give you the right to receive all or part of your spouse's or former spouse's retirement benefits. You can choose to have the payment made to you or you can instruct the plan to make a direct rollover to a traditional IRA or to your employer's qualified plan if it accepts rollovers. Alternatively, if the distribution is paid to you, 20% withholding will apply. You may complete a rollover within 60 days under the rules for personal rollovers discussed earlier. If you do not make the rollover, the distribution you receive is taxable, but you may be able to elect special averaging if averaging would have been allowed had it been received by your spouse or former spouse; *see 7.12*. If only part of the distribution is rolled over, the balance is taxed as ordinary income in the year of receipt. In figuring your tax, you are allowed a prorated share of your former spouse's cost investment, if any. You may not elect averaging or capital gain treatment for the portion not rolled over. You are *not* subject to the 10% penalty for premature distributions even if under age 59½.

Nonspouse beneficiaries. Distributions made before 2007 to a nonspouse beneficiary could not be rolled over. If you received a lump-sum distribution in 2006 as a nonspouse beneficiary, the distribution is taxable to you, but if the plan participant was born before January 2, 1936, you can elect 10-year averaging; *see 7.6*.

The Pension Protection Act of 2006 allows a nonspouse beneficiary to roll over a distribution after 2006 from a qualified plan, 403(b) plan, or governmental 457 plan to an IRA, but the IRA must be treated as an inherited IRA subject to the required minimum distribution rules for nonspouse beneficiaries discussed in *8.14*. The rollover to the inherited IRA must be made by means of a trustee-to-trustee transfer.

Law Alert

Nonspouse Beneficiary Can Roll Over to Inherited IRA After 2006

The Pension Protection Act of 2006 allows a nonspouse beneficiary to make a trustee-to-trustee transfer of a distribution after 2006 to an IRA, provided the IRA is treated as an inherited IRA. Required minimum distributions from the inherited IRA must be received under the rules for nonspouse beneficiaries discussed in *8.14*.

Court Decision

Stock Purchased With Cash Withdrawal Cannot Be Rolled Over

A taxpayer withdrew cash from his Keogh accounts and used most of the net distribution (after withholdings) to buy stock, which was then transferred to an IRA within 60 days of the withdrawal. He treated the entire distribution as a tax-free rollover but the IRS and Tax Court held it was taxable. The transfer of stock to the IRA was not a tax-free rollover; only the cash distribution itself could be rolled over. A negligence penalty was also imposed.

A direct rollover from the Keogh accounts to an IRA would have been tax free; the stock could then have been purchased through the new IRA.

7.9 Rollover of Proceeds From Sale of Property

A lump-sum distribution from a qualified plan may include property, such as non-employer stock; *see 7.10* for employer securities. If you plan to roll over the distribution, you may find that a bank or other plan trustee does not want to take the property. You cannot get tax-free rollover treatment by keeping the property and rolling over cash to the new plan. If you sell the property, you may roll over the sale proceeds to a traditional IRA as long as the sale and rollover occur within 60 days of receipt of the distribution. If you roll over all of the proceeds, you do not recognize a gain or loss from the sale; the proceeds are treated as part of the distribution. If you make a partial rollover of sale proceeds, you must report as capital gain the portion of the gain that is allocable to the retained sale proceeds.

If you receive cash and property, and you sell the property but only make a partial rollover, you must designate how much of the rolled-over cash is from the employer distribution and how much from the sale proceeds. The designation must be made by the time for filing your return (plus any extensions) and is irrevocable. If you do not make a timely designation, the IRS will allocate the rollover between cash and sales proceeds on a ratable basis; the allocation will determine tax on the retained amount.

7.10 Distribution of Employer Stock or Other Securities

If you are entitled to a distribution from an employer plan that includes employer stock (or other employer securities), you may be able to take advantage of a special exclusion rule. If you withdraw the stock from the plan as part of a lump-sum distribution and invest the stock in a taxable brokerage account instead of rolling it over to a traditional IRA, tax on the "net unrealized appreciation," or NUA, may be deferred until you sell the stock. To defer tax on the full NUA, the employer stock must be received in a lump-sum distribution, as discussed below. If the distribution is not a lump sum, a less favorable NUA exclusion is available, but only if you made after-tax contributions to buy the shares; *see* below.

Planning Reminder

Deferring Tax on NUA

If you receive a lump-sum distribution that includes appreciated employer securities, you may defer the tax on the net unrealized appreciation (NUA) in the securities.

Lump-sum distribution. If you receive appreciated stock or securities as part of a lump-sum distribution, net unrealized appreciation (increase in value since purchase of securities) is not subject to tax at the time of distribution unless you elect to treat it as taxable.

For purposes of the NUA exclusion, a lump-sum distribution is the payment within a single year of the plan participant's entire balance from all of the employer's qualified plans of the same kind (all of the employer's profit-sharing plans, or all pension or stock bonus plans). The distribution must be paid to: (1) a participant after reaching age 59½, (2) an employee-participant who separates from service (by retiring, resigning, changing employers, or being fired), (3) a self-employed participant who becomes totally and permanently disabled, or (4) a beneficiary of a deceased plan participant. If there is any plan balance at the end of the year, there is no lump sum and the NUA exclusion is not available.

Assuming you do not waive the NUA exclusion, you are taxed (at ordinary income rates) only on the original cost of the stock when contributed to the plan. Tax on the appreciation is delayed until the shares are later sold by you at a price exceeding cost basis and the gain attributable to the NUA will be taken at long-term capital gain rates *(5.3)*.

The NUA in employer's securities is shown in Box 6 of the Form 1099-R received from the payer. It is *not* included in the taxable amount in Box 2a.

If, when distributed, the shares are valued at below the cost contribution to the plan, the fair market value of the shares is subject to tax. If you contributed to the purchase of the shares and their value is less than your contribution, you do not realize a loss deduction on the distribution. You realize a loss only when the stock is sold for less than your cost or becomes worthless *(5.32)* at a later date. If a plan distributes worthless stock, you may deduct your contributions to the stock as a miscellaneous itemized deduction subject to the 2% of adjusted gross income floor.

EXAMPLES

1. *Shares valued below your cost contribution.* You contributed $500 and your employer contributed $300 to buy 10 shares of company stock having at the time a fair market value of $80 per share. When you retire, the fair market value of the stock is $40 per share, or a total of $400. You do not realize income on the distribution, and you do not have a deductible loss for the difference between your cost contribution and the lower fair market value. Your contribution to the stock is its basis. This is $50 per share. If you sell the stock for $40 per share, you have a capital loss of $10 per share. However, if you sell the stock for $60 per share, you have gain of $10 per share.
2. *Appreciated shares.* You receive 10 shares of company stock that was purchased entirely with the employer's funds. Your employer's cost was $50 a share. At the time of a lump-sum distribution, the shares are valued at $80 a share. Your employer's contribution of $50 a share, or $500, is included as part of your taxable distribution. The appreciation of $300 is not included, assuming you do not elect to be taxed currently on the appreciation. The cost basis of the shares in your hands is $500 (the amount currently taxable to

you). The holding period of the stock starts from the date of distribution. However, if you sell the shares for any amount exceeding $500 and up to $800, your profit is long-term capital gain regardless of how long you held the shares. If you sell for more than $800, the gain exceeding the original unrealized appreciation of $300 is subject to long-term capital gain treatment only if the sale is long term from the date of distribution. Thus, if within a month of the distribution you sold the shares for $900, $300 would be long-term gain; $100 would be short-term gain.

Election to waive tax-free treatment. You may elect to include the NUA in employer stock or securities as income. You might consider making this election when the NUA is not substantial or you want to accelerate income to the current year by taking into account the entire lump-sum distribution. If you were born before January 2, 1936, and are claiming averaging or capital gain treatment on Form 4972 *(7.4)*, follow the form instructions for adding the unrealized appreciation to the taxable distribution. If you are not filing Form 4972, the election to include the unrealized appreciation as ordinary income is made by reporting it on Line 16b (taxable pensions and annuities) of Form 1040 or Line 12b of Form 1040A.

Distribution not a lump sum. If you receive appreciated employer securities in a distribution that does not meet the lump-sum tests above, you report as ordinary income the amount of the employer's contribution to the purchase of the shares and the appreciation allocated to the employer's cost contribution. You do not report the amount of appreciation allocated to your own after-tax contribution to the purchase. In other words, tax is deferred only on the NUA attributable to your after-tax employee contributions. Net unrealized appreciation is shown in Box 6 of Form 1099-R. Cost contributions must be supplied by the company distributing the stock.

EXAMPLE

A qualified plan distributes 10 shares of company stock with an average cost of $100, of which the employee contributed $60 and the employer, $40. At the date of distribution, the stock had a fair market value of $180. The portion of the unrealized appreciation attributable to the employee's contribution is $48 (60% of $80); the employer's is $32 (40% of $80). The employee reports $72 as income: the employer's cost of $40 and the employer's share of appreciation, which is $32. For purposes of determining gain or loss on a later sale, the employee's basis for each share is $132, which includes the employee contribution of $60 and the $72 reported as taxable income.

7.11 Survivor Annuity for Spouse

If you have been married for at least a year as of the annuity starting date, the law generally requires that payments to you of vested benefits be in a specific annuity form to protect your surviving spouse. All defined benefit and money purchase pension plans must provide benefits in the form of a *qualified joint and survivor annuity (QJSA)* unless you, with the written consent of your spouse, elect a different form of benefit. A qualified joint and survivor annuity must also be provided by profit-sharing or stock bonus plans if you elect a life annuity payout or the plan does not provide that your nonforfeitable benefit is payable in full upon your death to your surviving spouse, or to another beneficiary if the spouse consents or there is no surviving spouse.

Under a QJSA, you receive an annuity for your life and your surviving spouse receives an annuity for his or her life that is no less than 50% of the amount payable during your joint lives. You may waive the QJSA only with your spouse's consent. Without the consent, you may not take a lump-sum distribution or a single life annuity ending when you die. A single life annuity pays higher monthly benefits during your lifetime than the qualified joint and survivor annuity. If benefits begin under a QJSA and you divorce the spouse to whom you were married as of the annuity starting date, that former spouse will be entitled to the QJSA survivor benefits if you die unless there is a contrary provision in a QDRO *(7.12)*.

The law also requires that a *qualified pre-retirement survivor annuity (QPSA)* be paid to your surviving spouse if you die before the date vested benefits first become payable or if you die after the earliest payment date but before retiring. The QPSA is automatic unless you, with your spouse's consent, agree to a different benefit.

Your plan should provide you with a written explanation of these annuity rules within a reasonable period before the annuity starting date, as well as the rules for electing to waive the joint and survivor annuity benefit and the pre-retirement survivor annuity.

Planning Reminder

Spouse Must Consent in Writing to Your Waiver

Your spouse must consent in writing to your waiver of a required annuity and the selection of a different type of distribution. A spouse's consent must be witnessed by a plan representative or notary public. An election to waive the qualified joint and survivor annuity may be made during the 90-day period ending on the annuity starting date. An election to waive the qualified pre-retirement survivor annuity may be made any time after the first day of the plan year in which you reach age 35. A waiver is revocable during the time permitted to make the election.

Plan may provide exception for marriages of less than one year. The terms of a plan may provide that a QJSA or QPSA will not be provided to a spouse of the plan participant if the couple has been married for less than one year as of the participant's annuity starting date (QJSA) or, if earlier, the date of the participant's death (QPSA).

Cash out of annuity. If the present value of the QJSA is $5,000 or less, your employer may "cash out" your interest without your consent or your spouse's consent by making a lump-sum distribution of the present value of the annuity before the annuity starting date. After the annuity starting date, you and your spouse must consent to a cash-out. Written consent is required for a cash-out if the present value of the annuity exceeds $5,000. Similar cash-out rules apply to a QPSA.

7.12 Court Distributions to Former Spouse Under a QDRO

As a part of a divorce-related property settlement, or to cover alimony or support obligations, a state domestic relations court can require that all or part of a plan participant's retirement benefits be paid to a spouse, former spouse, child, or other dependent. Administrators of pension, profit-sharing, or stock bonus plans are required to honor a qualified domestic relations order (QDRO) that meets specific tax law tests. For example, the QDRO generally may not alter the amount or form of benefits provided by the plan, but it may authorize payments after the participant reaches the earliest retirement age, even if he or she continues working. A QDRO may provide that the recipient spouse is entitled to all, some, or none of the spousal survivor benefits payable under the plan.

Caution

Drafting a QDRO

Drafting a QDRO involves technical details that legal counsel must carefully review. To ease the drafting burdens and reduce litigation over the effect of QDRO provisions, Congress passed a law requiring the IRS to provide sample language for inclusion in a QDRO that meets tax law requirements. The IRS sample language and a discussion of QDRO requirements is in IRS Notice 97-11.

QDRO distributions to spouse or former spouse. If you are the spouse or former spouse of an employee and you receive a distribution pursuant to a QDRO, the distribution is generally taxable to you. However, you may make a tax-free rollover to a traditional IRA or to an eligible employer plan, as discussed at *7.7*. If your spouse or former spouse (the plan participant) was born *before* 1936, a distribution to you of your entire share of the benefits may be eligible for special averaging, provided the distribution, if received by your spouse (or former spouse), would satisfy the lump-sum distribution tests at *7.2*. If the distribution qualifies, you may use Form 4972 to claim 10-year averaging, and possibly the 20% capital gain election; *see 7.4*. If your spouse (or former spouse) was born after 1935, you may *not* elect averaging or 20% capital gain treatment for the distribution. Transfers from a governmental or church plan pursuant to a qualifying domestic relations order are also eligible for special averaging or rollover treatment.

To create a valid QDRO, the court order must contain specific language. The recipient spouse (or former spouse) must be assigned rights to the plan participant's retirement benefits plan, and must be referred to as an "alternate payee" in the court decree. The decree must identify the retirement plan and indicate the amount and number of payments subject to the QDRO. Both spouses must be identified by name and address.

If the above information is not clearly provided in the decree, QDRO treatment may be denied and the plan participant taxed on the retirement plan distributions, rather than the spouse who actually receives payments.

Distributions to a child or other dependent. Payments from a QDRO are taxed to the plan participant, not to the dependent who actually receives them, where the recipient is not a spouse or former spouse.

7.13 When Retirement Benefits Must Begin

The longer you can delay taking retirement distributions from your company plan or self-employed Keogh plan, the greater will be the tax-deferred buildup of your retirement fund. To cut off this tax deferral, the law requires minimum distributions to begin no later than a specified date in order to avoid an IRS penalty. The required beginning date rules apply to distributions from all qualified corporate and self-employed Keogh plans, qualified annuity plans, and Section 457 plans of tax-exempt organizations and state and local government employers. The rules also apply to distributions from tax-sheltered annuities *(7.21)* but only for benefits accrued after 1986; there is no mandatory beginning date for tax-sheltered annuity benefits accrued before 1987.

Unless you are a more-than-5% owner for the plan year ending in the calendar year in which you reach age 70½, your required beginning date is generally the later of these dates: (1) April 1 following the year in which you reach age 70½ *or* (2) April 1 following the year in which you retire. For example, if you reach age 70½ in 2006, are not a more-than-5% owner in 2006, and do not retire until 2008, the first required minimum distribution from the plan does not have to be made to you until April 1, 2009, the year after the year of retirement.

If you are a more-than-5% owner for the plan year ending in the calendar year in which you reach age 70½, your required beginning date is April 1 of the year following the year in which you reach age 70½, even if you are still working. Being a more-than-5% owner means that you own over 5% of the capital or profits interest in the business.

However, an IRS regulation permits a plan to require all employees, and not just more-than-5% owners, to begin required minimum distributions no later than April 1 of the year after the year in which age 70½ is attained. Plans are allowed to offer in-service distributions at an earlier specified age, such as after attaining age 59½ in a profit-sharing plan, or at normal retirement age in a pension plan.

You do not have to figure your required minimum distributions. If you are not receiving an annuity, your plan administrator will determine the minimum amount that must be distributed each year from your account balance, based upon IRS regulations. The rules are similar to the traditional IRA rules discussed at *8.13*.

7.14 Payouts to Beneficiaries

As the beneficiary of an employee's qualified plan account, 403(b) tax-sheltered annuity, or Section 457 plan, your distribution options depend on the terms of the plan. You may prefer the option of receiving payments over your life expectancy but the plan may require that you receive a lump-sum distribution or allow installment payments over only a limited number of years.

Although IRS final regulations generally allow beneficiaries to use a life expectancy distribution method, the IRS rules represent the longest permissible payment period. Employer plans are allowed to require a shorter period and most do.

If you receive a lump-sum distribution, you generally may claim special averaging if the plan participant was born before January 2, 1936; *see 7.6*.

If you are a surviving spouse and receive a lump-sum distribution, you may make a tax-free rollover to another plan *(7.7)* whether or not special averaging is allowed for the distribution. Nonspouse beneficiaries could not make a tax-free rollover before 2007, but a new law allows a distribution after 2006 to be transferred (trustee to trustee) by a nonspouse beneficiary to an inherited IRA; *see 7.8*.

If the plan does give you the option of taking distributions over your life expectancy as allowed by the IRS rules, and you are the employee's surviving spouse, you may be able to delay the commencement of distributions for several years. If your spouse died before the year in which he or she attained age 70½, and you are the sole designated beneficiary of the account as of September 30 of the year following the year of death, you do not have to begin receiving distributions until the end of the year in which your spouse would have attained age 70½. This is an exception to the general rule that requires distributions under the life expectancy method to begin by the end of the year following the year in which the employee died.

7.15 Penalty for Distributions Before Age 59½

A 10% penalty generally applies to taxable distributions made to you before you reach age 59½ from a qualified corporate or Keogh plan, qualified annuity plan, and tax-sheltered annuity plan, but there are several exceptions. For example, the penalty does not apply to distributions made to you after separation from service if the separation occurs during or after the year in which you reach age 55. A full list of exceptions is shown below.

If no exception applies, the penalty is 10% of the taxable distribution. If you make a tax-free rollover *(7.7)*, the distribution is not taxable and not subject to the penalty. If a partial rollover is made, the part not rolled over is taxable and subject to the penalty.

A similar 10% penalty applies to IRA distributions before age 59½; *see 8.12* for IRA penalty rules. The penalty is 25% if a distribution before age 59½ is made from a SIMPLE IRA in the first two years of plan participation; *see 8.18*. The penalty for pre–age 59½ distributions from deferred annuities is at *7.23*. The penalty generally does *not* apply to Section 457 plans of tax-exempt employers or state or local governments. However, if a rollover is made to a governmental Section 457 plan from a qualified plan, 403(b) annuity, or IRA, a later distribution from the Section 457 plan is subject to the penalty to the extent of the rollover.

Exceptions to the penalty. The following distributions are exempt from the 10% penalty, even if made to you before age 59½. If your employer knows that an exception applies, a code for the exception will be entered in Box 7 of Form 1099-R on which the distribution is reported.

Law Alert

Penalty Exception for Qualified Hurricane Distributions

The 10% penalty on early withdrawals does not apply to qualified Hurricane Katrina, Rita, or Wilma distributions; *see 7.30*.

- ***Rollovers.*** Distributions that you roll over tax free under the "direct rollover" or "personal rollover" rules in *7.8 are not subject to the early distribution penalty.*
- ***Disability.*** Distributions made on account of your total disability do not subject you to the early distribution penalty.
- ***Separation from service if age 55 or older.*** The early distribution penalty does not apply to distributions after separation from service if you are age 55 or over in the year you retire or leave the company.
- ***Medical costs.*** Distributions are not subject to the early distribution penalty to the extent that you pay deductible medical expenses exceeding 7.5% of your adjusted gross income (whether or not an itemized deduction for medical expenses is claimed).
- ***Substantially equal payments.*** Distributions received after your separation from service that are part of a series of substantially equal payments (at least annually) over your life expectancy, or over the joint life expectancy of yourself and your designated beneficiary. If you claim the exception and begin to receive such a series of payments but then before age 59½ you receive a lump sum or change the distribution method and you are not totally disabled, a recapture penalty tax will generally apply. The recapture tax also applies to payments received before age 59½ if substantially equal payments are not received for at least five years. The recapture tax applies the 10% penalty to all amounts received before age 59½, as if the exception had never been allowed, plus interest for that period. However, the IRS allows taxpayers who have been receiving substantially equal payments under the fixed amortization or fixed annuitization method to switch without penalty to the required minimum distribution method; *see* Revenue Ruling 2002-62 for details. In private rulings, the IRS has allowed the annual distribution amount to be reduced without penalty after the account is divided in a divorce settlement.
- ***Beneficiaries.*** If you are the beneficiary of a deceased plan participant, you are not subject to the 10% penalty, regardless of your age or the participant's age.
- ***New law: Qualified reservist distribution.*** If you are a member of the reserves called to active military duty before December 31, 2007, for over 179 days, or indefinitely, distributions received during the active duty period that are attributable to elective deferrals (401(k) or 403(b) plan) are not subject to the early distribution penalty. Furthermore, a qualified reservist distribution may be recontributed to the plan within two years after the end of the active duty period. These rules apply retroactively to individuals called to active duty after September 11, 2001. If the two-year period for recontributions has expired, it is extended to August 17, 2008. A refund claim may be made on an amended return for a penalty paid on a qualified distribution or for tax paid on a recontributed distribution. If the amended return deadline has passed for a prior year *(47.2)*, you have until August 16, 2007, to file the amended return.
- ***New law: Public safety employees separated from service.*** The early distribution penalty does not apply to a distribution made after August 17, 2006, from a state or local defined benefit pension plan to a public safety officer (police, fire, emergency medical) who has separated from service in or after the year of reaching age 50.
- ***IRS levy.*** Involuntary distributions that result from an IRS levy on your plan account are not subject to the early distribution penalty.
- ***QDRO.*** Distributions paid to an alternate payee pursuant to a qualified domestic relations court order (QDRO) are not subject to the early distribution penalty.
- ***TEFRA designations.*** Distributions made before 1984 pursuant to a designation under the 1982 Tax Act (TEFRA).
- ***Separation from service before March 2, 1986.*** Distributions to an employee who separated from service by March 1, 1986, are not subject to the early distribution penalty, provided that accrued benefits were in pay status as of that date under a written election specifying the payout schedule.

Financial hardship distributions or distributions used for college or home-buying costs are subject to the penalty. The 10% penalty applies to a hardship distribution that you receive before age 59½ from a 401(k) plan *(7.19)* or 403(b) tax-sheltered annuity plan *(7.21)*. *Even* where it is used to pay tuition costs or to buy a principal residence, there is no penalty exception, although a penalty exception generally applies for IRA distributions used for such purposes (*see 8.12* for limitations).

A hardship distribution used to pay medical costs may qualify for an exception; *see* above.

Law Alert

New Exceptions to Early Distribution Penalty

The Pension Protection Act of 2006 provides penalty exceptions for qualified reservists on active duty and certain public safety officers who separate from service at age 50 or older; *see 7.15* for details.

Caution

Penalty Exception for Substantially Equal Payments

The substantially equal payments exception to the 10% early distribution penalty is generally revoked if qualifying payments are not received for at least five years. For example, you separate from service when you are age 57 and you begin to receive a series of qualifying substantially equal payments. When you are age 61, you stop the payments or modify the payment schedule so that it no longer qualifies. Unless the IRS permits an exception, the 10% penalty applies to the payments received before age $59^1/_2$ because the five-year test was not met.

Filing Instruction

Reporting the Early Distribution Penalty

If you received a distribution before age $59^1/_2$, do not qualify for a penalty exception, and Code 1 is shown in Box 7 of your Form 1099-R, multiply the taxable distribution by 10% and enter that amount as the penalty on Line 60 of Form 1040; write "no" next to Line 60 to indicate that Form 5329 does not have to be filed. If you are subject to the penalty and Code 1 is not entered in Box 7 of Form 1099-R, you must file Form 5329.

You may also have to file Form 5329 to claim a penalty exception. However, filing the form is not required if you qualify for the rollover exception or you qualify for another exception that is correctly coded in Box 7 of Form 1099-R.

Corrective distributions from 401(k) plans. If you are considered a highly compensated employee and excess elective deferrals or excess contributions are made on your behalf, a distribution of the excess to you is not subject to the penalty.

Filing Form 5329 for exceptions. If your employer correctly entered a penalty exception code in Box 7 of Form 1099-R, you do not have to file Form 5329 to claim the exception. You also do not have to file Form 5329 if you made a tax-free rollover of the entire taxable distribution. You must file Form 5329 if you qualify for an exception, other than the rollover exception, that is not indicated in Box 7 of Form 1099-R.

7.16 Restrictions on Loans From Company Plans

Within limits, you may receive a loan from a qualified company plan, annuity plan, 403(b) plan, or government plan without triggering tax consequences. The maximum loan you can receive without tax is the lesser of 50% of your vested account balance or $50,000, but the $50,000 limit is subject to reductions where there are other loans outstanding; *see* below. Loans must be repayable within five years, unless they are used for buying your principal residence. Loans that do not meet these guidelines are treated as taxable distributions from the plan. If the plan treats a loan as a taxable distribution, you should receive a Form 1099-R with Code L marked in Box 7.

See 7.31 for the special loan rules applicable to qualified hurricane victims.

If your vested accrued benefit is $20,000 or less, you are not taxed if the loan, when added to other outstanding loans from all plans of the employer, is $10,000 or less. However, as a practical matter, your maximum loan may not exceed 50% of your vested account balance because of a Labor Department rule that allows only up to 50% of the vested balance to be used as loan security. Loans in excess of the 50% cap are allowed only if additional collateral is provided.

If your vested accrued benefit exceeds $20,000, then the maximum tax-free loan depends on whether you borrowed from any employer plan within the one-year period ending on the day before the date of the new loan. If you did not borrow within the year, you are not taxed on a loan that does not exceed the lesser of $50,000 or 50% of the vested benefit.

If there were loans within the one-year period, the $50,000 limit must be further reduced. The loan, when added to the outstanding loan balance, may not exceed $50,000 less the excess of (1) the highest outstanding loan balance during the one-year period (ending the day before the new loan) over (2) the outstanding balance on the date of the new loan. This reduced $50,000 limit applies where it is less than 50% of the vested benefit; if 50% of the vested benefit was the smaller amount, that would be the maximum tax-free loan.

EXAMPLE

Your vested plan benefit is $200,000. Assume that in December 2006 you borrow $30,000 from the plan. On November 1, 2007, when the outstanding balance on the first loan is $20,000, you want to take another loan without incurring tax.

You may borrow an additional $20,000 without incurring tax: The $50,000 limit is first reduced by the outstanding loan balance of $20,000—leaving $30,000. The reduced $30,000 limit is in turn reduced by $10,000, the excess of $30,000 (the highest loan balance within one year of the new loan) over $20,000 (the loan balance as of November 1).

Repayment period. Generally, loans within the previously discussed limits must be repayable within five years to avoid being treated as a taxable distribution. However, if you use the loan to purchase a principal residence for yourself, the repayment period may be longer than five years; any reasonable period is allowed. This exception does not apply if the plan loan is used to improve your existing principal residence, to buy a second home, or to finance the purchase of a home or home improvements for other family members; such loans are subject to the five-year repayment rule.

Level loan amortization required. To avoid tax consequences on a plan loan, you must be required to repay using a level amortization schedule, with payments at least quarterly. According to Congressional committee reports, you may accelerate repayment, and the employer may use a variable interest rate and require full repayment if you leave the company.

Giving a demand note does not satisfy the repayment requirements. The IRS and Tax Court held the entire amount of an employee's loan to be a taxable distribution since his demand loan did not require level amortization of principal and interest with at least quarterly payments. It did not matter that the employee had paid interest quarterly and actually repaid the loan within five years.

Law Alert

More Favorable Loan Rules for Hurricane Victims

Higher loan limits than otherwise allowable under the rules at *7.16* apply to loans to Hurricane Katrina, Rita, or Wilma victims, and a delay is provided for repaying outstanding loans; *see 7.31*.

Caution

Unpaid Loan Taxable If You Leave Job Unless Rolled Over

If you leave your company before your loan is paid off, the company will reduce your vested account balance by the outstanding debt and report the defaulted amount as a taxable distribution on Form 1099-R.

For example, if your vested account balance is $100,000, and the outstanding loan is $20,000, your account balance is reduced to $80,000. If you elect to receive the balance, rather than choosing a direct rollover, $20,000 will be withheld (20% of the full $100,000) and you will receive only $60,000; *see 7.8*. However, the full $100,000 is treated as a taxable distribution. If you do not roll over *(7.8)* the entire $100,000 within 60 days, you will be taxed on the portion not rolled over, and possibly be subject to a 10% penalty if you were under age $59^1/_2$ at the time of the distribution *(see 7.15)*.

In other words, tax on the defaulted loan balance can be avoided by depositing that amount into a rollover IRA within 60 days of the date that the balance was treated as being in default.

If required installments are not made, the entire loan balance must be treated as a "deemed distribution" from the plan under IRS proposed regulations. However, the IRS allows the plan administrator to permit a grace period of up to one calendar quarter. If the missed installment is not paid by the end of the grace period, there is at that time a deemed distribution in the amount of the outstanding loan balance.

Under IRS regulations, loan repayments may be suspended for up to one year (or longer if you are in the uniformed services) if you take a leave of absence during which you are paid less than the installments due. However, the installments after the leave must at least equal the original required amount and the loan must be repaid by the end of the allowable repayment period (five years if not used to buy a principal residence). For example, on July 1, 2006, when his vested account balance is $80,000, Joe Smith takes out a $40,000 non–principal residence loan, to be repaid with interest in level monthly installments of $825 over five years. He makes nine payments and then takes a year of unpaid leave. When he returns to work he can either increase his monthly payment to make up for the missed payments or resume paying $825 a month and on June 30, 2011, repay the entire balance owed in a lump sum.

Spousal consent generally required to get a loan. All plans subject to the joint and survivor rules in *7.11* must require spousal consent in order to use your account balance as security for the loan in case you default. Check with your plan administrator for consent requirements.

Interest deduction limitations. If you want to borrow from your account to buy a first or second residence and you are not a "key" employee *(3.4)*, you can generally obtain a full interest deduction by using the residence as collateral for the loan; *see 15.2*. Your account balance may not be used to secure the loan. Key employees are not allowed any interest deduction for plan loans.

If you use a plan loan for investment purposes and are not a key employee, and the loan is not secured by your elective deferrals (or allocable income) to a 401(k) plan or tax-sheltered annuity, the loan account interest is deductible up to investment income; *see 15.10*. Interest on loans used for personal purposes is not deductible, unless your residence is the security for the loan.

401(k), 403(b), and Government Tax-Deferred Savings Plans

7.17 Tax Benefits of 401(k) Plans

If your company has a profit-sharing or stock bonus plan, it has the opportunity of giving you additional tax-sheltered pay. The tax law allows the company to add a cash or deferred pay plan, called a 401(k) plan.

Your company may offer to contribute to a 401(k) plan trust account on your behalf if you forego a salary increase, but in most plans, contributions take the form of salary-reduction deferrals. Under a salary-reduction agreement, you elect to contribute a specified percentage of your wages to the 401(k) plan instead of receiving it as regular salary. In addition, your company may match a portion of your contribution. A salary-reduction deferral is treated as a contribution by your employer that is not taxable to you if the annual contribution limits are not exceeded.

Employers have the option of amending their 401(k) plans to allow employees to designate part or all of their elective contributions as Roth contributions; *see 7.20*.

Salary-reduction deferrals. Making elective salary deferrals allows you to defer tax on salary and get a tax-free buildup of earnings within your 401(k) plan account until withdrawals are made.

An annual limit applies to salary-reduction deferrals from a 401(k) plan, and the same limit applies to 403(b) tax-sheltered annuities *(7.21)*, 457 plans *(7.22)*, and salary-reduction SEPs *(8.16)*. For 2006, the regular limit was $15,000 and an additional $5,000 contribution allowed for plan participants age 50 or older if the plan permitted the additional contributions. These limits may be increased for 2007 by an inflation adjustment; *see* the *e-Supplement*. The maximum deferral is lower for employees of "small" employers who adopt a SIMPLE 401(k); *see* below.

Elective deferrals within the annual limit are *pre-tax* contributions, so they are not subject to income tax withholding. However, the contributions are subject to Social Security and Medicare withholdings.

Your employer may not require you to make elective deferrals in order to obtain any other benefits, apart from matching contributions. For example, benefits provided under health plans or other compensation plans may not be conditioned on your making salary deferrals to a 401(k) plan.

Law Alert

Automatic 401(k) Plan Coverage

The Pension Protection Act of 2006 encourages employers to automatically enroll employees in a 401(k) plan. Unless employees affirmatively opt out, a specified percentage of their pay is contributed to the plan. Even though the employees do not make affirmative elections to contribute, such plans are qualified provided that the employees are given advance notice of their right either to receive cash or have the designated amount contributed by the employer to the plan.

Starting in 2008, the new law grants employers protection from nondiscrimination restrictions if they adopt automatic enrollment plans that include mandatory matching or non-elective employer contributions.

Distributions. Withdrawals from a 401(k) plan before age 59½ are restricted, as explained at *7.19*. For those born before January 2, 1936, a lump-sum distribution may be eligible for averaging under the rules in *7.4*. Mandatory 20% withholding applies to a lump sum as well as other distributions that are eligible for averaging; exceptions are at *7.7*.

Nondiscrimination rules. The law imposes strict contribution percentage tests to prevent discrimination in favor of employees who are highly compensated. If these tests are violated, the employer is subject to penalties and the plan could be disqualified unless the excess contributions (plus allocable income) are distributed back to the highly compensated employees within specified time limits.

SIMPLE 401(k). Nondiscrimination tests are eased for employers who adopt a 401(k) plan with SIMPLE contribution provisions. A SIMPLE 401(k) may be set up only by employers who in the preceding year had no more than 100 employees with compensation of at least $5,000. An employer who contributes to a SIMPLE 401(k) must report on a calendar-year basis and may not maintain another qualified plan for employees eligible to participate in the SIMPLE plan.

If the SIMPLE contribution requirements are met, the plan is considered to meet 401(k) nondiscrimination requirements. Employee elective deferrals may not exceed an annual limitation, which was $10,000 for 2006. For 2007 and later years, the $10,000 limit may be increased by a cost-of-living adjustment. The plan may also allow additional contributions by participants who are age 50 or older by the end of the year. The limit on the additional contribution was $2,500 for 2006 and may be increased for 2007 by a cost-of-living adjustment.

The employer must either match the employee deferral, up to 3% of compensation, or contribute 2% of compensation for all eligible employees, whether or not they make elective deferrals. All contributions are nonforfeitable. No other type of contribution is allowed. In figuring the 3% or 2% employer contribution, compensation is subject to an annual compensation ceiling; for 2006 it is $220,000.

Partnership plans. Partnership plans that allow partners to vary annual contributions are treated as 401(k) plans by the IRS. Thus, elective deferrals are subject to the annual limit *(7.18)* and the special 401(k) plan nondiscrimination rules apply.

7.18 Limit on Salary-Reduction Deferrals

Elective deferrals to a 401(k) plan must not exceed the annual tax-free ceiling; otherwise, the plan could be disqualified. If you also participate in a 403(b) tax-sheltered annuity plan *(7.21)* or simplified employee pension plan established before 1997 *(8.16)*, the limit applies to the total salary reductions for all the plans and any excess deferral should be withdrawn as discussed below. Certain highly compensated employees may be unable to take advantage of the maximum annual tax-free ceiling because of restrictions imposed by nondiscrimination tests.

The regular elective salary-deferral limit of $15,000 for 2006 is subject to cost-of-living increases for 2007 and later years. The "catch-up" contribution limit for plan participants age 50 or older (in plans that permit the additional catch-up contribution), which for 2006 was $5,000, is also subject to annual cost-of-living increases starting in 2007.

To avoid the strict nondiscrimination tests for employee elective deferrals and employer matching contributions, an employer may make contributions to a SIMPLE 401(k); *see 7.17*.

An employer may make matching or other contributions, provided the total contribution for the year, including the employee's pre-tax salary deferral and any employee after-tax contributions, does not exceed the annual limit for defined contribution plans, which for 2006 was the *lesser* of 100% of compensation or $44,000.

Caution

Reduced Deferral Limit for Highly Compensated Employees

To avoid discrimination problems an employer may set a lower limit for elective salary deferrals by highly compensated employees than the generally applicable ceiling.

If, after contributions are made, the plan fails to meet the nondiscrimination tests, the excess contributions will either be returned to the highly compensated employees or kept in the plan but recharacterized as after-tax contributions. In either case, the excess contribution is taxable. Form 1099-R will indicate the excess contribution.

Employers may avoid the nondiscrimination tests by meeting the SIMPLE plan contribution rules; *see 7.17*.

Starting in 2008, employers who adopt qualifying automatic enrollment features for their 401(k) plans are treated as meeting the nondiscrimination tests.

Withdrawing excess deferrals. A single plan must apply the annual limit on salary deferrals to maintain qualified status. If your deferrals to the plan for a year exceed the annual limit, the excess, plus allocable earnings, must be distributed to you or the plan risks disqualification. If you participated in more than one plan and the deferrals to all of the plans exceeded the limit, you should withdraw the excess, plus the allocable income, from any of the plans, by April 15 of the year following the year of the excess deferral.

Whether the excess deferrals were made to one or several plans, you must report the excess as wages for the year of the deferral on Line 7 of Form 1040. If you withdraw the excess by April 15 of the following year, it is not taxable again when you receive it. However, if the withdrawal of the excess is not received by the April 15 date, the excess is taxed again when received. The withdrawal of allocable earnings is always taxable in the year of the distribution. If a withdrawal of an excess deferral to a salary-reduction SEP (set up before 1997; *see 8.16*) is not withdrawn by the April 15 date, it is treated as a regular IRA contribution that could be subject to the penalty for excess IRA contributions *(see 8.7)*.

Excess deferrals (and earnings) distributed by the April 15 date are not subject to the 10% penalty for premature distributions *(7.15)* even if you are under age 59½ .

For the year in which the excess deferral and allocable earnings are distributed to you, the plan will send you a Form 1099-R. Box 7 will include a code designating the year for which the excess is taxable.

7.19 Withdrawals From 401(k) Plans Restricted

By law, you may not withdraw funds attributable to elective salary-reduction contributions to a 401(k) plan unless (1) you no longer work for the employer maintaining the plan; (2) you have reached age 59½; (3) you have become totally disabled; (4) you can show financial hardship; (5) you are the beneficiary of a deceased employee; or (6) the plan is terminated and no successor defined contribution plan (other than an employee stock ownership plan) is maintained by the employer. If a distribution is allowed and all of your plan contributions were pre-tax elective salary deferrals, the entire distribution is taxable unless it is rolled over to an eligible plan; *see 7.7*.

Under IRS rules, it is difficult to qualify for hardship withdrawals; *see* below. If you do qualify, the withdrawal is taxable, and if you are under age 59½ , it is subject to the 10% early distribution penalty unless you meet a penalty exception shown in *7.15*.

The hardship provision and age 59½ withdrawal allowance do not apply to certain "pre-ERISA" money purchase pension plans (in existence June 27, 1974).

An "involuntary" distribution resulting from an IRS levy on a 401(k) plan account is taxable to the employee (assuming only "pre-tax" contributions) but is not subject to the 10% penalty on pre-age 59½ distributions *(7.15)*.

Withdrawals before age 59½. Withdrawals for medical disability, financial hardship, or separation from service are subject to the 10% penalty for premature withdrawals unless you meet one of the exceptions listed at *7.15*.

Loans. If you are allowed to borrow from the plan, the loan restrictions at *7.16* apply.

Qualifying for hardship withdrawals. IRS regulations restrict hardship withdrawals of pre-tax salary deferrals. If you qualify under the following restrictive rules you may withdraw your elective deferrals. Income allocable to elective deferrals may be withdrawn as part of a hardship distribution only in limited circumstances. If the plan so provides, income may be withdrawn if it was credited to your account by a cut-off date that is no *later* than the end of the last plan year ending before July 1, 1989.

The IRS requires you to show an immediate and heavy financial need that cannot be met with other resources.

Financial need includes the following expenses (this list may be expanded by the IRS in rulings):

- Purchase of a principal residence for yourself (but not mortgage payments);
- Tuition, related fees and room and board for the next 12 months of post-secondary education for yourself, your spouse, children, or other dependents;
- Medical expenses previously incurred for yourself, your spouse, or dependents or expenses incurred to obtain medical care for such persons;
- Preventing your eviction or mortgage foreclosure; and
- Paying funeral expenses for a family member.

Even if you can show financial need, you may not make a hardship withdrawal if you have other resources to pay the expenses. You do not have to provide your employer with a detailed financial statement, but you must state to your employer that you cannot pay the expenses with: compensation, insurance, or reimbursements; liquidation of your assets without causing yourself hardship by virtue of the liquidation; stopping your contributions, including salary deferrals, to the plan; other distributions or nontaxable loans from plans of any employer; or borrowing from a commercial lender. Your spouse's assets, as well as those of your minor children, are considered to be yours unless you show that they are not available to you. For example, property held in trust for a child or under the Uniform Transfers (or Gifts) to Minors Act is not treated as your property.

Planning Reminder

Hardship Distribution Not Subject to Withholding

A hardship distribution from a 401(k) plan is not eligible for rollover *(7.7)* to an IRA or an eligible employer plan. Your employer will not apply 20% withholding to the distribution, as mandatory withholding applies only to rollover-eligible distributions *(7.7)*.

Under a special rule, you are considered to lack other resources if you have taken all available distributions from all plans of the employer, including nontaxable loans, and you suspend making any contributions to any of the employer's qualified and nonqualified deferred compensation plans for at least six months after receipt of the hardship distribution. Furthermore, all of the employer's plans must provide that for the year after the year of the hardship distribution, elective contributions must be limited to the excess of the annual salary deferral limitation over the elective contributions made for the year of the hardship distribution.

7.20 Designated Roth Contributions to 401(k) Plans

Employers with 401(k) plans may allow employees to irrevocably designate all or part of their pre-tax elective salary deferrals (and catch-up contributions if age 50 or older) as after-tax Roth contributions. The plan must be amended to allow Roth contributions. The Roth contributions, being after-tax, are treated as taxable wages subject to withholding.

The major incentive for employees to designate 401(k) plan contributions as Roth contributions is to obtain tax-free treatment for distributions under the qualified distribution rules applicable to Roth IRAs. That is, distributions of designated Roth contributions plus accrued earnings would be totally tax free if received after age 59½ and a five-year holding period; *see 8.23.*

Roth 401(k) contributions are available to individuals who might otherwise be unable to make annual contributions to a Roth IRA. Subject to 401(k) nondiscrimination tests, there are no income limitations on the right to make Roth 401(k) contributions, whereas contributions to a Roth IRA are barred if adjusted gross income exceeds an annual threshold; *see 8.20.*

Plans must segregate designated Roth contributions from regular 401(k) elective deferrals and maintain separate accounts for employees with both types of contributions. Gains, losses, and other credits or charges, as well as contribution and withdrawals, must be allocated between the accounts on a reasonable and consistent basis. Designated Roth contributions are subject to the 401(k) nonforfeitability and distribution restrictions and also to the nondiscrimination tests for pre-tax elective contributions.

Unless the employer provides otherwise in the adoption agreement, the plan will accept a rollover to a designated Roth account only if it is a direct rollover from another designated Roth account. A direct rollover of a distribution from a designated Roth account can be made only to a Roth IRA or to another designated Roth account.

403(b) plans. Under similar rules, designated Roth contributions may be made available under 403(b) plans *(7.21)* sponsored by public schools and tax-exempt organizations.

7.21 Annuities for Employees of Tax-Exempts and Schools (403(b) Plans)

If you are employed by a state or local government public school, or by a tax-exempt religious, charitable, scientific, or educational organization, or are on the civilian staff or faculty of the Uniformed Services University of the Health Sciences (Department of Defense), you may be able to arrange for the purchase of a nonforfeitable tax-sheltered annuity. Tax-sheltered annuities may also be purchased by self-employed ministers and by non-tax-exempt employers of ordained or licensed ministers or chaplains. Another name for a tax-sheltered annuity is a 403(b) plan. A 403(b) plan may invest funds for employees in mutual-fund shares as well as in annuity contracts.

The purchase of the annuity or mutual-fund shares is generally made through pre-tax salary-reduction contributions. Your plan may allow you to make after-tax contributions, and the employer may make non-elective contributions.

Note: As the following contribution rules for tax-sheltered annuities have been stated in general terms, we suggest that you also consult your employer or the issuer of the contract. IRS Publication 571 has detailed examples. Also, the IRS has proposed regulations that would remove investment options from participating employees; *see* the *e-Supplement* for an update.

Caution

Transfers May Be Blocked

The IRS has released proposed regulations that would eliminate the right of employees to make tax-free transfers of their accounts to vendors outside of the employer's 403(b) plan; *see* the *e-Supplement* for an update.

Limit on tax-free contributions. Tax-free salary reductions are limited to the annual ceiling for elective deferrals, and the plan may permit additional deferrals for participants who are age 50 or older; *see 7.18* for the deferral limits.

If, in addition to a tax-sheltered annuity, you make salary deferrals to a 401(k) plan, SIMPLE plan, or simplified employee pension plan, the annual salary-reduction limit applies to the total deferrals; *see 7.18*. If you defer more than the annual limit, the excess is taxable. Further, if a salary-reduction deferral in excess of the annual limit is made and the excess is not distributed to you by April 15 of the following year, the excess will be taxed twice—not only in the year of deferral but again in the year it is actually distributed. To avoid the double tax, any excess deferral plus the income attributable to such excess should be distributed no later than April 15 of the year following the year in which the excess deferral is made; *see 7.18*.

The annual salary-reduction ceiling is generally increased by $3,000 for employees of educational organizations, hospitals, churches, home health service agencies, and health and welfare service agencies who have completed 15 years of service. However, the extra $3,000 annual deferral may not be claimed indefinitely. There is a lifetime limit of $15,000 on the amount of extra deferrals allowed. Furthermore, the extra deferrals may not be claimed after lifetime elective deferrals to the plan exceed $5,000 multiplied by your years of service. Publication 571 has a worksheet for figuring the extra deferral.

The employee's salary reduction plus any after-tax contributions and any non-elective contributions made by the employer for the year are tax free only if they do not exceed the annual limit on contributions to a defined contribution plan, which for 2006 is the lesser of 100% of compensation or $44,000.

Distributions from tax-sheltered annuities. Distributions attributable to salary-reduction contributions to a 403(b) tax-sheltered annuity are allowed only when an employee reaches age 59½, has experienced a severance from employment, becomes disabled, suffers financial hardship, or dies. The hardship distribution rules are the same as for 401(k) plans; *see 7.19*. Annuity payments are taxed under the general rules for employees, discussed at *7.26*. Payments are fully taxable if the only contributions to the plan were salary-reduction contributions excluded from income (pre-tax contributions) under the annual limits discussed earlier in this section.

Non-annuity distributions from a tax-sheltered annuity do not qualify for special averaging *(7.4)*, but a tax-free rollover of a distribution may be made to another tax-sheltered annuity or traditional IRA unless the distribution is not eligible for rollover under the rules at *7.7*. An eligible rollover distribution *(7.7)* from a 403(b) plan may also be rolled over to a qualified plan or governmental Section 527 plan. However, if a rollover from a 403(b) plan to a qualified plan is made, a subsequent lump-sum distribution from the qualified plan will not be eligible for special averaging *(7.4)* or capital gain treatment *(7.5)* even if you were born before January 2, 1936, and those provisions would otherwise be available. If you do not choose to have the payer of the distribution make a direct rollover, mandatory 20% withholding will be applied. You may then personally make a rollover within 60 days, but you would have to include the withheld amount in the rolled-over amount to avoid tax on the entire distribution. *See 7.8* for further rollover and withholding details.

Benefits accruing after 1986 are subject to the required beginning date rules discussed at *7.13* and a penalty may be imposed for failure to take minimum required distributions. Benefits accrued before 1987 are not subject to the required minimum distribution rules until the year you reach age 75.

7.22 Government and Exempt Organization Deferred Pay Plans

Federal government civilian employees may make tax-deferred salary-reduction contributions to the Federal Thrift Savings Fund. Employees of state and local governments and of tax-exempt organizations may be able to make tax-free salary-reduction contributions to a Section 457 deferred compensation plan.

Federal employees. Federal employees may elect to defer up to 10% of their basic pay to the Federal Thrift Savings Fund, but no more than the limit on elective deferrals. The deferral limit is the same as for 401(k) plans; *see 7.18*. Deferrals are not taxed until distributed from the plan. The deferred amount is counted as wages for purposes of computing Social Security taxes and benefits.

Distributions from the Thrift Savings Fund are generally fully taxable. However, lump-sum distributions are eligible for special averaging under the rules discussed in *7.4*, or tax-free rollover treatment; *see 7.7*. If you separate from service before the year in which you reach age 55, you are subject to the 10% penalty for premature distributions unless you are disabled or qualify for the medical exception discussed at *7.15*.

Caution

Unforeseen Emergency Distributions

If you can show severe financial hardship arising from a sudden illness or accident, or loss of property due to events beyond your control, and you are unable to obtain funds elsewhere, you may make a withdrawal from your employer's Section 457 plan. However, the need to buy a home or pay college expenses does not qualify as an unforeseeable emergency.

Section 457 plans. State and local governments and tax-exempt organizations other than churches may set up Section 457 deferred compensation plans. Employees may annually defer compensation up to the 401(k) elective deferrable limit; *see 7.17*. Employees in state and local government 457 plans who are 50 or older may be permitted by the plan to make additional contributions; *see 7.17*. A limited "catch-up" provision may allow employees in the last three years before reaching normal retirement age to defer larger amounts. The "catch-up" rule allows up to double the regular limit to be deferred, provided that the full deferrable limit has not been used in prior years. For state and local government plan participants, the deferral limit under the three-year rule will never be less than the regular deferral limit for the year plus the additional contribution limit for participants age 50 or older.

Deferred compensation (and allocable income) under a Section 457 plan of a tax-exempt employer (non-governmental) is not taxed until paid or otherwise made available. Amounts deferred (and earnings) under state or local government 457 plans are taxed only when paid.

Distributions to employees or beneficiaries generally may not be made before the year the employee turns age 70½, has a severance from employment, or faces an "unforeseeable" emergency, assuming the plan allows payment in cases of emergency. Under IRS regulations, an unforeseeable emergency generally means severe financial hardship resulting from a sudden illness or accident of the employee or a dependent, or loss of property due to a casualty. If the employee can obtain funds by ceasing deferrals to the plan or by liquidating assets without causing himself or herself severe financial hardship, payment from the plan is not allowed. The regulations specifically prohibit payments from the plan to purchase a home or pay for a child's college tuition.

Eligible rollover distributions *(7.7)* from a governmental 457 plan (but not a nongovernmental plan) may be rolled over tax free to a traditional IRA, another governmental 457 plan, a qualified plan, or a 403(b) plan. Rollovers of eligible distributions may also be made to governmental 457 plans. If a rollover from a governmental 457 plan is made to a qualified plan, special averaging *(7.4)* and capital gain treatment *(7.5)* will *not* be allowed for a lump-sum distribution from the qualified plan even if such treatment would otherwise be available.

See 7.13 for required distribution starting dates after age 70½ and minimum payout rules.

Note: Check with your employer for other details on Section 457 contributions and distribution rules.

Reporting Commercial Annuities

7.23 Figuring the Taxable Part of Your Annuity

Tax treatment of a distribution depends on whether you receive it before or after the annuity starting date, and on the amount of your investment. A cash withdrawal before age 59½ from an annuity contract is generally subject to a 10% penalty, but there are exceptions; the penalty is discussed at the end of this section. If your annuity is from an employer plan, *see 7.26*.

The *annuity starting date* is either the first day of the first period for which you receive a payment or the date on which the obligation under the contract becomes fixed, whichever is later. If your right to an annuity was fixed on January 1, 2006, and your monthly payments started on July 1, 2006, for the period starting June 1, 2006, June 1, 2006, is your annuity starting date.

Filing Tip

Surrender of Contract

Payments on a complete surrender of the annuity contract or at maturity are taxable only to the extent they exceed your investment.

Payments before the annuity starting date. If your commercial annuity contract was purchased *after* August 13, 1982, withdrawals before the annuity starting date are taxable to the extent that the cash value of the contract (ignoring any surrender charge), immediately before the distribution, exceeds your investment in the contract at that time. Loans under the contract or pledges are treated as cash withdrawals.

If the contract was purchased before August 14, 1982, withdrawals *before* the annuity starting date are taxable only to the extent they exceed your investment. Loans are tax free and are not treated as withdrawals subject to this rule. Where additional investments were made after August 13, 1982, cash withdrawals are first considered to be tax-free distributions of the investment before August 14, 1982. If the withdrawal exceeds this investment, the balance is fully taxable to the extent of earnings on the contract, with any excess withdrawals treated as a tax-free recovery of the investment made after August 13, 1982.

Payments on or after the annuity starting date. If the withdrawal is a regular (not variable) annuity payment, that part of the annuity payment allocated to your cost investment is treated as a nontaxable return of the cost; the balance is taxable income earned on the investment. You may find the taxable part of your annuity payment by following the six steps listed below under "Taxable Portion of Commercial Annuity Payments." If you have a variable annuity, the computation of the tax-free portion is discussed following Step 6.

Payments on or after the annuity starting date that are not part of the annuity, such as dividends, are generally taxable, but there are exceptions. If the contract is a life insurance or endowment contract, withdrawals of earnings are tax free to the extent of your investment, unless the contract is a modified endowment contract.

Taxable Portion of Commercial Annuity Payments

If the payer of the contract does not provide the taxable amount in Box 2a of Form 1099-R, you can compute the taxable amount of your commercial annuity using the following steps.

Step 1: Figure your investment in the annuity contract. If you have no investment in the contract, annuity income is fully taxable; therefore, ignore Steps 2 through 6.

If your annuity is—	*Your cost is—*
Single premium annuity contract	The single premium paid.
Deferred annuity contract	The total premiums paid.
A gift	Your donor's cost.
An employee annuity	The total of your after-tax contributions to the plan plus your employer's contributions that you were required to report as income; *see 7.26.*
With a refund feature	The value of the refund feature.

From cost, you subtract the following items:

- Any premiums refunded, and rebates or dividends received on or before the annuity starting date.
- Additional premiums for double indemnity or disability benefits.
- Amounts received under the contract before the annuity starting date to the extent these amounts were not taxed; *see* above.
- Value of a refund feature; *see* below.

Value of refund feature. Your investment in the contract is reduced by the value, if any, of the refund feature.

Your annuity has a refund feature when these three requirements are present: (1) the refund under the contract depends, even in part, on the life expectancy of at least one person; (2) the contract provides for payments to a beneficiary or the annuitant's estate after the annuitant's death; and (3) the payments to the estate or beneficiary are a refund of the amount paid for the annuity.

The value of the refund feature is figured by using a life expectancy multiple that may be found in Treasury Table III or Table VII, depending on the date of your investment; the tables are in IRS Publication 939.

Where an employer paid part of the cost, the refund is figured on only the part paid by the employee.

The refund feature is considered to be zero if (1) for a joint and survivor annuity, both annuitants are age 74 or younger, the payments are guaranteed for less than 2½ years, and the survivor's annuity is at least 50% of the first annuitant's (retiree's) annuity or (2) for a single-life annuity without survivor benefits, the payments are guaranteed for less than 2½ years and you are age 57 or younger if using the new (unisex) annuity tables, age 42 or younger if male and using the old annuity tables, or age 47 or younger if female and using the old annuity tables.

Also subtract from cost any tax-free recovery of your investment received *before* the annuity starting date, as previously discussed.

Step 2: Find your expected return. This is the total of all the payments you are to receive. If the payments are to be made to you for life, your expected return is figured by multiplying the amount of the annual payment by your life expectancy as of the nearest birthday to the annuity starting date. The annuity starting date is the first day of the first period for which an annuity payment is received. For example, on January 1 you complete payment under an annuity contract providing for monthly payments starting on July 1 for the period beginning June 1. The annuity

Planning Reminder

Life Expectancy Tables

The life expectancy tables for figuring your expected return are in IRS Publication 939.

starting date is June 1. Use that date in computing your investment in the contract under Step 1 and your expected return.

If payments are for life, you find your life expectancy in IRS tables included in IRS Publication 939. If you have a single life annuity for which you made any investment after June 30, 1986, use IRS Table V from Publication 939, shown on page 174. Generally, Table 1 on page 174 is used if the entire investment was before July 1, 1986, but you may elect to use Table V; *see 7.24*. When using the single life table, your age is the age at the birthday nearest the annuity starting date. If you have a joint and survivor annuity and after your death the same payments are to be made to a second annuitant, the expected return is based on your joint life expectancy. Use Treasury Table II in IRS Publication 939 to get joint life expectancy if the entire investment was before July 1, 1986. Use Treasury Table VI if any investment was made after June 30, 1986. If your joint and survivor annuity provides for a different payment amount to the survivor, you must separately compute the expected return for each annuitant; this method is explained in Publication 939. Adjustments to the life expectancy multiple are required when your annuity is payable quarterly, semiannually, or annually. The required adjustment is discussed in *7.24*.

If the payments are for a fixed number of years or for life, whichever is shorter, find your expected return by multiplying your annual payments by a life expectancy multiple found in Treasury Table IV if your entire investment was before July 1, 1986, or Table VIII if any investment was made after June 30, 1986.

If payments are for a fixed number of years (as in an endowment contract) without regard to your life expectancy, find your expected return by multiplying your annual payment by the number of years.

Note: *See 7.24* for more information on the life expectancy tables.

Step 3: Divide the investment in the contract (Step 1) by the expected return (Step 2). This will give you the tax-free percentage of your yearly annuity payments. The tax-free percentage remains the same for the remaining years of the annuity, even if payments increase due to a cost-of-living adjustment. A different computation of the tax-free percentage applies to variable annuities; *see* below.

If your annuity started before 1987, and you live longer than your projected life expectancy (shown in the IRS table), you may continue to apply the same tax-free percentage to each payment you receive. Thus, you may exclude from income more than you paid. However, if your annuity starting date is after 1986, your lifetime exclusion may not exceed your net cost, generally your unrecovered investment as of the annuity starting date, without reduction for any refund feature. Once you have recovered your net cost, further payments are fully taxable.

If your annuity starting date is after July 1, 1986, and you die before recovering your net cost, a deduction is allowed on your final tax return for the unrecovered cost. If a refund of the investment is made under the contract to a beneficiary, the beneficiary is allowed the deduction. The deduction is claimed as a miscellaneous itemized deduction that is ***not*** subject to the 2% adjusted gross income floor; *see* Chapter 19.

Step 4: Find your total annuity payments for the year. For example, you received 10 monthly payments of $100 as your annuity began in March. Your total payments are $1,000, the monthly payment multiplied by 10.

Step 5: Nontaxable portion—multiply the percentage in Step 3 by the total in Step 4. The result is the nontaxable portion (or excludable amount) of your annuity payments.

Step 6: Taxable portion—subtract the amount in Step 5 from the amount in Step 4. This is the part of your annuity for the year that is subject to tax.

Note: An example of figuring the taxable and nontaxable portions for a single life annuity is in *7.24*.

Variable annuities. If you have a variable annuity that pays different benefits depending on cost-of-living indexes, profits earned by the annuity fund, or similar fluctuating standards, the tax-free portion of each payment is computed by dividing your investment in the contract (Step 1 above) by the total number of payments you expect to receive. If the annuity is for a definite period, the total number of payments equals the number of payments to be made each year multiplied by the number of years you will receive payments. If the annuity is for life, you divide the amount you invested in the contract by a multiple obtained from the appropriate life expectancy table; *see* Step 2. The result is the tax-free amount of annual annuity income.

If you receive a payment that is *less* than the nontaxable amount, you may elect when you receive the next payment to recalculate the nontaxable portion. The amount by which the prior nontaxable portion exceeded the payment you received is divided by the number of payments you expect as of the time of the next payment. The result is added to the previously calculated nontaxable portion, and the sum is the amount of each future payment to be excluded from tax. A statement must be attached to your return explaining the recomputation.

EXAMPLES

1. Andrew Taylor's total investment of $12,000 for a variable annuity was made after June 30, 1986. The annuity starting date was January 1, 2006. The annuity payments began July 1, 2006, in varying annual installments for life. Andrew's age (nearest birthday) at the January 1 starting date was 65. To figure the tax-free part of each payment, he uses a life expectancy multiple of 20.0, the amount shown in Table V on page 174 for a person age 65. The amount of each payment excluded from tax is:

Investment in the contract	$12,000
Multiple (from Table V)	20.0
Amount of each payment excluded from tax ($12,000 ÷ 20)	$600

   If the first payment is $920, then 320 ($920 – $600) will be included in Andrew's 2006 income.

2. Assume that, after receiving the 2006 payment of $920 in Example 1, Andrew receives $500 in 2007 and $1,200 in 2008. None of the 2007 payment is taxed, as $600 is excludable from each annual payment. Andrew may also elect to recompute his annual exclusion starting with the 2008 payment. The exclusion is recomputed as follows:

Amount excludable in 2006	$600
Amount received in 2006	500
Difference	$100
Multiple as of 1/1/2008 (*see* Table V on page 174 for age 67)	18.4
Amount added to previously determined annual exclusion ($100 ÷ 18.4)	$5.43
Revised annual exclusion for 2008 and later years ($600 + $5.43)	$605.43
Amount taxable in 2008 ($1,200 – $605.43)	$594.57

Penalty on Premature Withdrawals From Deferred Annuities

As discussed at the beginning of *7.23*, withdrawals before the annuity starting date may be taxable or tax free, depending on whether investments were made before or after August 13, 1982.

Withdrawals before age 59½ are also generally subject to a penalty of 10% of the amount includable in income; *see* the Filing Tip on the right. A withdrawal from an annuity contract is penalized unless:

1. You have reached age 59½ or have become totally disabled.
2. The distribution is part of a series of substantially equal payments, made at least annually over your life expectancy or over the joint life expectancies of you and a beneficiary. If you can avoid the penalty under this exception and you change to a nonqualifying distribution method within five years or before age 59½, such as where you receive a lump sum, a recapture tax will apply to the payments received before age 59½.
3. The payment is received by a beneficiary or estate after the policyholder's death.
4. Payment is from a qualified retirement plan, tax-sheltered annuity, or IRA; in this case the penalty rules of *7.15* (qualified plans) or *8.8* (IRAs) apply.
5. Payment is allocable to investments made before August 14, 1982.
6. Payment is from an annuity contract under a qualified personal injury settlement.
7. Payment is from a single-premium annuity where the starting date is no more than one year from the date of purchase.
8. Payment is from an annuity purchased by an employer upon the termination of a qualified retirement plan and held until you separated from service.

Filing Tip

Form 5329

If no exception to the early withdrawal penalty applies, you compute the 10% penalty in Part I of Form 5329. The penalty is 5% instead of 10% if as of March 1, 1986, you were receiving payments under a specific schedule pursuant to your written election. Attach an explanation to Form 5329 if you are applying the 5% rate.

Table 7-2 Life Expectancy Tables

TABLE I Investments Before July 1, 1986

Ages			Ages			Ages		
Male	*Female*	*Multiples*	*Male*	*Female*	*Multiples*	*Male*	*Female*	*Multiples*
6	11	65.0	41	46	33.0	76	81	9.1
7	12	64.1	42	47	32.1	77	82	8.7
8	13	63.2	43	48	31.2	78	83	8.3
9	14	62.3	44	49	30.4	79	84	7.8
10	15	61.4	45	50	29.6	80	85	7.5
11	16	60.4	46	51	28.7	81	86	7.1
12	17	59.5	47	52	27.9	82	87	6.7
13	18	58.6	48	53	27.1	83	88	6.3
14	19	57.7	49	54	26.3	84	89	6.0
15	20	56.7	50	55	25.5	85	90	5.7
16	21	55.8	51	56	24.7	86	91	5.4
17	22	54.9	52	57	24.0	87	92	5.1
18	23	53.9	53	58	23.2	88	93	4.8
19	24	53.0	54	59	22.4	89	94	4.5
20	25	52.1	55	60	21.7	90	95	4.2
21	26	51.1	56	61	21.0	91	96	4.0
22	27	50.2	57	62	20.3	92	97	3.7
23	28	49.3	58	63	19.6	93	98	3.5
24	29	48.3	59	64	18.9	94	99	3.3
25	30	47.4	60	65	18.2	95	100	3.1
26	31	46.5	61	66	17.5	96	101	2.9
27	32	45.6	62	67	16.9	97	102	2.7
28	33	44.6	63	68	16.2	98	103	2.5
29	34	43.7	64	69	15.6	99	104	2.3
30	35	42.8	65	70	15.0	100	105	2.1
31	36	41.9	66	71	14.4	101	106	1.9
32	37	41.0	67	72	13.8	102	107	1.7
33	38	40.0	68	73	13.2	103	108	1.5
34	39	39.1	69	74	12.6	104	109	1.3
35	40	38.2	70	75	12.1	105	110	1.2
36	41	37.3	71	76	11.6	106	111	1.0
37	42	36.5	72	77	11.0	107	112	0.8
38	43	35.6	73	78	10.5	108	113	0.7
39	44	34.7	74	79	10.1	109	114	0.6
40	45	33.8	75	80	9.6	110	115	0.5
						111	116	0.0

TABLE V Investments After June 30, 1986

Age	*Multiple*	*Age*	*Multiple*	*Age*	*Multiple*
5	76.6	42	40.6	79	10.0
6	75.6	43	39.6	80	9.5
7	74.7	44	38.7	81	8.9
8	73.7	45	37.7	82	8.4
9	72.7	46	36.8	83	7.9
10	71.7	47	35.9	84	7.4
11	70.7	48	34.9	85	6.9
12	69.7	49	34.0	86	6.5
13	68.8	50	33.1	87	6.1
14	67.8	51	32.2	88	5.7
15	66.8	52	31.3	89	5.3
16	65.8	53	30.4	90	5.0
17	64.8	54	29.5	91	4.7
18	63.9	55	28.6	92	4.4
19	62.9	56	27.7	93	4.1
20	61.9	57	26.8	94	3.9
21	60.9	58	25.9	95	3.7
22	59.9	59	25.0	96	3.4
23	59.0	60	24.2	97	3.2
24	58.0	61	23.3	98	3.0
25	57.0	62	22.5	99	2.8
26	56.0	63	21.6	100	2.7
27	55.1	64	20.8	101	2.5
28	54.1	65	20.0	102	2.3
29	53.1	66	19.2	103	2.1
30	52.2	67	18.4	104	1.9
31	51.2	68	17.6	105	1.8
32	50.2	69	16.8	106	1.6
33	49.3	70	16.0	107	1.4
34	48.3	71	15.3	108	1.3
35	47.3	72	14.6	109	1.1
36	46.4	73	13.9	110	1.0
37	45.4	74	13.2	111	0.9
38	44.4	75	12.5	112	0.8
39	43.5	76	11.9	113	0.7
40	42.5	77	11.2	114	0.6
41	41.5	78	10.6	115	0.5

Table 7-3 Multiple Adjustment Table

If the number of whole months from the annuity starting date to the first payment date is—	0–1	2	3	4	5	6	7	8	9	10	11	12
And payments under the contract are to be made:												
Annually	+0.5	+0.4	+0.3	+0.2	+0.1	0.0	0.0	–0.1	–0.2	–0.3	–0.4	–0.5
Semiannually	+0.2	+0.1	0.0	0.0	–0.1	–0.2						
Quarterly	+0.1	0.0	–0.1									

7.24 Life Expectancy Tables

IRS unisex actuarial tables must be used if you made *any* investment in a commercial annuity contract after June 30, 1986. Generally, life expectancies are longer under the unisex tables than under the prior male-female tables. The unisex life expectancy table for single life annuities is IRS Table V from Publication 939, shown on page 174. The unisex table for ordinary joint life and last survivor annuities is Table VI, in IRS Publication 939.

If your *entire* investment was before July 1, 1986, you use the older male/female tables. The tables, IRS Tables I through IV, are in Publication 939. Table I, shown on page 174, is for single life expectancies. Table II, for ordinary joint life and last survivor annuities, is in Publication 939.

You may make an irrevocable election to use the unisex tables for all payments received under the contract, even if you did not make an investment after June 30, 1986.

If you invested in the contract both before July 1, 1986, and after June 30, 1986, and you are the first person to receive annuity payments under the contract, you may make a special election to use the prior tables for the pre–July 1986 investment and the unisex tables for the post–June 1986 investment. *See* IRS Publication 939 for further information. Treasury Regulation 1.72-6(d) has examples showing how to figure the post–June 1986 and pre–July 1986 investments.

EXAMPLES

1. Bill Jones was 66 years old on April 14, 2006. On May 1, 2006, he received his first monthly annuity check of $1,000. This covered his annuity payment for April. Bill's annuity starting date was April 1, 2006, and his entire investment was before July 1, 1986.

   Looking at Table I on page 174 under "Male" at age 66 (age on birthday nearest April starting date), Bill finds the multiple 14.4. (He does not have to adjust that multiple because the payments are monthly.) Bill multiplies the 14.4 by $12,000 ($1,000 a month for a year) to find his expected return of $172,800. Assume there is no refund feature and Bill's net cost (*see* Step 3 in *7.23* above) is $129,600. He divides his expected return into the net cost and gets his exclusion percentage of 75%. Until Bill recovers his net cost, he receives tax free 75% of his annuity payments and is taxable on 25%. In 2006, Bill receives $8,000 ($1,000 in May through December) and reports $2,000 as the taxable amount:

Amount received	$8,000
Amount excludable (75%)	6,000
Taxable portion	$2,000

   For 2007, Bill will receive annuity payments for the full year. The amount received will be $12,000; amount excludable, $9,000; and taxable portion, $3,000. The excludable and taxable portions will remain the same in later years until Bill has excluded his net cost of $129,600. After that, the annuity payments will be fully taxable.

2. Same facts as in Example 1 except there was an investment after June 30, 1986, and Table V is used. Looking at Table V (on page 174) under age 66, Bill finds the multiple 19.2. The same multiple applies to males and females. Multiplying the 19.2 by $12,000 gives an expected return of $230,400. Using a net cost of $129,600, the exclusion percentage is 56.25% ($129,600 ÷ $230,400). For 2006, Bill reports annuity income as follows:

Amount received	$8,000
Amount excludable (56.25%)	4,500
Taxable portion	$3,500

   For 2007, $12,000 is received. The amount excludable will be $6,750 (56.25% × $12,000), and the taxable portion, $5,250. The same treatment will apply in later years until Bill has excluded his net cost of $129,600. Thereafter, all payments will be fully taxable.

3. You receive quarterly annuity payments. Your first payment comes on January 15, covering the first quarter of the year. Since the period between the starting date of January 1 and the payment date of January 15 is less than one month, you adjust the life expectancy multiple according to the table at the bottom of page 174, by adding 0.1. If the life expectancy multiple from the IRS table was 14.4, the adjusted multiple is 14.5.

Birthday nearest annuity starting date. In looking up single life or joint life expectancy in the applicable table, use your age (and the age of a joint annuitant) at the birthday nearest to the annuity starting date. The number in the table next to this age is the life expectancy multiple used to figure the tax-free and taxable portions of a monthly annuity; *see* the following Examples.

Adjustments for nonmonthly payments. An adjustment is required when your annuity payments are received quarterly, semiannually, or annually; *see* Example 3 below.

7.25 When You Convert Your Endowment Policy

When an endowment policy matures, you may elect to receive a lump sum, an annuity, an interest option, or a paid-up life insurance policy. If you elect—

A lump sum. You report the difference between your cost (premium payments less dividends) and what you receive.

An annuity before the policy matures or within 60 days after maturity. You report income in the years you receive your annuity. *See 7.23* for how to report annuity income. Use as your investment in the annuity contract the cost of the endowment policy less premiums paid for other benefits such as double indemnity or disability income. If you elect the annuity option more than 60 days after maturity, you report income on the matured policy as if you received the lump sum; *see* above rule. The lump sum is treated as the cost investment in the annuity contract.

An interest option before the policy matures. You report only the interest as it is received, provided you do not have the right to withdraw the policy proceeds. If you have the right to withdraw the proceeds, you are treated as in constructive receipt; the difference between your cost and what you receive would be taxed as if you had received a lump sum.

Paid-up insurance. You report the difference between the present value of the paid-up life insurance policy and the premium paid for the endowment policy. In figuring the value of the insurance policy, you do not use its cash surrender value, but the amount you would have to pay for a similar policy with the company at the date of exchange. Your insurance company can give you this figure. The difference is taxed at ordinary income tax rates.

Tax-free exchange rules apply to the policy exchanges listed at *6.12*.

Sales of endowment, annuity, or life insurance policies are taxable as ordinary income, not as capital gains.

The proceeds of a veteran's endowment policy paid before the veteran's death are not taxable.

Employee Annuities

7.26 Reporting Employee Annuities

Tax treatment of employee annuity payments from a qualified employee plan, qualified employee annuity, or tax-sheltered annuity *(7.21)* depends on the amount of your contributions and your annuity starting date. These rules are discussed in *7.26–7.29*. If payments are from a nonqualified employee plan, you must use the rules at *7.23* for commercial annuities.

Fully taxable payments if you have no investment in the plan. If you did not contribute to the cost of a pension or employee annuity, and you did not report as income your employer's contributions, you are fully taxed on payments after the annuity starting date. On your 2005 return, you report fully taxable payments on Line 16b of Form 1040 or Line 12b of Form 1040A.

An employee is taxed on the full value of a nonforfeitable annuity contract that the employer buys him or her if the employer does not have a qualified pension plan. Tax is imposed in the year the policy is purchased. A qualified plan is one approved by the IRS for special tax benefits.

Disability pension before minimum retirement age. Disability payments received before you reach the minimum retirement age (at which you would be entitled to a regular retirement annuity) are fully taxable as wages. After minimum retirement age, payments are treated as an annuity; *see 7.27*.

Partially taxable payments if you have an investment in the plan. If you and your employer both contributed to the cost of your annuity, the part of each payment allocable to your investment is tax free and the balance is taxable. You generally must use the simplified method to figure the tax-free portion allocable to your investment; *see 7.27* for details. For withdrawals before the annuity starting date, *see 7.29*.

Cost and cost adjustments are explained in *7.28*.

Filing Tip

Deducting Repaid Pension Overpayment

If you pay tax on a pension distribution and in the next year the plan determines that there was an overpayment, which you repay, the repayment may be deductible. If the repayment is $3,000 or less, it is deductible as a miscellaneous itemized deduction subject to the 2% floor *(see 19.1)*, which may limit or eliminate the deduction. If the repayment exceeds $3,000, you may claim either a miscellaneous deduction *not* subject to the 2% floor, or if it would provide a lower tax for the year of repayment, a tax credit based on a recomputation of the prior year's tax; *see 2.9*.

7.27 Simplified Method for Calculating Taxable Employee Annuity

If you have an investment in the plan and your annuity starting date is *after November 18, 1996*, you must use the simplified method explained below to figure the tax-free portion of your annuity payments from a qualified employer plan, qualified employee annuity, or 403(b) tax-sheltered annuity. The only exception is for an annuitant who is age 75 or older at the time payments begin and has payments guaranteed for at least five years; he or she must use the six-step method discussed at *7.23* for commercial annuities rather than the simplified method.

A beneficiary receiving a survivor annuity may use the simplified method.

If you have reported annuity payments using the prior law simplified method for annuities starting after July 1, 1986, and before November 19, 1996, continue using that method for figuring the tax-free part of your annual payments; *see* Table I below.

Figuring taxable and tax-free payments under the simplified method. Under the simplified method, a level tax-free portion is determined for each monthly payment with the following steps:

Step 1. Figure your investment in the contract as of the annuity starting date. Include premiums you paid and any after-tax contributions you made to the employer's pension plan; *see 7.28*.

Step 2. Divide the investment from Step 1 by the number of expected monthly payments shown in Table I or Table II below, using your age on the annuity starting date. The result is the tax-free recovery portion of each monthly payment. However, multiply this amount by three (3 months) to get the tax-free portion if payments are made quarterly rather than monthly. The tax-free portion remains the same if a spouse or other beneficiary receives payments under a joint and survivor annuity after the employee's death.

Use either Table I or Table II, described below. Table II is used for annuities based on more than one life if the annuity starting date is after December 31, 1997.

Table I: Use this table if the annuity starting date was after July 1, 1986, and before January 1, 1998, whether the annuity is based on your life only or is a joint and survivor annuity.

Also use Table I if the annuity starting date was after December 31, 1997, and the annuity is based on your life only.

Table II: Use this table if the annuity starting date is after December 31, 1997, and benefits are based on the life of *more than* one annuitant. For example, use this table if you started to receive payments in 2006 under a joint and survivor annuity. If there is more than one survivor annuitant, the primary annuitant's age plus the youngest survivor annuitant's age is the combined age used for Table II. If there is no primary annuitant and the annuity is payable to several survivor annuitants, the ages of the oldest and youngest are combined. Disregard a survivor annuitant whose entitlement to payment is contingent on something other than the primary annuitant's death.

Filing Instruction

Simplified Method Mandatory

If your annuity starting date was in 2006, you must use the simplified method discussed in *7.27* to figure the taxable part of your 2006 payments, unless on the annuity starting date you were age 75 or older and your payments are guaranteed for at least five years.

Table I

Age of primary annuitant at starting date	Number of expected monthly payments	
	Annuity starting date before November 19, 1996	*Annuity starting date after November 18, 1996*
55 and under	300	360
56–60	260	310
61–65	240	260
66–70	170	210
71 and over	120	160

Table II

Combined ages of annuitants at starting date	Number of expected monthly payments
110 and under	410
111–120	360
121–130	310
131–140	260
141 and over	210

Step 3. Multiply the Step 2 result by the number of monthly payments received during the year; this is the total tax-free payment for the current year. However, if any part of your cost was previously recovered tax free in years after 1986, the tax-free amount is limited to the excess of your investment from Step 1 over the prior year recoveries.

Step 4. Subtract the Step 3 tax-free payment from the total pension received this year; this is the taxable pension you must report on Form 1040 or Form 1040A. If the payer of the annuity shows a higher taxable amount on Form 1099-R, use the amount figured here.

EXAMPLE

Fred Smith, age 57, retires and beginning August 1, 2006, he receives payments under a joint and 50% survivor annuity with his wife Betty, also age 57. Fred receives an annuity of $1,500 per month and Betty will receive a survivor annuity of $750 per month after Fred's death. Fred's investment in the plan was $29,000. To figure the tax-free portion of each payment, Fred divides his $29,000 investment by 360, the number of expected monthly payments shown in Table II for two annuitants with a combined age of 114 years. The result, or $80.56, is the tax-free portion of each $1,500 payment. The balance of each payment , or $1,419.44 ($1,500 – $80.56), is taxable. On his 2006 return, Fred reports $7,097.20 (5 payments × $1,419.44) as taxable annuity payments.

If Fred dies before the receipt of 360 payments, Betty will also exclude $80.56 from each of her payments of $750 until a total of 360 payments (hers and Fred's) have been recovered. After 360 payments are received, all subsequent payments will be fully taxable. If Betty dies before the 360th payment, a deduction for the unrecovered investment is allowed on her final income tax return; the deduction is a miscellaneous itemized deduction *not* subject to the 2% AGI floor.

7.28 Employee's Cost in Annuity

For purposes of figuring the tax-free recovery of your investment under the general rules discussed in *7.23* or the simplified method discussed in *7.27*, include the following items paid as of the annuity starting date as your cost in an employee annuity:

- Premiums paid by you or by after-tax withholdings from your pay.
- Payments made by your employer and reported as additional pay.

Reduce the total by any refunded premiums that you received by the annuity starting date, or, if later, the date of your first payment.

Caution

Favorable Recovery Rules

Both of the favorable cost recovery rules discussed in *7.29* under "Exceptions" are complicated and you should consult your plan administrator to determine if the exceptions apply and how to make the required calculations.

7.29 Withdrawals Before Annuity Starting Date

You generally may not make tax-free withdrawals from your employer's qualified retirement plan, qualified employee annuity plan, or 403(b) plan before the annuity starting date, even if your withdrawals are less than your investment. On a withdrawal before the annuity starting date, you must pay tax on a portion of the withdrawal unless the exceptions below apply. The portion of the withdrawal allocable to your investment is recovered tax free; the portion allocable to employer contributions and income earned on the contract is taxed. To compute the tax-free recovery, multiply the withdrawal by this fraction:

$$\frac{\text{Your total investment}}{\text{Your vested account balance or accrued benefit}}$$

Your investment and vested benefit are determined as of the date of distribution.

Exceptions. More favorable investment recovery rules are allowed in the following cases:

1. *Employer plans in effect on May 5, 1986.* If on May 5, 1986, your employer's plan allowed distributions of employee contributions before separation from service, the above pro-rata recovery rule applies only to the extent that the withdrawal exceeds the total investment in the contract on December 31, 1986.

   For example, assume that as of December 31, 1986, you had an account balance of $9,750, which included $4,000 of your own contributions. If the plan on May 5, 1986, allowed pre-retirement distributions of employee contributions, you may receive withdrawals up to your $4,000 investment without incurring tax.

2. *Separate accounts for employee contributions.* A defined contribution plan (such as a profit-sharing plan) is allowed to account for employee contributions (and earnings on the contributions) separately from employer contributions. If separate accounting is maintained, withdrawals of employee contributions from the separate account may be made tax free. A defined benefit pension plan may also maintain employee contributions (and earnings) in a separate account to which actual earnings and losses are allocated.

Qualified Hurricane Distributions and Loans

7.30 Qualified Hurricane Distributions

Individuals whose principal residence was in the Hurricane Katrina disaster area (on 8/28/05), Hurricane Rita disaster area (on 9/23/05), or Hurricane Wilma disaster area (on 10/23/05) and who suffered an economic loss due to the applicable hurricane may apply favorable rules to withdrawals from and repayments to eligible employer retirement plans (such as 401(k) and 403(b) plans) and IRAs *(8.25)*. The distribution must have been made after August 24, 2005 (Katrina), September 22, 2005 (Rita), or October 22, 2005, and before 2007. The amount of the distribution does not have to correspond to the economic loss suffered.

The first $100,000 of qualified hurricane distributions are not subject to the penalty for pre–age 59½ distributions *(7.15)* and may be reported as income over a three-year period on Form 8915. If within the three-year period any amounts are recontributed back into the plan, the repayment is treated as a tax-free rollover and a refund claim may be made for tax paid on that amount.

Three-year reporting of qualified hurricane distributions on Form 8915. On Form 8915, you report your total retirement distributions and figure the amount subject to tax. The first $100,000 of qualified hurricane distributions are eligible for three-year reporting. The $100,000 limit applies to total distributions received from all eligible plans in 2005 and 2006. For example, if in 2005 you received a $50,000 distribution that you treated as a qualified hurricane distribution on Form 8915 filed with your 2005 Form 1040, and in 2006 you received a qualified distribution of $100,000, only $50,000 of the 2006 distribution can be treated as a qualified hurricane distribution on your Form 8915 for 2006.

If you did not receive qualified distributions in 2005 and in 2006 your qualified distributions exceed $100,000, and they are from different types of plans, such as an IRA and a 401(k) plan, you may allocate the $100,000 limit among the plans in any way you choose.

The three-year rule applies unless you elect not to use it. You "elect out" of the three-year method by checking a box on Form 8915 and reporting the entire distribution.

Repayments of qualified distributions within three years. You generally can avoid tax on a qualified distribution that is eligible for tax-free rollover by repaying it to an IRA or eligible employer plan within three years, starting on the day after the date of receipt.

If you are reporting a 2006 qualified distribution on Form 8915, any repayments made by the filing due date (including extensions) for your 2006 return reduce the amount subject to tax. A repayment made after the filing due date will reduce the amount of the qualified distributions subject to tax on your 2007 return.

If you reported a qualified distribution on your 2005 return and you repaid it in 2006 after the 2005 filing due date, the repayment offsets the amount includible as income for 2006. If the repayment exceeds the income for 2006, the excess may be carried forward to 2007 or an amended return for 2005 may be filed to carry back the excess and reduce the amount included in your 2005 income. *See* the instructions to the 2006 Form 8915.

7.31 Qualifying Loans to Hurricane Victims

If you were living in the Hurricane Katrina, Rita, or Wilma disaster area and suffered economic loss because of the applicable storm, you may qualify for a higher limit on tax-free loans received before 2007 from a qualified employer retirement plan and a one-year suspension of certain loan repayments. To qualify, your principal residence had to be in either the Hurricane Katrina disaster area on August 28, 2005, the Hurricane Rita disaster area on September 23, 2005, or the Hurricane Wilma disaster area on October 23, 2005.

Loan limit. For qualified individuals, the regular $50,000 limit on tax-free loans from a qualified employer plan *(7.16)* is increased to the lesser of $100,000 (reduced by the highest plan loan balance during the prior year) or 100% (up from 50%) of the vested account balance. This higher limit applies to loans made after September 23, 2005, and before 2007 for qualified individuals in the Katrina disaster area, and to loans made after December 20, 2005, and before 2007 to qualified individuals in the Rita and Wilma disaster areas.

One-year suspension for repayments. Loan repayments are suspended for one year for qualified individuals. The suspension applies to repayments otherwise due after August 24, 2005, and before 2007 in the case of qualified Hurricane Katrina individuals. For Hurricane Rita individuals, the suspension applies to repayments due after September 22, 2005, and before 2007, and for qualified Hurricane Wilma individuals, to repayments due after October 22, 2005, and before 2007. In Notice 2005-92, relating to qualified Hurricane Katrina individuals, the IRS provided a safe harbor to employers allowing them to end the suspension period before December 31, 2006.

At the end of the suspension period, loan payments must resume with the term of the loan extended and the amount of each monthly installment increased to reflect the interest accruing during the suspension period. If the loan is not a principal residence loan, the loan must be repaid within five years from the date of the loan, plus the suspension period.

Chapter 8

IRAs

There are several types of IRAs: Traditional IRAs, Roth IRAs, SIMPLE IRAs, and SEPs. You may personally set up a traditional or Roth IRA with your bank or broker. SIMPLE IRAs *(8.18)* and SEPs *(8.15)* are available only if your employer offers such plans.

For 2006, the contribution limit for both traditional and Roth IRAs is $4,000, or $5,000 for individuals who are age 50 or older; *see 8.2* and *8.20*.

Traditional IRA contributions may be fully deductible, partly deductible, or not deductible at all, depending on whether you (and your spouse) have retirement coverage where you work and if so, whether your income subjects you to the deduction phase-out rules; *see 8.4*.

Distribution rules for traditional IRAs and Roth IRAs are discussed in this chapter. Traditional IRA distributions are generally fully taxable and if made before age 59½, subject to a penalty; *see 8.12* for penalty exceptions. Minimum distributions from a traditional IRA must begin after you reach age 70½; *see 8.13*.

Roth IRAs are an alternative to traditional IRAs. Although contributions are not deductible, the major tax advantage of the Roth IRA is that tax-free withdrawals of earnings may be made after a five-year waiting period if you are over age 59½; *see 8.23*. Tax-free withdrawals of contributions may be made at any time. A traditional IRA may also be converted to a Roth IRA. If necessary, a Roth IRA may be recharacterized back to a traditional IRA, and subsequently reconverted to a Roth IRA. *See 8.20* for annual contributions, *8.21* for conversions, and *8.22* for recharacterizations and reconversions.

Low-to-moderate-income taxpayers may be able to claim a tax credit on Form 8880 for 2006 contributions to a traditional IRA, Roth IRA, SIMPLE IRA, or salary-reduction SEP, as well as deferrals to other employer-sponsored retirement plans. The credit is discussed in Chapter 25.

Also Refer to:

Starting and Contributing to a Traditional IRA

8.1 Starting a Traditional IRA

You may set up a traditional (non-Roth) IRA by making annual contributions *(see 8.2)* that may be deductible (*see 8.4* for deduction rules) or nondeductible *(see 8.6)*, or by rolling over a distribution received from a qualified employer plan or from another IRA. IRA accounts provide tax-free accumulation of earnings until withdrawals are made. On a rollover, you can avoid immediate tax when you receive a lump-sum payment upon retirement, changing jobs, or disability; *see 7.8.*

Your employer can set up a "deemed IRA" as a separate account under a qualified retirement plan. As long as the separate account otherwise meets IRA requirements, you can make voluntary employee contributions that will be treated as IRA contributions subject to the regular IRA rules. The separate account can be treated as a traditional IRA or Roth IRA *(8.19).*

Filing Tip

IRA Fees and Brokerage Commissions

Fees paid to set up or manage an IRA, and annual account maintenance fees, are not considered IRA contributions provided they are separately billed. They are investment expenses that may be deducted as a miscellaneous itemized deduction subject to the 2% of adjusted gross income floor; *see 19.1.* However, broker's commissions that are paid when you make investments for your IRA are not separately deductible, according to the IRS. They are considered IRA contributions subject to the $4,000 contribution limit ($5,000 if age 50 or older) for 2006.

Roth IRAs. Annual contributions to a Roth IRA and conversions of traditional IRAs to Roth IRAs are discussed at *8.19–8.21.*

Restrictions on traditional IRAs. You may not freely withdraw IRA funds until the year you reach age 59½ or become disabled. If you take money out before that time, you are subject to a penalty; *see 8.12.* Pledging the account as collateral is treated as a taxable distribution from the account; *see 8.8.* In the year you reach age 70½, you may no longer make traditional IRA contributions, and you must start to withdraw *(8.13)* from the account. All IRA withdrawals are fully taxable except for amounts allocable to nondeductible contributions; *see 8.8* and *8.9.* Special averaging for lump-sum distributions does not apply. Excess contributions *(8.7)* are penalized.

If your IRA loses value because of poor investments, you may not deduct the loss. A loss is allowed only if you make nondeductible contributions that you have not recovered when the account is depleted; *see 8.9.*

Types of traditional IRAs. You may set up an IRA as:

1. An individual retirement account with a bank, savings and loan association, federally insured credit union, or other qualified person as trustee or custodian. An individual retirement account is technically a trust or custodial account. Your contribution may be invested in vehicles such as certificates of deposit, mutual funds, and certain limited partnerships.
2. An individual retirement annuity by purchasing an annuity contract (including a joint and survivor contract for the benefit of you and your spouse) issued by an insurance company; no trustee or custodian is required. The contract, endorsed to meet the terms of an IRA, is all that is required. Contracts issued after November 6, 1978, must provide for flexible premiums up to the annual contribution limit, so that if your compensation changes, your payment may also change. As borrowing or pledging of the contract is not allowed under an IRA, the contracts will not contain loan provisions. Endowment contracts issued after November 6, 1978, that provide life insurance protection may not be used as individual retirement annuities.

Caution

Restrictions on Collectibles Investments

If you have a self-directed traditional IRA and you invest in collectibles, such as art works, gems, stamps, antiques, rugs, metals, guns, or certain coins, you will have to pay a tax on your investment. The investment is treated as a taxable distribution to you in the year you make it. Coins are treated as collectibles, except for state-issued coins or certain U.S. minted gold, silver, and platinum coins. There is also an exception for gold, silver, platinum, or palladium bullion held by the IRA trustee, provided the fineness of the metal meets commodity market standards. If bullion is stored with a company other than the IRA trustee, the investment is subject to the deemed distribution rule for collectibles.

You may set up one type of IRA one year and choose another form the next year. You also may split your contribution between two or more investment vehicles. For example, you are eligible to contribute $4,000 for 2006 if under age 50. You may choose to put $2,000 into an investment retirement annuity and $2,000 into an individual retirement account with a bank, mutual fund, or brokerage firm.

You do not have to file any forms with your tax return when you set up or make contributions to a deductible IRA. Form 8606 must be attached to Form 1040 or Form 1040A if you make nondeductible IRA contributions; *see 8.6.* The trustee or issuer of your IRA will report your contribution to the IRS on Form 5498, and you should receive a copy.

Self-Directed IRA. If you wish to take a more active role in managing your IRA investments, you may set up a "self-directed" IRA using an IRS model form. The model trust (Form 5305) and the model custodial account agreement (Form 5305-A) meet the requirements of an exempt individual retirement account and so do not require a ruling or determination letter approving the exemption of the account and the deductibility of contributions made to the account. If you use this method, you still have to find a bank or other institution or trustee to handle your account or investment. Investments in a self-directed IRA are subject to restrictions; *see* the Caution in *8.1.*

SIMPLE IRA. If you work for a company with 100 or fewer workers, your employer may set up a SIMPLE IRA to which you may make salary-reduction contributions; *see 8.17.*

Contributions allowed up until filing due date. You have until April 16, 2007 (the regular filing due date for your 2006 return) to make deductible or nondeductible IRA contributions for 2006. You must make your contribution by April 16, 2007, even if you get an extension to file your return. If you are short of cash, you may borrow the funds to make the contribution without jeopardizing the deduction. If an IRA deduction entitles you to a refund, you can file your return early, claim the IRA deduction, and if you receive the refund in time, apply it towards an IRA contribution before the due date.

8.2 Traditional IRA Contributions Must Be Based on Earnings

You may make contributions to a traditional IRA for 2006 of up to $4,000, $5,000 if you are age 50 or older in 2006, provided you have wage, salary, or net self-employment earnings and that you have not reached age 70½ by the end of the year. If your earned income is less than $4,000 ($5,000 if age 50 or older), the contribution limit is 100% of your pay or net earned income if self-employed. If you have more than one traditional IRA, the limit applies to total contributions to all of the IRAs for the year. Contributions for 2006 may be made up to the filing deadline of April 16, 2007, for 2006 returns; this is the deadline even if you obtain a filing extension for your 2006 return.

If you are married filing jointly, you may each contribute up to $4,000 (or $5,000 if age 50 or older) to an IRA for 2006, as long as your combined compensation covers the contributions; *see 8.3*.

Contributions up to these limits are ***fully deductible*** on your 2006 return if neither you nor your spouse is an active participant in an employer or self-employed retirement plan. Deductions for active plan participants are phased out for single persons with 2006 modified adjusted gross income over $50,000. The phase-out threshold on a joint return is generally $75,000 for 2006, but a more favorable $150,000 phase-out threshold applies to a jointly filing spouse who is not a plan participant; *see 8.3* and *8.4*.

Contribution limit for 2006 increased by $1,000 if age 50 or older. If you are age 50 or older by the end of 2006, an additional contribution of up to $1,000 may be made for 2006, increasing your contribution limit to the lesser of $5,000 or your taxable compensation. If you are an active participant in an employer retirement plan, the $5,000 limit is subject to the phaseout rule at 8.4.

Taxable compensation. Traditional IRA contributions, whether deductible or nondeductible, must be based on taxable compensation received for rendering personal services, such as salary, wages, commissions, tips, fees, bonuses, jury fees, or net earnings from self-employment (less Keogh plan contributions on behalf of the self-employed). An IRA contribution (deductible or nondeductible) may not be based upon:

1. Investment income such as interest, dividends, or profits from sales of property;
2. Deferred compensation, pensions, or annuities; or
3. Income earned abroad for which the foreign earned income exclusion is claimed.

EXAMPLE

A trader whose sole income was derived from stock dividends and gains in buying and selling stocks contributed to an IRA. The IRS disallowed the deduction on the grounds that his income was not earned income.

If you live in a community property state, the fact that one-half of your spouse's income is considered your income does not entitle you to make contributions to an IRA. The contributions must be based on pay earned through your services.

Working for spouse. If you work for your spouse, you may make an IRA contribution provided you actually perform services and receive an actual payment of wages. A wife who worked as a receptionist and assistant to her husband, a veterinarian, failed to meet the second test. Her husband did not pay her a salary. Instead, he deposited all income from his business into a joint bank account held with his wife. In addition, no federal income tax was withheld from her wages. In a ruling, the IRS held that the wife could not set up her own IRA, even though she performed

Law Alert

IRA Contribution Based on Tax-Free Combat Pay

The 2006 "Heroes Earned Retirement Opportunities Act" allows members of the armed services serving in a combat zone *(35.4)* to contribute to either a traditional IRA or a Roth IRA *(8.20)* based on their tax-free combat pay. Without the new law, members of the military who did not have any earnings apart from the combat zone pay could not make IRA contributions, which must be based on taxable compensation.

The new law applies retroactively for individuals who received tax-free combat pay in 2004 and 2005. They have until May 28, 2009, to make contributions to a traditional IRA or Roth IRA for 2004 and 2005. For those under age 50, the contribution limit was $3,000 for 2004 and $4,000 for 2005. For those age 50 and older, the limit was $3,500 for 2004 and $4,500 for 2005.

An overpayment of tax may result for 2004 and/or 2005 if a traditional IRA contribution for such year is deductible or a contribution (traditional or Roth) enables the service member to claim the retirement saver's credit *(25.16)*. A refund for the overpayment can be claimed within one year from the date the contribution is made even if the statute of limitations for claiming a refund *(47.2)* for that year has expired.

Law Alert

Contribution Limits After 2006

For individuals under age 50, the contribution limit for traditional and Roth IRAs will remain at $4,000 in 2007 and then increase to $5,000 for 2008, after which inflation adjustments to the $5,000 ceiling may be made. The additional contribution limit for individuals age 50 or older is scheduled to remain at $1,000 for 2007 and later years.

Caution

Broker's Restriction on IRA Transfers

Before you invest in an IRA, carefully review the terms of the agreement for restrictions. One investor who put his IRA in a brokerage account was not allowed by the trustee to transfer from one account to another. Furthermore, the trustee reserved some of the IRA funds to cover broker fees and other transfer costs. The investor asked the IRS if these restrictions violated the tax law. The IRS, in a private letter ruling, said there was no violation. An IRA is a contractual agreement between the IRA trustee and the participant. Although the tax laws do not place limitations on direct IRA-to-IRA transfers, the trustees of a particular account may restrict such transfers.

Planning Reminder

Roth IRA Contributions after Age 70½

Contributions to a traditional IRA may not be made after age 70½, but contributions to a Roth IRA may be made even if you are over age 70½, provided you have compensation *(8.2)* to support the contribution and your income is within the limit allowed under the Roth IRA contribution rules; *see 8.20.*

services; she failed to receive actual payment. Depositing business income into a joint account is neither actual nor constructive payment of the wife's salary. Furthermore, any deduction claimed for the wife's wages was disallowed.

Self-employed may make IRA contributions. IRA contributions may be based on net self-employment earnings *(45.1)*, after taking into account deductible Keogh or SEP retirement plan contributions *(41.5)* and the deduction for one-half of self-employment tax liability *(45.3)*. If you have a net loss for the year, you may not make an IRA contribution unless you also have wages.

If you have more than one self-employed activity, you must aggregate profits and losses from all of your self-employed businesses to determine if you have net income on which to base an IRA contribution. For example, if one self-employed business produces a net profit of $15,000 but another a net loss of $20,000, you may not make an IRA contribution based on the net profit of $15,000 since you have an overall loss. This netting rule does not apply to salary or wage income. If you are an employee who also has an unprofitable business, you may make an IRA contribution based on your salary.

If you have a self-employed retirement plan from your business, you are considered an active participant in a retirement plan for purposes of the adjusted gross income phase-out rules discussed at *8.4*.

Taxable alimony treated as compensation. A divorced spouse with little or no earnings may treat taxable alimony as compensation, giving a basis for deductible IRA contributions. If you are divorced, you generally may make an IRA contribution for 2006 equal to 100% of taxable alimony up to the $4,000 limit ($5,000 if age 50 or older). However, if you are an active participant in an employer plan and your adjusted gross income exceeds the $50,000 threshold for unmarried individuals, *see 8.4* for the phaseout of the deduction limit. Taxable alimony is alimony paid under a decree of divorce or legal separation, or a written agreement incident to such a decree; *see* Chapter 37. It does not include alimony payments made under a written agreement that is not incident to such a decree.

No contributions to traditional IRA allowed for those age 70½. Even if you still have earnings, you may not make contributions to a traditional IRA for the year in which you reach age 70½, or any later year. For example, if you were born in the last six months of 1935 or the first six months of 1936, you will reach age 70½ in 2006 and may not make any traditional IRA contributions for 2006 or later years.

If you have a nonworking spouse under age 70½, you may contribute to his or her IRA, even though no contribution may be made to your own traditional IRA because you have reached age 70½; *see 8.3.*

8.3 Contributions to a Traditional IRA If You Are Married

If both you and your spouse earned compensation in 2006 of at least $4,000 and are under age 50 at the end of the year, each of you may make a contribution of up to $4,000 to a traditional IRA for 2006 by April 16, 2007. Under the spousal IRA rule, the $4,000 per spouse contribution limit applies even if only one of you works, provided you file jointly and your combined compensation is at least $8,000. An additional contribution of up to $1,000 can be made for each spouse who is age 50 or older by the end of the year so long as there is compensation to cover it.

Contributions for 2006 are fully deductible up to the $4,000 limit ($5,000, if applicable) if neither you nor your spouse was covered by an employer retirement plan during the year. If either of you was an active plan participant, you are both considered active participants, and a deduction may be limited or disallowed depending on your modified adjusted gross income (MAGI). However, if you file jointly and only one of you was an active plan participant, a more favorable MAGI phase-out rule applies to the nonparticipant spouse, so that the spouse without coverage may be able to claim a deduction even if the participant spouse may not. The deduction phase-out rules are discussed below.

Spousal IRA contribution on joint return for nonworking or low-earning spouse. On a joint return for 2006, the contribution limit is $4,000 for each spouse as long as the combined compensation of both spouses is at least $8,000. If both spouses were age 50 or older by the end of 2006, the limit for each is raised to $5,000, so long as the combined compensation of both spouses is at least $10,000. This spousal IRA rule allows a spouse with minimal earnings to "borrow" compensation from his or her spouse in order to reach the maximum contribution limit.

In figuring their combined compensation for purposes of the "borrowing" rule, the higher earning spouse's compensation is reduced by his or her deductible IRA contribution and by any regular contributions made by the higher earning spouse to a Roth IRA for the year.

EXAMPLE

Rhonda and Elliot Richards file a joint return for 2006. Both are under age 50 in 2006. Rhonda had salary income of $56,000 in 2006. Elliot was a full-time student and had no compensation. Rhonda may contribute up to $4,000 to a traditional IRA for 2006. Even though Elliot did not work, he also may contribute up to $4,000 to a traditional IRA. Since Rhonda's earnings exceeded $8,000, $4,000 of her earnings may be credited to Elliot for contribution purposes.

If Rhonda and Elliot's modified adjusted gross income (MAGI; see 8.4) for 2006 does not exceed $75,000, contributions for each of them up to the $4,000 limit are fully deductible. If MAGI on their 2006 joint return exceeded $75,000 and if Rhonda were an active participant in her employer's retirement plan during 2006, her deduction would be phased out over a MAGI range of $75,000–$85,000. Elliot would be allowed a full $4,000 deduction so long as the joint return MAGI was less than $150,000. *See* the phase-out rule below.

Filing Tip

Deduction on Joint Return

If you and your spouse are each under age 50 at the end of 2006 and you have combined earnings of at least $8,000 and modified adjusted gross income (MAGI) on your 2006 joint return is $75,000 or less, each of you may claim an IRA deduction for contributions of up to $4,000. The limit for 2006 is increased to $5,000 for each spouse age 50 or older at the end of 2006. If MAGI for 2006 for exceeds $75,000, *see 8.4* for the deduction phaseout rules.

Deduction phase-out rule for spouses filing jointly for 2006. If either you or your spouse was an active participant in an employer retirement plan during 2006, the phase-out rule may limit or completely disallow an IRA deduction. However, even if one or both of you were active participants in an employer plan, the phase-out rule does not apply and you may each deduct contributions up to the $4,000 limit ($5,000 if age 50 or older) if your 2006 joint return modified adjusted gross income (MAGI; *see 8.4*) is $75,000 or less.

If both of you were active plan participants for 2006, the deduction limit is phased out if your joint return MAGI is more than $75,000 but less than $85,000. No deduction is allowed for either of you if your 2006 joint return MAGI is $85,000 or more.

If you were not an active plan participant in 2006 but your spouse was, a different phase-out rule applies to each of you. Your spouse, as an active plan participant, is subject to the deduction phaseout if MAGI on the joint return is between $75,000 and 85,000; no deduction is allowed if MAGI is $85,000 or more. However, as the nonparticipant spouse, your deduction limit is not subject to phaseout unless MAGI on the joint return is over $150,000. Your deduction is phased out if joint MAGI is between $150,000 and $160,000, and no deduction is allowed if MAGI is $160,000 or more.

See 8.4 for an example of how the reduced deduction limit is figured if MAGI is within the above phase-out ranges.

Planning Reminder

Phase-out Rule for Nonparticipant Spouses

If you are not covered by an employer retirement plan but your spouse is, and you file a joint return for 2006, your individual deduction limit is not subject to the phase-out rule unless modified adjusted gross income (MAGI) on the joint return is between $150,000 and $160,000. Your spouse, who is covered by an employer plan, is subject to the deduction phaseout for 2006 if modified adjusted gross income on the joint return is between $75,000 and $85,000.

Deduction phase-out rule for married persons filing separately for 2006. If you are married, live together at any time during 2006, file separately, and either of you is an active participant in an employer plan, the other spouse is also considered an active participant. Both of you are subject to the $0 to $10,000 MAGI deduction phaseout; *see 8.4*.

If you live apart for all of 2006, you each figure IRA deductions as if single. Thus, the more favorable deduction phase-out range of $50,000 to $60,000 applies if you are covered by an employer retirement plan; *see 8.4*. If you are not covered, you may claim a full deduction on your separate return.

Contributions for spouses under age 70½. If in 2006 you were age 70½ or over and had taxable compensation, you may contribute to a spousal IRA for 2006 if your spouse is nonworking and is under age 70½ at the end of the year. The entire contribution must be allocated to the nonworking spouse. No contribution may be made to your own traditional IRA for the year in which you reach age 70½, or any later year. However, you may contribute to a Roth IRA even if you are over age 70½, provided your compensation is within the Roth IRA limits; *see 8.20*.

8.4 IRA Deduction Restrictions for Active Participants in Employer Plan

If you are covered by an employer retirement plan, including a self-employed plan, you may be unable to make deductible IRA contributions to a traditional IRA. When you have coverage, your right to claim a full deduction, a limited deduction, or no deduction at all depends on your modified adjusted gross income (MAGI). If you are married, and your spouse has employer plan coverage for 2006, you are also considered to have coverage in most cases. However, if you file jointly and do not individually have employer plan coverage, a special MAGI phase-out rule may allow you to deduct IRA contributions even if a deduction for your spouse is limited or barred.

If you are unmarried and do not have employer plan coverage, or if you are married and neither of you has coverage, an IRA deduction of up to $4,000 ($5,000 if age 50 or older) for 2006 is allowed as long as you have compensation of $4,000 ($5,000 if age 50 or older) or more. The deduction phase-out rules do not apply, regardless of your income.

Are you an active plan participant? Generally, you are considered to be "covered" by a retirement plan if you are an active participant in the plan for any part of the plan year ending within your taxable year; see the Sara Wartes Example below. If you are an employee, your Form W-2 for 2006 should indicate whether you are covered for the year; if you are, the "Retirement plan" box within Box 13 of Form W-2 should be checked. Active participation in a self-employed Keogh plan or SEP (Chapter 41) is treated as employer plan coverage for purposes of the IRA deduction phase-out rules. Active participation is explained further at *8.5*.

EXAMPLE

Sara Wartes, a college teacher, quit her job in 1988 and withdrew all of the contributions she had made to her employee pension plan. The Tax Court held that Sara could not claim an IRA deduction in that year. Sara was an active participant in the college plan during 1988 and under the phase-out rules based upon adjusted gross income, no IRA deduction was allowed. The court noted that the active participation test is not made at the end of the year. Participation in a company plan at any time during the year triggers the deduction phase-out rules. This is true even where a person has forfeitable benefits.

You are not an active plan participant but your spouse is. Even if you were not an active participant in an employer retirement plan at any time in 2006, your IRA deduction limit for 2006 may be phased out because of your spouse's coverage. However, if you file jointly, your own deduction is not limited unless modified adjusted gross income (MAGI) on the 2006 joint return exceeds $150,000. For your spouse who has employer plan coverage, the rule is different: the phase-out threshold for his or her 2006 deduction is joint MAGI of $75,000, assuming you file jointly.

The deduction is phased out over the next $10,000 of MAGI exceeding the phase-out threshold. Thus, you as a nonparticipant are not allowed any deduction if MAGI on your joint return is $160,000 or more. A deduction for your spouse as an active participant is completely phased out if joint return MAGI for 2006 is $85,000 or more.

Stricter phase-out rules apply to married persons filing separately if they live together at any time during the year. If you lived with your spouse at any time during 2006 and either of you was an active plan participant in 2006, you are both subject to the $0 – $10,000 MAGI phase-out range on separate returns. Neither of you may claim an IRA deduction if the MAGI on your separate return is $10,000 or more.

If you are married filing separately and you lived apart for all of 2006, your spouse's plan participation does not affect your IRA deduction. Take into account only your own participation, if any, and if you are an active participant, your IRA deduction under the phase-out rules is figured as if you were single. If you are not an active participant, you may claim the full $4,000 deduction limit for 2006 ($5,000 if age 50 or older).

Modified adjusted gross income (MAGI) determines your deduction limit if you or your spouse is an active plan participant. If either you or your spouse is an active plan participant, you still may be allowed a full or limited deduction, but this will depend on whether your 2006 modified adjusted gross income (MAGI) is within the phase-out range that applies to you as shown below.

MAGI is generally equal to the adjusted gross income shown on your return plus any adjustments to income shown on your return, other than for IRA deductions. However, if you are claiming a deduction for student loan interest *(33.14)*, qualified college tuition and fees *(33.13)*, or domestic production activities income *(40.23)*, the deduction must be added back to adjusted gross income to get MAGI. If you are claiming an exclusion for employer-provided adoption assistance *(3.6)* or an exclusion for interest on U.S. EE Savings Bonds used for tuition *(33.4)*, you must add back that excluded amount to adjusted gross income to get MAGI. If you worked abroad and are claiming the foreign earned income exclusion *(36.1)*, or a foreign housing exclusion or deduction *(36.4)*, these amounts also must be added back to adjusted gross income to get MAGI.

Figuring Your 2006 IRA Deduction Under the Phase-Out Rules

If you are an active plan participant for 2006, or you file a joint return for 2006 and your spouse was an active participant, the full $4,000 (or $5,000 if age 50 or older) deduction limit is available to you only if your modified adjusted gross income (MAGI) is below a phase-out threshold shown below. The deduction limit is phased out over the first $10,000 of MAGI exceeding the threshold, so that if MAGI exceeds the phase-out threshold by $10,000 or more, no deduction is allowed. The phase-out threshold is $0 if you are married filing separately, you lived together at any time in 2006, and either of you was an active plan participant.

Phase-out threshold for 2006 returns. On 2006 returns, the $4,000 (or $5,000 if age 50 or older) deduction limit is subject to phaseout if modified adjusted gross income exceeds:

- $50,000 if you are single or head of household;
- $50,000 if you are married filing separately, you lived apart from your spouse for all of 2006, and you were an active plan participant during 2006. If you lived apart the entire year and you were not an active participant, you qualify for the full deduction limit; the phase-out rule is inapplicable to you even if your spouse was an active plan participant.
- $75,000 if you are married filing jointly and both you and your spouse were active plan participants during 2006, or you are a qualifying widow or widower and were an active plan participant during 2006;
- $75,000 if you are married filing jointly and you are an active plan participant during 2006 but your spouse was not. You use the $75,000 threshold; your spouse uses the $150,000 threshold;
- $150,000 if you are married filing jointly and you were not an active plan participant at any time during 2006 but your spouse was. You use the $150,000 threshold; your spouse uses the $75,000 threshold; and
- $0 if you are married filing separately, you lived with your spouse at any time in 2006, and either you or your spouse was an active plan participant during 2006. You and your spouse are both subject to the "0" threshold on 2006 returns so long as you lived together at any time in 2006 and either of you was an active plan participant during the year.

The phase-out applies to the first $9,999 of MAGI exceeding the $50,000, $75,000, $150,000, or zero phase-out threshold. If your MAGI exceeds the threshold by $10,000 or more, you are not allowed any IRA deduction.

Table 8-1 Phase-out Range for Deduction Limit on 2006 Returns

If your phase-out threshold (see above) is—	*Deduction limit is phased out if MAGI is—*	*No deduction if MAGI is—*
$50,000	Over $50,000 and under $60,000	$60,000 or more
$75,000	Over $75,000 and under $85,000	$85,000 or more
$150,000	Over $150,000 and under $160,000	$160,000 or more
$0	$0–$9,999	$10,000 or more

Figure your excess MAGI and compute the deduction limit under the phase-out rule. If your MAGI is within the $10,000 phase-out range, figure your excess MAGI by subtracting the phase-out threshold from your MAGI. If the excess MAGI is $10,000 or more, you are not allowed any IRA deduction; the entire deduction is phased out.

If the excess MAGI is less than $10,000, you are allowed a portion of the deduction limit. If you are under age 50 in 2006, the deduction limit generally equals $4,000 minus 40% of the MAGI in excess of the phase-out threshold. If age 50 or older by the end of 2006, the deduction limit is generally $5,000 minus 50% of the MAGI in excess of the phase-out threshold. A result that is not a multiple of $10 is rounded up to the next highest multiple of $10. If the rounded up amount is less than $200, it is increased to $200. You can figure the limit in your case by applying

Planning Reminder

Roth IRA vs. Deductible IRA

Even if you qualify for a full IRA deduction, you may want to consider making a nondeductible contribution to a Roth IRA *(8.20)*. For example, you may be willing to give up the current tax deduction in order to create a Roth IRA from which distributions will be completely tax free after age 59½ and a five-year waiting period has passed. If you choose to make a deductible contribution to a traditional IRA, distributions from the traditional IRA will be taxable. You may also prefer the Roth-IRA advantage of not having to take minimum distributions starting at age 70½, as is required with traditional IRAs.

Law Alert

Income Phase-out Limits After 2006

For single persons and heads of household, the $50,000 phaseout threshold that applied for 2006 will be adjusted for inflation beginning in 2007; *see* the *e-Supplement* for the adjusted amount. The phaseout threshold for married persons filing jointly has been scheduled to increase to $80,000 for 2007, but a new law will adjust the $80,000 amount for inflation as well as the $150,000 phaseout threshold for nonparticipant spouses. The adjusted thresholds for 2007 will be in the *e-Supplement*. After 2006, the phaseout range for married persons filing jointly and qualifying widows (or widowers) doubles to $20,000, while remaining $10,000 for all others.

the following four steps. The Examples below illustrate the computation.

1. Enter excess of your MAGI over your phase-out threshold. ________
2. Multiply Step 1 by 40%, or by 50% if you were age 50 or older at the end of 2006. ________
3. Subtract Step 2 from $4,000, or from $5,000 if you were age 50 or older at the end of 2006. ________
4. If Step 3 is not a multiple of $10, round it up to the next highest multiple of $10. If the result is under $200, increase it to $200. This is your deductible limit for 2006. ________

EXAMPLES

1. Rob Porter is single and under age 50 at the end of 2006. He is an active participant in an employer retirement plan. His salary for 2006 is $50,600 and his MAGI for 2006 is $51,343. His MAGI exceeds the $50,000 phase-out floor for single persons by $1,343. Rob figures a deduction limit for 2006 of $3,470.00 as follows:

1. Excess of MAGI over phase-out threshold for single persons ($51,343 – $50,000)	$1,343.00
2. 40% of Step 1	537.20
3. $4,000 minus Step 2	$3,462.80
4. Round Step 3 to the next highest multiple of $10. This is Rob's deductible limit.	3,470

2. Ted and Lynn Baker are both under age 50 at the end of 2006 and they file a 2006 joint return. They report wages of $32,000 for Ted and $34,250 for Lynn. Their modified adjusted gross income (MAGI) is $78,020. Ted and Lynn are both active participants in employer retirement plans in 2006 and so they are both subject to the $75,000 phase-out threshold. The deduction limit for each of them is $2,800, figured as follows:

1. Excess of MAGI over phase-out threshold for married couples filing jointly ($78,020 – $75,000)	$3,020.00
2. 40% of Step 1	1,208.00
3. $4,000 minus Step 2	$2,792.00
4. Round Step 3 to the next highest multiple of $10. This is the deductible limit for Ted and also for Lynn. On their joint return, they can each deduct IRA contributions of up to $2,800, for a total maximum deduction of $5,600.	$2,800

3. Assume the same facts as in Example 2 except that only Lynn was an active participant in an employer plan. Ted and Lynn must figure their deduction limitations separately using different phase-out thresholds

   For Lynn, the same $2,800 deduction limit applies as in Example 2. The $75,000 phase-out threshold applies, her excess MAGI is $3,020 ($78,020 MAGI on joint return – $75,000 threshold), and her deduction limit as shown in Example 2 is $2,800.

   For Ted, the special $150,000 threshold for nonparticipant spouses applies. Since joint return MAGI is well below the $150,000 threshold, he is not affected by the phase-out rules and may deduct IRA contributions up to the $4,000 ceiling for 2006.

Nondeductible contributions. Any contributions exceeding the amount allowed under the above rules may be treated as nondeductible IRA contributions. *See 8.6* for further details. Alternatively, the excess may be contributed to a Roth IRA if allowed under the rules at *8.20*.

Figuring your IRA deduction if you receive Social Security benefits. If you or your spouse *(8.3)* is an active participant in an employer plan and either of you receives Social Security benefits, you need to make an extra computation before you can figure whether an IRA deduction is allowed. Follow the rules discussed at *34.3* to determine if part of your Social Security benefits would be subject to tax, assuming no IRA deduction were claimed. If none of your benefits would be taxable, you follow the regular rules above for determining IRA deductions. If part of your Social Security benefits would be taxable, MAGI for IRA purposes is increased by the taxable benefits. The allowable IRA deduction is then taken into account to determine the actual amount of taxable Social Security. IRS Publication 590 has worksheets for making these computations.

8.5 Active Participation in Employer Plan

Active participants in an employer retirement plan are subject to the phase-out rules for deducting contributions discussed at *8.4*. When a married couple files jointly and only one of the spouses was an active plan participant for the taxable year, a more favorable phase-out range applies to the non-participant spouse than to the spouse who was an active participant; *see 8.4* for details.

An employer retirement plan means:

1. A qualified pension, profit-sharing, or stock bonus plan, including a qualified self-employed Keogh plan, SIMPLE IRA, or simplified employee pension (SEP) plan;
2. A qualified annuity plan;
3. A tax-sheltered annuity; and
4. A plan established for its employees by the United States, by a state or political subdivision, or by any agency or instrumentality of the United States or a state or political subdivision, but not eligible state Section 457 plans.

Caution

Active Participant Status

You are treated as an active participant in a 401(k) plan, profit-sharing plan, stock bonus plan, or money-purchase pension plan if contributions are made or allocated to your account for the plan year that ends within your tax year. Under this rule, you may be considered an active participant for a year during which no contributions by you or your employer are made to your account; *see* the Examples in this section.

Form W-2. If your employer checks the "Retirement plan" box within Box 13 of your 2006 Form W-2, this indicates that you were an active participant in your employer's retirement plan during the year. If you want to make a contribution before you receive your Form W-2, check the following guidelines and consult your plan administrator for your status.

Type of plan. Under any type of plan, if you are considered an active participant for any part of the plan year ending with or within your taxable year, you are treated as an active participant for the entire taxable year. Because of this plan year rule, you may be treated as an active participant even if you worked for the employer only part of the year. Under IRS guidelines, it is possible to be treated as an active participant in the year of retirement and even in the year after retirement if your employer maintains a fiscal year plan.

The plan year rule works differently for defined benefit pension plans than for defined contribution plans such as profit-sharing plans, 401(k) plans, money purchase pension plans, and stock bonus plans. These rules are discussed below.

If you are married, and either you or your spouse is treated as an active participant for 2006, *see 8.3* for the effect on the other spouse.

EXAMPLES

1. Pat O'Neil joins a company in February 2006 that has a 401(k) plan (a type of defined contribution plan) with a plan year starting July 1 and ending the following June 30. He is not eligible to participate in the plan year ending June 30, 2006. After he becomes eligible to participate in the second half of 2006, he elects to defer 6% of his 2006 salary to the 401(k) plan for the plan year ending June 30, 2007. Although he makes elective deferrals to the plan during 2006, he is not considered an active participant for 2006 because his contributions were made for the plan year ending in 2007. He will be considered an active participant in 2007, even if he decides not to defer any part of his 2007 salary for the plan year ending June 30, 2008.
2. Clarise Jones's employer has a defined benefit pension plan with a plan year starting July 1 and ending the following June 30. She is not excluded from participating. If she retired during September 2006, she is considered an active participant for 2006 because she was eligible to participate during the plan year ending during 2006. She will also be considered an active participant for 2007. Although she will retire before the end of the plan year starting July 1, 2006, and ending June 30, 2007, she will still be eligible to participate during part of that plan year (July 1, 2006, until retirement in September 2006), and since the 2006–2007 plan year ends within her 2007 tax year, she will be considered an active participant for 2007.

Defined benefit pension plans. You are treated as an active participant in a defined benefit pension plan if, for the plan year ending with or within your taxable year, you are eligible to participate in the plan. Under this rule, as long as you are eligible, you are treated as an active participant, even if you decline participation in the plan or you fail to make a mandatory contribution specified in the plan. Furthermore, you are treated as an active participant even if your rights to benefits are not vested.

Defined contribution plan. For a defined contribution plan, you are generally considered an active participant if "with respect to" the plan year ending with or within your taxable year (1) you make elective deferrals to the plan; (2) your employer contributes to your account; or (3) forfeitures are allocated to your account. If any of these events occur, you are treated as an active participant for that taxable year, even if you do not have a vested right to receive benefits from your account.

8.6 Nondeductible Contributions to Traditional IRAs

If you are not allowed to deduct any IRA contributions for 2006 because of the phase-out rule *(8.4)*, you may make *nondeductible* contributions of up to $4,000 ($5,000 if age 50 or over at the end of 2006) where you have compensation of at least that much. If the deduction limit is reduced under the phase-out rules of *8.4*, you may make a nondeductible contribution to the extent the maximum contribution limit of $4,000 (or $5,000) exceeds the deductible limit figured under *8.4*.

If you make contributions to a traditional IRA during the year, you may not know whether your active participation status *(8.5)* and modified adjusted gross income (MAGI) will permit you to claim a deduction under the phase-out rules at *8.4*. You can make your contribution and wait until you file your return to determine if you are eligible for a deduction. Assume that you make a contribution and after the end of the year you determine that you are eligible for only a portion of the deductible amount under the phase-out rule *(see 8.4)*. In that case, you can leave the nondeductible portion in a nondeductible traditional IRA (reporting it on Form 8606), or you may recharacterize *(8.22)* the nondeductible contribution as a Roth IRA contribution assuming you qualify to contribute to a Roth IRA *(see 8.20)*. On the other hand, you may decide to withdraw the nondeductible contribution as discussed below.

Roth IRA alternative. If you are not barred from making Roth IRA contributions *(see 8.20)* because of your income level, the Roth IRA has advantages over the nondeductible traditional IRA. Although both types of plans allow earnings to accumulate tax free until withdrawal, the Roth IRA has advantages at withdrawal. After a five-year period, completely tax-free withdrawals of earnings as well as contributions may be made from a Roth IRA if you are age 59½ or older, you are disabled, or you withdraw no more than $10,000 for first-time home-buyer expenses. Even within the first five-year period, contributions may be withdrawn tax free from a Roth IRA. On the other hand, withdrawals from a nondeductible traditional IRA are partially taxed if any deductible contributions to any traditional IRA were previously made. Even if only nondeductible contributions had been made, earnings from traditional IRAs are taxed at withdrawal. Furthermore, contributions after age 70½ may be made only to a Roth IRA, and mandatory required minimum distributions are not required from a Roth IRA, as they are from a traditional IRA. *See 8.19–8.24* for Roth IRA details.

Form 8606. If you made a nondeductible contribution to a traditional IRA for 2005, you must report it on Form 8606 unless you withdraw the contribution as discussed below. You must list on Form 8606 the value of all of your IRAs as of the end of the year, including amounts based on deductible contributions. If you are married and you and your spouse both make nondeductible contributions, you must each file a separate Form 8606. A $50 penalty may be imposed for not filing Form 8606 unless there is reasonable cause. Furthermore, if you overstate the amount of designated nondeductible contributions made for any taxable year, you are subject to a $100 penalty for each such overstatement unless you can demonstrate that the overstatement was due to reasonable cause. You may file an amended return for a taxable year and change the designation of IRA contributions from deductible to nondeductible or nondeductible to deductible.

Withdrawing nondeductible contributions. If you make an IRA contribution for 2005 and later realize it is not deductible, you may make a tax-free withdrawal of the contribution by the filing due date (plus extensions), instead of designating the contribution as nondeductible on Form 8606. To do this, you must also withdraw the earnings allocable to the withdrawn contribution and include the earnings as income on your 2006 return. If you file a timely 2006 return without making the withdrawal, you may do so by October 15, 2007, and report the related earnings on an amended return. Write "Filed pursuant to Section 301.9100-2" across the top of the amended return and attach an explanation of the withdrawal. You might want to make the withdrawal if you incorrectly determined that a contribution would be deductible and you do not want to leave nondeductible contributions in your account. However, making the withdrawal could subject you to bank penalties for premature withdrawals, or other withdrawal penalties imposed by the IRA trustee. Furthermore, if you are under age 59½, the 10% premature withdrawal penalty applies to the withdrawn earnings unless one of the exceptions at *8.12* is available.

Planning Reminder

Roth IRA Alternative

A Roth IRA is a nondeductible IRA that offers significant tax and retirement planning advantages. Contributions up to the annual limit may be made if modified adjusted gross income is below the annual phaseout threshold *(see 8.20)*. In general, after the five-year period beginning with the first taxable year for which a Roth IRA contribution was made, tax-free withdrawals may be made if you are age 59½ or older, you are disabled or you have qualifying first-time home-buyer expenses. Traditional IRAs may be rolled over to Roth IRAs if your modified adjusted gross income is $100,000 or less; *see 8.21* for further details.

Planning Reminder

Form 8606 for Traditional IRA Distributions

Keep a copy of each Form 8606 filed showing nondeductible contributions and keep a separate record of deductible contributions. When you make withdrawals from a traditional IRA, the portion of each withdrawal allocable to nondeductible contributions is not taxed. You may not completely avoid tax even if you withdraw an amount equal to your nondeductible contributions. The tax-free portion of the withdrawal is figured on Form 8606. The rules for figuring tax on withdrawals are at *8.9*.

8.7 Penalty for Excess Contributions to Traditional IRAs

If you contribute more than the allowable amount to a traditional IRA, whether deductible or nondeductible, the excess contribution may be subject to a penalty tax of 6%. The penalty tax is cumulative. That is, unless you correct the excess, you will be subject to another penalty on the excess contribution in the following year. The penalty tax is not deductible. The penalty is figured in Part III of Form 5329, which must be attached to Form 1040.

The 6% penalty may be avoided by withdrawing the excess contribution by the due date for your return, including extensions, plus any income earned on it. The withdrawn excess contribution is not taxable provided no deduction was allowed for it. The withdrawn earnings must be reported as income on your return for the year in which the excess contribution was made. The earnings should be reported to you as a taxable distribution on Form 1099-R. If you are under age 59½ (and not disabled) when you receive the income, the 10% premature withdrawal penalty applies to the income. Similar rules apply to withdrawals of excess employer contributions to a simplified employee pension plan *(8.15)* made by the due date for your return.

If an excess contribution for 2006 is not withdrawn by the due date (plus extensions) for your 2006 return, but you filed by the due date (with extensions), the IRS allows the withdrawal to be made no later than October 15, 2007 (six months after the original due date without extensions), provided the related earnings are reported on an amended return that explains the withdrawal; see the Form 5329 instructions for details. If the withdrawal is not made, the 6% penalty will apply to your 2006 return but it may be avoided for 2007 by withdrawing the excess by the end of 2007. Instead of withdrawing the excess contribution during 2007, you may also avoid a penalty for 2007 by reducing your allowable 2007 IRA contribution by the 2006 excess. *See* IRS Publication 590 and Form 5329 for details.

If you deducted an excess contribution in an earlier year for which total contributions were no more than the maximum deductible amount for that year ($3,000 for 2003–2004 or $4,000 for 2005, plus an additional $500 if age 50 or older by the end of the year), you may make a tax-free withdrawal of the excess by filing an amended return (*see 47.2* for deadline) to correct the excess deduction. However, the 6% penalty tax applies for each year that the excess was still in the account at the end of the year.

See IRS Publication 590 for further information on correcting excess contributions made in a prior year.

Roth IRAs. A similar 6% penalty applies on Form 5329 to excess contributions to a Roth IRA; *see* Form 5329 and IRS Publication 590 for further details.

Taking Money Out of a Traditional IRA

8.8 Taxable Distributions From Traditional IRAs

If all of your IRA contributions were deductible, any traditional IRA distribution you receive that you do not roll over or redeposit within 60 days *(8.10)* will be taxable, unless the special rules for qualified hurricane distributions *(see 8.25)* apply. Not only are distributions taxable, but the timing and amount of IRA payments is subject to these restrictions:

- Distributions before age 59½ are subject to a 10% tax penalty, unless you are totally disabled, meet exceptions for paying medical costs, receive annual payments under an annuity-type schedule or you qualify for another exception. The penalty and the exceptions are discussed at *8.12*.
- After you reach age 70½, you must start to receive annual distributions under a life-expectancy calculation. The required starting date is the April 1 of the year after the year in which you reach age 70½. For example, if you reach age 70½ during 2006 you must start taking IRA distributions by April 1, 2007. Failure to take the minimum required annual distribution can result in penalties. These rules are discussed in *8.13*.

Law Alert

Tax-Free Transfers From IRA to Charity in 2006/2007

If you are age 70½ or older, you can exclude from your 2006 income distributions of up to $100,000 from your traditional or Roth IRA that are transferred directly to a charity. The same exclusion applies for 2007 distributions.

How to report IRA distributions on your 2006 return. All IRA distributions are reported to you and to the IRS on Form 1099-R; see the guide to Form 1099-R on pages 149–150. Form 1099-R must be attached to your return only if federal tax has been withheld. You can avoid withholding by instructing the payer not to withhold using Form W-4P (or a substitute form); *see 26.11*.

If you have never made nondeductible contributions, your IRA withdrawals are fully taxable and should be reported on Line 15b of Form 1040 or Line 11b of Form 1040A. If you have made deductible and nondeductible contributions, complete Form 8606 to figure the nontaxable and

Law Alert

Tax-Favored Qualified Hurricane Distributions

Qualified hurricane distributions from a traditional IRA, SEP, SIMPLE IRA, or Roth IRA to residents in the Hurricane Katrina, Rita, or Wilma disaster areas may be reported as income over three years or repaid without tax within the three-year period; *see 8.25* and *8.26*.

Court Decision

Penalty on Garnished IRA

The Tax Court held that an IRA owner received a taxable distribution when a bank enforced a court's garnishment award for past-due child support by transferring his IRA to his ex-wife. The Tax Court found that the distribution to the owner's former wife was a discharge of indebtedness to her and was constructively received by him. Whether the transfer of funds was voluntary or in settlement of a legal obligation was held to be of no consequence. The 10% tax penalty for distributions before age 59½ also applied.

taxable portions as discussed in *8.9*. Then you report the total IRA withdrawal on Line 15a of Form 1040 or Line 11a of Form 1040A and enter only the taxable portion on Line 15b or Line 11b, respectively.

If you have an individual retirement annuity, your investment in the contract is treated as zero so all payments are fully taxable. Distributions from an endowment policy due to death are taxed as ordinary income to the extent allocable to retirement savings; to the extent allocable to life insurance, they are considered insurance proceeds.

Proceeds from U.S. retirement bonds (which were issued by the Treasury before May 1982) are taxable in the year the bonds are redeemed. However, you must report the full proceeds in the year you reach age 70½ even if you do not redeem the bonds.

Conversion to Roth IRA. A conversion of a traditional IRA to a Roth IRA is generally treated as a taxable distribution from the traditional IRA; *see 8.21* for conversion requirements and tax-treatment.

Tax-free distribution to charity in 2006 and 2007 if age 70½ or older. The Pension Protection Act of 2006 allows a direct transfer from a traditional or Roth IRA to a charity to be excluded from income, up to $100,000 per year in each of 2006 and 2007. You must be age 70½ or older on the date of the distribution, and it must be transferred directly by the IRA trustee to a qualifying charity other than a "supporting organization" or donor advised fund. A charitable deduction cannot be claimed for the amount of the excludable distribution. A qualifying charitable distribution counts against the required minimum distributions *(8.13)* that the IRA owner must otherwise receive.

The exclusion is not allowed unless the entire distribution would be deductible as a charitable contribution (had you received the distribution and contributed the proceeds), without regard to the annual percentage-of-income ceilings *(14.17)*.

Since a qualifying transfer is not included in adjusted gross income, you may be able to preserve eligibility for income-based tax breaks such as the right to convert a traditional IRA to a Roth IRA *(8.21)* and the $25,000 loss allowance under the passive loss rules *(10.2)*. The exclusion may also help limit the amount of Social Security benefits subject to tax *(34.3)*.

Loan treated as distribution. If you borrow from your IRA account or use it as security for a loan, you generally are considered to have received your entire interest. Borrowing will subject the account or the fair market value of the contract to tax at ordinary income rates as of the first day of the taxable year of the borrowing. Your IRA account loses its tax-exempt status. If you use the account or part of it as security for a loan, the portion that is pledged is treated as a distribution. However, under the rollover rules, a short-term loan may be made by withdrawing IRA funds and redepositing them in an IRA within 60 days, subject to the once-a-year rollover rule at *8.10*.

IRS seizure of IRA treated as distribution. The Tax Court has held that an IRS levy of an IRA to cover back taxes is a taxable distribution to the account owner, even though the funds are transferred directly from the account to the IRS and not actually received by the owner. Where the owner is under age 59½, the 10% penalty for early withdrawals (8.12) does *not* apply to involuntary distributions attributable to an IRS levy.

8.9 Partially Tax-Free Traditional IRA Distributions Allocable to Nondeductible Contributions

If you ever made a nondeductible contribution to a traditional IRA, you must file Form 8606 to report a 2006 distribution from any of your traditional IRAs, even if the distribution is from an IRA to which only nondeductible contributions were made. All of your traditional IRAs are treated as one contract. If you receive distributions from more than one IRA in the same year, they are combined for reporting purposes on Form 8606. When you withdraw an amount from any traditional IRA during a taxable year and you previously made both deductible and nondeductible IRA contributions, the part of your withdrawal that is allocable to your nondeductible contributions is tax-free; any balance is taxable. You may not claim that you are withdrawing only your tax-free contributions, even if your withdrawal is less than your nondeductible contributions. The six steps below reflect the IRS method used on Form 8606 to figure the nontaxable and taxable portions of the IRA distributions.

The rule requiring you to combine nondeductible and deductible IRAs when making IRA withdrawals does not apply to withdrawals from a Roth IRA. A Roth IRA is treated separately. After a five-year period, withdrawals after age 59½ from a Roth IRA are completely tax-free; *see 8.23.*

A bank or other payer of a distribution from a traditional IRA will not indicate on Form 1099-R whether any part of a distribution is a tax-free return of basis allocable to nondeductible contributions. It is up to you to keep records that show the nondeductible contributions you have made. IRS instructions require you to keep copies of all Forms 8606 on which nondeductible contributions have been designated, as well as copies of (1) your tax returns for years you made nondeductible contributions to traditional IRAs; (2) Forms 5498 showing all IRA contributions and showing the value of your IRAs for each year you received a distribution; and (3) Form 1099-R and Form W-2P showing IRA distributions. According to the IRS, you should keep such records until you have withdrawn all IRA funds.

Figuring the taxable portion of a traditional IRA distribution. If you received a distribution from a traditional IRA in 2006 and have ever made nondeductible contributions to any of your traditional IRAs, follow Steps 1–6 to determine the tax-free and taxable portions of the 2006 distribution. These steps assume that you did not convert a traditional IRA to a Roth IRA during 2006. If you did convert a traditional IRA to a Roth IRA, follow the instructions to Form 8606.

Step 1. Total IRA withdrawals during 2006.

Step 2. Total nondeductible contributions to all IRAs made by the end of 2006. Tax-free withdrawals of nondeductible contributions in prior years reduce the total. If you made any contributions to traditional IRAs for 2006 (including a contribution made between January 1 and April 16, 2007) that may be partly nondeductible because your modified adjusted gross income is within the deduction phase-out range shown in *8.4* for active plan participants, you should include the contributions in the Step 2 total.

Step 3. Add Step 1 to the value of all your IRAs (include SIMPLE IRAs and SEP IRAs) as of the end of 2006. If you received an IRA distribution within the last 60 days of 2006 that was rolled over to another IRA within the 60-day rollover period *(8.10) but* not until 2007, add the 2007 rollover to the year-end balance.

Step 4. Divide Step 2 by Step 3. This is the tax-free percentage of your IRA withdrawal.

Step 5. Multiply the Step 4 percentage by Step 1. This amount is tax free.

Step 6. Subtract Step 5 from Step 1. This amount is fully taxable.

EXAMPLE

In 2006, Nick James withdraws $5,000 from his traditional IRA, having made deductible IRA contributions of $8,000 and nondeductible contributions of $6,000 as follows:

Year	*Deductible*	*Nondeductible*
1991	$2,000	0
1992	2,000	0
1993	2,000	0
1994	1,000	$1,000
1995	1,000	1,000
1996	0	2,000
1997	0	2,000
	$8,000	$6,000

Assume that at the end of 2006, Nick's total IRA account balance, including earnings, is $17,500, and that this is his first IRA withdrawal. On Form 8606 for 2006, Nick figures that $1,350 of the $5,000 IRA withdrawal is tax free and $3,650 is taxable.

Step 1.	IRA withdrawal	$5,000
Step 2.	Nondeductible contributions	6,000
Step 3.	IRA balance at end of the year ($17,500) *plus* Step 1	22,500
Step 4.	Tax-free percentage: $6,000 ÷ $22,500	27%
Step 5.	Tax-free withdrawal: 27% × $5,000	1,350
Step 6.	Taxable withdrawal: $5,000 – $1,350	$3,650

The total $5,000 withdrawal should be reported on Line 15a of Form 1040 or on Line 11a of Form 1040A, and the taxable $3,650 portion should be entered on Line 15b (Form 1040) or on Line 11b (Form 1040A).

Planning Reminder

Deducting Loss

A loss on an IRA investment is deductible only if your basis in nondeductible contributions has not been received after the entire account has been distributed.

Deductible IRA loss based on unrecovered nondeductible contributions. According to the IRS, a loss is allowed if all IRA funds have been distributed and you have not recovered your basis in nondeductible contributions. However, the loss must be claimed as a miscellaneous itemized deduction subject to the 2%-of-adjusted-gross-income floor on Schedule A, Form 1040.

EXAMPLE

Paula Brown makes nondeductible IRA contributions of $10,000 from 1994–1998. In 2006, she withdraws $6,000. The year-end balance is $8,000. The tax-free portion of the withdrawal is $4,286 ($10,000 nondeductible contributions ÷ $14,000 total of withdrawal plus year-end balance × $6,000 withdrawal).

After the withdrawal, her account balance is $8,000; her basis is $5,714 ($10,000 – $4,286). If because of poor investments the value of the IRA fell to $3,000 by the end of 2006 and she withdrew the entire $3,000 balance, she could claim a $2,714 loss ($5,714 basis – $3,000 distribution), but only as a miscellaneous itemized deduction subject to the 2% floor (19.1) on Schedule A of Form 1040. Depending on her adjusted gross income and other miscellaneous itemized deductions, Paula may be unable to claim the loss on her IRA because of the 2% floor.

8.10 Tax-Free Rollovers and Direct Transfers to Traditional IRAs

There are two types of tax-free rollovers that you can make to a traditional IRA. You may roll over funds to a traditional IRA from a qualified company or self-employed retirement plan, 403(b) plan, or governmental 457 plan; *see 7.8*. You may also use a rollover to switch funds from one traditional IRA to another, although another option, a direct transfer, is a more advantageous way of changing IRA investments.

Planning Reminder

60-Day Loan From IRA

You can take advantage of the rollover rule to borrow funds from your IRA if you need a short-term loan to pay your taxes or other expenses. As long as you redeposit the amount in an IRA within 60 days you are not taxed on the withdrawal; the redeposit is considered a tax-free rollover. You may roll over the funds to a different IRA from the one from which the withdrawal was made. A second withdrawal from the same IRA within one year would be taxable; *see 8.10.*

Direct transfer from one IRA to another. A *direct transfer* is made by instructing the trustee of a traditional IRA to transfer all or part of your account to another IRA trustee. Direct transfers are tax free because you do not receive the funds. With a direct transfer, there is no risk of missing the 60-day deadline for rolling over a withdrawal into a new IRA. The tax law does not require a waiting period between direct transfers, whereas rollovers are subject to a once-a-year limitation, as discussed below.

For example, assume you have a traditional IRA at Bank "A" and decide to switch your account to Mutual Fund "ABC." The mutual fund will provide you with transfer request forms that you complete and return to the fund, which will then forward the forms to the bank to complete the direct transfer. The transfer from the bank to the mutual fund is tax free. Because the IRA funds were not paid to you, the transfer is not considered a rollover subject to the once-a-year rollover limitation. This means that if within one year you become unhappy with the performance of Mutual Fund "ABC," you may make another tax-free direct transfer of your IRA to Fund "XYZ" or to Bank "B."

Rollover within 60 days. If you withdraw funds from a traditional IRA, you have 60 days to make a tax-free rollover to another traditional IRA. The amount you receive from your old IRA must be transferred to the new plan by the 60th day after the day you received it. Amounts not rolled over within the 60-day period must be treated as a taxable distribution for the year you received the distribution (not the year in which the 60-day period expired, if that is later) and the 10% penalty for a distribution before age 59½ applies unless an exception *(8.12)* is available.

The IRS may waive the 60-day rollover deadline on equitable grounds if a distribution cannot be rolled over on time because of events beyond your reasonable control, such as illness, natural disaster, or a financial institution's error; see the IRS waiver guidlines below. An extension to the 60-day deadline is also allowed if your distribution is "frozen" and cannot be withdrawn from an insolvent or bankrupt financial institution; see below. The deadline is extended to 120 days if a distribution is taken to buy or build a qualifying "first home" and the deal falls through; *see* below.

Once you complete a rollover between traditional IRAs, you must wait one year before you can roll over the same funds; *see* below.

IRS may waive 60-day rollover deadline on equitable grounds. The IRS has discretion to waive the 60-day deadline for completing a rollover if failure to do so was due to events beyond your reasonable control and failure to waive the deadline would be against "equity or good conscience."

The IRS announced in Revenue Procedure 2003-16 that it will automatically waive the deadline if: (1) you deposit the rollover funds with a financial institution within the 60-day period, (2) you follow all of the institution's rollover procedures but the rollover account is not established on time solely because of the institution's error, and (3) the funds are actually deposited in a valid rollover account within one year of the start of the 60-day period.

In other hardship situations not eligible for the automatic waiver, you must apply to the IRS for a waiver by requesting a private letter ruling and paying the required user fee. You must show that failure to meet the 60-day deadline was beyond your reasonable control, such as where you were disabled, hospitalized, or there was a natural disaster, postal error, or error by the financial institution other than one qualifying for an automatic waiver. The IRS will take into account the length of the delay and whether you cashed a distribution paid to you by check.

For example, the IRS issued a private ruling allowing a waiver to a taxpayer whose IRA funds were stolen by his investment advisor. Without a rollover, the advisor's withdrawals would be treated as taxable distributions to the taxpayer. Since the taxpayer did not learn of the misappropriation until after the 60-day rollover period expired, a waiver was requested. The IRS agreed that not granting a waiver would be inequitable and it gave the taxpayer 30 days from the date of the ruling to make a cash rollover of the misappropriated amount.

However, the IRS has denied waivers to taxpayers who use an IRA distribution as a short-term loan to pay personal expenses but are unable to put back the funds into an IRA within 60 days. For example, an unemployed taxpayer withdrew money from his IRA to pay his mortgage and avoid a threatened foreclosure of the home. After he was turned down for loans by numerous mortgage companies, his mother borrowed against her home and loaned him the funds, which he redeposited into his IRA, but 102 days had passed since he received the distribution. The IRS in a private ruling denied his request for a waiver of the 60-day rollover deadline.

The once-a-year rollover rule applies separately to each of your IRAs. A tax-free rollover may occur only once in a one-year period starting on the date you receive the first distribution. If within that one-year period you receive a distribution from the previously rolled over IRA, the distribution is taxable and if you are under age 59½, could be subject to the 10% penalty for premature distributions; *see 8.12.* However, this rule applies separately to each of your traditional IRAs. For example, you have one traditional IRA invested in a bank and another invested in a mutual fund. Within the same one-year period, you may roll over the bank IRA to a different traditional IRA and you may also roll over the mutual-fund IRA to a different traditional IRA. However, neither of the new IRAs may be rolled over again within the one-year period starting on the date that you received the distribution from the original traditional IRA.

There is an exception to the one-year waiting period between rollovers if the second distribution is made from an insolvent financial institution by the FDIC (Federal Deposit Insurance Corporation) acting as receiver. The exception applies only if the receiver makes the distribution to you because it is unable to find a buyer for the insolvent institution.

Note: A *direct transfer* may be used as discussed above if you want to invest in another IRA within the one-year period.

Deposits in insolvent financial institutions. The 60-day limit for completing a rollover is extended if the funds are "frozen" and may not be withdrawn from a bankrupt or insolvent financial institution. The 60-day period is extended while the account is frozen and you have a minimum of 10 days after the release of the funds to complete the rollover.

If a government agency takes control of an insolvent bank, you might receive an "involuntary" distribution of your IRA account from the agency. According to the IRS and Tax Court, such a payment is subject to the regular IRA distribution rules. For example, a couple received payment for their $11,000 IRA balance from the Maryland Deposit Insurance Fund after the bank in which the funds were invested became insolvent. The Tax Court held that the payment was taxable, even though the distribution was from a state insurance fund and not from the bank itself. Furthermore, since they were under age 59½, the 10% penalty for early distributions *(8.12)* was imposed, even though the distribution was involuntary. The tax and penalty could have been avoided by making a rollover of the distribution within 60 days, but this was not done.

120-day rollover period after failure to acquire "first-time" home. As discussed in *8.12*, a "first-time" homebuyer may be able to limit or avoid a 10% penalty for a distribution before age 59½ by using the funds within 120 days to help buy, build, or rebuild a principal residence.

Filing Tip

Reporting a Rollover on Your 2006 Return

If in 2006 you rolled over a qualifying distribution from an employer plan to an IRA (7.8), report the total distribution on Line 16a of Form 1040 or Line 12a of Form 1040A. Enter zero as the taxable amount on Line 16b or Line 12b if the entire amount was rolled over. If only part of the distribution was rolled over, enter the portion not rolled over on Line 16b or Line 12b. Write "Rollover" next to the line.

If you rolled over funds from one IRA to another, the total distribution should be reported on Line 15a of Form 1040 or Line 11a of Form 1040A. If the entire distribution was rolled over, enter zero as the taxable amount on Line 15b or Line 11b. Otherwise, enter the amount not rolled over on Line 15b or Line 11b. Write "Rollover" next to the line.

If you made a tax-free direct transfer from one IRA to another, you do not have to report it on your return.

If the requirements of the exception cannot be met because the planned purchase or construction of the home falls through, the law allows the taxpayer to return the distribution to an IRA within 120 days after receiving the distribution. The extension of the tax-free rollover period from 60 days to 120 days is automatic if the requirements are met; a waiver of the 60-day deadline (as discussed above) from the IRS is not required. For example, a taxpayer withdrew IRA funds to buy a home and would have qualified as a "first-time" homebuyer, but his offer was rejected by the seller and approximately 72 days after the IRA withdrawal he put the amount of the distribution back into his IRA. The IRS in a private ruling held that the recontribution to the IRA was timely under the special 120-day rollover rule.

8.11 Transfer of Traditional IRA to Spouse at Divorce or Death

If you receive your former spouse's IRA pursuant to a divorce decree or written instrument incident to the decree, the transfer is not taxable to either of you. From the date of transfer the account is treated as your IRA. If you are legally separated, a transfer of your spouse's IRA to you is tax free if made under a decree of separate maintenance or written instrument incident to the decree. The transferred account is then treated as your IRA.

How to make a divorce-related transfer. If you are required to transfer IRA assets to your spouse or former spouse by a decree of divorce or separate maintenance, or a written instrument incident to such a decree, use one of these transfer methods to avoid being taxed on the transfer: (1) change the name on the IRA from your name to the name of your spouse or former spouse, or (2) direct your IRA trustee to transfer the IRA assets directly to the trustee of a new or existing IRA in the name of your spouse or former spouse.

If you simply withdraw money from your IRA and pay it to your spouse, you will be treated as having received a taxable distribution from your IRA. If you are under age 59½, you will be subject to the 10% early distribution penalty as well as regular tax on the withdrawal.

QDRO transfer of employer plan benefits to your IRA. If you receive your share of your spouse's or former spouse's benefits from an employer plan under a qualified domestic relations order (QDRO), the distribution is taxable to you unless you roll it over to a traditional IRA or another eligible retirement plan *(7.8)*. Special averaging may be available; *see 7.12*. If you roll over only part of a qualifying QDRO distribution, you figure the tax on the retained portion by taking into account a prorated share of your former spouse's cost investment.

Surviving spouse. If you inherit your spouse's IRA when he or she dies, you may elect to treat the IRA as your own, or you may receive distributions from the account as a beneficiary. *See 8.14* for a discussion of these options.

8.12 Penalty for Traditional IRA Withdrawals Before Age 59½

You have to pay a 10% penalty if you receive a distribution from a traditional IRA before you are age 59½, unless (1) you make a qualifying rollover to another IRA *(8.10)*, (2) you are totally disabled, (3) you pay medical expenses exceeding 7.5% of adjusted gross income, (4) you receive unemployment compensation for at least 12 consecutive weeks and pay medical insurance premiums, (5) you pay qualified higher education expenses, (6) the distribution is $10,000 or less and used for qualified first-time home-buyer expenses, (7) the distribution is one of a series of payments being made under one of several annuity-type methods, (8) you are a beneficiary receiving IRA distributions following the death of the owner, or (9) the distribution was due to an IRS levy on your IRA.

The penalty is 10% of the taxable IRA distribution. For example, if before age 59½ you withdraw $3,000 from your traditional IRA, you must include the $3,000 as part of your taxable income and, in addition, pay a $300 penalty tax. If part of a premature distribution is tax free because it is allocable to nondeductible contributions *(see 8.9)* or rolled over to another IRA *(8.10)*, the 10% penalty applies only to the taxable portion of the distribution.

If you are subject to the 10% early distribution penalty but not to the penalties discussed at *8.7* and *8.13*, the penalty is entered directly on Form 1040, Line 60.

Law Alert

Penalty Exception for Reservists Called to Active Duty

The Pension Protection Act of 2006 provides an exception to the early distribution penalty for reservists called to active duty after September 11, 2001, and before December 31, 2007, for over 179 days.

If you do not owe the penalty because you qualify for an exception, you may have to file Form 5329 with Form 1040, depending on whether the payer of the distribution correctly marked the exception in Box 7 of Form 1099-R. If you qualify for the annuity-method exception and the payer correctly indicated that exception by marking Code 2 in Box 7, you do not have to file Form 5329. Similarly, if you are the beneficiary of a deceased IRA owner and the payer has correctly noted that with Code 4 in Box 7, you do not have to file Form 5329 to claim the exception.

If you qualify for the disability exception (*see* below), it is unlikely that the payer will know of that fact and thus Code 3 (for the disability exception) will probably not be marked in Box 7 of Form 1099-R. In that case, you must file Form 5329 to claim the exception. You also must file Form 5329 if the annuity method or beneficiary exception applies but it is not coded in Box 7 of Form 1099-R.

If you rolled over your entire distribution within 60 days to another IRA *(8.10)*, the penalty does not apply and Form 5329 does not have to be filed.

Spousal beneficiaries. Beneficiaries are exempt from the pre–age 59½ penalty. If you inherit an IRA from your deceased spouse and elect to treat it as your own IRA as discussed at *8.14*, you are not eligible for the beneficiary exception; distributions from the account before you reach age 59½ will be subject to the penalty unless another exception applies. The beneficiary exception applies if the account is maintained in the name of your deceased spouse and you are receiving the distribution as a spousal beneficiary under the rules at *8.14*.

Disability exception. To qualify for the disability exception, you must be able to show that you have a physical or mental condition that can be expected to last indefinitely or result in death and that prevents you from engaging in "substantial gainful activity" similar to the type of work you were doing before the condition arose.

In one case, a 53-year-old stockbroker claimed that his IRA withdrawal of over $200,000 should be exempt from the 10% penalty because he suffered from mental depression. However, the Tax Court upheld the IRS imposition of the penalty because he continued to work as a stockbroker.

Medical expense exception. If you withdraw IRA funds in a year in which you pay substantial medical costs, part of the distribution may avoid the pre–age 59½ penalty. If your unreimbursed medical expenses in the year of the distribution exceed 7.5% of your adjusted gross income, the distribution, to the extent of the excess, is not subject to the penalty. The medical costs must be eligible for the itemized medical deduction *(see 17.2)*, but the IRA penalty exception applies whether you itemize or claim the standard deduction.

Unemployed person's medical insurance exceptions. There is no general penalty exception for being unemployed. However, if you are unemployed and received unemployment benefits under Federal or state law for at least 12 consecutive weeks, you may make penalty-free IRA withdrawals to the extent of medical insurance premiums paid during the year for you, your spouse, and your dependents. The withdrawals may be made in the year the 12-week unemployment test is met, or in the following year. However, the penalty exception does not apply to distributions made more than 60 days after you return to the work force.

Self-employed persons who are ineligible by law for unemployment benefits may be treated as meeting the 12-week test, and thus eligible for the exception, under regulations to be issued by the IRS.

Higher education expenses exception. A penalty exception is allowed for IRA distributions that do not exceed higher education expenses, including graduate school costs, for you, your spouse, your or your spouse's children, or your or your spouse's grandchildren that you paid during the year of the IRA distribution. Eligible expenses include tuition, fees, books, supplies, and equipment that are required for enrollment or attendance, plus room and board for a person who is at least a half-time student.

The penalty exception applies only if the withdrawal from the IRA and the payment of the qualified higher education expenses occur within the same year. For example, in one case, a taxpayer under age 59½ took IRA distributions in 2001 to pay credit card debt incurred in 1999 and 2000 to pay qualified higher education expenses for those years. Another taxpayer under age 59½ took IRA distributions in 2002 and used them to pay qualified expenses incurred in 2003 and 2004. In both cases, the Tax Court agreed with the IRS that the penalty exception was not available because the IRA withdrawals were not made in the same year that the qualified higher education expenses were incurred.

Law Alert

Penalty Exception for Hurricane Katrina Victims

The 10% penalty on early IRA withdrawals does not apply to qualified Hurricane Katrina distributions. *See 8.25.*

Planning Reminder

Annuity-Schedule Penalty Exceptions

If you are planning a series of payments to avoid the 10% early-distribution penalty, keep in mind that payments under this exception must continue for at least five years, or until you reach age 59½, whichever is the longer period.

Caution

Medical Expenses Exception

The medical expense exception to the 10% penalty applies only to the extent that in the year you receive the distribution, you pay deductible medical costs *(17.2)* in excess of 7.5% of your adjusted gross income. If the deductible medical expenses are not paid in the year the distribution is received, the exception is not available.

First-time home-buyer expense exception. A penalty exception is allowed for up to $10,000 of qualifying "first-time" home-buyer expenses. You are a qualifying first-time home-buyer if you did not have a present ownership interest in a principal residence in the two-year period ending on the acquisition date of the new home. If you are married, your spouse also must have had no such ownership interest within the two-year period. The penalty does not apply to IRA distributions that are used within 120 days to buy, construct, or reconstruct a principal residence for you, your spouse, child, grandchild, or ancestor of you or your spouse. Qualifying home acquisition costs include reasonable settlement, financing, or other closing costs. If you qualify, the exception applies only for $10,000 of home-buyer expenses. This is a lifetime cap per IRA owner and not an annual limit.

If you take a distribution, intending to use it for home acquisition costs that would qualify for the first-time buyer exception, but the transaction falls through, you have 120 days from the date you receive the distribution to roll it back to an IRA; *see 8.10*.

IRS levy. The 10% penalty does not apply to an "involuntary" distribution due to an IRS levy on your IRA.

New law: Qualified reservist distribution. If you are a member of the reserves called to active military duty before December 31, 2007, for over 179 days, or indefinitely, distributions received during the active duty period are not subject to the early distribution penalty. Furthermore, a qualified reservist distribution may be recontributed to the plan within two years after the end of your active duty period without regard to the regular limits on IRA contributions; a recontribution is not deductible. *See 7.15* for amended return and recontribution deadlines.

Table 8-2 Joint Life and Last Survivor Life Expectancy

(see "Required minimum distribution method" on page 199)

Ages	30	31	32	33	34	35	36	37	38	39	40	41	42	43	44	45	46	47	48	49	50	51	52	53	54	55	56	57	58	59
30	60.2	59.7	59.2	58.8	58.4	58.0	57.6	57.3	57.0	56.7	56.4	56.1	55.9	55.7	55.5	55.3	55.1	55.0	54.8	54.7	54.6	54.5	54.4	54.3	54.2	54.1	54.0	54.0	53.9	53.8
31	59.7	59.2	58.7	58.2	57.8	57.4	57.0	56.6	56.3	56.0	55.7	55.4	55.2	54.9	54.7	54.5	54.3	54.1	54.0	53.8	53.7	53.6	53.5	53.4	53.3	53.2	53.1	53.0	53.0	52.9
32	59.2	58.7	58.2	57.7	57.2	56.8	56.4	56.0	55.6	55.3	55.0	54.7	54.4	54.2	53.9	53.7	53.5	53.3	53.2	53.0	52.9	52.7	52.6	52.5	52.4	52.3	52.2	52.1	52.1	52.0
33	58.8	58.2	57.7	57.2	56.7	56.2	55.8	55.4	55.0	54.7	54.3	54.0	53.7	53.4	53.2	52.9	52.7	52.5	52.3	52.2	52.0	51.9	51.7	51.6	51.5	51.4	51.3	51.2	51.2	51.1
34	58.4	57.8	57.2	56.7	56.2	55.7	55.3	54.8	54.4	54.0	53.7	53.3	53.0	52.7	52.4	52.2	52.0	51.7	51.5	51.4	51.2	51.0	50.9	50.8	50.6	50.5	50.4	50.3	50.3	50.2
35	58.0	57.4	56.8	56.2	55.7	55.2	54.7	54.3	53.8	53.4	53.0	52.7	52.3	52.0	51.7	51.5	51.2	51.0	50.8	50.6	50.4	50.2	50.0	49.9	49.8	49.7	49.5	49.4	49.4	49.3
36	57.6	57.0	56.4	55.8	55.3	54.7	54.2	53.7	53.3	52.8	52.4	52.0	51.7	51.3	51.0	50.7	50.5	50.2	50.0	49.8	49.6	49.4	49.2	49.1	48.9	48.8	48.7	48.6	48.5	48.4
37	57.3	56.6	56.0	55.4	54.8	54.3	53.7	53.2	52.7	52.3	51.8	51.4	51.1	50.7	50.4	50.0	49.8	49.5	49.2	49.0	48.8	48.6	48.4	48.2	48.1	47.9	47.8	47.7	47.6	47.5
38	57.0	56.3	55.6	55.0	54.4	53.8	53.3	52.7	52.2	51.7	51.3	50.9	50.4	50.1	49.7	49.4	49.1	48.8	48.5	48.2	48.0	47.8	47.6	47.4	47.2	47.1	47.0	46.8	46.7	46.6
39	56.7	56.0	55.3	54.7	54.0	53.4	52.8	52.3	51.7	51.2	50.8	50.3	49.9	49.5	49.1	48.7	48.4	48.1	47.8	47.5	47.3	47.0	46.8	46.6	46.4	46.3	46.1	46.0	45.8	45.7
40	56.4	55.7	55.0	54.3	53.7	53.0	52.4	51.8	51.3	50.8	50.2	49.8	49.3	48.9	48.5	48.1	47.7	47.4	47.1	46.8	46.5	46.3	46.0	45.8	45.6	45.5	45.3	45.1	45.0	44.9
41	56.1	55.4	54.7	54.0	53.3	52.7	52.0	51.4	50.9	50.3	49.8	49.3	48.8	48.3	47.9	47.5	47.1	46.7	46.4	46.1	45.8	45.5	45.3	45.1	44.8	44.7	44.5	44.3	44.2	44.0
42	55.9	55.2	54.4	53.7	53.0	52.3	51.7	51.1	50.4	49.9	49.3	48.8	48.3	47.8	47.3	46.9	46.5	46.1	45.8	45.4	45.1	44.8	44.6	44.3	44.1	43.9	43.7	43.5	43.3	43.2
43	55.7	54.9	54.2	53.4	52.7	52.0	51.3	50.7	50.1	49.5	48.9	48.3	47.8	47.3	46.8	46.3	45.9	45.5	45.1	44.8	44.4	44.1	43.8	43.6	43.3	43.1	42.9	42.7	42.5	42.4
44	55.5	54.7	53.9	53.2	52.4	51.7	51.0	50.4	49.7	49.1	48.5	47.9	47.3	46.8	46.3	45.8	45.4	44.9	44.5	44.2	43.8	43.5	43.2	42.9	42.6	42.4	42.1	41.9	41.7	41.5
45	55.3	54.5	53.7	52.9	52.2	51.5	50.7	50.0	49.4	48.7	48.1	47.5	46.9	46.3	45.8	45.3	44.8	44.4	44.0	43.6	43.2	42.8	42.5	42.2	41.9	41.6	41.4	41.2	40.9	40.7
46	55.1	54.3	53.5	52.7	52.0	51.2	50.5	49.8	49.1	48.4	47.7	47.1	46.5	45.9	45.4	44.8	44.3	43.9	43.4	43.0	42.6	42.2	41.8	41.5	41.2	40.9	40.7	40.4	40.2	40.0
47	55.0	54.1	53.3	52.5	51.7	51.0	50.2	49.5	48.8	48.1	47.4	46.7	46.1	45.5	44.9	44.4	43.9	43.4	42.9	42.4	42.0	41.6	41.2	40.9	40.5	40.2	40.0	39.7	39.4	39.2
48	54.8	54.0	53.2	52.3	51.5	50.8	50.0	49.2	48.5	47.8	47.1	46.4	45.8	45.1	44.5	44.0	43.4	42.9	42.4	41.9	41.5	41.0	40.6	40.3	39.9	39.6	39.3	39.0	38.7	38.5
49	54.7	53.8	53.0	52.2	51.4	50.6	49.8	49.0	48.2	47.5	46.8	46.1	45.4	44.8	44.2	43.6	43.0	42.4	41.9	41.4	40.9	40.5	40.1	39.7	39.3	38.9	38.6	38.3	38.0	37.8
50	54.6	53.7	52.9	52.0	51.2	50.4	49.6	48.8	48.0	47.3	46.5	45.8	45.1	44.4	43.8	43.2	42.6	42.0	41.5	40.9	40.4	40.0	39.5	39.1	38.7	38.3	38.0	37.6	37.3	37.1
51	54.5	53.6	52.7	51.9	51.0	50.2	49.4	48.6	47.8	47.0	46.3	45.5	44.8	44.1	43.5	42.8	42.2	41.6	41.0	40.5	40.0	39.5	39.0	38.5	38.1	37.7	37.4	37.0	36.7	36.4
52	54.4	53.5	52.6	51.7	50.9	50.0	49.2	48.4	47.6	46.8	46.0	45.3	44.6	43.8	43.2	42.5	41.8	41.2	40.6	40.1	39.5	39.0	38.5	38.0	37.6	37.2	36.8	36.4	36.0	35.7
53	54.3	53.4	52.5	51.6	50.8	49.9	49.1	48.2	47.4	46.6	45.8	45.1	44.3	43.6	42.9	42.2	41.5	40.9	40.3	39.7	39.1	38.5	38.0	37.5	37.1	36.6	36.2	35.8	35.4	35.1
54	54.2	53.3	52.4	51.5	50.6	49.8	48.9	48.1	47.2	46.4	45.6	44.8	44.1	43.3	42.6	41.9	41.2	40.5	39.9	39.3	38.7	38.1	37.6	37.1	36.6	36.1	35.7	35.2	34.8	34.5
55	54.1	53.2	52.3	51.4	50.5	49.7	48.8	47.9	47.1	46.3	45.5	44.7	43.9	43.1	42.4	41.6	40.9	40.2	39.6	38.9	38.3	37.7	37.2	36.6	36.1	35.6	35.1	34.7	34.3	33.9
56	54.0	53.1	52.2	51.3	50.4	49.5	48.7	47.8	47.0	46.1	45.3	44.5	43.7	42.9	42.1	41.4	40.7	40.0	39.3	38.6	38.0	37.4	36.8	36.2	35.7	35.1	34.7	34.2	33.7	33.3
57	54.0	53.0	52.1	51.2	50.3	49.4	48.6	47.7	46.8	46.0	45.1	44.3	43.5	42.7	41.9	41.2	40.4	39.7	39.0	38.3	37.6	37.0	36.4	35.8	35.2	34.7	34.2	33.7	33.2	32.8
58	53.9	53.0	52.1	51.2	50.3	49.4	48.5	47.6	46.7	45.8	45.0	44.2	43.3	42.5	41.7	40.9	40.2	39.4	38.7	38.0	37.3	36.7	36.0	35.4	34.8	34.3	33.7	33.2	32.8	32.3
59	53.8	52.9	52.0	51.1	50.2	49.3	48.4	47.5	46.6	45.7	44.9	44.0	43.2	42.4	41.5	40.7	40.0	39.2	38.5	37.8	37.1	36.4	35.7	35.1	34.5	33.9	33.3	32.8	32.3	31.8

These rules apply retroactively to individuals called to active duty after September 11, 2001. If the two-year period for recontributions has expired, it is extended to August 17, 2008. A refund claim may be made on an amended return for a penalty paid on a qualified distribution or for tax paid on a recontributed distribution. If the amended return deadline has passed for a prior year *(47.2)*, you have until August 16, 2007, to file the amended return.

Annuity Schedule Payments Avoid 10% Penalty

You may avoid the penalty if you are willing to receive annual distributions under one of the three IRS-approved annuity-type methods discussed in this section. Before arranging an annuity-type schedule, consider these points: all of the payments will be taxable (unless allocable to nondeductible contributions, as discussed in *8.9*), and if you do not continue the payments for a minimum number of years, the IRS will impose the 10% penalty for all taxable payments received before age 59½, plus interest charges. The minimum payout period rules do not apply to totally disabled individuals or to beneficiaries of deceased IRA owners.

The payments must continue for at least five years, or until you reach age 59½, whichever period is longer. Thus, if you are in your 40s, you would have to continue the scheduled payments until you are age 59½. If you are in your mid-50s, the minimum payout period is not as serious a burden, as you only need to continue the scheduled payments for at least five years, starting with the date of the first distribution, provided that the period ends after you reach age 59½.

During this minimum period, the arranged annuity-type schedule generally may not be changed unless you become disabled. For example, taking a lump-sum distribution of your account balance before the end of the minimum payout period would trigger the retroactive penalty, plus interest charges. The penalty is triggered even if the change in distribution methods is made after you reach age 59½. However, the IRS may allow a reduction in payments during the minimum period, such as where part of an IRA has been transferred to an ex-spouse following a divorce. Also, as discussed below, the IRS allows a one-time irrevocable switch from the fixed amortization method or fixed annuitization method to the required minimum distribution method. After the minimum payout period, you can discontinue the payments or change the method without penalty.

IRS Alert

Division of IRA in Divorce

The IRS in private rulings has allowed a reduction in the scheduled payments from an IRA if part of the IRA is transferred to an ex-spouse as part of a divorce settlement. The reduction is not treated by the IRS as a "modification" that triggers the penalty.

Three approved payment methods. If you would like to take advantage of this penalty exception, you may apply one of the following three payout methods that have been approved by the IRS. With each method, you must receive at least one distribution annually. Under Method 1, the payment changes annually based on the value of the account. Under Methods 2 and 3 the annual payment is generally fixed when the payments begin, but in private rulings the IRS has approved payment schedules that from inception recalculate the amount to be withdrawn each year. Methods 2 and 3 require the assistance of a tax professional and financial advisor to plan the series of payments. The IRS allows taxpayers receiving payments under Method 2 or 3 to reduce the required annual amount without penalty by switching to Method 1; *see* the IRS Alert on the right.

1. ***Required minimum distribution method.*** This is the easiest method to figure but provides smaller annual payments than the other methods. Figure the annual withdrawal by dividing your account balance by your life expectancy or by the joint life and last survivor expectancy of you and your beneficiary.

For example, assume that you are age 50 in 2007 and have an IRA of $100,000 at the beginning of the year. If you use your single life expectancy, you may take a penalty-free payment of $2,924 in 2007 ($100,000 account balance ÷ 34.2 life expectancy). Single life expectancy is shown on the Beneficiary's Life Expectancy Table at *8.14*.

If instead of using your single life expectancy you used the joint life and last survivor expectancy of you and your beneficiary, the annual penalty-free amount would be smaller given the longer joint life expectancy. For example, if your beneficiary was age 45, your joint life and last survivor life expectancy would be 43.2 years (using ages 50 and 45), and the penalty-free withdrawal $2,315 ($100,000 account balance ÷ 43.2). *See* page 198 for a sample section of the IRS joint life and last survivor life expectancy table. The full IRS table showing joint life and last survivor life expectancy is in IRS Publication 590 and can also be obtained from your IRA trustee.

2. ***Fixed amortization method.*** Under this method, you amortize your IRA account balance like a mortgage, using the same life expectancy as under Method 1 (your single life expectancy or the joint life and last survivor expectancy of you and your beneficiary). For a series of payments beginning before 2003, any interest rate that was reasonable when the payments commenced could be used. However, for payment schedules starting after 2002, the IRS in Revenue Ruling 2002-62 limits the interest rate ceiling to no more than 120% of the federal mid-term rate for either of the

IRS Alert

IRS Allows Switch to Required Minimum Distribution Method

Because of stock market declines in the last few years, taxpayers who began a series of payments under the fixed amortization or annuitization factor method may have experienced a much more rapid decrease in their account balances than anticipated when the payments began. To avoid a premature depletion of the accounts, the IRS allows a one-time irrevocable switch without penalty to the required minimum distribution method. *See* Revenue Ruling 2002-62 for further details.

two months immediately preceding the month in which distributions begin. In private rulings, the IRS has approved proposed payment schedules that annually recalculate the payments to be received under the fixed amortization method.

3. *Fixed annuitization method.* This method is similar to the fixed amortization method, but an annuity factor from a mortality table is used. For payment schedules starting after 2002, Revenue Ruling 2002-62 provides the mortality table to be used. Revenue Ruling 2002-62 also provides that the maximum interest rate used for payment schedules starting after 2002 cannot exceed 120% of the federal mid-term rate for either of the two months immediately preceding the month in which distributions begin. In private rulings, the IRS has approved proposed payment schedules that annually recalculate the payments to be received under the fixed annuitization method.

8.13 Mandatory Distributions From a Traditional IRA After Age 70½

By April 1 of the year following the year in which you reach age 70½, you have to start receiving annual IRA distributions under a schedule that meets tax law tests. If you do not receive the minimum amount required by the tax law, a penalty tax of 50% applies to the difference between the minimum amount you should have received and the amount you did receive. The penalty is reported on Form 5329, which must be attached to Form 1040. The minimum distribution rules apply to account owners of traditional IRAs, as discussed in this section, and to beneficiaries of traditional IRAs, as discussed in *8.14*. Roth IRA owners *(8.19)* are not subject to minimum distribution requirements, but beneficiaries of Roth IRAs are *(8.24)*.

EXAMPLE

During 2006, Chris Calano reached age 70½ and received $3,000 from his traditional IRA. The required minimum distribution was $3,817. He must pay a penalty tax of $409 (50% of $817), unless it is waived by the IRS.

When must your first required minimum distribution be received? If you reached age 70½ during 2006, you may receive a minimum distribution for 2006 during 2006 or you may delay it until 2007 so long as it is received no later than April 1, 2007. You will also have to receive a minimum distribution for 2007 by December 31, 2007. Thus, if you do not take your first distribution during 2006, and wait until between January 1 and April 1, 2007, you will have to take two distributions in 2007, one by April 1 and another by December 31. This could increase your 2007 taxable income substantially. Distributions for later years must be taken by December 31 of each year.

If you reach age 70½ during 2007, your first required minimum distribution must be received no later than April 1, 2008. If you have an individual retirement annuity, your insurance company should gear your payments to meet minimum distribution requirements.

Do You Figure Your Required Minimum Distributions Yourself?

The trustee or custodian of your traditional IRA must calculate your required minimum distribution or offer to do so. If you reached age 70½ in 2006 or earlier, you should have received by January 31, 2006, a statement from the trustee or custodian of your traditional IRA showing the amount of your 2006 required minimum distribution or an offer to calculate the amount for you at your request.

If you are required to receive a required minimum distribution for 2007, the trustee or custodian must provide you with the amount by January 31, 2007, or offer to calculate it upon your request. By May 31, 2007, the trustee or custodian will send to you and the IRS copies of Form 5498 for 2006 ("IRA Contribution Information"). The fair market value of your account at the end of 2006 will be reported in Box 5 of Form 5498 and the box in Box 11 will be checked if you are due a required minimum distribution for 2007, but the amount does not have to be shown.

If the trustee or custodian calculates the required minimum distribution, the calculation may be based on the Uniform Lifetime Table (*see* page 203), which assumes that your beneficiary is 10 years younger than you are. However, if your sole beneficiary is your spouse who is more than 10 years younger than you, your required minimum distribution can be reduced by using the Joint Life and Last Survivor Expectancy Table (*see* page 204). If the trustee or custodian will not take the spousal exception into account, you can do so yourself by calculating the required minimum distribution under Steps 1–3 below.

If you have several traditional IRAs and each of the trustees or custodians provides you with the required minimum distribution, the total required amount may be taken from any one account or from any combination of the accounts.

Trustees or custodians are not currently obligated to calculate (or offer to calculate) the required minimum distribution for beneficiaries of inherited traditional IRAs, but the requirement may be imposed at a later date.

Importance of reviewing your beneficiary designations. The amount of required minimum distributions during your lifetime is not affected by the identity of your beneficiary (or beneficiaries) unless your sole beneficiary is your spouse who is more than 10 years younger than you are. However, after your death, your beneficiary designations assume importance not only for determining who will receive the funds but also for purposes of determining the maximum period of years over which distributions can be spread. You should review your beneficiary designations and if you have not done so, name a successor (contingent) beneficiary for each of your IRAs should your primary beneficiary predecease you. The maximum distribution period after your death will depend on the determination of the designated beneficiary as of September 30 of the year following the year of your death. For example, if the designated beneficary for the account is an individual, the maximum distribution period will be his or her life expectancy. However, if as of the September 30 determination date your estate was named as the beneficiary, the estate would not be a designated beneficiary and the heir who inherits the account through the estate could not extend distributions over his or her life expectancy. Depending on whether your death was before or after your required beginning date, the heir would have to withdraw the entire account within five years or over your remaining life expectancy figured as of the year of death. *See 8.14* for details on determining the designated beneficiary and the payout rules for inherited IRAs.

Figuring Your Required Minimum Distributions

As discussed above, the trustee or custodian of your traditional IRA must calculate the amount of your required minimum distribution or offer to do so. The calculation is based on final IRS regulations.

To make the calculation yourself, you can use the steps below, which reflect the final IRS regulations.

Steps for figuring your required minimum distribution. For each of your traditional IRAs, figure the required minimum distribution you must receive using the following steps. Keep in mind that once you have separately determined the required minimum distribution for each IRA, the IRS allows you to withdraw the total required minimum distribution for the year from any of the accounts in any combination you choose.

Step 1: Find the account balance of your IRA as of the previous December 31. If you reach age 70½ during 2006, the account balance to be used for figuring your first required minimum distribution is the account balance for December 31, 2005, even if the actual distribution for 2006 is not made until the first quarter of 2007 (January 1–April 1). For purposes of figuring your required minimum distribution for 2007, use the 2006 year-end balance, even if you took the first-year distribution in the first quarter of 2007.

The year-end account balance must be adjusted if toward the end of the year there is an outstanding rollover. For example, if in December of 2006 you withdraw funds from your IRA and you roll the funds back to the same IRA or a different one within 60 days but not until early in 2007, the rollover amount must be included as part of the December 31 account balance of the receiving IRA, even though it was not actually in any account on that date. Similarly, an adjustment is required if toward the end of 2006 you convert a traditional IRA to a Roth IRA but in 2007 you recharacterize the Roth IRA back to a traditional IRA *(see 8.22)*. For purposes of figuring the required minimum distribution for 2007, the account balance of the receiving traditional IRA (to which the recharacterization is made) is increased by the value of the Roth IRA on December 31, 2006.

Step 2: Divide the account balance (Step 1) by the applicable life expectancy. Your life expectancy under the IRS rules is taken from the Uniform Lifetime Table unless your sole beneficiary is your spouse who is more than 10 years younger than you are. The Uniform Lifetime

Filing Tip

Uniform Lifetime Table

To figure your required minimum distribution for the year you become age 70½ and later years, use the Uniform Lifetime Table on page 203, unless the exception for younger spouses applies, as explained on this page.

Table, shown on page 203, provides a joint life expectancy for you and a "deemed" beneficiary who is exactly 10 years younger than you are. Your beneficiary's actual age does not matter. The life expectancy period from the uniform table applies even if you have not named a beneficiary as of your required beginning date (April 1 of the year after the year you reach age 70½). Furthermore, you continue to use the Uniform Lifetime Table even if you change your beneficiary or beneficiaries after starting to receive minimum required distributions, unless the change results in the naming of your spouse as sole beneficiary for the entire year and you qualify to use the Joint Life and Last Survivor Expectancy Table because your spouse is more than 10 years younger than you are.

Your "deemed" life expectancy from the Uniform Lifetime Table is the number of years listed next to your age on your birthday in the year for which you are making the computation. For example, if you are figuring your required minimum distribution for 2006, and you are age 71 on your birthday in 2006, your life expectancy from the table, based on age 71, is 26.5 years. For 2007, your life expectancy from the table, using age 72, will be 25.6 years.

Exception for younger spouses. If the sole beneficiary of your IRA is your spouse and he or she is more than 10 years younger than you are, do not use the Uniform Lifetime Table. Use the actual joint life expectancy of you and your spouse, which will allow you to spread out distributions over an even longer period. *See* page 204 for Table 8-4, which has a sample section of the Joint Life and Last Survivor Expectancy Table from IRS Publication 590.

This rule applies only if your spouse meets the age test and is the sole beneficiary of your entire interest in the IRA at all times during the calendar year for which the required minimum distribution is being figured. If your spouse is named beneficiary during the year or he or she is one of several beneficiaries on the account, the Uniform Lifetime Table must be used for that year. Your spouse would not meet the sole beneficiary test. However, if you are married on January 1 of a year and during the year you divorce or your spouse dies, you are considered married for the entire year and may use the spousal exception to figure that year's required minimum distribution using the joint life table.

If the exception for spousal beneficiaries applies, find your joint life expectancy from the IRS table corresponding to both of your ages on your birthdays for the year of the computation. For example, if you are age 71 on your birthday in 2006 and your spouse on his or her birthday is age 58, use a joint life expectancy of 28.6 years (*see* Table 8-4 on page 204) to figure your required minimum distribution for 2006. This is more than the 26.5-year distribution period provided by the Uniform Lifetime Table for a 71-year-old.

Step 3: If you have more than one IRA, total the required minimum distributions for all the accounts. After figuring the required minimum distribution for each of your IRAs under Step 2, total the amounts. This is the minimum you must receive for the year; you are, of course, free to withdraw more than that. Although you must calculate the minimum required distribution separately for each account, you do not have to make withdrawals from each of them. The total minimum required distribution from all accounts may be taken from any one account, or more than one account if you prefer. For example, if you have five bank IRAs, you may take the entire required distribution from the bank where you have the largest balance, or from any other combination of banks. *See* Example 3 on page 203. The entire distribution is taxable unless part is allocable to nondeductible IRA contributions, as explained in *8.9*.

EXAMPLES

1. Joe Blake reached age 70½ in March 2006. A minimum distribution for 2006 must be received from his traditional IRA by April 1, 2007. As of December 31, 2005, Joe's IRA balance was $200,000. The 2005 year-end balance is used in the computation even if the distribution for 2006 is made in the first quarter of 2007 (by the April 1 deadline). Joe's beneficiary is his wife, who is age 63 on her birthday in 2006. On his birthday in September 2006, Joe is age 71. Here is how Joe figures his required minimum distribution for 2006:

   Step 1. Account balance of $200,000 as of December 31, 2005.

   Step 2. Based on Joe's age of 71, the life expectancy from the Uniform Lifetime Table is 26.5 years. The table assumes that Joe has a beneficiary who is age 61 (10 years younger than he is). The fact that his wife is age 63 does not matter.

   Step 3. Divide Step 1 by Step 2.

$200,000 ÷ 26.5 = $7,547. This is the minimum required distribution for 2006 that Joe must receive by April 1, 2007.

The second minimum distribution, due by December 31, 2007, is based upon the 2006 year-end account balance, even if the distribution for 2006 was not made until early 2007 (by April 1).

2. Same facts as Example 1, except that Joe's wife is age 56 on her birthday in 2006. Because Joe's wife is more than 10 years younger than Joe, he uses the joint life and last survivor expectancy table. Based on their ages of 71 and 56 (on their birthdays in 2006), the joint life expectancy from the table (*see* Table 8-4 on page 204) is 30.1 years. Joe's required minimum distribution for 2006 is $6,645 ($200,000 ÷ 30.1), which he must receive by April 1, 2007.
3. Cynthia Lowell has two IRAs. She reached age 70½ on January 15, 2006, and thus must receive her first distribution by April 1, 2007. The beneficiary of IRA-1 is her brother, who is age 61 on his birthday in 2006; the account balance of IRA-1 as of December 31, 2005, was $100,000. The beneficiary of IRA-2 is her husband, who was age 74 on his birthday in 2006; the account balance of IRA-2 at the end of 2005 was $10,000.

To figure her required minimum distribution for 2006, Cynthia uses the IRS's Uniform Lifetime Table shown below. The ages of her beneficiaries do not affect the computation.

IRA-1: The first minimum required distribution is $3,774. This is the account balance of $100,000 divided by 26.5, the life expectancy from the Uniform Lifetime Table for a person age 71 (Cynthia's age on her birthday in 2006).

IRA-2: The first minimum required distribution is $377, the account balance of $10,000 divided by 26.5, the life expectancy from the Uniform Lifetime Table, using age 71.

The total required distribution of $4,151 from both IRAs must be received by April 1, 2007. Cynthia may withdraw the money from either one or both of the IRAs.

Table 8-3 Uniform Lifetime Table*

IRA Owner's Age	*Distribution Period*	*IRA Owner's Age*	*Distribution Period*	*IRA Owner's Age*	*Distribution Period*
70	27.4	85	14.8	100	6.3
71	26.5	86	14.1	101	5.9
72	25.6	87	13.4	102	5.5
73	24.7	88	12.7	103	5.2
74	23.8	89	12.0	104	4.9
75	22.9	90	11.4	105	4.5
76	22.0	91	10.8	106	4.2
77	21.2	92	10.2	107	3.9
78	20.3	93	9.6	108	3.7
79	19.5	94	9.1	109	3.4
80	18.7	95	8.6	110	3.1
81	17.9	96	8.1	111	2.9
82	17.1	97	7.6	112	2.6
83	16.3	98	7.1	113	2.4
84	15.5	99	6.7	114	2.1
				115 and over	1.9

*Use this table unless your spouse is your sole IRA beneficiary and he or she is more than 10 years younger than you are. If the spousal beneficiary exception applies, use the IRS's joint life and last survivor expectancy table with the actual ages of both spouses (*see* Table 8-4 on the next page), which will provide a longer life expectancy distribution period than the above table provides.

Table 8-4 Joint Life and Last Survivor Expectancy Table (for use by owners whose spouses are more than 10 years younger)*

Age	70	71	72	73	74	75	76	77	78	79	80	81	82	83	84	85	86	87	88	89	90
35	48.7	48.7	48.7	48.6	48.6	48.6	48.6	48.6	48.6	48.6	48.5	48.5	48.5	48.5	48.5	48.5	48.5	48.5	48.5	48.5	48.5
36	47.8	47.7	47.7	47.7	47.7	47.7	47.6	47.6	47.6	47.6	47.6	47.6	47.6	47.6	47.6	47.5	47.5	47.5	47.5	47.5	47.5
37	46.8	46.8	46.8	46.7	46.7	46.7	46.7	46.7	46.6	46.6	46.6	46.6	46.6	46.6	46.6	46.6	46.6	46.6	46.6	46.6	46.6
38	45.9	45.9	45.8	45.8	45.8	45.7	45.7	45.7	45.7	45.7	45.7	45.7	45.6	45.6	45.6	45.6	45.6	45.6	45.6	45.6	45.6
39	44.9	44.9	44.9	44.8	44.8	44.8	44.8	44.8	44.7	44.7	44.7	44.7	44.7	44.7	44.7	44.7	44.6	44.6	44.6	44.6	44.6
40	44.0	44.0	43.9	43.9	43.9	43.8	43.8	43.8	43.8	43.8	43.7	43.7	43.7	43.7	43.7	43.7	43.7	43.7	43.7	43.7	43.7
41	43.1	43.0	43.0	43.0	42.9	42.9	42.9	42.9	42.8	42.8	42.8	42.8	42.8	42.8	42.7	42.7	42.7	42.7	42.7	42.7	42.7
42	42.2	42.1	42.1	42.0	42.0	42.0	41.9	41.9	41.9	41.9	41.8	41.8	41.8	41.8	41.8	41.8	41.8	41.8	41.8	41.7	41.7
43	41.3	41.2	41.1	41.1	41.1	41.0	41.0	41.0	40.9	40.9	40.9	40.9	40.9	40.9	40.8	40.8	40.8	40.8	40.8	40.8	40.8
44	40.3	40.3	40.2	40.2	40.1	40.1	40.1	40.0	40.0	40.0	40.0	39.9	39.9	39.9	39.9	39.9	39.9	39.9	39.9	39.8	39.8
45	39.4	39.4	39.3	39.3	39.2	39.2	39.1	39.1	39.1	39.1	39.0	39.0	39.0	39.0	39.0	38.9	38.9	38.9	38.9	38.9	38.9
46	38.6	38.5	38.4	38.4	38.3	38.3	38.2	38.2	38.2	38.1	38.1	38.1	38.1	38.0	38.0	38.0	38.0	38.0	38.0	38.0	38.0
47	37.7	37.6	37.5	37.5	37.4	37.4	37.3	37.3	37.2	37.2	37.2	37.2	37.1	37.1	37.1	37.1	37.1	37.0	37.0	37.0	37.0
48	36.8	36.7	36.6	36.6	36.5	36.5	36.4	36.4	36.3	36.3	36.3	36.2	36.2	36.2	36.2	36.2	36.1	36.1	36.1	36.1	36.1
49	35.9	35.9	35.8	35.7	35.6	35.6	35.5	35.5	35.4	35.4	35.4	35.3	35.3	35.3	35.3	35.2	35.2	35.2	35.2	35.2	35.2
50	35.1	35.0	34.9	34.8	34.8	34.7	34.6	34.6	34.5	34.5	34.5	34.4	34.4	34.4	34.3	34.3	34.3	34.3	34.3	34.3	34.2
51	34.3	34.2	34.1	34.0	33.9	33.8	33.8	33.7	33.6	33.6	33.6	33.5	33.5	33.5	33.4	33.4	33.4	33.4	33.4	33.3	33.3
52	33.4	33.3	33.2	33.1	33.0	33.0	32.9	32.8	32.8	32.7	32.7	32.6	32.6	32.6	32.5	32.5	32.5	32.5	32.5	32.4	32.4
53	32.6	32.5	32.4	32.3	32.2	32.1	32.0	32.0	31.9	31.8	31.8	31.8	31.7	31.7	31.7	31.6	31.6	31.6	31.6	31.5	31.5
54	31.8	31.7	31.6	31.5	31.4	31.3	31.2	31.1	31.0	31.0	30.9	30.9	30.8	30.8	30.8	30.7	30.7	30.7	30.7	30.7	30.6
55	31.1	30.9	30.8	30.6	30.5	30.4	30.3	30.3	30.2	30.1	30.1	30.0	30.0	29.9	29.9	29.9	29.8	29.8	29.8	29.8	29.8
56	30.3	30.1	30.0	29.8	29.7	29.6	29.5	29.4	29.3	29.3	29.2	29.2	29.1	29.1	29.0	29.0	29.0	28.9	28.9	28.9	28.9
57	29.5	29.4	29.2	29.1	28.9	28.8	28.7	28.6	28.5	28.4	28.4	28.3	28.3	28.2	28.2	28.1	28.1	28.1	28.0	28.0	28.0
58	28.8	28.6	28.4	28.3	28.1	28.0	27.9	27.8	27.7	27.6	27.5	27.5	27.4	27.4	27.3	27.3	27.2	27.2	27.2	27.2	27.1
59	28.1	27.9	27.7	27.5	27.4	27.2	27.1	27.0	26.9	26.8	26.7	26.6	26.6	26.5	26.5	26.4	26.4	26.4	26.3	26.3	26.3
60		27.2	27.0	26.8	26.6	26.5	26.3	26.2	26.1	26.0	25.9	25.8	25.8	25.7	25.6	25.6	25.5	25.5	25.5	25.4	25.4
61			26.3	26.1	25.9	25.7	25.6	25.4	25.3	25.2	25.1	25.0	24.9	24.9	24.8	24.8	24.7	24.7	24.6	24.6	24.6
62				25.4	25.2	25.0	24.8	24.7	24.6	24.4	24.3	24.2	24.1	24.1	24.0	23.9	23.9	23.8	23.8	23.8	23.7
63					24.5	24.3	24.1	23.9	23.8	23.7	23.6	23.4	23.4	23.3	23.2	23.1	23.1	23.0	23.0	22.9	22.9
64						23.6	23.4	23.2	23.1	22.9	22.8	22.7	22.6	22.5	22.4	22.3	22.3	22.2	22.2	22.1	22.1
65							22.7	22.5	22.4	22.2	22.1	21.9	21.8	21.7	21.6	21.6	21.5	21.4	21.4	21.3	21.3
66								21.8	21.7	21.5	21.3	21.2	21.1	21.0	20.9	20.8	20.7	20.7	20.6	20.5	20.5
67									21.0	20.8	20.6	20.5	20.4	20.2	20.1	20.1	20.0	19.9	19.8	19.8	19.7
68										20.1	20.0	19.8	19.7	19.5	19.4	19.3	19.2	19.2	19.1	19.0	19.0
69											19.3	19.1	19.0	18.8	18.7	18.6	18.5	18.4	18.3	18.3	18.2
70												18.5	18.3	18.2	18.0	17.9	17.8	17.7	17.6	17.6	17.5
71													17.7	17.5	17.4	17.3	17.1	17.0	16.9	16.9	16.8
72														16.9	16.7	16.6	16.5	16.4	16.3	16.2	16.1
73															16.1	16.0	15.8	15.7	15.6	15.5	15.4
74																15.4	15.2	15.1	15.0	14.9	14.8
75																	14.6	14.5	14.4	14.3	14.2
76																		13.9	13.8	13.7	13.6
77																			13.2	13.1	13.0
78																				12.6	12.4
79																					11.9

** This is a sample of the Joint Life and Last Survivor Expectancy Table shown in IRS Publication 590. Use this table to figure your required minimum distribution only if your spouse is your sole beneficiary and he or she is more than 10 years younger than you are; see "Exception for younger spouses" on page 202. Find your age (as of your birthday for the year you are making the computation) on the horizontal line and your spousal beneficiary's age in the vertical column. For example, if you are age 74 and your spousal beneficiary is 63, the life expectancy factor is 24.5 years. If your age or your spouse's age is not shown here, refer to IRS Publication 590.*

8.14 Inherited Traditional IRAs

Although inheritances are generally tax free *(11.4)*, distributions that you receive as a beneficiary of a traditional IRA are taxable. However, if the account owner made nondeductible contributions to the account, distributions allocable to those contributions on Form 8606 are tax free under the rules at *8.6*. Taxable distributions received as a beneficiary are not subject to the 10% penalty for distributions received before age 59½ *(8.12)*.

Beneficiaries must receive required minimum distributions from the inherited account for years after the year of the owner's death. If you are the "designated beneficiary" as determined under the final IRS regulations discussed below, distributions may be spread over your life expectancy. If the required minimum distribution for a year is not received, you are subject to a penalty tax of 50% on the difference between the required minimum amount and the amount actually received. You may, of course, accelerate payments and receive more than the required minimum distribution.

A surviving spouse who is the sole beneficiary of a deceased spouse's IRA may elect to treat the account as his or her own IRA or roll it over to his or her own IRA. By becoming the owner, the surviving spouse determines his or her required minimum distributions under the regular owner rules at *8.13*, rather than under the beneficiary rules discussed in this section.

A nonspouse beneficiary may not elect to be treated as the owner or make a rollover. However, the IRS allows a nonspouse beneficiary to make a trustee-to-trustee transfer of the IRA to another financial institution as long as the IRA into which the funds are moved is set up and maintained in the name of the deceased IRA owner for the benefit of the nonspouse beneficiary. Whether or not the account is transferred, a nonspouse beneficiary must receive required minimum distributions under the beneficiary rules below. The financial institution holding the account will change the Social Security number on the account from the deceased owner's number to the number of the beneficiary for purposes of tracking required minimum distributions. However, a nonspouse beneficiary must make sure that the deceased owner's name remains on the account. Putting the account in the nonspouse beneficiary's name would be treated by the IRS as a prohibited rollover, resulting in a taxable distribution, as if the beneficiary had received a total distribution of his or her share of the IRA. For example, if John Smith inherits his sister Jane's IRA, the account should indicate that the IRA is held for the benefit of (FBO) John as beneficiary, with wording such as this: "Jane Smith IRA, deceased November 16, 2006, FBO John Smith, beneficiary."

A beneficiary of a Roth IRA must also receive required minimum distributions but under different rules. Furthermore, the distributions are generally taxable only if the Roth IRA owner dies within the first five years after establishing the Roth IRA and account earnings are received by the beneficiary within the five-year period; *see 8.24*.

Caution

Estate as Beneficiary

If you name your estate as beneficiary of your IRA and you die before your required beginning date, the entire account must be withdrawn by the fifth year following the year of your death. If you die on or after the required beginning date, the account can be distributed over the balance of your single life expectancy, determined by your age in the year of death. *See* the single life expectancy table on page 208.

Distribution period depends on identity of designated beneficiary as of September 30 of year following year of IRA owner's death. Any individual named by the IRA owner as a beneficiary can be a designated beneficiary, but for purposes of determining the maximum period over which required minimum distributions are payable, there can be only one "designated" beneficiary for each traditional IRA. Under the final IRS regulations, the determination of the designated beneficiary is not made until September 30 of the year following the year of the IRA owner's death.

A designated beneficiary must be an individual named by the account owner or designated under the plan as of the date of death. A beneficiary named through an estate, either under the owner's will or by state law, cannot be a designated beneficiary for required minimum distribution purposes. An estate or a charity cannot be a designated beneficiary. Trust beneficiaries may qualify if certain tests are met, as discussed below.

The delay in determining the designated beneficiary does *not* mean that new beneficiaries can be added after the owner's death. However, after the account owner's death and prior to the September 30 determination date, a beneficiary named as of the date of death can be eliminated by means of the beneficiary's qualified disclaimer or distribution of the beneficiary's benefit. A beneficiary's interest can be cashed out by the September 30 determination date, leaving the balance to other co-beneficiaries named by the owner. For example, if a charity and an individual are named as co-beneficiaries, and the charity's interest is cashed out by the September 30 determination date, the remaining beneficiary can use his or her life expectancy to figure required minimum distributions.

Qualified disclaimer. A qualified written disclaimer made no later than nine months after the IRA owner's death can be used by an older primary beneficiary to pass all or part of an IRA to a younger contingent beneficiary. The disclaimer, made by the September 30 determination date, leaves the younger beneficiary as the designated beneficiary, thereby allowing required minimum distributions to be spread out over his or her longer life expectancy. Of course, a younger primary beneficiary may also disclaim in favor of an older contingent beneficiary. An estate may *not* disclaim its interest in order to create a designated beneficiary.

One of the requirements for a qualified disclaimer is that the person making the disclaimer must not have accepted the property prior to the disclaimer. The IRS in Revenue Ruling 2005-36 held that this rule does not prevent a beneficiary from making a disclaimer after taking the required minimum distribution for the year of the death (where the owner dies before receiving it). The act of taking the required minimum distribution is treated as an acceptance of that portion of the property, plus the income attributable to the distribution. However, after receiving the required minimum distribution, the beneficiary may make a qualified disclaimer (by the nine-month deadline) of all or part of the balance of the account, except for the income allocable to the required distribution. The disclaimed amount and the income allocable to the disclaimed amount must either be paid outright to the successor beneficiary entitled to receive it following the disclaimer or be segregated in a separate IRA for the benefit of that beneficiary. *See* Revenue Ruling 2005-36 for further details.

Splitting account among multiple individual beneficiaries. If a traditional IRA has several beneficiaries, all of whom are individuals, the general rule under the regulations is that the oldest beneficiary with the shortest life expectancy is considered to be the designated beneficiary, and that life expectancy is the period over which all the beneficiaries must receive required minimum distributions. This result can be avoided by splitting the IRA into separate IRAs, one for each beneficiary. Each beneficiary can then spread distributions over his or her individual life expectancy.

If the IRA account owner did not split the account into separate IRAs, the regulations allow the beneficiaries to do so by December 31 of the year after the year of the owner's death. This is three months later than the date for determining the designated beneficiary, or September 30 of the year following the year of the IRA owner's death. Given the inconsistency, it is advisable to split the IRA into separate accounts by the September 30 designated determination date.

If the account is split in the year following the year of the owner's death, whether by the September 30 date or December 31 date, each beneficiary may compute the required distribution for that year using his or her own life expectancy as determined by their ages in that year. That life expectancy is reduced by one year for each subsequent-year required distribution.

Individual and non-individual beneficiary for same account. If as of the September 30 determination date there is a *non-individual* beneficiary other than a qualifying trust, as well as one or more individual beneficiaries, the owner is treated as *not* having a designated beneficiary. If the owner's death was after his or her required beginning date (April 1 of the year after the year age 70½ is reached), the regulations require minimum distributions to be made over the owner's remaining life expectancy. Use the owner's life expectancy as of his or her birthday in the year of death and reduce it by one year for each subsequent year.

If the owner died before the required beginning date without a designated beneficiary, the entire account must be distributed by the end of the fifth year following the year of death. If the interest of the non-individual beneficiary is distributed from the plan and separate accounts are established for the individual beneficiaries by the September 30 deadline, the individual beneficiaries can base required minimum distributions on their own life expectancies starting in the next year.

Trust as beneficiary. If a trust is named the beneficiary of the account, the trust beneficiaries may be treated as designated beneficiaries if certain tests are met. The trust must be irrevocable or become irrevocable upon the account owner's death. Documentation of the trust beneficiaries must be provided to the IRA trustee or plan administrator. The deadline under the regulations for providing the documentation is October 31 of the year following the year of the owner's death. However, the regulations do not allow separate accounts to be created for the trust beneficiaries. All of the trust beneficiaries must receive required minimum distributions over the life expectancy of the oldest beneficiary.

Beneficiary's death before September 30 determination date. If an individual named as a beneficiary by the account owner dies after the owner but before the September 30 date for determining the designated beneficiary, that individual continues to be treated as a designated beneficiary under the final regulations. This rule allows his or her life expectancy to be used by a successor beneficiary named by the original beneficiary or who inherits the account through the estate of the original beneficiary.

Owner's death on or after required beginning date. If an owner dies on or after the required beginning date (April 1 of the year after the year the owner reaches age 70½), and there is a designated beneficiary, required minimum distributions are generally payable over the beneficiary's life expectancy. However, if on the date of the owner's death the designated beneficiary is older than the owner, the final regulations allow the beneficiary to receive required minimum distributions over the owner's remaining life expectancy rather than over the beneficiary's shorter life expectancy.

If the owner did not receive his or her required minimum distribution for the year of death, the beneficiary must receive that amount in the year of death or as soon as possible in the next year.

The first required beneficiary distribution must be received in the year following the year of the owner's death. The required distribution is the year-end account balance for the year of death divided by the designated beneficiary's life expectancy in the year following the year of death, taken from the Beneficiary's Single Life Expectancy Table, shown on page 208. For example, assume an IRA owner dies in 2006, after receiving the required minimum distribution for 2006. The designated beneficiary is his son, who is age 47 in 2007. The life expectancy table provides a life expectancy of 37 years for a 47-year-old. If the account balance at the end of 2006 was $100,000, the son must receive a required minimum distribution in 2007 of $2,703 ($100,000 ÷ 37). That is the minimum distribution required by the IRS rules; he can choose to withdraw more than that. The initial 37-year life expectancy is reduced by one year for each succeeding year when making the computation for the later years. The required minimum distribution for each subsequent year is figured by dividing the applicable life expectancy into the account balance at the end of the prior year.

Owner's death before required beginning date. If an owner dies before the required beginning date and there is an individual designated beneficiary, the period for receiving required minimum distributions is generally the life expectancy of the designated beneficiary. The life expectancy method is the "default" rule under the final regulations, but the plan may require application of the five-year rule, although this is unlikely, or the plan may allow the account owner or beneficiary to elect the five-year rule. Under the five-year rule, the entire account must be distributed by the end of the fifth year after the year of the owner's death; no distribution is required for any year prior to that fifth year. The five-year rule always applies if the owner dies before the required beginning date and there is no designated beneficiary.

Surviving spouse's rollover or election to treat IRA as his or her own. A surviving spouse who is the sole beneficiary of an IRA with unlimited withdrawal rights may elect to treat the IRA as his or her own by retitling the IRA in his or her name. If the surviving spouse contributes to the IRA or does not receive a timely required minimum distribution under the beneficiary rules, the surviving spouse is deemed to have made the election. The final regulations confirm that to make the election, the surviving spouse must take the required minimum distribution for the year of the owner's death to the extent that it was not received by the owner.

A surviving-spouse beneficiary may also make a spousal rollover by authorizing a direct transfer (trustee-to-trustee) of the IRA, or rolling over a distribution within 60 days of receiving it, to his or her own IRA. However, if the deceased IRA owner did not receive the required minimum distribution for the year of death, the surviving spouse must receive and pay tax on that required distribution; that amount cannot be rolled over (or directly transferred).

If the surviving spouse elects to treat the inherited IRA as his or her own or makes a spousal roll over, the surviving spouse is then subject to the same rules as any IRA owner. The surviving spouse should immediately name a new beneficiary for the IRA. The regular distribution rules apply, including the 10% penalty for taxable distributions received before age 59½ *(8.8)*. If the surviving spouse is under age 70½, required minimum distributions may be delayed until April 1 of the year following the year in which he or she reaches age 70½, at which time distributions will be based on the Uniform Lifetime Table for owners *(8.13)*.

Planning Reminder

Surviving Spouse Under Age 70½

If you inherit your spouse's traditional IRA and you are under age 70½, you may delay the start of required minimum distributions by treating the IRA as your own.

Surviving spouse as sole beneficiary. If the election to treat an inherited IRA or spousal rollover is not made, a surviving spouse must receive required minimum distributions as a beneficiary. A surviving spouse who is under age 59½ and needs the funds from the IRA may prefer this option because withdrawals, although taxable (unless allocable to nondeductible contributions made by the deceased spouse), are not subject to the 10% penalty for pre-59½ distributions *(8.12)*.

If the surviving spouse is the sole designated beneficiary, required minimum distributions are based on his or her life expectancy from the Beneficiary's Single Life Expectancy Table. Each year, life expectancy is recalculated using the spouse's attained age during the year. A spousal beneficiary is the only beneficiary who may recalculate life expectancy. Others must reduce their life expectancy from the Single Life Table for the year after the year of the owner's death by one year in each succeeding year.

If a surviving spouse is the sole designated beneficiary and the deceased spouse died before the year in which he or she would have reached age 70½, the surviving spouse does not have to begin receiving required minimum distributions until the year that the deceased spouse would have reached age 70½.

Even if the surviving spouse begins receiving required minimum distributions, a spousal rollover may be made at a later date.

Table 8-5 Beneficiary's Single Life Expectancy Table

Age	Life expectancy	Age	Life expectancy
0	82.4	56	28.7
1	81.6	57	27.9
2	80.6	58	27.0
3	79.7	59	26.1
4	78.7	60	25.2
5	77.7	61	24.4
6	76.7	62	23.5
7	75.8	63	22.7
8	74.8	64	21.8
9	73.8	65	21.0
10	72.8	66	20.2
11	71.8	67	19.4
12	70.8	68	18.6
13	69.9	69	17.8
14	68.9	70	17.0
15	67.9	71	16.3
16	66.9	72	15.5
17	66.0	73	14.8
18	65.0	74	14.1
19	64.0	75	13.4
20	63.0	76	12.7
21	62.1	77	12.1
22	61.1	78	11.4
23	60.1	79	10.8
24	59.1	80	10.2
25	58.2	81	9.7
26	57.2	82	9.1
27	56.2	83	8.6
28	55.3	84	8.1
29	54.3	85	7.6
30	53.3	86	7.1
31	52.4	87	6.7
32	51.4	88	6.3
33	50.4	89	5.9
34	49.4	90	5.5
35	48.5	91	5.2
36	47.5	92	4.9
37	46.5	93	4.6
38	45.6	94	4.3
39	44.6	95	4.1
40	43.6	96	3.8
41	42.7	97	3.6
42	41.7	98	3.4
43	40.7	99	3.1
44	39.8	100	2.9
45	38.8	101	2.7
46	37.9	102	2.5
47	37.0	103	2.3
48	36.0	104	2.1
49	35.1	105	1.9
50	34.2	106	1.7
51	33.3	107	1.5
52	32.3	108	1.4
53	31.4	109	1.2
54	30.5	110	1.1
55	29.6	111+	1.0

Simplified Employee Pension Plans (SEPs)

8.15 SEP Basics

A simplified employee pension plan (SEP) set up by an employer allows the employer to contribute to an employee's IRA account more money than is allowed under regular IRA rules. For 2006, your employer generally could contribute and deduct up to 25% of your compensation or $44,000, whichever is less. Your employer's SEP contributions are excluded from your pay and are not included on Form W-2 unless they exceed the limit. If contributions exceed the limit, the excess is included in your gross income and a 6% penalty tax may be imposed unless the excess (plus allocable income) is withdrawn by the due date of the return, plus extensions; *see 8.7*. If you are under age 59½, the 10% early distribution penalty may apply to the withdrawal of income earned on the excess contributions; *see 8.12*.

Caution

Employees over Age 70½

An employee over age 70½ may still participate in an employer SEP plan. Minimum distributions from the plan must begin as discussed in *7.13*.

Self-employed plans. Self-employed individuals may set up a SEP as an alternative to a Keogh plan; *see* Chapter 41.

Eligibility. A SEP must cover all employees who are at least age 21, earn over $450 (this amount may be adjusted after 2006 for inflation), and who have worked for the employer at any time during at least three of the past five years. Union employees covered by union agreements may generally be excluded.

SEP salary-reduction arrangements. If a qualifying small employer set up a salary-reduction SEP before 1997, employees may contribute a portion of their pay to the plan instead of receiving it in cash; *see 8.16*.

SEP distributions. Distributions from a SEP, including salary-reduction SEPs established before 1997, are subject to the regular distribution rules for traditional IRAs discussed at *8.8*. Tax-favored withdrawal and repayment rules for qualified hurricane distributions are discussed at *8.25–8.26*.

8.16 Salary-Reduction SEP Set Up Before 1997

Qualifying small employers may offer employees the option of deferring a portion of their salary to an IRA. There are two types of salary-reduction IRAs, with different eligibility and contribution rules: (1) salary-reduction SEPs established before 1997 and (2) "SIMPLE" IRA accounts established after 1996.

After 1996, an employer may establish a SIMPLE plan but not a salary-reduction SEP. Rules for SIMPLE IRAs established after 1996 are at *8.17–8.18*. A salary-reduction SEP that was established before 1997 may continue to receive contributions under the prior law rules discussed below, and employees hired after 1996 may participate in the plan, subject to those rules.

Salary-reduction SEPs established before 1997. Salary reductions are allowed for a year only if the employer had no more than 25 employees eligible to participate in the SEP at any time during the prior taxable year. Furthermore, at least 50% of the eligible employees must elect the salary-reduction option, and the deferral percentage for highly compensated employees may not exceed 125% of the average contribution of regular employees.

If salary reductions are allowed, the maximum salary-reduction contribution for 2006 was $15,000 ($20,000 for participants age 50 or older if the plan permitted the extra deferral). These are the same limits as for 401(k) plans *(7.18)*. Deferrals over $15,000 ($20,000 if extra deferral for participants age 50 or older was allowed) are taxable, and if not timely distributed to the employee, can be taxed again when distributed from the plan. For years after 2006, there may be a cost-of-living adjustment to the limits.

If an employee contributes to both a SEP and a 401(k) plan, the annual limit applies to the total salary reductions from both plans. If an employee makes salary-reduction contributions to a SEP and also to a tax-sheltered annuity plan *(7.21)*, the annual limit generally applies to the total salary reductions to both plans. In some cases, employees with at least 15 years of service may be able to defer an additional $3,000 to the tax-sheltered annuity plan as discussed at *7.21*.

SIMPLE IRAs

8.17 Who Is Eligible for a SIMPLE IRA?

A SIMPLE IRA is a salary-reduction retirement plan that qualifying small employers may offer their employees. For 2006, the maximum salary-reduction contribution was $10,000, or $12,500 for participants age 50 or older if the plan allowed the additional contributions. The limits may be increased for years after 2006 by a cost-of-living adjustment. Employers are required to make matching contributions or a flat contribution, as discussed in *8.18*.

Qualifying employers. A SIMPLE IRA may be maintained only by an employer that (1) in the previous calendar year had no more than 100 employees who earned compensation of $5,000 or more and (2) does not maintain any other retirement plan (unless the other plan is for collective bargaining employees). A self-employed individual who meets these tests may set up a SIMPLE IRA, as discussed in Chapter 41.

Planning Reminder

401(k) SIMPLE Plans

An employer with a 401(k) plan that reports on the calendar year may avoid the regular 401(k) nondiscrimination tests by following the contribution rules for SIMPLE IRAs; *see 7.17*.

In determining whether the 100-employee test is met for the prior year, all employees under the common control of the employer must be counted. For example, Joe Smith owned two businesses in 2006—a computer rental company with 80 employees and a computer repair company with 60 employees. If they all earned at least $5,000, they all count towards the 100 limit, so if Joe decides in 2007 to set up a retirement plan for his businesses, a different type of plan must be used. He may not establish a SIMPLE IRA for either business under the 100-employee limit.

If a SIMPLE IRA is established but the employer in a later year grows beyond the 100-employee limit, the employer generally has a two-year "grace period" during which contributions may continue to be made.

Eligible employees. In general, an employee must be allowed to contribute to a SIMPLE IRA for a year in which he or she is reasonably expected to earn $5,000 or more, provided at least $5,000 of compensation was received in any two prior years, whether or not consecutive. If the employer owns more than one business (under common control rules) and sets up a SIMPLE IRA for one of them, employees of the other business must also be allowed to participate if they meet the $5,000 compensation tests. Employees who are covered by a collective bargaining agreement may be excluded if retirement benefits were the subject of good-faith negotiations.

The employer may lower or eliminate the $5,000 compensation requirement in order to broaden participation in the plan. No other conditions on eligibility, such as age or hours of work, are permitted.

Deadline for setting up a SIMPLE IRA. An employer generally may establish a SIMPLE IRA effective on any date between January 1 and October 1 of a year. If the employer (or a predecessor employer) previously maintained a SIMPLE IRA, a new SIMPLE IRA may be effective only on January 1 of a year. A new employer that comes into existence after October 1 of a year may establish a SIMPLE IRA for that year if the plan is established as soon as administratively feasible after the start of the business.

The employer may use a model SIMPLE IRA approved by the IRS to set up a SIMPLE IRA. Form 5304-SIMPLE allows employees to select a financial institution to which the contributions will be made. With Form 5305-SIMPLE, the employer selects the financial institution to which contributions are initially deposited, but employees have the right to subsequently transfer their account balances without cost or penalty to another SIMPLE-IRA at a financial institution of their own choosing. Use of the IRS model forms is optional; other documents satisfying the statutory requirements for a SIMPLE IRA may be used.

SIMPLE IRA contributions and distributions. Contribution and distribution rules for SIMPLE IRAs are discussed in *8.18*.

8.18 SIMPLE IRA Contributions and Distributions

The only contributions that may be made to a SIMPLE IRA are elective salary-reduction contributions by employees and matching or non-elective contributions by employers. All contributions are fully vested and nonforfeitable when made.

Regardless of compensation, eligible employees *(see 8.17)* may elect each year to make salary-reduction contributions to the plan up to the annual SIMPLE IRA limit; *see 8.17*. Salary-reduction contributions are excluded from the employee's taxable pay on Form W-2 and not subject to federal tax withholding. They are subject to FICA withholding for Social Security and Medicare tax.

Eligible employees must be given notice by the employer of their right to elect salary-reduction contributions and at least 60 days to make the election. After the first year of eligibility, the election to defer for the upcoming year is made during the last 60 days (at minimum) of the prior calendar year. If the employer uses model IRS Form 5304-SIMPLE or 5305-SIMPLE, a notification document is included.

If an employee contributes to a SIMPLE IRA and also to a 401(k) plan, 403(b) or salary-reduction SEP of another employer for the same year, the salary-reduction contributions to the SIMPLE IRA count toward the overall annual limit on tax-free salary-reduction deferrals *(see 7.17)*. Deferrals over the annual limit are taxable and must be removed to avoid being taxed again when distributed from the plan; *see 7.18*.

Planning Reminder

Employer's Intended Contributions

The IRS model notification included with Form 5304-SIMPLE or 5305-SIMPLE requires the employer to tell employees how much the employer will be contributing for the upcoming year.

Employer contributions. Each year, the employer must make either a matching contribution or a fixed "non-elective" contribution. If the employer chooses matching contributions, the employee's elective salary-reduction contribution generally must be matched, up to a limit of 3% of the employee's compensation. For up to two years in any five-year period, the 3% matching limit may be reduced to as low as 1% for each eligible employee.

Instead of making either the 3% or reduced (between 1% and 3%) limit matching contribution, the employer may make a "non-elective" contribution equal to 2% of each eligible employee's compensation. If this option is chosen, the 2% contribution must be made for eligible employees whether or not they elect to make salary-reduction contributions for the year. The 2% contribution is subject to an annual compensation limit, which for 2006 was $220,000. Thus, for 2006, the maximum 2% non-elective contribution was $4,400 (2% of $220,000) even if an employee earned more than $220,000. The 3% matching contribution is not subject to the annual compensation limit, but only to the annual salary-reduction limit *(8.17)*. The employer must notify eligible employees of the type of contribution it will be making for the upcoming year prior to the employees' 60-day election period for making elective salary-reduction contributions. The employer must make the matching or non-elective contributions by the due date for filing the employer's tax return (plus extensions) for the year.

Caution

Increased Pre–Age 59½ Penalty

In the first two years of SIMPLE IRA participation, the penalty for distributions before age 59½ is increased from 10% to 25%. Proposals to eliminate the higher 25% penalty have not been approved by Congress.

EXAMPLE

Martin's 2007 salary is $90,000. He elects to make a $10,000 salary-reduction contribution to his employer's SIMPLE IRA plan. If his employer elects the 3% matching rule, the matching contribution is limited to $2,700, 3% of Martin's compensation.

Distributions from a SIMPLE IRA. A distribution from a SIMPLE IRA is fully taxable unless a tax-free rollover or trustee-to-trustee transfer is made. The penalty for distributions before age 59½ *(see 8.12)* is increased to 25% from 10%, assuming no penalty exception applies, if the distribution is received during the two-year period starting with the employee's initial participation in the plan. *See* the *e-Supplement* for an update on a proposal to eliminate the higher 25% penalty amount. After the first two years, the regular 10% penalty applies.

In the initial two-year period, a tax-free rollover or direct trustee-to-trustee transfer *(see 8.10)* of a SIMPLE IRA may be made to another SIMPLE IRA. After two years of participation, a tax-free rollover or direct transfer may be made to a traditional IRA, qualified plan, 403(b) plan, or state or local government 457 plan, as well as to a SIMPLE IRA. The mandatory distribution rules that apply to regular IRAs after age 70½ also apply to SIMPLE IRAs *(see 8.13)*.

Roth IRAs

8.19 Roth IRA Advantages

As with traditional IRAs, earnings accumulate within a Roth IRA tax free until distributions are made. The key benefit of the Roth IRA is that tax-free withdrawals of contributions may be made at any time and earnings may be withdrawn tax free after a five-year holding period by an individual who is age 59½ or older, is disabled, or who pays qualifying first-time home-buyer expenses.

If you have taxable compensation *(8.20)*, contributions after age 70½ may be made to a Roth IRA, but not to a traditional IRA, and the minimum required distribution rules that apply to traditional IRAs after age 70½ *(8.13)* do not apply to Roth IRAs. Thus, a Roth IRA can remain intact after age

Caution

Roth IRA Contribution Deadline

The deadline for making Roth IRA contributions for 2006 is April 16, 2007, the regular due date for your 2006 return. This is the contribution deadline even if you obtain a filing extension for your 2006 return.

Law Alert

Direct Rollover From Employer Plan to Roth IRA After 2007

The Pension Protection Act of 2006 allows distributions made after 2007 from qualified employer plans, 403(b) plans, and governmental 457 plans to be rolled over directly to a Roth IRA, without first being rolled over to a traditional IRA. A direct rollover will be subject to the rules in *8.21* for converting a traditional IRA to a Roth IRA. Thus, a direct rollover will not be allowed if the $100,000 MAGI limit for years before 2010 is exceeded and, if allowed, a direct rollover will be treated as a taxable transaction except to the extent that the transfer is allocable to after-tax contributions.

70½ and continue to grow tax free. The balance of the account not withdrawn during the owner's lifetime generally may be paid out to the beneficiaries tax free over their life expectancies, thereby providing a substantial tax-deferred buildup within the plan over an extended period *(8.24)*.

The opportunity to obtain such benefits makes the Roth IRA an attractive retirement planning and estate planning option. However, certain high-income taxpayers are not eligible to make Roth IRA contributions.

There are currently two ways in which you may establish a Roth IRA: (1) by making annual nondeductible contributions or (2) by converting a traditional IRA, SEP, or SIMPLE IRA to a Roth IRA. Each alternative is subject to an income limitation. Individuals with modified adjusted gross income up to $100,000 may convert a traditional IRA to a Roth IRA by paying a current tax, as discussed in *8.21*. Nondeductible annual contributions may be made to a Roth IRA subject to an income limitation as discussed at *8.20*. Individuals who qualify for deductible IRA contributions *(8.4)* as well as the Roth IRA should consider whether the tax value of deductible contributions outweighs the advantage of future tax-free distributions from the Roth IRA; distributions from traditional deductible IRAs are taxable. Roth IRA distribution rules are at *8.23*. After 2007, a Roth IRA can be set up by rolling over a distribution to an employer plan; *see* the Law Alert in this section.

Your employer can set up a "deemed Roth IRA" as a separate account under a qualified retirement plan. As long as the separate account otherwise meets the Roth IRA rules, you can make voluntary employee contributions that will be subject only to the Roth IRA rules. A deemed IRA can also be set up as a traditional IRA *(8.1)*.

8.20 Annual Contributions to a Roth IRA

Annual contributions to a Roth IRA may be made if you have taxable compensation for personal services and your modified adjusted gross income (MAGI) does not exceed the upper end of the phase-out range. If your MAGI for 2006 is less than $95,000 if you are unmarried, or less than $150,000 if married filing jointly, you are under the phase-out threshold and may contribute up to the 2006 contribution ceiling. The contribution limit for 2006 is $4,000 if you are under age 50, or $5,000 if you are age 50 or older by the end of the year; *see* the Law Alert in this section for years after 2006. Contributions up to the annual limit are allowed if you have taxable compensation of at least that much, subject to the phase-out rules. The contribution limit for 2006 is phased out for unmarried taxpayers with MAGI between $95,000 and $110,000, and for joint filers with MAGI between $150,000 and $160,000. For a married person filing separately who lived with his or her spouse at any time during the year, the contribution limit is phased out for MAGI between $0 and $10,000. A married person filing separately who lived apart from his or her spouse for the entire year is treated as unmarried.

Law Alert

Roth IRA Contribution Limits After 2006

The maximum contribution limit for Roth IRAs will remain at $4,000 in 2007 and increase to $5,000 for 2008. After 2008, the $5,000 limit will be subject to inflation indexing. The additional contribution limit for individuals age 50 or older is scheduled to remain at $1,000 for years after 2006.

Because of the phaseout rules, high income individuals may be ineligible to contribute. The $95,000 and $150,000 phaseout thresholds *(see 8.20)* that apply in 2006 will be subject to an inflation adjustment for 2007 and later years.

The Roth IRA rules do not replace the traditional IRA nondeductible contribution rules *(8.6)*. For an individual who is unable to contribute to a Roth IRA because the contribution limit is phased out, and is unable to make deductible IRA contributions because of the phase-out rules for active plan participants *(8.4)*, nondeductible contributions may still be made to a traditional IRA under the rules at *8.6*.

Spousal contribution on joint return for nonworking or low-earning spouse. If you are married filing jointly, you generally may contribute up to the annual limit (*see* above) for each spouse to a Roth IRA so long as the total compensation of both spouses is at least double the limit. This is the same spousal contribution rule as for traditional IRAs *(8.3)*; the lower-earning spouse is allowed to "borrow" compensation of the higher-earning spouse for contribution purposes. However, the Roth IRA contribution limit may be reduced because of the MAGI phase-out rules, as discussed in the next paragraph.

MAGI phase-out of 2006 Roth IRA contribution limit. The $4,000 or $5,000 Roth IRA contribution limit for 2006 (*see* above) is phased out if your 2006 modified adjusted gross income (MAGI) is between:

- $150,000 and $160,000, if you are married filing jointly, or a qualifying widow(er);
- $95,000 and $110,000, if you are single, head of household, or married filing separately and you lived apart for the entire year;
- $0 and $10,000, if you are married filing separately and you lived with your spouse at any time during the year.

For 2007 (and later years), the $95,000/$150,000 phaseout thresholds will be subject to inflation indexing.

For purposes of the phase-out rule, MAGI is figured in the same way as under the traditional IRA deduction phase-out rules *(8.4)*, except that a taxable conversion *(8.21)* from a traditional IRA to a Roth IRA is disregarded and any deductible traditional IRA contribution is also disregarded. The MAGI phase-out rule applies to Roth IRA contributions regardless of whether you are covered by an employer retirement plan, unlike the deductible traditional IRA phase-out rules *(8.4)*, which apply only to active plan participants.

The MAGI formula reduces the contribution limit by an amount that bears the same ratio to the limit as your "excess MAGI" (MAGI over phase-out threshold) bears to the phaseout range (which is either $10,000 or $15,000, depending on your filing status as shown above). See the Example below for the way the phase-out limit is computed. If the phase-out formula results in a reduced contribution limit that is not a multiple of $10, round it up to the next highest $10. If the reduced limit is between $0 and $200, you are allowed a $200 contribution limit.

EXAMPLE

In 2006, Mark is under age 50 and single. His 2006 salary is $90,000 and modified adjusted gross income (MAGI) is $98,000, $3,000 more than the $95,000 phase-out threshold for a single person's Roth IRA contributions. Under the MAGI phase-out rule, Mark's Roth IRA contribution limit for 2006 is reduced by $800, from $4,000 to $3,200. The $800 reduction equals the $4,000 limit multiplied by the phase-out percentage of 20% ($3,000 MAGI over the phase-out threshold ($98,000 – $95,000) ÷ $15,000 phase-out range for single persons).

If Mark was age 50 or over in 2006, the $5,000 contribution limit would be reduced by $1,000 to $4,000 (20% phase-out percentage × $5,000 limit = $1,000 reduction).

Contributing to Roth IRA and traditional IRA for the same year. If you contribute to both a traditional IRA and Roth IRA for the same year, total contributions for the year to all the accounts are limited to the annual limit, or your compensation if that is less. The annual limit is applied first to the traditional IRA contributions and then to the Roth IRA contributions. Thus, the maximum contribution limit for 2006 to a Roth IRA is the lesser of (1) $4,000, or $5,000 if age 50 or older, or (2) taxable compensation, minus deductible *(8.4)* or nondeductible *(8.6)* contributions to traditional IRAs.

However, if you are subject to the MAGI phaseout for Roth IRA contributions, as discussed above, the maximum Roth IRA contribution limit is the lesser of these two amounts: (1) the annual contribution limit (*see* above) or, if less, compensation, minus contributions for the year to traditional IRAs, or (2) the contribution limit figured under the MAGI phase-out rule.

Excess contributions. If Roth IRA contributions exceed the allowable limit, the excess contribution is subject to a 6% penalty tax unless you withdraw the excess, plus any earnings on the excess contribution, by the filing due date including extensions. The earnings must be reported as income for the year the contribution was made.

Contribution deadline. Contributions to a Roth IRA for a year may be made by the filing due date, without extensions. For 2006 contributions, the deadline is April 16, 2007.

8.21 Converting a Traditional IRA to a Roth IRA

If your modified adjusted gross income (MAGI) is $100,000 or less (*see* below), and you are not married filing separately, you may make a taxable conversion of a traditional IRA to a Roth IRA. A conversion may be made by directing the trustee of your traditional IRA to make a trustee-to-trustee transfer of your IRA to a new Roth IRA trustee, or by keeping the account with the same trustee but instructing the trustee to change the registration of the account from a traditional IRA to a Roth IRA. You may also make a conversion by receiving a distribution from your traditional IRA and rolling it over to a Roth IRA; the rollover must be completed within 60 days from the time you receive the distribution.

Conversion from SEP or SIMPLE IRA. You may also convert a SEP *(8.15)* to a Roth IRA. A SIMPLE IRA *(8.18)* may be converted to a Roth IRA if more than two years have passed since you began participation in the SIMPLE IRA.

Law Alert

Roth IRA Contribution Based on Tax-Free Combat Pay

The 2006 "Heroes Earned Retirement Opportunities Act" allows members of the armed services serving in a combat zone *(35.4)* to contribute to either a Roth IRA or a traditional IRA *(8.2)* based on their tax-free combat pay. Without the new law, members of the military who did not have any earnings apart from the combat zone pay could not make IRA contributions, which must be based on taxable compensation.

The new law applies retroactively for individuals who received tax-free combat pay in 2004 and 2005. They have until May 28, 2009, to make contributions to a Roth IRA (or traditional IRA) for 2004 and 2005. For those under age 50, the contribution limit was $3,000 for 2004 and $4,000 for 2005. For those age 50 and older, the limit was $3,500 for 2004 and $4,500 for 2005.

An overpayment of tax may result for 2004 and/or 2005 if a Roth IRA (or traditional IRA) contribution for such year enables the service member to claim the retirement saver's credit *(25.16)*. A refund for the overpayment can be claimed within one year from the date the contribution is made even if the statute of limitations for claiming a refund *(47.2)* for that year has expired.

Planning Reminder

Contributions After Age 70½

That you are over 70½ years of age is no bar to setting up and contributing to a Roth IRA. For an annual contribution, you must have taxable compensation and not be subject to the MAGI phaseout. To convert a traditional IRA to a Roth IRA, your income must be below the $100,000 ceiling; *see 8.21*.

Caution

Consider the Tax Cost of a Conversion

If your modified adjusted gross income is $100,000 or less *(see 8.21)*, you may roll over or convert a traditional IRA to a Roth IRA. If you do so, the entire rollover or conversion is taxable, except for any portion that is allocable to nondeductible contributions; *see* Form 8606.

If you plan to convert a traditional IRA to a Roth IRA, figure the tax due on the conversion and then weigh (1) whether you have sufficient funds outside the plan to pay the tax and (2), where there is a substantial tax due on the conversion, whether you want to give up the future income that would be earned on the funds used to pay the tax.

To reduce the tax due on a substantial conversion, you could do smaller conversions spaced out over several years. Also *see* the Law Alert in this section for the special ratable inclusion rule that will apply to conversions made in 2010.

Law Alert

Conversions to Roth IRA Encouraged in 2010

The Tax Increase Prevention and Reconciliation Act of 2005 (which was actually enacted in 2006) provides a tax planning opportunity in the guise of a revenue raiser. The $100,000 MAGI ceiling for making a conversion will be eliminated for tax years after 2009. Furthermore, a favorable income inclusion applies to conversions made in 2010. Unless a converting taxpayer elects otherwise, none of the income for a conversion made in 2010 will be taxable for that year; half of the income will be taxable in 2011 and half in 2012. This reporting break applies only for 2010 conversions. By extending the right to convert a traditional IRA to a Roth IRA to previously barred high-income taxpayers, and making it easier to pay the tax due on the conversion, Congress expects to garner a short-term revenue windfall as newly eligible taxpayers rush to convert in 2010. However, there is a potential cloud that could dampen the expected tax break on a 2010 conversion. There is uncertainty concerning the tax rates that will apply in 2011 and 2012 when the ratable inclusions would be made. The tax rates that apply under current law (ranging from 10% to 35%; *see 1.2*) are scheduled to "sunset" after 2010, and then be replaced with the rate structure that applied before 2001 (with rates ranging from 15% to 39.6%). The results of the 2008 presidential election are likely to determine what happens to tax rates.

$100,000 MAGI limit. For years before 2010, the transfer to a Roth IRA is allowed only if your modified adjusted gross income (MAGI) for the year of the rollover or conversion is $100,000 or less. If you are married, a conversion to a Roth IRA is generally allowed only if you file a joint return. The $100,000 MAGI ceiling applies to the combined MAGI of both spouses on the joint return. If you file a separate return and lived with your spouse at any time during the year, a conversion to a Roth IRA is not allowed, regardless of your income. If you lived apart from your spouse for the entire year, you may make a conversion to a Roth IRA if the MAGI reported on your separate return does not exceed the $100,000 MAGI ceiling.

The amount of the rollover or conversion is not taken into account in determining if the $100,000 MAGI limit is exceeded. However, the transferred amount is included in income for regular tax purposes; *see* below.

A law taking effect in 2005 has made it easier for an individual age 70½ or older to meet the $100,000 MAGI limit for a conversion. For 2005 and later years, required minimum distributions *(8.13)* from traditional IRAs are disregarded for purposes of the $100,000 MAGI limit, although the distributions themselves are still taxable. Before 2005, required minimum distributions were counted towards the $100,000 MAGI conversion ceiling.

If a conversion to a Roth IRA is made towards the end of the year by taking a withdrawal from a traditional IRA and then rolling it over to the Roth IRA within 60 days, the income for the year of the withdrawal, rather than the income for the year the rollover is completed, is used when determining if the $100,000 MAGI conversion ceiling is exceeded. The conversion contribution is considered made for the year in which the withdrawal from the traditional IRA is made.

For a taxpayer who is eligible to make deductible contributions to a traditional IRA, MAGI is not reduced by the deductible contribution when applying the $100,000 MAGI limit.

MAGI ceiling will be lifted—but not until 2010. The Tax Increase Prevention and Reconciliation Act eliminates the $100,000 MAGI ceiling for tax years beginning after 2009. For a conversion made in 2010, none of the conversion income will have to be included in 2010 income. Half of the conversion income will be taxable in 2011 and half in 2012, unless an election is made to report all of the income for 2010 rather than applying the two-year spread.

Required minimum distributions may not be converted. If you are age 70½ or older, you may not convert to a Roth IRA amounts that represent required minimum distributions *(8.13)* from a traditional IRA.The required minimum distribution is not eligible for conversion and if you make a conversion to a Roth IRA before receiving your required minimum distribution for the year of conversion, an amount equal to the required minimum distribution is treated as a taxable distribution from the traditional IRA, followed by a regular annual contribution to a Roth IRA subject to the contribution limit *(8.20)*. Amounts over the annual limit would be an excess contribution subject to a 6% penalty tax unless the excess is withdrawn.

How a conversion is taxed. You must report the conversion of a traditional IRA to a Roth IRA on Form 8606 as a taxable distribution, except to the extent that the converted amount was allocable to nondeductible contributions (under the rules at *8.9*). The conversion is taxable in the year it is made unless you "undo" the conversion with a timely recharacterization, as discussed in *8.22*. If you make a transfer by withdrawing funds from a traditional IRA towards the end of 2006 and in 2007 you complete a rollover to a Roth IRA within 60 days of the withdrawal, this is treated as a 2006 conversion that is taxable on your 2006 return, except for any part allocable to nondeductible traditional IRA contributions and any recharacterized *(8.22)* amount.

The increase in your regular adjusted gross income from the conversion could reduce the itemized deductions *(13.7)*, personal exemptions *(21.12)*, or rental losses *(10.2)* you may claim. The increase could also trigger tax on Social Security benefits *(34.3)* or subject more of the benefits to tax.

If properly and timely completed, a conversion from a traditional IRA to a Roth IRA is exempt from the 10% penalty on taxable distributions received before age 59½ *(8.12)*.

8.22 Recharacterizations and Reconversions

If you convert a traditional IRA to a Roth IRA and it turns out that your modified adjusted gross income exceeds the $100,000 ceiling *(8.21)*, the conversion is considered a "failed" conversion that will result in tax penalties unless the converted amount is recharacterized. A conversion made by a married taxpayer who files a separate return is also considered a failed conversion; separate filers are ineligible for a conversion to a Roth IRA unless the spouses lived apart for the entire year *(8.21)*. Without a recharacterization, a failed conversion is treated as a regular contribution to the Roth IRA, subject to the 6% excess contribution penalty unless the excess is withdrawn; *see 8.20*. In addition to regular tax on the distribution from the traditional IRA, you may be subject to the 10% penalty for distributions before age 59½.

These penalties may be avoided by recharacterizing the contribution, in effect "undoing" the failed conversion. This is done by making a direct trustee-to-trustee transfer of the Roth IRA contribution, plus the allocable earnings, to a traditional IRA, or by transferring the Roth IRA to a traditional IRA within the same financial institution (same trustee). The effect of the recharacterization is to disregard the conversion to the Roth IRA and to treat the original transfer from the traditional IRA as having been originally contributed to the transferee IRA.

There are also other types of recharacterizations. You may want to recharacterize your Roth IRA if the value of the account has dropped substantially since the conversion. You may recharacterize the Roth IRA contribution as part of a plan to reconvert back to a Roth IRA when the taxable conversion value is lower; *see* the discussion of reconversions below. You also may recharacterize a regular Roth IRA contribution as a traditional IRA contribution, or a traditional IRA contribution as a regular Roth IRA contribution; *see* the Planning Reminder on this page.

To make an election to recharacterize, notify the trustee of the account being recharacterized and the transferee trustee (if different) of your intent to recharacterize, specifically identify the amounts subject to the election, and direct the transferor trustee to make the transfer.

Deadline for recharacterization. IRS regulations generally require that a recharacterization election and the actual transfer be made on or before the due date, including extensions, for filing the tax return for the year of the conversion. However, the IRS allows timely filers an automatic extension of six months from the original filing due date, excluding extensions. To recharacterize a conversion made in 2006, you have until October 15, 2007, provided that you timely filed your 2006 return, including any extension. *See* the instructions to Form 8606 for how to report the conversion and the recharacterization. If you file a timely 2006 return and pay tax on the converted amount, and then recharacterize by the October 15 deadline, you must file an amended return. For example, by April 16, 2007, you file your 2006 return, which includes a taxable conversion made in 2006, and then by October 15, 2007, you recharacterize the converted amount back to a traditional IRA. You must file an amended 2006 return to report the recharacterization and claim a refund for the tax paid on the conversion. The amended return must be filed, within the regular amendment period, generally three years; *see 47.1*. On the amended return, write "Filed pursuant to Section 301.9100-2."

What if you miss the IRS recharacterization deadlines? A regulation gives the IRS authority to grant an extension if an "innocent" mistake was made and you act in good faith by promptly asking the IRS for the additional time after discovering the error (Reg. Sec. 301.9100-3). In several private rulings, the IRS has allowed the extra extension to taxpayers who missed the deadline and who requested recharacterization relief before the IRS discovered that they did not qualify for the conversion or that the attempted recharacterization had not been timely made. At the time of each request, the statute of limitations had not yet passed; if it had, the IRS would almost surely have denied the requests. In one private ruling, the IRS allowed extra time to recharacterize a Roth IRA back to a traditional IRA after an IRS audit uncovered additional income that pushed a taxpayer over the $100,000 MAGI limit. The taxpayer, according to the IRS, had acted reasonably and was not aware of the excess income.

Reconverting to a Roth IRA after a recharacterization. As discussed above, a traditional IRA that has been converted to a Roth IRA may be transferred back to a traditional IRA in a recharacterization. That amount may subsequently be reconverted back to a Roth IRA. This recharacterization/reconversion rule may allow an IRA owner to lower the tax due on a conversion to a Roth IRA. For example, if you convert a traditional IRA to a Roth IRA and the value of the account drops as a result of a stock market decline, you may be able to reduce the taxable conversion amount value by recharacterizing the account as a traditional IRA and then reconverting to a Roth IRA at a time when the value of the account is lower. The amount that you must include in income from the conversion is based on the value of the account as of the date of the reconversion.

However, the IRS has imposed a waiting period before a reconversion may be made. You may not convert to a Roth IRA, recharacterize back to a traditional IRA, and reconvert the same funds to a Roth IRA in the same calendar year. If you converted a traditional IRA to a Roth IRA and also

Planning Reminder

Recharacterization of Roth IRA to Traditional IRA and Vice Versa

The recharacterization rule is not limited to reversing a failed conversion to a Roth IRA. A regular Roth IRA contribution (up to the annual limit) may be recharacterized as a contribution to a traditional IRA if, for example, doing so would allow you to claim an IRA deduction under the rules discussed at *8.4*. Similarly, if you contribute to a traditional IRA and decide that you would like to switch to a Roth IRA, you may recharacterize the contribution by transferring the contribution plus allocable income to a Roth IRA. A recharacterization generally must be made by the filing due date, but an extension may be allowed, as discussed in *8.22*. If you recharacterize a traditional IRA contribution to a Roth IRA, the transfer is treated as if it were made to the Roth IRA on January 1 of the year in which the original traditional IRA contribution was made, regardless of when the recharacterization occurred. This may be an advantage for purposes of establishing the beginning of the five-year holding period for tax-free distributions of Roth IRA earnings; *see 8.23*.

Caution

Limits on Reconversions to Roth IRA

After converting a traditional IRA to a Roth IRA, you may undo the conversion by recharacterizing the account as a traditional IRA. If you want to reconvert to a Roth IRA, you must stay within the IRS guidelines. A reconversion may not be made until the year following the year of the original conversion. *See 8.22* for further details.

recharacterized that amount back to a traditional IRA during 2006, you may not reconvert those same funds to a Roth IRA until 2007. If the recharacterization was made in the last 30 days of 2006, you must wait until the 30th day following the date of the recharacterization before a valid reconversion may be made in early 2007.

The more-than-30-day waiting period also applies if in 2007 you recharacterize a conversion made in 2006; *see* the Joe Smith Example below. A reconversion after the 2007 recharacterization is treated as a new conversion in 2007, subject to the $100,000 MAGI ceiling and other conversion qualification rules discussed in *8.21*.

The effect of the waiting period is to make it impossible to take immediate advantage of a stock market decline that lowers the value of a Roth IRA. If you want to recharacterize back to a traditional IRA and then reconvert to a Roth IRA in order to lower the taxable conversion amount, you will have to wait a minimum of 30 days before reconverting. By that time, the value of the reconverted account may be as high, or higher, than it was at the time of the recharacterization.

If a reconversion is attempted before the end of the waiting period, the attempt will be treated as a "failed" conversion. A failed conversion is treated as a taxable distribution from the traditional IRA followed by a regular contribution to a Roth IRA. The pre–age 59½ early distribution penalty could apply to the taxable distribution *(8.12)* and the deemed regular contribution to the Roth IRA would be subject to the 6% excess contribution penalty *(8.7)*. A failed conversion may be remedied by making a timely recharacterization to a traditional IRA.

EXAMPLE

Joe Smith converts a traditional IRA to a Roth IRA during 2006. In early 2007, he realizes that his modified adjusted gross income (MAGI) for 2006 exceeds the $100,000 ceiling, making him ineligible for a conversion. He recharacterizes the Roth IRA as a traditional IRA on January 24, 2007. Joe may not reconvert that amount to a Roth IRA until February 23, 2007. This is the first day after the 30-day period that began on January 24, 2007, the date of the recharacterization, and ended on February 22, 2007.

If Joe attempts to reconvert before February 23, 2007, the transfer will be treated as a "failed" conversion. Unless the failed conversion amount is recharacterized back to a traditional IRA, it will be treated as a taxable distribution from the traditional IRA; the 10% penalty for pre–age 59½ distributions could also apply. It will also be treated as a regular contribution to a Roth IRA and the amount over the annual limit (8.20) would be subject to the 6% excess contribution penalty tax. To avoid these tax consequences, Joe may recharacterize the failed conversion back to a traditional IRA and later reconvert it to a Roth IRA at any time on or after February 23, 2007. Assume that Joe reconverts to a Roth IRA on March 1, 2007. The transfer is considered a 2007 conversion that will be valid only if Joe's 2007 MAGI does not exceed the $100,000 ceiling. If Joe recharacterizes the March 1 conversion amount back to a traditional IRA during 2007, he must wait until 2008 before he may reconvert that amount again.

8.23 Distributions From a Roth IRA

A distribution from a Roth IRA is tax free if it is a *qualified* distribution, as discussed below. Even if a distribution is not a qualified distribution, it is tax free to the extent it does not exceed your regular Roth IRA contributions *(8.20)* and conversion contributions *(8.21)*. The part of a non-qualified distribution allocable to earnings is taxable, but distributions are considered to be from contributions first and then from earnings; *see* the ordering rule below for the allocation between contributions and earnings.

You may make a tax-free direct transfer from one Roth IRA to another. A tax-free rollover of a Roth IRA distribution may be made to another Roth IRA if you complete the rollover within 60 days.

You do not have to receive minimum required distributions from a Roth IRA after you reach age 70½ as you would from a traditional IRA *(see 8.13)*. No Roth IRA distributions at all are required during your lifetime. After your death, your beneficiaries will be subject to a minimum distribution requirement; *see 8.24*.

Filing Instruction

Form 8606

IRS Form 8606 must be filed to report Roth IRA distributions. It is also used to report a conversion to a Roth IRA. If you recharacterized part of the converted amount, you must report the non-recharacterized amount on Form 8606. The recharacterized portion is not reported on Form 8606, but an explanation must be attached to your return; follow the Form 8606 instructions.

Qualified Roth IRA distributions are tax free. Two tests must be met for a Roth IRA distribution to be "qualified," and thus completely tax free: (1) the distribution must be made after the end of the five-year period beginning with the first day of the first taxable year for which any Roth IRA contribution was made and (2) one of the following conditions must be met:

- you are age 59½ or older when the distribution is made,
- you are disabled,
- you use the distribution to pay up to $10,000 of qualifying first-time home-buyer expenses as discussed below, *or*
- you are a beneficiary receiving distributions following the death of the account owner.

Five-year holding period. Even if you are age 59½ or older or meet one of the other tests for qualified distributions, you must also satisfy the five-year holding period test in order to make tax-free withdrawals of earnings from a Roth IRA. The five-year holding period begins with January 1 (assuming you are a calendar-year taxpayer) of the first year for which any Roth IRA contribution is made.

You have only one five-year period regardless of the number of Roth IRAs you have. Once you satisfy the five-year test for one Roth IRA, you also meet it for all subsequently established Roth IRAs. For example, if you converted a traditional IRA to a Roth IRA during 1998 (the first year Roth IRA contributions were allowed), or made a regular Roth IRA contribution for 1998 at any time between January 1, 1998, and April 15, 1999, your five-year holding period began January 1, 1998. If in a later year you converted *(8.21)* a traditional IRA to a Roth IRA, or made a regular Roth IRA contribution *(8.20)*, that did not begin a new five-year holding period for that Roth IRA. In this case, the five-year period for all your Roth IRAs began January 1, 1998, and ended December 31, 2002. If your first Roth IRA contribution was a regular contribution for 2002 (by April 15, 2003) or a conversion made during 2002, your five-year period for all your Roth IRAs ends December 31, 2006.

If you receive a Roth IRA distribution *after* the end of your five-year holding period, and you also meet one of the other qualified distribution requirements such as being age 59½ or older, the distribution is completely tax free. If you receive a distribution before satisfying both the five-year holding period requirement and one of the other qualified distribution requirements, and the withdrawal exceeds your contributions, the excess (i.e., earnings) is taxable and possibly subject to the 10% penalty for pre–age 59½ distributions *(see 8.12)*. Under the ordering rules discussed below, Roth IRA distributions are treated as being made first from contributions and then from earnings.

Ordering rules for distributions. Even if a distribution is not fully tax free as a qualified distribution, it is not taxable to the extent of your Roth IRA contributions. All of your Roth IRAs are treated as one account for purposes of determining if contributions or earnings have been withdrawn. If a distribution does not exceed total contributions to all of your Roth IRAs, it is not taxable.

Where you have made both regular annual contributions and conversion contributions to a Roth IRA, the regular contributions are considered to be withdrawn first. Then, conversion contributions are considered to be withdrawn in the order in which they were made. If part of a conversion contribution was not treated as a taxable distribution (because it was allocable to nondeductible contributions in the converted traditional IRA), the taxable part of the conversion is deemed withdrawn before the nontaxable part. Taking into account the taxable part of a conversion contribution before the nontaxable part (if any) of the conversion contribution may be important for purposes of determining whether the 10% early distribution penalty applies to the withdrawal of a conversion contribution within five years of the conversion (*see* below).

Earnings on Roth IRA contributions are considered to be withdrawn last, after all contributions are taken into account. If the distribution is not a qualified distribution, the withdrawn earnings are subject to tax and if you are under age 59½, to the 10% early distribution penalty (*see 8.12* for penalty exceptions).

Withdrawals before age 59½ and within five years of conversion to Roth IRAs. The regular 10% early withdrawal penalty applies if withdrawals from a conversion Roth IRA are made by taxpayers under age 59½ before January 1 of the fifth year after the year of the conversion. Unless a penalty exception is available, the 10% penalty applies to the extent that a withdrawal within the five-year period is allocable under the ordering rule (*see* above) to the taxable part of the conversion. The taxable conversion amount will be 100% of the conversion unless the converted IRA had nondeductible contributions. Under the ordering rule for Roth IRA distributions, the entire withdrawal may be tax free because it does not exceed regular Roth IRA contributions, plus conversion contributions, but the 10% penalty still applies if a taxable conversion amount is

Planning Reminder

Meeting the Five-Year Holding Test

For a withdrawal of earnings from a Roth IRA to be tax free, the five-year holding period test must be met and the taxpayer must be at least age 59½ or meet one of the other conditions for a qualified distribution. For example, a taxpayer whose first Roth IRA contribution was for 2002 satisfies the five-year test at the end of 2006, so a distribution received after age 59½ in 2007 (or later) will be a tax-free qualified distribution.

IRS Alert

Loss on Liquidation of Roth IRA

You may have a loss on your Roth IRA investment because of declines in the stock market. If you liquidate all of your Roth IRA accounts, and the total distribution is less than your contributions to all of the Roth IRAs, you may be able to claim the difference as a deductible loss. However, the deduction is allowed only as a miscellaneous itemized deduction subject to the 2%-of-adjusted-gross-income floor *(19.1)* on Schedule A.

Caution

Early Withdrawal From Conversion IRA

The 10% penalty *(8.12)* for pre–age 591/2 distributions may apply if within five years of making a conversion to a Roth IRA, a distribution from that Roth IRA is received. The penalty applies to the portion of the withdrawal allocable to the conversion amount that was taxable in the year of the conversion. This is so even if the withdrawal is tax free under the ordering rule for Roth IRA distributions.

deemed to be withdrawn before the end of the five-year period. The five-year period for purposes of this penalty rule is figured separately for each conversion contribution. If you made a conversion in 2002, the five-year holding period for avoiding the early distribution penalty on a withdrawal from that Roth IRA ends December 31, 2006.

Distribution used for up to $10,000 of first-time home-buyer expenses. Tax-free treatment will apply to a Roth IRA distribution received after the first five-year period and used for up to $10,000 of qualifying "first-time" home-buyer expenses. The $10,000 limit is a lifetime cap per IRA owner, not an annual limitation. Expenses qualify if they are used within 120 days of the distribution to pay the acquisition costs of a principal residence for you, your spouse, your child, or your grandchild, or an ancestor of you or your spouse. The residence does not have to be the homeowner's "first" home. A qualifying first-time home-buyer is considered to be someone who did not have a present ownership interest in a principal residence in the two-year period ending on the acquisition date of the new home. If the home-buyer is married, both spouses must satisfy the two-year test. Eligible acquisition costs include buying, constructing, or reconstructing the principal residence, including reasonable settlement, financing, and closing costs.

8.24 Distributions to Roth IRA Beneficiaries

If you are the surviving spouse of the Roth IRA owner and you are the owner's sole Roth IRA beneficiary, you may elect to treat the inherited account as your own Roth IRA. If you treat the account as your own, you do not have to take distributions from the account at any time, since a Roth IRA owner is not subject to minimum distribution requirements. If you take some distributions, you are not locked into a specific distribution schedule unless you agree to that schedule.

Surviving spouses who do not elect to treat an inherited Roth IRA as their own, and beneficiaries other than surviving spouses, must receive required minimum distributions. If there is an individual designated beneficiary under the final IRS regulations as of September 30 of the year following the year of the Roth IRA owner's death *(see 8.14)*, distributions are generally payable over the life expectancy of the designated beneficiary; *see* the Single Life Expectancy table at the end of *8.14*. Although it is unlikely, the plan document may require distributions under the five-year rule, which requires that the entire account be distributed by December 31 of the fifth year following the year of the owner's death. The plan may allow a choice between the life expectancy rule and the five-year rule. Of course, a beneficiary may choose to receive more than the minimum amount required under the life expectancy rule, or, if applicable, the five-year rule.

When distributions to beneficiary must start under life expectancy rule. For a nonspouse beneficiary, required minimum distributions must begin by the end of the year following the year of the Roth IRA owner's death. This is also the starting date for a surviving spouse who is a co-beneficiary of the account along with other individuals.

If you are the surviving spouse and are sole beneficiary of the Roth IRA, you may elect to treat the Roth IRA as your own. If you do not treat it as your own, you may delay the start of required minimum distributions until whichever is later: December 31 of the year your spouse would have reached age 70½, or December 31 of the year following the year of your spouse's death.

If there is no designated beneficiary under the IRS rules, such as where the Roth IRA owner's estate is the beneficiary *(see 8.14)*, the entire account must be paid out by the end of the fifth year following the year of the owner's death.

Five-year holding period for tax-free treatment. The same five-year holding period for receiving fully tax-free distributions that applied to the account owner *(8.23)* also applies to you as the beneficiary. The five-year holding period began on January 1 of the year for which the owner's first Roth IRA contribution was made. If you receive distributions before the end of the five-year holding period, the distributions will be tax free to the extent that they are a recovery of the owner's Roth IRA contributions and taxable to the extent they are earnings; *see* the adjacent Caution. Distributions you receive after the end of the five-year holding period are completely tax free.

Caution

Some Distributions Partly Taxable to Beneficiary

Tax treatment of a distribution you receive as the beneficiary of a Roth IRA depends on whether it would have been a qualified distribution had the owner been alive to receive it on the distribution date. If you receive the distribution before the end of the owner's five-year holding period *(8.23)*, and part of the distribution is allocable to earnings under the ordering rules *(8.23)*, you must include that amount in your taxable income. However, even if you receive a taxable distribution and are under age 59½, you are not subject to the 10% early distribution penalty.

8.25 Qualified Hurricane Distributions Taxable Over Three Years

Up to $100,000 of qualified hurricane distributions may be reported as income over a three-year period and are exempt from the penalty for distributions before age 59½ *(7.15)*. These rules apply to qualifying taxable distributions from a traditional IRA, Roth IRA, SEP, SIMPLE IRA, or an eligible employer plan such as a 401(k) or 403(b) plan.

A distribution can be a qualified hurricane distribution only if received by an individual whose principal residence was in the Hurricane Katrina disaster area (on 8/28/05), Hurricane Rita disaster area (on 9/23/05), or Hurricane Wilma disaster area (on 10/23/05), and who suffered an economic loss due to the applicable hurricane. The distribution must have been made after August 24, 2005 (Katrina), September 22, 2005 (Rita), or October 22, 2005, and before 2007. The amount of the distribution does not have to correspond to the economic loss sustained.

As discussed below, the first $100,000 of qualified hurricane distributions may be reported as income over a three-year period on Form 8915. If within the three-year period any amounts are recontributed back into the plan, the repayment is treated as a tax-free rollover and a refund claim may be made for tax paid on that amount; *see 8.26.*

Three-year reporting of qualified hurricane distributions on Form 8915. On Form 8915, you report your total retirement distributions and figure the amount subject to tax. The first $100,000 of qualified hurricane distributions from all eligible retirement plans received in 2005 and 2006 is includible in your income in equal amounts over three years unless you elect otherwise. For example, if in 2005 you received a $50,000 distribution that you treated as a qualified hurricane distribution on Form 8915 filed with your 2005 Form 1040, and in 2006 you received a qualified distribution of $100,000, only $50,000 of the 2006 distribution can be treated as a qualified hurricane distribution on your Form 8915 for 2006.

If you did not receive qualified distributions in 2005 and in 2006 your qualified distributions exceed $100,000, and they are from different types of plans, such as an IRA and a 401(k) plan, you may allocate the $100,000 limit among the plans in any way you choose.

The three-year rule applies unless you elect not to use it. You "elect out" of the three-year method by checking a box on Form 8915 and reporting the entire distribution.

8.26 Repayments of Qualified Hurricane Distributions Within Three Years

You generally can avoid tax on a qualified hurricane distribution *(8.25)* that is eligible for tax-free rollover treatment by repaying it to an IRA or eligible employer plan within three years, starting on the day after the date of receipt.

If you are reporting a 2006 qualified hurricane distribution on Form 8915, any repayments made by the filing due date (including extensions) for your 2006 return reduce the amount subject to tax. A repayment made after the filing due date will reduce the amount of the qualified distributions subject to tax on your 2007 return.

If you reported a qualified distribution on your 2005 return and you repaid it in 2006 after the 2005 filing due date, the repayment offsets the amount includible as income for 2006. If the repayment exceeds the income for 2006, the excess may be carried forward to 2007 or an amended return for 2005 may be filed to carry back the excess and reduce the amount included in your 2005 income.

See the instructions to Form 8915 for further details on the repayment rules.

Chapter 9

Income From Rents and Royalties

Use Schedule E of Form 1040 to report real estate rental income and expenses. You must also file Form 4562 to claim depreciation deductions for buildings you acquired in 2006.

Use Schedule C instead of Schedule E if you provide additional services for the convenience of the tenants, such as maid service. That is, Schedule C is used to report payments received for the use and occupancy of rooms or other areas in a hotel, motel, boarding house, apartment, tourist home, or trailer court where services are provided primarily for the occupant.

If you rent out an apartment or room in the same building in which you live, you report the rent income less expenses allocated to the rental property; *see 9.4*.

The law prevents most homeowners from deducting losses (expenses in excess of income) on the rental of a personal vacation home or personal residence if the owner or close relatives personally use the premises during the year. Tests based on days of personal and rental use determine whether you may deduct losses, as explained in *9.7*.

Rental losses may also be limited by the passive activity rules discussed in Chapter 10. Real estate professionals may avoid the passive restrictions on rental income. An investor who actively manages property may deduct rental losses of up to $25,000 under an exception to the passive activity loss restrictions.

Use Schedule E to report royalties, but if you are a self-employed author, artist, or inventor, report royalty income and expenses on Schedule C.

Business rentals of equipment, vehicles, or similar personal property are reported on Schedule C, not Schedule E.

Rental Income and Deductions

9.1 Reporting Rental Income and Expenses

On the cash basis, you report rent income on your tax return for the year in which you receive payment or in which you "constructively" receive it, such as where payment is credited to your bank account.

On the accrual basis, you report income on your tax return for the year in which you are entitled to receive payment, even if it is not actually paid. However, you do not report accrued income if the financial condition of the tenant makes collection doubtful. If you sue for payment, you do not report income until you win a collectible judgment.

Advance rentals. Advance rentals or bonuses are reported in the year received, whether you are on the cash or accrual basis.

Tenant's payment of landlord's expenses. The tenant's payment of your taxes, interest, insurance, mortgage amortization (even if you are not personally liable on the mortgage), repairs, or other expenses is considered additional rental income to you. If your tenant pays your utility bills or your emergency repairs and deducts the amount from the rent payment, you must include as rental income the full rental amount, not the actual net payment. However, you can claim an offsetting deduction for expenses, such as repairs, that would have been deductible had you paid them.

Tenant's payment to cancel lease. A tenant's payment for cancelling a lease or modifying its terms is considered rental income in the year you receive it regardless of your method of accounting. You may deduct expenses incurred because of the cancellation or modification and any unamortized balance of expenses paid in negotiating the lease.

Insurance. Insurance proceeds for loss of rental income because of fire or other casualty are rental income.

Improvements by tenants. You do not realize taxable income when your tenant improves the leased premises, provided the improvements are not substitute rent payments. Furthermore, when you take possession of the improvements at the time the lease ends, you do not realize income. However, you may not depreciate the value of the improvements as the basis to you is considered zero.

Property or services. If you receive property or services instead of money, include the fair market value of such property or services as rental income.

If you agree upon a specified price for services rendered, that price is generally treated as the fair market value.

Rental losses. Rental income may be offset by deductions claimed for depreciation, mortgage interest, and repair and maintenance costs. However, if these expenses exceed rental income, the resulting loss is subject to the passive activity loss restrictions. If you do not qualify as a real estate professional *(10.3)*, you generally may not deduct rental losses from other income (such as salary, interest, and dividends). Rental losses may offset only other rental and passive activity income. However, if you perform some management role, you may deduct from other income *real estate* rental losses of up to $25,000, provided your adjusted gross income does not exceed $100,000 *(see 10.2)*. The passive activity restrictions have the positive effect of making rental income attractive. Consider purchasing rental property if you have passive tax losses that may be used to offset the rental income. *See Chapter 10 for details on the passive loss restrictions.*

Application of the passive activity loss rules and exceptions assumes that the property is not considered a residence under the personal-use rules at *9.7*. If it is, rental expenses are deductible from rental income *(see 9.9)* but a loss is not allowed for that property.

Caution

Security Deposits

Distinguish advance rentals, which are income, from security deposits, which are not. Security deposits are amounts deposited with you solely as security for the tenant's performance of the terms of the lease, and as such are usually not taxed, particularly where local law treats security deposits as trust funds. If the tenant breaches the lease, you are entitled to apply the sum as rent, at which time you report it as income. If both you and your tenant agree that a security deposit is to be used as a final rent payment, it is advance rent. Include it in your income when you receive it.

9.2 Checklist of Rental Deductions

The expenses in this section are deductible from rental income on Schedule E of Form 1040 in determining your profit.

Real estate taxes. However, special assessments for paving, sewer systems, or other local improvements are not deductible; they are added to the cost of the land. *See 16.6* through *16.9* for real estate tax deductions.

Court Decision

Co-Tenant's Deduction for Real Estate Taxes

The Tax Court allowed a co-tenant to deduct more than her proportionate share of real estate taxes. According to the court, the deduction test for real estate taxes is whether the payment satisfies a personal liability or protects a beneficial interest in the property. In the case of co-tenants, nonpayment of taxes by the other co-tenants could result in the property being lost or foreclosed. To prevent this, a co-tenant who pays the tax is protecting his or her beneficial interest and, therefore, is entitled to deduct the payment of the full tax, provided the payment is from his or her own funds.

Construction period interest and taxes. These expenses generally have to be capitalized and depreciated; *see 16.4.*

Depreciation of a rental building. You may start claiming depreciation in the month the building is ready for tenants. For example, you bought a house in May 2006 and spent June and July making repairs. The house is ready to rent in August and you advertise for tenants. You begin depreciation as of August, even if a tenant does not move in until September or some later month. The month the building is ready for tenants is the month that determines the first-year depreciation write-off under the mid-month convention. *See 9.5* for the monthly depreciation rates for residential rental property. Rates for nonresidential buildings are at *42.13.*

Depreciation for furniture and appliances. Furniture, carpeting, and appliances such as stoves and refrigerators used in residential rental property are considered five-year property for MACRS depreciation purposes. Furniture used in office buildings is considered seven-year property. *See 42.5* for MACRS rates.

Management expenses, such as a fee paid to a company for collecting the rent.

Maintenance expenses, such as heating, repairs, lighting, water, electricity, gas, telephone, coal, and other service costs; *see 9.3.*

Salaries and wages paid to superintendents, janitors, elevator operators, and service and maintenance personnel.

Traveling expenses to look after the properties. If you travel "away from home" to inspect or repair rental property, be prepared to show that this was the primary purpose of your trip, rather than vacationing or other personal purposes. Otherwise, the IRS may disallow deductions for round-trip travel costs.

Legal expenses for dispossessing tenants. But expenses of long-term leases are capital expenditures deductible over the term of the lease.

Interest on mortgages and other indebtedness. But expenses and fees for securing loans are nondeductible capital expenditures.

Commissions paid to collect rentals. But commissions paid to secure long-term rentals must be deducted over the life of the lease. Commissions paid to acquire the property are capitalized.

Premiums for fire, liability, and plate glass insurance. If payment is made in one year for insurance covering a period longer than one year, you amortize and deduct the premium over the life of the policy, even though you are on a cash basis.

Also deductible is a premium paid to secure a release from a mortgage in order to get a new loan.

Tax return preparation. You may deduct as a rental expense the part of a tax preparation fee allocable to Part 1 of Schedule E (income or loss from rentals or royalties). You may also deduct, as a rental expense, a fee paid to a tax consultant to resolve a tax underpayment related to your rental activities.

Charging below fair market rent. If you rent your property to a friend or relative for less than the fair rental value, you may deduct expenses and depreciation only to the extent of the rental income; *see 9.8.*

Co-tenants. One of two tenants-in-common may deduct only half of the maintenance expenses even if he or she pays the entire bill. A tenant-in-common who pays all of the expenses of the common property is entitled to reimbursement from the other co-tenant, so one-half of the bill is not his or her ordinary and necessary expense. Each co-tenant owns a separate property interest in the common property that produces separate income for each. Each tenant's deductible expense is that portion of the entire expense that each separate interest bears to the whole, and no more.

Costs of cancelling lease. A landlord may pay a tenant to cancel an unfavorable lease. The way the landlord treats the payment depends on the reason for the cancellation. If the purpose of the cancellation is to enable the landlord to construct a new building in place of the old, the cancellation payment is added to the basis of the new building. If the purpose is to sell the property, the payment is added to the cost of the property. If the landlord wants the premises for his or her own use, the payment is deducted over the remaining term of the old lease. If the landlord gets a new tenant to replace the old one, the cancellation payment is also generally deductible over the remaining term of the old lease.

EXAMPLE

Handlery Hotels, Inc., had to pay its lessee $85,000 to terminate a lease on a building three years before the lease term expired. Handlery entered into a new 20-year lease on more favorable terms with another lessee. Handlery amortized the $85,000 cancellation payment over the three-year unexpired term of the old lease. The IRS claimed that the payment had to be amortized over the 20-year term of the new lease because it was part of the cost of obtaining the new lease. A federal district court agreed with the IRS, but an appeals court sided with Handlery. Since the unexpired lease term is the major factor in determining the amount of the cancellation payment, the cost of cancellation should be amortized over that unexpired term.

9.3 Distinguishing Between a Repair and an Improvement

Maintenance and repair expenses are not treated in the same way as expenses for improvements and replacements. Only maintenance and incidental repair costs are deductible against rental income. Improvements that add to the value or prolong the life of the property or adapt it to new uses are capital improvements. Capital improvements may not be deducted currently but may be depreciated under the rules at *42.13*. If you make improvements to property before renting it out, add the cost of the improvements to your basis in the property.

A repair keeps your property in good operating condition. For example, repairs include painting, fixing gutters or floors, fixing leaks, plastering, and replacing broken windows. However, putting a recreation room in an unfinished basement, paneling a den, putting up a fence, putting in new plumbing or wiring, and paving a driveway are all examples of capital improvements depreciable under *42.13*. Putting on a new roof is generally a depreciable capital improvement; however, the Tax Court has allowed current deductions for roof replacements intended to prevent leaks; *see* Example 2 below.

Repairs may not be separated from capital expenditures when both are part of an improvement program; *see* Example 3 below.

Planning Reminder

Repairs and Improvements

What if repairs and improvements are unconnected and not part of an overall improvement program? Assume you repair the floors of one story and improve another story by cutting new windows. You probably may deduct the cost of repairing the floors provided you have separate bills for the jobs. To safeguard the deduction, schedule the work at separate times so that the two jobs are not lumped together as an overall improvement program.

EXAMPLES

1. The cost of painting the outside of a building used for business purposes and the cost of papering and painting the inside are repair costs and may be deducted. A change in the plumbing system is a capital expenditure that must be depreciated under MACRS; *see 42.13*.
2. Campbell owned a one-story house that she rented to a tenant. She paid $8,000 to repair the roof after the tenant complained of leaks. The contractor she employed removed the existing layers of roof and replaced them with fiberglass and asphalt; no structural changes were made. The Tax Court allowed Campbell to deduct the full amount of the payment to the contractor as an ordinary and necessary repair because the roof replacement merely restored the property to a leak-free condition and did not add to the value of the home.

   The Tax Court also allowed an owner of a commercial building with a leaky roof to fully deduct the $52,000 cost of stripping the roof layers, replacing them, and spraying the new ones with foam to prevent future leaks. These were repairs intended to keep the property in working condition and did not extend the life of the building.
3. You buy a dilapidated business building and has it renovated and repaired. The total cost comes to about $130,000, of which $17,800 is allocable to the repairs. The cost of the repairs is not deductible because the entire project is a capital expenditure. When a general improvement program is undertaken, you may not separate repairs from improvements. Both become an integral part of the overall betterment and are a capital investment, although a portion could be characterized as repairs when viewed independently.

Normal maintenance or major improvement? Normal maintenance expenses were distinguished from major improvement costs in a case involving a major hotel where improvements and maintenance were generally done at the same time. The operators of the hotel capitalized the cost of the improvements but claimed expense deductions for the cost of painting and repapering rooms. The IRS disallowed the deductions, claiming they were part of the improvement program. The operators claimed that the papering and painting were normal and usual maintenance work required to keep the hotel in first-class condition. The Tax Court disagreed and sided with the IRS. However, on appeal, the appeals court allowed the deduction. The "rehabilitation doctrine" does not apply where it can be shown that repairs are part of a normal range of ongoing maintenance. Here, the painting and papering only served to maintain the first-class status of the hotel. The fact that the work was done under a general improvement plan did not defeat the deduction. Any commercial enterprise, such as a hotel, that annually spends large sums of money on replacements and repairs must do so under a detailed plan and budget.

How To Report Rentals of Residential and Vacation Homes

9.4 Reporting Rents From a Multi-Unit Residence

If you rent out an apartment or room in a multi-unit residence in which you also live, you report rent receipts and deduct expenses allocated to the rented part of the property on Schedule E of Form 1040 whether or not you itemize deductions. You deduct interest and taxes on your personal share of the property as itemized deductions on Schedule A of Form 1040 if you itemize deductions. If you or close relatives personally use the rented portion during the year and expenses exceed income, loss deductions may be barred under the rules in *9.7*.

Even if a loss is not barred by the personal-use rules *(9.7)*, a loss shown on Schedule E is subject to the passive loss restrictions discussed in Chapter 10. The loss, if it comes within the $25,000 allowance *(10.2)* or the exception for real estate professionals *(10.3)*, may be deducted from any type of income. If your only passive activity losses are rental losses of $25,000 or less from actively managed rental real estate and your modified adjusted gross income is $100,000 or less, you do not have to use Form 8582 to deduct losses under the $25,000 allowance; *see 10.12*. If you are not a qualifying real estate professional and cannot claim the allowance, the loss may be deducted only from passive activity income.

Court Decision

Rented Rooms That Are Not Separate Dwelling Units

A rental loss was denied to an owner of a two-story, four-bedroom house when he rented out two bedrooms to separate tenants after he lost his job. Although individual locks were placed on the doors of the rented bedrooms, the tenants and the owner shared access to the kitchen, bathroom, and other parts of the house. The Tax Court held that the rented rooms were not separate and distinct from the rest of the house that the owner used. The house was a single dwelling unit shared by the owner and tenants and under the personal-use rules at *9.7*, the owner could not claim a rental loss.

EXAMPLE

You buy a three-family house in March 2006. You occupy one floor as your personal residence and starting in June 2006 you rent out the other two floors. The house cost you $300,000 ($270,000 for the building and $30,000 for the land). Two-thirds of the basis of the building is subject to depreciation, or $180,000 (2/3 of $270,000). For a building placed in service in June, the depreciation rate is 1.970%, as shown in Table 9-1 on page 225, so your depreciation deduction is $3,546 (1.970% $180,000). Assuming you paid property taxes of $6,000, mortgage interest of $3,900, and repairs of $3,000, this is how you deduct expenses for 2006:

	Total	*Deduct itemized deductions*	*Deduct on Schedule E*	*Not deductible*
Taxes	$6,000	$2,000	$4,000	
Interest	3,900	1,300	2,600	
Repairs	3,000		2,000	$1,000
Depreciation	3,546		3,546	
	$16,446	$3,300	$12,146	$1,000

The taxes and interest allocated to personal use are deductible on Schedule A if you itemize deductions. Repairs allocated to your apartment are nondeductible personal expenses.

9.5 Depreciation on Converting a Home to Rental Property

When you convert your residence to rental property, you may depreciate the building. You figure depreciation on the *lower* of:

- Fair market value of the building at the time you convert it to rental property; *or*
- Adjusted basis. This is your original cost for the building, exclusive of land, plus permanent improvements minus casualty or theft loss deductions claimed on prior tax returns.

You claim MACRS depreciation based on a 27½-year recovery period, which extends to 28 or 29 years due to the mid-month convention. The specific rate for the year of conversion is the rate for the month in which the property is ready for tenants. For example, you move out of your home in May and make some minor repairs. You advertise the house for rent in June. Depreciation starts in June because that is when the home is ready for rental, even if you do not actually obtain a tenant until a later month. Under a mid-month convention, the house is treated as placed in service during the middle of the month. This means that one-half of a full month's depreciation is allowed for that month. In Table 9-1 below, the monthly depreciation rates for the year the property is placed in service and later years are shown. The table incorporates the mid-month convention.

EXAMPLE

In 1992, you bought a house for $125,000, of which $100,000 is allocated to the house; the $25,000 balance is allocated to the land. In June 2006, you move out of the house and rent it. At that time, the fair market value of the house exclusive of the land is $150,000. The depreciable basis of the house is the lower adjusted basis of $100,000. The depreciation rate for placing the house in service in June is 1.970%, as shown in Table 9-1 below. Thus, your 2006 depreciation deduction is $1,970 ($100,000 × 1.970%). Your 2007 depreciation deduction is $3,636 ($100,000 × 3.636%).

Depreciating a rented cooperative apartment. If you rent out a co-op apartment, you may deduct your share of the total depreciation claimed by the cooperative corporation. The method for computing your share depends on whether you bought your co-op shares as part of the first offering. If you did, follow these steps: (1) Ask the co-op corporation officials for the total real estate depreciation deduction of the corporation, not counting depreciation for office space that cannot be lived in by tenant-shareholders. (2) Multiply Step 1 by the following fraction: number of your co-op shares divided by total shares outstanding. The result is your share of the co-op's depreciation, but you may not deduct more than your adjusted basis.

The computation is more complicated if you bought your co-op shares after the first offering. You must compute your depreciable basis as follows: Increase your cost for the co-op shares by your share of the co-op's total mortgage. Reduce this amount by your share of the value of the co-op's land and your share of the commercial space not available for occupancy by tenant-stockholders. Your "share" of the co-op's mortgage, land value, or commercial space is the co-op's total amount for such items multiplied by the fraction in Step 2 above, that is, the number of your shares divided by the total shares outstanding. After computing your depreciable basis, multiply that basis by the depreciation percentage for the month your apartment is ready for rental.

Planning Reminder

Obtain Appraisal

Have an appraiser estimate the fair market value of the house when it is rented. The appraisal will help support your basis for depreciation or a loss deduction on a sale if your return is examined.

Table 9-1 Depreciation: Use the Row for the Month the Residence Is Ready for Rental in the First Rental Year

Year	Month property placed in service											
	1	2	3	4	5	6	7	8	9	10	11	12
1	3.485%	3.182%	2.879%	2.576%	2.273%	1.970%	1.667%	1.364%	1.061%	0.758%	0.455%	0.152%
2–9	3.636	3.636	3.636	3.636	3.636	3.636	3.636	3.636	3.636	3.636	3.636	3.636
10	3.637	3.637	3.637	3.637	3.637	3.637	3.636	3.636	3.636	3.636	3.636	3.636
11	3.636	3.636	3.636	3.636	3.636	3.636	3.637	3.637	3.637	3.637	3.637	3.637
12	3.637	3.637	3.637	3.637	3.637	3.637	3.636	3.636	3.636	3.636	3.636	3.636
13	3.636	3.636	3.636	3.636	3.636	3.636	3.637	3.637	3.637	3.637	3.637	3.637
14	3.637	3.637	3.637	3.637	3.637	3.637	3.636	3.636	3.636	3.636	3.636	3.636
15	3.636	3.636	3.636	3.636	3.636	3.636	3.637	3.637	3.637	3.637	3.637	3.637
16	3.637	3.637	3.637	3.637	3.637	3.637	3.636	3.636	3.636	3.636	3.636	3.636
17	3.636	3.636	3.636	3.636	3.636	3.636	3.637	3.637	3.637	3.637	3.637	3.637
18	3.637	3.637	3.637	3.637	3.637	3.637	3.636	3.636	3.636	3.636	3.636	3.636
19	3.636	3.636	3.636	3.636	3.636	3.636	3.637	3.637	3.637	3.637	3.637	3.637
20	3.637	3.637	3.637	3.637	3.637	3.637	3.636	3.636	3.636	3.636	3.636	3.636
21	3.636	3.636	3.636	3.636	3.636	3.636	3.637	3.637	3.637	3.637	3.637	3.637
22	3.637	3.637	3.637	3.637	3.637	3.637	3.636	3.636	3.636	3.636	3.636	3.636
23	3.636	3.636	3.636	3.636	3.636	3.636	3.637	3.637	3.637	3.637	3.637	3.637
24	3.637	3.637	3.637	3.637	3.637	3.637	3.636	3.636	3.636	3.636	3.636	3.636
25	3.636	3.636	3.636	3.636	3.636	3.636	3.637	3.637	3.637	3.637	3.637	3.637
26	3.637	3.637	3.637	3.637	3.637	3.637	3.636	3.636	3.636	3.636	3.636	3.636
27	3.636	3.636	3.636	3.636	3.636	3.636	3.637	3.637	3.637	3.637	3.637	3.637
28	1.97	2.273	2.576	2.879	3.182	3.485	3.636	3.636	3.636	3.636	3.636	3.636
29							0.152	0.455	0.758	1.061	1.364	1.667

Basis to use when you sell a rented residence. For purposes of figuring gain, you use adjusted basis at the time of the conversion, plus subsequent capital improvements, and minus depreciation and casualty loss deductions. For purposes of figuring loss, you use the *lower* of adjusted basis and fair market value at the time of the conversion, plus subsequent improvements and minus depreciation and casualty losses. You may have neither gain nor loss to report; this would happen if you figure a loss when using the above basis rule for gains and you figure a gain when using the basis rule for losses.

Depreciation on a vacant residence. If you move from your house before it is sold, you generally may not deduct depreciation on the vacant residence while it is held for sale. The IRS will not allow the deduction, and, according to a Tax Court case, a deduction is possible only if you can show that you held the house expecting to make a profit on an increase in value over and above the value of the house when you moved from it. That is, you held the house for sale on the expectation of profiting on a future increase in value after abandoning the house as a residence.

9.6 Renting a Residence to a Relative

The tax law distinguishes between a rental of a unit used by a close relative as a principal residence and a rental of a unit that is not the relative's principal residence, such as a second home or vacation home. It is easier to deduct a rental loss on the principal residence rental.

On a fair market rental of a unit used by the close relative as a principal residence, your relative's use is *not* considered personal use by you that could bar a loss under the personal-use test in *9.7*. A relative's use of the unit as a second or vacation home *is* attributed to you in applying the personal-use test at *9.7*, even if you receive a fair market value rent.

Close relatives who come within these rules are: brothers and sisters, half-brothers and half-sisters, spouses, parents, grandparents, children, and grandchildren.

Fair market rental is the amount a person who is not related to you would be willing to pay. The most direct way to determine fair market rental is to ask a real estate agent in your neighborhood for comparative rentals.

9.7 Personal Use and Rental of a Residence During the Year

The number of personal-use days and fair-market-rental days for your residential unit determines how you must report rental income and expenses. If rental use exceeds 15 days and your personal use of the unit exceeds the 14 day/10% limit described below, the unit is treated as a residence rather than rental property. If it is treated as a residence, your rental expenses are deductible only to the extent of the rental income from the property.

List your days of use in 2006:
Fair market rental days:______________
Personal-use days:______________

Personal-use days may also include rental days to family members listed at *9.6* and use days under co-ownership agreements. *See 9.8* for details on personal-use days.

The daily-use tests apply to any "dwelling unit" you rent out that is also used as a residence during the year by yourself or other family members. A dwelling unit may be a house, apartment, condominium, cooperative, house trailer, mini motor home, boat, or similar property with basic living accommodations, including any appurtenant structure such as a garage. A dwelling unit does not include property used exclusively as a hotel, motel, inn, or similar establishment.

The hotel/motel/inn exception applies only to property that is used exclusively in such a business. The exception does not apply to the dual-use portion of a hotel, inn, or bed and breakfast. In one case, the Tax Court agreed with the IRS that the owners of a three-floor bed-and-breakfast could not claim business expense deductions for depreciation or interest on the areas that were used both in the B&B business as well as by them personally. The lobby, registration area, office, kitchen, and laundry room were used 75% of the time for the business and 25% of the time for personal purposes. Because these areas were not used solely for operating the B&B, they could not qualify for the hotel exception. The dual-use areas were treated as part of the owners' dwelling unit for purposes of the 14-day/10% personal-use test.

EXAMPLE

Barranti inherited a residence from her grandmother. The house was in a state of disrepair. A real estate agent estimated the fair market rental rate for the house to be between $700 and $750 per month. Barranti rented the house to her brother for $500 a month while he repaired the structure. After a year, he moved out and Barranti sold the house and claimed a rental loss and a loss on the sale. The Tax Court disallowed both losses. The below-market rental to Barranti's brother was treated as her own personal use of the house, preventing the rental loss deduction. The below-market rental was also treated as evidence that Barranti held the property for personal purposes and therefore she could not deduct the loss on the sale either.

Rented less than 15 days during the taxable year. If you rent the unit for fewer than 15 days in the taxable year, you do not report the rental income and the only deductions allowed are those you would be allowed anyway as a homeowner. That is, if you itemize deductions on Schedule A, you deduct mortgage interest, real estate taxes, and casualty losses, if any. No other rental expenses such as depreciation and maintenance expenses are deductible. Interest is generally fully deductible if the home qualifies as a first or second home under the mortgage interest rules discussed in Chapter 15.

14-day/10% personal-use test applies if unit rented 15 days or more in the taxable year. A daily-use test determines whether your use of the unit during the taxable year is treated as residential use that requires you to limit your deductions to the rental income under the rules in *9.9*. You are considered to have used the unit as a residence if your personal-use days during the year (determined under *9.8*) exceeded 14 days, or, if greater, 10% of the days on which the unit was rented to others at a fair market rental price.

When the unit is treated as a residence, rental expenses are deductible on Schedule E only to the extent of rental income, following the rules in *9.9*. Expenses not deductible in the current year under this limitation may be carried forward and will be deductible up to rental income in the following year. The deduction limit is irrelevant if your rental income exceeds expenses. You report the rental income and claim the deductible expenses on Schedule E.

If your personal-use days do *not* exceed 14 days or 10% of the fair market rental days, whichever is more, your rental deductions on Schedule E (Form 1040) are not limited by the personal-use test. However, a loss deduction is subject to the passive activity loss restrictions discussed at *10.1*. Furthermore, you lose part of the mortgage interest deduction because the unit is not a qualified second home for mortgage interest purposes if personal use does not exceed the greater of 14 days or 10% of the fair market rental days. The interest allocable to the rental use *(see 9.9)* is deductible against rental income on Schedule E, but the balance is nondeductible personal interest.

EXAMPLES

1. In 2006, you rented out a condominium unit in Florida at a fair market rental for 260 days. If you used the unit personally for 27 or more days, the condominium is considered a residence subject to the deduction limitation rules at *9.9* because your personal use exceeds 26 days, 10% of the fair market rental days. If you used the unit for 26 days or less, you may treat the unit for the taxable year as rental property and you may deduct a loss, if any, subject to the passive activity rules at *10.1. However, if personal use did not exceed 26 days, the mortgage interest allocable to the personal-use days would be nondeductible personal interest.*

   Where rental days exceed 140 days, as a rule of thumb, you can figure that for every 10 days of fair-rent use, you may use the unit personally for one day. Thus, if you rented a vacation unit for 11 months, you could personally use it for a month or so without jeopardizing a deduction of a rental loss (rental of 330 days would permit 33 days of personal use).
2. Assume the same unit as in Example 1 but you rented the unit for 130 days. If you used the unit personally for 14 days or less, you may treat the unit as a rental property. To treat it as a residence, your personal use would have to exceed 14 days, since 14 days is greater than 10% of the rental days.

Planning Reminder

Shared-Equity Financing Agreements

As an investor, you can help finance the purchase of a principal residence for a family member or other individual. The rental income you receive for your ownership share in the property may be offset by deductions for your share of the mortgage interest, taxes, and operating expenses you pay under the terms of the agreement, as well as depreciation deductions for your percentage share. Rental losses are subject to the passive loss restrictions in Chapter 10.

The other co-owner living in the house may claim itemized deductions for payment of his or her share of the mortgage interest and taxes.

9.8 Counting Personal-Use Days and Rental Days for a Residence

In applying the 14-day/10% personal-use test in *9.7,* personal-use days are:

- Days you used the residence for personal purposes other than days primarily spent making repairs or getting the property ready for tenants. If you use a residence for personal purposes on a day you rent it at fair market value, count that day as a personal day, not a rental day, in applying the 14-day/10% test.
- Days on which the residence is used by your spouse, children, grandchildren, parents, brothers, sisters, or grandparents. However, if such a relative pays you a fair rental value to use the home as a principal residence, the relative's use is not considered personal use by you. If you rent a vacation home to such relatives, their use is considered personal use by you even if they pay a fair rental value amount; *see* Example 1 below.

  The same rules apply to days of use by a relative of a co-owner of the property.
- Days on which the residence is used by any person under a reciprocal arrangement that allows you to use some other dwelling during the year.
- Days on which you rent the residence to any person for less than fair market value.
- Days that a co-owner of the property uses the residence, unless the co-owner's use is under a shared-equity financing agreement discussed later in this section.

An owner is not considered to have personally used a home that is used by an employee if the value of such use is tax-free lodging required as a condition of employment; *see 3.12.*

Shared-equity financing agreements for co-owners. Use by a co-owner is not considered personal use by you if you have a shared-equity financing agreement under which: (1) the co-owner pays you a fair rent for using the home as his or her principal residence; and (2) you and your co-owner each have undivided interests for more than 50 years in the entire home and in any appurtenant land acquired with the residence.

Any use by a co-owner that does not meet these two tests is considered personal use by you if, for any part of the day, the home is used by a co-owner or a holder of any interest in the home (other than a security interest or an interest under a lease for fair rental) for personal purposes. For this purpose, any other ownership interest existing at the time you have an interest in the home is counted, even if there are no immediate rights to possession and enjoyment of the home under such other interest. For example, you have a life estate in the home and your friend owns the remainder interest. Use by either of you is personal use.

EXAMPLES

1. A son rented a condominium in Florida to his parents, who split their time between the Florida apartment and the home they owned in Illinois. Although the parents paid a fair amount for the Florida condo, the son's rental deductions were limited by the IRS and the Tax Court to interest and real estate taxes that did not exceed the rental income. The parents' rental days were attributed to the son under the 14 day/10% rental day limit since the home in Illinois, and not the Florida apartment, was their principal residence.
2. You and your neighbor Joe are co-owners of a vacation condominium. You rent the unit out whenever possible; Joe uses the unit for two weeks every year. As Joe owns an interest in the unit, both of you are considered to have used the unit for personal purposes during those weeks.
3. You and your neighbor Tom are co-owners of a house under a shared-equity financing agreement. Tom lives in the house and pays you a fair rental price. Even though Tom has an interest in the house, the days he lives there are not counted as days of personal use by you because Tom rents the house as a main home under a shared-equity financing agreement.
4. You rent a beach house to Jane. Jane rents her house in the mountains to you. You each pay a fair rental price. You are using your house for personal purposes on the days that Jane uses it because your house is used by Jane under an arrangement that allows you to use her house.

Rental of principal residence prior to sale. You are not considered to have made any personal use of a principal residence that you rent or try to rent at a fair rental for (1) a consecutive period of 12 months or more *or* (2) a period of less than 12 months that ends with the sale or exchange of the residence. For example, you move out of your principal residence on May 31,

2006, offering it for rental as of June 1. You rent it from June 15 until mid-November, when you sell the house. Under the special rental period rule, your use of the house from January 1 until May 31, 2006, is *not* counted as personal use. This means that deductions for the rental period are not subject to the rental income limitation discussed in *9.9*.

Rental pool arrangements. In proposed regulations, the IRS holds that a rental pool is not a basis for counting fair rental days. However, the proposed regulations permit rental pool participants to elect to average the actual rental of their units. Unanimous consent is required to elect the averaging rule. If the election is made, the number of rental days for a unit is determined by multiplying the aggregate number of days that all units in the rental pool were rented at fair rental during the pool season by a fraction. The numerator of the fraction is the number of participation days of a particular unit; the denominator is the aggregate number of participation days of all the units.

The IRS may apply the rental pool rule to a rental guarantee option. The Tax Court supported the IRS position, but an appeals court did not, in the following Example.

Caution

Rental Pool Arrangements

Pool arrangements have been devised to avoid the loss restriction by attempting to increase the days the home is held for a fair rental value. They have not been successful. Courts have ruled that only days on which a home is actually rented count as fair rental days, not days of availability through the rental pool.

EXAMPLE

Razavi owned a condo in Florida and elected to take a rental guarantee option from the resort operator over a three-year period. The annual guaranteed rent was $21,000 plus 40% of rentals over $52,500. In 1987, the resort actually received gross rentals of $48,300 for the unit, but Razavi received $21,000 under the guarantee and claimed a rental loss deduction. The IRS disallowed the loss because it claimed that Razavi personally used the unit for 27 days, exceeding 10% of the 200 days the unit had actually been rented.

Razavi claimed that the 27 days were less than 10% of the 338 days covered by a rental guarantee. That is, the guarantee covered 365 days less 27 days of personal use. The Tax Court disagreed on the grounds that the guarantee was based on a rental period of between 142 days and 179 days and this was far below the 270 rental days needed to support his 27 personal-use days.

The Sixth Circuit allowed the loss. The $21,000 guarantee was a fair rental for the entire year based on rentals of comparable units. Although Razavi probably could have earned more than $21,000 with daily or weekly rentals, such short-term rentals also would have carried added risks and responsibilities that he was able to avoid by choosing the rent guarantee.

9.9 Allocating Expenses of a Residence to Rental Days

When you rent out your home or other dwelling unit *(9.7)* for part of the year at fair market value and also use it personally on some days during the taxable year, expenses are allocated between personal and rental use. By law, deductible rental expenses are limited by this fraction:

$$\frac{\text{Days of fair market rental}}{\text{Total days of rental and personal use}}$$

The days a unit is held out for rent but not actually rented are not counted as rental days. Any day for which the unit is rented at a fair rental price is counted as a rental day for allocation purposes even if in fact you use it for personal purposes on that day.

Filing Tip

Carryover of Disallowed Expenses

If your deductions for operating expenses and depreciation are limited by the personal-use rules, the disallowed amounts may be carried over to the following year.

Mortgage interest and real estate taxes. There is a conflict of opinion between the IRS and some courts over the issue of whether the above fractional formula applies also to interest and taxes. According to the IRS, it does. According to the Tax Court and two federal appeals courts, interest and taxes are allocated on a daily basis. Thus, if a house is rented for 61 days in the year, one-sixth of the deductible interest and taxes ($^{61}/_{365}$) is deducted first from the rental income. This rule allows a larger amount of other expenses to be deducted from rental income than is allowed under the IRS application of the formula; *see* Example 2 on page 230.

Claiming expenses on Schedule E if personal use bars a loss deduction. If your personal use of a residence exceeds the 14-day /10% test in *9.7*, the residence was rented for at least 15 days during the year, and the allocable rental expenses (including depreciation) exceed rental income, you cannot deduct the net loss from other income. The allocable rental expenses are deducted from rental income in a specific order:

1. The rental portion of the following expenses is fully deductible on Schedule E of Form 1040, even if the total exceeds rental income: deductible home mortgage interest *(15.1)*, real estate taxes, deductible casualty and theft losses (Chapter 18), and directly related rental expenses. Directly related

rental expenses are rental expenses not related to the use or maintenance of the residence itself, such as office supplies, rental agency fees, advertising, and depreciation on office equipment used in the rental activity.

2. If there is any rental income remaining after the income is reduced by the expenses in Step 1, the balance is next offset by the rental portion of operating expenses for the residence itself, such as utilities, repairs, and insurance. Do not include depreciation on the rental part of the home in this group.
3. If any rental income remains after Step 2, depreciation on the rental portion of the residence may be deducted from the balance.

Step 1 expenses, as well as the expenses from Steps 2 and 3 that offset rental income, are deducted on the applicable lines of Schedule E. Operating expenses from Step 2 and depreciation from Step 3 that exceed the balance of rental income are carried forward to the next year as rental expenses for the same property. In the next year, the carried-over expenses are deductible only to the extent of rental income from the property for that year, even if your personal use of the residence does *not* exceed the 14-day/10% test in *9.7* for that year.

If you itemize deductions, you claim the *personal-use* portion of deductible mortgage interest, real estate taxes, and casualty and theft losses on Schedule A of Form 1040.

Interest expenses. If you personally use a rental vacation home for more than the greater of 14 days or 10% of the fair market rental days *(9.7)*, the residence may be treated as a qualifying second residence under the mortgage interest rules; *see 15.1.* The interest on a qualifying second home is generally fully deductible and is not subject to disallowance under the passive activity restrictions in Chapter 10. As shown in Step 1 above, the portion of the deductible mortgage interest allocable to the rental portion is deducted from rental income (along with taxes) before other expenses.

EXAMPLES

1. You rent out your vacation home for June and July of 2006 (61 days), receiving rent of $2,000. You also use the home yourself for 61 days during the year. You may deduct expenses only up to the amount of rental income because your personal use exceeds the 14-day/10% rental test (*see 9.7*). Your expenses are mortgage interest of $1,600, real estate taxes of $800, and maintenance and utility costs of $1,200. Depreciation (based on 100% rental use) is $1,500. Assume the vacation home is a qualifying second home *(15.1)*, so that all the interest is deductible under the mortgage interest rules. Under the IRS method, one-half of all the expenses (61 rental days divided by 122 total days of use), including the interest and taxes, are deducted in this order:

Rent income		$2,000
Less: Interest (½ of $1,600)	$ 800	
Taxes (½ of $800)	400	1,200
		$ 800
Less: Maintenance (½ of $1,200)		600
Less: Depreciation (½ of $1,500, or $750,		$ 200
limited to $200 balance of rental income)		$ 200

Under the Tax Court's method of allocating interest and taxes, one-sixth of the interest and taxes (61/365) would be deducted from rental income, rather than one-half as under the IRS method. The balance of interest and taxes is deductible as itemized deductions provided you claim itemized deductions on Schedule A of Form 1040.

Depreciation not deductible because of the rental income limitation may be carried forward to the following year.

If the vacation home were not a qualifying second residence as discussed in *15.1*, the interest would not be deducted with taxes from the $2,000 of rental income, but would be treated as an operating expense and deducted along with the maintenance expenses.

2. The Boltons paid interest and property taxes totaling $3,475 on their vacation home. Maintenance expenses (not including depreciation) totaled $2,693. The Boltons stayed at the home 30 days and rented it for 91 days, receiving rents of $2,700. Because the personal use for 30 days exceeded the 14-day limit, the Boltons could deduct rental expenses only up to the gross rental income of $2,700, reduced by interest and taxes allocable to rental. In figuring the amount of interest and taxes deductible from rents, they divided the number of rental days, or 91, by 365, the number of days in the year.

Court Decision

Allocation of Taxes and Interest

The IRS position on allocating mortgage interest and real estate taxes to rental income is not as favorable as the position adopted by the Tax Court and several appeals courts; *see* Example 2 on the right.

This gave them an allocation of 25%. After subtracting $869 for interest and taxes (25% of $3,475) from rental income, they deducted $1,831 ($2,700 – $869) of maintenance expenses from rental income.

The IRS argued that 75% of the Boltons' interest and tax payments had to be allocated to the rental income. The IRS used an allocation base of 121 days of personal and rental use. Thus, the IRS allocated 75% ($^{91}/_{121}$) of the interest and taxes, or $2,606, to gross rental income of $2,700. This allocation allowed only $94 maintenance expenses to be deducted ($2,700 – $2,606).

The Tax Court sided with the Boltons and an appeals court (the Ninth Circuit) agreed. The IRS method of allocating interest and taxes to rental use is bizarre. Interest and taxes are expenses that accrue ratably over the year and are deductible even if a vacation home is not rented for a single day. Thus, the allocation to rental use should be based on a ratable portion of the annual expense by dividing the number of rental days by the number of days in a year.

The Tenth Circuit appeals court also supports the Tax Court allocation method.

9.10 Rentals Lacking Profit Motive

If you rent a residential unit for 15 days or more and a loss is not barred under the personal-use limitation in *9.7*, the IRS may attempt to disallow a loss by claiming that you had no profit motive in placing the unit up for rent. If the IRS makes such an argument, you must try to prove a profit motive, as discussed in *40.10*. Any loss disallowed on these grounds may not be carried over to a later year.

Planning Reminder

Profit Motive

A profit motive is presumed if you can show a profit for at least three of the last five years you engaged in rental activities. The IRS, however, may ***rebut*** this presumption. For a way to fight this rebuttal, consult *40.10*.

EXAMPLES

1. *(Loss allowed.)* In 1973, Clancy purchased a house and land in a coastal resort area of California. Prior to the purchase, Clancy was told by a renting agent that he could expect reasonable income and considerable appreciation from the property. Previously, he had sold similar property in the same development at a profit. After the purchase, Clancy spent $5,000 to prepare the house for rental, and gave a rental agency the exclusive right to offer the property for rent. The house was available for rent 95% of the time in 1973, and 100% of the time in 1974. However, rentals proved disappointing, totaling only $280 in 1973 and $1,244 in 1974, despite the active efforts of the agency to rent the property. However, the house did appreciate in value and was eventually sold at a profit of $14,000. In 1973 and 1974, Clancy deducted rental expenses of approximately $21,000, which the IRS disallowed. The IRS claimed that the house was not rental property used in a business. Furthermore, as Clancy knew that he could not make a profit from the rentals, he could not be considered to hold the property for the production of income.

   The Tax Court agreed that the expenses were not deductible business expenses. But this did not mean they were not deductible as expenses of income production. Although the rental income from the property was minimal, Clancy acquired and held the property expecting to make a profit on a sale. He had previously sold similar property at a profit and was told to expect considerable rental income as well as appreciation from the new house. Where an owner holds property, as Clancy did here, because he or she believes that it may appreciate in value, such property is held for the production of income. Further evidence that Clancy held the property to make a profit: He rarely used it for personal purposes and an agent actively sought to rent it.

2. *(Loss allowed.)* Nelson bought a condominium, hired a rental agent, and even advertised in the *Wall Street Journal* and *Indianapolis Star*. He also listed the unit for sale. During 1974, he was unable to rent the apartment but deducted expenses and depreciation of over $6,100, which the IRS disallowed. The IRS argued that he did not buy the unit to make a profit but to shelter substantial income from tax. The Tax Court disagreed. Although his efforts to rent were not successful in 1974, he was successful in later years in renting the unit. He rarely visited the apartment other than to initially furnish it. When he went on vacation, he went abroad or to other vacation spots.

3. *(Loss disallowed.)* The Lindows purchased a condominium that they rented out during the prime winter rental season. However, over an eight-year period their expenses consistently exceeded rental income. The Tax Court agreed with the IRS that expenses

in excess of rental income were not deductible. Substantial, repeated losses, even after the initial years of operation, indicated that the operation was not primarily profit-oriented. The rental return during the prime rental season could not return a profit. Even if the condominium were fully rented for the entire prime rental season, annual claimed expenses would exceed rent income. The couple also used the unit for several months and intended to live there on retirement. They did not consider putting the unit up for sale with an agent. Finally, that they had detailed records of income and expenses did not prove a business venture. Records, regardless of how detailed, are insufficient to permit the deduction of what are essentially personal expenses.

IRS may challenge losses claimed on temporary rental before sale. If you are unable to sell your home and must move, it may be advisable to put it up for rent. This way you may be able to deduct maintenance expenses and depreciation on the unit even if it remains vacant. However, the IRS has disallowed loss deductions for rentals preceding a sale on the ground that there was no "profit motive" for the rental under the rules discussed at *40.10.* Courts have allowed loss deductions in certain cases.

EXAMPLES

1. The IRS and Tax Court disallowed a loss deduction for rental expenses under the "profit-motive rules" *(40.10)* where a principal residence was rented for 10 months until it could be sold. According to the Tax Court, the temporary rental did not convert the residence to rental property. Since the sales effort was primary, there was no profit motive for the rental. Thus, no loss could be claimed; rental expenses were deductible only to the extent of rental income. The favorable side of the Tax Court position: Since the residence was not converted to rental property, the owners could under prior law rules defer tax on the gain from the sale by buying a new home. An appeals court reversed the Tax Court and allowed both tax deferral and a loss deduction. The rental loss was allowed since the old home was actually rented for a fair rental price. Furthermore, the owners had moved and could not return to the old home, which was rented almost continuously until sold.
2. In 1976, a couple bought a condo apartment in Pompano Beach, Florida. In 1983, they decided to move and listed the unit for either sale or rent with a local real estate broker. Sale of the unit was difficult because of the saturation of the Florida real estate market. Rental of the unit was also difficult because the condominium association's rules barred the rental of condominium units on a seasonal basis. The unit remained unrented until it was sold in 1986 for a substantial gain. In 1984, the couple deducted a $9,576 rental loss ($7,596 for maintenance expenses and $1,980 for depreciation). The IRS disallowed the deduction as not incurred in a bona fide rental activity. The Tax Court allowed the deduction. The couple made an honest and reasonable effort to rent the condominium. Lack of rental income was caused by a slack rental market and the condominium association rules prohibiting short-term rentals.

Royalty Income and Deductions

9.11 Reporting Royalty Income

Royalties are payment for use of patents or copyrights or for the use and exhaustion of mineral properties. Royalties are taxable as ordinary income and are reported on Schedule E (Form 1040). Depletion deductions relating to the royalties are also reported on Schedule E. If you own an operating oil, gas, or mineral interest, or are a self-employed writer, investor, or artist, you report royalty income, expenses, and depletion on Schedule C.

Planning Reminder

Passive Income Exception

Certain working oil and gas interests are exempt from the passive activity loss restrictions; *see 10.10.*

Examples of Royalty Income

License fees received for use, manufacture, or sale of a patented article.

Renting fees received from patents, copyrights, and depletable assets (such as oil wells).

Authors' royalties including advance royalties if not a loan.

Royalties for musical compositions, works of art, etc.

Proceeds of sale of part of your rights in an artistic composition or book, for example, sale of motion picture or television rights.

Royalties from oil, gas, or other similar interests; *see 9.16*. To have a royalty, you must retain an economic interest in the minerals deposited in the land you have leased to the producer. You usually have a royalty when payments are based on the amount of minerals produced. However, if you are paid regardless of the minerals produced, you have a sale that is taxed as capital gain if the proceeds exceed the basis of the transferred property interest. Bonuses and advance royalties that are paid to you before the production of minerals are taxable as royalty income and are entitled to an allowance for depletion. However, bonuses and advance royalties for gas and oil wells and geothermal deposits are not treated as gross income for purposes of calculating percentage depletion. If the lease is terminated without production and you received a bonus or advance royalty, you report as income previously claimed depletion deductions. You increase the basis of your property by the restored depletion deductions.

9.12 Production Costs of Books and Creative Properties

Freelance authors, artists, and photographers may deduct their costs of producing original works in the years that the expenses are paid or incurred. The uniform capitalization rules that generally apply to property that you produce *(see 40.3)* do not apply.

You qualify for current expense deductions if you are self-employed and you *personally create* literary manuscripts, musical or dance scores, paintings, pictures, sculptures, drawings, cartoons, graphic designs, original print editions, photographs, or photographic negatives or transparencies. However, the exception to the uniform capitalization rules does not apply to, and thus current deductions are not allowed for, expenses relating to motion picture films, videotapes, printing, photographic plates, or similar items.

If you conduct business as an owner-employee of a personal service corporation and you are a qualifying author, artist, or photographer, the corporation may claim current deductions related to your expenses in producing books or other eligible creative works. Substantially all of the corporation's stock must be owned by you and your relatives.

Caution

Hobby Loss Restrictions

Authors and artists with expenses exceeding income may be barred by the IRS from claiming loss deductions; *see 40.10*.

9.13 Deducting the Cost of Patents or Copyrights

If you create an artistic work or invention for which you get a government patent or copyright, you may depreciate your costs over the life of the patent or copyright. Basis for depreciation includes all expenses that you are required to capitalize in connection with creating the work, such as the cost of drawings, experimental models, stationery, and supplies; travel expenses to obtain material for a book; fees to counsel; government charges for patent or copyright; and litigation costs in protecting or perfecting title.

If you purchased the patent or artistic creation, depreciate your cost over the remaining life of the patent or copyright. If your cost for a patent is payable annually as a fixed percentage of the revenue derived from use of the patent, the depreciation deduction equals the royalty paid or incurred for that year. However, if a copyright or patent is acquired in connection with the acquisition of a business, the cost is amortizable over a 15-year period as a Section 197 intangible; *see 42.18*.

If you inherited the patent or rights to an artistic creation, your cost is the fair market value either at the time of death of the person from whom you inherited it *(5.17)* or the alternate valuation date if elected by the executor. You get this cost basis even if the decedent paid nothing for it. Figure your depreciation by dividing the fair market value by the number of years of remaining life.

If your patent or copyright becomes valueless, you may deduct your unrecovered cost or other basis in the year it became worthless.

9.14 Intangible Drilling Costs

Intangible drilling and development costs include wages, fuel, repairs, hauling, and supplies incident to and necessary for the preparation and drilling of wells for the production of oil or gas, and geothermal wells. For wells you are developing in the United States, you can elect to deduct the costs currently as business expenses or treat them as capital expenses subject to depreciation or depletion.

Electing current deductions. The election applies only to costs of drilling and developing items that do not have a salvage value. You must make this election by deducting the expenses on your income tax return for the first tax year in which you pay or incur the costs.

Caution

Drilling Expense Prepayments

Prepayments of drilling expenses are deductible by tax-shelter investors only if the well is "spudded" within 90 days after the close of the taxable year in which the prepayment was made, and the deduction is limited to the original amount of the investment.

Tax-shelter investors may deduct prepayments of drilling expenses only if the well is "spudded" within 90 days after the close of the taxable year in which the prepayment is made. The prepayment must also have a business purpose, not be a deposit, and not materially distort income. The investor's deduction is limited to his or her cash investment in the tax shelter. For purposes of this limitation, an investor's cash investment includes loans that are not secured by his or her shelter interest or the shelter's assets and loans that are not arranged by the organizer or promoter. If the above tests are not met, a deduction may be claimed only as actual drilling services are provided.

Recapture of intangible drilling costs for oil, gas, geothermal, or mineral property. Upon the disposition of oil, gas, geothermal, or other mineral property placed in service after 1986, ordinary income treatment applies to previously claimed deductions for intangible drilling and development costs for oil, gas, and geothermal wells, and to mineral development and exploration costs. Depletion deductions, discussed in *9.15*, are also generally subject to this ordinary income treatment upon disposition of the property.

For oil, gas, or geothermal property placed in service before 1987, ordinary income treatment applies on the disposition of a working or operating interest to the extent that intangible drilling and development cost deductions exceeded what would have been allowed if the costs had been deducted through cost depletion. Recapture for geothermal property applies only to wells commenced after September 30, 1978.

AMT and intangible drilling costs. If you are an independent oil or gas producer or royalty owner, intangible drilling costs for oil and gas production are not treated as tax preference items for purposes of alternative minimum tax (AMT). However, the reduction in your AMT income from not treating intangible drilling costs as a tax preference is limited. The reduction may not exceed 40% of your AMT income, figured as if excess intangible drilling costs were still a tax preference item and without regard to any AMT net operating loss deduction; *see* the instructions to Form 6251.

9.15 Depletion Deduction

Filing Tip

No AMT Adjustment

As an independent oil or gas producer, or royalty owner, you do not have to treat a portion of your depletion deduction as a preference item or adjustment for AMT purposes; *see* Chapter 23.

Properties subject to depletion deductions are mines, oil and gas wells, timber, and exhaustible natural deposits.

Two methods of computing depletion are: (1) cost depletion and (2) percentage depletion. If you are allowed to compute under either method, you must use the one that produces the *larger* deduction. In most cases, this will be percentage depletion. For timber, you must use cost depletion.

Cost depletion. The cost depletion of minerals is computed as follows: (1) divide the total number of units (such as tons or barrels) remaining in the deposit to be mined into the adjusted basis of the property; and (2) multiply the unit rate found in Step 1 by the number of units for which payment is received during the taxable year if you are on the cash basis, or by the number of units sold if you are on the accrual basis.

Adjusted basis is the original cost of the property, less depletion allowed, whether computed under the percentage or cost depletion method. It does not include nonmineral property such as mining equipment. Adjusted basis may not be less than zero.

Timber depletion is based on the cost of timber (or other basis in the owner's hands) and does not include any part of the cost of land. Depletion takes place when standing timber is cut. Depletion must be computed by the cost method, not by the percentage method. However, instead of claiming the cost depletion method, you may elect to treat the cutting of timber as a sale subject to capital gain or loss treatment. For further details, *see* IRS Publication 535.

Percentage depletion. Percentage depletion is based on a certain percentage rate applied to annual gross income derived from the resource. In determining gross income for percentage depletion, do not include any lease bonuses, advance royalties, or any other amount payable without regard to production. A deduction for percentage depletion is allowed even if the basis of the property is already fully recovered by prior depletion deductions. The percentage to be applied depends upon the mineral involved; the range is from 5% up to 22%. For example, the maximum 22% depletion deduction applies to sulphur, uranium, and U.S. deposits of lead, zinc, nickel, mica, and asbestos. A 15% depletion percentage applies to U.S. deposits of gold, silver, copper, iron ore, and shale.

Taxable income limit. For properties other than oil and gas, the percentage depletion deduction *may not exceed* 50% of taxable income from the property computed without the depletion deduction. In computing the 50% limitation, a net operating loss deduction is not deducted from gross income. A 100% taxable income limit applies to oil and gas properties; *see 9.16.*

Oil and gas property. Percentage depletion for oil and gas wells was repealed as of January 1, 1975, except for the following exemptions: (1) small independent producers and royalty owners and (2) for gas well production. *See 9.16* for these oil and gas percentage depletion exemptions.

9.16 Oil and Gas Percentage Depletion

Small independent producers and royalty owners generally are allowed to deduct percentage depletion at a 15% rate for domestic oil and gas production. However, a higher rate may be allowed for qualifying "marginal" production, as discussed below. The deduction is subject to a taxable income limit.

The 15% rate applies to a small producer exemption that equals the gross income from a maximum daily average of 1,000 barrels of oil or 6 million cubic feet of natural gas, or a combination of both. Gross income from the property does not include advance royalties or lease bonuses that are payable without regard to the actual production.

The depletable natural gas quantity depends on an election made annually by independent producers or royalty owners to apply part of their 1,000-barrel-per-day oil limitation to natural gas. The depletable quantity of natural gas is 6,000 cubic feet times the barrels of depletable oil for which an election has been made. The election is made on an original or amended return or on a claim for credit or refund. For example, if your average daily production is 1,200 barrels of oil and 6.2 million cubic feet of natural gas, your maximum depletable limit is 1,000 barrels of oil, which you may split between the oil and gas. You could claim depletion for 500 barrels of oil per day and for 3 million cubic feet of gas per day: 3 million cubic feet of gas is the equivalent of the remaining 500 barrels of oil limit (500 barrels × 6,000 cubic feet depletable gas quantity equals 3 million cubic feet of gas).

Transferees receiving "proven" properties after 1974 and before October 12, 1990, are not allowed percentage depletion unless the transfer was made because of the death of the prior owner, a tax-free transfer to a controlled corporation, a transfer between commonly controlled corporations, or changes in beneficiaries of a trust where the changes are due to births, adoptions, or deaths within a single family.

Ineligible retailers and refiners. The small producer exemption is not allowed to any producer who owns or controls a retail outlet for the sale of oil, natural gas, or petroleum products. A taxpayer is not treated as a retailer where gross sales of oil and gas products are less than $5 million in any one year or if all sales of oil or natural gas products occur outside the United States, and none of the taxpayer's domestic production is exported. Bulk sales of oil or natural gas to industrial or utility customers are not to be treated as retail sales.

The small producer exemption is not allowed to a refiner who refines (directly or through a related person) more than 75,000 barrels of crude oil on any day during the year. The limit is based on average (rather than actual) daily refinery runs for the tax year.

Figuring average daily domestic production. Average daily production is figured by dividing your aggregate production during the taxable year by the number of days in the taxable year. If you hold a partial interest in the production (including a partnership interest), production rate is found by multiplying total production of such property by your income percentage participation in such property.

The production over the entire year is averaged regardless of when production actually occurred. If average daily production for the year exceeds the 1,000-barrel or 6-million-cubic-feet limit, the exemption must be allocated among all the properties in which you have an interest.

Taxable income limits on percentage depletion. The percentage depletion deduction for a small producer or royalty owner may not exceed the *lesser* of (1) 100% of the net income from the property before the depletion allowance or (2) 65% of your net income from all sources computed without regard to the depletion deduction allowed under the small producer's exemption, any net operating loss carryback, and any capital loss carryback.

The above 100% limit was suspended for production from marginal production properties for taxable years starting after 1997 and before 2006; *see* the *e-Supplement* for a possible extension of the suspension for tax years beginning after 2005.

Limitations where family members or related businesses own interests. The daily exemption rate is allocated among members of the same family in proportion to their respective production of oil. Similar allocation is required where business entities are under common control. This affects interests owned by you, your spouse, and minor children; by corporations, estates, and trusts in which 50% of the beneficial interest is owned by the same or related persons; and by a corporation that is a member of the same controlled group.

Depletion for marginal production. Depending on the "reference price" for crude oil (*see* below), independent producers and royalty owners may be allowed a higher depletion rate for *marginal production,* defined as oil or natural gas from "stripper well property" or property producing substantially all "heavy" oil. A stripper well property is one from which average daily production, divided by the number of all producing wells on the property, is 15 or fewer "barrel equivalents." A barrel equivalent is a barrel of oil or 6,000 cubic feet of natural gas.

The 15% rate is increased by 1% for each whole dollar that the "reference price" (the average annual wellhead price as estimated by the IRS) of domestic crude oil for the previous year was below $20 per barrel. However, since the reference price for 2005 exceeded $20 per barrel, the basic 15% rate applies for marginal production in 2006.

Chapter 10

Loss Restrictions: Passive Activities and At-Risk Limits

The passive activity laws were intended to discourage tax-shelter investments, but their reach goes beyond tax shelters to cover all real estate investors and persons who invest in businesses as "silent partners" or who are not involved full time in the business. The passive activity rules prevent an investor from deducting what the law defines as a passive loss from salary, self-employment income, interest, dividends, sales of investment property, or retirement income. Such losses are deductible only from income from other passive activities. Losses disallowed by the passive activity rules are suspended and carried forward to later taxable years and become deductible only when passive income is realized or substantially all of the activity is sold.

Casualty and theft losses are not passive losses unless they are of the type usually occurring in a business, such as shoplifting theft losses.

On your tax return, passive income items and allowable deductible items are reported as regular income and deductions. For example, rental income and allowable deductions are reported on Schedule E. However, before you make these entries, you may have to prepare Form 8582, which identifies your passive income and losses and helps you to determine whether passive loss items are deductible.

At-risk rules generally limit losses for an activity to your cash investment and loans for which you are personally liable, as well as certain nonrecourse financing for real estate investments. *See 10.17.*

Passive Activity Restrictions

At-Risk Rules

10.1 Rental Activities

Rental activities (real estate or personal property) are ***automatically*** treated as passive unless you qualify as a real estate professional *(10.3)* or the rentals are considered by law to be business activity as discussed below. If "automatic" passive activity treatment applies, you may not deduct a rental loss against nonpassive income such as salary or investment income unless you can take advantage of the up-to-$25,000 allowance that applies to rental real estate losses *(10.2)*. Even where rental income or loss is not automatically treated as passive because you qualify as a real estate professional or because the activity is excluded from the rental category and treated as a business (*see* the list below), income or loss will still be "passive" unless you materially participate *(10.6)* in the business activity.

What is a rental activity? Except for activities specifically excluded from the rental category (*see* the list of rentals treated as businesses below), rentals include all activities in which a customer pays for the use of tangible property (real estate or personal property). Such activities include rentals of apartments and commercial office space (whether long- or short-term); long-term rentals of office equipment, automobiles, and/or a vessel under a bareboat charter or a plane under a dry lease (no pilot or captain and no fuel); and net-leased property. A property is under a net lease if the deductions (other than rents and reimbursed amounts) are less than 15% of rental income or where the lessor is guaranteed a specific return or is guaranteed against loss of income.

Planning Reminder

Vacation Home Rentals

If you rent out a vacation unit for an average rental period of seven days or less at a loss, the loss is treated as a business loss deductible from nonpassive income if you meet the material participation tests at *10.6*. If you do not materially participate, the loss is treated as a passive loss, deductible only from passive income. The loss does not qualify for the up-to-$25,000 rental loss allowance discussed in *10.2* because the property is not treated as rental property.

Rentals treated as business activity. Although rental activities are generally treated as "passive," the following six activities are excluded from the category of rental activity and thus losses from the activities are not deductible under the $25,000 rental real estate loss allowance *(10.2)*. The fact that these activities are not treated as rentals does not mean that the passive activity rules are inapplicable. Income or loss from these activities will still be treated as passive income or loss if you fail to meet one of the business material participation tests at *10.6*.

1. **The average period of customer use of the property is seven days or less.** Short-term rentals of vacation units, autos, videocassettes, tuxedos, and hotel and motel rooms are *not* considered rental activities if the average period of customer use is seven days or less. You figure the average period of customer use for the year by dividing the aggregate number of days in all rental periods that end during the tax year by the number of rentals. Each period during which a customer has a continuous or recurring right to use the property is treated as a separate rental.

   A loss from a seven-day-or-less real estate rental activity is *not* eligible for the up-to-$25,000 loss allowance *(10.2)*. Since it is not treated as a real estate rental activity, it may not be included in the election to aggregate rental real estate activities under the real estate professional rules at *10.3*.

EXAMPLE

The Toups purchased a cottage in Callaway Gardens, a vacation resort south of Atlanta, Georgia. The unit was rented for short-term periods of seven days or less during the year to resort guests. The resort's operator was the sole managing and rental agent. Over a three-year period, they deducted net losses of $46,848. Under the seven-days-or-less rule, the activity was not a rental activity, but the IRS disallowed their losses as passive activity losses because they were passive investors who did not materially participate in the activity. The Toups argued that they materially participated, spending more than 300 hours each year preparing an annual budget and cash flow analysis and meeting with other owners to set rental fees and inspect the grounds.

The Tax Court sided with the IRS. The losses were passive because the Toups did not materially participate in the resort operation. They had nothing to do with running the resort on a day-to-day basis. Their activity was merely that of investors.

2. **The average period of customer use of the property is more than seven days but is 30 days or less, and you provide significant personal services.** Personal services include only services performed by individuals and do not include (a) services necessary to permit the lawful use of the property; (b) construction or repair services that extend the useful life of the property for a period substantially longer than the average period of customer

use; and (c) services that are provided with long-term rentals of high-grade commercial or residential real property such as cleaning and maintenance of common areas, routine repairs, trash collection, elevator service, and security guards.

Note: For purposes of Exceptions 1 and 2, if more than one class of property is rented as part of the same activity, average period of customer use is figured separately for each class. The average period of customer use (as explained in Exception 2) is multiplied by the ratio of gross rental income from that class to the total rental income from the activity; *see* the Form 8582 instructions.

3. **Regardless of the average period of customer use, extraordinary personal services are provided so that rental is incidental.** In a rare case, it may be possible to avoid the passive loss disallowance rule by showing that "extraordinary personal services" were provided to tenants who rented the space primarily to obtain these services. IRS regulations give as examples the use by patients of a hospital's room and board facilities, which is incidental to the medical services provided, and the use by students of school dormitories, which is incidental to the teaching services provided.

   In one case, an attorney and her husband, a medical doctor, convinced the Tax Court that they met the "personal services" exception by providing legal support services to law firms who leased office space from their LLC. The attorney supervised three clerical employees in providing legal support services to the tenant firms, which included client intake, answering phones and taking messages, conducting legal research, typing briefs and memoranda, binding briefs, photocopying, taking dictation, express mailing, process serving, filing documents at the courthouse and state capital, maintaining a file room, law library, and conference facilities, and providing coffee service. Her husband provided consulting services to the attorneys, reviewing medical malpractice cases, serving as an expert medical witness, helping the attorneys prepare for accreditation reviews of health-care organizations, and providing quality assurance trainings.

   Before the Tax Court, the tenant firms testified that these support services, particularly the legal research, were unique and that they would not have moved into the LLC's building without them. The Tax Court held that the LLC's leasing activity was not a rental activity under the extraordinary services exception, but the taxpayers still had to prove that they "materially participated" in the leasing/support activities to avoid passive loss disallowance for the rental losses. They did so by showing that at least 500 hours were spent working on the activity; *see 10.6.*

4. **Rental is incidental to a nonrental activity.** A rental of property is excluded from the rental activity category if the property is held mainly for investment or for use in a business. A rental is considered incidental to an investment activity if the principal purpose of holding the property is to realize gain from its appreciation and the gross rental income from the property for the year is less than 2% of the unadjusted basis or fair market value of the property, whichever is less.

   A rental is incidental to a business activity if (1) you own an interest in the business during the year, (2) the rented property was predominately used in that business during the current year or during at least two of the immediately preceding five tax years, and (3) gross rental income from the property is less than 2% of the lower of the unadjusted basis of the property or its fair market value. Under test (2), a rental may qualify for the exception although it is not rented to the related business in the current year, so long as it was used in the business in two or more of the preceding five years.

EXAMPLE

Kyle Gail owns unimproved land with a fair market value of $400,000 and an unadjusted basis of $300,000. He holds it for the principal purpose of realizing gain from its appreciation. To help reduce the cost of holding the land, he leases it to a rancher for grazing purposes at an annual rental of $3,500. The gross rental income of $3,500 is less than 2% of the lower of the fair market value or the unadjusted basis of the land. The rental of the land is not a rental activity.

5. **Providing property to a partnership or S corporation that is not engaged in rentals.** If you own an interest in a partnership or S corporation and you contributed property to it as an owner, the contributed property is not considered a rental activity. For example, if as a partner you contribute property to a partnership, your distributive share of partnership income will not be considered as income from a rental activity. However, this exception will not apply if the partnership is engaged in a rental activity.

6. **The property is generally allowed for the non-exclusive use of customers during fixed business hours, such as operating a golf course.** The customers are treated as licensees, not lessees.

Planning Reminder

Rental of Personal Residence

Renting a personal residence is not treated as a passive rental activity if you personally use the home for more than the greater of (1) 14 days or (2) 10% of the days the home is rented for a fair market rental amount; *see 9.7.* On Schedule E, you may claim a full deduction for the rental portion of real estate taxes and mortgage interest, assuming the home is a principal residence or qualifying second home under the mortgage interest rules *(15.1).*

See 9.9 for limitations on deductions of other rental expenses.

Grouping rental and nonrental business activities. Where you conduct rental as well as nonrental business activities, you may not group a rental activity with a nonrental activity, unless they form an appropriate economic unit and one of the activities is considered insubstantial in relation to the other. No guidelines are provided for determining what is "substantial" or "insubstantial."

Under an exception, a rental of property to a business may be grouped together with the business, although one activity is not insubstantial to the other, provided each business owner has the same proportionate ownership in the rental activity and the activities are an appropriate economic unit.

Real property rentals and personal property rentals. An activity involving the rental of realty and one involving the rental of personal property may not be treated as a single activity, unless the personal property is provided in connection with the real property or the realty is provided in connection with the personal property.

10.2 Rental Real Estate Loss Allowance of up to $25,000

If you are not a real estate professional *(10.3)* but you actively participate by performing some management role in a real estate rental venture, you may deduct up to $25,000 of a real estate rental loss against your regular, nonpassive income such as wages. The allowance is phased out if your modified adjusted gross income (MAGI) is between $100,000 and $150,000. You generally take the allowance into account on Schedule E but Form 8582 is sometimes required; *see 10.12.* If you are married filing separately, you are not eligible for the special loss allowance unless you lived apart for the entire year, and in that case, the allowance is limited to $12,500; *see* below.

The allowance applies only to real estate rentals not excluded from the rental category by the rules at *10.1.* For example, short-term vacation home rentals averaging seven days or less do not qualify for the allowance. The allowance applies only to real estate rentals, not to any rentals of equipment or other personal property.

A trust may not qualify for the $25,000 allowance. Thus, you may not circumvent the $25,000 ceiling or multiply the number of $25,000 allowances by transferring rental real properties to one or more trusts. However, an estate may qualify for the allowance if the decedent actively participated in the operation. The estate is treated as an active participant for two years following the death of the owner.

Married filing separately. If you file separately and at any time during the taxable year live with your spouse, you may not claim the allowance. If you are married but live apart from your spouse for the entire year and file a separate return, the $25,000 allowance and the adjusted gross income phase-out range are reduced by 50%. Thus, the maximum allowance on your separate return is $12,500 and this amount is phased out by 50% of MAGI over $50,000. Therefore, if your MAGI exceeds $75,000, no allowance is allowed.

Active participation test must be met. To qualify for the allowance, you must meet an *active participation test.* Having an agent manage your property does not prevent you from meeting the test, but you must show that you or your spouse participates in management decisions, such as selecting tenants, setting rental terms, and reviewing expenses. The IRS may not recognize your activity as meeting the test if you merely ratify your manager's decisions. You (together with your spouse) must also have at least a 10% interest in the property. Limited partners are not considered active participants and do not qualify for the allowance.

If a decedent actively participated in property held by an estate, the estate is deemed to actively participate for the two years following the death of the taxpayer.

EXAMPLES

1. You live in NewYork and own a condominium in Florida that you rent through an agent. You set the rental terms and give final approval to any rental arrangement. You also have final approval over any repairs ordered by the agent. You are an active participant and may claim the $25,000 rental allowance.
2. A married couple who owned a time-share interest in an ocean-front condominium rented the condo during their allotted period to vacationers. They claimed a rental loss that the IRS held did not qualify for the up-to-$25,000 allowance. Since the average rental period for their unit was seven days or less, the rentals were excluded from the category of rental activity; *see 10.1.*

Figuring the $25,000 allowance. First match income and loss from all of your rental real estate activities in which you actively participate. A net loss from these activities is then applied to net passive income (if any) from other activities to determine the $25,000 allowance. Gains from pre-1987 installment sales are passive income if the sold property was from an activity that would have been considered passive had the passive activity rules been in effect before 1987. If you rent out a personal residence, rental income or loss may be exempt from the passive activity rules; *see* the Planning Reminder on page 234. The allowance may not be used against carryover losses from prior taxable years when you were not an active participant.

EXAMPLE

David Chung is single and for 2006 has a $90,000 salary, $15,000 income from a limited partnership, and a $26,000 loss from rental real estate in which he actively participated. The $26,000 loss is first reduced by the $15,000 of passive income from the partnership. Since he actively participated in the rental real estate activities, the remaining balance of the $11,000 rental loss can be deducted from his nonpassive salary income. David's loss allowance is not subject to phaseout *(see below)* because his modified adjusted gross income (MAGI) is under $100,000. The partnership income and rental loss, which are passive, are disregarded in figuring MAGI.

Phaseout of the allowance. The maximum loss allowance of $25,000 ($12,500 if married filing separately and living apart for the entire year) is reduced by 50 cents for every dollar of modified adjusted gross income (MAGI) over $100,000 (or $50,000 if married filing separately). For purposes of the allowance phaseout, MAGI is adjusted gross income shown on your return, but you should disregard:

- Any passive activity income or loss.
- Any loss allowed under *10.3* for real estate professionals.
- Taxable Social Security and railroad retirement payments (Chapter 34). For example, if your adjusted gross income on Form 1040 is $90,000, and that includes $5,000 of taxable Social Security benefits, your modified adjusted gross income is $85,000.
- Deductible IRA contributions (Chapter 8).
- The deduction on Form 1040 for one-half of self-employment tax liability (Chapter 45).
- Deductible student loan interest (Chapter 33).
- Overall loss from a publicly traded partnership (*see* instructions to Form 8582).
- Excluded interest on U.S. Savings Bonds used for paying tuition in the year the bonds are redeemed. If you are allowed to exclude the interest from income for regular tax purposes (Chapter 33), the interest must still be included for purposes of the allowance phaseout.
- Employer-provided adoption assistance that is a tax-free fringe benefit (Chapter 3). The assistance must be included in MAGI for purposes of applying the allowance phase-out rule.

A rental loss that is carried over because it exceeds the allowance may be deductible in a later year if you continue to meet the active participation rule.

EXAMPLES

1. In 2006, Liz Blake had $120,000 in salary, $5,000 of partnership income from a limited partnership, and a $31,000 loss from a rental building in which she actively participates. She may deduct only $15,000 of the rental loss. The remaining $11,000 must be carried over to 2007. The $5,000 limited partnership income and the $31,000 rental loss are disregarded in figuring MAGI because they are passive. Her deduction and carryover are computed as follows:

Modified adjusted gross income	$120,000
Less: amount not subject to phaseout	$100,000
Amount subject to phaseout	$ 20,000
Phase-out percentage	50%
Portion of allowance phased out	$ 10,000
Maximum rental allowance offset	$ 25,000
Less: Amount phased out	$ 10,000
Deductible rental loss allowance offset in 2006	$ 15,000
Passive loss from rental real estate	$ 31,000
Less: Passive income from partnership	$ 5,000

Filing Tip

Rental Allowance Based on Income

The rental loss allowance is phased out when your modified adjusted gross income is over $100,000. For every dollar of income over $100,000, the loss allowance is reduced by 50 cents. When your modified adjusted gross income reaches $150,000, the allowance is completely phased out. An explanation of modified adjusted gross income and an example of how the phaseout works is under the heading "Phaseout of the allowance" on this page.

If modified AGI is–	Loss allowance is–
Up to $100,000	$25,000
110,000	20,000
120,000	15,000
130,000	10,000
140,000	5,000
150,000 or more	0

Planning Reminder

Proving Management Activities

To take advantage of the $25,000 loan allowance, make sure you have proof of active management, such as approving leases and repairs.

Passive activity loss	$ 26,000
Less: Deductible rental loss allowance in 2006	$ 15,000
Carryover loss to 2007	$ 11,000

2. In 2007, Liz's modified adjusted gross income is below the phase-out range and she continues to actively participate in the rental building, which incurred a loss of $5,000. Under the allowance, she may deduct a rental loss of $16,000 (the current loss plus the carryover loss).

Real estate allowance for tax credits. On Form 8582-CR, a deduction equivalent of up to $25,000 may allow a credit that otherwise would be disallowed. You must meet the active participation test in the year the credit arose. The $25,000 allowance is generally subject to the regular MAGI phase-out rule.

To claim low-income housing and rehabilitation credits, you need not meet the active participation test. Furthermore, for rehabilitation credits and credits for low-income housing property placed in service before 1990, the phaseout for the $25,000 allowance starts at MAGI of $200,000 ($100,000 if married filing separately and living apart the entire year); thus, the deduction equivalent is completely disallowed when MAGI reaches $250,000. The phaseout is figured on Form 8582-CR. There is no MAGI phaseout for low-income housing property placed in service after 1989, unless you have a pass-through interest in a partnership or S corporation that you acquired before 1990.

The *deduction equivalent* of a credit is the amount which, if allowed as a deduction, would reduce your tax by an amount equal to the credit. For example, a tax credit of $1,000 for a taxpayer in the 25% bracket equals a deduction of $4,000 and would come within the $25,000 allowance provided you actively participated. In the 25% bracket, the equivalent of a $25,000 deduction is a tax credit of $6,250 ($25,000 × 25%). Thus, if you have a rehabilitation credit of $7,000 and you are in the 25% bracket, the $25,000 allowance may allow you to claim $6,250 of the credit, while the balance of the credit would be carried forward to the following year.

If in one year you have both losses and tax credits, the $25,000 allowance applies first to the losses, then to tax credits from rental real estate with active participation, then to tax credits for rehabilitation or low-income housing placed in service before 1990, and finally to tax credits for low-income housing placed in service after 1989.

The allowance and net operating losses. If losses are allowed by the $25,000 allowance but your nonpassive income and other income are less than the loss, the balance of the loss may be treated as a net operating loss and may be carried back and forward; *see 40.18* for further details.

Planning Reminder

Tax Break for Real Estate Professionals

Proving professional status and material participation allows you to avoid passive loss limitations. You may improve your ability to meet the material participation tests in *10.6* by aggregating your rental real estate activities. However, you may not want to aggregate activities if you have passive losses from non–real estate activities and have rental income from an operation that, if treated as passive income, could be offset by the losses.

Also be aware that if you elect to group all of your rental real estate activities as one activity and later sell one of the rental properties, you will probably be unable to deduct suspended losses from that property because of the rule that requires "substantially all" of your interest in an activity (here, the combined activity) to be disposed of in order to deduct suspended losses; *see 10.13*.

10.3 Real Estate Professionals

Real estate rental activities are automatically passive *(10.1)* for all taxpayers except qualifying real estate professionals. You qualify as a real estate professional if you meet both parts of Test 1 below. If you qualify, any rental real estate activity in which you materially participate (Test 2) is *not* a passive activity. Income or loss from the rental real estate is reported as nonpassive on Schedule E (Form 1040).

Test 1: Qualifying as a real estate professional. You must meet both of the following two activity tests for the tax year:

1. More than 50% of your personal services in all of your businesses must be performed in real property businesses in which you materially participate *(10.6)*. For this purpose, a real property business means any real property development, redevelopment, construction, reconstruction, acquisition, conversion, rental operation, management, leasing, or brokerage trade or business. Real estate financing is not included. Personal services performed as an employee are *not* treated as performed in a real estate business unless you are considered a "more than 5% owner" in the employer. That is, you must own more than 5% of the outstanding stock or more than 5% of total combined voting powers of all stock issued by the corporation. In a noncorporate employer such as a partnership, you must own more than a 5% capital or profit interest.
2. More than 750 hours of your services are in real property businesses in which you materially participate *(10.6)*.

For purposes of determining hours of material participation under (1) and (2) above, each interest in rental real estate property is treated as a separate activity unless you elect to treat all of your interests as one rental activity as discussed below. If, under the rules in *10.1*, you group a rental real estate activity with a business activity, that rental activity is not treated as rental real estate for purposes of the real estate professional rules.

Attorneys who specialize in real estate practice while participating in a rental business may not treat the legal practice as material participation for purposes of qualifying as real estate professionals.

For a married couple filing jointly, both the "50% of services test" and the "750 hours test" must be met by one of the spouses individually, without regard to the other spouse's services.

A closely held C corporation qualifies under the real estate professional rules if in a taxable year more than 50% of the gross receipts of the corporation are from a real property business in which the corporation materially participates under the rules at *10.15*.

Test 2: Rental real estate activity material participation. If you qualify as a real estate professional under Test 1 above, you must still show that you materially participate *(10.6)* in your rental real estate activity(ies) to avoid passive activity treatment. If you have more than one rental real estate activity and elect to aggregate (*see* below), total participation in all of the activities is combined in applying the material participation tests in *10.6*. If an election to aggregate has not been made, material participation must be determined separately for each rental property.

Election to aggregate rental real estate activities. If in a prior year rental real estate activities were treated separately, you may elect to aggregate activities for any year you qualify as a real estate professional by attaching a statement to your original tax return for that year. The statement must contain a declaration that you are a qualifying real estate professional and are treating all of your rental real estate activities as a single activity under Internal Revenue Code Section 469(c)(7)(A). The election is binding for all future years in which you qualify as a real estate professional, even if there are intervening years in which you do not qualify. In the nonqualifying years, the election has no effect. You may not revoke the election in a later year unless there has been a material change in circumstances that you explain in a statement attached to your original return for the year of revocation. That the election no longer gives you a tax advantage is not a basis for a revocation.

EXAMPLE

Kosonen owned seven rental properties. In 1994, he worked on all his properties a total of 877 hours, which qualified him as a real estate professional. But he could not meet the material participation test for each of the individual properties. If he could aggregate the activities, the material participation test would be met for the combined activity, allowing him to deduct his net rental losses against nonpassive income.

On his 1994 return, he reported the losses from all the activities as an aggregate deduction and treated it as nonpassive. The IRS disallowed the deduction because he had not made a specific election to aggregate. Kosonen argued that by claiming on his return the total of his losses, he had put the IRS on notice that he was aggregating his rental activities.

The Tax Court disagreed. A specific election is required to put the IRS on notice that a taxpayer is a qualifying real estate professional making the election to aggregate rental activities. Reporting the net losses on his return as an aggregate active (nonpassive) loss was not enough because Kosonen could also have reported his net losses as active if he had materially participated in each of the seven activities and had not elected to aggregate.

If the election to aggregate is made and there is net income for the aggregated activity, the income may be offset by prior year suspended losses from any of the aggregated rental real estate activities regardless of which of the rental activities produced the income.

Rental loss allowance may apply to nonqualifying rental activity. A real estate professional may also be able to claim all or part of the $25,000 rental loss allowance *(10.2)*. For example, you are a real estate professional and meet the material participation test for one rental real estate activity but not for another and do not elect to aggregate. Losses from the nonqualifying activity qualify for the rental allowance. Furthermore, suspended prior year losses from the qualifying activity may also be deductible under the rental loss allowance, as illustrated in the following Example.

Caution

Consistent Treatment Required

Once you treat activities separately or group them together as a single activity, the IRS generally requires you to continue the same treatment in later taxable years. You can regroup activities only if the original treatment was "clearly inappropriate" or has become clearly inappropriate because of a material change in circumstances.

EXAMPLE

Jane Morton owns a rental building in Manhattan and a rental building in Newark. In 2006, she qualifies as a real estate professional. She does not elect to treat the two buildings as one activity. She materially participates in the operations of the Manhattan building, which has $100,000 of disallowed passive losses from prior years and a $20,000 loss for 2006. She does not materially participate in the operation of the Newark building, which has $40,000 of rental income for 2006. Jane also has $50,000 of income from other nonpassive sources.

The $20,000 loss from the Manhattan building is treated as nonpassive and offsets $20,000 of the $50,000 nonpassive income from other sources.

Jane can also use $40,000 of the $100,000 prior year suspended losses from the Manhattan building to offset the $40,000 of passive income from the Newark building in 2006. Of the $60,000 remaining suspended loss, $25,000 may be deducted under the rental loss allowance provided Jane's MAGI is under $100,000, the phase-out threshold for the allowance *(10.2)*.

The rental loss allowance is deducted from the $30,000 of remaining nonpassive income, leaving Jane with $5,000 of nonpassive income for 2006. The balance of suspended losses of $35,000 ($60,000 – $25,000 rental allowance) may be used in 2007 to offset income from the Newark building or passive income from other sources.

Interests in S corporations and partnerships. Your interest in rental real estate held by a partnership or an S corporation is treated as a single interest in rental real estate if the entity grouped its rental real estate as one rental activity. If not, each rental real estate activity of the entity is treated as a separate interest in rental real estate. However, you may elect to treat all interests in rental real estate, including the rental real estate interests held by an S corporation or partnership, as a single rental real estate activity.

If you hold a 50% or greater interest in the capital, income, gain, loss, deduction, or credit in a partnership or S corporation for the taxable year, each interest in rental real estate held by the entity is treated as a separate interest in rental real estate, regardless of the entity's grouping of activities. However, you may elect to treat all interests in rental real estate, including your share of the rental real estate interests held by the entities, as a single rental real estate activity.

Limited partners. Generally, a person who has a limited partnership interest in rental real estate must establish material participation by participating for more than 500 hours during the year or meeting Test 5 or Test 6 at *10.6*. This material participation rule also generally applies if an election is made to aggregate limited partnership interests in rental real estate with other rental real estate interests. However, these more stringent rules may be avoided if the election to aggregate is made and less than 10% of the gross rental income for the taxable year from all rental real estate activities is attributed to limited partnership interests. In such a case, you may make the election to aggregate all rental real estate activities and determine material participation under any of the seven tests at *10.6*.

10.4 Participation May Avoid Passive Loss Restrictions

To avoid passive activity treatment of income and loss from a business investment, you must show material participation in that activity. The word "activity" does not necessarily relate to one specific business. If you invest in several businesses, you may be able to treat all or some of those activities as one activity or treat each separately.

Determining aggregate or separate treatment for your activities is discussed at *10.5* and material participation tests are discussed at *10.6*.

For a rental activity, material participation tests apply only if you are trying to qualify for the passive activity exception for real estate professionals at *10.3*. For other rental real estate operators or investors, an "active" participation test that requires only certain management duties may allow you to deduct rental losses of up to $25,000; see *10.2*.

10.5 Classifying Business Activities as One or Several

If you are in more than one activity, determining aggregate or separate treatment is important for:

Deducting suspended losses when you dispose of an activity. If the activity is considered separate from the others, you may deduct a suspended loss incurred from that activity when you dispose of it. If it is not separate from the others, the suspended loss is deductible only if you dispose of substantially all of your investment; *see 10.13.*

Applying the material participation rules of *10.6*. If activities are separate and apart from each other, the material participation tests are applied to each activity separately. If the activities are aggregated as one activity, material participation in one activity applies to all.

Determining if you meet the 10% interest requirement for active participation under the rules discussed at *10.2.*

Grouping activities together. You may use any reasonable method under the facts and circumstances of your situation to determine if several business activities should be grouped together or treated separately. To be grouped together, the IRS says that the activities should be "an appropriate economic unit" for measuring gain or loss. For making this determination, the IRS sets these general guidelines: (1) similarities and differences in types of business; (2) the extent of common control; (3) geographic location; (4) the extent of common ownership; and (5) interdependencies among the activities. Interdependency is measured by the extent to which several business activities buy or sell among themselves, use the same products or services, have the same customers and employees, or use a single set of books and records.

The IRS will not require that all five factors be present for grouping for multiple activities.

Rental activities. Rental activities may not be grouped with business activities unless one of the exceptions discussed at *10.1* applies.

EXAMPLE

Lance Jones has a significant interest in a bakery and a movie theater at a shopping mall in Baltimore and in a bakery and a movie theater in Philadelphia. The IRS does not explain what constitutes a significant interest. In grouping his activities into appropriate economic units based on the relevant facts and circumstances, Jones could: (1) group the theaters and bakeries into a single activity; (2) place the two theaters into one group and the bakeries into a second group; (3) put his Baltimore businesses into one group and his Philadelphia businesses in another group; or (4) treat the two bakeries and two movie theaters as four separate activities.

Once he chooses a grouping, he must consistently use that grouping for all future years unless a material change makes the grouping inappropriate. His decision is also subject to IRS review and, if questioned, he must show the factual basis for his grouping.

IRS may regroup activities. The IRS may regroup your activities if your grouping does not reflect one or more appropriate economic units and a primary purpose of the grouping is to circumvent the passive loss rules.

EXAMPLE

Five doctors operate separate medical practices and also invest in tax shelters that generate passive losses. They form a partnership to operate X-ray equipment. In exchange for the equipment contributed to the partnership, each doctor receives limited partnership interests. The partnership is managed by a general partner selected by the doctors. Partnership services are provided to the doctors in proportion to their interests in the partnership and service fees are set at a level to offset the income generated by the partnership against individual passive losses. Under these facts, the IRS will not allow the medical practices and the partnership to be treated as separate activities as this would circumvent the passive loss limitations by generating passive income from the partnership to offset the tax-shelter losses. The IRS will require each doctor to treat his or her medical practice and interests in the partnership as a single activity.

Partnerships and S corporations. A partnership or S corporation must group its activities under the facts and circumstances test. Once a partnership or S corporation determines its activities, the partners or shareholders are bound by that decision and may not regroup them. The partners and shareholders then apply the facts and circumstances test to combine the partnership or S corporation activities with, or separate them from, their other activities.

Special rule for certain limited partners and limited entrepreneurs. A limited entrepreneur is a person with an ownership interest who does not actively participate in management. A limited entrepreneur or limited partner in films, videotapes, farming, oil and gas, or the renting of depreciable property generally may combine each such activity only with another of such activities in the same type of business, and only if he or she is a limited entrepreneur or partner in both. Grouping of such activities with other activities in the same type of business in which he or she is not a limited partner or entrepreneur is allowed if the grouping is appropriate under the general facts and circumstances test.

10.6 Material Participation Tests for Business

The IRS has seven tests for determining material participation in a business. Some tests require only a minimum amount of work, such as 500 hours a year, and others only 100 hours. You need to meet only one of the seven tests to qualify as a material participant. If you do, then the income and loss from that business is treated as *nonpassive*.

The tests apply whether you do business as a sole proprietor or in an S corporation or partnership. Losses and credits passed through S corporations and partnerships are subject to passive activity rules.

If you are a limited partner, you are by law not a material participant unless you satisfy certain conditions discussed at *10.11*.

Your tax position towards the IRS participation rules will depend on whether the particular activity produces income or loss. If you have passive activity losses from other activities, you may prefer to have a profitable business activity treated as a passive activity in order to offset the income by the losses from passive activities. On the other hand, if the business activity operates at a loss and you do not have passive income from other sources, you may want to meet the material participation test for that business activity in order to claim current loss deductions. IRS strategy in reviewing your activities would be the opposite. If your return were under audit, an agent would attempt to prevent you from treating income from a business activity as passive. For example, the IRS, by applying Tests 5 and 6, can prevent a retired person from treating post-retirement income from a prior business or profession as passive income to offset passive losses from another activity. If you realize a loss in one passive activity, Test 4 may prevent you from generating passive income by merely reducing your participation in another activity.

Planning Reminder

Proof of Material Participation

Material participation must be determined on an annual basis. Show proof of your participation by keeping an appointment book, calendar, or log of the days and time spent in the operation. If you want to treat contacts by phone as material activity, keep a log of phone calls showing the time and purpose of the calls.

Caution

Overcoming Investor Status

The IRS will not recognize time spent as an investor as "participation" unless you can show you are involved in daily operations or management of the activity. According to the IRS, this requires you to be at the business site on a regular basis. Even if you do appear daily, the IRS may ignore such evidence if there is an on-site manager or you have full-time business obligations at another site. Activity of an investor includes the studying and reviewing of financial reports for your own use that are considered unrelated to management decisions. If you invest in a business that is out of state or a distance from your home, you may also find it difficult to prove material participation.

Material participation results in nonpassive treatment. There are two key terms: material participation and significant participation. If you materially participate by meeting one of the seven IRS tests, your activity is not a passive activity. For example, under Test 1, work for more than 500 hours in an activity is considered material participation. Under Test 4, significant participation is work for more than 100 hours but less than 500 hours at an activity in which you do not otherwise materially participate. The IRS applies a significant participation rule to convert passive activity income into nonpassive income and to convert several significant participation activities into material participation if the total participation in those activities exceeds 500 hours; *see* Test 4.

IRS Tests for Material Participation

If you meet one of the following tests for the year in question, you are considered to have materially participated in that activity, and therefore the activity is considered *nonpassive* for that year. Tests 5 and 6 prevent retired individuals from treating post-retirement income as passive income.

Work by you or your spouse that counts as participation. Any work you do in a business in which you have an ownership interest is treated as "participation." If you are married, work by your spouse in the activity during the tax year is treated, for purposes of Tests 1–6, as participation by you. This is true even if your spouse does not own an interest in the business or if you file separately. However, the following type of work is not treated as participation:

1. Work that is not of a type customarily done by an owner of an activity, if one of the principal reasons for the performance of the work is to avoid the passive loss rules (*see* the Example below).
2. An investor's review of financial statements or analysis that is unrelated to day-to-day management or operation of the activity; *see* the Caution on the left.

EXAMPLE

An attorney owns an interest in a professional football team for which he performs no services. He anticipates a net loss from the football activity and to qualify as a material participant, he hires his wife to work 15 hours a week as an office receptionist for the team. Although a spouse's participation in an activity generally qualifies as participation by both spouses, the receptionist work here does not qualify as participation because (1) it is not the type of work customarily done by an owner of a football team and (2) the attorney hired his spouse to avoid disallowance of a passive loss.

Test 1. You participate in the activity for more than 500 hours during the tax year.
Test 2. Your participation in the activity for the tax year constitutes substantially all of the participation in the activity of all individuals including non-owners for the year.
Test 3. You participate in the activity for more than 100 hours during the tax year, and your participation is at least as great as that of any other person including non-owners for that year.

EXAMPLE

Joan Brown and Pat Collins are partners in a moving van business that they conduct entirely on weekends with the help of two employees. They both work for eight hours each weekend. Although neither partner participates for more than 500 hours (Test 1) and do not meet Test 2, they are both treated as material participants under Test 3 because they each participate for more than 100 hours and no one else participates more.

Test 4. You are active in several enterprises but each activity does not in itself qualify as material participation. However, if you spend more than 100 hours in each activity and the total hours of these more-than-100-hour activities exceeds 500, you are treated as a material participant in each of these activities. This test is referred to as the "significant participation" test.

EXAMPLES

1. Mike Smith is a full-time accountant with ownership interests in a restaurant and shoe store. He works 150 hours in the shoe store and 360 hours in the restaurant. Under the significant participation test (Test 4), Smith is considered a material participant in both activities, as the total hours of both exceed 500.
2. Carl Young invests in five businesses. In activity (a) he works 110 hours; in activity (b), 100 hours; in activity (c), 125 hours; in activity (d), 120 hours; and in activity (e), 140 hours. He does not qualify under the significant participation test (Test 4). Although his total hours in the five activities exceed 500, activity (b) is ignored in the total count because the hours did not exceed 100. The total of the four other activities is 495.
3. Assume that Young worked one hour more for activity (b). It and all of the other activities would be considered as meeting the significant material participation test. The total hours are 596. Assuming that activity (a) totaled 125 hours and activity (b) remained at 100 hours or less, he would meet the test for all of the activities except for activity (b), which did not exceed 100 hours. The total of the four qualified activities is 510 hours.

Test 5. You materially participated in the activity for any five tax years during the 10 tax years preceding the tax year in question. The five tax years do not have to be consecutive. Thus, if you are retired but meet the five-out-of-10-year participation test, you are currently considered a material participant, with the result that net income is treated as nonpassive, rather than passive. If you retired from a personal service profession, an even stricter rule applies; *see* Test 6.

Test 6. In a personal service activity, you materially participated for any three tax years preceding the tax year in question. The three years do not have to be consecutive. Examples of personal services within this test are the professions of health, law, engineering, architecture, accounting, actuarial science, the performing arts, consulting, or any other trade or business in which capital is not a material income-producing factor.

Test 7. Under the facts and circumstances test, you participate in the activity on a regular, continuous, and substantial basis. *According to the IRS, you do not come within this test if you participate less than 100 hours in the activity.*

For limited partner rules, *see 10.11*. For participation rules for personal service and closely held corporations, *see 10.15*.

Caution

Retired Farmers

Retired or disabled farmers are treated as materially participating in a farming activity if they materially participated for five of the eight years preceding their retirement or disability. A surviving spouse is also treated as materially participating in a farming activity if the real property used in the activity meets the estate tax rules for special valuation of farm property passed from a qualified decedent and the surviving spouse actively manages the farm.

10.7 Tax Credits of Passive Activities Limited

You may generally not claim a tax credit from a passive activity unless you report and pay taxes on income from a passive activity. Furthermore, the tax allocated to that income must be at least as much as the credit. If the tax credit exceeds your tax liability on income allocable to passive activities, the excess credit is not allowed. Use Form 8582-CR to figure the allowable credit. Suspended credits are not allowed when property is disposed of. The credits may be used only when passive income is earned.

EXAMPLE

Ben Wall has a $1,000 credit from a passive activity. He does not report income from any passive activity. He may not claim the credit because no part of his tax is attributed to passive activity income. The credit is suspended until he has income from a passive activity and he incurs tax on that income. All or part of the credit may then be claimed to offset the tax. If he disposed of his interest before using a suspended credit, the credit may no longer be claimed but the election to reduce basis, discussed below, could be made.

Credits for real estate activities. As discussed at *10.2*, more favorable tax credit rules apply to real estate activities.

Basis adjustment for suspended credits. If the basis of property was reduced by tax credits, you may elect on Form 8582-CR to add back a suspended credit to the basis when your entire interest in an activity is disposed of. If the property is disposed of in a transaction that is not treated as a fully taxable disposition as discussed at *10.13*, then no basis adjustment is allowed.

EXAMPLE

Mark places in service rehabilitation credit property and claims an allowable credit of $50, which also reduces basis by $50. However, under the passive loss rule, he is prevented from claiming the credit. In a later year, he disposes of his entire interest in the activity, including the property whose basis was reduced. He may elect to increase basis of the property by the amount of the original basis adjustment.

10.8 Determining Passive or Nonpassive Income and Loss

Filing Tip

Portfolio Income Accounting

You cannot deduct passive losses from portfolio income. The tax law broadly defines "portfolio income" to include nonbusiness types of income including interest, dividends, and profits on the sale of investment property.

The purpose of the passive loss rules is to prevent you from deducting passive losses from nonpassive income. Passive losses are losses from business activities in which you do not materially participate *(10.6)* or losses from rental activities that are not deductible under the $25,000 allowance *(10.2)* or which do not qualify you as a real estate professional *(10.3)*. In some cases, as explained in *10.9*, passive income may be recharacterized as nonpassive income.

Where you do not materially participate in a business activity, passive income or loss is determined by matching income and expenses of that activity. Portfolio income (*see* below) earned by the activity or any pay that you earn is not included to determine passive income or loss.

Portfolio income. Portfolio income is nonpassive income and broadly defined as income that is not derived in the ordinary course of business of the activity. Portfolio income includes interest, dividends, annuities, and royalties from property held for investment. However, interest income on loans and investments made in the business of lending money or received on business accounts receivable is generally not treated as portfolio income; *see 10.9* for special recharacterization rules. Similarly, royalties derived from a business of licensing property are not portfolio income to the person who created the property or performed substantial services or incurred substantial costs.

Portfolio income also includes gains from the sale of properties that produce portfolio income or are held for investment.

Expenses allocable to portfolio income, including interest expenses, do not enter into the computation of passive income or loss.

Sale of property used in activity. Gain realized on the sale of property used in the activity is generally treated as passive activity income if at the time of disposition the activity was passive. Under this rule, if you transact an installment sale, the treatment of installment payments depends on your status at the time of the initial sale. If you were not a material participant in the year of sale, installment payments in a later year are treated as passive income, even if you become a material participant in the later year. However, an exception to the year-of-sale status rule applies to certain sales of property formerly used in a passive activity; *see 10.16.*

Installment payments from a pre-1987 installment sale are treated as passive income if the activity would have been considered passive had the passive activity rules been in effect before 1987.

Although gain on the sale of property is generally passive income if the activity is passive at the time of sale, there is an exception that could recharacterize the gain as nonpassive income if the property was formerly used in a nonpassive activity; *see 10.16* for details.

Compensation for personal services is not passive activity income. The term "compensation for personal services" includes only (1) earned income, including certain payments made by a partnership to a partner and representing compensation for the services of the partner; (2) amounts included in gross income involving the transfer of property in exchange for the performance of services; (3) amounts distributed under qualified plans; (4) amounts distributed under retirement, pension, and other arrangements for deferred compensation of services; and (5) Social Security benefits includible in gross income.

Passive activity gross income also does not include (1) income from patent, copyright, or literary, musical, or artistic compositions, if your personal efforts significantly contributed to the creation of the property; (2) income from a qualified low-income housing project; (3) income tax refunds; and (4) payments on a covenant not to compete.

Passive activity deductions. Deductible expenses that offset passive income of an activity must be related to the passive activity, such as real property taxes. The following are not considered passive activity deductions:

Casualty and theft losses if similar losses do not recur regularly in the activity.
Charitable deductions.
Miscellaneous itemized deductions subject to the 2% AGI floor.
State, local, and foreign income taxes.
Carryovers of net operating losses or capital losses.
Expenses clearly and directly allocable to portfolio income.
Loss on the sale of property producing portfolio income.
Loss on the sale of your entire interest in a passive activity to an unrelated party. The loss is allowed in full; *see 10.13.*

Interest deductions. Interest expenses attributable to passive activities are treated as passive activity deductions and are not subject to the investment interest limitations. For example, if you have net passive loss of $100, $40 of which is of interest expense, the entire $100 is a passive loss. $40 of the loss is not subject to the investment interest limitation discussed in *15.10.* Similarly, income and loss from passive activities generally are not treated as investment income or loss in figuring the investment interest limitation.

If you rent out a vacation home that you personally use for more than the greater of 14 days or 10% of the fair market rental days *(9.7)*, you may treat the residence as a qualified second residence under the mortgage interest rules; *see 15.1.* Interest on such a qualifying second home is generally fully deductible, and the deductible interest *(15.1)* is not treated as a passive activity deduction. The rental portion of the interest is deducted on Schedule E of Form 1040 and the personal-use portion on Schedule A if itemized deductions are claimed; *see 9.9.*

Self-charged management fees or interest. For an individual with interests in several business entities, the payment of management fees by one of the entities to another is in effect a payment by the owner to himself. However, if the taxpayer materially participates in the entity providing the management services but not in the entity that pays the fees, the passive loss rules prevent the "self-charged" expense from offsetting the income from the payment. IRS final regulations allow a netting deduction *only* for self-charged interest but not for any other self-charged expense.

EXAMPLE

As an employee of his S corporation, Hillman provided real estate management services to rental real estate partnerships in which he had invested. On his personal return, he reported the management fees as passed-through S corporation income and deducted his allocable share of the fee payments by the partnership. The IRS disallowed the deduction: Since Hillman materially participated in the S corporation but not the partnerships, the fee payments by the partnerships were passive activity expenses that could not be deducted against the S corporation's nonpassive fee income. The fact that IRS regulations allow a deduction for self-charged interest does not mean that other self-charged passive expenses should also be deductible.

The Tax Court agreed with Hillman that there is no difference between interest and other self-charged expenses. The legislative history indicates a Congressional intent to allow deductions for self-charged expenses because they do not result in a net accretion to the taxpayer's wealth.

However, the Fourth Circuit, while sympathetic to Hillman's situation, reversed the Tax Court. Nothing in the tax law allows self-charged expenses to be deducted against nonpassive income. Although there is no reason why management fees should be distinguished from interest, the legislative history on self-charged expenses specifically mentioned only interest as an exception to the general statutory rule. The Congressional Committee reports that gave the IRS discretion to provide a deduction for other self-charged expenses did not limit that discretion. Unless the IRS changes its regulations, relief must come from Congress. The Fourth Circuit noted that while the denial of a deduction in this situation appears harsh, the deduction is not completely lost; the fee payments may be carried forward to later years as a passive expense.

After the Fourth Circuit ruled against him, Hillman went back to the Tax Court and tried an alternative argument in an attempt to deduct the management fees paid by the partnerships. He argued that the fees were nonpassive deductions that could offset the nonpassive income from the S corporation because the payment of the fees, by itself, constituted a separate business distinguishable from the passive rental activities of the partnerships. The Tax Court disagreed. The management fees were incurred in connection with the rental activities and thus were passive deductions. The Tax Court again acknowledged the unfairness of denying a deduction for the "self-charged" fees. Hillman's plight is lamentable, but as the Fourth Circuit ruled, relief can only come from Congress if the IRS does not liberalize its regulation on self-charged expenses.

10.9 Passive Income Recharacterized as Nonpassive Income

There is an advantage in treating income as passive income when you have passive losses that may offset the income. However, the law may prevent you from treating certain income as passive income. The conversion of passive income to nonpassive income is technically called "recharacterization." This may occur when you do not materially participate in the business activity, but are sufficiently active for the IRS to consider your participation as significant. Recharacterization may also occur when you rent property to a business in which you materially participate, rent nondepreciable property, or sell development rental property.

Caution

"Recharacterization" of Passive Income

As discussed at *10.16*, gain on the sale of property used in a passive activity may be recharacterized as nonpassive income if the property was formerly used in a nonpassive activity.

Significant participation. The IRS compares income and losses from all of your activities in which you work more than 100 hours but less than 500 and that are not considered material participation under the law. If you show a net aggregate gain, part of your gain is treated as nonpassive income according to the computation illustrated in the following Example.

EXAMPLE

Carol Warren invests in three business activities—A, B, and C. She does not materially participate in any of the activities during the year but participates in Activity A for 105 hours, in Activity B for 160 hours, and in Activity C for 125 hours. Her net passive income or loss from the three activities is:

	A	B	C	Total
Passive activity gross income	$600	$700	$900	$2,200
Passive activity deductions	(200)	(1,000)	(300)	(1,500)
Net passive activity income	$400	($300)	$600	$700

Carol's passive activity gross income from significant participation passive activities of $2,200 exceeds passive activity deductions of $1,500. A ratable portion of her gross income from significant participation activities with net passive income for the tax year (Activities A and C) is treated as gross income that is not from a passive activity. The ratable portion is figured by dividing:

1. The excess of her passive activity gross income from significant participation over passive activity deductions from such activities (here $700) by
2. The net passive income of only the significant participation passive activities having net passive income (here $1,000). The ratable portion is 70%.

Thus, $280 of gross income from Activity A ($400 × 70%) and $420 of gross income from Activity C ($600 × 70%) is treated as nonpassive gross income. This adjustment prevents $700 from being offset by passive losses from another activity.

Net interest income from passive equity-financed lending. Gross income from "equity-financed lending activity" is treated as nonpassive income to the extent of the lesser of the equity-financed interest income or net passive income. An activity is an "equity-financed lending activity" for a tax year if (1) the activity involves a trade or business of lending money and (2) the average outstanding balance of the liabilities incurred in the activity for the tax year does not exceed 80% of the average outstanding balance of the interest-bearing assets held in the activity.

Incidental rental of property by development activity. Where gains on the sale of rental property are attributable to recent development, passive income treatment may be lost if the sale comes within the following tests: (1) the rental started less than 12 months before the date of disposition; and (2) you materially participated or significantly participated in the performance of services enhancing the value of the property. The 12-month period starts at the completion of the development services that increased the property's value.

Self-rental rule: Renting to your business. If you rent a building to your business, the rental income, normally treated as passive income, may be recharacterized by the IRS as nonpassive income where you also have losses from other rentals. Recharacterization prevents you from deducting the rental losses against the net rental income. Although not specifically written into the law, the recharacterization rules are incorporated in IRS regulations. For the recharacterization rule to apply, you must "materially participate" in the business renting the property; *see* the following Example.

Caution

Property Rented to Nonpassive Activity (Self-Rental Property)

You may not generate passive income by renting property to a business in which you materially participate. *See* "Self-rental rule: Renting to your business" on this page.

EXAMPLES

1. Krukowski, an attorney who operated two businesses through wholly owned C corporations, claimed that the IRS's recharacterization regulations were arbitrary and capricious. He rented personally owned buildings to the corporations, one of which ran a health club and the other the attorney's law firm. He reported net income of $175,149 from the rental to the law firm and a $69,100 net loss from the rental to the health club. He deducted the loss from the income and reported net rental income of $106,049. The IRS disallowed the loss offset by recharacterizing the rental income from the law firm as nonpassive income. Recharacterization could be applied under the regulations because the time spent by the attorney in the law firm was material participation. The attorney had to report rental income of $175,149; the health club rental loss was treated as a "suspended" passive loss.

   Before the Tax Court, the attorney claimed that the recharacterization rule was arbitrary and contrary to the passive loss statute. The Court disagreed. The law authorizes the IRS to write regulations interpreting the law. Further, Congressional committee reports contemplate that the IRS would define nonpassive income in such a way as to prevent a taxpayer from offsetting active business income with passive business losses.

   The Seventh Circuit Court of Appeals affirmed the Tax Court. The IRS was given authority by Congress to enact the self-rental rule as a way of eliminating tax shelters. Two other appeals courts, the First and Fifth Circuits, have also upheld the IRS regulation.

2. Carlos argued that he could avoid the IRS's self-rental rule by grouping together *(10.5)* as a single rental activity two rental properties. He operated a steel company and a restaurant through wholly owned S corporations. He leased one of his personally owned buildings to the steel company and another to the restaurant. He had substantial rental income from the steel company lease but a loss on the restaurant lease because the restaurant did not pay the agreed upon rent. On his tax returns for 1999 and 2000, Carlos grouped both properties together as a single activity and on Schedule E netted the loss from the restaurant rental against the net income from the steel company rental.

Applying the self-rental rule, the IRS required the income from the steel company rental to be reported, while disallowing the losses from the restaurant rental. The income from the steel company rental that would otherwise be treated as passive was recharacterized as nonpassive income since Carlos materially participated in the steel company. After the recharacterization, there was no passive income to be offset by the passive losses from the restaurant rental. The passive losses can be carried forward.

The Tax Court rejected Carlos's argument that his grouping of passive income and loss within a single activity precluded application of the self-rental recharacterization rule. To allow netting in this situation would defeat Congressional intent that a taxpayer not be able to use self-rentals as a means of sheltering nonpassive income from an active business with passive losses.

Rental of property with an insubstantial depreciable basis. This rule prevents you from generating passive rental income with vacant land or land on which a unit is constructed that has a value substantially less than the land. If less than 30% of the unadjusted basis *(5.16)* of rental property is depreciable, and you have net passive income from rentals (taking into account carried-over passive losses from prior years), the net passive income is treated as nonpassive income.

EXAMPLES

1. A limited partnership buys vacant land for $300,000, constructs improvements on the land at a cost of $100,000, and leases the entire property. After the rental period, the partnership sells the property for $600,000, realizing a gain. The unadjusted basis of the depreciable improvements of $100,000 is only 25% of the basis of the property of $400,000. The rent and the gain allocated to the improvements are treated as nonpassive income.
2. Shirley offset a passive rental loss from an investment in a limited partnership, LP, which was a substantial owner of a general partnership, GP, against rental income from an investment in a joint venture, JV. JV had leased to GP land on which GP constructed a shopping center. The IRS held that the rental income from JV was nonpassive rental income within the 30% test and could not be offset by the passive rental loss. The Tax Court agreed and also rejected Shirley's attempt to aggregate her investment activities in JV and LP as one activity. The operations of each group, JV, LP, and GP, were separate and not owned by the same person. She was not the direct owner of any of the units. Further, the aggregation rule does not apply to property falling within the 30% test.

Licensing of intangible property. Your share of royalty income in a partnership, S corporation, estate, or trust is treated as nonpassive income if you invested after the organization created the intangible property, performed substantial services, or incurred substantial costs in the development or marketing of it. *See* Publication 925 for further details.

10.10 Working Interests in Oil and Gas Wells

Working interests are generally not treated as passive activities. This is true whether you hold your interest directly or through an entity, provided your liability is not limited. As long as you have unlimited liability, you need not materially participate in the activity. A working interest is one burdened with the financial risk of developing and operating the property, such as a share in tort liability (for example, uninsured losses from a fire); some responsibility to share in additional costs; responsibility for authorizing expenses; receiving periodic reports about drilling, completion, and expected production; and the possession of voting rights and rights to continue operations if the present operator steps out.

Limited liability. If you hold a working interest through any of the following entities, the entity is considered to limit your liability and you are subject to the passive loss rules: (1) a limited partnership interest in a partnership in which you are not a general partner; (2) stock in a corporation; or (3) an interest in any entity other than a limited partnership or corporation that, under applicable state law, limits the liability of a holder of such interest for all obligations of the entity to a determinable fixed amount.

Working interests are considered on a well-by-well basis. Rights to overriding royalties or production payments, and contract rights to extract or share in oil and gas profits without liability for a share of production costs, are not working interests.

Planning Reminder

Limited Liability for Oil or Gas Well

A working interest in an oil or gas well is exempt from the passive activity restrictions if your liability is not limited. The following forms of loss protection are disregarded and, thus, are not treated as limiting your liability: protection against loss by an indemnification agreement; a stop-loss agreement; insurance; or any similar arrangement or combination of agreements.

10.11 Partnership Rules

If you are a partner, your level of personal participation in partnership activity during the partnership year determines whether your share of income or loss is passive or nonpassive. Generally, limited partners are subject to passive activity treatment, but there are some exceptions. On Schedule K-1 of Form 1065, the partnership will identify each activity it conducts and specify the income, loss, deductions, and credits from each activity.

EXAMPLE

Don Bailey is a general partner of a fiscal year partnership that ends on March 31, 2006. During that fiscal year he was inactive. Since he did not materially participate, his share of partnership income or loss reported in 2006 is passive activity income or loss, even if he becomes active from April 1, 2006, to the end of 2006.

Not treated as passive income are payments for services and certain guaranteed payments made in liquidation of a retiring or deceased partner's interest unless attributed to unrealized receivables and goodwill at a time the partner was passive.

Gain or loss on the disposition of a partnership interest may be attributed to different trade, investment, or rental activities of the partnership. The allocation is made according to a complicated formula included in IRS regulations.

Payments to a retired partner. Gain or loss is treated as passive only to the extent that it would be treated as such at the start of the liquidation of the partner's interest.

Limited partners. A limited partner is generally not considered to be a material participant in a partnership activity, and, thus, treats income or loss as passive, except in these cases:

1. The limited partner participates for more than 500 hours during the tax year; *see* Test 1 in *10.6*.
2. The limited partner materially participated in the partnership during prior years under either Test 5 or Test 6 at *10.6*.
3. The limited partner is also a general partner at all times during the partnership tax year that ends with or within the partner's taxable year and any of the material participation tests *(10.6)* are met.

To determine material participation in rental real estate activities under the special rules for real estate professionals, Test 1 or Test 5 of *10.6* must generally be met, but *see* the exception at *10.3*.

A limited partner is not considered to be an "active participant" and thus does not qualify for the $25,000 rental loss allowance discussed in *10.2*.

Planning Reminder

Publicly Traded Partnerships (PTPs)

A PTP is a partnership whose interests are traded on established securities exchanges or are readily tradable in secondary markets. PTPs that are not treated as corporations for tax purposes are subject to special rules that allow losses to be used only to offset income from the same PTP. *See* the instructions to Form 8582.

10.12 Form 8582

The purpose of Form 8582 is to assemble in one place items of income and expenses from passive activities in order to determine the effect of the passive loss rules on these items. After this determination, income and allowable deductions are reported as regular income and deductions in appropriate schedules attached to your tax return. For example, net profits of a self-employed person who is not active in the business are reported on Schedule C, sales of capital assets of a passive activity are reported on Schedule D, your share of partnership income and allowable deductions is reported on Schedule E, and rental income and allowable deductions are reported on Schedule E.

Schedule D or Form 4797. Gains or losses from the sale of assets from a passive activity or from the sale of a partial interest that is less than "substantially all" of your entire interest in a passive activity are reported on Schedule D or on Form 4797 (sale of business property, *see* Chapter 44). The gain is also entered on Form 8582. Losses must first be entered on Form 8582 to see how much, if any, is allowable under the passive loss restrictions before an amount can be entered as a loss on Schedule D or Form 4797.

A disposition of an insubstantial part of your interest in the activity does not allow a deduction of suspended passive losses from prior years. When you dispose of your *entire* interest in a passive activity to a nonrelated party in a fully taxable transaction, your losses for the year plus prior year suspended losses from the activity are fully deductible. The same rule applies to a partial disposition only if you are disposing of *substantially all* of the activity and you have proof of the current year and prior year suspended losses allocable to the disposed-of portion. You net the gain or loss from the disposition with the net income or loss from current year operations and any prior year suspended passive losses. If the netting gives you an overall gain, you need to file Form 8582 only if you have other passive activities. If you have an overall loss after the netting, you do not file Form 8582.

Schedule E. If you have a net profit from rental property or other passive activity reported on Schedule E and you also have losses from other passive activities, the income reported on Schedule E is also entered on Form 8582. A net loss from rental activities generally must be entered on Form 8582 but Form 8582 is not needed if you qualify for the full $25,000 allowance *(10.2)* for rental real estate losses and meet these tests:

Your only passive activities are rental real estate activities and you have no suspended prior year passive losses from such activities;

You have no credits related to passive activities;

You actively participated in the rental real estate operations;

Your total losses from the rental real estate activities are $25,000 or less ($12,500 or less if married filing separately and you lived apart from your spouse all year);

Your modified adjusted gross income is $100,000 or less ($50,000 or less if married filing separately and you lived apart from your spouse all year); and

You do not own any interest in a rental real estate activity as a limited partner or beneficiary of a trust or estate.

If you have a loss from a passive interest in a partnership, trust, estate, or S corporation, you first determine on Form 8582 whether the loss is deductible on Schedule E.

Schedule F. A passive activity farm loss is entered on Form 8582 to determine the deductible loss. If only part of the loss is allowed, only that portion is claimed on Schedule F. A net profit from passive farm activities is also entered on Form 8582 to offset losses from other passive activities.

Other tax forms. Other forms tied to Form 8582 are Form 4797 (sale of business assets or equipment), Form 4835 (farm rental income), and Form 4952 (investment interest deductions). For further details see Form 8582; also *see* IRS Publication 925 for filled-in sample forms.

10.13 Suspended Losses Allowed on Disposition of Your Interest

Losses and credits that may not be claimed in one year because of the passive activity limitations are suspended and carried forward to later years. The carryover lasts indefinitely, until you have passive income against which to claim the losses and credits. No carryback is allowed. What if you have suspended losses and later materially participate in the business in which the loss was realized? The losses remain as passive losses but may offset nonpassive income of that activity.

Caution

Partial Disposition

To deduct suspended passive losses on a disposition of part of an activity, the part disposed of must constitute substantially all of the activity; *see 10.13.*

EXAMPLE

In 2005, Nick Milo was not a material participant in a business activity and his share of losses was $10,000, which was suspended because he had no passive income. In 2006, he becomes a material participant in the business and his share of income is $1,000. The $1,000 is treated as nonpassive income, and he may apply $1,000 of the suspended loss to offset that income.

Allocation of suspended loss. If your suspended loss is incurred from several activities, you allocate the loss among the activities using the worksheets accompanying Form 8582. The loss is allocated among the activities in proportion to the total loss. If you have net income from significant participation activities (Test 4 at *10.6*), such activities may be treated as one single activity in making the allocation; *see* the instructions to Form 8582.

Disposition of a passive interest. A fully taxable sale of your entire interest to a nonrelated person will allow you to claim suspended deductions from the activity. Worthlessness of a security in a passive activity is treated as a disposition. An abandonment also releases suspended losses.

On a disposition, the suspended losses plus any current year income or loss from the activity are combined with the gain or loss from the disposition; *see* the Examples below and follow the instructions to Form 8582 for reporting the net gain or loss.

Partial disposition. You may for the taxable year in which there is a disposition of *substantially all* of an activity treat the part disposed of as a separate activity. You must show: (1) the amount of prior year suspended deductions and credits allocable to that part of the activity for the taxable year, and (2) the amount of gross income and any other deductions and credits allocable to that part of the activity for the taxable year.

EXAMPLES

1. Jill Stein has a 5% interest in a limited partnership with an adjusted basis of $42,000. In 2006, she sells her interest in the partnership to an unrelated person for $50,000. For 2006, she has a current year loss from the partnership (shown on Schedule K-1) of $3,000. She also has $2,000 of suspended passive losses from prior years that have been carried forward to 2006. Jill's $8,000 gain from the sale of her interest is combined on Form 8582 with the current year loss and suspended losses giving her an overall gain of $3,000, figured as follows:

Sales price	$50,000	
Less: Adjusted basis	$42,000	
Gain	$8,000	
Less: Current year loss	$3,000	
Suspended losses	$2,000	$5,000
Overall gain		$3,000

If Jill has *other* passive activities, the $8,000 gain would be reported as current year income on Form 8582. The $3,000 current year loss and $2,000 suspended losses would also be entered on Form 8582.

If this was Jill's *only* passive activity, she does not have to file Form 8582. The gain from the sale is reported on Schedule D and the current year and suspended losses are reported as nonpassive losses on Schedule E.

2. Assume that Jill's suspended losses from prior years were $10,000 instead of $2,000. She has an overall loss of $5,000 after combining the gain from the sale of $8,000, the current year loss of $3,000, and the suspended losses of $10,000.

Since there is an overall loss after combining the gain and losses, Jill does not file Form 8582. The current year loss plus the suspended losses are reported as nonpassive losses on Schedule E and the gain from the disposition on Schedule D.

3. Assume in Example 1 that Jill sold her interest for $30,000 instead of $50,000. She would have a $12,000 loss on the sale ($42,000 adjusted basis less $30,000 sales price). Combining the loss with the current year loss of $3,000 and the $2,000 of suspended losses, she has an overall loss of $17,000.

Since there is an overall loss, Jill does not file Form 8582. The current year loss plus the suspended losses are reported as nonpassive losses on Schedule E. The $12,000 loss on the sale is reported on Schedule D as a capital loss. Under the regular rules for capital losses, the loss will offset capital gains for 2006 and any excess will be deductible only up to $3,000 *(5.4)*. Assuming the $3,000 limit applies, Jill has a $9,000 capital loss carryover to 2007.

Caution

$3,000 Capital Loss Limit

Capital losses incurred on a disposition of a passive interest are also subject to the general $3,000 loss limitation ($1,500 if married filing separately) discussed at *5.4*.

Gifts. When a passive activity interest is given away, you may not deduct suspended passive losses. The donee's basis in the property is increased by the suspended loss if he or she sells the property at a gain. If a loss is realized by the donee on a sale of the interest, the donee's basis may not exceed fair market value of the gift at the time of the donation.

Death. On the death of an investor in a passive interest, suspended losses are deductible on the decedent's final tax return, to the extent the suspended loss exceeds the amount by which the basis of the interest in the hands of the heir is increased.

EXAMPLE

An owner dies holding an interest in a passive activity with a suspended loss of $8,000. After the owner's death, the heir's stepped-up basis for the property (equal to fair market value) is $6,000 greater than the decedent's basis. On the decedent's final return, $2,000 of the loss is deductible ($8,000 – $6,000).

Installment sales. If you sell your entire interest in a passive activity at a profit on the installment basis, suspended losses are deducted over the installment period in the same ratio as the gain recognized each year bears to the gain remaining to be recognized as of the start of the year. For example, if you realize a gain of $10,000 and report $2,000 of gain each year for five years, in the year of sale you report 20% of your total gain under the installment method, and 20% of your suspended losses are also allowed. In the second year, you report $2,000 of the remaining $8,000 gain and 25% of the remaining losses ($2,000 ÷ $8,000) are allowed.

Filing Tip

Installment Sale of Your Interest

If you sell your passive activity interest at a profit and have suspended losses, you may deduct a percentage of the losses each year during the installment period; *see 10.13*.

10.14 Suspended Tax Credits

If you have tax credits that were barred under the passive activity rules, they may be claimed only in future years when you have tax liability attributable to passive income. However, in the year you dispose of your interest, a special election may be available to decrease your gain by the amount of your suspended credit; *see* below.

Basis election for suspended credits. If you qualify for an investment credit (under transition rules) or a rehabilitation credit, you are required to reduce the basis of the property even if you are unable to claim the credit because of the passive activity rules. If this occurs and you later dispose of your entire interest in the passive activity, including the property whose basis was reduced, your gain will be increased by virtue of the basis reduction although you never benefitted from the credit. To prevent this, you may reduce the taxable gain by electing to increase the pre-transfer basis of the property by the amount of the unused credit. The election is made on Form 8582-CR.

EXAMPLE

Dan Brown places in service rehabilitated credit property qualifying for a $50 credit, but the credit is not allowed under the passive loss rules. However, his basis is still reduced by $50. In a later year, Brown makes a taxable disposition of his entire interest in the activity and in the rehabilitation property. Assuming that no part of the suspended $50 credit has been used, Brown may elect on Form 8582-CR to increase his basis in the property by the unused $50 credit.

10.15 Personal Service and Closely Held Corporations

To prevent avoidance of the passive activity rules through use of corporations, the law imposes restrictions on income and loss offsets in closely held C corporations and personal service corporations.

Unless the material participation tests discussed in this section are met, the activities of a personal service corporation or a closely held corporation are considered passive activities, subject to the restrictions on loss deductions and tax credits. For purposes of these passive activity rules, a closely held C corporation is a corporation in which more than 50% in value of the stock is owned by five or fewer persons during the last half of the tax year.

A personal service corporation is a C corporation the principal activity of which is the performance of personal services by the employee-owners. Personal services are services in the fields of health, law, engineering, architecture, accounting, actuarial sciences, performing arts, or consulting. An employee-owner is any employee who on any day in the tax year owns any stock in the corporation. If an individual owns any stock in a corporation which in turn owns stock in another corporation, the individual is deemed to own a proportionate part of the stock in the other corporation. Further, more than 10% of the corporation's stock by value must be owned by owner- employees for the corporation to be a personal service corporation.

Filing Tip

Stockholder Activity

A stockholder may be treated as materially participating in his company's business; *see* the tests in *10.15*.

Material participation. A personal service corporation or closely held corporation is treated as materially participating in an activity during a tax year *only if* either:

1. One or more stockholders are treated as materially participating in the activity and they directly or indirectly hold in the aggregate more than 50% of the value of the corporation's outstanding shares; *or*
2. The corporation is a closely held corporation and in the 12-month period ending on the last day of the tax year, the corporation had at least one full-time manager, three full-time employees, none of whom own more than 5% of the stock, and business deductions exceeded 15% of gross income from the activity.

A stockholder is treated as materially participating or significantly participating in the activity of a corporation if he or she satisfies one of the seven tests in *10.6* for material participation. For purposes of applying the significant participation test (Test 4 at *10.6*), an activity of a personal service or closely held corporation will be treated as a significant participation activity for a tax year *only if*:

1. The corporation is not treated as materially participating in the activity for the tax year; and

2. One or more individuals, each of whom is treated as significantly participating in the activity directly or indirectly, hold in the aggregate more than 50% of the value of the outstanding stock of the corporation. Furthermore, in applying the seven participation tests, all activities of the corporation are treated as activities in which the individual holds an interest in determining whether the individual participates in an activity of the corporation; and the individual's participation in all activities other than activities of the corporation is disregarded in determining whether his or her participation in an activity of the corporation is treated as material participation under the significant participation test (Test 4 at *10.6*).

Closely held corporation's computation of passive loss. Even if a closely held corporation does not meet the material participation tests above, it still qualifies for a slight break from the passive loss restrictions. A closely held corporation may use passive activity deductions to offset not only passive activity gross income but also *net active income.* Generally, net active income is taxable income from business operations, disregarding passive activity income and expenses, and also disregarding portfolio income and expenses; *see 10.8.* Passive activity losses cannot offset portfolio income.

If a corporation stops being closely held, its passive losses and credits from prior years are not allowable against portfolio income but continue to be allowable only against passive income and net active income.

Tax liability on net active income may be offset by passive activity credits.

10.16 Sales of Property and of Passive Activity Interests

Gain on the sale or disposition of property is generally passive or nonpassive, depending on whether your activity is passive or nonpassive in the year of sale or disposition. Thus, gain on the sale of property used in a rental activity is generally treated as passive income, as is the gain on property used in a nonrental business if you did not materially participate in the business in the year of sale. On the other hand, gain on the sale of property is generally nonpassive if the property was used in a business that you materially participated in during the year of sale. However, exceptions described below may change this treatment.

Where you transact an installment sale, treatment of gain in later years depends on your status in the year of sale. For example, if you were considered a material participant in a business, all gain is treated as nonpassive income, including gain for later installments. If you were in a rental activity or were not a material participant in a nonrental business, the gain is treated as passive income, unless the exceptions in this section apply.

Gain on substantially appreciated property formerly used in nonpassive activity. Even if an activity is passive in the year that you sell substantially appreciated property, gain on the sale is treated as nonpassive unless the property was used in a passive activity for either 20% of its holding period or the entire 24-month period ending on the date of the disposition. Property is substantially appreciated if fair market value exceeds 120% of its adjusted basis.

EXAMPLE

In 1991, Andy Jones buys a building for use in a business in which he materially participates until March 31, 2005. On April 1, 2005, he rents the building. On December 31, 2006, he sells the building for more than 120% of its adjusted basis. Gain from the sale is treated as nonpassive although the building was used in a passive rental activity in the year of the sale. The building was used in a passive rental activity for 21 months before disposition (April 1, 2005, through December 31, 2006). Thus, it was not used in a passive activity for the entire 24-month period ending on the date of the sale. Further, the 21-month period during which the building was used in a passive activity is less than 20% of Jones's holding period of 14 years.

Property used in more than one activity in a 12-month period preceding disposition. You are required to allocate the amount realized on the disposition and the adjusted basis of the property among the activities in which the property was used during a 12-month period preceding the disposition. For purposes of this rule, the term "activity" includes personal use and holding for investment. The allocation may be based on the period for which the property is used in each activity during the 12-month period. However, if during the 12-month period the value of the property does not exceed the lesser of $10,000 or 10% of the value of all property used in the activity at the time of disposition, gain may be allocated to the predominant use.

EXAMPLE

Joe Smith sells a personal computer for $8,000. During the 12-month period that ended on the date of the sale, 70% of Smith's use of the computer was in a passive activity. Immediately before the sale, the fair market value of all property used in the passive activity, including the personal computer, was $200,000. The computer was predominantly used in the passive activity during the 12-month period ending on the date of the sale. The value of the computer, $8,000, did not exceed the lesser of $10,000 or 10% of the $200,000 value of all property used in the activity immediately before the sale. Thus, the amount realized and the adjusted basis are allocated to the passive activity.

Disposition of partnership and S corporation interests. Gain or loss from the disposition of an interest in a partnership and S corporation is generally allocated among the entity's activities in proportion to the amount that the entity would have allocated to the partner or shareholder for each of its activities if the entity had sold its interest in the activities on "applicable valuation date."

Gain is allocated only to appreciated activities. Loss is allocated only to depreciated activities. The entity may select either the beginning of its tax year in which the holder's disposition occurs or the date of the disposition as the applicable valuation date.

Claiming suspended loss on disposition of interest in passive activity. A fully taxable sale of your entire interest or of substantially all of your interest to a nonrelated person will allow you to claim suspended loss deductions from the activity. These rules are fully discussed in *10.13*.

Dealer's sale of property similar to property sold in the ordinary course of business. IRS regulations set down complex tests that determine whether the result of the sale is treated as passive or nonpassive income or loss.

At-Risk Rules

10.17 At-Risk Limits

The at-risk rules prevent investors from claiming losses in excess of their actual tax investment by barring them from including nonrecourse liabilities as part of the tax basis for their interest. Almost all ventures are subject to the at-risk limits. Real estate placed in service after 1986 is subject to the at-risk rules as well, but most real estate nonrecourse financing can qualify for an exception; *see 10.18*.

EXAMPLE

Crystal Parker invests cash of $1,000 in a venture and signs a nonrecourse note for $8,000. In 2006, her share of the venture's loss is $1,200. The at-risk rules limit her deduction to $1,000, the amount of her cash investment; as she is not personally liable on the note, the amount of the liability is not included as part of her basis for loss purposes.

Losses disallowed under the at-risk rules are carried over to the following year; *see 10.21*.

Form 6198. If you have amounts that are not at risk, you must file Form 6198 to figure your deductible loss. A separate form must be filed for each activity. However, if you have an interest in a partnership or S corporation that has more than one investment in any of the following four categories, the IRS currently allows you to aggregate all of the partnership or S corporation activities within each category. For example, all partnership or S corporation films and videotapes may be treated as one activity in determining amounts at risk. The aggregation rules may be changed by the IRS; *see* the instructions to Form 6198.

1. Holding, producing, or distributing motion picture films or videotapes;
2. Exploring for or exploiting oil or gas properties;
3. Exploring for, or exploiting, geothermal deposits (for wells commenced on or after October 1, 1978); *and*
4. Farming. For this purpose, farming is defined as the cultivation of land and the raising or harvesting of any agricultural or horticultural commodity—including raising, shearing, breeding, caring for, or management of animals. Forestry and timber activities are not included, but

Caution

At-Risk Rules Limit Loss Deductions

The purpose of at-risk rules is to keep you from deducting losses from investments in which you have little cash invested and no personal liability for debts.

orchards bearing fruits and nuts are within the definition of farming. Certain activities carried on within the physical boundaries of the farm may not necessarily be treated as farming.

In addition to the previous categories, the law treats as a single activity all leased depreciable business equipment (Section 1245 property) that is placed in service during any year by a partnership or S corporation.

Exempt from the at-risk rules are C corporations which meet active business tests and are not in the equipment leasing business or any business involving master sound recording, films, videotapes, or other artistic, literary, or musical property. For details on the active business tests, as well as a special at-risk exception for equipment leasing activities of closely held corporations, *see* IRS Publication 925.

The at-risk limitation applies only to tax losses produced by expense deductions that are not disallowed by reason of another provision of the law. For example, if a prepaid interest expense is deferred under the prepaid interest limitation *(15.14)*, the interest will not be included in the loss subject to the risk limitation. When the interest accrues and becomes deductible, the expense may be considered within the at-risk provision. Similarly, if a deduction is deferred because of farming syndicate rules, that deduction will enter into the computation of the tax loss subject to the risk limitation only when it becomes deductible under the farming syndicate rules.

Effect of passive loss rules. Where a loss is also subject to the at-risk rules, you apply the at-risk rules first. If the loss is deductible under the at-risk rules, the passive activity rules then apply. On Form 6198 (at risk), you figure the deductible loss allowed as at risk and then carry the loss over to Form 8582 to determine the passive activity loss.

Filing Tip

Form 6198

If you have invested an amount for which you are not at risk, such as a nonrecourse loan, you generally must file Form 6198 to figure a deductible loss. However, nonrecourse financing for real estate that secures the loan is treated as an at-risk investment in most cases; *see 10.18.*

10.18 What Is At Risk?

The following amounts are considered at risk in determining your tax position in a business or investment:

Cash;
Adjusted basis of property that you contribute; and
Borrowed funds for which you are personally liable for repayment.

Personal liability alone does not assure that the borrowed funds are considered at risk. The lender generally must have no interest in the venture other than as a creditor and must not be related to a person (other than the borrower) with an interest in the activity other than that of a creditor. Under final IRS regulations, a lender or person related to the lender is considered to have an interest other than that of a creditor only if the person has a capital interest in the activity or an interest in the net profits of the activity. However, even if the lender has such an interest, a loan after May 3, 2004, for which you are personally liable is treated as at risk if: (1) the loan is secured by real estate used in the activity and (2) the loan, were it nonrecourse, would be qualified nonrecourse financing, as discussed below.

At-risk basis is figured as of the end of the year. Any loss allowed for a year reduces the at-risk amount as of the start of the next year. Therefore, if a loss exceeds your at-risk investment, the excess loss will not be deductible in later years unless you increase your at-risk investment; *see* the Example below and *10.21.*

EXAMPLE

Julie Kahn, an investor, pays a promoter of a book purchase plan $45,000 for a limited partnership interest. The promoter is the general partner. Kahn pays $30,000 cash and gives a note for $15,000 on which she is personally liable. Her amount at risk is $30,000; the $15,000 personal liability note is not counted because it is owed to the general partner.

Qualified nonrecourse financing for real estate considered at risk. Generally, you are not considered at risk for nonrecourse financing, that is, loans for which you are not personally liable, unless the loan is secured by property not used in the activity. However, for real property other than mineral property placed in service after 1986, you may treat nonrecourse financing from unrelated commercial lenders or from government agencies as amounts at risk if the financing is secured by the real estate. This "security" requirement is considered met if in addition to the real estate used in the activity, the financing is also secured by other property valued at less than 10% of the total value of all property securing the financing, or if the other property is incidental to the activity of holding real property. Loans from the seller or promoter do not qualify. Third-party nonrecourse debt from a related lender, other than the seller or promoter, may also be treated as at risk, providing the terms of the loan are commercially reasonable and on substantially the same terms as loans involving unrelated persons.

If you acquired an interest after 1986 in a partnership or S corporation, the above at-risk rules apply to your share of real estate losses, regardless of when the partnership or S corporation placed the property in service.

Pledges of other property. If you pledge personally owned real estate used outside the activity to secure a nonrecourse debt and invest the proceeds in an at-risk activity, the proceeds may be considered part of your at-risk investment. The proceeds included in basis are limited by the fair market value of the property used as collateral (determined as of the date the property is pledged as security) less any prior (or superior) claims to which the collateral is subject.

Partners. A partner is treated as at-risk to the extent that basis in the partnership is increased by the share of partnership income. That partnership income is then used to reduce the partnership's nonrecourse indebtedness will have no effect on a partner's amount at risk. If the partnership makes actual distributions of the income in the taxable year, the amount distributed reduces the partner's amount at risk. A buy-sell agreement, effective at a partner's death or retirement, is not considered for at-risk purposes.

10.19 Amounts Not At Risk

The following may not be treated as part of basis for at-risk purposes in determining your tax position in a business or investment:

Liabilities for which you have no personal liability, except in the case of certain real estate financing; *see 10.18.*

Liabilities for which you have personal liability, but the lender also has a capital or profit-sharing interest in the venture; but *see* the exception at *10.18.*

Recourse liabilities convertible to a nonrecourse basis.

Money borrowed from a relative listed at *5.6* who has an interest in the venture, other than as a creditor, or from a partnership in which you own more than a 10% interest.

Funds borrowed from a person whose recourse is solely your interest in the activity or property used in the activity.

Amounts for which your economic loss is limited by a nonrecourse financing guarantee, stop-loss agreement, or other similar arrangement.

Investments protected by insurance or loss reimbursement agreement between you and another person. If you are personally liable on a mortgage but you separately obtain insurance to compensate you for any mortgage payments, you are at risk only to the extent of the uninsured portion of the personal liability. You may, however, include as at risk any amount of premium paid from your personal assets. Taking out casualty insurance or insurance protecting you against tort liability is not considered within the at-risk provisions, and such insurance does not affect your investment basis.

Caution

Lender Has Interest

Even if you are personally liable for a debt, you may not be considered at risk if the lender has an interest in the activity other than as a creditor; *see 10.18.*

EXAMPLES

1. Some commercial feedlots in livestock feeding operations may reimburse investors against any loss sustained on sales of the livestock above a stated dollar amount per head. Under such "stop-loss" orders, an investor is at risk only to the extent of the portion of his or her capital against which he or she is not entitled to reimbursement. Where a limited partnership makes an agreement with a limited partner that, at the partner's election, his or her partnership interest will be bought at a stated minimum dollar amount (usually less than the investor's original capital contribution), the partner is considered at risk only to the extent of his or her investment exceeding the guaranteed repurchase price.
2. A TV film promoter sold half-hour TV series programs to individual investors. Each investor gave a cash down payment and a note for which he or she was personally liable for the balance. Each investor's note, which was identical in face amount, terms, and maturity date, was payable out of the distribution proceeds from the film. Each investor also bought from the promoter the right to the unpaid balance on another investor's note. The promoter arranged the distribution of the films as a unit and was to apportion the sales proceeds equally among the investors.

The IRS held that each investor is not at risk on the investment evidenced by the note. Upon maturity, each may receive a payment from another investor equal to the one that he or she owes.

3. A gold mine investment offered tax write-offs of four times the cash invested. For $10,000 cash, an investor bought from a foreign mining company a seven-year mineral claim lease to a gold reserve. Under the lease, he could develop and extract all of the gold in the reserve. At the same time, he agreed to spend $40,000 to develop the lease before the end of the year. To fund this commitment, the investor authorized the promoter to sell an option for $30,000 to a third party who was to buy all the gold to be extracted. The $30,000 along with the $10,000 down payment was to be used to develop the reserve. The promoter advised the investor that he could claim a $40,000 deduction for certain development costs.

   The IRS ruled that $30,000 was not deductible because the amount was not "risk capital." The investor got $30,000 by selling an option that could be exercised only if gold were found. If no gold were found, he would be under no obligation to the option holder. The investor's risk position for the $30,000 was substantially the same as if he had borrowed from the option holder on a nonrecourse basis repayable only from his interest in the activity.

   The Tax Court struck down a similar plan on different grounds. Without deciding the question of what was at risk, the court held that the option was only a right of first refusal. Thus, $30,000 was taxable income to the investor in the year of the arranged sale.

4. David Krepp, an investor, purchases cattle from a rancher for $10,000 cash and a $30,000 note payable to the rancher. Krepp is personally liable on the note. In a separate agreement, the rancher agrees to care for the cattle for 6% of Krepp's net profits from the cattle activity. Krepp is considered at risk for $10,000; he may not increase the amount at risk by the $30,000 borrowed from the rancher.

Limited partner's potential cash call. Under the terms of a partnership agreement, limited partners may be required to make additional capital contributions under specified circumstances. Whether such a potential cash call increases the limited partner's at-risk amount has been a matter of dispute.

In one case, the IRS and Tax Court held that a limited partner was not at risk with respect to a partnership note where, under the terms of the partnership agreement, he could be required to make additional capital contributions if the general partners did not pay off the note at maturity. The possibility of such a potential cash call was too uncertain; the partnership might earn profits to pay off the note and even if there were losses, the general partners might not demand additional contributions from the limited partners.

However, a federal appeals court reversed, holding that the limited partner was at risk because his obligation was mandatory and "economic reality" insured that the general partners would insure their rights by requiring the additional capital contribution.

In another case, limited partners relied upon the earlier favorable federal appeals court decision to argue that they were at risk where they could be required by the general partners to make additional cash contributions, but only in order to cover liabilities or expenses that could not be paid out of partnership assets. So long as the partnership was solvent, the limited partners could "elect out" of the call provision. Because of this election, the Tax Court held that the limited partners' obligation was contingent, rather than unavoidable as in the earlier federal appeals court case. Thus, the cash call provision did not increase their at-risk amount.

10.20 At-Risk Investment in Several Activities

If you invest in several activities, each is generally treated separately when applying the at-risk limitation on Form 6198. You generally may not aggregate basis, gains, and losses from the activities for purposes of at-risk limitations. Thus, income from one activity may not be offset by losses from another; the income from one must be reported while the losses from the other may be nondeductible because of at-risk limitations.

However, you may aggregate activities that are part of a business you actively manage. Activities of a business carried on by a partnership or S corporation qualify if 65% or more of losses for the year are allocable to persons who actively participate in management.

The law allows partnerships and S corporations to treat as a single activity all depreciable equipment (Section 1245 property) that is leased or held for lease and placed in service in any tax year. Furthermore, you may aggregate all partnership or S corporation activities within the four categories of films and videotapes, oil and gas properties, geothermal properties, and farms; *see 10.17*.

10.21 Carryover of Disallowed Losses

Filing Tip

Carryover Losses

Losses disallowed by at-risk rules are carried over and may be deductible in a later year.

A loss disallowed in a current year by the at-risk limitation may be carried over and deducted in the next taxable year, provided it does not fall within the at-risk limits or the passive loss limits in that year. The loss is subject to an unlimited carryover period until there is an at-risk basis to support the deduction. This may occur when additional contributions are made to the business or when the activity has income which has not been distributed.

Gain from the disposition of property used in an at-risk activity is treated as income from the activity. In general, the reporting of gain will allow a deduction for losses disallowed in previous years to be claimed in the year of disposition.

10.22 Recapture of Losses Where At Risk Is Less Than Zero

To prevent manipulation of at-risk basis after a loss is claimed, there is a special recapture rule. If the amount at risk in an activity is reduced to below zero because of a distribution or a change in the status of an indebtedness from recourse to nonrecourse, income may be realized to the extent of the negative at-risk amount. The taxable amount may not exceed the amount of losses previously deducted.

The recaptured amount is not treated as income from the activity for purposes of determining whether current or suspended losses are allowable.

The recaptured amount is treated as a deduction allocable to that activity in the following year.

See IRS Publication 925 for further details.

Chapter 11

Other Income

This chapter discusses various types of payments you may receive; some are taxable and others are not taxable. Examples of taxable items include:

- Taxable state tax refunds, which are reported on Line 10 of Form1040.
- Prizes, gambling winnings, and awards, which are reported on Line 21 of Form 1040.
- Cancellations of debt, which are reported on Line 21 of Form 1040.
- Your share of partnership, S corporation, trust, or estate income or loss, which is reported in Schedule E according to Schedule K-1 statements provided you by the entity, and then transferred to Line 17 of Form 1040.

Further reporting details are discussed in this chapter.

Prizes; Lottery and Gambling Winnings

11.1 Prizes and Awards

Prizes and awards are taxable income except for an award or prize that meets *all* these four tests:

1. It is primarily in recognition of religious, charitable, scientific, educational, artistic, literary, or civic achievement.
2. You were selected without any action on your part.
3. You do not have to perform services.
4. You assign the prize or award to a government unit or tax-exempt charitable organization. You must make the assignment before you use or benefit from the award. You may not claim a charitable deduction for the assignment.

Filing Tip

Winnings Paid in Installments

Gambling losses are deductible as miscellaneous deductions up to the amount of your gambling winnings. Lottery winnings paid in installments qualify as such gambling winnings. If you receive lottery winnings in 2006, for instance, you may deduct any gambling losses incurred in 2006 up to the amount of that installment. Lottery winnings paid in installments do not lose their characteristic as gambling winnings.

Prize taxed at fair market value. A prize of merchandise is taxable at fair market value. For example, where a prize of first-class steamship tickets was exchanged for tourist-class tickets for a winner's family, the taxable value of the prize was the price of the tourist tickets. What is the taxable fair market value of an automobile won as a prize? In one case, the Tax Court held that the taxable value was what the recipient could realize on an immediate resale of the car.

Employee achievement awards. The above restrictions on tax-free treatment do not apply to awards from employers for length of service or safety achievement. The rules for such employee awards are at *3.11* and *20.25*.

11.2 Lottery and Sweepstake Winnings

Sweepstake, lottery, and raffle winnings are taxable as "other income" on Line 21 of Form 1040. The cost of tickets is deductible only to the extent you report winnings, and only if you itemize deductions. The deduction is claimed on Schedule A as a miscellaneous deduction that is *not* subject to the 2% adjusted gross income (AGI) floor (Chapter 19). For example, if you buy state lottery tickets and win a 2006 drawing, you may deduct the cost of your losing tickets in 2006 up to the amount of your winnings.

When a minor wins a state lottery and the prize is held by his or her parents as custodians under the Uniform Transfers to Minors Act, the prize is taxed to the minor in the year the prize is won.

Court Decision

Assignment of Future Lottery Payments

Courts have agreed with the IRS that a lump sum received for assigning the rights to future state lottery payments is taxed as ordinary income, not capital gain. The right to receive annual lottery payments is not a capital asset.

Installment payments. If lottery or sweepstakes winnings or casino jackpots are payable in installments, you pay tax only as installments are received. If within 60 days of winning a prize you have an option to choose a discounted lump-sum payment instead of an annuity, and you elect the annuity, you are taxed as the annuity payments are received. Merely having the cash option does not make the present value of the annuity taxable in the year the prize is won.

11.3 Gambling Winnings and Losses

Gambling winnings are taxable. Losses from gambling are deductible only up to the gains from gambling. You may not deduct a net gambling loss even though a particular state says gambling is legal. Nor does it matter that your business is gambling. You may not deduct the loss even if you are a professional gambler.

If you are not a professional gambler, gambling income is included on Form 1040 as "other income" on Line 21. Gambling losses (not exceeding the amount of the gains) are deductible as "miscellaneous deductions" on Schedule A. The losses are *not* subject to the 2% AGI floor (Chapter 19). According to the IRS, professional gamblers who bet only for their own account are not in a business and must deduct losses (up to gains) as itemized deductions. However, the Supreme Court has held that full-time gamblers may deduct losses as business expenses even if they place wagers only for themselves. According to the Supreme Court, in order to be considered engaged in a business, a gambler must prove that he or she gambles full time to earn a livelihood and not merely as a hobby. A professional gambler reports winnings and losses (lost wages and gambling transaction expenses) on Schedule C; the losses are deductible only to extent of the winnings.

To prove your losses in the event your return is questioned, you must retain evidence of loss.

EXAMPLES

1. To appear on *Wheel of Fortune,* Whitten traveled from Chicago to Los Angeles, spending $1,820 for transportation, meals, and lodging. When he won cash prizes of $14,850 plus an automobile, he tried to offset his winnings by the travel costs, claiming they were gambling losses on Schedule A not subject to the 2% AGI floor. The IRS and Tax Court disagreed; travel costs are not like wager or bet losses.
2. Trump Casino in Atlantic City gave Libutti, a high roller at its gaming tables, over $2.5 million in "comps" during a three-year period in which he lost over $8 million. The comps included 10 expensive automobiles, jewelry, European vacations, and tickets to sporting events. Libutti reported the comps as income and then claimed a matching miscellaneous deduction for gambling losses not subject to the 2% floor. The IRS disallowed the deduction, claiming that the comps were not gambling income because they were perks given to stimulate his desire to gamble at Trump's, and not winnings from the success of his wagers.

   The Tax Court disagreed. Libutti would not have received the comps unless he gambled at high stakes in Trump's casino. Although the comps did not directly hinge on the success or failure of his wagers, the comps were sufficiently related to his gambling losses to allow the deduction.

Court Decision

Gambler Not Taxed on Cancelled Gambling Debt

The federal appeals court for the Third Circuit (New Jersey, Pennsylvania, and Delaware) held that the settlement by an Atlantic City casino of a gambler's $3.4 million debt for $500,000 was not taxable. The debt was not enforceable under New Jersey law because the casino did not comply with state regulations on issuance of credit. Furthermore, the gambling chips were not "property" securing the debt; they had no economic value outside the casino.

11.4 Gifts and Inheritances

Gifts and inheritances you *receive* are not taxable. However, distributions taken from an inherited traditional IRA *(8.14),* and distributions from inherited qualified plan accounts such as 401(k) and profit-sharing plan accounts, are taxable, except for amounts attributable to nondeductible contributions made by the deceased account owner.

Income earned from gift or inherited property after you receive it is taxable.

Describing a payment as a gift or inheritance will not necessarily shield it from tax if it is, in fact, a payment for your services. Treatment of gifts to employees is covered at *2.4.*

A sale of an expected inheritance from a living person is taxable as ordinary income.

EXAMPLES

1. An employee is promised by his employer that he will be remembered in his will if he continues to work for him. The employer dies but fails to mention the employee in his will. The employee sues the estate, which settles his claim. The settlement is taxable.
2. A nephew left his uncle a bequest of $200,000. In another clause of the will, the uncle was appointed executor, and the bequest of the $200,000 was described as being made in lieu of all commissions to which he would otherwise be entitled as executor. The bequest is considered tax-free income. It was not conditioned upon the uncle performing as executor. If the will had made the bequest contingent upon the uncle's acting as executor, the $200,000 would have been taxed.
3. An attorney performed services for a friend without expectation of pay. The friend died and in his will left the attorney a bequest in appreciation for his services. The payment was considered a tax-free bequest. The amount was not bargained for.
4. A lawyer agreed to handle a client's legal affairs without charge; she promised to leave him securities. Twenty years later, under her will, the lawyer inherited the securities. The IRS taxed the bequest as pay. Both he and the client expected that he would be paid for legal services. If the client meant to make a bequest from their agreement, she should have said so in her will.

Planning Reminder

Gifts You Make

You may have to file a gift tax return if your gifts to an individual within the year exceed the annual gift tax exclusion, which for 2006 was $12,000; *see 39.2.*

State Tax Refunds and Other Recovered Deductions

11.5 Refunds of State and Local Income Tax Deductions

A refund of state or local income tax is not taxable if you did not previously claim the tax as an itemized deduction in a prior year. For example, if you claimed the standard deduction on your 2005 return and in 2006 you received a refund for state tax withheld from your 2005 wages, the refund is not taxable on your 2006 return.

Refund of 2004 or 2005 deduction for state/local income taxes or state/local general sales taxes. If in 2006 you received a refund for state or local income tax that you claimed as an itemized deduction for 2004 or 2005, the taxable portion of the refund depends on the amount of the state/local general sales tax that you could have deducted in lieu of the state/local income tax *(16.3)*. In general, the full amount of the refund is taxable for 2006 if it is less than the excess of the state/local income tax claimed as a deduction in the prior year over the state/local general sales tax that you could have but did not deduct. If the refund is more than the excess, the amount subject to tax is limited to the excess. For example, on your 2005 return, you claimed an itemized deduction for $11,000 in state/local income taxes, as this exceeded your payment of $10,000 in state/local general sales taxes. If in 2006 you received a $750 refund of 2005 state income tax, the entire refund would be taxable, since it is less than the $1,000 excess of the state/local income taxes over the state/local general sales taxes for 2005. However, if the refund had been $2,500 instead of $750, only $1,000 of the refund would be includible in 2006 income ($11,000 deduction minus $10,000 in state sales tax that could have been deducted).

Similarly, if in 2004 or 2005 you deducted state/local general sales taxes in lieu of state/local income taxes, and you received a sales tax refund in 2006, the IRS generally requires you to include the entire sales tax refund in your income if it is less than the excess of your sales tax deduction over the income tax deduction that could have been deducted.

The amount subject to tax could be further reduced because of the standard deduction limit discussed below.

Note: If your itemized deductions in the earlier year were subject to the 3% reduction *(13.7)*, follow the IRS method in Publication 525 for determining the taxable portion of a refund.

If AMT applied in year of deduction. If the refunded state tax was claimed as an itemized deduction but you were subject to the alternative minimum tax (AMT) for that year, the deduction was not allowable for AMT purposes; *see 23.2*. The refund is taxable only if the deduction gave you a tax benefit in the prior year. To determine if there was a tax benefit, you must recompute regular tax liability and AMT for the prior year after increasing your income by the refunded amount. If the recomputation does not increase your total tax, there was no tax benefit and the refund is not taxable. If your total tax increases by any amount, the deduction gave you a tax benefit and the refund is taxable to the extent that the deduction reduced your tax in the prior year.

Planning Reminder

Refund of State and Local Tax

A state and local tax refund received in 2005 is taxable only if you claimed the tax as an itemized deduction, and only to the extent that your itemized deductions in that year exceeded the standard deduction you could have claimed.

To help you figure the taxable portion of 2005 itemized deductions recovered in 2006, 2005 standard deduction amounts are shown on the next page.

Standard deduction limit. The taxable portion of a refunded state tax cannot exceed the standard deduction limit. You include in income the lesser of the refund or the excess of your itemized deductions for the prior year over the standard deduction that could have been claimed.

The standard deduction limit applies to your total recoveries where you had other recoveries in addition to a refund of state tax; *see 11.6*.

EXAMPLE

On your 2005 return, you filed as a single taxpayer. You claimed itemized deductions of $5,250, of which $3,150 was for state and local income taxes, $1,500 was for mortgage interest, and $600 was for charitable contributions. Your deductions exceeded by $250 the $5,000 standard deduction you could have claimed. The deductions were not subject to the 3% reduction discussed at *13.7* and you were not subject to alternative minimum tax.

In 2006, you received from the state a $750 refund for 2005 state income tax. The $3,150 deduction for state and local income tax exceeded your 2005 state and local general sales taxes by more than $750. You must report $250 of the refund as income on your 2006 Form 1040. The taxable recovery is limited to the $250 difference between the claimed itemized deductions of $5,250 and the $5,000 standard deduction for 2005.

If you had a negative taxable income in 2005, the taxable recovery figured under the above rule is reduced by the negative amount. If you had a negative taxable income of $100 in 2005, only $150 of the refund would be taxable.

Allocating a refund recovery. If in 2006 you received a refund of state or local income taxes and also a recovery of other deductions, and only part of the total recovery is taxable, you allocate the taxable amount of the recovery according to the ratio between the state income tax refund and the other recovery. You do this by first dividing the state income tax refund by the total of all itemized deductions recovered. The resulting percentage is then applied to the taxable recovery to find the amount to report as the unrefunded state income tax on Line 10 of Form 1040; other taxable recoveries are reported on Line 21.

EXAMPLE

In 2006, you received a refund of state income taxes of $500 and a recovery of other itemized expenses of $2,000 deducted for 2005. You figure that only $1,500 of the recovery is taxable because your total 2005 itemized deductions were $1,500 more than the standard deduction you could have claimed. As a state income tax refund is reported separately from other recoveries, you must find how much of the taxable recovery is attributed to the refund. By dividing the state income tax refund by the amount of the total recovery, you find that 20% is attributed to the refund ($500/$2,500). Thus, 20% of the taxable recovery, or $300 (20% of $1,500), is reported as a state income tax refund on Line 10, Form 1040, and the balance of $1,200 on Line 21, Form 1040. Also attach a statement showing that the allocation of recoveries required the reporting on Line 10, Form 1040, of an amount less than the actual state income tax refund shown on Form 1099-G.

Table 11-1 2005 Standard Deduction
(For Determining Whether Recovery of 2005 Itemized Deductions Is Taxable)

If you were—	*2005 standard deduction was—*
Married filing jointly	$ 10,000
Single	5,000
Head of household	7,300
Married filing separately	5,000
Qualifying widow or widower	10,000
Single age 65 or over	6,250
Single and blind	6,250
Single age 65 or over and also blind	7,500
Married filing jointly with:	
One spouse age 65 or over	11,000
Both spouses age 65 or over	12,000
One spouse blind under age 65	11,000
Both spouses blind under age 65	12,000
One spouse age 65 or over and also blind	12,000
One spouse age 65 or over and other spouse blind and under age 65	12,000
One spouse age 65 or over and also blind; other spouse blind and under age 65	13,000
Both spouses age 65 or over and also blind	14,000
Qualifying widow or widower age 65 or over	11,000
Qualifying widow or widower and blind	11,000
Qualifying widow or widower age 65 or over and also blind	12,000
Head of household age 65 or over	8,550
Head of household and blind	8,550
Head of household age 65 or over and also blind	9,800
Married filing separately age 65 or over*	6,000
Married filing separately and blind*	6,000
Married filing separately age 65 or over and also blind*	7,000

**If on your 2005 return you claimed your spouse as an exemption (21.2), add $1,000 if he or she was either blind or age 65 or older; add $2,000 if he or she was both blind and age 65 or older.*

Filing Instruction

Negative Taxable Income

If your taxable income was a negative amount in the year in which the recovered item was deducted, you reduce the recovery includible in income by the negative amount. For example, if the taxable recovery would be $1,700 but you had a negative taxable income of $500 for the year the deduction was claimed, only $1,200 is taxable.

Refund of state tax paid in installments over two tax years. If you pay estimated state or local income taxes, your last tax installment may be in the year you receive a refund. In this case, you allocate the refund between the two years; *see* the following Example.

EXAMPLE

Your estimated state income tax for 2005 was $4,000, which you paid in four equal installments. You made your fourth payment in January 2006. No state income tax was withheld during 2005. In 2006, you received a state income tax refund of $400 for 2005. You claimed itemized deductions on your 2005 and 2004 federal returns. You allocate the $400 refund between 2005 and 2004. As you paid 75% ($3,000 ÷ $4,000) of the estimated tax in 2005, 75% of the $400 refund, or $300, is treated as a recovery of taxes paid in 2005. On your 2006 return, you include $300 as income on Line 10, Form 1040. You also attach a statement explaining that the amount on Line 10 is less than the $400 refund shown on the Form 1099-G received from the state in 2006 because of the allocation required for the estimated tax installment made in January 2006.

When you figure your 2006 deduction for state income taxes, you reduce the $1,000 paid in January by $100, the portion of the refund attributed to your January 2006 payment of estimated state income tax. Your 2006 deduction for state income taxes will include the January net amount of $900 plus any estimated state income taxes paid in 2006 for 2006, any state income tax withheld during 2006, and any state income tax for 2005 that you paid when you filed your 2005 state return in 2006.

Note: If the $300 refund allocated to 2005 in the previous Example was more than the excess of your 2005 itemized deductions over the 2005 standard deduction you could have claimed, you report only that excess as income on your 2006 return.

11.6 Other Recovered Deductions

The rules in *11.5* for determining whether a refund of state sales tax is taxable also apply to the recovery of other items for which you claimed a tax deduction, such as a refund of real estate taxes *(16.1)* adjustable rate mortgage interest *(15.1)*, reimbursement of a deducted medical expense *(17.4)*, a reimbursed casualty loss *(18.2)*, a return of donated property that was claimed as a charitable deduction *(14.1)*, and a payment of debt previously claimed as a bad debt *(5.33)*.

EXAMPLE

You filed a joint return for 2005 and claimed itemized deductions of $11,000, which exceeded your standard deduction of $10,000. You were not subject to the 3% reduction to itemized deductions or to the alternative minimum tax. In 2006, you received the following recoveries for amounts deducted for 2005:

Medical expenses	$ 200
State income tax refund	400
Interest expense	325
Total	$ 925

The $400 state income tax refund was less than the difference between the state income tax you deducted and your state general sales taxes. The total recovery of $925 is taxable on your 2006 return. It is less than $1,000, the excess of your 2005 itemized deductions over the allowable standard deduction ($11,000 – 10,000). You report the state and local income tax refund of $400 on Line 10, Form 1040, and the balance of $525 on Line 21, Form 1040.

If the total recovery had been $2,500 instead of $925, $1,000 would be taxable (the excess of $11,000 over $10,000). The $1,500 balance would be tax free.

Tax credit in prior year. If you recover an item deducted in a prior year in which tax credits exceeded your tax, you refigure the prior year tax to determine if the recovery is taxable. Add the amount of the recovery to taxable income of the prior year and figure the tax on the increased taxable income. If your tax credit exceeds the recomputed tax, do not include the recovery in income. If the tax credit is less than the recomputed tax, include the recovery in income to the extent the recovery reduced your tax in the prior year. The recovery may reduce an available credit carryforward to a later year.

Alternative minimum tax in the prior year. If you were subject to the alternative minimum tax (AMT) in the year the recovered deduction was claimed, recompute your regular and AMT tax for the prior year based on the taxable income you reported plus the recovered amount. If inclusion of the recovery does not change your total tax, you do not include the recovery in income. If your total tax increases by any amount, the recovered deduction gave you a tax benefit and you must include the recovery in income to the extent the deduction reduced your tax in the prior year. The recovery may reduce a carryforward of a tax credit based on prior year AMT.

Recovery of previously deducted items used to figure carryover. A deductible expense may not reduce your tax because you have an overall loss. If in a later year the expense is repaid or the obligation giving rise to the expense is cancelled, the deduction of that expense will be treated as having produced a tax reduction if it increased a carryover that has not expired by the beginning of the taxable year in which the forgiveness occurs. For example, you are on the accrual basis and deducted but did not pay rent in 2005. The rent obligation is forgiven in 2006. The 2005 rent deduction is treated as having produced a reduction in tax, even if it resulted in no tax savings in 2005, if it figured in the calculation of a net operating loss that has not expired or been used by the beginning of 2006, the year of forgiveness. The same rule applies to other carryovers such as the investment credit carryover.

Damages and Debt Cancellation

11.7 How Legal Damages Are Taxed

Compensatory damages for physical injury or physical sickness are tax free, whether fixed by a court or in a negotiated settlement. Damages for *nonphysical* personal injuries, such as for discrimination, back pay, or injury to reputation, are taxable; a limited exception for certain emotional distress damages may be available as discussed below. Damages for lost profits, breach of contract, or interference with business operations are taxable. Interest added to an award is taxable, even if the award is tax-free damages for physical injury.

When damages compensate for the loss of property, you have taxable gain if the damages exceed adjusted basis of the property. A deductible loss will generally be allowed when the recovery is less than adjusted basis. The nature of the gain or loss takes on the same character (that is, capital gain or loss or ordinary income gain or loss) as the property lost.

Emotional distress. Damages for emotional distress are tax free if attributable to a physical injury or sickness. If emotional distress damages are due to an injury other than a physical injury or sickness, as in a discrimination action, the damages are taxable with one exception: Damages up to the amount of actual medical care expenses attributable to emotional distress are tax free. Apart from the medical expenses exception, damages for emotional distress are taxable when received for a personal injury other than a physical injury or sickness. This is true even where the emotional distress damages cover physical symptoms such as insomnia, headaches, and stomach disorders. The emotional distress by itself is not treated as a physical injury or sickness.

Punitive damages. Punitive damages are taxable, even if they relate to a physical injury or sickness. An exception in the law allows an exclusion from income for punitive damages awarded under a state wrongful death statute if the punitive damages are the only damages that may be awarded.

Holocaust restitution payments. There is a broad exclusion from gross income for Holocaust restitution payments. Tax-free treatment applies to payments received after December 31, 1999, by persons persecuted by Nazi Germany or any Nazi-controlled or allied country, as well as to payments received by heirs or estates of such persecuted persons. Persecution on the basis of race, religion, physical or mental disability, or sexual orientation is covered.

Excludable restitution includes compensation for assets that were stolen or lost before, during, or immediately after World War II and to life insurance issued by European insurers immediately before and during the war. Tax-free treatment also applies to interest earned on escrow accounts and funds established in settlement of Holocaust victim claims against European banks or corporations.

Attorney's contingent fee paid from taxable award. If you receive taxable damages, such as back pay in an employment dispute, and a percentage goes directly to your attorney under a contingent fee agreement, can you exclude from your income the contingent fee payment, so that you are only taxed on the net amount you receive?

Law Alert

Legal Fees

If your damages are tax free, you may not deduct your litigation costs. If your damages are taxable, including the contingency fee portion of a taxable recovery *(see 11.7)*, you may be able to deduct your legal fees. A business expense deduction may be claimed on Schedule C for legal fees to recover taxable business income. The American Jobs Creation Act of 2004 allows an above-the-line deduction (directly from gross income) for legal fees in employment discrimination suits, certain other unlawful discrimination cases and federal False Claims Act cases paid after October 22, 2004, with respect to settlements or judgments occurring after that date. The above-the-line deduction is claimed on Line 36 of Form 1040 *(see 12.2)*.

Legal fees not eligible for the above-the-line deduction or Schedule C deduction may be claimed only as miscellaneous itemized deductions on Schedule A subject to the 2% adjusted gross income floor and the limitation on itemized deductions for higher-income taxpayers. The miscellaneous itemized deduction is not allowed at all for alternative minimum tax (AMT) purposes.

The answer from the Supreme Court is no. The Supreme Court held in its 2005 *Banks* decision that the contingency-fee portion of a taxable damages award or settlement generally must be included in the litigant's gross income. The Court's decision did not resolve whether attorney fees paid pursuant to a statutory fee-shifting provision must be included in income, but it suggested that such statutory fees might in some cases be excludable. However, a subsequent Tax Court decision held that the attorney-fee portion of a taxable settlement was includible in the litigant's income where attorney fees were awarded under a California fee-shifting statute. Since the Supreme Court had not decided that issue, the Tax Court relied on its own prior decisions and precedent of the Ninth Circuit (where appeal would lie), which required inclusion of the fee portion of a settlement where a contingency-fee obligation was satisfied by a fee-shifting statute.

Note: If the contingency-fee portion of a taxable award in an unlawful employment discrimination case must be included in gross income under the Supreme Court decision, and the fees were paid after October 22, 2004, with respect to a judgment or settlement occurring after that date, the inclusion of the fees can be offset by an above-the-line deduction; *see* the Law Alert in *11.7*.

11.8 Cancellation of Debts You Owe

If a debt is cancelled or forgiven other than as a gift or a bequest the debtor generally must include the cancelled amount in gross income for tax purposes. Exclusions are allowed for discharges of farm or business real estate debt and debts of insolvent and bankrupt persons, as explained below.

Law Alert

Debt Cancelled as a Result of Hurricane Katrina

If a government agency or financial institution canceled your debt after August 24, 2005, and before January 1, 2007, the debt discharge is excludable from your income provided your principal residence was within the core Hurricane Katrina disaster area on August 25, 2005. The exclusion also applies if you lived within the Hurricane Katrina disaster area but outside the core disaster area on August 25, 2005, if you suffered economic loss because of Hurricane Katrina. The exclusion does not apply to any indebtedness to the extent that real property constituting security for such indebtedness is located outside the Hurricane Katrina disaster area. *See* IRS Publication 4492 for further details.

Form 1099-C. You should receive Form 1099-C from a federal government agency, credit union, or bank that cancels or forgives a debt you owe of $600 or more. The IRS receives a copy of the form. Generally, the amount of cancelled debt shown in Box 2 of Form 1099-C must be reported as "other income" on Line 21 of Form 1040, unless one of the exclusions discussed below applies.

Discounted mortgage repayment. A prepayment of a home mortgage at a discount is taxable. The income is reported on Line 21, Form 1040. The tax treatment of a foreclosure sale or voluntary conveyance to a creditor is discussed at *31.9*.

EXAMPLE

A bank allows a homeowner to prepay a low-interest mortgage of $20,000 for $18,000. The discount of $2,000 is taxable as ordinary income.

Foreclosure sale. If a creditor forecloses on your property or you voluntarily convey property to avoid a foreclosure sale, you may realize ordinary cancellation-of-debt income as well as capital gain or loss; *see 31.9*.

Cancellation of student loans. A cancelled student loan is taxable income with this exception: If a loan by a government agency, by a government-funded loan program of an education organization, or by a qualified hospital organization is cancelled because you worked for a period of time in certain geographical areas in certain professions, such as practicing medicine in rural areas or teaching in inner-city schools, then the cancelled amount is not taxable.

Planning Reminder

Loans Cancelled by Foundations

Student loans cancelled by educational organizations may be tax free if the loan was made under a program that encourages students to provide public service by working in occupations or areas with unmet needs. The services must be under the direction of a governmental unit or tax-exempt charity. Services to the lender organization do not qualify.

Debts cancelled in bankruptcy. Debt cancelled in a bankruptcy case is not included in your gross income. Instead, certain losses, credits, and basis of property must be reduced by the amount excluded from income. These losses, credits, and basis of property are called "tax attributes." The amount of cancelled debt is used to reduce the tax attributes in the order listed below:

1. Net operating losses and carryovers—dollar for dollar of debt discharge;
2. Carryovers of the general business credit—$33^1/_3$ cents for each dollar of debt discharge;
3. AMT minimum tax credit as of the beginning of the year immediately after the taxable year of the discharge—$33^1/_3$ cents for each dollar of debt discharge;
4. Net capital losses and carryovers—dollar for dollar of debt discharge;
5. Basis of depreciable and nondepreciable assets—dollar for dollar of debt discharge (but not below the amount of your total undischarged liabilities);
6. Passive activity loss and credit carryovers—dollar for dollar of debt discharge for passive losses; $33^1/_3$ cents for each dollar of debt discharge in the case of passive credits; and
7. Foreign tax credit carryovers—$33^1/_3$ cents for each dollar of debt discharge.

After these reductions, any remaining balance of the debt discharge is disregarded. On Form 982, you may make a special election to first reduce the basis of any depreciable assets before reducing other tax attributes in the order above. Realty held for sale to customers may be treated as depreciable assets for purposes of the election. The election allows you to preserve your current deductions, such as a net operating loss carryover or capital loss carryover, for use in the following year. The election also will have the effect of reducing your depreciation deductions for years following the year of debt cancellation. If you later sell the depreciable property at a gain, the gain attributable to the basis reduction will be taxable as ordinary income under the depreciation recapture rules discussed at *44.1*.

Separate bankruptcy estate. If you are an individual debtor who files for bankruptcy under Chapter 7 or 11 of the Bankruptcy Code, a separate "estate" is created consisting of property that belonged to you before the filing date. This bankruptcy estate is a new taxable entity, completely separate from you as a taxpayer. The estate is represented by a trustee who manages the estate for the benefit of any creditors. The estate earns its own income and incurs expenses. The trustee reports the estate's income or loss on a separate return (Form 1041). The creation of a separate bankruptcy estate also gives you a "fresh start"; with certain exceptions, wages you earn and property you acquire after the bankruptcy case has begun belong to you and do not become part of the bankruptcy estate.

A separate estate is not created for an individual who files for bankruptcy under Chapter 12 or 13.

In a Chapter 7 or 11 case, the tax attribute reductions are made to the attributes in the bankruptcy estate. Reductions are not made to attributes of an individual debtor that come into existence after the bankruptcy case begins or that are treated as exempt property under bankruptcy rules. Basis reduction does apply to property transferred by the bankruptcy estate to the individual.

Debts discharged while you are insolvent. If your debt is cancelled outside of bankruptcy while you are insolvent, the cancellation does not result in taxable income to the extent of the insolvency. Insolvency means that liabilities exceed the fair market value of your assets immediately before the discharge of the debt. The IRS and Tax Court hold that in determining whether liabilities exceed the value of assets at the time of a debt discharge, a taxpayer must include assets that are shielded from creditors under state law. This is true even though for federal bankruptcy purposes creditor-exempt assets do not have to be counted in determining whether an individual seeking bankruptcy protection is insolvent.

If liabilities do exceed the value of assets, the discharged debt is not taxed to the extent of your insolvency and is applied to the reduction of tax attributes on Form 982 in the same manner as to a bankrupt individual. If the cancelled debt exceeds the insolvency, any remaining balance is treated as if it were a debt cancellation of a solvent person and, thus, it is taxable unless it is a qualifying farming debt or business real estate debt as discussed later in this section.

See the Example below for the IRS approach to figuring insolvency upon a debt cancellation.

EXAMPLE

In 1998, Jones borrowed $1,000,000 from Chester and signed a note payable for that amount. Jones was not personally liable on the note, which was secured by an office building valued at $1,000,000 that he bought from Baker with the proceeds of Chester's loan. In 2006, when the value of the building declined to $800,000, Chester agreed to reduce the principal of the loan to $825,000. At the time, Jones held other assets valued at $100,000 and owed another person $50,000.

To determine the extent of Jones's insolvency, the IRS compares the value of Jones's assets and liabilities immediately before the discharge. According to the IRS, his assets total $900,000: the building valued at $800,000 plus other assets of $100,000. His liabilities total $1,025,000: the other debt of $50,000 plus the liability on the note, which the IRS considered to be $975,000, equal to the $800,000 value of the building and the discharged debt of $175,000. Jones is insolvent by $125,000 ($1,025,000 in liabilities less $900,000 in assets). As $175,000 was the amount of the discharged debt and Jones was insolvent to the extent of $125,000, only $50,000 is treated as taxable income.

Partnership debts. When a partnership's debt is discharged because of bankruptcy, insolvency, or if it is qualified farm debt or business real estate debt that is cancelled, the discharged amount is allocated among the partners. Bankruptcy or insolvency is tested not at the partnership level, but separately for each partner. Thus, a bankrupt or insolvent partner applies the allocated amount to reduce the specified tax attributes as previously discussed. A solvent partner may not take advantage of the rules applied to insolvent or bankrupt partners, even if the partnership is insolvent or bankrupt.

Court Decision

Credit Card Insurance Payments Taxable

Insurance can be purchased to cover a portion of credit card debt in the event you become unemployed or disabled, or you die. The Tax Court held that insurance payments of an unemployed credit card holder's debt were a taxable cancellation of debt to the extent the payments exceeded the premiums paid.

Filing Tip

Bankrupt Persons

Special rules apply to debt cancellations under bankruptcy law. A debt cancelled in a bankruptcy case is not included in your income, but certain losses, credits, and basis of property must be reduced by the amount of excluded income.

S corporation debts. The tax consequences of a debt discharge are determined at the corporate level. The Job Creation and Worker Assistance Act of 2002 overrode a 2001 Supreme Court decision that had allowed discharged debt of an insolvent S corporation to pass through to the shareholders as tax-exempt income. As a result of the pass-through, a stockholder could increase his or her basis in the S corporation, which in turn could allow a deduction for suspended losses. However, under the 2002 Act, a debt discharge after October 11, 2001, that is excludable from the S corporation's income because of insolvency or bankruptcy does not pass through to the shareholders and thus does not increase the shareholders' basis.

Purchase price adjustment for solvent debtors. If you buy property on credit and the seller reduces or cancels the debt arising out of the purchase, the reduction is generally treated as a purchase price adjustment (reducing your basis in the property). Since the reduction is not treated as a debt cancellation, you do not realize taxable income on the price adjustment. This favorable price adjustment rule applies only if you are solvent and not in bankruptcy, you have not transferred the property to a third party, and the seller has not transferred the debt to a third party, such as with the sale of your installment contract to a collection company.

Filing Instruction

Price Adjustments Not Taxed

If you bought property on credit and the seller cancels or reduces your purchase-related debt, this is a price adjustment, not a taxable cancellation of debt.

Qualified farm debt. A solvent farmer may avoid tax from a discharge of indebtedness by an unrelated lender, including any federal, state, or local government agency, if the debt was incurred in operating a farm business. This relief is available only if 50% or more of your total gross receipts for the preceding three taxable years was derived from farming. The excluded amount first reduces tax attributes such as net operating loss carryovers and business tax credits, next reduces basis in all property other than farmland, and then reduces the basis in land used in the farming business. *See* IRS Publication 225 for details.

Business real estate debt. A solvent taxpayer may elect to avoid tax on a discharge of qualifying real property business debt. Such a discharge may occur where the fair market value of the property securing the debt has fallen in value. The debt must have been incurred or assumed in connection with business real property and must be secured by such property. A debt incurred or assumed after 1992 must be incurred or assumed to buy, construct, or substantially improve real property used in a business, or to refinance such acquisition debt (up to the refinanced amount). Debt incurred after 1992 to refinance a pre-1993 business real property debt (up to the refinanced amount) also qualifies. The debt must be secured by the property. Discharges of farm indebtedness do not qualify but may be tax free under the separate rules discussed earlier.

The maximum amount that can be excluded from income is the excess of the outstanding loan principal (immediately before the discharge) over the fair market value (immediately before the discharge) of the real property securing the debt, less any other outstanding qualifying real property business debts secured by the property. The excludable amount also may not exceed the taxpayer's adjusted basis for all depreciable real property held before the discharge. The excluded amount reduces basis in all depreciable real property.

Effect of basis reduction on later disposition of property. A reduction of basis is treated as a depreciation deduction so that a profitable sale of the property at a later date may be subject to the rules of recapture of depreciation; *see 44.1*.

Partners, S Corporation Shareholders, and Trust and Estate Beneficiaries

11.9 Schedule K-1

Although partnerships, S corporations, trusts, and estates are different types of tax entities, they share a common tax-reporting characteristic. The entity itself generally does not pay income taxes. As a partner, shareholder, or beneficiary, you report your share of the entity's income or loss. The entity files a Schedule K-1 with the IRS that indicates your share of the income, deductions, and credits passed through from the entity. You will receive a copy of the Schedule K-1, which you should keep for your records; it does not have to be attached to your tax return.

To ensure that Schedule K-1 income is being reported, IRS computers match the information shown on the schedules with the tax returns of partners, S corporation shareholders, and beneficiaries.

11.10 How Partners Report Partnership Profit and Loss

A partnership files Form 1065, which informs the IRS of partnership profit or loss and each partner's share on Schedule K-1. The partnership pays no tax on partnership income; each partner reports his or her share of partnership net profit or loss and special deductions and credits, whether or not distributions are received from the partnership, as shown on Schedule K-1. Income that is not distributed or withdrawn increases the basis of a partner's partnership interest.

Your share reported to you on Schedule K-1 (Form 1065) is generally based on your proportionate capital interest in the partnership, unless the partnership agreement provides for another allocation.

Your partnership must give you a copy of Schedule K-1 (Form 1065), which lists your share of income, loss, deduction, and credit items, and where to report them on your return. For example, your share of income or loss from a business or real estate activity is reported on Schedule E and is subject to passive activity adjustments, if any. Interest and dividends are reported on Schedule B, royalties on Schedule E, and capital gains and losses on Schedule D. Your share of charitable donations is claimed on Schedule A if you itemize deductions. Tax preference items for alternative minimum tax purposes are also listed.

Health insurance premiums. A partnership that pays premiums for health insurance for partners has a choice. It may treat the premium as a reduction in distributions to the partners. Alternatively, it may deduct the premium as an expense and charge each partner's share as a guaranteed salary payment taxable to the partner. The partner reports the guaranteed payment shown on Schedule K-1 as nonpassive income on Schedule E and may deduct 100% of the premium on Line 29, Form 1040, as an above-the-line deduction from gross income; *see 12.2.*

Guaranteed salary and interest. A guaranteed salary that is fixed without regard to partnership income is taxable as ordinary wages and not as partnership earnings. If you receive a percentage of the partnership income with a stipulated minimum payment, the guaranteed payment is the amount by which the minimum guarantee exceeds your share of the partnership income before taking into account the minimum guarantee.

Interest on capital is reported as interest income.

Self-employment tax. As a partner, you pay self-employment tax on your net partnership income, including guaranteed salary and other guaranteed payments. The self-employment tax is explained in Chapter 45. Limited partners do not pay self-employment tax, unless guaranteed payments are received; *see 45.2.*

Special allocations. Partners may agree to special allocations of gain, income, loss, deductions, or credits disproportionate to their capital contributions. The allocation should have a substantial economic effect to avoid an IRS disallowance. The IRS will not issue an advance ruling on whether an allocation has a substantial economic effect. If the allocation is rejected, a partner's share is determined by his or her partnership interest.

To have substantial economic effect, a special allocation must be reflected by adjustments to the partners' capital accounts; liquidation proceeds must be distributed in accordance with the partners' capital accounts, and following a liquidating distribution, the partners must be liable to the partnership to restore any deficit in their capital.

If there is a change of partnership interests during the year, items are allocated to a partner for that part of the year he or she is a member of the partnership. Thus, a partner who acquires an interest late in the year is barred from deducting partnership expenses incurred prior to his entry into the partnership. If the partners agree to give an incoming partner a disproportionate share of partnership losses for the period after he or she becomes a member, the allocation must meet the substantial economic effect test to avoid IRS disallowance.

See IRS regulations to Code Section 704, IRS Publication 541, and Form 1065 instructions for further details.

Reporting transfers of interest to IRS. If you transfer a partnership interest that includes an interest in partnership receivables and appreciated inventory, you must report the disposition to the partnership within 30 days, or, if earlier, by January 15 of the calendar year after the year of the transfer. The partnership in turn files a report with the IRS on Form 8308. You must also attach a statement to your income tax return describing the transaction and allocating basis to the receivables and inventory items. The IRS wants to keep track of such dispositions because partners have to pay ordinary income tax on the portion of profit attributable to the receivables and inventory.

Filing Instruction

Partnership Elections

The partnership, not the individual partners, makes elections affecting the computation of partnership income such as the election to defer involuntary conversion gains, to amortize organization and start-up costs, and to choose depreciation methods, including first-year expensing. An election to claim a foreign tax credit is made by the partners.

Caution

Partner May Be Taxed on Pre-Contribution Gain

The rules subjecting partners to tax on pre-contribution gain when they contribute property and the partnership makes a later distribution are complicated and hedged with restrictions. Consult a tax advisor before making transfers of appreciated property to, or taking distributions from, a partnership.

Within 30 days of your transfer, provide the partnership with a statement that includes the date of the exchange and identifies the transferee (include Social Security number if known). You can be penalized for failure to notify the partnership. You and your transferee should receive a copy of the Form 8308 that the partnership will send to the IRS along with its Form 1065.

Generally, the partnership must file a separate Form 8308 for each transfer but the IRS may allow a composite Form 8308 for the calendar year if there were at least 25 reportable transfers.

Recognition of gain by partner on distribution of contributed property. Under a restrictive law (Code Section 737), a partner who contributes appreciated property to a partnership may incur tax on the pre-contribution gain if within seven years *other* property is received from the partnership that is valued at more than the partner's basis in the partnership. Under another law (Code Section 704(c)(1)(B)), if appreciated property contributed by a partner is distributed to a *different* partner within seven years of the contribution, the contributing partner is taxed on the pre-contribution gain as if the property had been sold at fair market value on the date of distribution.

11.11 When a Partner Reports Income or Loss

You report your share of the partnership gain or loss for the partnership year that ends in your tax reporting year. If you and the partnership are on a calendar-year basis, you report your share of the 2006 partnership income on your 2006 income tax return. If the partnership is on a fiscal year ending March 31, for example, and you report on a calendar year, you report on your 2006 return your share of the partnership income for the whole fiscal year ending March 31, 2006—that is, partnership income for the fiscal year April 1, 2005, through March 31, 2006.

If a Section 444 election of a fiscal year is made on Form 8716, a special tax payment must be computed for each fiscal year and if the computed payment exceeds $500, it must be paid to the IRS. The tax payment is figured and reported on Form 8752. The tax does not apply to the first tax year of a partnership's existence but Form 8752 must still be filed. In later years, a refund of prior payments is available to the extent the prior payments exceed the payment required for the current fiscal year. For example, if the required payment was $12,000 for the fiscal year July 1, 2006–June 30, 2007, and the required payment for the fiscal year starting July 1, 2007, is $10,000, a $2,000 refund may be claimed on Form 8752. Refunds of prior year payments also are available if the fiscal-year election is terminated and a calendar year adopted or if the partnership liquidates.

See *IRS Publication 541 for further information on partnership reporting.*

11.12 Partnership Loss Limitations

Your share of partnership losses may not exceed the adjusted basis of your partnership interest. If the loss exceeds basis, the excess loss may not be deducted until you have partnership earnings to cover the loss or contribute capital to cover the loss. The basis of your partnership interest is generally the amount paid for the interest (either through contribution or purchase) less withdrawals plus accumulated taxed earnings that have not been withdrawn. You also have a basis in loans to the partnership for which you are personally liable.

A partner's basis is not increased by accrued but unpaid expenses such as interest costs and accounts payable unless the partnership uses the accrual accounting method. However, basis is increased by capitalized items allocable to future periods such as organization and construction period expenses.

Partners are subject to the "at-risk" loss limitation rules. These rules limit the amount of loss that may be deducted to the amount each partner personally has at stake in the partnership, such as contributions of property and loans for which the partner is personally liable. *See 10.17* for a discussion of the "at-risk" rules. Furthermore, if the IRS determines that a tax-shelter partnership is not operated to make a profit, deductions may be disallowed even where there is an "at-risk" investment. Finally, any loss not barred by these limitations may be disallowed under the passive activity rules discussed in Chapter 10.

Court Decision

Settlements Need Not Be Consistent

Neither the IRS nor the Department of Justice is required to offer consistent settlements to audited partners so long as they do not discriminate for arbitrary reasons.

11.13 Unified Tax Audits of Partnerships

Tax audits of both a partnership of more than 10 partners and its partners must be at the partnership level. To challenge the partnership treatment of an item, the IRS must generally audit the partnership, not the individual partner. To avoid a personal audit of a partnership item, a partner should report partnership items as shown on the partnership return or identify any inconsistent treatment on his or her return. Otherwise, the IRS may assess a deficiency without auditing the partnership.

For a partnership-level audit, the partnership names a "tax matters partner" (TMP) to receive notice of the audit. If one is not named, the IRS will treat as a TMP the general partner having the largest interest in partnership profits at the end of the taxable year involved in the audit. Notice of the audit must also be given to the other partners. All partners may participate in the partnership audit. If the IRS settles with some partners, it is not required to offer consistent settlement terms. However, the IRS is required to apply the tax law consistently.

Within 90 days after the IRS mails its final determination, the TMP may appeal to the Tax Court; individual partners have an additional 60 days to file a court petition if the TMP does not do so. An appeal may also be filed in a federal district court or the claims court if the petitioning partner first deposits with the IRS an amount equal to the tax that would be owed if the IRS determination were sustained. A Tax Court petition takes precedence over petitions filed in other courts. The first Tax Court petition filed is heard; if other partners have also filed petitions, their cases will be dismissed. If no Tax Court petitions are filed, the first petition filed in federal district court or the claims court takes precedence. Regardless of which petition takes precedence, all partners who hold an interest during the taxable year involved will be bound by the decision (unless the statute of limitations with respect to that partner has run out).

Exception for 10 or fewer partners. The unified audit rules do not apply if there are 10 or fewer partners. The exception applies if all the partners are individuals (but not nonresident aliens), estates of deceased partners, or C corporations. A husband and wife (and their estates) are treated as one partner.

11.14 Stockholder Reporting of S Corporation Income and Loss

S corporations are subject to tax reporting rules similar to those applied to partnerships. However, shareholders who work for the corporation are treated as employees for payroll tax purposes. They do not pay self-employment tax on their salary income or other receipts from the corporation.

Your company must give you a copy of Schedule K-1 (Form 1120-S), which lists your share of income or loss, deductions, and credits that must be reported on your return. For example, your share of business income or loss is reported on Schedule E and is subject to passive activity adjustments, if any. Interest and dividends from other corporations are reported on Schedule B, capital gains and losses on Schedule D, Section 1231 gains or losses on Form 4797, and charitable donations on Schedule A. Tax preference items for alternative minimum tax purposes are also listed.

Health insurance premimums paid by an S corporation for more-than-2% stockholders are treated as wages, deductible on Form 1120-S by the corporation and reported to the stockholder on Form W-2. A more-than-2% shareholder who reports premiums as wages for 2006 may deduct the premiums on Line 29 of Form 1040 as an adjustment to income.

Allocation to shareholders. The following items are allocated to and pass through to the shareholders based on the proportion of stock held in the corporation:

- Gains and losses from the sale and exchange of capital assets and Section 1231 property, as well as interest and dividends on corporate investments and losses. Investment interest expenses subject to the rules discussed at *15.10* also pass through.
- Tax-exempt interest. Tax-exempt interest remains tax free in the hands of the stockholders but increases the basis of their stock. Dividends from other companies may qualify for the exclusion.
- First-year expense deduction (Section 179 deduction).
- Charitable contributions made by the corporation.
- Foreign income or loss.
- Foreign taxes paid by the corporation. Each stockholder elects whether to claim these as a credit or deduction.
- Tax preference items.
- Recovery of bad debts and prior taxes.

If your interest changed during the year, your pro rata share must reflect the time you held the stock.

IRS Alert

IRS Previews Guidance on Family S Corp Election

The American Jobs Creation Act of 2004 increased the maximum number of S corporation shareholders to 100 (from 75) and allowed family members to elect to treat all members of the family as one shareholder for purposes of the limit. The new rules apply to S corporation taxable years beginning after December 1, 2004, but the IRS has been slow in issuing guidance. When this book went to press, the IRS was in the process of preparing guidelines on the family election. In the interim, taxpayers may rely on the rules in Notice 2005-91.

The Tax Court and several federal appeals courts have held that an S corporation shareholder's basis is not increased by guaranteeing a loan to the corporation where there is no actual economic outlay. The Tax Court disagrees with the approach of another federal appeals court that allowed an increased basis where the lender looked to the guarantor-shareholder as the primary obligor on the guaranteed loan. *See also 11.8* for treatment of debt cancellations.

Planning Reminder

Basis Limits Loss Deductions

Deductible losses may not exceed your basis in S corporation stock and loans to the corporation. If losses exceed basis, the excess loss is carried over and becomes deductible when you invest or lend an equivalent amount of money to the corporation. This rule may allow for timing a loss deduction. In a year in which you want to deduct the loss, you may contribute capital to the corporation. If a carryover loss exists when an S election terminates, a limited loss deduction may be allowed.

Passive activity rules limit loss deductions. Losses allocated to you may be disallowed under the passive activity rules discussed in Chapter 10.

Basis adjustments. Because of the nature of S corporation reporting, the basis of each shareholder's stock is subject to change. Basis is increased by the pass-through of income items and by loans to the S corporation for which the shareholder is personally liable, and basis is reduced by the pass-through of loss items and the receipt of certain distributions. Because income and loss items pass through to stockholders, an S corporation has no current earnings and profits. An income item will not increase basis, unless you actually report the amount on your tax return. The specific details and order of basis adjustments are listed in the instructions to Schedule K-1 of Form 1120S.

EXAMPLES

1. A calendar-year corporation incurs a loss of $10,000. Smith and Jones each own 50% of the stock. On May 1, Smith sells all of his stock to Harris. For the year, Smith was a shareholder for 120 days, Jones for 365 days, and Harris for 245 days. The loss is allocated on a daily basis; the daily basis of the loss is $27.3973 ($10,000 divided by 365 days). The allocation is as follows:

   Smith: $1,644 ($27.3973 × 120 days × 50% interest)

   Jones: $5,000 ($27.3973 × 365 days × 50% interest)

   Harris: $3,356 ($27.3973 × 245 days × 50% interest)

2. Same facts as in Example 1, except that on May 1, Smith sells only 50% of his stock to Harris. The allocation for Smith accounts for his 50% interest for 120 days and his 25% interest for the remainder of the year.

   Smith: $3,322 ($27.3973 × 120 days × 50% plus $27.3973 × 245 days × 25%)

   Jones: $5,000 (as above)

   Harris: $1,678 ($27.3973 × 245 days × 25%)

   $\frac{\$1,000}{\$1,500} \times \$390 = \$260$

11.15 How Beneficiaries Report Estate or Trust Income

Trust or estate income is treated as if you had received the income directly from the original source instead of from the estate or trust. This means capital gain remains capital gain, ordinary income is fully taxed, and tax-exempt income remains tax free. Tax preference items of a trust or estate are apportioned between the estate or trust and beneficiaries, according to allocation of income.

You report your share of trust or estate income on Schedule B as shown on the Schedule K-1 (Form 1041) sent to you by the trustee. Dividends and interest from the trust are reported on Schedule B of Form 1040 and capital gains on Schedule D. Income or loss from real estate or business activities shown on Schedule K-1 is reported by you on Schedule E, subject to the passive activity restrictions discussed in Chapter 10.

Filing Instruction

Consistent Reporting by Beneficiaries

Beneficiaries of trusts and estates must report items consistently with the Schedule K-1 provided by the trust or estate. If an item is treated inconsistently and a statement identifying the inconsistency is not attached to the return, the IRS may make a summary assessment for additional tax without issuing a deficiency notice.

Reporting rule for revocable grantor trusts. A grantor who sets up a revocable trust or keeps certain powers over trust income or corpus must report all of the trust income, deductions, and credits. This rule applies if a grantor retains a reversionary interest in the trust that is valued at more than 5% of the trust (valued at the time the trust is set up); *see 39.6.* If a grantor is also a trustee of a revocable trust and all the trust assets are in the United States, filing Form 1041 is not necessary. The grantor simply reports the trust income, deductions, and credits on Form 1040. *See* the Form 1041 instructions for reporting requirements.

Income in Respect of a Decedent

11.16 Reporting Income in Respect of a Decedent (IRD)

If you receive income that was earned by but not paid to a decedent before death, such as wages, IRA and qualified plan distributions, lottery prize winnings, or installment sale proceeds, you are said to have "income in respect of a decedent," or IRD. You report the IRD on your return. Where the purchaser of a deferred annuity contract dies before the annuity starting date, payments to a beneficiary in excess of the purchaser's investment are IRD, whether payable in a lump sum or as periodic payments.

If the decedent's estate paid federal estate tax that was attributable to the IRD you received, you may claim an itemized deduction for the estate tax paid on that income; *see 11.17.*

Filing Instruction

Lump-Sum Distributions From Qualified Retirement Plans

When a beneficiary receiving a lump-sum distribution because of an employee's death reports the distribution using the special averaging method (Chapter 7), the taxable amount of the distribution must be reduced by the estate taxes attributable to the distribution. *See* the Form 4972 instructions when calculating the tax under averaging.

11.17 Deduction for Estate Tax Attributable to IRD

A beneficiary can claim an itemized deduction for the amount, if any, of federal estate tax paid on income in respect of a decedent (IRD). The deduction is allowed to the IRD recipient only for the year in which the recipient reports the IRD income. No deduction is allowed for state death taxes paid on IRD. If you receive IRD, ask the executor of the decedent's estate for the amount of federal estate tax paid and the portion of the estate that the IRD represented to help you compute the deduction.

The itemized deduction is a miscellaneous deduction claimed on Line 27 of Schedule A. The Line 27 deduction is not subject to the 2% AGI floor that applies to most miscellaneous itemized deductions.

However, if the IRD you receive is long-term capital gain, such as an installment payment on a sale transacted before a decedent's death, the estate tax attributed to the capital gain item is not claimed as a miscellaneous deduction. The deduction is treated as if it were an expense of sale and, thus, reduces the amount of gain, but not below zero.

EXAMPLE

When Jim Bennett's uncle died, he was owed a fee of $1,000. He also had not collected accrued bond interest of $500. Bennett, as the sole heir, will collect both items and pay income tax on them. These items are called "income in respect of a decedent." Assume that an estate tax of $390 was paid on the $1,500. Bennett collects the $1,000, which he reports on his income tax return. If he itemizes deductions, he may deduct $260, computed as follows:

$$\frac{\$1,000}{\$1,500} \times \$390 = \$260$$

When he collects the $500, he will deduct the balance, or $130 ($390 – $260).

Life Insurance Proceeds

11.18 How Life Insurance Proceeds Are Taxed to a Beneficiary

Life insurance proceeds received upon the death of the insured are generally tax free. However, insurance proceeds may be subject to estate tax so that the beneficiary actually receives a reduced amount; *see 39.8.*

Interest paid on proceeds left with the insurer is taxable except in this case: A surviving spouse who elects to receive installments rather than a lump sum does not pay tax on the first $1,000 of interest received each year if the decedent died before October 23, 1986.

Read the following checklist to find how your insurance receipts are taxed—

A lump-sum payment of the full face value of a life insurance policy: The proceeds are generally tax free. The tax-free exclusion also covers death benefit payments made under endowment contracts, workers' compensation insurance contracts, employers' group insurance plans, or accident and health insurance contracts. The exclusion does not apply to a policy combined with a nonrefund life annuity contract where a single premium equal to the face value of the insurance is paid.

Planning Reminder

Accelerated Death Benefits

A person who is terminally ill may withdraw without tax life insurance proceeds to pay medical bills and other living expenses. For policies lacking an accelerated benefits clause, it is possible to sell a life insurance policy without incurring tax to a viatical settlement company; *see 17.16.*

Insurance proceeds may be taxable where the policy was transferred for valuable consideration. Exceptions to this rule are made for transfers among partners and corporations and their stockholders and officers.

Installment payments spread over your life under a policy that could have been paid in a lump sum: Part of each installment attributed to interest may be taxed. Divide the face amount of the policy by the number of years the installments are to be paid. The result is the amount that is received tax free each year.

If you are still receiving installments as the surviving spouse of an insured who died before October 23, 1986, up to $1,000 of interest paid with the annual installment is also tax free. You are treated as a spouse even if you were separated from the insured at the date of his or her death, but not if divorced. (If you receive payments under a policy with a "family income rider," *see 11.19*.) The $1,000 interest exclusion is not allowed where the insured died after October 22, 1986.

EXAMPLE

Alice is the wife and beneficiary under her husband John's life insurance policy of $200,000. He died September 30, 1986. She elected to take installment payments for the rest of her life. Alice's life expectancy is 25 years. Thus, $8,000 ($200,000 ÷ 25) is the principal amount spread to each year. The first $9,000 received each year ($8,000 principal plus $1,000 of the spouse's special interest exclusion) is exempt from tax. If Alice lives more than 25 years, she may continue to treat up to $9,000 of annual payments as tax-free receipts.

If the policy guarantees payments to a secondary beneficiary if you should die before receiving a specified number of payments, the tax-free amount is reduced by the present value of the secondary beneficiary's interest in the policy. The insurance company can give you this figure.

Installment payments for a fixed number of years under a policy that could have been paid in a lump sum. Divide the full face amount of the policy by the number of years you are to receive the installments. The result is the amount that is received tax free each year.

EXAMPLE

Fran is the beneficiary of her husband's $100,000 life insurance policy. She elects to take installment payments for 10 years. Each year she may receive tax-free principal of $10,000 ($100,000 ÷ 10).

Installment payments when there is no lump-sum option in the policy: You must find the discounted value of the policy at the date of the insured's death and use that as the principal amount. The insurance company can give you that figure. After you find the discounted value, you divide it by the number of years you are to receive installments. The result is the amount that is tax free. The remainder is taxed.

EXAMPLE

The insured died in 2006. Under an insurance policy, the surviving wife is entitled to $5,000 a year for life. Her life expectancy is 20 years. There is no lump sum stated in the policy. Say the discounted value of the wife's rights is $60,000. The principal amount spread to each year for the wife is $3,000 ($60,000 ÷ 20). Subtracting $3,000 from each annual $5,000 payment gives her taxable income of $2,000.

Payments to you along with other beneficiaries under the same policy, by lump-sum or varying installments. *See* the following Example for the way multiple beneficiaries may be taxed.

EXAMPLE

Under one life insurance policy of an insured man who died in 2006, a surviving wife, daughter, and nephew are all beneficiaries. The wife is entitled to a lump sum of $60,000. The daughter and nephew are each entitled to a lump sum of $35,000. Under the installment options, the wife chooses to receive $5,000 a year for the rest of her life. (She has a 20-year life expectancy.) The daughter and the nephew each choose a yearly payment of $5,000 for 10 years. This is how each yearly installment is taxed:

Wife: The principal amount spread to each year is $3,000. Subtracting $3,000 from the yearly $5,000 payment gives the wife taxable income of $2,000.

Daughter and Nephew: Both are taxed the same way. The principal amount spread to each of the 10 years is $3,500. Subtracting this $3,500 from the yearly $5,000 installment gives the daughter and the nephew taxable income of $1,500 each.

Interest only option. When proceeds are left on deposit under the "interest only" option, distributions of interest are fully taxed. A surviving spouse of an insured who died before October 23, 1986, may not exclude $1,000 interest under the "interest only" option. However, if the surviving spouse later elects to receive proceeds from the policy in installments, the interest exclusion applies from the time of the election.

11.19 A Policy With a Family Income Rider

Payments received under a family income rider are taxed under a special rule. A family income rider provides additional term insurance coverage for a fixed number of years from the date of the basic policy. Under the terms of a rider, if the insured dies at any time during the term period, the beneficiary receives monthly payments during the balance of the term period, and then at the end of the term period, receives the lump-sum proceeds of the basic policy. If the insured dies after the end of the term period, the beneficiary receives only the lump sum from the basic policy.

When the insured dies during the term period, part of each monthly payment received during the term period includes interest on the lump-sum proceeds of the basic policy (which is held by the company until the end of the term period). That interest is fully taxed. The balance of the monthly payment consists of an installment (principal plus interest) of the proceeds from the term insurance purchased under the family income rider. You may exclude from this balance: (1) a prorated portion of the present value of the lump sum under the basic policy and (2) an additional amount of up to $1,000 attributable to interest if you are a surviving spouse of an insured who died before October 23, 1986. The lump sum under the basic policy is tax free when you eventually receive it.

The rules here also apply to an integrated family income policy and to family maintenance policies, whether integrated or with an attached rider.

In figuring your taxable portions, ask the insurance company for its interest rate and the present value of term payments.

11.20 How Other Insurance Proceeds Are Taxed

Dividends paid by the insurance company as reduction of premiums (taken in cash, left as interest with the company, or used to accelerate the maturity of the policy) are not taxable. They serve to reduce the cost basis of your policy, thus increasing gain sometimes computed upon maturity of some policies. However, interest on such "dividends" is generally taxable, although the interest on GI insurance dividends left on deposit with the VA is tax free.

Matured endowment policies. You generally report as income the difference between the proceeds received and your investment; *see 7.25.* The payment on an endowment contract because of the insured's death is treated as the payment of tax-free life insurance proceeds provided the policy meets certain technical definitions not discussed in this book.

Sale of an endowment contract before maturity. Taxed as ordinary income; *see 7.25.*

Collection of proceeds on policy purchased by or assigned to you on the life of someone else. Where a policy is transferred for valuable consideration, only the amount paid and the premiums paid after the transfer are tax free when collected; the balance is taxed. There is no tax on life insurance proceeds paid under contracts that have been transferred to a partner or to a corporation in which the insured was a shareholder or officer.

Caution

Surrender of Policy for Cash

If the cash received on the surrender of a policy exceeds the premiums paid less dividends received, the excess is taxed as ordinary income (not capital gain). If you take, instead, a paid-up policy, you may avoid tax; *see 6.12.* You get no deduction if there is a loss on the surrender of a policy.

Tax may be avoided by a terminally ill individual on the surrender of a policy under an accelerated death benefit clause or on a sale of the policy to a viatical settlement company; *see 17.16.*

PART 3

Claiming Deductions

In this part, you will learn how to reduce your tax liability by claiming deductions from gross income, and either the standard deduction or itemized deductions. Pay special attention to—

- Deductions you may claim directly from gross income in arriving at adjusted gross income. These are allowed even if you claim the standard deduction. *See* Chapter 12.
- The standard deduction. Although the standard deduction (*see* Chapter 13) may provide an automatic tax reduction, read the chapters on itemized deductions to see that you have not overlooked itemized deductions for charitable donations, interest expenses, state and local taxes, medical expenses, casualty and theft losses, miscellaneous expenses for job costs, and investment expenses.
- The 3% reduction of certain itemized deductions if your 2006 adjusted gross income, or AGI (Line 37 of Form 1040), exceeds $150,500 (or $75,250 if you are married and file separate returns). *See* Chapter 13.
- Personal exemptions. Each personal exemption claimed on your 2006 return—for yourself, your spouse, your children, and other dependents, is the equivalent of a $3,300 deduction. *See* Chapter 21 for exemption rules, including the phaseout of exemptions for certain high-income taxpayers.
- Other deductions that are discussed in the following chapters:

Chapter 40	Business expenses
Chapter 9	Rental expenses
Chapter 43	Automobile expenses

Chapter 12

Deductions Allowed in Figuring Adjusted Gross Income

Adjusted gross income (AGI) is the amount used in figuring the 7.5% floor for medical expense deductions *(17.1)*, the 10% floor for personal casualty and theft losses *(18.11)*, the 2% floor for miscellaneous itemized deductions *(19.1)*, the charitable contribution percentage limitations *(14.17)*, and the 3% reduction of itemized deductions *(13.7)*.

If you follow the instructions and order of the tax return, you will arrive at adjusted gross income automatically. But if you are planning the tax consequences of a transaction in advance of preparing your return, *12.1* will explain how to figure adjusted gross income (AGI).

There is an advantage in being able to claim deductions directly from gross income in arriving at adjusted gross income, since such deductions are allowed even if you claim the standard deduction and do not itemize deductions on Schedule A of Form 1040. Another advantage of such deductions is that they also reduce state income tax for taxpayers residing in states that compute tax based on federal adjusted gross income. This chapter will explain the deductions that qualify for the direct deduction from gross income.

Expenses Deductible Directly From Gross Income

12.1 Figuring Adjusted Gross Income (AGI)

Adjusted gross income is the difference between gross income in Step 1 and the deductions listed in Step 2.

Step 1. Figure gross income. This is all income received by you from any source, such as wages, salary, tips, gross business income, income from sales and exchanges of property, interest and dividends, rents, royalties, annuities, pensions, etc. But gross income does not include such items as tax-free interest from state or local bonds *(4.24)*, tax-free parsonage allowance *(3.13)*, tax-free insurance proceeds (Chapter 11), gifts and inheritances *(11.4)*, Social Security benefits that are not subject to tax under the rules at *34.3*, tax-free scholarship grants *(33.1)*, tax-free board and lodging *(3.12)*, and other tax-free fringe benefits (Chapter 3).

Step 2. Deduct from your 2006 gross income only the following items:

Repayment of supplemental unemployment benefits required because of receipt of trade readjustment allowances *(2.9)*

Forfeiture-of-interest penalties because of premature withdrawals *(4.16)*

Capital loss deduction up to $3,000 *(5.4)*

IRA contributions *(8.4)*

Rent and royalty expenses *(9.2)*

50% of self-employed tax liability *(12.2)*

Health insurance deduction if self-employed *(12.2)*

Jury duty pay turned over to your employer *(12.2)*

Performing artist's qualifying expenses *(12.2)*

Reforestation expenses *(12.2)*

Reservists' travel costs *(12.2)*

State and local official expenses *(12.2)*

Moving expenses *(12.3)*

Health savings account (HSA) contributions *(12.9)*

Archer MSA contributions *(12.12)*

Alimony payments *(37.1)*

Student loan interest *(33.6)*

Domestic production activities deduction *(40.23)*

Business expenses *(40.7)*

Net operating losses *(40.19)*

Keogh or SEP retirement plan contributions for yourself *(41.5)*

Note: The laws authorizing the tuition and fees deduction *(33.13)* and educator expenses *(12.2)* had not yet been extended to 2006 by Congress when this book went to press, but the extension was expected; *see* the *e-Supplement.*

Step 3. The difference between Steps 1 and 2 is adjusted gross income.

12.2 Claiming Deductions From Gross Income

Many deductions taken directly from gross income in arriving at adjusted gross income are deducted on Form 1040 schedules devoted to a specific activity, such as business deductions claimed on Schedule C (Chapter 40), capital losses claimed on Schedule D (Chapter 5), and real estate rental expenses claimed on Schedule E (Chapter 9). Other expenses are claimed directly from gross income on Form 1040. These deductions are referred to as "above-the-line" deductions, as they are allowed in figuring adjusted gross income and do not have to be claimed as itemized deductions.

On Form 1040A, you may deduct traditional IRA contributions and student loan interest. The deductions for tuition/fees and educator expenses might also be available on Form 1040A if they are allowed for 2006 by Congress; *see* the *e-Supplement.*

Extensions of deductions for tuition/fees and educator expenses pending when this book went to press. Congress was expected to extend to 2006 the laws authorizing the deductions for tuition/fees and educator expenses but had not yet done so when this book went to press.

Assuming the deductions are extended, the following rules will apply. *See* the *e-Supplement* for an update.

Educator expenses. If you were a teacher, instructor, counselor, principal, or aide in a private or public elementary or secondary school (kindergarten through grade 12) for at least 900 hours during the school year in 2006, you generally may deduct up to $250 of out-of-pocket costs for books and classroom supplies. Eligible expenses include computer equipment, including related software and services, other equipment, and supplementary materials used in the classroom. For courses in health or physical education, supplies must be related to athletics to qualify. If you are married filing jointly and you and your spouse both qualify as educators, each of you may deduct up to $250 of eligible costs, for a $500 maximum on your joint return.

If eligible expenses exceed the $250 limit, the excess may be deductible as a miscellaneous itemized expense; *see 19.1*.

The $250 deduction limit may have to be reduced or eliminated completely if certain tax-free amounts are received during the year. The deduction is reduced by tax-free interest on savings bonds used for tuition *(33.4)* and tax-free distributions from qualified tuition programs *(33.5)* and Coverdell education savings accounts *(33.12)*.

Tuition and fees. Up to $4,000 of college tuition and fees paid in 2006 may be deducted if MAGI does not exceed $65,000 for single and head of household filers and $130,000 for joint returns. A deduction of up to $2,000 is allowed for single and head of household filers with MAGI exceeding $65,000 but not $80,000 and for joint filers with MAGI exceeding $130,000 but not $160,000. *See 33.13* for details.

Overnight travel costs of Reservists and National Guard members. Armed Forces Reservists and National Guard members who travel over 100 miles and stay overnight to attend Reserve and Guard meetings may deduct their travel expenses as an above-the-line-deduction to the extent of the Federal Government *per diem* rate for that locality; *see 35.8*.

Expenses of performing artists. As a performing artist, you may deduct job expenses from gross income, whether or not itemized deductions are claimed, if you have:

1. Two or more employers in the performing arts during 2006 with at least $200 of earnings from at least two of them.
2. Expenses from acting or other services in the performing arts that exceed 10% of gross income from such work; and
3. Adjusted gross income (before deducting these expenses) that does not exceed $16,000.

If you are married, a joint return must be filed to claim the deduction, unless you lived apart from your spouse during the whole year. The $16,000 adjusted gross income limitation applies to your combined incomes. If both spouses are performing artists, the $16,000 adjusted income limit applies to the combined incomes, but each spouse must separately meet the two-employer test and 10% expense test for his or her job expenses to be deductible on the joint return.

You report the performing artist expenses on Form 2106 (or Form 2106-EZ where eligible) and enter the total on Line 24 of Form 1040, instead of on Schedule A. If you do not meet the tests, the expenses are deducted on Schedule A subject to the 2% AGI floor *(19.1)*.

State and local officials. State and local officials paid on a fee basis may deduct from gross income unreimbursed business expenses.

Health savings account (HSA) deduction. If you have coverage under a high-deductible health plan, are not entitled to Medicare benefits, and are not the dependent of another taxpayer, you generally can deduct contributions to an HSA within the limits discussed at *12.10*.

Moving expenses. Deductible moving expenses are discussed in this chapter at *12.3–12.8*.

50% of self-employment tax. After you figure your self-employment tax liability on Schedule SE, you deduct 50% of it here as an income tax deduction. *See 45.3–45.4* for the calculation of self-employment tax.

Keogh plan contributions and self-employed SEP or SIMPLE deductions. *See* Chapter 41 for further details.

Caution

Reduction of Self-Employed Health Insurance Deduction

The 100% health insurance deduction may not be claimed for any month during 2006 that you were eligible to participate in an employer's subsidized health plan, including a plan of your spouse's employer. If the deduction would be barred for any month because of such eligibility and you have long-term care coverage that is not employer subsidized, you may claim the 100% deduction for the portion of the long-term-care premiums that is deductible for your age, as shown at *17.15*.

Self-employed health insurance deduction. If you were self-employed in 2006, you may claim 100% of premiums paid in 2006 for medical and dental insurance, and qualified (*see* below) long-term-care insurance, for yourself, your spouse, and your dependents. The deduction is also allowed if you are a general partner in a partnership, a limited partner receiving guaranteed payments, or you received wages from an S corporation in which you were a more-than-2% shareholder. As a sole proprietor, you may claim the 100% above-the-line deduction whether the policy is purchased in your own name or the name of the business. However, if you are the sole shareholder-employee of an S corporation, the IRS position is that the above-the-line deduction is allowed only if the policy is purchased in the name of the corporation.

If you have a qualified long-term-care policy, part of the premium is deductible depending on your age *(see 17.15)* and this amount is included in the above-the-line deduction on Line 29.

The 100% deduction may not exceed your net profit from the business under which the health premiums are paid, less deductions claimed on Line 27 (50% of self-employment tax) and Line 28 (Keogh, SEP, or SIMPLE retirement plan contributions). Also *see* the Caution on the left.

Penalty on early savings withdrawals. *See 4.16.*

Alimony paid. *See* Chapter 37.

Traditional IRA contribution. The deductible limits, including the phase-out rules for individuals covered by employer retirement plans, are explained at *8.3–8.4*.

Student loan interest. Within limits, you may deduct interest you pay on a qualified student loan. *See 33.14* for details.

Domestic production activities deduction. *See 40.23–40.25.*

Attorney fees in employment discrimination cases. Attorney fees and court costs in actions involving unlawful discrimination claims are deductible on Line 36 of Form 1040 if they were paid after October 22, 2004, with respect to settlements or judgments occurring after that date. The deduction may not exceed the amount included in income as a result of the judgment or settlement. Also *see* the Law Alert in *11.7*.

Archer MSA contribution. If you are self-employed or employed by a qualifying small business and have high-deductible health coverage, a deduction for contributions to an Archer MSA account may be deductible. The deduction is figured on Form 8853 and then entered on Form 1040. *See 12.12* for further details.

Jury duty pay turned over to employer. If you receive your regular pay while on jury duty and turn over your jury duty fees to your employer, report the fees as other income on Line 21, Form 1040 and claim an offsetting deduction.

Repayment of supplemental unemployment benefits. As explained at *2.9*, you may claim a deduction from gross income for the repayment or in some cases a tax credit. Claim the deduction on Line 36 of Form 1040 and on the adjacent dotted line write the amount and label it "subpay TRA" (trade readjustment allowances).

Reforestation amortization. If you do not have to file Schedule C or F to report income from a timber activity, an amortization deduction for qualifying reforestation expenses may be claimed over an 84-month period; *see* Code Section 194 for details. On Line 36 of Form 1040, the amortization deduction should be labeled "RFST."

Costs of Moving to a New Job Location

12.3 What Moving Costs Are Deductible?

You may deduct unreimbursed expenses of moving your household goods and traveling to a new job location, provided you meet

- A 50-mile distance test *(12.4)*, and
- A 39-week or 78-week work test for remaining in the new location *(12.5–12.6)*. A deduction may be claimed even if the work test has not been met by the filing due date; *see 12.7*.

You claim the moving expense deduction as an adjustment to gross income on Form 1040, Line 26, whether you claim the standard deduction or itemized deductions.

If your expenses are reimbursed, you do not have to report the reimbursement, provided your employer reimburses you under an accountable plan; *see 20.31* and *12.8*.

If the tests are met, you may deduct on your 2006 return the following unreimbursed moving expenses incurred during 2006:

1. ***Traveling costs of yourself and members of your household en route from your old to the new locality.*** Here, you include the costs of transportation and lodging for yourself and household members while traveling to your new residence. Lodging before departure for one day after the old residence is unusable and lodging for the day of arrival at the new locality are included. If you use your own car, you may either deduct your actual costs of gas, oil, and repairs (but not depreciation) during the trip or take a deduction based on the rate of 18 cents per mile. Also add parking fees and tolls. Meal expenses are not a deductible moving expense.
2. ***The actual cost of moving your personal effects and household goods.*** This includes the cost of packing, crating, and transporting furniture and household belongings, in-transit storage up to 30 consecutive days, insurance costs for the goods, and the cost of moving a pet or shipping an automobile to your new residence. You may also deduct expenses of moving your personal effects from a place other than your former home, but only up to the estimated cost of such a move from your former home. Also deduct the cost of connecting or disconnecting utilities when moving household appliances. The cost of connecting a telephone in your new home is not deductible.

In one case, a moving expense deduction was allowed for the cost of shipping a sailboat. The IRS had disallowed the deduction, claiming the sailboat was not a "personal effect." The Tax Court, however, allowed the deduction based on these facts: the couple were active sailors and frequently used the boat; they lived on the sailboat for two weeks immediately before they moved and also for nine weeks after they arrived in the new location; and they kept on board personal effects such as a refrigerator, kitchen utensils, and chairs. According to the court, the boat was so "intimately related" to their lifestyle that it should be considered a deductible personal effect.

Filing Tip

Family Move

It is not necessary for you and members of your household to travel together, or at the same time, to claim a deduction for the expenses incurred by each family member.

Delay in moving to new job location. You may delay moving to the area of a new job location. A delay of up to one year does not jeopardize a deduction for moving expenses. Furthermore, if you move to the new job area within one year, your family may stay in the old residence for a longer period. Their later moving expenses will generally be deductible, even though incurred after one year. For example, the IRS allowed a moving expense deduction to a husband who immediately moved to a new job location, although his wife and children did not join him until 30 months after he began the new job. They delayed so that the children could complete their education. The IRS held that since part of the moving expenses were incurred within one year, the moving expenses incurred later were also deductible.

Nondeductible expenses. You may not deduct the cost of travel incurred for a maid, nurse, chauffeur, or similar domestic help (unless the person is also your dependent), expenses of refitting rugs and drapes, forfeited tuition, car tags or driver's license for the state you move to, losses on disposing of memberships in clubs, mortgage penalties, expenses for trips to sell your old house, or loss on the sale of the house. Furthermore, when your employer reimburses you for such costs, you realize taxable income equal to the amount of the reimbursement.

You may not deduct the cost of transporting furniture that you purchased en route from your old home.

You may not deduct the cost of pre-move house-hunting trips, temporary living expenses, or expenses of selling, purchasing, or leasing the old or new residence, such as attorneys' fees, real estate fees, or costs of settling an unexpired lease. Meal expenses while traveling to your new residence are not deductible.

12.4 The Distance Test

The distance between your new job location and your former home must be at least 50 miles more than the distance between your old job location and your former home. For this purpose, your home may be a house, apartment, trailer, or even a houseboat, but not a seasonal residence such as a summer cottage. If you had no previous job or you return to full-time work after a long period of unemployment or part-time work, the new job location must be at least 50 miles from your former home. Self-employed individuals are also subject to the mileage test.

Filing Tip

Meeting the Mileage Test

Use the following worksheet to see if your move satisfies the 50-mile test. Find the shortest of the most commonly traveled routes in measuring the distances.

Distance between	*In miles*
1. Old residence and new job location	______
2. Old residence and old job location	______
3. Difference (must be at least 50 miles)	______

The location of your new residence is not considered in applying the mileage test. However, if the distance between your new residence and the new job location is more than the distance between your old residence and new job location, your moving expenses may be disallowed unless you can show (1) you are required to live there as a condition of employment or (2) an actual decrease in commuting time or expense results.

If you worked for more than one employer, you find the shortest of the most commonly traveled routes from your old residence to your former principal place of employment.

Your job location is where you spend most of your working time. If you work at various locations, the job location is where you report to work. If you work for several employers on a short-term basis and get jobs through a union hall system, the union hall is considered your job location.

Moving overseas. A member of the Armed Forces may deduct the cost of moving his or her family to an overseas post.

If you take a new job overseas and qualify for the foreign earned income exclusion, moving expenses allocable to the excluded income are not deductible; *see 36.6*.

Alien moving to the U.S. The deduction is not limited to U.S. citizens and residents. An alien may deduct the cost of travel here to work at a full-time position.

EXAMPLES

1. Your company's office is in the center of a metropolitan area. You live 18 miles from your office. You are transferred to a new office and buy a new house. To deduct moving costs, you must show that the location of the new office is at least 50 miles from your previous residence.
2. Your old job was four miles from your former residence and your new job is 55 miles from your former residence. You move to a house that is less than 50 miles from your old house. Nevertheless, you have met the 50-mile test since your new job is 51 miles further from your former home than your old job was.

12.5 The 39-Week Test for Employees

In addition to meeting the distance test *(12.4)*, you must work in the locality of the new job as a full-time employee for at least 39 weeks during the 12-month period immediately following your arrival at the new job location. You do not need to have a job prior to your arrival at the new location. Your family does not have to arrive with you. The 39 weeks of work need not be consecutive or with the same employer. You may change jobs provided you remain in the same general commuting area for 39 weeks. The 39-week test does not apply to employees who become disabled and lose their jobs, or who die.

If you are temporarily absent from work through no fault of your own, due to illness, strikes, shutouts, layoffs, or natural disasters, your temporary absence counts toward the 39-week requirement as full-time employment.

Planning Reminder

Loss of Job

If you lose your job for reasons other than your willful misconduct, the 39-week requirement is waived. Should you resign or lose your job for willful misconduct, a part-time job will not satisfy the 39-week test. The time test is not waived because you reach mandatory retirement age first where this retirement was anticipated.

EXAMPLE

You accept a position with a company 600 miles from your former position. You move to the new location. After you have worked in the new position 14 weeks, you resign and take another job with a nearby company. You may add the 14 weeks of work with the first company to 25 weeks with the second company to meet the 39-week requirement.

Job transfers. The 39-week period is also waived if you are transferred from your new job for your employer's benefit. However, it must be shown that you could have satisfied the 39-week test except for the transfer.

What if *you* initiate the transfer? The IRS held in a ruling that the 39-week test is not waived if an employee initiates the transfer, even if the employer approves. An individual was not allowed to deduct the costs of moving across the country to take a government position when, within 39 weeks of taking the position, he applied for and took another government job in another area. The IRS disallowed the deduction, although the government reimbursed part of the employee's moving expenses to the new job post, thereby indicating that it considered the transfer to be in the government's interest. According to the IRS, the waiver of the 39-week test applies to transfers initiated by employers, not by employees.

Filing Tip

Job Status

For purposes of the 39-week test, full-time status is determined by the customary practices of your occupation in the area. If work is seasonal, off-season weeks count as work weeks if the off-season period is less than six months and you have an employment agreement covering the off-season.

Joint returns. On a joint return, either spouse may meet the time test. But the work time of one spouse may not be added to the time of the other spouse.

EXAMPLE

Smith moves from New York to a new job in Denver. After working full time for 30 weeks, he resigns from his job and cannot find another position during the rest of the 12-month period. He may not deduct his moving expenses. But assume that Mrs. Smith also finds a job in Denver at the same time as her husband and continues to work for at least 39 weeks. Since she has met the 39-week test, the moving expenses from New York to Denver paid by her husband are deductible, provided they file a joint return. However, if Mrs. Smith had worked for only nine weeks, her work period could not be added to her husband's to meet the 39-week test.

12.6 The 78-Week Test for the Self-Employed and Partners

In addition to meeting the distance test *(12.4)*, you must work full time in the area of the new business for at least 78 weeks during the 24 months immediately following your arrival, of which at least 39 weeks occur in the first 12 months. The full-time work requirement may prevent semi-retired hobbyists, students, or others who work only a few hours a week in self-employed trades or occupations from claiming the deduction.

You are considered to have obtained employment at a new principal place of work when you have made substantial arrangements to begin such work.

The time test is waived if disability or death prevents compliance.

Change of employee or self-employed status. If you start work at a new location as an employee and then become self-employed before meeting the 39-week employee time test, you must meet the 78-week test. Time spent as an employee is counted along with the time spent self-employed in meeting the test.

If, during the first 12 months, you change from working as a self-employed person to working as an employee, you may qualify under the 39-week employee time test, provided you have 39 weeks of work as an *employee*. If you do not have 39 weeks as an employee in the first 12 months, you must meet the 78-week test.

Joint returns. Where you file a joint return, you deduct moving expenses if either you or your spouse can satisfy the time test based on individual work records.

12.7 Claiming Deductible Moving Expenses

Qualifying unreimbursed moving expenses *(12.3)* incurred during 2006 are deductible on your 2006 return whether you claim the standard deduction or itemize deductions. Report your expenses and nontaxable employer reimbursements on Form 3903. Qualifying unreimbursed moving expenses from Form 3903 are then deducted on Form 1040, Line 26, as an adjustment to gross income.

Claiming the deduction before meeting the time test. If the due date for filing your tax return arrives before you can satisfy the 39-week *(12.5)* or 78-week *(12.6)* work test, you may, nevertheless, deduct unreimbursed moving expenses. If you subsequently fail to complete the work requirement, you have to file an amended return or report income; *see* the Example below. If you file your return without taking the deduction, you may file an amended return after meeting the time test to claim the deduction.

EXAMPLE

You move to a new location on November 1, 2006. At the end of the year, you have worked in your new position only nine weeks. You deduct your moving expenses on your 2006 tax return even though you did not complete the 39- or 78-week period of work. But if, after you file the 2006 return, you move from the location before completing the applicable 39-week or 78-week work period, you must report as income the amount of moving expenses deducted in 2006 on the return for the year you move from the location. Alternatively, you may file an amended 2006 return on which you eliminate the deduction.

Caution

Reimbursement for Loss on Sale of a Home

To encourage or facilitate an employee's move, an employer may reimburse the employee for a loss incurred on the sale of his or her home. The IRS taxes such reimbursements as pay.

12.8 Reimbursements of Moving Expenses

If your employer reimburses you for deductible moving expenses *(12.3)* under an accountable plan, the reimbursement should not be reported as salary or wage income on Form W-2. The requirements for an accountable plan are similar to those discussed for business travel expenses at *20.31*.

Qualified moving expenses an employer pays to a third party, such as to a moving company, are not reported on Form W-2.

A reimbursement for expenses that do *not* qualify for a deduction, such as pre-move house-hunting costs, temporary living expenses, meal costs, or real estate expenses, is reported as compensation on your Form W-2.

On Form 3903, you report your deductible expenses in excess of nontaxable reimbursements, and enter the deductible amount on Form 1040, Line 26, as an adjustment to gross income.

If in 2006 you had deductible moving expenses that you claim on your 2006 return and you receive a reimbursement for the expenses in 2007, you report your employer's reimbursement as compensation in 2007. Alternatively, you may prefer to delay the deduction until 2007. You may deduct on your 2007 return the excess of your 2006 expenses over the nontaxable reimbursement received in 2007.

Health Savings Accounts and Archer MSAs

12.9 Health Savings Account (HSA) Basics

Health savings accounts (HSAs) can be used by individuals covered by a high-deductible health plan (HDHP) to save for health-care costs on a tax-free basis in an IRA-like account. HSAs are intended to supplant Archer MSAs; *see 12.12* for Archer MSA rules.

The HSA provides a tax-sheltered account for paying routine medical expenses that fall below the deductible set by the HDHP. To contribute to an HSA, you must not be enrolled in Medicare Part A or Part B and you must not be a dependent of another taxpayer.

A qualifying HDHP must have a minimum annual deductible and a maximum annual limit on out-of-pocket costs (*see* below). For 2006, the minimum annual HDHP deductible was $1,050 for self-only coverage and $2,100 for family coverage. The limit on out-of-pocket costs for 2006 was $5,250 for self-only coverage and $10,500 for family coverage. The limit applies to co-payments, deductibles, and other payments but not premiums. The 2006 minimum annual deductible and limit on out-of-pocket costs may be increased for 2007 by a cost-of-living adjustment.

Generally, contributions to an HSA are not allowed if the taxpayer has coverage under any health plan that does not meet the "high deductible" requirement of an HDHP, but there are exceptions. A plan that otherwise satisfies HDHP rules may provide preventive care benefits without a deductible or with a deductible below the minimum annual deductible. Benefits may also be provided under certain types of "permitted" coverage and insurance before the deductible of the HDHP is satisfied. Permitted coverage includes coverage for vision, dental or long-term care, accidents, and disability. Permitted insurance includes *per diem* insurance while hospitalized, insurance for a specific disease or illness (such as cancer, diabetes, asthma, or heart failure), and insurance relating to workers' compensation liability, tort liability, or liabilities relating to owning or using a car or other property.

Filing Instruction

Report HSA Contributions and Distributions on Form 8889

Report your HSA contributions on Form 8889 and follow the instructions to figure any limitations on the amount you may deduct. Also use Form 8889 to report an HSA distribution and figure the amount, if any, that is taxable. Form 8889 must be attached to your Form 1040.

HSA contributions and distributions. Taxpayers who are eligible under the above tests can make a deductible annual contribution to an HSA based on the amount of the deductible set by the HDHP, subject to a cap. An additional contribution can be made if age 55 or older. The allowable contribution is deductible "above the line" from gross income on Line 25 of Form 1040. Contribution limits are discussed further at *12.10*. Earnings accumulate tax free within an HSA, as with an IRA.

Distributions from an HSA are not taxable to the extent used to pay qualified medical expenses of the account owner, his or her spouse, or dependents; *see 12.11*.

Note: *HSA contributions and distributions are reported on Form 8889.* See *the instructions to Form 8889 for further details not covered in* 12.10 *and* 12.11.

12.10 Limits on Deductible HSA Contributions

If you are an eligible individual (*see 12.9* for eligibility tests), you can set up an HSA with an insurance company, bank, or other financial institution that has been approved by the IRS for this purpose. HSA contributions are reported to the IRS on Form 5498-SA.

As with an IRA, HSA contributions can be made in a lump sum or in several payments over the year. The deductible annual contribution limit discussed below must be prorated for each month of HSA eligibility *(see 12.9)*, determined as of the first day of each month. Contributions can be made up until the due date for filing your tax return (without extensions). Thus, HSA contributions for 2006 can be made through April 16, 2007.

For 2006, the maximum deductible contribution limit for an individual with self-only HDHP coverage is the *lesser* of the amount of the deductible under the HDHP or $2,700. For an individual with family coverage, the maximum deductible contribution for 2006 is the *lesser* of the deductible under the HDHP or $5,450. If a married couple has family HDHP coverage and both spouses are eligible for an HSA, they can decide between themselves how to allocate HSA contributions; *see* Example 4 below. If each spouse has family coverage under a separate HDHP, both are treated as being covered under the plan with the lower deductible for purposes of figuring the contribution limit.

The contribution limit is increased for an account owner who is at least age 55 by the end of the year and who has not enrolled in Medicare. For 2006, the "catch-up" contribution limit is $700. Starting with the month that an individual enrolls in Medicare Part A or B (generally at age 65), no further contributions, including catch-up contributions, can be made to his or her HSA.

If HDHP coverage began during the year or eligibility was otherwise limited to some months during 2006, $^{1}/_{12}$ of the above limits are allowed for each month of eligibility; *see* the Examples below.

The $2,700 and $5,450 caps are subject to cost-of-living increases; *see* the *e-Supplement*. The additional contribution limit for account owners age 55 and older increases to $800 in 2007, $900 in 2008, and $1,000 in 2009 and later years.

You may have more than one HSA, but the above maximum annual contribution limit applies to the aggregate contributions to all of the HSAs.

If you are an employee eligible to contribute and your employer contributes to an HSA on your behalf, employer contributions within the limit are excludable from your income; *see 3.2*. If your employer's contribution is below the applicable limit, you may contribute to your HSA but the totals of all the contributions cannot exceed the applicable limit.

Contributions exceeding your applicable HSA limit are not deductible and are subject to a 6% excise tax. Contributions by an employer to an employee's HSA in excess of the limit are includible in the employee's income and subject to the excise tax. However, the excise tax can be avoided by a timely withdrawal of the excess contribution and any allocable income. The withdrawal deadline is generally the filing due date including extensions, or April 16, 2007, for an excess 2006 contribution. However, if you timely file without making the withdrawal, you may do so by October 15, 2007. On a timely withdrawal, the income is taxed in the year withdrawn but the excise tax does not apply and the distribution of the excess contribution is not taxed. *See* the instructions to Form 5329 for further details.

Use Form 8889 to report your HSA contributions and figure your deduction. You must report your HSA contributions for 2006 and apply the deduction limits on Form 8889, which must be attached to Form 1040. The deduction from Form 8889 is entered on Line 25 of Form 1040, where it is deductible above the line from gross income.

EXAMPLES

1. Josephine Jones is self-employed. On June 1, 2006, she enrolls in an HDHP providing self-only coverage with an annual deductible of $3,000. For calendar year 2006, she is enrolled in a qualifying HDHP for seven months. For the full year, the deductible HSA contribution limit would be $2,700, the lesser of the $3,000 HDHP deductible or the annual cap of $2,700 for self-only coverage in 2006. Since she was eligible for only seven months, Josephine's deductible contribution limit for the year is $1,575 ($2,700 × 7 months ÷12).
2. Starting in January 2006, Anthony Smith has self-only coverage under an HDHP with an annual deductible of $1,050. He attains age 65 in July 2006 and applies for and begins to receive Social Security benefits, which automatically enrolls him in Medicare. As of July 1, 2006, Anthony is no longer an eligible individual and may not contribute to an HSA. He may contribute for January through June. The annual contribution limit is $1,750 (the lesser of the $1,050 deductible or $2,700, plus a $700 catch-up contribution for being age 55 or older). Anthony's deductible contribution limit for January through June is $875 ($1,750 × 6 months ÷ 12).

IRS Alert

Transition Relief for State-Mandated Deductibles Ended

A state could require health plans to provide benefits without regard to a deductible or with a deductible below the minimum annual deductible for an HDHP ($1,050 for a self-only plan and $2,100 for family coverage in 2006). The IRS provided relief to individuals in these states while giving the states until January 1, 2006, to modify their laws to conform to HDHP requirements. Health plans that failed to qualify as HDHPs solely because of state laws in effect at the beginning of 2004 were treated as HDHPs by the IRS for months before 2006.

A further extension was provided to non-calendar-year health plans that complied with state deductible requirements as of their most recent plan renewal date before 2006. The IRS treated such non-calendar-year plans as HDHPs until their renewal date in 2006.

3. Assume that in Example 2 Anthony is covered under his employer's HDHP. He continues to work beyond age 65 and does not apply for Social Security or Medicare. Although he is "eligible" for Medicare due to his age, he is not "entitled" to Medicare because he has not applied for benefits by enrolling in Medicare Part A or Part B. Assuming he otherwise remains eligible, he can continue to make HSA contributions.
4. Mark and Jane marry in March 2006 and starting in April they have HDHP family coverage with a $2,400 deductible. For January through March, Mark had self-only HDHP coverage with a $1,200 deductible. Their contribution limit for the nine months of family coverage eligibility is $1,800 (9/12 of the $2,400 deductible). The $1,800 can go into an HSA for either Mark or Jane or be divided in any manner between the two accounts. For his first three months of self-only coverage, Mark's HSA contribution limit is $300 (3/12 of the $1,200 deductible). The $300 can only go into his HSA; Jane was not eligible until April.

12.11 Distributions From HSAs

Distributions from an HSA used exclusively to pay or reimburse qualified medical expenses of the account owner, his or her spouse, or dependents are not taxable. Distributions used for anything other than qualified medical expenses are taxable. Taxable distributions are also subject to a 10% penalty unless the distribution is made after the account owner becomes disabled, reaches age 65, or dies.

Distributions need not be taken in the year in which the expense is incurred to be tax free; they can be taken in the following year or in any later year. This may be necessary if there are insufficient funds to cover the expense at the time it is incurred. For example, an HSA account holder who incurs a $1,500 medical expense on December 1, 2006, can wait until June 2007 (or later) when the account balance exceeds $1,500. The distribution is tax free so long as records are kept to show that the distribution was used to reimburse qualified medical expenses that were not covered by insurance or otherwise reimbursed and not claimed in a prior year as an itemized deduction. The HSA must have been set up prior to the incurrence of the expense.

For tax-free distribution purposes, a "qualified medical expense" is generally a non-reimbursed payment for medical care that would otherwise be eligible for an itemized deduction; *see 17.2*. However, health-care premiums generally do not qualify for HSA purposes, but there are exceptions. An HSA can pay for premiums for long-term-care insurance, COBRA health-care continuation coverage, health coverage while an individual is receiving unemployment compensation, and for individuals over age 65, Medicare Part A or B, Medicare HMO, and the employee share of premiums for employer-sponsored health insurance including retiree health insurance. HSA distributions used to pay or reimburse long-term-care premiums are tax free only to the extent of the age-based deductible limit for such premiums; *see 17.5*. For example, if a person age 41 uses HSA funds to pay long-term-care premiums of $1,800 in 2006, only $530 (the deductible limit for those age 41 through 50 in 2006) is tax free. The balance is taxable and subject to a 10% penalty for withdrawal of funds prior to age 65.

A qualified medical expense may be for the care of the account owner, his or her spouse, or dependents, without regard to whether they are eligible to make HSA contributions. In the case of a married couple where both spouses have HSAs, one spouse may use a distribution from his or her HSA to pay or reimburse the qualified medical costs of the other spouse. However, both HSAs may not reimburse the same expense.

If an HSA account holder mistakenly takes a distribution such as to reimburse an expense he or she reasonably but mistakenly believes is a qualified medical expense, the funds can be repaid to the HSA in order to avoid tax on the withdrawn amount, assuming the plan accepts a return of mistaken distributions. The funds must be returned by April 15 of the year following the first year that the account holder knew or should have known of the mistake.

Inherited HSAs. If the beneficiary of an HSA is the surviving spouse of the deceased account owner, the surviving spouse becomes the owner of the account and will be subject to tax only on distributions that are not used for qualified medical expenses. If the beneficiary is not the surviving spouse, the account ceases to be an HSA as of the date of the owner's death and the date-of-death value of the HSA assets must be included in the beneficiary's income. The beneficiary (other than the decedent's estate) may reduce the taxable amount by any HSA payments for the decedent's medical expenses made within one year after death. A beneficiary is not subject to the 10% penalty for taxable distributions.

Report HSA distributions on Form 8889. You must report an HSA distribution on Part II of Form 8889, which must be attached to Form 1040. A taxable distribution, if any, from Form 8889 is reported on Line 21 of Form 1040 ("Other income"). On the dotted line next to Line 21 enter "HSA" and the amount. If there is a taxable distribution and no exception to the 10% penalty is available, the 10% penalty is entered on Form 8889 and reported on Line 63 of Form 1040 ("Total tax"). On the dotted line next to Line 63, enter "HSA" and the amount. The HSA custodian or trustee will report the distribution to the IRS on Form 1099-SA.

12.12 Archer MSAs

Archer MSAs (medical savings accounts) are in the process of being replaced by health savings accounts (HSAs); *see 12.9.* When this book went to press, the law authorizing the establishment of new Archer MSAs had not been extended beyond 2005. If the law is not extended, a self-employed individual may only contribute to an MSA set up before 2006; rules for employees are at *3.2. See* the *e-Supplement* for a legislative update.

An Archer MSA can be rolled over to an HSA. Contributions may not be made to an Archer MSA or to an HSA after you become entitled to Medicare benefits.

For 2006, a high-deductible health plan for self-only coverage must have a deductible of at least $1,800 and no more than $2,700. For family coverage, the deductible must be at least $3,650 and no more than $5,450. The high-deductible plan must limit out-of-pocket costs (other than premiums) for 2006 to $3,650 for self-only coverage and $6,650 for family coverage. You generally may not have any other coverage in addition to the high-deductible plan, but separate policies are allowed for disability, vision or dental care, long-term care, accidental injuries, specific diseases or illnesses, fixed payments during hospitalization, workers' compensation liability, tort liability, and liabilities arising from the ownership or use of property.

Deductible contribution limit. If you are self-employed, the maximum deductible contribution for 2006 is 65% of the annual policy deductible if you have self-only coverage under a high-deductible plan, and 75% of the annual policy deductible if you have family coverage. To deduct the maximum amount, you must have the policy for the entire year. Otherwise one-twelfth of the limit may be deducted for each full month of coverage. The deduction may not exceed your self-employment income from the business through which you have the high-deductible insurance.

If you are an employee of an MSA-participating employer and your employer makes any contributions to your Archer MSA, you are barred from making a deductible contribution; also *see* the Caution on employer contributions to a spouse's Archer MSA. As discussed at *3.2,* your employer's contribution to your Archer MSA is not taxable to you if it is within the 65%/75% limit discussed above.

Report contributions to your Archer MSA on Form 8853, which must be attached to your Form 1040. The deductible contribution shown on Form 8853 is entered on Form 1040 as a deduction from gross income ("above the line").

Distributions from Archer MSA. You can take a distribution from your Archer MSA to pay for medical expenses that are not reimbursable under your high-deductible plan. A distribution is tax free if it is used for qualifying medical expenses of you, your spouse, or your dependents. Generally, these are costs that could be claimed as an itemized deduction if you paid them directly. Premiums for long-term care insurance, for health coverage while you are receiving unemployment benefits, or for continuing coverage (COBRA) from a former employer qualify; other insurance premiums do not. Tax may be imposed on a distribution used to pay medical expenses of someone who was not covered by a high-deductible plan when the expenses were incurred; see Form 8853 for details.

Archer MSA distributions are reported on Part III of Form 8853, which must be attached to Form 1040. A taxable distribution from Form 8853 is reported on Line 21 of Form 1040 as "other income." A taxable distribution is also subject to a 15% penalty on Form 8853 unless you are age 65 or older, or disabled.

Caution

Employer Contribution to Spouse's MSA

If you and your spouse are covered under a high-deductible health plan with family coverage, employer contributions to either of your Archer MSAs bar both of you from making Archer MSA contributions for that year. If you each have self-only coverage under a high-deductible health plan, employer contributions to one of your Archer MSAs do not prevent the other from making MSA contributions.

Planning Reminder

MSA Contribution Deadline

You have until April 16, 2007, to make a deductible contribution to an Archer MSA for 2006.

Filing Instruction

Report Archer MSA Contributions and Distributions on Form 8853

Report your Archer MSA contribution on Form 8853 and follow the instructions to figure any limitations on the amount you may deduct and for the rules on handling excess contributions. Form 8853 must be attached to your Form 1040.

Chapter 13

Claiming the Standard Deduction or Itemized Deductions

Claim the standard deduction only if it exceeds your allowable itemized deductions for mortgage interest, property taxes, medical costs, charitable donations, casualty losses, and miscellaneous deductions for job costs and investment expenses. Generally, a single person may claim a 2006 standard deduction of $5,150; a head of household, $7,550; a married couple filing jointly or a qualifying widow(er), $10,300; and a married person filing separately, $5,150. Larger standard deductions are allowed to those who are age 65 or over or blind, and lower standard deductions are allowed to dependents with only investment income.

Before deciding whether to itemize or claim the standard deduction, read Chapters 14 through 20 to see that you have not overlooked any itemized deductions. To itemize, you must file Form 1040 and report your deductions on Schedule A.

Table 13-1 Itemized Deductions and the Standard Deduction for 2006

Item—	*Explanation—*	*Limitations and Examples—*
Standard deduction	The standard deduction is fixed by law according to your filing status and age. The standard deduction in 2006 is: $10,300 if you are married filing jointly or a qualifying widow or widower. $5,150 if you are single. $7,550 if you are a head of household. $5,150 if you are married filing separately. If you are age 65 or over or blind, your standard deduction is substantially larger; *see 13.4.*	A married person filing separately may not use the standard deduction if his or her spouse itemizes deductions; *see 13.3.* The standard deduction may not be claimed by a nonresident or dual-status alien or on a return filed for a short taxable year caused by a change in accounting period. A lower standard deduction of $850 is allowed to dependents with only unearned income; *see 13.5.*
Itemized deductions	You should itemize deductions on Schedule A of Form 1040 if your deductions exceed the standard deduction for your filing status. Itemized deductions include charitable contributions, interest expenses, local and state taxes, medical and dental costs, casualty and theft losses, job and investment expenses, and educational costs.	Individual itemized deductions are subject to limitations and some higher-income taxpayers are subject to an overall reduction, as explained below. **EXAMPLE** You are single and may claim the standard deduction of $5,150 for 2006. However, your allowable itemized deductions are $5,500. You claim $5,500 on Schedule A of Form 1040.
Reduction of certain itemized deductions	If your 2006 adjusted gross income (AGI) exceeds $150,500, itemized deductions other than medical expenses, casualty and theft losses, gambling losses, and investment interest expenses are generally reduced by 2% of the excess AGI over $150,500. If you are married filing separately, the reduction applies if your AGI exceeds $75,250; *see 13.7.*	**EXAMPLE** Your joint return adjusted gross income (AGI) for 2006 is $184,450. Your itemized deductions for mortgage interest, state income taxes, and charitable donations are $20,000. The AGI excess over $150,500 is $33,950. Therefore, itemized deductions are reduced by $679 (2% of $33,950). On Schedule A you may deduct $19,321 ($20,000 – $679).
Charitable contributions	If you itemize, you may deduct donations to religious, charitable, educational, and other philanthropic organizations that have been approved to receive deductible contributions; *see 14.1.*	The contribution deduction is generally limited to 50% of adjusted gross income *(14.17)*. Lower ceilings apply to property donations and contributions to foundations. The deductible amount is included in the reduction explained above. *See* Chapter 14 for details on charitable contributions.
Interest expenses	If you itemize, you may deduct interest on qualified home mortgages, points, home equity loans, and interest on loans to carry investments.	Interest on investment loans is deductible only to the extent of net investment income *(15.10)*. Interest on personal and consumer loans is not deductible. Interest on home mortgages that do not meet the tests at *15.1* is not deductible. Deductions for home mortgage interest and points are included in the reduction explained above. *See* Chapter 15 for details on interest deductions.
Taxes	If you itemize, you can deduct state and local income taxes. If extension legislation is enacted, state and local general sales taxes may be deducted in lieu of state and local income taxes; *see 16.3.* You may also deduct payments of state, local, and foreign real property taxes, and state and local personal property taxes. You claim your deduction for real estate taxes on the tax return of the year in which you paid the taxes, unless you report on the accrual basis; *see 16.6.*	Total deductible taxes are included in the reduction explained above. *See* Chapter 16 for details on deductible taxes.
Medical expenses	You may deduct payments of medical expenses for yourself, your spouse, and your dependents *(17.1)*. A checklist of deductible medical items is at *17.2.* With the exception of insulin, drugs are deductible *only* if they require a prescription by a physician.	Only expenses in excess of 7.5% of adjusted gross income are deductible. *See* Chapter 17 for details.

Table 13-1 Itemized Deductions and the Standard Deduction for 2006 (continued)

Casualty and theft losses	You may deduct personal property losses caused by storms, fires, and other natural events and as the result of theft *(18.1)*.	Each individual casualty loss must exceed $100 and the total of all losses during the year must exceed 10% of adjusted gross income; *see 18.11. See* Chapter 18 for casualty and theft loss details.
Job expenses	You may deduct unreimbursed costs of union dues, job educational courses, work clothes, entertainment, travel, and looking for a new job.	Included as miscellaneous expenses of which only the excess over 2% of adjusted gross income is deductible; *see 19.1.*The 2% floor does not apply to performing artists *(12.2)*, handicapped employees, or job-related moving expenses *(12.3)*.The deductible amount is included in the reduction explained above. *See* Chapter 19 for details.
Investment expenses and tax preparation costs	You may deduct investment expenses and other expenses of producing and collecting income, expenses of maintaining income-producing property, expenses of preparing your tax return or refund claims, and IRS audits.	Included as miscellaneous expenses of which only the excess over 2% of adjusted gross income is deductible; *see 19.1.* The deductible amount is included in the reduction explained above. *See* Chapter 19 for details.

13.1 Claiming the Standard Deduction

On your 2006 Form 1040, 1040A, or 1040EZ, you are allowed a standard deduction, which is an "automatic" deduction you may claim regardless of your actual expenses. The standard deduction reduces adjusted gross income (AGI). If you file Form 1040, choose the standard deduction if it exceeds the itemized deductions that could be claimed on Schedule A.

The ***basic standard deduction*** is allowed if you are under age 65 and not blind. The amount is adjusted each year to reflect inflation. For 2006, the basic standard deduction is:

$10,300 if married filing jointly or a qualifying widow(er);
$7,550 if filing as a head of household;
$5,150 if single; *and*
$5,150 if married filing separately.

A married person filing separately must itemize deductions and may not claim any standard deduction if the other spouse itemizes on a separate return; *see 13.3.*

EXAMPLE

Ben Green is age 25 and single. In 2006, he has salary income of $43,625 and receives mutual fund distributions *(32.4)* of $748. He makes a tax deductible contribution of $4,000 to a traditional IRA. Ben reduces his adjusted gross income of $40,373 by the $5,150 standard deduction because it exceeds his allowable itemized deductions for the year.

Gross income:		
Salary	$43,625	
Mutual fund income	748	$44,373
Deduction from gross income:		
IRA *(8.4)*		4,000
Adjusted gross income		$40,373
Less: Standard deduction		5,150
		$35,223
Less: Exemption *(21.1)*		3,300
Taxable income		$31,923

Age 65 or older or blind. For taxpayers age 65 or over, or taxpayers of any age who are blind, the basic standard deduction is increased by an additional amount; *see 13.4.*

Dependents. Individuals who may be claimed as dependents by other taxpayers are generally limited to an $850 standard deduction for 2006, unless they have earned income; *see 13.5.*

Dual-status alien. You are generally not entitled to any standard deduction if for part of the year you are a nonresident and part of the year a resident alien. However, a standard deduction may be claimed on a joint return if your spouse is a U.S. citizen or resident and you elect to be taxed on your worldwide income; *see 1.5.*

13.2 When To Itemize

Claim the standard deduction only if it exceeds your allowable itemized deductions for charitable donations, certain local taxes, interest, allowable casualty losses, miscellaneous expenses, and medical expenses. If your deductions exceed your standard deduction, you elect to itemize by claiming the deductions on Schedule A of Form 1040. However, if you are married filing separately and your spouse itemizes deductions, you also must itemize, even if the standard deduction exceeds your itemized deductions; *see 13.3.*

Filing Instruction

Changing an Election

If you filed your return using the standard deduction and want to change to itemized deductions, or you itemized and want to change to the standard deduction, you may do so within the three-year period allowed for amending your return. If you are married and filing separately, each of you must consent to and make the same change; you both must either itemize or claim the standard deduction.

EXAMPLE

Ellen Bates is single and her 2006 adjusted gross income is $48,000. Her itemized deductions total $5,650. As the $5,150 standard deduction is less than her itemized deductions, she claims itemized deductions of $5,650 on Schedule A.

13.3 Husbands and Wives Filing Separate Returns

If you and your spouse file separate returns *(1.3)* for 2006, and neither of you is a qualifying head of household *(1.12)*, you must both claim itemized deductions or limit yourselves to a standard deduction of $5,150 each. You must both make the same election; when one of you itemizes the other is not entitled to any standard deduction. That is, if your spouse has itemized deductions exceeding $5,150 and elects to itemize, you must also itemize, even if your itemized deductions are less than $5,150.

On a separate return, each spouse may deduct only those itemized expenses for which he or she is liable and pays. This is true even if one spouse pays expenses for the other. For example, if a wife owns property, then the interest and taxes imposed on the property are her deductions, not her husband's. If he pays them, neither one may deduct them on separate returns. The husband may not because they were not his liability. The wife may not because she did not pay them. This is true also of casualty or theft losses.

No restrictions if divorced or legally separated. Following a divorce or legal separation under a decree of divorce or separate maintenance, you and your former spouse are free to compute your tax as you each see fit, without reference to the way the other files. Both of you are treated as single. If you have itemized deductions, you may elect to claim them, and your former spouse is not required to itemize. Head of household tax rates may be available under the rules at *1.12.*

Head of household possibility if you live apart from your spouse. If you are separated but do not have a decree of divorce or separate maintenance, both of you must either itemize or claim the standard deduction of $5,150 for 2006. However, if you are married and live apart from your spouse and meet the following conditions, you may file your 2006 return as a head of household *(1.12)* and may choose between a $7,550 standard deduction and itemizing deductions:

- Your spouse was not a member of your household during the last six months of 2006.
- You paid over half of the costs of maintaining a home that for more than half of 2006 was the principal residence for you and a qualifying child or qualifying relative whom you may claim as your dependent. *See* Test 2 at *1.12* for details.

As a head of household, you may elect to itemize whether your spouse itemizes or not. If you elect not to itemize, your 2006 standard deduction as a head of household is $7,550 if you are under age 65 and not blind. If you are age 65 or over or blind, your standard deduction is increased by $1,250; *see 13.4.* The filing status of your spouse remains married filing separately. He or she must itemize deductions if you itemize. If you claim the $7,550 standard deduction for a head of household (or $8,800 if age 65 or older, or blind), he or she can itemize or claim the $5,150 standard deduction for married persons filing separately.

13.4 Standard Deduction If 65 or Older or Blind

A larger standard deduction is provided for persons who are age 65 or over or who are blind. The larger deduction for blindness is allowed regardless of age.

Age and blindness are determined as of December 31, 2006. However, if your 65th birthday is January 1, 2007, the IRS treats you as reaching age 65 on the last day of 2006, allowing you to claim the standard deduction for those age 65 or over on your 2006 return.

Your total standard deduction consists of two parts: (1) The basic standard deduction shown in *13.1* for your filing status plus (2) an extra standard deduction for being age 65 or older or blind. The amount of the extra deduction for 2006 is $1,250 if you are filing as single or head of household; and $1,000 if you are married, whether filing jointly or separately, or your filing status is qualifying widow(er). The chart below lists the total standard deduction, including the extra amount.

If you are married filing separately, you may claim the standard deduction only if your spouse also claims the standard deduction on his or her return; *see 13.3.*

Check applicable boxes

	65 or older	Blind
Yourself	☐	☐
Your spouse if you file a joint return	☐	☐
Your spouse if you file separately and can claim an exemption for your spouse *(21.2)*	☐	☐
Total checks____		

If you are—	*Number of checks are—*	*Standard deduction for 2006 is—*
Single	1	$ 6,400
	2	7,650
Married filing jointly *(1.4)* or qualifying widow or widower *(1.11)*	1	11,300
	2	12,300
	3	13,300
	4	14,300
Married filing separately *(13.3)*	1	6,150
	2	7,150
	3	8,150
	4	9,150
Head of household *(1.12)*	1	8,800
	2	10,050

1040 *Filing Instruction*

Total or Partial Blindness

An additional standard deduction is allowed to a person who is completely blind as of December 31, 2006. You also qualify if you are partially blind and attach a letter certified by your doctor stating that you cannot see better than 20/200 in your better eye with lenses or that your field of vision is 20 degrees or less. Keep a copy of this letter. If the certification states that your vision will never improve beyond these limits, you will not have to file a new certification in later years; you will only have to attach a statement referring to the earlier certification.

13.5 Standard Deduction for Dependents

If someone can claim you as a dependent for 2006 under the tests at *21.1*, your standard deduction is determined under the following rules. You may elect to itemize deductions if these exceed the allowable standard deduction. If you are married and your spouse itemizes on a separate return, you *must* itemize; *see 13.3.*

Dependent under age 65 and not blind. If you can be claimed as another taxpayer's dependent for 2006, your standard deduction is the greater of $850 *or* earned income plus $300, but no more than the basic standard deduction shown in *13.1* for your filing status.

EXAMPLE

1. Susan, age 17, is claimed as a dependent by her parents. For 2006, she has earned income of $475 and interest income of $220. Her standard deduction is $850, the greater of $850 or $775, the total of her earned income ($475) and $300.
2. Assume that Susan's earned income is $2,000 rather than $475. Her standard deduction for 2006 is $2,300, the greater of $850 or $2,300, the total of her earned income ($2,000) and $300.

Dependents age 65 or older or blind. Your standard deduction for 2006 is the total of these two steps:

Step 1. The greater of $850 *or* earned income plus $300; *plus*

Step 2. $1,000 if you are married or a qualifying widow or widower, or $1,250 if single or head of household. If you are age 65 or older *and* you are also blind, multiply the applicable figure, $1,000 or $1,250, by two.

The worksheets below incorporate these steps for computing your 2006 standard deduction.

Caution

Determine Dependency Status First

The reduced standard deduction rules apply to you if you *may* be claimed as a dependent on another tax return, such as by your parents. If you can be claimed as a dependent under the rules at *21.1*, it does not matter if you are actually claimed as a dependent.

Table 13-2 Standard Deduction for Dependents in 2006

Dependents With Earned Income* of $550 or Less

If your filing status is—	*Standard deduction is—*
Single or head of household	
Under age 65 and not blind	$ 850
Age 65 or older or blind	2,100
Age 65 or older and blind	3,350
Married, or qualifying widow(er)	
Under age 65 and not blind	$ 850
Age 65 or older or blind	1,850
Age 65 or older and blind	2,850

Dependents Under Age 65 and Not Blind With Earned Income* Exceeding $550

1. Enter your earned income *plus* $300. $ ________
2. Enter:
   $5,150 if you are single,
   $7,550 if head of household,
   $10,300 if qualifying widow(er) or married filing jointly, or
   $5,150 if married filing separately. ________
3. Enter the smaller of Lines 1 and 2. This is your standard deduction. ________

Dependents Age 65 or Older or Blind With Earned Income* Exceeding $550

1. Enter your earned income *plus* $300. $ ________
2. Enter:
   $5,150 if you are single,
   $7,550 if head of household,
   $10,300 if qualifying widow(er) or married filing jointly, or
   $5,150 if married filing separately. ________
3. Enter the smaller of Lines 1 and 2. ________

Filing Tip

Higher Standard Deduction for Dependents With Earned Income

For 2006, an individual who may be claimed as a dependent may add $300 to earned income in figuring the allowable standard deduction; *see* the worksheets in *13.5*.

4. Enter:

   $1,250 if you are single or head of household and are either age 65 or older or blind.

   $1,000 if you are married filing jointly or separately, or a qualifying widow(er) and are either age 65 or older or blind.

   If both age 65 or older and blind, the $1,250 or $1,000 amounts are doubled to $2,500 and $2,000, respectively. ________

5. Add Lines 3 and 4. This is your standard deduction. ________

**Include pay for services and taxable scholarships* (33.1): *Include net earnings from self-employment and then subtract 50% of self-employment tax liability* (45.3) *when figuring earned income. However, if your gross income (earned and unearned) is $3,300 or more, you may be claimed as a dependent only if you are the qualifying child of another taxpayer;* see 21.1.

EXAMPLES

Jane Dell claims her widowed mother, Beth, who is age 67, as her dependent for 2006. For 2006, Beth has interest income of $400, wages of $2,000, and Social Security benefits of $10,000 that are exempt from tax under the rules discussed at *34.3.* Beth's standard deduction is $3,550: $2,300 (the greater of $850 or her wage income of $2,000 plus $300) plus $1,250, the additional deduction for a single person over age 65. Beth's taxable income is zero. Although her gross income of $2,400 is below the filing threshold (*see* filing tests for dependents on page 4), she should file a tax return to obtain a refund of income tax withheld from her wages.

13.6 Prepaying or Postponing Itemized Expenses

Planning Reminder

Prepaying Deductible Expenses May Allow You To Itemize

As the end of the year approaches, check your records for payments of deductible itemized expenses. If these payments are slightly less than the allowable standard deduction for the year, making a year-end payment of a deductible expense that you would otherwise pay in the following year could allow you to itemize.

Before the end of the year, check your records for payments of deductible itemized expenses. If you find that your payments up to that time are slightly less than the allowable standard deduction for that year, accelerating payment of an expense that you would otherwise pay in the following year could allow you to itemize. For example, at the end of 2006, you may make an additional charitable contribution, or pay a state or local tax bill not due until 2007, or extend by one year professional association dues or job-related subscriptions. You cannot deduct prepayments of interest, insurance premiums, or rent on investment property.

On the other hand, making the year-end payment might still not increase your deductions enough to itemize. In that case, you would get no tax benefit from the payment. By postponing the payment until the next year, you may make it easier to itemize on that year's return.

If your year-to-year payments of itemized expenses have consistently been below the standard deduction, a prepayment or postponement strategy may allow you to itemize in at least one of two consecutive years, enabling you to reduce your taxes over the two-year period without increasing your overall expenditures.

13.7 Itemized Deduction Reduction

If your 2006 adjusted gross income (AGI) exceeds $150,500 ($75,250 if married filing separately) some of your itemized deductions are disallowed. First figure your itemized deductions under the regular rules; *see* Chapters 14 through 20 for details and limitations on specific types of expenses. Then reduce the total of otherwise allowable itemized deductions by the following, which are *not* subject to reduction:

- Medical and dental expenses
- Investment interest
- Casualty losses
- Theft losses
- Gambling losses

The balance of your 2006 itemized deductions is reduced. In most cases, the effect of the reduction formula is to reduce the balance by 2% of the excess of your AGI over the $150,500 (or $75,250) threshold. Use the worksheet below to figure the reduction. The reduction creates an added tax cost to earning additional income; *see 28.3.*

Table 13-3 Worksheet for Reduction

1.	Enter your 2006 adjusted gross income.	$________
2.	Enter $150,500 ($75,250 if married filing separately).	________
3.	Subtract Line 2 from Line 1.	________
4.	Multiply the amount on Line 3 by 3% (.03).	________
5.	Enter total allowable itemized deductions from Schedule A	________
6.	Enter the amount included on Line 5 for allowable medical and dental expenses, investment interest, casualty or theft losses, and gambling losses. These deductions are *not* subject to the reduction.	________
7.	Subtract Line 6 from Line 5.*	________
8.	Multiply the amount on Line 7 by 80% (.80).	________
9.	Enter the smaller of Line 4 or Line 8.	________
10.	Multiply Line 9 by 2/3 (0.6666). This is the disallowed amount.	________
11.	Subtract Line 10 from Line 5. This is the net amount of itemized deductions you may claim on Line 28 of Schedule A for 2006.	$________

**If the amount on Line 7 is zero, the reduction does not apply.*

Law Alert

Phaseout of Required Reduction

Starting in 2006, the required reduction to overall itemized deductions is being phased out. For 2006 and 2007, the reduction is only two-thirds of the reduction that was required for 2005. For 2008 and 2009, the reduction will be only one-third of the otherwise required reduction. Starting in 2010, the reduction rules will no longer apply.

EXAMPLE

Dan Sommer is single and his 2006 adjusted gross income on Form 1040 is $216,350. On Schedule A, Dan reports $31,000 of itemized expenses, after applying the 7.5% floor for itemized medical costs and the 2% floor for miscellaneous itemized deductions. Since his AGI exceeds $150,500, part of his itemized deductions will be disallowed.

Medical expense deduction (after 7.5% floor)	$ 700
State and local income taxes	13,000
Real estate taxes	2,341
Home mortgage interest	5,000
Charitable donation	9,000
Miscellaneous expenses (after 2% floor)	959
Total	$ 31,000

All of the deductions except medical expenses are subject to the reduction.

Following the steps of the worksheet shown above, Dan figures that $1,317 of his deductions are disallowed, leaving a net deduction of $29,683:

1.	Adjusted gross income	$ 216,350
2.	*Less:* threshold	150,500
3.	Excess	65,850
4.	3% of Line 3	1,976
5.	Itemized deductions	31,000
6.	*Less:* medical deductions (not subject to the reduction)	700
7.	Itemized deductions subject to the reduction	30,300
8.	80% of Line 7	24,240
9.	Smaller of (4) or (8)	1,976
10.	Multiply Line 9 by 0.6666. This is the amount disallowed.	1,317
11.	Net itemized deductions allowable on Schedule A (Line 5 *less* Line 10)	29,683

Chapter 14

Charitable Contribution Deductions

By making deductible donations, you help your favorite philanthropy and at the same time receive a tax benefit. For example, if you are in the 25% tax bracket, a donation of $1,000 reduces your taxes by $250.

If you contributed at least $250 to a charity in 2006, you must get a written receipt from the organization to substantiate the donation. A cancelled check is not sufficient evidence for a cash donation of $250 or more; *see 14.15.*

If you donated a car (or other vehicle) valued at over $500, you must attach Copy B of Form 1098-C to your return. Your deduction is generally limited to the gross sales proceeds received by the charity on a sale of the vehicle, even if you could substantiate a higher fair market value; *see 14.7.*

If you claim deductions for property valued at more than $500, you also must attach Form 8283 to Form 1040. If the value you claimed exceeds $5,000, you also may have to obtain a written appraisal; *see 14.12.*

There are deduction ceilings depending on the type of donation and the nature of the charity, and an annual ceiling based on adjusted gross income; *see 14.17.*

If your adjusted gross income for 2006 exceeds $150,500 ($75,250 if married filing separately), your charitable contribution deduction is subject to the reduction of itemized deductions explained in *13.7.*

Qualifying Charitable Donations

Donations of Property

Reporting Charitable Contributions

Qualifying Charitable Donations

14.1 Deductible Contributions

Charitable contributions are deductible only as itemized deductions on Schedule A of Form 1040. The deduction is subject to the 3% reduction of total itemized deductions explained at *13.7* if your adjusted gross income exceeds $150,500 ($75,250 if married filing separately).

You may deduct donations to religious, charitable, educational, and other philanthropic organizations approved by the IRS to receive deductible contributions; *see* the listing later in this section. If you are unsure of the tax status of a philanthropy, ask the organization about its status, or check the IRS list of tax-exempt organizations (IRS Publication 78). Donations to the federal, state, and local government are also deductible.

Substantiating your 2006 donations. Keep a cancelled check or receipt from the charity as proof of donations under $250. For donations of $250 or more, you need to obtain a written acknowledgment that notes any benefits or goods that you received in exchange; *see 14.15* for details.

For a donated car, other motor vehicle, boat, or airplane valued at over $500, you must obtain an acknowledgment on Form 1098-C (or equivalent substitute) that you must attach to your return; *see 14.7*.

Year-end donations. You deduct donations on the tax return filed for the year in which you paid them in cash or property. A contribution by check is deductible in the year you give the check, even if it is cashed in the following year. A check mailed and dated on the last day of 2006 is deductible in 2006. A postdated check with a 2007 date is not deductible until 2007. For checks of $250 or more, get a written receipt by the filing due date of your return (the cancelled check is not sufficient substantiation; *see 14.15*). A pledge or a note is not deductible until paid. Donations made through a credit card are deductible in the year the charge is made. Donations made through a pay-by-phone bank account are not deductible until the payment date shown on the bank statement.

Delivering securities. If you are planning to donate appreciated securities near the end of the year, make sure that you consider these delivery rules in timing the donation. If you unconditionally deliver or mail a properly endorsed stock certificate to the donee or its agent, the gift is considered completed on the date of delivery or mailing, provided it is received in the ordinary course of the mails. If you deliver the certificate to your bank or broker as your agent, or to the issuing corporation or its agent, your gift is not complete until the stock is transferred to the donee's name on the corporation's books. This transfer may take several weeks, so, if possible, make the delivery at least three weeks before the end of the year to assure a current deduction.

Debts. You may assign to a charity a debt payable to you. A deductible contribution may be claimed in the year your debtor pays the charity.

Limits on deduction. Depending on the nature of the organization and the donated property, a deduction ceiling of 50%, 30%, or 20% of adjusted gross income applies. In general, the deduction ceiling is 50% for cash contributions and 30% for contributions of appreciated property held long term. *See 14.17* for details on the deduction ceilings. Where donations in one year exceed the percentage limits, a five-year carryover of the excess may be allowed; *see 14.18*.

A deduction may also be limited under the 3% reduction rule discussed at *13.7*.

Law Alert

Direct Transfer From IRA to Charity in 2006 and 2007

Taxpayers age 70½ or older may exclude from gross income in 2006 and 2007 direct transfers from an IRA to a 50% limit charitable organization (other than a "supporting organization" or donor advised fund), up to a limit of $100,000 each year; *see 8.8.* No charitable deduction is allowed for a direct transfer that is excludable from income. An excludable transfer is not taken into account in applying the deduction ceilings of *14.17* to other charitable contributions.

Filing Tip

Donating Appreciated Securities

You get a tax deduction for the full market value when you donate appreciated securities traded on an established securities market that you have held more than one year. In addition, you also avoid paying capital gains tax on the securities' appreciation.

Organizations Qualifying for Deductible Donations

The following types of organizations may qualify to receive deductible contributions:

A domestic nonprofit organization, trust, community chest, fund, or foundation that is operated exclusively for one of the following purposes:

Religious. Payments for pew rents, assessments, and dues to churches and synagogues are deductible.

Charitable. In this class are organizations such as Boy Scouts, Girl Scouts, American Red Cross, Community Funds, Cancer Societies, CARE, Salvation Army, Y.M.C.A., and Y.W.C.A.

Scientific, literary, and educational. Included in this group are hospitals, research organizations, colleges, universities, and other schools that do not maintain racially discriminatory policies; and leagues or associations set up for education or to combat crime, improve public morals, and aid public welfare.

Prevention of cruelty to children or animals.

Fostering amateur sports competition. However, the organization's activities may not provide athletic facilities or equipment.

Domestic nonprofit veterans' organizations or auxiliary units.

A domestic fraternal group operating under the lodge system. The contributions must be used exclusively for religious, charitable, scientific, literary, or educational purposes; or for the prevention of cruelty to children or animals.

Nonprofit cemetery and burial companies, where the voluntary contribution benefits the whole cemetery, not only your plot.

Legal services corporations established under the Legal Services Corporation Act. Such corporations provide legal assistance to financially needy people in noncriminal proceedings.

The United States, a U.S. possession, a state, city, or town or Indian tribal government. The gift must be for public purposes. The gift may be directed to a government unit, or it may be to a government agency such as a state university, a fire department, a civil defense group, or a committee to raise funds to develop land into a public park. Donations may be made to the Social Security system (Federal Old Age and Survivors Insurance Trust Fund). Donations may be made to the federal government to help reduce the national debt; checks should be made payable to "Bureau of the Public Debt."

14.2 Nondeductible Contributions

Caution

Foreign Charities

You may deduct donations to domestic organizations that distribute funds to charities in foreign countries, as long as the U.S. organization controls the distribution of the funds overseas. An outright contribution to a foreign charitable organization is not deductible. Some exceptions to this ban are provided by international treaties. For example, if you have income from Canadian, Mexican, or Israeli sources, contributions to certain organizations in those countries are deductible subject to limitations. For details, *see* IRS Publication 526.

The following types of contributions are not deductible:

1. Donations to or on behalf of specific individuals, even if needy or worthy. Generally, scholarships for specific students, or gifts to organizations to benefit only certain groups. However, the IRS in private rulings has allowed deductions for scholarship funds that are limited to members of a particular religion, so long as that religion is open to all on a racially nondiscriminatory basis, and to scholarship funds open only to male students.
2. Payments to political campaign committees or political action committees.
3. Payments to an organization that devotes a substantial part of its activities to lobbying, trying to influence legislation, or carrying on propaganda or whose lobbying activities exceed certain limits set by the law, causing the organization to lose its tax-exempt status. The IRS has disallowed contributions to a civic group opposing saloons, nightclubs, and gambling places, although the group also aided libraries, churches, and other public programs.
4. Gifts to organizations such as:
   Fraternal groups—except when they set up special organizations exclusively devoted to charitable, educational, or other approved purposes.
   Professional groups such as those organized by accountants, lawyers, and physicians—except when they are specially created for exclusive charitable, educational, or other philanthropic purposes. The IRS will disallow unrestricted gifts made to state bar associations, although such organizations may have some public purposes. Some courts have allowed deductions for donations to bar associations on the ground that their activities benefit the general public. However, an appeals court disallowed deductible donations to a bar association that rates candidates for judicial office.
   Clubs for social purposes—fraternities and sororities are generally in this class. Unless an organization is exclusively operated for a charitable, religious, or other approved purpose, you may not deduct your contribution, even though your funds are used for a charitable or religious purpose.
5. Donations to civic leagues, communist or communist-front organizations, chambers of commerce, business leagues, or labor unions.
6. Contributions to a hospital or school operated for profit.
7. Purchase price of church building bond. To claim a deduction, you must donate the bond to the church. The amount of the deduction is the fair market value of the bond when you make the donation. Interest on the bond is income each year, under the original issue discount rules discussed in *4.19*, where no interest will be paid until the bond matures.
8. Donations of blood to the Red Cross or other blood banks.
9. Contributions to foreign charitable organizations or directly to foreign governments. Thus, a contribution to the State of Israel was disallowed.

Donation of services. You may not deduct the value of volunteer work you perform for charities. But you can deduct unreimbursed expenses incurred during such work; *see 14.4*.

Free use of property. You may not deduct the rental value of property you allow a charity to use without charge. That is, if you allow a charity rent-free use of an office in your building, you may not deduct the fair rental value. You also have no deduction when you lend money to a charity without charging interest.

To raise money for a charity, supporters of the organization may donate rental time for their vacation home, to be auctioned off to the public. No deduction is allowed for donating the rental time; *see 14.10*.

Parents' support payments of children serving as Mormon missionaries. According to the Supreme Court, support payments made by parents directly to their children who serve as missionaries are not deductible because the church does not control the funds.

14.3 Contributions That Provide You With Benefits

A contribution to a qualifying organization *(14.1)* is generally deductible only to the extent that you intend to give more than the value of benefits you receive and actually do so.

If you contribute $75 or less and receive benefits, the organization may tell you the value of the benefits. If your contribution exceeds $75, the organization by law *must* give you a written statement that estimates the value of the benefits provided to you and instructs you to deduct only the portion of your contribution that *exceeds* the benefits. However, the disclosure statement does not have to be provided to you if you receive only token benefits, or if you receive from a religious organization only "intangible religious benefits."

Caution

Tuition or Other Benefits Received

Except for certain token benefits and memberships that are disregarded for tax purposes, you may not deduct a contribution to a qualified charity to the extent that you receive goods, services, or financial benefits in exchange; *see 14.3*.

The Tax Court and Ninth Circuit Court of Appeals agree with the IRS that you may not deduct tuition payments to a religious school for the education of your children if secular courses that lead to a recognized degree are provided, unless the payments exceed the usual tuition charged for a secular education in your area.

Fees paid to a tax-exempt rest home in which you live, or to a hospital for the care of a particular patient, are not deductible if any benefit is received from the contribution. A gift to a retirement home, over and above monthly fees, is not deductible if your accommodations are dependent on the size of your gift.

EXAMPLES

1. You contribute $200 to a philanthropy and receive a book that you have seen on sale for prices ranging between $18 and $25. The charity estimates the value at $20. As the estimate is between the typical retail prices, it is acceptable to the IRS. Although the book sold at a price as high as $25, you may treat the $20 estimate as fair market value and claim a deduction of $180.
2. A charitable organization sponsors an art auction and provides a catalogue that lists the items being auctioned and estimates of fair market value. The catalogue lists the value of a vase at $100. At the auction, you bid and pay $500 for the vase. Because you were aware of the estimate before the auction and paid more for the vase, you may deduct $400.

Dues. Dues paid to a qualified tax-exempt organization are deductible to the extent they exceed the value of benefits from the organization, such as monthly journals, use of a library, or the right to attend luncheons and lectures. As discussed above, you generally must be provided with an estimate of any benefits you received if your donation exceeds $75.

If dues are paid to a social club with the understanding that a specified part goes to a qualifying charity *(14.1)*, you may claim a charitable deduction for dues earmarked for the charity. If the treasurer of your club is actually the agent of the charity, you take the deduction in the year you give him or her the money. If the treasurer is merely your agent, you may take the deduction only in the year the money is remitted to the charity.

Benefit tickets. Tickets to theater events, tours, concerts, and other entertainments are often sold by charitable organizations at prices higher than the regular admission charge. The difference between the regular admission and the higher amount you pay is deductible as a charitable contribution. If you decline to accept the ticket or return it to the charity for resale, your deduction is the price you paid.

The charity should explain to you how much is deductible. The charity must provide an explanation if you paid more than $75; *see* the discussion above.

If the ticket is at or below its normal cost, no deduction is allowed unless you decline the ticket or return it to the charity.

If tickets were purchased for a charity-sponsored series of events and the average cost of a single event is equal to or less than the cost of an individual performance, then a deduction for a returned ticket is based upon the time the ticket was held. Generally, you may deduct only your cost. However, if you have held the ticket for more than a year, you may deduct the price the charity will charge on resale of the ticket.

EXAMPLE

A couple claimed a full deduction for regular-price tickets to a high-school fund-raising event that they did not attend. They argued that they were entitled to the deduction because they received no benefit from their ticket purchase. The IRS disallowed the deduction and the Tax

Court agreed, holding that a donor receives a benefit by merely having the right to attend the event. To claim a deduction for the price of the tickets the couple should have returned them to the charity.

Caution

Bingo and Lotteries

You may not deduct the cost of raffle tickets, bingo games, or tickets for other types of lotteries organized by charities.

Donation for the right to buy athletic stadium tickets. If you contribute to a public or nonprofit college or university and receive the right to buy preferential seating at the school's athletic complexes, you may deduct 80% of the contribution to the school. The 80% deduction also applies where your contribution gives you the right to buy seating in stadium skyboxes, suites, or special viewing areas. The cost of any tickets you buy is not deductible. The deduction is allowed only to the extent that you receive the right to buy tickets rather than the tickets themselves. For example, if in exchange for a substantial donation you receive a season ticket worth $200, your payment is reduced by $200 before applying the 80% deductible percentage.

Token Items and Membership Benefits That Do Not Reduce Your Deduction

Token items. Popular fund-raising campaigns, such as those for museums, zoos, and public TV, offer token items such as calendars, tote bags, tee shirts, and other items carrying the organization's logo. You are allowed a full deduction for your contribution if the item is considered to be of insubstantial value under IRS guidelines.

The charity must tell you how much of your contribution is deductible in the solicitation that offers the token item. If the items are insubstantial in value, the charity should tell you that your payment is fully deductible. For example, if in 2006 you contributed at least $43, and the offered items cost the charity no more than $8.60, the value of the benefits is ignored and a full 2006 deduction is allowed. A full deduction for 2006 is also allowed if the items were worth no more than 2% of the contribution or $86, whichever is less. The $43, $8.60, and $86 amounts change annually for inflation.

Filing Tip

Estimated Value of Benefits

You may rely on a written estimate from the organization of the value of any benefits given to you unless it seems unreasonable. Although the value of benefits received generally reduces your deductible contribution, certain token items and membership benefits do not reduce the amount of your deduction.

Newsletters or program guides that are not of commercial quality are treated as token items having no fair market value or cost if their primary purpose is to inform members about the organization's activities, and they are not available to nonmembers by paid subscription or through newsstand sales.

Publications with articles written for compensation and advertising are treated as commercial-quality publications for which the organization must figure value to determine if a full deduction is allowed under the "insubstantial value" test. Professional journals, whether or not they have such articles and advertising, will generally be treated as commercial-quality publications that must be valued.

Membership benefits. If you contribute $75 or less for an annual membership in a qualified charity *(see 14.1)* and you receive only the following benefits, the benefits can be disregarded and you may deduct your entire payment:

1. Privileges that can be exercised frequently, such as free or discounted parking or admission, or discounts on gift shop or mail order merchandise, *or*
2. Admission to events that are open only to members and the organization's reasonably projected cost per person for each event excluding overhead (as of the time the membership package is offered) is no more than the annual limit for "low cost articles." For 2006, the "low cost article" limit is $8.60.

14.4 Unreimbursed Expenses of Volunteer Workers

If you work without pay for an organization listed at *14.1*, you may deduct as charitable contributions your unreimbursed expenses in providing the services. This includes commuting expenses to and from its place of operations, and meals and lodging on a trip away from home *(20.6)* for the organization.

To qualify for the deduction, the expenses must be incurred for a domestic organization that authorizes you to travel. You may not deduct the value of your donated services.

Keep records, such as cancelled checks, to substantiate the amount of your 2006 out-of-pocket expenses. To deduct an unreimbursed expense for 2006 of $250 or more, such as for a plane ticket or a luncheon you hosted on behalf of the organization, obtain for each such expense a statement from the charitable organization that acknowledges the services you provided. The acknowledgment must describe the services, and state whether you were provided any goods or services by the charity. If so, an estimate of their value must be given unless the benefits are "intangible religious benefits." The acknowledgment must be obtained by the date you file your return, but if you file after the due date (or extended due date if you get an extension), the acknowledgment must be obtained by the due date of your return, including extensions. For 2006 returns, the due date is April 16, 2007, unless you get an extension.

Car expenses. If you used your car (or other motor vehicle) during 2006 to provide volunteer services for a charity, you may deduct either the actual vehicle operating costs (such as gas and oil) that are directly related to your volunteer services, or you may claim a flat mileage rate.

The flat mileage rate for 2006 is set by statute and depends on whether the use of the vehicle is related to Hurricane Katrina relief activities. For non-Katrina-related services, the rate is just 14 cents per mile. For Katrina-related mileage, the rate is 32 cents per mile; this is 70% of the business mileage rate of 44.5 cents *(43.1)* rounded to the next highest cent.

If you are reimbursed in 2006 for using your car, van, pickup truck, or panel truck in connection with Katrina-related relief, you are not taxed on reimbursements up to the 44.5-cents-per-mile business rate.

Parking fees and tolls are deductible whether you claim actual expenses or the flat mileage rate.

After 2006, the mileage rate for all volunteer services will be 14 cents per mile; the special Katrina-related rates will no longer apply. The special reimbursement exclusion for Katrina-related services also will be inapplicable for years after 2006.

EXAMPLE

In the course of doing volunteer work for a charity in 2006, Jill Patton drove her car 1,000 miles. She may claim a contribution deduction of $140 (14 cents a mile), plus tolls and parking.

If Jill's volunteer work related to Hurricane Katrina relief, her deduction would be $320 (.32 × 1000 miles).

Planning Reminder

Foster Parent Expenses

If you receive payments from a state agency to reimburse you for the costs of caring for a foster child in your home, and you can show that your costs of caring for the child exceed the reimbursements, the excess is deductible as a charitable contribution. Keep detailed records to substantiate your support payments.

Also deductible as charitable contributions are:

- Uniform costs required in serving the organization
- Cost of telephone calls, and cost of materials and supplies you furnished such as stamps or stationery
- Travel expenses, including meals and lodging on overnight trips away from home as an official delegate to a convention of a church, charitable, veteran, or other similar organization. If you are a member but not a delegate, you may not deduct travel costs, but you may deduct expenses paid for the benefit of your organization at the convention.
- All related expenses in hosting a fund-raiser are deductible, from the invitations to the food and drink.

The IRS does not allow a deduction for "babysitting" expenses of charity volunteer workers. Although incurred to make the volunteer work possible, babysitting costs are a nondeductible personal expense. Furthermore, the expense is not a dependent care cost; it is not related to a paying job.

Recreational purposes may bar travel expense deduction. To claim a charitable deduction for travel expenses of a research project for a charitable organization, you must show the trip had no significant element of personal pleasure, recreation, or vacation.

EXAMPLES

1. Al Jones sails from one Caribbean island to another and spends eight hours a day counting whales and other forms of marine life as part of a project sponsored by a charitable organization. According to the IRS, he may not claim a charitable deduction for the cost of the trip.
2. Sara Smith works on an archaeological excavation sponsored by a charitable organization for several hours each morning, with the rest of the day free for recreation and sightseeing. According to the IRS, she may not deduct the cost of the trip.
3. Myra Scott, a member of a chapter of a local charitable organization, travels to New York City and spends the entire day at the required regional meeting. According to the IRS, she may deduct her travel expenses as a charitable donation, even if she attends a theater in the evening.

14.5 Support of a Student in Your Home

A limited charitable deduction is allowed for support of an elementary or high-school student in your home under an educational program arranged by a charitable organization. If the student is not a relative or your dependent, you may deduct as a charitable contribution your support payments up to $50 for each month the student stays in your home. For this purpose, 15 days or more of a calendar month is considered a full month. You may not deduct any payments received from the charitable organization if any reimbursements are received for the student's maintenance. The only exception is that if you prepay a "one-time" expense such as a hospital bill or vacation for the child at the request of the child's parents or the sponsoring charity, and you are later reimbursed for part of your payment, you may deduct your unreimbursed expenses.

To support the deduction, be prepared to show a written agreement between you and the organization relating to the support arrangement. Keep records of amounts spent for such items as food, clothing, medical and dental care, tuition, books, and recreation in order to substantiate your deduction. No deduction is allowed for depreciation on your house.

Donations of Property

Filing Instruction

Long-Term Holding Period

In this chapter, property held "long term" is property held more than one year by the donor.

14.6 What Kind of Property Are You Donating?

Generally, a deduction for the fair market value of donated property may be claimed, but the tax law does not treat all donations of appreciated property in the same way. Whether the full amount of the fair market value of the property is deductible depends on the type of property donated, your holding period, the nature of the philanthropy, and the use to which the property is put by the philanthropy. For donations of motor vehicles, boats, or airplanes valued at over $500, special deduction restrictions and substantiation restrictions apply; *see 14.7*.

Save records to support the market value and cost of donated property. Get a receipt or letter from the charitable organization acknowledging and describing the gift. You *must* get a receipt for donations of property valued at $250 or more; *see 14.15*. Lack of substantiation may disqualify an otherwise valid deduction. Furthermore, if the total claimed value of your 2006 property donations exceeds $500, you must report the donation on Form 8283, which you attach to Schedule A, Form 1040. *See also 14.12* for when you need an appraisal of the value of the property.

Figuring value. When donating securities listed on a public exchange, fair market value is readily ascertainable from newspaper listings of stock prices. It is the average of the high and low sales price on the date of the donation.

To value other property, such as real estate or works of art, you will need the services of an experienced appraiser. Fees paid to an appraiser are not deductible as a charitable contribution, but rather as a miscellaneous itemized deduction *(19.1)* subject to the 2% adjusted gross income floor on Schedule A.

Fair market value deductible for appreciated intangible personal property (such as securities) and real estate held long term. Fair market value is deductible where you have held such property long term (longer than one year) and you give it to a publicly supported charity or to a private foundation that qualifies as a 50% limit organization, but you may not deduct more than 30% of adjusted gross income, as discussed at *14.17*. A five-year carryover for the excess is allowed; *see 14.18*. If the donation exceeds the 30% ceiling, you may consider a special election that allows you to apply the 50% ceiling; *see 14.19*.

A contribution of appreciated securities or real estate held long term has two tax advantages that reduce the real cost of making the contribution:

1. Your taxes are reduced by the deduction of the fair market value of the property. For example, you donate appreciated stock that is selling at $1,000. You are in the 25% tax bracket. The deduction for the donation reduces your taxes by $250.
2. You avoid the tax you would have paid on a sale of the stock. Assume that your cost for the stock was $400 and that your regular top bracket is 25%. On a sale at $1,000, you would pay tax of $90 (15% capital gain rate on $600 profit). By donating the stock, you save that $90 plus $250 from the $1,000 deduction, for a total tax savings of $340. Your "cost" for donating the $1,000 asset is $660 ($1,000 – $340).

Caution

Appraisal Fees

A fee paid for an appraisal of donated real estate or art is not deductible as a charitable contribution. It may be claimed only as a miscellaneous itemized deduction subject to the 2% floor *(see 19.1)*.

The IRS ruled that you may not claim a deduction on donated stock if you retain the voting rights, even though the charity has the right to receive dividends and sell the stock. The right to vote is considered a substantial interest and is crucial in protecting a stockholder's investment.

If you are planning a year-end donation of securities, keep in mind that the gift is generally not considered complete until the properly endorsed securities are mailed or delivered to the charity or its agent; *see 14.1*.

Deduction limited to cost for appreciated property not held long term and ordinary income property. This is property that, if sold by you at its fair market value, would not result in long-term capital gain. The deduction for donations of this kind is restricted to your cost for the property. Examples include: stock and other capital assets held by you for one year or less, inventory items donated by business, farm crops, Section 306 stock (preferred stock received as a tax-free stock dividend, usually in a closely held corporation), and works of art, books, letters, and memoranda donated by the person who prepared or created them. *See 14.9* for art objects. For example, a former Congressman claimed a charitable deduction for the donation of his papers. His deduction was disallowed. His papers were ordinary income property, and since his cost basis in the papers was zero, he could claim no deduction. Depreciable business property is considered ordinary income property to the extent that depreciation would be recaptured as ordinary income on a sale *(see 44.1–44.3)*. If the cost of the property was fully deducted under first-year expensing *(42.3)*, you have no cost basis and you may not claim a deduction.

EXAMPLE

Bob James holds stock that cost him $1,000. It is now worth $1,500. If he holds it for one year or less and donates it to a philanthropy, his deduction would be limited to $1,000. He would get no tax benefit for the appreciation of $500. On the other hand, if the stock were held over a year, he could claim a deduction for the full market value of the stock on its donation.

Fair market value or cost may be deductible for appreciated tangible personal property held long term. If you donate appreciated tangible personal property held long term, such as works of art *(see 14.9)*, jewelry, furniture, books, equipment, fixtures (severed from realty), and antique cars, the deduction limit depends on how the charitable organization uses the property. If the property is used by the organization for purposes related to its tax-exempt purpose or function, you may deduct the fair market value. If the organization puts the property to a use that is unrelated to its tax-exempt purpose or function, the deduction is limited to your cost basis because the fair market value must be reduced by the amount of long-term capital gain that would have been realized if the property had been sold at fair market value. If the charity sells your gift to obtain cash for its exempt purposes, your donation is generally treated as being put to a nonrelated use by the charity, and your deduction must be reduced by the long-term gain element; *see* the Example below and the Law Alert on this page.

If the donation of tangible personal property is to a 50% deduction limit organization such as a church or college, and you must reduce the deduction as a *nonrelated* gift, the reduced gift is then subject to the 50% annual deduction ceiling discussed at *14.17*. If the organization's use of the property is *related* to its tax-exempt charitable purposes, and it is a 50% limit organization, you may deduct the property's fair market value subject to the 30% of adjusted gross income deduction ceiling; *see 14.17*. Alternatively, you may elect to deduct up to 50% of adjusted gross income by reducing the deduction by the long-term gain; *see 14.19*.

EXAMPLE

In August 2006, you contribute a painting held long term to a college that displays it in a library where art students may study it. The college's use of the painting is related to its tax-exempt educational purposes and you may deduct fair market value. However, if the college sells the painting and uses the proceeds for educational purposes, its use would be treated as nonrelated, and you would have to reduce your deduction by the long-term capital gain element, unless on the date of the donation you could reasonably anticipate that the painting would not be sold (or put to another nonrelated use).

New law caution: For a donation made after September 1, 2006, the deduction is limited to cost basis or is recaptured if the charity sells the property within three years, unless the charity makes a qualifying certification; *see* the Law Alert on this page.

Caution

Tangible Personal Property

When you donate appreciated collectibles and artwork held long term, you get a full deduction for the fair market value of the property if the items are used in connection with the charity's main activity or tax-exempt purpose. However, a deduction for fair market value is not available for certain contributions of taxidermy property; *see* IRS Publication 526.

If the charity sells your property, your deduction is limited to your basis in the property (what you paid for it, rather than its appreciated value). Protect a deduction for fair market value by obtaining a letter from the charity stating that it intends to use your gift in connection with its tax-exempt purposes.

Law Alert

Recapture of Deduction for Property Sold Within Three Years

If you donate appreciated tangible personal property held long term after September 1, 2006, for which you claim a deduction exceeding $5,000, and it is sold by the charity by the end of the year of the contribution, the deduction is limited to your cost basis (and not fair market value) unless the charity makes a written certification to the IRS and gives you a copy. The certification, signed by an officer of the charity under penalty of perjury, must either explain how the charity's use of the property furthered its tax-exempt purpose or function, or state that a related use of the property was intended at the time of the donation but it became impossible or unfeasible to implement such intent.

If you deduct fair market value for the property and the charity sells the property after the year of the contribution but within three years of the contribution, and the charity does not provide the above certification, you must recapture the benefit of the previously claimed deduction. In the year of the sale, you must report as ordinary income the excess of the deduction over your cost basis for the property at the time of the donation.

Donating mortgaged property. A donation of mortgaged property may be taxable. Before you give mortgaged property to a charity, have an attorney review the transaction. You may deduct the excess of fair market value over the amount of the outstanding mortgage. However, you may realize a taxable gain. The IRS and Tax Court treat the transferred mortgage debt as cash received in a part-gift, part-sale subject to the bargain-sale rules discussed at *14.8*. You will realize a taxable gain if the transferred mortgage exceeds the portion of basis allocated to the sale part of the transaction. This is true even if the charity does not assume the mortgage.

EXAMPLE

Bob Hill donates to a college land held over a year that is worth $250,000 and subject to a $100,000 mortgage. His basis is $150,000. Hill's charitable contribution deduction is $150,000 ($250,000 – $100,000). He also is considered to have made a bargain sale for $100,000 (transferred mortgage debt) on which he realized $40,000 long-term capital gain. 40% of the transaction is treated as a bargain sale:

$$\frac{\$100{,}000 \text{ (amount of mortgage)}}{\$250{,}000 \text{ (fair market value)}} = 40\%$$

Basis allocated to sale: 40% of $150,000, or $60,000

Amount realized	$100,000
Allocated basis	60,000
Gain	$ 40,000

Donating capital gain property to private non-operating foundations. You generally may not deduct the full fair market value of gifts of capital gain property to private non-operating foundations that are subject to the 20% deduction ceiling for non–50% limit organizations discussed at *14.17*. (Capital gain property is property that, if sold by you at fair market value, would result in long-term capital gain.) The deduction must be reduced by the long-term gain that would have been realized if the property had been sold at fair market value. In other words, your deduction is limited to your cost basis.

An exception is available for certain contributions of stock to a private non-operating foundation; *see* below.

Stock donation to private non-operating foundation. A deduction for fair market value is allowed on a donation to a non-operating private foundation of appreciated publicly traded stock held long term. To qualify, there must be readily available market quotations on an established securities market for the stock on the date of the contribution. If you or family members donated more than 10% of a corporation's stock, the fair market value deduction is allowed only for the first 10%. Under the family aggregation rule, your contributions of stock in a particular publicly traded corporation are aggregated with those of your spouse, brothers, sisters, parents and grandparents, children, grandchildren, and great-grandchildren to all private non-operating foundations, whether the foundations are related or not. If the 10% limit is exceeded, the excess contributions are subject to the cost basis deduction limitation.

The IRS has ruled that for purposes of applying the 10% limit, you must take into account previous stock contributions that the private foundation sold before the new contributions were made. Once publicly traded stock is donated to a private foundation, it must be counted toward the 10% limit, even if it is later disposed of. Furthermore, the value of each contribution at the time it is made is the value taken into account for applying the 10% limitation; prior contributions are not revalued each time there is a new contribution.

Patents and other intellectual property. If you donate patents or other intellectual property to charity, such as trademarks, trade names, trade secrets, know-how, and certain copyrights and software, you can claim an initial charitable contribution deduction for your cost basis in the property (assuming that is less than its fair market value). Additional deductions may be claimed in the year of the donation and in later years, based on a percentage of the income that the charity realizes from the property.

The additional deductions are allowed on a sliding scale percentage basis for the 10-year period beginning on the date of the contribution. In order to obtain the additional deductions, you must accompany the donation with a written statement that includes your name, address, and taxpayer identification number, a description of the intellectual property, and the date of the contribution. You must attach a statement that you intend to treat the contribution as a qualified intellectual property contribution and will claim additional deductions for the allowable annual percentage of the charity's income from the property.

For each year that the charity realizes net income from the property in the 10-year period beginning on the date of the contribution, the charity must report the income to the IRS on Form 8899. A copy of Form 8899 is sent to you and the income shown may be used as the basis for claiming an additional contribution deduction.

For further details, *see* the instructions to Form 8899 and IRS Publication 526.

U.S. Saving Bonds. You may not donate U.S. Saving Bonds, such as EE bonds, because you may not transfer them. They are nonnegotiable. You must first cash the bonds and then give the proceeds to the charity, or surrender the bonds and have new ones registered in the donee's name. When you do this, you have to report the accrued interest on your tax return. Of course, you will get a charitable deduction for the cash gift.

Gift of installment obligations. You may deduct your donation of installment notes to a qualified philanthropy. However, if you received them on your sale of property that you reported on the installment basis, you may realize gain or loss on the gift of the notes; *see 5.28*. The amount of the contribution is the fair market value of the obligation, not the face amount of the notes.

14.7 Cars, Clothing, and Other Property Valued Below Cost

If you donate property whose value has declined below your cost, your deduction generally is limited to the fair market value. However, the rules for cars, trucks, boats, and airplanes are more complicated. To prevent donors from claiming inflated deductions for donated vehicles where the charity actually received much less on a sale to raise cash, the American Jobs Creation Act of 2004 restricted the allowable deduction and imposed stringent substantiation requirements for donations after 2004 where the claimed value exceeds $500; *see* below.

If you are planning a donation of stock or other investment or business property worth less than your basis *(5.20)*, consider selling the property and then donating the proceeds. If you donate the property, your deduction is limited to the fair market value and you cannot deduct a loss. If you first sell the property, you can claim a loss on the sale and then claim a charitable contribution on your donation of the sale proceeds; *see* the Example below.

If the property is personal-use property such as a car, clothing, furniture, or appliances, a loss on the sale is not deductible. It generally makes no difference whether you sell the property for fair market value and donate the proceeds or donate the property. Your charitable deduction will be the value of the property, except that in the case of a car or other vehicle subject to the new restrictions, the deduction on a straight donation may be less than the fair market value if the charity sells the vehicle for less; *see* below.

EXAMPLE

Betty Dunn owns securities that cost $20,000 several years ago but have declined in value to $5,000. A donation of these securities gives a charitable contribution deduction of $5,000. If Betty sold the securities for $5,000, she could claim a long-term capital loss of $15,000. She could then donate the sales proceeds and claim a $5,000 charitable deduction for the cash contribution.

Cars, other motor vehicles, boats, and airplanes. You must obtain a timely written acknowledgment from the charity to substantiate a deduction for a car or other motor vehicle, boat, or airplane with a *claimed value of over $500*. The required acknowledgment must be on Form 1098-C or an equivalent statement from the charity. Copy B of the Form 1098-C (or equivalent acknowledgment) must be attached to your return; if you do not attach the form to your return, the IRS will disallow your deduction. You also must attach Form 8283 if your total deduction for all property donations exceeds $500; *see 14.12*. Vehicles held primarily for sale, such as dealer inventory, are not subject to the acknowledgment rules or the deduction restrictions in the following paragraphs; *see 14.13*.

Law Alert

Donating Used Clothing or Household Items

If you donate used clothing, furniture, or household appliances, deduct their fair market value, which is usually much less than your original cost. Prices paid in thrift shops for similar items are an indication of fair market value.

For contributions made after August 17, 2006, of used clothing or household items (furniture or furnishings, linens, appliances, or electronics, but not antiques, art, or jewelry), a deduction is barred unless the item is in good used condition or better. In addition, Congress wants the IRS to write regulations denying a deduction for clothing or household items that have minimal value. If an item is valued at over $500 in a qualified appraisal that is attached to the donor's return, a deduction is allowed even if the item is not in good used condition or better.

If the charity sells the vehicle to a buyer other than a needy individual (*see* below) without having put it to a significant intervening use, or without materially improving it, your deduction is limited to the gross sales proceeds. You must be sent the Form 1098-C (or equivalent substitute) within 30 days of the sale. The charity must certify in Box 4a that the sale was made in an arm's-length transaction to an unrelated party. The amount of the gross proceeds (not reduced by expenses or fees) will be shown in Box 4c.

If the charity intends to significantly use the vehicle in furtherance of its regularly conducted activities or to materially improve it before selling it, Form 1098-C (or other acknowledgment) must be provided to you within 30 days of the donation. In Box 5a, the charity must certify its intent and in Box 5c it must certify a detailed description of the planned use or improvement, including the intended duration of such use or improvement. If Box 5a is checked, you may take a deduction equal to the fair market value of the vehicle on the date of contribution.

Fair market value is also deductible if the charity checks Box 5b to certify that the donated vehicle will be given to a needy individual, or sold to such to an individual for significantly less than fair market value, in furtherance of the organization's charitable purpose.

Copy B of Form 1098-C states that the deduction may not exceed the gross sales proceeds unless Box 5a or 5b is checked. If fair market value is deductible because Box 5a or 5b is checked, value may be based on an established used-vehicle-pricing guide, provided the amount is for a comparable model in similar condition and sold in the same area.

In Boxes 6a–6c of Form 1098-C, the charity indicates whether any goods or services were provided to the donor and, if so, they are described and a good faith estimate of their fair market value is shown. The deduction must be reduced by the value of the goods/services provided, with one exception. If the only benefits provided to the donor are intangible religious benefits (such as admission to a religious ceremony), Box 6c will be checked and the deduction does not have to be reduced by such benefits.

If the claimed value of the vehicle is at least $250 but not over $500. If the claimed value of a car, other motor vehicle, boat, or airplane (but not dealer property) is at least $250 but not over $500, the contribution is not acknowledged on Form 1098-C (or equivalent), but a written acknowledgment meeting the general substantiation rules at *14.15* must be received by the due date for filing.

If the charity sells the donated vehicle (other than a sale to a needy person in furtherance of charitable purposes) without a significant intervening use or material improvement, and the gross sale proceeds are $500 or less, IRS guidelines allow a deduction to be claimed for fair market value if that exceeds the proceeds, but no more than $500 can be deducted. For example, if the gross sale proceeds are $400 but the donor can substantiate a fair market value of $450, a deduction of $450 would be allowed, provided a qualified acknowledgment *(14.15)* is obtained. If the donor could substantiate a fair market value exceeding $500, the deduction would be limited to $500.

14.8 Bargain Sales of Appreciated Property

A sale of appreciated property to a philanthropy for less than fair market value allows you to claim a charitable deduction while receiving proceeds from the sale. However, you must pay a tax on part of the gain attributed to the sale. That is, the transaction is broken down into two parts: the sale and the gift.

To compute gain on the sale, you allocate the adjusted basis of the property between the sale and the gift following these steps:

Step 1. Divide the sales proceeds by the fair market value of the property. If the property is mortgaged, include the outstanding debt as sale proceeds.

Step 2. Apply the Step 1 percentage to the adjusted basis of the property. This is the portion of basis allocated to the sale.

Step 3. Deduct the resulting basis of Step 2 from the sales proceeds to find the gain.

You may deduct the donated appreciation if full market value would be deductible on a straight donation (no sale) under the rules at *14.6*. Thus, the donated appreciation is deductible if the property is securities or real estate held long term or long-term tangible personal property related to the charity's exempt function; *see* Example 1 below. However, if a deduction for the property (assuming no sale) would be reduced to cost basis as discussed in *14.6*, your charitable deduction on the sale is also reduced; *see* Example 2 below. This reduction affects sales of capital gain property held short term; ordinary income property; tangible personal property not related to the charity's exempt function; depreciable personal property subject to recapture; and sales of capital gain property to private non-operating foundations.

EXAMPLES

1. Lana Briggs sells to a university for $12,000 stock she held over a year. The adjusted basis of the stock is $12,000, and the fair market value is $20,000. On the sale, she recouped her investment and donated the appreciation of $8,000, but, at the same time, she realized taxable gain of $4,800 computed as follows: The percentage of basis applied to the sale is 60% ($12,000 sale proceeds ÷ $20,000 fair market value). Thus, 60% of the $12,000 basis, or $7,200, is allocated to the sale. Gain on the sale equals the $12,000 sale proceeds less the $7,200 allocated basis, or $4,800.
2. Joel Marx sells to his church stock held short term for his basis of $4,000. The stock is worth $10,000. Using the allocation method in Example 1, 40% ($4,000 sale proceeds ÷ $10,000 fair market value) of his $4,000 basis, or $1,600, is allocated to the sale. Thus, he has a short-term capital gain of $2,400 ($4,000 sale proceeds – $1,600 allocated basis). Furthermore, his deductible charitable contribution is also $2,400, equal to the 60% of basis allocated to the gift (60% of $4,000 = $2,400).

Basis allocation applies even if a deduction is barred by the annual ceiling. The basis allocation rules for determining gain on a bargain sale apply even if the annual deduction ceilings *(14.17)* bar a deduction in the year of the donation and in the five-year carryover period.

EXAMPLE

The Hodgdons contributed real estate valued at $3.9 million but subject to mortgage debt of $2.6 million. The IRS treated the mortgage debt as sales proceeds and figured gain based on the difference between the debt and the portion of basis allocated to the sale element. The Hodgdons claimed that the basis allocation rule, which increased the amount of their gain, should not apply. Earlier in the year, they had made another donation that used up their charitable deduction ceiling for that year as well as for the following five-year carryover period. The Tax Court held that the basis allocation rule applied because a charitable deduction was "allowable," even if the contribution did not actually result in a deduction in the carryover period.

14.9 Art Objects

You may claim a charitable deduction for a painting or other art object donated to a charity. The amount of the deduction depends on (1) whether you are the artist; (2) if you are not the artist, how long you owned it; and (3) the type of organization receiving the gift.

If you owned the art work short term, your deduction is limited to cost, under the rules applying to donations of ordinary income property at *14.6*.

If you owned the art work long term *(see 14.6)*, your deduction depends on the way the charity uses the property. If the charity uses it for its exempt purposes, you may deduct the fair market value. However, if the charity uses it for unrelated purposes, your deduction is reduced by 100% of the appreciation. A donation of art work to a general fund-raising agency would be reduced because the agency would have no direct use for it. It would have to sell the art work and use the cash for its exempt purposes.

For donations of art (or other appreciated tangible personal property) after September 1, 2006, a deduction for fair market value may be recaptured if the charity sells the property within three years; *see* the Law Alert in *14.6*.

Appraisals. Be prepared to support your deduction with detailed proof of cost, the date of acquisition, and how value was appraised. The appraisal fee is treated as a "miscellaneous" itemized deduction subject to the 2% adjusted gross income floor; *see 19.1. See also 14.12* for appraisal requirements.

The IRS has its own art advisory panel to assess whether the fair market value claimed for donated art works is reasonable.

Caution

Donations of Personal Creative Works

If you are the artist, your deduction is limited to cost regardless of how long you held the art work or to what use the charity puts it. In the case of a painting, the deduction would be the lower of the cost for canvas and paints and the fair market value.

Filing Instruction

Appraisal Required

If you claim a deduction for art of $20,000 or more, you must attach a copy of a signed qualifying appraisal to Form 8283 and file it with your return; *see 14.12* for further details.

Law Alert

Recapture of Deductions for Certain Fractional Interests

If a fractional interest in art or other tangible personal property *(14.6)* is donated after August 17, 2006, and the charity does not receive complete ownership of the item within 10 years of the initial contribution, or, if earlier, the death of the donor, all prior charitable deductions for the property will have to be recaptured, and interest charges plus a 10% penalty will be imposed.

Requesting advance valuation of art from the IRS. To avoid a later dispute, you may ask the IRS for an advance valuation of art that you have had appraised at $50,000 or more. A request for an IRS Statement of Value (SOV) may be submitted for income tax, gift tax, or estate tax purposes. The IRS has the discretion to value items appraised at less than $50,000 if the SOV request includes at least one item appraised at $50,000 or more, and the IRS determines that the valuation is in the best interest of efficient tax administration.

A request for an SOV must be submitted to the IRS before filing the tax return reporting the donation. The request must include a copy of an appraisal for the item of art and a $2,500 fee, which pays for an SOV for up to three items of art. There is an additional charge of $250 for each item of art over three. It takes the IRS between six and 12 months to issue an SOV.

If the IRS agrees with the value reported on the appraisal, the IRS will issue an SOV approving the appraisal. If the IRS disagrees, the IRS will issue an SOV indicating its own valuation and stating the reasons it disagrees with the appraised amount. Regardless of whether you agree with the IRS appraisal, the SOV must be attached to and filed with the return reporting the donation. If you file the return before the SOV is issued, a copy of your request for the SOV must be attached to your return and on receipt of the SOV, an amended return must be filed with the SOV attached. For further SOV details, *see* IRS Publication 561 and Revenue Procedure 96-15.

Donating a partial interest in an art collection. You may deduct the value of a donated partial interest in an art collection, such as where you give a museum the right to exhibit the works for a specific period during the year. The deduction is allowed even if the museum does not take possession of the art works, provided it has the right to take possession. However, if a fractional interest is donated after August 17, 2006, a new law restricts the deduction for additional contributions of an interest in the same property. Furthermore, if the donor does not transfer all of his or her entire remaining interest to the same charity within 10 years of the initial fractional donation, or, if earlier, the date of the donor's death, the donor's charitable contributions will have to be recaptured, plus interest, and a penalty equal to 10% of the recaptured amount will be imposed. *See* Publication 526 for further details of the new law.

EXAMPLES

1. You give your college a painting that you have owned for many years. Its cost was $1,000 but it is now worth $10,000. The school displays the painting in its library for study by students. This use is related to the school's educational purposes. Your donation is deductible at fair market value. If, however, the school told you it was going to sell the painting and use the proceeds for general education purposes, its use would not be considered related. Your deduction would be reduced by the $9,000 appreciation to $1,000.

   As discussed in *14.6,* a sale by the charity within three years of a donation made after September 1, 2006, will trigger a recapture of a deduction for fair market value, unless the charity makes a qualifying certification.
2. You donate to the Community Fund a collection of first edition books held for many years and worth $5,000. Your cost is $1,000. Since the charity is a general fund-raising organization, its use of your gift is not related. Your deduction would be $1,000 ($5,000 less $4,000).
3. You contribute to a charity antique furnishings you owned for years. The antiques cost you $500 and are now worth $5,000. The charity uses the furnishings in its office in the course of carrying on its functions. This is a related use. Your contribution deduction is $5,000.

Keeping a reversionary interest. The IRS may challenge a charitable deduction where you retain some control over the donated property. However, if the possibility of the property reverting back to you is considered to be remote, a deduction may be allowed. For example, a taxpayer who donated her art collection to a museum was allowed to claim a charitable deduction even though she retained the right to decide where and how the art would be displayed. Disputes concerning art displays would be settled by a mutually acceptable museum curator. If the museum breached a condition, it had a period of time to cure the violation. If the violation was not cured, the ownership would revert back to the donor. The IRS allowed the deduction; the retained rights were fiduciary in nature and the possibility of the art reverting to the donor was so remote as to be negligible.

14.10 Interests in Real Estate

No deduction is allowed for the rental value of property you allow a charity to use free of charge. This is the case even if the property is used directly in furtherance of the organization's charitable purpose; *see* the Example below.

If you donate an undivided fractional part of your entire interest, a deduction will be allowed for the fair market value of the proportionate interest donated.

A donation of an option is not deductible until the year the option to buy the property is exercised.

Remainder interest in home or farm. You may claim a charitable deduction for a gift of the remainder value of a residence or farm donated to a charity, even though you reserve the use of the property for yourself and your spouse for a term of years or life. Remainder gifts generally must be made in trust. However, where a residence or farm is donated, the remainder interest must be conveyed outright, not in trust. A remainder interest in a vacation home or in a "hobby" farm is also deductible. There is no requirement that the home be your principal residence or that the farm be profitable.

Contribution of real property for conservation purposes. A deduction may be claimed for the contribution of certain partial interests in real property to government agencies or publicly supported charities for exclusively conservational purposes. Qualified conservation contributions include: (1) your entire interest in real property other than retained rights to subsurface oil, gas, or other minerals; (2) a remainder interest; or (3) an easement, restrictive covenant, or similar property restriction granted in perpetuity. The contribution must be in perpetuity and further at least one of the following "conservation purposes"—preservation of land areas for outdoor recreation, education, or scenic enjoyment; preservation of historically important land areas or structures; or the protection of plant, fish, and wildlife habitats or similar natural ecosystems.

To obtain the deduction, there must be legally enforceable restrictions that prevent you from using your retained interest in the property in a way contrary to the intended conservation purpose. The donee organization must be prohibited from transferring the contributed interest except to other organizations that will hold the property for exclusively conservational purposes. If you retain an interest in subsurface oil, gas, or minerals, surface mining must generally be specifically prohibited. However, there is a limited exception where the mineral rights and surface interests have been separately owned since June 12, 1976. A deduction will be allowed if the probability of surface mining is so remote as to be considered negligible. The exception does not apply if you are related to the owner of the surface interest or if you received the mineral interest (directly or indirectly) from the surface owner.

New law: *See* the Law Alert on this page for new deduction restrictions on certain easements. Also *see* the Law Alert in *14.17* for the favorable new law that increases the deduction ceiling for qualified conservation contributions made in 2006 and 2007.

EXAMPLE

To help a charity raise money, one owner allowed the charity to auction off a week's stay in his vacation home, and the highest bidder paid the charity a fair rental. The IRS ruled that not only was the owner's donation not deductible, but the one week stay by the bidder was considered personal use by the owner for purposes of figuring deductions for rental expenses. True, if the owner had directly rented the property to the bidder, the bidder's payment of a fair rental value would have been counted as a rental day and not a personal use day. However, the donation for charitable use is not a business rental, and the bidder's rental payment to the charity is not considered a payment to the owner.

Furthermore, the bidder's use of the home pushed the owner over the personal-use ceiling, which in turn prevented him from deducting a rental loss. A rental loss may not be claimed if personal use of a home exceeds the greater of 14 days and 10% of the number of days the home is rented at fair rental value *(9.7)*. Here, the owner personally used the home for 14 days and rented the home for 80 days. The rental expenses exceeded rental income. If the bidder's use of the home was not considered his personal use, the owner could have deducted the loss because his personal use did not exceed the 14-day limit (which was more than 10% of the 80 rental days). However, by adding the bidder's seven days of use to the owner's 14 days, the resulting 21 days of personal use exceeded the 14-day ceiling.

Caution

Donating Vacation Home Use Not Advisable

To raise funds, a charitable organization may ask contributors who own vacation homes to donate use of the property, which the charity then auctions off to the public. Be warned that if you offer your home in this way you will not only be denied a charitable deduction for your generosity, but you may jeopardize your deduction for rental expenses. A deduction is not allowed for giving a charity the free use of your property. *See* the Example at the end of *14.10*.

Law Alert

Restrictions on Easement Donations

Historic building façade easements. A donation after July 25, 2006, of a façade easement with respect to a building in a registered historic district, other than one listed in the National Register, is allowed only if the easement preserves the entire exterior, including the space above as well as the front, rear, and sides of the building. The easement must bar exterior changes inconsistent with the historical character of the building. A written agreement between the donor and the donee must certify that the donee is a qualifying historic preservation organization with the resources and commitment to enforce the easement.

For contributions after 2006, the donor must attach to his or her tax return a qualified appraisal of the easement, photographs of the building exterior, and a description of all zoning laws and similar restrictions on development.

If a deduction of over $10,000 is claimed for a façade easement donated on or after February 13, 2007, a $500 fee must be included with the donor's return or no deduction will be allowed.

Reduction for prior rehabilitation credit. The deduction for a historic building easement donated after August 17, 2006, must be reduced if a rehabilitation tax credit *(31.8)* was claimed for the building in the five years preceding the donation.

14.11 Life Insurance

You may deduct the value of a life insurance policy if the charity is irrevocably named as beneficiary and you make both a legal assignment and a complete delivery of the policy. A deduction may be disallowed where you reserve the right to change the beneficiary.

The amount of your deduction generally depends on the type of policy donated. Your insurance company can furnish you with the information necessary to calculate your deduction. In addition, you may deduct premiums you pay after you assign the policy.

Deducting premium payments on donated policy. If you assign a life insurance policy to a charity and continue to pay the premiums, you generally may deduct the premiums. However, in states where charities do not have an "insurable interest" in the donor's life, the IRS may challenge income tax and gift tax deductions for the premium payments. The IRS took this position in a private ruling interpreting New York law. In response, New York amended its insurance code to allow individuals to buy a life insurance policy and immediately transfer it to a charity. The IRS then revoked the earlier ruling but it did not announce a change in its position. Thus, the IRS may challenge premium deductions of donors in other states where a charity's insurable interest is not clearly provided by state law.

Caution

Split-Dollar Insurance Arrangements

No deduction is allowed for giving a charitable organization money with the understanding that it will be used to pay premiums on life insurance, annuities, or endowment contracts for your benefit or that of a beneficiary designated by you.

14.12 Form 8283 and Written Appraisal Requirements

Attach Form 8283 to your Form 1040 for 2006 if the total deduction claimed for all of your donations of property exceeds $500. The IRS may disallow your deduction if you fail to attach Form 8283.

If you are claiming a deduction exceeding $5,000 for an item, or for a group of similar items (such as paintings, buildings, coins, stamps, or books), you generally need a written appraisal from a qualified appraiser. The appraiser must sign a declaration in Part III of Section B of Form 8283 that he or she is unrelated to you and meets the other requirements for qualified appraisers. The appraisal must be made no earlier than 60 days before your donation, and you must receive it by the due date (including extensions) of the return on which you claim the deduction.

You do not need an appraisal for a car, boat, or airplane if your deduction is limited to the gross proceeds from its sale under *14.7*, or for publicly traded securities, non-publicly-traded securities of $10,000 or less, intellectual property *(14.6)*, or business inventory.

Whether or not a written appraisal is required, you must describe the property, value it, and provide your cost and other acquisition details in Section B, Part 1 of Form 8283.

The appraisal itself should be kept with your records and does not have to be attached to your return except in two situations: If you are claiming a deduction of $20,000 or more for art, you must attach a complete copy of the appraisal to Form 8283 and you may be asked by the IRS to submit a color photograph (8" × 10") or a slide (4" × 5") of the art. If the claimed deduction exceeds $500,000, the qualified appraisal must be attached to your return (assuming no exception to the appraisal requirement). *See* the Form 8283 instructions for further details on the appraisal requirements.

Caution

Charity Reports Transfer Within Three Years

If the charity sells or otherwise disposes of appraised property within three years after your gift, it must notify the IRS on Form 8282 and send you a copy. The sale might trigger the recapture of a deduction claimed for a contribution made after September 1, 2006; *see* the Law Alert in *14.6*. Reporting on Form 8282 is not required by the charity if in Part II, Section B of Form 8283 you indicated that the appraised value of the item was not more than $500. Similar items such as a collection of books by the same author, stereo components, or place settings of silverware may be treated as one item. Reporting is also not required for donated property that the organization uses or distributes without consideration, if this use furthers the organization's tax-exempt function or purpose.

Donee acknowledgment. For property donations exceeding $5,000, the donee organization must acknowledge the receipt of the property in Section B, Part IV of Form 8283.

Penalty for overvaluation. You may be penalized for a substantial overvaluation of donated property; *see 14.16*.

Appraisal fees. A fee paid to an appraiser is not considered a charitable deduction but is deductible as a "miscellaneous" expense subject to the 2% adjusted gross income floor; *see 19.1*.

14.13 Business Inventory

Self-employed business owners generally may not deduct more than cost for donations of inventory. If a charitable deduction is claimed, costs incurred in a year prior to the year of donation must be removed from opening inventory and excluded from the cost of goods sold when figuring business gross profit for the year of the contribution.

No contribution deduction is allowed for a gift of merchandise that was produced or acquired in the year donated. Instead, the cost is added to the cost of goods sold to figure gross profit for the year of the contribution. Business deductions are not subject to the percentage limitation applied to donations.

14.14 Donations Through Trusts

Outright gifts are not the only way to make deductible gifts to charities. You may transfer property to a charitable lead trust or a charitable remainder trust to provide funds for charity.

A charitable lead trust involves your transfer of property to a trust directed to pay income to a charity you name, for the term of the trust, and then to return the property to you or to someone else. A charitable remainder trust is one that provides income for you or another beneficiary for life, after which the property passes to a charity.

Trust arrangements require the services of an experienced attorney who will draft the trust in appropriate form and advise you of the tax consequences.

Deductions for gifts of income interests in trust. Current law is designed to prevent a donor from claiming an immediate deduction for the present value of trust income payable to a charity for a term of years. In limited situations, you may claim a deduction if either: (1) You give away all of your interests in the property to qualifying *(14.1)* organizations. For example, you put your property in trust, giving an income interest for 20 years to a church and the remainder to a college. A deduction is allowed for the value of the property. Or (2) you create a unitrust or annuity trust, and are taxed on the income. A unitrust for this purpose provides that a fixed percentage of trust assets is payable to the charitable income beneficiary each year. An annuity trust provides for payment of a guaranteed dollar amount to the charitable income beneficiary each year. A deduction is allowed for the present value of the unitrust or annuity trust interest.

Because income remains taxable to the grantor, alternative (2) will probably not be chosen, unless the income of the trust is from tax-exempt securities. If such a trust is created, a tax may be due if the donor dies before the trust ends or is no longer the taxable owner of trust income. The law provides for recapture of part of the tax deduction, even where the income was tax exempt.

Charitable remainder trusts. A charitable deduction is allowable for transfers of property to charitable remainder trusts only if the trust meets these requirements: The income payable for a noncharitable income beneficiary's life or a term of up to 20 years must be guaranteed under a unitrust or annuity trust. If a donor gives all of his or her interests in the property to the charities, the annuity or unitrust requirements need not be satisfied. The value of the charitable deduction allowable for a gift in trust is determined by IRS tables.

Planning Reminder

Life Income Plans

A philanthropy may offer a life income plan (pooled income fund) to which you transfer property or money in return for a guaranteed income for life. After your death, the philanthropy has full control over the property. If you enter such a plan, ask the philanthropy for the amount of the deduction that you may claim for the value of your gift.

Reporting Charitable Contributions

14.15 Records Needed To Substantiate Your 2006 Contributions

The type of records you must keep to substantiate your donations generally depends on their amount and whether you are contributing cash or property. As discussed below, the requirements are stricter for contributions of $250 or more than for smaller contributions. In addition, even stricter substantiationrequirements apply to donations valued at over $500 of motor vehicles, boats, or airplanes; *see 14.7* for these rules.

Caution: Cash contributions made after 2006, regardless of the amount, must be substantiated by a bank record or receipt from the charity; *see* the Law Alert on this page.

Contributions under $250. A cancelled check, dated receipt, or other contemporaneous written record is proof of a donation under $250. For a property donation, your receipt should contain a description of the property. You should keep records showing the fair market value of the property and your cost basis.

You need a written acknowledgment from the charity for contributions of $250 or more. A written acknowledgment is necessary to prove charitable contributions of $250 or more; *see* below for content details. You may not rely on a cancelled check to document a cash contribution of $250 or more. The acknowledgment requirement does not apply if the donation is less than $250, but if the contribution exceeds $75, you must be given a disclosure statement from the charity estimating the value of any benefits you received in return for the donation.

The IRS exempts from the acknowledgment requirement grantors of a charitable lead trust, charitable remainder annuity trust, or charitable remainder unitrust. Since a specific charity does

Law Alert

All Cash Contributions After 2006 Need Bank Record or Receipt

All charitable contributions of money after 2006, regardless of the amount, must be substantiated by a cancelled check, bank record, or acknowledgment from the charity showing the name of the organization and the date and amount of the contribution. Other written records do not qualify.

not have to be designated as beneficiary at the time the trust transfer is made, there may be no organization available to provide an acknowledgment.

Caution: *See 14.7* for the special acknowledgment requirements for donated cars (and other motor vehicles), boats, and airplanes with a claimed value of over $500. The acknowledgment rules in this section *(14.15)* do not apply to the vehicle donations subject to the special restrictions discussed in *14.7*.

Content of acknowledgment. An acknowledgment for a donation of $250 or more may be a letter, e-mail, computer-generated form, or postcard. If you gave cash, the amount of the donation must be shown. If you gave property, the property must be described in the acknowledgment, but the charity does not have to value it.

The acknowledgment must state whether or not you have received any goods or services from the charity in exchange for the contribution. If you have, the receipt must include a statement describing such benefits and estimating their value. However, "token" items and certain membership benefits, as described in *14.3*, do not have to be described or valued. There is also an exception if the contribution is to a religious organization and the *only* benefits received are "intangible" religious benefits, such as admission to religious ceremonies; these do not have to be described or valued, but the statement must indicate that they are the sole benefits provided.

Payments throughout the year. For purposes of the $250 threshold for an acknowledgment, each payment is generally considered separate. Thus, for small donations made during the year, you do not have to obtain an acknowledgment even if they total $250 or more.

Table 14-1 What You Need To Substantiate Donations Made in 2006

For each individual contribution of—	*You need—*
$75 or less	A cancelled check, receipt from the charity, or other contemporaneous written record.
More than $75 but less than $250	A cancelled check or receipt from the charity. If you received benefits, the charity is required to give you a "disclosure" statement that estimates the value of any benefits you received, such as concert tickets or books. The statement will tell you to deduct only the excess of your contribution over the value of the benefits. If a required disclosure statement is not provided when contributions are solicited, it must be provided when you make a contribution exceeding $75. The disclosure statement is not required if the only benefits you receive are "token items" or membership benefits that can be disregarded, as discussed in *14.3.* Nor is it required where you contribute to a religious organization and the only benefits you receive are "intangible religious benefits." An example of an intangible religious benefit would be admission to religious ceremonies. A Congressional committee report also suggests that tuition for wholly religious education that does not lead to a recognized degree would qualify.
$250 or more	A written acknowledgment from the charity. You may not rely on a cancelled check to document a cash contribution of $250 or more. A written acknowledgment is also required for a donation of property if you are claiming a deduction of $250 or more, but the charity does not have to value the property, just describe it. If you received any goods or services from the charity in exchange for the contribution, the acknowledgment must estimate their value unless you receive only "token" items or "intangible religious benefits" as discussed in the preceding paragraph. The deadline for obtaining acknowledgments is the date you file your return. If you file after the filing due date or extended due date, get the acknowledgment by the due date or extended due date. Where the contribution is $250 or more, and both the acknowledgment requirement and the disclosure requirement apply, the charity may satisfy both requirements with the same document. Keep the statement from the charity with your tax records; do not attach it to your tax return. If your total deduction for all property donations exceeds $500, you must report each of the contributions on Form 8283 (not just those valued over $500). If you are not allowed to deduct fair market value for a property donation under the rules at *14.6*, you must attach a statement to Form 8283 explaining the reduction for the appreciation. For property deductions exceeding $5,000, you need a written appraisal, as discussed in *14.12.*
More than $500 in the case of a donated car, other motor vehicle, boat, or airplane	*See 14.7* for the special acknowledgment rules that apply where the claimed value of the vehicle exceeds $500.

If contributions are made by payroll deductions from your wages, the amount withheld from each paycheck is treated separately. An acknowledgment is not required unless withholding on a single paycheck is at least $250. A pay stub or Form W-2 from the employer indicating the amount of a single withholding over $249 is considered a valid "acknowledgment"; a pledge card or other document from the charity must state that you have not received benefits in exchange for the payroll deduction contribution.

Deadline for 2006 donation acknowledgments. For a 2006 contribution, the deadline for obtaining an acknowledgment is the date you file your 2006 return but no later than the April 16, 2007, filing due date, or if you obtain a filing extension, the extended due date.

A charity must provide a disclosure statement if you contribute more than $75 and receive benefits. If you contribute more than $75 but less than $250 to a charity, you do not have to get a written receipt but the charity is required to give you a "disclosure" statement that estimates the value of any benefits you received, such as concert tickets or books. The statement will tell you to deduct only the excess of your contribution over the value of the benefits. Certain "token" items and membership benefits, and "intangible" religious benefits, can be disregarded; *see* "What You Need To Prove Your Donations" below. If a required disclosure statement is not provided when contributions are solicited, it must be provided when you make a contribution exceeding $75.

14.16 Penalty for Substantial Overvaluation of Property

If the IRS disallows a portion of your claimed deduction for appreciated property on the grounds that you have overvalued it, you may be subject to a penalty as well as additional tax. Depending on the extent of the overvaluation, a 20% or 40% penalty may apply. The thresholds for imposing both penalties have been lowered for tax returns filed after August 17, 2006. No penalty is imposed unless the overvaluation results in a tax underpayment exceeding $5,000.

20% penalty. If the claimed value of donated property is 150% or more of the correct value on a return filed after August 17, 2006, the penalty is 20% of the tax underpayment resulting from the overvaluation, provided the underpayment exceeds $5,000. For a return filed on or before August 17, 2006, the overvaluation threshold was 200% instead of 150%.

40% penalty. If the claimed value of donated property is 200% or more of the correct value on a return filed after August 17, 2006, the penalty is 40% of the tax underpayment resulting from the overvaluation, provided the underpayment exceeds $5,000. For a return filed on or before August 17, 2006, the overvaluation threshold was 400% instead of 200%.

Reasonable cause exception for relying on appraisal. On a return filed after August 17, 2006, the 20% penalty (but not the 40%) may be avoided under a reasonable cause exception if you relied on a qualified appraisal prepared by a qualified appraiser and, in addition, you made a good faith investigation of the value of the property. On a return filed on or before August 17, 2006, the reasonable cause exception applied to both the 20% and 40% penalty.

14.17 Ceiling on Charitable Contributions

Unless you make donations that are very substantial in relation to your adjusted gross income (Line 37, Form 1040), you do not have to be concerned with the deduction ceilings discussed in this section. For cash contributions, the deduction ceiling is generally 50% of adjusted gross income, but in some cases a 30% limit applies. For property donations, the deduction limit is generally 30% of adjusted gross income, although it sometimes is 50% or even 20%. As detailed below, the specific limit for each donation depends on whether it is made to a "50% limit organization" and whether it is capital gain property. Where you have made contributions subject to different ceilings, the ceilings are applied in a specific order and are subject to an overall ceiling of 50% of adjusted gross income. If your deduction is limited by any of the ceilings, a five-year carryover is allowed for the excess; *see 14.18.*

Even if your charitable contributions are within the ceilings, your overall charitable deduction is subject to the reduction to itemized deductions if your 2006 adjusted gross income exceeds $150,500 ($75,250 if married filing separately); *see 13.7.*

Filing Tip

Right To Buy Athletic Stadium Tickets

The IRS considers 20% of the amount paid for the right to buy college or university athletic seating to be the fair market value of the right. You may deduct 80% *(see 14.3)*. When your payment is $312.50 or more, you are considered to have made a contribution of at least $250 ($250 = 80% of $312.50), requiring a written acknowledgment from the charity.

Planning Reminder

Advance Valuation of Art From IRS

To protect against the possibility of a valuation dispute that could lead to a penalty where you are claiming a deduction of at least $50,000 for a work of art, you may request a valuation from the IRS prior to the time you file. *See 14.9* for obtaining the IRS valuation.

Law Alert

Direct Donations From IRAs in 2006 and 2007

Taxpayers age 70½ or older may exclude from gross income in 2006 and 2007 direct transfers from an IRA to a 50% limit charitable organization (other than a "supporting organization" or donor advised fund), up to a limit of $100,000 each year; *see 8.8.* No charitable deduction is allowed for a direct transfer that is excludable from income. An excludable transfer is not taken into account in applying the deduction ceilings of *14.17* to other charitable contributions.

Volunteer expenses. The deduction ceiling for unreimbursed expenses you incur doing volunteer work for a charity *(14.4)* is 50% of adjusted gross income if your services were for a 50% limit organization such as a church or college (*see* the list below), or 30% of adjusted gross income if the services were on behalf of an organization other than a 50% limit organization.

30% limit for contributions for the use of an organization. If a donation is treated as for the use of, rather than directly to, any organization, it is deductible under the 30% ceiling described below for contributions to organizations that are not 50% limit organizations.

This 30% ceiling applies to a charitable unitrust or annuity trust income interest that is deductible under the rules discussed at *14.14*. A charitable remainder trust transfer is also subject to the 30% limit if the trust provides that after the death of the income beneficiary, the property is to be held in the trust for the benefit of the charity, rather than distributed to the charity.

Deductible expenses for supporting a student in your home *(see 14.5)* are considered to be for the use of a charitable organization and thus subject to the 30% ceiling for contributions to organizations that are *not* 50% limit organizations.

Contributions to 50% Limit Organizations

Organizations in the 50% limit category include churches, schools, publicly supported charities, and private foundations in the list below. Cash contributions to such organizations are deductible up to 50% of adjusted gross income and contributions of capital gain property held long term generally are deductible up to 30% of adjusted gross income.

The 50% deduction ceiling also applies to donations to the United States, Puerto Rico, a U.S. possession, a state, a political subdivision of a state or U.S. possession, or an Indian tribal government.

Filing Tip

Cash Gifts

A donation of cash to a church, college, or publicly supported charity is deductible up to 50% of your adjusted gross income; *see* the list of 50% limit organization in *14.17*.

50% ceiling. Contributions of cash, ordinary income property, and capital gain property held short term are deductible up to 50% of adjusted gross income if made to the following types of charitable organizations:

- Churches, synagogues, mosques, and other religious organizations.
- Schools, colleges, and other educational organizations that normally have regular faculties and student bodies in attendance on site.
- Hospitals and medical research organizations associated with hospitals.
- Government-supported or publicly supported foundations for state and municipal universities and colleges.
- Religious, charitable, educational, scientific, or literary organizations that receive a substantial part of their financial support from the general public or a government unit. Libraries, museums, drama, opera, ballet and orchestral societies, community funds, the American Red Cross, the Heart Fund, and the United Way are in this category. Also included are organizations to prevent cruelty to children or animals, or to foster amateur sports (provided they do not provide athletic facilities or equipment).
- Private operating foundations.
- Private non-operating foundations that distribute their contributions annually to qualified charities within 2 months after the end of their taxable year.
- Private non-operating foundations that pool donations and allow donors to designate the charities to receive their gifts, if the foundation pays out all income within 2 months after the end of the tax year.
- Organizations that normally receive more than one-third of their support from the general public or governmental units.

Filing Instruction

Appreciated Securities and Real Estate

When you contribute appreciated securities or real estate that you have held for more than a year to a church, college, or other organization treated as a 50% limit organization, your deduction for the property donation is limited to 30% of your adjusted gross income unless you elect the 50% ceiling as discussed at *14.19*.

Carryover to 2006 of qualified contributions exempted from 50% limit for 2005. In the wake of Hurricanes Katrina, Rita, and Wilma, the Gulf Opportunity Zone Act allowed individuals to waive the regular 50% limit for cash contributions made to most 50%-limit organizations between August 28, 2005, and the end of 2005. The contributions did not have to be for Hurricane Katrina, Rita, or Wilma relief. By making an election on Line 15b of Schedule A to waive the ceiling, the deduction ceiling for qualified contributions was increased to adjusted gross income (AGI) minus the deduction for all other 2005 contributions.

If you made the election but your 2005 qualified contributions exceeded the increased limit, the excess is carried over to 2006 and treated as a contribution subject to the 50% limit on your 2006 return.

30% ceiling for capital gain property held long term. The deduction ceiling is generally 30% (not 50%) of adjusted gross income where you donate to a 50% limit organization property that would have resulted in long-term capital gain had you sold it at fair market value.

The 30% ceiling applies where the fair market value of the property is deductible under the rules discussed in *14.6*. This includes donations of appreciated securities and real estate held long term. It also includes donations of appreciated tangible personal property (such as furniture or art) held long term where the organization's use of your gift is directly related to its tax-exempt charitable purposes.

However, you may elect to apply the 50% ceiling instead of the 30% ceiling to such property donations if you reduce the fair market value of the property by the appreciation; *see 14.19*.

If you donate tangible personal property held long term that is *not* used by the organization for its tax-exempt charitable purposes, so that your deduction must be reduced for the appreciation *(14.6)*, the reduced amount is deductible under the 50% ceiling.

Contributions to Non–50% Limit Organizations

If a contribution is made to a qualifying organization that is *not* in the above list of 50% limit organizations, a 30% or 20% deduction ceiling applies. Organizations in this category include veterans' organizations, fraternal societies, nonprofit cemeteries and private non-operating foundations that do not meet the payout requirements for 50% limit status.

The 30% limit applies to contributions of cash, ordinary income property, and capital gain property held short term. The 20% limit applies to contributions of capital gain property held long term (more than one year). However, the actual ceiling may be less than 30% or 20% of adjusted gross income where in the same year you have made contributions to 50% limit organizations. In that case, follow Steps 2 and 4 of the following section on applying the deduction ceilings.

Applying the Deduction Ceilings

The various deduction ceilings are applied in a specific order, with the total deduction for the year limited to 50% of adjusted gross income. Check above for the ceilings that apply to your donations and then apply the ceilings in the following order. *See 14.18* for carryover rules if a portion of your deduction is barred by the deduction ceilings.

1. 50% of adjusted gross income ceiling for contributions to 50% limit organizations.
2. 30% of adjusted gross income ceiling for contributions to organizations that are *not* 50% limit organizations, except for contributions of capital gain property subject to the 20% ceiling under Step 4 below.

   If any contributions to 50% limit organizations were made, including donations of capital gain property that are subject to the 30% ceiling under Step 3 below, this Step 2 ceiling is the lesser of (1) 30% of adjusted gross income or (2) 50% of adjusted gross income minus the contributions to the 50% limit organizations.
3. 30% of adjusted gross income ceiling for contributions of capital gain property to 50% limit organizations.

   If contributions qualifying for the 50% ceiling (Step 1) were made, your deduction for these 30% limit contributions is the lesser of (1) 30% of adjusted gross income or (2) 50% of adjusted gross income minus the contributions qualifying for the 50% ceiling.
4. 20% of adjusted gross income ceiling for contributions of capital gain property to organizations that are not 50% limit organizations.

   If contributions are deductible under any of the other ceilings (Steps 1–3), you may deduct contributions subject to the 20% ceiling only to the extent that there is any adjusted gross income remaining under the overall 50% adjusted gross limit.

EXAMPLES

1. Linda Jones in 2006 contributes to a church $22,000 in cash and land held long term valued at $35,000. Her adjusted gross income is $100,000, so the total deduction for the year may not exceed $50,000 under the 50% overall limit. Since the $22,000 cash contribution subject to the 50% ceiling is considered first, the deduction for the land (subject to the 30% ceiling under Step 3 above) is limited to $28,000, the difference between the $50,000 overall limit and the $22,000 cash gift. Jones may carry over the unused $7,000 donation attributable to the land.

Law Alert

Increased Ceiling for Qualified Conservation Contributions

Instead of the generally applicable ceiling for capital gain property of 30% of adjusted gross income, a higher deduction ceiling for qualified conservation contributions *(14.10)* made in 2006 and in 2007 may be available. The fair market value of a qualified conservation contribution to a 50% limit organization in 2006 and 2007 may be deducted to the extent that 50% of adjusted gross income exceeds the deduction allowed for all other charitable contributions. If the donor is a qualified farmer or rancher, a qualified conservation contribution is allowable to the extent that 100% of adjusted gross income exceeds the deduction allowed for all other charitable contributions. If the donated property had been used in agriculture or livestock production, the 100% limit applies only if there is a requirement that the property remain generally available for such production. Qualified contributions in excess of the 50% or 100% limit can be carried forward for up to 15 years.

Filing Instruction

Carryover for Excess Contributions

If you contribute cash and property in the same year, your deductions may be subject to different limits, such as 50% of adjusted gross income for the cash and 30% for the property. Follow the steps and Examples at the end of this section for applying the ceilings.

If your donation exceeds the limits, you may carry over the excess for five years.

2. Earl Smith in 2006 has an adjusted gross income of $100,000. He contributes land worth $40,000 to a college, deductible under the 30% ceiling of Step 3 above. He also contributes $30,000 in cash to a non-operating private foundation subject to the 30% ceiling discussed in Step 2 above. The 30% limitation for cash gifts to non-operating private foundations is applied before the 30% limitation applicable to gifts of capital gain property to public charities. The deduction for the cash gift is reduced to $10,000 (50% of $100,000 adjusted gross income, or $50,000, minus $40,000 gift to college). The deduction for the land is limited to $30,000 (30% of $100,000). Accordingly, Smith's charitable contribution deduction for 2004 is $40,000 ($10,000 + $30,000).

   Smith is allowed to carry over *(14.18)* the amounts disallowed by the ceilings: $20,000 ($30,000 – $10,000) for the cash gift and $10,000 ($40,000– $30,000) for the land.

Filing Instruction

Different Ceilings

If you made charitable contributions subject to several deduction ceilings, the deductions are applied against adjusted gross income in the specific order shown under "Applying the Deduction Ceilings" in *14.17*.

14.18 Five-Year Carryover for Excess Donations

If you make donations that are not deductible because they exceed the 50%, 30%, or 20% of adjusted gross income ceilings discussed in *14.17*, you may carry the excess over the next five years. In each carryover year, the original percentage ceiling applies. For example, where contributions of appreciated long-term intangible personal property or real estate (or tangible personal property put to a related use by the charity) exceed the 30% ceiling for capital gain property *(14.17)*, the excess remains subject to the 30% ceiling in the carryover years.

In any carryover year, you must first figure your deduction for contributions in the current year under the applicable 50%, 30%, or 20% ceilings. For each category of property carried over, the carryover contributions are deductible only after the deduction for current year donations is figured. The total deduction in the carryover year, for both current year and carryover contributions, cannot exceed 50% of adjusted gross income for the carryover year.

Note: There is a special 15-year carryforward for donations in 2006 and 2007 of qualified conservation contributions; *see* the Law Alert on qualified conservation contributions in *14.17*.

Planning Reminder

Project Your Income

When planning substantial donations that may exceed the annual ceiling, make a projection of your income for at least five years. Although the carryover period of five years will probably absorb most excess donations, it is possible that the excess may be so large that it will not be completely absorbed during the year of the contribution and the five-year carryover period. It is also possible that your income may drop in the future so that you cannot adequately take advantage of the excess.

EXAMPLE

In 2006, you contribute to a university stock held over a year with a fair market value of $19,000. The contribution is subject to the 30% ceiling for capital gain property *(14.17)*. You also have a $2,000 carryover from 2005 for a cash gift to your church subject to the 50% ceiling. Your 2006 adjusted gross income is $40,000. Under the 30% ceiling, the deduction for the contribution of stock is limited to $12,000 (30% of $40,000 adjusted gross income). Since the overall deduction limit is $20,000 (50% of $40,000 adjusted gross income), the $2,000 carryover from 2005 is fully deductible. The total deduction on your 2006 return is $14,000 ($12,000 plus $2,000 carryover). You carry over to 2007 the $7,000 balance from the gift of stock that was subject to the 30% ceiling.

14.19 Election To Reduce Property Gift Appreciation

Although the 30% ceiling generally applies to long-term intangible property (such as securities) and real estate contributed to 50% limit organizations *(see 14.17)*, you may elect the 50% ceiling, provided you reduce the fair market value of the property by 100% of the appreciation on all such donations during the year. The reduction also applies to donations of tangible personal property related in use to the organization's charitable function. In most cases, this election should be made only where the amount of appreciation is negligible. Where there is substantial appreciation, the increase in the deduction may not make up or exceed the required 100% reduction, which allows you to claim a deduction only for your cost basis in the property. If the election is made in a year in which there are carryovers of capital gain property subject to the 30% ceiling, the carryovers are subject to reduction; *see* IRS Publication 526.

The election of the 50% ceiling is made by attaching a statement to your original return or amended return filed by the original due date. Even where no formal electing statement is made, claiming a deduction without the appreciation in order to come within the 50% ceiling is treated as an election. A formal or "informal" election is not revocable unless a material mistake is shown. A revocation based on a reconsideration of tax consequences is not considered sufficient grounds.

Chapter 15

Itemized Deduction for Interest Expenses

On Schedule A of Form 1040, you may deduct three types of interest charges:

- Home mortgage interest
- Points
- Investment interest

These deductions are also subject to limitations:

- Home mortgage interest and points are subject to the 3% reduction of itemized deductions if your adjusted gross income (AGI) exceeds $150,500 ($75,250 for married persons filing separate returns).
- Investment interest is deductible only up to the amount of net investment income *(15.10)* but is not included in the 3% reduction computation. The 3% reduction rule is discussed at *13.7*.

Interest on personal loans (such as loans to buy autos and other personal items and credit card finance charges) is not deductible with the exception of qualifying student loan interest; *see* Chapter 33.

Interest on loans for business purposes is fully deductible on Schedule C. Interest on loans related to rental property is fully deductible from rental income on Schedule E. Whether interest is a business, investment, or a personal expense generally depends upon the use made of the money borrowed, not on the kind of property used to secure the loan. However, interest on a loan secured by a first or second home may be deductible as home equity mortgage interest regardless of the way you use the loan.

Interest on a loan used to finance an investment in a passive activity is subject to the limitations discussed in Chapter 10. However, if you rent out a second home that qualifies as a second residence, the portion of mortgage interest allocable to rental use is deductible as qualified mortgage interest and is not treated as a passive activity expense.

Home Mortgage Loans

Investment Loans

Timing of Interest Deductions

Home Mortgage Loans

Planning Reminder

Home Acquisition Loan Limits

Interest is deductible on up to $1 million of home acquisition loans taken out after October 13, 1987 ($500,000 limit if married filing separately). Mortgage loans taken out before October 14, 1987, are not subject to the $1,000,000 (or $500,000) limit. However, outstanding loans from before October 14, 1987, reduce the $1 million (or $500,000) ceiling for post–October 13, 1987, loans.

Planning Reminder

Mortgage Interest on a Third Home

Interest on debt secured by a residence *other than* your principal or second home may still be deductible, if you use the proceeds for investment or business purposes; *see 15.12.*

15.1 Home Mortgage Interest

You generally may deduct on Schedule A (Form 1040) qualifying mortgage interest on up to two residences (*see* two-residence limit, below). However, if your 2006 adjusted gross income exceeds $150,500 ($75,250 if married filing separately), your mortgage interest deduction is subject to the 3% reduction of itemized deductions; *see 13.7.*

Mortgage loan obtained after October 13, 1987. Whether you can take a full mortgage interest deduction for a loan taken out after October 13, 1987, depends on the amount of the mortgage debt and how you use the proceeds. Loans used to buy, construct, or improve a first or second home are called *home acquisition loans*, and up to $1 million of such debt qualifies for a mortgage interest deduction, $500,000 if married filing separately. Loans used for any other purpose are called *home equity loans* by the tax law, and up to $100,000 of such debt qualifies for an interest deduction; the home equity limit is $50,000 for married persons filing separately.

Loan must be secured by residence. To deduct interest on a home acquisition or home equity loan, the loan must be secured by your main home or a second home. For the loan to be "secured," it must be recorded or satisfy similar requirements under state law. For example, if a relative gives you a loan to help you purchase a home, the relative must take the legal steps required to record the loan with local authorities; otherwise, you may not deduct interest on the loan. The IRS, in a private ruling, held that interest paid by a homeowners' association on a loan to rebuild the common area is not deductible by the individual homeowners where their residences are not pledged as collateral.

Home acquisition loans are further discussed at *15.2. Home equity loans* are discussed at *15.3.*

If you *refinance your mortgage, see 15.7.*

Mortgage loan obtained before October 14, 1987. You may deduct all of the interest on a loan secured by a first or second home if the loan was obtained before October 14, 1987. Technically, such loans are considered home acquisition debt, but they are treated as "grandfathered debt," exempt from the $1 million loan limit ($500,000 for married persons filing separately).

However, the amount of your pre–October 14, 1987, loan reduces the $1 million (or $500,000) limit on home acquisition debt after October 13, 1987; *see 15.2.* It also reduces the fair market value limit for home equity debt; *see 15.3.* If you refinance your loan, *see 15.7.*

Two-residence limit for qualifying mortgage debt. The rules for deducting qualifying acquisition debt or home equity debt apply to loans secured by your principal residence and one other residence. A residence may be a condominium or cooperative unit, houseboat, mobile home, or house trailer that has sleeping, cooking, and toilet facilities. If you own more than two houses, you decide which residence will be considered your second residence. Interest debt secured by the second residence is deductible under the rules for acquisition debt *(15.2)* or home equity debt *(15.3).*

A residence that you rent out for any part of the year may be treated as a second residence only if you use it for personal nonrental purposes for more than the greater of 14 days or 10% of the rental days. In counting rental days, include days that the home is held out for rental or listed for resale. In counting days of personal use, use by close relatives generally qualifies as your personal use; *see 9.6.*

Interest on debt secured by a residence other than your principal or second home may still be deductible, but only if you use the proceeds for investment or business purposes; *see 15.12.*

Interest on mortgage credit certificates. Under special state and local programs, you may obtain a "mortgage credit certificate" to finance the purchase of a principal residence or to borrow funds for certain home improvements. A tax credit for interest paid on the mortgage may be claimed. The credit is computed on Form 8396 and claimed on Line 54 of Form 1040. The credit equals the interest paid multiplied by the certificate rate set by the governmental authority, but the maximum annual credit is $2,000. If you claim the credit, your home mortgage interest deduction is reduced by the amount of the current year credit claimed on Form 8396. If you buy a home using a qualifying mortgage credit certificate and sell that home within nine years, you may have to recapture part of the tax credit on Form 8828.

EXAMPLE

You pay $5,000 interest for a mortgage issued under a qualifying mortgage credit certificate. Under its terms, you are allowed a tax credit of $750. You may claim the balance of your mortgage interest, or $4,250 ($5,000 – $750), as an itemized deduction. If the allowable credit exceeds tax liability, a three-year carryover is allowed for the excess credit.

15.2 Home Acquisition Loans

Under the mortgage interest rules, a qualifying "home acquisition loan" is a loan used to buy, build, or substantially improve your principal residence or second home, provided the debt is secured by that same residence.

Interest paid on such home acquisition loans is fully deductible if the total debt does not exceed $1,000,000, or $500,000 if you are married filing separately. The $1,000,000 (or $500,000) limit applies to acquisition loans taken out after October 13, 1987.

If your mortgages taken after October 13, 1987, exceed the $1,000,000 (or $500,000) limit, you must use IRS worksheets included in Publication 936 to figure the amount of your deductible interest. Furthermore, if you incurred substantial loans before October 14, 1987, and later purchase a new home, your deduction for the mortgage for the new home may be limited. The $1 million limit for acquisition debt after October 13, 1987, is reduced by the amount of outstanding pre–October 14, 1987, debt.

Although interest on a pre–October 14, 1987, debt is generally fully deductible regardless of the size of the loan, refinancing a pre–October 14, 1987, debt for more than the existing balance subjects the excess to the $1 million ceiling; *see 15.7*.

Generally, a debt qualifies as being incurred in buying, constructing, or improving a residence if you satisfy IRS tracing rules *(15.12)* that prove the use of the loan proceeds for such residential purposes. Even if you cannot prove under the tracing rules that a loan was used to buy a residence, a loan will be treated by the IRS as incurred for buying a home to the extent you can show acquisition expenses within 90 days before or 90 days after incurring the loan. Special construction loan and improvement loan rules are discussed in *15.4* and *15.5*.

Interest on a mortgage to buy or build a home other than your principal residence or qualifying second home is treated as nondeductible personal interest. If a nonqualifying home is rented out, the part of the mortgage interest that is allocable to the rental activity is treated as passive activity interest subject to the limitations discussed in Chapter 10; the interest allocable to your personal use is nondeductible personal interest.

A married couple filing jointly may designate as a second residence a home owned or used by either spouse.

If a married couple files separately, each spouse may generally deduct interest on debt secured by one residence. However, both spouses may agree in writing to allow one of them to deduct the interest on a principal residence plus a designated second residence.

Cooperatives. In the case of housing cooperatives, debt secured by stock as a tenant-stockholder is treated as secured by a residence. The cooperative should provide you with the proper amount of your deductible interest. If the stock cannot be used to secure the debt because of restrictions under local law or the cooperative agreement, the debt is still considered to be secured by the stock if the loan was used to buy the stock. For further details on allocation rules, *see* IRS Publication 936.

Line-of-credit mortgages. If you had a line-of-credit mortgage on your home on October 13, 1987, and you borrowed additional amounts on this line of credit after that date, the additional borrowed amounts are treated as a mortgage taken out after October 13, 1987. If the newly borrowed amounts are used to buy, build, or improve your first or second home, they are treated as home acquisition debt subject to the $1 million or $500,000 limit. If used for any other purpose, the amounts are subject to the home equity debt rules at *15.3*.

Mortgage interest paid after house destroyed. If your principal residence or second home *(15.1)* is destroyed and the land is sold within a reasonable period of time following the destruction, the IRS treats the property as a residence for purposes of deducting interest payments on the mortgage during the period between the destruction of the residence and the sale of the land. In one case, the IRS allowed the interest deduction where a sale of land took place 26 months after the destruction of a home by a tornado.

Court Decision

Family Financing of Residence

The Tax Court allowed a taxpayer to deduct mortgage interest payments on a loan that his brother obtained when the taxpayer's poor credit rating prevented him from obtaining a mortgage loan. The taxpayer's brother bought the house but allowed the taxpayer and his wife to live there on the condition that they make the mortgage payments directly to the bank.

The IRS disallowed the taxpayer's deduction for the mortgage interest on the grounds that he was not liable for the mortgage debt; his brother was. However, the Tax Court allowed the deduction, holding that the taxpayer was the equitable owner of the home and that he was legally obligated to his brother to pay off the mortgage.

If the destroyed residence is reconstructed and reoccupied within a reasonable period of time following the destruction, the property will continue to be treated as a residence during that period, and the interest payments on the mortgage on the property will be deductible. The IRS allowed an interest deduction where reconstruction began 18 months after, and was completed 34 months after, destruction of the home.

15.3 Home Equity Loans

For interest deduction purposes, qualifying home equity debt is the *lesser* of:

1. $100,000, or $50,000 if married filing separately, *or*
2. The fair market value of your principal residence and second home *(15.1)*, reduced by the amount of acquisition debt *(15.2)* and by any "grandfathered" pre–October 14, 1987, mortgages *(15.1)*. According to the IRS, fair market value, acquisition debt, and grandfathered debt are determined on the date that the last debt was secured by the home.

The debt must be secured by your first or second home *(15.1)* to qualify. If you have a second home as well as a principal residence, the above limitation under (1) and (2) applies to the total debt for both homes. Interest on a qualifying home equity loan is deductible regardless of the way you spend the proceeds, unless it is used to buy tax-exempt obligations *(15.11)*.

On loans exceeding the home equity debt limit, interest may be deductible if the proceeds are used for investment or business purposes. Otherwise, interest on the excess is nondeductible personal interest.

Planning Reminder

Home Equity Loan To Pay Consumer Debts

Interest on consumer loans is not deductible, but you can use a home equity line-of-credit mortgage to pay off existing consumer debts and finance future consumer expenses. However, although interest on a home equity loan is fully deductible for regular tax purposes if within the $100,000 limit, the interest is not deductible for purposes of alternative minimum tax, unless the loan proceeds were used to improve your first or second home; *see 23.2.*

EXAMPLES

1. You bought your house for $200,000 subject to a mortgage of $150,000. When the mortgage principal is $120,000 and the fair market value of the house is $210,000, you take out a home equity loan. Interest on a home equity loan of up to $90,000 is fully deductible. Qualifying home equity debt may not exceed the difference between the fair market value of the house ($210,000) and the current acquisition debt ($120,000). If the value of the house exceeded $220,000, you could have borrowed up to the $100,000 limit as a qualifying home equity loan.
2. The fair market value of your house is $200,000 and the current mortgage is $160,000. You may deduct interest on a home equity loan of up to $40,000 ($200,000 – $160,000).

A loan may qualify partially as acquisition debt and partially as home equity debt where part of it is used to refinance an existing acquisition debt. The refinanced amount is still considered acquisition debt. Debt in excess of the refinanced amount is either home equity debt subject to the $100,000 ceiling or home acquisition debt subject to the $1 million ceiling, depending on the way the proceeds are used; *see 15.7.*

15.4 Home Construction Loans

Interest on a home construction loan may be fully deductible from the time construction begins for a period of up to 24 months while construction takes place. Within the 24-month period, the loan is considered acquisition debt subject to the $1 million ceiling *(15.2)*, provided that the home is a principal residence or second home when it is actually ready for occupancy. Furthermore, the loan proceeds must be directly traceable to home construction expenses, including the purchase of a lot, and the loan must be secured by the lot to be treated as acquisition debt. According to the IRS, if construction begins before a loan is incurred, the loan is treated as acquisition debt to the extent of construction expenses within the 24-month period *before* the loan. In determining when a loan is "incurred" for purposes of this 24-month rule, you can treat the date of a written loan application as the date the loan was "incurred," provided you receive the loan within 30 days after loan approval.

Interest incurred on the loan before construction begins is treated as nondeductible personal interest (*see* Example 1 in this section). If construction lasts more than 24 months, interest after the 24-month period also is treated as nondeductible personal interest.

Interest on loans taken out within 90 days *after* construction is completed may qualify for a full deduction. The loan is treated as acquisition debt to the extent of construction expenses within the last 24 months before the residence was completed, plus expenses through the date of the loan (*see* Example 2 below). For purposes of the 90-day rule, the loan proceeds generally are treated as received on the loan closing date. However, a debt may be considered "incurred" on the date a

Filing Tip

Mortgage Fees Not Deductible

You may not deduct expenses incurred in obtaining a mortgage loan, such as loan assumption fees or costs of an appraisal or credit report.

written loan application is made, provided the loan proceeds are actually received within 30 days after loan approval. If a loan application is made within the 90-day period and it is rejected, and a new application with another lender is made within a reasonable time after the rejection, a loan from the second lender will be considered timely even if more than 90 days have passed since the end of construction.

EXAMPLES

1. On January 12, 2006, you borrow $100,000 to buy a residential lot. The loan is secured by the lot. You begin construction of a principal residence on January 1, 2007, and use $250,000 of your own funds for construction expenses. The residence is completed December 31, 2008.
   The interest paid in 2006 is nondeductible personal interest. It was paid before the 24-month qualifying construction period that started January 1, 2007, and ended December 31, 2008.
   Interest paid in 2007 and 2008 is fully deductible as the $100,000 loan is treated as acquisition debt for the 24-month construction period.
2. Same facts as in Example 1, but on March 17, 2008, you take out a $300,000 mortgage on the completed house to raise funds. You use $100,000 of the loan proceeds to pay off the $100,000 loan on the lot and keep the balance.
   All of the interest on the $300,000 loan is fully deductible because the loan qualifies as acquisition debt; $100,000 of the debt is treated as acquisition debt used for construction, since it was used to refinance the original 2006 debt to purchase the lot. The $200,000 balance is also treated as a construction loan under the 90-day rule. It was borrowed within 90 days after the residence was completed, and it reimbursed construction expenses of at least $200,000 incurred within 24 months before the completion date.
3. On January 12, 2006, you purchased a residential lot and began building a home on the lot using $45,000 of your personal funds. The home was completed on October 31, 2006. On November 24, 2006, you received a loan of $36,000 that was secured by the home. The debt may be treated as taken out to build the home as it was taken out no later than 90 days after the home was completed, and expenditures of at least $36,000 were made within the period of 24 months before the home was completed.

15.5 Home Improvement Loans

Loans used for substantial home improvements are treated as acquisition debt subject to the $1 million ceiling for loans after October 13, 1987; *see 15.2.* Include only the cost of home improvements that must be added to the basis of the property because they add to the value of the home or prolong useful life. Repair costs are not considered.

EXAMPLE

Your current acquisition mortgage is $100,000. You borrow $20,000 to build a new room. Your qualifying acquisition debt is now $120,000.

If substantial improvements to a home are begun but not completed before a loan is incurred, the loan will be treated as acquisition debt (assuming the debt is secured by the home) to the extent of improvement expenses made within 24 months before the loan. If the loan is incurred within 90 days after an improvement is completed, the loan is treated as acquisition debt (assuming the debt is secured by the home) to the extent of improvement expenses made within the period starting 24 months before completion of the improvement and ending on the date of the loan.

Caution

Mortgage Interest Reported on Form 1098

Banks and other lending institutions report mortgage interest payments of $600 or more to the IRS on Form 1098. You should receive a copy of Form 1098 or a similar statement by January 31, 2007, showing your mortgage payments in 2006. Deductible points *(15.8)* paid on the purchase of a principal home are included on Form 1098.

15.6 Mortgage Payment Rules

Payments to the bank or lending institution holding your mortgage may include interest, principal payments, taxes, and fire insurance premiums. Deduct only interest and tax payments. You may not deduct the payments of mortgage principal and insurance premiums.

In the year you sell your home, check your settlement papers for interest charged up to the date of sale; this amount is deductible.

Mortgage credit. If you qualify for the special tax credit for interest on qualified home mortgage certificates, you only deduct interest in excess of the allowable credit; *see 15.1.*

Prepayment penalty. A penalty for prepayment of a mortgage is deductible as interest.

Mortgage assistance payments. You may not deduct interest paid on your behalf under Section 235 of the National Housing Act.

Delinquency charges for late payment. According to the IRS, a late payment charge is deductible as mortgage interest if it was not for a specific service provided by the mortgage holder. In one case, the Tax Court agreed with the IRS that delinquency charges imposed by a bank were not interest where they were a flat percentage of the installment due, regardless of how late payment was. The late charges were primarily imposed by the bank to recoup costs related to collection efforts, such as telephone calls, letters, and supervisory reviews. They were also intended to discourage untimely payments by imposing a penalty.

Graduated payment mortgages. Monthly payments are initially smaller than under the standard mortgage on the same amount of principal, but payments increase each year over the first five- or 10-year period and continue at the increased monthly amount for the balance of the mortgage term. As a cash-basis taxpayer, you deduct the amount of interest actually paid even though, during the early years of the mortgage, payments are less than the interest owed on the loan. The unpaid interest is added to the loan principal, and future interest is figured on the increased unpaid mortgage loan balance. The bank, in a year-end statement, will identify the amount of interest actually paid. (An accrual-basis taxpayer may deduct the accrued interest each year.)

Reverse mortgage loan. Homeowners who own their homes outright may in certain states cash in on their equity by taking a "reverse mortgage loan." Typically, 80% of the value of the home is paid by a bank to a homeowner in a lump sum or in installments. Principal is due when the home is sold or when the homeowner dies; interest is added to the loan and is payable when the principal is paid. The IRS has ruled that an interest deduction may be claimed by a cash-basis home-owner only when the interest is paid, not when the interest is added to the outstanding loan balance.

Filing Tip

Joint Liability on Mortgage

If you do not personally receive a Form 1098 but a person (other than your spouse with whom you file a joint return) who is also liable for and paid interest on the mortgage received a Form 1098, you deduct your share of the interest and attach a statement to your Schedule A showing the name and address of the person who received the form. If you are the payer of record on a mortgage on which there are other borrowers entitled to a deduction for the interest shown on the Form 1098 you received, provide them with information on their share of the deductible amount.

The Tax Court has allowed a joint obligor to deduct his or her payment of another obligor's share of the mortgage interest if the payment is made to avoid the loss of the property, and payment is made with his or her separate funds.

Shared appreciation mortgage. Under a shared appreciation mortgage (SAM) for a personal residence, the lender agrees to charge a fixed rate of interest that is lower than the prevailing market rate. In return, the homeowner promises to pay a percentage of the appreciation on the property at a later date to make up the difference. The fixed-rate interest is deductible when paid and the percentage of appreciation is also treated as interest that you can deduct in the year of payment, subject to the limits discussed at *15.2*. For example, you agree to pay interest of 5% plus 40% of the appreciation in the value of the property within 10 years or earlier if you sell the home or pay off the mortgage. If, at the end of 10 years, the residence is not sold or the loan repaid, you may refinance at the prevailing rate the outstanding balance plus the interest based on the appreciation. If you refinance with the same lender, you may not claim an immediate deduction for the extra interest. The execution of a note is not considered payment. The amount covering the extra interest is deducted ratably over the period of the new loan. If you refinance with another lender and use the funds to pay off the old loan plus the extra interest, the extra interest is deductible in the year of payment, subject to the limits of *15.2*.

Redeemable ground rents. In a ground rent arrangement, you lease rather than buy the land on which your home is located. Ground rent is deductible as mortgage interest if: (1) the land you lease is for a term exceeding 15 years (including renewal periods) and is freely assignable; (2) you have a present or future right to end the lease and buy the entire interest; and (3) the lessor's interest in the land is primarily a security interest. Payments to end the lease and buy the lessor's interest are not deductible ground rents.

15.7 Interest on Refinanced Loans

When you refinance a mortgage on a first or second home *(15.1)* for the same amount as the remaining principal balance on the old loan, there is no change in the tax treatment of interest. In other words, if interest was fully deductible on the old loan, then it is fully deductible on the new loan.

If you refinance a home mortgage for more than the existing balance, the deductibility of interest on the excess amount depends upon how you use the funds and the amount of refinancing. If the excess amount is used to buy, build, or substantially improve your first or second home, then it is considered home acquisition debt; *see 15.2.* If the excess plus all other home acquisition loans does not exceed $1 million ($500,000 if married filing separately), the interest is fully deductible. If the excess is used for any other purpose, such as to pay off credit card debt or to finance a child's education, the excess is considered home equity debt; *see 15.3.* If the excess plus all other home equity loans does not exceed $100,000 ($50,000 if married filing separately), the interest is fully deductible. If the refinanced loan is partly home acquisition debt and partly home equity debt, the overall limit of $1.1 million applies ($1 million home acquisition debt and $100,000 home equity debt) or, if married filing separately, $550,000 ($500,000 home acquisition debt and $50,000 home equity debt).

Interest paid on loans in excess of home acquisition and home equity debt ceilings is generally treated as nondeductible personal interest unless the proceeds are used for business or investment purposes; *see 15.12.*

EXAMPLE

In 1998, Robert and Michelle Stein purchased a home for $250,000. They put $50,000 down and obtained a $200,000, 30-year mortgage secured by the home. In 2006, when their house is worth $300,000 and there is a $175,000 principal balance on the mortgage, they refinance to take advantage of lower interest rates. The refinanced mortgage is for $225,000, payable over 20 years. The Steins use $175,000 to pay off the old mortgage, $30,000 to purchase a car and to pay off credit card debt, and the remaining $20,000 to build a new deck on their home.

The interest on up to $175,000 of the debt incurred to pay off the old mortgage is fully deductible; the amount equals the outstanding balance before refinancing and also falls within the $1 million home acquisition debt ceiling. The $20,000 used to remodel the house is also treated as home acquisition debt. Interest on this amount is fully deductible; the amount falls within the $1 million ceiling when added to the $175,000.

The $30,000 used to buy a car and pay off credit cards is treated as home equity debt. Interest on this amount is fully deductible; the amount falls within the $100,000 ceiling.

Pre–October 14, 1987, loans. Refinanced pre–October 14, 1987, loans are not subject to the $1 million home acquisition and $100,000 home equity debt ceilings during the period of the original loan term. However, after the end of the loan term, the ceilings apply to the refinanced amount as explained above. Furthermore, where a refinanced pre–October 14, 1987, debt exceeds the remaining principal balance, the excess is also subject to the $1 million home acquisition and $100,000 home equity debt ceilings.

Points Paid on Refinancing

The IRS does not allow a current deduction for points on a refinanced mortgage. According to the IRS, the points must be deducted ratably over the loan period, unless part of the new loan is used for home improvements. Thus, if you pay points of $2,400 when refinancing a 20-year loan on your principal residence, the IRS allows you to deduct only $10 a month, or $120 each full year.

A federal appeals court rejected the IRS allocation rule where points are paid on a long-term mortgage that replaces a short-term loan; *see* the Court Decision in *15.7.*

If part of a refinancing is used for home improvements to a principal residence, the IRS allows a deduction for a portion of the points allocable to the home improvements.

EXAMPLE

In June 2006, Craig Smith refinances his home mortgage, which has a principal of $80,000 outstanding. The new loan is for $100,000, payable over 15 years starting in July 2006. He uses $80,000 to pay off the old $80,000 balance and the remaining $20,000 is used for home improvements. Assume that at the closing of the new loan, Smith pays points of $2,000 from his separate funds. In the year of payment he may deduct $400 allocable to the 20% of the loan used for home improvements. He may also deduct the ratable portion of the $1,600 balance of the points, which must be deducted over the period of the new loan. The ratable portion is $53 ($1,600 ÷ 180-month loan term × 6 months in 2006). Thus, Craig's total deduction for points in 2006 is $453 ($400 + $53).

Mortgage ends early. If you are ratably deducting points on a refinanced loan and you refinance again with a different lender, or the mortgage ends early because you prepay it or the lender forecloses, you can deduct the remaining points in the year the mortgage ends; *see 15.8.*

Court Decision

Current Deduction for Points on Refinancing

Huntsman replaced a three-year loan used to purchase his principal residence with a 30-year mortgage. He deducted $4,400 of points paid on the new mortgage. The IRS and the Tax Court held that the points had to be deducted over the 30-year loan term.

The Federal Appeals Court for the Eighth Circuit disagreed and allowed a full deduction in the year the points were paid. The first loan was temporary and merely a step in obtaining permanent financing for the purchase of the principal residence.

The IRS has announced that in areas outside of the Eighth Circuit, it will continue to disallow full deductions in the year of payment for points paid on refinancings. The Eighth Circuit includes only these states: Minnesota, Iowa, North and South Dakota, Nebraska, Missouri, and Arkansas. In these states, the IRS will not challenge deductions for points on refinancing agreements similar to Huntsman's that replace short-term financing with long-term permanent financing.

In a later case, the Tax Court held that the *Huntsman* exception does not apply where a borrower refinances a long-term mortgage to take advantage of lower interest rates; the points must be deducted over the term of the new mortgage.

15.8 "Points"

Lenders sometimes charge "points" in addition to the stated interest rate. The points increase the lender's upfront fees, but in return borrowers generally are charged a lower interest rate over the loan term. Points are either treated as a type of prepaid interest *(15.14)* or as a nondeductible service fee, depending on what the charge covers. If the points qualify as interest, they are deductible over the term of the loan unless they are paid on the purchase or improvement of your principal residence, in which case they are deductible in the year they are paid, as discussed below. If you pay points on a loan to purchase or improve a second home, you must deduct the points ratably over the term of the loan.

Points are treated as interest if your payment is solely for your use of the money and is not for specific services performed by the lender that are separately charged. Whether a payment is called "points" or a "loan origination fee" does not affect its deductibility if it is actually a charge for the use of money. The purpose of the charge—that is, for the use of the money or the services rendered—will be controlling. For example, you may not deduct points that are fees for services, such as appraisal fees, preparation of a mortgage note or deed of trust, settlement fees, notary fees, abstract fees, commissions, and recording fees.

If you are *selling* property and you assume the buyer's liability for points, do not deduct the payment as interest but include it as a selling expense that reduces the amount realized on the sale.

Caution

Service Fees Are Not Deductible Points

You may not deduct as points amounts that are for specific lender services. To be deductible, points on the purchase of a principal residence must be prepaid interest for the use of the loan money.

Deduction for Points on Purchase or Improvement of Principal Residence

Points are generally treated as prepaid interest *(15.14)* that must be deducted over the period of the loan. However, there is an exception for points you pay on a loan to buy, build, or improve your principal residence. The points on such loans are deductible in the year paid if these tests are met: (1) the loan is secured by your principal residence; (2) the charging of points is an established business practice in the geographic area in which the loan is made; (3) the points charged do not exceed the points generally charged in the area; (4) the amount of points is computed as a percentage of the loan and specifically earmarked on the loan closing statement as "points," "loan origination fees," or "loan discount"; and (5) you pay the points directly to the lender; *see* "Points withheld from the principal," below.

Filing Tip

Amortize Points Starting in Second Year

A married couple purchased a principal residence and paid points late in the year. For the year of the purchase, their standard deduction exceeded their itemized deductions. The IRS ruled that claiming the standard deduction for the year the points are paid would not entirely forfeit the deduction for points. The points may be amortized starting in the second year. Assuming that they itemize deductions starting in the second year, the allocable portion of the points may be deducted each year over the remaining loan term.

Points paid by seller are deductible by buyer. The seller's payment is treated as an adjustment to the purchase price that the seller gives to you as the buyer and that you then turn over to the lender to pay off the points. You must reduce your cost basis for the home by the seller-paid points.

Points withheld from the principal. Points withheld from the principal of a loan used to buy your principal residence are treated as if you paid them directly to the lender if, at or before closing, you have made a down payment, escrow deposit, or earnest money payment that is at least equal to the amount of points withheld. These payments must have been from your own funds and not from funds that have been borrowed from the lender as part of the overall transaction.

If the loan is used to *improve* your principal residence, the points are not immediately deductible if withheld from the loan principal. You must pay the points with funds that have not been obtained from the lender to claim the full deduction in the year of payment. Otherwise, the deduction must be spread over the loan term.

Caution

Points Reported to the IRS

Points you paid in 2006 on the purchase of your principal residence will be reported to the IRS by the lender on Form 1098 if they meet the five tests for a deduction listed in *15.8*. Seller-paid points are also included on Form 1098. Form 1098 is used by the IRS to check on the deduction you claim for points on Line 10 of Schedule A. Points paid on an improvement loan for your principal residence are deductible on Line 12 of Schedule A if they meet the tests; they are not shown on Form 1098.

Points on second home. If you pay points on a mortgage secured by a second home or a vacation home, the points are not fully deductible in the year of payment; you must claim the deduction ratably over the loan term.

Points paid on refinancing. The IRS does not allow a current deduction for points on a refinanced mortgage (*see 15.7* for further information).

Deduct balance of points if mortgage ends early. If you are deducting points over the term of the loan because a full first-year deduction is not allowed, you are allowed to deduct the balance in the year the mortgage ends, such as when you prepay the loan, or the lender forecloses. If the mortgage ends early because you refinance the mortgage with a different lender, you may deduct the balance of the points. For example, if you refinanced your mortgage in 1998 and paid points, those points had to be amortized over the loan term *(15.7)*. If in 2006 you refinance again with a different lender and pay points again, the balance of the points from the 1998 loan are deductible on your 2006 return, and the points on the new loan must be amortized over the loan term. If you refinanced with the same lender, the balance of the points from the 1998 loan must be deducted over the term of the new loan.

15.9 Cooperative and Condominium Apartments

Cooperative apartments. If you are a tenant-stockholder of a cooperative apartment, you may deduct your portion of:

- Interest paid by the cooperative on its debts, provided you do not pay interest on more than two residences; *see 15.1*. This includes your pro rata share of the permanent financing expenses (points) of the cooperative on its mortgage covering the housing project.
- Taxes paid by the cooperative *(16.6)*. However, if the cooperative does not own the land and building but merely leases them and is required to pay real estate taxes under the terms of the lease, you may not deduct your share of the tax payment.

In some localities, such as New York City, rent control rules allow tenants of a building converted to a cooperative to remain in their apartments even if they do not buy into the co-op. A holdover tenant may prevent some co-op purchasers from occupying an apartment. The IRS ruled that the fact that a holdover tenant stays in the apartment will not bar the owner from deducting his or her share of the co-op's interest and taxes.

Condominiums. If you own an apartment in a condominium, you have a direct ownership interest in the property and are treated, for tax purposes, just as any other property owner. You may deduct your payments of real estate taxes and mortgage interest. You may also deduct taxes and interest paid on the mortgage debt of the project allocable to your share of the property. The deduction of interest from condominium ownership is also subject to the two-residence limit discussed at *15.1*. If your condominium is used part of the time for rental purposes, you may deduct expenses of maintenance and repairs and claim depreciation deductions subject to the rules in *9.7*.

Investment Loans

15.10 Investment Interest Limitations

Interest paid on margin accounts and debts to buy or carry other investments is deductible on Schedule A up to the amount of net investment income. If you do not have investment income such as interest, you may not deduct investment interest. Investment income for purposes of the deduction generally does not include net capital gains or qualified dividends, but you may elect to include them in order to increase your investment interest deduction. If you make the election, the elected amount will not be eligible for the favorable 5% or 15% capital gain rates; *see* "Computing the Deduction" below. Investment interest in excess of net investment income may be carried forward and deducted from next year's net investment income.

You compute the deduction for investment interest on Form 4952, which must be attached along with Schedule A to Form 1040. The deduction is *not* subject to the 3% reduction of itemized deductions that applies on Schedule A if your adjusted gross income exceeds $150,500 ($75,250 if married filing separately); *see 13.7*.

Caution

Interest on Loans To Buy Market Discount Bonds and Treasury Bills

Limits apply to the deduction for interest on loans used to buy or carry market discount bonds *(4.20)* and Treasury bills *(4.27)*.

What is investment interest? It is all interest paid or accrued on debts incurred or continued to buy or carry investment property such as interest on securities in a margin account. However, interest on loans to buy tax-exempt securities is not deductible; *see 15.11*.

Investment interest does not include any qualified residence interest *(15.1)*, production period interest that is capitalized *(16.4)*, or interest related to a passive activity *(10.8)*.

Investment property includes property producing portfolio income (interest, dividends, or royalties not realized in the ordinary course of business) under the passive activity rules discussed in Chapter 10, and property in activities that are not treated as passive activities, even if you do not materially participate, such as working interests in oil and gas wells.

Passive activity interest is not investment interest. Interest expenses incurred in a passive activity such as rental real estate *(10.1)*, or a limited partnership or S corporation in which you do not materially participate *(10.6)*, are taken into account on Form 8582 when figuring net passive income or loss. This includes interest incurred on loans used to finance your investment in a passive activity. Do not treat passive activity interest as investment interest on Form 4952.

However, interest expenses allocable to *portfolio* income (non–business activity interest, dividends, or royalties) from a limited partnership or S corporation are investment interest and not passive interest. The investment interest will be listed separately on Schedule K-1 received from the partnership or corporation.

Computing the Deduction

Deductible investment interest is limited to net investment income. Net investment income is the excess of investment income over investment expenses. The key terms *investment income* and *investment expenses* are defined below.

Caution

Electing To Treat Long-Term Gains or Dividends as Investment Income

If you elect on Form 4952 to treat net capital gains or qualified dividends as investment income in order to increase your 2006 investment interest deduction, that amount is not eligible to be taxed at favorable capital gain rates *(5.3)*.

Investment income. Investment income is generally gross income from property held for investment, such as interest, dividends, other than qualified dividends, annuities, and royalties. Income or expenses considered in figuring profit or loss of a passive activity *(10.8)* is not considered investment income or expenses. Property subject to a net lease is not treated as investment property, as it is within the passive activity rules.

If you have net capital gains (net long-term capital gains exceeding net short-term losses) from the sale of investment property such as stocks or mutual-fund shares, or capital gain distributions from mutual funds, such gains and distributions are not treated as investment income unless you specifically elect to include them in investment income on Form 4952. You may elect to include all or part of them. The same election rule applies to qualified dividends *(4.1)* that are subject to net capital gain tax rates. An election must be made on Form 4952 to include qualified dividends in investment income. If you make this election, you may not apply preferential capital gain rates *(5.3)* to the amount of the net capital gains (and capital gain distributions) or qualified dividends treated as investment interest on Form 4952. If you make the election on Form 4952, the elected amount is subtracted from net capital gains when applying the capital gain tax rates on the IRS worksheets *(5.3)*.

Investment expenses. There are expenses, other than interest, directly connected with the production of investment income. However, for purposes of determining net investment income, only those investment expenses (other than interest) allowable after figuring the 2% floor for miscellaneous itemized deductions *(19.1)* are taken into account. The 2% floor will bar a deduction for some of the miscellaneous itemized deductions. For purposes of this net investment income computation, assume that miscellaneous itemized deductions other than investment expenses are disallowed first.

Net investment income. Reducing investment income by investment expenses gives you net investment income. Your deduction for investment interest expenses is limited to this amount; any excess interest expense for 2006 may be carried over to 2007, as discussed below.

Where to enter the deduction on your return. The deduction figured on Form 4952 is generally entered on Line 13 of Schedule A as investment interest. However, if the interest is attributable to royalties, you may have to enter the interest on Schedule E; follow the Form 4952 instructions. Furthermore, there is an additional complication if you have investment interest for an activity for which you are not "at risk" *(10.18)*. After figuring the investment interest deduction on Form 4952, you must enter the portion of the interest that is attributable to the at-risk activity on Form 6198. The amount carried over to Form 6198 is subtracted from the investment interest deduction claimed on Form 4952.

Carryover to 2007 and future years. Investment interest in excess of net investment income for 2006 may be carried forward to 2007 and is deductible in 2007 to the extent that when added to 2007 investment interest expenses it does not exceed net investment income. If not used in 2007, the carryforward extends indefinitely to 2008 and future years.

EXAMPLE

For 2006, Larry Jones has $10,000 of interest income. He has investment expenses, other than interest, of $3,200, after taking into account the 2% floor on miscellaneous itemized deductions. His investment interest expense from securities margin account loans is $8,000. Jones also has income of $2,000 from a passive partnership investment.

Jones's net investment income is $6,800: $10,000 of interest income less $3,200 of non-interest investment expenses. The passive activity income from the partnership is not included in investment income.

Jones's investment interest deduction for 2006 is limited to the $6,800 of net investment income. The $1,200 of investment interest in excess of net investment income ($8,000 – $6,800) is carried forward to 2007.

15.11 Debts To Carry Tax-Exempt Obligations

When you borrow money in order to buy or carry tax-exempt bonds, you may not deduct any interest paid on your loan. Application of this disallowance rule is clear where there is actual evidence that loan proceeds were used to buy tax-exempts or that tax-exempts were used as collateral. But sometimes the relationship between a loan and the purchase of tax-exempts is less obvious, as where you hold tax-exempts and borrow to carry other securities or investments. IRS guidelines explain when a direct relationship between the debt and an investment in tax-exempts will be inferred so that no interest deduction is allowed. The IRS will *not* infer a direct relationship between a debt and an investment in tax-exempts in these cases:

1. The investment in tax-exempts is not substantial. That is, it is not more than 2% of the adjusted basis of the investment portfolio and any assets held in an actively conducted business.
2. The debt is incurred for a personal purpose. For example, an investor may take out a home mortgage instead of selling his tax-exempts and using the proceeds to finance the home purchase. Interest on the mortgage is deductible under the rules at *15.1*.
3. The debt is incurred in connection with the active conduct of a business and does not exceed business needs. But if a person reasonably could have foreseen when the tax-exempts were purchased that he or she would have to borrow funds to meet ordinary and recurrent business needs, the interest expenses are not deductible.

The guidelines infer a direct relationship between the debt and an investment in tax-exempts in this type of case: An investor in tax-exempts has outstanding debts not directly related to personal expenses or to his or her business. The interest will be disallowed even if the debt appears to have been incurred to purchase other portfolio investments. Portfolio investments include transactions entered into for profit, including investments in real estate, that are not connected with the active conduct of a business; *see* the Example below.

EXAMPLE

An investor owning $360,000 in tax-exempt bonds purchased real estate in a joint venture, giving a purchase money mortgage and cash for the price. He deducted interest on the mortgage. The IRS disallowed the deduction, claiming the debt was incurred to carry tax-exempts. A court allowed the deduction. A mortgage is the customary manner of financing such a purchase. Furthermore, since the purchase was part of a joint venture, the other parties' desires in the manner of financing had to be considered.

Caution

Tax-Exempt Income From Mutual Fund

You may not deduct interest on loans used to buy or carry tax-exempt securities. If you receive exempt-interest dividends from a mutual fund during the year, you may deduct interest on a loan used to buy or carry the mutual-fund shares only to the extent that the proceeds can be allocated to taxable dividends you also receive.

15.12 Earmarking Use of Loan Proceeds

The IRS has set down complex record keeping and allocation rules for claiming interest deductions on loans used for business or investment purposes, or for passive activities. The rules deal primarily with the use of loan proceeds for more than one purpose and the commingling of loan proceeds in an account with unborrowed funds. The thrust of the rules is to base deductibility of interest on the *use* of the borrowed funds. The allocation rules do not affect mortgage interest deductions on loans secured by a qualifying first or second home; *see 15.1*.

Keep separate accounts for business, personal, and investment borrowing. For example, if you borrow for investment purposes, keep the proceeds of the loan in a separate account and use the proceeds only for investment purposes. Do not use the funds to pay for personal expenses; interest is not deductible on personal loans other than qualifying student loans (Chapter 33). Furthermore, do not deposit loan proceeds in an account funded with unborrowed money, unless you intend to use the proceeds within 30 days of the deposit. By following these directions, you can identify your use of the proceeds with a specific expenditure, such as for investment, personal, or business purposes, and the interest on the loan may be treated as incurred for that purpose. The 30-day rule is discussed below.

The IRS treats undisbursed loan proceeds deposited in an account as investment property, even though the account does not bear interest. When proceeds are disbursed from the account, the use of the proceeds determines how interest is treated; *see* Examples 1 and 2 below.

30-day disbursement rule. If you deposit borrowed funds in an account with unborrowed funds, a special 30-day rule allows you to treat payments from the account as made from the loan proceeds. Where you make more than one disbursement from such an account, you may treat any expenses paid within 30 days before or after deposit of the loan proceeds as if made from the loan proceeds. Thus, you may allocate interest on the loan to that disbursement, even if earlier payments from the account have been made; *see* Example 3 below. If you make the disbursement after 30 days, the IRS requires you to allocate interest on the loan to the first disbursement; *see* Example 4 below. Furthermore, if an account includes only loan proceeds and interest earned on the proceeds, disbursements may be allocated first to the interest income and then to the loan proceeds.

Planning Reminder

Keep Loans Separate

To safeguard your investment and business interest deductions, you must earmark and keep a record of your loans. You should avoid using loan proceeds to fund different types of expenditures.

Allocation period. Interest is allocated to an expenditure for the period *beginning* on the date the loan proceeds are used or treated as used and *ending* on the earlier of either the date the debt is repaid or the date it is reallocated.

Accrued interest is treated as a debt until it is paid, and any interest accruing on unpaid interest is allocated in the same manner as the unpaid interest is allocated. Compound interest accruing on such debt, other than compound interest accruing on interest that accrued before the beginning of the year, may be allocated between the original expenditure and any new expenditure from the same account on a straight-line basis. That is done by allocating an equal amount of such interest expense to each day during the taxable year. In addition, you may treat a year as *twelve 30-day months* for purposes of allocating interest on a straight-line basis.

Payments from a checking account. A disbursement from a checking account is treated as made at the time the check is written on the account, provided the check is delivered or mailed to the payee within a reasonable period after the writing of the check. You may treat checks written on the same day as written in any order. A check is presumed to be written on the date appearing on the check and to be delivered or mailed to the payee within a reasonable period thereafter. However, the presumption may not apply if the check does not clear within a reasonable period after the date appearing on the check.

Change in use of property. You must reallocate interest if you convert debt-financed property to a different use; for example, when you buy a business auto with an installment loan, interest paid on the auto is business interest, but if during the year you convert the auto to personal use, interest paid after the conversion is personal interest.

Order of repayment. If you used loan proceeds to repay several different kinds of debt, the debts being repaid are assumed to be repaid in the following order: (1) personal debt; (2) investment debt and passive activity debt other than active real estate debt; (3) debt from a real estate activity in which you actively participate; (4) former passive activity debt; and (5) business debt. *See* Example 5 below. Payments made on the same day may be treated as made in any order.

Planning Reminder

Using Borrowed Funds To Pay Interest

To get an interest deduction you must pay the interest; you may not claim a deduction by having the creditor add the interest to the debt. If you do not have funds to pay the interest, you may borrow money to pay the interest. The borrowed funds must be from a different creditor. The IRS disallows deductions where a debtor borrows from the same creditor to make interest payments on an earlier loan. The second loan is considered a device for getting an interest expense deduction without actually making payments. The Tax Court and several federal appeals courts have sided with the IRS.

EXAMPLES

1. On January 1, you borrow $10,000 and deposit the proceeds in a non–interest-bearing checking account. No other amounts are deposited in the account during the year and no part of the loan is repaid during the year. On April 1, you invest $2,000 of the proceeds in a real estate venture. On September 1, you use $4,000 to buy furniture.

   From January 1 through March 31, interest on the entire undisbursed $10,000 is treated as investment interest. From April 1 through August 31, interest on $2,000 of the debt is treated as passive activity interest and interest on $8,000 of the debt is treated as investment interest. From September 1 through December 31, interest on $4,000 of the debt is treated as personal interest; interest on $2,000 is treated as passive activity interest; and interest on $4,000 is treated as investment interest.

2. On September 1, you borrow money for business purposes and deposit it in a checking account. On October 15, you disburse the proceeds for business purposes. Interest incurred on the loan before the disbursement of the funds is treated as investment interest expense. Interest starting on October 15 is treated as business interest. However, you may elect to treat the starting date for business interest as of the first of the month in

which the disbursement was made—that is, October 1—provided all other disbursements from the account during the same month are similarly treated.

3. On September 1, you borrow $5,000 to invest in stock and deposit the proceeds in your regular checking account. On September 10, you buy a TV and stereo for $2,500 and on September 11 invest $5,000 in stock, using funds from the account. As the stock investment was made within 30 days of depositing the loan proceeds in the account, interest on the entire loan is treated as incurred for investment purposes.
4. Same facts as in Example 3, but the TV and stereo were bought on October 1 and the stock on October 31. As the stock investment was not made within 30 days, the IRS requires you to treat the purchase of the TV and the stereo for $2,500 as the first purchase made with the loan proceeds of $5,000. Thus, the 50% of loan interest that is allocated to the stereo purchase is nondeductible.
5. On July 12, Smith borrows $100,000 and immediately deposits the proceeds in an account. He uses the proceeds as follows:

August 31	$40,000 for passive activity
October 5	$20,000 for rental activity
December 24	$40,000 for personal use

On January 19 of the following year, Smith repays $90,000. Of the repayment, $40,000 is allocated as a repayment of the personal expenditure, $40,000 of the passive activity, and $10,000 of the rental activity. The outstanding $10,000 is treated as debt incurred in a rental activity.

Timing of Interest Deductions

15.13 Year To Claim an Interest Deduction

As a cash-basis taxpayer, you deduct interest in the year of payment except for prepayments of interest; *see 15.14*. Giving a promissory note is not considered payment. Increasing the amount of a loan by interest owed, as with insurance loans, is also not considered payment and will not support a deduction. If a person pays your interest obligation with the understanding you will repay him or her, you take the deduction in the year the interest is paid, not when you repay him or her. However, an accrual-basis taxpayer generally deducts interest in the year the interest accrues; *see 40.3*.

Here is how a cash-basis taxpayer treats interest in the following situations:

On a life insurance loan, where proceeds are used for a deductible (nonpersonal) purpose, you claim a deduction in the year in which the interest is paid. You may not claim a deduction when the insurance company adds the interest to your debt. You may not deduct your payment of interest on an insurance loan after you assign the policy.

On a margin account with a broker, interest is deductible in the year in which it is paid or your account is credited after the interest has been charged. But an interest charge to your account is not payment if you do not pay it in cash or the broker has not collected dividends, interest, or security sales proceeds that may be applied against the interest due. Note that the interest deduction on margin accounts is subject to investment interest limitations; *see 15.10*.

For partial payment of a loan used for a deductible (nonpersonal) purpose, interest is deductible in the year the payment is credited against interest due. When a loan has no provision for allocating payments between principal and income, the law presumes that a partial payment is applied first to interest and then to principal, unless you agree otherwise. Where the payment is in full settlement of the debt, the payment is applied first to principal, unless you agree otherwise. Where there is an involuntary payment, such as that following a foreclosure sale of collateral, sales proceeds are applied first to principal, unless you agree to the contrary. *See also 15.12* for the effect of payments on the allocation of debt proceeds.

Note renewed. You may not deduct interest by merely giving a new note. You claim a deduction in the year the renewed note is paid. The giving of a new note or increasing the amount due is not payment. The same is true when past due interest is deducted from the proceeds of a new loan; this is not a payment of the interest.

15.14 Prepaid Interest

If you prepay interest on a loan used for *investment* or *business* purposes you may not deduct interest allocable to any period falling in a later taxable year. The prepaid interest must be deducted over the period of the loan, whether you are a cash-basis or accrual-basis taxpayer.

Points paid on the purchase of a *principal residence* are generally fully deductible in the year paid; *see 15.8*. Points paid on refinancing generally are not deductible; *see 15.7*.

Planning Reminder

Business or Investment Loans

If you prepay business or investment loan interest, you must spread the interest deduction over the period of the loan. In the year of payment, you may deduct only the interest allocable to that year.

Treatment of interest included in a level payment schedule. Where payments of principal and interest are equal, a large amount of interest allocated to the payments made in early years of a loan will generally not be considered prepaid interest. However, if the loan calls for a variable interest rate, the IRS may treat interest payments as consisting partly of interest, computed under an average level effective rate, and partly of prepaid interest allocable to later years of the loan. An interest rate that varies with the "prime rate" does not necessarily indicate a prepaid interest element.

When you borrow money for a deductible purpose and give a note to the lender, the amount of your loan proceeds may be less than the face value of the note. The difference between the proceeds and the face amount is interest discount. For loans that do not fall within the OID rules in *4.18*, such as loans of a year or less, interest is deductible in the year of payment if you are on the cash basis. If you use the accrual basis, the interest is deductible as it accrues. For loans that fall within OID rules, your lender should provide a statement showing the interest element and the tax treatment of the interest.

EXAMPLE

In February 2006, you borrow $1,000 for an investment and receive $900 in return for your $1,000 one-year note. You repay the full loan in January 2007. You are on the cash basis. You do not deduct the interest of $100 when the note is given. The $100 interest is treated as investment interest *(15.10)* when the loan is paid in 2007.

Chapter 16

Deductions for Taxes

If you itemize deductions on Schedule A, you may deduct your 2006 payments of state, local, and foreign income taxes and real property taxes, as well as state and local personal property taxes. *See 16.3* for state and local general sales taxes.

To increase your deduction for state and local taxes, consider making a year-end prepayment of estimated tax liability. You also may be able to increase withholdings from your pay to increase your deduction.

If you pay transfer taxes on the sale of securities or investment real estate, the taxes are not deductible. However, they increase your cost basis when figuring your profit or loss.

Taxes paid in operating a business are generally deductible, except for sales taxes, which are added to the cost of the property.

Taxes claimed as itemized deductions are subject to the reduction of itemized deductions if your adjusted gross income exceeds $150,500, or $75,250 if married filing separately; *see 13.7*.

16.1 Deductible Taxes

If you itemize deductions for 2006 on Schedule A (Form 1040), you may deduct your 2006 payments of:

- State, local, and foreign income taxes
- State, local, and foreign real property taxes
- State and local personal property taxes

See 16.3 for the election to deduct general sales taxes in lieu of state and local income taxes.

In figuring deductible state or local income taxes, include the amount of state or local income tax withheld from your 2006 pay, any state or local estimated tax you paid in 2006, and any part of a prior year refund that you credited to your 2006 state or local tax. Also, do not forget to include tax that you paid in 2006 when you filed your 2005 state and local tax returns.

Taxes incurred in your business are generally deductible on Schedule C; *see 16.9*.

If your 2006 adjusted gross income exceeds $150,500, or $75,250 if married filing separately, your deduction for taxes is subject to the reduction computation explained at *13.7*.

Claim the deduction for deductible taxes on the tax return for the year in which you paid the taxes, unless you report on the accrual basis; *see 16.7*.

Filing Tip

State Income Tax Paid in 2006

In figuring your 2006 itemized deduction for state and local income taxes paid, remember to include tax that you paid in 2006 when you filed your 2005 state and local tax returns.

Table 16-1 Checklist of Taxes

Type of tax—	*Deductible as itemized deduction—*
Admission	No
Alcoholic beverage	No
Assessments for local benefits	No
Automobile license fees not qualifying as personal property tax	No
Cigarette	No
Customs duties	No
Driver's license	No
Estate—federal or state	No*
Excise—federal or state, for example, on telephone service	No
Gasoline—federal	No
Gasoline and other motor fuel—state and local	No
Gift taxes—federal and state	No
Income—federal (including alternative minimum tax)	No
Income—state, local, or foreign	Yes
Inheritance tax	No
Mortgage tax	No
Personal property—state or local	Yes
Poll	No
Real estate (state, local, or foreign)	Yes
Regulatory license fees (dog licenses, parking meter fees, hunting and fishing licenses)	No
Social Security	No
Tolls	No
Transfer taxes on securities and real estate	No

* But *see 11.17* for miscellaneous itemized deduction for estate tax paid on "income in respect of a decedent."

16.2 Nondeductible Taxes

Sales tax. Sales taxes on personal property are not deductible unless you make the election to claim them in lieu of state and local income taxes; *see 16.3.*

Transfer taxes. Transfer taxes paid on the sale of securities or investment real estate are not separately deductible, but you may increase your cost basis by the transfer tax in figuring profit or loss on Schedule D; *see* Chapter 5.

A transfer tax (which may be called an excise tax in some states) on the sale of a personal residence is not deductible as a real estate tax; it is imposed on the transaction and not on the value of the property. Transfer taxes are added to cost basis by the buyer or treated as an expense of sale by the seller.

Gasoline taxes. State and local taxes on gasoline used for personal purposes are not deductible. If you travel for business, the taxes are deductible as part of your gasoline expenses.

16.3 State and Local Income Taxes or General Sales Taxes

Note: The option to deduct state and local general sales taxes in lieu of state and local income taxes expired at the end of 2005, and Congress had not yet extended it to 2006 when this book went to press. The extension is likely, and the following discussion assumes that the option to deduct state and local general sales taxes will be available on 2006 returns. Check the **e-Supplement** ***for a legislation update.***

State and local income taxes. You may deduct on your 2006 return state and local income taxes withheld from your pay and estimated state and local taxes paid in 2006. Also deduct the balance of your 2005 state and local taxes you paid during 2006. If in 2007 you pay additional state income tax on your 2006 income, you deduct the payment on your 2007 tax return.

State income taxes may be claimed only as itemized deductions, even if attributed solely to business income. That is, state income taxes may not be deducted as business expenses from gross income.

To increase your itemized deductions on your 2006 return, consider prepaying state income taxes before the end of 2006. The prepayment is deductible provided the state tax authority accepts prepayments and state law recognizes them as tax payments. The IRS has ruled, however, that prepayments are not deductible if you do not reasonably believe that you owe additional state tax. Do not make prepayments if you may be subject to alternative minimum tax; *see* Chapter 23.

If you report on the accrual basis and you contest a tax liability, claim the deduction in the year of payment.

You may deduct on your federal return state and local income taxes allocable to interest income that is exempt from federal tax but not state and local income tax. However, state and local taxes that are allocated to other federal exempt income are not deductible. For example, state income tax allocated to a cost-of-living allowance exempt from federal income tax is not deductible as a state tax.

The IRS has held that mandatory employee contributions to state disability or unemployment insurance funds are deductible as state income taxes in these states: California, New Jersey, New York, Rhode Island, and West Virginia.

However, employee contributions to a private or voluntary disability plan in California, New Jersey, or New York have been held by the IRS to be nondeductible.

Mandatory employee contributions to a state unemployment fund are deductible.

Note: A refund of state income taxes claimed as an itemized deduction may have to be reported as income; *see 11.5.*

State and local general sales taxes. To figure your deductible state and local general sales taxes, you can use your credit card receipts and other records for non-business purchases during 2006 or use the optional tables provided by the IRS in the Schedule A instructions. The worksheet in the IRS instructions provides the procedure for claiming local general sales taxes.

State and local sales taxes paid on a motor vehicle may be added to the amount from the table but only to the extent the amount does not exceed the general sales tax rate. General sales taxes on a home (or major renovation or home-building materials), boat, or airplane may also be added; follow the IRS instructions.

Law Alert

Election To Deduct State and Local Sales Tax

When this book went to press, Congress had not yet extended to 2006 the law authorizing the option to deduct state and local general sales taxes in lieu of state and local income taxes. Without an extension, state and local sales taxes will not be deductible on 2006 returns. However, an extension is quite likely; *see* the *e-Supplement* for an update.

Filing Tip

Refund Credited to State Estimated Tax

If you were entitled to a refund on your 2005 state tax return and you credited the overpayment towards your 2006 estimated state tax, do not forget to include the credited amount with other 2006 payments of state and local income tax on your 2006 Schedule A.

16.4 Deducting Real Estate Taxes

Your payments of state, local, or foreign real estate taxes on your non-business property are deductible on Schedule A (Form 1040). The tax must be based on the assessed value of the property and the assessment must be based on a uniform rate imposed for public purposes. *See 16.5* for deductible and nondeductible assessments for local benefits.

The monthly mortgage payment to a bank or other mortgage holder generally includes amounts allocated to real estate taxes, which are paid to the taxing authority on their due date. Mortgage payments allocated to real estate taxes are deductible in the year you make the payments only if the mortgage holder actually pays the taxes to the tax authority by the end of that year. Typically, banks will furnish you with a year-end statement of disbursements to taxing authorities, indicating dates of payment.

See 16.5–16.7 for further details on real estate taxes.

Who may deduct real property taxes. A person who pays a property tax must have an ownership interest in the property to deduct the payment. The following table summarizes who may deduct payments of real property taxes.

Filing Tip

Cooperative Apartments

Tenant-stockholders of a cooperative housing corporation may deduct their share of the real estate taxes paid by the corporation. However, no deduction is allowed if the corporation does not own the land and building but merely leases them and pays taxes under the lease agreement. *See also 15.9.*

Table 16-2 Who Claims the Deduction?

If the tax is paid by—	*Then it is deductible by—*
You, for your spouse	Neither, if your spouse has title to the property, and you each file a separate return. This is true even if the mortgage requires you to pay the taxes. The tax is deductible on a joint return.
You, as owner of a condominium	You deduct real estate tax paid on your separate unit. You also deduct your share of the tax paid on the common property.
Your cooperative apartment or corporation	You deduct your share of real estate tax paid on the property; *see 15.9.* But if the organization leases the land and building and pays the tax under the terms of the lease, you may not deduct your share.
A life tenant	A court allowed the deduction to a widow required to pay the taxes under a will for the privilege of occupying the house during her life.
A tenant	The tenant of a business lease may deduct the payment of tax as additional rent, not tax. The tenant of a personal residence may not deduct the payment as either a tax or rent expense, unless placed on the real estate assessment rolls so that the tax is assessed directly against him or her; *see 16.6.*
You, as a local benefit tax to maintain, repair, or meet interest costs arising from local benefits	You deduct only that part of the tax that you can show is for maintenance, repair, or interest. If you cannot make the allocation, no deduction is allowed. If the benefit increases the value of the property, you add the non-deductible assessment to the basis of the property.
You, where your property was foreclosed for failure to pay taxes	You may not deduct the taxes paid out of the proceeds of the foreclosure sale if your interest in the property ended with the foreclosure.
Tenant by the entirety or joint tenant	The tenant who is jointly and severally liable and who pays the tax. If real property is owned by husband and wife as tenants by the entirety or joint tenants, either spouse may deduct the taxes paid on a separate return or a joint return.
Tenant in common	When property is owned as a tenancy in common, under an IRS rule, a tenant may deduct only his or her share of the tax, even if the entire tax was paid. However, the Tax Court has allowed a deduction for the full amount where a co-tenant's payment protected her against the possibility of foreclosure in the event the other co-tenants failed to pay their share of the taxes; *see 9.2.*
A mortgagee	No deduction. If tax is paid before the foreclosure, it is added to the loan. If paid after the foreclosure, it is added to the cost of property.

16.5 Assessments

Assessments by homeowner's association not deductible as taxes. Assessments paid to a local homeowner's association for the purpose of maintaining the common areas of the residential project and for promoting the recreation, health, and safety of the residents are not deductible as real property taxes.

Assessments for government services. If property is used solely as your residence, you may not deduct charges for municipal water bills (even if described as a "tax"), sewer assessments, assessments for sanitation service, or title registration fees. A permit fee to build or improve a personal residence is added to the cost basis of the house.

Assessments for local benefits are deductible if they cover maintenance or repairs of streets, sidewalks, or water or sewer systems, or interest costs on such maintenance. However, assessments for construction of streets, sidewalks, or other local improvements that tend to increase the value of your property are not deductible as real estate taxes. You add such assessments to your cost basis for the property.

If you are billed a single amount, you may deduct the portion allocable to assessments for maintenance or repairs. The burden is on you to support the allocation.

16.6 Tenants' Payment of Taxes

You generally may not deduct a portion of your rent as property taxes. This is so even where state or local law identifies a portion of the rent as being tied to tax increases.

Tenants have been allowed a deduction for property taxes in the following areas: In Hawaii tenants with leases of 15 years or more may deduct the portion of the rent representing taxes. In California, tenants who have their names placed on the tax rolls and who pay the taxes directly to the taxing authority may claim a deduction.

In New York, liability for tax is placed directly on the tenant and the landlord is a collecting agent for paying over the tax to the taxing authorities; the landlord also remains liable for the tax. The IRS ruled that it will not permit tenants to deduct a portion of rent as a payment of taxes.

EXAMPLE

A municipal rent control ordinance allowed landlords to charge real property tax increases to the tenants as a monthly "tax surcharge." The ordinance stated that the surcharge was not to be considered rent for purposes of computing cost-of-living rental increases. The IRS ruled that the tenant may not deduct the "tax surcharge" as a property tax. The tax is imposed on the landlord, not on the tenant. The city ordinance, which permitted the landlord to pass on the tax increases to a tenant, did not shift liability for the property taxes from the landlord to the tenant. For federal tax purposes, the surcharge is merely an additional rental payment by the tenant. Similarly, "rates tax" or "renters' tax" imposed on tenants was ruled to be nondeductible because the tax is imposed on the person using the property rather than the property itself.

16.7 Allocating Taxes When You Sell or Buy Realty

When property is sold, the buyer and seller apportion the real estate taxes imposed on the property during the "real property year." A "real property year" is the period that a real estate tax covers. This allocation is provided for you in a settlement statement at the time of closing. If you want to figure your own allocations, your local tax authority can give you the "real property year" of the taxes you plan to apportion. If you are the ***seller***, you deduct that portion of the tax covering the beginning of the real property year through the day before the sale. If you are the ***buyer***, you deduct the part of the tax covering the date of the sale through the end of the real property year.

EXAMPLE

The real property year in East County starts April 1 and ends March 31. On July 2, 2006, you sell realty located in East County to Jones. Assume the real estate tax for the real property year ending March 31, 2007, is $1,000. You deduct $252 ($^{92}/_{365}$ of $1,000, since there are 92 days in the period beginning April 1 and ending July 1, 2006). Jones deducts $748 ($^{273}/_{365}$ of $1,000, since there are 273 days in the period beginning July 2, 2006, and ending March 31, 2007).

The allocation of taxes between the buyer and seller is mandatory whether or not your contract provides for an allocation. However, you do not allocate taxes of a real property year when property is sold before the real property year. This rule prevents the seller from deducting any part of the tax for that year, even though it became a personal liability or lien while he or she owned the property. The buyer gets the deduction because he or she owns the property for the entire real property year. You also do not allocate taxes when property is sold after the real property year. This rule prevents the buyer from deducting the tax for that year even though it becomes a personal liability or lien after he or she takes possession of the property. The seller gets the deduction because the tax covers the property year in which the seller owns the property. The allocation is limited to a tax covering a property year during which both the seller and the buyer own the property.

IRS Alert

Form 1099-S for Sale of Principal Residence

A sale of a principal residence generally does not have to be reported on Form 1099-S if the seller gives the real estate agent responsible for the closing written assurance that the home was the seller's principal residence and that the full gain on the sale is excludable from income (*see* Chapter 29).

Form 1099-S. If Form 1099-S is filed by the mortgage lender or real estate broker responsible for the closing, Box 5 will show the buyer's share of the real estate tax paid in advance by the seller. For example, Smith sells her house in Green County, where the real estate tax is paid annually in advance. In the year of sale she paid $1,200 in real estate taxes. Assuming that the home is sold at the end of the ninth month of the real property tax year, the amount of the real estate tax allocable to the buyer is $300 ($100 per month × 3 months). This amount, which is shown as paid by the seller in advance on an HUD-1 (Uniform Settlement Statement) form provided at the closing, is reported as the buyer's share of the real estate tax in Box 5 of Form 1099-S.

When to deduct allocated taxes. After you have made the allocation based on the "real property year," you then must fix the year in which you deduct your share of the allocated tax. Here you consider your method of reporting your income—cash or accrual basis—and the date on which either you or the other party became liable for the tax or paid the tax. If neither you nor the other party is liable for the tax under local law, then the party who holds the property at the time the tax became a lien on the property is considered liable. Check the following rules to determine when you deduct the apportioned tax:

Seller on the cash basis—If the buyer is liable for the tax under local law, the seller may deduct his or her share of the allocated tax either in the year of the sale or a later year when the tax is actually paid. If the seller is liable for the tax under local law, and the tax is not payable until after the sale date, the seller may deduct the tax either in the year of sale or in the year he or she pays the tax.

Buyer on the cash basis—If the seller is liable for the tax under local law, the buyer may deduct the tax either in the year of sale or when the tax is actually paid. If the buyer is liable for the tax, he or she deducts the tax in the year the tax is paid.

Seller on the accrual basis—The seller accrues his or her share of the tax on the date of the sale, unless taxes have been accrued ratably over the years. If this is so, the last accrual is the sale date.

Buyer on the accrual basis—If the seller is liable for the tax, the buyer accrues his or her share of the tax on the date of the sale, unless taxes are accrued ratably. If taxes are accrued ratably, the accrual begins with the date of sale. If the buyer is liable for the tax, he or she deducts the tax in the return for the year the tax accrues unless an election is made to accrue ratably from the date of sale.

Filing Instruction

Buyer's Share of Real Estate Tax

If you sold a house in 2006 and received Form 1099-S, check Box 5 for the amount of real estate tax that you paid in advance and that is allocable to the buyer. The buyer may deduct this amount. You subtract it from the amount you paid when claiming your 2006 itemized deduction for real estate taxes.

Seller's deduction in excess of the allocated amount is taxed. If, in the year before the sale, the seller deducts an amount for taxes in excess of the allocated amount, the excess must be reported as income in the year of the sale. This may happen when the seller is on the cash basis and pays the tax in the year before the sale.

EXAMPLE

A real property tax of $1,000 is due and payable on November 30 for the following calendar year. On November 30, 2005, Keith Jones, who uses the cash basis and reports on a calendar year, pays the 2006 tax. On June 30, 2006, he sells the real property. Under the apportionment rule, Jones is allowed to deduct only $493 ($^{180}/_{365}$ of $1,000, since there are 180 days in the period from January 1 to June 29, 2006) of the tax for the 2006 real property tax year. But Jones has already deducted the full amount in the 2005 return. Therefore, he reports as income that part of the tax deduction that he was not entitled to under the apportionment.

Buyer may not deduct payment of seller's back taxes. The back taxes paid are added to the cost of the newly purchased property. The amount realized by the seller is increased by the buyer's payment of back taxes.

Seller's payment upon buyer's failure to pay. If a buyer is obligated to pay taxes under a land contract but fails to pay, the owner who pays the tax may deduct the payment if the tax is assessed to him or her.

Buyer of foreclosed property. If you buy realty at a tax sale and you do not receive immediate title to the property under state law until after a redemption period, you may not be able to deduct payment of realty taxes for several years.

16.8 Automobile License Fees

You may not deduct an auto license fee based on weight, model, year, or horsepower. But you may deduct a fee based on the value of the car as a state personal property tax if these three tests are met: (1) the fee is an *ad valorem* tax, based on a percentage of value of the property; (2) it is imposed on an annual basis, even though it is collected more or less frequently; and (3) it is imposed on personal property. This third test is met even though the tax is imposed on the exercise of a privilege of registering a car or for using a car on the road.

The majority of state motor vehicle registration fees are not *ad valorem* taxes and do not qualify for the deduction. Various states and localities impose *ad valorem* or personal property taxes on motor vehicles that may qualify for the deduction. Contact a state or local authority to determine whether a license fee qualifies.

Filing Tip

Value Portion of Auto License Fee

If an automobile license fee is based partly on value and partly on weight or other tests, the tax attributed to the value is deductible. For example, assume a registration fee based on 1% of value, plus 40¢ per hundred-weight. The part of the tax equal to 1% of value qualifies as an *ad valorem* tax and is deductible as a personal property tax on Schedule A.

16.9 Taxes Deductible as Business Expenses

That a tax is not deductible as an itemized deduction does not mean you may not deduct it elsewhere on your return. For example, you may generally deduct property taxes incurred as a cost of doing business on Schedule C. Here are some other examples:

If you pay excise taxes on merchandise you sell in your business, you deduct the tax as a business expense.

If you pay Social Security taxes (FICA) on your employees' wages, you deduct the tax as a business expense on Schedule C.

If you pay sales tax on business property, you add the tax to the cost of the property for depreciation purposes. If the tax is paid on nondepreciable property, the tax is included in the currently deductible cost.

If you pay sales tax on a deductible business meal, the tax is deductible as part of the meal costs, subject to the cost limit discussed at *20.24*.

50% self-employment tax deduction. One-half of the self-employment tax figured on Schedule SE is deductible from gross income on Line 27 of Form 1040, rather than on Schedule C; *see 45.3*.

Note: If you are not a material participant in the business, your Schedule C expenses are subject to passive activity limitations; *see* Chapter 10.

16.10 Foreign Taxes

You may deduct your payment of foreign real property taxes and income and excess profits taxes as itemized deductions. Where you pay foreign income or excess profits tax, you have an election of either claiming the tax as a deduction or a credit. Claiming the credit may provide a larger tax savings; *see 36.14*.

Chapter 17

Medical and Dental Expense Deductions

Tax relief for the high cost of medical care is limited. Medical expenses are deductible only if you itemize and only if you have expenses exceeding 7.5% of your adjusted gross income. Expenses up to 7.5% of AGI are not deductible. There is an exception for health insurance premiums paid by self-employed individuals. The self-employed do not have to itemize any premiums; 100% of their premiums is an above-the-line deduction that can be claimed directly from gross income; *see 12.2.*

Carefully review the list of deductible expenses in this chapter so that you do not overlook any deductible expenses. Include payments of doctors' fees, health-care premiums, prescription medicines, travel costs for obtaining medical care, and eligible home improvements.

If you are married, both you and your spouse work, and one of you has substantial medical expenses, filing separate returns may result in a lower overall tax.

Deductible medical expenses are *not* subject to the 3% reduction of itemized deductions that applies on 2006 returns if adjusted gross income exceeds $150,500 ($75,250 if married filing separately).

Qualifying long-term-care expenses may be treated as medical expenses subject to the 7.5% of AGI floor, including a specified deductible amount of premiums paid for a qualifying long-term-care contract; *see 17.15.*

Deductible contributions to health savings accounts (HSAs) and Archer MSAs may be available to individuals covered by high deductible health plans; *see* Chapter 12.

Workers displaced from jobs by import competition may claim a refundable tax credit for health insurance premiums. The credit is claimed on Form 8885; *see 25.17.*

Also *see*

17.1 Medical Expenses Must Exceed 7.5% of AGI

The tax law provides only a limited opportunity to deduct medical costs for you, your spouse, and your dependents *(17.7)*. A wide range of expenses, such as those listed on page 347, qualify as deductible medical expenses if you itemize expenses on Schedule A of Form 1040. However, you may not be able to claim the deduction because of a percentage floor. You may deduct only expenses exceeding 7.5% of your adjusted gross income (AGI). Adjusted gross income is explained at *12.1*. For 2006, adjusted gross income is shown on Line 37 and Line 38 of Form 1040.

Married persons filing joint returns apply the 7.5% floor to their combined adjusted gross income.

On your 2006 return, you may deduct expenses paid in 2006 by cash or check (unless the check is postdated to 2007) for yourself, your spouse *(17.6)*, or dependents *(17.7)*. If you borrow to pay medical or dental expenses, you claim the deduction in the year you use the loan proceeds to pay the bill, not in the later year when you repay the loan. If you paid medical or dental expenses by credit card in 2006, the deduction is allowed in 2006, although you do not pay the charge bill until 2007.

Caution

Only Unreimbursed Expenses Are Deductible

You may not deduct medical expenses for which you have been reimbursed by insurance or other awards *(17.4)*. Furthermore, reimbursement of medical expenses deducted in prior tax years may be taxable income *(11.6)*.

EXAMPLES

1. Frank Ryan's adjusted gross income (AGI; *see 12.1*) is $40,000 for 2006. His unreimbursed medical expenses were $2,000 for doctor and dentist visits, $420 for prescribed drugs and medicines, and $1,250 for medical insurance premiums. If he itemizes deductions on Schedule A, he may deduct medical expenses of $670, figured this way:

Unreimbursed expenses	$2,000
Premiums	1,250
Drugs	420
Total	$3,670
Less: 7.5% of adjusted gross income (7.5% of $40,000)	3,000
Medical expense deduction	$670

2. Same as facts as in Example 1 except that Frank's AGI is $50,000, not $40,000. Here, Frank may not claim any medical deduction because his expenses of $3,670 do not exceed $3,750, 7.5% of his AGI.

17.2 Allowable Medical Care Costs

In determining whether you have paid deductible medical expenses exceeding the 7.5% AGI floor *(17.1)*, include the cost of diagnosis, cure, mitigation, treatment, or prevention of disease or any treatment that affects a part or function of your body. Also include qualifying costs you paid for your spouse *(17.6)* and your dependents *(17.7)*. *See* the checklist of deductible expenses on page 347.

Expenses that are *solely* for cosmetic reasons are not deductible. Also, expenses incurred to benefit your general health are not deductible even if recommended by a physician; *see 17.3*.

Caution

Over-the-Counter Drugs

OTC drugs, even if prescribed by a doctor, are not deductible, with the exception of insulin.

Medicine and drugs. To be deductible, medicines and drugs other than insulin must be obtainable solely through a prescription by a doctor. Insulin is deductible even though a prescription may not be required. You may not deduct the cost of over-the-counter medicines and drugs, such as aspirin and other cold remedies, even if you have a doctor's prescription.

Marijuana is not deductible even if prescribed by a doctor in a state allowing the prescription.

A prescribed drug brought in or shipped into the U.S. from another country is not deductible unless the FDA (Food and Drug Administration) allows that drug to be legally imported by individuals.

IRS Alert

Weight-Loss Program for Obesity

The IRS allows a deduction for the costs of joining a weight-loss program and fees for follow-up meetings if a physician has made a diagnosis of obesity.

Stop-smoking programs. The cost of smoking cessation programs is a deductible medical expense, as well as nicotine withdrawal drugs that require a physician's prescription. Over-the-counter nicotine patches and gums are not deductible.

Exercise and weight-reduction programs. If you incur costs for such programs to improve your *general* health, the costs are not deductible even if your doctor has recommended them. However, if your doctor has recommended a program as treatment for a *specific* condition, such as heart disease or hypertension, the IRS allows a deduction for the cost.

Filing Tip

Childbirth Classes

A mother-to-be may deduct the cost of classes instructing her in Lamaze breathing and relaxation techniques, stages of labor, and delivery procedures. If her husband or other childbirth "coach" also attends the classes, the portion of the fee allocable to the coach is not deductible. Costs of classes on early pregnancy, fetal development, or caring for newborns also are not deductible.

Caution

Deducting Costs of Health Improvement Programs

Exercise and weight-reduction programs are deductible as treatments for specific conditions, but not as ways to improve your general health, even if your doctor has recommended them; *see 17.2.*

The IRS considers obesity a disease. If a physician has made a diagnosis of obesity, the costs of joining a weight-loss program and additional fees for meetings are eligible medical expenses. However, reduced-calorie diet foods that are substitutes for foods normally consumed are not deductible even if they are part of the program; *see* "Special foods" below.

Special foods. According to the IRS, the cost of special foods or beverages is not a deductible medical expense if the food or beverages substitute for those normally consumed.

EXAMPLE

To alleviate an ulcer, your doctor puts you on a special diet. According to the IRS, the cost of your food and beverages is not deductible. The special diet replaces the food you normally eat.

The Tax Court has set its own standard for deducting the extra cost of special foods as medical costs. The test is to show a medical need for taking the special food and the extra cost of the health food over ordinary food. Only the extra cost is deductible.

EXAMPLES

1. Anna Von Kalb suffered from hypoglycemia and her physician prescribed a special high protein diet, which required her to consume twice as much protein as an average person and exclude all processed foods and carbohydrates. She spent $3,483 for food, and deducted 30%, or $1,045, as the extra cost of her high protein diet. The IRS disallowed the deduction, claiming that the protein supplements were a substitute for foods normally consumed. The Tax Court disagreed. The high protein food did not substitute for her usual diet but helped alleviate her hypoglycemia. Thus, she may deduct its additional expense.
2. The Bechers suffered from allergies and were advised by a physician to eat organically grown food to avoid the chemicals in commercial food. The Bechers claimed a medical expense deduction of $2,255, the extra cost of buying organic food.

   The IRS disallowed the deduction and the Tax Court agreed. They did not present evidence that their allergies could be cured by limiting their diet to organic food. That the food was beneficial to their general health and was prescribed by a doctor is not sufficient for a deduction.

Portion of monthly service fees paid to retirement community. The portion of the monthly fees that is allocable to medical care is a deductible medical expense; *see 34.10.*

Advance payment for lifetime care in retirement community. The portion of a life-care fee or "founder's fee" that you pay in a lump sum or monthly to a retirement community for lifetime care may be included as a current medical expense to the extent that it is allocable to future medical care; *see 34.10.*

Advance payments for lifetime care of disabled dependent. You can treat as a current medical expense a nonrefundable advance payment to a private institution for the lifetime care and treatment of your physically or mentally impaired child upon your death or when you become unable to provide care. The nonrefundable payment must be a condition for the institution's future acceptance of your child.

EXAMPLE

Parents contracted with an institution to care for their handicapped child after their death. The contract provided for payments as follows: 20% on signing, 10% within 12 months, 10% within 24 months, and the balance when the child enters. Payment of specified amounts at specified intervals was a condition imposed by the institution for its agreement to accept the child for lifetime care. Since the obligation to pay was incurred at the time payments were made, the IRS held that they were deductible as medical expenses, although the medical services were not to be performed until a future time, if at all.

Table 17-1 Deductible Medical Expenses

Professional Services

Chiropodist
Chiropractor
Christian Science practitioner
Dermatologist
Dentist
Gynecologist
Neurologist
Obstetrician
Ophthalmologist
Optician
Optometrist
Orthopedist
Osteopath
Pediatrician
Physician
Physiotherapist
Plastic surgeon; but *see 17.3.*
Podiatrist
Practical or other nonprofessional nurse for medical services only, not for care of a healthy person or a child who is not ill. Costs for medical care of elderly person unable to get about or person subject to spells are deductible; *see 17.12.*
Psychiatrist
Psychoanalyst
Psychologist
Registered nurse
Surgeon
Unlicensed practitioner services are deductible if the type and quality of the services are not illegal.

Dental Services

Artificial teeth
Cleaning teeth
Dental X-rays
Extracting teeth
Filling teeth
Gum treatment
Oral surgery
Straightening teeth

Equipment and Supplies

Abdominal supports
Air conditioner where necessary for relief from an allergy or for relieving difficulty in breathing; *see 17.13.*
Ambulance hire
Arches
Artificial eyes, limbs
Autoette (auto device for handicapped person)
Back supports
Braces
Contact lenses and solutions
Cost of installing stair-seat elevator for person with heart condition; *see 17.13.*
Crutches
Elastic hosiery
Eyeglasses
Fluoridation unit in home
Hearing aids
Heating devices
Invalid chair
Iron lung
Orthopedic shoes—excess cost over cost of regular shoes
Oxygen or oxygen equipment to relieve breathing problems caused by a medical condition
Reclining chair if prescribed by doctor
Repair of special telephone equipment for the deaf
Sacroiliac belt
Special mattress and plywood bed boards for relief of arthritis or spine
Splints
Truss
Wheelchair
Wig advised by doctor as essential to mental health of person who lost all hair from disease

Medical Treatments

Abortion
Acupuncture
Blood transfusion
Childbirth delivery
Diathermy
Electric shock treatments
Hearing services
Hydrotherapy (water treatments)
Injections
Insulin treatments
Laser eye surgery or radial keratotomy to improve vision
Navajo healing ceremonies ("sings")
Nursing
Organ transplant
Prenatal and postnatal treatments
Psychotherapy
Sterilization
Radial keratotomy
Radium therapy
Ultraviolet ray treatments
Vasectomy
Whirlpool baths
X-ray treatments

Medicines and Drugs

Cost of prescriptions only; over-the-counter medicine is not deductible.

Laboratory Examinations and Tests

Blood tests
Cardiographs
Metabolism tests
Spinal fluid tests
Sputum tests
Stool examinations
Urine analyses
X-ray examinations

Hospital Services

Anesthetist
Hospital bills
Oxygen mask, tent
Use of operating room
Vaccines
X-ray technician

Premiums for Medical Care Policies

See 17.5 for the way to deduct:
Blue Cross and Blue Shield
Contact lens replacement insurance
Federal Voluntary Medicare (Part B) and Federal Medicare (Part A) by persons not covered by Social Security
Health insurance covering hospital, surgical, and other medical expenses
Membership in medical service cooperative

Miscellaneous

Alcoholic inpatient care costs
Birth control pills or other birth control items prescribed by your doctor
Braille books—excess cost of Braille works over cost of regular editions
Childbirth classes for expectant mother
Clarinet lessons advised by dentist for treatment of tooth defects
Convalescent home—for medical treatment only
Drug treatment center—inpatient care costs
Fees paid to health institute where the exercises, rubdowns, etc., taken there are prescribed by a physician as treatments necessary to alleviate a physical or mental defect or illness
Kidney donor's or possible kidney donor's expenses
Lead-based paint removal to prevent a child who has had lead poisoning from eating the paint. Repainting the scraped area is not deductible.
Legal fees for guardianship of mentally ill spouse where commitment was necessary for medical treatment
Lifetime care—advance payments made either monthly or as a lump sum under an agreement with a retirement home; *see 34.10.*
Long-term care costs for chronically ill; *see 17.15.*
Nurse's board and wages, including Social Security taxes paid on wages
Remedial reading for child suffering from dyslexia
School—payments to a special school for a mentally or physically impaired person if the main reason for using the school is its resources for relieving the disability; *see 17.10.*
"Seeing-eye" dog and its maintenance
Smoking cessation programs
Special school costs for physically and mentally handicapped children; *see 17.10.*
Telephone-teletype costs and television adapter for closed caption service for deaf person
Travel to obtain medical care; *see 17.9.*
Wages of guide for a blind person
Weight-loss program to treat obesity or other specific disease; *see 17.2.*

Table 17-2 Nondeductible Medical Expenses

- Antiseptic diaper service
- Athletic club expenses
- Babysitting fees to enable you to make doctor's visits
- Boarding school fees paid for healthy child while parent is recuperating from illness
- Bottled water bought to avoid drinking fluoridated city water
- Cost of divorce recommended by a psychiatrist
- Cost of hotel room suggested for sex therapy
- Cost of moving away from airport noise by person suffering a nervous breakdown
- Cost of trips prescribed by a doctor for a "change of environment" to boost an ailing person's morale
- Dance lessons advised by a doctor as general physical and mental therapy
- Divorced spouse's medical bills
- Domestic help; but *see 17.12* if nursing duties are performed.
- Ear piercing
- Funeral, cremation, burial, cemetery plot, monument, or mausoleum
- Health programs offered by resort hotels, health clubs, and gyms
- Illegal operations and drugs
- Marijuana, even if prescribed by a physician in a state permitting the prescription
- Marriage counseling fees
- Massages recommended by physician for general stress reduction
- Maternity clothes
- Premiums on policies guaranteeing you a specified amount of money each week in the event hospitalization
- Scientology fees
- Special food or beverage substitutes; but *see 17.2.*
- Tattooing
- Teeth whitening to reverse age-related discoloration
- Toothpaste
- Transportation costs of a disabled person to and from work
- Travel costs to favorable climate when you can live there permanently
- Travel costs to look for a new place to live—on a doctor's advice
- Tuition and travel expenses to send a problem child to a particular school for a beneficial change in environment; *see 17.10.*
- Weight-loss program to improve general health; *see 17.2.*

Table 17-3 How Your Medical Expense Deduction Is Reduced by the 7.5% Floor

	Your medical expenses are													
If your adjusted gross income is	*$1,000*	*$1,500*	*$2,000*	*$2,500*	*$3,000*	*$3,500*	*$4,000*	*$4,500*	*$5,000*	*$5,500*	*$6,000*	*$6,500*	*$7,000*	*$7,500*
	You may deduct													
$15,000	0	375	875	1,375	1,875	2,375	2,875	3,375	3,875	4,375	4,875	5,375	5,875	6,375
$20,000	0	0	500	1,000	1,500	2,000	2,500	3,000	3,500	4,000	4,500	5,000	5,500	6,000
$25,000	0	0	125	625	1,125	1,625	2,125	2,625	3,125	3,625	4,125	4,625	5,125	5,625
$30,000	0	0	0	250	750	1,250	1,750	2,250	2,750	3,250	3,750	4,250	4,750	5,250
$35,000	0	0	0	0	375	875	1,375	1,875	2,375	2,875	3,375	3,875	4,375	4,875
$40,000	0	0	0	0	0	500	1,000	1,500	2,000	2,500	3,000	3,500	4,000	4,500
$45,000	0	0	0	0	0	125	625	1,125	1,625	2,125	2,625	3,125	3,625	4,125
$50,000	0	0	0	0	0	0	250	750	1,250	1,750	2,250	2,750	3,250	3,750
$55,000	0	0	0	0	0	0	0	375	875	1,375	1,875	2,375	2,875	3,375
$60,000	0	0	0	0	0	0	0	0	500	1,000	1,500	2,000	2,500	3,000
$65,000	0	0	0	0	0	0	0	0	125	625	1,125	1,625	2,125	2,625
$70,000	0	0	0	0	0	0	0	0	0	250	750	1,250	1,750	2,250
$75,000	0	0	0	0	0	0	0	0	0	0	375	875	1,375	1,875
$80,000	0	0	0	0	0	0	0	0	0	0	0	500	1,000	1,500
$85,000	0	0	0	0	0	0	0	0	0	0	0	125	625	1,125
$90,000	0	0	0	0	0	0	0	0	0	0	0	0	250	750
$95,000	0	0	0	0	0	0	0	0	0	0	0	0	0	375
$100,000	0	0	0	0	0	0	0	0	0	0	0	0	0	0

17.3 Nondeductible Medical Expenses

The most common nondeductible medical expense is the cost of over-the-counter medicines and drugs, such as aspirin and other cold remedies. A deduction for over-the-counter medicines is disallowed even if you have a doctor's prescription; *see 17.2.* Expenses incurred to improve your general health, such as exercise programs not related to a specific condition, are not deductible. Also *see* the checklist on page 348.

Cosmetic procedures. A medical expense deduction is allowed for cosmetic surgery if it is necessary to improve a disfigurement related to a congenital abnormality, disfiguring disease, or an accidental injury.

You may not deduct the cost of cosmetic surgery or other procedures that do not have a medical purpose. Thus, face lifts, hair transplants, electrolysis, teeth-whitening procedures, and liposuction intended to improve appearance are generally not deductible. However, in one case, the Tax Court allowed an exotic dancer to claim a depreciation deduction for breast implants essential for her business; *see 19.8.*

Future medical care. Generally, you cannot include as a current medical expense payment for medical care that is to be provided substantially beyond the end of the year. However, advance payments for the care of a disabled dependent or the portion of a life-care fee or "founder's fee" to a retirement community that is allocable to future medical care is a currently deductible expense; *see 17.2.*

IRS Alert

Sex Change Operation Not Deductible

In a 2006 legal memorandum, IRS Chief Counsel determined that gender reassignment surgery (GRS) is nondeductible. It does not fit the narrow definition of allowable cosmetic procedures intended to correct a disfigurement arising from a disease, accident, or congenital abnormality. It could be argued that GRS is treatment for an illness or disease and, as such, is a deductible medical expense. However, Chief Counsel refused to go that far given the controversy surrounding this issue and the lack of favorable IRS guidance.

17.4 Reimbursements Reduce Deductible Expenses

Insurance or other reimbursements of your medical costs reduce your potential medical deduction. Reimbursements for loss of earnings or damages for personal injuries and mental suffering do not have to be taken into account. A reimbursement first reduces the medical expense for which it is paid. The excess is then applied to your other deductible medical costs. *See* Example 1 below.

Personal injury settlements or awards. Generally, a cash settlement recovered in a personal injury suit does not reduce your medical expense deduction. The settlement is not treated as reimbursement of your medical bills. But when part of the settlement is specifically earmarked by a court or by law for payment of hospital bills, the medical expense deduction is reduced.

If you receive a settlement for a personal injury that is partly allocable to future medical expenses, you reduce medical expenses for these injuries by the allocated amount until it is used up.

Fake claims. Medical reimbursements for fake injury claims are treated as taxable income; *see* Example 2 below.

EXAMPLES

1. Gail Hurz paid $2,400 in medical insurance premiums. She paid doctor and hospital bills totaling $1,200 and purchased prescription drugs costing $750. Group hospitalization insurance reimbursed $800 for doctors and hospital bills and $375 for medicines and drugs. Her adjusted gross income is $32,100. If Gail itemizes, she can claim a medical expense deduction of $767, computed as follows:

Prescription drugs	$750
Medical care expenses	1,200
Premiums	2,400
Total	$4,350
Less reimbursement	1,175
	$3,175
Less: 7.5% of $32,100	2,408
Medical expense deduction	$767

2. Dodge, with the aid of a "friendly" doctor, arranged to be hospitalized for alleged back injuries and realized over $200,000 from HIP policies. The IRS charged that the insurance proceeds were taxable income. Dodge argued they were tax-free reimbursements of medical costs.

   The Tax Court sided with the IRS. The tax-free rules cover the payment of legitimate medical costs. Here there were no legitimate medical costs of actual injuries. Dodge took out the policies in a scam arrangement with the doctor.

Caution

Reimbursements Exceeding Expenses

If you have more than one policy and receive reimbursements that exceed your total medical expenses for the year, you must pay tax on all or part of the reimbursement where your employer paid premiums on the policies; *see* Examples 1–4 on this page.

Reimbursements in excess of your medical expenses. If you paid the entire premium for health insurance, you are not taxed on payments from the plan even if they exceed your medical expenses for the year. If you and your employer each contributed to the policy, you generally have to include in income that part of the excess reimbursement that is attributable to employer premium contributions not included in your gross income; *see* Examples 2–4 below. The taxable excess reimbursement must be reported as "Other income" on Line 21 of Form 1040.

However, you do not have to report any excess reimbursements that are tax-free payments for permanent disfigurement or loss of bodily functions, as discussed in *3.2.*

If your employer paid the total cost of the policy and the contributions were not taxed to you, you report as income all of your excess reimbursement, unless it covers payment for permanent injury or disfigurement *(3.2).*

For the treatment of insurance reimbursements of long-term care costs, *see 17.15.*

EXAMPLES

1. Henry Knight pays premiums of $240 and $120 for two personal health insurance policies. His total medical expenses are $900. He receives $700 from one insurance company and $500 from the other. The excess reimbursement of $300 ($1,200 – $900) is not taxable because he paid the entire premium on the policy.

2. Lionel Guest's employer paid premiums of $1,800 for two employee health insurance policies covering medical expenses. Guest's medical expenses in one year are $900. He receives $1,200 from the two companies. The entire $300 excess is taxable because Guest's employer paid the total cost of the policy and the contributions were not taxed to him.

3. Kay Brown's employer paid a premium of $1,000 for a group health policy covering Brown, and Brown herself paid $300 for a personal health policy. Her medical expenses are $900. She receives reimbursements of $1,200, $700 under her employer's policy and $500 under her own policy. Brown's reimbursements exceed expenses by $300, but the taxable portion attributed to her employer's premium contribution is $175, computed this way:

Reimbursement allocated to Brown's policy ($500 ÷ $1,200) × $900	$375
Reimbursement allocated to employer's policy ($700 ÷ $1,200) × $900	$525
Taxable excess allocated to employer's policy ($700 – $525)	$175

4. Mike Green's employer paid $1,200 for a health insurance policy but contributed only $450 and deducted $750 from Green's wages. Green also paid $300 for a personal health insurance policy. His medical expenses are $900. He recovered $700 from the employer's policy and $500 from his personal policy. The excess attributable to the employer's policy is $175 (computed as in Example 3 above). However, the taxable portion is only $65.63. Both Green and his employer contributed to the cost of the employer's policy and a further allocation is necessary:

Green's contribution	$750
Employer's contribution	450
Total cost of policy	$1,200
Ratio of employer's contribution to annual cost of policy (450 ÷ 1,200, or 37.50%)	
Taxable portion: 37.50% of excess reimbursement of $175	$65.63

Reimbursement in a later year may be taxed. If you took a medical expense deduction in one year and are reimbursed for all or part of the expense in a later year, the reimbursement may be taxed in the year received. The reimbursement is generally taxable income to the extent the deduction reduced your tax in the prior year. For further details for figuring taxable income on a recovery of a prior deduction, *see 11.6.*

EXAMPLES

1. In 2005, Anna Gurchani had adjusted gross income of $32,000. She claimed itemized deductions that exceeded her allowable standard deduction by $1,000; on her Schedule A, Gurchani listed medical expenses of $3,800. She deducted $1,400 for 2005, computed as follows:

Medical expenses	$3,800
Less: 7.5% of $32,000	2,400
Allowable deduction	$1,400

   In 2006 she collects $300 from insurance, reimbursing part of her 2005 medical expenses. If she had collected that amount in 2005, her medical expense deduction would have been $1,100. The entire reimbursement of $300 is subject to tax in 2006. It is the amount by which the 2005 deduction of $1,400 exceeds the deduction of $1,100 that would have been allowed if the reimbursement had been received in 2005.

2. Same facts as in Example 1 above, but Anna did not deduct medical expenses in 2005 because she did not itemize deductions. The reimbursement in 2006 is not taxable.

17.5 Premiums of Medical Care Policies

Unless you are self-employed and qualify for the 100% above-the-line deduction (discussed below), health insurance premiums are deductible only as an itemized medical expense on Schedule A (Form 1040), subject to the overall 7.5% AGI floor. Include premiums you paid for health insurance that covers hospital, surgical, drug costs, and other medical expenses for you, your spouse *(17.6)*, and your dependents *(17.7)*. Also deductible are premiums paid for contact lens replacement insurance. Include premiums for Medicare Part B supplemental insurance. Payment for voluntary coverage under Medicare (Part A) is deductible by those over age 65 who are not covered by Social Security. Deductions may be claimed for membership payments in associations furnishing cooperative or free-choice medical services, group hospitalization, or clinical care policies, including HMOs (health maintenance organizations) and medical care premiums paid to colleges as part of a tuition bill, if the amount is separately stated in the bill.

Premiums paid before you reach age 65 for medical care insurance for protection after you reach age 65 are deductible in the year paid if they are payable on a level payment basis under the contract (1) for a period of 10 years or more or (2) until the year you reach age 65 (but in no case for a period of less than five years).

Premiums for qualifying long-term care policies are deductible subject to the limits explained in *17.15*.

Nondeductible premiums. You may *not* deduct premiums for a policy guaranteeing you a specified amount each week (not to exceed a specified number of weeks) in the event you are hospitalized. Also, no deduction may be claimed for premiums paid for a policy that compensates you for loss of earnings while ill or injured, or for loss of life, limb, or sight. If your policy covers both medical care and loss of income or loss of life, limb, or sight, no part of the premium is deductible unless (1) the contract or separate statement from the insurance company states what part of the premium is allocated to medical care and (2) the premium allocated to medical care is reasonable.

You may not deduct part of the car insurance premiums for medical insurance coverage for persons injured by or in your car where the premium covering you, your spouse *(17.6)*, or your dependents *(17.7)* is not stated separately from the premium covering medical care for others.

Self-employed deduction. If you were self-employed in 2006, you may claim a special deduction on Form 1040, Line 29, for 100% of health insurance premiums paid in 2006 for yourself, your spouse, and your dependents. The deduction is also allowed if you received wages from an S corporation in which you were more than a 2% shareholder, you were a general partner, or were a limited partner who received guaranteed payments.

The above-the-line deduction may not be claimed for any month during 2006 that you were eligible for coverage under an employer's subsidized health plan, including a plan of your spouse's employer. Also, the deduction may not exceed your net earnings from the business under which the health premiums are paid. *See 12.2* for further details on the above-the-line deduction.

Any balance of premiums not deductible because you had coverage under a subsidized employer health plan may be claimed as an itemized medical expense subject to the 7.5% income floor *(17.1)*.

Filing Instruction

Long-Term Care Premiums

The amount of deductible premiums for a qualifying long-term care policy depends on your age; *see 17.15*.

Filing Tip

Should Spouses File Separately?

If you are married and both you and your spouse have separate incomes, and one of you has substantial medical expenses, consider filing separate returns. This way the 7.5% floor will apply separately to your individual incomes, not to the higher joint income. To make sure which option to take—filing jointly or separately—you compute your tax on both types of returns and choose the one giving the lower overall tax; *see 1.3*.

17.6 Expenses of Your Spouse

Subject to the 7.5% floor, you may deduct as medical expenses your payments of medical bills for your spouse if you were married either at the time the expenses were incurred or at the time the bills were paid. That is, you may deduct your payment of your spouse's medical bills even though you are divorced or widowed, if, at the time the expenses were incurred, you were married. Furthermore, if your spouse incurred medical expenses before you married and you pay the bills after you marry, you may deduct the expense.

EXAMPLES

1. Your spouse has doctor bills covering an operation performed in 2005, before you were married. You married in 2006. You pay those bills in 2006. You may claim a 2006 medical expense deduction for your payment.
2. In October 2005, your spouse had dental work done. In February 2006, you are divorced; in April 2006, you pay your former spouse's dental bills. You may deduct the payment on your 2006 tax return.
3. In 2006, you pay medical expenses for your spouse who died in 2005. You remarry in 2006. On a 2006 joint return filed with your new spouse, you may deduct your payment of your deceased spouse's medical expenses.

Filing separately in community property states. If you and your spouse file separately and live in a community property state, any medical expenses paid out of community funds are treated as paid 50% by each of you. Medical expenses paid out of separate funds of one spouse can be deducted only by that spouse.

Filing Instruction

Multiple Support Agreement

If you may claim a person as your dependent under a multiple support agreement, include with your medical expenses only the amount you actually pay for the dependent's medical expenses. If you are reimbursed by others who signed the multiple support agreement, you must reduce your deduction by the amount of reimbursement.

17.7 Expenses of Your Dependents

You may deduct your payment of medical bills for your children or other dependents, subject to the 7.5% floor at *17.1*. You may deduct the expenses of a person who was your dependent either at the time the medical services were provided or at the time you paid the expenses. In determining dependent status for medical expense purposes, some of the regular exemption tests for dependents at *21.1* can be disregarded. You may deduct the medical costs of qualifying children or relatives who *cannot* be claimed as your dependents because: (1) they are claimed by the other parent under the special rules *(21.7)* for divorced/separated parents; *see* below, (2) their gross income exceeds the limit for qualifying relatives ($3,300 for 2006), (3) they file a joint return with their spouse, or (4) you are the dependent of another taxpayer and thus are barred from claiming any dependents on your return. The qualifying child or relative must be a U.S. citizen or national, or a resident of the United States, Canada, or Mexico, unless he or she is an adopted child who lives with you. *See* Examples 1–3 below. A child may not deduct medical expenses paid with his or her parent's welfare payments; *see* Example 4 below.

Divorced and separated parents. You may be able to deduct your payment of your child's medical costs, even though your ex-spouse is entitled to claim the child as a dependent under the rules in *21.7*. For purposes of the medical deduction, the child is considered to be the dependent of *both* parents if (1) they are divorced or legally separated under a court agreement, separated under a written agreement, or married but living apart during the last six months of 2006; (2) the child was in the custody of one or both parents for more than half of 2006; and (3) more than half of the child's 2006 support was provided by both parents.

EXAMPLES

1. You contribute more than half of your married son's support, including a payment of a medical expense of $800. Because he filed a joint return with his wife, you may not claim him as a dependent *(21.1)*. But you still may include your payment of the $800 medical expense with your other qualifying medical expenses since you contributed more than half of his support.
2. Your mother, a U.S. citizen, underwent an operation in November 2005. You paid for the operation in February 2006. You may deduct the cost of the operation in 2006 if you furnished more than one-half of your mother's support in either 2005 or 2006.

3. Same facts as Example 2, except your mother is a citizen and resident of Italy. You may not deduct the cost of the operation. She is not a U.S. citizen or a resident of the United States, Canada, or Mexico and thus does not qualify as a dependent for exemption purposes *(21.8)* or for medical deduction purposes.
4. A son is the legal guardian of his mother who is mentally incompetent. As guardian, he received his mother's state welfare and Social Security benefits, which he deposited in his personal bank account and used to pay part of his mother's medical expenses. On his tax return, he claimed a deduction for the total medical expenses paid on behalf of his mother. The court held that he could deduct only medical expenses in excess of the amounts received as welfare and Social Security payments. The benefits, to the extent used to pay medical expenses, represented the mother's payments in her own behalf.

Adopted children. You may deduct medical expenses of an adopted child if you may claim the child as a dependent either when the medical services are rendered or when you pay the expenses. An adopted child is treated as your child for dependent purposes when a court has approved the adoption or the child is lawfully placed with you for legal adoption.

If you reimburse an adoption agency for medical expenses it paid under an agreement with you, you are considered to have paid the expenses. But reimbursement of expenses incurred and paid before adoption negotiations does not qualify them as your medical expenses and you may not deduct them.

You may not deduct medical expenses for services rendered to the natural mother of the child you adopt.

Multiple support agreements. If you may claim a person as your dependent under a multiple support agreement *(21.6)*, your unreimbursed payments of that person's medical expenses are deductible. Even if you may not claim the dependent exception for 2006 because the person has a gross income of $3,300 or more, you may still deduct your payment of medical expenses provided the other multiple support agreement tests are met.

EXAMPLE

Ingrid Fromm and her brother and sister share equally in the support of their mother. Part of their mother's support includes medical expenses. Should the three of them share in the payment of the bills or should only one of them pay the bills? The answer: Payment should be made by the person who may claim the mother as a dependent under a multiple support agreement. Only that person may deduct the payment. If Ingrid is going to claim her as an exemption, she should pay the bill. She may deduct the payment although she did not contribute more than half of her mother's support. If her brother and sister reimburse her for part of the bill, she may include only the unreimbursed portion in her medical expenses. Neither Ingrid's brother nor her sister may deduct this share. Thus, a deduction is lost for these amounts.

17.8 Decedent's Medical Expenses

If you pay the medical expenses of your deceased spouse or dependent *(17.7)*, you may claim the payment as a medical expense in the year you pay the expenses, whether that is before or after the person's death.

If the executor or administrator of the estate pays the decedent's medical expenses within one year after the date of death, an election may be made to treat the expenses as if the deceased had paid them in the year the medical services were provided. The executor or administrator may file an amended return for the year the services were provided and claim them as a medical deduction for that year, assuming the period for filing the amended return *(47.2)* has not passed.

If the election is made by the executor to claim the expenses as an income tax deduction, they may not be claimed as a deduction on the estate tax return. The executor must file a statement with the decedent's income tax return that the expenses have not been deducted on the estate tax return and the estate waives its right to deduct them for estate tax purposes.

If medical expenses are claimed as an income tax deduction, the portion of the expenses that are below the 7.5% floor, and, therefore, not deductible, may not be deducted on the estate tax return. Although the expenses were not actually deducted, the IRS considers them to be part of the overall income tax deduction.

EXAMPLE

Oscar Reyes incurred medical expenses of $5,000 in 2005 and $3,000 in 2006. He died June 1, 2006, without having paid these expenses. He had already filed his 2005 return before the due date. In August 2006, his executor pays the $8,000 in medical expenses. The executor may file an amended return for 2005, claim a medical expense deduction for the $5,000, and get a refund for the increased deductions. The executor may claim the remaining $3,000 as a medical expense deduction on Reyes's final return for 2006.

17.9 Travel Costs May Be Medical Deductions

Filing Tip

Deductible Travel Costs

The costs of trips to receive medical treatment are deductible as medical expenses subject to the 7.5% AGI floor. The costs of a trip to a conference to learn about medical treatment may be deductible if recommended by a doctor.

Travel costs to a doctor's office, hospital, or clinic where you, your spouse, or your dependents receive medical care are deductible medical expenses, subject to the 7.5% AGI floor. Commuting to work is not a medical expense, even if your condition requires you to make special travel arrangements.

Deductible travel includes fares for buses, taxis or trains, and the costs of hiring a car service or ambulance to obtain medical care. Plane fares to another city are allowed by the IRS so long as obtaining medical care is the primary purpose of the trip; *see* below for lodging expense rule. If you used your automobile in 2006 to obtain medical care, you may deduct a flat rate of 18 cents a mile. In addition, you may deduct parking fees and tolls. If, however, auto expenses exceed this standard mileage rate, you may deduct your actual out-of-pocket costs for gas, oil, repairs, tolls, and parking fees. Do not include depreciation, general maintenance, or car insurance. The cost, as well as the operating and repair costs, of a wheelchair, autoette, or special auto device for a handicapped person is deductible if not used mainly for commuting.

EXAMPLE

In 2006, you drove your car to a doctor's office for treatment 40 times. Each round trip was 25 miles. If you use the IRS's flat mileage rate, you include $180 (1,000 miles × 18 cents) with your other medical expenses in computing your deduction for 2006. If you incurred tolls or parking fees during the trips, add these expenses to the mileage costs.

Medical conferences. Travel costs and admission fees to a medical conference are deductible medical expenses if an illness suffered by you, your spouse, or your dependents is the subject of the conference. For example, the IRS allowed a parent to deduct the registration fees and cost of traveling to a medical conference dealing with treatment options for a disease suffered by her dependent child. The child's doctor had recommended the conference. During the conference, most of the parent's time was spent attending sessions on her child's condition. Any recreational activities were secondary. If the parent had attended the conference because of her own condition the same deductions would have been allowed.

Lodging and meals while attending the conference are not deductible; these are allowed only if treatment is received at a licensed hospital or similar facility, as discussed below.

Caution

Meal Costs of Medical Trip

While transportation to receive medical care is a deductible medical expense subject to the 7.5% AGI floor, meals while on a trip for medical treatment are not deductible. They simply replace the meals you normally would eat. However, if you are hospitalized, the cost of meals while an inpatient is a deductible expense.

Lodging expenses. If you are receiving inpatient care at a hospital or similar facility, your expenses, including lodging and meals, are deductible. If you are not an inpatient, lodging expenses while away from home are deductible as medical expenses if the trip is primarily to receive treatment from a doctor in a licensed hospital, hospital-related outpatient facility, or a facility equivalent to a hospital. Meal expenses are not deductible unless they are paid as part of inpatient care.

EXAMPLE

Polyak spent the winter in Florida on the advice of her doctor to alleviate a chronic heart and lung condition. While in Florida, she stayed in a rented trailer that cost $1,426. She saw a physician for treatment of an infection and to renew medications. She deducted the trailer costs as a medical deduction, which the IRS and Tax Court disallowed. Although her Florida trip was primarily for mitigating her condition, she did not travel to receive medical care from a physician in a licensed hospital or related outpatient facility. The medical care was routine and incidental to her travel to Florida. Her deduction for transportation costs to Florida was not contested by the IRS, which conceded that the trip was primarily for and essential to her health.

The deduction for lodging while receiving treatment as an outpatient at a licensed hospital, clinic, or hospital-equivalent facility is limited to $50 per night per person. For example, the limit is $100 if a parent travels with a sick child. The IRS ruled that the $50 allowance could be claimed by a parent for a six-week hotel stay while her eight-year-old daughter was treated in a nearby hospital for serious injuries received in an automobile accident. The mother's presence was necessary so that she could sign release forms.

Deductible Transportation Costs

Examples of travel costs that have been treated as medical expenses by IRS rulings or court decisions are:

- Nurse's fare if nurse is required on trip
- Parent's fare if parent is needed to accompany child who requires medical care
- Parent's fare to visit his child at an institution where the visits are prescribed by a doctor
- Trip to visit specialist in another city
- Airplane fare to a distant city in which a patient used to live to have a checkup by a family doctor living there. That he could have received the same examination in the city in which he presently lived did not bar his deduction.
- Trip to escape a climate that is bad for a specific condition. For example, the cost of a trip from a northern state to Florida during the winter on the advice of a doctor to relieve a chronic heart condition is deductible. The cost of a trip made solely to improve a post-operative condition by a person recovering from a throat operation was ruled deductible.
- Travel to an Alcoholics Anonymous club meeting if membership in the group has been advised by a doctor
- Disabled veteran's commuting expenses where a doctor prescribed work and driving as therapy
- Wife's trip to provide nursing care for an ailing husband in a distant city. The trip was ordered by her husband's doctor as a necessity.
- Driving prescribed as therapy
- Travel costs of kidney transplant donor or prospective donor

Nondeductible Transportation Costs

- Commuting to work
- Trip for the general improvement of your health
- Traveling to areas of favorable climates during the year for general health reasons, rather than living permanently in a locality suitable for your health
- Meals while on a trip for outpatient medical treatment—even if cost of transportation is a valid medical cost. However, a court has allowed the deduction of the extra cost of specially prepared food.
- Trip to get "spiritual" rather than medical aid. For example, the cost of a trip to the Shrine of Our Lady of Lourdes is not deductible.
- Moving a family to a climate more suitable to an ill mother's condition. Only the mother's travel costs are deductible.
- Moving household furnishings to area advised by physician
- Operating an auto or special vehicle to go to work because of a disability
- Convalescence cruise advised by a doctor for a patient recovering from pneumonia
- Loss on sale of car bought for medical travel
- Medical seminar cruise taken by patient whose condition was reviewed by physicians taking the cruise

17.10 Schooling for the Mentally or Physically Disabled

You may include as medical expenses subject to the 7.5% floor the costs of sending on a doctor's recommendation a mentally or physically disabled dependent to a school or institution with special programs to overcome or alleviate his or her disability. Such costs may cover:

- Teaching of Braille or lip reading
- Training, caring for, supervising, and treating a mentally retarded person
- Training for a child with dyslexia

Caution

Counseling at a Private School

The parent of a child with psychological problems may deduct only that part of a private school fee directly related to psychological aid given to the child.

- Cost of meals and lodgings, if boarding is required at the school
- Costs of regular education courses also taught at the school, provided they are incidental to the special courses and services provided to overcome the disability

The school must have professional staff competent to design and supervise a program for helping your dependent overcome his or her disability. The fact that a particular school or camp is recommended for an emotionally disturbed child by a psychiatrist will not qualify the tuition as a deduction if the school or camp has no special program geared to the child's specific personal problem. The IRS allows a deduction for the costs of maintaining a mentally handicapped person in a home specially selected to meet the standards set by a psychiatrist to aid in an adjustment from life in a mental hospital to community living.

Payment for future medical care expenses is deductible if immediate payment is required by contract.

EXAMPLES

1. An emotionally disturbed child was sent to a private school maintaining a staff of three psychologists. His father deducted the school fee of $6,270 as a medical expense. The IRS disallowed the amount, claiming that the child, who was neither mentally impaired nor handicapped, was sent to school primarily for an education. The Tax Court allowed the father to deduct $3,000 covering the psychological treatment.
2. A mentally handicapped boy had been excluded from several schools for the mentally handicapped because he needed close attention. The director of a military academy had extensive experience in training young boys. Although it was not the usual practice of the academy to enroll mentally handicapped children, the director accepted the boy on a day-to-day basis as a personal challenge. The Tax Court held that the cost of both tuition and transportation to bring the boy to and from the school were deductible medical expenses. The primary purpose of the training given the boy was not ordinary education but remedial training designed to overcome his handicap. But note that, in other cases, a deduction for tuition of a military school to which a child was sent in order to remove him from a tense family environment, and the cost of a blind boy's attendance at a regular private school that made a special effort to accommodate his Braille equipment, were disallowed.

17.11 Nursing Homes

A payment for medical services, meals, and lodging to a nursing home, convalescent home, home for the aged, or sanitarium is treated as a medical expense subject to the 7.5% floor if you, your spouse, or dependent is confined for medical treatment.

If obtaining medical care is not the main reason for admission, but you can show the part of the cost covering actual medical and nursing care, that amount is deductible, but not the cost of meals and lodging.

Establishing medical purpose. The following facts are helpful in establishing the full deductibility of payments to a nursing home, convalescent home, home for the aged, or sanitarium:

- The patient entered the institution on the direction or suggestion of a doctor.
- Attendance or treatment at the institution had a direct therapeutic effect on the condition suffered by the patient.
- The attendance at the institution was for a specific ailment rather than for a "general" health condition. Simply showing that the patient suffers from an ailment is not sufficient proof that he or she is in the home for treatment.

In an unusual case, a court allowed a medical expense deduction for apartment rent of an aged parent; *see* the following Example.

Filing Tip

Meal Costs at a Nursing Home

If the patient entered a nursing home to receive medical care, a deduction may be taken for meals and lodging while there, in addition to medical care costs.

EXAMPLE

A doctor recommended to Ungar that his 90-year-old mother, convalescing from a brain hemorrhage, could receive better care at less expense in accommodations away from a hospital. A two-room apartment was rented, hospital equipment installed, and nurses engaged for seven months. The rent totaled $1,400. Ungar's sister, who worked in her husband's shoe store, nursed her mother for six weeks. Ungar paid the wages of a clerk who was hired to substitute for his sister in the store. Ungar deducted both the rent and wages as medical expenses. The IRS disallowed them; a Tax Court reversed the IRS's decision. The apartment rent was no less a medical expense than the cost of a hospital room. As for the clerk's wages, they too were deductible medical costs. The clerk was hired specifically to allow the daughter to nurse her mother, thereby avoiding the larger, though more direct, medical expense of hiring a nurse.

17.12 Nurses' Wages

Wages or fees paid for nursing services are medical expenses subject to the 7.5% floor. Include any Social Security or Medicare (FICA) tax, federal unemployment (FUTA) and state unemployment tax that you pay for the nurse. A nurse does not have to be registered or licensed so long as he or she provides you with medical services. Medical services include giving medications, changing dressings, and bathing and grooming the patient. If the nurse also performs personal or household services, you generally can deduct only that part of the pay attributable to medical services for the patient. However, if the patient is considered chronically ill, certain maintenance or personal care services are deductible as long-term care services; *see 17.15*.

The cost of an attendant's meals is included in your medical expenses. Divide total food costs among the household members to determine the attendant's share.

Costs eligible for tax credit. If, in order to work, you pay a nurse to look after a physically or mentally disabled dependent, you may be able to claim a credit for all or part of the nurse's wages as a dependent care expense. You may not, however, claim both a credit and a medical expense deduction. First, you claim the nurse's wages as a dependent care cost. If not all of the wages are allowed as care costs because of the expense limits (Chapter 25), the remaining balance is deductible as a medical expense.

The salary of a clerk hired specifically to relieve a wife from working in her husband's store in order to care for her ill mother was allowed as a medical expense; *see* the Ungar Example in *17.11*.

EXAMPLE

Dodge's wife was arthritic. He was advised by her doctor to have someone take care of her to prevent her from falling. He moved her to his daughter's home and paid the daughter to care for her mother. He deducted the payments to his daughter. The IRS disallowed the deduction, claiming that the daughter was not a trained nurse. The Tax Court allowed that part of the deduction specifically attributed to nursing aid. Whether a medical service has been rendered depends on the nature of the services rendered, not on the qualifications or title of the person who renders them. Here, the daughter's services, following the doctor's advice, qualify as medical care.

Caution

Nurse's Services

The cost of a nurse's services is a deductible medical expense, even if the nurse is not licensed or registered, so long as he or she provides the patient with medical services. If household services are also provided, only the portion of the nurse's pay attributable to the provision of medical services qualifies.

17.13 Home Improvements as Medical Expenses

A disease or ailment may require the construction or installation of special equipment or facilities in a home: A heart patient may need an elevator to carry him or her upstairs; a polio patient, a pool; and an asthmatic patient, an air cleaning system.

Subject to the 7.5% floor, you may deduct the full cost of minor equipment installed for a medical reason if it does not increase the value of your property, as, for example, the cost of a detachable window air conditioner. Where equipment or home improvement increases the value of your property, only the cost in excess of the increase in value to the home may be treated as a medical expense. This increased-value test does not apply to certain structural changes to a residence made to accommodate a disabling condition, as discussed below. If the equipment does not increase the value of the property, its entire cost is deductible, even though it is permanently fixed to the property.

The expense of maintaining and operating equipment installed for medical reasons may be claimed as a medical expense. This is true even if some or all of the cost does not qualify for a deduction because it must be reduced by the increase in value to your home. For example, if a heart patient installs an elevator in his home on the advice of his doctor, but an appraisal shows that the elevator increased the value of the home by more than the cost of the elevator, the cost would not be a medical expense. However, the cost of electricity to operate it and any maintenance costs are medical expenses as long as the medical reason for the elevator continues.

Caution

Does Equipment Increase Value of Home?

When special equipment is installed in your home to alleviate a disease or ailment, you must determine if it increases the value of your home. You generally may claim a medical deduction only to the extent that the cost of the equipment exceeds the increase in value. However, if you install a ramp or railing, widen doorways or hallways, or add similar improvements to cope with a disability, these are usually treated by the IRS as not adding to the value of the home.

EXAMPLE

Mike Gerard's daughter suffered from cystic fibrosis. While there is no known cure for the disease, doctors attempt to prolong life by preventing pulmonary infection. One approach is to maintain a constant temperature and high humidity. A doctor recommended that Gerard install a central air-conditioning unit in his home for his daughter. It cost $1,300 and increased the value of his home by $800. The $500 balance was a deductible medical expense.

Certain structural improvements to accommodate disability fully taken into account. The increased-value test does not apply to structural changes made to a residence to accommodate your disabled condition, or the condition of your spouse or dependents who live with you. Eligible expenses include adding ramps, modifying doorways and stairways, installing railings and support bars, and altering cabinets, outlets, fixtures, and warning systems. Such improvements are treated for medical deduction purposes as not increasing the value of the home. Lifts, but not elevators, also are in this category. The full cost of such improvements is added to other deductible expenses and the total is deductible to the extent that it exceeds the 7.5% AGI floor.

Prepaid home construction costs. Zipkin suffered from multiple chemical sensitivity syndrome and built a house with special filtering and ventilation systems. The cost of the special features exceeded the fair market value of the home by $645,000. She claimed a deduction for the full amount when the house was completed. The IRS disallowed the deduction for the construction costs incurred in the years before the home was completed. Zipkin successfully argued before a federal district court that the construction costs should be treated as prepaid medical expenses that are deductible in the year medical benefits are received. The federal court allowed Zipkin to deduct the full amount in the year the home became habitable.

Deducting the cost of a swimming pool. If swimming is prescribed as physical therapy, the cost of constructing a home swimming pool may be partly deductible as a medical expense but only to the extent the cost exceeds the increase in value to the house. However, the IRS is likely to question any deduction because of the possibility that the pool may be used for recreation. If you can show that the pool is specially equipped to alleviate your condition and is not generally suited for recreation, the IRS will allow the deduction unless the expense is considered to be "lavish or extravagant." For example, the IRS allowed a deduction for a pool constructed by an osteoarthritis patient. His physician prescribed swimming several times a day as treatment. He built an indoor lap pool with specially designed stairs and a hydrotherapy device. Given these features, the IRS concluded that the pool was specially designed to provide medical treatment.

In one case the IRS tried to limit the cost of a luxury indoor pool built for therapeutic reasons to the least expensive construction. The Tax Court rejected the IRS position, holding that a medical expense is not to be limited to the cheapest form of treatment; on appeal, the IRS position was adopted.

If, instead of building a pool, you buy a home with a pool, can you deduct the part of the purchase price allocated to the pool? The Tax Court said no. The purchase price of the house includes the fair market value of the pool. Therefore, there is no extra cost above the increase in the home's value that would support a medical expense deduction.

The operating costs of an indoor pool were allowed by the Tax Court as a deduction to an emphysema sufferer.

A deduction is barred where the primary purpose of the improvement is for personal convenience rather than medical necessity.

Filing Tip

Disability-Related Job Costs

If you are disabled and incur costs to enable you to work, the payments may be treated as a deductible business expense rather than as a medical expense.

EXAMPLES

1. Ken Cherry was advised by his doctor to swim to relieve his severe emphysema and bronchitis. He could not swim at local health spas; they did not open early enough or stay open late enough to allow him to swim before or after work. His home was too small for a pool. He bought a lot and built a new house with an indoor pool. He used the pool several times a day, and swimming improved his condition; if he did not swim, his symptoms returned. Cherry deducted pool operating costs of $4,000 for fuel, electricity, insurance, and repairs. The IRS disallowed the deductions, claiming that the pool was used for personal recreation. Besides, it did not have special medical equipment. The Tax Court allowed the deduction. Cherry built the pool to swim in order to exercise his lungs. That there was no special equipment is irrelevant; Cherry did not need special ramps, railings, a shallow floor, or whirlpool. Finally, his family rarely used the pool.

2. Doug Haines broke his leg in a skiing accident and underwent various forms of physical therapy, including swimming. To aid his recovery, his physician recommended that he install a swimming pool at his home. The Tax Court agreed with the IRS that the cost of the pool was not deductible. Although swimming was beneficial to his condition, he needed special therapy only for a limited period of time, and he could have gotten it at less cost at a nearby public pool. Finally, because of weather conditions, the pool could not be used for about half of the year.

17.14 Costs Deductible as Business Expenses

In some cases, expenses may be deductible as business expenses rather than as medical expenses. Claiming a business deduction is preferable because the deduction is not subject to the 7.5% adjusted gross income floor. However, the cost of a checkup required by your employer is a miscellaneous job expense subject to the 2% of adjusted gross income floor *(19.3)*.

EXAMPLE

An airline pilot is required by his company to take a semi-annual physical exam at his own expense. If he fails to produce a resultant certificate of good health, he is subject to discharge. The cost of such checkups certifying physical fitness for a job is an ordinary and necessary business expense. If the doctor prescribes a treatment or further examinations to maintain the pilot's physical condition, the cost of these subsequent treatments or examinations may be deducted only as medical expenses, even though they are needed to maintain the physical standards required by the job. Thus, a professional singer who consults a throat specialist may not deduct the fee as a business expense. The fee is a medical expense subject to the 7.5% AGI floor.

The Tax Court allowed a licensed social worker working as a therapist to deduct psychoanalysis costs as an education expense; *see 33.15*.

Impairment-related work expenses. Some expenses incurred by a physically or mentally disabled person may be deductible as business expenses rather than as medical expenses. A business expense deduction may be allowed if the expense is necessary for you to satisfactorily perform your job and is not required or used, except incidentally, for personal purposes.

If you are self-employed, claim the deduction on Schedule C *(40.6)*.

If you are an employee, the expenses are listed on Form 2106 and if not reimbursed, entered on Schedule A; *see 19.4*. The expenses are a fully deductible miscellaneous itemized deduction; the 2% AGI floor does *not* apply.

EXAMPLES

1. A professor is paralyzed from the waist down and confined to a wheelchair. When he attends out-of-town business meetings, he has his wife, a friend, or a colleague accompany him to help him with baggage, stairs, narrow doors, and to sit with him on airplanes when airlines will not allow wheelchair passengers without an attendant. While he does not pay them a salary, he does pay their travel costs. He may deduct these costs as business expenses. They are incurred solely because of his occupation.
2. An attorney uses prostheses due to bilateral amputation of his legs and takes medication several times a day for other ailments. On both personal and business trips, his wife or a neighbor accompanies him to help him travel and receive medication. He may deduct the out-of-town expenses paid for his neighbor only as a medical expense. The neighbor's services are not business expenses because assistance in personal activities is regularly provided. When his wife accompanies him, he may deduct her transportation costs as a medical expense; her food and lodging are nondeductible ordinary living expenses.

17.15 Long-Term Care

You may include as medical expenses (subject to the 7.5% adjusted gross income floor) your unreimbursed expenses for qualifying long-term care services that you require because you are "chronically ill" or because your spouse or dependent is chronically ill. Also deductible are premiums paid for qualified long-term care policies; the amount depends on your age.

Filing Tip

Long-Term Care Insurance

Unreimbursed expenses for long-term care services to care for a chronically ill patient are deductible medical expenses subject to the 7.5% AGI floor. Depending on your age, all or part of premiums paid for a qualifying policy are includible in your medical expenses.

Filing Instruction

Form 8853

If you received payments in 2006 from a qualified long-term care policy, you must figure the amount of taxable payments, if any, on Form 8853.

Qualifying long-term-care services for a chronically ill individual. A chronically ill person is someone who has been certified by a licensed health-care practitioner within the preceding 12 months as being unable to perform for a period of at least 90 days at least two of the following activities without substantial assistance: eating, toileting, dressing, bathing, continence, or transferring. Also qualifying as chronically ill is someone who requires substantial supervision because of severe cognitive impairment, such as from Alzheimer's disease.

Qualifying long-term-care services for a chronically ill individual are broadly defined as necessary diagnostic, preventive, therapeutic, curing, treating, mitigation, and rehabilitative services, and also maintenance or personal care services. The services must be provided under a plan of care prescribed by a licensed health-care practitioner, who may be a physician, a registered nurse, a licensed social worker, or other individual meeting Treasury requirements. Services provided by a spouse or relative are deductible only if that person is a licensed professional; services provided by a related corporation or partnership do not qualify.

Deductible premium costs of long-term-care policies. Depending on your age, all or part of your premium payments for a qualified long-term-care policy may be included as deductible medical expenses, subject to the 7.5% adjusted gross income floor. To qualify, the policy must provide for long-term-care services for the chronically ill (*see* above). The amount of the deductible premium depends on your age at the end of the year. For 2006, the maximum deductible premium amount for *each* person covered under the policy is: $280 if you are age 40 or younger at the end of 2006; $530 for those age 41 through 50; $1,060 for those age 51 through 60; $2,830 for those age 61 through 70; and $3,530 for those over age 70. These limits may be increased for 2007 by an inflation factor; *see* the *e-Supplement.*

If you are considering purchase of a long-term-care insurance policy, make sure that it qualifies for the tax treatment explained in this section. A qualified contract must provide only for coverage of qualified long-term-care services and be guaranteed renewable; it may not provide for a cash surrender value or money that can be assigned, pledged, or borrowed; it may not reimburse expenses covered by Medicare except where Medicare is a secondary payer or the contract makes *per diem* payments without regard to expenses.

Benefits paid by qualified long-term-care policies. Benefits from a qualified long-term-care insurance contract (other than dividends) are generally excludable from income. If payments are made on a *per diem* or other periodic basis, meaning that they are made without regard to actual expenses incurred, there is an annual limitation on the amount that can be excluded. For 2006, *per diem* payments of up to $250 per day are tax free. If *per diem* payments exceed the $250 limit, the excess is tax free only to the extent of unreimbursed expenses for qualified long-term-care services. The *per diem* limit must be allocated among all policyholders who own qualified long-term-care insurance contracts for the same insured.

You should receive a Form 1099-LTC showing any payments to you from a long-term-care insurance contract. Box 3 of Form 1099-LTC should indicate whether the payments were made on a *per diem* basis or were reimbursements of actual long-term-care expenses. *Per diem* payments and reimbursements must be reported on Form 8853 to determine if any of the *per diem* payments are taxable.

17.16 Life Insurance Used By Chronically ill

A person who is terminally ill may be forced to cash in a life insurance policy to pay medical bills and other living expenses. Insurance companies have developed life insurance policies with accelerated death benefit clauses to help terminally ill patients meet the high cost of medical care. Where a policy lacks an accelerated payment clause, it is also possible to sell a life insurance policy to a viatical settlement company that specializes in buying policies from ill persons who require funds to pay expenses.

Accelerated death benefits and viatical settlement proceeds received by terminally ill individuals are *not taxed.*

Payment of long-term care costs. A chronically ill individual may sell a life insurance policy to a viatical settlement company to pay for long-term-care costs. However, tax-free treatment is determined under the tax rules applied to long-term-care policies in *17.15*. Thus, if the proceeds exceed the $250 *per diem* limit for 2006 and also exceed actual long-term care costs, the excess is taxable on Form 8853. Accelerated life insurance proceeds paid under a long-term-care rider are also subject to the rules in *17.15*.

Chapter 18

Casualty and Theft Losses and Involuntary Conversions

All casualty and theft losses are claimed on Form 4684. The tax treatment of an unreimbursed casualty or theft loss depends on the purpose for which you held the damaged, destroyed, or stolen property. A loss of property held for:

- *Personal purposes* is subject to the sudden events test *(18.1)*. The deduction is reduced by $100 and also by 10% of your adjusted gross income *(18.12)* on Form 4684, unless the loss was caused by Hurricane Katrina, Rita, or Wilma. If the 10% floor applies, you may be unable to deduct a casualty or theft loss unless the loss is quite substantial.

  The itemized deduction claimed for personal-use property is not subject to the 3% reduction computation; *see 13.7.*
- *Income-producing purposes,* such as negotiable securities, should be claimed on Form 4684 and then entered on Line 27 of Schedule A. The loss deduction is not subject to the 2% AGI floor *(19.1)* or the 3% reduction *(13.7)* that applies to a loss deduction for income-producing property.
- *Business or rental purposes* is claimed on Form 4684 and then as a loss on Form 4797. It is not subject to any floor or the sudden event test. Follow the instructions to Form 4684.

If you have realized a gain, you may defer tax by replacing or repairing the property; *see 18.19.*

Appraisal fees and other incidental costs, such as taking photos to establish the amount of the loss, are claimed as a miscellaneous itemized deduction on Line 22 of Schedule A, Form 1040.

Deductible Casualty Losses

Deductible Theft Losses

How To Figure and Claim Your Casualty or Theft Loss

Taxable Gain From Involuntary Conversions

Deductible Casualty Losses

18.1 Sudden Event Test for Casualty Losses

To be a deductible casualty loss, property must be damaged or destroyed as the result of a sudden, unexpected, or unusual event. A sudden event is one that is swift, not gradual or progressive. An unexpected event is one that is ordinarily unanticipated and unintended. An unusual event is one that is not a day-to-day occurrence and that is not typical of the activity in which you were engaged. Chance or a natural phenomenon must be present. Examples include earthquakes, hurricanes, tornadoes, floods, severe storms, landslides, and fires. Loss due to vandalism during riots or civil disorders also is treated as a casualty loss. Damage to your car from an accident is generally deductible; *see 18.7.* Courts have allowed deductions for other types of accidents; *see* Example 2 below. The requirement of suddenness is designed to bar deductions for damage caused by a natural action such as erosion, corrosion, and termite infestation occurring over a period of time.

The IRS and the courts have generally disallowed casualty deductions based on a loss in property value due to permanent buyer resistance rather than actual physical damage; *see* Examples 4 and 5 below.

EXAMPLES

1. A homeowner claimed a loss for water damage to wallpaper and plaster. The water entered through the window frame. The loss was disallowed. He gave no evidence that the damage came from a sudden or destructive force, such as a storm. The damage may have been caused by progressive deterioration.
2. Mr. White accidentally slammed the car door on his wife's hand. In pain, she shook her hand vigorously. A diamond flew out of her ring's setting, which was loosened by the impact. The diamond was never found. The IRS disallowed the deduction, contending that a casualty loss requires a cataclysmic event. The Tax Court disagreed. A deductible casualty loss occurs whenever an accidental force is exerted against property, and its owner is powerless to prevent the damage because of the suddenness. The IRS has accepted the decision.
3. A boat, which was in a poor state of repair, was equipped with a pump that automatically began operating when the water in the hull rose above a certain level. One day, the dockside power source failed, and the boat sank at its mooring within four hours. The IRS claimed that no deductible casualty occurred because the leakage was a chronic problem. The Tax Court allowed the deduction. The sinking was not a direct result of the boat's leaking hull, but of the failure of the on-board water pump.
4. A Brentwood couple, whose home was near the O.J. Simpson house, filed for a refund in federal district court to claim a $400,000 casualty loss deduction. The couple claimed that the double murder and the media frenzy surrounding the Simpson trial caused permanent buyer resistance in their neighborhood, lowering the value of their home by at least $400,000. The district court denied the refund. The couple relied on a 1986 case in which the Eleventh Circuit appeals court allowed Finkbohner a casualty loss deduction based on permanent buyer resistance when 12 nearby homes were razed by local authorities following severe floods and the lots were required to be kept as open space. However, the Brentwood couple's case was appealable to the Ninth Circuit, and the Ninth Circuit requires that a casualty loss be based on actual physical damage caused by a fire, storm, or other sudden unusual event and not merely buyer resistance. Therefore, the claim for a casualty loss deduction for the Brentwood home was denied.

   In a similar case, the Tax Court denied a casualty loss deduction to O.J. Simpson's next-door neighbors, who claimed they had suffered a permanent devaluation of their home's value due to the trial publicity. The Tax Court holds that actual physical damage is required for a deduction.
5. A 1983 avalanche caused $9,000 of physical damage to the Lunds' vacation home in Sundance, Utah, but they claimed a $221,000 deduction. They argued that there was a permanent loss in property value due to the avalanche risk in the area. Local authorities blocked road access during heavy snowfalls and some neighbors had decided not to rebuild destroyed homes. A federal district court agreed with the IRS that their loss could not exceed the actual physical damage. There may have been temporary buyer resistance following the avalanche, but not a permanent change in the area itself as there was in the Eleventh Circuit *Finkbohner* case mentioned above in Example 4.

Is drought damage deductible? The IRS does not generally allow deductions for drought damage. An agent may argue that the loss resulted from progressive deterioration, which does not fit the legal definition of a personal casualty loss. Courts have allowed deductions for severe drought where the damages occur in the same year as the drought.

If the damage becomes noticeable a year later, a court will view this as evidence of progressive deterioration that does not qualify as a deductible casualty. Where there are drought conditions, inspect your property for damage before the end of the year and claim a deduction for the damage in that year to negate an IRS argument that damage was caused by progressive deterioration.

Damage to surrounding property. Loss due to buyer resistance because of damage to surrounding property is generally not deductible. However, the Eleventh Circuit allowed a deduction. *See* Example 4 above.

Damage to trees. The destruction of trees by southern pine beetles over a period of 5 to 10 days was held by the IRS to be a casualty. One court decided similarly where the destruction occurred over a 30-day period. For figuring the casualty deduction for tree and shrub damage, *see 18.6.*

Deduction despite faulty construction. A plumber stepped on a pipe that was improperly installed. Resulting underground flooding caused damage of over $20,000. The IRS argued that this was caused by a construction fault and thus was not a casualty loss. The Tax Court disagreed. The plumber caused the damage. Improper construction was only an element in the causative chain.

Foreseeable events and preventable accidents. The IRS may disallow a deduction by claiming that the loss was foreseeable and therefore not a deductible casualty loss; *see* the following Examples.

EXAMPLES

1. Heyn owned a hillside lot on which he contracted for the building of a home. A soil test showed a high proportion of fine-grain dense sandstone, which is unstable. His construction contract called for appropriate shoring up and support. But, because of the contractor's negligence, a landslide occurred. The IRS disallowed the loss on the ground that it was not a "casualty" because the danger was known before Heyn undertook the project and because of the negligence involved. The court disagreed. The contractor's negligence is not a factor in determining whether there was a casualty. For example, an automobile collision is considered a casualty, even if caused by negligent driving. Foreseeability is not a factor. A weather report may warn property owners to take protective steps against an approaching hurricane, but losses caused by the hurricane are deductible. The IRS has agreed to accept the decision.
2. Mrs. Kane placed her dirty ring in a glass of ammonia. Not knowing the contents of the glass, her husband emptied it into the sink and started the automatic garbage disposal, crushing the ring. The court allowed a full deduction for the loss, which it said resulted from a destructive force. That Mr. Kane was negligent has no bearing on whether the event was a casualty.
3. At Christmastime in 1982, Hananel left his 1974 Plymouth Valiant in Chicago in an area in which the city was towing away cars to make room for construction work. When he returned a week later, he found that his car was missing and reported it stolen. A month later, he learned that the city pound had towed the car away and then crushed it because its ownership could not be determined. He claimed a casualty loss for the car. The IRS disallowed the deduction, claiming that the towing and crushing were not an unforeseeable event, and thus did not qualify as a casualty.

   The Tax Court agreed that Hananel could have foreseen that leaving the car on the street subjected it to being towed. He was negligent. However, the penalty for this is a towing charge. He could not have foreseen its destruction. Therefore, the destruction occurred from an unusual and unexpected event, and he was allowed to claim a casualty loss deduction.
4. Destruction of a lawn through the careless use of weed killer was held by the Tax Court to be a casualty.

Caution

Loss Prevention Measures

The cost of preventive measures, such as burglar alarms or smoke detectors, or the cost of boarding up property against a storm, is not deductible.

Caution

Loss From Termites

Termite damage is generally nondeductible since it often results from long periods of termite infestation. Proving a sudden action in the sense of fixing the approximate moment of the termite invasion is difficult. Some courts have allowed a deduction, but the IRS will bar deductions for termite damage under any conditions based on a study that found that serious termite damage results only after an infestation of three to eight years. Examples of other nondeductible casualty losses are at *18.11.*

18.2 When To Deduct a Casualty Loss

Generally, you deduct a casualty loss in the year the casualty occurs, regardless of when you repair or replace damaged or destroyed property. However, for a qualifying disaster area loss *(18.3)*, you have the option of claiming the loss on your return for the year immediately preceding the year in which the disaster occurred. If a casualty occurs in one year and you do not discover the damage until a later year, or you know damage has been inflicted, but you do not know the full extent of the loss because you expect reimbursement in a later year, here is what to do:

If you reasonably expect reimbursement in a later year. You should deduct in the year the casualty occurred only that part of your loss (after applying the personal property floors discussed in *18.12*) for which you do not expect reimbursement. For example, if you expect a full insurance recovery in 2007 for a 2006 loss, you would take no deduction on your 2006 return.

If you do not expect any reimbursement and deduct a loss in 2006, but you receive insurance or other reimbursement in 2007, the reimbursement is taxable in 2007 to the extent that the 2006 deduction gave you a tax benefit by reducing your 2006 taxable income; *see 11.6*. You may not amend your 2006 tax return.

You must file a timely insurance claim if your property is covered by insurance. Otherwise, the amount covered by the insurance cannot be taken into account when figuring your deductible casualty loss; *see 18.13* and *18.16*.

Caution

Deducting Loss in Proper Year

Read the rules on this page to insure that you deduct your casualty loss in the correct year.

EXAMPLE

In 1969, Hurricane Camille destroyed oceanfront real estate owned jointly by two brothers. The buildings were insured under two policies that included wind damage but not losses resulting from floods, tidal waves, or water. The insurers, claiming the tidal wave had caused the destruction, denied their claim. The brothers consulted an attorney about the possibility of suit against the insurance companies, but there seemed to be little likelihood of recovery, so the brothers deducted their shares of the casualty loss in 1969. However, in January 1970, the adjusters of both companies changed their decisions, reimbursing the brothers for more than two-thirds of their loss. One of the brothers filed an amended 1969 tax return, reducing the previously reported casualty loss.

The IRS claimed that the insurance recovery was taxable in the year of receipt, 1970, to the extent that the prior deduction reduced 1969 income. The brother claimed that he made an error in claiming the deduction in 1969 because he had a reasonable prospect of reimbursement. Thus it was proper to reduce the deduction by the reimbursement on an amended return.

The Tax Court disagreed. Tax liability is based on facts as they exist at the end of each year. A recovery in a later tax year does not prove that a reasonable prospect of recovery existed in the earlier year. Amendments to previously filed tax returns may be made only to correct mathematical errors or miscalculations, not to rearrange facts and readjust income for two years.

If your reimbursement is less or more than you expected. Assume you took no loss deduction in 2005 because you expected to recover your entire loss in 2006—but the insurance company refuses to pay your claim. When do you deduct your loss? You deduct your loss in the year you find that you have no reasonable prospect of recovery. For example, you sue the company in 2006, with a reasonable prospect of winning your claim. However, in 2007, a court rules against you. You deduct your loss in 2007, subject to the personal property floors in *18.12*. If you, as lessee, are liable to the lessor for damage to property, you may deduct the loss in the year you pay the lessor.

If you claimed a loss in 2005 and in 2006 you receive a larger insurance reimbursement than expected, you must include the recovery as 2006 income to the extent the deduction reduced your 2005 taxable income; *see 11.6*.

If you do not discover the loss until a later year. In this case, IRS regulations do not specifically allow a deduction for the loss in the year it is discovered, but court decisions have. In one case, an unseasonable blizzard damaged a windbreak planted to protect a house, buildings, and livestock. The damage to the evergreens did not become apparent until the next year, when about half of the trees died and the others were of little value. The court held that the loss occurred in the later year. In another case, hurricane damage did not become apparent for two years. The Tax Court allowed the deduction in the later year. Where drought damage occurs, *see 18.1*.

If your loss is in a federal disaster area. If your property is damaged in an area eligible for federal disaster assistance, you have a choice of years for which the loss may be claimed; *see 18.3.*

If reimbursements exceed your adjusted basis for the property. Receiving reimbursements in excess of adjusted basis results in a gain that you must report on your return unless you acquire qualifying replacement property and elect to defer the gain; *see 18.19.* If a loss is claimed in one year and in a later year you receive reimbursements that exceed your adjusted basis, the gain is included in income for the later year to the extent the original deduction reduced your taxable income; *see 11.6.* The remainder of the gain is taxable unless you buy replacement property that enables you to defer the gain as discussed in *18.19.*

18.3 Disaster Losses

If you suffer a loss from a disaster in an area declared by the President as warranting federal assistance, you may deduct the loss either on the return for the year of the loss or on the return of the prior tax year. *See 18.13* for figuring the deductible loss.

You may elect to claim the deduction on a tax return for the previous year any time on or before the *later* of (1) the due date (without extensions) of the return for the year of the disaster *or* (2) the due date considering any extension for filing the return for the prior tax year. For a 2006 disaster loss, you generally have until April 16, 2007, to amend a 2005 tax return to claim the 2006 loss for 2005. In the case of a 2007 disaster loss, you generally have until April 15, 2008, to amend a 2006 tax return to claim the 2007 loss for 2006.

Revoking new year election. You have 90 days in which to revoke an election to deduct a disaster loss for the previous year. After the 90-day period, the election becomes irrevocable. However, where an early election is made, you have until the due date for filing your return for the year of the disaster to change your election. Your revocation of an election is not effective unless you repay any credit or refund resulting from the election within the revocation period. A revocation made before you receive a refund will not be effective unless you repay the refund within 30 days after you receive it.

Homeowners forced to relocate. If you were forced to relocate or demolish your home in a disaster area, you may be able to claim a loss even though the damage, such as from erosion, does not meet the sudden event test in *18.1.* For example, after a severe storm, there is danger to a group of homes from nearby mudslides. State officials order homeowners to evacuate and relocate their homes. Disaster loss treatment is allowed provided: (1) the President has determined that the area warrants federal disaster relief; (2) within 120 days of the President's order, you are ordered by the state or local government to demolish or relocate your residence; and (3) the home was rendered unsafe by the erosion or other disaster. The law applies to vacation homes and rental properties, as well as to principal residences.

If these tests are met, the loss in value to your home is treated as a disaster loss so that you may elect to deduct the loss either in the year the demolition or relocation order is made or in the prior taxable year.

Fiscal year. If you are on a fiscal year, an election may be made for disaster losses occurring after the close of a fiscal year on the return for that year. For example, if your fiscal year ends June 30, and you suffer a disaster loss at any time between July 1, 2006, and June 30, 2007, you may elect to deduct it on your return for the fiscal year ending June 30, 2006.

Disaster relief grants and loans. Cancellation of part of a federal disaster loan under the Disaster Relief and Emergency Assistance Act is treated as a reimbursement that reduces your loss; *see 18.16.* If you receive a post-disaster grant under the Disaster Relief Act to help you meet medical, dental, housing, transportation, personal property, or funeral expenses, the grant is excludable from income. However, to the extent the grant specifically reimburses a casualty loss or medical expense *(17.2),* that expense is not deductible. Unemployment assistance payments under the Disaster Relief Act are taxable unemployment benefits; *see 2.6.*

Disaster grants for business property losses. Payments by the federal government or a state or local government to a business for property losses may not be excluded from business gross income. The IRS has ruled that the disaster relief exclusion that applies to government payments made to individuals to promote the general welfare (*see* the Law Alert on this page) does not apply to business property losses. The business realizes a taxable gain to the extent the grant exceeds the adjusted basis in the damaged or destroyed property, but that gain can be deferred under the

Filing Tip

Accelerating a Tax Refund With Disaster Loss

Disaster loss rules give you a chance to deduct a loss earlier than under general rules. This may result in a tax refund for the prior year. You may make an election to claim the loss for the prior year in a signed statement attached to an amended return for that year if the original return has already been filed. List the date of the disaster and where the property was located (city, town, county, and state). To amend a filed return for the prior year, use Form 1040X. Consider making the election if the deduction on the return of the prior year gives a greater tax reduction than if claimed on the return for the year in which the loss occurred, or if you need the refund for the prior year tax and do not want to wait until you file your return for the year of the disaster to claim the loss.

Law Alert

Tax-Free Disaster Relief Payments to Individuals

You are not taxed on disaster relief payments from any source that reimburses or pays you for unreimbursed costs of repairing or rehabilitating your personal residence, or replacing its contents, as a result of a Presidentially declared disaster.

You are not taxed on payments, regardless of the source, that cover reasonable and necessary personal, family, living, or funeral expenses as a result of a Presidentially declared disaster, so long as they are not otherwise paid by insurance or other reimbursement. The exclusion also applies to payments made by the federal, state, or local government to individuals affected by a Presidentially declared disaster in order to promote the general welfare.

Filing Tip

Refund Opportunity for Nontaxable Disaster Mitigation Payments

Under a 2005 law, property owners are not taxed on qualified disaster mitigation payments from FEMA (Federal Emergency Management Agency) to elevate or relocate flood-prone homes and businesses or build hurricane shelters. If you included such payments in income on a prior year's return, and the time limit for filing an amended return *(47.2)* has not expired, you can file for a refund on Form 1040X.

Planning Reminder

IRS Interest Abatement

If the IRS extends the due date to file tax returns and pay taxes for a person in an area declared to be a disaster area by the President, the IRS will abate interest on past-due taxes for the period covered by the extension.

involuntary conversion rules *(18.19)* by making a timely reinvestment of the payments in qualified replacement property. The replacement period for damaged or destroyed business property is two years; *see 18.22.*

IRS interest abatement. For declared disasters, the IRS will abate interest on taxes due for the period covered by an extension to file tax returns and pay taxes.

Insurance Proceeds for Damaged or Destroyed Residence

Destruction of principal residence and contents. Generally, you have a taxable gain if you receive insurance proceeds in excess of your adjusted basis for damaged or destroyed property *(18.19)*. However, where your principal residence is destroyed, any gain from the receipt of insurance proceeds may generally be excluded from gross income under the $250,000 ($500,000 if married filing jointly) home sale exclusion; *see 29.1.* If the home sale exclusion is not available to you or if the gain exceeds your exclusion, the nonexcludable gain may be deferred under the involuntary conversion rules if you buy a replacement residence; *see 18.19.*

Where your principal residence is damaged or destroyed in a Presidentially declared disaster, favorable involuntary conversion rules eliminate tax on some of the gain and make it easier to defer the balance. These rules apply to renters as well as home owners.

1. You do not have to pay tax on gain from insurance proceeds received for "unscheduled" personal property in your principal residence (rented or owned). Personal property is unscheduled if it is not separately listed on a schedule or rider to the basic insurance policy.
2. Insurance proceeds received for the home itself or for *scheduled* property are treated as received for a single item of property. Gain on this combined insurance pool may be deferred by reinvesting in replacement property that is similar or related in service or use to either the damaged residence or its contents. If the cost of a new principal residence and/or contents equals or exceeds the combined insurance pool, you may elect to defer any gain attributable to the insurance recovery; *see 18.21* for making the election. The deferred gain reduces your basis in the replacement property. The period for purchasing replacement property generally ends four years after the end of the first tax year in which any part of your gain is realized. However, for a principal residence destroyed or damaged by Hurricane Katrina, or as a result of the September 11 attacks in the New York Liberty Zone, there is a five-year replacement period (instead of four years), provided that the replacement residence is used in the Hurricane Katrina disaster area or in New York City. If the cost of the replacement property is less than the combined insurance pool, your gain is taxed to the extent of the unspent reimbursement.

EXAMPLE

You rent an apartment as your principal residence. Your apartment and its contents were completely destroyed by a hurricane in 2006; the county in which your apartment was located was declared a disaster area. You received insurance proceeds of $17,000 for unscheduled personal property in your apartment. The proceeds are not taxable.

Sale of land underlying destroyed principal residence or second home. If your principal residence is destroyed in a Presidentially declared disaster, and you decide to relocate elsewhere and sell the underlying land, the IRS treats the sale and the destruction as a single involuntary conversion. If you have a gain that is not excludable under the home sale exclusion rules (Chapter 29), the land sale proceeds are combined with your insurance recovery for purposes of figuring deferrable gain under the involuntary conversion replacement rules *(18.19)*. All of the gain resulting from the insurance recovery may be deferred if a new principal residence is purchased within the four-year replacement period and it costs at least as much as the combined insurance and sales proceeds. The replacement period ends four years after the close of the first year in which any part of your gain is realized. The replacement period is extended from four to five years for a principal residence destroyed as a result of Hurricane Katrina or the September 11 attacks in the New York Liberty Zone, but only if the replacement residence is in the Hurricane Katrina disaster area or in New York City.

The above "single conversion" rule also applies if a second residence such as a vacation home that qualifies for a mortgage interest deduction *(15.1)* is destroyed, but in that case the replacement period *(18.22)* is two years (instead of four years), unless the five-year replacement period for Hurricane Katrina property or New York Liberty Zone property applies.

Note: The IRS treats the sale of land and destruction of a residence as a single involuntary conversion even if the destruction was *not* in a Presidentially declared disaster area. In this case, a two-year (rather than four-year) replacement period applies.

18.4 Who May Deduct a Casualty Loss

A casualty loss deduction may be claimed only by the owner of the property. For example, a husband filing a separate return may not deduct damage to a car belonging to his wife; only she may deduct it on her separate return.

On jointly owned property, the loss is divided among the owners. If you and your spouse own the property jointly, you deduct the entire loss on a joint return. If you file separately, each owner deducts his or her share of the loss on each separate return.

If you have a legal life estate in the property, the loss is apportioned between yourself and those who will get the property after your death. The apportionment may be based on actuarial tables that consider your life expectancy.

You may claim a casualty loss for property lost or destroyed by your dependent if you own the property. You may not claim a loss deduction for destroyed property that belongs to your child who has reached majority, even though he or she is still your dependent.

Caution

Damage to Nearby Property

The casualty must have caused damage to your property. Damage to a nearby area that lowered the value of your property does not give you a loss deduction.

Lessee. A person leasing property may be allowed to deduct payments to a lessor that compensate for a casualty loss. A tenant was allowed to deduct as a casualty loss payment of a judgment obtained by the landlord for fire damage to the rented premises that had to be returned in the same condition as at the start of the lease. However, the Tax Court does not allow a deduction for the cost of repairing a rented car, as the lessee has no basis in the car.

EXAMPLE

You buy or lease a lot on which to build a cottage. Along with your purchase or lease, you have the privilege of using a nearby lake. The lake is later destroyed by a storm and the value of your property drops. You may not deduct the loss. The lake is not your property. You only had a privilege to use it, and this is not an ownership right that supports a casualty loss deduction.

18.5 Bank Deposit Losses

If a bank or other financial institution in which you deposit funds fails and your loss is not covered by insurance, generally you may claim your loss either as a bad debt deduction or casualty loss. Alternatively, if none of the deposits were federally insured, an investment loss may be claimed. A casualty loss deduction may not be claimed for lost deposits in foreign financial institutions that are not organized and supervised under federal or state law. Neither the casualty loss nor the investment loss option is available to stockholders of the bank with more than a 1% interest, officers of the bank, or relatives of shareholders or officers.

Filing Tip

Lost Bank Deposit

If you have other miscellaneous deductions that exceed 2% of adjusted gross income, claiming investment loss treatment may be preferable to treating the loss as a casualty subject to the 10% floor or a bad debt subject to the $3,000 limit.

Bad debt. You may claim a bad debt deduction for a loss of a bank deposit in the year there is no reasonable prospect of recovery from the insolvent or bankrupt bank. You claim the loss as a short-term capital loss on Schedule D (Form 1040) unless the deposit was made in your business. A nonbusiness bad debt deduction is deductible from capital gains. If you do not have capital gains or the bad debt loss exceeds capital gains, only $3,000 of the loss may offset other income. The remaining loss is carried over. A lost deposit of business funds is claimed as a business bad debt; *see 5.33*.

Casualty loss. You may elect to take a casualty loss deduction for the year in which the loss can be reasonably estimated. A loss of personal funds is subject to the $100/10% AGI floors for personal-use property losses; *see 18.12*. Once the casualty loss election is made, it is irrevocable and will apply to all other losses on deposits in the same financial institution.

The casualty loss election may allow you to claim the loss in an earlier year because you do not have to wait until the year there is no prospect of recovery as required in the case of bad debts. The casualty loss election may also be advisable if other casualty losses may absorb all or part of the 10% AGI floor.

Investment loss. If *none* of your deposits were federally insured and you reasonably estimate that you will not recover the funds, up to $20,000 ($10,000 if married filing separately) may be claimed on Schedule A (Form 1040) as an investment loss subject to the 2% adjusted gross income floor for miscellaneous itemized deductions *(19.1)*. The $20,000 limit (or $10,000) applies to total losses from any one financial institution, regardless of the number of accounts you have. A separate $20,000 deduction limit applies to each financial institution. The $20,000 (or $10,000) limit is reduced by any insurance proceeds authorized by *state* law that you reasonably expect to receive. If you claimed a bad debt deduction for a lost deposit in a prior year and you qualify for the investment loss, you may file an amended return to claim the investment loss if the statute of limitations has not passed.

Reasonable estimate of casualty or investment loss. Generally, the trustees of the troubled bank will provide depositors with an estimate of the expected recovery and loss. In the year of that determination, you may claim the estimated loss deduction. If you deduct an estimated loss that is less than you are entitled to, you may claim the additional loss in the year of the final determination as a bad debt. If you deduct more than the actual loss, the excess loss must be reported as income in the year of the final determination. Failure to claim the loss in the year in which the loss can first be reasonably estimated does not bar a deduction in a later year.

For any particular year, only one election may be made for losses in the same bank. If you elect the up-to-$20,000 investment loss for losses in one bank and your loss exceeds the limit, the balance may not be claimed as a casualty deduction. Similarly, if you elect casualty loss treatment, the amount that is not deductible because of the $100 and 10% of adjusted gross income floors *(18.12)* is not deductible under the $20,000 investment loss rule.

18.6 Damage to Trees and Shrubs

Not all damage to trees and shrubs qualifies as a casualty loss. The damage must be occasioned by a sudden event; *see 18.1.* Destruction of trees over a period of 5–10 days by southern pine beetles is deductible. One court allowed a deduction for similar destruction over a 30-day period. However, damage by Dutch Elm disease or lethal yellowing disease has been held to be gradual destruction not qualifying as a casualty loss. The Tax Court has allowed a deduction for the cost of removing infested trees, but denied a deduction for the loss of trees after a horse ate the bark.

If shrubbery and trees on *personal-use property* are damaged by a sudden casualty, you figure the loss on the value of the entire property before and after the casualty. You treat the buildings, land, and shrubs as one complete unit; *see* Example 2 below.

In fixing the loss on *business* or *income-producing property,* however, shrubs and trees are valued separately from the building; *see* Example 1 below.

EXAMPLES

1. Wayne Smith bought an office building for $90,000. The purchase price was allocated between the land ($18,000) and the building ($72,000). Smith planted trees and ornamental shrubs on the grounds surrounding the building at a cost of $1,200. When the basis of the building had been depreciated to $66,000, a hurricane caused extensive property damage. The fair market value of the land and building immediately before the hurricane was $18,000 and $80,000; immediately afterwards it was $18,000 and $52,000. The fair market value of the trees and shrubs immediately before the casualty was $2,000 and immediately afterwards, $400. Insurance of $15,000 is received to cover damage to the building. Deductible losses are figured separately for the building and the trees and shrubs. The deduction for the building is $13,000, computed as follows:

Value of building immediately before casualty	$80,000
Less: Value immediately after casualty	52,000
Loss in value	$28,000
Less: Insurance received	15,000
Deduction allowed	$13,000

The deduction for the trees and shrubs is $1,200:

Value immediately before casualty	$2,000
Less: Value of trees immediately after casualty	400
Loss in value	$1,600*

*However, the deductible loss cannot exceed the adjusted basis of the property, $1,200.

2. Same facts as in Example 1, except that Smith purchases a personal residence instead of an office building. Smith's adjusted gross income is $25,000, and this is his only loss. No allocation of the purchase price is necessary for the land and house because the property is not depreciable. Likewise, no individual evaluation of the fair market values

Court Decision

Failure To Winterize Car

The Tax Court held that the loss of an engine because of a failure to use antifreeze is not deductible as a casualty loss since the damage is not the result of a destructive force or accident but of personal neglect.

of the land, house, trees, and shrubs is necessary. The amount of the deduction for the land, house, trees, and shrubs is $12,000, computed as follows:

Value of property immediately before casualty		$100,000
Less: Value of property immediately after casualty		70,400
Loss in value		$29,600
Less: Insurance received	$15,000	
10% floor ($2,500) and $100 floors	2,600	17,600
Deduction allowed		$12,000

18.7 Deducting Damage to Your Car

Damage to your car in an accident may be a deductible casualty loss unless caused by your willful conduct, such as drunken driving.

You may not deduct legal fees and costs of a court action for damages or money paid for damages to another's property because of your negligence while driving for commuting or other personal purposes. But if at the time of the accident you were using your car on business, you may deduct as a business loss a payment of damages to the other party's car. For purposes of a business loss deduction, driving between two locations of the same business is considered business driving but driving between locations of two separate businesses is considered personal driving. Therefore, the payment of damages arising from an accident while driving between two separate businesses is not deductible as a business expense.

A court has allowed casualty deductions for damage resulting from a child starting a car and from flying stones while driving over a temporary road. In a private letter ruling, the IRS disallowed a loss for damage to a race car by an amateur racer on the ground that in races, crashes are not an unusual event and so do not constitute a casualty.

If the deduction is questioned, be prepared to show the amount, if any, of your insurance recovery. A deduction is allowed only for uninsured losses. Not only must the loss be proved, but also that it was not compensated by insurance.

Towing costs are not included as part of the casualty loss.

A parent may not claim a casualty loss deduction for damage to a car registered in a child's name, although the parent provided funds for the purchase of the car.

Expenses of personal injuries arising from a car accident are not a deductible casualty loss.

Filing Tip

Auto Damage

Unreimbursed accident damage may be a deductible casualty loss.

Automobile used partly for business. When you use an automobile partly for personal use and partly for business, your loss is computed as though two separate pieces of property were damaged—one business and the other personal. The $100 and 10% floors reduce only the loss on the part used for personal purposes.

18.8 Proving a Casualty Loss

If your return is audited, you will have to prove that the casualty occurred and the amount of the loss. The time to collect your evidence is as soon after the casualty as possible. Table 18-1, Proving a Casualty Loss, below, indicates the information that you will need when computing your loss under the steps explained in *18.13*.

Table 18-1 Proving a Casualty Loss

To prove—	*You need this information—*
That a casualty actually occurred	With a well-known casualty, like regional floods, you will have no difficulty proving the casualty occurred, but you must prove it affected your property. Photographs of the area, before and after, and newspaper stories placing the damage in your neighborhood are helpful. If only your property is damaged, there may be a newspaper item on it. Some papers list all the fire alarms answered the previous day. Police, fire, and other municipal departments may have reports on the casualty.
The cost of repairing the property	Cost of repairs is allowed as a measure of loss of repairing the value if it is not excessive and the repair merely restored your property to its condition immediately before the casualty. Save cancelled checks, bills, receipts, and vouchers for expenses of clearing debris and restoring the property to its condition before the casualty.

Table 18-1 Proving a Casualty Loss (continued)

The value immediately before and after the casualty	Appraisals by a competent expert are important. Get them in writing—in the form of an affidavit, deposition, estimate, appraisal, etc. The expert—an appraiser, engineer, or architect—should be qualified to judge local values. Any records of offers to buy your property, either before or after the casualty, are helpful. Automobile "blue books" may be used as guides in fixing the value of a car. But an amount offered for your car as a trade-in on a new car is not usually an acceptable measure of value.
Cost or other basis of your property—the deductible loss cannot be more than that	A deed, contract, bill of sale, or other document probably shows your original cost. Bills, receipts, and cancelled checks probably show the cost of improvements. One court refused to allow a deduction because an owner failed to prove the original cost of a destroyed house and its value before the fire. In another case, estimates were allowed where a fire destroyed records of cost. A court held that the homeowner could not be expected to prove cost by documents lost in the fire that destroyed her property. She made inventories after the fire and again at a later date. Her reliance on memory to establish cost, even though inflated, was no bar to the deduction. The court estimated the market value based on her inventories. If you acquired the property by gift or inheritance, you must establish an adjusted basis in the property from records of the donor or the executor of the estate; *see 5.17* and *5.18.*

Deductible Theft Losses

18.9 Theft Losses

You can deduct a theft loss in the year you discover that your property was stolen. The taking of property must be illegal under state law to support a theft loss deduction. That property is missing is not sufficient evidence to sustain a theft deduction. It may have been lost or misplaced. So if all you can prove is that an article is missing or lost, your deduction may be disallowed. Sometimes, of course, the facts surrounding the disappearance of an article indicate that it is reasonable to assume that a theft took place. A deduction has been allowed for the theft of trees.

If you expect to be reimbursed by insurance, you must subtract the expected reimbursement when you figure your deductible loss; *see 18.13.*

A legal fee paid to recover stolen property has been held to be deductible as part of the theft loss.

To figure the amount of a theft loss deduction, *see 18.13.*

Fraud by building contractors. A deduction was allowed when a building contractor ran away with a payment he received to build a residence. The would-be homeowner was allowed a theft loss deduction for the difference between the money he advanced to the contractor and the value of the partially completed house. In another case, a theft deduction was allowed for payments to subcontractors. The main contractor had fraudulently claimed that he had paid them before he went bankrupt.

Embezzlement losses are deductible as theft losses in the year the theft is discovered. However, if you report on a cash basis, you may not take a deduction for the embezzlement of income you have not reported. For example, an agent embezzled royalties of $46,000 due an author. The author's theft deduction was disallowed. The author had not previously reported the royalties as income; therefore, she could not get the deduction.

Fraudulent sales offers. Worthless stock purchases made on the representation of false and fraudulent sales offers are deductible as theft losses in the year there is no reasonable prospect of recovery. However, the illegal sale of unregistered stock does not support a theft loss deduction. In addition, buying stock from a bad tip and losing money is not deductible.

Kidnapping ransom. Payment of ransom to a kidnapper is generally a deductible theft loss. However, the expense of trying to find an abducted child is not a theft loss.

Fortune tellers. The Tax Court allowed a theft loss deduction in New York, where fortune telling is by law a theft-related offense. The law assumes that telling fortunes or promising to control occult forces is a form of fraud. An exception is made for fortune telling at shows for the purpose of entertaining or amusement. That a person voluntarily asks for advice does not bar the deduction. According to the court, a gullible person who gives money to fortune tellers in the belief that he or she will be helped is still defrauded or swindled. Theft is a broad term and includes theft by swindling, false pretenses, and any other form of guile. In this case, the taxpayer, who was suffering from depression, had become attached to two fortune tellers whom he claimed took him for over $19,000.

Filing Instruction

If Stolen Property Is Recovered

If you claim a theft loss and in a later year the property is returned to you, you must refigure your loss deduction. If the refigured deduction is lower than the amount you claimed, the difference must be reported as income in the year of the recovery. To recalculate the loss, follow the steps in *18.13* for figuring deductible losses, but in Step 1, compute the loss in fair market value from the time the property was stolen until you recovered it. The lower of this loss in value, if any, or your adjusted basis for the property is then reduced by insurance reimbursements and the personal-use floors *(18.12)* to get the recalculated loss.

Riot losses. Losses caused by fire, theft, and vandalism occurring during riots and civil disorders are deductible. To support your claim of a riot loss, keep evidence of the damage suffered and the cost of repairs. Photographs taken prior to repairs or replacement, lists of damaged or missing property, and police reports would help to establish and uphold your loss deduction.

Foreign government confiscations. The IRS and courts have disallowed casualty deductions for confiscations of personal property by foreign governments. This includes deposits in foreign banks; the loss is limited to a short-term capital loss.

Swindled by friend. A theft loss deduction was allowed to a widow who gave her old beau over $2 million to acquire stock for her in his bank. He used the money to pay his personal debts. The IRS barred the theft loss, arguing that the widow failed to prove fraud. A district court disagreed and allowed the deduction. Under Oklahoma state law, a person who makes a promise in return for cash has committed larceny by fraud if he never intended to return the funds or make good on the promise. Here, that the widow gave him the money voluntarily does not bar a theft loss deduction. She parted with the funds based upon his false claim that he would invest the money for her when he had no intention of doing so, but planned all along to pay off his debts with the funds.

Caution

Stock Devaluation Due to Corporate Misconduct

The IRS has warned shareholders who suffer a loss in the value of their stock due to the fraud, misappropriation, or other misconduct of corporate officers or directors that their loss is not a deductible theft loss. A decline in stock value is not a theft if the stock was purchased on the open market rather than directly from the corporate officials accused of misconduct. The loss is deductible only as a capital loss when the stock is sold or becomes worthless; *see 5.4* for the limits on capital losses.

The Tax Court took the same approach in holding that a taxpayer who bought stock on the open market could not support a theft loss under California law because there was no "privity" relationship between the taxpayer and the corporate officers accused of wrongdoing, and so it could not be shown that there was intent to obtain the taxpayer's property.

18.10 Proving a Theft Loss

Get statements from witnesses who saw the theft or police records documenting a break-in to your house or car. A newspaper account of the crime might also help.

When you suspect a theft, make a report to the police. Even though your reporting does not prove that a theft was committed, it may be inferred from your failure to report that you were not sure that your property was stolen. But a theft loss was allowed where the loss of a ring was not reported to the police or an attempt made to demand its return from the suspect, a domestic employee. The owner feared being charged with false arrest.

How To Figure and Claim Your Casualty or Theft Loss

18.11 Nondeductible Losses

Review the rules in *18.1* and *18.9* to make sure you have a deductible casualty or theft. Certain losses, though "casualties" for you, may not be deducted if they are not due to theft, fire, or from some other sudden natural phenomenon. The following have been held to be nondeductible losses:

- Termite damage; *see 18.1*
- Carpet beetle damage
- Dry rot damage
- Damages for personal injuries or property damage to others caused by your negligence
- Legal expenses in defending a suit for your negligent operation of your personal automobile
- Legal expenses to recover personal property wrongfully seized by the police
- Expenses of moving to and rental of temporary quarters
- Loss of personal property while in storage or in transit
- Loss of passenger's luggage put aboard a ship. The passenger missed the boat and the luggage could not be traced.
- Accidental loss of a ring from your finger
- Injuries resulting from tripping over a wire
- Loss by husband of joint property taken by his wife when she left him
- Loss of a valuable dog (or family pet) that strayed and was not found
- Steady weakening of a building due to normal wind and weather conditions
- Damage to a crop caused by plant diseases, insects, or fungi
- Damage to property from drought in an area where a dry spell is normal and usual
- Damage to property caused by excavations on adjoining property
- Damage from rust or corroding of understructure of house
- Moth damage
- Dry well
- Losses occasioned by water pockets, erosion, inundation at still water levels, and other natural phenomena (there was no sudden destruction.)
- Death of a saddle horse after eating a silk hat
- A watch or spectacles dropped on the ground
- Sudden drop in the value of securities
- Loss of contingent interest in property due to the unexpected death of a child

Filing Tip

$100 Floor for Married Couples

Where a husband and wife file a joint return, only one $100 floor applies to a casualty loss suffered by either spouse, whether the property is owned jointly or separately. If separate returns are filed, each spouse must reduce his or her half of the loss on jointly owned property by $100. If the property is owned by one spouse, only that spouse can claim a casualty loss on a separate return.

- Improper police seizure of private liquor stock
- Chinaware broken by a family pet
- Temporary fluctuation of property value
- Damage to property from local government construction project
- Fire purposely set by owner
- Engine damage due to failure to use antifreeze

Note: Some of the above items may be allowed as business expenses.

18.12 Floors for Personal-Use Property Losses

Casualty and theft losses to personal-use property are subject to "floors" that will reduce, and in some cases eliminate, your deduction. For each casualty or theft, a $100 reduction applies after the loss is computed under the steps at *18.13*. In addition, total personal casualty and theft losses (after the $100 reduction) are deductible only to the extent they exceed 10% of your adjusted gross income. However, neither the $100 reduction nor the 10% of adjusted gross income floor applies to personal losses attributable to Hurricane Katrina, Rita, or Wilma.

Filing Tip

Hurricane Katrina/Rita/Wilma Losses Not Subject to Reductions

Personal casualty or theft losses that were caused by 2005 Hurricane Katrina, Rita, or Wilma are not subject to the $100 per casualty/theft reduction and also are not subject to the 10% of adjusted gross income floor. Line 11 of Form 4684 specifically exempts these hurricane losses from the $100 reduction, and on Line 17 they are excluded from the 10% of adjusted gross income floor that otherwise applies on Line 19.

The $100 floor. The $100 floor reduces casualty and theft losses of property used for personal purposes; *see* Step 5 in *18.13*. The $100 floor does not apply to losses of business property or property held for the production of income such as securities. If property used both in business and personal activities is damaged, the $100 offset applies only to the loss allocated to personal use.

For each casualty or theft during the year, a separate $100 reduction applies. For example, if you are involved in five different casualties during the year, there will be a $100 offset applied to each of the five losses. But when two or more items of property are destroyed in one event, only one $100 offset is applied to the total loss. For example, a storm damages your residence and also your car parked in the driveway. You figure the loss on the residence and car separately, but only one $100 offset applies to the total loss.

The $100 floor is applied after taking into account insurance proceeds received and insurance you expect to receive in a later year.

The $100 floor applies separately to the loss of each individual whose property has been damaged by a single casualty, even where the damaged property is owned by two or more individuals. The only exception is for a married couple filing jointly who apply only one $100 floor to their losses from a single casualty.

EXAMPLES

1. Two sisters own and occupy a house that is damaged in a storm. Each sister applies the $100 floor to figure her separate deduction.
2. Your house is partially damaged by a fire that also damages the personal property of a houseguest. You are subject to one $100 floor and the houseguest is subject to a separate $100 floor.

10% AGI floor. The 10% adjusted gross income (AGI) floor applies to the total of all casualty and theft losses occurring during the taxable year to personal-use property. You must deduct 10% of your AGI from the total loss to determine your deduction. The Example below illustrates the application of the $100 floor to each separate casualty event and the 10% AGI floor to the total losses.

Filing Instruction

Reporting on Form 4684

If you are claiming a loss for personal-use property, use Section A on page 1 of Form 4684. If you suffered more than one casualty or theft during the year, use a separate Form 4684 for each one. The total deductible casualty or theft loss from Section A of Form 4684 is then entered on Line 19, Schedule A of Form 1040.

EXAMPLE

In January 2006, you have an uninsured jewelry theft loss of $1,000, and in July 2006 uninsured damage of $3,000 to your personal car. Your adjusted gross income is $25,000. If you itemize deductions, you may claim a deductible loss on Form 4684 of $1,300, figured as follows:

Theft loss	$1,000	
Less	100	$ 900
Car damage	3,000	
Less	100	2,900
Total loss		3,800
Less 10% of $25,000		2,500
Deductible loss		$1,300

Form **4684** | **Casualties and Thefts** | OMB No. 1545-0177

Department of the Treasury
Internal Revenue Service

▶ See separate instructions.
▶ Attach to your tax return.
▶ Use a separate Form 4684 for each casualty or theft.

2006
Attachment Sequence No. **26**

Name(s) shown on tax return | **Identifying number**

SECTION A—Personal Use Property (Use this section to report casualties and thefts of property **not** used in a trade or business or for income-producing purposes.)

1 Description of properties (show type, location, and date acquired for each property). Use a separate line for each property lost or damaged from the same casualty or theft.

Property **A** Residence 2-8-1979
Property **B** Furniture 3-15-1990
Property **C**
Property **D**

		Properties A	B	C	D
2 Cost or other basis of each property	2	76,000	5,000		
3 Insurance or other reimbursement (whether or not you filed a claim) (see instructions)	3	10,000	1,000		
Note: *If line 2 is* ***more*** *than line 3, skip line 4.*					
4 Gain from casualty or theft. If line 3 is **more** than line 2, enter the difference here and skip lines 5 through 9 for that column. See instructions if line 3 includes insurance or other reimbursement you did not claim, or you received payment for your loss in a later tax year.	4				
5 Fair market value **before** casualty or theft	5	217,500	2,500		
6 Fair market value **after** casualty or theft	6	202,500	-0-		
7 Subtract line 6 from line 5	7	15,000	2,500		
8 Enter the **smaller** of line 2 or line 7	8	15,000	2,500		
9 Subtract line 3 from line 8. If zero or less, enter -0-	9	5,000	1,500		

10 Casualty or theft loss. Add the amounts on line 9 in columns A through D	10	6,500
11 Enter the **smaller** of line 10 or $100. But if the loss arose in the Hurricane Katrina disaster area after August 24, 2005; Hurricane Rita disaster area after September 22, 2005; or Hurricane Wilma disaster area after October 22, 2005, and was caused by that particular hurricane, enter -0-	11	100
12 Subtract line 11 from line 10	12	6,400
Caution: *Use only one Form 4684 for lines 13 through 21.*		
13 Add the amounts on line 12 of all Forms 4684	13	6,400
14 Add the amounts on line 4 of all Forms 4684	14	-0-
15 • If line 14 is **more** than line 13, enter the difference here and on Schedule D. **Do not** complete the rest of this section (see instructions). • If line 14 is **less** than line 13, enter -0- here and go to line 16. • If line 14 is **equal** to line 13, enter -0- here. **Do not** complete the rest of this section.	15	-0-
16 If line 14 is **less** than line 13, enter the difference	16	6,400
17 Add the amounts on line 12 of all Forms 4684 on which you entered -0- on line 11	17	-0-
18 Is line 17 less than line 16? ☐ **No.** Stop. Enter the amount from line 16 on Schedule A (Form 1040), line 19. Estates and trusts, enter the amount from line 16 on the "Other deductions" line of your tax return. ☑ **Yes.** Subtract line 17 from line 16.	18	6,400
19 Enter 10% of your adjusted gross income from Form 1040, line 38. Estates and trusts, see instructions	19	4,800
20 Subtract line 19 from line 18. If zero or less, enter -0-	20	1,600
21 Add lines 17 and 20. Also enter the result on Schedule A (Form 1040), line 19. Estates and trusts, enter the result on the "Other deductions" line of your tax return	21	1,600

For Paperwork Reduction Act Notice, see page 4 of the instructions. Cat. No. 12997O Form **4684** (2006)

Exception for Hurricane Katrina, Rita, and Wilma casualty/theft losses. Personal casualty or theft losses attributable to Hurricane Katrina, Rita, or Wilma are deductible without regard to the $100 and 10% AGI floor floors. *See* the Filing Tip in *18.12* and follow the Form 4684 instructions.

18.13 Figuring Your Loss on Form 4684

Form 4684 is used to report casualties or thefts of personal-use property, business property, or income-producing property. The deductible loss is usually the difference between the fair market value of the property before and after the casualty or theft *less* (1) reimbursements received for the loss and (2) $100 if the property was used for personal purposes. However, the loss may not exceed your adjusted basis *(5.20)* for the property, which for many items will be your cost. If your adjusted basis is less than the loss in value, your deduction is limited to basis, less reimbursements and the $100 floor for personal-use assets. After figuring all allowable casualty and theft losses for personal-use property, the total is deductible only to the extent it exceeds the 10% adjusted gross income floor *(18.12)*.

Losses attributable to Hurricanes Katrina, Rita, and Wilma are *not subject to* the $100 reduction or the 10% of adjusted gross income floor; *see 18.12*.

Use the following five-step method for figuring the deductible amount.

Steps for calculating your deductible loss. The following five steps reflect the procedure on Form 4684 for computing a casualty or theft loss. If your loss is to business inventory, you do not have to use Form 4684, but may take the loss into account when figuring the cost of goods sold; *see* "Inventory losses" later in this section.

To figure your deductible loss, follow these five steps:

Step 1. Compute the loss in fair market value of the property. This is the difference between the fair market value immediately before and immediately after the casualty. You do *not* have to compute the loss in fair market value for business or income-producing property (such as a rental property) that has been *completely* destroyed or stolen; go to Step 2.

You will need written appraisals to support your claim for loss of value. You may not claim sentimental or aesthetic values or a fluctuation in property values caused by a casualty; you must deal with cost or market values of what has been lost. If the value of your property has been lowered because of damage to a nearby area, you do not have a deductible loss since your own property has not been damaged. No deduction may be claimed for estimated decline in value based on buyer resistance in an area subject to landslides.

For household items, the Tax Court has allowed losses based on cost less depreciation, rather than on the decrease in fair market value.

Step 2. Compute your adjusted basis for the property. This is usually the cost of the property plus the cost of improvements, less previous casualty loss deductions and depreciation if the property is used in business or for income-producing purposes. Unadjusted basis of property acquired other than by purchase is explained at *5.16*. Adjusted basis is explained at *5.20*.

Step 3. Take the lower amount of Step 1 or 2. For business or income-producing property that was stolen or completely destroyed, reduce adjusted basis from Step 2 by any salvage value.

Step 4. Reduce the loss in Step 3 by the insurance proceeds or other compensation for the loss; *see 18.16*. This is your deductible loss for business or income-producing property. If the property was used for personal purposes, apply the reductions in Step 5.

Step 5. If the property was used for personal purposes, the loss from Step 4 must be reduced by $100 and you may only deduct the balance to the extent it exceeds 10% of your adjusted gross income. Neither the $100 floor nor the 10% of AGI floor applies to losses from Hurricane Katrina, Rita, or Wilma. If you have more than one personal casualty or theft, reduce the total combined loss by 10% of adjusted gross income; only the excess is deductible; *see 18.12* and the Examples below.

Filing Tip

Business or Income-Producing Property

If you are claiming a loss for property used in your business or income-producing activity, use Section B on page 2 of Form 4684 (not shown here). Losses from income-producing property are entered on Line 27 of Schedule A as "other miscellaneous deductions" and are not subject to the 2% adjusted gross income floor.

EXAMPLES

1. Your home, which cost $76,000 in 1979, was damaged by a fire in 2006. The value of the house before the disaster was $217,500, but afterwards $202,500. Furniture that cost $5,000 in 1990 and was valued at $2,500 before the fire was totally destroyed. The insurance company reimbursed you $10,000 for your house damage and $1,000 for your furnishings. This was the only casualty for the year. Your adjusted gross income is $48,000. You figure your loss for the furniture separately from the loss on the house but apply only one $100 reduction *(18.11)* because the damage was from a single casualty. *See* the sample Form 4684 on page 373 for how this loss is reported.

1. Decrease in home's fair market value:	
Value of house before fire	$217,500
Value of house after fire	202,500
Decrease in value	$15,000
2. Adjusted basis:	$76,000
3. Loss sustained (lower of 1 or 2)	$15,000
Less: Insurance	10,000
Loss on house	$5,000
4. Loss on furnishings (decreased value)*	$2,500
Less: Insurance	1,000
Loss on furnishings	$1,500
5. Total loss ($5,000 and $1,500)	$6,500
Less: $100 floor	100
Casualty loss (subject to 10% floor)	$6,400
6. 10% AGI floor (10% of $48,000 AGI)	$4,800
7. Casualty loss ($6,400 – $4,800)	$1,600

*The loss for the furnishings on Line 4 is $2,500, the decrease in fair market value, as this is lower than the $5,000 basis.

2. Depreciable business property with a fair market value of $1,500 and an adjusted basis of $2,000 is totally destroyed. Because property used in your business was totally destroyed (*see* Step 3 on page 374), your loss is measured by your adjusted basis of $2,000, which is larger than the $1,500 loss in fair market value. Salvage value, if any, reduces your deduction, but you disregard the $100 floor applied to casualty losses on personal property. If the property was used for personal purposes, the loss would have been limited to the $1,500 loss in market value less $100, leaving a loss of $1,400 subject to the 10% adjusted gross income floor.

Business losses. Losses from business property are generally netted against gains from casualties or thefts on Form 4684 and the net gain or loss is entered on Form 4797. Follow the instructions to Form 4684 .

Inventory losses. A casualty or theft loss of inventory is automatically reflected on Schedule C in the cost of goods sold, which includes the lost items as part of your opening inventory. Any insurance or other reimbursement received for the loss must be included as sales income.

You may separately claim the inventory loss as a casualty or theft loss on Form 4684 instead of automatically claiming it as part of the cost of goods sold. If you do this, you must eliminate the items from inventory by lowering either opening inventory or purchases when figuring the cost of goods sold.

Cost less depreciation method for household items. The Tax Court has allowed casualty loss deductions based on cost less depreciation, rather than on the difference in fair market value immediately before and after the casualty. *See* the following Example.

EXAMPLE

Basing a deduction on the difference between the value of furnishings immediately before and immediately after a casualty may limit your deduction to the going price for secondhand furnishings. A homeowner whose furniture was destroyed by fire claimed that the fair market value immediately before the fire should be original cost less depreciation. He based his figures on an inventory prepared by certified public adjusters describing each item, its cost and age. The deduction figured this way came to approximately $27,500 ($55,000 cost, less $13,000 depreciation, a $14,400 insurance recovery, and the $100 floor).

Caution

Incidental Expenses

Expenses that are incidental to a casualty or theft, such as medical treatment for personal injury, temporary housing, fuel, moving, or rentals for temporary living quarters, are not deductible as casualty losses.

Filing Tip

Appraisals for Disaster Relief

The IRS may accept an appraisal that is used to obtain federal loans or loan guarantees following a Presidentially declared disaster as proof of the amount of a casualty loss.

The IRS estimated that the furniture was worth $15,304 before the fire and limited the deduction to $804 after accounting for the insurance and the $100 floor. The Tax Court disagreed. The householder's method of valuing his furniture is consistent with methods used by insurance adjusters who have an interest in keeping values low. He is not limited to the amount his property would bring if "hawked off by a secondhand dealer or at a forced sale." However, in another case, the court refused to allow the cost less depreciation formula where the homeowner's inventory list was based on memory.

18.14 Personal and Business Use of Property

For property held partly for personal use and partly for business or income-producing purposes, a casualty or theft loss deduction is computed as if two separate pieces of property were damaged, destroyed, or stolen. Follow the steps in *18.13* for figuring the allowable loss, but apply the $100 and 10% of adjusted gross income floors only to the personal part of the loss.

EXAMPLE

A building with two apartments, one used by the owner as his home and the other rented to a tenant, is damaged by a fire. The fair market value of the building before the fire was $169,000 and after the fire, $136,000. Its cost basis was $120,000. Depreciation taken before the fire was $14,000. The insurance company paid $20,000. The owner has adjusted gross income of $40,000. This is his only loss this year. He has a business casualty loss of $6,500 and a deductible personal casualty loss of $2,400 figured as follows:

	Business	*Personal*
1. Decrease in value of building:		
Value before fire ($169,000)	$84,500	$84,500
Value after fire ($136,000)	(68,000)	(68,000)
Decrease in value	$16,500	$16,500
2. Adjusted basis of building:	$60,000	$60,000
Less: Depreciation	(14,000)	
Adjusted basis	$46,000	$60,000
3. Loss sustained (lower of 1 or 2)	$16,500	$16,500
Less: Insurance (total $20,000)	($10,000)	($10,000)
4. Loss	$6,500	$6,500
Less: $100 floor and 10% of adjusted gross income	–	(4,100)
Deductible casualty loss	$6,500	$2,400

18.15 Repairs May Be a "Measure of Loss"

The cost of repairs may be treated as evidence of the loss of value (Step 1 in *18.13*), if the amount is not excessive and the repairs do nothing more than restore the property to its condition before the casualty. An estimate for repairs will not suffice; only actual repairs may be used as a measure of loss. However, where you measure your loss by comparing appraisals of value for before and after the casualty, repairs may be considered in arriving at a post-casualty value even though no actual repairs are made.

Deduction not limited to repairs. A casualty loss deduction is not limited to repair expenses where the decline in market value is greater, according to a federal appeals court; *see* the following Example.

Planning Reminder

Keep Records of Deductible Losses

If your property is damaged, you must reduce the basis of the damaged property by the casualty loss deduction and compensation received for the loss; *see 5.20.* When you later sell the property, gain or loss is the difference between the selling price and the reduced basis.

EXAMPLE

Connor claimed that the market value of his house dropped $93,000 after it was damaged by fire. His $52,000 cash outlay in repairing the house was reimbursed by insurance. He claimed a casualty loss of approximately $40,000, the uncompensated drop in market value. The IRS barred the deduction. The house was restored to pre-casualty condition. The cost of the repairs is a realistic measure of the loss, and, as the expense was fully compensated by insurance, Connor suffered no loss. A federal appeals court disagreed. The house dropped $70,000 in market value, of which $20,000 was uncompensated by insurance. The deduction is measured by the uncompensated difference in value before and after the casualty. It is not limited to the cost of repairs, even where the repair expense is less than the difference in fair market values. Had the repairs cost more than this difference, the IRS would not have allowed a larger deduction.

18.16 Insurance Reimbursements

You reduce the amount of your loss *(18.13)* by insurance proceeds, voluntary payments received from your employer for damage to your property, and cash or property received from the Red Cross. Also reduce your loss by reimbursements you expect to receive in a later year; *see 18.2.* However, cash gifts from friends and relatives to help defray the cost of repairs do not reduce the loss where there are no conditions on the use of the gift. Also, gifts of food, clothing, medical supplies, and other forms of subsistence do not reduce the loss deduction nor are they taxable income.

Cancellation of part of a disaster loan under the Disaster Relief Act is treated as a partial reimbursement of the loss and reduces the amount of the loss. Payments from an urban renewal agency to acquire your damaged property under the Federal Relocation Act of 1970 are considered reimbursements reducing the loss.

Insurance payments for the cost of added living expenses because of damage to a home do not reduce a casualty loss. The payments are treated as separate and apart from payments for property damage. Payments for excess living costs are generally not taxable; *see 18.17.*

Passive activity property loss reimbursements. A reimbursement of a casualty or theft loss deduction is not considered passive activity income if the original loss was not treated as a passive deduction; *see 10.1.* The reimbursement may be taxed under the rule discussed at *11.6.*

Realizing a gain from insurance. If you receive insurance proceeds in excess of your adjusted basis for the property, you generally realize a gain, which you may be able to defer by buying replacement property; *see 18.19.*

Caution

Failure To Make an Insurance Claim

If you are insured for your full loss and do not file a claim because you do not want to risk cancellation of liability coverage, you may not claim a deduction. If you do not file an insurance claim but your loss exceeds the coverage, the noncovered loss may be deductible. For example, if you have a $2,500 deductible on your personal automobile insurance policy, a loss of up to $2,500 would be reduced by the $100 floor and the balance would be deductible only to the extent the 10% of adjusted gross income floor was exceeded (*see* Step 5 in *18.13*).

18.17 Excess Living Costs Paid by Insurance Are Not Taxable

Your insurance contract may reimburse you for excess living costs when a casualty or a threat of casualty forces you to vacate your house. The payment is tax free if these tests are met:

1. Your principal residence is damaged or destroyed by fire, storm, or other casualty or you are denied use of it by a governmental order because of the occurrence or threat of the casualty.
2. You are paid under an insurance contract for living expenses resulting from the loss of occupancy or use of the residence.

Whether you have a taxable or tax-free reimbursement is figured at the end of the period you were unable to use your residence. Thus, if the dislocation covers more than one taxable year, the taxable income, if any, will be reported in the taxable year in which the dislocation ended.

The tax-free amount includes only excess living costs paid by the insurance company. The excess is the difference between (1) the actual living expenses incurred during the time you could not use or occupy your house and (2) the normal living expenses that you would have incurred for yourself and members of your household during the period. Living expenses during the period may include the cost of renting suitable housing and extraordinary expenses for transportation, food, utilities, and miscellaneous services. The expenses must be incurred for items and services (such as laundry) needed to maintain your standard of living that you enjoyed before the loss and must be covered by the policy.

Where a lump-sum settlement does not identify the amount covering living expenses, an allocation is required to determine the tax-free portion. In the case of uncontested claims, the tax-free portion is that part of the settlement that bears the same ratio to total recovery as increased living expense bears to total loss and expense. If your claim is contested, you must show the amount reasonably allocable to increased living expenses consistent with the terms of the insurance contract, but not in excess of coverage limitations specified in the contract.

The exclusion from income does not cover insurance reimbursements for loss of rental income or for loss of or damage to real or personal property; such reimbursements for property damage reduce your casualty loss; *see 18.16.*

If your home is used for both residential and business purposes, the exclusion does not apply to insurance proceeds and expenses attributable to the nonresidential portion of the house. There is no exclusion for insurance recovered for expenses resulting from governmental condemnation or order unrelated to a casualty or threat of casualty.

The insurance reimbursement may cover part of your normal living expenses as well as the excess expenses due to the casualty. The part covering normal expenses is income; it does not reduce your casualty loss.

EXAMPLES

1. On March 1, your home was damaged by fire. While it was being repaired, you and your spouse lived at a motel and ate meals at restaurants. Costs are $1,200 at the motel, $1,000 for meals, and $75 for laundry services. You make the required March payment of $790 on your home mortgage. Your customary $40 commuting expense is $20 less for the month because the motel is closer to your work. Your usual commuting expense is therefore treated as not being incurred to the extent of the $20 decrease. Furthermore, you do not incur your customary $700 food expense for meals at home, $75 for utilities, and $60 for laundry at home. Your insurance company pays you $1,700 for expenses. The tax-free exclusion for insurance payments is limited to $1,420, computed in the third column below. On Line 21 of Form 1040 ("Other income") you must report as income $280 ($1,700 – $1,420).

	Expenses from casualty	*Expenses not incurred*	*Increase (Decrease)*
Housing	$1,200		$1,200
Utilities		$75	(75)
Meals	1,000	700	300
Transportation		20	(20)
Laundry	75	60	15
Total	$2,275	$855	$1,420

2. Same facts as in Example 1 except that you rented the residence for $400 per month and the risk of loss was to the landlord. You did not pay the March rent. The excludable amount is $1,020 ($1,420 less $400 normal rent not incurred). You would have to report as income the excess of the insurance received over the $1,020 exclusion.

18.18 Do Your Casualty or Theft Losses Exceed Your Income?

If your 2006 casualty or theft losses exceed your income, you pay no tax in 2006. You may also carry the excess loss back to 2003 and file a refund claim for that year. Any remaining loss may be carried back to 2004 and 2005 and carried forward to 2007 through 2026, or you may just carry your loss forward 20 years until it is used up. The excess casualty loss is carried back or forward as a net operating loss. *See 40.18* for net operating loss rules.

Note: The $100 and 10% of adjusted gross income floors for personal casualty losses apply only in the year of loss; you do not again reduce your loss in the carryback or carryover years.

Taxable Gain From Involuntary Conversions

Filing Tip

Involuntary Conversion of Personal Residence

Gain on the conversion may escape tax under the rules discussed in Chapter 29. If not, tax may be deferred under the involuntary conversion replacement rules.

18.19 Defer Gain by Replacing Property

If your property is destroyed, damaged, stolen, or taken by a government authority, this is considered to be an *involuntary conversion* for tax purposes. If upon an involuntary conversion you receive insurance or other compensation that exceeds the adjusted basis of the property, you realize a gain that is taxable unless you may defer gain under the rules in *18.20–18.24* or, in the case of a principal residence, you may exclude gain under the rules in Chapter 29.

You may elect to postpone tax on the full gain provided you invest the proceeds in replacement property the cost of which is equal to or exceeds the net proceeds from the conversion. Buying a replacement from a related party generally qualifies only if your gains from involuntary conversions are $100,000 or less *(see 18.23)*. Gain realized on a destroyed or condemned principal residence that exceeds the allowable exclusion under the rules in Chapter 29 may be postponed by reinvesting at least the conversion proceeds minus the excluded gain. Reinvestment requirements are discussed at *18.20–18.24*. The replacement period for personal-use property is two years; for business and investment property it is two or three years depending on the type of involuntary conversion; for a residence and its contents involuntarily converted due to a Presidentially declared disaster *(see 18.3)* it is four years. The replacement period is extended to five years for property damaged by Hurricane Katrina, or by the September 11 attacks in the New York Liberty Zone, provided substantially all of the use of the replacement property is in the Hurricane Katrina disaster area or in New York City. *See 18.22* for further replacement period details.

Basis in replacement property. Your basis in the replacement property is its replacement cost, minus any postponed gain. If you find that you cannot buy a replacement by the end of the period, ask the IRS for an extension of time *(see 18.22)*.

18.20 Involuntary Conversions Qualifying for Tax Deferral

For purposes of an election to defer tax on gains, "involuntary conversion" is more broadly defined than "casualty loss." You have an involuntary conversion when your property is:

Damaged or destroyed by some outside force.

Stolen, seized, requisitioned, or condemned by a governmental authority. If you voluntarily sell land made useless to you by the condemnation of your adjacent land, the sale may also qualify as a conversion. Condemnation of property as unfit for human habitation does not qualify. Condemnation, as used by the tax law, refers to the taking of private property for public use, not to the condemnation of property for noncompliance with housing and health regulations. Similarly, a tax sale to pay delinquent taxes is not an involuntary conversion.

Sold under a threat of seizure, condemnation, or requisition. The threat must be made by an authority qualified to take property for public use. A sale following a threat of condemnation made by a government employee is a conversion if you reasonably believe he or she speaks with authority and could and would carry out the threat to have your property condemned. If you learn of the plan of an imminent condemnation from a newspaper or other news media, the IRS requires you to confirm the report from a government official before you act on the news.

Farmers. Farmers also have involuntary conversions when:

Land is sold within an irrigation project to meet federal acreage limitations ;

Cattle are destroyed by disease or sold because of disease; *or*

Draft, breeding, or dairy livestock is sold because of drought. The election to treat the sale as a conversion is limited to livestock sold over the number that would have been sold but for the drought.

In some cases, livestock may be replaced with other farm property where there has been soil or other environmental contamination.

Should you elect to postpone gain? An election gives an immediate advantage: tax on gain is postponed and the funds that would have been spent to pay the tax may be used for other investments.

However, as a condition of deferring tax, the basis of the replacement property is generally fixed at the same adjusted basis as the converted property. If your reinvestment exceeds the insurance proceeds, the excess increases the basis of the replacement property. As long as the value of the replacement property does not decline, tax on the original gain is finally incurred when the property is sold.

Special rules for federally declared disaster areas are discussed at *18.3*.

EXAMPLE

Assume a rental building is destroyed by fire and a proper replacement is made. Assume that gain on the receipt of the insurance proceeds is taxable as capital gain. An election is generally not advisable if you have capital losses to offset the gain. However, even if you have no capital losses, you may still decide not to make the election and pay tax in order to fix, for purposes of depreciation, the basis of the new property at its purchase price, if the future depreciation deductions will offset income taxable at a higher rate than the current tax. If there is little or no difference between the two rates so that a net after-tax benefit from the depreciation would not arise, an election might be made solely to postpone the payment of tax.

18.21 How To Elect To Defer Tax

To defer tax on your gain, do not report the gain as income for the year it is realized. Attach to your return a statement giving details of the transaction, including computation of the gain and your intention to buy a replacement if you have not yet done so. *See 18.22* for replacement periods and IRS notification requirements.

Planning Reminder

Basis Reduction

Consider whether postponement of gain at the expense of a reduced basis for property is advisable, compared to the tax consequences of reporting the gain in the year it is realized.

Law Alert

Sale of Property Under Hazard Mitigation Program

A sale or other transfer of vulnerable property to federal, state, or local authorities (or Indian tribal governments) under a hazard mitigation program is treated as an involuntary conversion, thereby allowing a gain to be deferred if a qualifying replacement *(see 18.19)* is made.

If your property is condemned and you are given similar property, no election is necessary. Postponement of tax on the gain is required. For example, the city condemns a store building and gives you another store building the value of which exceeds the cost basis of the old one; gain is not taxed.

Partnerships. The election to defer gain must be made at the partnership level. Individual partners may not make separate elections unless the partnership has terminated, with all partnership affairs wound up. Dissolution under state law is not a termination for tax purposes.

18.22 Time Period for Buying Replacement Property

To defer tax, you generally must buy property similar or related in use *(18.23)* to the converted property within a fixed time period. The replacement period is either two, three, four years or five:

1. A two-year replacement period applies for destroyed, damaged, or stolen property, whether used for business, investment, or personal purposes, but there is a four-year period for principal residences in Presidentially declared disaster areas *(18.3)*. The two-year period for damaged, destroyed, and stolen property *starts* on the date the property was destroyed, damaged, or stolen, and *ends* two years after the end of the year in which any part of your gain is realized. A two-year period also applies to a condemned residence.
2. A three-year replacement period applies for condemned business or investment real estate, excluding inventory. However, the two-year and not the three-year period applies if the condemned business or investment real estate is replaced by your acquiring control of a corporation that owns the replacement property.
3. A four-year replacement period applies for a principal residence or its contents involuntarily converted as a result of a Presidentially declared disaster; *see 18.3*. The four-year replacement period *starts* on the date the residence is involuntarily converted and *ends* four years after the end of the first taxable year in which any part of the gain is realized.
4. A five-year replacement period applies for property in the New York Liberty Zone that was damaged or destroyed as a result of the September 11, 2001, terrorist attacks, but only if substantially all of the use of the replacement property is in New York City.
5. A five-year replacement period applies for property damaged or destroyed by Hurricane Katrina, but only if substantially all of the use of the replacement property is in the Hurricane Katrina disaster area.

Planning Reminder

Extension of Time To Replace

Within the time limits, you must buy replacement property rather than merely contracting to do so. If you cannot replace property within the time required, ask your local IRS area director for additional time. Apply for an extension before the end of the period. If you apply for an extension within a reasonable time after the statutory period has run out, you must have a reasonable cause for the delay in asking for the extension.

Replacing condemned property. For condemnations, the replacement period starts on the earlier of (1) the date you receive notification of the condemnation threat or (2) the date you dispose of the condemned property. Depending on the replacement period (*see* above), the period ends two, three, four, or five years after the end of the first year in which any part of the gain on the condemnation is realized. You may make a replacement after a threat of condemnation. If you buy property before the actual threat, it will not qualify as a replacement even though you still own it at the time of the actual condemnation.

EXAMPLES

1. On January 10, 2006, a parcel of investment real estate is condemned; the parcel cost $15,000. On February 28, 2006, you received a check for $23,500 from the state. You may defer the tax on the gain of $8,500 if you invest at least $23,500 in other real estate not later than December 31, 2009, the end of the three-year replacement period.
2. Business property was contaminated by dangerous chemicals, and after the Environmental Protection Agency ordered businesses and residents to relocate, the property was sold to the local government under a threat of condemnation. The owner was paid the full pre-contamination fair market value for the property. The owner wanted to defer gain under the three-year replacement rule for condemnations. However, the IRS said that part of the gain was deferrable under the two-year rule and part under the three-year rule. There were two conversions: (1) the contamination, subject to the two-year replacement rule; and (2) the later condemnation, subject to the three-year rule.

   To determine the amount eligible for deferral for each period, an allocation must be made between the proceeds allocable to the destruction of the property and the proceeds allocable to the condemnation.

   According to the IRS, the burden for making the allocation between the two conversions rests with the owner. The government's payments are allocable to the condemnation and, therefore, eligible for the three-year replacement rule, only to the extent of the post-contamination value. Practically speaking, it may be advisable to make the replacement within the two-year period, as it may be difficult to show the contaminated land had any value after the contamination.

Advance payment of award. Gain is realized in the year compensation for the converted property exceeds the basis of the converted property. An advance payment of an award that exceeds the adjusted basis of the property starts the running of the replacement period.

An award is treated as received in the year that it is made available to you without restrictions, even if you contest the amount.

Replacement by an estate. A person whose property was involuntarily converted may die before he or she makes a replacement. According to the IRS, his or her estate may not reinvest the proceeds within the allowed time and postpone tax on the gain. The Tax Court rejects the IRS position and has allowed tax deferral where the replacement was made by the deceased owner's estate. However, the Tax Court agreed with the IRS that a surviving spouse's investment in land did not defer tax on gain realized by her deceased husband on an involuntary conversion of his land. She had received his property as survivor of joint tenancy and could not, in making the investment, be considered as acting for his estate.

Giving IRS notice of replacement. If you have not bought replacement property by the time you file your return for the year of the involuntary conversion but you intend to do so, attach a statement to your return describing the conversion and the computation of gain, and state that you intend to make a timely replacement. Then, on the return for the year of replacement, attach a statement giving the details of your replacement property. This notice starts the running of the period of limitations for any tax on the gain. Failure to give notice keeps the period open. Similarly, a failure to give notice of an intention not to replace also keeps the period open. When you do not buy replacement property after making an election to postpone tax on the gain, file an amended return for the year in which gain was realized and pay the tax (if any) on the gain.

Assume you have a gain from an involuntary conversion and do not expect to reinvest the proceeds. You report the gain and pay the tax. In a later year, but within the prescribed time limits, you buy similar property. You may make an election to defer tax on the gain and file a claim for tax refund.

Caution

Nullifying Deferral Election on Amended Return

If you elect to defer tax on a gain, intending to buy replacement property, but you fail to make a replacement within the time limit, you must file an amended return for the year of the gain and pay the tax that you had elected to defer. You also must file an amended return and report the gain not eligible for deferral if you invest in property that does not qualify as a replacement, or which costs less than the amount realized from the involuntary conversion.

However, if you elect to defer and make a timely qualifying replacement, you may not change your mind and pay tax on the gain in order to obtain a higher basis *(18.20)* for the replacement property. The Tax Court has agreed with the IRS that the election to defer is irrevocable once a qualified replacement is made within the time limits. Similarly, once you report to the IRS *(18.22)* that a qualified replacement has been made, you may not substitute other replacement property, even if the replacement period has not yet expired.

18.23 Types of Qualifying Replacement Property

Although exact duplication is not required, the replacement generally must be *similar* or *related in service or use* to the property that was involuntarily converted in order to defer tax. Where *real property* held for productive use in a business or for investment is converted through a *condemnation* or threat of condemnation, the replacement test is more liberal. A replacement merely has to be of a *like kind* to the converted property.

Under the *like-kind* test, the replacement of condemned real estate with other real estate qualifies. Improved real property may be replaced by unimproved real property; *see 6.1*. Foreign and U.S. real property are considered to be of like kind for purposes of this test.

Under the *related-service/use* test, the replacement of unimproved land for improved land does not qualify. A replacement generally must be closely related in function to the destroyed property. For example, a condemned personal residence must be replaced with another personal residence. The replacement of a house rented to a tenant with a house used as a personal residence does not qualify for tax deferral; the new house is not being used for the same purpose as the condemned one. This functional test, however, is not strictly applied to conversions of rental property. Here, the role of the owner toward the properties, rather than the functional use of the buildings, is reviewed. If an owner held both properties as investments and offered similar services and took similar business risks in both, the replacement may qualify.

You may own several parcels of property, one of which is condemned. You may want to use the condemnation award to make improvements on the other land such as drainage and grading. The IRS generally will not accept the improvements as a qualified replacement. However, an appeals court has rejected the IRS approach in one case.

If it is not feasible to reinvest the proceeds from the conversion of livestock because of soil contamination or other environmental contamination, then other property (including real property) used for farming purposes is treated as similar or related and qualifies as replacement property.

Caution

Buying Replacement From Relative

Buying a replacement from a relative or related business organization will not defer gain unless total gains from involuntary conversions for the year are $100,000 or less.

Deferral may be barred when buying a replacement from a relative. The gain deferral rules do not apply if you buy a replacement from a close relative or a related business organization unless the total gain you realized for the year on all involuntary conversions on which there are realized gains is $100,000 or less. In determining whether gains exceed $100,000, gains are not offset by losses. Affected related parties are the same as defined for loss transactions discussed at *5.6*.

Buying controlling interest in acorporation. The replacement test may be satisfied by purchasing a controlling interest (80%) in a corporation owning property that is similar or related in service to the converted property.

Business and investment property in a disaster area. The similar or related-use tests do not have to be met when replacing business or investment property damaged or destroyed in a Presidentially declared disaster area. You may make a qualified replacement by buying any tangible property held for business use.

18.24 Cost of Replacement Property Determines Postponed Gain

To fully defer tax on the replacement of involuntarily converted property *(18.20)*, the cost of the replacement property must be equal to or exceed the net proceeds from the conversion. If replacement cost is no more than the adjusted basis of the converted property, you report the entire gain. If replacement cost is less than the amount realized on the conversion but more than the basis of the converted property, the difference between the amount realized and the cost of the replacement is reported as gain; you may elect to postpone tax on the balance of the gain. *See* Examples 1–3 below.

Condemnation award. The award received from a state authority may be reduced by expenses of getting the award such as legal, engineering, and appraisal fees. The treatment of special assessments and severance damages received when part of your property is condemned is explained at *18.25*. Payments made directly by the authority to your mortgagee may not be deducted from the gross award.

Do not include as part of the award interest paid on the award for delay in its payment; you report the interest as interest income. The IRS may treat as interest part of an award paid late, even though the award does not make any allocation for interest.

Relocation payments are not considered part of the condemnation award and are not treated as taxable income to the extent that they are spent for purposes of relocation; they increase basis of the newly acquired property.

Distinguish between insurance proceeds compensating you for loss of profits because of business interruption and those compensating you for the loss of property. Business interruption proceeds are fully taxed as ordinary income and may not be treated as proceeds of an involuntary conversion.

A single standard fire insurance policy may cover several assets. Assume a fire occurs, and in a settlement the proceeds are allocated to each destroyed item according to its fair market value before the fire. In comparing the allocated proceeds to the tax basis of each item, you find that on some items, you have realized a gain; that is, the proceeds exceed basis. On the other items, you have a loss; the proceeds are less than basis. According to the IRS, you may elect to defer tax on the gain items by buying replacement property. You do not treat the proceeds paid under the single policy as a unit, but as separate payments made for each covered item.

EXAMPLES

1. The cost basis of your four-family apartment house is $175,000. It is condemned to make way for a thruway. After expenses, the net award from the state is $200,000. Your gain is $25,000. If you buy a similar apartment house for $175,000 or less, you report the entire $25,000 gain.
2. Same facts as in Example 1, except that you buy an apartment house for $185,000. Of the gain of $25,000, you report $15,000 as taxable gain ($200,000 – $185,000). You may elect to postpone the tax on the balance of the gain, or $10,000. If you elect deferral, your basis for the new building is $175,000 ($185,000 – $10,000 postponed gain).
3. Same facts as in Example 1, but you buy an apartment house for $200,000. You may elect to postpone tax on the entire gain because you have invested all of the award in replacement property.

18.25 Special Assessments and Severance Damages

When only part of a property parcel is *condemned* for a public improvement, the condemning authority may:

1. Levy a special assessment against the remaining property, claiming that it is benefitted by the improvement. The authority usually deducts the assessment from the condemnation award.
2. Grant an award for severance damages if the condemnation of part of your property causes a loss in value or damage to the remaining property that you keep.

Special assessments reduce the amount of the gross condemnation award. If they exceed the award, the excess is added to the basis of the property. An assessment levied after the award is made may not be deducted from the award.

EXAMPLE

Two acres of a 10-acre tract are condemned for a new highway. The adjusted basis of the land is $30,000, or $3,000 per acre. The condemnation award is $10,000; the special assessment against the remaining eight acres is $2,500. The net gain on the condemnation is $1,500:

Condemnation award		$10,000
Less:		
Basis of two condemned acres	$6,000	
Special assessment	2,500	8,500
Net gain		$1,500

When both the condemnation award and severance damages are received, the condemnation is treated as two separate involuntary conversions: (1) A conversion of the condemned land. Here, the condemnation award is applied against the basis of the condemned land to determine gain or loss on its conversion; and (2) a conversion of part of the remaining land in the sense that its utility has been reduced by condemnation, for which severance damages are paid.

Net severance damages reduce the basis of the retained property. Net severance damages are the total severance damages, reduced by expenses in obtaining the damages and by any special assessment withheld from the condemnation award. If the damages exceed basis, gain is realized. Tax may be deferred on the gain through the purchase of replacement property under the "similar or related in service or use" test at *18.23*, such as adjacent land or restoration of the property to its original condition.

Allocating the proceeds between the condemnation award and severance damages will either reduce the gain or increase the loss realized on the condemned land. The IRS will allow such a division only when the condemnation authority specifically identifies part of the award as severance damage in the contract or in an itemized statement or closing sheet. The Tax Court, however, has allowed an allocation in the absence of earmarking where the state considered severance damages, and the value of the condemned land was small in comparison to the damages suffered by the remaining property. To avoid a dispute with the IRS, make sure the authority makes this breakdown. Without such identification, the IRS will treat the entire proceeds as consideration for the condemned property.

18.26 Reporting Gains From Casualties

If an involuntary conversion was the result of a *theft* or *casualty*, you have to prepare Form 4684. To report net gains, Form 4684 will direct you to Form 1040, Schedule D, or Form 4797, depending on the type of property involved. Generally, use of Form 4797 reflects the netting requirements for involuntary conversions of business, rental, or royalty property under Section 1231; *see 44.8*.

If the conversion occurred because of a *condemnation*, you use Form 4797 for business or investment property and Schedule D for personal-use property.

1040 *Filing Instruction*

Business and Income-Producing Property

Follow the instructions to Form 4684 for reporting gains or losses from casualties and thefts of property used in a business or held for the production of income.

Chapter 19

Deducting Job Costs and Other Miscellaneous Expenses

On Schedule A (Form 1040), you may be able to deduct a portion of miscellaneous expenses covering a wide and varied range of items, such as employee travel and entertainment expenses, work clothes expenses, union and employee professional dues, investment expenses, legal expenses, tax preparation expenses, and educational expenses. They share a significant limitation: the 2% of adjusted gross income (AGI) floor. If your expenses do not exceed this floor, you may not deduct them. If the expenses exceed the floor, only the excess is deductible on Schedule A, as explained in *19.1*. Some miscellaneous expenses, such as gambling losses and impairment-related work expenses, are not subject to the 2% AGI floor.

In addition to the 2% AGI floor, employees who incur unreimbursed meal and entertainment costs face this further restriction: Only 50% of meal and entertainment costs are deductible.

Finally, miscellaneous deductions, except for gambling losses, are subject to the 3% reduction to itemized deductions *(13.7)* if your adjusted gross income exceeds $150,500 ($75,250 if you are married and file separate returns).

Miscellaneous Expenses on Schedule A

19.1 2% AGI Floor Reduces Most Miscellaneous Expenses

A floor of 2% of adjusted gross income (AGI) applies to the total of most miscellaneous deductions that are claimed on Schedule A of Form 1040. AGI is the amount on Lines 37 and 38 of Form 1040. The purpose of the floor is to reduce or eliminate such deductions. Only expenses above the floor are deductible.

If your 2006 AGI exceeds $150,500, or $75,250 if married filing separately, deductible miscellaneous expenses (after applying the 2% AGI floor) are then subject to a further reduction under the 3% reduction computation discussed at *13.7*.

Caution

AMT Disallowance

Even if you are able to deduct for regular tax purposes a portion of miscellaneous expenses because they exceed the 2% AGI floor, you will lose the benefit of that deduction if you are subject to alternative minimum tax (AMT). The deduction from Schedule A for miscellaneous expenses (after the 2% floor) must be added back to income in determining whether you are liable for AMT; *see 23.2.*

Miscellaneous expenses subject to the 2% AGI floor include:

- Unreimbursed travel, meals, and entertainment expenses of employees on trips away from home, *20.1* and *20.30*
- Taxable reimbursements of job expenses or taxable expense allowances under non-accountable plans, *20.34*
- Unreimbursed local transportation costs of visiting clients or customers, *19.8*
- Union dues, *19.5*
- Professional and business association dues, *19.5*
- Work clothes expenses, *19.6*
- Cost of looking for a new job, *19.7*
- Job agency fees, *19.7*
- Tax advice and preparation fees, *19.16*
- Appraisal fees related to casualty losses and charitable property contributions, *19.16*
- Investment costs, e.g, IRA custodial fees, safe-deposit rentals, and fees to investment counselors, *19.15*
- Employee home office expenses, *19.13*
- Legal fees for recovering taxable job-related or personal damages, *19.17*
- Work-related education costs, *33.15*
- Business bad debt on a loan made to your employer to protect your job, *5.33*

Miscellaneous expenses not subject to the 2% AGI floor include:

- Casualty and theft losses from income-producing property, *18.13*
- Impairment-related work expenses for disabled employees, *19.4*
- Gambling losses up to gambling income, *11.3*
- Estate tax attributable to income in respect of a decedent, *11.16*
- The deduction for repayment of amounts held under a claim of right, *2.8*
- Amortizable bond premium on bonds purchased before October 23, 1986, *4.17*
- Unrecovered investments in pension on deceased retiree's final return, *7.22*

Caution

2% AGI Floor

Most miscellaneous deductions are subject to a floor of 2% of your adjusted gross income (AGI), which may limit or bar a deduction. Your AGI is the amount on Line 37 of Form 1040; it is shown again on Line 38.

EXAMPLES

1. You pay union dues of $380, work clothes costs of $400, and $150 for the preparation of your tax return. Your adjusted gross income (AGI) is $35,000. Your miscellaneous deduction on Schedule A after applying the 2% floor is $230:

Union dues	$380
Work clothes	400
Tax preparation	150
	$930
Less: 2% of $35,000	700
Deductible amount	$230

2. Your adjusted gross income (AGI) is $90,000. You pay the following deductible miscellaneous expenses:

Professional dues	$100
Investment counsel fee	300
Safe-deposit box	50
Tax preparation fee	500
Unreimbursed travel expenses	800
	$1,750

Since the 2% floor of $1,800 (2% × $90,000) exceeds your miscellaneous expenses, none of the expenses are deductible.

19.2 Effect of 2% AGI Floor on Deductions

The table below shows the effect of the 2% AGI floor on miscellaneous deductible expenses. A higher bracket taxpayer may also be subject to the 3% reduction to itemized deductions discussed at *13.7*.

If your adjusted gross income (AGI) is—	*Only miscellaneous expenses exceeding this amount are deductible—*
$10,000	$200
20,000	400
30,000	600
40,000	800
50,000	1,000
60,000	1,200
70,000	1,400
80,000	1,600
90,000	1,800
100,000	2,000
200,000	4,000

Job Expenses

19.3 Checklist of Job Expenses Subject to the 2% AGI Floor

The following expenses that are job related—ranging from professional dues and subscriptions to employment agency fees—are subject to the 2% AGI floor and so you may be unable to deduct them; *see 19.2.* Generally, you must file Form 2106 to claim job-related expenses that were not reimbursed by your employer. You enter your expenses and any reimbursements on Form 2106, and the allowable amount is then transferred to Line 20 of Schedule A (unreimbursed employee expenses), where it is subject to the 2% AGI floor along with other miscellaneous deductions; *see 19.1.* If you are using the standard mileage rate *(43.1)* for 2006 vehicle expenses, and you were not reimbursed by your employer for any job expenses, you may file Form 2106-EZ to report your auto and other job expenses.

You may enter your unreimbursed expenses directly on Line 20 of Schedule A without having to complete Form 2106 or Form 2106-EZ if you are not claiming any job-related travel, local transportation, meal, or entertainment expenses and you received no employer reimbursement at all for any of your other job costs (such as education expenses, union dues, or uniforms).

Filing Instruction

Form 2106 or 2106-EZ

You generally must report your job-related expenses, and any employer reimbursements, on Form 2106. Form 2106-EZ is a shorter form that you may use if none of your job expenses are reimbursed and you deduct car expenses, if any, using the IRS flat mileage allowance.

Airfares, *20.5*
Auto club membership, *43.2*
Auto expenses, *19.4, 43.1*
Books used on the job, *19.5*
Bond costs, *19.15*
Business bad debt for loan to employer, *5.33*
Car insurance premiums, *43.2*
Cleaning costs, *19.6*
Commerce association dues, *19.5*
Commuting costs, *20.2*
Computers, *19.10*
Convention trips, *20.12* and *20.14*
Correspondence course, *19.16*
Depreciation, *42.1*
Dues, *19.5*
Educational expenses, *33.13*
Employment agency fees, *19.7*
Entertainment expenses, *20.15–20.29*
Equipment, *19.10–19.12*
Foreign travel costs, *20.11* and *20.14*
Furniture, *19.13*
Garage rent, *43.2*
Gasoline, *43.2*
Gasoline taxes, *43.2*
Gifts, *20.25*
Home office expenses, *19.13*
Hotel costs, *20.5*
Job-hunting costs, *19.7*
Labor union dues, *19.5*
Laundry, *19.6*
Legal expenses, *19.17*
Local transportation and travel away from home, *20.1*
Lodging, *20.5*
Magazines, *19.5*
Malpractice liability premiums, *40.6*
Meals, *20.3* and *20.4*
Medical examinations, *17.2*
Membership dues and fees, *19.5*
Motel charges, *20.5*
Moving expenses, *12.7*
Parking fees, *43.2*
Passport fees for business travel, *20.11*
Pay turned over to employer, *2.9*
Periodicals, *19.5*
Protective clothing, *19.6*
Rail fares, *20.5*
Reimbursed expenses, *20.30–20.34*
Safety helmets, *19.6*
Safety shoes, *19.6*
Secretarial convention, *20.12*
Subscriptions, *19.5*
Taxi fares, *20.5*
Telephone calls, *19.14*
Toll charges, *43.2*
Tools, *19.12*
Trade association dues, *19.5*
Tuition, *33.13*
Typewriter, *19.11*
Uniforms, *19.6*
Union dues, *19.5*
Work clothes, *19.6*

19.4 Job Expenses Not Subject to the 2% AGI Floor

Expenses of teachers, instructors, counselors, principals, or aides. Legislation allowing the education expense deduction to be claimed for 2006 had not yet been enacted when this book went to press, although an extension was expected. If the extension occurs, eligible costs may be claimed subject to the limitations discussed in *12.2*. *See* the *e-Supplement* for a legislation update.

Impairment-related work expenses. Unreimbursed impairment-related work expenses are reported on Form 2106 (or Form 2106-EZ where eligible) and then the unreimbursed portion is entered on Line 27 of Schedule A as a miscellaneous itemized deduction that is *not* subject to the 2% AGI floor. You have to show:

1. You are physically or mentally disabled. The physical or mental disability must result in a functional limitation of employment that substantially limits one or more major life activities. Generally, showing blindness or deafness will meet this test, but other disabilities that impair your ability to walk, speak, breathe, or perform manual tasks also may qualify if they limit the ability to work.
2. You incur the expenses in order to work. The expenses must be ordinary and necessary to allow you to work. Attendant care services at a place of employment that are necessary for you to work are also deductible.

Expenses of performing artists. As a performing artist, you may deduct job expenses from gross income, whether or not itemized deductions are claimed, *see 12.2*.

You report the performing artist expenses on Form 2106 (or Form 2106-EZ where eligible) and enter the total on Line 24 of Form 1040, instead of on Schedule A. If you do not meet the tests, the expenses are deducted on Schedule A subject to the 2% AGI floor.

Moving expenses. Moving expenses to a new job location, although job related, are deducted directly from gross income on Form 1040, Line 26, and not as an itemized deduction on Schedule A.

Filing Tip

Life Insurance Agents and Food Deliverers

Statutory employees, such as full-time life insurance salespersons, may deduct expenses on Schedule C and so avoid the 2% AGI floor; *see 40.6* for further details.

19.5 Dues and Subscriptions

You may deduct as miscellaneous itemized deductions, subject to the 2% AGI floor on Schedule A, dues paid to a:

- Professional society if you are a salaried lawyer, accountant, teacher, physician, or other professional
- Trade association when conducted for the purpose of furthering the business interests of its members
- Stock exchange if you are a securities dealer
- Community "booster" club conducted to attract tourists and settlers to the locality where the members do business
- Chamber of Commerce if it is conducted to advance the business interests of its members

Union costs. Union members may deduct as "miscellaneous" itemized deductions union dues and initiation fees. Similarly, non-union employees may deduct monthly service charges to a union. An assessment paid for unemployment benefits is deductible if payment is required as a condition of remaining in the union and holding a union job. Voluntary payments to a union unemployment benefit or strike fund are not deductible.

No deduction is allowed for mandatory contributions to a union pension fund applied toward the purchase of a retirement annuity; the contributions are treated as the cost of the annuity. Furthermore, to the extent that an assessment covers sick, accident, or death benefits payable to you or your family, it is not deductible. Similarly, an assessment for a construction fund to build union recreation centers was disallowed by the Tax Court, even though the payment was required for keeping the job.

Campaign costs for running for union office are not deductible.

Subscriptions. Subject to the 2% AGI floor, you may claim as miscellaneous itemized deductions unreimbursed payments for job-related subscriptions to professional journals and trade magazines.

19.6 Uniforms and Work Clothes

The cost of uniforms and other apparel, including their cleaning, laundering, and repair, is deductible *only* if the clothes are:

1. Required to keep your job; *and*
2. Not suitable for wear when not working.

The deduction is subject to the 2% AGI floor; *see 19.1.*

Special work clothes. Courts have held that the cost of special work clothes that protect you from injury is deductible even if you are not required to wear them to keep your job. However, you may not deduct the cost of special clothing, such as aprons and overalls, that protect your regular street clothing. Nor may you deduct the cost of ordinary clothes used as work clothes on the grounds that: (1) they get harder use than customary garments receive; (2) they are soiled after a day's work and cannot be worn socially; or (3) they were purchased for your convenience to save wear and tear on your better clothes. For example, a sanitation inspector, a machinist's helper, a carpenter, and a telephone repairman were not allowed to deduct the cost of their work clothes.

Employer allowance. An allowance paid by your employer for work clothes or a uniform is not reported as income, unless you do not substantiate the expenses to your employer. If you do substantiate the expenses, those exceeding the reimbursement are reported on Form 2106, and the deduction is subject to the 2% AGI floor; *see 20.30.*

High-fashion work clothes. That your job requires you to wear expensive clothing is not a basis for deducting the cost of the clothes if the clothing is suitable for wear off the job.

Deductions allowed. Deductions for costs of uniforms and work clothes have been allowed to:

Airline pilot
Bakery salesperson—for a uniform with a company label
Baseball player
Bus driver
Cement finisher for gloves, overshoes, and rubber boots
Civilian faculty members of a military school
Commercial fisherman for protective clothing, such as oil cloths, gloves, and boots
Dairy worker for rubber boots, white shirts, trousers, and cap worn only while inside the dairy
Entertainer for theatrical clothing used solely for performances
Exotic dancer for breast implants used as a "stage prop" essential to her business; *see* Example 7 in *19.9*
Factory foreman for white coat bearing the word "foreman" and the name of the company
Factory worker for safety shoes
Firefighter
Hospital attendant for work clothes; he came in contact with patients having contagious diseases
Jockey
Letter carrier
Meat cutter for special white shoes
Musician for formal wear
Paint machine operator for high top shoes and long leather gloves
Plumber for special shoes and gloves
Police officer
Railroad conductor
Railroad firefighter for boots, leather gloves, raincoat, caps, and work gloves

EXAMPLES

1. A painter may not deduct the cost of work clothing consisting of a white cap, a white shirt, white bib overalls, and standard work shoes. The clothing is not distinctive in character as a uniform would be. That his union requires him to wear such clothing does not make it a deductible expense.
2. A tennis pro who taught at private clubs was not allowed to deduct the cost of tennis outfits or shoes required for his job. He did not wear them outside of work and argued that he replaced the shoes every few weeks to reduce the chances of injury. However, the Tax Court upheld the IRS's disallowance of his deductions because the clothes and shoes are suitable for everyday wear; warm-up suits and tennis clothes are fashionable and frequently worn as casual wear. Furthermore, there was no evidence that his tennis shoes reduced chances of injury.

Filing Tip

Uniform Required

Your claim of a work clothes deduction is helped if your employer requires you to wear a uniform. Uniform costs of reservists and service persons, in excess of any uniform allowance, are deductible if you are prohibited from wearing the uniform off duty.

Filing Tip

Cleaning and Laundering

If you are allowed to deduct the cost of work clothes and uniforms, you also may deduct the cost of cleaning and laundering them. Also, courts have allowed the cost of cleaning and laundering to be deducted in situations where:

- The clothes could only be worn one day at a time because they became too dirty.
- Dirty clothes were a hazard; they became baggy and might have gotten caught in machinery.
- Clothes were worn only at work and a place for changing clothes was provided by the employer.
- A meat cutter had to wear clean work clothes at all times.

19.7 Expenses of Looking for a New Job

Subject to the 2% AGI floor, you may deduct expenses of looking for a new job in the *same line of work,* whether or not a new job is found. If you are unemployed when seeking a new job, and the period of unemployment has been substantial, the IRS may disallow the deduction.

EXAMPLE

The IRS disallowed the driving expenses of an unemployed secretary on the ground that she was not currently employed. The Tax Court disagreed and held that for purposes of deducting job-hunting expenses, she could still be considered in the business of being a secretary. She had worked as an administrative secretary with Toyota in San Francisco. The firm relocated, resulting in a 100-mile-per-day commute. She quit her job at the end of January 1984. From February to November 1984, she drove her Cadillac El Dorado over 4,600 miles looking for a new job. The Tax Court allowed her a depreciation deduction of $2,880 and $981 for car operating costs.

Expenses of seeking your *first job* are not deductible, even if a job is obtained. Also, expenses of looking for a job in a different line of work are not deductible, even if you get the job.

The IRS may also dispute the deduction of search expenses of a previously employed professional who forms a partnership.

EXAMPLE

A CPA working for a firm decided to go out on his own. After a period of investigation, he formed a partnership with another CPA. The IRS disallowed his deduction of search expenses, claiming his expenses were incurred in a new business. As an employee he was in a different business from that of a self-employed practitioner. Thus, the expenses should be capitalized as a cost of setting up or organizing the partnership. The Tax Court disagreed, allowing the deduction. The travel expenses were incurred to seek work as a CPA, whether as a self-employed or employed CPA.

Travel expenses. If you travel to find a new job in the same line of work, such as an interview in a distant city, you may deduct travel expenses, including meals and lodging. If, during the trip, you also do personal visiting, you may deduct the transportation expenses to and from the area if the trip was primarily related to your job search. Time spent on personal activity is compared with time spent looking for a job to determine the primary purpose of the trip. If the transportation expenses to and from the destination are not deductible because the trip was primarily personal, you may still deduct the expenses of seeking a new job while you are away.

Are you between jobs? If you are between jobs and you continue to see and entertain your former customers, the IRS holds that you may not deduct the cost of entertainment and other business expenses during this period on the ground that you are not in business and earning income. However, the Tax Court in the following case allowed the deduction.

EXAMPLE

Haft was a successful jewelry salesman earning as much as $60,000 a year. In the fall of one year, he left his employer and started to look for a new connection. During the following year, he continued to maintain contacts with his former customers by entertaining buyers and their representatives. He deducted the expenses of entertaining and other business costs. The IRS disallowed the deduction, claiming he was not in business. The Tax Court disagreed. His lack of business income was temporary and resulted from a period of transition that lasted a reasonable time.

19.8 Local Transportation Costs

Unreimbursed local transportation costs to see your employer's clients or customers, such as taxi, bus, or train fares, are miscellaneous itemized deductions subject to the 2% AGI floor. Transportation from your regular job to a second job on the same day is also deductible. You may not deduct the cost of commuting from home to a regular job or second job, but commuting to a temporary work location *(20.2)* is deductible.

Caution

First Job

You may not deduct the expenses of seeking your first job.

Filing Tip

Employment Agency Fee

If your new employer pays the fee under an agreement with an agency, you may disregard the payment for tax purposes. However, if you pay the fee and deduct it as a job search expense and in a later year you are reimbursed by your employer, you must report the reimbursement as taxable income to the extent you received a tax benefit from the earlier deduction; *see 11.6.*

A company interested in your services may invite you to a job interview and agree to pay all of the trip expenses to its office, even if you are not hired. The company payment is tax free up to your actual expenses.

If you use your own car for job-related travel, you may deduct unreimbursed out-of-pocket costs for gasoline, tolls, and parking. The IRS mileage allowance *(43.1)* is available for the occasional business use of your personal car if you elected the allowance for the first year you used the car for business purposes; *see* the instructions to Form 2106 or Form 2106-EZ.

19.9 Unusual Job Expenses

The following are not typical deductible expenses. However, deductions in the following cases have been allowed.

EXAMPLES

1. *Shoeshine expense of a pilot.* Company rules required a commercial airline pilot to look neat, keep his hair cut, and wear conservative black shoes, properly shined. The pilot deducted as a business expense $100 for his haircuts and $25 for his shoe shines. The IRS disallowed the deductions, but the Tax Court allowed the cost of the shoe shines. The shoes were of a military type which he wore only with his pilot's uniform. The cost of keeping up a uniform is deductible. The haircuts were merely nondeductible personal expenses.
2. *Depreciation on furnishings bought by executive for his company office.* Following a quarrel with an interior decorator, a sales manager bought his own office furniture when his firm moved to new quarters. Rather than complain or ask for reimbursement, he footed the bill and deducted depreciation. The IRS disallowed the deduction, claiming the expense was that of his company. The Tax Court allowed the deduction. The manager's action was unusual, but prudent. He did not want to cause difficulties, and at the same time had to maintain his image as a successful manager. His expenses for furniture were appropriate and helpful.
3. *Salesman's cost of operating a private plane.* Sherman flew his own plane to visit clients in six southern states and deducted $18,000 as operating costs of the plane. The IRS disallowed the deduction, claiming there was no business reason for the plane. He could have taken commercial flights or used a company car to reach his clients. Furthermore, his company did not reimburse him for the private airplane costs, although it would cover costs of his car and commercial air travel. Finally, the amount of airplane expenses was unreasonable compared to his salary of $25,000. Sherman convinced the Tax Court that use of a private airplane was the only reasonable way he could cover his six-state sales area. He showed that most of his clients were not near commercial airports. Although the airplane costs were large in relation to his salary, they were still reasonable and, therefore, deductible.
4. *Executive's purchase of blazers for sales force.* Jetty, the president of an oil equipment manufacturing firm, thought that he could generate goodwill for the company if employees who attended industrial trade shows wore a blazer and vest set in the company colors. He personally paid and deducted $6,725 for 27 blazers and vests. The IRS disallowed the deduction on the grounds that it was a company expense and that Jetty should have sought reimbursement from the company.

   The Tax Court allowed the deduction. Paying for the clothes was a legitimate business expense for Jetty since he depended on bonuses for a large portion of his pay, and, as company president, he had responsibility for seeing to it that there were profits to share in. Furthermore, the outlay was not the type of expense covered by the company's manual on expense reimbursements.
5. *Repayment of layoff benefits to restore pension credit.* When he was laid off, an employee received a lump-sum payment from his company based on his salary and years of service. When he was rehired a year later, he repaid the lump sum in order to restore his pension credits and other benefit rights. The IRS ruled that he may deduct the repayment as a condition of being rehired; the repayment was required to restore employee benefits.
6. *Politician's expenses.* Elected officials may incur out-of-pocket expenses in excess of the allowances received from the government. They may deduct as miscellaneous deductions their payment of office expenses such as salaries, office rent, and supplies. Part-time officials may claim the deduction. The expenses are deductible even if they exceed the official's income.

7. *Depreciation for exotic dancer's breast implants.* Hess, an exotic dancer, enlarged her breasts to the abnormal size of 56N and claimed a $2,088 depreciation deduction for their cost. The IRS disallowed the deduction, claiming that cosmetic surgery is a personal expense. The Tax Court disagreed. Hess's expenses were incurred solely in furtherance of her business and not for her own personal benefit. The breast implants were not of the kind that women usually get to enhance their appearance. Rather, Hess enlarged her breasts to a "freakish" size to substantially increase her annual income, which she did. The court also compared the implants to special work clothes *(19.6)*, required for a job and not for personal wear. As an exotic dancer, Hess's large breasts are like a "costume" needed to keep her job. Although she could not remove them daily, she would have, if possible, because they caused her serious medical problems.

Computers, Phones, and Home Office Costs of Employees

19.10 Computers and Cellular Phones

Computers (and peripherals) and cellular phones are treated as "listed property" subject to deduction restrictions: To get a first-year expensing deduction *(42.3)* or to claim any type of depreciation, the computer or cellular phone must be used for the convenience of your employer, which means your use of the equipment satisfies a substantial business need of your employer. The equipment must also be required as a condition of your job, which means that you cannot properly do your job without it. The IRS strictly interprets these requirements.

Computer. A letter from your employer stating that a computer is needed for your position does not by itself satisfy the deduction tests. Even where your employer encourages use of a personal computer that is used for basic job requirements, the IRS requires proof that you need your own computer to do your job because your employer does not provide one, or because the computer supplied by your employer is not adequate for your job. In the following Examples, the IRS disallowed depreciation writeoffs.

EXAMPLES

1. An electric company offered to help pay for its engineers' personal computers where this would improve productivity. Qualifying engineers received extra pay and had to buy a computer meeting company specifications, take approved computer courses, and agree to restrictions on resale of the computer. An engineer bought a computer and used it 95% of the time for writing business memos and reports, and studying business flow charts. He did not use the computer for entertainment.

   The IRS held that although the engineer's computer was work related and benefitted his employer, buying a computer was not required for his job; it was not "inextricably related" to proper job performance. Further, his participation in the employer's computer program was optional, not mandatory.

2. A professor of nursing, trying to keep her temporary position, bought a personal computer, needing a word processor for independent research papers and to document her qualifications for research grants. The research and external grant support were implied university requirements for faculty appointments. She did not have access to university word-processing equipment during regular work hours; and because of her classroom responsibilities, her research and grant development work had to be done on her own time. To help her pursue outside grants, the university bought her a "modem" that allowed a phone hook-up with its computer at night. Her computer was used 100% for research and grant work.

   As in Example 1, the IRS held that use of the computer was not "inextricably related" to proper job performance and did not qualify for a depreciation writeoff. Furthermore, there was no evidence that employees who did not use computers were professionally disadvantaged.

3. The IRS held that an insurance agent could not deduct depreciation for a laptop computer he used to help develop insurance plans for clients. The insurance company encouraged its agents to buy the computer because office computers were not generally accessible.

Court Decision

Tax Court Allows Computer Deduction

The Tax Court allowed a first-year expensing deduction to a working couple who used the same home computer given these facts: The husband, a professor, used it to store historical data; the wife, a state transportation planner, used it to do extensive number crunching. What apparently won the decision for the couple was evidence that (1) the husband did not have access to a computer at the university, and (2) the state office in which the wife worked did not have funds to buy a computer. The court held that the use of the computer was necessary for them to properly do their jobs, and as the purchase of a computer spared their employers from having to provide them with computers, the purchase was for the employers' convenience.

In a later case, a telemarketing sales manager was allowed a first-year expensing deduction for a home computer and printer used to prepare reports. The key to winning the deduction was her supervisor's testimony that as a mid-level manager, she could not enter the office after regular hours to use a company computer, and that she was able to keep up with the volume of sales reports she was required to submit by using her home computer and accessing information via modem.

According to the IRS, it is not enough that the agent's productivity increased or that he used the computer solely for business. Purchasing the computer was optional, not a mandatory job requirement. Employees who did not purchase computers were not professionally disadvantaged.

4. The IRS barred a third-grade teacher from deducting the cost of a Macintosh computer because it was not required for her job. She bought the computer using an interest-free loan from the school after the school decided that report cards and student evaluations would have to be prepared on a Macintosh instead of being written. The Tax Court and an appeals court sided with the IRS. It may have been convenient for the teacher to use a home computer but it was not required. Other teachers were able to timely complete their duties using school computers.

Cellular phones. The IRS has not released specific guidelines or rulings covering deduction requirements for cellular phones. In general, the "convenience of the employer" and "job condition" tests must be met to claim first-year expensing or depreciation. In addition, you need detailed records to support your claimed business use if you are deducting the cost of the equipment or service charges. Keep records showing the amount, time, place, and business purpose of your calls to satisfy the stringent substantiation requirements for "listed property."

Caution

Deducting Cellular Phone Costs

Cellular phone equipment must be used for the convenience of the employer and be a condition of your employment for you to be able to claim first-year expensing or a depreciation deduction for the cost.

Claiming a deduction. If you can meet the "convenience of the employer" and "job condition" tests for a computer or cellular phone purchased in 2006, and you have records to prove that the unit is used more than 50% of the time for your job, you may write off the cost under first-year expensing (the limit for 2006 is generally $108,000; *see 42.3*), or accelerated five-year MACRS depreciation rates *(42.5)* may be used. If business use of the unit is 50% or less, you may not use first-year expensing or regular MACRS but you may claim straight-line depreciation.

First-year expensing or depreciation is claimed on Form 4562 and then entered on Form 2106 or Form 2106-EZ along with other job-related costs. The deduction from Form 2106 or Form 2106-EZ is subject to the 2% AGI floor for miscellaneous deductions on Schedule A; *see 19.1.* If you use first-year expensing or accelerated MACRS and business use in a later year is 50% or less, *see* Example 2 at *42.10* for recapture rules.

You need to keep records documenting your percentage of business use for a computer or cellular phone.

19.11 Calculators, Copiers, Fax Machines, and Typewriters

The listed property requirements applied to computers and cellular phones *(19.9)* do not apply to calculators, copiers, fax machines, adding machines, and typewriters. This means that the restrictive convenience of the employer and job condition rules do not apply. However, to depreciate the cost of such equipment, you should be ready to prove that you need the equipment for your job, and keep a record of the time it is used for business. To claim first-year expensing *(42.3)*, rather than regular depreciation, you must use the equipment *more* than 50% of the time for business.

Filing Instruction

Office for Sideline Business

If you are an employee and also have a sideline business for which you use a home office, the office expenses are deductible if the office is used regularly and exclusively as your principal place of business or a meeting place with clients, customers, or patients. If the tests are met, you claim your home office expenses as a self-employed person on Form 8829, which you attach to Schedule C. The deduction may not exceed your income from the sideline business. *See* Chapter 40 for a sample Form 8829 and other deduction details.

19.12 Small Tools

If you furnished your own small tools used on your job, you may deduct their cost if they are not expected to last beyond a year. The deduction is subject to the 2% AGI floor. The cost of tools with a useful life of more than a year must be recovered through depreciation or first-year expensing; *see 42.3.* Be prepared to substantiate your deduction with receipts showing the cost and type of tools purchased, and the business necessity for them.

19.13 Employee Home Office Deductions

The tax law has been drafted to prevent employees from deducting the expenses of an office at a home. The tests for deducting home office expenses are discussed at *40.12.* Even if an employee should meet one of the tests, such as doing administrative work at home, the employee must also show that the home office was required for the "convenience of his or her employer" in order to claim the deduction.

EXAMPLE

Charlie, a teacher, has a small office at school where he can grade papers and tests, work on lesson plans, and meet with parents and students. The school does not require him to work at home, but he prefers to use the office he has set up in his home, and does not use the office the school provides. Although Charlie's home office is used for the administrative duties of teaching, Charlie may not deduct his home office expenses because he does not meet the convenience of the employer test. His employer provides him with an office at school and does not require him to work at home.

19.14 Telephone Costs

For business calls made outside of your employer's office or at home, keep a record or diary of business calls to support your deduction. To avoid the problem of allocating the costs of a single phone for both business and personal use, consider a separate phone for business use only.

Deduction barred for basic charge of first phone line. You may not claim as a deductible home office expense any part of the standard monthly charge for the first telephone line into your home. This disallowance rule only applies to the first telephone line. If you have more than one telephone line and use additional lines in a home office, costs for these lines remain deductible, subject to the restrictions at *19.13*. The restriction does not affect deductibility of long-distance calls, phone rentals, or optional services such as call waiting, call forwarding, three-way calling, or extra directory listings.

Caution

Deducting Telephone Costs

To support your deduction, keep a record of business calls made at home or anywhere outside your employer's office.

Investment, Legal, and Tax Advice Expenses

19.15 Checklist of Deductible Investment Expenses

The following investment expenses are deductible as miscellaneous expenses on Schedule A subject to the 2% adjusted gross income (AGI) floor. In addition, the 3% reduction for total itemized deductions applies if your 2006 adjusted gross income exceeds $150,500, or $75,250 if married filing separately; *see 13.7*.

- Accounting fees for keeping records of investment income.
- Bank deposit loss if not federally insured; *see 18.5*.
- Casualty or theft losses of income-producing property such as stock certificates, but not rental or royalty property; the deduction is figured on Form 4684 and entered on Schedule A.
- Fees for collecting interest and dividends. Also deductible are fees paid to a bank that acts as dividend agent in an automatic dividend reinvestment plan of a publicly owned corporation. Costs of collecting tax-exempt interest are not deductible; expenses deducted on an estate tax return are also not deductible. Fees paid to a broker to acquire securities are not deductible but are added to the cost of the securities. Commissions and fees paid by an investor on the sale of securities reduce the selling price; a dealer, however, may deduct selling commissions as business expenses.
- Fees to set up or administer an IRA. The fees must be billed and paid separately from the regular IRA contribution.
- Guardian fees or fees of committee for a ward or minor incurred in producing or collecting income belonging to the ward or minor or in managing income-producing property of the ward or minor.
- Investment management or investment planner's fees. However, fees allocated to advice dealing with tax-exempt obligations are not deductible.
- Investment fees from non–publicly offered mutual fund, shown in Box 5 of Form 1099-DIV.
- Legal costs; *see 19.17*.
- Premiums and expenses on indemnity bonds for the replacement of missing securities. If part of the expenses are refunded in the year the expenses are paid, only the excess expense is deductible. A refund in a later year is taxable income to the extent the expenses were deducted and reduced your tax; *see 11.6*.
- Proxy fight expenses where the dispute involves legitimate corporate policy issues, not a frivolous desire to gain membership on the board.
- Safe-deposit box rental fee or home safe to hold your securities, unless used to hold personal effects or tax-exempt securities.
- Salary of a secretary, bookkeeper, or other employee hired to keep track of your investment income.
- Subscriptions to investment services.

Planning Reminder

Travel to Check Investments

Travel costs of a trip away from home *(20.6)* to look after investments, or to confer with your attorney, accountant, trustee, or investment counsel about the production of income, may be deducted as miscellaneous itemized deductions subject to the 2% of adjusted gross income floor. If you have investment property in a resort area, keep proof that the trip was taken primarily to check your investment property, not to vacation.

Computer used to manage investments. Subject to the 2% floor, depreciation may be claimed; *see 42.10.*

Managing investment property. Expenses incurred in managing property held for income are deductible, even if the property does not currently produce income. Similarly, expenses incurred to avoid further losses or to reduce anticipated losses on such property are deductible.

Rental or royalty expenses. Expenses of earning royalty or rental income are deducted directly from the income, rather than as itemized deductions subject to the 2% AGI floor.

EXAMPLE

You pay deductible investment management fees of $1,500, a tax preparation fee of $500, and a safe-deposit box fee of $40. Your other miscellaneous expense deductions subject to the 2% floor are $500 for unreimbursed job expenses. Your adjusted gross income is $80,000. Your deduction after applying the 2% AGI floor is $940, figured as follows:

Investment management fees	$1,500
Tax preparation fee	500
Safe-deposit box fee	40
Other miscellaneous expenses	500
	$2,540
Less: 2% of $80,000	1,600
Total deductible	$ 940

Caution

Investment Seminars

You may not deduct the cost of an investment or financial planning seminar or similar meeting.

Nondeductible travel costs. Investors may not deduct the costs of these types of trips:

- Trips to investigate prospective rental property.
- Trips to attend a convention, seminar, or similar meeting that deals with investment, financial planning, or the production or collection of income. Convention costs are deductible only in the case of a business activity; *see 20.12.*
- Trips to attend stockholder meetings. However, in a private letter ruling, one stockholder was allowed a deduction. He owned substantial stockholdings that had lost value because his corporation had been issuing stock to the public at prices below book value. He went to the annual shareholders' meeting to present a resolution requesting management to stop the practice; the resolution passed. Under such circumstances, the IRS held that the trip was directly related to his stockholdings and allowed him the deduction. The IRS distinguished his case from a ruling that bars most stockholders from deducting the cost of travel to an annual meeting. Here the stockholder's purpose in getting the resolution passed was more closely related to his investment activities than if he had attended the meeting, as most stockholders do, to pick up data for future investment moves.

Hobby expenses. For the limitations on deducting hobby expenses, *see 40.10.*

Home office of an investor. An investor may not deduct the costs of an office at home unless investing constitutes a business. For example, you get no deduction for use of a home office in your residence where you manage your investments and read financial periodicals and reports. These activities are not considered a business.

EXAMPLE

In his home office, Moller spent 40 hours a week managing four stock portfolios worth over $13 million. However, an appeals court held he could not deduct home office expenses despite the time spent there managing his investment. To deduct home office expenses, Moller had to show he was a trader. A trader is in a business; an investor is not. A trader buys and sells frequently to catch daily market swings. An investor buys securities for capital appreciation and income without regard to daily market developments. Here, Moller was an investor. He was primarily interested in the long-term growth potential of stock. He did not earn his income from the short-term stock turnovers. He had no significant trading profits.

19.16 Costs of Tax Return Preparation and Audits

You may deduct your payment of fees charged for the services listed below, subject to the 2% AGI floor and the 3% reduction if AGI exceeds $150,500 ($75,250 if married filing separately); *see 13.7.*

- Preparing your tax return or refund claim involving any tax;
- Preparing and obtaining a private IRS ruling, including IRS filing fees; *and*
- Representing you before any examination, trial, or other type of hearing involving any tax.

Tax preparation fees include the cost of tax publications and tax preparation software programs. Any fee paid to electronically file your return is also included. The term "any tax" covers not only income taxes but also gift, property, estate, or any other tax, whether the taxing authority be federal, state, or municipal.

Tax practitioner's fees. Deductible fees for services of tax practitioners are claimed on Schedule A as miscellaneous itemized deductions (subject to the 2% AGI floor) on the tax return for the year in which the fee was paid. For example, if in March 2006 you paid an accountant to prepare your 2005 return, the fee is deductible on your 2006 return.

You deduct fees related to preparing Schedule C or F (and related business Schedules) on the Schedule C or F, thereby avoiding the 2% AGI floor on Schedule A. In one case, the Tax Court allowed a Schedule C deduction for a $55 tax preparation fee claimed by a self-employed lumberjack, although nonbusiness income was also reported on his return. Any allocation to the nonbusiness income would have been minimal. The Court noted that the IRS's position in disallowing the deduction reflected misguided zeal and was not only petty but impractical.

If you report rental or royalty income or loss on Schedule E, you deduct the allocated tax preparation fee on Schedule E.

An accountant's fee for arranging the purchase of real estate was deductible where the purchase was part of a plan to cut taxes; *see* the Collins Example below.

Personal checking account fees. These are nondeductible, even though the checks are used for tax records. Similarly, the per-check fee on an interest-bearing NOW account is nondeductible. However, fees charged on a bank money-market account may be deductible if check writing is severely limited and writing excess checks forfeits the status of the account as a money-market account.

Appraisal fees. Appraisals for determining a casualty loss or charitable donation are miscellaneous expenses.

EXAMPLES

1. Stockholders of a closely held corporation negotiated with a publicly held company for a tax-free exchange of their stock. An accounting firm asked the IRS for a ruling to determine whether the exchange would be taxable or tax free. The accounting fee was $8,602. Of this, $7,602 was for the ruling and $1,000 was for fixing the basis of the new stock. The stockholders deducted the full fee, which the IRS disallowed because the fee was not charged for the preparation of a tax return nor for representation at a contest of a tax liability.

   The Tax Court disagreed in part. The fee paid for the ruling was deductible; it was connected with determining the extent of the stockholders' liability, if any, in the proposed exchange. But a deduction could not be allowed for the $1,000 charged to determine the basis of the new stock. This was computed for the stockholders' information, not for determining tax liability. The disallowed fee could be added to the cost basis of the stock.
2. Collins paid an accountant $4,511 for tax advice to reduce his tax on a sweepstakes winning. He was advised to buy an apartment house under a contract obligation to make a large prepayment of interest (which was deductible under prior law). The accountant helped prepare contracts, escrow agreements, and other documents to implement the plan. Collins's deduction of his accountant's fee was disallowed. The IRS held that the fee was a capital expense in acquiring the property. The Tax Court disagreed. The accountant was hired to minimize Collins's income tax through the purchase of the building and the terms of the purchase. Therefore, his fee was deductible.

Filing Tip

Tax Advice and Tax Return Preparation

You may deduct legal fees paid in 2006 for preparing your tax return or refund claim, or for representing you in a trial, examination, or hearing involving any tax; *see 19.16.* Legal fees incurred in defending against a tax imposed by a foreign country are also deductible. However, legal fees incurred in reducing an assessment on property to pay for local benefits are not deductible; the fees are capital expenses which are added to basis.

Caution

Credit Card Fees Not Deductible

Companies authorized by the IRS to process credit card payments of taxes charge a convenience fee. The fee is not deductible as a tax preparation expense. Expenses for figuring tax liability are deductible but this is a fee to enable the payment of one's liability after it has been determined.

Filing Tip

Deducting the Cost of This Book

The purchase of *Your Income Tax* in 2006 may be claimed as a miscellaneous expense deduction on your 2006 return. The cost, when included with other miscellaneous expenses, is subject to the 2% AGI floor. If you purchase the book in 2007, include the cost with your other miscellaneous expenses on your 2007 return.

Planning Reminder

Allocate Fees for Tax Advice

There have been disputes over the deductibility of fees charged for general tax advice unconnected to the preparation of a return or a tax controversy. A deduction for fees charged for general tax advice not within these areas may be disallowed, unless the fee can be related to the production of business or investment income or the management of income-producing property. *See* the Examples in *19.16*.

Planning Reminder

Lawyer's Bill Should Be Itemized

Your lawyer should bill you separately or itemize fees for services connected with deductible items (collection of taxable alimony or separate maintenance payments; or preparation of tax returns, tax audits, and tax litigation) and nondeductible capital items (expenses incurred in purchase of property or dispute over title).

19.17 Deducting Legal Costs

A legal expense is generally deductible if the dispute or issue arose in the course of your business or employment or involves income-producing property. Legal expenses for personal lawsuits are not deductible unless you recover taxable damages. Legal fees incurred in obtaining an award of tax-free damages, such as for physical injuries *(11.7)*, are not deductible.

If you are self-employed, your deduction for legal fees arising from a business-related dispute is claimed on Schedule C. Legal expenses related to your job as an employee or to investment activities are claimed as miscellaneous itemized deductions subject to the 2% AGI floor, except for fees relating to employment discrimination claims, which may qualify for an above-the-line deduction; *see 19.18.* The IRS may disallow the deduction on the ground that the legal dispute does not directly arise from the business or income activity. Thus, for example, the cost of contesting the suspension of a driver's license for drunken driving is not deductible despite a business need for the license; the suspension arose out of a personal rather than a business-related activity. A deduction may also be disallowed where the dispute involves title to property; *see* below.

For the deductibility of legal fees in organizing a new business, *see 40.11.*

Employment suits. The following Examples illustrate when legal costs for job-related matters may be deductible.

EXAMPLES

1. An Army officer was allowed to deduct the cost of successfully contesting a court martial based on charges of misrepresentations in official statements and reports. He would have lost his position had he been convicted.
2. Tellier, a securities dealer, was convicted of mail fraud and securities fraud. He was allowed to deduct legal fees as business expenses related to his securities business. That he was found guilty of the criminal charge does not affect the deductibility of the expense. The deduction of legal expenses is not disallowed on public policy grounds since a defendant has a constitutional right to an attorney.
3. In an alimony action, Gilmore was successful in preventing his wife from securing stock and taking control of corporations from which he earned practically all his income. He was not allowed to deduct his legal costs. The dispute did not arise from an income-producing activity; the fact that an adverse determination of the dispute might affect his income did not make the legal expenses deductible.
4. A doctor who attempted to bribe a judge to suspend his sentence for tax evasion was convicted of the bribe attempt and lost his license to practice medicine. He could not deduct his defense costs. His practice of medicine did not give rise to his need for an attorney. The fact that the conviction affected his ability to earn income was merely a consequence of personal litigation.
5. Siket, a police officer, was not allowed to deduct expenses of successfully defending a criminal charge of assault while off duty. The origin of the claim was personal, even though a conviction might have been detrimental to his position as a police officer. The arrest did not occur within the performance of his duties; he was off duty and in a different municipality at the time of the arrest.
6. A resort company instructed its staff to stop serving drinks to intoxicated patrons and to encourage the patrons to either take a taxi home or to stay on the premises at a reduced rate. One of the company's executives attempted to deduct legal defense fees when he was charged with criminal sexual assault, arguing that the assault allegation arose from his business duty to procure a room for three intoxicated guests. The IRS and the Tax Court denied the deduction on the grounds that the allegation arose from the executive's second visit to the guests' room, not from the time he placed them in the room. Even if the alleged assault had occurred during the first visit, the executive personally violated company policy by not stopping the guests from drinking when they were already drunk.

Will contests and wrongful death actions. Legal costs of a will contest are generally not deductible because an inheritance is not taxable income. Similarly, legal fees incurred to collect a wrongful death award (which is tax-free income) are not deductible.

EXAMPLE

Parker, an heir who was left out of his grandmother's estate, sued to recover his inheritance. In a settlement, he received his share of his grandmother's property plus income earned on that property. The allocable portion of legal fees attributed to the income, which was taxable, was deductible; the balance of the fees was not deductible.

Title issues or disputes. Legal costs related to the acquisition of property or to the determination of title to property, whether such property is business or personal, are nondeductible capital expenditures. They are added to the basis of the property. For example, litigation costs to fix the value of shares of dissident shareholders are not deductible because they are related to the purchase of the stock and are part of the cost of acquisition.

Legal fees incurred to acquire title to stock are also nondeductible.

Where a dispute over property does not involve title, such as in a recovery of income-producing securities loaned as collateral, the Tax Court holds that legal fees are deductible.

Personal injury actions. Where you recover taxable damages, the legal fees are deductible above the line (from gross income) in unlawful discrimination cases or as a miscellaneous itemized deduction subject to the 2% floor in other cases; *see 19.18* and *12.2*. If the damages are not taxable, legal fees are not deductible; *see 11.7*.

Legal expenses incurred in marital actions. *See 37.8*.

Collecting Social Security. If you hire an attorney to press a claim for disputed benefits, such as disability benefits, you may deduct the legal fees only to the extent that your benefits are taxable under the rules of *34.3*. For example, if 50% of your Social Security benefits are taxable, 50% of your legal fees are treated as miscellaneous expenses subject to the 2% AGI floor.

Estate tax planning fee. All or part of an attorney's fee for estate tax planning services may be deductible subject to the 2% AGI floor. Estate tax planning usually involves tax and non-tax matters. To the extent that the services do not cover tax advice or income-producing property, the fee is not deductible. A bill allocating a fee between deductible and nondeductible services may help support a deduction claimed for the deductible portion of the fee.

Recovery of attorneys' fees from government. *See* Chapter 47.

19.18 Contingent Fees Paid Out of Taxable Awards

As discussed at *11.7*, contingent attorney fees paid to recover taxable damages have been held by the Supreme Court to be includible in the litigant's income. An offsetting deduction for the fees may be available. An above-the-line deduction (directly from gross income) is allowed for attorneys' fees and court costs in employment discrimination suits, certain other unlawful discrimination actions, and Federal False Claims Act cases settled or decided after October 22, 2004. The deduction, claimed on Line 36 of Form 1040 *(12.2)*, is limited to the amount of the judgment or settlement reported as taxable income for the year.

If the above-the-line deduction does *not* apply, fees for recovering taxable personal damages or job-related damages *(19.17)* are allowed only as a miscellaneous itemized deduction subject to the 2% AGI floor *(19.1)*. Any amount allowed after the application of the 2% AGI floor may be further reduced by the overall 3% reduction to itemized deductions *(13.7)* imposed on higher-income taxpayers. Finally, if the alternative minimum tax (AMT) applies, fees claimed as a miscellaneous itemized deduction for regular tax purposes must be added back to income in calculating AMT *(23.2)*, so the benefit of the deduction is lost.

Fees incurred in recovering lost business income *(19.17)* are deductible on Schedule C.

Chapter 20

Travel and Entertainment Expense Deductions

Unreimbursed employee travel expenses are deductible but are subject to the 2% of adjusted gross income (AGI) floor on Schedule A. If you are self-employed, the 2% floor does not apply to travel expenses claimed on Schedule C. The types of deductible travel expenses are highlighted in the key to deductible travel and transportation expenses at the beginning of this chapter. Generally, you must be away from home to deduct travel expenses on business trips. On one-day business trips within the general area of your employment, only transportation costs may be deducted; meals may not.

To support your travel expense deductions, keep records that comply with IRS rules as explained at *20.26.* To avoid the 2% AGI floor, consider an "accountable" reimbursement arrangement of your travel expenses with your employer; *see 20.31.*

You report unreimbursed employee transportation and travel expenses on Form 2106 or on short form 2106-EZ if you are not reimbursed by your company and you do not claim depreciation on a car used for business.

Unreimbursed expenses from Form 2106 or 2106-EZ are entered on Schedule A, where they are subject to the 2% AGI floor.

An expense allowance for travel costs is not reported as income on Form W-2 if you substantiated the expenses to your employer and returned any unsubstantiated portion of the allowance; *see 20.31* for details.

If you are self-employed, you deduct travel costs on Schedule C. The 2% AGI floor does not apply, but only 50% of meal and entertainment expenses are deductible.

Commuting and Meal Expenses

20.1 Deduction Guide for Travel and Transportation Expenses

The following chart summarizes the rules for deducting local business transportation costs and travel expenses while "away from home" on business trips; *see 20.6* for when you are away from home. Generally, commuting expenses from your home to your place of business are not deductible; *see 20.2.* However, you may be able to claim a deduction for daily transportation expenses incurred in commuting to a temporary job location; *see* Table 20-1 and *20.2.*

See 20.28 for how to report deductible expenses if you are self-employed, and *20.29* if you are an employee.

20.2 Commuting Expenses

The cost of travel between your home and place of work is generally not deductible, even if the work location is in a remote area not serviced by public transportation. Nor can you justify the deduction by showing you need a car for faster trips to work or for emergency trips. Travel from a union hall to an assigned job is also considered commuting. If you join a car pool, you may not deduct expenses of gasoline, repairs, or other costs of driving you and your passengers to work.

According to the IRS, if you install a telephone in your car and make calls to clients or business associates while driving to your office, you are still commuting and your expenses are not deductible. Similarly, the deduction is not allowed if you drive passengers to work and discuss business.

Deductible commuting expenses. The IRS allows these exceptions to its blanket ban on commuting expense deductions.

If you are on a business trip out of town, you may deduct taxi fares or other transportation costs from your hotel to the first business call of the day and all other transportation costs between business calls.

If you use your car to carry tools to work, you may deduct transportation costs where you can prove that they were incurred in addition to the ordinary, nondeductible commuting expenses. The deduction will be allowed even if you would use a car in any event to commute; *see* the Examples below.

EXAMPLES

1. Jones commuted to and from work by public transportation before he had to carry tools. Public transportation cost $2 per day to commute to and from work. When he had to use the car to carry the tools, the cost of driving was $3 a day and $5 a day to rent a trailer to carry the tools. Jones may deduct only the cost of renting the trailer. The IRS does not allow a deduction for the additional $1 a day cost of operating the car. It is not considered related to the carrying of the tools. It is treated as part of the cost of commuting, which is not deductible.
2. Same facts as above, but Jones does not rent a trailer. He uses the car trunk to store his tools. He may not claim a deduction because he incurs no additional cost for carrying the tools.
3. Smith uses his car regardless of the need to transport tools. He rents a trailer for $5 a day to carry tools. He may deduct $5 a day under the "additional-cost" rule.

Commuting to a temporary place of work. Whether you can deduct commuting expenses to a temporary place of work may depend on the location of the temporary assignment and whether you have a regular place of business or a home office that is your principal place of business. According to the IRS, if you have a *regular* place of work outside of your home, or you have a home office that is your principal place of business, you may deduct the cost of commuting between your home and a temporary (*see* below) work location, regardless of where the temporary location is. If you do not have a regular place of work but normally work at several locations in the metropolitan area where you live, you may deduct the costs of commuting to a temporary location that is outside that metropolitan area, but not to a temporary location within the metropolitan area.

If you do not have a regular place of work and all of your jobs are outside the metropolitan area where you live, none of your commuting costs are deductible under the IRS rule. In one case, a commuting cost deduction was denied to an iron worker who lived in Yuba City, California,

Court Decision

Self-Employed Person's Office at Home

If you are self-employed and your regular office is outside your home, you may not deduct the cost of commuting to the office or from that office to your home even if you work at home at a second job. However, in several cases, the Tax Court allowed self-employed persons whose home office was their principal place of business *(40.12)* to deduct travel costs beginning with the first business call of the day. The IRS now agrees with this approach.

and who obtained temporary work assignments at a union hall in Sacramento, 40 miles from her home. All of the temporary jobs were in or near Sacramento. The Tax Court agreed with the IRS that none of her commuting costs to the temporary locations were deductible because she did not work in the Yuba City area where she lived. Since all of her assignments were in other cities, her decision to live in Yuba City was for personal, not business, reasons.

Caution

IRS Definition of "Temporary"

The IRS considers a work location temporary if the period of employment is realistically expected to last, and actually does last, one year or less. If you take an assignment expected to last more than a year but it actually lasts less than a year, your assignment is *not* considered temporary and commuting costs are not deductible.

What is a temporary place of work? A temporary work location is one at which your employment is realistically expected to last, and actually does last, for one year or less. If at first you realistically expect an assignment to last for no more than one year but that expectation changes, the IRS will generally treat the employment as temporary until the date that it became realistic to expect that the work would exceed one year.

Accountants, architects, engineers, and other professionals often have to travel to job sites of their clients. If such work at the site is temporary and they can show they also have a regular work office, they may deduct commuting expenses from their homes to their work sites.

EXAMPLE

The IRS ruled that a professional who spent 25–27% of his time at his employer's field office satisfied the regular place of business test. His remaining time was spent at client locations. These were considered temporary because he went to each client location only once every two years for two to three weeks at a time. He was allowed to deduct his unreimbursed costs of driving between his home and the client locations.

20.3 Overnight-Sleep Test Limits Deduction of Meal Costs

The overnight-sleep rule prevents the deduction of meal costs on one-day business trips. To be deductible, meal costs must be incurred while "away from home" and this test requires that they be on a business trip that lasts longer than a regular working day (but not necessarily 24 hours) and requires time off to sleep (not just to eat or rest) before returning home. Taking a nap in a parked car off the road does not meet the overnight-sleep test.

EXAMPLES

1. A New Yorker flies to Washington, D.C., which is about 250 miles away, to see a client. He arrives at noon, eats lunch, and then visits the client. He flies back to New York. He may deduct the cost of the plane fare, but not the cost of the lunch. He was not away overnight nor was he required to take time out to sleep before returning home.
2. Same facts as above except he sleeps overnight in a Washington hotel. He eats breakfast there, and then sees another client and returns home to New York in the afternoon. He may deduct not only the cost of the plane fare but also the cost of the meals while on the trip and the cost of the hotel, since he was away overnight.
3. A trucker's run is from Seattle to Portland and back. He leaves at about 2:00 A.M. and returns to Seattle the same day, getting in at about 6:00 P.M. While in Portland, he is released from duty for about four hours layover time to get necessary sleep before returning to Seattle. He may deduct the cost of meals because he is released at a layover location to obtain necessary sleep. Official release from duty, however, is not a prerequisite for satisfying the sleep or rest test.

Several courts held that the IRS rule was unreasonable and outdated in the world of supersonic travel, and they would have allowed the New Yorker on the one-day trip to Washington, D.C., to deduct the cost of his lunch. The Supreme Court disagreed and upheld the IRS rule as a fair administrative approach.

Meal costs during overtime. Such costs are not deductible if you are not away from your place of business. Thus, for example, a resident physician could not deduct the cost of meals and sleeping quarters at the hospital during overnight or weekend duty.

Table 20-1 Deductible Travel and Transportation Expenses

Your Travel Status—	*Tax Rule—*
Trips to see customers and clients	You may deduct your transportation expenses but not the cost of personal meals on one-day business trips within the general area of your tax home. On out-of-town business trips "away from home," lodging and meals are deductible as well as transportation costs.
Two job locations for one employer in the same area **EXAMPLE:** Your employer has two business locations in the city in which you live. You work about half of the time in each place—at one location in the morning and at the other in the afternoon.	You deduct transportation expenses from one location to the other. However, if, for personal reasons, such as the choice of a place for eating lunch, you do not go directly from one location to the other, you may deduct your transportation expenses only to the extent that they do not exceed the cost of going directly from the first location to the second. But say your employer has several locations in the same city, but you do not move from one location to another in the same day. You spend the entire day at one place. You may not deduct transportation expenses between your home and the various locations, even if you report to a different location each day.
Two different jobs in the same area **EXAMPLE:** You work for two different employers in the city in which you live. Most of the time you work a full work shift at your principal place of employment. Then you work a part-time shift for your second employer some distance away.	You may deduct the transportation expenses from one job to another within the same working day. But you may not claim the deduction if you return home after the first job and then, after supper, go to your second job.
Permanent job in an area other than where you have your residence **EXAMPLE:** You live with your family in Chicago, but work in Milwaukee. During the week, you stay in a hotel in Milwaukee and eat meals in a restaurant. You return to your family in Chicago every weekend.	Milwaukee is your "home" for tax purposes; *see 20.6.* Thus, your expenses for traveling to Milwaukee and your meals and lodging there are personal, nondeductible expenses.
Temporary assignment in an area other than where you have your residence **EXAMPLE:** You live in Kansas City, where you work. You have been assigned to duty in Omaha for 60 days. Occasionally, you return to Kansas City on your days off, but most of the time you stay in Omaha.	You may deduct the necessary expenses for traveling from Kansas City to Omaha and returning to Kansas City after your temporary assignment is completed. You may also deduct expenses for meals and lodging (even for your days off) while you are in Omaha. As discussed at *20.9,* deductions are not allowed on temporary assignments that are *expected* to last more than one year.
Weekend trip home from temporary assignment **EXAMPLE:** Same facts as in the Example above except that you return home to Kansas City during the weekend.	You are not "away from home" while you are in Kansas City on your days off and your meals and lodging while you are there are not deductible. However, you may deduct your traveling expenses (including meals and lodging, if any) from Omaha to Kansas City and back if they are no more than the amount it would have cost you for your meals and lodging if you had stayed in Omaha. If they are more, your deduction is limited to the amount you would have spent in Omaha. If you retain your room in Omaha while in Kansas City, your expenses of returning to Kansas City on days off are deductible only to the extent of the amount you would have spent for your meals had you stayed in Omaha.
Temporary job location away from home where there are no living accommodations **EXAMPLE:** You live and work in Chicago. You have been assigned for three months to a construction job located 20 miles outside Nashville. There are no living facilities near the job site and you have to stay at a hotel in Nashville.	Under these circumstances, your necessary expenses in getting to and from your temporary job are business expenses and not commuting expenses. If you were employed at the site for an indefinite period *(20.9),* then the costs of commuting would be nondeductible, regardless of the distance; *see 20.2.*

Table 20-1 Deductible Travel and Transportation Expenses (continued)

Your Travel Status—	Tax Rule—
Taxi trips between customers' locations	The cab fares are deductible; *see 20.2.*
Seasonal jobs in different areas **EXAMPLE:** You live in Cincinnati, where you work for eight months each year. You earn the greater share of your annual income from that job. For the remaining four months of the year, you work in Miami. When in Miami, you eat and sleep in a hotel. You have been working on both of these jobs for several years and expect to continue to do so.	You have two recurring seasonal places of employment. Cincinnati is your principal place of employment. You may deduct the costs of your traveling expenses while away from Cincinnati working at your minor place of employment in Miami, including meals and lodging in Miami.
Trailer home moved to different job sites **EXAMPLE:** You are a construction welder. You live in a trailer that you move from city to city, where you work on construction projects. You have no other established home.	You may not deduct your expenses for meals and lodging. Each place where you locate becomes your principal place of business and, therefore, you are not "away from home."
Travel to school after work to take job-related courses	You may deduct travel costs if you meet the rules discussed at *33.17.*
Finding a new job in the same line of work **EXAMPLE:** You live in New York. You travel to Chicago for an interview for a new position.	You may deduct the cost of the trip and living expenses in Chicago; *see 19.7.*
Convention trip	You may deduct costs of travel to a business convention under the rules in *20.12.* If you are a delegate to a charitable or veterans' convention, you may claim a charitable deduction for the travel costs; *see 14.4.*
Trip to out-of-town college for educational courses	You deduct the cost of the trip if you meet the rules at *33.17.*
Trip for health reasons	You may deduct the cost of the trip as a medical expense if you meet the rules at *17.9.*

20.4 IRS Meal Allowance

If you find it difficult to keep records of meal costs while away from home *(20.3)* on business trips, you may prefer to claim an IRS meal allowance. In government tables, the allowance is referred to as the "M&IE" rate (meals and incidental expenses). In addition to meals and tips for food servers, the allowance (M&IE rate) includes a limited number of "incidental" expenses such as fees and tips for porters, baggage carriers, hotel maids, or room stewards. Self-employed individuals may claim the M&IE allowance as well as employees who are not reimbursed for meals under an "accountable" plan; *see 20.31.* However, the meal allowance may not be used if your employer is your brother, sister, spouse, parent, child, grandparent, or grandchild, or if you own more than 10% of the employer's outstanding stock.

Meal allowance on 2006 tax returns. For travel within the continental U.S. (referred to as CONUS locations), the standard meal allowance (M&IE) for 2006 is usually $39 per day, but higher rates apply in certain high-cost areas designated by the government. The high-cost-areas are generally major metropolitan cities or resort areas. The basic and high-cost-area meal rates are determined by the federal government's General Services Administration (GSA) and the IRS allows taxpayers to use the applicable rates in figuring their meal allowance deduction.

You must keep a record of the time, place, and business purpose of the trips. As long as you have this proof, you may claim the allowance even if your actual costs are less than the allowance.

The IRS provides the CONUS M&IE rates in Publication 1542, available online at www.irs.gov/formspubs. Publication 1542 is available only online; print copies can no longer be ordered. Publication 1542 shows the CONUS M&IE rates in tables that coincide with the start of a new fiscal year for the federal government each October. For example, Table 4 of the May 2006, revision of Publication 1542 shows the rates applicable for business trips from October 1, 2005, through

September 30, 2006 (Table 3 shows the rates for the prior one-year period). When the GSA changes the nationwide rates for the fiscal year starting October 1, 2006, the IRS will revise Publication 1542 and the rates for October 1, 2006, through September 30, 2007, will be shown in a new Table 4 and the rates for the first nine months of 2006 will be in Table 3. The IRS will post other online revisions to Publication 1542 throughout the year following GSA rate changes for particular localities. You can find alerts to these changes by linking from www.irs.gov/formspubs to the IRS's "What's Hot in Tax Forms, Publications, and Other Tax Products" webpage.

The CONUS rates can also be obtained from the GSA website at www.gsa.gov; click on "Per Diem Rates."

In computing your meal allowance (M&IE) deduction for 2006 business trips, you can apply the rates that were in effect for the first nine months of the year to business trips in the last three months. You may use the first set of rates for the first nine months and the updated rates for the last three months. For trips within the last three months, you must consistently use either the rates in effect for the first nine months or the revised rates that took effect on October 1; you cannot switch between the sets of rates on a trip-by-trip basis. If you travel to more than one city on the same day, use the meal allowance for the area where you stay overnight.

Travel outside the continental United States. Different rates apply for travel in Alaska, Hawaii, Puerto Rico, and U.S. possessions, as well as for travel to foreign countries. These rates (OCONUS) can be obtained by using links from the GSA website at www.gsa.gov.

Transportation industry workers. Employees or self-employed persons in the transportation industry may elect to claim a special M&IE rate. For the first nine months of 2006, the rate is $52 per day for any CONUS location and $58 per day for any OCONUS location. The rates may change effective October 1, 2006; *see* the *e-Supplement* for an update.The special rate avoids the need to apply the CONUS or OCONUS rates on a locality-by-locality basis. You cannot combine the two methods. If the special rate is used for one trip, it must be used for all trips during the same year.

Claiming the allowance. The allowance is prorated for the first and last day of a trip. You may claim 75% of the allowance for the days you depart and return. Alternatively, you may claim 100% of the allowance if you are away for a regular "9-to-5" business day.

If you are an employee and claim a deduction based on the allowance, you must reduce the deduction by 50% on Form 2106 or Form 2106-EZ. Furthermore, if you are an employee, the balance, when added to your other miscellaneous deductions, is subject to the 2% AGI floor on Schedule A. If you are self-employed, the allowance is claimed on Schedule C, where it is subject only to the 50% reduction; *see 40.6.* Interstate truck drivers, pilots, railroad operators, and other transportation industry employees subject to Department of Transportation hours of service limits are allowed to deduct 75% for meals (instead of 50%) consumed in 2006.

IRS Alert

Incidental Expenses

The IRS standard meal allowance (M&IE rate) does not include laundry, cleaning, and pressing of clothing. If you have receipts to substantiate laundry and cleaning costs, you may deduct them separately from the M&IE allowance, which includes as incidental expenses fees and tips for porters, baggage carriers, hotel maids, and room stewards.

If you do *not* pay or incur any meal expenses for a particular day on a trip away from home but you do have qualifying incidental expenses on that day, you have the option of deducting the actual costs or an allowance of $3 per day for the incidental expenses. The $3-per-day allowance must be prorated for the first and last days of the trip, as discussed at the end of *20.4* ("Claiming the allowance").

Deducting Travel Expenses Away From Home

20.5 Business Trip Deductions

The following expenses of a business trip *away from home (20.6)* are deductible if not reimbursed by your employer:

- Plane, railroad, taxi, and other transportation fares between your home and your business destination
- Hotel and other lodging expenses. You need receipts or similar evidence for lodging expenses; there is no IRS standard lodging allowance as there is for meals *(20.4)*.
- Meal costs. You may claim your actual meal costs if you maintain records, or you may use the standard meal allowance discussed in *20.4*. Only 50% of the cost of the meal is generally deductible; *see 20.24.*
- Tips, telephone, and telegraph costs
- Laundry and cleaning expenses
- Baggage charges (including insurance)
- Cab fares or other costs of transportation to and from the airport or station and your hotel. Also deductible are cab fares or other transportation costs, beginning with your first business call of the day, of getting from one customer to another, or from one place of business to another.
- Travel costs to find a new job are deductible; *see 19.7.*
- Entertainment expenses incurred while traveling away from home are deductible under the rules at *20.6.*

Cruise ship. If you travel by cruise ship on a business trip, your deductible cruise costs are limited to twice the highest federal *per diem* rate for travel in the United States on that date multiplied by the number of days in transit.

EXAMPLE

You sail to Europe on business. While you are away, the highest *per diem* federal rate is $346 and the trip lasts five days. The maximum deduction for the cost of the trip is $3,460 (2 × $346 × 5). The double *per diem* rule applies without regard to the 50% limit on meal costs if meals are not separately stated in your bill. If a separate amount for meals or entertainment is included, such amount must be reduced by 50%.

The double *per diem* rule does not apply to cruise ship convention costs that are deductible up to $2,000 a year if all the ports of call are in the U.S. or U.S. possessions and if the ship is registered in the United States; *see 20.14.*

Important: Record-keeping requirements. *See* the section beginning at *20.26* for record-keeping rules to support a deduction for unreimbursed travel expenses or to avoid being taxed on employer reimbursements.

20.6 When Are You Away From Home?

You have to meet the "away from home" test to deduct the cost of meals (only 50% deductible) and lodging while traveling. You have to satisfy the overnight-sleep rule at *20.3* to be "away from home."

Law Alert

Tax Home Defined

For travel expense purposes, your home is your place of business, employment, or post of duty, regardless of where you maintain your family residence. This tax home includes the entire city or general area of your business premises or place of employment. The area of your residence may be your tax home if your job requires you to work at widely scattered locations, you have no fixed place of work, and your residence is in a location economically suited to your work.

EXAMPLES

1. Your residence is in a suburb within commuting distance of New York City where you work full time. Your personal home and tax home are the same, that is, within the metropolitan area of New York City. You are away from home when you leave this area, say for Philadelphia. Meals and lodging are deductible only if you meet the overnight-sleep test; *see 20.3.*
2. Your residence is in New York City, but you work in Baltimore. Your tax home is Baltimore; you may not deduct living expenses there. But you may deduct travel expenses on a temporary assignment to New York City even while living at your home there.
3. A construction worker works for a utility company on construction sites in a 12-state area. Assignments are sent from his employer's regional office; he is not required to report to the office. The IRS ruled that his residence, which is in a city in the 12-state area, is his tax home.

Are you constantly on the road? If you move from job to job and do not work within any particular locality, an IRS agent may disallow your travel deductions on the grounds that your tax home is wherever you work; thus, you are never "away from home." You are considered a transient worker.

If your deduction is questioned because you have no regular or main place of business, you may be able to show that your tax home is the area of your residence. If you meet the following three tests, the IRS will treat your residence as your tax home: (1) you do some work in the vicinity of your residence, house, apartment, or room and live there while performing services in the area; (2) you have mortgage expenses or pay rent for the residence while away on the road; and (3) the residence is in an area where you were raised or lived for a long time, or a member of your immediate family such as your parent or child lives in the residence, or you frequently return there.

According to the IRS, if you meet only two of these three tests, it will decide on a case-by-case basis if your residence is your tax home. If you meet less than two of the tests, the IRS will not allow a deduction; each of your work locations is treated as your tax home.

If you live in a trailer at each job assignment and have no other home, each job location is your principal place of business and you are not "away from home."

Permanent duty station of service members. The Supreme Court held that a member of the Armed Forces is not away from home when he or she is at a permanent duty station. This is true even if the service member has to maintain a separate home for family members who are not permitted to live at the duty station.

20.7 Fixing a Tax Home If You Work in Different Locations

If you regularly work in two or more separate areas, your tax home is the area of your principal place of business or employment. You are away from home when you are away from the area of your principal place of business or employment. Therefore, you may deduct your transportation costs to and from your minor place of business and your living costs there.

Professional sports players, coaches, and managers. When the only business of such persons is the professional sport, their home is the "club town." But if they are in another business in addition to their professional playing, how much time is spent and how much is earned at each place determines whether their club's hometown or the place of their off-season business is their tax home. If it is the club's hometown, they deduct travel and living expenses while away from that town—including the time they are where the second business is. (If the second place is where their families also live, they may not deduct the families' expenses there.) If the town where the other business is located is the tax home, then expenses in the club's hometown may be deducted.

Airline pilots. It is important for airline pilots who fly in and out of various locations to determine a tax home for income and deduction purposes. Generally, the IRS considers an airline pilot's tax home to be the airport at which the pilot is regularly based. For example, in one case the IRS barred a pilot from claiming the foreign earned income exclusion *(36.1)* because his tax home was deemed to be his base in New York, rather than in London, where he and his wife actually lived.

Planning Reminder

Determining Your Principal Place of Business

If you have more than one regular place of business, your tax home is your principal place of business. Your principal place of business or employment is determined by comparing: (1) the time ordinarily spent working in each area; (2) the degree of your business activity in each area; (3) the amount of your income from each area; (4) the taxpayer's permanent residence; and (5) whether employment at one location is temporary or indefinite.

No single factor is determinative. The relative importance of each factor will vary depending on the facts of a particular case. For example, where there are no substantial differences between incomes earned in two places of employment, your tax home is probably the area in which you spend more of your time. Where there are substantial income differences, your tax home is probably the area in which you earn more of your income.

EXAMPLES

1. Sherman lived in Worcester, Mass., where he managed a factory. He opened his own sales agency in New York. He continued to manage the factory and spent considerable time in Worcester. The larger part of his income came from the New York business. However, he was allowed to treat New York as his minor place of business and to deduct his travel expenses to New York and his living expenses there because he spent most of his time in Worcester and his income there was substantial.
2. Benson, a consulting engineer, maintained a combination residence-business office in a home he owned in New York. He also taught four days a week at a Technological Institute in West Virginia under a temporary nine-month appointment. He spent three-day weekends, holidays, and part of the summer at his New York address. At the Institute, he rented a room in the student union building. The IRS disallowed transportation expenses between New York and West Virginia and meals and lodging there as not incurred while away from home. The Tax Court disagreed. A taxpayer may have more than one occupation in more than one city. When his occupations require him to spend a substantial amount of time in each place, he may deduct his travel expenses, including meals and lodging, at the place away from his permanent residence. That Benson's teaching salary happened to exceed his income from his private practice does not change the result.

20.8 Tax Home of Married Couple Working in Different Cities

When a husband and wife work and live in different cities during the week, one of them may seek to deduct travel expenses away from home. Such deductions have generally been disallowed, but courts have allowed some exceptions. Although for common law purposes the domicile of the husband may be the domicile of the wife, for tax purposes when each spouse works in a different city, each may have a separate tax home.

EXAMPLES

1. Robert worked in Wilmington, Delaware; his wife, Margaret, worked in New York City. During the weekend, she traveled to Wilmington and deducted, as travel expenses away from home, her living costs in New York and weekend travel expenses to Wilmington. She argued that because she and her husband filed a joint return, they were a single taxable unit, and the tax home of this unit was Wilmington where her husband lived. The deduction was disallowed. That a couple can file a joint return does not give them deductions that are not otherwise available to them as individuals. Margaret's tax home was New York, where she worked. Therefore, her expenses there are not deductible. And, as the weekend trips to Wilmington had no relationship to her job, they, too, were not deductible.

2. Hundt and his wife lived in Arlington, Va., but he wrote and directed films in various parts of the country. He wrote screenplays either at his Arlington home or on location, but most of his business came from New York City, where he lived in hotels. One year, he spent 175 days in New York City on business and rented an apartment for $1,200 because it was cheaper than a hotel. He deducted half the annual rent for the New York apartment, the costs of traveling between Arlington and New York, and the cost of meals in New York. The IRS disallowed the expenses, finding New York to be his tax home. The Tax Court disagreed. Arlington was Hundt's tax home because (1) part of his income came from his creative writing in Arlington; and (2) his travel to other parts of the country was temporary. The fact that most of his income came from New York did not make New York his tax home.

20.9 Deducting Living Costs on Temporary Assignment

A business trip or job assignment away from home *(20.6)* at a single location may last a few days, weeks, or months. If your assignment is considered *temporary,* you may deduct travel costs (*see* below) while there because your tax home has not changed. An assignment is considered temporary by the IRS if you realistically expect it to last for one year or less and it actually does last no more than one year. If an assignment is realistically expected to last more than a year it is considered *indefinite,* and you cannot deduct your living costs at the area of the assignment because that location becomes your tax home. This is true even if the assignment actually lasts only a year or less. That is, you can be away for a year or less and still be barred from claiming a deduction if at the time you started the assignment you realistically expected it to last for more than a year. Likewise, employment that is initially temporary may become indefinite due to changed circumstances; *see* the Examples below.

Planning Reminder

Federal Crime Investigations

Federal employees such as FBI agents and prosecutors who are certified by the Attorney General as traveling on behalf of the federal government in a temporary duty status to investigate, prosecute, or provide support services for the investigation or prosecution of a federal crime are not subject to the one-year limitation on deductibility of expenses while away from home on temporary assignments.

EXAMPLES

1. You are on a job assignment away from home in a single location that is expected to last (and it does in fact last) for one year or less. The IRS will treat the employment as temporary, unless facts and circumstances indicate otherwise. Expenses are deductible.
2. You are sent on a job assignment away from home at a *single* location. You expected that the job would last 18 months. However, due to financial difficulties you were transferred home after 11 months. Even though your assignment actually lasted for less than one year the IRS treats the employment as indefinite because you realistically expected it to last more than one year. Thus, your travel and living expenses while away from home are not deductible.
3. You are sent on a job assignment away from home at a *single* location. You expected that the job would last only nine months. However, due to changed circumstances occurring after eight months, you were asked to remain on the assignment for six more months. The IRS treats the assignment as temporary for eight months, and indefinite for the remaining time you are away from home. Thus, travel and living expenses you paid or incurred during the first eight months are deductible; expenses paid or incurred thereafter are not.

Deductible travel costs on temporary trip. While on a temporary job assignment expected to last a year or less, you may deduct the cost of meals and lodging there, even for your days off. If you return home, say for weekends, your living expenses at home are not deductible. You may deduct travel expenses, meals, and lodging en route between your home and your job assignment provided they do not exceed your living expenses had you stayed at the temporary job location. If you keep a hotel room at the temporary location while you return home, you may deduct your round-trip expenses for the trip home only up to the amount you would have spent for meals had you stayed at the temporary workplace.

Caution

Taking Your Family With You

If you take your family with you to a temporary job site, an IRS agent may argue that this is evidence that you considered the assignment to be indefinite. In the Michaels Example on this page, however, such a move was not considered detrimental to a deduction of living expenses at the job location.

EXAMPLE

Michaels, a cost analyst for Boeing, lived in Seattle. He traveled for Boeing, but was generally not away from home for more than five weeks. Michaels agreed to go to Los Angeles for a year to service Boeing's suppliers in that area. He rented his Seattle house and brought his family with him to Los Angeles. Ten months later, Boeing opened a permanent office in Los Angeles and asked Michaels to remain there permanently. Michaels argued that his expenses for food and lodging during the 10-month period were deductible as "away from home" expenses. The IRS contended that the Los Angeles assignment was for an indefinite period.

The Tax Court sided with Michaels. He was told that the stay was for a year only. He leased his Seattle house to a tenant for one year, planning to return to it. He regarded his work in Los Angeles as temporary until Boeing changed its plans. The one-year period justified his taking the family but did not alter the temporary nature of the assignment.

Separate assignments over a period over a year. Where over a period of years you work on several separate assignments for one client, the IRS may attempt to treat the separate assignments as amounting to a permanent assignment and disallow living costs away from home, as in Mitchell's situation, below.

EXAMPLE

Mitchell, a publishing consultant who lived and worked out of his home in Illinois, advised a publisher of a magazine with offices in California. Over a five-year period, from 1991 to 1995, he worked on short job assignments that averaged 130 days a year for the magazine. Some assignments arose because of unforeseen events, such as the abrupt firing of a novice editor, the hiring of a new editor, and the editor's later absence because of cancer and her death. In 1994 and 1995, when working in California, he rented an apartment because it was cheaper than a hotel. He claimed lodging and meal expenses in California that the IRS disallowed on the grounds that his employment in California was not temporary; it lasted more than one year.

The Tax Court disagrees. Just because an independent contractor returns to the same general location in more than one year does not mean that he is employed there on an indefinite basis. Mitchell's work followed an on again, off again pattern. Each job assignment that lasted less than a year ended with no expectation of future employment. Throughout the five-year period, his consultancy services were required by unexpected events.

No regular job where you live. That you do not have regular employment where you live may prevent a deduction of living costs at a temporary job in another city. The IRS may disallow the deduction on the grounds that the expenses are not incurred while you are away from home; the temporary job site is the tax home.

Deducting Expenses of a Business-Vacation Trip

20.10 Business-Vacation Trips Within the United States

On a business trip to a resort area, you may also spend time vacationing. If the *primary purpose* of the trip is to transact business and the area is within the United States (50 states and the District of Columbia) you may deduct all of the costs of your transportation to and from the area, lodging, and 50% of meal expenses, even if you do spend time vacationing. If the main purpose of the trip is personal, you may not deduct any part of your travel costs to and from the area. The amount of time spent on business as opposed to sightseeing or personal visits is the most important issue in determining your primary purpose. Regardless of the primary purpose of your trip, you are allowed to deduct expenses related to the business you transacted while in the area.

No deductions will be allowed if you attend a convention or seminar where you are given videotapes to view at your own convenience and no other business-related activities or lectures occur during the convention. The trip is considered a vacation.

If your trip is primarily for business, and while at the business destination you extend your stay for a few days for nonbusiness reasons, such as to visit relatives, you deduct travel expenses to and from the business destination.

EXAMPLE

You work in Atlanta and make a business trip to New Orleans. You stay in New Orleans for six days and your total costs, including round-trip transportation to and from New Orleans, meals, and lodging, is $600, which you may deduct subject to the 50% limit for meals. If, on your way home, you spend three days in Mobile visiting relatives and incur an additional $200 in travel costs, your deduction is limited to the $600 (less 50% of meals) you would have spent had you gone home directly from New Orleans.

Caution

Primary Business Purpose

If your return is examined, proving the business purpose of your trip depends on presenting evidence to convince an examining agent that the trip, despite your vacationing, was planned primarily to transact business. Keep a log or diary to substantiate business activities.

Reimbursement for weekend travel. If your employer extends your business trip over a weekend to take advantage of discount airfares that require a Saturday night stayover, you may deduct the cost of meals, lodging, and other incidental expenses incurred for the additional night. The reason for the stayover has a business purpose: to cut travel costs. If your employer pays for the expenses directly or if you are reimbursed under an accountable plan *(20.31)*, the payment is not taxable to you.

20.11 Business-Vacation Trips Outside the United States

On a business trip abroad, you may deduct your travel expenses (the 50% limit applies for meals), even though you take time out to vacation, provided you can prove: (1) the primary purpose of the trip was business and (2) you did not have control over the assignment of the trip.

Fixing the date of the trip does not mean that you had control over the assignment. IRS regulations assume that when you travel for your company under a reimbursement or allowance arrangement, you do not control the trip arrangements, provided also that you are not: (1) a managing executive of the company; (2) related to your employer *(see 20.4)*; or (3) have more than a 10% stock interest in the company. You are considered a managing executive if you are authorized without effective veto procedures to decide on the necessity of the trip. You are related to your employer if the employer is your spouse, parent, child, brother, sister, grandparent, or grandchild.

Caution

Vacation Areas

If the IRS determines that you were primarily on vacation, it will disallow all travel costs except for costs directly related to your business in the area such as registration fees at a foreign business convention; *see 20.14*.

Rule for managing executives and self-employed persons. If you are a managing executive, self-employed, related to your employer, or have a more-than-10% stock interest, your deduction for transportation costs to and from your business destination may be limited. However, a full deduction for transportation costs is allowed if:

1. The trip outside the United States took a week or less, not counting the day you left the U.S. but counting the day you returned,
2. If the trip abroad lasted more than a week, you spent less than 25% of your time, counting the days your trip began and ended, on vacation or other personal activities, *or*
3. In planning the trip you did not place a major emphasis on taking a vacation.

If the vacationing and other personal activities took up 25% or more of your time on a trip lasting more than one week, and you cannot prove that the vacation was a minor consideration in planning the trip, you must allocate travel expenses between the time spent on business and that spent on personal affairs. The part allocated to business is deductible; the balance is not. To allocate, count the number of days spent on the trip outside the United States, including the day you leave the U.S. and the day you return. Then divide this total into the number of days on which you had business activities; include days of travel to and from a business destination.

If you vacation at, near, or beyond the city in which you do business, the expense subject to allocation is the cost of travel from the place of departure to the business destination and back. For example, you travel from New York to London on business and then vacation in Paris before returning to New York. The expense subject to allocation is the cost of traveling from New York to London and back; *see* Example 2 below. However, if from London you vacationed in Dublin before returning to New York, you would allocate the round-trip fare between New York and Dublin and also deduct the difference between that round-trip fare and the fare between New York and London; *see* Example 3 below.

EXAMPLES

1. You fly from New York to Paris to attend a business meeting for one day. You spend the next two days sightseeing and then fly back to New York. The entire trip, including two days for travel en route, took five days. The plane fare is deductible. The trip did not exceed one week.
2. You fly from Chicago to New York, where you spend six days on business. You then fly to London, where you conduct business for two days. You then fly to Paris for a five-day vacation after which you fly back to Chicago. You would not have made the trip except for the business that you had to transact in London. The nine days of travel outside the United States away from home, including two days for travel en route, exceeded a week, and the five days devoted to vacationing were not less than 25% of the total travel time outside the U.S. The two days spent traveling between Chicago and New York, and the six days spent in New York, are not counted in determining whether the travel outside the United States exceeded a week and whether the time devoted to personal activities was less than 25%.

Assume you are unable to prove either that you did not have substantial control over the arrangements of the trip or that an opportunity for taking a personal vacation was not a major consideration in your decision to take the trip. Thus, $^5/_9$ (five nonbusiness days out of nine days outside the U.S.) of the plane fare from New York to London and from London to New York is not deductible. You may deduct $^4/_9$ of the New-York-to-London round-trip fare, plus lodging, 50% of meals, and other allowable travel costs while in London. No deduction is allowed for any part of the costs of the trip from London to Paris.

3. Same facts as in Example 2, except that the vacation is in Dublin, which is closer to the U.S. than London. The allocation is based on the round-trip fare between New York and Dublin. Thus, $^4/_9$ of the New York to Dublin fare is deductible and $^5/_9$ is not deductible. Further, the IRS allows a deduction for the excess of the New-York-to-London fare over the New-York-to-Dublin fare.

Filing Tip

Weekend Expenses

If your business trip is extended over a weekend to take advantage of reduced airfares, the additional cost of meals, lodging, and other incidental expenses is deductible.

Weekends, holidays, and business standby days. If you have business meetings scheduled before and after a weekend or holiday, the days in between the meetings are treated as days spent on business for purposes of the 25% business test just discussed. This is true although you spend the days for sightseeing or other personal travel. A similar rule applies if you have business meetings on Friday and the next scheduled meeting is the following Tuesday; Saturday through Monday are treated as business days. If your trip is extended over a weekend to take advantage of reduced airfares, the additional expense of meals, lodging, and other incidental expenses is deductible; *see 20.10.*

20.12 Deducting Expenses of Business Conventions

Conventions and seminars at resort areas usually combine business with pleasure. Therefore, the IRS scrutinizes deductions claimed for attending a business convention where opportunities exist for vacationing. Especially questioned are trips where you are accompanied by your spouse and other members of your family. Foreign conventions are discussed at *20.14.*

Generally, you may not deduct expenses of attending investment conventions and seminars; *see 19.15.* You also may not deduct the costs of business conventions or seminars where you merely receive a videotape of business lectures to be viewed at your convenience and no other business-related activities occur during the event.

In claiming a deduction for convention expenses, be prepared to show that the convention was connected with your business. Cases and IRS rulings have upheld deductions for doctors, lawyers, and dentists attending professional conventions. One case allowed a deduction to a legal secretary for her costs at a secretaries' convention. If you are a delegate to a business convention, make sure you prove you attended to serve primarily your own business interests, not those of the association. However, it is not necessary for you to show that the convention dealt specifically with your job. It is sufficient that attendance at the convention may advance or benefit your position. If you fail to prove business purpose, the IRS will allocate your expenses between the time spent on your business and the time spent as a delegate. You then deduct only the expenses attributed to your business activities.

EXAMPLES

1. An attorney with a general law practice was interested in international law and relations. He was appointed a delegate to represent the American branch of the International Law Association at a convention in Paris. The attorney deducted the cost of the trip and convention as business expenses which the IRS and a court disallowed. He failed to prove that attending the conference on international law helped his general practice. He did not get any business referrals as a result of his attendance at the convention. Nor did he prove the chance of getting any potential business from the conference.
2. An insurance agent doing business in Texas attended his company's convention in New York. One morning of the six-day convention was devoted to a business meeting and luncheon; the rest of the time was spent in sightseeing and entertainment. The company paid for the cost of the trip. The IRS added the reimbursement to the agent's pay and would not let him deduct the amount. The convention in New York served no business purpose. It was merely a method of entertaining company personnel. If there was any valid business to be transacted, the company could have called a meeting in Texas, the area of his home office.

Caution

Substantiate Convention Business

Keep a copy of the convention program and a record of the business sessions you attend. If the convention provides a sign-in book, sign it. In addition, keep a record of all of your business expenses as explained in *20.26.*

3. A plywood company could not deduct the costs of entertaining 116 customers and employees at a New Orleans hotel during a Superbowl weekend. The company did not reserve conference rooms or make any other arrangements for organized business meetings. The IRS and two federal courts held that although business discussions may have occurred on a random basis, these were secondary to entertainment.

What expenses are deductible? If the convention trip is primarily for business, you may deduct travel costs both to and from the convention, food costs, tips, display expenses (such as sample room costs), and hotel bills. If you entertain business clients or customers, you may deduct these amounts too.

Food and beverage costs are subject to the 50% cost limitation rule as explained in *20.24*.

EXAMPLE

You attend a business convention held in a coastal resort city primarily for business reasons. During the convention period, you do some local sightseeing, social entertaining, and visiting—all unrelated to your business. You may deduct your traveling expenses to and from the resort, your living expenses at the resort, and other expenses such as business entertaining, sample displays, etc. But you may not deduct the cost of sightseeing, personal entertaining, and social visiting.

Keep records of your payments identifying expenses directly connected with your business dealings at the convention and those that are part of your personal activity, such as sightseeing, social visiting, and entertaining. Recreation costs are not deductible even though a part of your overall convention costs.

Fraternal organizations. You may not deduct expenses at conventions held by fraternal organizations, such as the American Legion, Shriners, etc., even though incidental business was carried on. However, delegates to fraternal conventions may in some instances deduct expenses as charitable contributions; *see 14.4*.

20.13 Travel Expenses of a Spouse or Dependents

Travel costs of a spouse, dependent, or any other individual who is not a business associate and who accompanies you on a business trip are not deductible unless that person is also your employee and has a bona fide business reason for taking the trip that would justify claiming a deduction if the person took the trip on his or her own.

Even though the travel costs of a non-employee spouse or other person are not deductible, you may deduct the cost of such person's participation in the entertainment of business clients at conventions or business trips if the trip or entertainment meets the tests at *20.21*. Generally, you may deduct the cost of goodwill entertaining of associates immediately before or after convention business meetings. A convention meeting qualifies as a bona fide business meeting.

Filing Tip

How Much To Deduct for Spouse

If your spouse accompanied you on a business trip, your bills will probably show costs for both of you. These usually are less than twice the cost for a single person. To find what you may deduct where your spouse's presence is for personal and not qualifying business reasons, do not divide the bill in half. Figure what accommodations and transportation would have cost you alone and deduct that. The excess over the single person's costs is not deductible.

EXAMPLES

1. You and your spouse travel by car to a convention. You pay $200 a day for a double room. A single room would have cost $150 a day. Your spouse's presence at the convention was for social reasons. You may deduct the total cost of operating your car to and from the convention city. You may deduct $150 a day for your room. If you traveled by plane or railroad, you would deduct only your own fare.
2. Connie worked with her husband operating a home improvement contracting business. With him, she attended trade shows and conventions, where they ran a display booth. There, she talked about their company's services and solicited new business. The IRS disallowed the company's deduction of her travel expenses as having no business purpose. The Tax Court disagreed. Both Connie and her husband were officers and employees of the company. They attended the conferences together. As the IRS allowed her husband's expenses, it should have also allowed expenses attributed to her participation, especially as they were incurred together as employees.

20.14 Restrictions on Foreign Conventions and Cruises

You may not deduct expenses at a foreign convention outside the North American area unless you satisfy the rules at *20.11* and also can show the convention is directly related to your business and it was as reasonable for the meeting to be held outside the North American area as within it.

Apart from the United States, the North American area includes Mexico, Canada, Puerto Rico, U.S. Virgin Islands, American Samoa, Northern Mariana Islands, Guam, Marshall Islands, Micronesia, Palau and U.S. island possessions.

Conventions may also be held in eligible Caribbean countries that agree to exchange certain data with the U.S. and do not discriminate against conventions held in the United States. Antigua and Barbuda, Barbados, Bermuda, Costa Rica, Dominica, Dominican Republic, Grenada, Guyana, Honduras, Jamaica, Saint Lucia, and Trinidad and Tobago have qualified and are considered to be within the North American area.

Check with the convention operator about whether the country in which your convention is being held has qualified.

Limited cruise ship deduction. Up to $2,000 a year is allowed for attending cruise ship conventions if all the ports of call are in the U.S. or U.S. possessions and if the ship is registered in the United States. A deduction is allowed only if you attach to your return statements signed by you and by an officer of the convention sponsor that detail the daily schedule of business activities, the number of hours you attended these activities, and the total days of the trip. Do not confuse the $2,000 limitation with the *per diem* limitation for cruise ship costs discussed at *20.5*. The *per diem* limitation does not apply to cruises that meet the tests for the up-to-$2,000 deduction.

Meals and Entertainment Expenses for Clients, Customers, or Employees

20.15 50% Deduction Limit

To be deductible at all, dining and entertainment costs for clients, customers, or employees must meet one of the restrictive tests at *20.16*. Even if the expenses qualify under one of the tests, only 50% of unreimbursed expenses are generally deductible and this 50% balance is reduced by the 2% AGI floor if you are an employee. Furthermore, all entertainment costs, including meals, must be backed up with records. If you do not keep adequate records, your deductions will be disallowed. The 50% deduction limit and exceptions to the limit are discussed at *20.24*.

20.16 The Restrictive Tests for Meals and Entertainment

Meal and entertainment costs are deductible, subject to the 50% limit *(20.24)*, if they are ordinary and necessary to your business, and also are either:

1. Directly related to the active conduct of your business *(20.17), or*
2. Directly preceding or following a substantial and bona fide business discussion on a subject associated with the active conduct of your business. This test applies to dining and entertainment in which you seek new business or to goodwill entertainment to encourage the continuation of an existing business relationship. Under this test, you may entertain business associates in nonbusiness settings such as restaurants, theaters, sports arenas, and nightclubs, provided the entertainment directly precedes or follows the business discussion. Business associates are: established or prospective customers, clients, suppliers, employees, agents, partners, or professional advisers, whether established or prospective; *see 20.18.*

Ordinary and necessary expenses are those considered helpful and common practice in your business or profession; they do not have to be indispensable to your business.

20.17 Directly Related Dining and Entertainment

The directly related test limits the deduction of dining and entertainment costs at restaurants, nightclubs, on yachts, at sporting events, on hunting trips, and during social events.

The directly related test for dining and entertainment costs may be met in one of three ways: (1) under the generally related test; (2) as expenses incurred in a clear business setting; or (3) as expenses incurred for services performed. If dining or entertainment fails to meet the directly related tests, it may qualify under the rules discussed in *20.18*, which require the holding of a business discussion before or after the entertainment.

Planning Reminder

Scheduling Entertainment and Business Discussions

A business discussion generally must take place the same day as the dining or entertainment. If not, and your deduction is questioned, you must give an acceptable reason for the interval between the discussion and the dining or entertainment. IRS regulations recognize that a day may separate a business meeting and the entertainment of an out-of-town customer. He or she may come to your office to discuss business one day and you provide entertainment the next day, or you provide the entertainment on the first day and discuss business the day after.

The IRS does not estimate how long a business discussion should last. But it does warn that a meeting must involve a discussion or negotiation to obtain income or business benefits. It does not require that more time be devoted to the meeting than to the entertainment.

Caution

Hunting or Fishing Trips

The IRS presumes that entertainment during a hunting or fishing trip or on a yacht is not conducive to business discussion or activity. You must prove otherwise.

In one case, a printing-press-parts manufacturer convinced a federal appeals court (Eighth Circuit) that there was a business purpose for the annual fishing trips it held for factory workers and sales personnel following its sales conference. Specific company business was discussed during the trips. Salespersons gave feedback to factory employees concerning manufacturing problems that increased the need for repairs, parts distribution issues were discussed, and plans made to counter competitors.

Generally related test. Under this test, you must show a business motive for the dining or entertainment and business activity during the entertainment. You must show that you had more than a general expectation of getting future income or other specific business benefit (other than goodwill). Although you do not have to prove that income or other business benefit actually resulted from the expense, such evidence will help support your claim. What type of business activity will an IRS agent look for? The agent will seek proof that a business meeting, negotiation, or discussion took place during the period of dining or entertainment. It is not necessary that more time be devoted to business than to entertainment. What if you did not talk business? You must prove that you would have done so except for reasons beyond your control.

Clear business setting test. Expenses incurred in a clear business setting meet the directly related test provided also that you had no significant motive for incurring the expenses other than to further your business. Entertainment of people with whom you have no personal or social relationship is usually considered to have occurred in a clear business setting. For example, entertainment of business representatives and civic leaders at the opening of a new hotel or theatrical production to obtain business publicity rather than goodwill is considered to be entertainment in a clear business setting. Also, entertainment that involves a price rebate is considered to have occurred in a clear business setting, as, for example, when a hotel owner provides occasional free dinners at the hotel for a customer who patronizes the hotel.

The cost of a hospitality room displaying company products at a convention is also a directly related expense.

Entertainment occurring under the following circumstances or in the following places is generally *not* considered as directly related:

- You are not present during the entertainment.
- The distractions are substantial, as at nightclubs, sporting events, or during a social gathering such as a cocktail party.
- You meet with a group that includes persons other than business associates at cocktail lounges, country clubs, golf and athletic clubs, or at vacation resorts.

Services performed test. An expense is directly related if it was directly or indirectly made for the benefit of an individual (other than an employee) either as taxable compensation for services he or she rendered or as a taxable prize or award.

EXAMPLE

A manufacturer provides a vacation trip for retailers whose sales of his products exceed quotas. The value of the vacation is a taxable prize to the retailers. The vacation cost is a directly related entertainment expense for the manufacturer.

20.18 Goodwill Entertainment

Goodwill entertaining may qualify as deductible entertainment. Dining and entertainment costs may be deductible if a substantial and *bona fide* business discussion directly preceded or followed the dining or entertainment.

An officially scheduled meeting at a convention is generally considered a bona fide business discussion.

EXAMPLES

1. During the day, you negotiate with a group of business associates. In the evening, you entertain the group and their spouses at a theater and nightclub. The cost of the entertainment is deductible, even though arranged to promote goodwill.
2. In the evening after a business meeting at a convention, you entertain associates or prospective customers and their spouses. You may deduct the entertainment costs.

20.19 Home Entertaining

The cost of entertaining business customers or clients at home is deductible provided a business discussion occurs before, during, or after the meal. When you claim such a deduction, be ready to prove that your motive for dining with them was business rather than social. Have a record of the entertainment costs, names of the guests, and their business affiliations.

20.20 Your Personal Share of Entertainment Costs

If the entertaining occurred while on a business trip away from home, you deduct your own meal costs as travel expenses away from home *(20.6)*. If the entertaining occurred within the locality of your regular place of business, whether you will be allowed a deduction for your share will depend on the agent examining your return. The IRS said in a ruling that an agent will not disallow your deduction of your own part of the meal cost unless he or she finds that you are claiming a substantial amount that includes personal living expenses. In such a case, which generally is limited to situations where personal meals are regularly claimed as part of an "abusive" pattern, the agent will follow the stricter Tax Court rule (sometimes referred to as the "Sutter" rule) and allow only that part of the meal cost that exceeds what you would usually spend on yourself when alone.

Filing Tip

Allocating Payment Covering Lodging and Meals

A hotel may include meals in a room charge. In such cases, the room charge must be allocated between the meals/entertainment and lodging. The amount allocated to meals and entertainment is subject to the 50% cost limitation. If you receive a *per diem* allowance from your employer covering both lodging and meals under an accountable reimbursement plan, you may have to allocate part of the reimbursement to meals in order to deduct expenses in excess of the reimbursement; *see 20.31.*

20.21 Entertainment Costs of Spouses

A deduction is allowed for the spouses' share of the entertainment costs if they were present during entertainment that qualified as directly related entertainment under the general rule discussed in *20.17*. For goodwill entertainment, the cost of entertainment of the spouses is deductible if your share and the business associate's share of the entertainment is deductible. The IRS recognizes that when an out-of-town customer is accompanied by his or her spouse, it may be impracticable to entertain the customer without the spouse. Under such circumstances, the cost of the spouse's entertainment is deductible if the customer's entertainment costs are also deductible. Furthermore, if your spouse joined the party because the customer's spouse was present, the expenses of your spouse are also deductible.

20.22 Entertainment Facilities and Club Dues

You may not deduct the expenses of maintaining and operating facilities used to entertain clients and customers. By law, entertainment facilities are not considered business assets. Examples of entertainment facilities are yachts, hunting lodges, fishing camps, swimming pools, tennis courts, automobiles, airplanes, apartments, hotel suites, or homes in a vacation area. A season box seat or pass at a sporting event or theater is *not* considered an entertainment facility; *see* the special rule at *20.24* for skybox rentals.

The disallowance rule applies to operating expenses such as rent, utilities, and security, and also to depreciation, but not to such expenses as interest, taxes, and casualty losses that are deductible without having to show business purpose.

Exceptions. A deduction may be allowed for expenses such as the cost of food and drinks incurred at an entertainment facility, if they meet the rules discussed in *20.16* through *20.21*.

Club dues. You may not deduct dues for country clubs, golf and athletic clubs, airline clubs, hotel clubs, business luncheon clubs, and other clubs organized for business, pleasure, recreation, or other social purposes. However, IRS regulations generally allow a deduction for dues paid to (1) civic or public service organizations such as Kiwanis, Lions, and Rotary clubs; (2) professional organizations such as medical or bar associations; and (3) chambers of commerce, trade associations, business leagues, real estate boards, and boards of trade. The deduction for dues is allowed provided that the organization in (1)–(3) does not have a principal purpose of providing entertainment for members or their guests.

20.23 Restrictive Test Exception for Reimbursements

As an employer, you can deduct expense allowances or other reimbursements of employee expenses that you treat as compensation and from which you withhold federal tax. You are not subject to the 50% deduction limit for meals and entertainment; the employee is, when claiming the meals on Form 2106.

A similar rule applies to meal allowances or reimbursements that you give to an independent contractor and that you report as compensation on Form 1099-MISC where the contractor does not adequately account for the expenses.

The restrictive tests in *20.16* do not apply to such reimbursements. They are deductible if they are "ordinary and necessary" business expenses, and you have records to back up the deduction.

Law Alert

Transportation Industry Workers

Individuals subject to Department of Transportation limitations on hours of service, such as interstate truck and bus drivers, pilots and other air transportation workers, and train crews, may claim a higher deductible percentage of food and beverage costs when working away from home. The deductible amount is 75% in 2006 and 2007, and 80% for 2008 and later years.

Filing Tip

Meals Provided to Employees

An employer who provides meals to employees on employer premises is allowed a full deduction for all the meals provided that more than half of the employees who are provided meals are furnished them for substantial noncompensatory business reasons.

20.24 50% Cost Limitation on Meals and Entertainment

You generally may not deduct the full amount of your deductible expenses for business meals and entertainment expenses, such as tickets to sports events. Unless one of the exceptions below applies, only 50% of the otherwise allowable amount for food, beverages, and entertainment is deductible. A higher deductible percentage is allowed to workers subject to the Department of Transportation's "hours of service" limits; *see* the Law Alert on this page.

Taxes and tips are considered part of the cost subject to the 50% limit. If your employer reimburses your expenses, the 50% limit applies to the employer.

The 50% limit applies to both employees and the self-employed. It applies to the IRS meal allowance deduction; *see 20.4*. For employee expenses the limit is taken into account on Form 2106 or 2106-EZ (if you are not reimbursed by your employer and do not claim depreciation for a business car), and on Schedule C for self-employment expenses.

EXAMPLES

1. You pay meal and entertainment costs of $5,000. Only $2,500 ($5,000 × 50%) is considered deductible.
2. Same facts as above, but your employer reimburses your costs after you account for the expenses. The employer's deduction is limited to $2,500. You have no deduction.

Tickets. The deductible amount for a ticket treated as an entertainment expense is generally restricted to the face value of the ticket. Amounts in excess of face value paid to ticket agencies or scalpers are not deductible. Also *see* the special rule for skybox rental costs below. The deductible cost of tickets is also generally subject to the 50% limitation. However, a full deduction is allowed for tickets to qualifying charitable sporting events; *see* Exception 7 below.

EXAMPLE

You buy from a ticket broker five tickets to entertain clients. The face value of the five tickets is $500. You paid $600 for them. The deductible amount is $250 (50% × $500).

Exceptions to 50% cost limitation. In the following cases, you may claim a full deduction for meals and entertainment; the 50% limitation does not apply:

1. As an employer, you pay for an employee's meals and entertainment that are treated as taxable compensation to the employee and as wages for purposes of withholding of income tax.
2. You reimburse an independent contractor for meal and entertainment expenses he or she incurs on your behalf and the contractor does not adequately account for the expenses. You deduct the reimbursements as compensation if they are ordinary and necessary business expenses.
3. As an employer, you incur expenses for recreational, social, or similar activities (including facilities) primarily for the benefit of employees who are not highly compensated employees. For example, the expenses of food, beverages, and entertainment for a company-wide summer party are not subject to the 50% limit.
4. Expenses for meals and entertainment, including the use of facilities made available to the general public, such as a free concert, for advertising or goodwill purposes. For example, the IRS allowed a real-estate broker to fully deduct the cost of free dinners it provided to potential investors who attended its sales presentations. The 50% deduction limitation for meals does not apply to promotional activities that are made available to the general public. The IRS relied on the following example in a 1986 Congressional committee report for purposes of allowing a 100% deduction: A wine merchant provides customers with wine and food to demonstrate the suitability of the wine with certain types of meals. The committee report indicated that the cost of the wine, food, and other costs associated with the wine-tasting function would be fully deductible.
5. Expenses for meals and entertainment sold to the public in your business, such as meal expenses if you run a restaurant, or the cost of providing entertainment if you run a nightclub. These expenses are fully deductible.
6. Food or beverage provided to your employees as a tax-free *de minimis* fringe benefit *(3.10)*. This would include expenses of a cafeteria on your premises for employees where meal charges cover the direct operating cost of the cafeteria. The *de minimis* benefit exception allows a full deduction for all meals

provided to employees on employer premises if more than half of the employees who are provided meals are furnished them for the employer's convenience (substantial noncompensatory business purpose). If the more-than-half test is met, the meals are tax free to all the employees; *see 3.12*.

7. The price of tickets to charitable sports events (including amounts in excess of face value) provided the ticket package includes admission to the event. To qualify, a charitable sports event must: (1) be organized for the primary purpose of benefitting a tax-exempt organization; (2) contribute 100% of its net proceeds to such organization; and (3) use volunteers for substantially all work performed in carrying out the event. According to Congressional committee reports, a golf tournament that donates all its proceeds to charity is eligible to qualify under this exception, even if it offers prize money to the golfers who participate or uses paid concessionaires or security personnel. However, tickets to a college football game or similar scholastic events generally do not qualify because they do not satisfy the requirement that substantially all work be performed by volunteers.

Skybox rental costs. A skybox is a private luxury seating area at a sports arena. Skybox seats are generally rented for the season or for a series of games such as the World Series. The deductible amount for a rental covering more than one game or performance may not exceed the sum of the face values of non-luxury box seat tickets for the number of seats in the box. The allowable amount is also subject to the 50% cost limitation. Separately stated charges for food or beverages at the skybox are deductible as entertainment expenses and are subject to the 50% cost rule. For example, assume that for two games, you paid $1,480 for a skybox containing 10 seats—$740 per game. The cost of 10 non-luxury box seat tickets for each game was $200, or $400 total. You may deduct 50% of the $400 non-luxury face value, or $200. If you had rented the skybox for one game, you could deduct $370 (50% of $740) for that skybox because the special limitation applies only where the rental is for more than one game or other performance.

20.25 Business Gift Deductions Are Limited

Deductions for gifts to business customers and clients are restricted. Your deduction for gifts is limited to $25 a person. You and your spouse are treated as one person in figuring this limitation even if you do not file a joint return and even if you have separate business connections with the recipient. The $25 limitation also applies to partnerships; thus a gift by the partnership to one person may not exceed $25, regardless of the number of partners.

In figuring the $25 limitation to each business associate, do not include the following items:

1. A gift of a specialty advertising item that costs $4 or less on which your name is clearly and permanently imprinted. This exception saves you the trouble of having to keep records of such items as pens, desk sets, plastic bags, and cases on which you have your name imprinted for business promotion.
2. Signs, displays, racks, or other promotional material that is used on business premises by the person to whom you gave the material.
3. Incidental costs of wrapping, insuring, mailing, or delivering the gift. However, the cost of an ornamental basket or container must be included if it has a substantial value in relation to the goods it contains.

If you made a gift to the spouse of a business associate, it is considered as made to the associate. If the spouse has an independent bona fide business connection with you, the gift is not considered as made to the associate unless it is intended for the associate's eventual use.

If you made a gift to a corporation or other business group intended for the personal use of an employee, stockholder, or other owner of the corporation, the gift generally is considered as made to that individual.

Packaged food or drink given to a business associate is a gift if it is to be consumed at a later time. Theater or sporting event tickets given to business associates are entertainment, not gift, expenses if you accompany them. If you do not accompany them, you may elect to treat the tickets either as gifts, which are subject to the $25 limitation, or as entertainment expenses subject to the entertainment expense rules, such as the requirement to show a business conference before or after the entertainment and the 50% cost limitation.

Gifts not coming within the $25 limit are: (1) scholarships that are tax free under the rules in Chapter 33; (2) prizes and awards that are tax free under the rules in *11.1*; and (3) awards to employees, discussed below.

Awards to employees. There is an exception to the $25 gift deduction limitation for achievement awards of tangible personal property given to your employees in recognition of length of service or safety achievement. Special deduction limits apply to such achievement awards provided they are given as part of a presentation under circumstances indicating that they are not a form of disguised compensation. For example, awards will not qualify if given at the time of annual salary adjustments, or as a substitute for a prior program of cash bonuses, or if awards discriminate on behalf of highly compensated employees.

The amount of your deduction depends on whether the achievement award is considered a qualified plan award. You may deduct up to $1,600 for all qualified plan awards (safety and length of service) given to the same employee during the taxable year. If the award is not a qualified plan award, the annual deduction ceiling for each employee is $400. The $1,600 overall limit applies if the same employee receives some qualified plan awards and some non-qualified awards during the same year.

To be a qualified plan award, the award for length of service or safety achievement must be given under an established written plan or program that does not discriminate in favor of highly compensated employees. The average cost of all awards under the plan for the year (to all employees) must not exceed $400. In determining this $400 average cost, awards of nominal value are not to be taken into account. In case of a partnership, the deduction limitation applies to the partnership as well as to each partner.

Caution

Employee Bonuses

Employee bonuses should not be labeled as gifts. An IRS agent examining your records may, with this description, limit the deduction to $25 unless you can prove the excess over $25 was compensation. By describing the payment as a gift, you are inviting an IRS disallowance of the excess over $25. This was the experience of an attorney who gave his secretary $200 at Christmas. The IRS disallowed $175 of his deduction. The Tax Court refused to reverse the IRS. The attorney could not prove that the payment was for services.

Safety and length of service. A length of service award does not qualify as an employee achievement award if it is given during the employee's first five years. Furthermore, only one length of service award every five years is considered an employee achievement award.

Safety awards granted to managers, administrators, clerical employees, or professional employees are not considered employee achievement awards. Furthermore, if during the year more than 10% of other employees (not counting managers, administrators, clerical employees, or professional employees) previously received safety awards, none of the later awards are subject to the employee achievement award rules.

Employee's tax. The employer's deductible amount for an employee achievement award is tax free to the employee; *see 3.12.* For example, you give a qualified plan award costing $1,800 to an employee. You may deduct only $1,600. The employee is not taxed on the award up to $1,600; the $200 balance is taxable.

Documenting Your T&E Expenses and Reporting Your Expenses

20.26 Record-Keeping Requirements

Your testimony—even if accepted by an IRS agent or a judge as truthful—is not sufficient to support a deduction of travel and entertainment expenses. By law, your personal claim must be supported by other evidence such as records or witnesses. The most direct and acceptable way is to have records that meet IRS rules discussed below. Failure to have adequate records will generally result in an examination of your return and in a disallowance of your travel and entertainment expense deductions. Only in unusual circumstances will evidence other than records provide all of the required details of proof. If your expenses are reimbursed by your company, you must keep records to support the reimbursement arrangement with your company; *see 20.30.*

Planning Reminder

Credit Cards

Credit card charge statements for traveling and entertainment expenses meet the IRS tests, provided the business purpose of the expense is also shown. Credit card statements provide space for inserting the names of people entertained, their business relationship, the business purpose of the expense, and the portion of the expense to be allocated to business and personal purposes. These statements generally meet the IRS requirements of accounting to your employer for reimbursed expenses *(20.31)*, provided a responsible company official reviews them. The IRS will not accept a credit card statement as substantiation of a lodging expense.

20.27 Proving Travel and Entertainment Expenses

To satisfy the IRS requirements and to substantiate your expense deductions in the event of an audit, you need two types of records:

1. A computer log, diary, account book, or similar record to list the time, place, and business purpose of your travel and entertainment expenses; and
2. Receipts, itemized paid bills, or similar statements for lodging regardless of the amount, and for other expenses of $75 or more. But note these exceptions:
    - A receipt for transportation expenses of $75 or more is required only when it is readily obtainable. For example, for air travel a receipt or a boarding pass is usually provided.
    - A cancelled check by itself is not an acceptable voucher. If you cannot produce a bill or voucher, you may have to present other evidence such as a statement in writing from witnesses to prove business purpose of the expense.

A receipted bill or voucher must show (1) the amount of the expense; (2) the date the expense was incurred; (3) where the expense was incurred; and (4) the nature of the expense.

A hotel bill must show the name, location, date, and separate amounts for charges such as lodgings, meals, and telephone calls. A receipt for lodging is not needed if its cost is covered by a *per diem* allowance; *see 20.32*. The IRS will not allow a credit card statement to substitute for a lodging receipt. The IRS wants detailed receipts to catch personal items such as personal phone calls or the purchase of gifts.

A restaurant bill must show the restaurant's name and location, the date and amount of the expense, and, when a charge is made for items other than meals or beverages, a description of the charge.

Account book or computer entries. Your records do not have to duplicate data recorded on a receipt, provided that a notation in your record is connected to the receipt. You are also not required to record amounts your company pays directly for any ticket or fare. Credit card charges should be recorded.

Your records for entertainment costs must also show (1) the names of those you entertained; (2) the business purpose served by the entertainment; (3) the business relationship between you and your guests; and (4) the place of entertainment. Inattention to these details of substantiation can cost you the deduction. For example, an executive's company treasurer verified that the executive was required to incur entertainment expenses beyond reimbursed amounts. He also kept a cash diary in which he made contemporaneous notes of the amounts he spent. But he failed to note place, purpose, and business relationship. Consequently, there was no record that tied the expenses to his employment and the deduction was disallowed.

Planning Reminder

Sampling Can Support Deduction

If an adequate record of expenses is kept for part of a tax year, and that period is representative of the whole year, the IRS will accept those records as proof of expenses for the entire year. For example, if you keep records for the first week of each month that show that 75% of the use of your car is for business purposes, and your invoices and bills show the same business pattern for the rest of each month, the IRS will treat your partial record as proof of 75% business use for the whole year.

Excuses for Inadequate Records

Substantial compliance. If you have made a "good faith" effort to comply with the IRS rules, you will not be penalized if your records do not satisfy every requirement. For example, you would not automatically be denied a deduction merely because you did not keep a receipt.

Accidental destruction of records. If receipts or records are lost through circumstances beyond your control, you may substantiate deductions by reasonable reconstruction of your expenditures.

Exceptional circumstances. If, by reason of the "inherent nature of the situation," you are unable to keep adequate records, you may substantially comply by presenting the next best evidence. A supporting memorandum from your files and a statement from the persons entertained may be an adequate substitute. IRS regulations do not explain the meaning of "inherent nature of the situation."

EXAMPLES

1. Bryan's 1966 records were lost by a moving company. He claimed a T&E deduction of $15,301.87. The IRS estimated his T&E and other business expenses as $8,669 on the basis of his 1971 expense records. The Tax Court affirmed the IRS's approach. True, Bryan's loss of records made his burden of proof difficult, but he had to provide a reasonable reconstruction of his records to support his claimed deduction. His testimony of what he incurred in 1966 was not sufficient. A more accurate method was the IRS's use of his 1971 records and receipts.
2. Jackson claimed the IRS lost his records. He left his records with the IRS when he was audited, and the records were never returned. The Tax Court held that to be a good excuse for not producing his records and allowed a deduction on the basis of reconstructed records. Evidence that the IRS lost them: The IRS discovered Jackson's worksheet a year after the audit interview.
3. Murray claimed he lost his records when he was evicted from his apartment for failure to pay rent for a month. The Tax Court accepted his excuse on proof that he had kept records before they were lost. The eviction was beyond his control. However, if the records had been lost during a voluntary move, the loss would not have been excused, as in Example 1.

Court Decision

Ask for Reimbursement

If you are entitled to reimbursement from your employer, make sure you ask for reimbursement. Failure to be reimbursed may prevent you from deducting your out-of-pocket expenses. A supervisor whose responsibility was to maintain good relations with his district and store managers entertained them and their families and also distributed gifts among them. His cost was $2,500, for which he could have been reimbursed by his company, but he made no claim. Consequently, the Tax Court disallowed the cost as a deduction on his return. The expense was the company's; any goodwill he created benefitted it. But because he failed to seek reimbursement, he was not allowed to convert company expenses into his own.

20.28 Reporting T&E Expenses If You Are Self-Employed

You must keep travel and entertainment (T&E) records following the rules in *20.27*. You may claim the meal allowance at *20.4* on overnight business trips. The reimbursement rules discussed in *20.30* do not apply to you.

In preparing your tax return, you report your expenses on the appropriate lines of Schedule C or Schedule C-EZ (if you qualify). You do not use Form 2106. An advantage of reporting on Schedule C (or C-EZ) is that your travel and entertainment expenses (T&E) are not subject to the 2% adjusted gross income (AGI) floor. Only 50% of meals and entertainment costs are deductible; *see 20.24* for exceptions.

20.29 Employee Reporting of Unreimbursed T&E Expenses

If you are paid a salary with the understanding that you will pay your own expenses and you pay all of your travel and entertainment (T&E) expenses *without* reimbursement, you report all of your salary or commission income as shown on Form W-2. You report your expenses on Form 2106 or Form 2106-EZ (if other tests are met). Meals and entertainment are only 50% deductible. You must also keep records as required by *20.27* to support your deduction. The deductible amount from Form 2106 or Form 2106-EZ is entered on Schedule A as a miscellaneous expense subject to the 2% AGI floor. Therefore, if your total miscellaneous expenses, including the unreimbursed T&E costs, do not exceed 2% of adjusted gross income, none of the miscellaneous expenses will be deductible.

If your employer has a reimbursement plan but the rules for accountable plans are *not* met, reimbursements are treated as part of your taxable pay; *see 20.34*.

Employer Reimbursement Plans

20.30 Tax Treatment of Reimbursements

Compliance rules are imposed on employees and employers for reporting reimbursed travel and entertainment expenses in order to prevent reimbursement arrangements from being used to avoid the 2% of adjusted gross income (AGI) floor for employee miscellaneous expenses. Plans that allow reimbursements that *do not* comply with the IRS rules are called *non-accountable plans*. All reimbursements under a non-accountable plan are reported as salary or wage income on Form W-2. You then deduct your expenses as miscellaneous deductions subject to the 2% AGI floor; *see 20.34*.

If a plan meets the IRS rules, the plan is called an *accountable plan* and reimbursements made by the plan are not reported on Form W-2 as taxable wages. You also do not have to deduct expenses, assuming the reimbursement equals your expenses. In other words, there is a bookkeeping "wash" in which the full amount of expenses offsets the reimbursement without being reduced by the 2% AGI floor, and in the case of meal and entertainment costs, by the 50% reduction. Even though the employer may only deduct 50% of qualifying meal and entertainment expenses, you are not taxed on any part of a reimbursement of such costs if the accountable plan rules are met.

To qualify a plan as accountable, your employer must see to it that you submit adequate proof of your expenditures, and that you return any excess advances; *see 20.31*. To reduce record-keeping for actual costs, the company may reimburse you according to certain fixed *per diem* allowance rates; *see 20.32*. Your company must also determine how much of the advance or reimbursement, if any, is to be reported on your Form W-2.

EXAMPLE

Your adjusted gross income is $85,000, and you incur T&E expenses of $1,600 that are reimbursed by your company. If the reimbursement arrangement does not meet the IRS rules, the $1,600 reimbursement is reported as wage income on your Form W-2. You may report the expenses on Form 2106 and after reducing meal and entertainment costs by 50%, enter the balance as a deduction on Schedule A as a miscellaneous expense subject to the 2% AGI floor. However, if these are your only miscellaneous expenses, you will not get the benefit of a deduction because they do not exceed 2% of $86,600 ($85,000 + $1,600), or $1,732. The $1,600 is fully taxable although spent for T&E.

If your reimbursement arrangement qualified as an accountable plan, and you made an adequate reporting to your employer, the $1,600 would not be reported as income on your Form W-2, and you would not have to be concerned with the 2% floor for miscellaneous itemized deductions. There is a bookkeeping "wash." In other words, you receive a full deduction by substantiating the expenses to your employer.

Reimbursements of club dues or spousal travel costs. If you are reimbursed for nondeductible club dues *(20.22)* or nondeductible travel costs of a spouse or other person *(20.13)*, the reimbursement may be treated by your employer as taxable wages. If it is, you are not allowed an offsetting deduction. If the reimbursement is not treated as taxable wages by your employer, and you substantiate a business purpose for the club dues or for a travel companion's presence, the reimbursement is considered to be a tax-free working condition fringe benefit *(3.9)*.

EXAMPLE

A company pays for the country club dues of an executive. It reimbursed dues of $20,000, and the executive used the club for business purposes 40% of the time. If the company does not treat the reimbursement as taxable wages but as a fringe benefit, $8,000 of the reimbursement is tax free to the executive; the $12,000 allocated to personal use is taxable.

20.31 What Is an Accountable Plan?

A reimbursement or allowance arrangement is an accountable plan *(see 20.30)* if you must:

- Adequately account to your employer for your expenses; *and*
- Return to your employer any excess reimbursement or allowance that you do not show was spent for ordinary and necessary business expenses.

If these terms are met and your expenses are fully reimbursed, you do not report the expenses or the reimbursement on your return. If the reimbursement is less than your payment of expenses, you use Form 2106 and Schedule A to claim a deduction for the unreimbursed expenses. The unreimbursed expenses are subject to the 2% AGI floor on Schedule A.

What is an adequate accounting? You adequately account to your employer by submitting bills and an account book, diary, or similar record in which you entered each expense at or near the time you had it. You must account to your employer for all amounts received as advances, reimbursements, or allowances, including amounts charged on a company credit card. Your records and supporting information must meet the rules discussed in *20.27*. You must also pay back reimbursements or allowances that exceed the expenses that you adequately accounted for, or the nonreturned excess will be taxable under the rules at *20.34* for non-accountable plans.

The accounting requirements are eased if you are reimbursed under a *per diem* arrangement covering meals, lodging, and incidental expenses *(20.32)* or you receive a flat mileage allowance *(20.33)*.

Time limits for receiving advances, substantiating expenses, and returning excess payments. The general rule is that these events must occur within a reasonable time. Under an IRS "safe harbor," the following payments are considered to be within a reasonable time:

- Advance payments—if given to you within 30 days before you reasonably anticipate to pay or incur expenses;
- Substantiation of expenses—if provided to your employer within 60 days after the expense is paid or incurred; and
- Return of excess—if done within 120 days after you pay or incur expense.

An employer may set up a "periodic statement method" to meet IRS rules. Here, an employer gives each employee periodic statements (at least quarterly) that list the amounts paid in excess of expenses substantiated by the employee and request substantiation of the additional amounts paid, or a return of the excess, within 120 days of the date of the statement. Substantiation or return within the 120-day period satisfies the reasonable time test.

Allocating reimbursements to meals and entertainment. Only 50% of meals and entertainment expenses are deductible. Therefore, if you adequately account for your expenses, and receive a flat reimbursement that is partly for meals and entertainment, and partly for other

Filing Tip

Failure To Timely Return Excess

If you fail to return excess payments within a reasonable time but you meet all of the other tests applied to an accountable plan, such as providing proof of the expenses, only the retained excess is taxed to you as if paid outside of an accountable plan.

expenses, you must allocate part of the reimbursement to meals and entertainment if the employer has not provided an item-by-item breakdown. You must make this allocation if you want to deduct expenses exceeding reimbursements because on Form 2106, you must separately list meals and entertainment costs and reimbursements for meals and entertainment. The Form 2106 instructions have a worksheet for allocating the reimbursement based on the percentage that your meal costs bear to the total T&E expenses.

EXAMPLE

You receive an allowance of $1,000 for travel expenses and have total expenses of $1,500, including $300 for meals. The percentage of your meals to total expenses is 20% (300 ÷ 1,500). On Form 2106, you show 20% of the allowance, or $200, as the allocable reimbursement for meals and $800 as the allocable reimbursement to the non-meal expenses. The balance of the non-meal expenses, or $400 ($1,200 – $800), is deductible. The unreimbursed $100 balance for meals ($300 – $200) must be reduced to $50 by the 50% reduction for meals. The total deductible amount of $450 ($50 for meals and $400 for other expenses) is transferred from Form 2106 to Schedule A, where it is deductible as a miscellaneous itemized expense subject to the 2% AGI floor.

20.32 *Per Diem* Travel Allowance Under Accountable Plans

Instead of providing a straight reimbursement for substantiated out-of-pocket travel expenses, an employer may use a *per diem* allowance to cover meals, lodging, and incidental *(20.4)* expenses of employees on business trips away from home. If you are not related to the employer, you do not have to give your employer proof of your actual expenses if you receive a *per diem* allowance or reimbursement that is equal to or less than the federal travel rate for the particular area. You do have to account for the time, place, and business purpose of your travel. If you do not provide such an accounting for some travel days, you must be required to return the *per diem* allowance received for such days in order for the employer's plan to qualify. If these tests are met, the allowance satisfies the accountable plan *(20.31)* requirements and it does not have to be reported as income on your Form W-2.

Planning Reminder

Importance of Adequate Accounting

If you adequately report expenses to your employer and return excess reimbursements, you are treated as being reimbursed under an accountable plan and generally do not have to report any reimbursement on your return; *see 20.31.*

Tables published by the government show the federal travel rate for areas within the continental U.S. (called CONUS locations) and for areas outside the continental U.S., including Hawaii and Alaska (called OCONUS locations). As discussed in *20.4*, new CONUS tables are released every October, effective for the government's October 1–September 30 fiscal year. The best way to obtain the CONUS *per diem* rates is from IRS Publication 1542, available online at www.irs.gov/formspubs. The rates are also available from the General Services Administration website at www.gsa.gov. The OCONUS rates can also be accessed from the GSA website.

High-low rate. For business trips within the continental United States (CONUS), employers may use the IRS's "high-low" method to reimburse employees for lodging, meals, and incidental expenses instead of using the locality-by-locality *per diem* CONUS rates set by the General Services Administration (GSA) for federal government workers. For each employee, either the federal *per diem* rates or the high-low method must be used for the entire year.

For the first nine months of 2006, the rate for most areas was $141 per day and the rate for designated high-cost areas was $226 per day. For employer deduction purposes, $58 of the $226 high-cost-area rate, and $45 of the $141 rate for other localities, must be allocated to meals. Only 50% of the allocated meals portion is generally deductible. The deduction percentage is 75% for 2006 meal costs of transportation workers such as pilots and interstate truck/bus drivers who are subject to Department of Transportation limits on service hours.

Planning Reminder

High-Low Method

An employer that uses the high-low method to reimburse an employee for the first nine months of the year must continue to do so for the rest of the year. Although the rates and high-cost localities list may change on October 1, the pre-October rates and high-cost localities may be used for the rest of the year as long as this is done consistently for all employees.

The $141 and $226 rates, and the areas treated as high-cost areas are scheduled to change, effective October 1, 2006. After the IRS announces the changes, it will revise Publication 1542, which is available only online at www.irs.gov/forms/pubs. The revised Publication will have tables showing the high-cost areas for the period before October 1 and the period beginning October 1. An employer that used the high-low method before October 1, 2006, to reimburse an employee must continue to do so for the rest of 2006. However, the pre-October rates and high-cost localities list may be used for the rest of the year as long as this is done consistently for all employees. Employers that did not use the high-low method for an employee before October 1 may not do so until 2007.

Employees related to the employer. The IRS *per diem* rules that allow you to avoid accounting for actual expenses do not apply if you work for a brother, sister, spouse, parent, child, grandparent, or grandchild. They also do not apply if you are an employee-stockholder who owns more than 10% of the company's stock.

Reporting a *per diem* allowance. If the allowance does not exceed the federal travel rate or IRS high-low rate, the reimbursement is not reported on Form W-2. If your expenses do not exceed the reimbursement, you do not have to report the expenses or the reimbursement on your tax return; *see* Example 1 below. If your expenses exceed the allowance, you may deduct the excess by reporting the expenses and reimbursement on Form 2106. The net amount from Form 2106, after applying the 50% reduction for meals, is claimed on Schedule A as a miscellaneous expense subject to the 2% AGI floor; *see* Example 2 below.

If the allowance exceeds the federal rate, the allowance up to the federal rate is reported by the employer in Box 12 of your Form W-2. This amount is not taxable. However, the excess allowance will be included as wages in Box 1 of your Form W-2; *see* Example 3 below.

EXAMPLES

1. You take a three-day business trip to a locality at a time when the federal travel rate for the area is $106 per day. You account for the date, place, and business purpose of the trip. Your employer reimburses you at the federal rate of $106 a day for lodging, meals, and incidental expenses, for a total of $318. Your actual expenses do not exceed this amount. Your employer does not report the reimbursement on your Form W-2. You do not have to report the reimbursement or deduct any expenses on your return.
2. Same facts as in Example 1, except that the reimbursement is less than your actual expenses of $450, for which you have records. On Form 2106, you report the $318 reimbursement and your $450 of expenses and also must allocate part of the allowance to meals and entertainment to apply the 50% limit. The instructions to Form 2106 have a worksheet for making the allocation. The net amount from Form 2106 is deductible on Schedule A as a miscellaneous expense subject to the 2% AGI limit.
3. Same facts as in Example 1, except that you receive a *per diem* allowance of $114 per day—$8 per day more than the federal travel rate. If you do not return the excess of $24 ($8 × 3 days) within a reasonable time *(20.31)*, your employer must report the $24 as income in Box 1 of your Form W-2. The amount up to the federal travel rate, or $318, will be reported in Box 12 of Form W-2 with Code L, but not included as income.

Meal allowance only. If your employer gives you a *per diem* allowance covering only meals and incidental expenses, it is not taxable to you if you are not related to the employer and the allowance does not exceed the IRS meal allowance rates discussed at *20.4*.

20.33 Automobile Mileage Allowance

If your employer paid you a fixed mileage allowance in 2006 of up to 44.5 cents per mile, the amount of your automobile expenses is treated as substantiated, provided you show the time, place, and business purpose of your travel. If the allowance is in the form of an advance, it must be given within a reasonable period before the anticipated travel and you must also be required to return within a reasonable period *(20.31)* any portion of the allowance that covers mileage that you have not substantiated.

If these tests are met, the allowance will not be reported as income on Form W-2, and you will not have to report the allowance or expenses on your return; *see* Example 1 below. If you do not prove to your employer the time, place, and purpose of your travel, the entire reimbursement is treated as paid from a non-accountable plan and will be reported as income on Form W-2.

Your employer may reimburse you for any parking fees and tolls in addition to the mileage allowance.

EXAMPLES

1. In 2006 you drove 12,000 miles for business. You accounted to your employer for the time, place, and business purpose of each trip. Your employer reimbursed you at the IRS rate of 44.5 cents per mile. None of the reimbursements will be reported as income on your Form W-2, and you do not have to report the reimbursements or any expenses on your return if your expenses do not exceed 44.5 cents per mile.

Planning Reminder

Online Revisions to IRS Publication 1542

As changes to *per diem* rates are announced by the General Services Administration (GSA), a *What's Hot* article on the IRS website will announce the new rates. Go to www.irs.gov/formspubs; then go to the "What's Hot in Tax Forms, Publications and Other Tax Products" page for updates to Publication 1542.

Caution

Excess *Per Diem* Allowances

If a *per diem* allowance exceeds the federal travel rate or the IRS high-low rate, the excess will be reported as income on your Form W-2, unless you return the excess; *see* Example 3 on the left. The excess reportable on Form W-2 is also subject to income tax and FICA tax withholding.

Caution

Allowance Exceeding IRS Rate

If you were given mileage allowance for 2006 in excess of 44.5 cents per mile, the excess will be included as wages on your Form W-2; *see* Example 2 in *20.33*. If your allowance was less than 44.5 cents per mile, you may deduct the difference as a miscellaneous itemized deduction subject to the 2% AGI floor; *see* Example 3 in *20.33*.

2. Same facts as in Example 1, except that you were reimbursed at 48 cents per mile for your travel. The amount using the IRS rate, or $5,340 (.445 x 12,000 miles), is $420 less than the reimbursement of $5,760 (.48 x 12,000). The $420 excess over the IRS rate will be reported as wages on your Form W-2.

   If you had records substantiating expenses over 44.5 cents per mile, you could claim them on Form 2106. The excess of your expenses over the IRS rate is shown on Form 2106, and that excess is claimed on Schedule A as a miscellaneous itemized deduction subject to the 2% AGI floor.
3. Same facts as in Example 1, except that you were reimbursed only 35 cents per mile. The reimbursements will not be reported as income on your Form W-2. You may be able to deduct expenses up to the IRS rate by reporting the expenses and the reimbursements on Form 2106. The amount using the IRS rates is $5,340 (.445 x 12,000). This is $1,140 more than the reimbursement of $4,200 (.35 x 12,000). The $1,140 excess of the IRS allowance over your reimbursements is shown on Form 2106 and then may be claimed as a miscellaneous itemized deduction on Schedule A subject to the 2% AGI floor.

   If you had records showing actual expenses of more than $5,340, you would claim those expenses on Form 2106 and not use the IRS fixed mileage allowance rate to figure your deduction.

Fixed and variable rate allowance (FAVR). In lieu of setting the allowance at the IRS standard mileage rate, an employer may use a fixed and variable rate allowance, called a FAVR, that gives employees a cents-per-mile rate to cover gas and other operating costs, plus a flat amount to cover fixed costs such as depreciation or lease payments, insurance, and registration. A FAVR allowance must reflect local driving costs and allows employers to set reimbursements at a rate that more closely approximates employee expenses. If your employer sets up a qualifying FAVR under IRS guidelines, you will be required to provide records substantiating your mileage and certain car ownership information. Expenses up to the FAVR limits are deemed substantiated and will not be reported as wages on your Form W-2.

20.34 Reimbursements Under Non-Accountable Plans

A non-accountable plan is one that either does not require you to adequately account for your expenses or allows you to keep any excess reimbursement or allowances over the expenses for which you did adequately account.

Your employer reports allowances or reimbursements for a non-accountable plan as part of your salary income in Box 1 of your Form W-2. The allowance or reimbursement is also subject to income tax and FICA tax (Social Security) withholding. To claim deductions, you must use Form 2106 and itemize your deductions on Schedule A. Your expenses are subject to the 2% AGI floor and thus you may be unable to offset the taxable reimbursement (allowance) included on your Form W-2.

Chapter 21

Personal Exemptions

Each personal exemption you claim on your 2006 return is the equivalent of a $3,300 deduction. Exemptions for children, parents, and other dependents are allowed if the tests in this chapter are met.

If you have a high adjusted gross income, you may lose the benefit of your deduction under the phase-out rule discussed in *21.12*.

Number of Exemptions	*Deduction Allowed*
1	$ 3,300
2	6,600
3	9,900
4	13,200
5	16,500
6	19,800
7	23,100
8	26,400
9	29,700
10	33,000

21.1 How Many Exemptions May You Claim?

On your 2006 return, you may claim a $3,300 exemption for each of the following, provided you are not subject to the phaseout of exemptions for high income taxpayers *(see 21.12)*:

- **Yourself.** You claim an exemption for yourself unless you are the dependent of another taxpayer. If someone else can claim you as a dependent for 2006, you may not claim a personal exemption for yourself on your own return; this is true even if the other person does not actually claim you as a dependent. This rule prevents your child or other dependent from claiming an exemption on his or her return if you may claim an exemption for the child or other dependent.
- **Your spouse.** You claim your spouse as an exemption when you file a joint return. If you file a separate return, you claim your spouse as an exemption if he or she has no income and is not a dependent of another person; *see 21.2.*
- **Your dependents.** There are two categories of dependents: qualifying children and qualifying relatives. You may not claim any dependents if you can be claimed as a dependent by another taxpayer. In addition, a qualifying child or relative must meet a citizen or resident test, and, if married, must generally not file a joint return; *see* below.

Qualifying children. A qualifying child is your child or stepchild (by blood or adoption), foster child, sibling, or step-sibling, or the descendants of any of these (such as your grandchildren, nieces, or nephews), provided the following tests are met:

1. The child had the same principal place of abode (residence) as you did for more than half of 2006. Temporary absences are disregarded.
2. The child is under age 19 at the end of 2006, or under age 24 at the end of 2006 if a full-time student for at least five months during the year. The age test does not apply to a child who is permanently and totally disabled at any time during the year.
3. The child did not provide more than half of his or her own support for 2006.

See 21.3 for further details on the qualifying child rules.

Qualifying relatives. An individual is your qualified relative for 2006 if the following tests are met:

1. The individual is your relative other than a qualifying child or is a member of your household.
2. The individual had gross income for 2006 of under $3,300.
3. You contributed over half of the individual's support for 2006 or more than 10% of his or her support under the multiple support test discussed in *21.6.*

See 21.4 for further details on the qualifying relative rules.

Additional tests for claiming dependents. Even if a person is your qualifying child or relative, you cannot claim that person as your dependent if any of the following apply:

1. You, or your spouse if filing jointly, could be claimed as a dependent by another taxpayer for the taxable year;
2. The child/relative is not a U.S. citizen or national, or a resident of the U.S., Canada, or Mexico for at least some part of the year; there is an exception for certain adopted children; *see 21.8;*
3. If married, the child/relative files a joint return, unless the return is only a claim for refund and neither spouse would owe tax on a separate return; *see 21.9.*

Special rules for divorced or separated parents. *See 21.7* for determining which parent may claim the exemption for their children.

Death of dependent during the year. If a dependent who otherwise met the tests for a qualifying child or relative died during the year, you can claim an exemption for that dependent.

Social Security numbers checked by IRS. The IRS verifies the Social Security numbers for both spouses on a joint return and for all claimed dependents; *see 21.10* and *21.11.*

Law Alert

Exemption for Housing Hurricane Katrina Victim

On Form 8914 you can claim an additional exemption of $500 for each person displaced by Hurricane Katrina, other than your spouse or dependent, for whom you provide free housing in your principal residence for at least 60 days. The additional $500 exemption is allowed for up to four displaced persons, for a maximum of $2,000 (but no more than $1,000 if married filing separately). The $2,000 limit applies to both 2005 and 2006, so any additional exemptions claimed on your 2005 return reduce the $2,000 maximum for 2006.

Filing Instruction

You Must Report I.D. Numbers for Dependents

You must obtain and report on your return the Social Security number of each dependent claimed. Nonresident and resident aliens not eligible for Social Security numbers must have an individual taxpayer identification number; *see 21.11.*

21.2 Your Spouse as an Exemption

Your spouse is not your dependent for tax purposes. An exemption for a spouse is based on the marital relationship, not support. On a joint return, each spouse receives an exemption as a taxpayer. The name and Social Security number of each spouse listed on a joint return will be matched by the IRS against computer records of the Social Security Administration. If there is a mismatch, the exemption for that spouse will be disallowed; *see 21.10.*

On a separate return (as married filing separately or as head of household), you may claim your spouse as an exemption if he or she has no gross income and cannot be claimed as a dependent by another taxpayer. You may not claim an exemption for your spouse who has income, *unless you file a joint return that includes that income.* For example, if a wife files a separate return, her husband may not claim her as an exemption, even if she filed the return merely for a refund of taxes withheld on her wages.

If your spouse is a nonresident alien, has no income from U.S. sources, and is not a dependent of another person, you may claim an exemption for your spouse on a separate return.

If divorced or legally separated during the year. You may not claim your former spouse as an exemption if you are divorced or legally separated under a *final* decree of divorce or separate maintenance, even if you provided his or her entire support. However, an interlocutory (not final) decree does not bar you from claiming your spouse as an exemption.

EXAMPLE

An interlocutory (not final) decree of divorce is entered in 2006, and a final decree in 2007. For 2006, the couple may file a joint return on which exemptions for both are claimed. A marriage is not dissolved until a final decree is entered, which in this case is in 2007.

Your spouse died during the year. If you did not remarry and your deceased spouse had gross income, you may claim an exemption for your spouse only if you file a joint return that includes his or her income. You may claim the exemption on a separate return only if your spouse had no gross income and was not a dependent of another taxpayer.

EXAMPLE

Sylvia Smith dies on June 27. Her husband, Steve Smith, may file a joint return and claim Sylvia as an exemption. They were married as of the date of Sylvia's death. The joint return includes all of Steve's income for the year, but only that part of Sylvia's income earned up to June 27; *see 1.10.*

If you remarry before the end of the year in which your spouse died, you may not claim an exemption for your deceased spouse. If you file a joint return with your new spouse, you may be claimed as an exemption on that return. If you had *no* income for the year, you may be claimed as an exemption on both your deceased spouse's separate return and on a separate return filed by your new spouse, provided no one else may claim you as a dependent.

Caution

Spouses' Social Security Numbers and Names

Make sure that the names used when you and your spouse file your joint return match the names you have provided to the Social Security Administration. If there is a mismatch between a name and Social Security number, the IRS will disallow the exemption and then send you a notice that allows you to explain the discrepancy and restore the deduction; *see 21.10.*

21.3 Qualifying Children

You may claim an exemption for your qualifying children provided you (and your spouse if you file jointly) cannot be claimed as a dependent by someone else and the citizenship or resident *(21.8)* and joint return *(21.9)* tests applicable to all dependents also are met.

Qualifying children include your children, siblings, and their descendants (*see* the relationship test below) if a residence test and age or student test are also met. If the tests for a qualifying child are met, you do not have to show that you provided more than half of the child's support, as is required for a qualifying relative *(21.4)*. However, a child is not a qualifying child if he or she provides over half of his or her own support. For a qualifying child, there is *no* gross income test; he or she may earn any amount and still be claimed as your dependent.

Note: Even if a child is not a qualifying child, as where the age/student test or place of abode test is not met, you may still be able to claim an exemption for the child as a "qualifying relative"; *see 21.4.*

Relationship test. Your children, stepchildren, and their descendants (your grandchildren and great-grandchildren), and your siblings, including step- and half-brothers and -sisters and their descendants (your nieces and nephews), meet the relationship test. A legally adopted child or a child lawfully placed with you for adoption is treated as your child, as is a foster child placed with you by a court order or by an authorized placement agency.

You may claim a full $3,300 exemption for a child born at the end of 2006 if the other dependency tests are met. The exemption is allowed for a child who was born alive even if he or she lived only for a moment. No exemption is allowed for a stillborn child.

Residence test (abode test). The qualifying child must have the same principal place of abode as you for more than half the year. You do not have to own the home or pay the maintenance costs, but the child must live with you for over half the year.

Planning Reminder

Qualifying Children

If a child or sibling (or his or her descendant) is your qualifying child under *21.3*, his or her gross income does not matter. You also do not have to provide over half of the child's support. You may claim the exemption if the other tests for an exemption are met as explained at *21.3.*

Temporary absences disregarded. Congressional committee reports indicate that temporary absences due to special circumstances, such as for education or illness, can be disregarded in applying the principal place of abode test. However, the IRS has not defined the parameters of the temporary absence exception.

Kidnapped child. The principal place of abode test is considered met for a child under age 18 who met the test prior to being kidnapped by a non–family member.

Age or student test. A qualifying child must be under age 19 at the end of the year, a full-time student under age 24 at the end of the year, or permanently and totally disabled, regardless of age.

Qualifying as a full-time student. A full-time student is one who attends school full time during at least five calendar months in the tax year. For example: attendance from February through some part of June—or from February through May and then at least one month from September through December—qualifies. The five months do not have to run consecutively. Attendance at a vocational, trade, or technical school for the five-month period qualifies, but not correspondence schools or on-the-job training courses.

Night school. Your child who attends school at night is considered a full-time student only if he or she is enrolled for the number of hours or classes that is considered full-time attendance.

Tie-breaker rules. The law provides tie-breaker rules to determine who can treat a child as a qualifying child when the qualifying child tests are met by more than one taxpayer and the taxpayers cannot agree as to which of them should claim the child. If more than one taxpayer claims the exemption for a child and the child is a qualifying child for each taxpayer, the tie-breaker depends on who the claimants are.

If only one of the taxpayers is the parent of the child, the child is treated as the qualifying child of that parent. This situation could arise, for example, where a parent and infant child live with the child's grandparent for more than half the year. Both the child's parent and grandparent would meet the principal place of abode test and relationship test with respect to the child, but under the tie-breaker rule, the child is treated as the qualifying child of the parent.

If both parents claim an exemption for the child on separate returns, first determine if the noncustodial parent is entitled to the exemption under the special rule discussed in *21.7* for divorced or separated parents. If the special *21.7* rule applies, the tie-breaker rules do not apply. If the special rule in *21.7* does not apply and the child is a qualifying child of both parents under the above tests, the tie-breaker rule deems the child to be the qualifying child of the parent with whom the child has resided for the longer period during the year. If the residency period with both parents is the same, the parent with the higher adjusted gross income is entitled to treat the child as a qualifying child.

If none of the taxpayers claiming the exemption is a parent of the child, the claimant with the highest adjusted gross income is entitled to claim the child as a qualifying child.

21.4 Qualifying Relatives

On your 2006 return, you may claim an exemption for a qualifying relative who is not your qualifying child *(21.3)* and is not the qualifying child of any other taxpayer for 2006, provided you cannot be claimed as a dependent (nor your spouse if you file jointly) by another taxpayer and the citizenship/resident test *(21.8)* and joint return test *(21.9)* are also met.

Assuming a person meets the relationship test, you must provide over 50% of his or her support and his or her gross income must be under the exemption amount ($3,300 for 2006) for you to claim that person as a qualifying relative.

Relationship test. Relatives listed below meet the relationship test; they do not have to live with you. Unrelated or distantly related persons not on this list meet the relationship test if they live with you as discussed below.

Children, grandchildren, and great-grandchildren who are not qualifying children. Your children, grandchildren, and great-grandchildren can meet the relationship test for a qualifying relative only if they are not your qualifying children or the qualifying children of any other taxpayer under the rules discussed in *21.3*. For example, if your child is not your qualifying child for 2006 because he or she does not meet the age/student test or the principal place of abode test in *21.3*, you may still be able to claim an exemption for the child as your qualifying relative, but only if he or she has gross income under the $3,300 limit and you provide over 50% of his or her support for the year.

Filing Tip

Nephew, Niece, Uncle, and Aunt

Nephews, nieces, uncles, and aunts must be your blood relatives to qualify under the relationship test. For example, the brother or sister of your father or mother qualifies as your relative; their spouses do not. You may not claim your spouse's nephews, nieces, uncles, or aunts as your qualifying relatives unless you file a joint return.

Brothers, sisters, and their children. The same considerations discussed above for children, grandchildren, and great-grandchildren apply for your siblings (including half- or step-siblings) and their children. They can be your qualifying relatives only if they are not qualifying children under *21.3*.

Parents, grandparents, and other relatives. The following individuals also meet the relationship test: your parent, grandparent, great-grandparent, step-parent, son- or daughter-in-law, father- or mother-in-law, and brother- or sister-in-law. If related by blood, aunts and uncles also qualify.

Stepchild's husband or wife or child. Your stepchild's spouse does not meet the relationship test. Nor may you claim an exemption for a step-grandchild if you file a separate return. But you may claim them on a joint return as qualifying relatives if the other exemption tests are met. On a joint return, it is not necessary that the close relationship exist between the dependent and the spouse who furnishes the chief support. It is sufficient that the relationship exists with either spouse.

EXAMPLE

You contribute more than half of the support of the sister of your wife's mother (your wife's aunt). If you and your wife file a joint return, her aunt meets the relationship test. But your wife's aunt's husband is not related by blood to you or your wife. You cannot claim an exemption for him, even on a joint return, unless he is a member of your household under the rules discussed below and other exemption tests are met.

In-laws. Brother-in-law, sister-in-law, father-in-law, mother-in-law, son-in-law, and daughter-in-law are relatives by marriage. They meet the relationship test and you may claim them as exemptions if the other tests for qualifying relatives are satisfied.

An in-law who was related to you by marriage and whom you continue to support after divorce or the death of your spouse meets the relationship test.

EXAMPLE

For many years, Allen has contributed all the support of his father-in-law, who has no gross income. Allen's wife died in 2005. Allen continued to be the sole support of his wife's father in 2006. Allen may claim him as a qualifying relative in 2006.

Death during the year. If a relative died during 2005 but was supported by you while alive, and the other tests for an exemption are met you may claim an exemption for the relative.

EXAMPLE

On January 21, 2006, your father died. Until that date, you contributed all of his support. He had no gross income for 2006. You may claim him as an exemption for 2006. The full deduction is taken; exemptions are not prorated.

Member-of-household test for unrelated or distantly related dependents living with you. A relative not listed above, such as a cousin, meets the relationship test if he or she is a member of your household *and* your home is his or her principal home for the entire year, except for temporary absences due to schooling, vacationing, being away on business, serving in the military, or being confined to a hospital. A friend or mate living with you does not meet the member-of-household test if the relationship violates local law. For example, if you live with a person married to someone else and the relationship violates the law of the state where you live, you cannot claim an exemption for that person.

Under the tax law, one spouse is not considered a dependent of the other; *see 21.2*. If you are divorced or legally separated during the year, your former spouse cannot be your qualifying relative even if he or she is a member of your household for the whole year.

Gross income limit. A person meeting the above relationship test cannot be claimed as your qualifying relative if he or she had gross income for 2006 of $3,300 or more. This is true even if you provide most or all of that person's support. The $3,300 limit, equal to the exemption amount, is subject to annual increases for inflation.

Caution

Students Age 24 or Older

The gross income test does not apply to qualifying children *(21.3)*, including full-time students who are under age 24 as of the end of the year. If your child was age 24 or older at the end of 2006 and had gross income of $3,300 or more, you may not claim him or her as a dependent.

Keep in mind that the gross income test does *not* apply to qualifying children meeting the tests at *21.3*. However, if a child does not meet the age/student test or principal place of abode test, and thus is not a qualifying child *(21.3)*, he or she must have gross income under the $3,300 limit to be claimed as a dependent under the qualifying relative rules.

Gross income here means taxable income items includible in the dependent's tax return. It does not include nontaxable items such as gifts and tax-exempt bond interest. Gross income for a service-type business is gross receipts without deductions of expenses and for a manufacturing or merchandising business is total sales less cost of goods sold. A partner's share of partnership gross income, not the share of net income, is treated as gross income.

Social Security benefits are treated as gross income only to the extent they are taxable under the rules discussed at *34.3*.

Exception for disabled student working at sheltered workshop. For purposes of the gross income test gross income does not include income earned by a totally and permanently disabled individual at a school operated by a government agency or tax-exempt organization, if the school provides special instruction for alleviating the disability and the income is incidental to medical care received.

Support test. A person cannot be your qualifying relative unless you provide over half of his or her total support for the year. The support test applies to a child who does not meet the tests for a qualifying child at *21.3*. *See 21.5* for how to count total support and your contribution to the total.

21.5 Meeting the Support Test for a Qualifying Relative

To claim an exemption for a dependent as a qualifying relative *(21.4)*, you must contribute more than 50% of the dependent's total support for the year. The support test does not apply for qualifying children under the rules at *21.3*.

Meeting the support test. Follow these steps to figure support: (1) Total the value of the support contributed by you, by the dependent, and by others for the dependent. Use the checklists later in this section for determining what to include in total support and what to exclude. (2) Determine your share of the total. If your share is more than 50% of the dependent's total support, you meet the support test. It does not matter how many months or days you provided the support; only the total cost of the support is considered. You may not take the exemption if the dependent contributed 50% or more of his or her own support or 50% or more was contributed by others, including government sources.

Multiple support agreement. If the dependent or someone else did not contribute 50% or more of the support, and you contributed more than 10% of the total support, you may be able to claim the exemption under a multiple support agreement; *see 21.6*.

Divorced or separated parents contributing to support of their children should follow the special rules at *21.7*.

EXAMPLE

Eric Hill receives Social Security benefits of $6,000 and also $300 in bank interest in 2006. He has no other income. Eric spends $4,400 on food, clothes, transportation, and recreation. The $4,400 spent is his contribution to his own support. Eric's rent, utilities, unreimbursed medical expenses, and other necessities are paid by his son, Mike. If Mike's payments exceed $4,400, and no one else contributes to Eric's support, Mike may claim Eric as a dependent.

Planning Reminder

Dependents in the Armed Forces

If your dependent joins the military, the value of food, lodging, clothing, and educational assistance provided by the government constitutes government support.

Checklist of Support Items

- Food and lodging; see below.
- Clothing
- Medical and dental expenses, including premiums paid for health insurance policies and supplementary Medicare
- Education expenses such as tuition, books, and supplies. If your child receives a student loan and is the primary obligor, the loan proceeds are considered his or her own support contribution. This is true even if you are a guarantor of the loan. Scholarships received by full-time students are not treated as support; *see* the checklist of nonsupport items in this section.

- Cars and transportation expenses. Include the cost of a car bought for a dependent as support. If you buy a car but register it in your own name, the cost of the car is *not* support provided by you, but any out-of-pocket expenses you have for operating the car are part of your support contribution.
- Recreation and entertainment. A computer or TV set bought for your child or other dependent is support. Also include costs of summer camp, singing and dancing lessons, and musical instruments, as well as wedding expenses.

Personal savings and tax-exempt income may be support. In figuring a person's total support, include his or her tax-exempt income and personal savings if actually used for support items such as food, lodging, or clothing. Also include support items that are financed by loans. Income that is invested and not actually spent for support is not included in the earner's total support.

Social Security. Social Security benefits paid to children of deceased workers that are used for their support are treated as the children's contribution to their own support. Follow this rule even though benefits are paid to you as the child's parent or custodian. If the Social Security benefits used for a child's support are more than half of the child's total support, no one may claim the child as a dependent.

Where husband and wife are paid Social Security benefits in one check made out in their joint names, 50% is considered to be used by each spouse unless shown otherwise.

Government benefits. In figuring whether you have provided more than 50% of the dependent's support, you have to consider certain government benefits as support provided by a third party. For example, welfare, food stamps, or housing payments based on need are state support payments if they are used for support items. G.I. Bill education assistance is support provided by the government.

Foster care payments by a child placement agency to parents are support provided by the agency and not by the parents. The value of board, lodging, and education provided to a child in a state juvenile home is treated as support provided by the state.

When a person joins the Armed Forces, the value of board, lodging, and clothing he or she receives is treated as the government's support contribution. However, if *you* are in the Armed Forces, dependency allotments withheld from your pay and used to support your dependents are included in *your* support contributions for them. Also included in your support contribution is a military quarters allowance covering a dependent.

Planning Reminder

Savings and Investments as Support

Income that is invested is not treated as support. However, personal savings are treated as support if they are used for food, clothing, lodging, or other support items.

Lodging and food as support. You count as support the *fair rental value* of a room, apartment, or house in which the dependent lives. In your estimate, you include a reasonable allowance for the rental value of furnishings and appliances, and for heat and other utilities. You do *not* add payments of rent, taxes, interest, depreciation, paint, insurance, and utilities. These are presumed to be accounted for in the fair rental estimate. The fair rental value of lodging you furnish a dependent is the amount you could reasonably expect to receive from a stranger for the lodging.

Does dependent live in his or her own home? If a dependent listed at *21.4* lives in his or her own home, treat the total fair rental value as his or her own contribution to support. However, if you help maintain the home by giving cash, or you directly pay such expenses as the mortgage, real estate taxes, fire insurance premiums, and repairs, you reduce the total fair rental value of the home by the amount you contributed when figuring his or her own support contributions; *see* the Example below.

If you lived with your dependent rent-free in his or her home, the fair rental value of lodging furnished to you must be offset against the amounts you spent for your dependent in determining the net amount of your contribution to the dependent's support.

Food and other similar household expenses. If the dependent lives with you, you divide your total food expenses equally among all the members of your household, unless you have records showing the exact amount spent on the dependent; *see* the Examples at the end of this section. If he or she does not live with you, you count the actual amount of food expenses spent by or for that dependent.

Do you pay for a relative's care in a health facility? If you pay part of a relative's expenses for care in a nursing home or other facility, your payment is a support contribution. If you make a lump-sum contribution covering a relative's stay in an old-age home or other care facility, you prorate your payment over the relative's life expectancy to determine the current support contribution.

Planning Reminder

Lump-Sum Payment to Care Facilities

A lump-sum contribution covering a relative's stay in a long-term care facility is prorated over the relative's life expectancy to determine your current support contribution.

EXAMPLE

You contribute $7,000 as support to your father who lives in his own home, which has a fair rental value of $8,000 a year. He uses $4,600 of the money you give him to pay real estate taxes and $2,400 for food. He spends $3,000 of his Social Security for recreation and invests the rest. He has no gross income *(21.4)* and receives no other support. Your father's contribution to his own support is $6,400:

Fair rental value of house ($8,000 *less* $4,600 you gave for taxes)	3,400
Social Security spent	3,000
Father's contribution to his own support	$6,400

You may claim your father as a dependent because your contribution of $7,000 exceeds half of his total support of $13,400 (your $7,000 contribution and his $6,400 contribution).

Checklist of Items Not Counted as Support

- Federal, state, and local income taxes and Social Security taxes paid by the dependent from his or her own income
- Funeral expenses
- Life insurance premiums
- Medicare Part A (basic Medicare) and Part B (Supplementary Medicare benefits). In one case the IRS argued that Medicaid benefits were includible in total support but the Tax Court disagreed, holding that Medicaid is similar to excludable Medicare benefits.
- Medical insurance benefits received by the dependent
- Scholarships received by your child, stepchild, or legally adopted child who is a full-time student for at least five calendar months during the year. Scholarship aid is counted as support contributed by the child if he or she is not a full-time student for at least five months. Naval R.O.T.C. payments and payments made under the War Orphans Educational Assistance Act are scholarships that are not counted as support. State aid to a disabled child for education or training, including room and board, is a scholarship.

Allocating Support

The Examples below illustrate how you should allocate various support items when your contributions benefit more than one person or when your dependent provides part of his or her own support.

Filing Tip

Households with Several Dependents

If your contribution does not exceed 50% of total household support, earmark contributions to at least one of the dependents. This will allow you to claim at least one exemption. Without proper records, however, the IRS treats your contributions as divided among the members of the household.

Earmarking support to one dependent. If you are contributing funds to a household consisting of several persons and the amount you contribute does not exceed 50% of the total household support, you may be able to claim an exemption for at least one dependent by earmarking your support to his or her use. Your earmarked contributions must exceed 50% of this dependent's support costs. Mark your checks for the benefit of the dependent, or provide the dependents with a written statement of your support arrangement at the time you start your payments. If you do not designate for whom you are providing support, your contribution is allocated equally among all members of a household.

EXAMPLES

1. Your father lives in your home with you, your spouse, and your three children. He receives Social Security benefits of $9,800, which are not subject to tax *(34.3)* and half of which ($4,900) he spends for his own clothing, travel, and recreation. You spend $6,600 for food during the year. You also paid his dental bill of $500. You estimate the annual fair rental value of the room furnished him as $3,600. Your father's total support is:

Social Security used for support	$4,900
Share of food costs ($^1/_6$ of $6,600)	1,100
Dental bill paid by you	500
Rental value of room	3,600
	$10,100

You meet the support test. You contributed more than half his total support, or $5,200 ($3,600 for lodging, $500 for the dental bill, and $1,100 for food).

2. Your parents live with you, your spouse, and your two children in a house you rent. The annual fair rental value of their room is $3,000. Your father receives a tax-free government pension of $5,200, all of which he spent equally for your mother and himself for clothing and recreation. Your parents' only other income was $500 of tax-exempt interest. They did not make any other contributions toward their own support. Your total expense in providing food for the household is $6,000. You pay heat and utility bills of $1,200. You paid your mother's medical expenses of $600. Your father's total support from all sources is $5,100 and your mother's is $5,700, figured as follows:

	Father	*Mother*
Fair rental value of room	$1,500	$1,500
Pension used for their support	2,600	2,600
Share of food costs ($^{1}/_{6}$ of $6,000)	1,000	1,000
Medical expenses for mother		600
	$5,100	$5,700

In figuring your parents' total support, you do not include the cost of heat and utilities, because these are presumed to be included in the fair rental value of the room ($3,000). The support you furnish your father, $2,500 (lodging, $1,500; food, $1,000), is not over half of his total support of $5,100. The support you furnish your mother, $3,100 (lodging, $1,500; food, $1,000; medical, $600), is over half of her total support of $5,700. You meet the support test for your mother but not your father. Since she did not have taxable income, the gross income test *(21.4)* is satisfied.

21.6 Multiple Support Agreements

Are you and others sharing the support of one person, but with no one individual providing more than 50% *(21.5)* of his or her total support? You are treated as meeting the support test for a qualifying relative *(21.4)* if:

1. You gave more than 10% of the support;
2. The amount contributed by you and others to the dependent's support equals more than half the support;
3. Each contributor could have claimed the exemption—except that he or she gave less than half the support; *and*
4. Each contributor who gave more than 10% agrees to let you take the exemption. Each signs a Form 2120, "Multiple Support Declaration." You then attach the forms to your return.

EXAMPLES

1. You and your two brothers contribute $2,000 each toward the support of your mother. She contributes $1,000 of her own to support herself. Your two sisters contribute $500 each. Thus, the total support comes to $8,000. Of this, you and your brothers each gave 25% ($2,000 ÷ $8,000), for a total of 75%. Each sister gave 6¼% ($500 ÷ $8,000). You or one of your brothers may claim the exemption, assuming the other tests for a qualifying relative *(21.4)* are met. Since each of you contributed more than 10% and the total of your contributions is more than half of your mother's support, you may decide among yourselves which of the three of you will claim the exemption. If you claim the exemption, your brothers must sign Forms 2120, which you attach to your return. If one of your brothers claims the exemption, you sign a Form 2120, which is attached to the return of the brother who claims the exemption. Since neither of your sisters furnished more than 10%, neither can claim the exemption; they need not sign Forms 2120.
2. Your mother's support totals $10,000; you contribute $3,000; your brother, $2,000; your father, $1,600; and your mother from her savings contributes $3,400. Assume your father does not file a tax return claiming your mother as an exemption. You and your brother cannot use your father's contribution to meet the more than 50% test required by Rule 2 above. Your father may not join in a multiple support agreement because your mother is not his dependent for tax purposes, although an exemption may be claimed for a wife on the basis of the marital relationship; *see 21.2.*

Filing Instruction

Multiple Support Agreement

If you contribute more than 10% of a person's support and all other more-than-10% contributors agree to let you claim the exemption, each of them should sign a consent on separate Forms 2120 that you attach to your return.

Planning Reminder

Form 8332 Waiver Applies to Child Tax Credit

If a custodial parent releases the right to claim a dependency exemption for his or her child on Form 8332 (or substitute statement), the release also gives the noncustodial parent the right to claim the child tax credit and the additional child tax credit, assuming the credits are not phased out; *see 25.2.*

Caution

Should Married Dependents File Separately?

When a married dependent files a joint return, the parent cannot claim an exemption. The loss of the exemption may cost a parent more than the joint return saves the couple. In such a case, it may be advisable for the couple to file separate returns so that the parent may benefit from the larger tax saving.

If the couple decides to revoke their election to file jointly and then file separately in order to preserve the exemption for a parent, they must do so before the filing date for the return. Once a joint return is filed, the couple may not, after the filing deadline, file separate returns for the same year.

21.7 Special Rule for Divorced or Separated Parents

A special rule applies where divorced or separated parents together provide more than half of their child's total support and one or both of them have custody of the child for more than half the year. Specifically, the special rule applies only if these threshold conditions are met: (1) the child receives over one-half of his or her total support for the year from one or both parents, (2) the parents are divorced or legally separated under a decree of divorce or separate maintenance, separated under a written separation agreement, or live apart at all times during the last six months of the year (this includes parents who were never married to each other), and (3) the child is in the custody of one or both parents for more than half the year.

The first condition is not met, and the special rule does not apply, if a parent and other individuals contributing more than 10% of the child's support enter into a multiple support agreement *(21.6)* authorizing the parent to claim the exemption.

How the special rule works. If the above threshold conditions are met, the noncustodial parent may claim the exemption for a child only if (1) the custodial parent provides a written waiver (Form 8332 or substitute) and the waiver is attached to the noncustodial parent's return, or (2) a pre-1985 agreement gives the exemption to the noncustodial parent and at least $600 of the child's support is provided by the noncustodial parent.

The custodial parent is the parent who had custody of the child for the greater part of the year.

A post-1984 decree or agreement that gives the noncustodial parent the right to claim the exemption is not enough; the waiver from the custodial parent must be obtained and attached to the noncustodial parent's return.

21.8 The Dependent Must Meet a Citizen or Resident Test

To claim a 2006 exemption for a dependent, the dependent must have at some time during 2006 qualified as a:

- Citizen or resident of the United States;
- United States national (one who owes permanent allegiance to the U.S.; principally, a person born in American Samoa who has not become a naturalized American citizen); *or*
- Resident of Canada or Mexico.

Child born abroad. A child born in a foreign country, one of whose parents is a nonresident alien and whose other parent is a U.S. citizen, qualifies as a U.S. citizen and thus as a dependent if the other tests are met.

If you are a U.S. citizen who has legally adopted a child who is not a U.S. citizen or resident, or the child was lawfully placed with you for adoption, you may claim the child as your dependent if for the entire year your home is the child's principal residence and he or she is a member of your household.

21.9 The Dependent Does Not File a Joint Return

You may not claim an exemption for a dependent who files a joint return with another. For example, if you meet the other tests entitling you to an exemption for your married daughter as your dependent, but she files a joint return with her husband, you may not claim her as your dependent on your tax return.

Exception. Even if your dependent files a joint return, you may claim the exemption where the income of each spouse is under the income limit required for filing a return and the couple files a joint return merely to obtain a refund of withheld taxes. Under these circumstances, the dependent's return is considered a refund claim, and you may claim the dependency exemption.

21.10 Spouses' Names and Social Security Numbers on Joint Return

The IRS checks the Social Security number (SSN) of each spouse on a joint return. If the SSN and name on the return do not match IRS/Social Security Administration records, the IRS will disallow the exemption for that spouse.

The most common reason for a mismatch is when, after marriage, one spouse takes the other spouse's last name, or a hyphenated name is used. An updated Social Security card should be obtained using Form SS-5, available from the Social Security Administration website at www.ssa.gov, or calling 1-800-772-1213.

If a new name is used on the return but Social Security Administration records have not been updated, the IRS will disallow that spouse's exemption unless the new name is shown on an enclosed Form W-2 or the name change is explained and documented, such as by enclosing a copy of a new driver's license or marriage certificate.

If a spouse's exemption is disallowed, the IRS will mail the taxpayers an explanatory notice. By contacting the IRS and verifying a name change, the exemption can be restored.

21.11 Reporting Social Security Numbers of Dependents

On your 2006 return, you must list the Social Security number (SSN) of each dependent you claim. Include the SSNs of parents or other adults you claim as dependents, as well as those of children.

An SSN may be obtained from the Social Security Administration for U.S. citizens and aliens who have been lawfully admitted for permanent residence or employment. If a dependent is a resident alien or nonresident alien ineligible to obtain an SSN, an individual taxpayer identification number (ITIN) must be obtained from the IRS by filing Form W-7.

If you are in the process of legally adopting a U.S. citizen or resident child who has been placed in your home by an authorized placement agency, and you cannot obtain a Social Security number for the child in time to file your tax return, you may use Form W-7A to apply to the IRS for a temporary adoption taxpayer identification number (ATIN).

If you fail to include a correct SSN or ITIN for a dependent claimed on your return, the IRS may disallow the exemption, although it may contact you and give you an opportunity to provide the number. If an exemption is disallowed, the IRS may assess the extra tax using a summary assessment procedure if you fail to request abatement of the assessment within 60 days of receiving notice; this procedure does not require issuance of a deficiency notice, so there is no appeal to the Tax Court.

To obtain a Social Security number for a dependent child, file Form SS-5 with your local Social Security Administration office. Parents of newborn children may request a number when filling out hospital birth-registration records.

Planning Reminder

Filing for SSN or ITIN

If you are planning to claim an exemption for a dependent who as of the end of 2006 does not have the required Social Security number or individual taxpayer identification number, either you or that person should file Form SS-5 with the Social Security Administration or Form W-7 with the IRS (for an ITIN) as soon as possible so the number may be obtained before the April 16, 2007, filing deadline for your 2006 return. If you do not have the SSN by the filing due date, you should file Form 4868 for an automatic extension to file; *see 46.3*.

Religious beliefs. Religious beliefs against applying for and using SSN numbers for their children do not excuse taxpayers from the obligation to provide them. That's what the Tax Court told the Millers, who had refused to use SSN numbers for claiming their two children as exemptions. They argued that SSNs are universal numerical identifiers equal to the "mark of the Beast," as described in the New Testament. However, they were willing to use Individual Taxpayer Identification Numbers (ITINs).

The Court held that the IRS properly refused to issue ITINs in this case because ITINs are issued only to taxpayers who are ineligible to receive SSNs, which are issued by the Social Security Administration. The couple had argued that the requirement to use SSNs "substantially burdened" their First Amendment right to free exercise of religion, which entitled them to relief under the Religious Freedom Restoration Act of 1993. The Court held that it did not have to decide the "burden" issue because the IRS was able to show that the SSN requirement furthers a compelling governmental interest and is the least restrictive means of achieving this interest. Here, the Government has a compelling interest in effectively tracking claimed dependency exemptions and administering the tax system in a uniform and mandatory way. Moreover, the requirement to supply SSNs for dependent children has significantly reduced the improper claiming of dependents. Allowing the use of ITINs would be a less effective means of detecting fraud than requiring SSNs. If an individual entitled to an SSN was issued an ITIN, an SSN could later be obtained, allowing duplicate exemption claims to be made.

21.12 Phaseout of Personal Exemptions

You will lose part or all of the $3,300 deduction for each 2006 personal exemption if your adjusted gross income (AGI) exceeds the threshold amount for your filing status. *Adjusted gross income* is explained at *12.1*. On your 2006 Form 1040, adjusted gross income is shown on Lines 37 and 38.

If your 2006 status is—	Phaseout applies if AGI exceeds*—	Exemptions completely phased out if AGI exceeds—
Married filing jointly or Qualifying widow(er)	$225,750	$348,250
Head of household	188,150	310,650
Single	150,500	273,000
Married filing separately	112,875	174,125

**These thresholds are adjusted annually for inflation.*

Caution

Phaseout of Exemptions

On a 2006 return, you are not allowed to claim any deduction for personal exemptions if your adjusted gross income exceeds $273,000 if you are single, $348,250 if you are married filing jointly, 310,650 if you file as head of household, and $174,125 if you are married filing separately.

Law Alert

Scheduled Reduction of Phaseout

The phaseout of exemptions is being gradually eliminated between 2006 and 2010. For 2006 and 2007, the amount of the phaseout is two-thirds of the "full" phaseout that was required on 2005 returns. For 2008 and 2009, only one-third of the phaseout will apply, and after 2009, there will not be any phaseout of exemptions.

How the phaseout increases your marginal tax rate. The phaseout *increases* the effective marginal rate on earnings within the $122,500 phase-out range ($61,250 for married filing separately); *see* the Example below. The marginal rate increases with the number of exemptions.

Exemption Reduction Worksheet

1. Multiply $3,300 by the number of exemptions claimed on Form 1040, Line 6d. 1______
2. Enter adjusted gross income (Line 37, Form 1040). 2______
3. Enter phase-out threshold for your filing status:
   - Joint return or Qualifying widow(er): $225,750
   - Single: $150,500
   - Head of household: $188,150
   - Married filing separately: $112,875 3______
4. Subtract Line 3 from Line 2.* 4______
5. Divide Line 4 by $2,500 ($1,250 if married filing separately). Round up to next higher whole number if result is not a whole number (for example, round .005 to 1). 5______
6. Multiply Line 5 by 2% and enter the number as a decimal. 6______
7. Multiply Line 1 by Line 6. 7______
8. Multiply Line 7 by $^2/_3$ (0.6666). **This amount is disallowed.** 8______
9. Subtract Line 8 from Line 1. **This is the amount that you deduct for exemptions on Line 42, Form 1040.** 9______

**If Line 4 is zero or less, your exemptions are not reduced. Enter the amount from Line 1 on Form 1040, Line 42. If Line 4 is over $122,500 ($61,250 if married filing separately), you may not claim any deductions for exemptions. If Line 4 is more than zero but no more than $122,500 ($61,250 if married filing separately), proceed to Line 5.*

EXAMPLE

Howard and Jessica are married. For 2006, they filed a joint return and claimed four exemptions. They reported adjusted gross income of $229,550 on Line 37 of Form 1040. Their exemptions are reduced by $352 to $12,848, figured as follows:

1. $3,300 × 4	$13,200
2. Adjusted gross income	$229,550
3. Phaseout threshold for joint return	225,750
4. AGI in excess of threshold	3,800
5. $3,800 (Line 4) ÷ 2,500 (1.52 rounded up to 2)	2
6. 2 (Line 5) × 2%	.04 (4%)
7. $13,200 (Line 1) × 4% (Line 6)	528
8. $528 (Line 7) × $^{2}/_{3}$ (0.6666) is disallowed	352
9. Deduction for exemptions allowed (Line 1 *less* Line 8 ($13,200 – $352))	12,848

Earning $3,800 over the phase-out threshold has cost Howard and Jessica a $352 deduction, which in their top 33% bracket is worth $116 (33% × $352). This $116 tax cost is in addition to the $1,254 regular tax on the excess earnings (33% × 3,800). The total tax liability attributed to the $3,800 earnings, or $1,370 ($1,254 + $116), represents an effective marginal tax rate of 36.05%:

$$\frac{\$1{,}370}{\$3{,}800} = 36.05\%$$

PART 4

Personal Tax Computations

In this part, you will learn how to:

- ***Figure your regular tax.*** After claiming the standard deduction or itemized deductions *(13.1)* and deducting your allowable personal exemptions *(21.1)*, you figure your regular tax either by looking up the tax in the Tax Table or by figuring the tax using the Tax Computation Worksheet; *see* Chapter 22.
- ***Apply the alternative minimum tax.*** If you have reduced your taxable income by certain deductions and tax benefits, you may be subject to the alternative minimum tax (AMT); for further details, *see* Chapter 23.
- ***Reduce your tax liability with tax credits.*** You may be entitled to tax credits that lower your regular tax as well as any AMT; *see 22.6.*
- ***Figure estimated tax payments.*** If you have investment and self-employment income, you generally have to pay quarterly estimated tax; *see 27.1.*
- ***Compute the "kiddie tax."*** If your child under age 18 has investment income exceeding $1,700, you must compute tax on that income as if it were your own. "Kiddie tax" rules are discussed in Chapter 24.

Chapter 22

Figuring Your Regular Income Tax Liability

There are two types of income tax rates: (1) regular rates, which apply to all taxpayers, and (2) alternative minimum tax (AMT) rates, which apply only if certain tax benefits, when added back to your income, result in an AMT tax that exceeds your regular tax.

Most taxpayers do not have to compute the regular tax. They find the tax for their income and filing status in the IRS Tax Table if their taxable income is less than $100,000; *see 22.2.* The Tax Computation Worksheet must be used to figure your regular income tax if taxable income is $100,000 or more; *see 22.3.* However, if you have net capital gain or qualified dividends, do not use the Tax Table or the Tax Computation Worksheet. Instead, figure your regular tax liability on the applicable capital gains worksheet in the IRS instructions; *see 22.4.*

Computation of the alternative minimum tax is more complicated and requires the preparation of Form 6251. AMT is discussed in Chapter 23.

22.1 Taxable Income and Regular Income Tax Liability

The way you determine your regular tax liability depends on the amount of your taxable income and in some cases the type of income you have. If your taxable income is less than $100,000, you must use the IRS Tax Table to look up your tax; *see 22.2.* If your taxable income is $100,000 or more, you use the Tax Computation Worksheet to determine the tax; *see 22.3.* However, if you have net capital gain or qualified dividends, you generally figure your tax on the Qualified Dividends and Capital Gain Tax Worksheet in the IRS instructions for Form 1040; *see 22.4.* Tax is figured on Form 8615 if the "kiddie tax" computation *(24.4)* must be made.

Taxable income is your adjusted gross income *(12.1)* minus the following: (1) your standard deduction or itemized deductions, whichever you claim (*see* Chapter 13), and (2) deductions for personal exemptions allowed under the rules discussed in Chapter 21. On Form 1040 for 2006, taxable income is entered on Line 43.

On Form 1040A and Form 1040EZ, the computation of taxable income generally takes fewer steps because only limited types of income and deductions may be reported. Itemized deductions may not be claimed. Personal exemptions for dependents may be claimed on Form 1040A but not on Form 1040EZ. *See* the table on page 7 for the types of income and deductions that may not be reported on these forms.

On Form 1040A for 2006, taxable income is entered on Line 27; on Form 1040EZ, it is on Line 6.

Caution: regardless of how your regular tax liability is determined, you may also be liable for alternative minimum tax (AMT), which is figured on Form 6251; *see 23.1.*

Filing Instruction

Taxable Income Under $100,000

If you do not have net capital gains on Schedule D *(see 22.4),* and are not using Form 8615 to compute the "kiddie tax" for a child under age 18 *(24.4),* the IRS requires you to use the Tax Table to determine the regular tax on your taxable income if it is less than $100,000.

22.2 Using the Tax Table

If you file Form 1040EZ or Form 1040A, you use the Tax Table in Part 8 to look up your regular income tax liability. If you file Form 1040, you also use the Tax Table if your taxable income is *less* than $100,000; if your taxable income is $100,000 or more, you use the Tax Computation Worksheet; *see 22.3.* However, use the special capital gain worksheets discussed in *22.4* if you have net capital gain or qualified dividends.

If you use the Tax Table, you do not have to compute your tax mathematically. To use the Table you first figure your taxable income *(see 22.1),* then turn to your income bracket and look for the tax liability listed in the column for your filing status. Filing status (single, married filing jointly, head of household, married filing separately, and qualifying widow(er)) is discussed in Chapter 1.

EXAMPLES

1. You are single and have an adjusted gross income of $36,595 for 2006. You claim one personal exemption and the standard deduction.

Adjusted gross income		$36,595
Less: Standard deduction	$5,150	
Exemption	3,300	8,450
Taxable income		$28,145

Your tax liability from the Tax Table is $3,841. The tax is shown in the column for single persons with taxable income of at least $28,100 but less than $28,150.

2. You are married filing jointly and have 2006 adjusted gross income of $48,440, itemized deductions of $10,900, and three exemptions.

Adjusted gross income		$48,440
Less: Itemized deductions	$10,900	
Exemptions (3 × $3,300)	9,900	20,800
Taxable income		$27,640

Your tax liability from the Tax Table is $3,389.

22.3 Tax Computation Worksheet

If your taxable income is $100,000 or more and you do not have net capital gain or qualified dividends *(see 22.4)*, you must figure your 2006 regular tax liability on the Tax Computation Worksheet shown in Part 8. The Tax Computation Worksheet has replaced the tax rate schedules but provides the same result.

There are six tax rate brackets for 2006: 10%, 15%, 25%, 28%, 33%, and 35%. At the top of page 11, we show the amount of taxable income subject to each tax bracket for each filing status in 2006. However, since the Tax Computation Worksheet applies only to taxable incomes of $100,000 and more, it only shows the brackets that a taxpayer with taxable income of at least $100,000 can be subject to. These brackets vary with each filing status.

To figure regular income tax liability using the Tax Computation Worksheet, follow the column-by-column instructions. First go to the section corresponding to your filing status and find the (horizontal) row that includes your taxable income. On that row, multiply your taxable income by your top tax rate shown in column (b), enter the result in column (c), and then reduce it by the subtraction amount shown in column (d) to obtain the regular tax liability that you enter on Form 1040.

EXAMPLE

You and your spouse file a joint return reporting taxable income of $130,000 for 2006. By following the column-by-column- instructions of the Tax Computation Worksheet, you figure your regular tax liability of $25,804:

$130,000 × 28% rate from column (b)	$36,400.00
Less subtraction amount from column (d)	10,596.00
Tax	$ 25,804.00

22.4 Tax Calculation If You Have Net Capital Gain or Qualified Dividends

If a portion of your taxable income consists of net capital gain (net long-term capital gain in excess of net short-term capital loss; *see 5.3*) or qualified dividends *(4.1)*, you should figure your regular tax liability on the Qualified Dividends and Capital Gain Tax Worksheet in the IRS instruction booklet. On the Worksheet, you can apply the favorable capital gain rates *(5.3)* to your net gain and qualified dividends. *See 5.8* for an example of how to report transactions on Schedule D (Form 1040) and a filled-in sample of the Qualified Dividends and Capital Gain Tax Worksheet from the Form 1040 instructions that illustrates the computation of tax liability. You may be able to figure your liability on the Qualified Dividends and Capital Gain Tax Worksheet without having to file Schedule D if you have capital gain distributions from Box 2a of Form 1099-DIV *(see 32.8)* and/or qualified dividends and no other capital gains or losses.

However, you use a different worksheet if you report any 28% rate gains or unrecaptured Section 1250 gain on Schedule D. In this case, you must use the Schedule D Tax Worksheet in the Schedule D instructions to figure tax liability.

22.5 Income Averaging for Farmers and Fishermen

A farmer or fisherman may elect to average 2006 farm or fishing income over three years on Schedule J of Form 1040. On Schedule J, one-third of elected farm or fishing income is allocated to each of 2003, 2004, and 2005. The tax for 2006 equals the tax liability figured without elected farm or fishing income plus increases in tax liability for the three prior years by including allocated elected farm or fishing income. Income averaging is available only to individual farmers or fishermen and may not be elected by estates or trusts engaged in the farming or fishing business.

Elected farm or fishing income is taxable income attributable to a farming or fishing business. A farming business is generally any business that involves cultivating land or raising or harvesting agricultural or horticultural commodities. A fishing business is generally any business involving the actual or attempted catching, taking, or harvesting of fish. *See* the Schedule J instructions.

Filing Tip

Negative Taxable Income in Prior Three Years

When figuring your tax under the averaging method on Schedule J, you may use negative taxable income for a base year (any of the three preceding years) for which deductions exceeded gross income. *See* the Schedule J instructions for details.

Filing Tip

IRS Definition of "Fish"

The word "fish" means finfish, mollusks, crustaceans, and all other forms of marine animal and plant life other than marine mammals and birds.

A previous election to average farm income may by revoked or the elected farm income may be changed by filing an amended return within the period of limitations for a refund claim *(see 47.2)*.

AMT relief for averaging. When computing AMT on Form 6251, a farmer's regular tax liability is determined without regard to averaging. Since AMT liability is based on the excess of tentative AMT over regular tax, ignoring the reduction to the regular tax from averaging limits or eliminates the AMT.

22.6 Tax Credits

After applying the Tax Table or Tax Computation Worksheet to get your 2006 regular tax liability, you may be able to reduce that liability as well as AMT liability (Chapter 23) by claiming tax credits. The child tax credit, the dependent care credit, alternative motor vehicle credit, earned income credit, adoption credit, credit for retirement savings contributions, health insurance credit, mortgage interest credit, and the District of Columbia First-Time Homebuyer Credit are discussed in Chapter 25. The education tax credits are discussed in Chapter 33. The credit for the elderly is discussed in Chapter 34 and the foreign tax credit in Chapter 36. The business tax credits are discussed in Chapter 40. The credit for prior year AMT liability is discussed at *23.5*.

If you worked for more than one employer in 2006 and Social Security taxes of more than $5,840.40 were withheld from your wages, the excess may be claimed as a credit in the "Payments" section of Form 1040; *see 26.10*.

Refund for federal telephone long-distance tax. The IRS is refunding to taxpayers the federal excise tax collected after February 28, 2003, and before August 1, 2006, on long-distance telephone service. The refund is obtained by claiming a credit for it in the "Payments" section of your 2006 tax return. You can claim either the safe harbor amount allowed by the IRS or the actual tax paid if you can document the amount. To claim the actual long-distance tax paid, you must complete Form 8913 and attach it to your return. Taxpayers whose income is below the 2006 filing threshold can obtain the refund of the telephone tax by filing Form 1040EZ-T. *Also see 46.4.*

Chapter 23

Alternative Minimum Tax (AMT)

The purpose of AMT is to effectively take back some of the tax breaks allowed for regular tax purposes. The AMT is an additional tax that you may owe if for regular tax purposes you claimed:

- Itemized deductions, such as taxes, interest on home equity loans used for nonresidential purposes, medical expenses, and miscellaneous job and investment expenses.
- Certain tax-exempt interest, accelerated depreciation, and incentive stock option benefits.
- A substantial number of exemptions for dependents.

There are no specific tests to determine whether or not you are liable for AMT. You must first figure your regular income tax and then see whether tax benefit items must be added back to taxable income to figure alternative minimum taxable income, on which the AMT is figured. If after claiming the AMT exemption and applying the AMT rates of 26% and 28% the tentative alternative minimum tax exceeds your regular income tax, the excess is your AMT liability, which is added to the regular tax on your return. In other words, your tax liability for the year will be the greater of your regular tax or your AMT.

AMT liability is figured on Form 6251 and is attached to Form 1040. If you file Form 1040A, AMT liability, if any, is figured on a worksheet and the AMT is entered on the line for total tax on Form 1040A.

Table 23-1 Key to AMT Rules for 2006

Item—	AMT Rule—
Tax rate	A 26% rate applies to AMT taxable income of $175,000 or less (after the AMT exemption), $87,500 or less if married filing separately. A 28% rate applies to AMT income exceeding the $175,000 or $87,500 threshold.
AMT taxable income	Regular taxable income without personal exemptions, increased or decreased by adjustments and increased by preferences.
AMT exemption	$62,550 if married filing a joint return (or a qualifying widow(er)); $42,500 if single or head of household; *or* $31,275 if married filing a separate return. Under a phase-out rule, these exemption amounts are reduced by 25¢ for each $1 that AMT taxable income (AMTI) exceeds $150,000 for joint filers or a qualifying widow(er), $112,500 if you file as a single person or head of household, and $75,000 for a married person filing separately. The exemption is completely phased out at $400,200 on a joint return and $282,500 on a single or head of household return. On a married person's separate return, the exemption is eliminated if AMT taxable income is $200,100 or more. Further, a married person filing separately must increase AMTI by 25% of AMTI exceeding $200,100.
AMT adjustments	Itemized deductions for taxes, certain interest, and most miscellaneous deductions are not allowed. Personal exemptions and the standard deduction are not allowed. MACRS depreciation is figured under the alternative MACRS system for real estate using 40-year straight-line recovery, and, for personal property, the 150% declining balance method. For incentive stock options; *see 23.2.* Mining exploration and development costs are allowable costs amortized over 10 years. For long-term contracts entered into after February 28, 1986, income is figured under the percentage-of-completion method. Pollution control facilities amortization is figured under alternate MACRS. Alternative tax net operating loss is allowed with adjustments. Circulation expenditures must be amortized ratably over three years. Research and experimental expenditures must be amortized ratably over 10 years. Passive activity losses are recomputed; certain tax-shelter farm losses may not be allowed.
AMT preference items	Tax-exempt interest from private activity bonds issued after August 7,1986, *except* for qualifying 501(c)(3) bonds. Accelerated depreciation on real property and leased personal property placed in service before 1987—excess depreciation or amortization taken over straight-line deduction. If you sell qualified small business stock that qualifies for an exclusion *(5.7)*, 7% of the exclusion is a preference item.
Adjusted gross income	In making AMT computations involving adjusted gross income limitations, use adjusted gross income as computed for regular tax purposes.
Partnership AMT	If you are a partner, include for AMT your distributive share of the partnership's adjustments and tax preference items. These are reported on Schedule K-1 (Form 1065). The partnership itself does not pay alternative minimum tax
Trust or estate AMT	If you are a beneficiary of an estate or trust, consider for AMT your share of distributable net alternative minimum taxable income shown on Schedule K-1 (Form 1041). The estate or trust must pay tax on any remaining alternative minimum taxable income.
S corporation stockholder	If you are a shareholder, consider for AMT your share of the adjustments and tax preference items reported on Schedule K-1 (Form 1120-S).
Children subject to "kiddie tax"	Children under age 14 who are subject to the "kiddie tax" *(24.3)* may have to compute AMT liability on Form 6251. The 2005 AMT exemption for a child subject to the "kiddie tax" equals the child's earned income plus $6,050, but no more than the regular AMT $42,500 exemption for single persons.

23.1 Computing Alternative Minimum Tax on Form 6251

You use Form 6251 to compute AMT liability, if any. The checklist below gives an indication as to when you may have to use Form 6251. The checklist items are discussed at *23.2–23.5*.

If you check any of the items on the list, you should complete Form 6251 to determine if you are liable for AMT. These items are AMT adjustments and preferences and generally are added back to regular taxable income to calculate alternative minimum taxable income (AMTI). The items that most commonly get added back to income when calculating AMTI are personal exemptions, state and local taxes, and miscellaneous itemized deductions.

AMTI is reduced by the allowable AMT exemption. Subject to the phase-out rule discussed in the "Key to AMT Rules for 2006" on the preceding page, the exemption is $42,500 if single or head of household, $62,550 if married filing jointly or qualifying widow(er), or $31,275 if married filing separately.

After reducing AMTI by the allowable exemption, a 26% AMT rate generally applies to the first $175,000 of AMT income ($87,500 if married filing separately), and a 28% rate applies to any balance of the AMT income. However, if you had net capital gains that qualify for reduced capital gains rates *(5.3)*, you apply the same capital gains rate for AMT purposes as for regular income tax purposes.

The resulting tax, less any AMT foreign tax credit, is the tentative AMT, which applies only to the extent it *exceeds* your regular income tax. For this purpose, regular income tax is the tax on your taxable income, without taking into account personal credits (such as the child tax credit or education credits), *minus* any special averaging tax on a lump-sum distribution or any regular foreign tax credit. The excess of tentative AMT over this regular tax, if any, is the AMT liability that you must report as an additional tax on Line 45 of Form 1040.

Follow the line-by-line instructions to Form 6251 to figure your AMT liability, if any.

Items subject to AMT:	**Check: ✓**
1. Personal exemptions	❑
2. Standard deduction	❑
3. Itemized deductions for taxes, miscellaneous expenses, and medical expenses	❑
4. Interest on home equity debt used for nonresidential purposes	❑
5. Accelerated depreciation in excess of straight line	❑
6. Income from the exercise of incentive stock options	❑
7. Tax-exempt interest from private activity bonds	❑
8. Intangible drilling costs	❑
9. Depletion	❑
10. Circulation expenses	❑
11. Mining exploration and development costs	❑
12. Research and experimental costs	❑
13. Pollution control facility amortization	❑
14. Tax-shelter farm income or loss	❑
15. Passive income or loss	❑
16. Certain installment sale income	❑
17. Income from long-term contracts computed under percentage-of-income method	❑
18. Net operating loss deduction	❑
19. Foreign tax credit	❑
20. Investment expenses	❑
21. Gain on small business stock qualifying for 50% exclusion	❑

Law Alert

Higher AMT Exemption for 2006 Only

The Tax Increase Prevention and Reconciliation Act increased the AMT exemption for 2006 to $62,550 for joint filers (from $58,000), $42,500 for single filers and heads of household (from $40,250), and $31,275 for married persons filing separately (from $29,000).

The increase is a one-year "patch" that Congress settled on to prevent millions of middle class taxpayers from becoming subject to the AMT for 2006. Unless further legislative relief is enacted, the AMT exemption will fall back in 2007 to $45,000 for joint filers, $33,750 for single filers and heads of household, and $22,500 for married persons filing separately.

EXAMPLE

You are married filing jointly and for 2006 you have adjusted gross income of $135,500. You claim itemized deductions of $45,046 and five personal exemptions. For individuals who itemize deductions for regular tax purposes, the starting point for figuring AMT on Form 6251 is the amount shown on Line 41 of Form 1040 (AGI minus itemized deductions). This is $90,454, your AGI of $135,500 minus $45,046 of itemized deductions. Your personal exemptions are ignored for AMT purposes. The itemized deductions include $34,000 for state and local taxes and interest of $6,500 on a home equity mortgage loan used for non-residential purposes *(23.2)*. These deductions are adjustments for AMT purposes. You also have an MACRS depreciation adjustment of $1,000. Before figuring AMT on Form 6251, you complete Form 1040 and compute tax liability of $11,609 on taxable income of $73,954 ($135,500 AGI – $45,046 itemized deductions – $16,500 for five exemptions). You prepare Form 6251 *(see* below) and figure alternative minimum taxable income of $131,954 ($90,454 + $34,000 + $6,500 + $1,000). This is reduced by your AMT exemption of $62,550 and the balance of $69,404 is multiplied by the 26% AMT rate to give a tentative minimum tax of $18,045. You must pay as AMT $6,436, the excess of the tentative minimum tax over the regular tax ($18,045 – $11,609). You must pay the $6,436 in addition to your regular income tax. Enter the AMT on Line 45 of Form 1040.

Form **6251** Department of the Treasury Internal Revenue Service (99)

Alternative Minimum Tax—Individuals

▶ See separate instructions.

▶ Attach to Form 1040 or Form 1040NR.

OMB No. 1545-0074 **2006** Attachment Sequence No. 32

Name(s) shown on Form 1040 | Your social security number

Part I Alternative Minimum Taxable Income (See instructions for how to complete each line.)

		Line	Amount
1	If filing Schedule A (Form 1040), enter the amount from Form 1040, line 41 (minus any amount on Form 8914, line 6), and go to line 2. Otherwise, enter the amount from Form 1040, line 38 (minus any amount on Form 8914, line 6), and go to line 7. (If less than zero, enter as a negative amount.)	1	90,454
2	Medical and dental. Enter the **smaller** of Schedule A (Form 1040), line 4, **or** 2½% of Form 1040, line 38	2	
3	Taxes from Schedule A (Form 1040), line 9	3	34,000
4	Enter the home mortgage interest adjustment, if any, from line 6 of the worksheet on page 2 of the instructions	4	6,500
5	Miscellaneous deductions from Schedule A (Form 1040), line 26	5	
6	If Form 1040, line 38, is over $150,500 (over $75,250 if married filing separately), enter the amount from line 11 of the **Itemized Deductions Worksheet** on page A-6 of the Instructions for Schedule A (Form 1040)	6	( )
7	Tax refund from Form 1040, line 10 or line 21	7	( )
8	Investment interest expense (difference between regular tax and AMT)	8	
9	Depletion (difference between regular tax and AMT)	9	
10	Net operating loss deduction from Form 1040, line 21. Enter as a positive amount	10	
11	Interest from specified private activity bonds exempt from the regular tax	11	
12	Qualified small business stock (7% of gain excluded under section 1202)	12	
13	Exercise of incentive stock options (excess of AMT income over regular tax income)	13	
14	Estates and trusts (amount from Schedule K-1 (Form 1041), box 12, code A)	14	
15	Electing large partnerships (amount from Schedule K-1 (Form 1065-B), box 6)	15	
16	Disposition of property (difference between AMT and regular tax gain or loss)	16	
17	Depreciation on assets placed in service after 1986 (difference between regular tax and AMT)	17	1,000
18	Passive activities (difference between AMT and regular tax income or loss)	18	
19	Loss limitations (difference between AMT and regular tax income or loss)	19	
20	Circulation costs (difference between regular tax and AMT)	20	
21	Long-term contracts (difference between AMT and regular tax income)	21	
22	Mining costs (difference between regular tax and AMT)	22	
23	Research and experimental costs (difference between regular tax and AMT)	23	
24	Income from certain installment sales before January 1, 1987	24	( )
25	Intangible drilling costs preference	25	
26	Other adjustments, including income-based related adjustments	26	
27	Alternative tax net operating loss deduction	27	( )
28	**Alternative minimum taxable income.** Combine lines 1 through 27. (If married filing separately and line 28 is more than $200,100, see page 7 of the instructions.)	28	131,954

Part II Alternative Minimum Tax

29 Exemption. (If this form is for a child under age 18, see page 7 of the instructions.)

IF your filing status is . . .	AND line 28 is not over . . .	THEN enter on line 29 . . .
Single or head of household	$112,500	$42,500
Married filing jointly or qualifying widow(er)	150,000	62,550
Married filing separately	75,000	31,275

If line 28 is **over** the amount shown above for your filing status, see page 7 of the instructions.

		Line	Amount
29	Exemption (from table above)	29	62,550
30	Subtract line 29 from line 28. If more than zero **or** you are filing Form 2555 or 2555-EZ, go to line 31. If zero or less and you are not filing Form 2555 or 2555-EZ, enter -0- on lines 33 and 35 and skip the rest of Part II	30	69,404
31	• If you are filing Form 2555 or 2555-EZ, see page 8 of the instructions for the amount to enter. • If you reported capital gain distributions directly on Form 1040, line 13; you reported qualified dividends on Form 1040, line 9b; **or** you had a gain on both lines 15 and 16 of Schedule D (Form 1040) (as refigured for the AMT, if necessary), complete Part III on the back and enter the amount from line 55 here. • **All others:** If line 30 is $175,000 or less ($87,500 or less if married filing separately), multiply line 30 by 26% (.26). Otherwise, multiply line 30 by 28% (.28) and subtract $3,500 ($1,750 if married filing separately) from the result.	31	18,045
32	Alternative minimum tax foreign tax credit (see page 7 of the instructions)	32	
33	Tentative minimum tax. Subtract line 32 from line 31	33	18,045
34	Tax from Form 1040, line 44 (minus any tax from Form 4972 and any foreign tax credit from Form 1040, line 47). If you used Schedule J to figure your tax, the amount for line 44 of Form 1040 must be refigured without using Schedule J (see page 9 of the instructions)	34	11,609
35	**Alternative minimum tax.** Subtract line 34 from line 33. If zero or less, enter -0-. Enter here and on Form 1040, line 45	35	6,436

For Paperwork Reduction Act Notice, see page 9 of the instructions. Cat. No. 13600G Form **6251** (2006)

23.2 Adjustments for AMT

The starting point for figuring AMT is your adjusted gross income from Form 1040. This amount will generally be increased by adjustments on Form 6251.

Standard deduction and personal exemptions not allowed. If you claimed the standard deduction for regular tax purposes, the deduction is disregarded when figuring AMT liability. You also must disregard the personal exemptions claimed for regular tax purposes. *See* the Filing Instruction and Court Decision on this page.

Certain itemized deductions disallowed for AMT purposes. Some key itemized deductions claimed on Schedule A are disallowed or reduced when figuring alternative minimum taxable income (AMTI) on Form 6251. For example, no AMT deduction is allowed for state and local income (or, if elected, sales) taxes, real property taxes, or personal property taxes, or for foreign income or real property taxes. Also not allowed for AMT purposes are miscellaneous itemized deductions that were allowed on Schedule A after application of the 2% AGI floor. A smaller deduction for medical expenses is allowed for AMT than for regular tax purposes. The deduction for interest on home equity mortgage loans may have to be reduced. Investment interest may have to be refigured for AMT.

The required AMT adjustments for these deductions are discussed in the following paragraphs.

On the other hand, if some of your itemized deductions were disallowed on Schedule A by the 3% reduction rule for taxpayers with adjusted gross income over $150,500 ($75,250 if married filing separately), the disallowed amount is entered as a negative adjustment to AMTI.

Mortgage interest. Less interest may be deductible for AMT purposes than for regular tax purposes. If an interest deduction is claimed on Schedule A for debt that does not qualify under the AMT rules, that interest is added back as an adjustment on Form 6251.

No AMT adjustment is required for home mortgage interest paid on a debt incurred to buy, construct, or substantially rehabilitate your principal residence or qualifying second residence. The residence may be a house, apartment, cooperative apartment, condominium, or mobile home not used on a transient basis. Nor is an adjustment required for interest on a debt incurred before July 1, 1982, provided that the mortgage was secured at the time it was taken out by your principal residence or any other home used by you or a family member.

An adjustment is required for home mortgage interest on a loan taken out after June 30, 1982 if the loan proceeds were used for any purpose other than to buy, build, or substantially improve your principal residence or second residence. If your Schedule A deduction includes interest on a refinanced loan taken out after June 30, 1982 (including a second or later refinancing), you must treat as an AMT adjustment any interest on the new mortgage balance that exceeded the balance of the prior debt immediately before the refinancing (whether it was the balance of the original debt or balance of a prior refinancing).

The instructions to Form 6251 have a worksheet for figuring the home mortgage interest adjustment.

Taxes. State, local, and foreign taxes deducted on Schedule A must be added back to income in figuring AMT. If you received in 2006 a refund of taxes deducted in a prior year and the refund is reported as income on your 2006 Form 1040 *(11.5–11.6)*, you enter the refund on Form 6251 (Line 7) as a negative adjustment in figuring alternative minimum taxable income.

Medical Expenses. If medical expenses in excess of the 7.5% AGI floor are deducted for regular tax purposes, you must add back to income on Form 6251 the smaller of the allowable medical deduction from Schedule A or 2.5% of adjusted gross income. The effect of this adjustment is to allow medical expenses as an AMT deduction only to the extent that they exceed 10% of AGI.

Miscellaneous deductions. In figuring alternative minimum taxable income (AMTI), you may not deduct miscellaneous itemized deductions in excess of 2% of adjusted gross income that you claim on Schedule A. These include unreimbursed job expenses *(19.3)*, tax preparation fees *(19.16)*, and contingent legal fees paid to recover taxable damages in employment or personal legal actions *(19.18)*.

Investment interest. If for regular tax purposes you claimed an itemized deduction (Schedule A) for investment interest on Form 4952, you must complete a second Form 4952 to determine if your allowable deduction for AMT is more or less than the itemized deduction, taking into account AMT adjustments and preferences. The difference between the regular tax deduction and

Filing Instruction

Standard Deduction and Exemptions Disallowed for AMT

If you claimed the standard deduction instead of itemizing deductions on Form 1040, you may not claim the standard deduction as an AMT deduction. Exemptions for yourself and your dependents are also not allowed for AMT purposes. The standard deduction and personal exemptions are not added back to income. They are indirectly disallowed by using adjusted gross income as the starting point for figuring AMT on Form 6251, However. the extra exemption allowed on Form 8914 for housing a person displaced by Hurricane Katrina *(21.1)* is an allowable AMT deduction on Form 6251.

Court Decision

10 Children Subject Parents to AMT

A married couple found themselves paying AMT tax when their regular tax deduction of 12 personal exemptions for themselves and their 10 children was disregarded for AMT purposes. In the Tax Court, they argued that AMT was not intended to apply to taxpayers merely because they had large families. The Tax Court disagreed. Congress specifically wrote the law considering the effect of personal exemptions on AMT tax liability. The Tenth Circuit appeals court, although more sympathetic to the couple, agreed with the Tax Court that their situation fit within the AMT rules.

the allowable AMT deduction is entered on Form 6251 as a positive adjustment if the regular tax deduction is more, or as a negative adjustment if the AMT amount is more. For example, if you paid interest on a home equity loan whose proceeds were invested in stocks or bonds, that interest is not treated as investment interest on Form 4952 when figuring the itemized deduction for regular tax purposes, but it is included as investment interest on the second Form 4952 used to figure the allowable AMT amount.

MACRS depreciation. Depreciation allowed for AMT may differ from that allowed for regular tax purposes. For tangible personal property (such as cars or furniture) placed in service before 1999, the AMT depreciation rate is the 150% declining balance method over the alternative depreciation system recovery period (ADS; *see 42.9*), switching to the straight-line method once it provides a larger deduction than the 150% method. For tangible personal property placed in service after 1998, the AMT deduction is figured using the 150% declining balance rate (switching to straight line when it gives a larger deduction) over the general depreciation system (GDS) recovery periods of three, five, seven, or 10 years *(42.4)*. Real property acquired after 1986 is depreciated for AMT over a 40-year period using the straight-line method. Depreciation deductions for films, videotapes, and sound recordings under the unit-of-production method or other method not based on a term of years are not adjusted under AMT.

If, for regular tax purposes, you use the regular 200% declining balance method to depreciate business equipment with a recovery period of three, five, seven, or 10 years, the difference between the regular depreciation and the 150% rate for AMT is an adjustment. For real estate, the adjustment is the difference between the straight-line depreciation claimed for regular tax purposes using the recovery period discussed at *42.13* and the straight-line recovery over the AMT 40-year recovery period.

The adjustment for MACRS may result in providing more depreciation for AMT purposes where the AMT depreciation computation towards the latter part of the useful life of the property provides larger deductions than the regular MACRS deduction. If the AMT deduction exceeds the regular tax deduction, the difference is entered as a negative adjustment that reduces alternative minimum taxable income.

Property placed in service before 1987, unless it qualifies under the MACRS transitional rules, is subject to prior law tax preference rules. Prior law creates tax preference items when the ACRS deduction exceeds regular straight-line depreciation; *see 23.3*. A tax preference item always increases AMT taxable income.

Basis adjustment affects AMT gain or loss. When post-1986 depreciable assets are sold, gain for AMT purposes is figured on the basis of the property as adjusted by depreciation claimed for AMT purposes. This gain or loss will be different from the gain or loss figured for regular tax purposes where regular MACRS depreciation was used. (This AMT basis rule does not apply to property placed in service before 1987 except for transitional property within the post-1986 rules).

Caution

Selling ISO Stock to Avoid AMT Adjustment

If you exercise an incentive stock option and your rights in the acquired stock are transferable and not subject to a substantial risk of forfeiture, you have to treat as an AMT adjustment the excess of the fair-market value of the stock when the option was exercised over the option price. Unless you sell the stock by the end of that same year, you must report an AMT adjustment based on the value of the stock when the option was exercised, *even if* the value later declines substantially. You avoid the AMT adjustment if you sell the stock in the same year the option was exercised.

Incentive stock option (ISO). For regular tax purposes, you are not taxed when you exercise an incentive stock option (ISO); *see 2.16*. However, the exercise of an ISO can result in a substantial AMT liability. You generally must increase AMT income by including on Form 6251 the excess, if any, of:

1. The fair market value of the stock acquired through exercise of the option (determined without regard to any lapse restriction) when your rights in the acquired stock first become transferable or when these rights are no longer subject to a substantial risk of forfeiture, over
2. The amount you paid for the stock, including any amount you paid for the ISO used to acquire the stock.

If your rights in the acquired ISO stock are not transferable and are subject to a substantial risk of forfeiture in the year you exercise the ISO, you do not report the AMT adjustment until the year your rights become transferable or are no longer forfeitable. However, within 30 days of the transfer to you of the stock acquired through exercise of the ISO, you may elect to include in AMT income for that year the excess of the stock's fair market value (determined without regard to any lapse restriction) over the exercise price; *see* the discussion of the Section 83(b) election at *2.17*.

Note: If you acquire stock by exercising an ISO and you dispose of that stock in the *same* year, the tax treatment under the regular tax and the AMT is the same. No AMT adjustment is required.

If you report an AMT adjustment for stock acquired through the exercise of an ISO, increase the AMT basis of the stock by the amount of the adjustment. Since the AMT basis in stock acquired through an ISO is likely to be significantly higher than your regular tax basis, you may have a larger gain for regular tax purposes and a larger loss for AMT purposes in the year you sell the stock. This would produce a negative adjustment for AMT. Follow the instructions to Line 16 ("Disposition of Property") of Form 6251.

Mining exploration and development costs. The deduction allowed for regular tax purposes for mining exploration and development costs is amortized ratably over a 10-year period for AMT purposes.

If a mine is abandoned as worthless, all mining exploration and development costs that have not been written off are deductible in the year of abandonment.

Circulation costs. Circulation costs deducted in full for regular tax purposes must be amortized over three years for the AMT. The difference between the two allowable deductions must be reported as an adjustment on Form 6251.

Long-term contracts. The use of the completed contract method of accounting or certain other methods of accounting for long-term contracts is generally not allowable. For AMT, the percentage of completion method must be used. However, there is an exception for home construction contracts.

Amortization of certified pollution control facilities. For AMT purposes, the amortization deduction for a certified pollution control facility placed in service after 1986 is determined under alternative MACRS; *see 42.9*.

Research and experimental expenditures. Costs must be amortized over 10 years for AMT purposes if incurred in a business in which you are not a material participant. The difference between the regular tax and AMT deductions must be entered as an adjustment on Form 6251.

Passive tax-shelter farm losses. Generally, no AMT loss is deductible for any tax-shelter farm activity. A tax-shelter farm activity is any farming syndicate or any farming activity in which you do not materially participate. You may be treated as a material participant if a member of your family materially participates or you meet certain retirement or disability tests discussed at *10.6*.

Gains and losses reported for regular tax purposes from tax-shelter farm activities must be refigured by taking into account any AMT adjustments and preferences. However, a refigured loss is not allowed for AMT purposes except to the extent that you are insolvent at the end of the year. This means that you deduct the loss to the extent of your insolvency. Insolvency is the excess of liabilities over fair market value of assets. Any AMT-disallowed loss is carried forward to later years in which there is gain from that same activity, or until you dispose of the activity.

Passive losses from nonfarming activities. These are adjusted for preference or adjustment items not allowed for AMT purposes. For example, an adjustment for MACRS depreciation is made directly against the passive loss and is not treated as a separate AMT adjustment item. The loss allowed for AMT purposes is increased by the amount by which you are insolvent at the end of the year. *See* the instructions to Form 6251, which suggest that the AMT adjustment of passive losses be figured on a separate Form 8582 that you do not file.

Planning Reminder

Incentive Stock Options

Your AMT basis in stock acquired through the exercise of an ISO is increased by the amount of the required AMT adjustment. Keep basis records for both AMT and regular tax purposes, since in the year the stock is sold, the higher AMT basis will reduce (or even eliminate in some cases) the gain reportable for AMT purposes.

23.3 Tax Preference Items

The following are tax preference items that increase the amount of 2006 AMT taxable income.

Tax-exempt interest on nonessential private activity bonds. For AMT purposes, you must include as a tax preference item the tax-exempt interest on qualified private activity bonds issued after August 7, 1986, except for qualified 501(c)(3) bonds, New York Liberty bonds, and qualified Gulf Opportunity Zone bonds. Generally, private activity bonds issued after August 7, 1986, are subject to AMT, but for certain bonds meeting specific tests, the AMT rule applies to bonds issued on or after September 1, 1986. Interest paid on buying or carrying such bonds is deductible for AMT purposes.

EXAMPLE

You received $5,000 interest income from a private activity bond issued in 1992. You also had $100 of investment expense related to this bond. You enter $4,900 on Form 6251.

Exclusion on qualifying small business stock. If you sold small business stock qualifying for the 50% or 60% exclusion *(5.7)*, 7% of the excluded gain is treated as an AMT preference item.

Accelerated depreciation of property acquired before 1987. For real property placed in service before 1987, the difference between the depreciation that would have been allowable if the straight-line method had been used and accelerated depreciation claimed on real property during the taxable year is a tax preference item. The excess is computed separately for each asset depreciated through an accelerated method. For example, if you use ACRS 15-year, 18-year, or 19-year accelerated rates for regular tax purposes, figure the deduction for each such property under the straight-line method and report the excess of your regular tax deduction over the straight-line amount as a preference item.

For personal property leased to others before 1987, the preference item is the excess of the regular tax deduction over the depreciation that would have been allowed under the straight-line method, without regard to salvage value. The excess is computed separately for each asset. For 10-year property, a 15-year recovery period is used.

Note: *See 23.2* for the MACRS adjustment rules for post-1986 assets.

Oil and gas preference items. Independent oil and gas producers and royalty owners do not have to compute preference items for excess percentage depletion deductions. Excess intangible drilling costs (IDC) are generally not treated as a preference item unless they exceed 40% of AMT income; *see* the instructions to Form 6251.

23.4 Net Operating Losses

A net operating loss (NOL) claimed for regular tax purposes must be recomputed for AMT after all other AMT adjustments and preference items are taken into account. The alternative tax net operating loss deduction allowed for AMT purposes is generally the amount of the regular net operating loss except that in figuring the nonbusiness deduction adjustment *(40.19)* only AMT itemized deductions are taken into account. Thus, state and local taxes and other itemized deductions that are not allowable AMT deductions *(23.2)* do not reduce nonbusiness income in figuring the alternative tax net operating loss deduction.

The AMT net operating loss may be limited to 90% of alternative minimum taxable income; follow the instructions to Form 6251 for further details on computing the alternative tax net operating loss deduction.

23.5 Tax Credits Allowed Against AMT

The only tax credit allowed in computing tentative alternative minimum tax liability on Form 6251 is a revised version of the foreign tax credit allowed for regular tax purposes. The allowable credit is generally based on foreign source AMT income. The AMT foreign tax credit reduces the tentative AMT figured on Form 6251 before comparing it to the regular tax liability (actual AMT is the excess if any, of tentative AMT over the regular tax). If the AMT foreign tax credit exceeds the limits detailed in the Form 6251 instructions, the unused amount generally may be carried back or forward; follow the Form 6251 instructions.

If there is an AMT liability on Form 6251, that AMT is added to regular tax liability on Form 1040. Various tax credits may be claimed against the AMT as well as the regular tax. For 2006, the Tax Increase Prevention and Reconciliation Act allows all nonrefundable personal credits to offset AMT as well as regular tax; this same rule applied for 2000 through 2005. If this law is not extended beyond 2006, the only nonrefundable credits that will be allowed against the AMT as well as regular tax in 2007 are the child tax credit, the adoption credit, and the retirement savings credit. Without legislative relief, other nonrefundable personal credits, including the dependent care credit, educational (Hope and Lifetime Learning) credits, credit for the elderly and disabled, and mortgage interest credit, will be allowed after 2006 only to the extent of the excess, if any, of regular tax liability over tentative AMT figured on Form 6251.

23.6 AMT Tax Credit From Regular Tax

You may be able to reduce your regular 2006 tax by a tax credit based on AMT incurred in prior years. The prior-year AMT had to be attributable to "deferral items" such as the ISO adjustment or depreciation that provide only a temporary reduction to taxable income. Furthermore, the credit, which is computed on Form 8801, is allowed only to the extent that your regular 2006 tax liability (as reduced by allowable tax credits) exceeds 2006 tentative alternative minimum tax liability computed on Form 6251. Follow the instructions to Form 8801.

23.7 Avoiding AMT

If you are within the range of the AMT tax, review periodically your income and expenses to determine whether to postpone or accelerate income, defer the payment of expenses, and/or make certain tax elections.

There are elections, such as the election of alternative straight-line MACRS depreciation, that may avoid AMT adjustments. However, such elections will increase your regular tax. Similarly, adjustment treatment for mining exploration and development costs, circulation expenses, and research expenses can be avoided by elections to amortize; *see 23.2.*

The following steps may also avoid or soften the impact of the AMT tax:

- If your income is increasing, defer deductible expense items to the next year if your regular tax bracket in the next year is likely to exceed your AMT tax rate (either 26% or 28% depending on your AMT income). Consider deferring payment of home mortgage interest and large medical bills. Do not prepay state income tax. You will get a larger tax benefit from the deductions in the later year.
- Spread out the exercise of incentive stock options (ISOs) over more than one year to limit the AMT adjustment for the bargain element (the difference between the option price and the fair market value of the stock on the date of exercise). If you exercise an ISO and hold the acquired stock beyond the end of the year, the bargain element is subject to AMT *(23.2).* You may find yourself with an unexpected tax liability and if the stock has depreciated in value since the date of exercise, you may find yourself short of funds to pay the liability even after selling the stock. To limit the AMT adjustment, you can stagger the exercise of options over more than one year. You can avoid the adjustment completely by selling the stock in the same year that the option was exercised, but if you do, any gain on the sale will be taxed as ordinary income and not at the favorable rate for long-term capital gains.

Accelerating income. If you find that you will be subject to AMT in a current year, you may want to subject additional income in that year to the 26% or 28% AMT tax rate. In such a case, consider accelerating the receipt of income to that year. If you are in business, you might ask for earlier payments from customers or clients. If you control a small corporation, you might prepay salary or pay larger bonuses. But here be careful not to run afoul of reasonable compensation rules. You might also consider paying dividends.

Chapter 24

Computing the "Kiddie Tax" for Children Under Age 18

For 2006, investment income over $1,700 earned by a child under age 18 is taxed at the child's parent's tax rate. The child's parent or legal representative generally makes this tax computation, which is nicknamed the "kiddie tax." Application of the kiddie tax to children under age 18 is the result of a retroactive 2006 law change. For years before 2006, the kiddie tax applied only to children under age 14. Under the new law, the kiddie tax does not apply to a child under 18 who is married and files a joint return.

The kiddie tax applies only to investment income, such as interest, dividends, rents, royalties, and profits on the sale of property. Income from wages and self-employment is not subject to the kiddie tax.

As the child's parent, you generally must use Form 8615 to report the income of a child under age 18. On Form 8615, the kiddie tax rules are applied and the tax is reported on the child's personal income tax return. The Form 8615 computation has no effect on the treatment of items on your own return or on your tax computation. You may instead elect on Form 8814 to report the child's investment income on your own return, provided the child received only interest and dividend income. If you elect on Form 8814 to report the child's investment income on your own return, your adjusted gross income will increase and this could adversely affect your right to claim various deductions; *see 24.5*.

If you are married but file separately, the parent with the larger amount of taxable income is responsible for the kiddie tax computation. If parents are divorced, separated, unmarried, or living apart for the last six months of the year, the parent who has custody of the child for the greater part of 2006 computes the tax. If a child cannot get tax information directly from a parent, the legal representative of the child may ask the IRS for the necessary information.

24.1 Filing Your Child's Return

To discourage substantial income splitting of investment income between parents and minor children, the tax law has complicated income reporting for parents and children by—

1. Imposing a "kiddie tax" that taxes a child's investment income over an annual floor ($1,700 for 2006) at the parent's tax bracket if the child is under 18 years of age at the end of the taxable year; *see 24.2.* A favorable IRS rule treats a child reaching age 18 on January 1 as if his or her birthday were on the last day of the preceding year.
2. Barring a dependent child from claiming a personal exemption on his or her own tax return.
3. Limiting the standard deduction for a dependent child who has only investment income. For 2006 the deduction is $850; *see 13.5.*

Does your child have to file? For a child who can be claimed as a dependent, the income filing threshold is generally $850. If your dependent child has gross income (earned and investment income) of $850 or less for 2006, he or she is not subject to tax and does not have to file a tax return.

A 2006 return must be filed for a dependent child with investment income exceeding $300 and gross income of more than $850. If a dependent child has salary or other earned income but no investment income, a return does not have to be filed unless such earned income exceeds $5,150 in 2006. If your child's only income is from interest and dividends, you may be able to make an election to report the income on your own return; *see 24.4.*

Although a dependent child may not claim a personal exemption on his or her 2006 tax return, the child is allowed to claim at least an $850 standard deduction. A dependent child with earned income over $850 may claim a standard deduction up to those earnings plus an additional $300, but no more than the basic standard deduction, which is generally $5,150; *see 13.1.*

Filing Instruction

Child 18 or Over

The "kiddie tax" does not apply to a child who was 18 years old or older on January 1, 2007, or to a child under age 18 who is married and files a joint return; *see 23.2.*

How to file a 2006 return for your child. If your child was under age 18 as of January 1, 2007, and had investment income of $1,700 or less, follow the regular filing rules and use Form 1040EZ, 1040A, or Form 1040 to report the child's income and deductions. The "kiddie tax" computation does not apply, so all of the child's income will be taxed at his or her own tax rate. If your child is unable to sign his or her tax return, you must do so; *see 1.13.*

If your child's investment income exceeded $1,700, the kiddie tax computation applies; *see 24.2.* Form 8615 must be filed to compute the kiddie tax unless your child's only income is interest and dividends and you elect to report your child's investment earnings on your own return as discussed at *24.4.* On Form 8615 you must provide your tax identification number and taxable income. Form 8615 is attached to the child's tax return; *see 24.3.*

If your child was age 18 or older as of January 1, 2007, your child should file Form 1040EZ, 1040A, or 1040, depending on the type of income and deductions he or she has. The special kiddie tax rules do not apply.

Child's AMT liability. A child who has substantial tax-exempt interest, tax preferences, or tax adjustments subject to the alternative minimum tax must compute tentative AMT liability on Form 6251; *see* Chapter 23.

EXAMPLES

1. Your daughter, whom you claim as your dependent, has interest income of $480 and no other income for 2006. She has no income tax liability and does not have to file a return.

Interest income	$480
Less: standard deduction *(13.5)*	850
Tax liability	0

2. At the end of 2006, your son, whom you claim as your dependent, is age 18. He has interest income of $1,400 and salary income of $950 from his part-time job. His standard deduction is $1,250, the greater of earned income plus $300 *(see 13.5)* or $850. No personal exemption may be claimed. Assuming he has no itemized deductions, taxable income is $1,100 ($2,350 gross income – $1,250 standard deduction). The kiddie tax computation based on your top rate does not apply because your son is at least age 18 at the end of the year.

3. In 2006, your 12-year-old daughter has investment income of $900. Taxable income of $50 is subject to tax at her own tax rate.

Interest income	$900
Less: standard deduction	850
Taxable income	$50

The kiddie tax computation does not apply because investment income does not exceed $1,700.

24.2 Children Under Age 18 Subject to the "Kiddie Tax"

The "kiddie tax" subjects a portion of your child's investment income to tax at your tax rate, where your child's tax rate is lower than yours. For 2006 tax returns, the kiddie tax applies if all of the following are true:

- Your child was under age 18 on January 1, 2007. Technically, the kiddie tax applies to children under age 18 at the end of the tax year, but for a child reaching age 18 on January 1, 2007, the IRS applies a favorable rule that treats the child as having reached age 18 on the last day of 2006, so the kiddie tax does not apply for 2006.
- Your child had more than $1,700 of investment income. The $1,700 floor is increased, as discussed below, if the child has itemized deductions exceeding $850 that are directly connected to the production of investment income.
- If married, your child filed separately from his or her spouse.

If both a child's parents were deceased at the end of 2006, the kiddie tax computation does not apply, and the child's tax is figured under the regular rules.

Law Alert

Age Limit for Kiddie Tax Increased to 18

The Tax Increase Prevention and Reconciliation Act applies the kiddie tax to investment income of children age under age 18 as of the end of the year, effective for 2006 and later tax years. Previously, only children under age 14 were subject to the kiddie tax.

New law retroactively raises kiddie tax age limit to include children under 18. The Tax Increase Prevention and Reconciliation Act (TIPRA), enacted in May 2006, increased the age limit for the kiddie tax by applying it to children under age 18, rather than children under age 14 as under the pre-TIPRA rules. The change was made retroactive to January 1, 2006, thereby affecting tax returns for 2006 and later years.

The increase in the kiddie tax age limit foils the investment planning of parents who assumed that assets held in their child's name could be sold after age 14, with the gain taxed at the child's tax rate. Investment income of a child age 14 through 17 is now subject to the kiddie tax if the rules otherwise apply.

The retroactive change hits parents who sold their child's assets early in 2006 (prior to enactment of TIPRA) on the assumption that the kiddie tax was no longer applicable. For example, if in early 2006 you sold stocks held in your child's custodial account because your child was turning age 14 during the year and you expected (based on the pre-TIPRA rule) the gains to be taxed at your child's low rate, that expectation was dashed by the retroactive law change; the kiddie tax applies and the gains over $1,700 are subject to tax at your tax rate.

Exceptions for children filing jointly and distributions from qualified disability trusts. TIPRA provides two new exceptions to the kiddie tax for 2006 and later tax years. The kiddie tax does not apply to a child under age 18 who is married and files a joint return for the tax year. The exception does not apply if the child is married filing separately.

If a child is a beneficiary of a qualified disability trust, distributions of investment income from the trust are treated as earned income and thus not subject to the kiddie tax rules.

Planning Reminder

Investment Strategies for Children Under Age 18

The reach of the kiddie tax can be reduced or eliminated if investments held in the name of children under age 18 earn little or no current taxable income, as in the case of growth stocks or tax-exempt municipal bonds. Interest on U.S. savings bonds can be deferred until after a child reaches age 18 and the kiddie tax no longer applies.

Figuring kiddie tax on child's or parent's return. The kiddie tax computation is generally made on Form 8615, which must be attached to your child's return. However, if the only income of your child who is under age 18 is interest and dividends and other tests are met, you may elect on Form 8814 to include your child's investment income on your own tax return, instead of computing the kiddie tax on Form 8615; *see 24.4*.

Kiddie tax on Form 8615 applies to investment income exceeding $1,700 floor. If your child files his or her own return, the "kiddie tax" computation on Form 8615 applies to the child's *net investment income*. For purposes of this rule, *net investment income* equals gross investment income minus $1,700 if your child does not itemize deductions on Schedule A. Thus, if your child does not itemize, the first $1,700 of investment income is exempt from the special computation. Investment income exceeding $1,700 is considered net investment income subject to the special computation; *see* Example 1 in this section.

Investment income includes all taxable income that is not earned income (compensation for personal services). Include taxable interest income (but not tax-exempt interest), dividends, capital gains, royalties, rents, and taxable pension payments. Payments from a trust are generally included to the extent of distributable net income, but, as noted earlier, there is an exception for distributions from qualified disability trusts, which, for tax years beginning after 2005, are treated as earned income, and thus not subject to the kiddie tax. Income in custodial accounts is treated as the child's income and is subject to the kiddie tax computation. Capital losses first offset capital gains, and any excess loss offsets up to $3,000 of other investment income.

Investment income on all of your child's property must be considered, even if the property was a gift from you or someone else, or if the property was produced from your child's wages, such as a bank account into which the wages were deposited. The wages themselves, or self-employment earnings, are not considered.

If your child does itemize deductions, and has more than $850 of deductions that are directly connected to the production of investment income, the $1,700 floor is increased. The floor is $850 plus the directly connected deductions. If the directly connected deductions are $850 or less, the regular $1,700 kiddie tax exemption applies, as in Example 2 in this section. Directly connected itemized deductions are expenses paid to produce or collect income or to manage, conserve, or maintain income-producing property. Only the part of the total expenses exceeding the 2% AGI floor may be deducted. These expenses include custodian fees and service charges, service fees to collect interest and dividends, and investment counsel fees. If, after you subtract the itemized deductions, your child's net investment income exceeds his or her taxable income, you apply the tax to the lower taxable income, rather than to the net investment income.

EXAMPLES

(In the following Examples, assume the child is your dependent for 2006 and under age 18 on January 1, 2007.)

1. For 2006, your son has dividend income of $1,850. After taking into account a standard deduction of $850, taxable income is $1,000, of which $150 is subject to the kiddie tax computation based on your tax bracket on Form 8615.

Figuring taxable income:

Dividend income	$1,850
Less: standard deduction	850
	$1,000

Income subject to tax at your rate:

Investment income	$1,850
Less: $1,700	1,700
	$150

As an alternative to computing kiddie tax on $150 on Form 8615, you may elect to report your son's dividend income on his return; *see 24.4.*

2. Your daughter has $300 of wages and $1,750 of dividends and mutual-fund capital gain distributions for 2006. On Schedule A, your daughter claims itemized deductions of $400 related to investment income after the 2% AGI floor. She also has $500 of other itemized deductions. Itemized deductions of $900 are claimed; they exceed the $850 standard deduction.

Figuring taxable income:

Gross income	$2,050
Less: itemized deductions	900
Taxable income	$1,150

Income subject to tax at parent's rate:

Investment income	$1,750
Less: greater of (1) $1,700 or (2) the sum of $850 and directly related expenses of $400	1,700
Net investment income subject to tax at parent's rate on Form 8615 *(24.3)*; *see 24.4* for parent's alternative election	$50

24.3 Computing "Kiddie Tax" on Child's Return

If your child is subject to the "kiddie tax" under *24.2*, the tax is computed on Form 8615, which is attached to his or her return, unless you make the parent's election at *24.5*. Before your child's Form 8615 can be completed, your own taxable income must be determined. On Form 8615, your taxable income is added to the child's net investment income in excess of $1,700.

As parents, the kiddie tax computation on Form 8615 does not affect your tax liability or the way you compute any limitation on deductions or credits. For example, the addition of the child's net investment income to your taxable income on Form 8615 does *not* affect the adjusted gross income floors for purposes of figuring your deduction for IRA contributions, medical expenses, or miscellaneous expenses.

Planning Reminder

Prepare Your Return First

Before your child can complete Form 8615, or you prepare it for the child, your own taxable income must be determined.

Which parent's return to use. If the parents file a *joint return*, their joint taxable income is entered on Form 8615, along with the net investment income *(24.2)* of all their children under age 18. If the parents file *separate returns*, the larger of the parents' separate taxable incomes is used on the child's Form 8615.

Where parents are legally separated or divorced and custody of the child is shared, Form 8615 should be completed using the taxable income of the parent who has custody for the greater part of the year. If parents are married but living apart, and the custodial parent qualifies as unmarried under Test 1 at *1.12*, that parent's taxable income is used on Form 8615. If the custodial parent is not considered unmarried, the income of the parent with the larger taxable income is used. If the custodial parent has remarried and files a joint return with a new spouse, their joint return taxable income is used on the child's Form 8615. If the parents were never married but they live together with the child, the income of the parent with the larger taxable income is used; if the parents live apart, the income of the parent with custody for most of the year is used on Form 8615.

More than one child subject to kiddie tax. You file a separate Form 8615 for each child and on each form net investment income of all the children subject to the tax is included. The computed tax is allocated to each of your children, according to his or her share of their combined net investment income. This computation is incorporated in the steps of Form 8615 and by following the order of the form, you will make the proper allocation.

Planning Reminder

Estimating Tax on Form 8615

If you are unable to file your 2006 return by April 16, 2007, but your child's return is filed by the April 16 deadline, the child's Form 8615 may be based on an estimate of your tax liability. When you have the completed income information, file an amended return.

Estimating the kiddie tax in case of filing delay. If you are unable to file your return by April 16, 2007, the child's tax on Form 8615 may be based on an estimate. You may make a reasonable estimate of your taxable income on Form 8615 or may estimate the net investment income of children under age 18 if that information is not yet available. When you have the complete income details, file an amended return on Form 1040X.

A reasonable estimate may be based on your 2005 taxable income and the 2005 investment income of the child. If a refund is due, the IRS will pay interest from April 16, 2007, or, if the return was filed late, from the filing date. If additional tax is due on the amended return, interest will be charged from April 16, but no penalty will be imposed.

Instead of estimating the kiddie tax, you may file Form 4868 to get a six-month extension *(46.3)* for your return on which the kiddie tax is included. However, interest will be charged on any tax due that was not paid by the original filing date, and late payment penalties may also apply; *see 46.3*.

24.4 Parent's Election To Report Child's Dividends and Interest

Instead of filing a separate return for your child *(24.3)* whose income is subject to the "kiddie tax," you may elect on Form 8814 to compute the kiddie tax on your return if all of the following tests are met:

- The child's only income is from interest and dividends (including mutual-fund capital gain distributions and Alaska Permanent Fund dividends);
- The total interest and dividends are over $850 but less than $8,500;
- Estimated tax payments were not made in the child's name and Social Security number for 2006, and there was no overpayment from the child's 2005 return applied to his or her 2006 estimated tax; *and*
- The child was not subject to 2006 backup withholding.

Caution

Reporting Child's Income on Your Return

Including the child's income on your return could be disadvantageous not only by subjecting the income to a higher tax rate (than on the child's own return), but also by making it more difficult for you to claim certain deductions and raising your state and local taxes.

By making this election, and following the steps of Form 8814, you include in your income the child's interest and dividends to the extent they exceed $1,700; report the excess on Line 21 of your Form 1040. You also figure an additional tax equal to the smaller of $85 or 10% of your child's income over $850, which is included in the tax liability you enter on Line 44 of your Form 1040.

If the parents are married filing separately, or are divorced, separated, unmarried, or living apart for the last six months of the year, the parent whose taxable income would be taken into account on Form 8615 *(24.3)* is the parent who may elect to report the income on his or her own return.

In figuring whether you owe alternative minimum tax (AMT), you must include as a tax preference item interest income your child receives from specified private activity bonds; *see 23.3* and Form 6251 instructions.

Should you make the election? The only advantage in making the election is to skip the paperwork involved in preparing a return in the child's name or returns in your children's names. This could save you money in the form of reduced tax preparation costs. However, including the child's income as your own increases your AGI, which may create these disadvantages:

- Subject you to the exemption phaseout *(21.12)* and 3% reduction computation *(13.7)* for itemized deductions.
- Make it more difficult to deduct job expenses and other miscellaneous itemized deductions, which are subject to a 2% AGI floor *(19.1)*, and medical deductions, subject to a 7.5% AGI floor *(17.1)*.
- Limit a deduction for IRA contributions under the phase-out rules *(8.4)*.
- Limit your ability to claim the special $25,000 rental loss allowance under the passive activity rules *(10.2)*.
- Increase local and state tax liability.

Finally, if you elect to report the child's income on your own return, you may not claim any deductions that your child would have been able to claim on his or her return such as investment expenses or a penalty on premature withdrawals from a savings account. On the other hand, reporting your child's interest or dividends increases your net investment income, which may allow you to claim a larger deduction for investment interest; *see 15.10*. Also, your ceiling for charitable donations may be increased. If you plan to report your child's income on your 2007 return, provide for the tax in your estimated tax payments or withholdings during 2007.

Chapter 25

Personal Tax Credits Reduce Your Tax Liability

The following tax credits are discussed in this chapter: child tax credit, dependent care credit, earned income credit (EIC), adoption credit, retirement savings credit, health coverage credit, mortgage interest credit, the District of Columbia first-time homebuyer credit, the new credit for hybrid vehicles, and the temporary credits for residential energy improvements. Education tax credits are discussed in Chapter 33.

The child tax credit is $1,000 for each qualifying dependent child under age 17. To claim the credit, you must follow the steps on the "Child Tax Credit Worksheet." There is a phaseout of the credit, as explained in *25.3*. If the credit exceeds your tax liability, you may be entitled to a refundable credit called the "additional child credit" on Form 8812.

The dependent care credit is for working people who pay care costs that allow them the freedom to work. Depending on your income, the credit is 20% to 35% of up to $3,000 of care expenses for one dependent and up to $6,000 of expenses for two or more dependents. If your adjusted gross income exceeds $43,000, the maximum credit is $600 for one dependent and $1,200 for two or more dependents.

The earned income credit (EIC) is provided to low-income workers who support children, and a limited credit is allowed to certain workers without qualifying children; *see 25.10*.

An adoption credit of up to $10,960 may be claimed in 2006 for costs of adopting a child under the age of 18 or a disabled person incapable of self-care.

Personal Credits

25.1 Overview of Personal Tax Credits

After you determine your regular tax liability using the tax table *(22.2)* or Tax Computation Worksheet *(22.3)*, and your AMT liability if any *(see 23.1)*, you may be able to reduce that liability by claiming one or more tax credits. Most personal tax credits are allowed to the full extent of your regular tax liability and alternative minimum tax (AMT; *see 23.1*) but are not refundable if they exceed your liability. Nonrefundable credits include the child tax credit, dependent care credit, adoption credit, education credits, retirement savings credit, credit for the elderly and disabled, mortgage interest credit, and D.C. first-time homebuyer credit.

The additional child tax credit, earned income credit, and the health coverage credit are refundable, meaning that if the credit exceeds your tax liability you will receive a refund for the excess.

Eligibility rules and credit limitations for many of the personal credits are discussed in this chapter, while some are discussed in other chapters as shown below. Business tax credits are in Chapter 40.

Child tax credit and additional child tax credit. *See 25.2–25.3.*

Child and dependent care credit. *See 25.4–25.9.*

Earned income credit. *See 25.10–25.13.*

Adoption credit. *See 25.14–25.15.*

Qualified retirement savings contributions credit. *See 25.16.*

Health coverage credit. *See 25.17.*

Mortgage interest credit. *See 25.18.*

District of Columbia first-time homebuyer credit. *See 25.19.*

Education credits. *See 33.7–33.10* for details of the Hope credit and the Lifetime Learning credit.

Credit for elderly or disabled. *See 34.7–34.9.*

Foreign tax credit. *See 36.14.*

Prior-year AMT credit. *See 23.6.*

Residential energy tax credits. *See 25.20.*

Hybrid and electric vehicle credit. *See 25.21.*

Credit for excess Social Security or Railroad Retirement withholdings. *See 26.10.*

Credit for tax on mutual-fund undistributed capital gain. *See 32.8.*

Credit for federal telephone excise tax. *See 25.22.*

Law Alert

Nonrefundable Personal Credits

The law allowing all nonrefundable personal credits to offset regular income tax and AMT liability was extended through 2006.

Child Tax Credit

25.2 Child Tax Credit for Children Under Age 17

For 2006, you generally may claim a tax credit of $1,000 for each qualifying child who is under age 17 at the end of 2006. To figure the exact amount of your credit, however, you must complete the "Child Tax Credit Worksheet" in the IRS instructions to Form 1040 or 1040A to determine if the credit is limited by your tax liability. Even if the credit does exceed your tax liability, part or all of the credit may be refundable as an additional credit on Form 8812 if your earned income for 2006 exceeds $11,300 or you have three or more children; *see 25.3.*

The credit may also be limited if your adjusted gross income (AGI) exceeds the $55,000, $75,000, or $110,000 phase-out threshold shown below for your filing status. If your AGI exceeds the threshold, the IRS instructions direct you to the worksheet in Publication 972, where the phase-out rules and the other credit limitations are applied.

Law Alert

Child Tax Credit

The $1,000 maximum child tax credit per qualifying child applies through 2010.

Filing Instruction

Filing Form 8901 If Qualifying Child Is Not a Dependent

You can claim the child tax credit for a child who is a qualifying child *(25.2)* even though he or she cannot be claimed as your dependent because (1) you, or your spouse if filing jointly, can be claimed as a dependent by another taxpayer, or (2) the child is married and files a joint return, and the exception at *21.9* does not apply.

To claim the child tax credit for such a non-dependent child, you must complete Form 8901 and attach it to your Form 1040 or Form 1040A.

Law Alert

Refundable Credit

The refundable portion of the child tax credit for 2006 is 15% of taxable earned income in excess of $11,300. Combat pay that is otherwise excluded from income *(see 35.4)* is treated as taxable earned income for purposes of figuring the refundable amount.

Qualifying child. The credit may be claimed for a child under age 17 at the end of 2006 who meets the definition of a "qualifying child" under the dependency exemption rules in *21.3*. This includes your child, stepchild, grandchild, great-grandchild, brother, sister, stepbrother, stepsister, half-brother or -sister, or the descendant of any of these. An adopted child qualifies if placed with you by an authorized agency for legal adoption, even if the adoption is not final by the end of 2006. A foster child placed with you by a court or an authorized agency qualifies. Such a child must live with you for over half the year and not provide over half of his or her own support; *see 21.3*. The child also must be a U.S. citizen, resident, or national in order for you to claim the child tax credit for him or her.

Phaseout of credit. The credit is limited or eliminated if your adjusted gross income is above a threshold amount for your filing status. In applying the phaseout, AGI is increased by any foreign earned income exclusion, foreign housing exclusion or deduction, or possession exclusion for American Samoa residents. If your income exceeds the following threshold for your filing status, *see 25.3*.

Filing status	*Phaseout applies if MAGI exceeds*
Married filing jointly	$110,000
Head of household	75,000
Single	75,000
Qualifying widow(er)	75,000
Married filing separately	55,000

Changing your withholding. If you can claim the child tax credit, you may have too much tax withheld from your wages during the year. If so, you can claim more withholding allowances. File the new Form W-4 with your employer so that less income tax will be withheld.

25.3 Figuring the Child Tax Credit

You use the Child Tax Credit Worksheet in the IRS instruction booklet or in Publication 972 to figure the credit. You do not attach the worksheet to your return.

Phase-out formula. If your income exceeds the phase-out threshold shown in *25.2*, the maximum credit of $1,000 per qualifying child is reduced by $50 for each $1,000 (or fraction of $1,000) that your AGI exceeds the phase-out threshold *(25.2)* for your filing status. The computation is made on the worksheet in Publication 972. *See* Example 2 below.

Liability limitation. The IRS worksheet limits the child tax credit to your tax liability (regular tax plus alternative minimum tax, if any). If you are subject to the phase-out rule, the amount of the credit allowed after the phase-out computation is subject to the liability limitation. Tax liability is reduced if you claim the child and dependent care credit, education credits, retirement savings credit, foreign tax credit, or credit for the elderly or disabled. If your credit exceeds your liability, the credit is limited to the liability but you can probably claim the "additional child tax credit" on Form 8812 to receive a refund; *see* below.

Refundable portion of credit claimed as additional child tax credit. If the full amount of the credit cannot be claimed on the Child Tax Credit Worksheet because of the tax liability limitation, you may be able to obtain a refund for the balance on Form 8812, Additional Child Tax Credit. The credit is refundable for 2006 to the extent of 15% of your taxable earned income plus tax-free combat pay *(35.4)* in excess of $11,300. If your earned income is *not* over $11,300, a refundable credit may still be available if you have three or more qualifying children and you paid Social Security taxes that exceed your earned income credit *(25.13)*, if any. Follow the instructions to Form 8812. Any portion of the credit that is phased out as discussed above is "lost" and is not eligible for the additional credit on Form 8812. The $11,300 earned income threshold is subject to annual inflation adjustments.

EXAMPLES

1. Carl and Abby's only children, twin daughters, were born in 2006. Carl and Abby file a joint return for 2006, report AGI of $44,000, and claim the standard deduction. Their AGI is well below the $110,000 phase-out threshold *(see 25.2)*. They may claim the full child tax credit of $2,000 ($1,000 per child), as it does not exceed their tax liability.

2. Jane is single and has two dependent children, ages six and three. She files her 2006 return as head of household. Her 2006 AGI is $77,500. Because her AGI exceeds the $75,000 phase-out threshold for a head of household, her credit for 2006 is reduced on the worksheet in Publication 972. Jane's credit limit of $2,000 is reduced by $50 for each $1,000 or fraction of $1,000 of excess AGI. The excess income of $2,500 is rounded up to $3,000 (next multiple of $1,000) and multiplied by the phase-out percentage of 5%, resulting in a credit reduction of $150 ($3,000 × 5%). Jane may claim a child tax credit of $1,850 ($2,000 – $150) on her 2006 return. She is not subject to the liability limitation as her liability exceeds the $1,850 credit.

Dependent Care Credit

25.4 Qualifying for Child and Dependent Care Credit

Did you hire someone to care for your children or other dependents while you work? If so, you may qualify for a tax credit for the expenses. You may claim the credit even if you work part time. The credit is generally available to the extent you have earnings from employment. Your employer may have a plan qualifying for tax-free child care and, if you are covered, you may be unable to claim a tax credit; *see 25.8*.

Caution

Nonrefundable Credit

The dependent care credit is limited to your tax liability. In other words, if the credit amount exceeds the tax that you owe, you will not be given a refund of the difference.

Where to claim the credit. The credit is claimed on Form 2441 if you file Form 1040, or on Form 1040A, Schedule 2. The size of the credit depends on the amount of your care expenses, number of dependents, and income. Depending on your adjusted gross income, the credit is 20% to 35% of up to $3,000 of care expenses for one dependent and up to $6,000 of expenses for two or more dependents. The minimum credit percentage of 20% applies if your adjusted gross income exceeds $43,000. *See* the chart in *25.5*.

Credit requirements for 2006. To qualify for the credit on your 2006 return, you must:

1. Incur expenses to care for a qualifying person *(25.7)* in order to earn income. In the case of a married couple, this requires both spouses to work either at full- or part-time positions. An exception to the earned income rule is made for a spouse who is a full-time student or incapacitated *(25.6)*. Qualifying care expenses are discussed at *25.8*. Limits on the amount of qualifying costs are discussed at *25.5*.
2. File jointly if you are married, unless you are separated under the rules discussed at *25.9*.
3. Hire a care provider *other than* your child who is under age 19 at the end of the year, your spouse, or a person you can claim as a dependent; *see 25.8*.
4. Have qualifying expenses in excess of tax-free reimbursements received from your employer; *see 25.8*.
5. Report on your tax return the name, address, and taxpayer identification number (Social Security number for individuals) of the child-care provider; *see* below.

Identifying care provider on your return. You must list the name, address, and taxpayer identification number of the person you paid to care for your dependent on Form 2441 if you file Form 1040, or on Form 1040A, Schedule 2. You do not need the taxpayer identification number if a tax-exempt charity provides the dependent care services. Failure to list the correct name, address, and number may result in a disallowance of the credit. To avoid this possibility, ask the provider to fill out Form W-10 or get the identifying information from a Social Security card, driver's license, or business letterhead or invoice. If a household employee has filled out Form W-4 for you, this may act as a backup record.

Withholding tax for a housekeeper. Where you employ help to care for your dependent in your home, you may be liable for FICA (Social Security) and FUTA (unemployment) taxes; *see 38.3*.

25.5 Limits on the Dependent Care Credit

The credit is a percentage of expenses paid for the care of a qualifying person *(25.7)* to allow you to work and earn income. Qualifying expenses are discussed at *25.8*. The credit percentage depends on your income.

Limit on expenses. In figuring the credit for 2006, you take into account qualifying expenses *(25.8)* up to a limit of $3,000 for one dependent, or $6,000 for two or more dependents. The $3,000 or $6,000 limit applies even if your actual expenses are much greater. Further, the $3,000 or $6,000 limit must be reduced by tax-free benefits received from an employer's dependent care plan. Finally, if your earned income is less than the $3,000 or $6,000 limit, your credit is figured on the lower income amount.

Take into account only payments in 2006 for 2006 services. Your credit for 2006 must be based on payments made in 2006 for care services provided in 2006. If you paid for 2005 services in 2006, you may be able to claim an additional credit on your 2006 return, but only in limited circumstances, as discussed at the end of this section. If in 2006 you prepay for 2007 services, you must allocate your payment. Only payments for 2006 services should be counted toward the $3,000 or $6,000 limit when figuring your 2006 credit.

Credit percentage. Depending on your income, a credit percentage of 20% to 35% applies to your expenses up to the $3,000 (one dependent) or $6,000 (two or more dependents) limit. The maximum credit is 35% for families with adjusted gross income of $15,000 or less. For adjusted gross income over $15,000, the 35% credit is reduced by 1% for each $2,000 of adjusted gross income or fraction of $2,000 over $15,000, but not below 20%. The 20% credit applies to adjusted gross incomes exceeding $43,000.

The dependent care credit is nonrefundable. It is limited to your regular income tax liability plus any alternative minimum tax minus any foreign tax credit; follow the IRS instructions.

Table 25-1 Allowable Credit*

Adjusted gross income	*Credit percentage*	*Maximum credit for one dependent**	*Maximum credit for two or more dependents**
$15,000 or less	35%	$1,050	$2,100
15,001–17,000	34	1,020	2,040
17,001–19,000	33	990	1,980
19,001–21,000	32	960	1,920
21,001–23,000	31	930	1,860
23,001–25,000	30	900	1,800
25,001–27,000	29	870	1,740
27,001–29,000	28	840	1,680
29,001–31,000	27	810	1,620
31,001–33,000	26	780	1,560
33,001–35,000	25	750	1,500
35,001–37,000	24	720	1,440
37,001–39,000	23	690	1,380
39,001–41,000	22	660	1,320
41,001–43,000	21	630	1,260
43,001 and over	20	600	1,200

*Maximum credit assumes qualifying expenses are at least $3,000 for one dependent, or $6,000 for two or more dependents. If qualifying expenses are less than the $3,000/$6,000 maximum, your credit is the credit percentage multiplied by the expenses.

Filing Tip

Employer Reimbursements Reduce Credit

Expenses qualifying for the dependent care credit are reduced by any tax-free reimbursements under a qualified employer dependent care program. That is, the reimbursements reduce the $3,000 expense limit for one dependent, or the $6,000 expense limit for two or more qualifying dependents; *see 25.8.* Your employer will report reimbursements in Box 10 of your Form W-2. You figure the tax-free portion of the reimbursement, and any reduction to the credit expense base, on Form 2441 if you file Form 1040 or on Schedule 2 if you file Form 1040A.

EXAMPLES

1. You pay $6,500 in 2006 to a neighbor to care for your two children while you work. Your adjusted gross income is $34,824. The credit percentage of 25% is applied to the maximum expense limit of $6,000, giving you a credit of $1,500.
2. Same as above, except you receive a tax-free reimbursement of $2,500 from your employer's plan. The reimbursement reduces the $6,000 expense limit to $3,500 ($6,000 – $2,500); *see 25.8.* Your credit is $875 (25% of $3,500). If the tax-free reimbursement were $5,000 or more (the maximum allowable exclusion), the credit would be $250 (25% × $1,000 ($6,000 – $5,000)).

Additional credit for 2006 payment of 2005 dependent care expenses. Payments made in 2006 for 2005 services may be eligible for an additional credit but only if you did not use up the $3,000 or $6,000 expense limit that applied for the 2005 credit. Follow the instructions for Form 2441 or Schedule 2 of Form 1040A to figure the additional credit.

25.6 Earned Income Test for Dependent Care Credit

To claim the credit, you must earn wage, salary, or self-employment income figured without regard to community property laws. Expenses for dependent care incurred while looking for a job may be included. However, you must have earnings during the year to claim the credit.

Earned income rule for married couples. Generally, both spouses must work at least part time, unless one is incapable of self-care or is a full-time student. If either you or your spouse earns less than the maximum $3,000 or $6,000 credit base *(25.5)*, the base is limited to the smaller income.

EXAMPLE

John and Mary are married. In 2006, John earns $5,300. Mary earns $33,000. They incur care costs of $6,200 for their two children, ages 5 and 7. Their adjusted gross income including interest earnings is $38,575; their credit percentage is 23%. The maximum $6,000 credit base (for two or more dependents) is limited to John's lower income of $5,300. They may claim a credit of $1,219 ($5,300 × 23%).

Spouses who are students or disabled. An incapacitated spouse or a spouse who is a full-time student is considered to have earned income of $250 a month if expenses are incurred for one dependent, or $500 a month for two or more dependents.

A full-time student is one who attends school full time during each of five calendar months during the year.

EXAMPLE

Same facts as in the Example above, except John was a full-time student for nine months and earned no income for the year. The credit base is limited to $4,500 ($500 × 9).

Filing Tip

No Credit if Neither Spouse Works

If both husband and wife are full-time students and neither works, they may not claim the credit for dependent care costs. While one student-spouse is considered to have earned income of $250 ($500 if more than one qualified person is cared for) each month, the other spouse's earned income is zero. Care costs eligible for the credit are limited to the lesser amount of earned income, which in this case is zero.

25.7 Credit Allowed for Care of Qualifying Persons

To claim a credit for 2006, you must incur employment-related expenses *(25.8)* for at least one of the following qualifying persons who lives with you more than half the year:

1. A dependent *under the age of 13* who is a "qualifying child" under *21.3.* If you are divorced or separated, and you resided with the child for a longer time during the year than the other parent, you may be able to claim the credit even if the other parent is entitled to claim the child as a dependent; *see 25.9.*
2. Your spouse, if physically or mentally incapable of caring for him- or herself.
3. A dependent, regardless of age, who is physically or mentally incapable of caring for himself or herself. For example, he or she needs help to dress or to take care of personal hygiene or nutritional needs, or requires constant attention to avoid hurting him- or herself or others. Generally, you must be able to claim the person as a dependent, either as a qualifying child *(21.3)* or qualifying relative *(21.4)*, but even if the person cannot be claimed as your qualifying relative because he or she has gross income of $3,300 or more for 2006, you may still claim a credit for his or her care costs. Also, if you cannot claim an exemption for the person because you (or your spouse if you file jointly) can be claimed as a dependent by another taxpayer, a credit can still be claimed for the person's care costs.

EXAMPLE

You live with your mother, who is physically incapable of caring for herself. You hire a practical nurse to care for her in the home while you are at work. Payments to the nurse qualify as care costs. However, if you placed her in a nursing home, the cost of the nursing home would not qualify as a dependent care cost; but *see 17.11* for a possible medical expense deduction.

If your child becomes age 13 during the year. Take into account expenses incurred for his or her care prior to the 13th birthday. However, you do not prorate the $3,000 limitation. For example, if your child becomes age 13 on May 1, 2006, and you incurred $3,000 or more in care expenses between January 1 and April 30, the entire $3,000 qualifies for the 2006 credit.

25.8 Expenses Qualifying for the Dependent Care Credit

If you do not receive tax-free dependent care benefits from an employer's plan, you may take into account up to $3,000 of the following types of expenses paid in 2006 when figuring the credit for one dependent, or up to $6,000 for two or more dependents. If you receive employer-financed dependent care, tax-free reimbursements reduce the $3,000 or $6,000 base.

1. Costs of caring for your qualifying child under age 13, incapacitated spouse, or incapacitated dependent in your home; *see 25.7.* If you pay FICA or FUTA taxes on your housekeeper's wages *(38.3)*, you may include your share of the tax (employer) as part of the wages when entering your qualifying expenses. Also include your housekeeper's share of FICA tax if you pay it. Note that these taxes may more than offset your allowable credit.

   The manner of care need not be the least expensive alternative. For example, where a grandparent resides with you and may provide adequate care for your child to enable you to work, the cost of hiring someone to care for the child is still eligible for the credit.
2. Ordinary domestic services in your home, such as laundry, cleaning, and cooking (but not payments to a gardener or chauffeur) that are partly for the care of the qualifying person. Expenses for the dependent's food, clothing, or entertainment do not qualify. Food costs for a housekeeper who eats in your home may be added to qualifying expenses. Extra expenses for a housekeeper's lodging (extra rent or utilities) also qualify.
3. Outside-the-home care costs for a child under age 13, as in a day-care center, day camp (including a specialty camp such as a computer or soccer camp), nursery school, or in the home of a babysitter. Outside-the-home care costs also qualify if incurred for a handicapped dependent, regardless of age, provided he or she regularly spends at least eight hours per day in your home. However, the cost of schooling in the first grade or higher does not qualify for the credit. Costs for sleep-away camp also do not qualify for the credit.

   Proposed IRS regulations treat the cost of transportation by the care provider to or from a day-care center as a qualifying expense. However, if you provide the transportation, the cost of transportation does not qualify.

Filing Tip

Day-Care Center or Nursery School

The amount you pay to a day-care center or nursery school for a dependent child under age 13 is eligible for the credit, even if it covers such incidental benefits as lunch. However, tuition for a child in first grade or higher is not taken into account. If the dependent is not your child, costs for care outside the home qualify only if the dependent regularly spends at least eight hours per day in your home. Up to $3,000 a year of outside-the-home care expenses may be taken into account in figuring the credit for one dependent, and up to $6,000 for two or more.

Payments to relatives. No credit may be claimed for payments made to persons you may claim as your dependents *(21.1)*. Thus, if you pay your mother to care for your child and you cannot claim your mother as a dependent, such payments qualify for the credit. The same rule applies for payments to unrelated persons who live with you and qualify as your dependents; *see 21.4.*

No credit may be claimed for payments to your child who is under 19 years of age at the close of the tax year, whether or not you may claim the child as a dependent.

Allocating expenses when employed less than an entire year. When an expense covers a period, part of which you were gainfully employed or in active search of gainful employment and part of which you were not employed or seeking employment, you must allocate expenses on a daily basis.

EXAMPLE

You are employed for only two months and 10 days. Monthly care expenses are $300. Eligible care expenses amount to $700 ($300 × 2 months, plus $^1/_3$ of $300).

Employer-financed dependent care reduces credit base. Tax-free reimbursements under an employer's dependent care program reduce the $3,000 or $6,000 credit base. For example, if you have one child and you receive a $1,500 reimbursement of child-care costs from your company's plan, the amount eligible for the tax credit is reduced to $1,500 ($3,000 – $1,500). A reimbursement of $3,000 or more would bar any credit. The $6,000 credit expense limit for two or more dependents is similarly reduced by dependent care benefits from your employer. On your Form W-2, your employer will report the amount of tax-free reimbursement; *see 3.4.*

If your employer's plan allows you to fund a reimbursement account with salary-reduction contributions that are excluded from taxable pay *(3.14)*, reimbursements from the account are considered employer-financed payments that reduce the $3,000 or $6,000 credit base. In deciding whether to make salary-reduction contributions, you should determine whether the tax-free reduction will provide a larger tax savings than that provided by the credit. You may find that the salary reduction provides the larger tax savings, taking into consideration not only the decrease in federal income tax, but also the Social Security tax and state and local taxes avoided by using the salary reduction. Further, by lowering your adjusted gross income, a salary reduction may enable you to claim a larger IRA deduction if you are subject to the deduction phase-out rule *(8.4)*, or a larger deduction for miscellaneous itemized deductions subject to the 2% floor *(19.1)*.

Filing Tip

Care Costs Qualifying as Medical Expenses

Care costs, such as a nurse's wages, may also qualify as medical expenses, but you may not claim both the dependent care credit and the medical expense deduction. If you use the expenses to figure the credit and your care costs exceed the amount allowed as dependent care costs, the excess, to the extent it qualifies as a medical expense, may be added to other deductible medical costs.

Allocation if expenses cover noncare services. If a portion of expenses is for other than dependent care or household services, only the portion allocable to dependent care or household services qualifies. No allocation is required if the non–dependent care services are minimal.

EXAMPLES

1. A person accepts a full-time position and sends his 12-year-old child to boarding school. The expenses paid to the school must be allocated. The part representing care of the child qualifies; the part representing tuition does not.
2. A full-time housekeeper is hired to care for two children, ages 9 and 12. The housekeeper also drives the mother to and from work each day. The driving takes no longer than 30 minutes. No allocation is required because the non–dependent care services of chauffeuring are minimal.

25.9 Dependent Care Credit Rules for Separated Couples

A married person generally must file a joint return to claim the dependent care credit *(25.4)*, but if you are living apart from your spouse you may claim the credit on a separate return if you meet the following tests:

1. You maintain as your home a household that a qualifying person *(25.7)* lives in for more than half the year;
2. You furnish over half the cost of maintaining the household for the entire year; *and*
3. Your spouse was not a member of the household during the *last six months* of the year.

If you satisfy these tests, you are treated as unmarried and may claim the credit on a separate return. You do not have to take your spouse's income into account or show that he or she is employed in order to claim a credit.

Your child may be your qualifying person for purposes of a 2006 credit even if you cannot claim the child as your dependent under the rules at *21.7*. This favorable rule applies if: you are legally divorced or separated, separated under a written agreement, or you lived apart from your spouse during the last six months of 2006; you or you and the other parent had custody of the child for more than half the year and provided more than half of the child's support; and you are the *custodial parent* (lived with the child longer than the other parent). If these tests are met, you may claim the credit for care of a dependent child who is under age 13 or physically or mentally incapable of caring for himself or herself even though the noncustodial parent has the right to the exemption under *21.7*. The noncustodial parent may not claim the credit even if he or she is allowed the exemption.

Earned Income Credit (EIC)

25.10 Qualifying Tests for EIC

The earned income credit (EIC) may be claimed not only by workers with qualifying children who meet the tests below, but also, in limited cases, by childless workers. For 2006, the EIC can be as much as $2,747 if you have one qualifying child, $4,536 if you have more than one qualifying child, and $412 if you do not have a qualifying child. There is a phaseout of the credit; *see 25.11.* You look up the credit amount in IRS tables included in the tax form instructions. The EIC is "refundable"; you will receive a refund from the IRS if the credit exceeds your tax liability.

Caution

Denial of Future Credits for Recklessness or Fraud

A taxpayer who negligently or fraudulently claims the EIC is prohibited from claiming future credits over a period of several years. The credit is disallowed for two years from the tax year for which it is determined that the EIC claim was claimed recklessly or in disregard of the rules. The period increases to 10 years from the most recent tax year for which it is found that the EIC was claimed fraudulently.

Claiming the EIC for 2006 With Qualifying Children

You may claim the EIC on a 2006 return if you:

- Have earned income, such as wages and self-employment earnings, and also adjusted gross income of under $32,001 ($34,001 if married filing jointly) if you have one qualifying child or under $36,348 ($38,348 if married filing jointly) if you have two or more qualifying children. However, the maximum credit begins to phase out at much lower income levels; *see 25.11* for the credit phaseout rules.
- Have a qualifying child who lived with you in your main home in the U.S. for more than six months in 2006; *see* below.
- File a joint return if married. Married persons filing separately may not claim the EIC. If you lived apart from your spouse for the last half of the year, you may be able to claim the credit as a head of household.
- File Schedule EIC with your Form 1040 or Form 1040A. On Schedule EIC, you identify and provide information about a qualifying child. Your child's Social Security number must be entered on Schedule EIC.
- Are not a qualifying child of another person.
- Include on your return your Social Security number and, if married, that of your spouse.

A qualifying child. A qualifying child is your son, daughter, adopted child, grandchild, stepchild, or descendents of any of these who at the end of 2006 is under age 19 or under age 24 and a full-time student (enrolled full time during any five months), or any age if permanently and totally disabled. The qualifying person must live with you for over half the year. Your brother, sister, step- or half-brother or step- or half-sister, or their descendents, who meet the age 19 or 24 test and live with you more than half the year also qualify. A foster child who lives with you for more than half the year qualifies if the child was placed with you by a court order or by an authorized placement agency.

Household requirement. The qualifying child must have lived with you in your main home in the U.S. for more than six months. Temporary absences for school, vacation, medical care, or detention in a juvenile facility count as time lived at home.

A person in the U.S. Armed Forces who is stationed outside the U.S. on extended active duty is treated as maintaining a main residence within the U.S.

If you are married, you must file a joint return with your spouse to claim the credit. However, if your spouse did not live in your household for the last six months of the year, and you maintained a home for a child who lived with you for more than half of the year, you may claim the credit as a head of household; *see 1.12.*

Permanently and totally disabled. A person is permanently and totally disabled if: (1) he or she cannot engage in any substantial gainful activity because of a physical or mental condition and (2) a physician determines that the condition has lasted or is expected to last for at least a year or lead to death.

Qualifying child of two or more people. "Tie-breaking" rules determine who can take the EIC if a child is a qualifying child of more than one person.

If both parents are eligible to claim the credit for the same qualifying child and they do not file a 2006 joint return, the parent with whom the child resided for the longer period during the year may claim the child. If the child lived with each parent for the same amount of time, the child will be treated as the qualifying child of the parent who had the higher adjusted gross income (AGI) for 2006.

If a parent and one or more nonparents are otherwise entitled to claim the child as a qualifying child, only the parent may claim the credit for the child. If none of the persons otherwise entitled to treat the child as a qualifying child are the child's parent, the child will be treated as the qualifying child of the person who had the highest AGI for 2006.

Married child. If your child was married at the end of 2006, he or she is your qualifying child only if you can claim an exemption for the child under the rules at *21.3,* or you would be so entitled except that the noncustodial parent is given the exemption under the rules at *21.7*.

Nonresident aliens. An individual who is a nonresident alien for any part of the year is not eligible for the credit unless he or she is married and an election is made by the couple to have all of their worldwide income subject to U.S. tax.

Claiming the Credit for 2006 Without Qualifying Children

If you do not have a qualifying child, you may claim the EIC on a 2006 return if you:

- Have earned income, such as wages and self-employment earnings and also adjusted gross income under $12,120 ($14,120 if married filing jointly). However, *see 25.11* for the credit phaseout rule.
- Have your main home in the U.S. for more than six months in 2006.
- Are at least 25 but under age 65 at the end of 2006. If filing a joint return, either you or your spouse must satisfy this age test.
- File a joint return if married, unless you lived apart for the last six months and qualify to file as a head of household.
- Are not a dependent of another taxpayer. If filing jointly, your spouse also must not be another taxpayer's dependent.
- Are not a qualifying child of another taxpayer. If filing jointly, your spouse also must not be another taxpayer's qualifying child.
- Include your Social Security number on your return, and, if married, that of your spouse.

25.11 Income Tests for Earned Income Credit (EIC)

For purposes of the credit, earned income includes wages, salary, tips, commissions, jury duty pay, union strike benefits, certain disability pensions, and net earnings from self-employment. An election may be made to include combat pay that is otherwise excluded from 2006 income *(35.4)* as earned income for 2006 EIC purposes. Apart from such combat pay, nontaxable employee compensation, such as salary deferrals, or excludable dependent care benefits, is not considered when computing the credit.

Disqualifying income. For 2006, an individual is not eligible for the earned income credit if he or she has "disqualified income" exceeding $2,800. Disqualified income includes interest (taxable and tax-exempt), dividends, net rent and royalty income, net capital gain income, and net passive income that is not self-employment income.

Credit phases out with income. There are two different phase-out ranges, one for married couples filing jointly and another for taxpayers filing as single, head of household, or qualifying widow(er).

If you have only one qualifying child *(25.10),* the 2006 credit begins to phase out in the EIC Table *(25.12)* if either earned income or adjusted gross income is at least $14,850 if filing as single, head of household, or qualifying widow(er). The phase-out threshold is $16,850 if filing jointly. No credit is allowed if either earned income or AGI is $32,000 or more if filing as single, head of household, or qualifying widow(er), or $34,000 or more if filing jointly.

If you have two or more qualifying children, the credit begins to phase out if either earned income or adjusted gross income is at least $14,850 if filing as single or head of household or $16,850 if filing jointly. The credit is completely phased out if either earned income or AGI is at least $36,348 or $38,348 (joint return).

If you do not have any qualifying children, the phaseout of the credit begins when either earned income or AGI is at least $6,750 ($8,750 if married filing jointly), and the credit is completely phased out if either amount is $12,120 or more ($14,120 or more if married filing jointly).

Filing Tip

Definition of Earned Income for EIC Purposes

Earned income does *not* include nontaxable employee compensation such as salary deferrals and reductions, excludable dependent care benefits, and excludable education assistance.

Caution

Recertification Required if EIC Denied

If the IRS denies an EIC by issuing a deficiency notice, the credit may not be claimed in a future tax year unless you show on Form 8862 that you are eligible to take the credit. If the IRS recertifies eligibility, Form 8862 does not have to be filed again in subsequent tax years unless the IRS again denies the EIC in a deficiency proceeding.

Self-employed. If you were self-employed in 2006, your earned income for credit purposes is the net earnings shown on Schedule SE, *less* the income tax deduction for 50% of self-employment tax claimed on Line 27 of Form 1040. If your net earnings were less than $400, the net amount is your earned income for purposes of the credit. If you had a net loss, the loss is subtracted from any wages or other employee earned income. If you are a statutory employee, the income reported on Schedule C qualifies for the credit.

Foreign earned income. If you work abroad and claim the foreign income exclusion, you may *not* take the credit.

25.12 Look up EIC in Government Tables

After completing a worksheet in the IRS instructions that determines whether your earned income credit (EIC) is based on your earned income or adjusted gross income *(25.11)*, you then look up the amount of your credit in the EIC Table, which is shown in Part 8.

EXAMPLE

Jane is divorced. Her only income in 2006 is wages of $25,143. She supports her eight-year-old daughter, who lives with her for the entire year.

To find her credit, Jane turns to the 2006 EIC Table. In the table, the credit shown for her income bracket is $1,099.

25.13 Advance Payment of Earned Income Credit

If you believe you are entitled to an earned income credit, you may file a certificate, Form W-5, with your employer to have a portion of the credit added to your paycheck throughout the year. To get advanced earned income payments you must have a qualifying child *(25.10)*.

If you receive any advance payments, you must report them on Form 1040 or Form 1040A; your employer will include the amount in Box 9 of your Form W-2. If you receive advance payments in excess of the credit you are entitled to, the excess is treated as a tax you owe when you file your return. If the credit you are entitled to exceeds the advance payments, the excess credit reduces any other tax you owe. If the credit exceeds your liability, the difference is refunded to you.

Adoption Credit

25.14 Qualifying for the Adoption Credit

A tax credit of up to $10,960 may be available on your 2006 return for the qualifying costs of adopting a child under age 18, or a person who is physically and mentally incapable of self-care. The credit is phased out ratably for those with modified adjusted gross income between $164,410 and $204,410.

The credit is claimed on Form 8839. If you paid qualifying adoption costs in 2006 but the adoption was not final at the end of the year, the credit may *not* be claimed on your 2006 return; *see 25.15* for the credit timing rules.

Employer plans. As discussed at *3.6*, an exclusion from income is also available to employees if adoption expenses are paid through a qualifying employer program, subject to rules similar to that of the credit. If you receive employer adoption benefits that are less than your qualifying adoption expenses, you may be able to claim the credit on Form 8839.

25.15 Claiming the Adoption Credit on Form 8839

The fact that you paid qualified adoption expenses during 2006 does not mean that you can claim a credit for those costs on your 2006 return. A 2006 credit is not allowed for 2006 expenses unless the adoption was finalized by the end of the year. Under the credit timing rules discussed below, you may claim a 2006 credit for expenses incurred in 2005 if the eligible child was a U.S. citizen or resident when the adoption effort began. If the child was not a U.S. citizen or resident when the adoption effort began, a credit is not allowed until the year the adoption is finalized even if you incurred expenses in one or more previous years.

If a credit is allowed for 2006, figure it on Form 8839 and attach the form to your Form 1040 or Form 1040A. You must enter an identification number for the child on Form 8839. Generally this is a Social Security number (SSN), but if you are in the process of adopting a child who is U.S. citizen or resident and you cannot get an SSN for the child before you file your return, you should apply for an adoption taxpayer identification number (ATIN) on IRS Form W-7A. If the child is not eligible for an SSN, apply for an individual identification number (ITIN) on Form W-7.

Credit limitations. The maximum credit on a 2006 return is $10,960 per eligible child. The $10,960 limit is not an annual limit on qualified expenses but an overall limit for each effort to adopt an eligible child *(25.14)*. If under the credit timing rules you are allowed a 2006 credit for more than one child, a separate $10,960 limit applies for each. However, if an adoption of a child with special needs is finalized in 2006, the maximum $10,960 credit is allowed even if this amount exceeds your qualified adoption expenses; *see* below. For years after 2006, an inflation adjustment may raise the $10,960 maximum credit.

The credit may be reduced or eliminated by a phase-out rule based on modified adjusted gross income (MAGI). For 2006, the phaseout applies if MAGI is over $164,410, and the credit is completely phased out if MAGI is $204,410 or more. For years after 2006, the phase-out range may be adjusted for inflation.

If you are married, you generally must file a joint return to take the adoption credit or exclusion. You may take the credit or exclusion on a separate return if you are legally separated under a decree of divorce or separate maintenance, or if you lived apart from your spouse for the last six months of the tax year and (1) your home is the eligible child's home for more than half the year and (2) you pay more than half the cost of keeping up your home for the year.

Filing Tip

Unused Credit Carryforward

The amount of your allowable adoption credit for a year cannot be more than your tax liability for that year; follow the Form 8839 instructions. If your credit is more than this limit, you can carry forward any unused credit for the next five years, or until used, whichever comes first.

Qualified adoption expenses. Qualifying adoption expenses are reasonable and necessary adoption fees, court costs, attorney fees, travel expenses away from home, and other expenses directly related to, and whose principal purpose is for, the legal adoption of an eligible child *(25.14)*. Do not include expenses paid or reimbursed by your employer or any other person or organization. You may not claim a credit for the costs of a surrogate parenting arrangement or for adopting your spouse's child.

When to claim the adoption credit for a child who is a U.S. citizen or resident. If at the time the adoption effort begins the child is a U.S. citizen or resident and you pay qualifying expenses in any year before the year the adoption becomes final, the credit is delayed one year. The credit is allowed in the year after the year of the payment, whether or not the adoption is final in that year. If you pay qualifying expenses in the year the adoption becomes final, the credit for those expenses is claimed in that year. If qualifying expenses are paid in any year after the year in which the adoption becomes final, the credit is claimed in the year of payment.

When to claim the adoption credit for a foreign child. If you adopt a child who is not a U.S. citizen or resident at the time the adoption effort begins, a credit may not be claimed until the year the adoption becomes final. If adoption expenses are paid after the tax year in which the adoption became finalized, a credit for such expenses is allowed for the tax year of payment.

The IRS has released safe harbors for determining the finality of an adoption of a foreign-born child and thereby the timing of a credit. These safe harbors apply only to adoptions of foreign-born children who receive an "immediate relative" (IR) visa from the State Department. IR visas are issued to a foreign-born child entering the U.S. after a foreign court or government agency (with authority over child welfare) has granted an adoption or guardianship decree.

Adoptive parents who bring a foreign-born child into the U.S. with an IR-2 visa, an IR-3 visa, or an IR-4 (if a "simple" adoption) visa may treat the adoption as final in either the taxable year in which the foreign court or agency enters the adoption decree or in the taxable year in which a court in the parents' home state enters a decree of "re-adoption" or the home state otherwise recognizes the foreign adoption decree, provided this occurs in one of the two years after the year in which the foreign court or agency enters its decree. If the child receives an IR-4 visa under a guardianship or legal custody arrangement, the adoption may not be treated as final for tax purposes until the year in which a court in the parents' home state enters a decree of adoption.

Special needs adoption. An adoption is considered a "special needs" adoption if the child is a U.S. citizen or resident when the adoption process begins, and a state (or District of Columbia) determines that the child cannot or should not be returned to his or her parents and that because of special factors, assistance is required to place the child with adoptive parents.

A special rule allows qualifying expenses to be grossed up to the maximum credit in the year the adoption is finalized where the aggregate of qualifying expenses for that year and all prior years is under the maximum. For example, if a special needs adoption is initiated in 2005 and finalized in 2006 and actual qualifying expenses for both years are $8,000, a $10,960 credit may be claimed for 2006. Total expenses are deemed to be the $10,960 maximum, so the credit for 2006 includes not only the $8,000 of actual expenses, but also an additional $2,960, the excess of $10,960 over the actual expenses. This special rule applies only to finalized special needs adoptions.

Miscellaneous Personal Credits

25.16 Retirement Savings Contributions Credit

You may be eligible for the saver's tax credit if you made retirement plan contributions for 2006. To qualify, your 2006 adjusted gross income cannot exceed $50,000 if you are married filing jointly, $37,500 if you are a head of household, or $25,000 if you are single, married filing separately, or a qualified widow(er). Furthermore, you are ineligible for a credit if you were born after January 1, 1989, are claimed as a dependent on another taxpayer's 2006 return, or were a full-time student during five or more months in 2006.

The credit is claimed on Form 8880 and attached to your Form 1040 or 1040A. Depending on your 2006 adjusted gross income, a credit percentage of 50%, 20%, or 10% applies, as shown in the following chart. Adjusted gross income is incresed by any exclusion for foreign earned income or income from Puerto rico or American Samoa, or foriegn housing exclusion or deduction.

Law Alert

Saver's Credit Made Permanent

The credit for qualified retirement savings contributions had been scheduled to expire at the end of 2006, but it was made permanent by the Pension Protection Act of 2006.

The income ranges for the three credit rates may be raised by an inflation adjustment starting in 2007.

Table 25-2 Adjusted Gross Income for 2006

Credit Rate	*Married Filing Jointly*	*Head of Household*	*Others*
50%	up to $30,000	up to $22,500	up to $15,000
20%	$30,001 – $32,500	$22,501 – $24,375	$15,001 – $16,250
10%	$32,501 – $50,000	$24,376 – $37,500	$16,251 – $25,000

For 2007, the income limits may be increased by an inflation adjustment; *see* the *e-Supplement* for an update.

Figuring the credit on Form 8880. The maximum credit equals the applicable income-dependent rate shown in Table 25-2 (50%, 20%, or 10%) multiplied by the first $2,000 of eligible retirement contributions made for 2006. If you are married filing jointly, you and your spouse may each take into account up to $2,000 of eligible contributions.

Eligible contributions include: (1) traditional IRA or Roth IRA contributions, (2) salary-reduction contributions to a 401(k) plan (including a SIMPLE 401(k)), 403(b) plan, SIMPLE IRA, governmental Section 457 plan, or salary-reduction SEP, or (3) voluntary after-tax contributions to a qualified plan or 403(b) plan.

Withdrawals can eliminate the credit. A credit can be lost because you have withdrawn money from a retirement plan. In figuring a credit for 2006, your eligible contributions for 2006 must be reduced by the total of distributions you received (and also your spouse if filing jointly) after 2003 and *before* the due date of your 2006 return (including extensions) from traditional IRAs and Roth IRAs, 401(k) plans, SEPs, SIMPLE plans, 403(b) plans, and other qualified retirement plans. Do not count tax-free rollovers, direct transfers (trustee-to-trustee), conversions of a traditional IRA to a Roth IRA, distributions of excess contributions or deferrals, or returned contributions; *see* the instructions to Form 8880.

The credit is not refundable. It is limited to your tax liability (regular tax plus AMT, if any), reduced by certain other nonrefundable credits such as the child tax credit, the dependent care credit or the Hope or Lifetime Learning credit.

Although the intent of the law was apparently to allow lower-income savers a maximum credit of $1,000, or $2,000 to married joint filers, it is impossible for anyone to obtain a $1,000 or $2,000 credit, given the way the credit is structured and the nonrefundable feature. Taxpayers eligible for the 50% credit bracket (adjusted gross income up to $15,000, $22,500, or $30,000, depending on filing status) will not have a high enough tax liability to absorb a $1,000 or $2,000 (joint return) credit.

25.17 Health Coverage Credit

Displaced workers who have lost jobs due to foreign competition and are receiving Trade Adjustment Assistance (TAA) benefits as well as Pension Benefit Guaranty Corporation (PBGC) pension beneficiaries age 55 or older are generally entitled to a health insurance credit. An eligible individual may claim a tax credit on Form 8885 for 65% of the premiums paid for COBRA contribution coverage and in some cases coverage under a spouse's employer group plan or state-sponsored health plan. Premiums for individual health insurance qualify if the eligible individual was enrolled in the plan for at least 30 days before becoming unemployed and thereby eligible for the credit. However, even if you purchase qualifying health insurance, the credit is not allowed if you have other specified coverage, such as Medicare.

The credit from Form 8885 is refundable; claim it on Form 1040, Line 70c.

Claim the credit in advance. Your state workforce agency or the PBGC can provide instructions for enrolling in the advanced tax credit plan. Once your eligibility and health coverage are confirmed, you only have to pay 35% of the premium and the Treasury Department will then pay it plus the other 65% to your insurer. Advance payments made on your behalf will be reported to you on Form 1099-H. The advance payments reduce the amount of the credit that can be claimed on Form 8885.

25.18 Mortgage Interest Credit

Under special state and local programs, you may obtain a "mortgage credit certificate" to finance the purchase of a principal residence or to borrow funds for certain home improvements. Generally, a qualifying principal residence may not cost more than 90% of the average area purchase price, 110% in certain targeted areas. A tax credit for interest paid on the mortgage may be claimed. The credit is computed on Form 8396 and claimed on Line 54a of Form 1040. The credit equals the interest paid multiplied by the certificate rate set by the governmental authority, but if the credit rate is over 20%, the credit is limited to $2,000.

Liability limit and carryover. The mortgage interest credit is nonrefundable. The credit for 2006 cannot exceed your 2006 regular tax plus alternative minimum tax (if any) reduced by other personal credits such as the child tax credit, child and dependent care credits, and the education credits. The tax liability limitation is figured on Form 8396. However, if your allowable credit exceeds the liability limitation, the unused credit can be carried forward for up to three years.

Mortgage interest deduction must be reduced. If you itemize deductions, you must reduce your home mortgage interest deduction *(15.1)* by the current year mortgage interest credit claimed on Line 3 of Form 8396 (certificate credit rate multiplied by interest paid, subject to the $2,000 limit). The reduction to the mortgage interest deduction applies even if part of the Line 3 credit is carried forward to the next tax year.

Caution

Recapture of Mortgage Subsidy

If within nine years of receiving a mortgage credit certificate you sell or dispose of your home at a gain, the mortgage subsidy you received generally must be recaptured as income. *See* Form 8828 for details.

25.19 District of Columbia First-Time Homebuyer Credit

When this book went to press, Congress had not yet extended the District of Columbia first-time homebuyer credit to purchases after 2005. However, an extension is likely. The following paragraphs assume that legislation extending the credit for 2006 will be enacted.* See the e-Supplement *for an update.

If you bought a home in the District of Columbia in 2006 and neither you nor your spouse owned a home in the District during the one-year period preceding your purchase, you may be entitled to a tax credit of up to $5,000 ($2,500 if married filing separately). On Form 8859, the credit is phased out for modified adjusted gross income between $110,000 and $130,000 if married filing jointly and between $70,000 and $90,000 for other taxpayers.

The credit is limited to regular tax liability plus alternative minimum tax (if any), reduced by other personal credits. A carryforward is allowed for any portion of the credit that may not be claimed because of the tax liability limitation; *see* Form 8859.

25.20 Residential Energy Tax Credits

The Energy Policy Act of 2005 created a number of limited tax credits for individuals who make energy savings improvements to their homes in 2006 or 2007. The residential energy credits are claimed on Form 5695, which must be attached to Form 1040.

Caution

Exterior Siding

The IRS announced that siding does not qualify for the credit. However, because some consumers had purchased siding based on a manufacturer's certification that a credit was available, the IRS said that homeowners who installed siding before December 1, 2006, could rely on such a certification and claim the credit.

Eligible home energy improvements. Tax credits are available for many types of home improvements placed in service after 2005 and before 2008. These include: insulation to walls, ceilings, high-efficiency water heaters, furnaces and boilers, high-efficiency central air-conditioning units, and high-efficiency fans for cooling and heating. Also qualifying for the credit are purchases of exterior windows (including skylights), exterior doors, and metal roofs with appropriate pigmented coating.

The maximum credit for all eligible improvements combined over both 2006 and 2007 is $500, of which no more than $200 can be for windows, but there are also separate caps on the credit for specific improvements; *see* "Credit limits" below. Improvements must be installed in or on the taxpayer's principal residence in the United States. The increase in the basis of the residence due to the improvement is reduced by the amount of the credit.

Some consumers are also eligible for utility or state rebates, as well as state tax incentives for energy-efficient homes and equipment. Your state energy office website may have more information on specific state tax information, or go to www.dsire.org to search by state.

Manufacturers offering energy-efficient items, such as insulation or storm windows, can assure their customers that their energy-efficient items qualify for the tax credit if certain energy-efficiency requirements are met. To qualify, a component must meet or exceed the criteria established by the 2000 International Energy Conservation Code (including supplements). Specific information regarding materials and equipment that qualify for the credit can be found at www.energystar.com. Obtain the manufacturer's certification of the item at the time of purchase.

Credit limits. In figuring the allowable credit on Form 5695, there are specific limitations for certain items and an overall limitation:

- 10% of the cost of insulation materials, exterior doors, and metal roofs with pigmented coating, but no more than $500 for both 2006 and 2007 expenditures
- 10% of the cost of exterior windows (including storm windows and skylights), but no more than $200 for window costs in both 2006 and 2007
- $300 for any qualifying water heater or heat pump
- $300 for any qualifying central air conditioner
- $150 for any qualifying furnace or boiler
- $50 for any qualifying fan used in a furnace

The cost of labor for onsite preparation, assembly, and installation can be included when applying the $300, $150, and $50 per item limits. Credits for $300, $150, and $50 limit expenditures are also subject to the overall $500 limit on qualifying costs over both 2006 and 2007. Of the overall $500 limit for both years, the amount for window expenses cannot exceed the lesser of 10% of cost or $200.

There is also a tax liability limitation. The energy credit can be claimed against your tax liability (regular tax plus AMT) as reduced by other specified personal credits; *see* Form 5695. Any excess energy credit is not allowed and cannot be carried over to 2007.

Solar panels, solar water heaters, and fuel cell power plants. In addition to any credit claimed for the improvements listed above, a credit may be claimed on Form 5695 for adding qualified solar panels, solar water heating equipment, or a fuel cell power plant to a U.S. residence (*see* below) in 2006 or 2007.

The credit is 30% of the qualified investment in solar panels up to a maximum annual credit of $2,000 for 2006 or 2007. The same annual limit applies for an investment in a certified solar water heating system if at least half of the energy used by the system comes from the sun. Both credits are available for a principal residence or vacation home in the United States. No credit can be claimed for expenditures used to heat a swimming pool or hot tub.

There is also a 30% tax credit for the purchase of a qualified fuel cell power plant that is installed in a principal residence located in the United States. The credit may not exceed $500 for each half-kilowatt of capacity produced by the fuel cell power plant.

For each of these credits, a qualified investment includes the cost of labor for onsite preparation, assembly, and installation.

If the property is used for business as well as residential purposes, and the residential use is at least 80%, 100% of the qualifying expenditures can be taken into account in figuring the credit. An allocation must be made to residential use if the residential use is less than 80%.

If the credits for 2006 exceed tax liability as reduced by most other personal credits, a carryover of the excess is allowed to 2007; *see* Form 5695.

25.21 Tax Credit for Hybrid Vehicles and Other Alternative Fuel Vehicles

The alternative motor vehicle credit includes separate credits for four distinct categories of vehicles purchased after 2005: hybrid vehicles, alternative fuel vehicles, fuel cell vehicles, and advanced lean burn technology vehicles. When this book went to press, credit certifications had been made for numerous hybrid vehicles and two alternative fuel vehicles; *see* below. The alternative motor vehicle credit replaces the deduction for hybrid vehicles that applied before 2006.

The IRS acknowledges certifications made by vehicle manufacturers that certain models qualify for a credit. The IRS acknowledgment allows the manufacturers to certify to consumers that these models qualify for a credit equal to the certified amount. The credit for qualifying vehicles is claimed on Form 8910. Unless the credit is reduced under the phaseout rule discussed below, there is no computation required on your part; the credit is simply the full amount fixed for the particular vehicle.

For hybrid passenger automobiles and light trucks with a gross vehicle weight rating of no more than 8,500 pounds, the amount of the credit depends on the vehicle's fuel economy and the projected lifetime fuel savings. The maximum hybrid vehicle credit under the law is $3,400, but thus far, the highest certification has been $3,150; *see* the list below. Because of the phaseout rule (*see* below), the full credit is only available for a limited time, depending on the manufacturer and when you buy.

Qualifying for the hybrid credit. Only the original purchaser of a new qualifying hybrid vehicle may claim the hybrid vehicle credit. A credit is not allowed for a used hybrid vehicle. If you lease a qualifying vehicle, only the leasing company (and not you) may claim the credit. The vehicle must be placed in service after December 31, 2005, and purchased on or before December 31, 2010. It must be used predominantly within the United States.

Hybrid credit is subject to phaseout on a manufacturer-by-manufacturer basis. Once a manufacturer sells its 60,000th hybrid vehicle after 2005 (all models), the tax credit for any of that manufacturer's certified hybrids is reduced as follows: For the second and third calendar quarters after the quarter in which the 60,000th qualifying vehicle is sold, you may claim 50% of the credit. For the fourth and fifth calendar quarters, you may claim 25% of the credit; no credit is allowed after the fifth quarter.

EXAMPLE

Toyota (including its Lexus division) sold its 60,000th hybrid vehicle in the second quarter of 2006. A Toyota Prius for model year 2006 qualifies for a credit of $3,150. The full credit can be claimed only for a 2006 Prius purchased from January 1, 2006, through September 30, 2006. The full credit for other Toyota and Lexus certified hybrids (*see* below) also applies only to purchases made before October 1, 2006.

For purchases after September 30, 2006, and through March 31, 2007, only one-half of the certified credit amount for the Prius or any other Toyota or Lexus model is allowed. For purchases between April 1, 2007, and September 30, 2007, the credit for any Toyota or Lexus hybrid will be 25% of the certified credit amount and for purchases after September 30, 2007, no credit will be allowed for a Toyota or Lexus model — unless Congress modifies the 60,000 vehicle credit phaseout rule.

How to claim the credit. Use Form 8910, Alternative Motor Vehicle Credit, to claim a hybrid vehicle or alternative fuel vehicle credit for 2006. If you are eligible for nonrefundable personal tax credits besides the alternative motor vehicle credit, the other personal credits are taken into account first, reducing the regular tax liability against which the alternative motor vehicle credit for personal use can be claimed. In addition, the reduced amount of regular tax liability must be further reduced by your tentative minimum tax as figured on Form 6251 (regardless of whether you owe AMT). The reduced liability, if any, is the maximum dollar limit on the credit for personal use of the vehicle. If your alternative motor vehicle tax credit exceeds your maximum dollar limit, the excess is not refundable, and the excess cannot be carried over to another year.

If the vehicle is used for business, the credit for the business use of a qualifying hybrid vehicle is figured on Form 8910 and entered on Form 3880, General Business Credit *(40.26)*.

Caution

How the AMT Affects the Credit

The alternative motor vehicle tax credit cannot be used to reduce your alternative minimum tax *(23.5)*. Even if you are not liable for AMT, you must figure your tentative AMT on Form 6251 to figure your credit for personal use of a qualifying vehicle on Form 8910. The tentative AMT reduces the regular tax liability against which the vehicle credit can be claimed. As a result, the benefit of the hybrid vehicle tax credit may be substantially reduced or eliminated because of the tentative AMT.

EXAMPLE

In 2006, an individual claims a child tax credit and dependent care credit that reduce her tax liability to zero. She purchases a 2006 Ford Escape Hybrid with two-wheel drive that is eligible for a $2,600 credit. Because her tax liability is zero, she cannot claim any hybrid vehicle credit and she cannot carry forward the unused credit.

Certified hybrid vehicles. When this book went to press, the following hybrid models had been certified for the credit in the following amounts:

- Toyota Prius (2005 and 2006 models)—$3,150
- Toyota Highlander 2WD or 4WD Hybrid (2006 model)—$2,600
- Toyota Camry Hybrid (2007 model)—$2,600
- Ford Escape Hybrid 2WD (2006 and 2007 models)—$2,600
- Lexus RX400h 2WD and 4WD (2006 model)—$2,200
- Honda Civic Hybrid CVT (2006 model)—$2,100
- Mercury Mariner Hybrid 4WD (2006 and 2007 models)—$1,950
- Ford Escape Hybrid 4WD (2006 and 2007 models)—$1,950
- Honda Civic Hybrid CVT (2005 model) and MT (2005 model)—$1,700
- Lexus GS 450h (2007 model)—$1,550
- Honda Insight CVT (2005 and 2006 models)—$1,450
- Honda Accord Hybrid AT and Navi AT with updated calibration (2006 model)—$1,300
- Honda Accord Hybrid AT and Navi AT without updated calibration (2006 model)—$650
- Honda Accord Hybrid AT and Navi AT (2005 model)—$650
- GMC Sierra, four-wheel drive, Hybrid pickup truck (model years 2006 and 2007)—$650
- Chevrolet Silverado, four-wheel drive, Hybrid pickup truck (model years 2006 and 2007) —$650
- Saturn Vue Green Line (model year 2007)—$650
- GMC Sierra, two-wheel drive, Hybrid pickup truck (model years 2006 and 2007)—$250
- Chevrolet Silverado, two-wheel drive, Hybrid pickup truck (model years 2006 and 2007) —$250

Filing Tip

IRS List of Qualifying Hybrid Vehicles

A complete and updated list of qualifying hybrid vehicles can be found at www.irs.gov/newsroom/topic/index.html. Click on "Hybrid Cars and Alternative Motor Vehicles."

Hybrid heavy trucks. For qualifying hybrid motor vehicles weighing more than 8,500 pounds, the maximum credit depends on the weight. *See* the instructions to Form 8910.

Credit for alternative fuel vehicles. A credit is allowed on Form 8910 for alternative fuel vehicles, which include those fueled by compressed natural gas, liquefied natural gas, liquefied petroleum gas, hydrogen, and any liquid that is at least 85% methanol.

Two vehicles powered by compressed natural gas (CNG) have been certified for the credit: Honda Civic GX model year 2005 and Honda Civic GX model year 2006, each for a credit of $4,000.

Electric vehicles. Vehicles powered solely by electricity that are purchased and placed in service in 2006 qualify for a separate tax credit; this credit is separate from the alternative fuel motor vehicle credit. The maximum electric vehicle credit in 2006 is 2.5% (.025) of up to $40,000, for a top credit of $1,000. The credit is claimed on Form 8834. Unless Congress extends the law authorizing the credit for electric vehicles, no credit will be allowed after 2006.

25.22 Credit for Federal Telephone Excise Tax

Taxpayers can obtain a refund of federal excise tax paid on long-distance service, including interest, billed to them after February 28, 2003, and before August 1, 2006. Individuals and Schedule C filers can claim the refund based on actual excise tax payments or an IRS-created safe harbor. Either way, the refund must be claimed on a 2006 tax return. Those with income below the threshold requiring them to file a tax return can use Form 1040 EZ-T to claim the refund.

For more information on how to claim the refund and whether to claim the safe harbor or actual taxes paid, *see 46.4*, "Getting Your Refund."

Chapter 26

Tax Withholdings

Withholding taxes gives the Government part of your income before you have a chance to use it. Withholding tax is imposed on salary and wage income, tip income, certain gambling winnings, pensions, and retirement distributions, but you may avoid withholding on retirement payments; *see 26.10.* Withholding is also imposed on interest and dividends if you do not give your taxpayer identification number to a payer of interest or dividend income.

You may increase or decrease withholdings on your wages by submitting a new Form W-4 to your employer. Withholdings may be reduced by claiming allowances based on tax deductions and credits.

Make sure that tax withholdings meet or help you meet the estimated tax rules that require withholdings plus estimated tax payments to equal 90% of your current year liability or the required percentage of the prior year's liability; *see* Chapter 27.

A 20% withholding rate applies to eligible rollover distributions from an employer retirement plan. You may avoid the withholding by instructing your employer to directly transfer the funds to an IRA or the plan of your new employer; *see 26.10.*

26.1 Withholdings Should Cover Estimated Tax

In fixing the rate of withholding on your wages, pay attention to the tests for determining whether sufficient income taxes have been withheld from your pay. A penalty will apply if your wage withholdings plus estimated tax payments (including prior year overpayments credited to current estimated tax) do not equal the lesser of 90% of your current tax liability or the required percentage of the prior year's tax; *see 27.1.*

Taxes are withheld from payments made to you for services that you perform as an employee; *see 26.2* for exceptions. By filing Form W-4, you claim allowances for yourself, your spouse, and dependents. The number of allowances claimed will either decrease or increase the amount of withholding. On Form W-4, you also may claim withholding allowances for itemized deductions and credits such as the child tax credit, child and dependent care credit, education tax credits, adoption credit, retirement savings credit, prior-year AMT credit, credit for the elderly and disabled, the foreign tax credit, credit for home mortgage interest, the general business credit, and earned income credit (if you have not filed for an advance payment of the credit on Form W-5).

If you need to increase your withholding, such as to cover investment or self-employment income, you can choose not to claim all of the allowances allowed on Form W-4. You can also direct your employer on Form W-4 to withhold an additional flat amount from each paycheck.

You can change your withholdings, either increasing or decreasing them, if your financial or family situation changes; *see 26.5.*

26.2 Income Taxes Withheld on Wages

The amount of income tax withheld for your wage bracket depends on your marital status and the number of allowances you claim. You file a withholding certificate, Form W-4, with your employer, indicating your status and allowances. Without a Form W-4, your employer must withhold tax as if you are a single person with no exemptions.

Cash payments or the cash value of benefits paid to an employee by an employer are subject to withholding, unless the payments are specifically excluded.

Filing Instruction

Adjust Withholdings

If you do not expect withholdings to meet your final tax liability, ask your employer to withhold a greater amount of tax; *see 26.1.* On the other hand, if the withholding rate applied to your wages results in overwithholding, you may claim extra withholding allowances to reduce withholding during the year; *see 26.4* and *26.5.*

Income Taxes Are Withheld on:

- Payments to employees as salaries, wages, fees, commissions, pensions, retirement pay, vacation allowances, dismissal pay, etc. (whether paid in cash or goods). If bonuses, commissions, overtime pay accumulated, leave, or taxable expense allowances (under nonaccountable plans) are separately identified from regular wages, an employer may withhold at a flat rate of 25% instead of using the regular withholding tables. *See 26.10* for withholding on pensions and annuities.
- Sick pay paid by your employer. If a third party pays you sick pay on a plan funded by your employer, you may request withholding by filing Form W-4S.
- Taxable group insurance coverage over $50,000.
- Reimbursements of expenses that do not meet qualifying rules of accountable plans discussed at *20.31.* Also, reimbursements from accountable plans that exceed federal rates if the employee does not return the reimbursement or show that it is substantiated by proof of expenses.
- Pay to members of the U.S. Armed Forces.
- Prize awarded to a salesperson in a contest run by his or her employer.
- Retroactive pay and overtime under the Fair Labor Standards Act.
- Taxable supplemental unemployment compensation benefits.

Income Taxes Are Not Withheld on:

- Payments to household workers. However, although income tax withholding is not required, the worker and the employer may make a voluntary withholding agreement; *see* Chapter 38.
- Payments to agricultural workers, college domestics, ministers of the gospel (except chaplains in the Armed Forces), casual workers, nonresident aliens, public officials who receive fees directly from the public, notaries, jurors, witnesses, precinct workers, etc.
- Pay for newspaper home delivery by children under age 18.
- Advances for traveling expenses if the employee substantiates expenses to the employer and if the employee returns any unsubstantiated amount; *see 20.31.*
- Value of tax-free board and lodging furnished by an employer.
- Fringe benefits not subject to tax.
- Substantiated reimbursements for deductible moving expenses or medical care benefits under a self-insured medical reimbursement plan.
- Death benefit payments to beneficiary of employee; wages due but unpaid at employee's death and paid to estate or beneficiary.

- Pay for U.S. citizen working abroad or in U.S. possessions to the extent that the pay is tax free; *see* Chapter 36 for rules.
- Earnings of self-employed persons; they may pay estimated tax installments throughout the year.

Form W-2. By January 31, 2007, your employer must give you duplicate copies of your 2006 Form W-2, which is a record of your pay and the withheld income and Social Security taxes. If you leave your job during the year, you may ask your employer for a Form W-2 by making a written request within 30 days of leaving the job.

26.3 Low Earners May Be Exempt From Withholding

If you had no income tax liability in 2006 and expect none for 2007, you may be exempt from income tax withholdings on your 2007 wages. If eligible, students working for the summer, retired persons, and other part-time workers do not have to wait for a refund of withheld taxes they do not owe. The exemption applies only to income tax withholding, not to withholdings for Social Security and Medicare *(26.9)*. However, if you can be claimed as a dependent on another person's tax return, you may not claim this special exemption if you expect total income (wages plus investments) to be more than $850 *(13.5)* and investment income to be more than $300. If the $850 and $300 amounts are increased due to an inflation factor, the higher amounts will be on the 2007 version of Form W-4.

If you cannot be claimed as a dependent by another person, you can claim the exemption from withholding if your total income is expected to be no more than the sum of your personal exemption and the standard deduction for your filing status.

To claim an exemption for 2007, you must file a withholding exemption certificate, Form W-4, with your employer. If you will file a joint return for 2007, do not claim an exemption on Form W-4 if the joint return will show a tax liability. An exemption claimed during 2007 will expire February 15, 2008.

26.4 Are You Withholding the Right Amount?

You do not want to withhold too little from your pay and you do not want to withhold too much. You may need to withhold more to avoid a large tax payment or an estimated tax penalty *(26.1)* when you file your return, especially if you have substantial income from investments or a business. On the other hand, if you have been receiving large refunds from the IRS, you may want to consider reducing your Form W-4 allowances to avoid over-withholding. Balance the loss of the use of your earnings during the year against the value of receiving a substantial refund check from the IRS after you file your return.

If you are starting a new job or if you have not changed your withholding allowances in several years, review the Form W-4 worksheets to help you determine if you are withholding the right amount.

Working couples filing jointly should figure withholding allowances on their combined wage income, deductions, adjustments, and credits, but can divide the total number of allowances between them in any way they wish. On separate returns, the allowances must be figured separately.

If you work for only one employer and are unmarried, you may claim an additional withholding allowance. If you are married, you may claim the additional allowance if you work for only one employer and your spouse does not work, or your wages from a second job or your spouse's wages are $1,000 or less. This special allowance is only for withholding purposes. You may not claim it on your tax return.

If you work for two or more employers at the same time, you figure your withholding allowances based on the total income, and then split the allowances between the two jobs in any way you wish. Do not claim the same allowances with more than one employer at the same time.

File a new Form W-4 each year for withholding allowances based on your anticipated deductions and credits. Furthermore, you may have to file a new form to increase your withholding if withholding allowances you had been claiming are no longer allowed; *see 26.5*.

IRS review of Form W-4. Employers are not required to submit Forms W-4 to the IRS for review unless the IRS sends written notice directing the employer to provide the W-4 forms of specified employees. The IRS uses the information on Form W-2 wage statements to spot employees who are not withholding enough federal income tax from their income. If the IRS determines that too many withholding allowances are being claimed, the IRS can issue a "lock-in letter" requiring your employer to limit the number of allowances to a specified maximum. You will receive a copy

Planning Reminder

When To Change Withholdings

Adjust withholding if there will be a significant change in the tax you owe for 2007. Credits such as the child tax credit, Hope scholarship credit, and lifetime learning credit may reduce your 2007 tax. By decreasing your withholding now, you can get the benefit of the lower taxes throughout the year. On the other hand, a withholding increase may be advisable if previously claimed deductions or credits will not be available to you, or if you expect an increase in nonwage income such as capital gains. Check the instructions to Forms W-4 and 1040-ES for 2007 to help you adjust your withholdings.

Planning Reminder

Part-Year Employees May Avoid Overwithholding

Starting a new job in the middle of a year presents a withholding problem. The amount of tax withheld from your paycheck is figured by taking your weekly pay and multiplying this by a 52-week pay period. For example, if as a recent graduate you start a job on July 1 and your weekly pay is $1,000 for 26 weeks (July 1–December 31), your withholding will be based on an annual income of $52,000 ($1,000 × 52 weeks) and not the $26,000 you will actually earn that year. This will result in overwithholding. To alleviate this problem, you may ask your employer to calculate withholdings on what is known as the "part year" method if your work days during the year are expected to be 245 or fewer. This formula calculates withholding based on actual earnings rather than expected earnings over a full year of employment. As an alternative, you may elect to claim extra exemptions on Form W-4, which has the same effect of reducing the amount withheld each week from your paycheck.

of the "lock-in letter" and be given an opportunity to dispute the IRS determination before your employer adjusts your withholding.

The IRS may impose a $500 civil penalty if you did not have a reasonable basis for claiming allowances that reduced your withholding on Form W-4. There is also a criminal penalty of up to $1,000 plus a jail sentence upon conviction for willfully supplying false information.

26.5 When To File a New Form W-4

You should file a new Form W-4 any time the number of your exemptions or withholding allowances increases or decreases, such as when a child is born or adopted, you marry, you get a divorce, or your deductible expenses change.

Your employer may make the new Form W-4 effective with the next payment of wages. However, an employer may postpone the new withholding rate until the start of the first payroll period ending on or after the 30th day from the day you submit the revised form.

You must file a new Form W-4 within 10 days if the number of allowances previously claimed by you decreases, such as where you divorce or legally separate, or a person who has been claimed as your dependent no longer qualifies.

The death of a spouse or a dependent in a current year does not affect your withholding until the next year but requires the filing of a new certificate, if possible, by the first business day in December, or within 10 days if the death is in December. However, a widow or widower entitled to joint return rates in the next two years as a qualifying widow or widower with a dependent child *(1.11)* need not file a new withholding certificate.

When you file on or before December 1, your employer must reduce your withholding as of January 1 of the next year.

26.6 Voluntary Withholding on Certain Government Payments

You can choose to have income tax withheld from Social Security benefits (and equivalent tier 1 Railroad Retirement benefits), unemployment compensation, crop damage payments, and Commodity Credit Corporation loans. The withholding request is made on Form W-4V. Electing to have tax withheld may eliminate the need to make estimated tax installments; *see 27.2.*

For unemployment compensation you may choose a withholding rate of 10%. For the other government payments, you may select a withholding rate of 7%, 10%, 15%, or 25%.

26.7 When Tips Are Subject to Withholding

Tips are subject to income tax and FICA (Social Security and Medicare) withholdings. If you receive cash tips amounting to $20 or more in a month, you must report the total amount of tips received during the month to your employer on Form 4070 (or a similar written report). Include cash tips paid to you in your own behalf. If you "split" or share tips with others, you include in your report only your share. You do not include tips received in the form of merchandise or your share of service charges turned over to you by your employer. Make the report on or before the 10th day after the end of the month in which the tips are received. (If the 10th day is a Saturday, Sunday, or legal holiday, you must submit the report by the next business day.) For example, tips amounting to $20 or more that are received during January 2007 are reported by February 10, 2007. Your employer may require more frequent reporting.

You are considered to have income from tips when you receive the tips, even if they are not reported to the employer.

Your employer withholds the Social Security, Medicare, and income tax due on the tips from your wages or from funds you give him or her for withholding purposes. If the taxes due cannot be collected on the tips, either from your wages or from voluntary contributions, by the 10th day after the end of the month in which tips are reported, you have to pay the tax when you file your income tax return.

Penalty for failure to report tips. Failure to report tip income of $20 or more received during the month to your employer may subject you to a penalty of 50% of the Social Security and Medicare tax due on the unreported tips, unless your failure was due to reasonable cause rather than to willful neglect.

Tips of less than $20 per month are taxable but not subject to withholding.

Filing Instruction

Tip Reporting

If you have not reported tips of $20 or more in any month, or tips are allocated to you under the special tip allocation rules, you must compute Social Security and Medicare tax on that amount on Form 4137 and enter it as a tax due on Line 59 of Form 1040; attach Form 4137 to Form 1040. The unreported tips must be included as wages on Line 7 of Form 1040.

Tip allocation reporting by large restaurants. To help the IRS audit the reporting of tip income, restaurants employing at least 10 people must make a special report of income and allocate tips based on gross receipts. For purposes of the allocation, the law assumes tip income of at least 8%. If you voluntarily report tips equal to your allocable share of 8% of the restaurant's gross receipts, no allocation will be made to you. However, if the total tips reported by all employees is less than 8% of gross receipts and you do not report your share of the 8%, your employer must make an allocation based on the difference between the amount you reported and your share of the 8% amount. The allocated amount is shown on Form W-2. However, taxes are not withheld on the allocated amount. Taxes are withheld only on amounts actually reported by employees. An employer or majority of employees may ask the IRS to apply a tip percentage of less than 8%, but no lower than 2%.

Reporting allocated tips. Your employer will show allocated tips in Box 8 of your Form W-2. However, this amount will not be included in Box 1 wages and you must add it to income yourself by reporting it on Line 7 of Form 1040. You also must compute Social Security and Medicare tax on the allocated tips on Form 4137 and enter the tax from Form 4137 on Line 59 of Form 1040. You may not use Form 1040A or Form 1040EZ.

Filing Instruction

Uncollected Social Security and Medicare Taxes

If your employer is unable to collect enough money from your wages during the year to cover the Social Security or Medicare tax on the tips you reported, the uncollected amount is shown on your Form W-2 in Box 12 with Code A next to it for Social Security or Code B for Medicare. You must report the uncollected amount on Line 63 of Form 1040 (total tax) as an additional tax due; write "UT" and show the amount next to Line 63.

26.8 Withholding on Gambling Winnings

Gambling winnings are generally reported by the payer to the IRS and to the winner on Form W-2G if the amount paid is $600 or more and at least 300 times the amount of the wager; the payer has the option of taking into account the wager in applying the $600 test. Different reporting rules apply to winnings from keno, bingo, and slot machines. Keno winnings are reported on Form W-2G if they are $1,500 or more, *reduced* by the wager. Winnings from bingo or slot machines of $1,200 or more, *not* reduced by the wager, are reported on Form W-2G.

Your winnings from gambling are subject to 25% withholding if your winnings exceed:

1. $5,000 from lotteries, sweepstakes, and wagering pools (whether or not state-conducted), including church raffles, *pari-mutuel* betting pools and on- and off-track racing pools; or
2. $5,000 from other wagering transactions, if the proceeds are at least 300 times as large as the amount wagered, such as from wagers on horse races, dog races, or jai alai.

If your winnings exceed the $5,000 threshold, withholding applies to your gross winnings less your wagers, and not just the amounts over $5,000. Any withholdings will be shown on Form W-2G.

The IRS requires you to tell the payers of gambling winnings if you are also receiving winnings from identical wagers; winnings from identical wagers must be added together to determine if withholding is required.

If you have agreed to share your winnings with another person, give the payer a Form 5754. The payer will then prepare separate Forms W-2G for each of you.

Caution

Backup Gambling Withholding

Winnings from bingo, keno, and slot machines are not subject to income tax withholding. However, if you do not provide a taxpayer identification number, the payer will withhold tax at the 28% backup withholding rate *(26.12)*.

26.9 FICA Withholdings

FICA withholdings are employee contributions for Social Security and Medicare coverage. Your employer is liable for the tax if he or she fails to make proper withholdings. The amount withheld is figured on your wages and is not affected by your marital status, number of exemptions, or the fact that you may be over age 65 and collecting Social Security. On Form W-2, Social Security withholdings are shown in Box 4 and Medicare withholdings in Box 6.

Subject to FICA tax are your regular salary, commissions, bonuses, vacation pay, cash tips, group-term insurance coverage over $50,000, the first six months of sick pay, and contributions to cash or deferred (401(k)) pay plans or salary-reduction contributions to a simplified employee pension (SEP), SIMPLE IRA, or tax-sheltered annuity. Not subject to tax are the value of tax-free meals and lodgings, as discussed in *3.11,* and reimbursements for substantiated travel or entertainment expenses or for moving expenses.

Excess Social Security and Railroad Retirement withholding. If you have worked for more than one employer during 2006, attach all Copies B of Form W-2 to your return. Check to see that the total withheld in 2006 by your employers does not exceed your liability for Social Security taxes. The maximum 2006 liability for Social Security is $5,840.40, 6.2% on the first $94,200 of salary income. If too much was withheld, claim the excess as a payment on Line 67 of your 2006 Form 1040. On Form 1040A, the excess is included on the line for total tax payments; you cannot claim the excess on Form 1040-EZ.

Medicare tax is withheld at a rate of 1.45% on *all* salary and wage income.

Planning Reminder

Wages Paid to Household Employees

See Chapter 38 for FICA withholding on wages paid to household employees.

Caution

Employer Plan Distributions

Your employer must withhold 20% from a distribution paid to you if the distribution was eligible for tax-free rollover; *see 7.8.*

Planning Reminder

Rollover From Employer Plan

20% withholding does not apply to a distribution eligible for rollover *(7.8)* if you have the employer make a direct rollover to a qualified plan or IRA.

Employees covered by the Railroad Retirement Tax Act (RRTA) receive Form W-2, which lists total wages paid and withholdings of income and Railroad Retirement taxes. Follow tax form instructions for claiming a credit for excess Railroad Retirement withholding.

If any one employer withheld too much Social Security or Railroad Retirement tax, you cannot claim the excess on your income tax return. You must ask that employer for a refund of the excess.

Wages you pay to your spouse or child. Wages you pay to your spouse for working in your business are subject to FICA tax and income tax withholding. Wages you pay to your child for working in your business are subject to income tax withholding but exempt from FICA if the child is under age 18. Wages you pay to your child under age 21 or to your spouse for domestic work or child care in your own home are exempt from FICA.

Student employees exempt from FICA. A statutory exemption from FICA taxes covers students who work for schools, colleges, and universities. The exemption benefits students whose work is incidental to their studies, as opposed to "career" employees who take courses while working for a school. IRS Revenue Procedure 2005-11 provides a safe harbor for the student FICA exception. The safe harbor standards reflect final regulations adopted at the end of 2004.

26.10 Withholding on Retirement Distributions

Retirement distributions are subject to withholding taxes, but you may avoid withholdings. The method of avoiding withholding varies with the type of payment.

Periodic payments. If you receive periodic payments, such as an annuity, withholding is required unless you elect to avoid withholding on Form W-4P, or on a substitute form furnished by the payer. If you are a U.S. citizen or resident alien, withholding may not be avoided on pensions or other distributions paid outside the U.S. or U.S. possessions. Payment must be to your home address within the U.S. (or in a U.S. possession) to avoid withholding.

Unless you tell the payer otherwise, wage withholding tables are used to figure withholdings on periodic payments as if you were married and claiming three withholding exemptions. Withholding allowances may be claimed on Form W-4P for estimated itemized deductions, alimony payments, student loan interest, and deductible IRA contributions.

You may also request that the payer withhold a specific amount of additional tax for each payment.

Nonperiodic payments from IRAs and commercial annuities. Nonperiodic payments are subject to withholding at a flat 10% rate unless you elect to avoid withholding on Form W-4P (or substitute form). IRA distributions that are payable upon demand are considered nonperiodic and, thus, subject to the 10% withholding rule.

Nonperiodic payments from qualified employer plans. Employers must withhold 20% from nonperiodic payments, such as lump-sum distributions that are eligible for tax-free rollover but which are paid directly to you. To avoid withholding you must direct your employer to make a direct rollover *(7.8)* of the funds to an IRA or to a defined contribution plan of your new employer. If you do not instruct your employer to make the direct transfer and elect to personally receive the distribution, 20% will be withheld before payment is made to you.

See 7.8 for a further explanation and an Example showing the effects of the withholding rule where you receive the distribution and then decide to make a rollover yourself.

26.11 Backup Withholding

Backup withholding is designed to pressure taxpayers to report interest and dividend income. You may be subject to backup withholding if you do not give your taxpayer identification number to parties paying you interest or dividend income, you give an incorrect number, or you ignore IRS notices stating that you have underreported interest or dividends. Your taxpayer identification number generally is your Social Security number or your employer identification number. The backup withholding rate is 28%.

Backup withholding will apply to fees of $600 or more (Form 1099-MISC) for work you do as an independent contractor, payments from brokers (Form 1099-B), royalty payments (Form 1099-MISC), and certain gambling winnings *(see 26.8)* if you do not give the payer your taxpayer identification number.

Civil and criminal penalties can be imposed if you provide false information to avoid backup withholding.

Chapter 27

Estimated Tax Payments

Income taxes are collected on a pay-as-you-go basis through withholding on wages and pensions, as well as quarterly estimated tax payments on other income. Where all or most of your income is from wages, pensions, and annuities, you will generally not have to pay estimated tax, because your estimated tax liability has been satisfied by withholding. But do not assume you are not required to pay simply because taxes have been withheld from your wages. Always check your estimated tax liability. Withholding may not cover your tax; the withholding tax rate may be below your actual tax rate when considering other income such as interest, dividends, business income, and capital gains.

Your estimated tax must also include liability for self-employment tax, alternative minimum tax (AMT), and FICA withholding tax for household employees.

If you expect your 2007 tax liability to be $1,000 or more after taking into account withholding taxes and credits, you should make quarterly estimated tax payments unless you expect the withholdings and credits to be at least 90% of your 2007 liability, or, if less, 100% or 110% of your liability for 2006. The 100% test applies if your 2006 adjusted gross income (AGI) was $150,000 or less, $75,000 or less if married filing separately in 2007. The 110% test applies if your 2006 AGI exceeded the $150,000 or $75,000 threshold.

Failure to pay a required estimated tax installment will subject you to a penalty based on the prevailing IRS interest rate applied to tax deficiences.

27.1 Do You Owe an Estimated Tax Penalty for 2006?

When you have computed the exact amount of your 2006 tax liability on your 2006 return, you can determine whether you are subject to an estimated tax penalty. If you owe less than $1,000 on your 2006 return after taking into account withheld taxes, you are not subject to a penalty. If the tax owed after withholdings is $1,000 or more, you can now determine whether your 2006 withholdings plus estimated tax installments were at least 90% ($66^2/_3$% for farmers and fishermen) of your 2006 total tax (regular tax plus alternative minimum tax and penalty taxes) *minus* certain tax credits. If you met the 90% test, you are not subject to an estimated tax penalty for 2006.

Even if the 90% test was not met, you may still generally avoid an estimated tax penalty if your withholdings and estimated tax installments for 2006 were at least 100% of the total tax on your 2005 return. This exception requires that the 2005 return covered all 12 months. However, if your 2005 adjusted gross income exceeded $150,000 ($75,000 if you are married filing separately for 2006), your withholdings plus estimated tax installments for 2006 had to be at least 110% of your 2005 total tax (not 100%) to qualify for this prior year liability exception.

To completely avoid a penalty for 2006 under either the 90% current year exception or the 100%/110% prior year exception, you must have paid at least 25% of the amount required under the applicable exception by each of the four payment dates. The penalty is figured separately for each payment period; *see* below.

Even if you owe $1,000 or more (after withholdings) on your 2006 return and you do not qualify for either the 90% current year exception or 100%/110% prior year exception, you are not subject to an estimated tax penalty for 2006 if you did not have to file a 2005 return or your 2005 total tax was zero. This exception applies only if you were a U.S. citizen or resident for all of 2005 and your 2005 tax year included 12 full months.

Planning Reminder

Credit Card Payments

You may charge estimated tax payments using a Visa, MasterCard, American Express, or Discover Card. *See* the Form 1040-ES instructions. If you charge estimated tax payments, you do not have to file Form 1040-ES vouchers.

If you underestimated your 2006 liability because of an unexpected increase in income during 2006, or if you did not earn income evenly throughout 2006, such as where you operated a seasonal business, you may be able to lower or eliminate the penalty by using the *annualized income installment method.* Under this exception, you may avoid a penalty for an estimated tax installment by figuring the installment that would be due if the income (and deductions) earned before the date for the installment were *annualized.* Form 2210 and IRS Publication 505 have worksheets for applying the annualized income exception. The computation is complicated and its use may be discouraged by the complexity, despite the potential benefits.

Penalties are figured separately for each payment period. Separate penalty determinations must be made for each of the four 2006 estimated tax payment periods, as of the applicable installment dates: April 17, June 15, and September 15 in 2006, and January 16, 2007). This means that if, after taking into account withholdings from your pay, you underpaid an installment, you may owe a penalty for that period even though you overpaid later installments to make up the difference. The penalty for each period, which is based on the prevailing IRS interest rate for deficiencies *(see 46.7)*, runs from the installment due date until the amount is paid or until the regular filing date for the final tax return, whichever is earlier.

Withholding payments are treated as if they were payments of estimated tax. In applying them, the total withholdings of the year are divided equally between each installment period unless you elect on Form 2210 to apply them to the periods in which they were actually withheld.

Figure the 2006 penalty for yourself on Form 2210 or let the IRS do it. You can use Form 2210 to determine any 2006 penalty, but the IRS encourages taxpayers to let the IRS compute any penalty. The IRS will figure the amount of any penalty and bill you for the amount if you do not complete Form 2210.

There is no penalty and you do not have to file Form 2210 if the tax liability shown on your 2006 return is less than $1,000, after taking into account withholdings. There also is no penalty if you had no tax liability for 2005, you were a U.S. citizen or resident for all of 2005, and your 2005 taxable year included 12 full months.

You *must* attach Form 2210 to your 2006 return if: (1) you use the annualized income exception; (2) you do not allocate wage withholdings in four equal amounts; (3) your required estimated tax payment for 2006 is based on the applicable percentage (100% or 110%) of the 2005 tax and a joint return is filed for either 2005 or 2006 but not both; or (4) you claim a penalty waiver; *see* below for waiver rules.

If you *underpaid* for any payment period, the amount of the underpayment reduces the payment made in the following period. That is, an underpayment of one period is carried over to succeeding periods on Form 2210. If you underpay for a period, any payment you make after that installment date will be applied first to the earlier underpayment. Thus, even if you make the required payment for a period, you could still be subject to a penalty for that period because your payment is applied to a prior underpayment.

If you *overpaid* for any period, the excess carries over to the next period. The excess cannot be used to make up for an underpayment of the prior period if the payments were made electronically, with Form 1040-ES vouchers or by credit card. However, withholdings are allocated equally over the year so that withholdings late in the year can reduce an underpayment for an earlier payment period.

Waiver of penalty for hardship, retirement, or disability. The IRS may waive the penalty if you can show you failed to pay the estimated tax because of casualty, disaster, or other unusual circumstances.

The IRS may also waive a penalty for a 2006 underpayment if in 2006 or 2005 you retired after reaching age 62 or became disabled, and you failed to make a payment due to reasonable cause and not due to willful neglect. To apply for the waiver, attach an explanation on Form 2210 that documents the circumstances supporting your waiver request.

Farmers and fishermen. Farmers or fishermen who earned at least $^2/_3$ of their 2005 or 2006 gross income from farming or fishing can use Form 2210-F to determine whether they owe an estimated penalty for 2006, but generally the form does not have to be filed; *see* the Form 2210-F instructions.

27.2 Planning Estimated Tax Payments for 2007

In planning your payments for 2007, you do not want to pay more than is necessary to avoid a penalty. If you expect your 2007 income and deductions to be about the same as in 2006, apply 2007 tax rates (the 2007 tax brackets will be in the *e-Supplement* and in the 2007 instructions to Form 1040-ES) to your 2006 taxable income and base your 2007 withholdings and quarterly estimated tax installments on 90% of that tax. If you were subject to self-employment tax or alternative minimum tax in 2006, add 90% of such taxes to your 2007 estimate.

Safe harbor for 2007 based on 2006 tax. If you are uncertain of the amount of your 2007 income and deductions, you can play it safe and avoid a possible penalty for 2007 by having withholdings and quarterly estimated tax installments equal to your 2006 tax liability if your 2006 adjusted gross income is $150,000 or less ($75,000 or less if married filing separately for 2007), provided you filed a 2006 return covering a full 12 months. If your 2006 AGI exceeds the $150,000 (or $75,000) threshold, your payments for 2007 must be at least 110% of your 2006 tax.

If an accurate estimate for 2007 is possible, it is generally advantageous to base your estimated payments on the 90% test rather than the 100%/110% prior year test, as using this prior year test will probably result in an overestimation of your liability unless the 2007 tax turns out to be substantially larger than the 2006 tax.

You may use the worksheet and the tax rate schedule included in the 2007 Form 1040-ES to figure your estimated tax liability and the required annual payment to avoid a penalty under either the 90% current year or prior year liability tests just discussed.

Reduce your 2007estimated tax liability by expected withholdings from wages, pensions, and annuities. If after withholdings your estimated tax is $1,000 or more, you must make estimated tax payments unless the withholdings will cover at least 90% of your estimated 2007 liability or 100%/110% of your 2006 liability. If withholdings will not cover the amount required under the 90% or 100%/110% tests, you may pay the balance of the estimated tax with Form 1040-ES vouchers or by credit card. You may schedule electronic payments using the Electronic Federal Tax Payment System (EFTPS), or you can make one 2007 estimated tax payment by direct debit from your checking or savings account if you electronically file your 2006 return. *See* the 2007 Form 1040-ES instructions for details on the payment options.

Crediting 2006 refund to 2007 estimated tax. If you are due a refund when you file your 2006 return, it may be credited to your 2007 estimated tax. You may also split up the amount due you.

Planning Reminder

Annualized Income Method

If your income typically fluctuates throughout the year, or if your income unexpectedly changes during the year, you may base installment payments on the annualized income method. This method allows you to avoid a penalty for installment periods during which less income is earned by reducing the required estimated tax payment for such periods. To figure your installment payments, use the Annualized Estimated Tax Worksheet in IRS Publication 505. If you base installment payments on the annualized method, you must file Form 2210 with your return to determine if you are subject to an estimated tax penalty.

Planning Reminder

Withholdings Cover Prior Underpayment

You have a choice in allocating withholdings from pay or other income that is subject to withholding: (1) You may treat your entire year's withholdings as having been withheld in equal amounts for each of the four payment periods or (2) you may allocate to each payment period the actual withholdings paid for that period. Also, if toward the end of the year you find that you have underestimated for an earlier period, ask your employer to withhold an extra amount that may be allocated equally over the four periods. This way, you may eliminate the underestimate for the earlier periods.

You may take part of the overpayment as a refund. The other part may be credited to your estimate of 2007 taxes. The IRS will credit the refund to the April installment of 2007 estimated tax unless you attach a statement to your return instructing the IRS to apply the refund to later installments.

Check your arithmetic before you apply an overpayment as a credit on your next year's estimate. If you apply too much, the amount credited may not be used to offset any additional tax due that the IRS determines you owe. For example, your 2006 return shows a $500 refund due, and you apply it towards your 2007 estimated tax. However, the IRS determines that you overpaid $200, not $500. You will be billed for the additional $300 tax, plus interest due; you may not offset the extra tax with the credited amount.

Farmers or fishermen. In figuring the required annual payment to avoid a penalty for 2007, a farmer or fisherman has to pay only $66^2/_3$% of the 2007 estimated liability, rather than 90%. A penalty may also be avoided by paying 100% of the 2006 tax, provided a tax return covering a 12-month period was filed for 2006; the 110% test for higher-income taxpayers does not apply to a farmer or fisherman. To qualify as a farmer or fisherman under these rules, at least two-thirds of gross income for 2006 or 2007 must be from farming or fishing.

27.3 Dates for Paying Estimated Tax Installments for 2007

The four installment dates for 2007 estimated tax are: April 16, 2007; June 15, 2007; September 17, 2007; and January 15, 2008. Later installments may be used to amend earlier ones; *see 27.1*. You do not have to file the January 15, 2008, voucher if you file your 2007 tax return and pay the balance of tax due by January 31, 2008.

If you use a fiscal year. A fiscal year is any year other than the calendar year. If you file using a fiscal year, your first estimated installment is due on or before the 15th day of the fourth month of your fiscal year. The second and third installments are due on or before the 15th day of the sixth and ninth months of your fiscal year with the final installment due by the 15th day of the first month of your next fiscal year.

Farmers and fishermen. Farmers only have to make one installment payment, generally by January 15 of the following year. The payment for 2007 must be made by January 15, 2008, or farmers may file their 2007 returns by March 3, 2008, instead of making an estimated tax payment. To qualify under these rules, a farmer must receive two-thirds of his or her 2006 or 2007 gross income from farming.

Fishermen who expect to receive at least two-thirds of their gross income from fishing pay estimated taxes as farmers do.

27.4 Estimates by Husband and Wife

A married couple may pay joint or separate estimated taxes. The nature of the estimated tax does not control the kind of final return you file.

Where a joint estimated tax is paid but separate tax returns are filed, you and your spouse can decide on how to divide the estimated payments between you. Either one of you can claim the whole amount, or you can agree to divide it in any proportion. If you cannot agree, the IRS will allocate the estimated taxes proportionally according to the percentage of total tax each spouse owes.

If separate estimated taxes are paid, overpayment by one spouse is not applied against an underpayment by the other when separate final returns are filed.

A joint estimated tax may be made by a husband and wife only if they are both citizens or residents of the United States. Both must have the same taxable year. A joint estimate may not be made by a couple who are divorced or legally separated under a decree. If a joint estimate is made and the spouses are divorced or legally separated later in that year, they may divide the joint payments between them under the above rule for spouses who file separately.

Responsibility for paying estimated tax rests upon each spouse individually. Each must pay if individually required by the rules.

If a joint estimated tax is made and one spouse dies, the estate does not continue to make installment payments. The surviving spouse is required to pay the remaining installments unless he or she amends the joint estimate. Amounts paid on the joint estimate may be divided as agreed upon by the spouse and the estate of the deceased. If they do not agree, the IRS will apportion the payments according to the percentage of the total tax owed by each spouse.

27.5 Adjusting Your Payments During the Year

If, during the year, your income, expenses, or exemptions change, refigure your estimated tax liability and adjust your payment schedule as shown in the following Examples. Increasing an installment payment cannot make up for an underpayment in a prior period; *see* Example 2. However, withholdings from pay, pensions, and IRA withdrawals can be allocated equally over all four periods and, thus, withholding increased at the end of the year may be applied to earlier periods.

If taxes paid in the previous installments total more than your revised estimate, you cannot obtain a refund at that time. You must wait until you file your final return showing that a refund is due.

EXAMPLES

1. Smith, who is self-employed, figures that to avoid a penalty for 2007 under the estimated tax rules discussed above, he must make estimated tax installments of $6,000. By April 16, 2007, he pays an installment of $1,500. In June, he amends his estimate, showing a tax of $3,000 instead of $6,000. He refigures the installment schedule by dividing $3,000 by 4, which gives a payment rate of $750 for each period. As he paid $1,500 in April, the $750 overpayment covers his June obligation. By September 17, 2007, he pays $750; by January 15, 2008, he pays $750.

2. In September 2007, Jones finds that his estimated 2007 tax liability should be $25,000 rather than his original estimate of $20,000. He paid $5,000 as his April and June installments ($10,000 total). Under the amended schedule, he should have paid $6,250 per period ($25,000 ÷ 4), $6,250 by April 16 and $6,250 by June 15. Thus, there is a $2,500 underpayment ($12,500 – 10,000) for the first two periods.

   To cover the underpayment of $2,500, which carries over to the third payment period (June 1 through August 31), Jones's installment by September 17 must be at least $8,750 ($6,250 + $2,500). If less than $8,750 is paid, there will be an underpayment for the third payment period, as payments in that period are applied first to the carried-over underpayment of $2,500. If at least $8,750 is paid by September 17, there is no third period underpayment to be carried over, so the required installment for the fourth period (September 1 through December 31), due by January 15, 2008, will be $6,250. Unless an exception *(27.1)* applies, the underpayments for the first two periods will be subject to a penalty.

PART 5

Tax Planning

The chapters in this part will alert you to special tax situations. They will point out tax-saving opportunities and show you how to take advantage of tax-saving ideas and planning strategies.

Chapter 28

Tax Planning Overview

Tax planning is a year-round activity. By planning income and deduction strategies, you may be able to reduce your tax. You may realize capital gain income subject to lower capital gain rates, defer certain income to a later year in which you expect to pay a lower tax, and accelerate deductions to a higher tax year. Tax-free investments are available and, within limits, income splitting with family members may be possible.

This chapter illustrates basic tax-planning strategies. In subsequent chapters, tax-savings plans for homeowners, families, investors, and executives are discussed.

28.1 Tax-Saving Opportunities

The table below highlights some of the tax-saving opportunities discussed in this book.

Table 28-1 Tax-Saving Opportunities

Objective—	*Explanation—*
Realizing long-term capital gains	Long-term capital gains are taxed at lower rates than short-term gains and regular income. *See* Chapter 5 for basic capital gain rules. *See* Chapters 30 and 31 for discussions of special investment situations
Earn qualifying dividends	Qualifying corporate dividends are now subject to the same reduced tax rates as long-term capital gains; *see 4.1.*
Earning tax-free income	You can earn tax-free income by— 1. Investing in tax-exempt securities. However, before you invest, determine whether the tax-free return will exceed the after-tax return of taxed income; *see 30.12.* 2. Taking a position in a company that pays tax-free fringe benefits, such as health and life insurance protection. For a complete discussion of tax-free fringe benefits, *see* Chapter 3. 3. Seeking tax-free education benefits with scholarship arrangements and educational IRAs; *see* Chapter 33. 4. Taking a position overseas to earn excludable foreign earned income; *see* Chapter 36. 5. Investing in Roth IRAs; *see* Chapter 8.
Deferring income	You can defer income to years when you will pay less tax through— 1. Deferred pay plans, which are discussed in Chapter 2. 2. Qualified retirement plans such as 401(k) plans (*see* Chapter 7), Keogh plans (Chapter 41), and traditional IRA and Roth IRA plans (Chapter 8). 3. The year-end planning techniques explained in *28.2.* 4. Transacting installment sales when you sell property; *see 5.21.* 5. Investing in U.S. Savings EE bonds or I-bonds; *see 4.28 and 4.29, 30.14,* and *30.15.*
Income splitting	Through income splitting you divide your income among several persons or taxpaying entities that will pay an aggregate tax lower than the tax that you would pay if you reported all of the income. Although the tax law limits income-splitting opportunities, certain business and family income planning through the use of trusts and custodian accounts can provide tax savings; *see* Chapters 24 and 39.
Tax-free exchanges	You can defer tax on appreciated property by transacting tax-free exchanges as discussed at *6.1* and *31.3*
Buying a personal residence rather than renting	Homeowners are favored by the tax law. 1. Rather than paying rent, buy a home, condominium, or cooperative apartment. You may deduct interest and taxes. When you sell your home, you may avoid tax on gains of up to $250,000 if single and up to $500,000 if married filing jointly; *see* Chapter 29. 2. Homeowners can borrow on their home equity and deduct interest expenses; *see 15.3.*
Take advantage of special personal tax breaks for education	The tax law provides several breaks for education expenses; *see* Chapter 33, which discusses scholarships, grants, tuition plans, savings bond tuition plans, education credits, Coverdell Education Savings Accounts, and student loan interest deduction.
Take advantage of personal tax credits	*See* Chapter 25 for personal tax credits such as the child tax credit, dependent care credit, and adoption credit that can reduce your tax liability.

28.2 When To Defer Income and Accelerate Deductions

Your tax bracket may shift from year to year because of fluctuations in income or expenses. If you expect to pay less tax in the following year than in the current year, consider deferring income and accelerating deductible expenses and losses. Even if you expect your tax bracket to remain the same, you may want to accelerate deductions to reduce tax for the current year or defer income, if possible, to delay the payment of tax.

In planning to defer income and accelerate deductions, watch these tax-rule limitations.

Postponing income. You may not defer salary income by not cashing a paycheck or not taking salary that you have earned and that you can receive without restrictions. Under certain conditions, you may contract with your employer to defer the taxable receipt of current compensation to future years. To defer pay to a future period you must take some risk. You cannot have any control over your deferred pay account. If you are not confident of your employer's ability to pay in the future, you should not defer pay.

Accelerating deductions. In accelerating deductions, there are these limitations: You may not deduct prepaid interest and rent. Prepaid interest must be deducted over the period of the loan. Rentals must also be deducted over the rental period. You can generally deduct prepayments of state income tax, but prepayment should not be made if it would trigger AMT liability; *see 23.2.* Annual subscriptions to professional journals and business magazines can be renewed before the end of the year. If the subscription is for more than a year, you may deduct only the first-year prepayment. The cost of the later subscription must be deducted in the later year. Business and investment expenses charged to credit card accounts are deductible in the year of charge, even though you do not pay your charge account bill until the next year. You can also realize losses by selling business or investment property that has lost value in the year you want to incur the loss.

Planning Reminder

Deferring Business Income

If you are self-employed and are on the cash basis, you can defer income by delaying your billing at the end of the year or extending the time of collection. If you own a closely held corporation, you can time the payment of dividends and bonuses.

Making an extra charitable donation at the end of the year also may provide an added deduction that may lower your tax. You may deduct a charitable gift made by check on the last day of the year, even if the check is not cashed until the new year begins. A credit card donation is deductible in the year of the charge. Charitable donations may be timed to give you the largest possible tax savings. If, toward the end of the year, you find that you need an extra deduction, you may make a deductible donation in late December. Doing so would be especially beneficial if you know that your tax bracket will be lower the following year; *see* Chapter 14 for further planning details.

Also *see* Chapter 13 for claiming the standard deduction and itemizing deductions in alternate years, and Chapter 23 for planning steps when you may be subject to alternative minimum tax.

Deferring interest income to next year. Buying six-month certificates after June 30 can defer interest reporting to the next year. As a general rule, you have to report interest credited to your savings account for 2006, even if the account is a passbook account and you did not present the passbook to have the amount entered. Similarly, interest coupons due and payable in 2006 are taxable on your 2006 return, regardless of when they were presented for collection. For example, a coupon due in December 2006, but presented for payment in 2007, is taxable in 2006. However, there are opportunities to defer interest in the following ways:

1. Buy a savings certificate after June 30 with a maturity of one year or less. Interest is taxable in the next year when the certificate matures, provided that interest is specifically deferred until the following year by the terms of the certificate.

2. Buy Treasury bills that come due next year. 26-week bills bought after June 30 will mature in the next year.

3. Buy Series EE bonds. These bonds may be cashed for their purchase price, plus an increase in their value over stated periods of time. The increase in redemption value is taxed as interest. You may defer the interest income until the year you cash the bond or the year the bond finally matures, whichever is earlier. Income deferral is also available for investments in U.S. "I-bonds"; *see 30.15.*

Planning Reminder

Year-End Securities Sales

If you have realized capital gains during the year and have paper losses, realizing losses can offset the gains plus up to $3,000 of other income. If you previously realized losses and have paper gains, you can selectively realize gains that can be offset by the losses. *See 30.1* and *30.2* for planning securities transactions.

Timing sales of property. A sale is generally taxable in the year title to the property passes to the buyer. Since you can control the year title passes, you can usually defer income realized on the sale to the year in which you will pay less tax. Year-end sales of securities are discussed at *30.1.*

28.3 Earning Over the Thresholds for the Exemption Phaseout and Itemized Deduction Reduction

In figuring the tax cost of earning additional income, consider the phaseout of personal exemptions *(21.12)* or the 3% reduction to itemized deductions *(13.7)*. When extra income, such as from a bonus, a freelance assignment, or a year-end sale of stock, pushes you over the *threshold* for the exemption phaseout or the 3% reduction, or if you already are over the threshold, your taxable income is increased not only by the earnings but also by the amounts disallowed by the phaseout or the 3% reduction. *See 21.12* for an example of how the effective tax rate on earnings is increased by the exemption phaseout.

For the 3% itemized deduction reduction on 2006 returns, the adjusted gross income (AGI) threshold is $150,500, except for married persons filing separately, who are subject to a $75,250 threshold. For the exemption phaseout, the AGI threshold is $150,250 for single persons, $188,150 for heads of household, $225,750 for married persons filing jointly and qualifying widow(er)s, and $112,875 for married persons filing separately.

You can estimate the amount of the increase in the effective rate on the additional income due to the exemption phaseout or 3% itemized deduction reduction by this equation:

$$\text{Increase in effective rate} = \frac{\text{Top bracket} \times \text{disallowed amount}}{\text{Excess income over threshold}}$$

Chapter 29

Tax Savings for Residence Sales

You may avoid tax on gain on the sale of a principal residence if you owned and used it for at least two years during the five-year period ending on the date of sale. If you are single, you may avoid tax on up to $250,000 of gain, $500,000 if you are married and file jointly.

If you used the residence for less than two years, you may avoid tax if you sold because of a change of job location, poor health or unforeseen circumstance; *see 29.4*.

You may not deduct a loss on the sale of a personal residence. Losses on the sale of property devoted to personal use are nondeductible. However, *see 29.9* and *29.10*, which explain under what conditions you may claim a loss deduction on the sale of a residence.

If you rent out a residential property and you or family members also use the residence during the year, rental expenses are subject to the special restrictions discussed at *9.7*.

$250,000/$500,000 Exclusion

Filing Instruction

Reporting Home Sale Gain

If the entire gain on the sale of your principal residence is excludable from income under the rules discussed in *29.1–29.7,* you do not have to report the sale at all on your return. This is true even if you receive a Form 1099-S from the settlement agent showing a sales price exceeding the maximum $250,000/$500,000 exclusion. So long as your allowable exclusion equals or exceeds your gain, the sale does not have to be reported, regardless of the sales price.

If you have any gain that cannot be excluded, or you decide not to claim the exclusion for excludable gain, you must report the entire gain on Schedule D. If some of the gain is excludable, the exclusion is entered as a loss, reducing the reported gain. For example, if you have a gain of $650,000 and qualify for the maximum $500,000 exclusion on a joint return, the details of the sale would be reported on Line 8 of Schedule D. Directly below the $650,000 gain shown in column (f) of Line 8, you would subtract the $500,000 exclusion as if it were a loss; label it "Section 121 exclusion."

Planning Reminder

Form 1099-S

The settlement agent responsible for closing the sale of your principal residence must report the sale to the IRS on Form 1099-S if the sales price exceeded $250,000, or $500,000 if you are married filing jointly. If the price was $250,000/$500,000 or less and you provide a written, signed certification that the full amount of your gain qualifies for the exclusion, the settlement agent may rely on the certification and not file the Form 1099-S or may choose to file the form anyway. IRS Revenue Procedure 98-20 has a sample certification form.

29.1 Avoiding Tax on Sale of Principal Residence

If you sell (or exchange) your principal residence at a gain *(29.5),* up to $250,000 of the gain may be excluded from income if you owned and occupied it as a principal residence for an aggregate of at least two years in the five-year period ending on the date of sale and did not claim an exclusion on another sale within the prior two years. *See 29.2* for the two-out-of-five-year ownership and use tests. If you are married filing jointly, you may be able to exclude up to $500,000 of gain; *see 29.3.* Even if you do not meet the two-out-of-five-year ownership and use tests, you are entitled to a reduced maximum exclusion limit if the primary reason for your sale was a change in the place of employment, health reasons, or unforeseen circumstances; *see 29.4.*

Frequency of exclusion. If you meet the ownership and use tests for a principal residence *(see 29.2),* you may claim the exclusion when you sell it although you previously claimed the exclusion for another residence, provided that the sales are more than two years apart. If you claim the exclusion on a sale and within two years of the first sale you sell another principal residence, an exclusion may not be claimed on the second sale even if you meet the ownership and use tests for that residence. There is an exception if the second sale was due to a change in employment, health reasons, or unforeseen circumstances. In that case, a prorated exclusion limit is allowed; *see 29.4.*

Principal residence. A principal residence is not restricted to one-family houses but includes a mobile home, trailer, houseboat, and condominium apartment used as a principal residence. An investment in a retirement community does not qualify as a principal residence unless you receive equity in the property. In the case of a tenant-stockholder of a cooperative housing corporation, the residence ownership requirement applies to the ownership of the stock and the use requirement applies to the house or apartment that the stockholder occupies; *see 29.2.*

Multiple homes. If you have more than one home, you may exclude gain only on the sale of your principal residence and only if you meet the ownership and use tests *(see 29.2)* for that residence. Your "principal residence" is determined on a year-to-year basis, based primarily on where you live most of the time. However, the IRS may also consider such factors as the primary residence of your family members, your place of employment, mailing address, the address listed on your tax returns, driver's license and automobile and voter registration, and the location of your bank.

Vacant land. Vacant land owned and used as part of a taxpayer's principal residence may qualify for the exclusion. The vacant land must be adjacent to the residence and the sale of the residence must be within two years before or after the sale of the land. Qualifying sales of land and residence are treated as one sale, so the $250,000 exclusion limit ($500,000 for qualifying joint filers) applies to the combined sales. If the sales occur in different years, the exclusion limit applies first to the residence sale.

Business or rental use. If part of your home was rented out or used for business, *see 29.7.*

Home destroyed or condemned. If your home is destroyed or condemned, any gain realized on the conversion may qualify for the exclusion. Any part of the gain that may not be excluded (because it exceeds the limit) may be postponed under the rules explained in *18.19.*

Sale of remainder interest. You may choose to exclude gain from the sale of a remainder interest in your home. If you do, you may not choose to exclude gain from your sale of any other interest in the home that you sell separately. Also, you may not exclude gain from the sale of a remainder interest to a related party. Related parties include your brothers and sisters, half-brothers and half-sisters, spouse, ancestors (parents, grandparents, etc.), and lineal descendents (children, grandchildren, etc.). Related parties also include certain corporations, partnerships, trusts, and exempt organizations.

Expatriates. You may not claim the exclusion if Section 877(a)(1) of the Internal Revenue Code applies to you. That section applies to U.S. citizens who have renounced their citizenship (and long-term residents who have ended their residency) if one of their principal purposes was to avoid U.S. taxes.

The exclusion is not mandatory. You do not have to apply the exclusion to a particular qualifying sale. For example, you are unable to sell a residence when you acquire a new residence. When you finally are able to find a buyer for the first home, you also decide to sell the second residence. Assume both sales may qualify for the exclusion, but the potential gain on the first house will be less than the potential gain on the sale of the second home. You will not want to apply the exclusion to the sale of the first home if doing so will prevent you from applying the exclusion to the second sale because of the rule allowing an exclusion for only one sale every two years.

Federal subsidy recapture. If your home was financed with the proceeds of a tax-exempt bond or a qualified mortgage credit certificate *(15.1)* and you sell or dispose of the home within nine years of the financing, you may have to recapture the federal subsidy received. Use Form 8828 to figure the amount of the recapture tax, which is reported on Form 1040 as a separate tax.

29.2 Meeting the Ownership and Use Tests

To qualify for the up-to-$250,000 exclusion, you must have owned and occupied a home as your principal residence for at least two years during the five-year period ending on the date of sale. The periods of ownership and use do not have to be continuous. The ownership and use tests may be met in different two-year periods, provided both tests are met during the five-year period ending on the date of sale. You qualify if you can show that you owned the home and lived in it as your principal residence for 24 full months or for 730 days (365 × 2) during the five-year period ending on the date of sale. If you or your spouse serve on qualified official extended duty as a member of the uniformed services or Foreign Service of the United States, you can suspend the five-year test period for the years of qualified service; *see* below.

If you are a joint owner of the residence and file a separate return, the up-to-$250,000 exclusions applies to your share of the gain, assuming you meet the ownership and use tests.

If you are married and file a joint return, you may claim an exclusion of up to $500,000 if one of you meets the ownership test and both of you meet the use test; *see 29.3*.

If the ownership and use tests are *not* met but the primary reason for the sale was a change in the place of employment, health reasons, or unforeseen circumstances, an exclusion is allowed under the reduced maximum exclusion rules in *29.4*.

In counting the period of ownership and use of a residence that you bought as a replacement residence under the prior law rollover rules, you may include the ownership and use of all the prior residences bought under the rollover rules.

Even if the ownership and use tests are met, the exclusion is not allowed for a sale if within the two-year period ending on the date of sale, you sold another principal residence for which you claimed the exclusion. However, a reduced exclusion limit may be available under the rules at *29.4*.

Filing Tip

Short Absences

Short temporary absences for vacations count as time you used the residence. This is true even if you rent out your residence during the vacation period.

EXAMPLES

1. From 1999 through August 2006, Janet lived with her parents in a house that her parents owned. In September 2006, she bought this house from her parents. She continued to live there until December 15, 2006, when she sold it at a gain. Although Janet lived in the home for more than two years, she did not own it for at least two years. She may not exclude any part of her gain on the sale, unless she sold because of a change in her place of employment, health reasons, or unforeseen circumstances as discussed in *29.4*.
2. John bought and moved into a house in January 2004. He lived in it as his principal residence continuously until October 1, 2005, when he went abroad for a one-year sabbatical leave. On October 1, 2006, he sold the house. He does not meet the two-year use test. Because his leave was not a short, temporary absence, he may not include the period of leave in his period of use in order to meet the two-year use test. He may avoid tax on gain if he sold because of a changed job location unforeseen circumstances, or poor health; *see 29.4*.
3. Since 1991, Jonah lived in an apartment building that was changed to a condominium. He bought the apartment on December 1, 2002. In 2004, he became ill and on April 14 of that year he moved to his son's home. On July 10, 2006 while still living there, he sold the apartment.

Caution

Residence Acquired in Like-Kind Exchange

A residence acquired in a like-kind exchange must be owned for at least five years before gain on its sale can qualify for the exclusion. The five-year ownership requirement applies to sales after October 22, 2004.

He may exclude gain on the sale because he met the ownership and use tests. The five-year period is from July 11, 2001, to July 10, 2006, the date of the sale of the apartment. He owned the apartment from December 1, 2002, to July 10, 2006 (over two years). He lived in the apartment from July 11, 2001 (the beginning of the five-year period) to April 14, 2004, a period of use of over two years.

4. On May 30, 2000, Amy moved into a home she bought and she lived in it until May 31, 2002, when she moved and put it up for rent. The house was rented from June 1, 2002, to March 31, 2004. Amy moved back into the house on April 1, 2004, and lived there until she sold it on January 31, 2006. During the five-year period ending on the date of the sale (February 1, 2001–January 31, 2006), Amy owned and lived in the house for 38 months, more than the two-year period (24 months) required for the exclusion.

Five-year period—	*Home use (months)—*	*Rental use (months)—*
2/1/01–5/31/02	16	
6/1/02–3/31/04		22
4/1/04–1/31/06	22	
Total	38	22

Since she met the ownership and use tests, Amy may exclude gain up to $250,000 on the January 31, 2006, sale.

5. In 1996, Carol bought a house and lived in it until January 31, 2003, when she moved and put it up for rent. The house was rented from February 1, 2003, until May 31, 2006. Carol moved back into the house on June 1, 2006, and lived there until she sold it on September 30, 2006. During the five-year period ending on the date of the sale (October 1, 2001 – September 30, 2006), Carol lived in the house for less than two years.

Five-year period—	*Home use (months)—*	*Rental use (months)—*
10/1/01–1/31/03	16	
2/1/03–5/31/06		40
6/1/06–9/30/06	4	
Total	20	40

Carol may not exclude any of the gain on the sale, unless she sold the house for health or employment reasons or due to unforeseen circumstances; *see 29.4.*

Military and Foreign Service personnel can suspend five-year period. You may elect to suspend the running of the five-year ownership and use period while you or your spouse is on qualified official extended duty as a member of the uniformed services or Foreign Service of the United States. The suspension can be for up to 10 years. It is allowed for only one residence at a time. By making the election and disregarding up to 10 years of qualifying service, you can claim an exclusion where the two-year use test is met before you began the qualifying service and after your return; *see* the Example below. Qualifying service means active duty for over 90 days or for an indefinite period with a branch of the U.S. Armed Forces at a duty station at least 50 miles from your principal residence or in Government-mandated quarters. Members of the Foreign Service, commissioned corps of the National Oceanic and Atmospheric Administration, and commissioned corps of the Public Health Service who meet the active duty tests also qualify.

The law authorizing the suspension rule was enacted in November 2003 but it applies retroactively, so you may be able to file for a refund on an amended return for a sale that did not qualify for an exclusion under the regular two-out-of-five-year test. The refund claim must be filed within the time limits at *47.2* so it is generally too late to file a refund claim for a sale before 2003.

EXAMPLE

Michael bought a home in Maryland in 1996 that he lived in for three years before moving to Brazil in November 1999 as a member of the Foreign Service of the United States. He serves there on qualified official extended duty for eight years, until the end of 2007. In January 2008, he sells the Maryland home at a gain. He did not use the home as his principal residence for two out of the five years preceding the sale and so does not qualify for an exclusion under the regular rule. However, Michael can exclude gain of up to $250,000 by electing to suspend the running of the five-year test period while he was abroad with the

Foreign Service. Under the election, his eight years of service are disregarded and his three years of use from 1996—1999 are considered to be within the five-year period preceding the sale. He thus meets the two-out-of-five-year test and can claim the exclusion.

Cooperative apartments. If you sell your stock in a cooperative housing corporation, you meet the ownership and use tests if, during the five-year period ending on the date of sale, you:

1. Owned stock for at least two years, *and*
2. Used the house or apartment that the stock entitles you to occupy as your principal residence for at least two years.

Incapacitated homeowner. A homeowner who becomes physically or mentally incapable of self-care is deemed to use a residence as a principal residence during the time in which the individual owns the residence and resides in a licensed care facility. For this rule to apply, the homeowner must have owned and used the residence as a principal residence for an aggregate period of at least one year during the five years preceding the sale.

If you meet this disability exception, you still have to meet the two-out-of-five-year ownership test to claim the exclusion.

Previous home destroyed or condemned. For the ownership and use tests, you may add time you owned and lived in a previous home that was destroyed or condemned if any part of the basis of the current home sold depended on the basis of the destroyed or condemned home under the involuntary conversion rules; *see 18.19.*

29.3 Home Sales by Married Persons

Where a married couple owned and lived in their principal residence for at least two years during the five-year period ending on the date of sale, they may claim an exclusion of up to $500,000 of gain on a joint return.

Under the law, the up-to-$500,000 exclusion may be claimed on a joint return provided that during the five-year period ending on the date of sale: (1) *either* spouse owned the residence for at least two years, (2) *both* spouses lived in the house as their principal residence for at least two years, and (3) *neither* spouse is ineligible to claim the exclusion because an exclusion was previously claimed on a sale of a principal residence within the two-year period ending on the date of this sale. If Tests 1 and 3 are met but only one of you meets Test 2, your exclusion limit on a joint return is $250,000.

Caution

Exclusion for Married Couple

For a recently married couple, the exclusion limit on a joint return is $250,000, not $500,000, where only one of the spouses has satisfied the ownership and use tests before a sale. Gain in excess of the $250,000 exclusion is reported on Schedule D; *see* the Filing Instruction on page 494.

EXAMPLES

1. You and your wife owned and occupied your principal residence for 10 years. In December 2006, you sell the house for a gain of $450,000. If you file jointly, none of the gain is taxable as the up-to-$500,000 exclusion applies.
2. As a widower, you used and owned your principal residence from June 2002 through the end of 2005. In January 2006 you remarried and you and your wife lived in the house for nine months. In October 2006, you sold the house and realized a gain of $350,000. You may claim an exclusion of $250,000 on your joint return; the balance of $100,000 is taxable. You meet the exclusion tests, but your wife does not. Thus, the exclusion is limited to $250,000.

Death of spouse before sale. If your spouse died before the date of sale, you are considered to have owned and used the property during any period of time when your spouse owned and used it as a principal home. This rule can enable you to satisfy the two-out-of-five-year ownership and use tests.

However, since the year of your spouse's death is the last year for which you may file a joint return, the sale must be completed by the end of that year to qualify for the up-to-$500,000 exclusion limit. If your spouse died late in the year and you do not complete a sale of the home until the following year, your exclusion limit is $250,000.

Divorce. If a residence is transferred to a taxpayer incident to divorce, the time during which the taxpayer's spouse or former spouse owned the residence is added to the taxpayer's period of ownership. If pursuant to a divorce or separation a taxpayer moves out of a home that he or she owns or jointly owns with the other spouse (or former spouse), the taxpayer who has moved out is treated as having used the home for any period that he/she retains an ownership interest in the residence while the other spouse or former spouse continues to use it as a principal residence under the terms of the divorce or separation agreement.

Separate residences. Where a husband and wife own and live in separate residences, each spouse is entitled to a separate exclusion limit of $250,000 on the sale of his or her residence. If both residences are sold in the same year and each spouse met the ownership and use test for his or her separate residence, two exclusions may be claimed (up to $250,000 each), either on a joint return or on separate returns.

29.4 Reduced Maximum Exclusion

Generally, no exclusion is allowed on a sale of a principal residence if you owned or used the home for less than two of the five years preceding the sale; *see 29.2.* Similarly, an exclusion is generally disallowed if within the two-year period ending on the date of sale, you sold another home at a gain that was wholly or partially excluded from your income.

However, even if a sale of a principal residence is made before meeting the ownership and use tests or it is within two years of a prior sale for which an exclusion was claimed, an exclusion is available if the primary reason for the sale is: (1) a change in the place of employment, (2) health, or (3) unforeseen circumstances. If the sale is for one of these qualifying reasons, you are entitled to a prorated portion of the regular $250,000 or $500,000 exclusion limit. The employment change, health problem, or unforeseen circumstance can be attributable to you or another "qualified individual," as defined below.

You automatically qualify for the reduced exclusion if your sale is within a safe harbor established by the IRS. If a safe harbor is not available, you may qualify by showing that the "facts and circumstances" of your situation establish that the primary reason for the sale was a change in the place of employment, health problem or unforeseen circumstances.

When you fall within a safe harbor or meet the primary reason test, you are allowed an allocable percentage of the regular $250,000 or $500,000 exclusion limit, depending on how much of the regular two-year ownership and use test was satisfied, or the time between this sale and a sale within the prior two years. For example, if you owned and lived in your home for 438 days before selling it to take a new job, you are entitled to 60% of the regular exclusion limit, which is based on 730 qualifying days (438/730 = 60%). Use the worksheet at the end of this section to figure your reduced exclusion limit. Although the maximum exclusion is reduced, this may not disadvantage you. If the reduced exclusion limit equals or exceeds your gain, none of your gain is subject to tax.

Qualified individual. In addition to yourself, the following persons are considered qualified individuals for purposes of qualifying for the reduced maximum exclusion: your spouse, a co-owner of the residence, or any person whose main home was your principal residence.

For purposes of the "health reasons" category, qualified individuals include not only the above individuals but also their family members: parents or step-parents, grandparents, children, stepchildren, adopted children, grandchildren, siblings (including step- or half-siblings), in-laws (mother/father, brother/sister, son/daughter), uncles, aunts, nephews, or nieces.

EXAMPLE

You bought and moved into your residence on April 1, 2005. In 2006, you move to a new job location in another state and sell your house at a gain of $50,000 on March 31, 2006. Since you owned and used your home for 365 days, your exclusion limit is reduced by 50%. You are single. Your reduced exclusion limit is $125,000 (50% of $250,000) and since the gain of $50,000 is totally covered by the exclusion it is not taxable.

IRS Alert

Amended Return to Claim Reduced Maximum Exclusion

The reduced maximum exclusion rules in *29.4* reflect IRS regulations that generally apply to sales after August 12, 2004, but an election can be made to apply the rules retroactively to earlier sales. If you reported gain on a sale that can be avoided under the reduced maximum exclusion rules for sales due to a change in place of employment, health, or unforeseen circumstances, a refund claim can be made on an amended return, provided the prior year is not closed by the statute of limitations; *see 47.2.*

Sale due to change in place of employment. The reduced exclusion limit applies if the primary reason for your sale is a change in the location of a qualified individual's employment; *see* the above definition of qualified individual. "Employment" includes working for the same employer at a different location or starting with a new employer. It also includes the commencement of self-employment or the continuation of self-employment at a new location.

The IRS provides a safe harbor based on distance. If a qualified individual's new place of employment is at least 50 miles farther from the sold home than the old place of employment was, the reduced exclusion limit is allowed so long as the change in employment occurred while you owned and used the home as your principal residence. If an unemployed qualified person obtains employment, the safe harbor applies if the sold home is at least 50 miles from the place of employment.

If the 50-mile safe harbor cannot be met, the facts and circumstances may indicate that a change in the place of employment was the primary reason for the sale, thereby allowing the reduced exclusion limit.

EXAMPLE

An emergency room physician buys a condominium in March 2005 that is five miles from the hospital where she works. In November 2006, she takes a new job at a hospital 51 miles away from her home. She sells her home and buys a townhouse that is four miles away from the new hospital. The sale does not qualify for the 50-mile safe harbor since the new hospital is only 46 miles further from the old home than the first hospital was. However, given the doctor's need to work unscheduled hours and to get to work quickly, the IRS allows the reduced exclusion limit; the facts show that her change in place of employment was the primary reason for the home sale.

Sale due to health problems. The reduced exclusion limit applies if a principal residence is sold primarily to obtain or facilitate the diagnosis, treatment, or mitigation of a qualified person's disease, illness or injury, or to obtain or provide medical or personal care for a qualified individual suffering from a disease, illness, or injury. A sale does not qualify if it is merely to improve general health. Note that for "health sales," the definition of qualified individual is broadened to include family members; *see* above.

A physician's recommendation of a change in residence for health reasons automatically qualifies under an IRS safe harbor.

EXAMPLES

1. One year after purchasing a home in Michigan, Smith is told by his doctor that moving to a warm, dry climate would mitigate his chronic asthma symptoms. Smith takes the advice, selling the house and moving to Arizona. The sale is within the doctor recommendation safe harbor and Smith may claim a reduced maximum exclusion for gain on the sale of the Michigan home.
2. In 2005, Mike and Kathy Anderson sell the house they bought in 2004 so they can move in with Kathy's father, who is chronically ill and unable to care for himself. The IRS allows the Andersons to claim a reduced maximum exclusion, as the primary reason for the sale is to provide care for Kathy's father, a qualified individual.

Sale due to unforeseen circumstances. A sale of a principal residence due to any of the following events fits within an IRS safe harbor for unforeseen circumstances and automatically qualifies for a reduced maximum exclusion:

(1) The involuntary conversion of the home;

(2) Damage to the residence from a natural or man-made disaster, war, or act of terrorism;

(3) Any of the following events involving a qualified individual (*see* above): death, divorce, or legal separation, becoming eligible for unemployment compensation, or change in employment or self-employment status that left the homeowner unable to pay housing costs and reasonable basic household expenses, or multiple births resulting from the same pregnancy.

The IRS may expand the list of safe harbors in generally applicable revenue rulings or in private rulings requested by individual taxpayers.

Sales not covered by a safe harbor can qualify if the facts and circumstances indicate that the home was sold primarily because of an event that could not have been reasonably anticipated before the residence was purchased and occupied. However, an improvement in financial circumstances does *not* qualify even if the improvement is the result of unforeseen events, such as receiving a promotion and a large salary increase.

Filing Tip

Jointly Owned Home

If you and your spouse sell your jointly owned home and file a joint return, you figure your gain or loss as one taxpayer. If you file separate returns, each of you must figure your own gain or loss according to your ownership interest in the home. Your ownership interest is determined by state law.

If you and a joint owner other than your spouse sell your jointly owned home, each of you must figure your own gain or loss according to your ownership interest in the home.

EXAMPLES

1. Three months after Jones buys a condominium as his principal residence, the condominium association replaces the roof and heating system and a few months later the monthly condominium fees are doubled. If Jones sells the condo because he cannot pay the higher fees and his monthly mortgage payment, the sale is considered to be due to unforeseen circumstances and Jones may claim a reduced maximum exclusion.
2. Tom and his fiancée, Alice, buy a house and live in it as their principal residence. The next year they break up and Tom moves out. The house is sold because Alice cannot afford to make the monthly payments alone. According to the IRS, the sale is due to unforeseen circumstances and Alice and Tom may each claim a reduced maximum exclusion.
3. A married couple purchased a home in a retirement community that had minimum age requirements for residents. Shortly after they moved in, their daughter lost her job and was in the process of getting a divorce. The daughter and her child wanted to move in but could not because of the community's age requirements. The couple sold the home and bought a new one in which their daughter and grandchild lived while the daughter looked for full-time employment. The IRS privately ruled that the sale of the retirement community home was due to unforeseen circumstances and the reduced maximum exclusion could be claimed.

Worksheet — **Reduced Maximum Exclusion**

Caution: *Complete this worksheet only if you qualify for a reduced maximum exclusion (under the rules at 29.4). Complete column (B) only if you are married filing a joint return.*		(A) **You**	(B) **Your Spouse**
1. Maximum amount	**1.**	$250,000.00	$250,000.00
2a. Enter the number of days (or months) that you used the property as a main home during the 5-year period* ending on the date of sale. (If married filing jointly, fill in columns (A) and (B))	**2a.**		
b. Enter the number of days (or months) that you owned the property during the 5-year period* ending on the date of sale. If you used days on line 2a, you must also use days on this line and on lines 3 and 5. If you used months on line 2a, you must also use months on this line and on lines 3 and 5. (If married filing jointly and one spouse owned the property longer than the other spouse, both spouses are treated as owning the property for the longer period)	**b.**		
c. Enter the smaller of line 2a or 2b	**c.**		
3. Have you (or your spouse, if filing jointly) excluded gain from the sale of another home during the 2-year period ending on the date of this sale? **NO.** Skip line 3 and enter the number of days (or months) from line 2c on line 4. **YES.** Enter the number of days (or months) between the date of the most recent sale of another home on which you excluded gain and the date of sale of this home	**3.**		
4. Enter the smaller of line 2c or 3	**4.**		
5. Divide the amount on line 4 by 730 days (or 24 months). Enter the result as a decimal (rounded to at least 3 places). But do not enter an amount greater than 1.000	**5.**		
6. Multiply the amount on line 1 by the decimal amount on line 5	**6.**		
7. Add the amounts in columns (A) and (B) of line 6. This is your **reduced maximum exclusion**. Enter it here and on *Worksheet 2*, line 8 (see page 503)	**7.**		

***If you or your spouse was a member of the uniformed services or Foreign Service during the time you owned the home,** *see 29.2*, **to determine your five-year period.**

29.5 Figuring Gain or Loss

To figure the gain or loss on the sale of your principal residence, you must determine the *selling price*, the *amount realized*, and the *adjusted basis*. Worksheet 2 on page 503 may be used to figure gain or loss on the sale of a principal residence.

Gain or loss. The difference between the amount realized and adjusted basis is your gain or loss. If the amount realized exceeds the adjusted basis, the difference is a gain that may be excluded under the rules at *29.1*. If amount realized is less than adjusted basis, the difference is a loss. A loss on the sale of your main home may not be deducted; *see 29.8*.

Foreclosure or repossession. If your home was foreclosed on or repossessed, you have a sale. *See* Chapter 31.

Selling price. This is the total amount received for your home. It includes money, all notes, mortgages, or other debts assumed by the buyer as part of the sale, and the fair market value of any other property or any services received. The selling price does not include receipts for personal property sold with your home. Personal property is property that is not a permanent part of the home, such as furniture, draperies, and lawn equipment.

If your employer pays you for a loss on the sale or for your selling expenses, do not include the payment as part of the selling price. Include the payment as wages on Line 7 of Form 1040. (Your employer includes the payment with the rest of your wages in Box 1 of your Form W-2.)

If you grant an option to buy your home and the option is exercised, add the amount received for the option to the selling price of your home. If the option is not exercised, you report the amount as ordinary income in the year the option expires. Report the amount on Line 21 of Form 1040.

Amount realized. This is the selling price minus selling expenses, including commissions, advertising fees, legal fees, and loan charges paid by the seller (e.g., loan placement fees or "points").

Adjusted basis. This is the cost basis of your home increased by the cost of improvements and decreased by deducted casualty losses, if any, as explained in *29.6*. Cost basis is generally what you paid for the residence. If you obtained possession through other means, such as a gift or inheritance, *see 5.17*.

Seller-paid points. If the person who sold you your residence paid points on your loan, you may have to reduce your basis in the home by the amount of the points. If you bought your residence after 1990 but before April 4, 1994, you reduce basis by the points only if you chose to deduct them as home mortgage interest in the year paid. If you bought the residence after April 3, 1994, you reduce basis by the points even if you did not deduct the points.

Settlement fees or closing costs. When buying your home, you may have to pay settlement fees or closing costs in addition to the contract price of the property. You may include in basis fees and closing costs that are for buying the home. You may not include in your basis the fees and costs of getting a mortgage loan. Settlement fees also do not include amounts placed in escrow for the future payment of items such as taxes and insurance.

Examples of the settlement fees or closing costs that you may include in the basis of your property are: (1) abstract fees (sometimes called abstract of title fees), (2) charges for installing utility services, (3) legal fees (including fees for the title search and preparing the sales contract and deed), (4) recording fees, (5) survey fees, (6) transfer taxes, (7) owner's title insurance, and (8) any amounts the seller owes that you agree to pay, such as certain real estate taxes, back interest, recording or mortgage fees, charges for improvements or repairs, and sales commissions.

Examples of settlement fees and closing costs *not* included in your basis are: (1) fire insurance premiums, (2) rent for occupancy of the home before closing, (3) charges for utilities or other services relating to occupancy of the home before closing, (4) any fee or cost that you deducted as a moving expense before 1994, (5) charges connected with getting a mortgage loan, such as mortgage insurance premiums (including VA funding fees), loan assumption fees, cost of a credit report, and fee for an appraisal required by a lender, and (6) fees for refinancing a mortgage.

Construction. If you contracted to have your residence built on land you own, your basis is the cost of the land plus the cost of building the home, including the cost of labor and materials, payments to a contractor, architect's fees, building permit charges, utility meter and connection charges, and legal fees directly connected with building the home.

Filing Tip

Form 1099-S

If you received Form 1099-S, Box 2 should show the gross proceeds from the sale of your home. However, Box 2 does not include the fair market value of any property other than cash or notes, or any services you received or will receive. For these, Box 4 will be checked. If you certify to the person responsible for closing the sale that your entire gain is excludable from your gross income, that person does not have to report the sale on Form 1099-S, but may choose to do so.

Caution

Repairs

These maintain your home in good condition but do not add to its value or prolong its life. You do not add their cost to the basis of your property. Examples of repairs include repainting your house inside or outside, fixing gutters or floors, repairing leaks or plastering, and replacing broken window panes. *See 9.3* when repairs tied to an improvement project may be capital improvements.

Cooperative apartment. Your basis in the apartment is usually the cost of your stock in the co-op housing corporation, which may include your share of a mortgage on the apartment building.

29.6 Figuring Adjusted Basis

Adjusted basis in your home is cost basis *(29.5)* adjusted for items discussed below. Worksheet 1 on page 503 may be used to figure adjusted basis.

Increases to cost basis include: improvements with a useful life of more than one year, special assessments for local improvements, and amounts spent after a casualty to restore damaged property.

Decreases to cost basis include: gain you postponed from the sale of a previous home before May 7, 1997, deductible casualty losses not covered by insurance, insurance payments you received or expect to receive for casualty losses, payments you received for granting an easement or right-of-way, depreciation allowed or allowable if you used your home for business or rental purposes, any allowable tax credit in 2006 or 2007 for a home energy improvement *(see 25.20)* that increases the basis of the home, residential energy credit (generally allowed from 1977 through 1987) claimed for the cost of energy improvements added to the basis of your home, adoption credit you claimed for improvements added to the basis of your home, nontaxable payments from an adoption assistance program of your employer that you used for improvements added to the basis of your home, first-time homebuyers credit (allowed to certain first-time buyers of a home in the District of Columbia), and an energy conservation subsidy excluded from your gross income because you received it (directly or indirectly) from a public utility after 1992 to buy or install any energy conservation measure. An an energy conservation measure is an installation or modification that is primarily designed either to reduce consumption of electricity or natural gas or to improve the management of energy demand for a home.

Planning Reminder

Gains Postponed Under Prior Law Rules

Gain on a previous home sale that you postponed under the prior law rollover rules reduces the basis of your current home if your current home was a qualifying replacement residence for the previous home. Postponed gains on several earlier sales may have to be taken into account under the basis reduction rule. The basis reduction will increase the gain on the sale of your current home.

Improvements. Improvements add to the value of your home, prolong its useful life, or adapt it to new uses. You add the cost of improvements to the basis of your property.

Examples of improvements include: bedroom, bathroom, deck, garage, porch, and patio additions, landscaping, paving driveway, walkway, fencing, retaining wall, sprinkler system, swimming pool, storm windows and doors, new roof, wiring upgrades, satellite dish, security system, heating system, central air conditioning, furnace, duct work, central humidifier, filtration system, septic system, water heater, soft water system, built-in appliances, kitchen modernization, flooring, wall-to-wall carpeting, attic, walls, and pipes.

Adjusted basis does not include the cost of any improvements that are no longer part of the home.

EXAMPLE

You installed wall-to-wall carpeting in your home 15 years ago. In 2006, you replace that carpeting with new wall-to-wall carpeting.The cost of the old carpeting is no longer part of adjusted basis.

Record-keeping. Ordinarily, you must keep records for three years after the due date for filing your return for the tax year in which you sold your home. But you should keep home records as long as they are needed for tax purposes to prove adjusted basis. These include: (1) proof of the home's purchase price and purchase expenses, (2) receipts and other records for all improvements, additions, and other items that affect the home's adjusted basis, (3) any worksheets you used to figure the adjusted basis of the home you sold, the gain or loss on the sale, the exclusion, and the taxable gain, and (4) any Form 2119 that you filed to postpone gain from a home sale before May 7, 1997.

Filing Tip

Refund Opportunity

If you reported taxable gain allocable to a home office on the sale of a home before 2003 that qualifies for the exclusion, you can file a refund claim (on Form 1040X), provided the statute of limitations for filing an amended return has not expired for the year of sale; *see 47.2.*

29.7 Personal and Business Use of a Home

If you sell a home that was used for business or rental as well as residential purposes, you may be able to exclude part or all of any gain realized on the sale. The excludable amount depends on whether the non-residential and residential areas were part of the same dwelling unit, whether the ownership and use tests *(29.2)* were met, and whether depreciation was claimed after May 6, 1997.

Home office or other non-residential use within the dwelling unit. Gain does not have to be allocated between non-residential and residential use if both the residential and

Worksheet 1. **Adjusted Basis of Home Sold**

1.	Enter the purchase price of the home sold. (If you filed Form 2119 when you originally acquired that home to postpone gain on the sale of a previous home before May 7, 1997, enter the adjusted basis of the new home from that Form 2119.)		**1.** ______
2.	Seller paid points for home bought after 1990. (See 29.5 for *seller-paid points.*) Do not include any seller-paid points you already subtracted to arrive at the amount entered on line 1		**2.** ______
3.	Subtract line 2 from line 1		**3.** ______
4.	Settlement fees or closing costs. If line 1 includes the adjusted basis of the new home from Form 2119, go to line 6.		
a.	Abstract and recording fees	**4a.** ______	
b.	Legal fees (including title search and preparing documents)	**4b.** ______	
c.	Surveys	**4c.** ______	
d.	Title insurance	**4d.** ______	
e.	Transfer or stamp taxes	**4e.** ______	
f.	Amounts that the seller owed that you agreed to pay (back taxes or interest, recording or mortgage fees, and sales commissions)	**4f.** ______	
g.	Other	**4g.** ______	
5.	Add lines 4a through 4g		**5.** ______
6.	Cost of additions and improvements. Do not include any additions and improvements included on line 1		**6.** ______
7.	Special tax assessments paid for local improvements, such as streets and sidewalks		**7.** ______
8.	Other increases to basis		**8.** ______
9.	Add lines 3, 5, 6, 7, and 8		**9.** ______
10.	Depreciation, related to the business use or rental of the home, claimed (or allowable)	**10.** ______	
11.	Other decreases to basis (See *29.6*)	**11.** ______	
12.	Add lines 10 and 11		**12.** ______
13.	**ADJUSTED BASIS OF HOME SOLD**. Subtract line 12 from line 9. Enter here and on *Worksheet 2*, line 4		**13.** ______

Worksheet 2. **Gain (or Loss), Exclusion, and Taxable Gain**

Part 1 – Gain (or Loss) on Sale		
1.	Selling price of home	**1.** ______
2.	Selling expenses	**2.** ______
3.	Subtract line 2 from line 1	**3.** ______
4.	Adjusted basis of home sold (from *Worksheet 1*, line 13)	**4.** ______
5.	Subtract line 4 from line 3. This is the **gain (or loss)** on the sale. If this is a loss, stop here	**5.** ______
Part 2 – Exclusion and Taxable Gain		
6.	Enter any depreciation allowed or allowable on the property for periods after May 6, 1997. If none, enter zero	**6.** ______
7.	Subtract line 6 from line 5. (If the result is less than zero, enter zero.)	**7.** ______
8.	If you qualify to exclude gain on the sale, enter your maximum exclusion. (See *29.2–29.4*.) If you do not qualify to exclude gain, enter -0-	**8.** ______
9.	Enter the smaller of line 7 or line 8. This is your **exclusion**	**9.** ______
10.	Subtract line 9 from line 5. This is your **taxable gain.** Report it on Line 1 or 8 of Schedule D depending on how long you owned the residence. Use Form 6252 if reporting the gain on the settlement sale method (5.21); enter any exclusion from Line 9 on Line 15 of Form 6252. If the amount on this line is zero, do not report the sale or exclusion on your tax return. **If the amount on Line 6 is more than zero, complete Line 11**	**10.** ______
11.	Enter the smaller of line 6 or line 10. Enter this amount on line 12 of the *Unrecaptured Section 1250 Gain Worksheet* in the instructions for Schedule D (Form 1040)	**11.** ______

non-residential portions are within the same dwelling unit. This rule allows a home office to be considered residential property. If the two-out-of-five- year ownership and use test *(29.2)* is met for the residential portion, you are also treated as meeting the two-year residential use test for the home office even if you used the area as a business office for your entire period of ownership. As a result, the gain on the entire residence is eligible for the exclusion, except for the gain allocable to depreciation for periods after May 6, 1997. The gain allocable to post–May 6, 1997, depreciation is never excludable; it must be reported on Schedule D (Form 1040) as unrecaptured Section 1250 gain. *See* Example 1 below.

Business or rental area in separate dwelling unit. If you sell property that was partly your home and partly business or rental property separate from your dwelling unit, and the business/rental use of that separate part exceeded three years during the five-year period ending on the date of the sale, treat the transaction as two sales. This situation could arise if you live in an apartment and rent out other apartments in the same building, you rent out an unattached garage or building elsewhere on your property, your apartment is upstairs from your business, you operate a business from a barn or other structure separate from the residence, or your home is located on a working farm.

Where the business/rental use of the separate part (the garage, barn, or separate apartment) exceeded three years in the five years before the sale, you must treat your sale as if two properties were sold. You must allocate the basis and amount realized between the part used as your home and the separate business/rental part. The gain allocable to the separate business/rental part is taxable and must be reported on Form 4797. The gain allocable to the residence qualifies for the exclusion and does not have to be reported to the IRS, assuming the two-out-of-five-year ownership and use tests for the exclusion were met *(29.2)* and there was no depreciation claimed for periods after May 6, 1997. If depreciation was claimed, gain to the extent of the depreciation is taxable and must be reported on Schedule D. In this case, the total gain is reported on Line 8 of Schedule D as a long-term gain and below it, the exclusion is shown as a loss. The gain attributable to the depreciation is unrecaptured Section 1250 gain, which must be entered on the Unrecaptured Section 1250 Gain Worksheet in the Schedule D instructions.

Even if you did not use the separate part for business/rental purposes for over three years in the five-year period ending on the date of the sale, the IRS requires that you make an allocation and report the gain for the separate part on Form 4797 if there was business/rental use of that separate part in the year of sale. Form 4797 is required although the gain allocable to the separate part qualifies for the exclusion; *see* Example 2 below. If there was no business/rental use of the separate part in the year of sale, you do not have to make an allocation or file Form 4797; *see* Example 3 below.

EXAMPLES

1. Alice Attorney buys a house in 2003 and uses part of it as a law office. Depreciation deductions for the office space totaling $2,000 are claimed for 2003 through 2006, when the home is sold. Assume that gain on the sale is $13,000. Since the office and residential area were in the same dwelling unit, Alice does not have to allocate gain to the office. She may exclude $11,000 of the $13,000 gain from income. The $2,000 of gain attributable to depreciation cannot be excluded. Alice reports her $13,000 gain on Line 8 of Schedule D (long-term gains and losses) and just below it, the $11,000 exclusion is shown as a loss. The $2,000 gain attributable to the depreciation is unrecaptured Section 1250 gain, which Alice enters on the Unrecaptured Section 1250 Gain Worksheet in the Schedule D instructions; *see 5.3.*
2. Thomas Smith buys a three-story townhouse in 2002. At the end of 2004, he converts the basement level, which has a separate entrance, into a separate apartment by installing a kitchen and bathroom and removing the interior stairway leading to the upper floors. In 2005 and 2006, Thomas rents out the basement apartment and uses the top two floors as his principal residence. He claims depreciation deductions totaling $2,000 for the rented apartment. On the sale of the entire property in December 2006, Thomas realizes a gain of $18,000.

   Since the rental apartment was a separate unit from the residence, and there was rental use in the year of sale, Thomas must allocate his basis, selling price, and selling expenses between the residential floors and the rental apartment. Assume that $^2/_3$ is allocable to the residential part and $^1/_3$ to the rental part. The $6,000 gain allocable to the rental part must be reported in Part III of Form 4797. However, since the rental use did not exceed three years in the five years preceding the sale, $4,000 of the gain is excludable: the $6,000 total gain minus the $2,000 of depreciation. The $4,000 exclusion is reported on Line 2 of Form 4797; see the Form 4797 instructions. The $2,000 gain attributable to depreciation is taxable.

The $12,000 of gain allocable to the residential floors is fully excludable under the two-out-of-five-year use test *(29.2)* and Thomas does not have to report it on his tax return.

3. Same facts as in Example 2, except that in December 2006, Thomas incorporates the basement level into his principal residence by removing the kitchen and building a new interior stairway to the upper floors. He then uses all three floors as his principal residence until he sells the townhouse in 2008 or a $20,000 gain. Since he used the entire townhouse as his principal residence for at least two of the five years preceding the sale, his entire gain may be excluded except for the $2,000 attributable to depreciation deductions. Thomas does not have to file Form 4797 because the two-year use test is met for the entire property and there was no rental use in the year of sale. However, Thomas must file Schedule D to report the $2,000 gain attributable to depreciation. On Line 8 of Schedule D he reports the $20,000 gain and just below it, he reports the $18,000 exclusion as a loss. The $2,000 taxable gain from depreciation is entered on the Unrecaptured Section 1250 Gain Worksheet in the Schedule D instructions; *see 5.3.*

Exclusion plus gain deferral on exchange of residence. A home originally used for personal purposes but converted to business or investment use (e.g., rental property) and exchanged for other property held for business or investment use can qualify for both the exclusion and deferral of gain.

EXAMPLE

Tom, who is single, bought a house in 2001 for $210,000 and uses it as his primary residence until 2005, when he converts it to rental property. The house is rented until 2007, when Tom exchanges it for a town house worth $460,000 to be used as rental property, plus cash of $10,000. His depreciation deductions for the 2005–2007 rental period total $20,000. His gain on the exchange is $280,000 ($470,000 amount realized [$460,000 + $10,000] minus $190,000 basis [$210,000 cost – $20,000 depreciation]). Since the house met the two-year ownership and use test prior to sale, Tom can apply the $250,000 exclusion to his gain. And since the house was investment property exchanged for other investment property in a like-kind exchange, the balance of his gain, or $30,000 ($280,000 – $250,000), which includes $20,000 depreciation, can be deferred. The $10,000 cash boot is not taxable because it does not exceed the excluded gain. Tom's basis in the town house is $430,000 ($190,000 basis in the relinquished house, plus the $250,000 of excluded gain and minus the $10,000 cash received).

Caution

Temporary Rental Before Sale

A rental loss may be barred on a temporary rental before sale. The IRS and Tax Court held that where a principal residence was rented for several months while being offered for sale, the rental did not convert the home to rental property. Deductions for rental expenses were limited to rental income; no loss could be claimed. A federal appeals court disagreed and allowed a rental loss deduction; also *see 9.7.*

Selling Your Home at a Loss

29.8 No Loss Allowed on Personal Residence

A loss on the sale of your principal residence is not deductible. If part of your principal residence was used for business in the year of sale, treat the sale as if two pieces of property were sold. Report the business part on Form 4797. A loss is deductible only on the business part.

Second home or vacation home. If you sell at a loss a second home or vacation home (not your principal residence) that was used entirely for personal purposes, you report the loss transaction on Schedule D, even though the loss is not deductible. Instead of entering the loss amount in column (f) of Schedule D, write "Personal Loss." If in the year of sale part of the home was rented out or used for business, allocate the sale between the personal part and the rental or business part; report the personal part on Schedule D and the rental or business part on Form 4797.

29.9 Loss on Residence Converted to Rental Property

You are not allowed to deduct a loss on the sale of your personal residence. If you convert the house from personal use to rental use you may claim a loss on a sale if the value has declined below the basis fixed for the residence as rental property.

To determine if you have a loss for tax purposes, you need to know the conversion date basis. This is the *lower* of (1) your adjusted basis *(29.6)* for the house at the time of conversion or (2) the fair market value at the time of conversion. *Add* to the lower amount the cost of capital improvements made after the conversion, and *subtract* depreciation and casualty loss deductions claimed after the conversion. To deduct a loss, you have to be able to show that this basis exceeds the sales price. For example, if you paid $200,000 for your home and convert it to rental property when the value has declined to $150,000, your conversion date basis for the rental property is $150,000. If the property continues to decline in value, and you sell for $125,000 after having deducted $10,000 for depreciation, you may claim a loss of $15,000 ($140,000 – $125,000). Your loss deduction will not reflect the $50,000 loss occurring before the conversion.

EXAMPLE

In 1988, Adams bought a house in Fort Worth, Texas. He paid $124,000, put in capital improvements, and lived there until he was forced to put it on the market when he lost his job. In 1989, he listed the house with a broker for $145,000. After receiving no offers, he decided to lease the house through 1990. By October of 1990 Adams owed $4,551 in property taxes and was three months behind on his mortgage payments. Fearing foreclosure, he sold the house for $130,000.

For purposes of figuring a loss, Adams assumed that the fair market value at the time of conversion was equal to the $145,000 list price. The adjusted basis of the house was $141,026. As this was less than the estimated fair market value of $145,000, he used the $141,026 adjusted basis to figure a loss of $11,026 ($130,000 – $141,026). The IRS claimed the fair market value at the time of conversion was equal to the actual sale price of $130,000. Since basis for the converted property is the lesser of fair market value ($130,000) or adjusted basis ($141,026), Adams had no loss on the sale.

However, the Tax Court allowed a $5,000 loss by fixing the fair market value at the time of conversion at $135,000. It held that Adams sold at a lower price because of his weak financial position of which the buyer took advantage. The court figured the $135,000 as follows: $129,000 fair market value in 1988 (based on an appraisal report, which both parties agree was correct), plus $6,000 of appreciation attributable to the capital improvements made to the property after it was converted.

Filing Tip

Loss Allowed

If you sell a house that has been converted from personal to rental use, and the sales price is less than the conversion date basis, a loss on the sale is deductible; *see 29.9.*

Partially rented home. If you rented part of your home for over three years during the five years preceding the sale, you must allocate the basis and amount realized between the portion used as your home and the rented portion; *see 29.7.* A loss on a sale is allowable on the rented portion, which is reported on Form 4797.

Profit-making purposes. Renting a residence is a changeover from personal to profit-making purposes. If the house is merely put up for rent or is rented for several months, the IRS may not recognize the house as rental property and may disallow the loss deduction. However, the Tax Court has approved a loss deduction where a house was rented on a 90-day lease with an option to buy. The court set down the following two tests for determining when a house is converted to rental property: (1) the rental charge returns a profit and (2) the lease prevents you from using or reoccupying the house during the lease period. Under the Tax Court approach, you have a conversion to rental property if you have a lease that gives possession of the house to the tenant during the lease period and if the rent, after deducting taxes, interest, insurance, repairs, depreciation, and other charges, returns you a profit.

Loss allowed on house bought for resale. A loss deduction is also allowed where you acquired the house as an investment with the intention of selling it at a profit, even though you occupied it incidentally as a residence prior to sale. For example, an owner bought a house with the intention of selling it. He lived in it for six years, but during that period it was for sale. He was allowed to deduct the loss on its sale by proving he lived in it to protect it from vandalism and to keep it in good condition so that it would attract possible buyers.

In another case, an architect and builder built a house and offered it for sale through an agent and advertisements. He had a home and no intention to occupy the new house. On a realtor's advice, he moved into the house to make it more saleable. Ten months later, he sold the house at a loss of $4,065 and promptly moved out. The loss was allowed on proof that his main purpose in building and occupying the house was to realize a profit by a sale; the residential use was incidental.

Gain on rented residence. You have a gain on the sale of rental property if you sell for more than your adjusted basis at the time of conversion, plus subsequent capital improvements, and minus depreciation and casualty loss deductions. The sale is subject to the rules in Chapter 44 for depreciable property.

Stock in cooperative apartment. Normally, you get no deduction for a loss on the sale of your stock in a cooperative housing corporation. It makes no difference that you occasionally sublet your apartment. It is still not considered property used in a business. But you may get a loss deduction when there were non-stockholder tenants in the cooperative housing corporation when you bought your stock. Then, you get a partial capital loss deduction if you sell your stock or if it becomes worthless. To figure capital loss:

1. First find the difference between your cost and your selling price. This would ordinarily be your capital loss.
2. Then find the percentage of non-stockholding tenants (based on rental values) in the housing corporation when you bought your stock.
3. Apply this percentage to the loss you figured above. This is the capital loss you are allowed.

See 9.5 for when depreciation may be taken on the basis of the cooperative stock ownership.

29.10 Loss on Residence Acquired by Gift or Inheritance

You may deduct a loss on the sale of a house received as an inheritance or gift if you personally did not use it and offered it for sale or rental immediately or within a few weeks after acquisition.

EXAMPLES

1. A couple owned a winter vacation home in Florida. When the husband died, his wife immediately put the house up for sale and never lived in it. It was sold at a loss. The IRS disallowed her capital loss deduction, claiming it was personal and nondeductible. The wife argued that her case was no different from the case of an heir inheriting and selling a home, since at the death of her husband her interest in the property was increased. The Tax Court agreed with her reasoning and allowed the capital loss deduction.
2. A widow inherited a house owned by her late husband and rented out by his estate. Shortly after getting title to the house, she sold it at a loss that she deducted as an ordinary loss. The IRS limited her to a capital loss deduction. The Tax Court agreed. She could not show any business activity. She did not negotiate the lease with the tenant who was in the house when she received title. She never arranged any maintenance or repairs for the building. Moreover, she sold the property shortly after receiving title, which indicates she viewed the house as investment, not rental, property.
3. An inherited residence was rented out by the owner to her brother for $500 a month when the fair market rental value was $700 to $750 per month. When she sold the residence at a loss, the IRS disallowed the loss, and the Tax Court agreed. The below-market rental was treated as evidence that she held the property for personal purposes, not as rental property or as investment property held for appreciation in value.

Planning Reminder

Inherited Residence

If you inherit a residence in which you do not intend to live, it may be advisable to put it up for rent to allow for an ordinary loss deduction on a later sale. If you merely try to sell, and you finally do so at a loss, you are limited to a capital loss.

Chapter 30

Tax Savings for Investors in Securities

You have the opportunity to control the taxable year in which to realize gains and losses. Gains and losses are realized when you sell, and if there are no market pressures, you can time sales to your advantage. To profit from the low 5% or 15% tax rate on long-term capital gains, pay attention to the more-than-one-year holding period for realizing long-term capital gains on the sale of securities. Realizing long-term capital gains will give you tax savings. However, do not overlook the fact that realizing substantial capital gains may subject you to the exemption phaseout and/or 3% reduction of itemized deductions. The 3% reduction increases the effective capital gain rate and, depending on the number of exemptions phased out, the effective rate will be still higher.

The $3,000 limitation ($1,500 if married filing separately) on deducting capital losses from other types of income is a substantial restriction. If you have capital losses exceeding the $3,000 (or $1,500) limit, it is advisable to realize capital gains income that can be offset by the losses.

Security Transactions

Savings Bonds

Traders in Securities

Security Transactions

30.1 Planning Year-End Securities Transactions

First establish your current gain and loss position for the year. List gains and losses already realized from completed transactions. Then review the records of earlier years to find any carryover capital losses. Include nonbusiness bad debts as short-term capital losses. Then review your paper gains and losses and determine what losses might now be realized to offset realized gains or what gains might be realized to be offset by realized losses.

If you have already realized net capital losses exceeding $3,000 ($1,500 if married filing separately), you may want to realize capital gains that will be absorbed by the excess loss. Remember, only up to $3,000 (or $1,500) of capital losses exceeding net capital gain may be deducted from other income such as salary, interest, and dividends. Also, project your tax-bracket ranges in the current and next tax year. For example, assume that you are close to the threshold for the phaseout of exemptions and that realizing substantial gains will place you in the exemption phase-out range *(21.16)*. You may want to defer gain transactions to a year in which you will be in a lower bracket or not subject to the phaseout.

Planning for losses. Realizing losses may pose a problem if you believe the security is due to increase in value sometime in the near future. Although the wash-sale rule *(30.6)* prevents you from taking the loss if you buy 30 days before or after the sale, the following possibilities are open to you.

- If you believe the security will go up, but not immediately, you can sell now, realize your loss, wait 31 days, and then recover your position by repurchasing before the expected rise.
- You can hedge by repurchasing similar securities immediately after the sale provided they are not substantially identical. They can be in the same industry and of the same quality without being considered substantially identical. Check with your broker to see if you can use a loss and still maintain your position. Some brokerage firms maintain recommended "switch" lists and suggest a practice of "doubling up"—that is, buying the stock of the same company and then 31 days later selling the original shares. Doubling up has disadvantages: It requires additional funds for the purchase of the second lot, exposes you to additional risks should the stock price fall, and the new shares take a new holding period.

EXAMPLE

You own 100 shares of Steel Co. stock that cost you $10,000. In November 2006, the stock is selling at $6,000 ($60 a share × 100 shares). You would like to realize the $4,000 loss but, at the same time, you want to hold on to the investment. You buy 100 shares at a market price of $60 a share (total investment $6,000) and 31 days later sell your original 100 shares, realizing the loss of $4,000. You retain your investment in the new lot.

Planning Reminder

December 29 Deadline for 2006 Gains and Losses

If you want to realize gains on publicly traded securities, you have until December 29, 2006, to transact the sale. Gain is reported in 2006, although cash is not received until the settlement date in 2007. If you do not want to realize the gain in 2006, delay the trade date until 2007.

Losses are also realized as of the trade date; a loss on a sale made by December 29, 2006, is reported on your 2006 return.

30.2 Earmarking Stock Lots

Keep a record of all your stock transactions, especially when you buy the stock of one company at varying prices. By keeping a record of each stock lot, you may control the amount of gain or loss on a sale of a part of your holdings. If you do not make an adequate identification, the IRS will treat the shares you bought first as the shares being sold under a first-in, first-out (FIFO) rule. You may *not* average the cost of stock lots; averaging is allowed only for mutual-fund shares *(32.10)*.

If your stock is held by your broker, the IRS considers that an adequate identification is made if you give instructions to your broker about which particular shares are to be sold, and you receive a written confirmation of your instructions from the broker or transfer agent within a reasonable time.

EXAMPLE

Over a three-year period, you bought the following shares of Acme Steel stock: In 1997, 100 shares at $77 per share; in 1998, 200 shares at $84 per share; and in 1999, 100 shares at $105 per share. When the stock is selling at $90, you plan to sell 100 shares. You may use the cost of your 1999 lot and get a $1,500 loss if, for example, you want to offset some gains or other income you have already earned this year. Or you may get capital gains by selling the 1997 lot or part of the 1998 lot.

You must clearly identify the lot you want to sell. Say you want a loss and sell the 1999 lot. Unless you identify it as the lot sold, the IRS will hold that you sold the 1997 lot under the "first-in, first-out" rule. This rule assumes that, when you have a number of identical items that you bought at different times, your sale of any of them is automatically the sale of the first you bought. So the cost of your first purchase is what you match against your selling price to find your gain or loss. Here is what to do to counteract the first-in, first-out rule: If you have stock certificates registered in your name, show that you delivered the 1999 stock certificates. If the broker is holding the stock, specifically identify the 1999 lot in your selling instructions and get a written confirmation. *See 32.10* for averaging cost on the sale of mutual-fund shares.

Table 30-1 How To Identify Securities

If your securities are—	*Identify them by—*
Registered in your own name	The number, your name, and any other identification that they bear.
In a margin account registered in a "street" name	A specified block or security bought on a designated day at a particular price. A mere intention to sell a particular share without informing the broker is without significance.
New certificates received for old in a recapitalization	Record the new certificate with the lowest number as being in exchange for the old certificate with the lowest number. Do this until all the new certificates are matched with all the old.
Shares exchanged for shares in a reorganization	Allocate each of the new certificates to each of the old in your records. Where the exchange involves several blocks of stock and there is no specific identification, the IRS says you must average your costs.
Shares received in a stock split	Match the new certificates with the old ones surrendered. Identifying the securities being sold as the "highest cost" or "lowest cost" stock is insufficient. You have to match at the time of the split-up.
Stock dividends	The lot of stock on which you received the dividend. The new stock is part of the old lot. But if you receive one certificate for more than one lot, you may have to apply the first-in, first-out rule when you sell.
Acquired by exercise of nontaxed stock rights	The number, or other identification, of the lot you receive by exercising the rights. Each lot you so acquire is considered a separate lot received on the date of subscription.

30.3 Sale of Stock Dividends

A sale of stock originally received as a dividend is treated as any other sale of stock. The holding period of a *taxable* stock dividend *(4.8)* begins on the day after the date of distribution. The holding period of a *tax-free* stock dividend or stock received in a *split (4.6)* starts from the time you acquired the original stock.

EXAMPLE

You bought 100 shares of X Co. stock on December 3, 1998. On August 15, 2006, you receive 10 shares of X Co. stock as a tax-free stock dividend. On December 12, 2006, you sell the 10 shares at a profit. You report the sale as long-term capital gain because the holding period of the 10 shares goes back to your original purchase date of December 3, 1998, not August 15, 2006.

Basis of tax-free dividend in the same class of stock. Assume you receive a common stock dividend on common stock. You divide the original cost by the total number of old shares and new shares to find the new basis per share.

EXAMPLE

You bought 100 shares of common stock for $1,000, so that each share has a basis of $10. You receive 100 shares of common stock as a tax-free stock dividend. The basis of your 200 shares remains $1,000. The new cost basis of each share is now $5 ($1,000 ÷ 200 shares). You sell 50 shares for $560. Your profit is $310 ($560 – $250).

Basis of tax-free dividend in a different class of stock. Assume you receive preferred stock dividends on common stock. You divide the basis of the old shares over the two classes in the ratio of their values at the time the stock dividend was distributed.

EXAMPLE

You bought 100 shares of common stock for $1,000. You receive a tax-free dividend of 10 shares of preferred stock. On the date of distribution, the market value of the common stock is $9 a share and that of the preferred stock is $30. That makes the market value of your common stock $900 and your preferred stock $300. So you allocate 75% ($900 ÷ $1,200) of your $1,000 original cost, or $750, to your common stock and 25% ($300 ÷ $1,200) of your cost to the preferred stock.

Basis of taxable stock dividend. The basis of a taxable stock dividend *(4.6)* is its fair market value at the time of the distribution. Its holding period begins on the date of distribution. The basis of the old stock remains unchanged.

EXAMPLE

You bought 1,000 shares of stock for $10,000. The company gives you a choice of a cash dividend or stock (one share for every hundred held). You elect the stock. On the date of the distribution, its market value was $15 a share. The basis of the new stock is $150 (10 × $15), the amount of the taxable dividend. The basis of the old stock remains $10,000.

Planning Reminder

Basis of Public Utility Stock Received Under Dividend Reinvestment Plan

For several years before 1986, an exclusion was allowed for stock dividends received from public utility companies if the dividends were reinvested in stock. If you claimed the exclusion, the stock takes a zero basis. If you sell the stock, the entire sales proceeds of the stock are reported as long-term capital gain.

30.4 Stock Rights

The tax consequences of the receipt of stock rights are discussed at *4.6*. The following is an explanation of how to treat the sale, exercise, or expiration of nontaxable stock rights. The basis of taxable rights is their fair market value at the time of distribution.

Expiration of nontaxable distributed stock rights. When you allow nontaxable rights to expire, you do not have a deductible loss; you have no basis in the rights.

Sale of nontaxable distributed stock rights. If you sell stock rights distributed on your stock, you treat the sale as the sale of a capital asset. The holding period begins from the date you acquired the original stock on which the rights were distributed.

Purchased rights. If you buy stock rights, your holding period starts the day after the date of the purchase. Your basis for the rights is the price paid; this basis is used in computing your capital gain or loss on the sale.

If you allow purchased rights to expire without sale or exercise, you realize a capital loss. The rights are treated as having been sold on the day of expiration. When purchased rights become worthless during the year prior to the year they lapse, you have a capital loss that is treated as having occurred on the last day of the year in which they became worthless.

Figuring the basis of nontaxable stock rights. Whether rights received by you as a stockholder have a basis depends on their fair market value when distributed. If the market value of rights is less than 15% of the market value of your old stock, the basis of your rights is zero, unless you elect to allocate the basis between the rights and your original stock. You make the election on your tax return for the year the rights are received by attaching to your return a statement that you are electing to divide basis. Keep a copy of the election and the return.

Planning Reminder

Exercise of Stock Rights

You realize no taxable income on the exercise of stock rights. Capital gain or loss on the new stock is recognized when you later sell the stock. The holding period of the new stock begins on the date you exercised the rights. Your basis for the new stock is the subscription price you paid plus your basis for the rights exercised.

If the market value of the rights is 15% or more of the market value of your old stock, you must divide the basis of the stock between the old stock and the rights, according to their respective values on the date of distribution.

No basis adjustment is required for stock rights that become worthless during the year of issue.

EXAMPLE

You own 100 shares of M Co. that cost $10 a share. On September 15, there is a distribution of stock rights allowing for the purchase of one additional share of common for each 10 rights held at a price of $13 a share. The common stock is now worth $15 (ex-rights). The rights have a market value of 20¢ each. This is less than 15% of the market value of the stock. You can either: (1) choose not to spread the tax cost of the stock between the old stock and the rights or (2) elect to spread the tax cost as follows:

Cost of your old stock, 100 shares at $10, or $1,000.

Fair market value of old stock, 100 shares at $15, or $1,500.

Market value of 100 rights at 20¢, or $20.

Market value of both old stock and rights, or $1,520.

Apportionment of old stock:

$$\frac{1,500}{1,520} \times 1,000 = 986.84$$

Your new basis of old stock is $986.84 for 100 shares, or $9.87 a share. The tax cost of the rights is then calculated:

$$\frac{20}{1,520} \times 1,000 = \$13.16$$

The basis of the rights is $13.16 for 100 rights.

When you exercise your rights and 10 shares are bought, your basis for the new stock is $130 plus the cost of the rights of $13.16, or $143.16.

If the option of allocation is not exercised, the rights have a basis of zero and the basis of the new stock is $130. The basis of the old stock remains $1,000.

30.5 Short Sales of Stock

A short sale is a sale of stock borrowed from a broker. The short sale is closed when you replace the borrowed stock by buying substantially identical stock and delivering it to the broker or by delivering stock that you held at the time of the short sale. One objective of a short sale is to profit from an anticipated drop in the market price of the stock; another objective may be to use the short sale as a hedge.

Tax rules applied to short sales are designed to prevent you from:

- Postponing gain to a later year when you sell short while holding an appreciated position in the same or substantially identical stock. This type of short sale is called "a sale against the box."
- Converting short-term gains to long-term gains.
- Converting long-term losses to short-term losses.

Year in which gain on short sale is realized. You report gain on a short sale in the year in which you close the short sale by delivering replacement stock, unless you execute a short sale while holding an appreciated position in the same stock (short sale against the box) or substantially identical stock is acquired to close an appreciated short position. In such cases, the short sale or acquisition of substantially identical stock is treated as a constructive sale of an appreciated financial position *(30.8)* and you must report the transaction in the year of the constructive sale, even though delivery of replacement stock is made in a later year; *see* Examples 2 and 3 below. However, there is this exception: The short sale is reported in the year of delivery of the replacement stock if you close the short sale before the end of the 30th day of the next year and continue to hold a similar position in the stock for at least 60 days after the closing of the short sale.

If the stock sold short becomes worthless before you close the short sale, you recognize taxable gain in the year the shares became worthless.

EXAMPLES

1. On May 3, 2006, you buy 100 shares of Auto Corp. stock for $1,000. On September 8, 2006, you borrow 100 shares of Auto Corp. from your broker and sell them short for $1,600. You make no subsequent transactions involving Auto Corp. stock. The short sale is treated as a constructive sale of an appreciated financial position because a sale of your Auto Corp. stock on September 8, the date of the short sale, would have resulted in a gain. You have a $600 short-term capital gain from the constructive sale and you have a new holding period for your Auto Corp. stock that begins on September 8, 2006.
2. In January 2006, you buy 100 shares of Steel Co. stock for $1,000 (100 × $10). In November 2006 when the stock is selling at $50, you execute a short sale of 100 shares (100 × $50 = $5,000). In February 2007, you deliver your shares to close the short sale. The tax law treats the short sale as a constructive sale of an appreciated financial position because a sale of your Steel Co. stock on the date of the short sale would have resulted in a gain. You report the gain of $4,000 ($5,000 – $1,000) in 2006, the year of the short sale, not in 2007 when you close the sale. To shift tax reporting to 2007, you would have had to close the short sale by the 30th of January and obtain similar stock, which you would have had to hold for at least 60 days after the closing of the short sale. Also *see* Example 3 and *30.8* for further details on constructive sales.
3. A taxpayer who does not own any shares of XYZ stock directs his broker in January of Year 1 to sell short borrowed XYZ shares. On December 31 of Year 1, when the value of XYZ shares has decreased, the taxpayer directs the broker to close the short sale by purchasing XYZ shares in a "regular-way" sale, with actual delivery of the shares taking place at the beginning of Year 2. The IRS ruled that the short position is an appreciated financial position as of December 31, given the decrease in the stock price since the short sale. The purchase of replacement shares on December 31 is a constructive sale of the appreciated position. Gain is taxable in Year 1, not in Year 2 when the shares were delivered.

Short-term or long-term gain or loss. Whether you have short-term or long-term capital gain or loss generally depends on your holding period for the property delivered to the broker to close the short sale. Furthermore, you must apply Rules 1 and 2 below if you answer "yes" to either of the following questions:

1. When you sold short, did you or your spouse hold for one year or less securities substantially identical to the securities sold short? (Substantially identical securities are described at *30.6*.)
2. After the short sale, did you or your spouse acquire substantially identical securities on or before the date of the closing of the short sale?

Rule 1. Gain realized on the closing of the short sale is short term. The gain is short term regardless of the period of time you have held the securities as of the closing date of the short sale.

Rule 2. The beginning date of the holding period of substantially identical stock is suspended. The holding period of substantially identical securities owned or bought under the facts of question (1) or (2) does not begin until the date of the closing of the short sale (or the date of the sale, gift, or other disposition of the securities, whichever date occurs first). But note that this rule applies only to the number of securities that do not exceed the quantity sold short.

Losses. A loss on a short sale is not deductible until shares closing the short sale are delivered to the broker. You may not realize a short-term loss on the closing of a short sale if you held substantially identical securities long term (that is, for more than a year) on the date of the short sale. The loss is long term even if the securities used to close the sale were held for one year or less. This rule prevents you from creating short-term losses when you held the covering stock long term. Loss deductions on short sales may be disallowed under the wash-sale rules in *30.6*.

EXAMPLES

1. On February 6, 2006, the stock of Oil Co., which you do not own, is selling at $90 per share. You expect the price to fall over the next year and sell short 500 shares borrowed from your broker for $45,000 (500 × $ 90). However, 13 months later, on March 9, 2007, after the price has risen to $110, you close the short sale by buying 500 shares of Oil Co. stock ($500 × $110 = $55,000 cost) and immediately delivering them to your broker. Your loss of $10,000 ($55,000 – $45,000) is treated as a short-term capital loss because your holding period for the delivered stock is less than one day.

Planning Reminder

Puts

The acquisition of a *put* (an option to sell) is treated as a short sale if you hold substantially identical securities short term at the time you buy the put. If you have held the underlying stock for one year or less at the time you buy the put, any gain on the exercise, sale, or expiration of the put is a short-term capital gain. The same is true if you buy the underlying stock after you buy the put but before its exercise, sale, or expiration. Your holding period for the underlying stock begins on the earliest of: (1) the date you dispose of the stock; (2) the date you exercise the put; (3) the date you sell the put; or (4) the date the put expires. However, the short-sale rules do not apply if on the same day you buy a put and stock that is identified as covered by the put. If you do not exercise the put that is identified with the stock, add its cost to the basis of the stock.

2. On February 6, 2006, you buy 100 shares ofTech Corp. stock for $1,000. On July 12, 2006, you sell short 100 shares ofTech Corp. for $1,600. You close the short sale on November 8, 2006, by buying 100 shares for $1,800 and delivering them to your broker. On the short sale, you realize a $ 200 short-term capital loss.

   On February 9, 2007, you sell for $1,900 your original lot of Tech Corp. stock bought on February 6, 2006. Although you have held these shares for more than one year, the $1,900 gain realized on the sale is treated as a short-term capital gain under Rule 2 above. Rule 2 applies because on the date of the short sale, the February 6 shares were held short term (one year or less). Under Rule 2, the holding period of the February 6 lot is considered to begin on November 8, 2006, the date the short sale was closed.

Expenses of short sales. Before you buy stock to close out a short sale, you pay the broker for dividends paid on stock you have sold short. If you itemize deductions, you may treat your payment as investment interest *(15.10)*, provided the short sale is held open at least 46 days, or more than a year in the case of extraordinary dividends. If the 46-day (or one-year) test is not met, the payment is generally not deductible and is added to basis; in counting the short-sale period, do not count any period during which you have an option to buy or are obligated to buy substantially identical securities, or are protected from the risk of loss from the short sale by a substantially similar position.

Under an exception to the 46-day test, if you receive compensation from the lender of the stock for the use of collateral and you report the compensation as ordinary income, your payment for dividends is deductible to the extent of the compensation; only the excess of your payment over the compensation is disallowed. This exception does not apply to payments with respect to extraordinary dividends.

An extraordinary dividend is generally a dividend that equals or exceeds the amount realized on the short sale by 10% for any common stock or by 5% for any preferred stock dividends. For purposes of this test, dividends on stock received within an 85-day period are aggregated; a one-year aggregation period applies if dividends exceed 20% of the adjusted basis in the stock.

Arbitrage transactions. Special holding period rules apply to short sales involved in identified arbitrage transactions in convertible securities and stock into which the securities are convertible. These rules can be found in Treasury regulations to Internal Revenue Code Section 1233.

30.6 Wash Sales

Planning Reminder

Basis Adjusted for New Stock

Although the loss deduction is barred if the wash-sale rule applies, the economic loss is not forfeited for tax purposes. The loss might be realized at a later date when the repurchased stock is sold, because after the disallowance of the loss, the cost basis of the new lot is fixed as the basis of the old lot and adjusted (up or down) for the difference between the selling price of the old stock and purchase price of the new stock; *see* the Examples in *30.6*.

The objective of the wash-sale rule is to disallow a loss deduction where you recover your market position in a security within a short period of time after the sale. Under the wash-sale rule, your loss deduction is barred if within 30 days of the sale you buy *substantially identical* stock or securities, or a "put" or "call" option on such securities. The wash-sale period is 61 days—running from 30 days before to 30 days after the date of sale. The end of a taxable year during this 61-day period does not affect the wash-sale rule. The loss is still denied. If you sell at a loss and your spouse buys substantially identical stock within this period, the loss is also barred.

The wash-sale rule does not apply to gains. It also does not apply to acquisitions by gift, inheritance, or tax-free exchange.

The wash-sale rule applies to investors and traders. It does not apply to dealers.

EXAMPLES

1. You bought common stock of Appliance Co. for $10,000 in 1993. On June 21, 2006, you sold the stock for $8,000, incurring a $2,000 loss. A week later, you repurchased the same number of shares of Appliance stock for $9,000. Your loss of $2,000 on the sale is disallowed because of the wash-sale rule. The basis of the new lot becomes $11,000. The basis of the old shares ($10,000) is increased by $1,000, which is the excess of the purchase price of the new shares ($9,000) over the selling price of the old shares ($8,000).

2. Assume the same facts as in Example 1, except that you repurchase the stock for $7,000. The basis of the new lot is $9,000. The basis of the old shares ($10,000) is decreased by $1,000, which is the excess of the selling price of the old shares ($8,000) over the purchase price of the new shares ($7,000).

3. Assume that in February 2007 you sell the new lot of stock acquired in Example 1 above for $9,000 and do not run afoul of the wash-sale rule. On the sale, you realize a loss of $2,000 ($11,000 – $9,000).

Loss on the sale of part of a stock lot bought less than 30 days ago. If you buy stock and then, within 30 days, sell some of those shares, a loss on the sale is deductible; the wash-sale disallowance rule does not apply.

EXAMPLE

You buy 200 shares of stock. Within 30 days, you sell 100 shares at a loss. The loss is not disallowed by the wash-sale rule. The wash-sale rule does not apply to a loss sustained in a bona fide sale made to reduce your market position. It does apply when you sustain a loss for tax purposes with the intent of recovering your position in the security within a short period. Thus if, after selling the 100 shares, you repurchase 100 shares of the same stock within 30 days after the sale, the loss is disallowed.

Oral sale-repurchase agreement. The wash-sale rule applies to an oral sale-repurchase agreement between business associates.

Defining "substantially identical." What is substantially identical stock or securities? Buying and selling General Motors stock is dealing in an identical security. Selling General Motors and buying Chrysler stock is not dealing in substantially identical securities.

Bonds of the same obligor are substantially identical if they carry the same rate of interest; that they have different issue dates and interest payment dates will not remove them from the wash-sale provisions. Different maturity dates will have no effect, unless the difference is economically significant. Where there is a long time span between the purchase date and the maturity date, a difference of several years between maturity dates may be considered insignificant. A difference of three years between maturity dates was held to be insignificant where the maturity dates of the bonds, measured from the time of purchase, were 45 and 48 years away. There was no significant difference where the maturity dates differed by less than one year, and the remaining life, measured from the time of purchase, was more than 15 years.

The wash-sale rules do not apply if you buy bonds of the same company with substantially different interest rates, buy bonds of a different company, or buy substantially identical bonds outside of the wash-sale period.

Warrants. A warrant falls within the wash-sale rule if it is an option to buy substantially identical stock. Consequently, a loss on the sale of common stocks of a corporation is disallowed when warrants for the common stock of the same corporation are bought within the period 30 days before or after the sale. But if the timing is reversed—that is, you sell warrants at a loss and simultaneously buy common stock of the same corporation—the wash-sale rules may or may not apply depending on whether the warrants are substantially identical to the purchased stock. This is determined by comparing the relative values of the stock and warrants. The wash-sale rule will apply only if the relative values and price changes are so similar that the warrants become fully convertible securities.

Repurchasing fewer shares. If the number of shares of stock reacquired in a wash sale is less than the amount sold, only a proportionate part of the loss is disallowed.

EXAMPLE

You bought 100 shares of Stock A for $10,000. On December 11, 2006, you sell the lot for $8,000, incurring a loss of $2,000. On January 8, 0007, you repurchase 75 shares of Stock A for $6,000. Three-quarters ($^{75}/_{100}$) of your loss is disallowed, or $1,500 ($^{3}/_{4}$ of $2,000). You deduct the remaining loss of $500 on your return for 2006. The basis of the new shares is $7,500 ($6,000 cost *plus* $1,500 disallowed loss).

Holding period of new stock. After a wash sale, the holding period of the new stock includes the holding period of the old lots. If you sold more than one old lot in wash sales, you add the holding periods of all the old lots to the holding period of the new lot. You do this even if your

Planning Reminder

Tax Advantage of Wash-Sale Rule

Sometimes the wash-sale rule can work to your advantage. Assume that during December you are negotiating a sale of real estate that will bring you a large capital gain. You want to offset a part of that gain by selling certain securities at a loss. You are unsure just when the gain transaction will go through. It may be on the last day of the year, at which point it may be too late to sell the loss securities before the end of the same year.

You can do this: Sell the loss securities during the last week of December. If the profitable deal goes through before the end of the year, you need not do anything further. If it does not, buy back the loss securities early in January. The December sale will be a wash sale and the loss disallowed. When the profitable real estate sale occurs next year, you can sell the loss securities again. This time the loss will be allowed and will offset the gain.

holding periods overlapped as you purchased another lot before you sold the first. You do not count the periods between the sale and purchase when you have no stock.

Losses on short sales. Losses incurred on short sales are subject to the wash-sale rules. A loss on the closing of a short sale is denied if you sell the stock or enter into a second short sale within the period beginning 30 days before and ending 30 days after the closing of the short sale.

30.7 Convertible Stocks and Bonds

You realize no gain or loss when you convert a bond into stock, or preferred stock into common stock of the same corporation, provided the conversion privilege was allowed by the bond or preferred stock certificate.

Holding period. Stock acquired through the conversion of bonds or preferred stock takes the same holding period as the securities exchanged. However, where the new stock is acquired partly for cash and partly by tax-free exchange, each new share of stock has a split holding period. The portion of each new share allocable to the ownership of the converted bonds (or preferred stock) includes the holding period of the bonds (or preferred stock). The portion of the new stock allocable to the cash purchase takes a holding period beginning with the day after acquisition of the stock.

Basis. Securities acquired through the conversion of bonds or preferred stock into common take the same basis as the securities exchanged. Where there is a partial cash payment, the basis of the portion of the stock attributable to the cash is the amount of cash paid; *see* Examples 1 and 2 below.

If you paid a premium for a convertible bond, you may not amortize the amount of the premium that is attributable to the conversion feature.

EXAMPLES

1. On January 5, you paid $100 for a debenture of A Co. Your holding period for the debenture begins on January 6; *see 5.9.* The debenture provides that the holder may receive one share of A Co. common stock upon surrender of one debenture and the payment of $50. On October 19, you convert the debenture to stock on payment of $50. For tax purposes, you realize no gain or loss upon the conversion regardless of whether the fair market value of the stock is more or less than $150 on the date of the conversion. The basis and holding period for the stock is as follows: $100 basis for the portion attributed to the ownership of the debenture with the holding period beginning January 6; and $50 basis attributed to the cash payment with the holding period for this portion beginning October 20.
2. Same facts as in the above Example, but you acquired the debenture on January 5 through the exercise of rights on that date. Since the holding period for the debenture includes the date of exercise of the rights, *see 30.4,* the portion of the stock allocable to the debenture takes a holding period beginning on January 6.

30.8 Constructive Sales of Appreciated Financial Positions

One aspect of a constructive sale of an appreciated financial position was discussed in *30.5,* dealing with short sales. The constructive sale rules apply not only to short sales of stock but also to other transactions such as an appreciated financial position in a partnership interest or certain debt obligations.

You have made a constructive sale of an appreciated financial position if you:

1. Enter into a short sale of the same or substantially identical property,
2. Enter into an offsetting notional principal contract relating to the same or substantially identical property,
3. Enter into a futures or forward contract to deliver the same or substantially identical property, *or*
4. Acquire the same or substantially identical property (if the appreciated financial position is a short sale, an offsetting notional principal contract, or a futures or forward contract).

You are also treated as having made a constructive sale of an appreciated financial position if a person related to you enters into any of the above transactions.

A contract for sale of any stock, debt instrument, or partnership interest that is not a marketable security is not a constructive sale if it settles within one year of the date you enter into it.

Tax treatment. If you are considered to have transacted a constructive sale, you must report as taxable income gain on the financial position as if the position was sold at its fair market value on the date of the constructive sale. The property held by you receives a new holding period starting on the date of the constructive sale and its basis is the fair market value at that date. Thus, under the constructive sale rule you are also treated as immediately repurchasing the position as of the date of the constructive sale.

Caution

Constructive Sales of Appreciated Position

If you are subject to the constructive sale rules, you will have to report income as if you had made a sale although you still hold the position.

Closing a short sale to avoid a constructive sale. You may avoid the constructive sale rule if:

1. You close the transaction before the end of the 30th day after the end of your tax year,
2. You hold the appreciated financial position throughout the 60-day period beginning on the date you close the transaction,
3. Your risk of loss is not reduced at any time during that 60-day period by holding certain other positions.

If a closed transaction is reestablished in a substantially similar position during the 60-day period beginning on the date the first transaction was closed, this exception still applies if the reestablished position is closed before the end of the 30th day after the end of your tax year in which the first transaction was closed and, after that closing, tests (2) and (3) apply.

EXAMPLE

On October 4, 2006, you buy 100 shares of Oil Co. for $60 a share. On December 5, 2006, you sell short 100 shares of Oil Co. for $80 a share. On January 8, 2007, you buy for $75 a share 100 shares of Oil Co. to close the short sale. You hold the October lot for over 60 days after January 8, 2007. The December 2006 short sale is not treated as a constructive sale in 2006. You realized a loss of $5 per share when you closed the short position.

An appreciated financial position. You have an appreciated financial position interest in stock, a partnership interest, or a debt instrument (including a futures or forward contract, a short sale, or an option) if disposing of the interest would result in a gain.

An appreciated financial position does not include any position that is marked to market, including Section 1256 contracts. It also does not include any position in a debt instrument if:

1. The debt unconditionally entitles the holder to receive a specified principal amount,
2. The interest payments on the debt (or other similar amounts) are payable at a fixed rate or a variable rate described in Section 1.860G-1(a)(3) of the Regulations, *and*
3. The debt is not convertible, either directly or indirectly, into stock of the issuer (or any related person).

For the constructive sale rules, an interest in an actively traded trust is treated as stock unless substantially all of the value of the property held by the trust is debt that qualifies for the debt exception above.

A transaction treated as a constructive sale of an appreciated financial position is not treated as a constructive sale of any other appreciated financial position, as long as you continue to hold the original position. However, if you hold another appreciated financial position and dispose of the original position before closing the transaction that resulted in the constructive sale, you are treated as if, at the same time, you constructively sold the other appreciated financial position.

30.9 Straddle Losses

Tax accounting rules generally match losses against unrealized gains in offsetting straddle positions. Straddle rules apply to commodities and to stock options used in straddle positions. Straddle positions include actively traded stock if at least one of the offsetting positions is: (1) a position on that stock or substantially similar or related property, or (2) the stock is in a corporation formed or used to take positions in personal property that offset positions taken by any shareholder. True *hedging* transactions are not subject to the straddle tax rules.

Filing Instruction

Form 6781

You use Form 6781 for reporting gains and losses on straddle positions and on Section 1256 contracts that are open at the end of the year but treated as sold under the marked-to-market rules discussed in this section.

Filing Tip

Carryback Election

If for 2004 you have a net loss on Section 1256 contracts, the loss may be carried back for three years under special rules. To carry back the net loss, you must make the election on Form 6781, file Form 1045 or an amended return (Form 1040X), and attach an amended Form 6781 for the applicable year. Follow the instructions to Form 6781.

Filing Instruction

Marked-to-Market Rules

Non-equity options and dealer equity options, which include options based on regulated stock indexes and interest rate futures, are taxed like regulated futures contracts. This means that they are reported annually under the marked-to-market accounting system. You treat all such options held at the end of the year as if they were disposed of at year-end for a price equal to fair market value. Any gain or loss is arbitrarily taxed as if it were 60% long term and 40% short term. It is advisable to ask your broker whether the specific options you hold come within this special rule.

You use Form 6781 to report 60/40% gains, which are then transferred to Schedule D.

A call option is not treated as part of a straddle position if it is considered a qualified covered call option. A *qualified covered call option* is an option that a stockholder who is not a dealer grants on stock traded on a national securities exchange. Furthermore, the option must be granted more than 30 days before its expiration date and must not be "deep-in-the-money." A covered call option will not qualify if gain on the sale of the stock to be purchased by the option is reported in a year after the year in which the option is closed, and the stock is not held for 30 days or more after the date on which the option is closed. In such a case, the option is subject to the straddle loss deferral rules. The same loss deferment rule applies where the stock is sold at a loss, and gain on the related option held less than 30 days is reported in the next year.

Loss on a qualified covered call option with a strike price less than its applicable stock price is treated as long-term capital loss if loss realized on the sale of the stock would be long term. The holding period for stock subject to the option does not include any period during which the taxpayer is the grantor of the option.

A "deep-in-the-money" option is an option with a strike or exercise price that is below the lowest qualified benchmark. The technical rules for determining these values are not discussed in this book.

Tax rules for straddles. The following paragraphs give a brief overview of the straddle rules, and if you have transacted straddles or are considering such transactions, we suggest that you see IRS Publication 550 and consult with an experienced tax practitioner.

Generally, a realized loss on a position that is part of a straddle is deductible on Form 6781 to the extent that it exceeds the unrecognized gains in offsetting positions as of the close of the taxable year. Any part of a loss that is not deductible is carried forward to the next year and subject to the same limitation. However, you may not deduct any loss from an identified position that was established in an identified straddle after October 21, 2004. Instead, you must increase the basis of the offsetting positions in the identified straddle that have unrecognized gain by the amount of the unallowed loss; *see* the Form 6781 instructions.

Straddle positions of related persons (such as a spouse or child) or controlled flow-through entities (such as a partnership or an S corporation) are considered in determining whether offsetting positions are held.

The loss deferral rule does *not* apply to positions in a regulated futures contract or other Section 1256 contract subject to the marked-to-market system explained later in this section.

The loss deferral rule also does not apply to businesses that must hedge in order to protect their supplies of inventory or financial capital. Hedging transactions are subject to ordinary income or loss treatment. Hedging transactions entered into by syndicates do not qualify for the exception and are subject to the loss deferral rule if more than 35% of losses for a taxable year are allocable to limited partners or entrepreneurs. Furthermore, hedging losses of limited partners or limited entrepreneurs are generally limited to their taxable income from the business to which the hedging transaction relates.

Conversion transactions. On certain so-called "conversion transactions," discussed at *30.10*, gain realized on the disposition of certain positions is treated as ordinary income instead of capital gain.

Marked-to-market rules for gain or loss on regulated futures contracts and other Section 1256 contracts. Gain or loss on regulated futures contracts is reported annually under the marked-to-market accounting system of regulated commodity exchanges. To settle margin requirements, regulated exchanges determine a party's account for futures contracts on a daily basis. Each regulated futures contract is treated as if sold at fair market value on the last day of the taxable year. Any capital gain or loss is arbitrarily allocated: 40% is short term and 60% is long term. Use Form 6781 to figure gains and losses on Section 1256 contracts that are open at the end of the year or that were closed out during the year. These amounts are then transferred from Form 6781 to Schedule D.

Under the law, a regulated futures contract is considered a Section 1256 contract. Other Section 1256 contracts subject to the marked-to-market rules are foreign currency contracts, dealer equity options, and non-equity options.

The marked-to-market rules do not apply to true hedging transactions executed in the normal course of business to reduce risks and that result in ordinary income or loss. Syndicates may generally not take advantage of this hedging exception if more than 35% of their losses during a taxable year are allocable to limited partners or entrepreneurs. Further, the ability of entrepreneurs or limited partners to deduct losses from hedging transactions is generally limited to taxable income from the business to which the hedging transaction relates.

Mixed straddle contracts. If you have a mixed straddle in which at least one but not all of the positions is a Section 1256 contract, the marked-to-market rules generally apply but you may elect to avoid this treatment and apply the regular straddle tax rules. The election, made on Form 6781, is irrevocable unless the IRS allows a revocation. Furthermore, the IRS allows an election to offset gains and losses from positions that are part of mixed straddles if you separately identify each mixed straddle or establish mixed straddle accounts for a class of activities for which gain and loss will be recognized and offset on a periodic basis.

Wash sales. Rules similar to wash-sale rules apply to losses arising from sales of shares that make up a straddle if within a 30-day period you acquire substantially identical shares; *see* IRS Publication 550 for further details.

Contract cancellations. Investors buying forward contracts for currency or securities may not realize ordinary loss by cancelling the unprofitable contract of the hedge transaction. Loss realized on a cancellation of the contract is treated as a capital loss.

Cash-and-carry transactions. You may not deduct carrying costs for any period during which the commodity or stock or option is part of a balanced position. The costs must be capitalized and added to basis. The rule does not apply to hedging straddles. Capitalized items are reduced by dividends on stock included in a straddle, market discounts, and acquisition discounts. These reductions, however, are limited to so much of the dividends and discounts as is included in income.

30.10 Capital Gain Restricted on Conversion Transactions

A "conversion transaction" is a transaction generally involving two or more positions taken with regard to the same or similar property. The investor is in the economic position of a lender who expects to receive income while undertaking no significant risks other than those of a lender. Where substantially all of your expected return is in the nature of interest on a loan from the following types of transactions, some or all of the income earned on the transaction is treated as ordinary income rather than capital gain:

- You acquire property and also agree to sell the property or substantially identical property for a determined price;
- You take offsetting positions on a straddle transaction; *or*
- You invest in a transaction marketed or sold as producing capital gain but your expected return is in the nature of interest on a loan.

Option dealers and commodity dealers are generally exempt from the new limitations.

Amount treated as ordinary income. In a conversion transaction, the amount of ordinary income is limited to an "applicable imputed income amount." This is generally the amount of interest that would have accrued on the net investment in the conversion transaction for the period ending on the date of disposition. To figure the interest element, 120% of the applicable federal rate, compounded semiannually, is used. The applicable rate is the federal short-term, mid-term, or long-term rate, depending on the term of the transaction. If the term is indefinite, the federal short-term rate is used. The federal rates are determined monthly and published in the Internal Revenue Bulletin.

EXAMPLE

On January 7, 2005, Jones buys stock for $100 and on the same day agrees to sell it to Brown for $115 on January 10, 2006. Assume the applicable federal interest rate is 5%. On January 10, 2006, Jones delivers the stock to Brown for $115. If the conversion transaction rule did not apply, Jones would recognize a capital gain of $15 ($115 sale price less $100 purchase price). However, under the conversion transaction rules, $12.36 of the gain is ordinary income ($12.36 is $100 times 6% compounded for two years; 6% is 120% of the 5% federal rate). The balance of the gain, or $2.64, is long-term capital gain ($15 *less* $12.36).

Where a loan finances a conversion transaction and interest is capitalized (under a provision applied to straddles), the amount of ordinary income reported is reduced.

If the conversion transaction involves a "built-in" loss, the loss is recognized without regard to the conversion rules. For example, if the loss is a capital loss, it remains a capital loss although the conversion rules apply to the transaction.

Filing Tip

Reporting Conversion Transactions

You report conversion transactions on Form 6781. The ordinary income element is not reported as interest income, but as an ordinary gain on Form 4797.

30.11 Puts and Calls and Index Options

You may buy options to buy and sell stock. On the stock exchange, these options are named *calls* and *puts*. A call gives you the right to require the seller of the option to sell you stock during the option period at a fixed price, called the exercise or strike price. A put gives you the right to require the seller of the option to buy stock you own at a fixed price during the option period. *See* the chart on the following page for an explanation of different option terms.

The option price depends on the value of the stock, the length of the option period, the volatility of the stock, and the demand and supply for options for the particular stock.

Puts may be treated as short sales. Be careful in using puts when you own stock covered by the put. If you have held the stock short term, the purchase of the put is a short sale. The exercise or expiration of the put will then be treated as the closing of the short sale. Short-sale rules, however, do not apply (1) when you hold stock long term, and (2) when you buy a put and the related stock on the same day and identify the stock with the put; *see 30.5*.

Planning Reminder

Speculate With Puts and Calls

Puts and calls allow you to speculate at the expense of a small investment—a call, for expected price rises, and a put, for expected price declines. They may also be used to protect paper profits or fix the amount of your losses on securities you own.

You do not have to exercise a put or call to realize your profit. You may sell the option to realize your profit. If you exercise a call, the cost of the call is added to the cost of the stock purchased. If you exercise a put, you reduce the selling price of stock sold by the cost of the put. If you do not exercise a call or put, you realize a capital loss.

Buyers of options. If you buy an option, the tax treatment of your investment in the option depends on what you do with it.

1. If you sell it, you realize short-term or long-term capital gain or loss, depending upon how long you held the option.
2. If you allow the option to expire without exercise, you incur a short-term or long-term capital loss, depending on the holding period of the option. The expiration date is treated as the date the option is disposed of.
3. If you exercise a call and buy the stock, you add the cost of the call to the basis of the stock. If you exercise a put, the cost of the put reduces your amount realized when figuring gain or loss on the sale of the underlying stock.

Grantors of options. If you write an option through the exchange, you do not treat the premium received for writing the option as income at the time of receipt. You do not realize profit or loss until the option transaction is closed. This may occur when the option expires or is exercised or when you "buy in" on the exchange an option similar to the one you gave to end your obligation to deliver the stock. Here are the rules for these events:

1. If the option is not exercised, you report the premium as short-term capital gain in the year the option expires.
2. If the option is exercised, you add the premium to the sales proceeds of the stock to determine gain or loss on the sale of the stock. Gain or loss is short term or long term depending upon the holding period of the stock.
3. If you "buy in" an equivalent option in a closing transaction, you realize profit or loss for the difference between the premium of the option you sold and the cost of the closing option. The profit or loss is treated as short-term capital gain or loss. However, a loss on a covered call that has a stated price below the stock price may be long-term capital loss if, at the time of the loss, long-term gain would be realized on the sale of the stock. Furthermore, the holding period of such stock is suspended during the period in which the option is open. Finally, year-end losses from covered call options are not deductible, unless the stock is held uncovered for more than 30 days following the date on which the option is closed.

Using a call as leverage. You expect a stock to appreciate in value but you do not have sufficient capital for a further investment. Instead of investing your limited amount of capital in an outright purchase, you might buy a call covering such stock. With a call, the same amount of capital allows you to speculate in many more shares than you could if you purchased stock outright. If the stock rises in value, your call also increases in value.

Table 30-2 Key to Option Terms

Item—	*Explanation—*
Call option	An option contract that gives the holder the right to buy a specified number of shares of the underlying stock at the given exercise price on or before the option expiration date.
Put option	An option contract that gives the holder the right to sell a specified number of shares of the underlying stock at the given exercise price on or before the option expiration date.
Strike price/exercise price	The stated price per share for which the underlying stock may be bought (in the case of a call) or sold (in the case of a put) by the option holder upon exercise of the option contract.
At-the-money	An option is at-the-money if the exercise price of the option is equal to the market price of the underlying security.
In-the-money	A call option is in-the-money if the exercise price is less than the market price of the underlying security. A put option is in-the-money if the exercise price is greater than the market price of the underlying security.
Out-of-the-money	A call option is out-of-the-money if the exercise price is greater than the market price of the underlying security. A put option is out-of-the-money if the strike price is less than the market price of the underlying security.
Premium	The price of the option contract determined in the competitive marketplace, which the buyer of the option pays to the option writer.
Intrinsic value	The amount by which the option is in-the-money.
Time value (premium-intrinsic value)	The portion of the premium that is attributable to the amount of time remaining until the option's expiration date and to the fact that the underlying components that determine the value of the option may change during that time.
Secondary market	A market that provides for the purchase or sale of previously sold or bought options through closing transactions.
Expiration date	The expiration date is the last day on which an option may be exercised.
Writer	The seller of an option contract.

30.12 Investing in Tax-Exempts

Interest on state and local obligations is not subject to federal income tax. It is also exempt from the tax of the state in which the obligations are issued. In comparing the interest return of a tax-exempt with that of a taxable bond, you figure the taxable return that is equivalent to the tax-free yield of the tax-exempt. This amount depends on your tax bracket. For example, a municipal bond of $5,000 yielding 3% is the equivalent of a taxable yield of 4.167% subject to the tax rate of 28%.

You can compare the value of tax-exempt interest to taxable interest for your tax bracket by using this formula:

$$\frac{\text{Tax-exempt interest rate}}{\text{1 minus your tax bracket}}$$

The denominator of the above fraction is:

0.85 if your tax bracket is 15%
0.75 if your tax bracket is 25%
0.72 if your tax bracket is 28%
0.67 if your tax bracket is 33%
0.65 if your tax bracket is 35%

Planning Reminder

Municipal Bond Funds

Instead of purchasing tax-exempts directly, you may consider investing in municipal bond funds. The funds invest in various municipal bonds and, thus, offer the safety of diversity. The value of fund shares will fluctuate with the bond markets. Also, an investment in the fund may be as small as $1,000 compared with the typical $5,000 municipal bond. Check on fees and other restrictions in municipal bond funds.

EXAMPLE

You are deciding between a tax-exempt bond and a taxable bond. You want to find which will give you more income after taxes. You have a choice between a tax-exempt bond paying 3.25% and a taxable bond paying 4%. Your tax bracket is 25%.

You find that the tax-exempt bond is a better buy in your tax bracket as it is the equivalent of a taxable bond paying 4.33%.

$$\text{Taxable Equivalent Rate (T)} = \frac{0.0325}{0.75\ (1.00 - 0.25)}$$

$$T = .0433, \text{ or } 4.33\%$$

Filing Instruction

Interest Subject to AMT

Interest on qualified private activity bonds issued after August 7, 1986, is tax free for regular tax purposes but is a tax preference item for alternative minimum tax (AMT) purposes; *see* Chapter 23.

Tax law restrictions. Most state and municipal bonds that are issued before July 1, 1983, except for housing issues, are in the form of bearer bonds; the owners are not identified, and interest coupons are cashed as they come due. However, state and municipal bonds issued after June 30, 1983, with a maturity of more than one year, as well as obligations of the federal government and its agencies, are in registered form. Principal and interest are transferable only through an entry on the books of the issuer.

In buying state or local bonds, check the prospectus for the issue date and tax status of the bond. The tax law treats bonds issued after August 7, 1986, as follows:

1. "Public-purpose" bonds. These include bonds issued directly by state or local governments or their agencies to meet essential government functions, such as highway construction and school financing. These bonds are generally tax exempt.
2. "Qualified private activity" bonds. These include bonds issued to finance housing and student loans. There are limits on the amount of qualifying private activity bonds an authority may issue. Interest on qualifying bonds issued after August 7, 1986 (or after August 31, 1986, for certain bonds), is tax free for regular income tax purposes, but is a preference item to be added to taxable income if you are subject to alternative minimum tax (Chapter 23). Because of the AMT, a nongovernment-purpose bond may pay slightly more interest than public-purpose bonds. Your broker can help you identify such bonds.
3. "Taxable" municipals. These are bonds issued for nonqualifying private purposes. They are subject to federal income tax, but may be exempt from state and local taxes in the states in which they are issued.

30.13 Ordinary Loss for Small Business Stock (Section 1244)

Shareholders of qualifying "small" corporations may claim within limits an ordinary loss, rather than a capital loss, on the sale or worthlessness of Section 1244 stock. An ordinary loss up to $50,000, or $100,000 on a joint return, may be claimed on Form 4797. On a joint return, the $100,000 limit applies even if only one spouse has a Section 1244 loss. Losses in excess of these limits are deductible as capital losses. Any gains on Section 1244 stock are reported as capital gain on Schedule D.

An ordinary loss may be claimed only by the original owner of the stock. If a partnership sells Section 1244 stock at a loss, an ordinary loss deduction may be claimed by individuals who were partners when the stock was issued. If a partnership distributes the Section 1244 stock to the partners, the partners may not claim an ordinary loss on their disposition of the stock.

If an S corporation sells Section 1244 stock at a loss, S corporation shareholders may not claim an ordinary loss deduction. The IRS with Tax Court approval limits shareholders' deductions to capital losses (which are deductible only against capital gains plus $3,000 ($1,500 if married filing separately); *see 5.4*).

To qualify as Section 1244 stock:

1. The corporation's equity may not exceed $1,000,000 at the time the stock is issued, including amounts received for the stock to be issued. Thus, if the corporation already has $600,000 equity from stock previously issued, it may not issue more than $400,000 worth of additional stock.

   If the $1,000,000 equity limit is exceeded, the corporation follows an IRS procedure for designating which shares qualify as Section 1244 stock.

   Preferred stock issued after July 18, 1984, may qualify for Section 1244 loss treatment, as well as common stock.

Planning Reminder

Record-Keeping for Section 1244 Stock

You must keep records that distinguish between Section 1244 stock and other stock interests. Your records must show that the corporation qualified as a small business corporation when the stock was issued, you are the original holder of the Section 1244 stock, and it was issued for money or property. Stock issued for services does not qualify. In addition, the records should also show the amount paid for the stock, information relating to any property transferred for the stock, any tax-free stock dividends issued on the stock, and the corporation's gross receipts data for the most recent five-year period.

Failure to keep these records will be grounds for disallowing a loss that is claimed on Section 1244 stock.

2. The stock must be issued for money or property (other than stock and securities).
3. The corporation for the five years preceding your loss must generally have derived more than half of its gross receipts from business operations and not from passive income such as rents, royalties, dividends, interest, annuities, or gains from the sales or exchanges of stock or securities. The five-year requirement is waived if the corporation's deductions (other than for dividends received or net operating losses) exceed gross income. If the corporation has not been in existence for the five years before your loss, then generally the period for which the corporation has been in existence is examined for the gross receipts test.

Savings Bonds

30.14 Series EE and E Bonds

Savings bond purchases give you an opportunity to defer tax; *see* below. EE bonds can be purchased for one-half the face value (ranging from $50 to a maximum of $10,000). *See 30.15* for I bonds.

EE bonds must be held 12 months from the issue date before they can be redeemed. Bonds cashed in any time before five years are subject to a three-month interest penalty; *see* the Example below.

Series EE savings bonds with an issue date on or after May 1, 2005, earn a fixed rate of interest. Interest accrues monthly and is compounded semiannually. EE bonds issued from May 1997 through April 2005 continue to earn market-based interest rates set at 90% of the average five-year Treasury securities yields for the preceding six months; these rates change every May 1 and November 1. EE bonds issued before May 1997 earn various rates depending on the date of issue.

EXAMPLE

You purchased series EE bonds in March 2005. If you cash them 24 months later, in March 2007, you get your original investment back plus 21 months of interest (instead of 24 months of interest) because of the three-month penalty for redemptions within the first five years of ownership.

Deferring tax on savings bond interest. Unless you report the interest annually, Series E and EE bond interest is deferred *(4.29)* until the year you redeem the bond or it reaches final maturity. When you redeem the bond, the accumulated interest is taxable on your federal return but *not* taxable on your state and local income tax return. If in the year of redemption you use the proceeds to pay for higher education or vocational school costs, the accumulated interest may be tax free for federal tax purposes; *see 33.4*.

Interest accrual dates for Series E and Series EE savings bonds. For EE bonds issued after April 1997, interest accrues on the first day of every month. However, for most EE bonds issued before May 1997 and for all E bonds, interest accrues only twice a year. The months of accrual depend on the issue date of the bond, as discussed below. When you cash a bond, you receive the value of the bond as of the last date that interest was added. If you cash a bond in between accrual months, you will not receive interest for the partial period. For example, if interest accrues in February and August, and you cash a bond in during July, you would earn interest only through February. By waiting until August 1 to cash the bond, you would earn another six months of interest.

Series E bond accrual dates. The only E bonds still earning interest are those that have not yet reached their 30-year final maturity. All E bonds issued December 1965–June 1980 (the last issue month for E bonds) stop earning interest when they reach final maturity 30 years after issue. E bonds issued before December 1965 reached final maturity 40 years after issue and no longer earn interest.

Until final maturity is reached, 30-year E bonds accrue interest on the first day of the issue month and the sixth month after the issue month. For example, if you own an E bond issued in May 1979, interest accrues every May 1 (month of issue) and every November 1 (six months after the May issue month).

Series EE bond accrual dates. In general, all EE bonds issued before May 1, 1997, accrue interest on the first day of the issue month and the sixth month after the issue month. For example, if you own an EE bond issued in August 1995, interest accrues every August 1 (month of issue) and every February 1 (six months after the August issue month).

An exception may apply for EE bonds issued March 1993 through April 1995. The twice-a-year accrual rule just discussed applies unless monthly increases are needed to guarantee a 4% return.

Caution

Timing Bond Redemptions

In the year you cash in a savings bond you could lose interest by cashing it in too soon. Interest accrues only twice a year on E bonds. Interest also accrues twice a year on EE bonds issued prior to May 1, 1997. The accrual months depend on the month of issue. If you cash your bonds before the accrual month that applies to your bond, you will lose interest. *See 30.14.*

Final maturity for savings bonds. Do not neglect the final maturity date for older bonds. After the final maturity date, no further interest will accrue. For example, E bonds issued in 1975 reached final maturity in 2005.

Bond	Issue Date	Final Maturity
Series E	May 1941–November 1965	40 years after issue
	December 1965–June 1980	30 years after issue
Series EE	January 1980 or later	30 years after issue
Savings notes (Freedom Shares)	May 1967–October 1970	30 years after issue
H bonds	February 1957–December 1979	30 years after issue
HH bonds	January 1980–August 2004	20 years after issue

Caution

HH Bonds No Longer Issued

Holders of Series E and EE bonds are no longer able to exchange their bonds for HH bonds. The Treasury discontinued HH offerings at the close of business on August 31, 2004. HH bonds issued on or before August 31, 2004, will continue to earn interest semiannually until they reach final maturity 20 years after issue.

Accrual dates for Series HH bonds. Taxable interest on HH bonds obtained before September 1, 2004 in exchange for savings bonds or savings notes accrues semiannually at a fixed rate. A fixed interest rate applies for the first 10 years you hold an HH bond and the rate is then reset for the next 10 years until final maturity 20 years after the date of issue. For HH bonds issued or entering an extended maturity period after 2002, the rate is 1.5% per year. Interest on HH bonds issued from March 1993 through December 2002 will retain their 4% rate until they enter extended maturity after the first 10 years, and will then earn 1.5% per year.

Accrual dates for Series H bonds. These bonds were available before 1980 and reach final maturity 30 years from original issue. They pay semiannual interest that is taxable when received. If you own Series H bonds purchased through the exchange of Series E bonds, *see 4.28* for reporting interest.

30.15 I Bonds

Treasury "I bonds" provide a return that rises and falls with inflation. I bonds are issued at face value in amounts of $50, $75, $100, $200, $500, $1,000, $5,000, and $10,000. You may buy up to $30,000 of I bonds in any calendar year. I bonds may be purchased from most banks, credit unions, or savings institutions or online from the Treasury at www.publicdebt.treas.gov. They earn interest for 30 years. Interest is added to a bond monthly and paid when the bond is redeemed.

I bonds are not redeemable within the first 12 months. You forfeit three months of interest if an I bond is redeemed within the first five years.

Rates. Interest on an I bond is determined by two rates. One rate, set by the Treasury Department, remains constant for the life of the bond. The second rate is a variable inflation rate announced each May and November by the Treasury Department to reflect changes reported by the Bureau of Labor Statistics in the Consumer Price Index. If deflation sets in, a decline in the Consumer Price Index does not reduce the redemption value of the bond, even if the deflation rate exceeds the fixed rate.

Income tax reporting. Investors may defer paying federal income taxes on I bond interest, which is automatically reinvested and added to the principal. Deferral applies to the fixed rate interest as well as the variable inflation rate interest. You may defer federal tax on the interest until you redeem the bond or the bond reaches maturity in thirty years. You may report the interest each year as it accrues instead of deferring the interest. I bond interest is exempt from state and local income taxes.

If an I bond is redeemed to pay for college tuition or other college fees, all or part of the interest may be excludable from income under the rules discussed in *33.4*.

Traders in Securities

30.16 Trader, Dealer, or Investor?

The tax law recognizes three types of individuals who may sell and buy securities. They are:

Investor. You are an investor if you buy and sell securities for long-term capital gains and to earn dividends and interest.

Trader. You may be a trader if you buy and sell securities to profit from daily market movements in the prices of securities and not from dividends, interest, or capital appreciation. Your buy and sell orders must be frequent, continuous, and substantial. There are at present no clearcut tests to determine the amount of sales volume that qualifies a person as a trader. The term "trader" is not defined in the Internal Revenue Code or Treasury regulations. The IRS has not issued rulings for determining trader status. The Tax Court has held that sporadic trading does not qualify; *see* the Example below.

Dealer. You are a dealer if you hold an inventory of securities to sell to others. Dealers report their profits and losses as business income and losses under special tax rules not discussed in this book.

EXAMPLE

While holding a full-time job as a computer chip engineer in 1999, Chen made 323 transactions, 94 percent of which occurred in February, March, and April; he did no trading in June or August through December. Most of the securities were held for less than a month. He had losses of nearly $85,000, which he reported as ordinary losses.

The Tax Court held that Chen was not a trader in securities and was limited to deducting $3,000 of his net 1999 loss against ordinary income. To be considered a trader, the purchases and sales of securities must amount to a trade or business. There is no exact number of trades or other clear standard used to make this determination. Rather, it is based on the taxpayer's intent, the nature of the income derived from trading, and the frequency, extent, and regularity of the transactions. During three months of the year, Chen bought and sold with frequency, but he failed to achieve trader status because, overall, his activities were not frequent, regular, and continuous. In prior cases, trader status has been found where such activities usually were frequent, regular, and continuous for a period of more than a single year. Because Chen could not claim trader status, he was ineligible to make a mark-to-market election.

Tax treatment of traders. The tax rules applied to traders are a hybrid of tax rules applied to investors and business persons, as discussed in the following paragraphs.

Reporting trader gains and losses. Unless a trader previously made a mark-to-market election, gains and losses are reported as capital gains and losses on Schedule D. As almost all or substantially all of a trader's sales are short-term, such gains are reported as short-term gains and losses as short-term losses. A net profit from Schedule D is *not* subject to self-employment tax *(45.1)*. Substantial losses subject to capital loss treatment are a tax disadvantage because capital losses in excess of capital gains are deductible only up to $3,000 of ordinary income in one tax year. True, carryover capital losses may offset capital gains in the next year, but your inability to deduct them immediately may subject you to paying a tax liability that might have been reduced or eliminated if the losses had been deductible for the year of the sale. If you are concerned about incurring substantial short-term capital losses that would be limited by capital loss treatment, you may consider a mark-to-market election *(see 30.17)*, which would allow you to treat your security gains and losses as ordinary income and loss.

Deducting trader expenses. Although a trader does not sell to customers but for his or her own account, a trader is considered to be in business. Expenses such as subscriptions and margin interest may be deducted as ordinary business losses on Schedule C of Form 1040. Home office expenses are deductible if the office is regularly and exclusively used as the principal place of conducting the trading business *(see 40.12)*; the deduction is computed on Form 8829 and entered on Schedule C.

An investor, on the other hand, may deduct margin interest only as an itemized deduction to the extent of net investment income *(15.10)*. Other investment expenses are allowed only as miscellaneous itemized deductions and only to the extent that, when added to other miscellaneous costs such as fees for tax preparation, they exceed 2% of adjusted gross income *(19.1)*. An investor's overall itemized deductions are also subject to the 3% reduction for higher-income taxpayers *(13.7)*. An investor may not deduct home office expenses since investment activities, no matter how extensive, are not considered a business; *see* the *Moller* decision discussed at *40.16*.

30.17 Mark-to-Market Election for Traders

A trader in securities may elect to have his gains and losses treated as ordinary gains and losses by making a mark-to-market election. As explained below, it is too late to make an election for 2005. In the absence of an election, gains and losses of a trader are treated as capital gains and losses on Schedule D.

If the mark-to-market election is made, you report trading gains and losses on closed transactions plus unrealized gains and losses on securities held in your trading business at the end of your taxable year as ordinary gains and losses on Form 4797. Trader profits reported on Form 4797 are *not* subject to self-employment tax *(45.1)*. Reported unrealized gain or loss on a security increases or reduces the basis of the security. For example, if you report an unrealized gain of $50 on stock with a cost of $100, you increase the basis of the stock to $150. If you later sell the stock for $90, you report a loss of $60 in the year of the sale. The requirement to report unrealized gains and losses at the end of the year and to adjust basis of shares is a change in accounting method that requires you to file Form 3115 with the IRS National Office and report required adjustments; *see* IRS Publication 550 and Revenue Procedure 99-17 for details.

Making the election is not proof that you are actually a trader in securities. If you are audited by the IRS, you must be able to prove that your activities are such that you are in the business of making money by buying and selling over short periods of time. As mentioned in *30.16*, there are no hard and fast rules that specify how many daily or short-term trades qualify you as a trader.

When to make the mark-to-market election. The IRS requires you to make the election by the due date (without extensions) of the tax return for the year prior to the year for which the election is to be effective. Under this prior year tax return rule, it is too late to make an election for 2006, as this had to be done by April 17, 2006, the due date for your 2005 return.

A regulation gives the IRS authority to grant an extension of time to file the mark-to-market election if the taxpayer has acted reasonably and in good faith and allowing relief does not prejudice the interests of the government. However, the IRS has refused to allow such extensions, claiming that a late election invariably results in prejudice to the interests of the government.

The Tax Court supported the IRS in a case where a taxpayer tried to file the election several years after the year it should have been filed. In another case, the Tax Court was more sympathetic, allowing an extension to a taxpayer who filed his election for 2000 on July 21, 2000, three months after the IRS deadline of April 17, 2000. He had left his law practice and became a trader in January 2000. The accountant who prepared his 1999 return did not know about the mark-to-mark election but a friend told him about it in June 2000 and in July the taxpayer hired a law firm, which filed the election for him and asked the IRS to allow the extension. The taxpayer did not conduct any trading activities between the date he should have filed the election and the date he actually filed it. Over IRS objection, the Tax Court allowed the late election on the grounds that the taxpayer had acted reasonably and in good faith by promptly employing the law firm after learning about the availability of the election. Since the taxpayer did not realize any further gains or losses between the date he should have filed the election and when he actually did so, the Court held that the interests of the government were not prejudiced.

How to make the mark-to-market election. An election for 2007 must be made by April 16, 2007, on a statement attached to your original 2006 return or on a request for an extension to file that return. The statement should specify that effective for the taxable year starting January 1, 2007, you are electing to report gains and losses from your trading business under the mark-to-market rules of Section 475(f). However, in the case of a new taxpayer, a different rule applies. A new taxpayer is defined as a taxpayer for which no federal tax return was required to be filed for the taxable year immediately preceding the election year. A new taxpayer, such as a newly organized partnership, would make the election by placing a statement of election in its books and records no later than two months and 15 days after the first day of the election year. A copy of the statement also must be attached to the original tax return filed for the election year.

One of the conditions of the election is that you must clearly distinguish between securities held for investment and trading purposes. Holding investment securities in a separate account is advisable.

An election may not be revoked in a later year except with IRS permission.

In light of the accounting requirements and the overall effect of reporting unrealized gains and losses, before making the election you should consult a professional experienced in the use of mark-to-market accounting.

See IRS Revenue Procedure 99-17 for details on making the mark-to-market election.

Chapter 31

Tax Savings for Investors in Real Estate

Real estate investors may take advantage of the following tax benefits:

- Sale of investment property may be taxed at capital gain rates.
- Depreciation can provide a source of temporary tax-free income; *see 31.1.*
- Rental income can be used to offset passive losses; *see* Chapter 10.
- Tax-free exchanges make it possible to defer tax on exchanges of real estate held for investment; *see 31.3.*

Losses on real estate transactions may be subject to the following disadvantages:

- Rental losses may not be deductible from other income such as salary, interest, and dividends unless you qualify as a real estate professional or for the special $25,000 rental loss allowance; *see* Chapter 10.
- Compromises of mortgage liability may subject you to tax; *see 31.10.*

Real Estate Investments

Foreclosures and Abandonments of Mortgaged Property

Real Estate Investments

31.1 Investing in Real Estate Ventures

A real estate investment should provide a current income return and an appreciation in the value of the original investment. As an additional incentive, a real estate investment may in the early years of the investment return income subject to little or no tax. That may happen when depreciation and other expense deductions reduce taxable income without reducing the amount of cash available for distribution. This tax savings is temporary and limited by the terms and the amount of the mortgage debt on the property. Payments allocated to amortization of mortgage principal reduce the amount of cash available to investors without an offsetting tax deduction. Thus, the amount of tax-free return depends on the extent to which depreciation deductions exceed the amortization payments.

To provide a higher return of tax-free income, at least during the early years of its operations, a venture must obtain a constant payment mortgage that provides for the payment of fixed annual amounts that are allocated to continually decreasing amounts of interest and increasing amounts of amortization payments. Consequently, in the early years, a tax-free return of income is high while the amortization payments are low, but as the amortization payments increase, nontaxable income decreases. When this tax-free return has been substantially reduced, a partnership must refinance the mortgage to reduce the amortization payments and once again increase the tax-free return; *see* Examples 1 and 2 below.

The tax-free return is based on the assumption that the building does not actually depreciate at as fast a rate as the tax depreciation rate. If the building is depreciating physically at a faster rate, the so-called tax-free return on investment does not exist. Distributions to investors (over and above current income return) that are labeled tax-free distributions are, in fact, a return of the investor's own capital.

Caution

Management Fees

The promoter may be taking a real estate commission by having a commission paid to a company that he or she controls. A reliable promoter should disclose this fact and be willing to collect the commission only after the investors have recovered their capital. Also check the reasonableness of prepaid management fees and loan fees and whether or not the sale of property to the syndicate is from a corporation in which the syndicator has an interest. If there is such a sale, check its terms, price, interest rates, and whether there is any prepaid interest that may conceal a cash profit payout to the syndicator.

EXAMPLES

1. A limited partnership of 100 investors owns a building that returns an annual income of \$100,000 after a deduction of operating expenses, but before a depreciation deduction of \$80,000. Thus, taxable income is \$20,000 (\$100,000 – \$80,000). Assuming that there is no mortgage on the building, all of the \$100,000 is available for distribution. (Since the depreciation requires no cash outlay, it does not reduce the cash available for distribution.) Each investor receives \$1,000. Taxable income being \$20,000, only 20% (\$20,000 ÷ \$100,000) of the distribution is taxable. Thus, each investor reports as income only \$200 of his or her \$1,000 distribution; \$800 is tax free.
2. Same facts as in Example 1, except that the building is mortgaged, and an annual amortization payment of \$40,000 is being made. Consequently, only \$60,000 is available for distribution, of which \$20,000 is taxable. Each investor receives \$600, of which $^1/_3$ (\$20,000 ÷ \$60,000), or \$200, is taxed, and \$400 is tax free. In other words, the \$60,000 distribution is tax free to the extent that the depreciation deduction of \$80,000 exceeds the amortization of \$40,000—namely \$40,000. If the amortization payment were increased to \$50,000, only \$30,000 of the distribution would be tax free (\$80,000 – \$50,000).

Real estate investment trusts (REITs). The tax treatment of real estate investment trusts resembles that of open-end mutual funds. Distributions generally are reported to the investors on Form 1099-DIV as dividend income. However, distributions generally do *not* qualify for the reduced tax rate on qualified dividends *(4.1)*. A distribution qualifies for the reduced rate only to the extent it represents previously taxed undistributed income or qualifying dividends received by the REIT (from stock investments) that are passed through to the investors. Capital gain distributions reported on Form 1099-DIV must be reported as long-term capital gains regardless of how long the REIT shares have been held; also *see 4.4*. If the trust operates at a loss, the loss may not be passed on to the investors.

REMICs. A real estate mortgage investment company (REMIC) holds a fixed pool of mortgages. Investors are treated as holding a regular or residual interest. A REMIC is not a taxable entity for federal income tax purposes. It is generally treated as a partnership, with the residual interest holders as partners.

Investors with regular REMIC interests are treated as holding debt obligations. Interest income is reported to them by the REMIC on Form 1099-INT and original issue discount (OID) on Form 1099-OID.

The net income of the REMIC, after payments to regular interest holders, is passed through to the holders of residual interests. A residual interest holder's share of the REMIC's taxable income or loss is reported by the REMIC to the interest holder each quarter on Schedule Q of Form 1066, and the investor reports his or her total share of the year in Part IV of Schedule E.

31.2 Sales of Subdivided Land—Dealer or Investor?

An investor faces a degree of uncertainty in determining the tax treatment of sales of subdivided realty. In some situations, investor status may be preferred, and in others, dealer status.

Capital gain on sale. Investor status allows capital gain treatment. Capital losses may offset the gains. For capital gain, an investor generally has to show that his or her activities were not those of a dealer but were steps taken in a liquidation of the investment. To convince an IRS agent or a court of investment activity, this type of evidence may present a favorable argument for capital gain treatment:

- The property was bought as an investment, to build a residence, or received as a gift or inheritance.
- No substantial improvements were added to the tract.
- The property was subdivided to liquidate the investment.
- Sales came through unsolicited offers. There was no advertising or agents.
- Sales were infrequent.
- There were no previous activities as a real estate dealer.
- The seller was in a business unrelated to real estate.
- The property was held for a long period of time.
- Sales proceeds were invested in other investment property.

Planning Reminder

Installment Sales

The distinction between an investor and dealer is significant if land is sold on the installment basis. Investor status is preferable if you want to elect the installment method. Dealers may not elect installment sale treatment; *see 5.21*.

Section 1237 capital gain opportunity. Section 1237 is a limited tax provision that provides a capital gain opportunity for subdivided lots only if arbitrary holding period rules and restrictions on substantial improvements are complied with. For example, the lots must generally be held at least five years before sale unless they were inherited. If the lots were previously held for sale to customers, or if other lots are so held in the year of sale, Section 1237 does not apply. Furthermore, substantial improvements must not have been made to the lots. According to the IRS, a disqualifying substantial improvement is one that increases the value of the property by more than 10%. The IRS considers buildings, hard surface roads, or utilities, such as sewers, water, gas, or electric lines, as substantial improvements.

Interest expense deductions. The distinction between an investor in land and a dealer is also important in the case of interest expenses. Dealer status is preferable here. Interest expenses incurred by an investor are subject to investment interest deduction limitations; *see* Chapter 15. On the other hand, interest expenses of a dealer in the course of business activities are fully deductible; *see* the Morley Example below.

Passive activity. Income from sales of lots is not considered passive activity income. Thus, losses from sales of land may offset salary and other investment income. If you hold rental property and also sell land, make sure that your accounts distinguish between and separate each type of income. This way income and losses from land sales will not be commingled with rent income subject to the passive activity restrictions discussed in Chapter 10. Your activity in real property development counts towards qualifying you as a real estate professional who may deduct rental losses from nonpassive income if material participation tests are met; *see 10.3*.

EXAMPLE

Morley was interested in buying farm acreage to resell at a profit. Two and a half million dollars was set as the purchase price. To swing the deal, Morley borrowed $600,000. A short time later, his attempts to resell the property failed, and he allowed the property to be foreclosed. While he held the property he incurred interest costs of over $400,000, which he deducted. The IRS held the interest was not fully deductible. It claimed the interest was investment interest subject to investment interest restrictions. That is, the debt was incurred to purchase and carry investment property. The IRS position was based on the so-called "one-bite" rule, which holds that a taxpayer who engages in only one venture may not under any circumstances be held to be in a business as to that venture. Morley argued that he bought the property not as an investment property but as business property for immediate resale.

The Tax Court sided with Morley, holding that he held the acreage as ordinary business property. The court rejected the "one-bite" rule. The fact that he had not previously sold business property did not mean that he could not prove that he held acreage for resale. Here, he intended promptly to resell it, and the facts supported his intention.

31.3 Exchanging Real Estate Without Tax

You may trade real estate held for investment for other investment real estate and incur no immediate tax. The potential tax on the gain is postponed to the time you sell the new property for more than your basis. A tax-free exchange may also defer a potential tax due on gain from depreciation recapture and might be considered where the depreciable basis of a building has been substantially written off. Here, the building may be exchanged for other property that will give larger tax deductions.

Planning Reminder

Exchanging a Building for Land

A tax-free exchange may be advantageous in the case of land. Land is not depreciable, but it may be exchanged for a depreciable rental building. The exchange is tax free and depreciation may be claimed on the building. However, be aware of a possible tax trap if you exchange rental property for land and the building was subject to depreciation recapture: The recapture provisions override the tax-free exchange rules. The "recapture element" will be taxable as ordinary income.

Fully tax-free exchanges. To transact a fully tax-free exchange, you must satisfy these conditions:

- The property traded must be solely for property of a "like kind." The words *like kind* are liberally interpreted. They refer to the nature or character of the property, not its grade, quality, or use. Some examples of like-kind exchanges are: farm or ranch for city property; unimproved land for improved real estate; rental house for a store building; and fee in business property for 30-year or more leasehold in the same type of property; *see 6.1*. You may not make a tax-free exchange of U.S. real estate for real estate in foreign countries.
- The property exchanged must have been held for productive use in your business or for investment and traded for property to be held for productive use in business or investment. Therefore, trades of property used, or to be used, for personal purposes, such as exchanging a residence for rental property, cannot receive tax-free treatment. Special rules, however, apply when you trade your residence for another home; *see* Chapter 29.
- The trade must generally occur within a 180-day period, and property identification must occur within 45 days of the first transfer; *see 6.4* for further details of this test.

A real estate dealer cannot transact a tax-free exchange of property held for sale to customers. Also, an exchange is not tax free if the property received is held for immediate resale.

Tax-free exchanges between related parties are subject to tax if either party disposes of the exchanged property within a two-year period; *see 6.6*.

Disadvantage of tax-free exchange. Although the postponement of tax from a tax-free exchange is equivalent to an interest-free loan from the government equal to the amount you would have owed in taxes had you sold the property, this tax advantage is offset by a disadvantage in the case of an exchange of depreciable real estate. You must carry over the basis of the old property to the new property; *see* the following Example.

EXAMPLE

You have property with a basis of $25,000, now valued at $50,000, that you exchange for another property worth $50,000. Your basis for depreciation for the new property is $25,000.

If—instead of making an exchange—you sell the old property and use the proceeds to buy similarly valued property, the tax basis for depreciation would be $50,000, giving you larger depreciation deductions than you would get in the exchange transaction. If increased depreciation deductions are desirable, then it may pay to sell the property and purchase new property. Tax may be spread by transacting an installment sale. Project the tax consequences of a sale and an exchange and choose the one giving the greater overall tax benefits. You may find it preferable to sell the property and purchase new property on which MACRS may be claimed.

Partially tax-free exchanges. To be completely tax-free, the exchange must be solely an exchange of like-kind properties. If you receive "boot," such as cash or property that is not of like kind, gain is taxed up to the amount of the boot.

If you trade mortgaged property, the mortgage released is treated as boot; *see 6.3*. When there are mortgages on both properties, the mortgages are netted. The party giving up the larger mortgage and getting the smaller mortgage treats the excess as boot. *See* the Example below and also the Example in *6.3*, which illustrates how to report an exchange on Form 8824.

If the amount of boot exceeds your actual gain, the entire gain is taxed; taxable boot cannot exceed the amount of your gain.

EXAMPLE

You own a small office building with a fair market value of $170,000, and an adjusted basis of $150,000. There is a $130,000 mortgage on the building. You exchange it for Low's building valued at $155,000, having a $120,000 mortgage, and for $5,000 in cash. You compute your gain in this way:

What you received		
Present value of Low's property		$155,000
Cash		5,000
Mortgage on building you traded		130,000
Total received		$290,000
Less:		
Adjusted basis of building traded	$150,000	
Mortgage assumed by you	120,000	270,000
Actual gain on the exchange		$20,000

However, your actual gain of $20,000 is taxed only up to the amount of boot, $15,000.

Figuring boot		
Cash received		$5,000
Mortgage on building traded	$130,000	
Less: Mortgage assumed on Low's property	120,000	10,000
Gain taxed to the extent of boot		$15,000

Planning Reminder

Loss Deduction

A tax-free exchange is not desirable if the transaction will result in a loss, since you may not deduct a loss in a tax-free exchange. To ensure the loss deduction, first sell the property and then buy new property with the proceeds.

31.4 Timing Your Real Property Sales

Generally, a taxable transaction occurs in the year in which title or possession to property passes to the buyer. By controlling the year title and possession pass, you may select the year in which to report profit or loss. For example, you intend to sell property this year, but you estimate that reporting the sale next year will incur less in taxes. You can postpone the transfer of title and possession to next year. Alternatively, you can transact an installment sale, giving title and possession this year but delaying the receipt of all or most of the sale proceeds until next year; *see 5.21.*

31.5 Cancellation of a Lease

Payments received by the tenant on the cancellation of a business lease held long term are treated as proceeds received in a Section 1231 transaction; *see 44.8.* Payments received by the tenant on cancellation of a lease on a personal residence or apartment are treated as proceeds of a capital asset transaction. Gain is long-term capital gain if the lease was held long term; losses are not deductible.

Payments received by a landlord from a tenant for cancelling a lease or modifying lease terms are reported as rental income when received; *see 9.1.*

Cancellation of a distributor's agreement is treated as a sale if you made a substantial capital investment in the distributorship. For example, you own facilities for storage, transporting, processing, or dealing with the physical product covered by the franchise. If you have an office mainly for clerical work, or where you handle just a small part of the goods covered by the franchise, the cancellation is not treated as a sale. Your gain or loss is ordinary income or loss. If the cancellation is treated as a sale, the sale is subject to Section 1231 treatment; *see 44.8.*

31.6 Sale of an Option

The tax treatment of the sale of an option depends on the tax classification of the property to which the option relates.

If the option is for the purchase of property that would be a capital asset in your hands, profit on the sale of the option is treated as capital gain. A loss is treated as a capital loss if the property subject to the option was investment property; if the property was personal property, the loss is not deductible. Whether the gain or loss is long term or short term depends on your holding period.

EXAMPLES

1. You pay $500 for an option to purchase a house. After holding the option for five months, you sell the option for $750. Your profit of $250 is short-term capital gain.
2. The same facts as in Example 1 above, except that you sell the option for $300. The loss is not deductible because the option is related to a sale of a personal residence.

If the option is for a "Section 1231 asset" *(44.8)*, gain or loss on the sale of the option is combined with other Section 1231 asset transactions to determine if there is capital gain or ordinary loss.

If the option relates to an ordinary income asset in your hands, then gain or loss would be ordinary income or loss.

If you fail to exercise an option and allow it to lapse, the option is considered to have been sold on the expiration date. Gain or loss is computed according to the rules just discussed.

The party granting the option realizes ordinary income on its expiration, regardless of the nature of the underlying property. If the option is exercised, the option payment is added to the selling price of the property when figuring gain or loss.

31.7 Granting of an Easement

Granting an easement presents a practical problem of determining whether all or part of the basis of the property is allocable to the easement proceeds. This requires an opinion as to whether the easement affects the entire property or just a part of the property. There is no hard and fast rule to determine whether an easement affects all or part of the property. The issue is factual. For example, an easement for electric lines will generally affect only the area over which the lines are suspended and for which the right of way is granted. In such a case, an allocation may be required; *see* Example 1 below. If the entire property is affected, no allocation is required and the proceeds reduce the basis of the property. If only part of the property is affected, then the proceeds are applied to the cost allocated to the area affected by the easement. If the proceeds exceed the amount allocated to basis, a gain is realized. Capital gain treatment generally applies to grants of easements. The granting of a perpetual easement that requires you to give up all or substantially all of a beneficial use of the area affected by the easement is treated as a sale. The contribution to a government body of a scenic easement in perpetuity is a charitable contribution *(14.10)*, not a sale.

Planning Reminder

Basis Allocation

In reviewing an easement, the IRS will generally try to find grounds for allocating part of a property owner's basis to easement proceeds, especially where the allocation will result in a taxable gain. In opposition, a property owner will generally argue that the easement affects the entire property or that it is impossible to make an allocation because of the nature of the easement or the particular nature of the property. If he or she can sustain an argument, the proceeds for granting the easement reduce the basis of the entire property; *see* the Examples in *31.7*.

Condemnation. If you realize a gain on a grant of an easement under a condemnation or threat of condemnation, you may defer tax by investing in replacement property; *see 18.19*.

EXAMPLES

1. The owner of a 600-acre farm was paid $5,000 by a power company for the right to put up poles and power lines. The right of way covered 20 acres along one boundary that the owner continued to farm. The cost basis of the farm was $60,000, or $100 an acre. The IRS ruled that he had to allocate the basis. At $100 an acre, the allocated basis for the 20 acres was $2,000. Thus, a gain of $3,000 was realized ($5,000 – $2,000).
2. The owner of a tract of unimproved land gave a state highway department a perpetual easement affecting only part of the land. He wanted to treat the payment as a reduction of the basis of the entire tract and so report no gain. The IRS ruled that he had to allocate basis to the portion affected by the road.
3. The owner of farmland gave a transmission company a 50-foot right of way for an underground pipeline that did not interfere with farming. During construction, the right of way was 150 feet. The owner received payments for damages covering loss of rental income during construction and for the 50-foot permanent right of way. The IRS ruled that the damage payment was taxable as ordinary income; the payment for the right of way was a taxable gain to the extent that it exceeded the basis allocated to the acreage within the 50-foot strip.

Release of a restrictive covenant. A payment received for a release of a restrictive covenant is treated as a capital gain if the release involves property held for investment.

EXAMPLE

You sell several acres of land held for investment to a construction company subject to a covenant that restricts construction to residential dwellings. Later, the company wants to erect structures other than individual homes and pays you for the release of the restrictive covenant in the deed. You realize capital gain on receipt of the payment. The restrictive covenant is a property interest and a capital asset in your hands.

31.8 Special Tax Credits for Real Estate Investments

To encourage certain real estate investments, the tax law offers the following tax credits:

Low-income housing credit. Qualifying investors are allowed to claim a tax credit in annual installments over 10 years for qualifying newly constructed low-income housing and also to certain existing structures that are substantially rehabilitated. The amount of the credit depends on whether the building is new and whether federal subsidies are received. To claim the credit, you, as the building owner, must receive a certification from an authorized housing credit agency. The agency allocates a credit to you on Form 8609, which you use to claim the credit on Form 8586. You must attach to your return Form 8586, and, in some cases, also Form 8609 and Schedule A, Form 8609.

Rehabilitation credit for pre-1936 buildings or certified historic structures. On Form 3468, you may claim a 10% tax credit for rehabilitating pre-1936 buildings or a 20% credit for rehabilitating certified historic structures. For both types of rehabilitation credits, you must generally incur rehabilitation expenses of $5,000 or your adjusted basis in the building, whichever is greater.

For purposes of figuring depreciation deductions, you must reduce basis by the full amount of either rehabilitation credit.

Both rehabilitation credits are subject to recapture if you dispose of the property within five years after it was placed in service or you change use of the property within the five-year period so it no longer qualifies for the credit; *see* Form 4255 for recapture details.

Gulf Opportunity Zone property. A higher rehabilitation credit is allowed on Form 3468 for rehabilitating buildings in the Gulf Opportunity Zone. For a pre-1936 building the credit percentage is increased from 10% to 13% and for a certified historic structure the percentage is increased from 20% to 26%. The higher credit applies to GO Zone expenditures paid or incurred after August 27, 2005, and before January 1, 2009.

Certified historic structure. A certified historic structure may be used for residential or nonresidential purposes. The National Park Service must certify that a planned rehabilitation is in keeping with the building's historic status designation for the credit to be available.

In one case, a developer who rehabilitated a certified historic structure and donated a conservation easement to a historic society in the same year was required to base the credit computation on the rehabilitation expenses minus the charitable deduction claimed. If the donation had been made in a later year, a portion of the original credit claimed would be subject to recapture.

Pre-1936 buildings. The 10% credit for pre-1936 buildings applies only to nonresidential property. A substantial portion of the building's original structure must be retained after the rehabilitation. At least 75% of the external walls must be intact, with at least 50% kept as external walls. At least 75% of the existing internal structural framework must be kept in place.

Tax credit limitations. Tax credits for low-income housing and rehabilitating historic or pre-1936 buildings may be limited by passive activity restrictions on Form 8582-CR (Chapter 10) and by tax liability limits for the general business credit (Chapter 40).

Law Alert

Donating Easement After Claiming Rehabilitation Credit

The charitable deduction for a historic building easement *(14.10)* donated after August 17, 2006, must be reduced if a rehabilitation credit was claimed for the building in the five years preceding the donation.

Court Decision

Rehabilitating Pre-1936 Building

In one case, the IRS and Tax Court interpreted the 75% external wall test for pre-1936 buildings as requiring that at least 75% of the existing external walls be retained in the same place, thereby denying the credit for a pre-1936 building that was relocated and then renovated. However, a federal appeals court disagreed, holding that there is no relocation restriction; the credit is allowed provided at least 75% of the external walls are retained as such after the renovation.

Foreclosures and Abandonments of Mortgaged Property

31.9 Foreclosures, Repossessions, and Voluntary Conveyances to Creditors

If you are unable to meet payments on a debt secured by property, the creditor may foreclose on the loan or repossess the property. A foreclosure sale or repossession, including a voluntary return by you of the property to the creditor, is treated as a sale of the property. If you are personally liable on the debt, and if the value of the property is less than the cancelled debt, you also generally realize ordinary income on the debt cancellation.

Figuring gain or loss on foreclosure or repossession. Gain or loss is the difference between your adjusted basis in the property and the amount realized. Determining the amount realized depends on your liability for the debt:

If you are *not* personally liable on the debt, the amount realized includes the full amount of the cancelled debt, regardless of the value of the property. You do not have ordinary income from the debt cancellation.

If you are personally liable, the amount realized includes the portion of the cancelled debt that equals the fair market value of the property. If the fair market value of the property is less than the debt, the foreclosure or voluntary conveyance back to the creditor is treated as two separate transactions:

1. A sale of property. Gain or loss is the difference between adjusted basis and the amount realized, including the cancelled debt up to the fair market value of the property.
2. The receipt of ordinary income upon the cancellation of the debt for less than the face amount of the debt. You generally have cancellation of debt income equal to the excess of the cancelled debt over the fair market value of the property. However, this income may not be taxable, if you come within the exclusion rules discussed at *11.8*, such as being insolvent at the time of the foreclosure. *See also 31.10* for the exclusion on restructurings of business real property debt.

EXAMPLES

1. Jones could not meet the mortgage payments on a condominium that cost him $85,000. He had paid cash of $20,000 and taken a mortgage loan of $65,000 on which he was personally liable. When the remaining balance of the loan was $62,000, he defaulted, and the bank accepted his voluntary conveyance of the unit, cancelling the loan. Similar units at the time were selling for $60,000. On the transaction, Jones incurred a loss of $25,000: the difference between his adjusted basis of $85,000 and the fair market value of the unit of $60,000. The loss is not deductible because the unit was held for personal purposes. Jones also recognizes income on the cancellation of the loan because the amount of the debt exceeded the fair market value of the unit by $2,000. This amount is taxable, unless Jones can show he was insolvent at the time of the transfer to the bank; *see 11.8.*
2. Brown invested in a vacant lot. He put down cash of $10,000 and assumed a mortgage of $20,000. When he could not make payments on the mortgage, the bank foreclosed. The net proceeds from the foreclosure sale were $32,000. Brown received $12,000 and realized a capital gain of $2,000 (the difference between his adjusted basis of $30,000 and the amount realized of $32,000). There is no income from cancellation of indebtedness because the debt was less than the value of the property.

Caution

Form 1099-A Notifies IRS

If your mortgaged property is foreclosed or repossessed, and the bank or other lender reacquires it, or if the lender knows that you have abandoned the property, you should receive from the lender Form 1099-A, which indicates the foreclosure bid price, the amount of your debt, and whether you were personally liable. The IRS may compare its copy of Form 1099-A with your return to check whether you have reported income from the foreclosure or abandonment.

If the lender also cancels your debt of $600 or more, you may instead receive Form 1099-C, on which the information about the foreclosure or repossession will be included.

Foreclosure proceeds less than outstanding mortgage. Where a foreclosure sale does not cancel the mortgage debt, how should the amount realized be computed? The Tax Court view is illustrated by the following case:

In 1982, Aizawa bought rental property for $120,000, paying $30,000 down and giving the seller a $90,000 recourse mortgage note, payable in five years. The Aizawas made timely monthly interest payments but failed to pay off the principal at the end of the fifth year. In 1987, the sellers sued and got a judgment of $133,507 for the original principal due of $90,000, attorneys' fees of $25,000, and extra interest charges. Then, at a foreclosure sale, the sellers bought back the property for $72,700. The judgment and foreclosure sale left a deficiency judgment of $60,807.

The Aizawas deducted a $70,898 loss. They claimed the deficiency judgment of $60,807 should be deducted from the mortgage of $90,000, leaving an amount realized of $29,193. The difference between this amount and the $100,091 undepreciated basis of the property gave them a $70,898 loss. The IRS claimed that the amount realized was $90,000, the amount of the mortgage principal, so that the loss was only $10,091 ($100,091 less $90,000).

The Tax Court disagreed with both sides. The court held that the amount realized was the $72,700 proceeds from the foreclosure sale, so that a loss of $27,391 ($100,091 less $72,700) was incurred. The Aizawas' approach is wrong; they reduced the amount realized by the deficiency award they had not paid. The IRS approach is wrong; it included in the amount realized part of the mortgage debt that the Aizawas still owed.

The court recognized that its approach gave the Aizawas an additional loss of $17,300 ($90,000 less $72,700) based on a debt they might not repay. However, this advantage may be eliminated by later events. If they pay off the remaining debt, they may not deduct any additional loss. If they are discharged from paying the balance of the debt, they may be required to report income on the discharge if they are solvent.

31.10 Restructuring Mortgage Debt

Rather than foreclose on a mortgage, a lender (mortgagee) may be willing to restructure the mortgage debt by cancelling either all or part of the debt. As a borrower (mortgagor), do not overlook the tax consequences of the new debt arrangement. A debt cancellation or reduction is taxable unless it fits within specific exceptions, such as insolvency or bankruptcy. As discussed at *11.8*, there is no tax if the debt is restructured by the seller of the property or where a debt is reduced by a third-party lender and you are either insolvent, bankrupt, or are a qualifying farmer. These rules apply also to a restructuring of a nonrecourse debt on which you are not personally liable; *see* the Jones Example below, which shows the IRS approach to figuring insolvency upon a debt cancellation.

In the case of partnership property, tax consequences of the restructuring of a third-party loan are determined at the partner level. This means that if you are a partner and are solvent *(11.8)* you may not avoid tax on the transaction, even if the partnership is insolvent.

EXAMPLE

In 2005, Jones borrowed $1,000,000 from Chester and signed a note payable for $1,000,000. Jones was not personally liable on the note, which was secured by an office building valued at $1,000,000 that he bought from Baker with the proceeds of Chester's loan. In 2006, when the value of the building declined to $800,000, Chester agreed to reduce the principal of the loan to $825,000. At the time, Jones held other assets valued at $100,000 and owed another person $50,000. In 2006, Jones realized income of $175,000 on the reduction of the debt, but he can avoid tax to the extent he is insolvent.

To determine the extent of Jones's insolvency, the IRS compares Jones's assets and liabilities immediately before the discharge. According to the IRS, his assets total $900,000: the building valued at $800,000 plus other assets of $100,000. His liabilities total $1,025,000: the debt of $50,000 plus the liability on the note, which the IRS considers to be $975,000, equal to the $800,000 value of the building and the $175,000 discharged debt. The difference between the assets of $900,000 and liabilities of $1,025,000 is $125,000, the amount by which Jones is insolvent. As Jones is insolvent by $125,000, only $50,000 of the $175,000 discharged debt is treated as taxable income.

Restructuring debt on business real estate. A solvent taxpayer may avoid tax on a restructuring of qualifying business real estate debt *(11.8)* by electing to reduce the basis of depreciable real property by the amount of the tax-free debt discharge. The election to reduce basis is made on Form 982.

EXAMPLE

Grant, who is solvent, owns a building worth $150,000 used in his business. It is subject to a first mortgage of $110,000 and a second mortgage of $90,000. Grant's basis in the building is $120,000. On July 10, 2006, the second mortgagee agrees to reduce the second mortgage to $30,000. This results in debt discharge of $60,000 ($90,000 – $30,000). The $60,000 is considered debt discharge income. But Grant may elect to exclude $50,000. He reports the remaining $10,000 of discharged debt as taxable income. The exclusion limit is calculated as follows:

2nd mortgage before discharge		$90,000
Less: Fair market value of building	$150,000	
Less: First mortgage	110,000	40,000
Excludable amount		$50,000

On Form 982, Grant may elect to exclude $50,000 from tax because the basis of the building is sufficient to absorb a basis reduction of $50,000.

Filing Tip

Reporting a Foreclosure or Voluntary Conveyance

You report a foreclosure sale or voluntary conveyance to a creditor on Schedule D if the property was held for personal or investment purposes.

Foreclosures and reconveyances of business assets are reported on Form 4797.

If income from cancellation of indebtness is realized and it is not excludable under the rules discussed at *11.8*, you report the taxable amount on Line 21, Form 1040.

31.11 Abandonments

On an abandonment of business or investment property, you may claim an ordinary loss for the property's adjusted basis (when abandoned) on Form 4797. However, if the abandoned property is later foreclosed or repossessed, you may realize a gain or loss under the rules in *31.9* for foreclosures or voluntary conveyances to creditors. For example, if an abandonment loss for mortgaged property is claimed in 2005 but in 2006 the property is foreclosed upon or repossessed by the lender, all or part of the cancelled debt will be treated as an amount realized by you on a sale in 2006. The amount realized depends on whether you were personally liable and the value of the property. If personally liable, you may also realize ordinary income from cancellation of the debt; *see 31.9*.

A loss is *not* deductible if the property was held for personal use. If the lender forecloses on the loan or repossesses the property, gain or loss must be figured, and ordinary income from cancellation of debt may be realized, as discussed at *31.9*.

Planning Reminder

Foreclosure After Abandonment

If, after the year the abandoned loss is claimed, the partnership's mortgaged holdings are foreclosed upon or reconveyed to the lender, each partner's share of the cancelled debt may be treated as an amount realized on a sale, or as ordinary cancellation of debt income; *see 31.9*.

Abandoning a partnership interest. Where real estate values have sharply declined, partnerships may be holding realty subject to mortgage debt that exceeds the current value of the property. Some investors in such partnerships have claimed that they can abandon their partnership interests and claim abandonment losses. In one case, an investor in a partnership holding land in Houston, Texas, argued that he abandoned his partnership interest by making an abandonment declaration at a meeting of partners, and also declaring that he would make no further payments. He offered his interest to the others, who refused his offer. The IRS held that he failed to prove abandonment of his partnership interest or that the partnership abandoned the land. The Tax Court sided with the IRS, emphasizing his failure to show that the partnership abandoned the land. However, the appeals court for the Fifth Circuit reversed and allowed the abandonment loss. It held that the emphasis should be on the partner's actions, not the actions of the partnership. Although neither state law nor the IRS regulations described how a partnership interest is to be abandoned, the appeals court held that the partner's acts and declaration were sufficient to effect an abandonment of his partnership interest. The appeals court also held that the loss on the partnership interest could have been sustained on the basis of the worthlessness of his interest. The partnership was insolvent beyond hope of rehabilitation: (1) the partnership's only asset was land with a fair market value less than the mortgage debt; (2) the partnership had no source of income; and (3) the partners refused to contribute more funds to keep the partnership afloat.

In a subsequent case, the Tax Court held that a doctor had abandoned a movie production partnership interest when he refused to advance any more money or to participate in the venture because he disapproved of the content of the film being produced and feared it might jeopardize his position at a hospital operated by a religious organization. Also, the limited partners had voted to dissolve.

31.12 Seller's Repossession After Buyer's Default on Mortgage

When you, as a seller, repossess realty on the buyer's default of a debt that the realty secures, you may realize gain or loss. (If the realty was a personal residence, the loss is not deductible.) A debt is secured by real property whenever you have the right to take title or possession or both in the event the buyer defaults on his or her obligation under the contract.

Figuring gain on the repossession. Gain on the repossession is the excess of: (1) payments received on the original sales contract prior to and on the repossession, including payments made by the buyer for your benefit to another party, over (2) the amount of taxable gain previously reported prior to the repossession.

Gain computed under these two steps may not be fully taxable. Taxable gain is limited to the amount of original profit less gain on the sale already reported as income for periods prior to the repossession and less your repossession costs.

The limitation on gain does not apply if the selling price cannot be computed at the time of sale as, for example, where the selling price is stated as a percentage of the profits to be realized from the development of the property sold.

These repossession gain rules do not apply if you repurchase the property by paying the buyer a sum in addition to the discharge of the debt, unless the repurchase and payment was provided for in the original sale contract, or the buyer has defaulted on his or her obligation, or default is imminent.

In such cases, gain or loss on the repossession, and basis in the repossessed property, must be determined under the different rules for personal property; *see* IRS Publication 537 for details.

EXAMPLE

Assume you sell land for $25,000. You take a $5,000 down payment plus a $20,000 mortgage, secured by the property, from the buyer, with principal payable at the rate of $4,000 annually plus 9% interest. The adjusted basis of the land was $20,000 and you elected to report the transaction on the installment basis. Your gross profit percentage is 20% ($5,000 profit divided by $25,000 selling price). In the year of sale, you include $1,000 in your income on the installment basis (20% of $5,000 down payment). The next year you reported profit of $800 (20% of $4,000 annual installment). In the third year, the buyer defaults, and you repossess the property. Your repossession costs are $500. The amount of gain on repossession is computed as follows:

1. Compute gain:		
Amount of money received ($5,000 *plus* $4,000)		$9,000
Less: Amount of gain taxed in prior years ($1,000 *plus* $800)		1,800
Gain		$7,200
2. Compute limit on taxable gain:		
Original profit		$5,000
Less:		
Gain reported as income	$1,800	
Repossession costs	500	2,300
Taxable gain on repossession		$2,700

Caution

Character of Gain

The gain limitation rules discussed at *31.12* do not affect the character of the gain. Thus, if you repossess property as a dealer, the gain is subject to ordinary income rates. If you, as an investor, repossess a tract originally held long term whose gain was reported on the installment method, the gain is capital gain.

The basis of repossessed property. This is the adjusted basis of the debt (face value of the debt less the unreported profits) secured by the property, figured as of the date of repossession, increased by (1) the taxable gain on repossession *and* (2) the legal fees and other repossession costs you paid.

EXAMPLE

Same facts as in the previous Example. The basis of the repossessed property is computed as follows:

1. Face value of debt ($20,000 note *less* $4,000 payment)		$16,000
2. *Less:* Unreported profit (20% of the $16,000 still due on the note)		3,200
3. Adjusted basis at date of repossession		$12,800
4. *Plus:* Gain on repossession	$2,700	
Repossession costs	500	3,200
5. Basis of repossessed property		$16,000

If you treated the debt as having become worthless or partially worthless before repossession, you are considered to receive, upon the repossession of the property securing the debt, an amount equal to the amount of the debt treated as worthless. You report as income the amount of any prior bad debt deduction and increase the basis of the debt by an amount equal to the amount reported as income.

If your debt is not fully discharged as a result of the repossession, the basis of the undischarged debt is zero. No loss may be claimed if the obligations subsequently become worthless. This rule applies to undischarged debts on the original obligation of the purchaser, a substituted obligation of the purchaser, a deficiency judgment entered in a court of law into which the purchaser's obligation was merged, and any other obligations arising from the transaction.

Principal residence. Special rules apply to repossessions and resales of a principal residence if you excluded all or part of the gain on your original sale of the residence *(29.1)*, and you resell it within a year after you repossess it.

The original sale and resale is treated as one transaction. You refigure the amount realized on the sale. You combine the selling price of the resale with the selling price of the original sale. From this total, you subtract selling expenses for both sales, the part of the original installment obligation that remains unpaid at the time of repossession, and repossession costs. The net is the amount realized on the combined sale-resale. Subtracting basis in the home from the amount realized gives the gain on the combined sale-resale before taking into account the exclusion rules. *See* Treasury Regulation Section 1.1038-2 for further details.

31.13 Foreclosure on Mortgages Other Than Purchase Money

If you, as a mortgagee (lender), bid in on a foreclosure sale to pay off a mortgage that is *not a purchase money mortgage*, your actual financial loss is the difference between the unpaid mortgage debt and the value of the property. For tax purposes, however, you may realize a capital gain or loss and a bad debt loss that are reportable *in the year of the foreclosure sale.*

Your bid is treated as consisting of two distinct transactions:

1. The repayment of your loan. To determine whether this results in a bad debt, the bid price is matched against the face amount of the mortgage.
2. A taxable exchange of your mortgage note for the foreclosed property, which may result in a capital gain or loss. This is determined by matching the bid price against the fair market value of the property.

Planning Reminder

Voluntary Conveyance

Instead of forcing you to foreclose, the mortgagor may voluntarily convey the property to you in consideration for your cancelling the mortgage debt. Your loss is the amount by which the mortgage debt plus accrued interest exceeds the fair market value of the property. If, however, the fair market value exceeds the mortgage debt plus accrued interest, the difference is taxable gain. The gain or loss is reportable in the year you receive the property. Your basis in the property is its fair market value when you receive it.

EXAMPLES

1. *Mortgagee's bid less than market value.* You hold a $40,000 mortgage on property having a fair market value of $30,000. You bid on the property at the foreclosure sale at $28,000. The expenses of the sale are $2,000, reducing the bid price to $26,000. The mortgagor is insolvent, so you have a bad debt loss of $14,000 ($40,000 – $26,000). You also have a $4,000 capital gain (the fair market value of the property of $30,000 – $26,000).
2. *Mortgagee's bid equal to market value.* Suppose your bid was $32,000, and you had $2,000 in expenses. The difference between the net bid price of $30,000 and the mortgage of $40,000 is $10,000. As the mortgagor is insolvent, there is a bad debt loss of $10,000. Since the net bid price equals the fair market value, there is neither capital gain nor loss.
3. *Mortgagee's bid greater than market value.* Suppose your bid was $36,000 and you had $2,000 in expenses. Your bad debt deduction is $6,000—the difference between the mortgage debt of $40,000 and the net bid price of $34,000. You also had a capital loss of $4,000 (the difference between the net bid price of $34,000 and the fair market value of $30,000).

Where the bid price equals the mortgage debt plus unreported but accrued interest, you report the interest as income. But where the accrued interest has been reported, the unpaid amount is added to the collection expenses.

31.14 Foreclosure Sale to Third Party

When a third party buys the property in a foreclosure, the mortgagee receives the purchase price to apply against the mortgage debt. If it is less than the debt, the mortgagee may proceed against the mortgagor for the difference. Foreclosure expenses are treated as offsets against the foreclosure proceeds and increase the bad debt loss.

You deduct your loss as a bad debt. The law distinguishes between two types of bad debt deductions: business bad debts and nonbusiness bad debts. A business bad debt is fully deductible. A nonbusiness bad debt is a short-term capital loss that can be offset only against capital gains, plus a limited amount of ordinary income *(5.33)*. In addition, you may deduct a partially worthless business bad debt, but you may not deduct a partially worthless nonbusiness bad debt. Remember this distinction if you are thinking of forgiving part of the mortgage debt as a settlement. If the debt

Planning Reminder

Keep Records

Preserve evidence of the property's fair market value. At a later date, the IRS may claim that the property was worth more than your bid and may tax you for the difference. Furthermore, be prepared to prove the worthlessness of the debt in order to support the bad debt deduction.

is a nonbusiness bad debt, you will not be able to take a deduction until the entire debt proves to be worthless. But whether you are deducting a business or a nonbusiness bad debt, your deduction will be allowed only if you show the debt to be uncollectible—for example, because a deficiency judgment is worthless or because the mortgagor is declared bankrupt.

EXAMPLE

You hold a $30,000 note and mortgage that are in default. You foreclose, and a third party buys the property for $20,000. Foreclosure expenses amount to $2,000. The deficiency is uncollectible. Your $12,000 loss is figured as follows:

Unpaid mortgage debt		$30,000
Foreclosure proceeds	$20,000	
Less: Expenses	2,000	
Net proceeds		18,000
Bad debt loss		$12,000

31.15 Transferring Mortgaged Realty

Mortgaging realty that has appreciated in value is one way of realizing cash on the appreciation without current tax consequences. The receipt of cash by mortgaging the property is not taxed; tax will generally be imposed only when the property is sold. However, there is a possible tax where the mortgage exceeds the adjusted basis of the property and the property is given away or transferred to a controlled corporation. Where the property is transferred to a controlled corporation, the excess is taxable gain. Further, if the IRS successfully charges that the transfer is part of a tax avoidance scheme, the taxable gain may be as high as the amount of the mortgage liability.

Charitable donations. The IRS holds that a donation of mortgaged property results in taxable income to the donor to the extent that the mortgage liability exceeds the donor's basis; *see 14.6.*

Chapter 32

Tax Pointers for Investors in Mutual Funds

Mutual-fund investments relieve you of the responsibility of making daily investment decisions for securities actively traded or affected by changing market conditions.

As a mutual-fund shareholder, you may receive several types of distributions, such as ordinary dividends, capital gain distributions, exempt-interest dividends, and return of capital distributions. The rules for reporting the different types of distributions are discussed in this chapter.

Different methods of identifying sold shares and determining the cost basis of those shares are also discussed. The choice of cost-basis methods will affect the computation of gain or loss on a sale of shares.

32.1 Investing in Mutual Funds

A mutual fund is a professionally managed pool of individual investors' contributions invested in a variety of securities. Mutual funds are either closed or open end. Open-end funds are much more popular than closed-end funds, and the term "mutual fund" generally refers to open-end funds. The value of and number of shares in the portfolio of an open-end fund change daily as investors purchase and redeem shares. A closed-end fund issues a fixed number of shares that trade like shares of publicly held corporations listed on the stock exchange. The daily price of its shares may be below or above the net value of its investment portfolio.

Funds are designed and marketed to meet different investor objectives. Money-market mutual funds allow investors to earn a return based on swings in the short-term money market for U.S. government obligations, CDs of commercial banks, bankers' acceptances, and commercial paper. Tax-free money-market funds invest in short-term obligations of state and local governments; investors of certain states may invest in funds paying dividends exempt from state and local, as well as federal, income tax. Income funds invest in either stocks paying high current dividends or bonds paying interest. Some funds focus on Treasury Inflation Protected Securities (TIPS). Growth funds invest in securities that are expected to appreciate over the long term. Some aggressive growth funds invest in small, developing companies with short track records. Other growth funds invest primarily in established firms. International funds invest in stocks of companies outside the United States. Sector funds specialize in specific industries, such as utilities, gold, or high technology companies. Balanced funds try to promote long-term growth by maintaining a mix of investments in bonds and stocks. Index funds buy the stocks that constitute a broad-based index to replicate the index's performance.

Do some research to find a fund that matches your investment objectives. Check the fund's performance over a substantial period of from five to 10 years. Keep in mind that yields fluctuate and are not guaranteed. In funds other than money market funds, the value per share also fluctuates. Gain or loss may be realized when you redeem shares in growth or income mutual funds. Also consider the rate at which a fund turns over its assets. A fund with a high turnover rate will realize frequent capital gains and losses, increasing the likelihood that capital gain distributions will be short term rather than long term. Short-term capital gain distributions are taxed as ordinary income dividends. Long-term capital gain distributions are subject to the rules for long-term capital gains.

Compare sales charges and redemption fees, if any, before you buy. No-load funds do not have a sales charge. Financial sections of major newspapers list prices of mutual-fund offerings. A no-load fund has the same purchase price and redemption price for fund shares; different prices for purchases and redemptions indicate a sales charge. Funds available through a broker may have a charge for commissions.

Planning Reminder

Exchange-Traded Funds (ETFs)

Exchange-traded funds (ETFs) are an alternative to mutual-fund index funds. ETFs provide diversification by closely tracking a particular market index (stocks, bonds, real estate securities, etc.). Unlike traditional open-end mutual funds, but like stocks or closed-end funds, ETFs trade on public exchanges. ETFs generally charge lower management fees than comparable open-end mutual funds. They are also generally more tax efficient than open-end funds, as they rarely have to make taxable capital gains distributions to investors. However, ETF investors pay broker commissions on every transaction, so for individuals who make small, regular investments, an open-end fund may be less costly.

32.2 Timing Your Investment

You may buy a tax liability if you invest in a mutual fund that has already realized significant capital gains during the year. For example, if a fund is about to make a large year-end capital gain distribution and you invest shortly before that, you will in effect have to pay tax on the return of your recently invested money.

You will be eligible to receive a forthcoming dividend or capital gain distribution if you are a shareholder of record on the "record date" set by the fund. On the "ex-dividend date," the net asset value per share will be reduced by the distribution amount per share. If you buy before the record date, the higher cost for your shares will be offset by the distributions you receive, but you will have to pay tax on the distributions. On the other hand, because you paid the higher pre-distribution price, your higher basis will reduce any capital gain on a later sale, or increase any capital loss.

If you want to limit your current tax and forego the basis increase, postpone your investment until after the record date for distributions. By that time, the value per share that determines the price will have been reduced by the distribution. Before investing, you may be able to find out from the fund when distributions for the year are expected; call the fund or check the fund's website for an estimate of projected distributions.

32.3 Reinvestment Plans

Funds allow you to reinvest dividends and capital gain distributions from the fund in new fund shares instead of receiving cash. You report such distributions as if you received them in cash. Form 1099-DIV sent to you by a fund reports the gross amount of taxable distributions that you must report on your return. *See 32.4* for how to report them.

Keep track of reinvested distributions. If you reinvest your mutual-fund distributions instead of taking them in cash, keep a record of the distributions and of the shares purchased with the reinvestment. The reinvested distributions are considered your cost basis for the acquired shares. You need a record of reinvestments to figure your cost when you sell your shares; *see 32.8* for calculating gain on the sale of mutual-fund shares.

Reinvested distribution can trigger wash sale. If you redeem fund shares at a loss within 30 days before or after a dividend distribution is reinvested into your account, a "wash sale" results, and the portion of the loss allocable to the reinvestment is not deductible *(30.6)*. The allocable loss is disallowed even though the wash sale was inadvertently caused by the reinvestment. The disallowed loss is actually deferred, as it is added to the cost basis of the replacement shares and will affect the computation of gain or loss on a later sale.

32.4 Mutual-Fund Distributions Reported on Form 1099-DIV

Mutual-fund distributions are reported to you and the IRS by the fund on Form 1099-DIV or substitute statement. Distributions that you reinvested to acquire additional shares are reported and taxed in the same way as distributions that are actually paid out to you.

Filing Tip

Reduced Rate for Qualified Dividends

Box 1b of Form 1099-DIV shows your qualified dividends, the portion of the amount in Box 1a (total ordinary dividends) that is eligible for the 15% or 5% capital gain rate.

Types of distributions. The Form 1099-DIV (or substitute statement) from your fund may show several kinds of distributions. Distributions that you reinvested *(32.3)* instead of receiving in cash are included on the Form 1099-DIV.

- ***Ordinary dividends***—are the most common type of dividend, payable out of the fund's earnings and profits. They are shown in Box 1a of Form 1099-DIV. Short-term capital gain distributions are reported as ordinary dividends.
- ***Qualified dividends***—are your share of the fund's qualified dividends *(4.1)* from U.S. corporations and qualified foreign corporations. This amount, shown in Box 1b of Form 1099-DIV, is eligible for the 15% capital gain rate (5% if the gain would otherwise be taxed in the 10% or 15% bracket), provided that you held your fund shares for at least 61 days during the 121-day period beginning 60 days before the ex-dividend date (also known as the reinvestment date).
- ***Capital gain distributions***—shown in Box 2a of Form 1099-DIV, are your share of the net long-term capital gains realized by the fund on sales of securities in its portfolio. These are taxable to you as long-term capital gain regardless of how long you have owned your fund shares.

  If the fund retained long-term capital gains and paid tax on them, your share will be reported to you on Form 2439, rather than Form 1099-DIV. *See 32.7.*
- Return of capital (nontaxable) distributions—shown in Box 3 of Form 1099-DIV, are a return of your investment that reduce your basis in your shares and are not taxed until basis has been reduced to zero.

  See* 32.8 *for details on how to report these distributions on your tax return.

Year-end dividends. Mutual funds sometimes declare dividends at the end of a calendar year but do not pay them until January of the following year. If the dividend is declared in October, November, or December, and paid in the following January, the fund will report the distribution as taxable in the year it is declared.

32.5 Tax-Exempt Bond Funds

Dividends from a bond fund that represent tax-exempt interest earned by the fund are not taxable, but capital gain distributions are taxable. The exempt-interest dividends are not shown by the fund on 1099-DIV, but are reported separately by the fund. You report exempt-interest dividends along with your other tax-exempt interest on Line 8b of Form 1040 or of Form 1040A. The amount on Line 8b is not taxable, but if you receive Social Security benefits, the amount may affect the amount of taxable benefits; *see 34.3.*

Capital gain distributions are shown on Form 1099-DIV and must be reported on your return; *see* Table 32-1 on page 544.

When you redeem your shares in a tax-exempt bond fund or exchange the fund shares for other shares in a different fund, you realize taxable capital gain or deductible loss.

If you received exempt-interest dividends on mutual-fund shares held for six months or less and sold those shares at a loss, the amount of your loss is reduced by the exempt-interest dividend. To reflect this adjustment, you increase the sales price reported on Line 1 in column (d) of Schedule D by the loss not allowed. Report the balance as a short-term capital loss.

EXAMPLE

In January 2007, you bought a mutual-fund share for $40. In February 2007, the mutual fund paid a $5 dividend from tax-exempt interest, which is not taxable to you. In March 2007, you sold the share for $34. If it were not for the tax-exempt dividend, your loss would be $6 ($40 – 34). However, you may deduct only $1, the part of the loss that exceeds the exempt-interest dividend ($6 – 5). On Schedule D in column (d), increase the sales price from $34 to $39 (the $5 nondeductible loss). You may deduct $1 as a short-term capital loss.

32.6 Fund Expenses

If you own shares in a *publicly offered* mutual fund, you do not pay tax on your share of the fund expenses. There should be no entry in Box 5 of your Form 1099-DIV. However, expenses of a *non–publicly offered* fund are included in Box 5 of Form 1099-DIV and must be reported as a taxable dividend, even though the amount has not actually been distributed to you. This amount is included as a fully taxable ordinary dividend in Box 1 of Form 1099-DIV. An offsetting deduction may be claimed on Schedule A as a miscellaneous itemized deduction, subject to the 2% adjusted gross income floor; *see 19.1.*

For purposes of figuring gain or loss when you redeem or exchange shares, load charges (sales fees) on the purchase of the shares may not be treated as part of your cost if you held the shares for 90 days or less and then reinvested the sales proceeds at a reduced load charge.

32.7 Tax Credits From Mutual Funds

Undistributed capital gains. Some mutual funds retain their long-term capital gains and pay capital gains tax on those amounts. Even though not actually received by you, you include as a capital gain distribution on your return the amount of the undistributed capital gain allocated to you by the fund. If the mutual fund paid a tax on the undistributed capital gain, you are entitled to a tax credit.

To claim the credit, check the Form 2439 sent to you by your fund, which lists your share of undistributed capital gain and the amount of tax paid on it by the fund. Enter your share of the tax the fund paid on this gain on Line 70 of Form 1040, and check the box for Form 2439. Attach Copy B of Form 2439 to your return to support your tax credit. Increase the basis of your stock by the excess of the undistributed capital gain over the amount of tax paid by the mutual fund, as reported on Form 2439.

Foreign tax credit or deduction. You may be able to claim a foreign tax credit (on Form 1116) or a deduction on Schedule A for your share of the fund's foreign taxes. In Box 6 of Form 1099-DIV, the fund will report your share of the foreign taxes paid by the fund, and in Box 7, the name of the foreign country. The fund should give you instructions for claiming the foreign tax credit or deduction; also *see 36.14.*

Filing Tip

Undistributed Capital Gains From REITs

The reporting and credit rules discussed at *32.7* for mutual funds also apply if you own shares in a REIT that has retained its long-term capital gains.

32.8 How To Report Mutual Fund Distributions

You cannot report mutual fund distributions on Form 1040EZ. Further, you must file Form 1040 and cannot use Form 1040A if you must report an undistributed capital gain on Schedule D or you must report a return of capital distribution on Schedule D because your basis in your fund shares has been reduced to zero.

Check Table 32-1 below for details on reporting distributions on your return.

Table 32-1 Reporting Mutual-Fund Distributions

Type of Distribution	*Shown by the Fund in*	*How To Report*
Ordinary dividends and short-term capital gain distributions.	Box 1a, Form 1099-DIV	Box 1a of Form 1099-DIV shows taxable ordinary dividends. The total includes ordinary dividends and short-term capital gain distributions, which are taxed as ordinary income, and also qualified dividends, if any, which are taxable at the 15% or 5% capital gain rate. The Box 1a total must be entered on Line 9 of Form 1040 or 1040A. If your ordinary dividends from all sources exceed $1,500 or if you received as a nominee ordinary dividends on behalf of another taxpayer, you must itemize the ordinary dividends on Line 5, Schedule B of Form 1040, or Line 5, Schedule 1 of Form 1040A.
Qualified dividends (eligible for 15% or 5% capital gain rate if you held your shares at least 61 days during the 121-day period beginning 60 days before the ex-dividend date).	Box 1b, Form 1099-DIV	Box 1b shows the portion of the Box 1a amount that is eligible for the 15% or 5% capital gain rate. Report these qualified dividends on Line 9b of Form 1040 or 1040A. Unless you have 28% rate gains or unrecaptured Section 1250 gains that have to be reported on the "Schedule D Tax Worksheet" in the Schedule D instructions, you may use the "Qualified Dividends and Capital Gain Tax Worksheet'" in the Form 1040 or Form 1040A instructions to figure your regular tax liability using the capital gain rates.
Capital gain distributions. (This represents your share of net long-term gains realized by a fund on sales made from its portfolio.)	Boxes 2a–2d, Form1099-DIV	Box 2a of Form 1099-DIV shows your total capital gain distributions. If your only capital gains are capital gain distributions, you do not have capital losses, and no amount is shown in Boxes 2b–2d of all your Forms 1099-DIV, you generally do not have to complete Schedule D (Form 1040) and may report the capital gain distributions from Box 2a directly on Line 13 of Form 1040 or Line 10 of Form 1040A. In that case, you use the Qualified Dividends and Capital Gain Tax Worksheet in the Form 1040 or 1040A instructions to figure your tax using the capital gain rates. If Schedule D is required, the total capital gain distributions from Box 2a must be reported on Line 13 of Schedule D and the rest of Schedule D completed. Box 2b shows the part of Box 2a that is unrecaptured Section 1250 gain from the sale of depreciable buildings. Box 2c shows the part of Box 2a that is Section 1202 gain eligible for a 50% exclusion. Box 2d shows the amount of Box 2a that is 28% rate gain from sales of collectibles. If you have an amount in Box 2b, 2c, or 2d, you must complete Schedule D.
Return of capital distributions (nontaxable)	Box 3, 1099-DIV	A return of capital distribution is not taxable income. However, if your basis for your shares has been reduced to zero by return of capital gain distributions, report additional nontaxable distributions as either long-term or short-term capital gain on Schedule D of Form 1040, depending on how long you held the shares.
Exempt-interest dividends	A separate statement; not included on Form 1099-DIV. This will be sent to you within 60 days after the close of the fund's taxable year.	Report along with other tax-exempt interest on Line 8b of Form 1040 or Form 1040A.
Undistributed capital gains	Undistributed gains shown on Form 2439, Box 1a Tax paid by fund shown on Form 2439, Box 2	Box 1 of Form 2439 shows your total share of undistributed long-term capital gains. The undistributed gains are reported on Line 11 of Schedule D. To get a tax credit for the tax paid by the fund, enter the tax on Line 70 of Form 1040. Increase the basis of your mutual-fund shares by the excess of the undistributed gains included on Schedule D over the tax credit claimed on Line 69 of Form 1040.
Fund expenses from non-publicly offered funds	Box 5, Form 1099-DIV	If you itemize deductions on Form 1040, the expenses are deductible as miscellaneous expenses, subject to the 2% adjusted gross income floor *(19.1).*
Foreign taxes	Box 6, Form 1099-DIV. Box 7 shows the country imposing the tax.	The foreign taxes may be claimed as a tax credit on Form 1116 or as an itemized deduction on Schedule A of Form 1040; *see 36.14.*

32.9 Redemptions and Exchanges of Fund Shares

When you ask the fund to redeem all or part of your shares, you have transacted a sale subject to capital gain or loss rules explained in Chapter 5. Exchanges of shares of one fund for shares of another fund within the same fund "family" are treated as sales. If you owned the shares for more than one year, your gain or loss is long term; if you held them for a year or less, your gain or loss is short term. However, if you received a capital gain distribution before selling shares held six months or less at a loss, your loss must be reported as a long-term capital loss to the extent of the capital gain distribution attributable to the sold shares. Any excess loss is reported as a short-term capital loss. This restriction does not apply to dispositions under periodic redemption plans.

EXAMPLE

In June 2006, you bought mutual-fund shares for $1,000. In August, you received a capital gain distribution of $50, and you sold the shares for $850 in September. Instead of reporting a $150 short-term capital loss ($1,000 cost – $850 proceeds), you must report a long-term capital loss of $50, the amount of the capital gain distribution; the remaining $100 of the loss is a short-term capital loss.

Caution

Wash-Sale Loss Disallowance

A loss on the redemption of fund shares is disallowed to the extent that within 30 days before or after the sale, you buy shares in the same fund. The wash-sale rule *(30.6)* is triggered even when the acquisition of new shares occurs automatically (within the 61-day period) under a dividend reinvestment plan.

Identifying the shares you sell. Determining which mutual-funds shares are being sold is necessary to figure your gain or loss and whether the gain or loss is short term or long term. *See 32.10* for the identification methods.

Holding period of fund shares. You determine your holding period by using the trade dates. The trade date is the date on which you contract to buy or redeem the mutual-fund shares. Do not confuse the trade date with the settlement date, which is the date by which the mutual-fund shares must be delivered and payment must be made. Most mutual funds will show the trade date on your purchase and redemption confirmation statements.

Your holding period starts on the day after the day you bought the shares. (The day you bought the shares is the trade date.) This same date of each succeeding month is the start of a new month regardless of the number of days in the month before. The day you dispose of the shares (trade date) is also part of your holding period.

32.10 Basis of Redeemed Shares

To figure gain or loss, you need to know the basis per share. Generally, your basis is the purchase price of the shares, including shares acquired by reinvesting distributions back into the fund, plus commission or load charges.

Load charges. Basis does not include load charges (sales fees) on the purchase of mutual-fund shares if you held the shares for 90 days or less and then exchanged them for shares in a different fund in the same family of funds at a reduced load charge.

EXAMPLE

You pay a $200 load charge on purchasing shares for $10,000 in Fund A. Within 90 days, you exchange the Fund A shares for Fund B shares. Because Fund A and Fund B are in the same family of funds, the $200 load charge that would otherwise be due on the purchase of the Fund B shares is waived. For purposes of figuring your gain or loss on the exchange of Fund A shares, your basis is $10,000, not $10,200. The disallowed $200 is added to the basis of the new Fund B shares, provided those shares are held more than 90 days. If the waived load charge on Fund B shares had been $100, basis for the original Fund A shares would be increased by $100, the excess of the original $200 load charge over the amount waived on the reinvestment.

Planning Reminder

Keeping Track of Cost Basis

Keep confirmation statements for purchases of shares as well as a record of distributions that are automatically reinvested in your account. These will show the cost basis for your shares. Your basis is increased by amounts reported to you by the fund on Form 2439, representing the difference between your share of undistributed capital gains that you were required to report as income and your share of the tax paid by the fund on undistributed gains. Your basis is reduced by nontaxable dividends that are a return of your investment. Keep copies of Form 2439 and information returns showing nontaxable dividends.

Identifying the sold shares. If your shares in a mutual fund were acquired at different times, you need to know the basis of the particular shares you are selling in order to determine gain or loss. There are several methods of identifying which shares you are selling:

- ***Specific Identification Method***—allows you to select exactly which shares are being sold, enabling you to determine your gain or loss and achieve a desired tax result (*see* Examples 1 and 2 below and Table 32-2 on page 548). You may not use this method if you have used the averaging cost basis method on a prior sale from the same fund.

Planning Reminder

Specific Identification Method

When you redeem part of your shares, the specific identification method of identifying the shares sold provides you the most flexibility. However, note the paperwork requirements for this method in Examples 1 and 2 in *32.10*.

Planning Reminder

Shares Received as Gift

To determine your original basis of mutual-fund shares you acquired by gift, you must know the donor's adjusted basis, the date of the gift, the fair market value of the shares at the time of the gift, and whether any gift tax was paid on the shares. *See 5.17.*

- ***Average Cost Basis Method***—averages your cost for all shares in the fund (*see* Example 3 below). Once you elect to use average basis, you must continue to do so for all accounts in the same fund; *see* Table 32-2 on page 548 for averaging details.
- ***First-in, first-out (FIFO) Method***—applies if you do not specifically identify the shares or elect the averaging method (*see* Examples 1 and 2 below).

See Table 32-2 on page 548 for details on these identification methods.

EXAMPLES

1. In 1995, you bought 100 shares of a mutual fund for $10 a share. In 1998, you bought another 200 shares for $11 a share, and in 1999, another 500 shares for $15 a share. In 2006, you sell 130 shares at $20 a share, but do not specifically identify the shares being sold. Under the IRS FIFO method, you are treated as having first sold the original 100 shares from 1995, then 30 of the shares bought in 1998. Your basis for the sold shares is $1,330:

100 shares from 1995 costing $10 each	$1,000
30 shares from 1998 costing $11 each	330
	$1,330

Your taxable gain is $1,270 ($2,600 sales price less $1,330 basis). Had you specifically designated shares from the most recent lot, which cost you more, you would have reduced the taxable gain. For example, if you had given the fund written instructions to sell 130 of the 500 shares that you bought in 1999 at $15 per share and the fund acknowledged in writing your instructions, your basis on the sale under the specific identification method would be $1,950 (130 × $15) instead of $1,330. Gain would be reduced from $1,270 to $650 ($2,600 sales price less $1,950 basis).

2. Hall sold by phone part of his holdings in two mutual funds acquired over a number of years without specifying the particular shares being sold. On his return, Hall claimed a net long-term capital loss of about $2,400 using a LIFO method (last-in, first-out). However, using the FIFO method, the IRS held that he had a long-term capital gain of $163,000. In the Tax Court, Hall argued that the specific identification rule applies only to stock certificates, not noncertificate shares left on deposit with a mutual fund. The court disagreed. Without specific identification, the IRS FIFO method is reasonable. If good records are kept, you can select the specific shares being sold at the time of sale. You cannot wait until you file your return to allot specific sales to gain a tax advantage.

   What if you give written instructions to a mutual fund that specific shares should be sold, but the fund does not acknowledge your specification in its written confirmation? Regulations require such a written confirmation within a reasonable time after the sale.

3. You bought 160 shares of the XYZ Mutual Fund on February 4, 2002, for $4,000. On August 5, 2002, you bought another 240 shares for $4,800. You obtained an additional 10 shares on December 16, 2002, when you reinvested a $300 dividend. On December 18, 2003, you obtained an additional 20 shares when you reinvested a $750 dividend. This was your last investment in the fund. You sell 200 shares of the fund on September 25, 2006, for $8,000.

   Using the average basis method, your average basis is $22.91 per share. Your total cost basis for all 430 shares is $9,850. Dividing $9,850 by 430 gives you an average basis per share of $22.91. Thus, your basis for the 200 sold shares is $4,582 (200 × $22.91 = $4,582).

   Under the average-basis method, the shares you acquired first are the shares deemed to be sold for purposes of determining your capital gain holding period. Thus, you are deemed to have sold the 160 shares bought on February 4, 2002, and 40 of the 240 shares bought on August 5, 2002. The sold shares were held long term on the sale date of September 25, 2006. You have a $3,418 long-term capital gain on the sale: $8,000 proceeds less $4,582 basis figured under the average-basis method.

32.11 Comparison of Basis Methods

As discussed at *32.10*, your choice of basis method can have a significant effect on the computation of capital gains and losses when you sell a portion of your shares in a mutual fund. The following example compares the single averaging method to the specific identification and FIFO methods.

Transaction history. Assume that on February 8, 1993, you made an initial investment of $4,500 for 375 shares in ABC Mutual Fund at $12 per share. Under the dividend reinvestment plan, you reinvested a $400 dividend, received in December 1993, for an additional 40 shares at $10 per share. On June 10, 1994, you bought 350 shares at $15 per share. In December 1994 you reinvested your dividend, this time for 25 shares at $12 per share. On September 14, 1995, you bought 200 shares at $16 per share. You did not reinvest your dividends received in 1995–2007 and did not buy any more shares. On October 22, 2007, you ask ABC Mutual Fund to redeem 200 shares and you receive $20 per share. The table below illustrates your transactions.

Date	*Action*	*Share Price*	*No. of Shares*	*Shares Owned*
2/8/1993	Invest $4,500	$12	375	375
12/20/1993	Reinvest $400 dividend	$10	40	415
6/10/1994	Invest $5,250	$15	350	765
12/14/1994	Reinvest $300 dividend	$12	25	790
9/14/1995	Invest $3,200	$16	200	990
10/22/2007	Redeem $4,000	$20	200	790

The following are three different ways to compute the basis of the shares redeemed on October 22, 2007.

Specific identification method. If you identify the shares you sold, you can use the adjusted basis of those shares to figure your gain or loss. You must specify the particular shares to be redeemed at the time of the sale, and must receive a written confirmation of your specification within a reasonable time. Depending on your situation, you may want to either maximize or minimize your gain or loss on the sale. Here, you will have a gain regardless of which shares are treated as being sold. Assuming you want to minimize your gain, then you would specify the 200 shares bought at $16 per share on September 14, 1995, as the shares sold. Since the shares were sold for $20 per share, the gain would be $4 per share, for a total of $800 of long-term capital gain ($4,000 – $3,200).

FIFO (first-in, first-out). If you do not identify which shares you sold or choose the averaging method, you must use the basis of the shares you acquired first as the basis of the shares sold. Therefore, the oldest shares still available, the February 8, 1993, shares, are considered sold first. Thus, the basis of the 200 shares sold would be $12 per share. Your long-term capital gain is $1,600 ($4,000 – $2,400).

Average cost. The ABC Mutual Fund may provide you with your average basis when you make the redemption. If it does not, you may compute the average basis for all shares owned at the time of disposition, regardless of how long you owned them, including shares acquired with reinvested dividends. The basis and gain is computed as follows: You total the number of shares owned prior to the sale, 990, and total your investment in these shares, which is $13,650. You divide $13,650 by 990, which gives an average cost of $13.79 per share and a total cost of $2,758 for the 200 shares. Your gain is $1,242 ($4,000 – $2,758). For holding period purposes, the shares sold are considered to be from the earliest lot in 1993, so your gain is long-term capital gain.

Result: The specific identification method gives you the lowest capital gain under this set of facts.

Caution

Get Written Confirmation for Specific Identification Method

If you want to take advantage of the specific identification method, make sure the fund sends you a written confirmation of your selling instructions.

The specific identification method allows you to designate specific shares as the shares sold, allowing you to minimize a gain on the sale or to select shares that, because of their basis, would give you a loss.

Table 32-2 Identifying Mutual-Fund Shares When You Sell

Method—	Tax Effect—
Specific identification of shares sold	If you sell some of your shares that have been left on deposit with an agent for the fund, and you identify the specific lot of shares being sold in your sell order, you can fix profit or loss on the sale, depending on the cost of the shares selected. *See* Example 1 in *32.10.* You should give the fund written instructions to sell shares that you bought on a particular date and at a particular price. Ask the fund for a written confirmation that acknowledges your instructions. The IRS requires that written confirmation of your instruction to sell particular shares be received within a reasonable time after the sale. The fund does not actually have to sell specific shares, just provide written confirmation that you instructed it to do so.
FIFO (First-in, first-out)	If you do not specifically identify the sold shares as just discussed, and you do not elect to average cost basis as discussed below, the IRS requires you to compute gain or loss as if shares were sold in the order that you acquired them. If the earliest acquired shares are treated as sold, taxable gain on a current sale will generally be higher than if the specific identification method was used, assuming that your least expensive shares were bought first; *see* Example 1 in *32.10.*
Averaging your basis	You may elect to average the cost of shares acquired at different times and prices. The election applies to mutual-fund shares held by an agent, usually a bank, in an account kept for the periodic acquisition or redemption of shares in the particular fund. You still need records of your total basis, but averaging avoids the difficult task of identifying the exact shares being sold. Many funds ease the record-keeping burden by providing to shareholders who have redeemed shares a statement showing their average cost basis under the single-category method. *See* Example 3 in *32.10.* The single-category method is easier to apply than the double-category method, as explained below. To elect either averaging method, attach a note to your return specifying the chosen method. Once you have elected a method, you must continue to apply the same method for all sales or exchanges of shares in the same fund. However, you may use the specific identification method or the FIFO method, or the other averaging method for shares of other funds in the same "family" of funds. For example, if you own shares in the XYZ Co. growth fund and also in the XYZ Co. bond fund, you may use an averaging method for the bond fund shares and the specific identification method for the growth fund shares. You can use the average cost basis for sales of shares in one mutual-fund family, and use the specific identification method for sales of shares of other fund families. ***Single-category averaging.*** You figure the average cost per share by dividing your total basis for all shares in the account by the number of shares. For example, if you bought 100 shares of a fund in 2002 at $20 per share and another 100 shares in 2003 at $30 per share, your average basis per share is $25 ($5,000 total cost ÷ 200 shares). If you sell 50 shares in 2006 for $35 a share, your basis for the sold shares is $1,250 (50 × $25 average basis) and your gain on the sale is $500 ($1,750 sales proceeds less $1,250 basis). For holding period purposes, you are treated as having sold shares in the order you acquired them (first-in, first-out). ***Double-category averaging.*** You have to separate your account shares into a long-term category for shares held more than one year and a short-term category for shares held one year or less. You figure the average cost per share in each category by dividing the total basis for all shares in that category by the number of shares in that category. You may specify to the agent handling share transactions the category from which you are selling. If you do not so specify, the long-term shares are deemed to have been sold first. If the number of shares sold exceeds the number in the long-term class, the excess shares are charged to the short-term class.

Chapter 33

Educational Tax Benefits

The tax law provides several tax benefits for people attending school. If you can take advantage of them, you are in effect receiving a government subsidy that lowers the cost of education.

The following benefit provisions can provide substantial tax savings, but are hedged with restrictions that may bar or limit their availability: Hope and lifetime learning education tax credits, a student loan interest deduction, and a deferral of taxes on interest earned on contributions to state-sponsored college tuition programs and Coverdell ESAs. An above-the-line deduction for higher education tuition and fees may be available if your income is too high to claim a Hope or lifetime learning credit; *see 33.13*.

Scholarships, Grants, and Excludable Savings Bond Interest

33.1 Scholarships and Grants

Scholarships and fellowships of a degree candidate are tax free to the extent that the grants pay for tuition and course-related fees, books, supplies, and equipment that are required for courses. Amounts for room, board, and incidental expenses are taxable. If you are not a candidate for a degree (*see* the degree test below), your entire grant is taxable.

Generally, you must pay tax on grants or tuition reductions that pay for teaching or other services required as a condition of receiving the grant. This is true even if all degree candidates are required to perform the services. Thus, if you are a graduate student and receive a stipend for teaching, those payments are taxable, subject to withholding, and reported by the school on Form W-2. Similarly, no tax-free exclusion is allowed for federal grants where the recipient agrees to do future work with the federal government. However, a grant or tuition reduction that represents payment for teaching, research, or other services is not taxable if it is paid under the National Health Services Corps Scholarship Program or the Armed Forces Health Professions Scholarship and Financial Assistance Program.

Degree test. Scholarships given to students attending a primary or secondary school, or to those pursuing a degree at a college or university, meet the degree test. Also qualifying are full-time or part-time scholarships for study at an educational institution that (1) provides an educational program acceptable for full-time credit towards a higher degree or offers a program of training to prepare students for gainful employment in a recognized occupation *and* (2) is authorized under federal or state law to provide such a program and is accredited by a nationally recognized accreditation agency.

Caution

Graduate Teaching and Research Assistants

If you must teach, do research, or provide other services to obtain a tuition reduction for graduate studies, a tuition reduction from the school is tax free if it is in addition to regular pay for the services. If the tuition reduction is your compensation, it is taxable, unless it is paid under the National Health Services Corps Scholarship Program or the Armed Forces Health Professions Scholarship and Financial Assistance Program.

33.2 Tuition Reductions for College Employees

Free or partially free tuition for *undergraduate* studies provided to a faculty member or school employee is generally not taxable. The tuition reduction may be for education at his or her own school or at a similar school. Tuition benefits may be taxable to highly compensated employees if the tuition plan discriminates in their favor. Tuition reductions that represent compensation for services are taxable unless paid under the National Health Services Corps Scholarship Program or the Armed Forces Health Professions Scholarship and Financial Assistance Program.

Tax-free tuition benefits may also be provided to the employee's spouse, dependent child, a former employee who retired or left on disability, a widow or widower of an individual who died while employed by the school, or a widow or widower of a retired or disabled employee.

A child under the age of 25 qualifies for a tax-free tuition reduction if both parents have died and one of the parents qualified for tax-free tuition benefits. If the child is age 25 or over, tuition reductions are taxed even if both parents are deceased.

33.3 How Fulbright Awards Are Taxed

Fulbright awards for teaching, lecturing, or research are taxable unless you can claim the foreign earned income exclusion to avoid tax on the grant (Chapter 36). If you do not qualify for the exclusion, your overseas stay is temporary, and you intend to return to your regular teaching position in the United States, you may deduct the cost of your travel, meals, and lodgings overseas.

33.4 U.S. Savings Bond Tuition Plans

Consider the use of Series EE bonds *(30.14)* or I bonds *(30.15)* to fund part of a college savings program. You can defer the interest income until final maturity (30 years) or report the interest annually. At redemption, the interest is not subject to state or local tax. For bonds purchased in your child's name, having your child report the interest annually may be advisable where it can be offset by the child's standard deduction or itemized deductions. To the extent interest is offset each year, it escapes tax; *see 4.29*.

Interest exclusion may be available if you redeem EE bonds issued after 1989 or I bonds. If you purchased EE bonds in your own name or jointly with your spouse after 1989 and have been deferring the reporting of interest income, you may be able to exclude accumulated interest from federal tax in the year you redeem the bonds if in that year you pay tuition and enrollment education fees or you contribute to a Coverdell ESA *(33.11)* or qualified tuition program *(33.5)*. The interest exclusion rule also applies to redemptions of I bonds. The exclusion, claimed on Form 8815, is subject to several limitations as discussed in the following paragraphs.

Who qualifies for the exclusion. You must be age 24 or over before the month in which the bonds are purchased, and the bonds must be issued solely in your name or in the joint names of you and your spouse. You may not claim the exclusion for bonds bought in your child's name or owned jointly with your child. In the year the bonds are redeemed you must pay tuition and enrollment fees or contribute to a Coverdell ESA or qualified tuition plan for yourself, your spouse, or your dependents for whom you claim an exemption on your return. Thus, grandparents may not claim the exclusion if they buy savings bonds to fund the college education of grandchildren unless the children are dependents of the grandparents in the year the bonds are cashed. Tuition and fees must be for a college, university, or vocational school that meets federal financial aid standards. Room and board are not eligible expenses. Married persons filing separately are *not* eligible for the exclusion.

Excludable amount and phase-out rule. The tax-free amount of EE or I bond interest is figured on Form 8815. The amount of the exclusion depends on the amount of qualified higher educational expenses you pay and your modified adjusted gross income (MAGI) in the year of redemption. However, no exclusion is allowed to a married person who files separately, regardless of income or amount of expenses.

On Form 8815, qualified expenses must be reduced by the amount of any nontaxable scholarship or fellowship grant, tax-free employer-provided educational assistance, educational expenses taken into account when figuring a Hope or lifetime learning credit *(see 33.7)*, and educational expenses taken into account when figuring the tax-free portion of a distribution from a qualified tuition plan *(33.6)* or a Coverdell ESA *(see 33.11)*.

If after required reductions qualified expenses equal or exceed the redemption proceeds, 100% of the interest is potentially excludable, subject to the phaseout based on MAGI. If the redemption amount exceeds the amount of educational expenses (after any required reduction), the excludable amount is based on the ratio of expenses to the redemption amount and the phaseout computation.

A full interest exclusion is allowed only to persons with MAGI below a phase-out threshold. For 2006, the MAGI phase-out ranges are $94,700 to $124,700 for married persons filing jointly and qualifying widow(er)s, and $63,100 to $78,100 for single persons and heads of household. For purposes of applying the phaseout, MAGI is generally your regular adjusted gross income plus the interest on the redeemed EE or I bonds, student loan interest *(33.14)*, or tuition and fees *(33.13)* that you deduct, and foreign income items and employer-provided adoption assistance that you excluded from income. *See* the Form 8815 instructions.

EXAMPLE

In November 2006, you redeem an I bond that you bought in September 2001 for $10,000 (face value). You receive $13,372, including $10,000 principal and $3,372 interest. In 2006, your qualified higher education expenses total $12,500. After taking into account $2,200 of expenses used to figure a Hope credit *(33.8)*, you show $10,300 of qualified higher education expenses on Form 8815. The excludable percentage of interest is 77.03% ($10,300 divided by $13,372). Thus, $2,597 (77.03% × $3,372) of the interest is potentially excludable from income, subject to the phase-out rules.

Assume that you are married filing jointly and have MAGI of $97,100 for 2006. On Form 8815, you divide your excess MAGI of $2,400 ($97,100 – 94,700 threshold) by the $30,000 phase-out range to get a phase-out percentage of 8%. Thus, 8% of the potential $2,597 exclusion, or $208, is phased out. The exclusion is limited to $2,389 ($2,597 – $208).

Qualified Tuition Programs (Section 529 Plans)

33.5 Contributing to a Qualified Tuition Program (Section 529 Plan)

Qualified tuition programs (QTPs), also known as Section 529 plans, allow you to either prepay a designated beneficiary's future qualified higher education expenses or to establish a savings plan from which such expenses can be paid. States can sponsor savings plans and prepayment plans.

Law Alert

QTP Provisions Made Permanent

The Pension Protection Act of 2006 has permanently extended QTP provisions that were scheduled to expire at the end of 2010, most prominently the rule that allows tax-free treatment for QTP distributions used to pay college costs. By removing the uncertainty over the post-2010 rules, the new law is expected to spur greater interest in QTPs among parents who may have held back from investing.

Private colleges, universities, and vocational schools can set up prepayment plans only. Qualified higher education costs include tuition, fees, books, supplies, and eligible room and board costs. As discussed at *33.6*, distributions are generally tax free to the extent of qualified higher education expenses.

In a prepayment plan, a parent or other relative can purchase tuition credits or certificates as a prepayment of a child's future college costs. Where the child will not start college for many years, prepaying tuition according to a set schedule can avoid higher inflation-based tuition costs down the road. In a state-sponsored savings plan, annual contributions are made to an account for the benefit of the designated beneficiary, earnings accumulate tax-free, and withdrawals can later be made to pay the beneficiary's qualified higher education costs.

Contribution details and other plan terms including investment options can vary greatly from plan to plan. If you are considering an investment, you should contact the state or educational institution maintaining the plan for details.

Contributions are not deductible for federal tax purposes. However, a state income tax deduction may be available to residents who contribute to a state-sponsored QTP.

You may contribute to both a QTP and a Coverdell ESA *(33.11)* in the same year on behalf of the same beneficiary.

Gift tax consequences. A contribution to a qualified tuition program is treated as a completed gift of a present interest passed from the contributor to the beneficiary at the time of contribution. Contributions are eligible for the annual gift tax exclusion, which is currently $12,000 for a contribution from an individual (or $24,000 for a married couple electing gift splitting). If your contribution exceeds the regular annual exclusion, you may elect to treat up to $60,000 of the contribution ($120,000 for a married couple who elect gift splitting) as if it were made ratably over a five-year period. If the election is made, you have to report as a taxable gift on Form 709 only 20% of the total contribution (up to the $60,000 or $120,000 limit) in the year of contribution. In each of the next four years an additional 20% is reported. If the contribution exceeds the $60,000 (or $120,000) limit, the excess must be reported as a taxable gift on Form 709 in the year of the contribution.

33.6 Distributions From Qualified Tuition Programs (Section 529 Plans)

The portion of a QTP distribution that is allocable to a recovery of contributions to the plan (basis) is not taxable. This is true whether the plan is a state QTP or a private educational institution QTP. A beneficiary who receives a distribution of earnings from a state or private QTP to pay college costs does not have to include the earnings in income if the total distribution does not exceed "adjusted qualified higher education expenses" for the year, as discussed below.

On Form 1099-Q, which you should receive from the plan paying the distribution, the gross distribution in Box 1 is divided between earnings in Box 2 and the return of investment (or basis) in Box 3.

Qualified higher education expenses. For purposes of figuring if part of a distribution from a QTP is taxable (*see* below), qualified higher education costs are tuition, fees, books, supplies, and equipment required for enrollment or attendance at an eligible educational institution, which is any college, university, vocational school, or other postsecondary school eligible to participate in federal student aid programs. Reasonable room and board costs for a designated beneficiary who is at least a half-time student also qualify. The limit that is considered reasonable for room and board expenses is the *greater* of the room and board allowance determined by the eligible institution for federal financial aid purposes or the actual amount charged for a student residing in housing that is owned and operated by the eligible educational institution. In the case of a special needs beneficiary, the definition of qualifying expenses includes all expenses that are necessary for that person's enrollment or attendance at an eligible institution.

Figuring the taxable portion of a distribution from a QTP. Whether or not a distribution of earnings from a QTP is taxable depends on whether the distribution exceeds adjusted qualified higher education expenses. The qualified higher education expenses paid during the year must be reduced by any tax-free assistance such as scholarships, Pell grants, veterans' assistance, and employer-paid expenses. If a Hope or lifetime learning credit is claimed for the year of the distribution, the expenses taken into account in determining the credit also reduce qualified higher education expenses. If after the reductions the resulting adjusted qualified higher education expenses equal or exceed the total QTP distribution, the entire distribution is tax free. If after the reductions the resulting adjusted qualified higher education costs are less than the total QTP distribution, part of the earnings (shown in Box 2 of Form 1099-Q) is taxable. The Example below illustrates the computation of the taxable amount.

If earnings are taxable, a 10% "additional tax" may also be due, but there are exceptions for distributions that are taxable merely because qualified expenses had to be reduced by tax-free education assistance or expenses taken into account in figuring a Hope or lifetime learning credit. The additional tax is figured on Form 5329.

EXAMPLE

In 1999, Marta's parents opened a savings QTP maintained by their state government. Over the years they contributed $18,000 to the account. The total balance in the account is $27,000 in June 2006 when a $3,600 distribution from the plan is made to Marta. In the summer of 2006, Marta enrolled in college and had $6,700 of qualified higher education expenses for the rest of the year. Marta was awarded a $3,000 scholarship. Towards the end of 2006, Marta received a $3,600 distribution from the QTP. On their 2006 return, Marta's parents claimed a Hope credit of $1,650 (the maximum credit per student for 2006; *see 33.8*).

Before Marta can determine the taxable portion of her withdrawal, she must reduce her total qualified higher education expenses. Note that the reduction for the Hope credit is $2,200, as $2,200 of expenses are taken into account in figuring a $1,650 credit *(33.8)*.

Total qualified higher education expenses	$6,700	
Less: Tax-free scholarship		–3,000
Less: Expenses taken into account in figuring Hope credit		–2,200
Equals: Adjusted qualified higher education expenses		$1,500

Since Marta's adjusted qualified expenses of $1,500 are less than the $3,600 QTP distribution, she must pay tax on the part of the distributed earnings that is not allocable to the expenses. She received a Form 1099-Q that showed that $2,400 of the QTP distribution was a recovery of basis and $1,200 was earnings. Marta figures the taxable part of distributed earnings as follows:

1. The tax-free portion of the earnings is $500: $1,200 distributed earnings × $1,500 expenses / $3,600 distribution.
2. The balance of the earnings, or $700 ($1,200 – $500), is taxable. Marta must report it as "other income" on Line 21 of Form 1040.

Coordination with Coverdell ESA distributions. If distributions from both a QTP and a Coverdell ESA *(33.11)* are received in the same year and the total distributions exceed the adjusted qualified higher education expenses, the expenses must be allocated between the distributions. Assume that in the above example Marta had withdrawn $3,000 from her QTP and $600 from her Coverdell ESA instead of taking the entire amount from her QTP. Marta would allocate $1,250 of the expenses to the QTP distribution ($3,000 QTP / $3,600 total distribution × $1,500 expenses = $1,250), and $250 of the expenses to the ESA ($600 ESA/$3,600 distribution × $1,500 expenses = $250). She would then figure the taxable portion of earnings from each distribution based on the allocable $1,250 or $250 of expenses.

Contributor's loss on QTP investment. If the entire account is distributed and the total investment in the account has not been recovered, the contributor may be able to claim a loss. However, the loss is a miscellaneous itemized deduction subject to the 2% of AGI floor on Schedule A, Form 1040.

Hope and Lifetime Learning Credits

33.7 Education Tax Credits

There are two tax credits for higher education tuition and qualified fees (discussed below): The Hope credit and the lifetime learning credit. They are both figured on Form 8863. You may not claim both credits for the same student for the same year; *see* the Caution in *33.7*. A key difference

Caution

Both Education Credits Not Allowed for the Same Student

Compare the benefits and limitations for the Hope credit and the lifetime learning credit before choosing which one to use for an eligible student. You may not claim both credits for the same student for the same tax year. This choice is only an issue for the first two years of post-secondary education, as the Hope credit is allowed only for those first two years *(see 33.8)*; for later years, only the lifetime learning credit may be claimed.

For example, if in 2006 you paid more than $2,200 of qualified expenses for your daughter's first year of college, you may not claim a $1,650 Hope credit based on the first $2,200 of expenses *(33.8)* and also claim a 20% lifetime learning credit for the balance of her expenses up to $10,000 *(see 33.9)*. For 2006, the lifetime learning credit is generally more advantageous if qualified expenses exceed $8,250. However, if you paid qualified expenses for more than one student, keep in mind that the maximum lifetime learning credit you may claim on your 2006 return is $2,000 *(33.9)*, regardless of how many students you paid expenses for, while the up-to-$1,650 Hope credit for 2006 is allowed for each eligible student. You can claim the Hope credit for one student and the lifetime learning credit for another student in the same year.

Law Alert

Liability Limitation on Education Credits

For 2006, nonrefundable personal credits, including the education credits, may offset both regular income tax and AMT liability. Liability is reduced by certain credits when figuring the limitation for the education credits on Form 8863.

is that the Hope credit is available only for the first two years of pursuing a degree at a post-secondary institution, whereas the lifetime learning credit may be claimed for any year of post-secondary education and for non-degree courses, such as classes to acquire or improve job skills. Another key difference is that the up-to-$1,650 Hope credit (for 2006) is per eligible student, whereas the lifetime learning credit is limited to $2,000 per return, regardless of how many students you pay tuition and eligible fees for.

Rules that apply to both credits are discussed in this section. The Hope credit is discussed further at *33.8* and the lifetime learning credit at *33.9*.

Gulf Opportunity Zone students. The education credits are expanded for students attending eligible educational institutions in the Gulf Opportunity Zone in 2005 and 2006; *see 33.8* (Hope credit) and *33.9* (lifetime learning credit) for details.

Rules Applicable to Both Hope Credit and Lifetime Learning Credit

Can you claim a credit? If you pay qualified higher education expenses (defined below) for you, your spouse, or a person you claim as a dependent (*see* Chapter 21) on your return, and you are not subject to the credit phaseout because of the amount of your income, you generally may claim a credit on Form 8863. However, the Hope credit can be claimed only twice for the same student; *see 33.8*. If married, you must file a joint return to claim either education credit. The phaseout applies if your 2006 MAGI is between $45,000 and $55,000 if filing as single, head of household, or qualifying widow(er), or between $90,000 and $110,000 if married filing jointly. *See 33.10* for how the credit is reduced if MAGI is within the phase-out range. The credit allowed under the phaseout rule is subject to a tax liability limitation; *see* the Law Alert on this page.

You may not claim a Hope credit or a lifetime learning credit and also claim the above-the-line tuition and fees deduction for the same student in the same year; *see 33.13*.

A credit and a business expense deduction for work-related courses may not be based on the same expenses; *see 33.15*.

Claiming credit for expenses paid by your child or other dependent. A dependent's expenses are treated as the expenses of the taxpayer claiming an exemption *(21.1)* for the dependent. For example, if your child is an eligible student and pays qualified expenses, and you claim an exemption for your child as a dependent on your tax return, only you can claim a credit for his or her expenses. Because you claim the child as your dependent, his or her payment of qualifying expenses is treated as your payment.

If a third party, such as the child's grandparent, pays tuition and related expenses for the child directly to a college, the student is treated as receiving the payment from the other person and making the payment to the school. If you claim a dependency exemption for your child, you treat the expenses as your own and may base a credit on the expenses. If the grandparent meets the support test for the child and claims the dependency exemption, the grandparent could use the expenses to claim a credit. The child can claim a credit based on the payment only if no one claims him or her as a dependent.

Qualified expenses paid directly to a school for a dependent under a court-approved divorce decree are also treated as paid by the dependent.

If you are eligible to claim the exemption for your child but do *not* do so, your child can claim a credit for qualifying expenses he or she pays as well as qualifying expenses that you paid. According to the IRS, this rule applies even if you cannot claim the exemption because your income is so high that the exemption on your return is phased out *(21.12)*. Although the deduction is phased out, you are still considered "eligible" for the exemption if you otherwise meet the dependency exemption tests.

What expenses qualify. Generally, the only qualified expenses are tuition and fees required for enrollment or attendance of an eligible student at an eligible educational institution (*see* below). However, for students attending schools in the Gulf Opportunity Zone, additional expenses also qualify for the credit (*see* below). A credit for 2006 can be based on your payment in 2006 of qualified expenses paid for yourself, your spouse, or your dependent (*see* the section above for dependent expenses). The payment can be by check, by credit card, in cash, or with borrowed funds. Qualified expenses do *not* include room and board, insurance, medical expenses, transportation, or other personal or family living expenses. The cost of books, supplies, equipment, and student activity fees may be included *only* if it must be paid to the educational institution as a condition of enrollment. Hobby- or sport-related courses and noncredit courses do not qualify for the Hope credit unless they are part of the student's degree program *(33.8)*. Such courses qualify for the lifetime learning credit if they are part of a degree program or are taken to acquire or improve job skills.

Qualified education costs must be reduced by tax-free scholarships received by an eligible student, as well as Pell grants or tax-free employer provided educational assistance *(3.7)*. However, you may base a credit on expenses paid from the earnings or personal savings of the eligible student (you, your spouse, or dependent), or from loans, gifts, or inheritances.

On Form 1098-T, the eligible education institution may report to the enrolled student the amount of qualified education expenses it received during the year, as well as the amount of scholarships or grants, reimbursements, and adjustments for prior years.

Expanded definition of qualified expenses for GO Zone students. For students attending an eligible institution in the Gulf Opportunity Zone (GO Zone) in 2005 and 2006, the expenses eligible for the credit include not only tuition and fees required for enrollment or attendance, but also reasonable room and board expenses if they are at least "half-time" students, and books, supplies, and equipment required for enrollment or attendance. Eligible room and board costs are limited to the greater of the allowance for room and board as determined by the education institution for financial aid purposes or the actual amount charged if the student is residing in housing owned or operated by the institution. For a special needs student in a GO Zone school, all expenses necessary for enrollment or attendance qualify for the credit.

Prepaid expenses. Generally, a Hope credit or lifetime learning credit must be based on payments within the year of qualified expenses for education furnished in academic periods beginning in that year. However, a prepayment that covers an academic period beginning in the first three months of the next year is treated as an expense for the year of payment. For example, if in December 2006 you paid qualified tuition for the semester beginning in January 2007, you include the payment as a 2006 expense in figuring your credit for 2006. The payment cannot be used to figure a credit for 2007. If the December 2006 payment were for an academic period starting after March 2007, it would not be an eligible expense for 2006 or 2007.

Eligible students and eligible educational institutions. You, your spouse, or an eligible dependent may qualify as an eligible student if enrolled at an eligible educational institution for at least one academic period (semester, trimester, quarter) during the year. An eligible dependent is a person for whom you claim a dependency exemption on your tax return; *see* Chapter 21.

An eligible educational institution generally includes any accredited public, nonprofit, or proprietary college, university, vocational school, or other *post-secondary* institution eligible to participate in the student aid programs administered by the Department of Education. The special GO Zone rules apply to students attending eligible educational institutions in various parishes in Louisiana and counties in Alabama and Mississippi. The instructions to Form 8863 list the qualifying areas.

If you pay qualified expenses for more than one eligible student in the same year, you may choose to take credits on a per-student, per-year basis. Thus, you can claim the Hope credit for one child and the lifetime learning credit for another child in the same tax year.

Coordination with Coverdell ESAs or a qualified tuition program. You may be able to receive a tax-free distribution from either a Coverdell ESA or a state qualified tuition program (QTP) in the same year that you claim a Hope credit or lifetime learning credit. The expenses taken into account as the basis of a Hope or lifetime learning credit reduce eligible expenses for purposes of figuring the tax-free part of an ESA or state QTP distribution.

Recapture of credit. If you claim a credit and after you file your return for that year you receive tax-free educational assistance for the prior year or receive a refund of an expense used to figure the prior-year credit, you have to refigure the original credit. If the refund or assistance would have reduced the original credit, the amount of the reduction must be added to your tax liability for the year you receive the refund or assistance; *see* the Form 8863 instructions.

Phase-out of credits. Both credits are reduced under a phase-out formula if your modified adjusted gross income (MAGI) comes within the rules discussed in *33.10*.

Law Alert

Higher Hope Credit for GO Zone Students

The maximum Hope credit is doubled for students attending an eligible GO Zone institution in 2005 or 2006. For 2006, the maximum credit per student, before application of the phaseout *(33.10)*, is $3,300, 100% of the first $2,200 of qualified expenses and 50% of the next $2,200. For 2005, the maximum credit per GO Zone student was $3,000,100% of the first $2,000 of qualified expenses and 50% of the next $2,000.The higher credit limit will not apply after 2006.

Law Alert

Higher Credit Percentage for GO Zone Students

For students attending an eligible GO Zone institution in 2005 or 2006, the lifetime learning credit (prior to the phaseout in *33.10*) is 40% of the first $10,000 of qualified expenses, double the normal limit. The higher limit will not apply after 2006.

33.8 Hope Credit

If you paid qualified tuition and related expenses in 2006 for an eligible student who at the beginning of 2006 had not yet completed the first two years of college or other post-secondary institution, you generally may figure a Hope credit on Form 8863 of up to $1,650 for the qualified tuition and fees paid in 2006 for the student. However, the Hope credit may only be claimed twice for a particular student, so if you claimed the credit for a student in more than one prior year, you may not claim a 2006 credit for that student, even if the first two years of college had not been completed as of the start of 2006.

An eligible student must meet the following requirements: (1) be enrolled in one of the first two years of postsecondary education (generally, the freshman or sophomore years of college), (2) be enrolled in a program that leads to a degree, certificate, or other recognized educational credential, (3) be taking at least one-half of the normal full-time workload for his or her course of study for at least one academic period beginning during the calendar year, and (4) not have any felony conviction for possessing or distributing a controlled substance.

The amount of the Hope credit for 2006 is generally 100% of the first $1,100 plus 50% of the next $1,100 paid for *each* eligible student's qualified tuition and related expenses. This means that you can claim the maximum $1,650 credit for each eligible student for whom you pay at least $2,200 of qualified expenses, subject to the phaseout rule at *33.10*. The $1,650 Hope credit limit may be indexed for inflation in 2007. For students attending an eligible GO Zone institution in 2006, the maximum Hope credit is doubled, to 100% of the first $2,200 of qualified expenses and 50% of the next $2,200 of qualified expenses for a maximum credit of $3,300 per GO Zone student, subject to the phaseout *(33.10)*.

If a student completed the second year of post-secondary education before 2006, or if the Hope credit was claimed in two prior years, the lifetime learning credit *(see 33.9)*, but not the Hope credit, may be claimed for that student's eligible 2006 expenses.

EXAMPLE

Lucy and Ricky are married and file a joint tax return. For 2006, they claim their daughter Sophia as a dependent on their tax return and their modified adjusted gross income is $70,000. Sophia started her sophomore (second) year of studies at the local university in September 2006. On their 2005 return, Lucy and Ricky claimed a Hope credit for their payment in 2005 of Sophia's freshman year expenses. In 2006 they paid tuition of $12,000 for Sophia. They can claim a $1,650 Hope credit for 2006, the maximum amount allowed. However, by electing the lifetime learning credit rather than the Hope credit for Sophia's 2006 expenses, Lucy and Ricky can increase their 2006 credit to $2,000. For the lifetime learning credit, 20% of the first $10,000 of expenses may be taken into account; *see 33.9*.

33.9 Lifetime Learning Credit

For academic expenses paid during 2006, you may claim on Form 8863 a lifetime learning credit of up to $2,000 for the total qualified expenses paid for yourself, your spouse, or your dependents enrolled in eligible educational institutions *(see 33.7)* during the year, subject to the income phaseout *(33.10)*. The maximum 2006 credit is doubled to $4,000 for students attending school in the Gulf Opportunity Zone (GO Zone).

In contrast to the Hope credit, the lifetime learning credit does not have a degree requirement or a workload requirement. The credit may be claimed for one or more courses at an eligible educational institution that are either part of a post-secondary degree program or part of a nondegree program taken to acquire or improve job skills. The lifetime learning credit is not limited to students in the first two years of postsecondary education, as is the Hope credit, and it covers expenses for graduate-level degree work. There is also no limit on the number of years for which the lifetime learning credit can be claimed for each eligible student.

The lifetime learning credit for 2006 is 20% of the first $10,000 paid in 2006 for qualified expenses for *all* eligible students in the family, excluding GO Zone students. Thus, the maximum lifetime learning credit you may claim for 2006 is $2,000 (20% of $10,000), subject to the income-based phaseout; *see 33.10*. Under current law, both the credit percentage (20%) and the expense limit ($10,000) are fixed and not eligible for an inflation adjustment. For 2006 returns, the credit percentage for GO Zone students is 40% (instead of 20%) of the first $10,000 of qualified expenses;

the same rule applied for 2005. If you paid qualified expenses in 2006 for both GO Zone students and non–GO Zone students, the qualified expenses taken into account for the GO Zone students reduce the expenses that can be taken into account for the other students on Form 8863.

The $2,000 limit applies regardless of the number of eligible students for whom you paid education expenses. This aspect of the lifetime learning credit differs from the Hope credit, which may be claimed for each eligible student, up to $1,650 each for 2006 *(see 33.8)*.

33.10 Income Phaseout of Education Credits

The Hope credit and the lifetime learning credit are phased out on Form 8863 for 2006 if your modified adjusted gross income is between $45,000 and $55,000 and you file as single, head of household, or qualifying widow(er), or between $90,000 and $110,000 on a joint return. For 2007, the MAGI phaseout ranges may be increased by an inflation adjustment. For most taxpayers, modified adjusted gross income is adjusted gross income (AGI) unless they have tax-free income earned abroad or from certain U.S. territories or possessions. If so, adjusted gross income is increased by such amounts.

Law Alert

Phaseout of Credits

You cannot claim any higher education credits for 2006 if your modified adjusted gross income exceeds $55,000 ($110,000 on a joint return). For 2007, these phaseout limits may again be indexed for inflation.

EXAMPLES

1. Ron and Jackie are married and file a joint tax return. Their MAGI for 2006 is $93,000. They pay $6,000 of qualifying expenses for their son, Leo, and $7,500 for their daughter, Ally. Both students are claimed as dependents on Ron and Jackie's joint return. A Hope credit of $3,300, $1,650 for each child, is allowed prior to taking the phaseout into account. On Form 8863, Ron and Jackie figure a $2,805 Hope credit after application of the phase-out rules. Their excess MAGI of $3,000 ($93,000 – $90,000 phase-out threshold) is 15% of the $20,000 phase-out range, so 15% of the tentative $3,300 credit is phased out and 85% is allowed.
2. John, unmarried, has MAGI of $46,000 for 2006. He pays $2,500 in qualified tuition and fees. He figures a lifetime learning credit of $500 (20% of qualified tuition and fees), before taking the phaseout into account. On Form 8863, he figures a $450 lifetime learning credit after application of the phase-out rules. John's excess MAGI of $1,000 ($46,000 – $45,000) is 10% of the $10,000 phase-out range, so he is allowed 90% of his tentative $500 credit and 10% is phased out.

Parent's option to forego child's exemption to let child claim credit. As discussed at *33.7*, your child may claim a credit if you are eligible to claim him or her as a dependent but do not do so. If you are not allowed a credit for your dependent child's expenses because of the MAGI phaseout, and your child has tax liability against which the credit may be claimed, you can forego claiming the child as a dependency exemption on your return, which would allow the credit to be claimed on the child's return. Consider which of the child's credit or your dependency exemption would provide the larger tax savings.

Coverdell Education Savings Accounts (Formerly Education IRAs)

33.11 Contributing to a Coverdell Education Savings Account (ESA)

A Coverdell Education Savings Account, or ESA, is a trust or custodial account set up specifically for the purpose of paying the qualified education expenses of the designated beneficiary of the account. A contribution cannot be made for a beneficiary after he or she reaches age 18 unless the beneficiary is a special needs beneficiary, as discussed below. Contributions must be in cash. Coverdell Education Savings Accounts were formerly known as Education IRAs.

Contribution limits. The maximum cash contribution that any individual (including the designated beneficiary) can make for a designated beneficiary for a particular year is $2,000. The limit is generally reduced if your modified adjusted gross income (MAGI) is between $95,000 and $110,000, or if you are married filing jointly, between $190,000 and $220,000. For most individuals, MAGI is the same as adjusted gross income (AGI), but if the foreign earned income exclusion or an exclusion of income from Puerto Rico or American Samoa is claimed, the exclusion is added back to AGI. You may not contribute to a beneficiary's Coverdell ESA if your MAGI is $110,000 or more, or $220,000 or more if filing a joint return.

Total annual contributions per beneficiary are also limited to $2,000. If more than one Coverdell ESA has been set up for a beneficiary, the total annual limit for all of the accounts is $2,000, regardless of how many persons contribute. The deadline for making a contribution for any year is the due date of your return for that year (not including extensions).

A 6% excise tax applies to Coverdell ESA contributions that exceed $2,000 for 2006 for any beneficiary. The penalty is imposed on the beneficiary (Form 5329). The excise tax does not apply if the excess contributions (and any earnings) are withdrawn before the first day of the sixth month (June 1) of the following year. The withdrawn earnings are taxable for the year in which you made the excess contribution.

Special needs beneficiary. Contributions to a Coverdell ESA for a special needs beneficiary may continue after the beneficiary reaches age 18. Also, the Coverdell ESA of a special needs beneficiary does not have to be emptied at age 30. The definition of "special needs" has not yet been established. Congress wants the IRS definition to include an individual who, because of a physical, mental, or emotional condition (including a learning disability), requires additional time to complete his or her education.

33.12 Distributions From Coverdell ESAs

A designated beneficiary of a Coverdell ESA is not taxed on withdrawals that do not exceed qualified education expenses. If the total withdrawals for a tax year exceed the qualified education expenses (*see* below), a portion of the withdrawals is taxable to the beneficiary. The taxable portion is the amount of the excess withdrawal allocable to earnings; *see* the Example below and the worksheet in IRS Publication 970.

If there are assets remaining in a Coverdell ESA when the designated beneficiary reaches age 30, the beneficiary must withdraw the assets within 30 days, unless he or she is a special needs beneficiary. The duration of the account can be extended by changing the designated beneficiary or rolling over the account to a member of the beneficiary's family who is under age 30; *see* below.

Filing Tip

Coordination With Education Credits

A Hope credit or lifetime learning credit may be claimed in the same year that a Coverdell ESA distribution is excluded from income as long as the distribution does not cover the same expenses for which a credit is claimed.

Qualified education expenses. In addition to qualified higher education expenses (as defined at *33.6* for QTPs), qualified expenses for Coverdell ESA purposes include contributions to a QTP *(33.5)* on behalf of the ESA beneficiary. Also qualifying are elementary and secondary education expenses, kindergarten through grade 12. The elementary or secondary school may be a public, private, or religious school.

Eligible expenses for elementary and secondary school students include tuition, fees, academic tutoring, special services for special needs beneficiaries, books, supplies, computers and peripheral equipment, Internet access, and software. Software designed for sports or hobbies must be predominately educational in nature. Qualified expenses also include room and board, uniforms, transportation, and supplementary items and services including extended day programs required or provided by the school.

Coordination with education credits. If a Hope credit or lifetime learning credit is claimed for 2006, qualified expenses for purposes of figuring tax-free Coverdell ESA distributions are reduced by the expenses taken into account when figuring the credit.

Figuring tax free and taxable part of distribution. If the adjusted qualified expenses of the beneficiary equal or exceed the distribution, the entire distribution is tax free. If a distribution exceeds adjusted qualified education expenses, then part of the earnings included in the distribution is taxable. To determine the amount of adjusted qualified educational expenses, reduce the total qualified education expenses (defined above) by any tax-free educational assistance such as excludable scholarships, Pell grants, veteran's educational assistance or employer-provided educational assistance. Any expenses taken into account when figuring a Hope credit or lifetime learning credit further reduce qualified expenses. The balance of qualifying expenses after subtracting tax-free educational assistance and credit-related expenses is the beneficiary's adjusted qualified educational expenses. The following Example shows how the taxable portion of the distribution is determined when the total distribution exceeds the adjusted qualified education expenses.

EXAMPLE

In 2006, Bianca Jane had $4,400 of qualified higher education expenses, her first year in college. She paid her college expenses from a variety of sources: a partial scholarship (excluded from gross income) of $1,500, a $1,000 Coverdell ESA withdrawal, a $500 gift from her parents, and $1,400 of earnings from a part-time job.

Of her $4,400 of qualified expenses, $2,700 was tuition and required fees that also qualified for a Hope credit. Bianca Jane's parents claimed a $1,650 Hope credit on their 2006 tax return.

Before Bianca Jane can determine the taxable portion of her ESA withdrawal, she must reduce her total qualified higher education expenses. Note that the reduction for the Hope credit is $2,200, as $2,200 of expenses are taken into account in figuring a $1,650 credit *(33.8)*.

Total qualified higher education expenses	$4,400
Less: Tax-free education benefits	–1,500
Less: Expenses taken into account in figuring Hope credit	–2,200
Equals: Adjusted qualified higher education expenses	$700

Since Bianca Jane's adjusted qualified education expenses of $700 are less than the $1,000 Coverdell ESA withdrawal, part of the withdrawal will be taxable. The balance in Bianca Jane's account before the $1,000 withdrawal was $2,800, to which $2,500 had been contributed. The Form 1099-Q sent to Bianca Jane shows that $893 of the $1,000 withdrawal is allocable to contributions (basis) and $107 to earnings. She must include $32 of the $107 earnings in her income, figured as follows:

1. The tax-free portion of the earnings used for qualified expenses is $75: $107 earnings × ($700 expenses / $1,000 distribution).
2. The balance of the earnings, or $32, is taxable, and must be reported as "other income" on Line 21 of Form 1040.

If Form 1099-Q had not provided Bianca with the breakdown between earnings and basis, she would need to rely on records showing her unrecovered contributions (basis) in order to figure the taxable part of the distribution. For example, Bianca's records show that total contributions to her account (none of which have previously been distributed) were $2,500. Dividing the $2,500 contributions by the $2,800 account balance and multiplying the result by the $1,000 distribution gives the $893 basis portion of the distribution ($1,000 x $2,500/$2,800= $893). The balance of the distribution, or $107 ($1,000 – $893), is the earnings portion of the distribution.

Law Alert

Additional Tax Exception for Service Academy Appointees

If a designated beneficiary is appointed to the U.S. Military Academy, Naval Academy, Air Force Academy, Coast Guard Academy, or Merchant Marine Academy, a distribution is not subject to the 10% additional tax to the extent of the costs of "advanced education" at such academy (as defined by Section 2005(e)(3) of Title 10, United States Code, in effect on November 11, 2003).

Additional tax on taxable distributions. Generally, a taxable distribution is subject to a 10% additional tax. The 10% additional tax does not apply to distributions that are: (1) made to a beneficiary (or to the estate of the designated beneficiary) on or after the death of the designated beneficiary, (2) made because the designated beneficiary is disabled, (3) made because the designated beneficiary received a tax-free scholarship or educational assistance allowance that equals or exceeds the distribution, or (4) taxable only because the qualified ESA education expenses were reduced by expenses used in figuring a Hope or lifetime learning credit.

The 10% additional tax also does not apply to the withdrawal of an excess contribution (and allocable earnings; *see 33.11*) before June 1 of the following year.

Rollovers and other transfers. Withdrawn assets may be rolled over tax free from one Coverdell ESA to another for the benefit of the same beneficiary or a member of the beneficiary's family if the recipient is under age 30. For example, if a beneficiary still has money in his or her account upon graduation from college, the Coverdell ESA can be rolled over tax free to the Coverdell ESA of a younger sibling. The withdrawal is considered rolled over if it is paid to another Coverdell ESA within 60 days. Only one rollover per Coverdell ESA is allowed during the 12-month period ending on the date of the payment or withdrawal. For rollover purposes, members of the beneficiary's family include the beneficiary's spouse, child, grandchild, stepchild, brother, sister (and a sibling's son or daughter), half-sister, half-brother, stepbrother, stepsister, father, mother (and siblings of parents), grandfather, grandmother, stepfather, stepmother, in-laws, and the spouses of any of the above.

The designated beneficiary can be changed to a member of the beneficiary's family (included in the above list) with no tax consequences if the new beneficiary is under age 30. The new beneficiary will have to withdraw the account balance no later than 30 days after reaching age 30, unless he or she is a special needs beneficiary.

If the beneficiary dies before age 30, the account balance generally must be distributed to the beneficiary's estate within 30 days of the date of death. However, if the Coverdell ESA is transferred to a surviving spouse or other family member (defined above) who is under age 30, the account may be maintained until he or she reaches age 30. The age 30 limitation will not apply if the new beneficiary is a special needs beneficiary.

Deductible Tuition/Fees and Student Loan Interest

33.13 Tuition and Fees Deduction

Note: The tuition and fees deduction expired at the end of 2005 and when this book went to press, Congress had not yet extended the deduction to 2006. Given the likelihood that Congress will extend the deduction, the following discussion assumes that the 2005 rules will apply to 2006 returns. Check the* e-Supplement *for an update on the expected extension legislation.

Depending on your income, you may be able to deduct up to $2,000 or $4,000 of qualifying higher education tuition and fees paid during 2006 on your 2006 return. The deduction is claimed directly from gross income on Form 1040 (whether or not you itemize), or on Form 1040A.

You may *not* claim the deduction for expenses of a dependent for whom a Hope credit or lifetime learning credit is claimed. You may *not* claim the credit for some of an eligible student's expenses and the deduction for the balance. If you qualify for both, you must choose between the credit and the deduction. A credit generally provides a larger tax savings, but the credit is phased out at a lower income level; *see 33.10*. If your income is too high to claim a credit or most of the credit is phased out because of your income *(33.10)*, you may be able to take advantage of the deduction.

Law Alert

Legislation Needed to Extend Deduction Beyond 2005

Legislation to extend the deduction for tuition and fees beyond 2005 is expected, but had not yet been enacted when this book went to press. *See* the *e-Supplement* for an update.

Deduction amount based on income. If your modified adjusted gross income (MAGI) for 2006 does not exceed $65,000 or $130,000 if you are filing jointly, your maximum tuition and fees deduction is $4,000. If MAGI is more than $65,000 or $130,000, but not more than $80,000 or $160,000 if filing jointly, your maximum tuition and fees deduction is $2,000. No deduction is allowed if MAGI exceeds $80,000 or $160,000.

For purposes of the deduction, MAGI is generally the same as the AGI shown on your return. AGI is increased by any exclusion for foreign earned income or income from Puerto Rico or American Samoa, or the foreign housing exclusion or deduction.

Ineligible taxpayers. You may not claim the deduction if you are married filing separately. You are also ineligible if you may be claimed as a dependent on another taxpayer's return, whether or not you are actually so claimed.

Qualified higher education expenses. Expenses eligible for the deduction are the same as those qualifying for the Hope or lifetime learning credit. That is, the deduction is limited to tuition and enrollment fees paid to an eligible educational institution for yourself, your spouse or your dependents; *see 33.7*. The costs of student activity fees and course-related books qualify if they must be paid to the school. The rules at *33.7* for claiming the expenses of a dependent also apply to the tuition and fees deduction. Eligible expenses paid in 2006 for an academic period starting in the first three months of 2007 are deductible for 2006. Eligible educational institutions include any college, university, vocational school, or other postsecondary institution eligible to participate in the financial aid programs of the Department of Education.

Filing Tip

Credit or Deduction?

When you have qualifying education expenses, check to determine whether or not you can claim either the Hope or Lifetime learning credit. A credit produces a dollar-for-dollar reduction of your tax liability, while a deduction only reduces your taxable income. Claim the credit if it provides you with a larger tax benefit. You may not claim a credit and tuition and fees deduction for the same student in the same year.

Deduction affected by excludable education benefits. Expenses eligible for the deduction are reduced by tax-free scholarships *(33.1)* and other tax-free educational assistance. If you receive tax-free interest from an EE or I savings bond used for tuition *(33.4)*, the excludable interest reduces the expenses eligible for the deduction. A tax-free distribution of earnings from a Coverdell ESA *(33.12)* or a QTP *(33.6)* reduces the deduction-eligible expenses.

Recapture of deduction. If after you file your return on which the deduction was claimed you receive tax-free educational assistance for that year or receive a refund of an expense used to figure the deduction, you may have to repay (recapture) all or part of the original deduction. Refigure the original deduction by reducing it by the refunded amount and also refigure tax liability for that year. To the extent of the increase in tax liability, you must include the refunded amount in your income for the year you receive it.

33.14 Student Loan Interest Deduction

If you paid interest on a qualified student loan in 2006, you may be able to claim an above-the-line (directly from gross income) deduction of up to $2,500. Eligibility for the deduction is phased out if you have 2006 modified adjusted gross income (MAGI, *see* below) between $50,000 and $65,000, or between $105,000 and $135,000 if married filing a joint return. On a joint return, the deduction limit remains $2,500 even if you and your spouse each pay interest on a qualified student loan. If you are claimed as a dependent by another taxpayer, or you are married filing separately, you may not claim the deduction regardless of your income. The deduction is claimed on Line 33 of Form 1040 or Line 18 of Form 1040A. A worksheet in the form instructions may be used to figure your student loan interest deduction.

Qualified loans and expenses. A qualified student loan is one taken out to pay qualified higher education expenses for you, your spouse, or a person who was your dependent when you took out the loan. The education expenses must be paid or incurred within a reasonable time before or after the loan was taken out, and the funds obtained must be used toward education furnished while the student is enrolled at least half-time in a program leading to a degree or other recognized educational credential at an eligible educational institution. Eligible institutions are colleges, universities, vocational schools, and other post-secondary educational institutions eligible to participate in Department of Education student aid programs. Graduate school programs are included. Also included are medical internships or residency programs leading to a degree or certificate from an educational institution or hospital offering postgraduate training.

Qualified higher education expenses include tuition, fees, room and board (within qualified limits discussed at *33.6*), books, equipment, and other necessary expenses such as transportation. These costs must be reduced by:

1. Nontaxable employer-provided educational assistance benefits.
2. Nontaxable Coverdell ESA or QTP distributions.
3. U.S. Savings Bond interest excluded from income because it is used to pay higher education expenses.
4. Qualified tax-free scholarships.
5. Veterans' educational assistance benefits.

Loan origination fees and capitalized interest (unpaid interest that accrues and is added to the balance of the loan) can be counted as interest. In general, a payment, regardless of its label, is treated first as a payment of interest to the extent that accrued interest remains unpaid, second as a payment of any loan origination fees or capitalized interest, until such amounts are reduced to zero, and third as a payment of principal.

Voluntary interest payments are deductible. You can deduct voluntary interest payments, such as when you have been granted a repayment deferment.

Dependents and married persons filing separately are ineligible. You may not claim a student loan interest deduction during any year in which someone claims you as a dependent. However, you may deduct interest payments made in a later year when you are no longer claimed as a dependent.

You may not claim a student loan interest deduction for any year in which you are married and file a separate tax return.

Other restrictions. A revolving line of credit is not a qualified loan unless you agree to use the funds solely to pay education costs.

You may not deduct interest paid on a loan from a relative as educational loan interest; *see 5.6*.

You may not deduct interest on a loan from a qualified employer plan.

You may not claim a student loan interest deduction for any amount you may deduct under any other tax law provision, for example home mortgage interest. You also cannot use the deduction if you use part of the borrowed money for purposes other than education, for instance to make improvements to your house.

Phaseout. The interest deduction is reduced or eliminated if your modified adjusted gross income (MAGI) exceeds phaseout limits. The reduction applies to your deduction for 2006 if MAGI is more than $50,000, or more than $105,000 on a joint return. If MAGI is more than $65,000, or more than $135,000 on a joint return, you may not claim a deduction for 2006. MAGI is the same as the adjusted gross income shown on your return (disregarding student loan interest) unless you claim a deduction for tuition and fees *(33.13)*, the exclusion for foreign earned income (Chapter 36), the domestic production activities deduction *(40.23)*, or certain other items of foreign income or expenses were excluded or deducted from your income. Such items generally must be added back to adjusted gross income.

If your MAGI is within the phase-out range, figure the reduction to the 2006 deduction by multiplying your deductible interest (up to the $2,500 limit) by a fraction, the numerator of which is your MAGI less $50,000, or $105,000 if married filing jointly, and the denominator of which is $15,000, or $30,000 if married filing jointly.

Caution

Deduction Lost for Student Dependent's Loan

If your parent or someone else claims you as a dependent on his or her return, you may not deduct interest on your return for student loan interest you paid. Furthermore, the person who claims you as a dependent may not deduct the interest where you are the borrower legally obligated to repay the loan.

The student loan deduction worksheet in the Form 1040 or Form 1040A instructions can be used to figure the phase-out reduction and the amount of your deduction.

EXAMPLES

1. In 2006 you paid $900 interest on a qualified student loan. Your MAGI is $110,000 on a joint return. Your deduction is reduced by $150. You can deduct $750 ($900 – $150).

   $$\$900 \times \frac{\$110{,}000 - \$105{,}000}{\$30{,}000} = \$150 \text{ reduction}$$

2. The same facts as in Example 1, except you paid $2,600 interest. The maximum deduction of $2,500 is reduced by $417. You can deduct $2,083 ($2,500 – $417).

   $$\$2{,}500 \times \frac{\$110{,}000 - \$105{,}000}{\$30{,}000} = \$417 \text{ reduction}$$

Business Deduction for Work-Related Education Expenses

33.15 Types of Deductible Work-Related Costs

If you improve your job or professional skills by attending continuing education or refresher classes, advanced academic courses, or vocational training, you may be able to treat your expenses as a business expense deduction. As a self-employed business owner or professional, allowable expenses are deductible on Schedule C and reduce income subject to self-employment tax *(45.1)* as well as income tax liability. However, as an employee, the tax benefit of an unreimbursed educational expense deduction is limited because the expenses are miscellaneous itemized deductions, which, together with any other miscellaneous expenses, are deductible on Schedule A only to the extent that the total exceeds 2% of your adjusted gross income; *see 19.1*.

Keep in mind that tuition and fees (but not transportation and usually not books or supplies) for work-related educational courses may also qualify for the lifetime learning credit *(33.9)* or the tuition and fees deduction *(33.13)*. The lifetime learning credit, by reducing tax liability rather than taxable income, is more valuable than a deduction for education costs. However, you may be unable to claim the credit because your income exceeds the phase-out limit for the credit *(33.10)*. The tuition and fees deduction is an above-the-line deduction available even if you claim itemized deductions. If you are an employee and are within the income range for the tuition and fees deduction *(33.13)*, it is preferable to an itemized job expense on Schedule A that may be limited or eliminated by the 2% floor.

Filing Tip

Lifetime Learning Credit or Tuition and Fees Deduction

If you have qualifying work-related education costs, check *33.9* to determine whether you can claim the lifetime learning credit. Also check *33.13* to see if you are eligible for the above-the-line deduction for tuition and fees. These tax breaks may be more valuable to you than a business or job expense deduction.

To deduct education costs on Schedule C (self-employed) or Schedule A (employee subject to the 2% AGI floor), you must show that the following conditions are met:

1. You are employed or self-employed;
2. You already meet the minimum requirements of your job, business, or profession;
3. The course maintains or improves your job or professional skills, or you are required by your employer or by law to take the course to keep your present salary or position; *and*
4. The course does *not* lead to qualification for a new profession or business. The cost of courses preparing you for a new profession is not deductible, even if you take them to improve your skills or to meet your employer's requirements. This rule prevents the deduction of law school costs. Furthermore, the cost of a bar review course or CPA review course is not deductible because it leads to a new profession as an attorney or CPA. If courses lead to qualification for a new business or profession, no deduction is allowed even if you keep your current position.

Filing Tip

Deducting Unreimbursed Employee Educational Costs

Unreimbursed education costs, such as for travel, tuition, books, fees, and meals, are deductible only if you claim itemized deductions. You generally must report your expenses on Form 2106 or in some cases Form 2106-EZ *(see 19.3)* before entering the deductible amount on Line 20 of Schedule A, where they and other miscellaneous itemized deductions are subject to the 2% AGI floor.

If your courses meet the above requirements you may deduct the following education costs on Schedule C if self-employed or on Schedule A subject to the 2% AGI floor if the courses are related to your job:

1. Tuition, textbooks, fees, equipment, and other aids required by the courses.
2. Local transportation costs as discussed at *33.17*.
3. Travel to and from a school away from home, and lodging and 50% of meals while at school away from home; *see 33.17*. The IRS will not disallow traveling expenses to attend a school away from home or in a foreign country merely because you could have taken the course in a local school. But it may disallow your board and lodging and expenses at the school if your stay lasts longer than a year.

Further details of the deduction requirements are explained at 33.16.

33.16 Work-Related Tests for Education Costs

Educational costs are not deductible on Schedule C (self-employed) or Schedule A (employee) if you are unemployed or inactive in a business or profession. The cost of "brush-up" courses taken in anticipation of resuming work is also not deductible.

You are not considered unemployed when you take courses during a temporary leave of absence lasting one year or less.

Course must not meet minimum standards. You may not deduct the cost of courses taken to meet the minimum requirements of your job. The minimum requirements of a position are based on a review of your employer's standards, the laws and regulations of the state you live in, and the standards of your profession or business. That you are presently employed does not in itself prove that you have met the minimum standards for your job.

If minimum standards change after you enter a job or profession, courses you take to meet the new standards are deductible.

Teachers. The minimum educational requirements are those that existed when you were hired. If your employer set no tests fixing a minimum educational level, you meet the minimum requirements when you become a member of the faculty. Whether you are a faculty member depends on the custom of your employer. You are ordinarily considered a faculty member if: (1) you have tenure, or your service is counted toward tenure; (2) the institution is contributing toward a retirement plan based on your employment (other than Social Security or a similar program); or (3) you have a vote in faculty affairs.

That you are already employed as a teacher, with all the responsibilities of a teacher, may not establish that you have met the minimum educational requirements. A school system that requires a bachelor's degree before granting a permanent teaching certificate may grant temporary or provisional certificates after a person has completed a number of college credits. Renewal of the provisional certificate may be conditioned on the teacher's continuing education for a bachelor's degree. In this case, the IRS will disallow a deduction for the educational costs. The minimum requirements are not met until the teacher has the degree.

Course must maintain or improve job skills. To be deductible, the education must maintain or improve your current job skills. That you are established in your position and that persons in similar positions usually pursue such education indicates that the courses are taken to maintain and improve job skills. However, the IRS may not allow a deduction for a general education course that is a prerequisite for a job-related course.

If the courses lead to a change of position or promotion within the same occupation, a deduction for their cost will usually be allowed if your new duties involve the same general type of work. If, as a consequence of taking a job-related course, you receive a substantial advancement and the IRS questions the deduction of the course costs, be prepared to prove that you took the course primarily to maintain or improve skills of your existing job. However, if the course leads to qualification for a new profession, the IRS will disallow a deduction even if the course also improves current job skills.

Courses must not lead to qualification for a new profession. If a course improves your current job skills but leads to qualification for a new profession, the course is not deductible, even if you have no intention of entering that business or profession. For example, a deduction is not allowed for the cost of law school or medical school courses since they prepare you for a new profession. This is true even if you do not intend to practice medicine or law. The IRS with Tax Court approval has also held that a deduction is not allowed for the cost of college courses that are part of a degree program, such as a bachelor of arts or science degree.

If you are practicing your profession, the cost of courses leading to a specialty within that profession is deductible. For example, a practicing attorney may deduct the cost of a master's of law degree program (LLM).

EXAMPLES

1. Allemeier was originally hired as a sales representative by a manufacturer of orthodontic appliances. An outstanding employee, he quickly advanced in the company and was given greater responsibilities, including sales strategizing and conducting seminars. While he was encouraged in his decision to pursue an MBA, the corporation neither required such a degree for advancement nor reimbursed employees for the expense.

Planning Reminder

Teacher's Job Change

Elementary and secondary school teachers may deduct the cost of courses taken to make any of the following job changes: (1) elementary to secondary school classroom teacher; (2) classroom teacher in one subject (such as mathematics) to classroom teacher in another subject (such as English or history); (3) classroom teacher to guidance counselor; or (4) classroom teacher to principal. These are not considered a change to a new business.

Caution

Are MBA Courses Deductible?

The cost of MBA courses is deductible if the courses enhance the skills required in your current position, are not a minimum job requirement, and do not qualify you for a new business. If an MBA degree is required to obtain a promotion to a new position, the MBA is a minimum job requirement and no deduction will be allowed. For a deduction, the courses must be related to your existing job responsibilities and not lead to qualification for a new business. The Tax Court has allowed deductions for MBA expenses where individuals with some managerial or administrative experience took the courses to improve skills needed for their existing jobs.

In one case, a college graduate who took a summer job before starting MBA courses was not allowed a deduction because he had not yet established himself in a business or employment; the summer position was just a temporary stage between schooling.

If your employer reimburses you for MBA courses that qualify for a deduction, the reimbursement is a tax-free working condition fringe benefit; *see 3.6*.

Allemeier was promoted to several higher positions before obtaining the MBA. The Tax Court determined that Allemeier's MBA did not lead to a new trade or business and therefore his tuition payments were deductible. The MBA merely enhanced the skills he already used on the job, specifically, giving him a better understanding of financials, cost analyses, marketing, and advertising. His job requirements did not significantly change after he obtained the MBA.

2. A practicing dentist returned to school full time to study orthodontics while continuing his practice on a part-time basis. When he finished his training, he limited his work to orthodontics. The IRS ruled he could deduct the cost of his studies. His post-graduate schooling improved his professional skills as a dentist. It did not qualify him for a new profession.
3. A practicing psychiatrist may deduct the cost of attending an accredited psychoanalytic institute to qualify to practice psychoanalysis. A social worker has also been allowed a deduction for the cost of learning psychoanalysis. In one case, the Tax Court allowed a psychiatrist to deduct the cost of personal therapy sessions conducted through telephone conversations and tape cassettes. The court was convinced that the therapy improved his job skills by eliminating psychological blind spots that prevented him from understanding his patients' problems.
4. A licensed practical nurse may not deduct the costs of a college program that qualifies him or her as a "physician's assistant," which is a new business. Physicians' assistants and practical nurses are subject to different registration and certification requirements under state law, and, more importantly, the physician's assistant may perform duties, such as physical examinations and minor surgery, which go beyond practical nursing duties.
5. Edward, a self-employed golf instructor without an undergraduate degree, earned an associate's degree in business from the Golf Academy of the South. The IRS and Tax Court disallowed his deduction for tuition and fees. It does not matter that the courses may have improved his skills as a golf instructor. No deduction was allowed because completing the associate's program was a first step in acquiring a basic undergraduate degree that would qualify Edward for a variety of trades or businesses other than that of a golf instructor.

Further education required by employer or law. If, to retain your present job or rate of pay, your employer requires you to obtain further education, you may deduct the cost of the courses. The fact that you also qualified for a raise in pay or a substantial advancement in your position after completing the courses should not bar the deduction.

The employer's requirement must be for a bona fide business reason, not merely to benefit you. Only the minimum courses necessary for the retention of your job or rate of pay are considered by the IRS as taken to meet your employer's requirement. You must show any courses beyond your employer's minimum requirements were taken to maintain or improve your job skills.

33.17 Local Transportation and Travel Away From Home To Take Courses

If your courses meet the requirements at *33.15* and *33.16*, costs of local transportation and travel away from home may be included in the business/job expense deduction.

Local transportation expenses. If your courses qualify for a deduction under *33.16*, you may deduct transportation costs of going from your job directly to school. Transportation costs include the actual costs of bus, subway, cab, or other fares, as well as the costs of using your car. According to the IRS, the return trip from school to home is also deductible if you are regularly employed and going to school on a *temporary* basis. According to the IRS, you are going to school on a temporary basis if your courses are realistically expected to last for one year or less and actually do last no more than one year. This is the same one-year test for determining whether you can deduct the cost of commuting to a "temporary" work location *(20.2)* or living costs while away from home on a "temporary" assignment *(20.9)*. The IRS position is illustrated in the following Examples.

EXAMPLES

1. You regularly work in Camden, New Jersey, and every night for three weeks you drive from home to attend a refresher course. The course is considered temporary. You may deduct the round-trip transportation costs between home and school. The deduction is allowed regardless of how far you travel.

   If you went directly from your job to the school, you may deduct transportation from work to school, and from school to home.
2. On six consecutive Saturdays, which are nonworkdays for you, you drive from home to attend a qualifying course. This is considered a temporary course. You are allowed a deduction for round-trip transportation between home and school, even though you are traveling on a nonworkday.
3. You regularly work in Camden, New Jersey, and after work you drive from home to take classes twice a week for 15 months. The IRS does not consider the course to be temporary. You may deduct the cost of going directly from work to school, but the costs of going between home and school are nondeductible.

Using your car. If you use your own car for transportation to school, you may deduct your actual expenses or use the standard business mileage rate to figure the deductible amount. The standard mileage rate for 2006 is 44.5 cents per mile. Regardless of the method you use, you may deduct parking fees and tolls.

Travel and living expenses away from home. "Away from home" as explained at *20.6* has a special tax meaning. You are not away from home unless you are away overnight. If you are away from home to attend a qualifying course, you may deduct the cost of travel to and from the site of the course, plus lodging and 50% of meals while you are there.

Expenses of sightseeing, social visiting, and entertaining while taking the courses are not deductible. If personal reasons are your main purpose in going to the vicinity of the school, such as to take a vacation, you may deduct only the cost of the courses and your living expenses while attending school. You may not deduct the rest of your travel costs.

To determine the purpose of your trip, an IRS agent will pay close attention to the amount of time devoted to personal activities relative to the time devoted to the courses.

Is travel itself a form of education? A teacher generally may not deduct the cost of an "educational" trip to another state or country as a job expense. Although a trip may have educational value in that the teacher learns about people, culture, or places related to the courses that he or she teaches, the IRS position is that a specific statute, Code Section 274(m)(2), bars a deduction for travel that is a form of education. There may be exceptions where specific research can only be accomplished at a particular location, but a trip for "general" educational purposes does not qualify according to the IRS.

The Tax Court took a different view of the statute in a decision that opens the door to a deduction for teachers who travel overseas to take highly organized courses with regular lectures, a structured syllabus, tours to historically and culturally relevant sites, and extensive reading assignments. The Court allowed a California high-school English teacher and department chair to deduct $5,334 for her airfare, lodging, meals, and tuition for an 18-day trip to Greece in 1995. She was also allowed to deduct $7,705 for a two-week trip to Southeast Asia in 1996. In Greece, she took a course on Greek myths and legends and on the Asian trip, a course on Buddhist and Hindu traditions. Her school required neither course. For the Tax Court, the key to the deduction was the organized nature of the courses, which were sponsored by the Berkeley extension program, taught by university professors, and qualified for undergraduate credit, although the teacher was not taking the courses for credit. The regular lectures, tours, and readings were focused educational activities, not the type of mere educational travel that Congress intended to make nondeductible. After holding that a deduction was not barred by Section 274(m)(2), the Court still had to find that the courses had the primary purpose of maintaining or improving the teacher's skills, but it had little difficulty in doing so. The courses improved her teaching skills and helped her to develop curriculum. The courses on Asian traditions also helped her relate better to the predominantly Asian student population in her school. She spent most of her time attending courses and related programs and had minimal free time.

Chapter 34

Special Tax Rules for Senior Citizens

All of your Social Security benefits are tax free if your "provisional income," explained at *34.3*, is $25,000 or less if you are single, or $32,000 or less if you are married and file a joint return. No more than 50% of your benefits are subject to tax if you file a joint return and your provisional income is over $32,000 but no more than $44,000, or if you are single and your provisional income is over $25,000 but no more than $34,000. When provisional income exceeds $34,000 or $44,000 (depending on your filing status), more than 50%, but no more than 85%, of your benefits are subject to tax. If you are married and filing separately, and did not live apart for the whole year, you compute the amount of taxable benefits without considering the base amounts allowed on joint and single returns. If you are married filing separately and you lived apart the entire year, are a head of household, or are a qualifying widow(er), use the $25,000 and $34,000 base amounts for single persons.

If you are receiving Social Security benefits but continue to earn wages or self-employed income, you must pay FICA taxes or self-employment tax on that income regardless of your age.

Social Security Benefits

34.1 Senior Citizens Get Certain Filing Breaks

The following special tax rules favor senior citizens:

- ***Higher filing thresholds.*** If you are single and age 65 or older on or before January 1, 2007, you do not have to file a 2006 return unless your gross income is $9,700 or over. This is $1,250 more than for younger taxpayers. If you are married and you and your spouse are both age 65 or older, a joint return does not have to be filed unless your gross income is $18,900 or over, or $17,900 or over if only one of you is age 65 or older; *see* the chart on page 3 for further details.
- ***Higher standard deduction.*** If you are age 65 or older on or before January 1, 2007, you receive an additional standard deduction allowance if you do not itemize deductions. If you are single you get an additional $1,250 on your 2006 return, or 1,000 if you are married or a qualifying widow(er); *see 13.4*. Your 2006 standard deduction is $6,400 if you are single. If married filing jointly, it is $11,300 if one of you is age 65 or over, or $12,300 if both of you are; *see 13.4.*
- ***Tax credit if age 65 or older.*** This is a limited tax credit for taxpayers age 65 or older who receive little or no Social Security or Railroad Retirement benefits. The credit may also be available to persons under age 65 who are totally disabled; *see 34.7*. For example, if you are single, or married but only you are eligible, and receive more than $416 each month from Social Security, you may not claim the credit. If you are married and both you and your spouse are eligible for the credit and file a joint return, you may not claim the credit if you receive more than $625 each month from Social Security.
- ***Social Security benefits may be exempt from tax.*** The taxable portion of Social Security benefits may vary from year to year because it depends on an amount called "provisional income," which is explained at *34.3*. If you are married and file jointly, none of your net Social Security benefits are taxable in 2006 if your provisional income is not more than a base amount of $32,000. The base amount is $25,000 if your filing status is single, head of household, qualifying widow(er), or you are married filing separately and did not live with your spouse at any time during 2006. Married persons who file separately and live together at any time during the year are not allowed any base amount; *see 34.3* for computing taxable Social Security benefits.

34.2 Social Security Benefits Subject to Tax

If you received or repaid Social Security benefits in 2006, you will receive Form SSA-1099 from the Social Security Administration, showing the total benefits paid to you and any benefits you repaid to the government in 2006. Total benefits include monthly survivor and disability benefits, but not Supplemental Security Income (SSI), which is not taxable. Amounts withheld for Medicare premiums, workers' compensation offset, or attorneys' fees are itemized and included in Box 3, benefits paid in 2006. Keep Form SSA-1099 for your records; do not attach it to your return.

The *net benefit* shown in Box 5 of Form SSA-1099 (benefits paid less benefits repaid) is the benefit amount used to determine the taxable portion of your benefits (if any) under *34.3*.

Railroad Retirement benefits. The portion of your Tier 1 Railroad Retirement benefits that is equivalent to Social Security retirement benefits is subject to the computation at *34.3* for determining taxable benefits. If any part of your 2006 Tier 1 benefits is equivalent to Social Security benefits, you will receive Form RRB-1099 from the government. The *net* Social Security Equivalent Benefit shown on Form RRB-1099 is the amount used to determine taxable benefits under *34.3*. Other Tier 1 Railroad Retirement benefits, as well as Tier 2 benefits, are treated as pension income and not as Social Security benefits for tax purposes.

Benefits paid on behalf of child or incompetent. If a child is entitled to Social Security benefits, such as after the death of a parent, the benefit is considered to be the child's regardless of who actually receives the payment. Whether the child's benefit is subject to tax will depend on the amount of the child's income.

Workers' compensation. If you are receiving Social Security disability payments and workers' compensation for the same disability, your Social Security benefits may be reduced by the workers' compensation. For example, you are entitled to Social Security disability benefits of $5,000 a year. After receiving a $1,000 workers' compensation award, your disability benefits are reduced to $4,000. For purposes of the computation steps at *34.3*, you treat the full $5,000 as Social Security benefits.

Planning Reminder

Voluntary Withholding on Social Security Benefits

You can use your Social Security benefits to meet your estimated and final tax liability by electing on Form W-4V to have tax withheld from benefits at a 7%, 10%, 15%, or 25% rate.

Net benefits. The net benefit shown in Box 5 of Form SSA-1099 is the amount used to determine the taxable portion of your benefits. If Box 5 shows a negative amount (a figure in parentheses), none of your benefits are taxable. If the negative amount is related to Social Security benefits included in gross income in a prior year, you may be entitled to a deduction or a credit; *see* IRS Publication 915 for further instructions on how to figure the deduction or credit when your repayments exceed your gross benefits.

Taxable Social Security benefits are not considered earnings and therefore may not be the basis of an IRA contribution *(8.2)*, earned income credit *(25.10)*, or foreign earned income exclusion *(36.2)*.

Caution

Married Filing Separately

If you are married filing separately and during 2006 you lived with your spouse at any time, you must include in your taxable income the lesser of (1) 85% of your net Social Security benefits shown on Line 1 of the worksheet or (2) 85% of the provisional income shown on Line 7 of the worksheet on this page.

Nonresident aliens. Unless provided otherwise by tax treaty, 85% of a nonresident alien's Social Security benefits will be subject to the 30% withholding tax imposed on U.S. source income that is not connected with a U.S. trade or business. *See* IRS Publication 519 for further details.

34.3 Computing Taxable Social Security Benefits

The taxable portion of your benefits depends on your *provisional income* and your filing status. Part of your net Social Security benefits will be subject to tax if your *provisional income* exceeds a base amount of $25,000 or $32,000. The *base amount* is $25,000 if your filing status is single, head of household, qualifying widow(er), or married filing separately and you lived apart from your spouse for all of 2006. The base amount is $32,000 if you are married filing jointly. You are not entitled to any base amount if you are married filing separately and you lived with your spouse at any time during 2006; *see* the Caution in this section.

Worksheet 1. **Figuring Your Taxable Benefits - See the Sam and Fran Baker Example in 34.3.**

Before you begin:

- If you are married filing separately and you lived apart from your spouse for all of 2006, enter "D" to the right of the word "benefits" on Form 1040, line 20a, or Form 1040A, line 14a.
- Do not use this worksheet if you repaid benefits in 2006 and your total repayments (box 4) were more than your gross benefits for 2006 (box 3). None of your benefits are taxable for 2006. For more information, see *Repayments More Than Gross Benefits.*

1. Enter the total amount from box 5 of ALL your Forms SSA-1099 and RRB-1099. Also enter this amount on Form 1040, line 20a, or Form 1040A, line 14a 1. 15,000
2. Enter one-half of line 1 . . . . . 2. 7,500
3. Enter the total of the amounts from:
   Form 1040: Lines 7, 8a, 8b, 9a, 10 through 14, 15b, 16b, 17 through 19, and 21
   Form 1040A: Lines 7, 8a, 8b, 9a, 10, 11b, 12b, and 13 . . . . . 3. 30,000
4. ***Form 1040 filers:*** Enter the total of any exclusions/adjustments for:
   - Qualified U.S. savings bond interest (Form 8815, line 14)
   - Adoption benefits (Form 8839, line 30)
   - Foreign earned income or housing (Form 2555, lines 45 and 50, or Form 2555-EZ, line 18), and
   - Certain income of bona fide residents of American Samoa (Form 4563, line 15) or Puerto Rico

   Form 1040A filers: Enter the total of any exclusions for:
   - Qualified U.S. savings bond interest (Form 8815, line 14)
   - Adoption benefits (Form 8839, line 30) . . . . . 4. - 0 -
5. Add lines 2, 3, and 4 . . . . . 5. 37,500
6. ***Form 1040 filers:*** Enter the amount from Form 1040, line 36, minus any amounts on Form 1040, lines 33 and 35*.
   Form 1040A filers: Enter the amount from Form 1040A, line 20, minus any amount on Form 1040A, line 18* . . . 6. - 0 -
7. Is the amount on line 6 less than the amount on line 5?
   No. STOP None of your social security benefits are taxable. Enter -0- on Form 1040, line 20b, or Form 1040A, line 14b.
   Yes. Subtract line 6 from line 5 . . . . . 7. 37,500
8. If you are:
   - Married filing jointly, enter $32,000
   - Single, head of household, qualifying widow(er), or married filing separately and you **lived apart** from your spouse for all of 2006, enter $25,000 . . . . . 8. 32,000

   Note. If you are married filing separately and you lived with your spouse at any time in 2006, skip lines 8 through 15; multiply line 7 by 85% (.85) and enter the result on line 16. Then go to line 17.
9. Is the amount on line 8 less than the amount on line 7?
   No. STOP None of your benefits are taxable. Enter -0- on Form 1040, line 20b, or on Form 1040A, line 14b. If you are married filing separately and you **lived apart** from your spouse for all of 2006, be sure you entered "D" to the right of the word "benefits" on Form 1040, line 20a, or on Form 1040A, line 14a.
   Yes. Subtract line 8 from line 7 . . . . . 9. 5,500
10. Enter $12,000 if married filing jointly; $9,000 if single, head of household, qualifying widow(er), or married filing separately and you **lived apart** from your spouse for all of 2006 . . . . . 10. 12,000
11. Subtract line 10 from line 9. If zero or less, enter -0- . . . . . 11. - 0 -
12. Enter the **smaller** of line 9 or line 10 . . . . . 12. 5,500
13. Enter one-half of line 12 . . . . . 13. 2,750
14. Enter the **smaller** of line 2 or line 13 . . . . . 14. 2,750
15. Multiply line 11 by 85% (.85). If line 11 is zero, enter -0- . . . . . 15. - 0 -
16. Add lines 14 and 15 . . . . . 16. 2,750
17. Multiply line 1 by 85% (.85) 17. 12,750
18. **Taxable benefits.** Enter the **smaller** of line 16 or line 17. Also enter this amount on Form 1040, line 20b, or Form 1040A, line 14b 18. 2,750

TIP *If you received a lump-sum payment in 2006 that was for an earlier year, also complete Worksheet 2 or 3 and Worksheet 4 to see if you can report a lower taxable benefit.*

* If the tuition and fees deduction is extended to 2006 by Congress *(see 33.13)*, that deduction would have to be added to the "**minus amounts**" on Line 6. *See* the *e-Supplement* and the IRS instructions.

To figure *provisional income*, you will have to increase the total income shown on your return by certain tax-exempt amounts, and also by 50% of your net Social Security benefits, before subtracting adjustments to income other than the student loan interest deduction *(33.14)*, the tuition and fees deduction *(33.13)*, and the domestic production activities deduction *(40.23)*. For example, *tax-exempt interest* reported on Line 8b of your return is included as part of provisional income for purposes of figuring the taxable part of your Social Security benefits, although this amount is not included when figuring your regular tax liability. On the worksheet above, provisional income is the amount computed for Line 7.

EXAMPLES

1. Frank Adams, who is single, has 2006 earnings of $15,000 from a part-time job, $3,000 of interest income, and $2,000 of dividends. He also receives $8,000 of net Social Security benefits (Box 5 of Form SSA-1099). Completing the worksheet, Frank's provisional income on Line 7 is $24,000 ($15,000 + 3,000 + 2,000 + 50% of the $8,000 net Social Security benefits). Since $24,000 does not exceed the $25,000 base amount on Line 8 of the worksheet, none of Frank's Social Security benefits are taxable.
2. Sam and Fran Baker receive in 2006 net Social Security benefits (Box 5 of Form SSA-1099) of $15,000. Their taxable interest, dividends, and capital gains are $20,000, and tax-exempt interest is $10,000. They file a joint return. Their provisional income from Line 7 of the worksheet is $37,500 ($20,000 + 10,000 + 50% of the $15,000 net Social Security benefits). Since $37,500 exceeds the $32,000 base amount on Line 8 of the worksheet, part of their Social Security benefits will be taxed. On the sample worksheet shown on page 568, Sam and Fran figure that $2,750 of their benefits are subject to tax.

IRA contributions. Do *not* use the worksheet on page 568 if you are an active participant in an employer retirement plan and you plan to make deductible IRA contributions *(8.4)*. You must use the worksheets printed in IRS Publication 590. With the worksheets, you first determine the amount of Social Security benefits that would be subject to tax, assuming you did not claim any IRA deduction. That amount is then used to figure the allowable IRA deduction, taking into account any limitations under the phase-out rules *(8.4)*, and, finally, the allowable IRA deduction is used to compute the taxable portion of your Social Security benefits.

If you are not covered by an employer retirement plan, you may use the worksheet to figure the taxable portion of your Social Security benefits.

34.4 Election for Lump-Sum Social Security Benefit Payment

If in 2006 you receive a lump-sum payment of benefits covering prior years, you have a choice as to how to determine the taxable portion of the benefits: (1) You may treat the entire payment as a 2006 benefit taxable under the rules in *34.3 or* (2) you may allocate the benefits between 2006 and the earlier years. Choose the method that provides the lowest required increase to income in the current year. For example, if you receive a 2006 lump-sum payment that includes benefits for 2005, you may find that an allocation of benefits is advantageous where your income over the two-year period has fluctuated and benefits allocated to 2005 would be subject to a lower taxable percentage than in 2006.

When you elect to allocate benefits to a prior year, you do not amend the return for that year. You compute the increase in income (if any) that would have resulted if the Social Security benefits had been received in that year. You then add that amount to the income of the current year.

See IRS Publication 915 for instructions and worksheets for making the allocation and figuring the amount to be reported on your return.

34.5 Retiring on Social Security Benefits

Retirement benefits are not paid automatically. You should file for Social Security retirement benefits three months before you want to start receiving benefits. The age for receiving full Social Security benefits, traditionally 65, is now increasing by a few months a year. For example, if your 65th birthday is in 2007, full benefits will not be available until you are 65 and 10 months; *see* the Law Alert on this page. Reduced benefits may be elected if you are at least age 62. Even though your full Social Security retirement age is over 65, you should register with the Social Security Administration three months before the month in which you turn age 65 to ensure Medicare coverage.

Law Alert

Social Security Retirement Age

The retirement age for receiving full Social Security benefits is gradually increasing, as shown below.

Birth year—	*Full Social Security retirement age—*
Before 1938	65
1938	65 and 2 months
1939	65 and 4 months
1940	65 and 6 months
1941	65 and 8 months
1942	65 and 10 months
1943–1954	66
1955	66 and 2 months
1956	66 and 4 months
1957	66 and 6 months
1958	66 and 8 months
1959	66 and 10 months
1960 and after	67

If you are at least age 62 and elect reduced benefits, the reduction depends on the number of months between the start date and your full Social Security retirement age. For example, if you elect benefits at age 62 in 2007, the benefit reduction is about 25%.

If you delay benefits beyond full Social Security retirement age, your potential Social Security benefit increases for each year you delay retirement. The yearly increase is 6.5% for those born in 1937 or 1938, 7% for those born in 1939 or 1940, 7.5% for those born in 1941 or 1942, and 8% for those born in 1943 or later.

Planning Reminder

Earnings Test

Benefit forfeitures for working while receiving benefits apply only to retirees under the full Social Security retirement age; *see 34.5* and the Law Alert on page 569. You receive full benefits starting in the month you reach full retirement age no matter how much you earn.

Benefits before reaching full retirement age may be reduced because of earnings. If you are under full retirement age (*see* the Law Alert on retirement age on page 569) and are receiving benefits, $1 of benefits will be deducted for each $2 earned above an annual limit. In 2006, the limit is $12,480 (the 2007 limit will be listed in the *e-Supplement*). For the year you reach full retirement age, $1 of benefits is deducted for each $3 earned over a different limit, which for 2006 is $33,240, but only earnings before the month you reach full retirement age are counted. Starting with the month in which you reach full retirement age, you are entitled to full benefits with no limit on how much you may earn.

There is also a favorable rule for the first year of retirement. A full benefit may be received for any month in which your earnings do not exceed $^1/_{12}$ of the annual limit, even if the yearly limit is exceeded.

Regardless of your age, you may receive any amount of income from sources other than work—for example, private pensions or investments—without affecting the amount of Social Security retirement benefits.

EXAMPLES

1. Jones retires and begins receiving reduced Social Security benefits in January 2006 at age 62. He is entitled to receive $600 a month ($7,200 annually). He works and earns $21,920, which is $9,440 over the $12,480 limit for 2006. Under the regular benefit reduction rule, Jones would lose $4,720 of benefits ($1 for every $2 over $12,480). However, since this is his first year of retirement, a full benefit would be paid for any month in which earnings were $1,040 ($^1/_{12}$ of $12,480) or less.
2. Smith, who began receiving benefits before 2006, reaches full retirement age of 65 and 6 months in August 2006. He is entitled to monthly benefits of $600. He was fully employed during the year, earning $34,440 before August and $22,500 for the remainder of the year. The benefit reduction applies to his pre-August benefits. He earned $1,200 over the $33,240 limit and loses $400 of benefits ($1 for every $3 earned over $33,240). Starting in August, he begins to receive his full benefits regardless of the amount of his earnings.

So long as you continue to work, you pay Social Security taxes on your earnings, regardless of your age.

Request an estimate of benefits and copy of earnings record. You can get an estimate of retirement benefits by sending for Form SSA-7004. After mailing in a completed Form SSA-7004, you will receive a Personal Earnings and Benefit Estimate Statement, showing your earnings history, Social Security tax payments, and an estimate of your retirement, disability, and survivor's benefits.

Form SSA-7004 is available at your local Social Security office. You can also request the form from the Social Security Administration by calling 1-800-772-1213 or obtain it from the Social Security Administration website at www.ssa.gov.

34.6 How Tax on Social Security Reduces Your Earnings

There is an added tax cost of earning income if the earnings will subject your Social Security benefits to tax. Therefore, if your benefits are not currently exposed to tax, you have to figure *not only* the tax on the extra income *but also* the amount of Social Security benefits subjected to tax by those earnings. If the additional earnings will put you over the base amount *(34.3)*, then you will not only have to pay tax on the additional earnings but also on the Social Security benefits that will be subject to tax.

EXAMPLES

1. You are over full Social Security retirement age *(see 34.5)* and you and your spouse receive net Social Security benefits of $8,000. You file jointly. You have pension income of $25,000 and $3,000 in tax-exempt interest. Your provisional income *(34.3)* is $32,000. No part of your Social Security benefits is taxable because your provisional income of $32,000 does not exceed the $32,000 base amount for married persons filing jointly.
2. Same facts as in Example 1, except that you take a part-time job paying $7,000. This increases your provisional income to $39,000 and subjects $3,500 of Social Security benefits to tax.

Provisional income	$39,000
Less: Base amount	32,000
Excess	$7,000
50% of excess taxable *(34.3)*	$3,500

The $7,000 of additional earnings increases your taxable income by $10,500, which is the $7,000 of earnings plus the $3,500 of Social Security benefits made taxable because of the increase in provisional income.

When earnings result in forfeiture of Social Security benefits. If you receive reduced Social Security benefits before full Social Security retirement age, it is possible under the current tax structure to earn extra income and yet have only a small gain or even lose money when considering the increased tax on the earnings and on Social Security benefits, and also the forfeiture of benefits when earnings exceed the annual retirement earnings test; *see 34.5*.

Therefore, before taking on work to earn extra income, you should compute the tax cost of the extra earnings and the loss of benefits. As a rule of thumb, you may figure the extra tax cost by multiplying the earnings by your top federal tax bracket and also by the FICA tax rate of 7.65% (Social Security and Medicare withholdings) and by your top rate for state or local taxes. But be aware that this composite rate ignores the effect of the increased tax from crossing the thresholds for taxing up to 50% or 85% of Social Security benefits. Therefore, in such cases, the tax cost will be greater than the estimated composite tax rate. For greater accuracy, figure your tax position as if you were preparing two tax returns: one that does not include the extra income and the other that does include the extra income. The tax difference is the extra income tax cost of earning the extra pay. Add to this cost the FICA tax on the extra earnings and any additional state or local taxes. Then figure the amount of benefits that will be forfeited. This will give you a net gain or in some cases a net loss. If you have a tax consultant, it may be advisable to ask the consultant to make the computations.

Tax Credit for the Elderly and Disabled

34.7 Claiming the Credit for the Elderly and Disabled

You may qualify for a tax credit for 2006 if you meet one of the following conditions:

- Your 65th birthday is on or before January 1, 2007; *or*
- You were under age 65 at the end of 2006, you retired before the end of 2006 because of permanent and total disability, and you received taxable disability income in 2006 from your former employer's disability plan. Disability income is taxable wages or payments in lieu of wages paid to you while you are absent from work because of permanent and total disability. Qualifying disability income does not include payments received after reaching mandatory retirement age.

However, even if you meet one of these tests, you will not be able to claim a credit if your Social Security benefits or adjusted gross income is too high, or if you have no tax liability; *see 34.9*.

Disabled. You are considered permanently and totally disabled if you are unable to engage in any substantial gainful activity by reason of any medically determinable physical or mental impairment that can be expected to result in death or that has lasted or can be expected to last for a continuous period of not less than 12 months.

For the first year you claim the credit, you need a physician's certification of your disability. For later years, new certifications are generally not required.

Law Alert

Lack of Inflation Adjustment Weakens Credit

Since 1983, the base amounts *(34.8)* and AGI phase-out thresholds *(34.9)* for figuring the credit for the elderly or disabled have remained the same while inflation adjustments and tax law changes have reduced tax liability. Since the credit cannot exceed tax liability, the number of taxpayers able to claim the credit has dropped drastically.

Nonresident aliens. You may not claim the credit if you are a nonresident alien at any time during 2006, unless you are married to a citizen or resident and you have elected to be treated as a resident; *see 1.5.*

Amount of credit. The amount of the credit is 15% times the base amount after reductions. The base amount for the credit is generally $7,500, $5,000, or $3,750, as shown in *34.8*. The base amount is reduced by nontaxable Social Security and other tax-free pensions, as well as by adjusted gross income exceeding specific limits as explained in *34.9*.

The credit is not refundable. That is, it is allowed only up to your tax liability; *see 34.9.*

How to claim the credit. You claim the credit on Schedule R if you file Form 1040. If you file Form 1040A, claim the credit on Part 3. You may not claim the credit on Form 1040EZ.

Married couples. A married couple may claim the credit only if they file a joint return. However, if a husband and wife live apart at all times during the taxable year and file separately, the credit may be claimed on a separate return.

34.8 Base Amount for the Elderly or Disabled Credit

The law specifies an initial base amount for figuring the credit. This base amount is reduced by certain tax-free benefits and excess adjusted gross income before applying the 15% credit amount and the tax liability limitation, if any, as explained in *34.9*.

The initial base amount is:

- $5,000, if you are single, head of household, or are a qualifying widow(er).
- $5,000, if you file a joint return and only one spouse is eligible for the credit.
- $7,500, if you file a joint return and both spouses are eligible for the credit. The credit is figured solely on this base; a separate computation is not made for each spouse.
- $3,750, if you are married and file a separate return. The credit may be claimed on a separate return only if you and your spouse have lived apart at all times during the year.

Base amount if disabled. If you are under age 65 and permanently and totally disabled, the base amount for figuring the credit is the *lower* of your 2006 taxable disability income or the initial base amount for your filing status shown above. For example, if you are single, under age 65, permanently and totally disabled, and received taxable disability income of $4,800, you figure the credit on $4,800, which is less than the base of $5,000 for single persons.

Joint return and both spouses qualify for the credit. If one spouse is age 65 or over and one spouse is under age 65 and receives disability income, the initial base amount is the lesser of (1) $7,500 or (2) $5,000 *plus* the disability income of the spouse under age 65. If both spouses are under age 65 and disabled, the initial base amount is the total of their disability income, not exceeding $7,500.

34.9 Reduction of the Base Amount and Liability Limitation for the Credit

Caution

Low Social Security Benefits Required for Credit

The tax credit for the elderly or disabled is not available to an unmarried individual who receives $5,000 or more of nontaxable Social Security benefits or nontaxable federal pensions such as from the Veterans Administration. The $5,000 limit also applies if you are married filing jointly and only one spouse qualifies for the credit. The limit is $7,500 if you file a joint return and both spouses qualify for the credit.

The $3,750, $5,000, or $7,500 credit base amount *(34.8)* is reduced by nontaxable pensions and Social Security, and also by "excess" adjusted gross income, figured as follows:

Nontaxable Social Security and pensions. The base amount is reduced by:

- Social Security and Railroad Retirement benefits that are *not taxable* under the rules in *34.3*; *and*
- Tax-free pension, annuity, or disability income paid under a law administered by the Veterans Administration or under other federal laws.

You do *not* reduce the base amount for: military disability pensions received for active service in the Armed Forces or in the Coast Guard and Geodetic Survey or Public Health Service; certain disability annuities paid under the Foreign Service Act of 1980; and workers' compensation benefits. However, if Social Security benefits are reduced by workers' compensation benefits, the amount of workers' compensation benefits is treated as Social Security benefits that reduce the base.

Excess adjusted gross income. You reduce the base amount by one-half of adjusted gross income (AGI) exceeding: $7,500 if you are single, head of household, or a qualified widow(er); $10,000 if you are married filing a joint return; or $5,000 if you are married, live apart from your spouse for the entire year, and file a separate return. Applying these income floors, the credit is no longer available to a single person when AGI reaches $17,500, $20,000 on a joint return where one spouse is eligible for the credit, $25,000 on a joint return where both spouses are eligible for the credit, and $12,500 where a married person files separately.

15% credit limited by tax liability. After reducing the credit base amount as just discussed for nontaxable Social Security and pensions and excess AGI, the remaining credit base is multiplied by 15%. This is the maximum credit but where this amount exceeds tax liability, the credit is limited to the lesser liability, as in the following Examples.

EXAMPLES

1. John Andrews is 58 years old and single. In 2002, he retired on permanent and total disability. In 2006, he receives a taxable disability pension of $9,400, nontaxable Social Security disability benefits of $2,500, and taxable interest of $100. Adjusted gross income (AGI) is $9,500 ($9,400 + $100). His taxable income after claiming the standard deduction ($5,150) and personal exemption ($3,300) is only $1,050. As shown below, the credit formula would allow a credit of $225, but the credit cannot exceed John's 2006 tax liability, which is $106 (based on taxable income of $1,050).

Initial base amount *(34.8)*	$5,000
Less: nontaxable Social Security disability	2,500
Less: 50% of AGI over $7,500	
(50% of ($9,500 *minus* $7,500))	1,000
Credit base amount	$1,500
Credit (15% of credit base amount)	$225
Tax liability limitation	$106

2. William White, age 53, retired in 1994 on permanent and total disability. In 2006, he received a taxable disability pension of $6,000 and nontaxable Social Security disability benefits of $3,000. He files a joint return with his wife, Helen, age 49, who had wages of $9,200 and a taxable disability pension of $2,000 from a job from which she retired on account of permanent and total disability. Their adjusted gross income (AGI) for 2006 is $17,200 ($6,000 + $9,200 + $2,000). Their taxable income (after the $10,300 standard deduction and $6,600 personal exemptions) is only $300 and their tax liability is just $31. Thus, the $135 credit allowed under the credit formula is limited to $31.

Initial base amount	
(Taxable disability income; *see 34.8*)	$7,500
Less: Nontaxable Social Security	3,000
Less: 50% of AGI over $10,000	
(50% of ($17,200 – $10,000))	3,600
Credit base amount	$900
Credit (15% of credit base amount)	$135
Tax liability limitation	$31

Continuing Care Communities

34.10 Tax Effects of Moving to a Continuing Care Facility

Senior citizens who move into "continuing care" or "life-care" facilities pay large upfront entrance fees upon admittance, as well as monthly fees thereafter in return for a residence, meals, and lifetime health care, including long-term skilled nursing care, should that become necessary. The payments raise several tax issues discussed in this section and in *34.11*.

Portion of monthly fees deductible as medical expense. Part of the monthly fees to a life-care community are allocable to health care, which you may deduct as an itemized medical expense subject to the 7.5% floor; *see 17.1*. Continuing care facilities generally send a statement to the residents specifying the portion of their monthly service fees that went towards health care.

The IRS and Tax Court have approved the use of a "percentage method" for allocating the community's medical expenses among the residents. In general, the annual medical expenses of the community are divided by total operating expenses to get the medical care allocation percentage. In a particular case, the IRS could contest how the allocation is figured or how the allocated amount is divided among the residents.

Caution

Charitable Contribution Deductions

Payments made to a tax-exempt organization that operates a life-care community are generally not deductible charitable contributions because you are receiving services in exchange. If you donate amounts over and above your regular monthly fees and do not receive any extra benefit as a result, you may deduct the excess payment as a charitable contribution; *see 14.3*.

For example, in a 2004 case (Baker, 122 TC 143), the IRS contested a couple's medical expense deduction for a portion of the monthly service fees paid for their two-bedroom duplex apartment, categorized as an "independent living unit" (ILU). Using a percentage method computation supplied by the resident council of their continuing care retirement community, the Bakers deducted $6,557 of their 1997 monthly service fees and $9,891 of their 1998 monthly fees as medical expenses. The IRS initially allowed a deduction for $4,488 of the 1997 fees and $5,142 of the 1998 fees using a different percentage method. Then, when the Bakers appealed to the Tax Court, the IRS argued that the deductible part of the service fees should be figured using an "actuarial method," which would increase the Bakers' two-year deduction by a few hundred dollars over what the examining agent had allowed.

However, the Tax Court refused to require use of the actuarial method, which requires projections of longevity and lifetime utilization of health-care services, and is so complicated that the IRS could not fully explain the method to the Court. The Court held that the percentage method is appropriate, noting that the IRS has approved use of the percentage method in rulings since 1967. However, in applying the percentage method to determine the Bakers' deductions, the Court had to resolve disputes over how certain expenses should be treated and how the allocated medical care percentage, once determined, should be split among the residents. For example, the Court held that the community's interest expenses, depreciation and amortization allowances should be included in both the numerator and denominator when dividing medical costs by operating costs to determine the medical care allocation percentage.

The Court calculated that 27.93% of the community's 1997 total costs and 30.07% of the 1998 costs were allocable to medical care. The Court then held that the Bakers could not simply multiply these percentages by the fees they paid to get their deductions. The same medical expense amount must be allocated to each ILU resident by multiplying the allocation percentage by a weighted average of the service fees paid each year by the ILU residents. The weighted average annual service fee for 1997 paid by the ILU residents was $13,902, which when multiplied by the allocation percentage of 27.93%, gave a medical care allocation of $3,883 per resident. For 1998, the weighted average annual service fee for ILU residents was $14,093, which when multiplied by the allocation percentage of 30.07%, gave a medical care allocation of $4,238 per resident. On their joint returns, the Bakers could treat double the per resident amounts as medical expenses; that is, $7,766 for 1997 and $8,476 for 1998.

Portion of nonrefundable entrance fee deductible as medical expense. What about the upfront payments required by life-care communities? If an entrance fee or founder's fee for lifetime care is nonrefundable, part may be treated as a medical expense *(17.1)* if you can prove what part of the lump sum is allocable to future medical coverage. The IRS recognizes that a deduction may be based on a showing that the life-care facility historically allocates a specified percentage of the fee to future medical care. With such proof there is a current obligation to pay and the allocable amount is treated as a deductible medical expense when the lump sum is paid. The same rules apply if the life-care or founder's fee is paid monthly rather than as a lump sum.

Separate sponsorship gift. In one case, an individual was allowed by the Tax Court and an appeals court to claim a charitable contribution deduction for a "sponsorship gift" paid to a life-care retirement facility where she and her husband were residents. The sponsorship gift was entirely separate from her entrance fee; it was not required for admission and did not entitle her to reduced monthly payments. She did not receive any extra benefit from her gift and was not entitled to a refund of any part of it.

34.11 Imputed Interest on Refundable Entrance Fees

You must pay a lump-sum entrance fee when you enter a continuing care community. Depending on the type of plan, a portion of the lump-sum fee may be refundable either to you if you move from the community or to your heirs upon your death. The payment of the fee may also reduce your monthly charges.

The refundable part of the entrance fee is generally considered a "loan" to the continuing care facility, so that imputed interest income could be charged to you under the rules in *4.31*.

However, the 2006 Tax Increase Prevention and Reconciliation Act (TIPRA) provides a complete exemption from the imputed interest rules for loans to qualified continuing care facilities if the loan is pursuant to a continuing care contract and the lender or lender's spouse is age 62 or older by the end of the year. The exemption applies for 2006 through 2010, and is retroactive, covering loans made prior to 2006.

To be a qualified continuing care facility, substantially all of the individual living unit residents must be covered by continuing care contracts with these features: (1) the contracting individual or his or her spouse is allowed to use the facility for life; (2) housing is provided in an independent living unit with outside facilities for meals and personal care, and, as available in the facility, in an assisted living facility or nursing facility; and (3) as is available in the facility, assisted living or nursing care will be provided as the health of the individual or his/her spouse requires.

If the exemption is not extended beyond 2010, then starting in 2011 the prior law rules will again apply, under which loans to qualified continuing care facilities were subject to imputed interest to the extent the loan exceeded an annual floor; for example, the floor for 2006 was scheduled to be $163,300 before the TIPRA exemption was enacted.

Law Alert

Continuing Care Facility Loans Exempted From Imputed Interest

For 2006–2010, a loan made to a qualified continuing care facility is exempt from imputed interest rules.

Chapter 35

Members of the Armed Forces

Special tax benefits are provided to Armed Forces personnel. A major tax-free benefit is the combat pay exclusion. Under this exclusion, members of the Armed Forces, including active duty reservists, may exclude from gross income all compensation for active service received for any month in which they served in a combat zone or were hospitalized as a result of any wound, injury, or disease incurred while serving in a combat zone. Commissioned officers are allowed an exclusion equal to the highest rate of basic pay at the top pay level for enlisted personnel, plus any hostile fire/imminent danger pay received for the month.

Other pay benefits may be tax free, and you may be able to get filing extensions and time extensions for home residence replacements. A list of tax-free benefits may be found at *35.2*. Filing extensions are discussed at *35.5*.

Combat zones include Iraq and neighboring areas in the "Arabian Peninsula," Afghanistan and the Balkans. *See 35.4*.

35.1 Taxable Armed Forces Pay and Benefits

Armed Forces personnel report as taxable pay the following items:

- Basic pay for active duty, attendance at a designated service school, back wages, drills, reserve training, and training duty
- Special pay for aviation career incentives, diving duty, foreign duty (for serving outside the 48 contiguous states and the District of Columbia), hazardous duty, medical and dental officers, nuclear-qualified officers, and special duty assignments
- Enlistment and reenlistment bonuses
- Payments for accrued leave, and personal money allowances paid to high-ranking officers
- Student loan repayment from programs such as the Department of Defense Educational Loan Repayment Program

Caution

Community Property

If you are married and your domicile (permanent home to which you intend to return) is in one of the following states, your military pay is subject to community property laws of that state: Arizona, California, Idaho, Louisiana, Nevada, New Mexico, Texas, Washington, and Wisconsin. *See 1.6* for community property reporting rules.

State income tax withholding. A state that makes a withholding agreement with the Secretary of the Treasury may subject members of the Armed Forces regularly stationed within that state to its payroll withholding provisions. National Guard members and reservists are not considered to be members of the Armed Forces for purposes of this section.

Where and when to file. Mail your return to the Internal Revenue Service Center for the place you are stationed. For example, you are stationed in Arizona but have a permanent home address in Missouri; you send your return to the Service Center for Arizona. For filing extensions on entering the service, *see 35.7*.

35.2 Tax-Free Armed Forces Benefits

The following benefits are *not* subject to tax:

- Combat pay; *see 35.4*
- Living allowances for BAH (Basic Allowance for Housing). You may deduct mortgage interest and real estate taxes on your home even if you pay these expenses with BAH funds.
- BAS (Basic Allowance for Subsistence) living allowances
- Housing and cost-of-living allowances abroad, whether paid by the U.S. Government or by a foreign government
- VHA (Variable Housing Allowance)
- Family allowances for educational expenses for dependents, emergencies, evacuation to a place of safety, and separation
- Death allowances for burial services, death gratuity payments to eligible survivors, and travel of dependents to burial site
- Dislocation allowance, intended to partially reimburse expenses such as lease forfeitures, temporary living charges in hotels, and other expenses incurred in relocating a household
- Temporary lodging expense allowance intended to partially offset the added living expenses of temporary lodging within the United States for up to 10 days and up to 60 days abroad
- A moving-in housing allowance, intended to defray costs, such as for rental agent fees, home-security improvements, and supplemental heating equipment, associated with occupying leased space outside the United States
- Travel allowances for annual round trip for dependent students, leave between consecutive overseas tours, reassignment in a dependent-restricted status, and transportation for you or your dependents during ship overhaul or inactivation
- Defense counseling payments
- ROTC educational and subsistence allowances
- Survivor and retirement protection plan premium payments
- Uniform allowances paid to officers and uniforms furnished to enlisted personnel
- Medical or hospital treatment provided by the United States in government hospitals
- Pay forfeited on order of a court martial
- Education, training, or subsistence allowances paid under any law administered by the Department of Veterans Affairs (VA). However, deductible education costs must be reduced by the VA allowance.
- Adjustments in pay to compensate for losses resulting from inflated foreign currency
- Payments to former prisoners of war from the U.S. Government in compensation for inhumane treatment suffered at the hands of an enemy government
- Benefits under Servicemembers' Group Life Insurance
- Dividends on GI insurance. These are a tax-free return of premiums paid.
- Interest on dividends left on deposit with the Department of Veterans Affairs (VA). The IRS has revoked a prior ruling that subjected such interest to tax.

Disability retirement pay. Your disability retirement pay may be tax free if you are a former member of the Armed Forces of any country, the Foreign Service, the Coast Guard, the National Oceanic and Atmospheric Administration, or the Public Health Service. Tax-free treatment of disability retirement pay is retroactive to the date of the application for benefits. But Social Security disability payments made on account of a combat-related injury are taxable to the same extent as Social Security retirement payments *(see 34.3)*.

Filing Tip

Away From Home Base

If your ship or squadron is away from your "home" port or base, you may be able to deduct travel expenses while away. However, you are not considered "away from home" if you are at your *permanent* duty station or you are a naval officer assigned to permanent duty aboard a ship; *see also 20.6*.

35.3 Deductions for Armed Forces Personnel

Members of the Armed Forces may deduct the items listed below as miscellaneous itemized deductions subject to the 2% adjusted gross income (AGI) floor; *see 19.1*:

- Board and lodging costs over those paid to you by the government while on temporary duty away from your home base
- Costs of rank insignia, collar devices, gold braids, etc., and the cost of altering rank insignia when promoted or demoted
- Contributions to a "Company" fund made according to Service regulations. But personal contributions made to stimulate interest and morale in a unit are not deductible.
- Court martial legal expenses in successfully defending against the charge of conduct unbecoming an officer
- Dues to professional societies. But you may not deduct dues for officers' and noncommissioned officers' clubs.
- Expense of obtaining increased retirement pay
- Out-of-pocket moving expenses for service-connected moves. The 50-mile test and the 39-week test generally required to deduct moving expenses do not have to be met; *see 12.3*.
- Subscriptions to professional journals
- Transportation, food, and lodging expenses while on official travel status. But you are taxed on mileage and *per diem* subsistence allowance.
- Uniforms. The cost and cleaning of uniforms are deductible if: (1) they must be worn on duty; (2) they cannot under military regulations be worn off duty; and (3) the cost exceeds any tax-free clothing allowance.

35.4 Tax-Free Pay for Service in Combat Zone or Hazardous Duty Area

If your grade is below commissioned officer and you serve in a designated combat zone or hazardous duty area during any part of a month, *all* of your qualifying military pay (*see* below) for that month is excluded from your taxable income. You may also exclude military pay earned during any part of a month that you are hospitalized as a result of wounds, disease, or injury incurred in a combat zone or hazardous duty area. The exclusion for military pay while hospitalized does not apply to any month that begins more than two years after the end of combat activities in that combat zone or hazardous duty area. Your hospitalization does not have to be in the combat zone or hazardous duty area.

Filing Tip

Who Qualifies for Exclusion?

Members of the U.S. Armed Forces qualifying for the exclusion include commissioned officers and enlisted personnel in all regular and reserve units under control of the Secretaries of Defense, Army, Navy, and Air Force, and the Coast Guard. Members of the U.S. Merchant Marines or the American Red Cross are not included.

Officers. If you are a commissioned officer, you may exclude up to the highest rate of basic pay at the highest pay grade that enlisted personnel receive per month plus any hostile fire/imminent danger pay received for each month during any part of which you served in a combat zone or hazardous duty area.

If you are a commissioned warrant officer, you are considered an enlisted person.

What is included as tax-free pay? The following military pay qualifies for tax-free treatment: (1) active duty pay earned in any month you served in a combat zone or hazardous duty area; (2) a dislocation allowance if the move begins or ends in a month you served in a combat zone or hazardous duty area; (3) a reenlistment bonus if the voluntary extension or reenlistment occurs in a month you served in a combat zone or hazardous duty area; (4) pay for accrued leave earned in any month you served in a combat zone or hazardous duty area (the Department of Defense must determine that the unused leave was earned during that period); (5) pay received for duties as a member of the Armed Forces in clubs, messes, post and station theaters, and other nonappropriated fund activities. The pay must be earned in a month you served in a combat zone or hazardous duty area; and (6) awards for suggestions, inventions, or scientific achievements you are entitled to because of a submission you made in a month you served in a combat zone or hazardous duty area.

Service in the combat zone or hazardous duty area includes any periods you are absent from duty because of sickness, wounds, or leave. If, as a result of serving in a combat zone, you become a prisoner of war or missing in action, you are considered to be serving in the combat zone as long as you keep that status for military pay purposes.

Retirement pay and pensions do not qualify for the combat zone exclusion. According to a Fourth Circuit Court of Appeals decision, a Navy severance pay package was taxable although the recipient became entitled to the payment while on active duty in the Persian Gulf. The court differentiated the package, which was provided in order to entice the man to leave the service, from a reenlistment bonus provided as compensation for active service.

Law Alert

IRA Contributions Based on Tax-Free Combat Pay

The "Heroes Earned Retirement Opportunities Act" allows members of the armed services serving in a combat zone to contribute to either a traditional IRA *(8.2)* or a Roth IRA *(8.20)* based on their tax-free combat pay. The new law applies retroactively for individuals who received tax-free combat pay in 2004 and 2005. They have until May 28, 2009, to make contributions to a traditional IRA or a Roth IRA for 2004 and 2005.

Combat zones and hazardous duty areas. A combat zone is any area the President of the United States designates by Executive Order as an area in which the U.S. Armed Forces are or have engaged in combat. An area becomes and ceases to be a combat zone on the dates designated by the President. At the time this book went to press, the following designations were still in place. For any changes, *see* IRS Publication 3 and tax form instructions.

The following Arabian Peninsula Areas (including airspace) have been designated combat zones since January 17, 1991: the total land areas of Iraq, Kuwait, Saudi Arabia, Oman, Bahrain, Qatar, and the United Arab Emirates; the Persian Gulf; the Red Sea; the Gulf of Oman; the part of the Arabian Sea that is north of 10 degrees north latitude and west of 68 degrees east longitude; and the Gulf of Aden.

In support of Operation Iraqi Freedom (in addition to the above Arabian Peninsula Areas), service in the following areas is considered to be in direct support of the operation and therefore treated as in the combat zone: service in Jordan on or after March 19, 2003, in Israel January 1 through July 31, 2003, in Egypt March 19 through April 20, 2003, in Turkey on or after January 1, 2003, and in the Mediterranean Sea east of 30 degrees east longitude from March 19 through July 31, 2003.

Afghanistan, including the airspace above, was designated a combat zone beginning September 19, 2001. Service in Jordan and Pakistan on or after September 19, 2001, in Kyrgyzstan and Uzbekistan on or after October 1, 2001, in the Philippines on or after January 9, 2002, in Yemen on or after April 10, 2002, and in Djibouti on or after July 1, 2002, is considered to be in direct support of the Afghanistan operations and is therefore treated as in the combat zone.

Effective March 24, 1999, the Kosovo area was designated a combat zone including: the Federal Republic of Yugoslavia (Serbia/Montenegro), Albania, the Ionian Sea north of the 39th parallel, and the Adriatic Sea. Airspace above these areas is also part of the zone. As of November 21, 1995, a special law designated Bosnia and Herzegovina, Croatia, and Macedonia as a qualified hazardous duty area.

Qualifying service outside a combat zone or hazardous duty area. Military service outside a combat zone or hazardous duty area is considered to be performed in a combat zone or hazardous duty area if: (1) the service is in direct support of military operations in the combat zone or hazardous duty area, and (2) the service qualifies you for special military pay for duty subject to hostile fire or imminent danger. Military pay received for this service will qualify for the pay exclusion if the other requirements are met. As mentioned above, service in Israel, Turkey, and the Mediterranean Sea has been certified as in direct support of Operation Iraqi Freedom, and service in Pakistan, Jordan, Tajikistan, Uzbekistan, and Kyrgyzstan meets these tests as supportive of the operations in Afghanistan.

Filing Tip

Spouses of Combat Zone Personnel

If your spouse serves in a combat zone or hazardous duty area, you are generally entitled to the same deadline extension as he or she is. However, any extra extension for your spouse's hospitalization within the United States is not available to you. Further, a spouse's extension does not apply to any year beginning more than two years after the end of combat or hazardous duty activities.

Nonqualifying service. The following military service does not qualify as service in a combat zone or hazardous duty area: (1) presence in a combat zone while on leave from a duty station located outside the combat zone; (2) passage over or through a combat zone during a trip between two points that are outside a combat zone; and (3) presence in a combat zone solely for your personal convenience. Such service will not qualify you for the pay exclusion.

Hospitalized while serving in a combat zone or hazardous duty area. If you are hospitalized while serving in a combat zone or hazardous duty area for a wound, disease, or injury, it will be presumed to have been incurred while serving in the combat zone or hazardous duty area unless there is clear evidence to the contrary.

EXAMPLES

1. You are hospitalized for a specific disease after serving in a combat zone for three weeks, and the disease for which you are hospitalized has an incubation period of two to four weeks. The disease is presumed to have been incurred while you were serving in the combat zone. On the other hand, if the incubation period of the disease is one year, the disease would not have been incurred while you were serving in the combat zone.
2. You were hospitalized for a specific disease three weeks after you left the combat zone. The incubation period of the disease is from two to four weeks. The disease is considered to have been incurred while serving in the combat zone.

IRS Alert

Combat Zone E-Mail Address

The IRS has established an e-mail address, combatzone@irs.gov, for military personnel to ask questions about filing returns, paying taxes, and combat zone status. Responses to general questions will be communicated via e-mail. However, answers to questions that reference an individual's account information will be mailed to the last address of record; such information cannot be provided over the Internet.

Form W-2. The wages shown in Box 1 of your Form W-2 should not include combat pay. Retirement pay is not combat pay.

35.5 Tax Deadlines Extended for Combat Zone or Hazardous Duty Area Service

You are allowed an extension of at least 180 days (*see* below) to take care of tax matters if you are a member of the Armed Forces who served in a combat zone or hazardous duty area. The extension applies to filing tax returns, paying taxes, filing a Tax Court petition, filing refund claims, and making an IRA contribution (*see* IRS Publication 3 for details). The time allowed for the IRS to begin an audit or take collection actions is also extended.

Support personnel. The deadline extension also applies if you are serving in a combat zone or hazardous duty area in support of the Armed Forces. This includes Red Cross personnel, accredited correspondents, and civilian personnel acting under the direction of the Armed Forces in support of those forces.

Extension is a minimum of 180 days. Your deadline for taking actions with the IRS is extended for at least 180 days after the later of: (1) the last day you are in a combat zone or hazardous duty area (or the last day it qualifies as a combat zone or hazardous duty area), or (2) the last day of any continuous qualified hospitalization for injury from service in the combat zone or hazardous duty area. Hospitalization may be outside the United States, or up to five years of hospitalization in the United States.

Time in a missing status (missing in action or prisoner of war) counts as time in a combat zone or hazardous duty area.

In addition to the 180 days, a filing deadline is also extended by the number of days you had left to file with the IRS when you entered a combat zone or hazardous duty area. If you entered the combat zone or hazardous duty area before the time to file began, the deadline is extended by the entire filing time.

35.6 Tax Forgiveness for Combat Zone or Hazardous Duty Area Deaths

If a member of the Armed Forces is killed in a combat zone or hazardous duty area or dies from wounds or disease incurred while in these zones or areas, any income tax liability for the year of death or any earlier year including service in such zones or areas is waived. In addition, the service member's estate is entitled to a refund for income tax paid while serving there.

If a member of the Armed Forces was a resident of a community property state and his or her spouse reported half of the military pay on a separate return, the spouse may get a refund of taxes paid on his or her share of the combat zone or hazardous duty area pay.

Forgiveness benefits apply to an Armed Forces member serving outside the zone or area if service: (1) was in direct support of military operations there, and (2) qualified the member for special military pay for duty subject to hostile fire or imminent danger.

Missing status. The date of death for a member of the Armed Forces who was in a missing status (missing in action or prisoner of war) is the date his or her name is removed from missing status for military pay purposes. This is true even if death occurred earlier.

How tax forgiveness is claimed. If the individual died in a combat zone or in a terroristic or military action, you file as the individual's representative: (1) Form 1040 if a U.S. individual income tax return (Form 1040, 1040A, or 1040EZ) has not been filed for the tax year. Form W-2, Wage and Tax Statement, must accompany the return. (2) Form 1040X if a U.S. individual income tax return has been filed. A separate Form 1040X must be filed for each year in question.

Check with your local IRS office for the address of the IRS office to which the return is filed.

An attachment should accompany any return or claim and should include a computation of the decedent's tax liability before any amount is forgiven and the amount that is to be forgiven.

The following documents must also accompany all returns and claims for refund: (1) Form 1310, Statement of Person Claiming Refund Due a Deceased Taxpayer; and (2) a certification from the Department of Defense. Department of State certification is required if the decedent was a civilian employee of an agency other than the Department of Defense.

Caution

Tax Forgiveness

Tax forgiveness does *not* apply to a U.S. civilian or military employee who dies as a result of an accident or a training exercise. Abatement also does not apply to terroristic action within the United States. However, abatement does apply if the individual dies in the U.S. from a wound or injury incurred in a terroristic or military action outside the United States.

Tax forgiveness for civilian or military personnel killed in terroristic or military action. Tax liability is waived for civilian or military U.S. government employees killed in terroristic or military actions outside the U.S., even if the President has not designated the area as a combat zone and it is not a hazardous duty area. Tax liability is waived for the period beginning with the taxable year before the year in which the injuries were incurred and ending with the year of death. Refund claims for prior years must generally be filed on Form 1040X by the later of three years from the time the original return was filed or two years from the time the tax was paid. However, if death occurred in a combat zone, the filing period is extended by the time served in the combat zone, plus the period of continuous hospitalization outside the U.S., plus an additional 180 days. The individual must also be a U.S. government employee both on the date of injury and date of death.

Filing Tip

Uniform Costs of Reservists

The cost and upkeep of uniforms is deductible only if you are prohibited from wearing them when off duty; *see 19.6*. A deduction allowed under this test must be reduced by any uniform allowance you receive, and the unreimbursed cost is subject to the 2% adjusted gross income (AGI) floor for miscellaneous itemized deductions.

Determination of death for Vietnam MIAs. Under prior law, MIAs were generally presumed dead as of December 31, 1982. Under current law, the date of death of service members missing in action in Vietnam is the date determined by the Armed Forces. Thus, under current law, tax abatement may be available for years after 1982. Furthermore, the date of death, as determined by the Armed Forces, also applies for such rules as whether to file as a surviving spouse, and for postponing the due date for filing returns and paying taxes.

35.7 Extension To Pay Your Tax When Entering the Service

If you are unable to pay your tax when you enter the Armed Forces, you may get an extension until six months after your initial period of service ends. Get a form at the IRS office of your District Director or write a letter to the District Director or to the IRS office requesting payment (your spouse or parent may do it for you). An extension, without interest, may be given if your income dropped after entering the military *and* you actually apply for the extension.

The extension does not cover your spouse, who must file a separate return and pay the tax due. But you and your spouse may file a joint return before the postponement period expires even though your spouse filed a separate return for that particular year. No interest is charged on this postponement of your tax.

Automatic extension of time to file your return. If you are on duty outside the U.S. or Puerto Rico on April 16, 2007, you get an automatic two-month extension to file your 2006 return; *see* page 6.

Interest charged on back taxes. If you do not show hardship qualifying you for the above interest-free payment extension, the IRS may reduce its interest rate on the deficiency. The maximum interest rate the IRS may charge for taxes incurred prior to your entry into active service is 6%. This reduced rate applies only to the period of your active duty.

Filing Tip

Overnight Travel to National Guard and Reserve Meetings

National Guard and Reserve members who travel over 100 miles and stay overnight to attend Guard or Reserve meetings may claim an above-the-line deduction from gross income for their meals, lodging, and incidental expenses, plus the standard mileage rate for driving costs and parking fees and tolls. The expenses are reported on Form 2106 and the amount attributable to the over-100-mile-away trips is entered on Line 24 of Form 1040 as an above-the-line deduction from gross income *(12.2)*. Other travel costs from Form 2106 are allowed only as miscellaneous itemized deductions, subject to the 2% of AGI floor.

35.8 Tax Information for Reservists

Transportation costs to reservist meetings generally are not deductible. A possible exception is the cost of traveling from your regular job location to a meeting held on a regular workday or traveling from home to a meeting outside the metropolitan area where you live and normally work. The cost would be deductible, subject to the 2% adjusted gross income (AGI) floor for miscellaneous itemized deductions; *see 19.1*.

Law Alert

Penalty-Free Withdrawals From Retirement Plans

A new law allows individuals who are called to active duty for over 179 days to withdraw IRA or qualified plan funds before age $59^1/_2$ without penalty; *see 35.8.*

If you travel overnight more than 100 miles away from your tax home *(20.6)* to a meeting or training camp, you may claim an above-the-line deduction for transportation, lodging, and meals (subject to the 50% reduction for meals); *see* the Filing Tip in this section.

If you are called for active duty away from your tax home, you may deduct travel expenses provided you keep your regular job while on active duty, return to it after you are released, and pay for those expenses at the military post. To the extent they exceed BAH (housing) and BAS (subsistence) allowances, the expenses are deductible only as a miscellaneous itemized deduction subject to the 2% AGI floor.

Deferring tax payments and reduction of IRS interest rate. If you owed a tax deficiency to the IRS before being called to active duty, the IRS may defer payment, without interest, if your ability to pay has been severely impaired by your call-up; *see 35.7.* If you are not allowed a deferment, the IRS will reduce its interest charge to 6% on the taxes you owed before your call-up.

Penalty-free withdrawals from retirement plans. If you are called to active military duty before December 31, 2007, for over 179 days, or indefinitely, distributions received during the active duty period are not subject to the 10% early distribution penalty. This applies to distributions from a traditional IRA and distributions attributable to elective deferrals you made to a 401(k) or 403(b) plan.

Furthermore, no tax (as well as no penalty) is due on a qualified reservist distribution if it is recontributed to the plan within two years after the end of the active duty period.

These rules apply retroactively to individuals called to active duty after September 11, 2001. If the two-year period for recontributions has expired, it is extended to August 17, 2008. A refund claim may be made on an amended return for a penalty paid on a qualified distribution or for tax paid on a recontributed distribution. If the amended return deadline has passed for a prior year *(47.2)*, you have until August 16, 2007, to file the amended return.

Chapter 36

How To Treat Foreign Earned Income

There is a tax incentive for working abroad—in 2006 up to $82,400 of income earned abroad may escape U.S. income taxes and you may be entitled to an exclusion or deduction for certain housing costs. In measuring the economic value of this tax savings, consider the extra cost of living abroad. In some areas, the high cost of living and currency exchange rates will erode your tax savings.

The exclusion does not apply to investment income or to any other earned income that does not meet the exclusion tests.

To claim a foreign income exclusion you must satisfy a foreign residence or physical presence test *(36.5)*.

Employees of the U.S. government may not claim an exclusion based on the government pay earned abroad.

36.1 Claiming the Foreign Earned Income Exclusion

If your tax home is in a foreign country and you meet either the foreign residence test or physical presence test *(36.3)*, you may exclude up to $82,400 of foreign earned income earned in 2006. You must file a U.S. return if your gross income *exceeds* the filing threshold for your personal status, even though all or part of your foreign earned income may be tax free. For years after 2006, the maximum $82,400 exclusion may be increased by an inflation adjustment. The exclusion is not automatic; you must elect it. You elect the foreign earned income exclusion on Form 2555, which you attach to Form 1040. The housing cost exclusion *(36.4)* is also elected on Form 2555.

You may file simplified Form 2555-EZ if your 2006 foreign wages are $82,400 or less, you do not have self-employment income, and you do not claim the foreign housing exclusion, housing deduction, business, or moving expenses.

A separate exclusion is allowed for the value of meals and lodging received by employees living in qualified camps; *see 36.8*.

If you claim the foreign income exclusion of $82,400, you may not:

- Claim business deductions allocable to the excluded income;
- Make a deductible traditional IRA or Roth IRA contribution based on the excluded income; *or*
- Claim foreign taxes paid on excluded income as a credit or deduction.

In deciding whether to claim the exclusion, compare the overall tax (1) with the exclusion and (2) without the exclusion but with the full foreign tax credit and allocable deductions. Choose whichever gives you the lower tax; *see 36.3* and *36.6*. Keep in mind that if you claim the exclusion, any taxable income not subject to the earned income and housing exclusions will be taxed at the same rates that would have applied had no exclusions been allowed. For example, if you elect to exclude $80,000 of foreign earned income and have, after deductions, $20,000 in other taxable income, the $20,000 will be taxed at the rate or rates (depending on filing status) applicable to taxable income in the range of $80,000 – $100,000.

Once you elect the exclusion, that election remains in effect for all future years unless you revoke it. If you revoke the election, you cannot elect the exclusion again during the next five years without IRS consent. A revocation is made in a statement attached to your return for the year you want it to take effect. The foreign earned income exclusion and the housing cost exclusion must be revoked separately.

Reinstating the exclusion. The IRS may consent to a reinstatement of the exclusion following a revocation under the following circumstances: you return for a period of time to the United States, you move to another foreign country with different tax rates, you change employers, or there has been substantial change in the tax law of the foreign country of residence or physical presence.

EXAMPLE

A U.S. citizen living abroad asked the IRS if the declaration of a tax holiday by a foreign country in 1999 was a substantial change of law. Prior to 1996, while working abroad he had claimed the foreign income exclusion. But in 1996 and 1997, he revoked the election and claimed a foreign tax credit for taxes paid on his foreign earnings. In 1999, he wanted to resume claiming the income exclusion due to the declaration of a tax holiday in the country in which he was employed. The IRS ruled that he can claim the exclusion. The declaration of a tax holiday is considered a substantial change of law because he went from being taxed to being exempt from tax.

Law Alert

New Exclusion Rules Effective for 2006

The inflation adjustment that had been scheduled to take effect in 2008 was accelerated to 2006, increasing the foreign earned income exclusion for 2006 to $82,400. However, the new law generally reduces the amount of housing costs that can be excluded from income; *see 36.4*.

The new law also increases the tax on any taxable income not covered by the foreign earned income and housing cost exclusions. Such other income is subject to tax at the higher rate (or rates) that would have applied had there been no exclusions, rather than at the lowest tax brackets, as under prior law.

Caution

Claiming Foreign Tax Credit Revokes Prior Election

If you have been claiming the exclusion and decide that it would be advantageous this year to forego the exclusion and instead claim the foreign tax credit for foreign earned income, be aware that claiming the credit is treated by the IRS as a revocation of the prior exclusion election. You may not claim an exclusion for the next five years unless the IRS allows you to reelect the exclusion.

Claiming a foreign tax credit also may revoke a prior election to claim the housing cost exclusion. Depending on the foreign earned income in the year the credit is claimed, the credit may be considered a revocation of a prior earned income exclusion election and also a prior housing cost exclusion election, or as a revocation of only one of the elections.

A good faith error in calculating foreign earned income that leads to claiming a foreign credit will not be treated as a revocation of prior elections.

36.2 What Is Foreign Earned Income?

For exclusion purposes, foreign earned income includes salaries, wages, commissions, professional fees, and bonuses for personal services performed while your tax home is in a foreign country and you meet either the foreign residence test or the physical presence test; *see 36.3*. Earned income also includes allowances from your employer for housing or other expenses, as well as the value of housing or a car provided by the employer. It may also include business profits, royalties, and rents, provided this income is tied to the performance of services. Earned income does not include pension or annuity income, payments for nonqualified employee trusts or nonqualified annuities, dividends, interest, capital gains, gambling winnings, alimony, or the value of tax-free meals or lodging under the rules at *3.12*. Foreign earned income does not include amounts earned in countries subject to U.S. government travel restrictions.

Foreign earned income eligible for the exclusion must be received no later than the taxable year after the year in which you perform the services. Pay is excludable in the year of receipt if you did not use the full exclusion in the year of the services.

U.S. government pay ineligible. If you are an employee of the U.S. government or its agencies, you may *not* exclude any part of your pay from your government employer. Courts have agreed with the IRS that U.S. government workers were U.S. employees even though they were paid from sources other than Congressionally appropriated funds. If you are not an employee of the U.S. government or any of its agencies, your pay is excludable even if paid by a government source. You are not an employee of the U.S. government if you work under a contract made between your employer and the government.

Under a special law, tax liability is waived for a civilian or military employee of the U.S. government killed in a military action overseas; *see 35.6.*

Profits from sole proprietorship or partnership. If your business consists solely of services (no capital investment), 100% of gross income is considered earned income. If services and capital are both income-producing factors, the value of your personal services, but no more than 30% of your share of the net profit, is considered earned income. Net profit is reduced by the deduction for 50% of self-employment tax *(12.2)* before figuring your 30% share.

If you do not contribute any services to a business (for example, you are a "silent partner"), your share of the net profits is *not* earned income.

If you do not have a net profit, the portion of your gross profit that represents a reasonable allowance for personal services is considered earned income.

EXAMPLES

1. A U.S. citizen resides in England. He invests in an English partnership that sells manufactured goods outside the U.S. He performs no services for the business. His share of net profits does not qualify as earned income.
2. Same facts as in Example 1, except he devotes his full time to the partnership business. Then up to 30% of his share of the net profits may qualify as earned income. Thus, if his share of profits is $50,000, earned income is $15,000 (30% of $50,000), assuming the value of his services is at least $15,000.
3. You and another person are consultants, operating as a partnership in Europe. Since capital is not an income-producing element, the entire gross income of the business is earned income.

Caution

Rental Income

Rental income is generally not earned income. However, if you perform personal services, for example as an owner-manager of a hotel or rooming house in a foreign country, then up to 30% of your net rents may be earned income.

The partnership agreement generally determines the tax status of partnership income in a U.S. partnership with a foreign branch. Thus, if the partnership agreement allocates foreign earnings to partners abroad, the allocation will be recognized unless it lacks substantial economic effect.

Fringe benefits. The value of fringe benefits, such as the right to use company property and facilities, is added to your compensation when figuring the amount of your earned income.

Royalties. Royalties from articles or books are earned income if you receive them for transferring all of your rights to your work, or you have contracted to write the articles or book for an amount in cash plus a royalty on sales.

Royalties from the leasing of oil and mineral lands and from patents are not earned income.

Reimbursement of employee expenses. Do not include reimbursement of expenses as earned income to the extent they equal expenses that you adequately accounted for to your employer; *see 20.31.* If your expenses exceed reimbursements, the excess is allocated according to the rules in *36.6.* If reimbursements exceed expenses, the excess is treated as earned income.

Straight commission salespersons or other employees who arrange with their employers, for withholding purposes, to consider a percentage of their commissions as attributable to their expenses treat such amounts as earned income.

Reimbursed moving expenses. Reimbursements of moving expenses are not reported as income if you adequately account to your employer for the expenses; *see 12.8.*

A reimbursement is taxable if received under a non-accountable plan or for moving expenses that are not deductible *(12.3)* or that you deducted in an earlier year. However, for purposes of claiming the earned income exclusion, the reimbursement may be considered to have been earned in a year other than the year of receipt. This is important because an exclusion is allowed only for the year income is earned. If the move is from the U.S. to a foreign country, the reimbursement is considered foreign earned income in the year of the move if you qualify under the foreign residence or physical presence test for at least 120 days during that tax year. Reimbursement of moving expenses from one foreign country to another is considered foreign earned income in the year of the move, if you qualify under the residency or physical presence test at the new location for at least 120 days during the tax year. If you do not meet one of these tests in the year of the move, the reimbursements are earned income that must be allocated between the year of the move and the following tax year.

A taxable reimbursement for a move back to the U.S. is considered income from U.S. sources if you continue to work for the same employer. If you move back to the U.S. and take a job with a new employer *or* if you retire and move back to the U.S. and your old employer reimburses your moving expenses under a prior written agreement or company policy, the reimbursement is considered to be for past services in the foreign country and qualifies as foreign earned income eligible for the exclusion. The reimbursement is considered earned in the year of the move if you qualified under the residency or physical presence test *(36.5)* for at least 120 days during the tax year. Otherwise, the reimbursement is allocated between the year of the move and the year preceding the move. *See* IRS Publication 54 for details.

36.3 Qualifying for the Foreign Earned Income Exclusion

You may elect the exclusion for foreign earned income only if your tax home is in a foreign country *and* you meet either the foreign residence test *or* the foreign physical presence test of 330 days. The foreign residence and physical presence tests are discussed at *36.5*. Tax home is discussed at *20.6–20.8*. If your tax home is in the U.S., you may not claim the exclusion but may claim the foreign tax credit and your living expenses while away from home if you meet the rules at *20.9* for temporary assignments that are expected to last, and actually do last, for one year or less. U.S. government employees may not claim either the earned income exclusion or housing exclusion based on government pay.

Caution

Countries Subject to Travel Restrictions

You may not claim the foreign earned income exclusion, or the housing exclusion or deduction, if you work in a country subject to U.S. government travel restrictions. You are not treated as a bona fide resident of, or as present in, a country subject to the travel ban. *See* Form 2555 for countries on the restricted list.

Exclusion prorated on a daily basis. If you qualify under the foreign residence or physical presence test for only part of 2006, the $82,400 exclusion limit is reduced on a daily basis.

EXAMPLES

1. You were a resident of France from February 20, 2004, until July 1, 2006. On July 2 you returned to the U.S. Since your period of foreign residency included all of 2005, thereby satisfying the foreign residence test, you may claim a prorated exclusion for 2006. As you were abroad for 182 of the 365 days in 2006, you exclude earnings up to $41,085, or $^{182}/_{365}$ of the $82,400 maximum exclusion. If you earned more than $41,085, the exclusion is limited to $41,085.
2. You worked in France from June 1, 2005, through September 30, 2006. Your only days outside France were a 15-day vacation to the U.S. in December 2005. You do not qualify for an exclusion under the foreign residence test because you were not abroad for a full taxable year; you were not abroad for either the full year of 2005 or 2006. However, you do qualify under the physical presence test; you were physically present abroad for at least 330 full days during a 12-month period. The 12-month period giving you the largest 2006 exclusion is the 12-month period starting October 21, 2005, and ending October 20, 2006. *See 36.5* for figuring the 12-month period. Since you were abroad for at least 330 full days during that 12-month period, you may claim an exclusion. In 2006, you were abroad for 293 days within the 12-month period (January 1 to October 20, 2006, is 293 days). Thus, you exclude earnings up to $^{293}/_{365}$ of the maximum exclusion. If your earnings in France for 2006 exceeded $82,400, your exclusion is limited to $66,142 ($82,400 × $^{293}/_{365}$).

If you are married and you and your spouse each have foreign earned income and meet the foreign residence or physical presence test, you may each claim a separate exclusion. If your permanent home is in a community property state, your earned income is not considered community property for purposes of the exclusion.

Foreign earnings from a prior year. Foreign income earned in a prior year but paid in 2006 does not qualify for the 2006 exclusion. However, if the income was attributable to foreign services performed in 2005, the pay is tax free in 2006 to the extent that you did not use the full 2005 exclusion of $80,000. Under another exception, payments received in 2006 for 2005 services are treated as 2006 income if the payment was within a normal payroll period of 16 days or less that included the last day of 2005. If the services were performed before 2005, no exclusion is available to shelter the pay.

Income for services performed in the U.S. does not qualify for the exclusion, even though it is paid to you while you are abroad.

Foreign tax credit. Foreign taxes paid on tax-free foreign earned income do not qualify for a credit or deduction. But if your foreign pay for 2006 exceeds $82,400, you may claim a foreign tax credit or deduction for the foreign taxes allocated to taxable income. The instructions to Forms 2555 and 1116 and IRS Publication 514 provide details for making the computation.

36.4 How To Treat Housing Costs

The housing costs of employees and self-employed persons are treated differently by the tax law. Employees get a housing exclusion; self-employed persons get a deduction from *taxable* foreign earned income. If you live in a special camp provided by your employer, all housing costs are excluded; *see 36.8*.

Filing Tip

Claiming the Housing Exclusion

On Form 2555, you figure the housing exclusion before the foreign income exclusion. The income exclusion is limited to the excess of foreign earned income over the housing exclusion.

Exclusion for employer-financed housing costs. The housing exclusion is the excess of the employer-financed reasonable housing expenses (*see* below) over a "base housing amount." For 2006 and later years, the base housing amount is 16% of the maximum foreign earned income exclusion multiplied by the number of qualifying days of foreign residence or presence for the year. Thus, for 2006, the base housing amount is $13,184 ($82,400 maximum foreign earned income exclusion × 16%) if you qualify under the foreign residence or physical presence test for the entire year. If you qualify under residence or presence test for only part of the year, the $13,184 maximum base amount is prorated on a daily basis.

In figuring housing expenses in excess of the base housing amount, there is a limit on the expenses that can be taken into account for years after 2005. The housing expenses cannot exceed 30% of the maximum earned income exclusion, prorated as applicable by the number of qualifying days of foreign residence or presence for the year. The IRS has the authority to annually adjust the 30% amount upward or downward to take into account geographic differences in housing costs relative to costs within the United States.

Law Alert

New Housing Exclusion Computation

Starting in 2006, the steps for computing the housing cost exclusion are changed. There is a new definition of the base housing amount and a limit is imposed on the amount of employer-financed housing costs that can be taken into account.

Thus, for 2006, the limit on housing expenses is $24,720 (30% × $82,400) and the maximum housing exclusion is $11,536 ($24, 720 – $13,184 maximum base amount).

On Form 2555, your foreign earned income exclusion is limited to the excess of your foreign earned income (including employer-financed housing costs) over your housing exclusion.

Reasonable housing expenses. Include rent, utilities other than telephone costs, insurance, parking, furniture rentals, and repairs for yourself, your spouse, and dependents living with you. The following expenses do not qualify: cost of purchasing a home, furniture, or accessories; home improvements; payments of mortgage principal; domestic labor; and depreciation on a home or on improvements to leased housing. Furthermore, interest and taxes that are otherwise deductible do not qualify for the exclusion.

You may include the costs of a separate household that you maintain outside the U.S. for your spouse and dependents because living conditions at your foreign home are adverse.

Self-employed persons. On Form 2555, self-employed individuals may claim a limited deduction for housing costs exceeding the base housing amount. You may claim this deduction only to the extent it offsets taxable foreign earned income. The deduction is claimed as an "adjustment to income" on Line 36 of Form 1040, even if you do not itemize deductions.

Where you may not deduct expenses because you do not have taxable foreign earned income, expenses may be carried forward one year and deducted in the next year to the extent of taxable foreign earned income.

If you are an employee and self-employed during the same year. Housing expenses above the base amount are partly excludable and partly deductible. For example, if half of your foreign earned income is from services as an employee, half of the excess housing expenses over the base amount are excludable. The remaining excess housing costs are deductible to the extent of taxable foreign earned income. Follow the instructions to Form 2555.

Countries ineligible for tax benefits. Housing expenses incurred in a country subject to a U.S. government travel restriction are not eligible for the tax benefits explained in this section. *See* Form 2555 instructions for a list of countries to which travel restrictions apply.

36.5 Meeting the Foreign Residence or Physical Presence Test

To qualify for the foreign earned income exclusion, you must be either a U.S. citizen (or U.S. resident entitled to tax treaty benefits) meeting the foreign residence test or a U.S. citizen or resident meeting the physical presence test in a foreign country. The following areas are not considered foreign countries: Puerto Rico, Virgin Islands, Guam, Commonwealth of the Northern Mariana Islands, American Samoa, or the Antarctic region.

Waiver of time test. If war or civil unrest prevented you from meeting the foreign residence or physical presence test, you may claim the exclusion for the period you actually were a resident or physically present abroad. Foreign locations and the time periods that qualify for the waiver of the residency and physical presence tests are listed in the instructions to Form 2555.

If, by the due date of your 2006 return (April 16, 2007), you have not yet satisfied the foreign residence or physical presence test, but you expect to meet either test after the filing date, you may either file on the due date and report your earnings or ask for a filing extension under the rules at *36.7*.

Caution

Residence or Domicile?

Residence does not have the same meaning as *domicile*. Your domicile is a permanent place of abode; it is the place to which you eventually plan to return wherever you go. You may have a residence in a place other than your domicile. Thus, you may go, say, to Amsterdam, and take up residence there and still intend to return to your domicile in the U.S. But your leaving your domicile does not, by itself, establish a bona fide residence in a new place. You must intend to make a new place your residence.

Foreign residence test. You must be a U.S. citizen who is a bona fide resident of a foreign country for an uninterrupted period that includes one full tax year; a full tax year is from January 1 through December 31 for individuals who file on a calendar-year basis. A U.S. resident alien who is a citizen or national of a country with which the U.S. has an income tax treaty and meets the full-year foreign residence test also qualifies. Business or vacation trips to the U.S. or another country will not disqualify you from satisfying the foreign residence test. If you are abroad more than one year but less than two, the entire period qualifies if it includes one full tax year.

EXAMPLE

You are a bona fide foreign resident from September 30, 2005, to March 25, 2007. The period includes your entire 2006 tax year. Therefore, up to $82,400 of your 2006 earnings is excludable. Your overseas earnings in 2005 and 2007 qualify for a proportionate part of the maximum exclusion allowed for those years.

To prove you are a foreign resident, you must show your intention to be a resident of the foreign country. Evidence tending to confirm your intention to stay in a foreign country includes: (1) your family accompanies you; (2) you buy a house or rent an apartment rather than a hotel room; (3) you participate in the foreign community activities; (4) you can speak the foreign language; (5) you have a permanent foreign address; (6) you join clubs there; or (7) you open charge accounts in stores in the foreign country.

You will not qualify if you take inconsistent positions toward your foreign residency. That is, you will *not* be treated as a bona fide resident of a foreign country if you have earned income from sources within that country, filed a statement with the authorities of that country that you are not a resident there, and have been held not subject to the income tax of that country. However, this rule does not prevent you from qualifying under the physical presence test.

If you cannot prove that you are a resident, check to determine if your stay qualifies under the physical presence test.

Physical presence test. To qualify under this test, you must show you were on foreign soil 330 days (about 11 months) during a 12-month period. Whether you were a resident or a transient is of no importance. You have to show you were physically present in a foreign country or countries for 330 full days during any 12-consecutive-month period. The 330 qualifying days do not have to be consecutive. The 12-month period may begin with any day. There is no requirement that it begin with your first full day abroad. It may begin before or after arrival in a foreign country and may end before or after departure from a foreign country. A *full* day is from midnight to midnight (24 consecutive hours). You must spend each of the 330 days on foreign soil. In departing from U.S. soil to go directly to the foreign country, or in returning directly to the U.S. from a foreign country, the time you spend on or over international waters does not count toward the 330-day total.

EXAMPLES

1. On August 9, you fly from New York City to London. You arrive there at 10 a.m. August 10. Your first full qualifying day toward the 330-day period is August 11.
   You may count in your 330-day period:
- Time spent traveling between foreign countries.
- Time spent on a vacation in foreign countries. There is no requirement that the 330 days must be spent on a job.
- Time spent in a foreign country while employed by the U.S. government counts towards the 330-day test, even though pay from the government does not qualify for the earned income exclusion.
- Time in foreign countries, territorial waters, or travel in the air over a foreign country. However, you will lose qualifying days if any part of such travel is on or over international waters and takes 24 hours or more, or any part of such travel is within the U.S. or its possessions.

2. You depart from Naples, Italy, by ship on June 10 at 6:00 p.m. and arrive at Haifa, Israel, at 7:00 a.m. on June 14. The trip exceeded 24 hours and passed through international waters. Therefore, you lose as qualifying days June 10, 11, 12, 13, and 14. Assuming you remain in Haifa, Israel, the next qualifying day is June 15.

Choosing the 12-month period. You qualify under the physical presence test if you were on foreign soil 330 days during any period of 12 consecutive months. Since there may be several 12-month periods during which you meet the 330-day test, you should choose the 12-month period allowing you the largest possible exclusion if you qualify under the physical presence test for only part of 2006.

Filing Tip

Overseas Moving Expenses

These expenses are generally treated as related to your foreign earnings. Thus, if you move to a foreign country and exclude your income, you may not deduct your moving expenses. If your earned income exceeds the exclusion limit, you allocate moving expenses between your tax-free and taxable earned income.

EXAMPLE

You worked in France from June 1, 2005, through September 30, 2006, and the next day you left the country. During this period, you left France only for a 15-day vacation to the U.S. during December 2005. You earned $85,000 for your work in France during 2006. Your maximum 2006 exclusion is figured as follows:

1. Start with your last full day, September 30, 2006, and count back 330 full days during which you were abroad. Not counting the vacation days, the 330th day is October 21, 2005. This is the first day of your 12-month period.
2. From October 21, 2005, count forward 12 months to October 20, 2006, which is the last day of your 12-month period.
3. Count the number of days in 2006 that fall within the 12-month period ending October 20, 2006. Here, the number of qualifying days is 293, from January 1 through October 20, 2006.
4. The maximum 2006 exclusion is $82,400 × $^{293}/_{365}$ or $66,142. You may exclude $66,142, the lesser of the maximum exclusion or your actual earnings of $85,000.

36.6 Claiming Deductions

You may not deduct expenses that are allocable to the foreign earned income and housing exclusions. If you elect the earned income exclusion, you deduct expenses as follows:

Personal or nonbusiness deductions, such as medical expenses, mortgage interest, and real estate taxes paid on a personal residence, are deductible if you itemize deductions. Business expenses that are attributable to earning excludable income are not deductible. Dependency exemptions are fully deductible; *see* Example 1 below.

If your foreign earnings exceed the exclusion ceiling, you allocate expenses between taxable and excludable income and deduct the amount allocated to taxable earned income; *see* Example 2 below.

EXAMPLES

1. You were a resident of Denmark and elect to exclude your wages of $70,000 from income. You also incurred unreimbursed travel expenses of $2,000. You may not deduct the travel expenses, since the amount is attributable to the earning of tax-free income.
2. You earn wages of $103,000 and satisfy the physical presence test. Your unreimbursed travel expenses for 2006 are $5,000, after reducing meals and entertainment by 50%. If you elect the $82,400 exclusion, 20% of the travel expenses, or $1,000, attributable to the taxable 20% of earnings, may be claimed as a miscellaneous itemized deduction on Schedule A (Form 1040) subject to the 2% AGI floor.

If your job expenses are reimbursed and the expenses are adequately accounted for to your employer *(20.30)*, the reimbursements are not reported as income on your Form W-2. If the reimbursement is less than expenses, the excess expenses are allocated as in Example 2 above.

You may have to allocate state income taxes paid on your income.

If either you or your spouse elects the earned income or housing exclusion, you may not claim an IRA deduction based on excluded income.

If you were reimbursed by your employer under a non-accountable plan, or if the reimbursement is for expenses that you deducted in an earlier year, the reimbursement is considered earned income in the year of receipt and is added to other earned income before taking the exclusion and making the allocation. *See 36.2* for allocating reimbursements between the year of the move and the following year for purposes of claiming the exclusion.

If, after working in a foreign country, your employer transfers you back to the U.S. or you move back to the U.S. to take a different job, your moving expenses are deductible under the general rules discussed in *12.3*. If your residence and principal place of work was outside the U.S. and you retire and move back to the U.S., your moving expenses are also deductible, except that you do not have to meet the 39-week test for employees or the 78-week test for the self-employed and partners.

Survivors of workers abroad returning to U.S. If you are the spouse or dependent of a worker who died while his or her principal place of work was outside the U.S., you may deduct your moving expenses back to the U.S. For the costs to be deductible, the move must begin within six months of the worker's death. The requirements for deducting moving expenses apply, except for the 39-week test for employees or the 78-week test for the self-employed and partners.

Compulsory home leave. Foreign service officers stationed abroad must periodically return to the U.S. to reorient themselves to American ways of life. Because the home leave is compulsory, foreign service officers may deduct their travel expenses; travel expenses of the officer's family are not deductible.

Filing Tip

Extension of Time To File

If you are living and working abroad on April 16, 2007, you have an automatic extension to June 15, 2007. For an additional four months, file Form 4868 by June 15, 2007, and pay the estimated tax to limit interest and late payment penalties. For a longer extension, in anticipation of owing no tax on your foreign income, you may file Form 2350 either with the Internal Revenue Service, Philadelphia, Pennsylvania 19255, or with a local IRS representative. File Form 2350 before the due date for filing your 2006 return, which is June 15, 2007, if you are abroad and are on a calendar year. Generally, you will be granted an extension for a period ending 30 days after the date you expect to qualify for the foreign earned income exclusion.

36.7 Exclusion Not Established When Your Return Is Due

When your 2006 return is due, you may not have been abroad long enough to qualify for the exclusion. If you expect to qualify under either the residence or physical presence test after the due date for your 2006 return, you may either (1) ask for an extension of time for filing your return on Form 2350 until after you qualify under either rule or (2) file your return on the due date, reporting the foreign income on the return, pay the full tax, and then file for a refund when you qualify.

If you will have tax to pay even after qualifying for the exclusion—for example, your earned income exceeds the exclusion—you may file for an extension to file but you will owe interest on the tax due. To avoid interest charges on the tax, you may take one of the following steps:

1. File a timely return and pay the total tax due without the application of the exclusion. When you do qualify, make sure you file a refund claim within the time limits discussed in Chapter 47; *or*
2. Pay the estimated tax liability when you apply for the extension to file on Form 2350. If the extension is granted, the payment is applied to the tax shown on your return when you file.

36.8 Tax-Free Meals and Lodging for Workers in Camps

If you must live in a camp provided by your employer, you may exclude from income the value of the lodging and meals furnished if the camp is (1) provided because you work in a remote area where satisfactory housing is not available; (2) located as near as is practical to the worksite; and (3) a common area not open to the public normally accommodating at least 10 employees.

You also may qualify for the earned income exclusion.

36.9 Virgin Islands, Samoa, Guam, and Northern Marianas

The Virgin Islands, Guam, American Samoa, and the Commonwealth of the Northern Mariana Islands have their own independent tax departments. Therefore, contact the particular tax authority for the proper treatment of your income and obtain a copy of IRS Publication 570, *Tax Guide for Individuals With Income From U.S. Possessions.*

For tax information from Guam, write to Department of Revenue and Taxation, Government of Guam, P.O. Box 23607, GMF, Guam 96921. For information from the Commonwealth of the Northern Mariana Islands, write to the Department of Revenue and Taxation, Commonwealth of the Northern Mariana Islands, P.O. Box 5234, CHRB, Saipan, MP 96950. For information from American Samoa, write to the Tax Division, Government of American Samoa, Pago Pago, American Samoa 96799. Also *see* IRS Publication 570.

For information about tax liability in the Virgin Islands, write to Virgin Islands Bureau of Internal Revenue, 9601 Estate Thomas, Charlotte Amalie, St. Thomas, U.S. Virgin Islands 00802. Also *see* IRS Publication 570.

Possession exclusion. A possession exclusion applies to bona fide residents of American Samoa for the entire year. On Form 4563, such residents may exclude for U.S. tax purposes their income from sources in American Samoa and income effectively connected with a business in these possessions.

Caution

Form 8898 To Report Change of Residence

You generally must file Form 8898 for a tax year in which you have worldwide income of over $75,000 and in which you become or cease to be a bona fide resident of a U.S. possession. A $1,000 penalty may be imposed for failure to file a required Form 8898.

36.10 Earnings in Puerto Rico

If you are a U.S. citizen who is also a resident of Puerto Rico for the entire year, you generally report all of your income on your Puerto Rico tax return. Where you report income from U.S. sources on the Puerto Rico tax return, a credit against the Puerto Rico tax may be claimed for income taxes paid to the United States.

If you are not a resident of Puerto Rico, you report on a Puerto Rico return only income from Puerto Rican sources. Wages earned for services performed in Puerto Rico for the U.S. government or for private employers are treated as income from Puerto Rican sources.

Planning Reminder

Information for Puerto Rico Filing

Information on Puerto Rico tax returns may be obtained at www.hacienda.gobierno.pr. Written requests may be sent to the Departamento de Hacienda, Negociado de Asistencia, Contributiva y Legislación, P.O. Box 9024140, San Juan, Puerto Rico, 00902-4140.

EXAMPLE

You and your spouse are bona fide residents of Puerto Rico during the entire year of 2006. You receive $25,000 in wages as an employee of the U.S. government working in Puerto Rico, a $100 dividend from a Puerto Rican corporation that does business in Puerto Rico, and a $500 dividend from a U.S. corporation that does business in the U.S. Your spouse earned $18,000 in wages from a Puerto Rican corporation for services performed in Puerto Rico. Your exempt and taxable income for U.S. federal tax purposes is as follows:

	Taxable	*Exempt*
Your wages	$25,000	
Your spouse's wages		$18,000
Puerto Rican corporation dividend		100
U.S. corporation dividend	500	
Totals	$25,500	$18,100

You file tax returns with both Puerto Rico and the U.S. You have gross income of $25,500 for U.S. tax purposes and $43,600 for Puerto Rican tax purposes. A tax credit may be claimed on the U.S. tax return for income taxes paid to Puerto Rico and on your Puerto Rico return for income taxes paid to the U.S on U.S. source income.

U.S. tax returns. As a U.S. citizen, you must file a U.S. tax return reporting income from all sources. But if you are a bona fide resident of Puerto Rico for an entire tax year, you do not report on a U.S. tax return any income earned in Puerto Rico during your residence there, except amounts received for services performed in Puerto Rico as an employee of the U.S. government. Similar rules apply if you have been a bona fide resident of Puerto Rico for at least two years before changing your residence from Puerto Rico. On a U.S. tax return, you may not deduct expenses or claim tax credits allocable to the excludable income. Personal exemptions are fully deductible.

If you are not a bona fide resident of Puerto Rico for the entire tax year, or were not a bona fide resident for two years prior to the tax year, you report on your U.S. tax return all income you earned in Puerto Rico, as well as all income from other sources. If you are required to report income earned in Puerto Rico on your U.S. tax return, you may claim a credit for income tax paid to Puerto Rico. You figure the credit on Form 1116. *See* IRS Publication 570.

36.11 Tax Treaties With Foreign Countries

Tax treaties between the United States and foreign countries modify some of the rules discussed in this chapter. The purpose of the treaties is to avoid double taxation. Consult your tax advisor about the effect of these treaties on your income. IRS Publication 901 has information about the tax treaties the U.S. maintains with foreign countries.

36.12 Exchange Rates and Blocked Currency

Income reported on your federal income tax return must be stated in U.S. dollars. Where you are paid in foreign currency, you report your pay in U.S. dollars on the basis of the exchange rates prevailing at the time the income is actually or constructively received. You use the rate that most closely reflects the value of the foreign currency—the official rate, the open market rate, or any other relevant rate. You may even be required to use the black market rate if that is the most accurate measure of the actual purchasing power of U.S. dollars in the foreign country. Be prepared to justify the rate you use.

Filing Tip

Currency Gains and Losses

A special statute, Section 988, governs the treatment of gain or loss on currency transactions. An individual who disposes of foreign currency in a personal transaction is not subject to tax under Section 988 on gain resulting from fluctuating exchange rates if the gain on the transaction is $200 or less.

Fulbright grants. If 70% or more of a Fulbright grant is paid in nonconvertible foreign currency, U.S. tax may be paid in the foreign currency. *See* IRS Publication 520 for details.

Blocked currency. A citizen or resident alien may be paid in a foreign currency that cannot be converted into American dollars and removed from the foreign country. If your income is in blocked currency, you may elect to defer the reporting of that income until: (1) the currency becomes convertible into dollars, (2) you actually convert it into dollars, or (3) you use it for personal expenses (for example, in the foreign country when you go there). Purchase of a business or investment in the foreign country is not the kind of use that is treated as a conversion. (4) You make a gift of it or leave it in your will. (5) You are a resident alien and you give up your U.S. residence.

If you use this method to defer the income, you may not deduct the expenses of earning it until you report it. You must continue to use this method after you choose it. You may only change with permission of the IRS.

You do not defer the reporting of capital losses incurred in a country having a blocked currency.

There may be these disadvantages in deferring income:

- Many years' income may accumulate and all be taxed in one year.
- You have no control over the year in which the blocked income becomes taxable. You usually cannot control the events that cause the income to become unblocked.

You choose to defer income in blocked currency by filing a tentative tax return reporting your blocked taxable income and explaining that you are deferring the payment of income tax because your income is not in dollars or in property or currency that is readily convertible into dollars. You must attach to your tentative return a regular return, reporting any unblocked taxable income received during the year or taxable income that became unblocked during the year. When the currency finally becomes unblocked or convertible into a currency or property convertible to dollars, you pay tax on the earnings at the rate prevailing in the year the currency became unblocked or convertible. On the tentative return, note at the top: "Report of Deferrable Foreign Income, pursuant to Revenue Ruling 74-351." File separate returns for each country from which blocked currency is received. The election must be made by the due date for filing a return for the year in which an election is sought.

36.13 Information Returns on Foreign Currency

If you have a financial interest in, or signature or other authority over, a foreign bank account, a foreign securities account, or any other foreign financial account, you must report this fact on Form TDF 90-22.1 (Report of Foreign Bank and Financial Accounts) if the aggregate value of the accounts at any time during the year exceeds $10,000. The form does not have to be filed if the accounts were with a U.S. military banking facility operated by a U.S. financial institution. Taxpayers filing Form 1040 must also indicate on Schedule B whether they had an interest in a foreign account during the year. Form TDF 90-22.1 is not filed with your income tax return. The form must be filed by June 30 of the year following the year in which you had this financial interest. Foreign accounts for 2006 must be reported by June 30, 2007.

Treasury regulations impose reporting and record-keeping requirements for currency transfers to and from the U.S. Generally, transactions involving a physical transfer of funds or monetary instruments into or outside the U.S. must be reported if the amount involved exceeds $10,000 on any one occasion; *see* Form 4790.

36.14 Foreign Tax Credit

You may claim an itemized deduction for qualified foreign taxes or you may claim a foreign tax credit. You must file Form 1116 to compute your credit unless the *de minimis* exception discussed in the Filing Tip on this page. You may not claim a foreign tax credit or deduction for taxes paid on income not subject to U.S. tax. If all of your foreign earned income is excluded, none of the foreign taxes paid on such income may be taken as a credit or deduction on your U.S. return. If you exclude only part of your foreign pay, you determine which foreign taxes are attributable to excluded income and thus barred as foreign tax credits by applying the fractional computation provided in the instructions to Form 1116 and IRS Publication 514.

In one tax year, you may not elect to deduct some foreign taxes and claim others as a credit. One method must be applied to all taxes paid or accrued during the tax year. If you are a cash-basis taxpayer, you may claim a credit for accrued foreign taxes, but you must consistently follow this method once elected.

Filing Tip

Exemption From Limit for *De Minimis* Foreign Taxes

An individual with $300 or less of creditable foreign taxes, $600 for married persons filing jointly, may elect to be exempt from the overall limitation on the credit, provided that the only foreign source income is qualified passive income. If the election is made, a foreign tax credit may be claimed directly on Line 47 of Form 1040 without filing Form 1116. *See* the instructions to Form 1116 for rules on making this election.

Credit disallowed. The credit may *not* be claimed if:

- You are a nonresident alien. However, under certain circumstances, an alien who is a bona fide resident for an entire taxable year in Puerto Rico may claim the credit. Also, a nonresident alien engaged in a U.S. trade or business may claim a credit if he or she receives income *effectively connected* to that business.
- You are a citizen of a U.S. possession (except Puerto Rico) but not a U.S. citizen or resident.

No credit is allowed for taxes imposed by a country designated by the government as engaging in terroristic activities; *see* IRS Publication 514 for a list of these countries.

Taxes qualifying for the credit. The credit is allowed only for foreign income tax, excess profits taxes, and similar taxes in the nature of an income tax. It is not allowed for any taxes paid to foreign countries on sales, gross receipts, production, the privilege to do business, personal property, or export of capital. But it may apply to a:

- Tax similar to a U.S. tax on income.
- Tax paid by a domestic taxpayer in lieu of the tax upon income, which would otherwise be imposed by any foreign country or by any U.S. possession.
- Tax of a foreign country imposing income tax, where for reasons growing out of the administrative difficulties of determining net income or basis within that country, the tax is measured by gross income, sales, and number of units produced.
- Pension, unemployment, or disability funds of a foreign country; certain foreign social security taxes do not qualify.

Filing Tip

Choosing Credit or Deduction

If you qualify for a credit or deduction, you will generally receive a larger tax reduction by claiming a tax credit rather than a deduction. A deduction is only a partial offset against your tax, whereas a credit is deducted in full from your tax. Also, taking a deduction may bar you from carrying back an excess credit from a later year. However, a deduction may give you a larger tax saving if the foreign tax is levied at a high rate and the proportion of foreign income to U.S. income is small. Compute your tax under both methods and choose the one providing the larger tax reduction.

Law Alert

Reduction to Two Credit Limitation Categories

For taxable years beginning after 2006, there will be only two credit limitation income categories: the passive income category and the general limitation income category.

Reporting foreign income on your return. You report the gross amount of your foreign income in terms of United States currency. You also attach a schedule showing how you figured the foreign income in United States currency.

Limit on credit. Your credit for foreign income taxes paid or accrued is subject to a limitation on Form 1116 unless you qualify for and elect the exemption for *de minimis* taxes referred to in the first Filing Tip in *36.14*. The limitation is your total U.S. regular tax liability multiplied by a fraction: the numerator is your taxable income from sources outside the U.S., and the denominator is your total taxable income from all sources. To determine the limit, you must separate your foreign source income into 10 separate categories, such as passive income, high withholding tax interest, and a general limitation category for salary and active business income not specified by another category. All foreign income and expenses within each separate category is treated as a single unit and the credit is limited to the U.S. income tax on the taxable income in that category from all non-U.S. sources. A separate Form 1116 must be used to figure the credit for each category of foreign source income and the various credits are summarized on one of the Forms 1116; *see* the Form 1116 instructions.

Carryback and carryover of excess foreign tax credit. If you are unable to claim a credit for all of the qualified foreign taxes paid or accrued during the year, the balance may be carried back one year and then carried forward 10 years. For further details, *see* IRS Publication 514 and the instructions to Form 1116.

Chapter 37

Planning Alimony and Marital Settlements

Alimony payments that meet tax law tests in this chapter are deductible if you pay them, and taxable if you receive them. Payments are not deductible by the payer unless taxable to the recipient.

You claim a deduction for deductible alimony that you pay on Line 31a of Form 1040. You deduct the payments even if you claim the standard deduction rather than itemizing deductions. You must enter the Social Security number of your ex-spouse. Otherwise, your deduction may be disallowed and you may have to pay a $50 penalty. If you pay deductible alimony to more than one ex-spouse, enter the Social Security number of one of them and provide similar information for the others on a separate statement attached to your return.

If you receive taxable alimony, report the payments on Line 11 of Form 1040. You must give your ex-spouse your Social Security number and could be subject to a $50 penalty if you fail to do so.

Transfers of property between spouses during marriage, as well as transfers incident to divorce, are generally treated as tax-free exchanges. The transferor-spouse does not realize gain or loss and the transferee takes the transferor's basis in the property; *see 6.7.*

Tax Rules for Alimony Payments

37.1 Planning Alimony Agreements

You can arrange beforehand the way in which the costs of a divorce are to be borne. You may specifically state in the decree or agreement that the alimony is neither taxable to the payee-spouse (under IRC Section 71) nor deductible by the payer-spouse (under IRC Section 215). Such a statement effectively disqualifies payments that otherwise would be taxable to the payee-spouse and deductible by the payer-spouse. A copy of the agreement that contains the statement must be attached to the tax return of the payee-spouse for each year the statement is applicable.

The first step in planning the after-tax consequences of alimony is convincing a couple that they may have a common financial interest; the second is projecting future tax consequences.

For example, assume that the husband is to make payments to the wife. If tax planning is approached from the viewpoint of each spouse separately, the tax deduction is an advantage for the husband; tax-free income is an advantage for the wife. However, both advantages cannot be achieved, and the couple must face the reality of the tax law, which allows the husband to deduct payments only if they are taxed as alimony to the wife. The husband and wife must compromise by setting amounts and tax consequences that balance their interests.

One approach is to view both spouses as a single economic tax unit. If this is done and the husband will be in a higher tax bracket during the payout period than the wife, an agreement should generally provide for taxable and deductible alimony. The tax savings provided by the deduction can conserve more of the husband's assets while providing funds required by the wife. The final amount of alimony to be paid depends on the spouses' tax brackets. Where tax brackets do not differ, there may be no advantage in making an agreement for taxable and deductible alimony when viewing the two parties as a unit.

If you agree that one spouse is to pay deductible alimony and the other spouse is to report the alimony as income, these rules must be met:

- The alimony must be paid under a decree of divorce or legal separation agreement or decree of support; *see 37.2.*
- The agreement must provide for cash payments; *see 37.3.* A noncash property settlement is not alimony. There is no minimum payout period for annual cash alimony payments of $15,000 or less. One payment of $15,000 can qualify as deductible and taxable alimony. There is also no minimum payout period for annual alimony payments exceeding $15,000. However, recapture of alimony deductions claimed in the first or second year may occur where annual payments of over $15,000 are scheduled and paid, but in the second or third year a reduced payment is made. To avoid recapture of deductions for payments over $15,000, carefully plan schedules of declining payments within the rules discussed at *37.7.*
- In providing for the support of children, a specific allocation to their support or the setting of certain contingencies disqualifies payments as deductible and alimony as taxable; *see 37.5.*
- Divorced and legally separated parties must not live in the same household when payments are made. If they live in the same household, alimony payments are not deductible or taxable. However, there are these exceptions: A spouse who makes payments while preparing to leave the common residence may deduct payments made within one month before the departure. Also, where you are separated under a written agreement, but not legally separated under a decree of divorce or separate maintenance, you may deduct alimony payments even if you both are members of the same household.
- The payer spouse's liability to pay alimony must end on the death of the payee spouse. The alimony agreement does not have to state expressly that payments end on death if liability ends under state law; *see 37.4.*

Filing Instruction

Reporting Alimony

If you paid alimony in 2006 meeting the deductible tests, claim your deduction on Line 31a of Form 1040, and enter the recipient's Social Security number. If you receive qualifying alimony payments, report them on Line 11 of Form 1040.

IRS Alert

Alimony Deductible Although Foreign Recipient Not Taxed

According to the IRS, an alimony payment to a foreign recipient is deductible by the payer even if the recipient is not subject to U.S. tax on the payment because of a treaty provision or statutory exemption.

Planning Reminder

Property Transfers

A property transfer to a former spouse that is incident to a divorce is generally treated as a tax-free exchange; *see 6.7* for details.

37.2 Decree or Agreement Required

Alimony, to be deductible and taxable, must be required by one of the following: (1) a decree of divorce or legal separation; (2) a written separation agreement; or (3) a decree of support. This rule applies to both pre-1985 and post-1984 decrees and agreements. Voluntary payments are not deductible or taxable.

Divorced or legally separated. The obligation to pay alimony must be imposed by the decree of divorce or separate maintenance or a written agreement incident to the divorce or separation.

Alimony paid under a Mexican divorce decree qualifies. Payments under a Mexican or state decree declared invalid by another jurisdiction do not qualify according to the IRS. Two appeals courts have rejected the IRS position.

Support payments ordered by a court in a wife's home state qualify as alimony, even though not provided for by an *ex parte* divorce decree obtained by the husband in another state. Similarly, payments qualified when a state court increased support originally ordered before the husband obtained an uncontested Mexican divorce.

Payments made under a separation approved by a Roman Catholic ecclesiastical board do not qualify.

When a decree of divorce or separate maintenance fails to mention alimony, payments qualify as long as they are made under a written agreement considered "incident to" the decree.

Payments made under an agreement amended after a divorce or legal separation may also qualify, if the amendment is considered "incident" to the divorce or separation. For example, the IRS agrees that a written amendment changing the amount of alimony payments is incident to the divorce where the legal obligation to support under the original agreement survived the divorce. However, payments under an amended agreement did not qualify where the original agreement settled all rights between the husband and wife and made no provision for future support. The legal obligation to support the wife did not survive the divorce and could not be revived by the new agreement.

Annulments. Payments made under an annulment decree qualify as deductible (and taxable) alimony.

Separated from spouse. Where a husband and wife are separated and living apart, alimony is deductible by the payer-spouse and taxable to the payee-spouse provided it is paid under either a written separation agreement or decree of support.

A decree of support. Any court decree or order requiring support payments qualifies, including alimony *pendente lite* (temporary alimony while the action is pending) and an interlocutory (not final) divorce decree.

In certain community property states, payments under a decree of alimony *pendente lite* which do not exceed the wife's interest in community income are neither deductible by the husband nor taxable to the wife; payments exceeding the wife's interest are taxable to her and deductible by the husband.

37.3 Cash Payments Required

Only payments of cash, checks, and money orders payable on demand qualify as taxable and deductible alimony. Your cash payment to a third party for a spouse qualifies if made under the terms of a divorce decree or separation instrument. For example, you pay the rent, mortgage, tax, medical expenses, or tuition liabilities of your former spouse. The payments qualify if made under the terms of the divorce or separation instrument. If taxable as alimony, your former spouse may deduct your payment of real estate taxes, mortgage interest, or medical expenses if he or she claims itemized deductions. You may not deduct payments to maintain property owned by you but used by your spouse. For example, you pay the mortgage expenses, real estate taxes, and insurance premiums for a house that you own and in which your former spouse lives. You may not deduct those payments as alimony even if they are required by a decree or agreement.

Providing services or transferring or providing property does not qualify. For example, you may not deduct as alimony your note, the assignment of a third party note, or an annuity contract.

Premiums paid for term or whole life insurance on your life made under a divorce or separation instrument qualify as deductible alimony to the extent your former spouse owns the policy.

Planning Reminder

Payments to a Third Party

Cash payments to a third party may be deducted as alimony if they are under the terms of a divorce decree or separation instrument. You may also deduct as alimony payments made to a third party at the written request of the payee spouse. For example, your former wife asks you to make a cash donation to a charitable organization instead of paying alimony installments to her. Her request must be in writing and state that both she and you intend the payment to be treated as alimony. You must receive the written request before you file your return for the taxable year in which the payment was made. Your former wife may deduct the payment as a charitable contribution if she claims itemized deductions.

37.4 Payments Must Stop at Death

Liability for a payment must end on the death of the payee-spouse. If all the payments must continue after the death of the payee-spouse, none of the payments, whether made before or after the payee's death, qualify as taxable (to payee-spouse) or deductible (by payer-spouse) alimony. If some payments must continue after the payee's death, that amount is not alimony regardless of when paid.

The divorce decree or separation agreement does not have to specifically state that payments end at death, if under state law the liability to pay ends on the death of the payee-spouse.

Table 37-1 Key to Alimony and Marital Settlement Issues

Item—	*Comments—*
Alimony	The same rules determine whether alimony is deductible and taxable. For example, if a husband makes deductible alimony payments to his ex-wife, the payments are taxable to her. He may not deduct payments that are not taxable to her. If you are currently planning an alimony agreement, consider the tax consequences to both spouses. As current tax rates may be as high as 35% for one spouse and as low as 10% for the other, there may be a substantial tax savings to the couple, when considered as an economic unit, in negotiating an agreement that qualifies the payments as deductible alimony; *see 37.1.* ***Note***: Prior tax rules that apply to pre-1985 agreements are not discussed in this chapter. If you have a problem involving a payment of alimony under a pre-1985 agreement, refer to a past issue of *Your Income Tax* or to IRS Publication 504.
Child support agreements	A payment fixed as payable for the support of your child does not qualify as deductible or taxable alimony; *see 37.5.*
Property settlements	Transfers of property between spouses that are incident to a divorce are treated as tax-free exchanges. There is no recognition of gain or loss. Future tax consequences should be considered by the spouse receiving appreciated property. When the property is sold, that spouse will be taxed on the appreciation. If this is so, that spouse may want to bargain for larger alimony payments or additional property to compensate for the projected future tax; *see 6.7.*
Alimony to nonresident alien	If you pay alimony payments to a nonresident alien, and you are a U.S. citizen or resident, you must withhold 30% (or a lower rate as set by treaty) on each payment for income tax purposes. *See* IRS Publications 504 and 515 for more information.
Exemptions for children	Exemptions for children of a divorced couple are governed by the rules explained at *21.7.* Further, where a spouse is in the income range requiring the phaseout or disallowance of personal exemptions *(21.12)*, there may be no advantage in providing the exemption to that spouse. The exemption should be given to the spouse who may claim a full deduction for the exemption.
Annuity or endowment policy	Funds for payments of alimony may be provided through the purchase of an annuity or endowment policy. You may not deduct payments made under the policies assigned or purchased for your spouse. For example, to meet an alimony obligation of $500 a month, you buy your spouse a commercial annuity contract. The full $500 a month received by him or her is taxable. You may not deduct these payments.
Trust to pay alimony	To meet your alimony obligations, you may transfer income-producing property to a trust that is to pay the income to your spouse. You may not deduct payments made by the trust. You are not taxable on the income earned by the trust, even though it meets your alimony obligations. This tax treatment is the equivalent of receiving a tax deduction for paying alimony. If you receive alimony from a trust, ask the trustee how to report such income. Tax treatment may depend on whether the trust was created before 1985 or after 1984. If the trust was set up after 1984, as a beneficiary you generally report trust income under the general trust reporting rules in Chapter 11. These general trust rules may not apply to certain alimony trusts created before 1985 that were subject to the prior alimony rules. Distributions from such trusts may be treated as taxable alimony regardless of whether the distributions are from income or principal. In any event, the trustee should provide you with the necessary tax information.
Retirement plans	A state court can allocate your interest in a qualified retirement plan to a former spouse in a qualified domestic relations order. The benefits are taxed to your former spouse when they are paid to her or him. Benefits paid to another beneficiary, such as a child, are taxable to you; *see 7.12.*
Remarriage's effect on pre-1985 agreement	The tax deduction allowed for alimony payments made under a pre-1985 decree or agreement hinges on the obligation to support. Once the spouse receiving alimony remarries, the obligation to support generally ends under state law. In these states, any payment after remarriage is not considered alimony and is not deductible. For example, payments to a former wife made after remarriage are considered tax-free gifts if the former husband knows of the remarriage and that he is no longer obligated to pay. If she does not inform him of her remarriage, his payments are taxable to her but are not deductible by him.
Voluntary payments in excess of required alimony	Voluntary payments in excess of required alimony are not deductible or taxable as alimony. Amending the decrees retroactively to cover an increase does not qualify the increase as deductible and taxable alimony. The increase has to be approved by the court before the increased payments are made.
Avoiding or limiting liability for previously filed joint returns	Even though you are no longer married, you remain liable for the tax on a previously filed joint return unless you qualify for innocent spouse or equitable relief; *see 1.7–1.9.*

To the extent that one or more payments are to begin, increase in amount, or accelerate after the death of the payee-spouse, such payments may be treated as a substitute for continuing payments after the death of the payee-spouse. Such substitute payments will be denied alimony treatment.

EXAMPLES

1. Under the terms of a divorce decree, Smith is obligated to make annual alimony payments of $30,000, terminating on the earlier of the end of six years or the death of Mrs. Smith. She also is to keep custody of their two minor children. The decree also provides that if on her death the children are still minors, Smith is to pay annually $10,000 to a trust each year. The trust income and corpus are to be used for the children until the youngest child reaches the age of majority. Under these facts, Smith's possible liability to make annual $10,000 payments to the trust is treated as a substitute for $10,000 of the $30,000 annual payments. $10,000 of each of the $30,000 annual payments does not qualify as alimony.
2. Same facts as in Example 1, but the alimony is to end on the earlier of the expiration of 15 years or the death of Mrs. Smith. Further, if Mrs. Smith dies before the end of the 15-year period, Smith will pay her estate the difference between the total amount that he would have paid had she survived and the amount actually paid. For example, if she dies at the end of the tenth year, he will pay her estate $150,000 ($450,000 – $300,000). Under these facts, his liability to make a lump-sum payment to the estate is a substitute for the full amount of each of the annual $30,000 payments. Accordingly, none of the annual $30,000 payments qualifies as alimony.

Attorneys' fees. Under the laws of many states, a court award of attorneys' fees remains enforceable after the death of the payee-spouse, thereby disqualifying a payer's alimony deduction for the payment and making it nontaxable to the payee-spouse. For example, a husband who was ordered by an Oklahoma court to pay his wife $154,000 for her attorneys' fees prior to the entry of a final divorce decree was unable to deduct his payment. The Tax Court and the Tenth Circuit Court of Appeals agreed with the IRS that under Oklahoma law, the husband's liability to pay the attorneys' fees would not have ended, as a hypothetical matter, had the wife died before the final decree was entered. The policy reason for the state law is to assure that attorneys get paid for their services, which will enable indigent clients to retain counsel in divorce actions.

In this situation, the payer can obtain a deduction if the attorneys' fees remain the liability of the payee-spouse and the court decree increases the amount of cash alimony to cover the fees, rather than having them paid separately. The cash alimony would be taxable to the payee-spouse. The payee-spouse's payment of the fees to the attorneys may be deductible, but only as a miscellaneous expense subject to the 2% of AGI floor.

37.5 Child Support Payments Are Not Alimony

A payment that is specifically designated as child support in the divorce or separation instrument is not deductible by the payer or taxable as alimony to the payee.

Even if there is not a specific allocation to child support, a payment will be presumed by the IRS to be payable for child support if it is to be reduced on the happening of a contingency relating to the child, such as: the child reaches a specific age or income level, or the child leaves school, marries, leaves the parent's household, or begins to work.

If both alimony and child support are specified and a payment is less than the total of the two amounts, then the payment is first allocated to child support.

Tax refund diversion for delinquent child support. The IRS can give your tax refund to a state that is paying support to your child if you fail to make support payments. The IRS will not notify you of the diversion until it is made to the state. However, the state agency must provide prior notice of the proposed offset and procedures for contesting it.

EXAMPLE

On July 1, 2006, Thomas and Tina are divorced when their children, John (born July 15, 1991), and Jane (born September 23, 1993), are ages 14 and 12. Under the divorce decree,

Caution

Alimony Reductions Tied to Child's Age

If a reduction in your payments is not specifically tied to your child's reaching majority age but the scheduled date for the reduction is within six months before or after your child reaches age 18 or 21 (or other age of majority under local law), the IRS holds that the reduction is tied to the child's age. The reduction amount will be treated as child support unless you can prove that the reduction is for some other purpose. The IRS makes the same presumption if you have more than one child and your alimony payments are to be reduced at least twice and each reduction is within one year of a different child's reaching a particular age between ages 18 and 24; *see* the Example in *37.5*.

Thomas is to make monthly alimony payments of $2,000. The monthly payments are to be reduced to $1,500 on January 1, 2012, and to $1,000 on January 1, 2016. On January 1, 2012, the date of the first reduction, John will be 20 years, 5 months, and 17 days old. On January 1, 2016, the date of the second reduction, Jane will be 22 years, 3 months, and 9 days old. As each reduction is to occur not more than one year before or after each child reaches the age of 21 years and four months, the IRS will presume that the reductions are associated with the happening of a contingency relating to the children. The two reductions total $1,000 per month and are treated as the amount fixed for the support of the children. Thus, $1,000 of the $2,000 monthly payment does not qualify as alimony. To avoid this result, Thomas must prove that the reductions were not related to the support of the children.

Minimum Payments and Recapture of Alimony

37.6 No Minimum Payment Period for Alimony

There is no minimum payment period, but a recapture rule applies where payments fall by more than $15,000 within the first three years; *see 37.7*.

37.7 3rd Year Recapture If Alimony Drops by More Than $15,000

The recapture rules are designed to prevent the so-called "front loading" of property settlement payments disguised as alimony. However, the rules apply even where no property settlement was intended if you come within their terms. Here are the rules: Deductible payments made in the first year or second year may be recaptured (that is, reported as income) in the third year where payments within the first three years decline by more than $15,000. The three years are called "post-separation years." The first post-separation year is the first calendar year in which you pay alimony under a decree of divorce or separation agreement. The period does not begin with the year of the decree or agreement if no payments are made. Recapture does not apply to temporary support payments made before the final decree or agreement. The second and third post-separation years are the next two calendar years after the first post-separation year whether or not payments are made during those years.

Payments made in the second post-separation year are recaptured if the payments exceed the payments made in the third post-separation year by more than $15,000. Payments made in the first post-separation year are recaptured if they exceed the average payments made in the second post-separation year and the third post-separation year by more than $15,000. The Examples below illustrate how to make these computations.

Filing Tip

Reporting Recapture on Your Return

The payer-spouse reports the recaptured amount as income in the third year and the payee-spouse claims a deduction for the same amount. The payer reports the recaptured amount on Form 1040, Line 11 (alimony received); cross out "received" and write "recapture" along with the payee-spouse's Social Security number.

The payee-spouse deducts the recaptured amount on Form 1040, Line 31a (alimony paid). He or she crosses out the word "paid" and writes "recapture," and also enters on that line the payer-spouse's Social Security number.

When recapture does not apply. Recapture is not triggered if payments in both the first and second post-separation years do not exceed $15,000. Recapture also does not apply to:

- Payments made under a continuing liability to pay for at least three years a fixed part of your income from a business or property or from a job or self-employed business or profession, *or*
- Payments that end because of your death or the death of your former spouse or the remarriage of your former spouse at any time before the end of the third post-separation year.

The steps of recapture are:

Step 1. Recapture for the second-year payment is computed first. This is the excess, if any, of the second-year payment over the third-year payment, *minus* $15,000.

Step 2. Recapture for the first-year payment is computed next. There is recapture if the first-year payment exceeds by more than $15,000 the average payment made in the second and third years. In figuring the average payment, reduce the second-year payment by any recapture amount for the second year figured under Step 1.

EXAMPLES

1. In 2004, Jones obtains a divorce and pays deductible alimony of $50,000. His wife reports $50,000 as income. In 2005 and 2006, he makes no payments. On his 2006 return, $35,000 of the first year 2004 deduction is recaptured ($50,000 – $15,000) and reported as income by Jones. His ex-spouse deducts $35,000.
2. In 2004, Smith makes his first alimony payment of $50,000; in 2005 he pays $20,000 and in 2006 he pays nothing. On his 2006 return, $32,500 is recaptured as follows:

Recapture of second-year payment:		
Payment in 2nd year		$20,000
Less: 3rd-year payment	$0	
Less: Allowance	15,000	15,000
Recapture for second year		$ 5,000
Recapture of first-year payment:		
Average calculation:		
Payment over the 2nd and 3rd years	$20,000	
Less: recapture in the 2nd year	$ 5,000	
	$15,000	
Average ($15,000 ÷ 2)	$ 7,500	
Payment in first year		$50,000
Less: Average	$ 7,500	
Less: Allowance	15,000	22,500
Recapture for first year		$27,500
Total recaptured in 2006:		
For second year		$ 5,000
For first year		$27,500
Total:		$32,500

37.8 Legal Fees of Marital Settlements

If you are receiving taxed alimony, you may deduct part of your legal fees. Ask your attorney to divide his or her fees into charges for arranging: (1) the divorce or separation and (2) details of the alimony payments.

You may be able to deduct the legal fees allocated to (2), but you may not deduct the fee attributed to the divorce or separation negotiation. However, the deduction is subject to the 2% adjusted gross income (AGI) floor on miscellaneous itemized deductions *(see 19.1)* and if you are subject to alternative minimum tax, the deduction is not allowed for AMT purposes *(see 23.2)*. If the alimony is not taxed to you, you may not deduct any part of the fee. However, part of a fee allocated to a property settlement may be added to the basis of the property.

If you are paying deductible alimony, you may not deduct legal fees paid for arranging a divorce or for resisting your spouse's demands for alimony. Furthermore, you may not deduct legal fees incurred in resisting your spouse's claims to income-producing property the loss of which would affect your earnings. That part of your legal fee that is identified as being paid for tax advice is allowed as a miscellaneous itemized deduction subject to the 2% AGI floor *(19.1),* but no deduction is allowed for AMT purposes. The following types of proof may support the miscellaneous itemized deduction:

- The fee is charged by a firm that limits its practice to state and federal tax matters and is engaged to advise on the consequences of a property settlement involving the transfer of property in exchange for other property and the release of the other spouse's marital rights in the property.
- The fee is charged by a firm engaged in general practice that assigns tax problems, such as the tax consequences of creating an alimony trust, to its special tax department. On the bill, an allocation is made for tax advice based on time, complexity of the case, and the amount of tax involved.
- An attorney handles the divorce for a fixed fee and also gives advice on the right to claim exemptions for the children following the divorce. The bill allocates part of the fee to the tax advice, based on time, and fees customarily charged in the locality for similar services.

Caution

Spouse's Legal Fees

You may not deduct your payment of your spouse's legal fees as a miscellaneous itemized deduction, even if the fees are only for tax advice. Furthermore, as discussed at *37.4,* a payment of your spouse's legal fees may not qualify as deductible alimony even if paid under court order because liability for the payment might survive the payee-spouse's death under state law.

Chapter 38

Household Employment Taxes ("Nanny Tax")

If you employ someone to care for your children or a disabled or elderly dependent in your home, clean your residence, cook, or provide other personal services in or around your home, you may be obligated to pay and withhold Social Security and Medicare (FICA) taxes and also to pay federal unemployment (FUTA) taxes.

The reporting requirements for FICA and FUTA are discussed in *38.2* and *38.4*.

38.1 Who Is a Household Employee?

If you hired someone to do household work and you were able to control what work he or she did and how it was done, you had a household employee. Such a worker is your employee regardless of whether the work is full or part time or whether you hired the worker through an agency or from a list provided by an agency or association. Also, it does not matter if the wages were paid for work done on an hourly, daily, weekly, or per-job basis.

Workers who are not your employees. Workers you hire through an agency are not your employees if the agency is responsible for who does the work and how it is done. If you use a placement agency that exercises control over what work is done and how it is done, the worker is not your employee. Self-employed workers are also not employees; in addition to maintaining control over how their work is done, self-employed workers usually provide their own tools and offer services to the general public.

Notable exceptions to the household employee definition. You do not have to file a Schedule H and report payments if the employee was your spouse, your parent, your child who was under age 21, or an individual under age 18 if providing household services was not his or her principal occupation. However, payments to parents are taxable if your child who lived with you was under age 18 and had a mental or physical disability that required personal care for at least four continuous weeks and you were divorced and not remarried, widowed, or married to and living with a person whose physical or mental condition prevented him or her from caring for the child during that four-week period.

Verifying employment status. It is unlawful to employ an alien who cannot legally work in the United States. If you hire a household employee to work for you on a regular basis, you and the employee must each complete part of the U.S. Citizenship and Immigration Services (USCIS) Form I-9, Employment Eligibility Verification. You must verify that the employee is either a U.S. citizen or an alien who can legally work in the U.S. and you must keep Form I-9 for your records. The form and a USCIS Handbook for Employers can be obtained at www.uscis.com or by calling 1-800-870-3676. For answers to other questions about the employment eligibility verification process or other immigration-related matters, contact the USCIS Office of Business Liaison at 1-800-357-2099.

Proof of eligibility. You are required to get each employee's name and Social Security number and enter them on Form W-2. This applies to both resident and nonresident alien employees. You may not accept an individual taxpayer identification number (ITIN) in place of an SSN. An ITIN is only available to resident and nonresident aliens who are ineligible to work in the U.S. and need identification for tax purposes. You may verify up to five names and numbers by contacting the Social Security Administration at 1-800-772-6270.

38.2 Social Security and Medicare (FICA) Taxes for Household Employees

Income tax withholding is not required for a household employee *(38.3)*, but generally you must withhold Social Security and Medicare (FICA) taxes from the employee's cash wages and also pay an equal amount yourself, unless the wages are below an annual threshold, which for 2006 was $1,500. You report and pay the FICA taxes on Schedule H, which you must attach to your Form 1040; *see 38.3*.

Once payments to a non-exempt employee *(38.1)* equal or exceed $1,500, the entire amount, including the first $1,500, is subject to FICA taxes. The $1,500 threshold may be increased for 2007 by an inflation adjustment.

Tax rates. As an employer, you are liable for FICA taxes at the rate of 6.2% for Social Security and 1.45% for Medicare on wages up to the annual Social Security wage base, which for 2006 is $94,200. Your household employee owes the same amount, which you are responsible for paying. You must either withhold your employee's share from his or her wages or pay it from your own funds. If wages exceed the annual Social Security wage base, you and the employee each owe Medicare tax of 1.45% on the entire excess with no ceiling.

If you do not withhold the employee's share of FICA taxes, you are liable for the full amount. If you pay the employee's share of FICA taxes from your own funds instead of deducting it from

Caution

January 31 W-2 Distribution Deadline

Even if you request an extension to file copies of Form W-2 with the Social Security Administration, you must still furnish Form W-2 to your employees by January 31, 2007.

wages, you must treat your payments as additional wages when you report the employee's wages on Form W-2, but the payment is not considered wages for Social Security, Medicare, or FUTA tax purposes; *see* the Example in *38.3*.

Estimated taxes. You may need to increase the federal income tax withheld from your pay or pay estimated taxes to avoid an estimated tax penalty based on your household employment taxes. However, you will not be penalized for failure to pay estimated taxes if you will not have federal income tax withheld from wages, pensions, or any other payments you receive and your income taxes, excluding your household employment taxes, would not be enough to require payment of estimated taxes.

Reporting options for self-employed persons who have regular business employees as well as household employees. Self-employed persons who have business employees in addition to household employees may use one of the following reporting options:

1. Report FICA and FUTA taxes and any income tax withholding for household employees annually on Schedule H, and report FICA taxes and any income tax withholding for other employees quarterly on Form 941 and FUTA taxes annually on Form 940 (or 940-EZ); or
2. Report FICA taxes and any income tax withholding for *all* employees (household employees as well as other employees) quarterly on Form 941 and report FUTA taxes annually on Form 940 or Form 940-EZ.

Small employers whose annual liability for Social Security, Medicare, and withheld federal income tax is $1,000 or less may be notified by the IRS that they must file Form 944 to report and pay the taxes only once a year, instead of quarterly on Form 941.

Employers of household employees must also give copies of Form W-2 (Wage and Tax Statement) to each employee and to the Social Security Administration, as discussed in *38.3*.

38.3 Filing Schedule H To Report Household Employment Taxes

You must file Schedule H with your 2006 Form 1040 if you paid any one household employee cash wages of $1,500 or more in 2006, or withheld federal income tax during 2006 for a household employee, or paid cash wages totaling $1,000 or more in any calendar quarter during 2005 or 2006 to all household employees. On Schedule H, you report the Social Security and Medicare taxes *(38.2)*, federal income taxes withheld, if any (*see* below), and federal unemployment taxes *(38.4)* for your household employees. Total household employment taxes from Schedule H are entered as an "Other Tax" on Line 62 of your Form 1040.

If you get an extension to file your return, file Schedule H with the return by the extended due date. If you are not required to file a 2006 tax return, you may file Schedule H by itself by the filing deadline, April 16, 2007. The completed Schedule H should be mailed to the same address that you would use for filing a return, along with a check or money order for the total household employment taxes due.

Withholding federal income taxes. Income tax withholding is not required for a household employee, but if the employee requests withholding and you agree, the employee must furnish you with a complete Form W-4, Withholding Allowance Certificate. *See* Publication 926, Household Employer's Guide, and Publication 15-A (Circular E), Employer's Tax Guide.

The earned income credit (EIC). An employee who qualifies for the earned income credit may receive advance payments by giving you Form W-5 *(25.13)*. You must notify your household employee about the EIC if you agreed to withhold federal income taxes from wages. An employee who qualifies for the earned income credit may receive advance payments by giving you a Form W-5.

Fringe benefits. All or part of the value of certain fringe benefits are specifically excluded from taxable income. If you provide a household employee with lodging or meals on your premises, the benefits will not be taxable if furnished for your convenience as a condition of employment. You may also provide tax free transportation assistance to an employee. For 2006, the tax-free limit is $105 monthly for rides in commuter highway vehicles or transit passes, or $205 monthly for qualified parking.

SCHEDULE H (Form 1040)
Department of the Treasury Internal Revenue Service (99)

Household Employment Taxes

(For Social Security, Medicare, Withheld Income, and Federal Unemployment (FUTA) Taxes)
▶ **Attach to Form 1040, 1040NR, 1040-SS, or 1041.**
▶ **See separate instructions.**

OMB No. 1545-1971
2006
Attachment Sequence No. **44**

Name of employer: Nancy Nixon

Social security number: X1X 00 0011

Employer identification number: 5 6 7 8 9 0 1 2 3

A Did you pay **any one** household employee cash wages of $1,500 or more in 2006? (If any household employee was your spouse, your child under age 21, your parent, or anyone under age 18, see the line A instructions on page H-3 before you answer this question.)

- ☑ **Yes.** Skip lines B and C and go to line 1.
- ☐ **No.** Go to line B.

B Did you withhold federal income tax during 2006 for any household employee?

- ☐ **Yes.** Skip line C and go to line 5.
- ☐ **No.** Go to line C.

C Did you pay **total** cash wages of $1,000 or more in **any** calendar **quarter** of 2005 or 2006 to **all** household employees? (**Do not** count cash wages paid in 2005 or 2006 to your spouse, your child under age 21, or your parent.)

- ☐ **No. Stop.** Do not file this schedule.
- ☐ **Yes.** Skip lines 1-9 and go to line 10 on the back. (Calendar year taxpayers having no household employees in 2006 **do not** have to complete this form for 2006.)

Part I **Social Security, Medicare, and Income Taxes**

1	Total cash wages subject to social security taxes (see page H-4)	1	2,200			
2	Social security taxes. Multiply line 1 by 12.4% (.124)			2	272	80
3	Total cash wages subject to Medicare taxes (see page H-4)	3	2,200			
4	Medicare taxes. Multiply line 3 by 2.9% (.029)			4	63	80
5	Federal income tax withheld, if any			5		
6	**Total social security, Medicare, and income taxes.** Add lines 2, 4, and 5			6	336	60
7	Advance earned income credit (EIC) payments, if any			7		
8	**Net taxes** (subtract line 7 from line 6)			8	336	60

9 Did you pay **total** cash wages of $1,000 or more in **any** calendar **quarter** of 2005 or 2006 to household employees? (**Do not** count cash wages paid in 2005 or 2006 to your spouse, your child under age 21, or your parent.)

- ☑ **No. Stop.** Enter the amount from line 8 above on Form 1040, line 62. If you are not required to file Form 1040, see the line 9 instructions on page H-4.
- ☐ **Yes.** Go to line 10 on the back.

For Privacy Act and Paperwork Reduction Act Notice, see page 7 of the separate instructions. Cat. No. 12187K **Schedule H (Form 1040) 2006**

Filing Tip

Check State Requirements for Employers

You may have to register and pay state unemployment tax for a household employee. Contact your state tax and labor departments for guidance.

EXAMPLE

On March 1, 2006, Nancy Nixon hired Eleanor Edwards to clean her house every Wednesday. She paid Eleanor $50 every Wednesday and did not withhold Eleanor's share of Social Security and Medicare (FICA) taxes from her wages. Instead, Nancy will pay Helen's share of Social Security and Medicare taxes out of pocket when she files Schedule H with her 2006 Form 1040. Nancy also did not withhold any federal income taxes because Eleanor did not give her a W-4 or in any other way request that income taxes be withheld. Eleanor didn't receive any advance earned income credit payments.

Eleanor worked for a total of 44 Wednesdays and received $2,200 (44 x $50) in total compensation from Nancy.

Eleanor's total cash wages	$2,200 ($50 x 44 weeks)	
Eleanor's share of employment taxes paid by Nancy:		
Social security tax	$136.40	($2,200 x 6.2%)
Medicare tax	$31.90	($2,200 x 1.45%)

Wages included in Box 1 of Eleanor's Form W-2 and Nancy's Form W-3:

Cash wages	$2,200.00
Eleanor's share of Social Security tax paid by Nancy	136.40
Eleanor's share of Medicare tax paid by Nancy	31.90
Total wages	$2,368.30

Nancy will report Eleanor's total wages of $2,368.30 in Box 1 of Eleanor's Form W-2. The total includes Nancy's payment of Eleanor's share of Social Security and Medicare (FICA) taxes. However, only the cash wages of $2,200 are subject to Social Security and Medicare (FICA) taxes. When she computes her liability for Social Security and Medicare taxes on Schedule H, Nancy does not include her payment on Eleanor's behalf.

Employer identification number (EIN). If you are a household employer, you will need an employer identification number (EIN) and you may have to pay employment taxes. You can obtain an EIN by completing Form SS-4, Application for an Employer Identification Number. The number can be obtained immediately by phone, over the Internet, or in four weeks if you apply by mail. If you are still waiting for your number, do not use your Social Security number as a substitute. Instead, enter "Applied For" and the date you applied for the EIN in the space provided for the number.

Forms W-2 and W-3. You need an EIN in order to properly file the necessary W-2 and W-3 forms. You must file a Form W-2 for each household employee to whom you paid $1,500 or more of cash wages in 2006 that are subject to Social Security and Medicare taxes. If the wages were not subject to those taxes but you withheld income taxes, you must file Form W-2 for the employee. Furnish copies B, C, and 2 of Form W-2 to your household employee by January 31, 2007.

If you file one or more Forms W-2, you must also file a Form W-3, Transmittal of Wage and Tax Statement. You must send Copy A of all Forms W-2 and W-3 to the Social Security Administration (SSA) by February 28, 2007 (March 31 if you file electronically).

38.4 Federal Unemployment Taxes (FUTA) for Household Employees

Caution

Reduced Credit for Some States

If you are in a state that owes money to the federal unemployment fund, your FUTA credit for state unemployment taxes is reduced on Schedule H.

As an employer, you are also liable for FUTA (federal unemployment taxes) if you pay cash wages of $1,000 or more for household services during any calendar quarter or if you did so in any quarter in the preceding year. You do not pay FUTA on wages paid to your spouse, your parents, or your children under age 21. Your employee is not liable for FUTA.

The FUTA rate for 2006 is 6.2% of the first $7,000 of cash wages. However, there is a credit of up to 5.4% for state unemployment taxes that reduces FUTA liability, resulting in a net tax of 0.8%. Only employers that pay all the required contributions for 2006 by April 16, 2007, will receive the entire credit; the credit for payments made after April 16, 2007, is limited to 90% of the pre-deadline credit.

For wages paid to a household employee in 2006, you will generally report FUTA on Schedule H, which you attach to your Form 1040. If you have regular business employees, *see 38.2* for more reporting options.

Chapter 39

Gift and Estate Tax Planning

Gift planning can be an important part of estate planning. This chapter provides an overview of the federal gift tax and estate tax. Developing an estate plan for your assets requires professional assistance, but the basic guidelines in this chapter can help you begin to estimate your potential estate and start thinking about property transfers that may reduce or avoid the estate tax.

Relatively small gifts can completely avoid gift tax because of the annual gift tax exclusion, which for 2006 was $12,000 per donee; *see 39.2.* Gifts to a spouse and certain gifts to pay educational or medical expenses also are not subject to the gift tax; *see 39.2.*

Gift tax generally does not have to be paid even on very substantial taxable gifts because the tax is offset by a tax credit that effectively exempts up to $1 million of lifetime taxable gifts from the tax; *see 39.4.*

The estate tax is in a state of legislative flux. Under the 2001 Economic Growth and Tax Relief Reconciliation Act, the estate tax exemption (and corresponding tax credit) are slated to be increased and the top tax rate decreased until 2009 prior to repeal of the estate tax in 2010, a repeal scheduled for just that one year, *see 39.11.* Efforts to make repeal permanent failed in mid-2006, and when this book went to press, Congress was considering proposals to retain the estate tax but broaden the exemption and lower the rates. *See the* e-Supplement *for legislative developments.*

Gift Planning

Estate Tax Planning

39.1 Gifts of Appreciated Property

Making a gift of appreciated property to a family member in advance of an anticipated sale can reduce the income tax liability for the family as a whole. By making a gift of interests in the property to several family members, it is possible to spread the profit and the tax among a number of taxpayers in the lowest tax bracket. Depending on the value of the property, you may or may not have to file a gift tax return; *see 39.2.*

Tax legislation enacted in 2006 (the Tax Increase Prevention and Reconciliation Act) has extended for two years the gift planning opportunity that Congress created in 2003 when it reduced the rates for net capital gains. Those favorable rates had been scheduled to apply through the year 2008, but the new law extends them through 2010. Thus, the 15% rate will apply through 2010 for taxpayers in brackets over 15%. For taxpayers in the 10% or 15% brackets, the current 5% rate will apply through 2007 and then fall to zero for 2008–2010. If you make a gift of appreciated property to a child or other family member who is age 18 or older (and thus not subject to the "kiddie tax"; *see 24.1*) and whose top bracket is 10% or 15%, he or she picks up your holding period and on a sale before 2008 can pay tax at the 5% capital gain rate. On a sale in 2008, 2009, or 2010, your transferee would owe no tax; the capital gain rate is zero in 2008–2010 for those in the 10% or 15% bracket. At the end of 2010, the 5% (or zero) and 15% capital gain rates will "sunset," and the rates for gains before May 6, 2003, will be reinstated, unless Congress again extends the favorable rates. *See 5.3* for further details on capital gain rates.

Warning: The IRS may claim that the gift was never completed if, after sale by the donee, you control the sales proceeds or have the use of them.

Do not make a gift of investment property such as stock that has decreased in value if you want a deduction for the loss. Once you give the property away, the loss deduction is gone forever. Neither you nor your donee can ever take advantage of it. The better way is first to sell the property, get a loss deduction, and then make a gift of the proceeds.

39.2 Gift Tax Basics

When you consider making gifts of cash or property, you must consider possible gift tax liability. However, it is possible to make substantial gifts without incurring gift tax liability because of exclusions allowed by the tax law. Even where a gift is technically subject to the gift tax, liability computed on Form 709 can generally be avoided by applying the lifetime credit, which effectively exempts up to $1 million of gifts from the tax; *see 39.4.*

Planning Reminder

Annual Gift Tax Exclusion

The annual exclusion exempts from gift tax the first $12,000 of gifts of present interests to each donee during 2006. If your spouse consents on Form 709 to split your gifts, the exclusion for each donee doubles to $24,000. Any change to the exclusion amount for gifts made after 2006 will be reported in the *e-Supplement.*

If you make gifts of present interests in trust for more than one beneficiary, each beneficiary is treated separately for purposes of the annual exclusion. Also, if you give a present interest in property to more than one person as joint tenants, the annual exclusion can be claimed for each donee.

The annual exclusion and other tax-free gifts. Gift tax liability may be avoided by making gifts that do not exceed the annual exclusion. The annual exclusion applies separately to each donee to whom you make gifts during a calendar year. For 2006, the per-donee exclusion is $12,000, or $24,000 if your spouse consents on Form 709 to "split" the gifts. The annual exclusion is allowed only for cash gifts or gifts of present interests in property; gifts of future interests do not qualify. For 2007, the amount of the annual exclusion may be increased above $12,000 by a cost-of-living adjustment; *see* the *e-Supplement.*

Gifts to your spouse are completely tax free under the gift tax marital deduction if your spouse is a U.S. citizen at the time of the gift. For gifts to a spouse who is not a U.S. citizen, there is an annual exclusion; for 2006 gifts, the exclusion is $132,000, provided that the $120,000 excess over the basic $12,000 annual exclusion otherwise qualifies for the marital deduction.

There is an unlimited gift tax exclusion for payments of another person's tuition or medical expenses, if you make the payment directly to the educational organization or care provider. The medical and educational exclusions are allowed without regard to the relationship between you and the donee for whom you are making the payments. The exclusion for directly paid educational expenses applies only to tuition, not to room and board, books, or supplies.

Contributions to a qualified tuition program (QTP; *see 33.5*) on behalf of a designated beneficiary do not qualify for the educational exclusion, but do qualify for an enhanced annual exclusion. You can elect to treat a QTP contribution over the basic annual exclusion as if it were made ratably over a five-year period, but only up to five times the annual exclusion. For example, a QTP contribution made in 2006 of up to $60,000 may be treated as if $^1/_5$, or $12,000, had been contributed in 2006 and in each of the next four years. Thus, the entire gift up to $60,000 can avoid gift tax and if your spouse consents to split the gift on Form 709 *(see 39.3)* the exclusion increases to $120,000. If you make QTP contributions for more than one person in the same year, you can make the special QTP election for each of them.

Taxable gifts. If you make a gift that exceeds the allowable annual exclusion and which is not otherwise exempt from the gift tax, you must report the gift on Form 709; *see 39.3.* Gift tax on Form 709 is computed using the same rates that apply for estate tax purposes; *see* the table at the end of this chapter. However, the unified credit shown in *39.4* will generally offset the gift tax liability figured on Form 709. Any unified credit you use against your gift tax in one year reduces the amount of credit that you can use against your gift tax in a later year. The total credit used during your lifetime to offset your gift tax reduces the credit available to use against your estate tax.

Basis for property received as gift. The basis for appreciated property received as a gift is generally the same as the donor's basis. If gift tax was paid by the donor, basis is increased; *see 5.17* for an explanation and examples of the basis computation

Caution

Generation-Skipping Tax

Complicated gift tax and estate rules apply to transfers of property that skip one or more generations, as where a grandparent gives property to a grandchild or great-grandchild. The generation-skipping transfer tax may apply in addition to regular gift tax or estate tax. The annual gift tax exclusion applies and there is an aggregate exemption that applies for lifetime gifts and transfers at death. The exemption equals the estate tax applicable exclusion amount shown at *39.11. See* the gift tax instructions for Schedule C of Form 709 and the estate tax instructions for Schedule R of Form 706. The assistance of an experienced tax practitioner is advised if you are planning "skip" transfers.

39.3 Filing a Gift Tax Return

A gift tax return generally must be filed on Form 709 for a gift made during 2006 to an individual other than your spouse if it exceeds $12,000 or is a gift of a future interest (regardless of value). A return does not have to be filed for gifts qualifying for the tuition or medical expense exclusion discussed in *39.2.*

Married couples who consent to split gifts of over $12,000 in 2006 to any one person must report the gifts to the IRS on Form 709. No gift tax is due under the annual exclusion if the "split" gift is $24,000 or less.

Form 709 generally must be filed by April 15th of the year following the year of the gift. If you get a filing extension for your income tax return, the extension also applies to the gift tax return. If you do not request an extension for your income tax return, you can use Form 8892 to request a filing extension for your gift tax return.

EXAMPLES

1. On July 12, 2006, Randall Johnson makes a gift of publicly traded stock to his son, Philip. He gives Philip 1,000 shares of stock valued at $20,000 ($20 per share). His cost basis for the 1,000 shares was $13,000. On Randall's Form 709, Randall's wife, Claire, consents to split the gift, thereby doubling the annual exclusion for the gift. Neither Randall nor Claire made any other gifts during 2006. As a result of the gift splitting, Randall's share of the gift is reduced to $10,000 and is offset by the annual exclusion. No gift tax is due.
2. Same facts as in Example 1 except that the value of the stock given to Philip was $40,000 instead of $20,000. After Claire consents to split Randall's gift, there is a taxable gift of $16,000 ($40,000 – $24,000 annual exclusion), of which half, or $8,000, is attributed to each of them. They each must file their own Form 709. Assuming that this is the first taxable gift for both Randall and Claire, they will each figure a gift tax of $1,440 on their $8,000 gift; *see* the Table at the end of this chapter. However, no tax is due because it is offset by a $1,440 credit. Randall and Claire each have a lifetime credit of $345,800 for gift tax purposes, which effectively exempts $1 million of lifetime taxable gifts from tax; *see 39.4.* The $1,440 credit used this year reduces the remaining lifetime credit for each of them to $344,360 ($345,800 – $1,440). They each have a remaining lifetime exemption of $992,000.

Caution

Gift Disclosure Starts Running of Statute of Limitations

To begin the running of the statute of limitations on gift valuation, the gift must be adequately disclosed on Form 709 filed for the year of the gift. Follow the disclosure instructions for Schedule A of Form 709. Given this statute of limitations consideration, even donors of property valued at under the $12,000 annual exclusion may want to report the gift on Form 709 in order to start the clock running on how long the IRS has to challenge valuation of the gift.

39.4 Gift Tax Credit

On Form 709, any gift tax that you owe is eliminated or reduced by a tax credit. A "unified" credit applies to both the gift tax and the estate tax. Any unified credit you use against your gift tax in one year reduces the amount of credit that you can use against your gift tax in a later year. The total amount used during your lifetime against your gift tax reduces the credit available to use against your estate tax.

For years before 2004, the same unified credit amount applied to both the gift tax and the estate tax. However, under the 2001 Economic Growth and Tax Relief Reconciliation Act, the credit against taxable gifts was set at $345,800 starting in 2002 and the credit will remain at $345,800

Law Alert

Lifetime Gift Tax Credit and Exemption

For 2002 and later years, a $345,800 lifetime credit is allowed, providing a lifetime exemption for $1 million of taxable gifts. If taxable gifts are made in one year, the amount of the credit used to offset the gift tax for that year reduces the credit available for use against gift tax in later years. The $345,800 credit and the $1 million exemption it provides will not increase even though the estate tax credit and exemption will increase through 2009; *see 39.4.* The maximum gift tax rate will be reduced along with the maximum estate tax rate *(39.11)* through 2009. Starting in 2010, the top gift tax rate will be the top rate for individual income tax, scheduled to be 35%. However, the post-2009 rules could be altered if Congress passes reform legislation. For example, when this book went to press, Congress was considering a proposal to reunify the gift and estate tax after 2009; *see* the Law Alert at *39.11.*

Planning Reminder

Custodial Securities Account

Purchase of securities through custodial accounts provides a practical method for making a gift of securities to a minor child, eliminating the need for a trust. The mechanics of opening a custodial account are simple. An adult opens a stock brokerage account for a minor child and registers the securities in the name of a custodian for the benefit of the child. The custodian may be a parent, a child's guardian, grandparent, brother, sister, uncle, or aunt. In some states, the custodian may be any adult or a bank or trust company. The custodian has the right to sell securities in the account and collect sales proceeds and investment income, and use them for the child's benefit or reinvestment. Tax treatment of custodial accounts is discussed in *39.5.*

(exempting $1 million from tax) even though the estate tax credit will increase through 2009. The following table shows the unified credit and applicable exclusion amount (the exemption from tax) for the calendar years in which a gift is made or an individual dies after 2005. A proposal to reunify the gift and estate tax after 2009 was under consideration when this book went to press; *see* the Law Alert in *39.11.*

Table 39-1 Gift / Estate Tax Credit and Exclusion

	For Gift Tax Purposes:		For Estate Tax Purposes:	
Year	**Unified Credit**	**Applicable Exclusion Amount**	**Unified Credit**	**Applicable Exclusion Amount**
2006, 2007, and 2008	345,800	1,000,000	780,800	2,000,000
2009	345,800	1,000,000	1,455,800	3,500,000

39.5 Custodial Accounts for Minors

A minor generally lacks the ability to manage property. You could create a formal trust, but this step may be costly. A practical alternative may be a custodial account under the Uniform Gifts to Minors Act (UGMA), or the Uniform Transfers to Minors Act (UTMA), which has replaced the UGMA in practically every state.

Custodial accounts set up in a bank, mutual fund, or brokerage firm can achieve income splitting; the tax consequences discussed below generally apply to such accounts. Trust accounts that are considered revocable under state law are ineffective in splitting income.

Although custodial accounts may be opened anywhere in the United States, the rules governing the accounts may vary from state to state. The differences between the laws of the states generally do not affect federal tax consequences.

There are limitations placed on the custodian. Proceeds from the sale of an investment or income from an investment may not be used to buy additional securities on margin. While a custodian should prudently seek reasonable income and capital preservation, he or she generally is not liable for losses unless they result from bad faith, intentional wrongdoing, or gross negligence.

When the minor reaches majority age (depending on state law), property in the custodial account is turned over to him or her. No formal accounting is required. The child, now an adult, may sign a simple release freeing the custodian from any liability. But on reaching majority, the child may request a formal accounting if there are any doubts as to the propriety of the custodian's actions while acting as custodian. For this reason, and also for tax record-keeping purposes, a separate bank account should be opened in which proceeds from sales of investments and investment income are deposited pending reinvestment on behalf of the child. Such an account will furnish a convenient record of sales proceeds, investment income, and reinvestment of the same.

Income tax treatment of custodian account. Income from a custodian account is generally taxable to the child. However, taxable income from a custodial account in excess of the annual "kiddie" tax floor ($1,700 in 2006) is taxed at the parent's tax rate if the child is under age 18; computation of the "kiddie tax" is discussed in Chapter 24.

If a parent is the donor of the custodial property or the custodian of the account and income from the account is used to discharge the parent's legal obligation to support the child, the account income is taxed to the parent.

Gift tax treatment of custodial account. When setting up a custodial account, you may have to pay a gift tax. A transfer of cash or securities to a custodial account is a gift. But you are not subject to a gift tax if you properly plan the cash contributions or purchase of securities for your children's accounts. You may make gifts that are shielded from gift tax by the annual exclusion. The exclusion applies each year to each person to whom you make a gift.

If your spouse consents to join with you in the gift, the annual exclusion is doubled. For gifts in 2006, the per-donee exclusion is $12,000, $24,000 if your spouse consents to split the gift.

If the custodial account is set up at the end of December, another tax-free transfer of up to the annual exclusion may be made in the first days of January of the following year. Assuming the annual exclusion in each year is $12,000, a total of $48,000 can be shifted within the two-month period with spousal consent.

Even if gifts exceeding the annual exclusion are made, gift tax liability may be offset by the unified credit applied to gift and estate taxes.

Estate tax treatment of custodial account. The value of a custodial account will be taxed in your estate if you die while acting as custodian of an account before your child reaches his or her majority. However, you may avoid the problem by naming someone other than yourself as custodian. If you should decide to act as custodian, taking the risk that the account will be taxed in your estate, remember that no estate tax is incurred if the tax on your estate is offset by the estate tax credit.

If you act as custodian and decide to terminate the custodianship, care should be taken to formally close the account. Otherwise, if you die while retaining power over the account, the IRS may try to tax the account in your estate.

39.6 Trusts in Family Planning

You establish a trust by transferring legal title to property to a trustee who manages the property for one or more beneficiaries. As the one who sets up the trust, you are called the *grantor* or *settlor* of the trust. The trustee may be one or more individuals or an institution such as a bank or a trust company.

You can create a trust during your lifetime or by your will. A trust created during your lifetime is called an *inter vivos* trust; one established in your will is a testamentary trust. An *inter vivos* trust can be revocable or irrevocable. An irrevocable trust does not allow for changes of heart; it requires a complete surrender of property. By conveying property irrevocably to a trust, you may relieve yourself of tax on the income from the trust principal. Furthermore, the property in trust usually is not subject to estate tax, although it may be subject to gift tax. A trust should be made irrevocable only if you are certain you will not need the trust property in a financial emergency.

Trust income. Where a child is a trust beneficiary, the child reports distributable net trust income as taxable income. If the child is under the age of 14, distributable net income is subject to the "kiddie tax," discussed at *24.3*. Income that is accumulated for the benefit of a minor child is generally not taxable and, thus, not subject to the kiddie tax.

Grantor trusts. The grantor of a grantor trust is taxed on the income of the trust. A trust is treated as a grantor trust where the grantor has a reversionary interest (at the time of the transfer) of more than 5% of the value of the property transferred to the trust. Under an exception, a grantor is not treated as having a reversionary interest if that interest can take effect only upon the death before age 21 of a beneficiary who is a lineal descendant of the grantor. The beneficiary must have the entire present interest in the trust or trust portion for this exception to apply.

Given the highly compressed tax brackets for trust income, a grantor may intentionally retain an interest in the trust property so that he or she will be taxed under the grantor trust rules. By setting up such a "defective" grantor trust, trust income may be subject to lower tax at the grantor's tax bracket than under the trust rate schedule.

Planning Reminder

Revocable Trusts

In a revocable trust, you retain control over the property by reserving the right to revoke the trust. As such, it is considered an incomplete gift and offers no present income tax savings. Furthermore, the trust property will be included as part of your estate. But a revocable trust minimizes delay in passing property to beneficiaries if you die while the trust is in force. When you transfer property to a trust, the property is generally not subject to probate, administration expenses, delays attendant on distributions of estates, or claims of creditors. The interests of trust beneficiaries are generally more secure than those of heirs under a will because a will may be denied probate if found invalid.

Estate Tax Planning

39.7 What Is the Estate Tax?

The estate you built up may not be entirely yours to give away. The federal government and, in most cases, at least one state government stand ready to claim their shares.

The federal estate tax is a tax on the act of transferring property at death. It is not a tax on the right of the beneficiary to receive the property; the estate and the estate alone pays the tax, although the property passing to individual beneficiaries may be diminished by the tax.

Understand what the word *estate* means in estate tax law so that you do not underestimate the value of your taxable estate. The estate includes not only your real estate (foreign and domestic), bank deposits, securities, and personal property such as art objects, but can also include insurance, your interest in trusts or jointly held property, and certain interests you have in other estates.

The general guide to federal estate taxation in this chapter will alert you to the potential extent of estate tax costs, and help you plan for estate tax savings that you may discuss with an experienced estate tax planning professional. Periodic re-evaluation of your estate plan is essential, expecially given the uncertainty as to whether the scheduled repeal of the estate tax for 2010 *(see 39.11)* will be made permanent.

39.8 Take Inventory

The first step in estate tax planning follows a simple business practice of taking inventory of everything you own. Listing your belongings takes thought, time, and a surprising amount of work. On your list you should include records of purchases, fire and theft insurance inventories, bankbooks, brokers' statements, etc. You should also include your cash, real estate (here and abroad), securities, mortgages, rights in property, trust accounts, personal effects, collections, and art works. Life insurance is includible if: (1) it is payable to your estate; (2) it is payable to others and you have kept "incidents of ownership" such as the right to change beneficiaries, surrender or assign the policy, or pledge it for a loan; or (3) you assign the policy and die within three years.

If you own property jointly with your spouse, your estate includes only one-half its value.

If you had appraisals made of specially treasured items or collections, or property of substantial value, file such appraisals with your estate papers and then enter the value on your inventory.

Planning Reminder

Life Insurance

If you are buying a new policy with yourself as the insured, and you want to keep the proceeds out of your gross estate, set up an irrevocable trust to buy the policy or have the individual beneficiary buy the policy. For example, a daughter applies for a $1 million policy on her father's life and is the policy owner under the terms of the policy. If the father pays the premiums, his payments are treated as gifts, but the proceeds paid at his death are not subject to estate tax because he never had ownership rights in the policy.

If you have an existing policy, you may assign your ownership rights, such as the right to change beneficiaries, the right to surrender or cancel the policy, the right to assign it, and the right to borrow against it, but the assignment must occur more than three years before death to exclude the proceeds from your estate.

Retirement benefits. The taxable estate generally includes benefits payable at your death from any of the following retirement plans: pension plan, profit-sharing plan, Keogh plan, individual retirement account, or annuity. However, the value of an annuity from an IRA or employer plan that is payable to a beneficiary other than your estate may qualify for a full or partial exclusion if IRA distributions began before 1985 or you separated from service before 1985; no exclusion is allowed to the extent of your own nondeductible contributions to the plan.

A full exclusion is allowed for IRA funds if you began taking distributions from the account before 1983 under a schedule that irrevocably set the form of benefits. If IRA distributions began in 1983 or 1984 and you irrevocably elected the form of benefits before July 18, 1984, a $100,000 exclusion is allowed.

If you began receiving distributions from an employer plan before 1983 under a schedule that irrevocably set the form of benefits, a full estate tax exclusion is allowed. If you separated from service in 1983 or 1984, a $100,000 exclusion is allowed if the form of benefits is not changed before death; this is true even if distributions did not begin until after 1984.

39.9 Finding the Value of Your Estate

When you have completed your inventory, assign to each asset what you consider to be its fair market value. This may be difficult to do for some assets. Resist the tendency to overvalue articles that arouse feelings of pride or sentiment and undervalue some articles of great intrinsic worth. For purposes of your initial estimate, it is better to err on the side of overvaluation. You can list ordinary personal effects at nominal value.

If you have a family business, your idea of its value and that of the IRS may vary greatly. Estate plans have been upset by the higher value placed on such a business by the IRS. You can protect your estate by anticipating and solving this problem with your business associates and counselors.

Caution

Trusts Includible in Estate

There are some assets that you might not ordinarily consider as part of your estate. Nevertheless, include in your inventory any trust arrangements created by you in which you have: (1) a life estate (the income or other use of property for life); (2) income that is to be used to pay your legal obligations (support of a child, for example); (3) the right to change the beneficiary or his or her interest (a power of appointment); (4) the right to revoke a trust transfer or gift; and (5) a reversionary interest (the possibility that the property can come back to you).

If your business is owned by a closely held corporation, and there is no ready or open market in which the stock can be valued, get some factual basis for a figure that will be reported on the estate tax return. One of the ways to do this is by arranging a buy-sell agreement with a potential purchaser. This agreement must fix the value of the stock. Generally, an agreement that binds both the estate and the purchaser and restricts lifetime sales of the stock will effectively fix the value of the stock for estate tax purposes. Another way would be to make a gift of some shares to a family member and have value established in gift tax proceedings.

If a substantial part of your estate is real estate used in farming or a closely held business, your executor may be able to elect, with the consent of heirs having an interest in the property, to value the property on the basis of its farming or business use, rather than its highest and best use. For estates of individuals dying in 2005, special use valuation may not reduce the gross estate by more than $870,000; the ceiling is subject to adjustment for inflation. This savings may be recaptured from your heir if he or she stops using the property in farming or business within 10 years of your death.

39.10 How the Estate Tax Is Applied

A single unified rate schedule applies to a decedent's estate and all post-1976 lifetime gifts *over* the annual gift tax exclusion. The 2006 rate schedule is shown at the end of this chapter, and scheduled reductions to the top rate are shown in *39.11*. Under the unified gift and estate tax rate, the overall tax on your property holdings is theoretically the same whether or not you make lifetime gifts. In actual cases, however, lifetime gifts may reduce the potential overall tax because of the annual gift tax exclusion *(39.2)*. The $1 million exemption for taxable gifts made after 2001 *(39.2)* is not increasing, although the exemption for estate tax gradually increases to $3.5 million as shown in *39.11*.

You may use IRS Form 706 to estimate what the estate tax would be on your estate. If you make no taxable gifts during your life, estimating estate tax on Form 706 is fairly easy. You start with the total market value of the property in the estate. This is called the *gross estate*. From the gross estate you subtract certain deductions. For example, administration expenses for the estate and charitable bequests are deductible. An unlimited marital deduction is allowed for bequests to a surviving spouse who is a U.S. citizen. The net amount after deductions is your taxable estate. A unified credit is subtracted from the tax calculated on the taxable estate *(see 39.11)* and other credits further reduce the federal estate tax on your estate. The state death tax credit allowed under pre-2005 law has been replaced with a deduction for state death taxes.

If you have made taxable gifts after 1976, estimating your estate tax is more complicated. The estate tax and gift tax are cumulative. That is, the tax rate is applied to the sum of (1) your taxable estate at death, and (2) taxable lifetime gifts made after 1976 (other than gifts included in your estate). The tax you figure on both (1) and (2) is reduced by gift taxes payable on gifts made after 1976. The unified or applicable credit and other credits are then subtracted from the remaining amount. *See* the Form 706 instructions for details.

Generation-skipping transfers. Transfers that "skip" a generation, such as a gift to a grandchild, are subject to a special tax (computed on Schedule R of Form 706) if they exceed an exemption, which for 2006 is $2 million. Because of other exceptions and the complexity of these rules, you should consult an experienced tax practitioner if you are planning "skip" transfers.

39.11 Estate Tax Reductions Prior to Scheduled Repeal

Estate tax computed on Form 706 is eliminated or reduced by a tax credit. As discussed at *39.4*, a "unified" credit applies to both the gift tax and the estate tax. Any unified credit used against lifetime gift taxes reduces the amount of credit available to use against your estate tax. The credit in effect provides an exemption that the tax law refers to as the "applicable exclusion amount." Under the 2001 Economic Growth and Tax Relief Reconciliation Act, the estate tax unified credit and applicable exclusion amounts are increasing in the years leading up to the scheduled repeal of the estate tax in 2010, as shown below. Scheduled reductions to the top tax rate under the 2001 Act are also shown below.

Despite numerous attempts in Congress to settle the fate of the estate tax after 2009, there was continuing uncertainty when this book went to press. Attempts to make repeal permanent had failed and the House and Senate could not agree on a reform package that would retain the estate tax after 2009 but significantly expand the exemption and lower the rates; *see* the Law Alert on this page.

Rate table. The same tax rate table applies for gift tax and estate tax purposes. The table for 2006 gift tax and estate tax is shown at the end of this chapter. Those rates will also apply through 2009, except for the scheduled reduction to the top rate as shown below. Rates below the top rate are not scheduled to change.

Law Alert

Will Congress Reform the Estate Tax?

When this book went to press, it was unclear if the House and Senate would be able in the near future to agree on a compromise plan to reform the estate tax. Republican-led efforts to make estate tax repeal permanent after 2009 passed the House but not the Senate in mid-2006. This was followed by attempts to enact a compromise reform plan. The House passed a bill that would reunify the estate and gift taxes starting in 2010 as part of a package that would also extend expiring tax provisions and increase the minimum wage. However, the plan did not gain Senate approval because of opposition by Senate Democrats to the estate tax provisions. The bill would increase the exemption for gift and estate tax purposes in stages to $5 million by 2015 (and then index it for inflation), and allow the unused portion of a deceased spouse's exemption to be used by the surviving spouse. The tax rate on taxable transfers up to $25 million would be the capital gains rate and transfers over $25 million would be taxed at a rate of 40% in 2010, with the rate decreasing by 2% a year until reaching 30% for 2015 and later years. After 2015, the $25 million threshold would be indexed for inflation.

When this book went to press, new efforts were underway to gain approval of the bill in the Senate, or possibly modify it in an attempt to win passage. *See* the *e-Supplement* for an update.

Table 39-2 Estate Tax Exclusion, Credit, and Top Rate

Individual dying in—	*Applicable exclusion amount [exemption] —*	*Unified credit—*	*Top estate tax rate—*
2006	$2 million	$780,800	46%
2007	$2 million	$780,800	45%
2008	$2 million	$780,800	45%
2009	$3.5 million	$1,455,800	45%
2010	If Congress does not change the law (*see* the Law Alert in *39.11*), total repeal of estate tax		
2011	If Congress does not change the law (*see* the Law Alert in *39.11*), then starting in 2011 the exclusion would be $1 million and the top estate tax rate would be 55%.		

Planning Reminder

Marital Deduction

To qualify for the marital deduction, the property must generally be given to the spouse outright or by other arrangements that are the legal equivalent of outright ownership. There is an exception for income interests in charitable remainder annuity or unitrusts and certain other qualified terminable interest property (QTIP) for which the executor makes an election.

39.12 Reducing or Eliminating a Potential Estate Tax

Here are general approaches to eliminating or reducing a potential estate tax: You can make direct lifetime gifts. Any appreciation on the property transferred will be removed from your estate. Furthermore, each gift, to the extent of the annual per donee exclusion ($12,000 in 2006), reduces your gross estate; *see 39.2.* Life insurance can be assigned to avoid estate tax, provided the assignment takes place more than three years before death; *see 39.8.* You can provide in your will for bequests that will qualify for the marital and charitable deductions.

The marital deduction. A married person may greatly reduce or eliminate estate tax by using the marital deduction. Property passing to a spouse is generally free from estate or gift tax because of an unlimited marital deduction.

Weigh carefully the tax consequences of leaving your spouse all of your property. For maximum tax savings, you may want to give your spouse only enough property to reduce your taxable estate to the exclusion floor *(see 39.11).* The unified credit amount will then eliminate tax on that amount at the time of your death. By leaving your spouse less than the maximum deductible amount, you may be able to reduce the estate tax at the time of his or her death.

Life insurance proceeds may qualify as marital deduction property. Name your spouse the unconditional beneficiary of the proceeds with unrestricted control over any unpaid proceeds. If your spouse is not given this control or general power of appointment, and there is no requirement that proceeds remaining on your spouse's death be payable to his or her estate, the insurance proceeds will not qualify for the marital deduction.

What should be done if you believe your spouse cannot manage property? You will not want to give complete and personal control. The law permits you to put the property in certain trust arrangements that are considered equivalent to complete ownership. Your attorney can explain how you can protect your spouse's interest and qualify the trust property for the marital deduction.

Marital deduction restrictions for noncitizen spouses. A marital deduction may not be claimed for property passing outright to a surviving spouse who is not a U.S. citizen. However, the marital deduction is allowed if the surviving spouse's interest is in a qualifying domestic trust (QDOT). At least one trustee must be an individual U.S. citizen or domestic corporation with power to withhold estate tax due from distributions of trust corpus. The trust must maintain sufficient assets as required by IRS regulations. For the marital deduction to apply, the executor must make an irrevocable election on the decedent's estate tax return. On Form 706-QDT, estate tax will apply to certain distributions of trust corpus made prior to the surviving spouse's death, and to the value of the QDOT property remaining at the surviving spouse's death. You should consult an experienced tax practitioner to set up a QDOT trust and plan for distribution provisions.

The estate of a nonresident alien is subject to estate tax only to the extent that the estate is located in the United States. A marital deduction may be claimed by the estate of a nonresident alien for property passing to a surviving spouse who is a U.S. citizen. If the surviving spouse is not a U.S. citizen, then the transferred interest must be in the form of a QDOT.

Periodically review your estate plan. No estate plan is ever really final. Economic conditions and inflation constantly change values. For this reason, your plan must be reviewed periodically as changes occur in your family and business, as when a birth or death occurs; when you receive a substantial increase or decrease in income; when you enter a new business venture or resign from an old one; or when you sell, retire from, or bring new persons into business. A member of your family may no longer need any part of your estate, while others may need more. Material changes may occur in the health or life expectancy of one of your beneficiaries. Furthermore, political conditions may affect the scheduled phaseout and repeal of the federal estate tax *(39.11)*.

39.13 Estate Tax Freeze Advisory

The object of an estate tax freeze is to reduce or eliminate estate tax on the inheritance of property by fixing the value through certain property arrangements. A complicated gift and estate tax law (IRC §§2701–2704) attempts to discourage such plans by applying special valuation rules. The rules cover not only common and preferred stock holdings within the family but also partnership interests, the deferral of dividend payments on preferred stock, life and remainder interests, and buy-sell agreements in family businesses.

The estate freeze rules impose gift tax and estate tax values for property transfers subject to the law. Because of the complexity of these rules and their effect on gift and estate values, we suggest that you seek professional advice in the following situations:

- As an owner of a family business, you plan to give common stock to family members while retaining preferred stock or recapitalize with common and preferred stock.
- You plan to give up a voting interest or liquidating rights attached to preferred stock in a family business.
- You defer payment of dividends in preferred stock in a family business.
- You plan to retain an interest for life in a transfer or purchase of property.
- You plan to give stock to a family member in a company in which you have a buy-sell agreement.

Caution

Get Expert Advice

Estate tax planning is not a do-it-yourself activity. You should contact experienced counsel for help in developing a plan for your future estate that will accomplish your tax and personal objectives.

Table 39-3 Gift and Estate Tax Rates for Gifts Made in 2006 and Estates of Individuals Dying in 2006*

If taxable amount is: over—	*But not over—*	*The tax is—*	*Plus %—*	*Of the amount over—*
$0	$10,000	$0	18	$0
10,000	20,000	1,800	20	10,000
20,000	40,000	3,800	22	20,000
40,000	60,000	8,200	24	40,000
60,000	80,000	13,000	26	60,000
80,000	100,000	18,200	28	80,000
100,000	150,000	23,800	30	100,000
150,000	250,000	38,800	32	150,000
250,000	500,000	70,800	34	250,000
500,000	750,000	155,800	37	500,000
750,000	1,000,000	248,300	39	750,000
1,000,000	1,250,000	345,800	41	1,000,000
1,250,000	1,500,000	448,300	43	1,250,000
1,500,000	2,000,000	555,800	45	1,500,000
2,000,000		780,800	46	2,000,000

** See 39.11 for the scheduled reduction in the top tax rate for 2006–2009.*

Part 6

Business Tax Planning

In this part, you will learn how to report your income from a business or profession, and how to reduce your tax liability by claiming expense deductions. Pay special attention to—

- Reporting rules for income and expenses on Schedule C (Chapter 40).
- Restrictions on deducting home office expenses. Your deduction may be limited by a restrictive income test (Chapter 40).
- The new deduction for qualified domestic production activities income (Chapter 40).
- Keogh, SEP, and SIMPLE retirement plan rules if you are self-employed. These plans offer tax deductions for contributions and tax-free accumulation of income within the plan. In some cases, special averaging for lump-sum distributions from a Keogh plan is allowed (Chapter 41).
- First-year expensing and depreciation write-offs for business assets (Chapter 42).
- The IRS mileage allowance as an alternative to claiming operating expenses and depreciation for your business automobile (Chapter 43).
- Computing and paying self-employment tax on self-employment earnings from a business or profession (Chapter 45).

Chapter 40

Income or Loss From Your Business or Profession

As a self-employed person, you report income and expenses from your business or profession separately from your other income, such as income from wages. On Schedule C, you report your business income and itemize your expenses. Any net profit is subject to self-employment tax, as well as regular tax. A net profit can also be the basis of deductible contributions to a SEP or Keogh retirement plan, as discussed in Chapter 41.

If you work out of your home, you may deduct home office expenses.

If you claim a loss on Schedule C, be prepared to show that you regularly and substantially participate in the business. Otherwise, your loss may be considered a passive loss deductible only from passive income, as discussed in Chapter 10.

If you have a business loss that exceeds your other income, you may carry back the loss and claim a refund. For a loss in a tax year ending in 2006, the carryback period is generally two years; *see 40.18*.

If you have no employees and business expenses of $5,000 or less, you may be able to file a simplified schedule called Schedule C-EZ; *see 40.6*.

Organizing Your Business

40.1 Forms of Doing Business

The legal form of your business determines the way you report business income and loss, the taxes you pay, the ability of the business to accumulate capital, and the extent of your personal liability. It is beyond the scope of this book to discuss the pros and cons of each form. The decision should be made with the services of a professional experienced in both the legal and tax consequences of doing business in a particular form as it applies to your current and future business prospects.

If you are going into business alone, your choices are: operating as a sole proprietor, incorporating, and forming a limited liability company (LLC). If you are going to operate with associates, you may choose to operate as a partnership, a corporation, or an LLC. If you are concerned with limiting your personal liability, your choice is between a corporation or an LLC. An LLC gives you the advantage of limited liability without having to incorporate.

As a sole proprietor, you report business profit or loss on your personal tax return, as explained in this chapter. If you are a partner, you report your share of partnership profit and loss as explained in Chapter 11. If you incorporate, the corporation pays tax on business income. You are taxable on salaries and dividends paid to you by the corporation. You may avoid this double corporate tax by making an S corporation election, which allows you to report corporate income and loss; *see 11.14.*

If you operate through an LLC with no co-owners, you report income and loss as a sole proprietor. If you operate an LLC with associates, the LLC reports as a partnership and you report your share of income and loss. However, under check-the-box rules, the LLC may elect on Form 8832 to report as an association taxable as a corporation.

40.2 Reporting Self-Employed Income

You file a separate Schedule C along with Form 1040 if you are a sole proprietor of a business or a professional in your own practice. If you do freelance work as an independent contractor, you are self-employed and use Schedule C. If you are an employee with a sideline business, report the self-employment income and expenses from that business on Schedule C. Do not file Schedule C if your business is operated through a partnership or corporation. A guide to Schedule C is in *40.6.*

On Schedule C, you deduct your allowable business expenses from your business income. Net business profit (or loss) figured on Schedule C is entered on Line 12, Page 1 of Form 1040. Thus, business profit (or loss) is added to (or subtracted from) nonbusiness income on Form 1040 to compute adjusted gross income. This procedure gives you the chance to deduct your business expenses, whether you claim itemized deductions or nonbusiness deductions on Schedule A, such as charitable contributions, taxes, and medical expenses, or you claim the standard deduction where it exceeds your allowable itemized deductions; *see 13.2.*

You may be able to file a simplified schedule, Schedule C-EZ, if your income and expenses are below certain limits; *see 40.6.*

Filing Tip

Did You Suffer a Loss?

Business persons and professionals with a 2006 net operating loss may get a refund of taxes paid in two prior tax years (more in some cases). If the loss is not fully eliminated by the income of the two prior years, the balance of the loss may be used to reduce your business income for up to 20 of the following years. *See 40.18* for details.

Passive loss restrictions. Pay special attention to the passive loss restrictions discussed in Chapter 10. Generally, if you do not regularly and substantially participate in your business, losses are considered passive and are deductible only against other passive income.

Tax ID number. As a sole proprietor, you usually do not need a separate tax ID number for Schedule C; you can use your Social Security number as your tax ID number. However, you must obtain an employer identification number if you have any employees and/or maintain a qualified retirement plan (you may also need one to open a business bank account). You can obtain your employer identification number online at www.irs.gov/businesses/small/index.html (click on "Employer ID Numbers" (EINs).

Table 40-1 Key to Reporting Business and Professional Income and Loss

Item—	*Comments—*
Tax return to file	If you are self-employed, prepare Schedule C to report business or professional income. If your business expenses are $5,000 or less, and you have no employees, you may be able to file a simplified Schedule C-EZ; *see 40.6.* If you are a farmer, use Schedule F. You attach Schedule C and/or F to Form 1040. If you operate as a partnership, use Form 1065; if you operate as a corporation, use Form 1120S or Form 1120.
Method of reporting income	The cash or accrual accounting rules determine when you report income and expenses. You must use the accrual basis if you sell a product that must be inventoried unless a safe harbor exception applies. The cash-basis and accrual-basis methods are discussed at *40.3.*
Tax reporting year	There are two general tax reporting years: calendar years that end on December 31 and fiscal years that end on the last day of any month other than December. Your taxable year must be the same for both your business and nonbusiness income. Most business income must be reported on a calendar-year basis. If, as a self-employed person, you report your business income on a fiscal-year basis, you must also report your nonbusiness income on a fiscal-year basis. Use of a fiscal year is restricted for partnerships and S corporations.
Office in home	To claim home office expenses as a self-employed person, you must use the home area exclusively and on a regular basis either as a place of business to meet or deal with patients, clients, or customers in the normal course of your business or as your principal place of business. Form 8829 must be used to compute the deduction; *see 40.12.*
Social Security coverage	If you have self-employment income, you may have to pay self-employment tax, which goes to financing Social Security and Medicare benefits; *see* Chapter 45.
Passive participation in a business	If you do not regularly, continuously, and substantially participate in the business, your business income or loss is subject to passive activity restrictions. A loss is deductible only against other passive activity income. The passive activity restrictions are discussed in detail in Chapter 10.
Self-employed Keogh plan	You may set up a retirement plan based on business or professional income. Individuals who are self-employed may contribute to a self-employed retirement plan, according to the rules in Chapter 41.
Depreciation	Under the increased first-year expensing deduction, you generally may deduct up to $108,000 for equipment placed in service in 2006; *see 42.3.* Depreciation rules for assets not deducted under first-year expensing are in Chapter 42. Cars and trucks are subject to special depreciation limits; *see* Chapter 43.
Health insurance	You may deduct 100% of premiums paid for health insurance coverage for yourself, spouse, and dependents. This deduction is claimed directly from gross income on Line 29 of Form 1040. You may also take advantage of a health savings account plan as explained in *17.17.*
Net operating losses	A loss incurred in your profession or business is deducted from other income reported on Form 1040. If the loss (plus any casualty loss) exceeds income, the excess may generally be first carried back two years, and then forward 20 years until it is used up. A loss carried back to a prior year reduces income of that year and entitles you to a refund. A loss applied to a later year reduces income for that year. In some cases a three-year or five-year carryback applies; *see 40.18.* You may elect to carry forward your loss for 20 years, foregoing the carryback; *see 40.22.*
Sideline business	You report business income of a sideline business following the rules that apply to full-time business. For example, if you are self-employed, you report business income on Schedule C or C-EZ. You may also have to pay self-employment tax on this income; *see* Chapter 45. You may also set up a self-employment retirement plan based on such income; *see* Chapter 41. If you incur losses over several years, the hobby loss rules discussed in *40.10* may limit your loss deduction.
Domestic production activities deduction	If your business makes something in the U.S., you may be eligible for a 3% deduction, which effectively reduces the tax rate you would otherwise pay on this income; *see 40.23.*

Accounting for Business Income

40.3 Accounting Methods for Reporting Business Income

Business income is reported on either the accrual or cash basis. If you have more than one business, you may have a different accounting method for each business.

Inventories. Unless the $10 million safe harbor discussed below applies, the IRS requires inventories at the beginning and end of every taxable year in which the production, purchase, or sale of merchandise is an income-producing factor. If you must keep inventories, you *must* use the accrual basis.

IRS Alert

Cash Method Safe Harbor

Businesses with average annual gross receipts of $10 million are eligible to use a cash method safe harbor.

Cash method. You report income items in the taxable year in which they are received; you deduct all expenses in the taxable year in which they are paid. Under the cash method, income is also reported if it is "constructively" received. You have "constructively" received income when an amount is credited to your account, subject to your control, or set apart for you and may be drawn by you at any time. For example, in 2006 you receive a check in payment of services, but you do not cash it until 2007. You have constructively received the income in 2006, and it is taxable in 2006.

On the cash basis, you deduct expenses in the year of payment. Expenses paid by credit card are deducted in the year they are charged. Expenses paid through a "pay by phone" account with a bank are deducted in the year the bank sends the check. This date is reported by the bank on its monthly statement.

Advance payments. Generally, no immediate deduction can be claimed for advance rent or premium covering charges of a later year. However, under a "12-month rule," you can claim an immediate deduction for prepayments that create rights or benefits that do not extend beyond the earlier of: (1) 12 months after the first date on which the taxpayer realizes rights or benefits attributable to the expenditure, or (2) the end of the taxable year following the taxable year in which the payment is made. However, prepayments of rent remain nondeductible for accrual-method taxpayers under the economic performance rules.

Cash method of accounting limited. The following may not use the cash method: a regular C corporation, a partnership with a C corporation as a partner, a tax shelter, or a tax-exempt trust with unrelated business income. Exceptions: A farming or tree-raising business may use the cash method even if it operates as a C corporation or a partnership with a C corporation as a partner. The cash method may also be used by personal service corporations in the fields of medicine, law, engineering, accounting, architecture, performing arts, actuarial science, or consulting. To qualify, substantially all of the stock must be owned directly or indirectly (through partnerships, S corporations, or personal service corporations) by employees.

Planning Reminder

Advantage of Cash-Basis Accounting

The cash basis has this advantage over other accounting methods: You may defer reporting income by postponing the receipt of income. But make certain that you avoid the constructive receipt rule. For example, if 2006 is a high income year or you might drop to a lower tax bracket in 2007, you might delay mailing some of your customers' bills so they do not receive them until 2007. You may also postpone the payment of presently due expenses to a year in which the deduction gives you a greater tax savings.

If the production, purchase, or sale of merchandise is *not* an income-producing factor, the cash method may be used by a C corporation or a partnership with a C corporation as a partner if the average annual gross receipts over the prior three-year period were $5 million or less.

Cash method safe harbor for businesses with average gross receipts of $10 million or less. Business owners with average annual gross receipts of $10 million or less can use the cash method even if they would otherwise have to account for inventories under the accrual method. If the safe harbor applies, items that are purchased for resale to customers or used as raw materials for producing finished goods may not be deducted until the year the items are provided to customers if that is later than the year of purchase. A qualifying small business that wants to apply the safe harbor guidelines must file for an accounting method change as explained in Revenue Procedure 2002-28.

The taxpayer's average annual gross receipts must be $10 million or less for the three taxable years ending with *each* prior taxable year ending on or after December 31, 2000. Thus, to qualify for 2006, the taxpayer's average annual gross receipts had to be $10 million or less for each of the following three-year periods: 2000–2002, 2001–2003, 2002–2004, and 2003–2005. If the test is not met, the cash method cannot be used for 2006 or any later year. If the business has not been in existence for three prior taxable years, including the period of any predecessor, the average is figured for the years it has been in existence.

The cash method safe harbor applies to service businesses, custom manufacturers, and any other taxpayer whose principal activity is not specifically ineligible under Revenue Procedure 2002-28. If a taxpayer's principal business activity is any of the following, Revenue Procedure 2002-28 bars the cash method safe harbor for *that* activity: retail or wholesale sales, manufacturing (other than eligible custom manufacturers), publishing, sound recording, or mining. The "principal" activity is the activity that produced the largest percentage of gross receipts in the prior year or the largest average percentage over the three prior years.

Where the taxpayer's principal activity is not in the prohibited group, the taxpayer may use the cash method for *all* of its businesses. Where the principal activity is in the prohibited group, the cash method safe harbor may not be used for *that* activity but it may be used for a separate secondary activity that does not fall within the ineligible group if a complete and separate set of books is maintained for it. For example, a plumbing contractor satisfies the prior-year principal activity test if in the prior year 60% of its gross receipts were from plumbing installations and 40% were from selling plumbing equipment at its retail store. Plumbing installation is a construction activity that is not within the prohibited group. The taxpayer may use the cash method for both the plumbing installation and retail businesses, subject to the timing rule for items purchased for resale and raw materials used to produce finished goods. If the principal activity had been retail sales, the cash method could not be used for that ineligible activity. However, if the taxpayer treats the two activities as separate businesses, each with it own complete set of books, the cash method could be used for the installation business assuming the $10 million gross receipts test is met.

Accrual method. On the accrual method, report income that has been earned, whether or not received, unless your right to collect the income is unsure because a substantial contingency may prevent payment; *see* the Example below.

Planning Reminder

Advantage of Accrual-Method Accounting

The accrual method has this advantage over the cash basis: It generally gives a more even and balanced financial report.

EXAMPLE

You report business income as a calendar-year accrual taxpayer. You sell several products on December 27, 2006, and bill the customer in January 2007. You report the sales income on your 2006 Schedule C, even though payment is not made until 2007. Under the accrual method, you are considered to earn the income when the products are sold and delivered to the customer.

Where you are prepaid for services to be performed in a later year, the IRS allows you to defer the prepayment until the next taxable year. Deferral cannot extend beyond the year following the year of payment even if the term of the agreement is for a longer period. *See* the following Examples and Revenue Procedure 2004-34 for further details.

EXAMPLES

1. In November 2006, you receive full payment under a one-year contract requiring you to provide 48 music lessons. In 2006, you give eight lessons, and report one-sixth ($^{8}/_{48}$) of the payment as income. In 2007, the remaining five-sixths of the payment must be reported, even if you do not actually give the required number of lessons by the end of 2007.
2. Assume in Example 1 that the contract is for two years, and eight lessons are provided in 2006, 48 lessons in 2007, and 40 lessons in 2008. You must report one-twelfth ($^{8}/_{96}$) of the 2006 payment as income for 2006 and the remaining eleven-twelfths of the payment as income for 2007.

Filing Tip

Changing Your Accounting Method

Generally, you must obtain the consent of the Internal Revenue Service prior to any change in accounting method. Apply for consent by filing Form 3115 as early as possible during the tax year for which you wish to make the change.

Expenses under the accrual method are deductible in the year your liability for payment is fixed, even though payment is made in a later year. To prevent manipulation of expense deductions, there are tax law tests for fixing the timing of accrual method expense deductions. The tests generally require that *economic performance* must occur before a deduction may be claimed, but there are exceptions, such as for "recurring expenses." These rules are discussed in IRS Publication 538.

Expenses owed by an accrual-method business owner to a related cash-basis taxpayer. A business expense owed to your spouse, brother, sister, parent, child, grandparent, or grandchild who reports on the cash basis may not be deducted by you until you make the payment and the relative includes it as income. The same rule applies to amounts owed to a controlled corporation (more than 50% ownership) and other related entities.

Long-term contracts. Section 460 of the Internal Revenue Code has a special percentage of completion method of accounting for long-term construction contractors.

Capitalize costs of business property you produce or buy for resale. A complicated statute (Code Section 263A) generally requires manufacturers and builders to capitalize certain indirect costs (such as administrative costs, interest expenses, storage fees, and insurance), as well as direct production expenses, by including them in inventory costs; *see* IRS Publication 538, Form 3115, and the regulations to Code Section 263A.

Non-accrual experience method (NAE) for deferring service income. Taxpayers using the accrual method who either provide services in the fields of health, law, accounting, actuarial science, engineering, architecture, performing arts, or consulting, or who meet a $5 million annual gross receipts test, can use the non-accrual experience method (NAE). If you qualify, you do not have to accrue amounts that on the basis of your experience will not be collected. However, if interest or a penalty is charged for a failure to make a timely payment for the services, income is reported when the amount is billed. Furthermore, if discounts for early payments are offered, the full amount of the bill must be accrued; the discount for early payment is treated as an adjustment to income in the year payment is made.

Regulation Section 1.448-2T allows four safe harbor NAE methods.

40.4 Tax Reporting Year for Self-Employed

Your taxable year must be the same for both your business and nonbusiness income. If you report your business income on a fiscal year basis, you must also report your nonbusiness income on a fiscal year basis.

Generally, you report the tax consequences of transactions that have occurred during a 12-month period. If the period ends on December 31, it is called a *calendar year*. If it ends on the last day of any month other than December, it is called a *fiscal year*. A reporting period, technically called a *taxable year*, can never be longer than 12 months unless you report on a 52-to-53-week fiscal year basis, details of which can be found in IRS Publication 538. A reporting period may be less than 12 months whenever you start or end your business in the middle of your regular taxable year, or change your taxable year.

To change from a calendar year to fiscal year reporting for self-employment income, you must ask the IRS for permission by filing Form 1128. Support your request with a business reason such as that the use of the fiscal year coincides with your business cycle. To use a fiscal year basis, you must keep your books and records following that fiscal year period.

Fiscal year restrictions. Restrictions on fiscal years for partnerships, personal service corporations, and S corporations are discussed in *11.11* and IRS Publication 538.

40.5 Reporting Business Cash Receipts to the IRS

Cash receipts of more than $10,000 in one business transaction or two or more related transactions must be reported on Form 8300. There are penalties for failure to file.

File Form 8300 with the IRS within 15 days of each cash transaction of over $10,000. Only cash payments are reported; do not report funds received by bank check or wire transfer where cash was not physically transferred. Foreign currency is considered cash. If multiple payments from a single payer (or a payer's agent) are received within a 24-hour period, the payments are aggregated, and the total must be reported if over $10,000.

The reporting requirement applies to individuals, corporations, partnerships, trusts, and estates, except for certain financial institutions that are already required to report cash transactions to the Treasury. Cash received in transactions occurring entirely outside the U.S. does not have to be reported.

The filing requirement applies to cash received for providing goods or services. Thus, an attorney, doctor, or other professional must report cash payments of over $10,000 from a client. Furthermore, cash received for setting up a trust of more than $10,000 for a client must be reported. The IRS has a program to assess penalties against attorneys who have disregarded the cash reporting rules. Courts have held that an attorney may not refuse to report large cash fees by invoking the attorney-client privilege. However, one appeals court held that disclosure of the name of a client who paid cash exceeding $10,000 was not required where disclosure would implicate the client or would reveal confidential communications made by the client to the attorney. The trial court in a closed hearing heard the attorney's claim and ruled against him, but the appeals court ruled in his favor; the circumstances were not disclosed because of their confidential nature.

Caution

Splitting Up a Transaction

The cash reporting requirement may not be avoided by splitting up a single transaction into separate transactions. Thus, a sale of property for $36,000 may not be broken down into four separate sales of $9,000 to avoid reporting. Similarly, an attorney who represents a client in a case must aggregate all cash payments by the client, although payments may be spread over several months. If the total exceeds $10,000, it must be reported.

On an installment sale of business property, you report each payment exceeding $10,000 within 15 days of receipt. If the initial installment is $10,000 or less, you aggregate it plus all payments received within one year of the initial payment. If the total exceeds $10,000, report the total within 15 days after the receipt of the payment that raised the total to over $10,000. In addition, if—after receiving single or aggregated reportable payments—subsequent payments within one year exceed $10,000 individually or in the aggregate, you must report the payments within 15 days.

EXAMPLE

On February 9, 2007, you receive an initial cash payment of $11,000. For the same transaction, you also receive cash of $4,000 on March 16, 2007; $6,000 on April 20, 2007; and $12,000 on June 14, 2007. You report the February payment by February 24, 2007. You also report the payments totaling $22,000 received from March 16, 2007, through June 14, 2007, by June 29, 2007, that is, within 15 days of the date (June 14) that the later payments, all received within a one-year period, exceeded $10,000.

Cash equivalents of $10,000 or less. Cash equivalents such as money orders, traveler's checks, cashier's checks, and bank drafts with a face value of $10,000 or less are treated as cash in sales of consumer durables, collectibles, and travel or entertainment services costing $10,000 or more. Common examples of consumer durables are autos, boats, and jewelry.

For example, if jewelry costing $12,000 is bought with $2,400 cash and traveler's checks of $9,600, the jeweler must file Form 8300 reporting the transaction. If the $2,400 were paid by personal check, the transaction would not have to be reported because personal checks are not treated as cash. Reporting exceptions are also allowed where the cash equivalent constitutes the proceeds of a bank loan, or where it is used as a down payment or promissory note payment under a payment plan used for all retail sales by the seller.

Form 8300. On Form 8300, you must provide the payer's home address and tax identification number to the IRS. You also must provide the payer with a copy of the form or a similar statement by January 31 of the following year.

There is an exception to the reporting requirement for persons who act as agents if they receive cash of over $10,000 from their principal and use it within 15 days in a cash transaction, provided they identify the principal to the payee in the cash transaction.

You must keep a copy of each Form 8300 you file with the IRS for five years from the date of filing.

Reporting Income and Expenses on Schedule C

40.6 Filing Schedule C

In this section are explanations of how a sole proprietor reports income and expenses on Schedule C, a sample of which is on page 626. If you have more than one sole proprietorship, use a separate Schedule C for each business.

Schedule C-EZ. This simple form is designed for persons on the cash basis who do not have a net business loss and have:

- Business expenses of $5,000 or less;
- No inventory at any time during the year;
- Only one sole proprietorship;
- No employees;
- No home office expense deduction;
- No prior year suspended passive activity losses from this business; *and*
- No depreciation to be reported on Form 4562.

Statutory employees. Statutory employees report income and expenses on Schedule C. Thus, expenses may be deducted in full on Schedule C rather than as a miscellaneous itemized deduction *(19.1)*, subject to the 2% adjusted gross income (AGI) floor on Schedule A. Statutory employees are full-time life insurance salespersons, agent or commission drivers distributing certain foods and beverages, pieceworkers, and full-time traveling or city salespersons who solicit on behalf of and transmit to their principals orders from wholesalers and retailers for merchandise for resale or for supplies.

SCHEDULE C (Form 1040)

Department of the Treasury Internal Revenue Service (99)

Profit or Loss From Business

(Sole Proprietorship)

▶ **Partnerships, joint ventures, etc., must file Form 1065 or 1065-B.**

▶ **Attach to Form 1040, 1040NR, or 1041.** ▶ **See Instructions for Schedule C (Form 1040).**

OMB No. 1545-0074

2006

Attachment Sequence No. **09**

Name of proprietor | **Social security number (SSN)**

A Principal business or profession, including product or service (see page C-2 of the instructions) | **B Enter code from pages C-8, 9, & 10** ▶

C Business name. If no separate business name, leave blank. | **D Employer ID number (EIN), if any**

E Business address (including suite or room no.) ▶
City, town or post office, state, and ZIP code

F Accounting method: (1) ☐ Cash (2) ☐ Accrual (3) ☐ Other (specify) ▶

G Did you "materially participate" in the operation of this business during 2006? If "No," see page C-2 for limit on losses ☐ **Yes** ☐ **No**

H If you started or acquired this business during 2006, check here . . . ▶ ☐

Part I Income

1	Gross receipts or sales. **Caution.** If this income was reported to you on Form W-2 and the "Statutory employee" box on that form was checked, see page C-3 and check here . . . ▶ ☐	**1**	
2	Returns and allowances	**2**	
3	Subtract line 2 from line 1	**3**	
4	Cost of goods sold (from line 42 on page 2)	**4**	
5	**Gross profit.** Subtract line 4 from line 3	**5**	
6	Other income, including federal and state gasoline or fuel tax credit or refund (see page C-3)	**6**	
7	**Gross income.** Add lines 5 and 6 . . . ▶	**7**	

Part II Expenses. Enter expenses for business use of your home **only** on line 30.

8	Advertising	**8**		**18**	Office expense	**18**	
9	Car and truck expenses (see page C-4)	**9**		**19**	Pension and profit-sharing plans	**19**	
10	Commissions and fees	**10**		**20**	Rent or lease (see page C-5):		
11	Contract labor (see page C-4)	**11**		**a**	Vehicles, machinery, and equipment	**20a**	
12	Depletion	**12**		**b**	Other business property	**20b**	
13	Depreciation and section 179 expense deduction (not included in Part III) (see page C-4)	**13**		**21**	Repairs and maintenance	**21**	
				22	Supplies (not included in Part III)	**22**	
				23	Taxes and licenses	**23**	
				24	Travel, meals, and entertainment:		
				a	Travel	**24a**	
14	Employee benefit programs (other than on line 19)	**14**		**b**	Deductible meals and entertainment (see page C-5)	**24b**	
15	Insurance (other than health)	**15**		**25**	Utilities	**25**	
16	Interest:			**26**	Wages (less employment credits)	**26**	
a	Mortgage (paid to banks, etc.)	**16a**		**27**	Other expenses (from line 48 on page 2)	**27**	
b	Other	**16b**					
17	Legal and professional services	**17**					

28	**Total expenses** before expenses for business use of home. Add lines 8 through 27 in columns . ▶	**28**	
29	Tentative profit (loss). Subtract line 28 from line 7	**29**	
30	Expenses for business use of your home. Attach **Form 8829**	**30**	
31	**Net profit or (loss).** Subtract line 30 from line 29. • If a profit, enter on **Form 1040, line 12,** and **also** on **Schedule SE, line 2** or **Form 1040NR, line 13** (statutory employees, see page C-6). Estates and trusts, enter on Form 1041, line 3. • If a loss, you **must** go to line 32.	**31**	
32	If you have a loss, check the box that describes your investment in this activity (see page C-6). • If you checked 32a, enter the loss on **Form 1040, line 12,** and **also** on **Schedule SE, line 2** or **Form 1040NR, line 13** (statutory employees, see page C-6). Estates and trusts, enter on Form 1041, line 3. • If you checked 32b, you **must** attach **Form 6198.** Your loss may be limited.	**32a** ☐ All investment is at risk. **32b** ☐ Some investment is not at risk.	

For Paperwork Reduction Act Notice, see page C-7 of the instructions. Cat. No. 11334P **Schedule C (Form 1040) 2006**

The term *full time* refers to an exclusive or principal business activity for a single company or person and not to the time spent on the job. If your principal activity is soliciting orders for one company, but you also solicit incidental orders for another company, you are a full-time salesperson for the primary company. Solicitations of orders are considered incidental to a principal business activity if you devote 20% or less of your time to the solicitation activity. A city or traveling salesperson is presumed to meet the principal business activity test in a calendar year in which he or she devotes 80% or more of working time to soliciting orders for one principal.

IRS regulations give this example: A salesperson's principal activity is getting orders from retail pharmacies for a wholesale drug company called Que Company. He occasionally takes orders for two other companies. He is a statutory employee only for Que Company.

If you are a statutory employee, your company checks Box 13 on Form W-2, identifying you as a statutory employee. Although a statutory employee may treat job expenses as business expenses, the employer withholds FICA (Social Security and Medicare) taxes on wages and commissions.

You must check a box on Line 1 of Schedule C (or C-EZ) to indicate statutory employee status. If you also have self-employment earnings from another business, you must report the self-employment earnings and statutory employee income on separate Schedules C. If both types of income are earned in the same business, allocate the expenses between the two activities on the separate schedules.

Filing Tip

Health Insurance Premiums

As a sole proprietor, you do not deduct health insurance premiums on Schedule C. Instead, you deduct 100% of health insurance costs for yourself, your spouse, and your dependents on Line 29, Form 1040. *See also 12.10* for the way to claim health savings account contributions on Line 25 of Form 1040.

Gross receipts or sales on Schedule C (Line 1). If you do not produce or sell goods, but provide only services, you do not determine cost of goods sold, but report only your receipts from services on Line 1.

Do not report as receipts on Schedule C the following items:

- Gains or losses on the sale of property used in your business or profession. These transactions are reported on Schedule D and Form 4797.
- Dividends from stock held in the ordinary course of your business. These are reported as dividends from stocks that are held for investment.

Caution

Interest on Business Tax Deficiency

Interest on a tax deficiency based on business income reporting is not a deductible business expense; interest on a tax deficiency is always nondeductible personal interest.

Deductions on Schedule C. You can usually deduct most expenses incurred in your business, although there may be limits on the amount or timing of deductions. The basic requirement for deductibility is that expenses must be ordinary and necessary to your business. An ordinary expense is one that is common and accepted in your business; a necessary expense is one that is helpful and appropriate to your business.

Deductible business expenses are claimed in Part II; the descriptive breakdown of items is generally self-explanatory. However, note these points:

Car and truck expenses (Line 9): In the year you place a car in service, you may choose between the IRS mileage allowance and deducting actual expenses, plus depreciation. You must also attach Form 4562 to support a depreciation deduction; *see* Chapter 43.

Depreciation (Line 13): Enter here the amount of your annual depreciation deduction. A complete discussion of depreciation may be found in Chapter 42. You must figure your depreciation deduction on Form 4562 for assets placed in service in 2006, or for cars, computers, or other "listed property," regardless of when the assets were placed in service.

Employee benefit programs including health insurance (Line 14): Enter your cost for the following programs you provide for your employees: accident or health plans; long-term care insurance coverage; wage continuation; self-insured medical reimbursement plans; educational assistance programs; supplemental unemployment benefits; and prepaid legal expenses. Retirement plan contributions, such as to pension and profit-sharing plans, are reported separately on Line 19.

Insurance other than health insurance (Line 15): Insurance policy premiums for the protection of your business, such as accident, burglary, embezzlement, marine risks, plate glass, public liability, workers' compensation, fire, storm, or theft, and indemnity bonds upon employees, are deductible. State unemployment insurance payments are deducted here or as taxes if they are considered taxes under state law.

Premiums paid on an insurance policy on the life of an employee or one financially interested in a business, for the purpose of protecting you from loss in the event of the death of the insured, are not deductible.

Under a "12-month" rule, prepaid premiums can be deducted in the year paid if the coverage term does not extend more than 12 months beyond the first date coverage is received, and also does not extend beyond the taxable year following the year in which the premium is paid.

Filing Tip

Security Trader's Operating Expenses

A security trader may deduct expenses of trading on Schedule C; for further details, *see 30.16.*

Filing Tip

Tax Advice and Tax Preparation Costs

On Line 17 of Schedule C, you deduct the portion of tax preparation costs allocable to preparing Schedule C and related tax forms. Also deduct on Line 17 fees for tax advice related to the business.

Caution

Employment Tax Responsibilities

If you have employees, you must comply with employment tax responsibilities, such as collecting and paying to the government income tax withholding from employee wages. For details, *see* IRS Publication 15, Circular E, Employer's Tax Guide.

Premiums for disability insurance to cover loss of earnings when out ill or injured are nondeductible personal expenses. But you may deduct premiums covering business overhead expenses.

Interest (Line 16): Include interest on business debts, but prepaid interest that applies to future years is not deductible.

Deductible interest on an insurance loan is limited if you borrow against a life insurance policy covering yourself as an employee or the life of any other employee, officer, or other person financially interested in your business. Interest on such a loan is deductible only if the policy covers an officer or 20% owner (no more than five such "key persons" can be counted) and the loan is no more than $50,000 per person. If you own policies covering the same employees (or other persons) in more than one business, the $50,000 limit applies on an aggregate basis to all the policies. The interest deduction limit applies even if a sole proprietor borrows against a policy on his or her own life and uses the proceeds in a business; interest is not deductible to the extent the loan exceeds $50,000.

Pension and profit-sharing plans (Line 19): Keogh plan or SEP contributions made for your employees are entered here; contributions made for your account are entered directly on Form 1040 as an adjustment to income. In addition, you may have to file an information return by the last day of the seventh month following the end of the plan year; *see 41.8.*

Rent on business property (Line 20): Rent paid for the use of lofts, buildings, trucks, and other equipment is deductible. Prepaid rents can be deducted by cash-method taxpayers in the year of payment if the rent term does not extend more than 12 months beyond the first day of the lease and also not beyond the end of the taxable year following the taxable year in which the prepayment is made. However, the economic performance rules prevent accrual-method taxpayers from deducting prepaid rent; economic performance occurs only ratably over the lease term.

Taxes on leased property that you pay to the lessor are deductible as additional rent.

Repairs (Line 21): The cost of repairs and maintenance is deductible provided they do not materially add to the value of the property or appreciably prolong its life. Expenses of replacements that arrest deterioration and appreciably increase the value of the property are capitalized and their cost recovered through depreciation.

Taxes (Line 23): Deduct real estate and personal property taxes on business assets here. Also deduct your share of Social Security and Medicare taxes paid on behalf of employees and payments of federal unemployment tax. Federal highway use tax is deductible. Federal import duties and excise and stamp taxes normally not deductible as itemized deductions are deductible as business taxes if incurred by the business. Taxes on business property, such as an *ad valorem* tax, must be deducted here; they are not to be treated as itemized deductions. However, the IRS holds that you may not deduct state income taxes on business income as a business expense. Its reasoning: Income taxes are personal taxes even when paid on business income. As such, you may deduct state income tax only as an itemized deduction on Schedule A. The Tax Court supports the IRS rule on the grounds that it reflects Congressional intent toward the treatment of state income taxes in figuring taxable income.

For purposes of computing a net operating loss, state income tax on business income is treated as a business deduction.

If you pay or accrue sales tax on the purchase of nondepreciable business property, the sales tax is a deductible business expense. If the property is depreciable, add the sales tax to the cost basis for purposes of computing depreciation deductions.

Travel, meals, and entertainment (Line 24): Travel expenses on overnight business trips while "away from home" *(20.5)* are claimed on Line 24a. Total meals and entertainment expenses, reduced by 50%, are claimed on Line 24b. The net amount after figuring the 50% reduction is reported on Line 24d. The 50% limit for meals and entertainment is increased to 75% for transportation industry workers subject to the Department of Transportation hours of service limits.

Self-employed persons may use the IRS meal allowance rates discussed at *20.4*, instead of claiming actual expenses. *See also 20.26–20.28* for record-keeping requirements for travel and entertainment expenses.

Utilities (Line 25): Deduct utilities such as gas, electric, and telephone expenses incurred in your business. However, if you have a home office *(40.12)*, you may *not* deduct the base rate (including taxes) of the first phone line into your home; *see 19.14.*

Wages (Line 26): You do not deduct wages paid to yourself. You may deduct reasonable wages paid to family members who work for you. If you have an employee who works in your office and also in your home, such as a domestic worker, you deduct that part of the salary allocated to the work in your office. If you claim an empowerment zone or Indian employment tax credit, the wage deduction is reduced by the credit.

Other expenses (Line 27): In Part V of Schedule C, you list deductible expenses not reported in Part II, such as amortizable business start-up costs *(40.11)*, and enter the total on Line 27.

40.7 Deductions for Professionals

The following expenses incurred by self-employed professionals in the course of their work are generally allowed as deductions from income when figuring profit (or loss) from their professional practices on Schedule C:

- Dues to professional societies
- Operating expenses and repairs of car used on professional calls
- Supplies
- Subscriptions to professional journals
- Rent for office space
- Cost of fuel, light, water, and telephone used in the office
- Salaries of assistants
- Malpractice insurance; *see 40.6*
- Cost of books, information services, professional instruments, and equipment with a useful life of one year or less. Professional libraries are depreciable if their value decreases with time. Depreciation rules are discussed at *42.1*.
- Fees paid to a tax preparer for preparing Schedule C and related business forms

Professionals as employees. Professionals who are not in their own practice may not deduct professional expenses on Schedule C. Salaried professionals may deduct professional expenses only as miscellaneous itemized deductions on Schedule A, subject to the 2% adjusted gross income (AGI) floor; *see 19.1*. However, "statutory" employees may use Schedule C; *see 40.6*.

The cost of preparing for a profession. You may not deduct the cost of a professional education; *see 33.16*.

The IRS does not allow a deduction for the cost of a license to practice. However, the Tax Court has allowed attorneys to amortize over their life expectancy bar admission fees paid to state authorities.

Payment of clients' expenses. An attorney may follow a practice of paying his or her clients' expenses in pending cases. The IRS will disallow a deduction claimed for these payments on the grounds that the expenses are those of the client, not the attorney. The courts agree with the IRS position where there is a net fee agreement. In a net fee agreement, expenses first reduce the recovery before the attorney takes a fee. However, where the attorney is paid under a gross fee agreement, an appeals court has reversed a Tax Court decision that disallowed the deduction of the attorney's payment of client expenses. Under a gross fee agreement, the attorney's fee is based on the gross award; the prior payment of expenses does not enter into the fee agreement and so is not reimbursed. Because he would not be reimbursed, an attorney claimed his payment of client expenses was deductible. An appeals court accepted this argument and allowed the deduction. The court allowed the deduction although California law disapproved of the practice of paying client expenses without a right of reimbursement. The court believed that there is no ethical difficulty with the practice and other jurisdictions approve of it. It is necessary for and it is the practice of personal injury firms to pay the costs of many of their clients.

If you are not allowed a current deduction for payment of clients' expenses, you may deduct your advance as a bad debt if the claim is worthless in another year; *see 40.6*.

An attorney might deduct a payment to a client reimbursing the client for a bad investment recommended by the attorney. A court upheld the deduction on the grounds that the reimbursement was required to protect the reputation of an established law practice. However, no deduction is allowed when malpractice insurance reimbursement is available but the attorney fails to make a claim.

Daily business lunches with associates have been held to lack business purpose. Courts agree with the IRS that professionals do not need to have lunch together every day to talk shop. The cost of the meals is therefore not deductible.

Filing Tip

New Deduction for Commercial Buildings

Owners and leaseholders of commercial buildings that are certified to meet certain energy-efficiency standards can qualify for a deduction of up to $1.80 per square foot.

Caution

Doctor's Malpractice Insurance

A self-employed doctor may deduct the premium costs of malpractice insurance. However, a doctor who is not self-employed but employed by someone else, say a hospital, may deduct the premium costs only as a miscellaneous itemized deduction subject to the 2% of adjusted gross income floor. Whether malpractice premiums paid to a physician-owned carrier are deductible depends on how the carrier is organized. If there is a sufficient number of policyholders who are not economically related and none of whom owns a controlling interest in the insuring company, a deduction is allowed provided the premiums are reasonable and are based on sound actuarial principles.

In one case, physicians set up a physician-owned carrier that was required by state insurance authorities to set up a surplus fund. The physicians contributed to the fund and received nontransferable certificates that were redeemable only if they retired, moved out of the state, or died. The IRS and Tax Court held the contributions to the fund were nondeductible capital expenses.

In another case, a professional corporation of anesthesiologists set up a trust to pay malpractice claims, up to specified limits. The IRS and Tax Court disallowed deductions for the trust contributions on the grounds that the PC remained potentially liable. Malpractice claims within the policy limits might exceed trust funds and the PC would be liable for the difference. Since risk of loss was not shifted to the trust, the trust was not a true insurance arrangement.

EXAMPLES

1. A law partnership deducted the meal costs of the staff attorneys who lunched every day at the same restaurant to discuss cases and court assignments. The deductions were disallowed as personal expenses. The Tax Court and an appeals court agreed with the IRS that daily lunches are not necessary. Co-workers generally do not need luncheons to provide social lubrication for business talk, as is true with clients.
2. A physician held luncheon meetings three or four times a week with other physicians. He argued that the purpose of the luncheons was to generate referrals. A court held that such frequent luncheons became a routine personal event not tied to specific business. The cost of the meals was not deductible.
3. A medical professional corporation (PC) deducted the cost of meals taken by its physician-stockholders at a hospital cafeteria. It argued that the doctors discussed patients and met other doctors who made referrals to them. The Tax Court agreed with the IRS that the meal costs were not deductible; doctors ate in the cafeteria for their personal convenience. Furthermore, the meal costs were taxed to the doctors as dividends. The court noted that the PC might have been able to claim a deduction had it treated the meal costs as taxable pay; however, the PC refused to take this position, unsuccessfully gambling that it could claim the costs as business deductions.

40.8 Nondeductible Expense Items

Caution

Penalties and Fines

Penalties or fines paid to a government agency because of a violation of any law are not deductible. You may deduct penalties imposed by a business contract for late performance or nonperformance.

Capital expenditures may not be deducted. Generally, the cost of acquiring an asset or of prolonging its life is a capital expenditure that must be amortized over its expected life. If the useful life of an item is less than a year, its cost, including sales tax on the purchase, is deductible. Otherwise, you generally may recover your cost only through depreciation except to the extent first-year expensing applies; *see 42.3*. As discussed in *40.3*, IRS regulations provide safe harbors, including a "12-month" rule, for expenditures relating to intangible assets or benefits.

EXAMPLE

A new roof is installed on your office building. If the roof increases the life of the building, its cost is a capital expenditure recovered by depreciation deductions. The cost of repairing a leak in the roof is a deductible operating expense. In several decisions, the Tax Court has allowed a deduction for the cost of a major roof renovation or replacement on evidence that the work was not designed to increase the value of the building but to prevent leaks and keep the property in working condition.

Expenses while you are not in business. You are not allowed to deduct business expenses incurred during the time you are not engaged in your business or profession.

EXAMPLE

A lawyer continued to maintain his office while he was employed by the government. During that time he did no private law work. He only kept the office to have it ready at such time as he quit the government job and returned to practice. His costs of keeping up his office while he was working for the government were not deductible.

Bribes and kickbacks. Bribes and kickbacks are not deductible if they are illegal under a federal or a generally enforced state law that subjects the payer to a criminal penalty or provides for the loss of license or privilege to engage in business. A kickback, even if not illegal, is not deductible by a physician or other person who has furnished items or services that are payable under the Medicare or Medicaid programs. A kickback includes payments for referral of a client, patient, or customer.

In one case, the IRS, with support from the Tax Court and a federal appeals court, disallowed a deduction for legal kickbacks paid by a subcontractor. The courts held that the kickbacks were not a "necessary" business expense because the contractor had obtained nearly all of its other contracts without paying kickbacks, including contracts from the same general contractor bribed here.

40.9 How Authors and Artists May Write Off Expenses

Self-employed authors, artists, photographers, and other qualifying creative professionals may write off business expenses as they are paid. The law (Code Section 263A) that requires expenses to be amortized over the period income is received does not apply to freelancers who personally create literary manuscripts, musical or dance scores, paintings, pictures, sculptures, drawings, cartoons, graphic designs, original print editions, photographs, or photographic negatives or transparencies. Furthermore, expenses of a personal service corporation do not have to be amortized if they directly relate to expenses of a qualifying author, artist, or photographer who owns (or whose relatives own) substantially all of the corporation's stock.

Current deductions are *not* allowed for expenses relating to motion picture films, videotapes, printing, photographic plates, or similar items.

An author or artist with expenses exceeding income may be barred by the IRS from claiming a loss under a profit motive test; in that case, the profit-presumption rule discussed at *40.10* may allow a deduction of the loss.

40.10 Deducting Expenses of a Sideline Business or Hobby

There is a one-way tax rule for hobbies: Income from a hobby is taxable as "other income" on Form 1040; expenses are deductible only to the extent you report hobby income, and the deduction is limited on Schedule A by the 2% adjusted gross income (AGI) floor for miscellaneous itemized deductions. Hobby losses are considered nondeductible personal losses. A profitable sale of a hobby collection or activity held long term is taxable as capital gain; losses are not deductible.

Planning Reminder

Hobby or Sideline Business

The question of whether an activity, such as dog breeding or collecting and selling coins and stamps, is a hobby or sideline business arises when losses are incurred. As long as you show a profit, you may deduct the expenses of the activity. But when expenses exceed income and your return is examined, an agent may allow expenses only up to the amount of your income and disallow the remaining expenses that make up your loss. At this point, to claim the loss, you may be able to take advantage of a "profit presumption" discussed in *40.10*, or you may have to prove that you are engaged in the activity to make a profit.

How to deduct hobby expenses. If the profit presumption discussed later does *not* apply and the activity is held *not* to be engaged in for profit, business operating expenses and depreciation are deductible only as miscellaneous itemized deductions and only up to the extent of income from the activity; a deduction for expenses exceeding the income is disallowed.

A special sequence is followed in determining which expenses are deductible from income. Deducted first on Schedule A are amounts allowable without regard to whether the activity is a business engaged in for profit, such as mortgage interest and state and local taxes, as well as casualty losses (after applying the $100 and 10% of AGI casualty floors *(18.12)*). These amounts are deductible in full on the appropriate lines of Schedule A without regard to income from the activity. However, they reduce gross income from the activity for purposes of figuring whether other deductions may be claimed. If after deducting these amounts from gross income there is any income remaining, "business" operating expenses such as wages, utilities, insurance premiums, interest, advertising, repairs, and maintenance may be claimed. Then deduct depreciation and excess casualty losses not allowed in the first step to the extent of remaining income. The "business" expenses, depreciation, and excess casualty losses are allowed only as miscellaneous itemized deductions subject to the 2% AGI floor; *see 19.1*. Thus, even if the expenses offset income from the activity, none of the expenses will be deductible unless your total miscellaneous expenses (including those from the activity) exceed 2% of your adjusted gross income.

Presumption of profit-seeking motive. You are *presumed to be* engaged in an activity for profit if you can show a profit in at least three of the last five years, including the current year. If the activity is horse breeding, training, racing, or showing, the profit presumption applies if you show profits in two of the last seven (including current) years. The presumption does not necessarily mean that losses will automatically be allowed; the IRS may try to rebut the presumption. You would then have to prove a profit motive by showing these types of facts: You spend considerable time in the activity; you keep businesslike records; you relied on expert advice; you expect the assets to appreciate in value; and losses are common in the start-up phase of your type of business.

Election postpones determination of profit presumption. If you have losses in the first few years of an activity and the IRS tries to disallow them as hobby losses, you have this option: You may make an election on Form 5213 to postpone the determination of whether the above profit presumption applies. The postponement is until after the end of the fourth taxable year (sixth year for a horse breeding, training, showing, or racing activity) following the first year of the activity. For example, if you enter a farming activity in 2006, you can elect to postpone the profit motive determination until after the end of 2010. Then, if you have realized profits in at least three of the five years (2006–2010), the profit presumption applies. When you make the election on Form 5213, you agree to waive the statute of limitations for all activity-related items in the taxable years involved. The waiver generally gives the IRS an additional two years after the filing due date for the last year in the presumption period to issue deficiencies related to the activity.

To make the election, you must file Form 5213 within three years of the due date of the return for the year you started the activity. If before the end of this three-year period you receive a deficiency notice from the IRS disallowing a loss from the activity and you have not yet made the election, you can still do so within 60 days of receiving the notice. These election rules apply to individuals, partnerships, and S corporations. An election by a partnership or S corporation is binding on all partners or S corporation shareholders holding interests during the presumption period.

40.11 Deducting Expenses of Looking for a New Business

When you are planning to invest in a business, you may incur preliminary expenses for traveling to look at the property and for legal or accounting advice. Expenses incurred during a general search or preliminary investigation of a business are not deductible, including expenses related to the decision whether or not to enter a transaction. However, when you go beyond a general search and actually go into business, you may elect to deduct or amortize your start-up costs.

Deductible or amortizable start-up costs. You can elect to deduct up to $5,000 of start-up costs on Schedule C in the taxable year in which your self-employed business begins. The $5,000 limit is reduced by the amount of start-up costs exceeding $50,000. Start-up costs over the first-year deduction limit may be amortized over 15 years. Start-up costs incurred before October 23, 2004, are amortizable over a period of not less than 60 months, beginning with the month the business begins (there is no $5,000 upfront deduction allowed). An election to amortize is made on a statement attached to Form 4562; the deduction from Form 4562 is then entered in Part V ("Other Expenses") of Schedule C.

Eligible costs include investigating and setting up the business, such as expenses of surveying potential markets, products, labor supply, and transportation facilities; travel and other expenses incurred in lining up prospective distributors, suppliers, or customers; salaries or fees paid to consultants or attorneys, and fees for similar professional services. The business may be one you acquire from someone else or a new business you create.

Caution

Nonqualifying Costs

You may *not* deduct or amortize the expenses incurred in acquiring or selling securities or partnership interests such as securities registration expenses or underwriters' commissions.

Organizational costs for a partnership or corporation. Costs incident to the creation of a partnership or corporation are also deductible or amortizable under the rules for start-up costs discussed above. For a partnership, qualifying expenses include legal fees for negotiating and preparing a partnership agreement, and management, consulting, or accounting fees in setting up the partnership. No deduction or amortization is allowed for syndication costs of issuing and marketing partnership interests such as brokerage and registration fees, fees of an underwriter, and costs of preparing a prospectus.

For a corporation, qualifying expenses include the cost of organizational meetings, incorporation fees, and accounting and legal fees for drafting corporate documents. Costs of selling stock or securities, such as commissions, do not qualify.

An election to amortize is made on Part VI of Form 4562 for the first year the partnership or corporation is in business. A statement attached to the return must describe the expenses and the amortization period. The election on Form 4562 and the required statement must be filed no later than the return due date, including extensions, for the year in which the business begins.

Nonqualifying expenses. Deductible and amortizable expenses are restricted to expenses incurred in investigating the acquisition or creation of an active business, and setting up such an active business. They do not include taxes or interest. Research and experimental costs are not start-up costs, but are separately deductible or amortizable; see IRS Publication 535 and Code Section 174. For rental activities to qualify as an active business, there must be significant furnishing of services incident to the rentals. For example, the operation of an apartment complex, an office building, or a shopping center would generally be considered an active business.

If you do not elect to deduct or amortize qualifying start-up costs, you treat the expenses as follows:

- Costs connected with the acquisition of capital assets are capitalized and depreciated; *and*
- Costs related to assets with unlimited or indeterminable useful lives are recovered only on the future sale or liquidation of the business.

If the acquisition fails. Where you have gone beyond a general search and have focused on the acquisition of a particular business, but the acquisition falls through, you may deduct the expenses as a capital loss.

EXAMPLES

1. In search of a business, you place newspaper advertisements and travel to investigate various prospective ventures. You pay for audits to evaluate the potential of some of the ventures. You then decide to purchase a specific business and hire a law firm to draft necessary documents. However, you change your mind and later abandon your plan to acquire the business. According to the IRS, you may not deduct the related expenses for advertisements, travel, and audits. These are considered investigatory. You may deduct the expense of hiring the law firm.
2. Domenie left his job to invest in a business. He advertised and was contacted by a party who wished to sell. He agreed to buy, hired an attorney, transferred funds to finance the business, and worked a month with the company manager to familiarize himself with the business. Discovering misrepresentations, he refused to buy the company and deducted over $5,000 for expenses, including travel and legal fees. The IRS disallowed the deduction as incurred in a business search. The Tax Court disagreed. Domenie thought he had found a business and acted as such in transferring funds and drawing legal papers for a takeover.

Job-hunting costs. For deducting the expenses of looking for a new job, *see 19.7.*

Business Use of a Home

40.12 Exclusive and Regular Use of a Home Office

If you operate your business from your home, using a room or other space as an office or area to assemble or prepare items for sale, you may be able to deduct expenses such as utilities, insurance, repairs, and depreciation allocated to your business use of the area. To deduct home office expenses, you must prove that you use the home area *exclusively* and *on a regular basis* either as:

1. ***A place of business to meet or deal with patients, clients, or customers in the normal course of your business (incidental or occasional meetings do not meet this test)****, or*
2. ***Your principal place of business.*** Your home office will qualify as your principal place of business if you spend most of your working time there and most of your business income is attributable to your activities there.

Administrative (record-keeping) activity. A home office meets the principal place of business test (Test 2) if: (1) you use it regularly and exclusively for administrative or management activities of your business and (2) you have no other fixed location where you do a substantial amount of such administrative work. Self-employed persons are the beneficiaries of this administrative/management rule. Employees usually may not take advantage of the rule because of the application of the convenience-of-the-employer test to an employee's use of a home office; *see* the Example at *19.13.* Examples of administrative and management activities include billing customers, clients, or patients; keeping books and records; ordering supplies; setting up appointments; forwarding orders; and writing reports.

According to the IRS, performance of management or administrative activities under the following conditions do not disqualify a home office as a principal place of business:

- You have a company send out your bills from its place of business (*see* Example 1 below).
- You do administrative or management activities at times from a hotel or automobile (*see* Example 2 below).
- You occasionally conduct minimal administrative or management activities at a fixed location outside your home.
- You have suitable space to do administrative or management work outside your home but choose to use your home office for such activities (*see* Example 3 below).

Filing Tip

Using a Home Office for Administrative Tasks

A home office deduction may be claimed if you regularly and exclusively use part of your home as the only place for conducting the administrative or management activities of your business, or if only minimal administrative work is done outside your home. The home area qualifies as your principal place of business even if you spend most of your working time providing services at outside locations.

Caution

Principal Place of Business Test

The tests for deducting office expenses will generally not present problems where the home area is the principal place of business or professional activity. For example, you are a doctor and see most of your patients at an office set aside in your home. A tax dispute may arise where you have a principal place of business elsewhere and use a part of your home for occasional work or administrative paperwork. Occasional use is not sufficient. If your deduction is questioned, you must prove that the area is used regularly and exclusively to meet with customers, clients, or patients or that the home office is the only place where administrative/management activities for the business are conducted. Have evidence that you have actual office facilities. Furnish the room as an office—with a desk, files, and a phone used only for business calls. Also keep a record of work done and business visitors.

Filing Instruction

Form 8829

You must report deductible 2006 home office expenses on Form 8829. Part I is used for showing the space allocated to business use *(40.14)*; Part II for reporting deductible expenses allocated to business use *(40.14)*; Part III for figuring depreciation on the business area *(40.13)*; and Part IV for carryover to 2007 of expenses not allowed in 2006 because of income limitations applied in Part II *(40.15)*. A sample copy of Form 8829 is on page 638.

EXAMPLES

1. A self-employed plumber does all of his repair and installation services outside of his home where he has a small office used to phone customers, order supplies, and keep his books. However, he uses a local bookkeeping service to bill his customers. He has no other fixed location for doing his administrative work. That he uses an outside billing service does not disqualify his home office as a principal place of business.
2. A self-employed sales representative for several products uses a home office to set up appointments and write up orders. When she is out of town, she writes up such orders from a hotel room. The occasional use of a hotel room to write up orders does not disqualify the home office as a principal place of business that otherwise meets the new tests.
3. A self-employed anesthesiologist spends most of his professional time at three local hospitals. One of the hospitals provides him with a small shared office where he could do administrative and management work; however, he does not use this space. He uses his home as an office to: contact patients, surgeons, and hospitals regarding schedules; prepare presentations; keep billing records and patient logs; and read medical journals and books. His use of the home office for administrative activities satisfies the principal place of business test. His choice to use his home office instead of the one provided by one hospital does not disqualify his home office as the principal place of business.

If you work at home and also outside of your home at other locations and you do not meet the administrative/management rule, deductions of home office expenses should be supported by evidence that your activities at home are relatively more important or time consuming than those outside your home.

Exclusive and regular business use of home area required. If you use a room, such as a den, both for business and family purposes, be prepared to show that a specific section of the den is used *exclusively* as office space. For example, a real estate operator was not allowed to deduct the cost of a home office, on evidence that he also used the office area for nonbusiness purposes. A partition or other physical separation of the office area is helpful but not required.

Under the regular basis test, expenses attributable to incidental or occasional trade or business use are not deductible, even if the room is used for no other purpose but business.

Even if you meet these tests, your deduction for allocable office expenses may be substantially limited or barred by a restrictive rule that limits deductions to the income from the office activity. This computation is made on Form 8829 and is illustrated in *40.15*.

Multiple business use of home office. If you use a home office for more than one business, make sure that the home office tests are met for all businesses before you claim deductions. If one business use qualifies and another use does not, the IRS will disallow deductions even for the qualifying use, *see* the following paragraph.

Employee with sideline business. Employees who use a home office for their job and for a sideline business also should be aware of this problem. Most employees are unable to show that their home office is the principal place of their work *(19.13)*. Claiming an unallowable deduction for employee home office use will jeopardize the deduction for sideline business use. This happened to Hamacher, who as a self-employed actor earned $24,600 over a two-year period from an Atlanta theater and a few radio and television commercials. He also earned $18,000 each year as the administrator of an acting school at the theater. For his job as administrator, Hamacher shared an office at the theater with other employees. He had access to this office during nonbusiness hours. He also used one of the six rooms in his apartment for an office. Because of interruptions at the theater, he used the home office to work on the school curriculum and select plays for the theater. In connection with his acting business, he used the home office to receive phone calls, to prepare for auditions, and rehearse for acting roles.

The IRS disallowed his deduction for both self-employment and employee purposes because Hamacher's office use as an employee did not qualify. The Tax Court agreed. A single-office space may be used for different business activities, but all of the uses must qualify for a deduction. Here, Hamacher's use of the home office as an employee did not qualify. He had suitable office space at the theater. He was not expected or required to do work at home. As the employee use of the home office did not qualify, the Tax Court did not have to determine if the sideline business use qualified. Even if it had qualified, no allocation of expenses between the two uses would have been made. By requiring that a home office be used "exclusively" as a principal place of business or place for seeing clients, patients, or customers, the law imposes an all-or-nothing test.

Separate structure. If in your business you use a separate structure not attached to your home, such as a studio adjacent but unattached to your home, the expenses are generally deductible if you satisfy the exclusive use and regular basis tests discussed earlier. A separate structure does not have to qualify as your principal place of business or a place for meeting patients, clients, or customers. However, the income limitation discussed at *40.15* applies. In one case, a taxpayer argued that an office located in a separate building in his backyard was not subject to the exclusive and regular business use tests and the gross income limitation. However, the IRS and Tax Court held that it was. The office building was "appurtenant" to the home and thus part of it, based on these facts: The office building was 12 feet away from the house and within the same fenced-in residential area; it did not have a separate address; it was included in the same title and subject to the same mortgage as the house; and all taxes, utilities, and insurance were paid as a unit for both buildings.

Day-care services. The exclusive-use test does not have to be met for business use of a home to provide day-care services for children and handicapped persons, or persons age 65 or older, provided certain state licensing requirements are met. If part of your home is *regularly* but not exclusively used to provide day-care services, you may deduct an allocable part of your home expenses. You allocate expenses by multiplying the total costs by two fractions: (1) The total square footage in the home that is available for day-care use throughout each business day and regularly so used, divided by the total square footage for the home. (2) The total hours of business operation divided by the total number of hours in the year (8,760 in 2006).

If the area *is* exclusively used for day-care services, only fraction (1) applies.

EXAMPLE

In 2006, Alice Jones operates a day-care center at home from 7 a.m. to 6 p.m., five days a week for 50 weeks, for a total of 2,750 business-use hours during the year. Her family uses the area the rest of the time. Annual home expenses total $10,000 ($5,000 for interest and taxes; $4,000 for electricity, gas, water, trash collection, maintenance, and insurance; and $1,000 for depreciation). The total floor area of the home is 2,000 square feet; 1,500 square feet are used for day-care purposes. Alice multiplies her $10,000 of expenses by 75%, the part of the home used for day-care purposes (1,500 square feet ÷ 2,000 square feet), and also by 31.39%, the percentage of business-use time (2,750 hours ÷ 8,760 hours). Thus, she may deduct $2,354: $10,000 × 75% × 31.39%. The full $2,354 is deductible only if net income generated from the day-care facility is at least that much.

In one case, the Tax Court held that utility rooms, such as a laundry and storage room and garage, may be counted as part of the day-care business area. The IRS had argued that because the children were not allowed in these areas, the space could not be considered as used for business. The Tax Court disagreed. The laundry room was used to wash the children's clothes; the storage room and garage were used to store play items and equipment. Thus, the space was considered as used for child care even though the rooms were off limits to the children.

Storage space and inventory. If your home is the only location of a business selling products, you may deduct expenses allocated to space regularly used for inventory storage, including product samples, if the space is separately identifiable and suitable for storage.

40.13 What Home Office Expenses Are Deductible?

For a home office that qualifies under *40.12*, deductible costs may include real estate taxes, mortgage interest, operating expenses (such as home insurance premiums and utility costs), and depreciation allocated to the area used for business. The deduction figured on Form 8829 may not exceed the net income derived from the business; *see 40.15*.

The deduction from Form 8829 is entered on Line 30 of Schedule C.

Expenses that affect only the business part of your home, such as repairs or painting of the home office only, are entered on Form 8829 as "direct" expenses. Expenses for running the entire home, including mortgage interest, taxes, utilities, and insurance, are deductible as "indirect" expenses to the extent of your business-use percentage; *see 40.14*.

Household expenses and repairs that do not benefit the office space are not deductible. However, a pro rata share of the cost of painting the outside of a house or repairing a roof is deductible. Costs of lawn care and landscaping are not deductible.

Filing Tip

If You Rent Your Home

If you rent rather than own your home, and you meet the home office tests in *40.12*, enter the rent you paid during the year on Column (b) of Line 20 (Other Expenses) of Form 8829.

Table 40-2 Nonresidential Real Property (39 years—Property placed in service after May 12, 1993)

Use the column for the month of taxable year placed in service.

Year	1	2	3	4	5	6	7	8	9	10	11	12
1	2.461%	2.247%	2.033%	1.819%	1.605%	1.391%	1.177%	0.963%	0.749%	0.535%	0.321%	0.107%
2–39	2.564	2.564	2.564	2.564	2.564	2.564	2.564	2.564	2.564	2.564	2.564	2.564
40	0.107	0.321	0.535	0.749	0.963	1.177	1.391	1.605	1.819	2.033	2.247	2.461

Filing Instruction

When To Figure Depreciation on a Home Office Using 27.5 Year Recovery

While depreciation of a home office usually is figured using a 39-year recovery period, a 27.5 year recovery period can be used by an on-site landlord of a building in which at least one dwelling unit is rented out and 80% or more of the gross rental income is rental income from dwelling units within the building. In applying the 80% test, the rental value of the entire landlord's unit is treated as gross rental income and the rental value of the landlord's residential space (but not the home office) is treated as rental income from a dwelling unit.

For example, where a landlord lived in one unit of his eight-unit building and used a room in his unit for a home office, the IRS allowed the home office to be depreciated over 27.5 years as residential rental property.

If you install a security system for all your home's windows and doors, the portion of your monthly maintenance fee that is allocable to the office area is a deductible operating expense. Furthermore, the business portion of your cost for the system is depreciable. Thus, if the office takes up 20% of your home *(40.14)* you may deduct, subject to the income limitation in *40.15*, 20% of the maintenance fee and a depreciation deduction for 20% of the cost.

Figuring depreciation. Even though a home is a residence, depreciation on a home office usually is figured as if it were commercial property using a 39-year recovery period (*see* Table 40-2 above). For depreciation purposes, the cost basis of the house is the lower of the fair market value of the house at the time you started to use a part of it for business or its adjusted basis, exclusive of the land. Only that part of the cost basis allocated to the office is depreciable. Form 8829 has a special section, Part III, for making this computation.

EXAMPLE

In April 2006, you start to use one room in your single family house exclusively and on a regular basis to meet with clients. This room is 10% of the square footage of your home. In 1990, you bought the property for $100,000, of which $90,000 was allocated to the house. The house has a fair market value of $185,000 in April 2006. You compute depreciation on the cost basis of $90,000, which is lower than the value. You multiply $90,000 by 10% (business-use percentage), which gives you $9,000 as the depreciable basis of the business part of the house. As you started business use in the fourth month of 2006, you multiply the depreciable basis of $9,000 by 1.819%. This percentage is listed for the fourth month in the depreciation rate table for 39-year property shown above. Your depreciation deduction is $163.71 (9,000 × 1.819%).

40.14 Allocating Expenses to Business Use

Allocate to home office use qualifying operating expenses *(40.13)* as follows: If the rooms are not equal or approximately equal in size, compare the number of square feet of space used for business with the total number of square feet in the home and then apply the resulting percentage to the total deductible expenses.

If all rooms in your home are approximately the same size, you may base the allocation on a comparison of the number of rooms used as an office to the total number of rooms.

EXAMPLE

A doctor rents a apartment using three rooms for his office and seven rooms for his residence. The rooms are not equal in size. The apartment has 2,000 square feet; the office has 600. He allocates 30% ($^{600}/_{2,000}$) of the following expenses to his office:

	Total	*Office*	*Residence*
Rent	$7,200	$2,160	$5,040
Light	600	180	420
Heat	1,000	300	700
Wages of domestic	2,000	600	1,400
	$10,800	$3,240	$7,560

The $3,240 of office expenses are deductible as indirect interest expenses on Form 8829, subject to the income limitation in *40.15*.

40.15 Business Income May Limit Home Office Deductions

Even if your home business use satisfies the deduction tests in *40.12*, deductions for the business portion *(40.14)* of utilities, maintenance, and insurance costs, as well as depreciation or rent deductions, may not exceed net business income after reducing the tentative profit from Schedule C by allocable mortgage interest, real estate taxes, and casualty deductions. To make sure that deductible expenses do not exceed income, the IRS requires you to use Form 8829. If you do not realize income during the year, no deduction is allowed. For example, you are a full-time writer and use an office in your home. You do not sell any of your work this year or receive any advances or royalties. Therefore, you may not claim a home office deduction for this year. *See also 40.9* on rules for writers and artists.

Part II of Form 8829 limits the deduction of home office expenses to net income derived from office use. You start with the tentative profit from Schedule C. If you sold your home during the year, increase the tentative profit by any net gain (or decrease tentative profit by any net loss) that is allocable to the office area and reported on Schedule D or Form 4797. The following expenses are listed first in Part II of Form 8829 for purposes of applying the income limit: Casualty losses affecting the residence, deductible mortgage interest, and real estate taxes. If there is income remaining after these expenses are subtracted from the Schedule C tentative profit, then home insurance premiums, repair and maintenance expenses for the residence, utility expenses, and rent are claimed against the remaining income. Depreciation is taken into account last, in Part III of Form 8829.

Business expenses not related to the home are deducted on the appropriate lines of Schedule C. For example, a salary paid to a secretary is deducted on Line 26 of Schedule C; the cost of depreciable business equipment used in your home is deducted on Line 13 of Schedule C.

The amount of real estate taxes, mortgage interest, or casualty losses not allocated to home office use may be claimed as itemized deductions on Schedule A.

Planning Reminder

Carryover Allowed

Expenses disallowed because of the income limitation may be carried forward and treated as home office expenses in a later tax year (Part IV, Form 8829). The carryover as well as the expenses of the later year are subject to the income limitation of that year. For example, tentative profit for 2006 on Line 29 of Schedule C is $1,000. Expenses allocated to the home office are $2,000. Only $1,000 of the expenses are deductible; $1,000 is carried over to 2007.

EXAMPLE

Samuel Brown does sideline business consulting from a home office in his single-family house that he uses exclusively for business for all of 2006. His income in 2006 from consulting services is $12,400. He paid $7,600 for a photocopy machine and a computer, and had office telephone expenses of $600 and office supply costs of $800.

In addition, his home costs are:

Mortgage interest	$10,000
Real estate taxes	4,000
Insurance	1,200
Utilities	1,800

His office space took up 20% of the area of his home, and he figured depreciation allocated to business use of $1,200.

On Schedule C he claims first-year expensing *(42.3)* for the copier and the computer, and also deducts the office phone costs and supplies. This gives a tentative profit of $3,400 ($12,400 – $9,000) on Line 29, Schedule C.

In Part I of Form 8829, he lists the total area of the home and the area used for business, showing 20% business use.

In Part II, he enters the home costs listed above. We have taken only the relevant lines of the Form 8829 as an illustration. Samuel Brown's Form 8829 is on page 638.

Form 8829 Line—

8.	Tentative profit from Schedule C, Line 29		$3,400
10b.	Mortgage interest	$10,000	
11b.	Real estate taxes	4,000	
12b.	Total	$14,000	
13 & 14.	Business portion of Line 12		2,800
15.	Remaining tentative profit		600
17b.	Insurance	1,200	
19b.	Utilities	1,800	
21b.	Total	3,000	
22, 24, & 25.	Business portion of Line 21		600
26.	Remaining tentative profit		0

No depreciation is deductible because there is no remaining business income and excess home office expenses may not generate a loss deduction. The depreciation is carried over to 2006. Home office expenses of $3,400 from Lines 14 and 25 are deducted on Line 30, Schedule C.

Form **8829** — Department of the Treasury, Internal Revenue Service (99)

Expenses for Business Use of Your Home

▶ File only with Schedule C (Form 1040). Use a separate Form 8829 for each home you used for business during the year.
▶ See separate instructions.

OMB No. 1545-0074 — **2006** — Attachment Sequence No. **66**

Name(s) of proprietor(s): Samuel Brown — Your social security number: X1X 01 1111

Part I Part of Your Home Used for Business

No.	Description			Line	Amount
1	Area used regularly and exclusively for business, regularly for daycare, or for storage of inventory or product samples (see instructions)			1	500 sq. ft.
2	Total area of home			2	2,500 sq. ft.
3	Divide line 1 by line 2. Enter the result as a percentage			3	20 %
	• **For daycare facilities not used exclusively for business, also complete lines 4–6.**				
	• **All others, skip lines 4–6 and enter the amount from line 3 on line 7.**				
4	Multiply days used for daycare during year by hours used per day	4	hr.		
5	Total hours available for use during the year (365 days × 24 hours) (see instructions)	5	8,760 hr.		
6	Divide line 4 by line 5. Enter the result as a decimal amount	6			
7	Business percentage. For daycare facilities not used exclusively for business, multiply line 6 by line 3 (enter the result as a percentage). All others, enter the amount from line 3 ▶			7	20 %

Part II Figure Your Allowable Deduction

No.	Description	Line	(a) Direct expenses	Line	(b) Indirect expenses	Line	Amount
8	Enter the amount from Schedule C, line 29, **plus** any net gain or (loss) derived from the business use of your home and shown on Schedule D or Form 4797. If more than one place of business, see instructions					8	3,400
	See instructions for columns (a) and (b) before completing lines 9–20.						
9	Casualty losses (see instructions)	9					
10	Deductible mortgage interest (see instructions)	10			10,000		
11	Real estate taxes (see instructions)	11			4,000		
12	Add lines 9, 10, and 11	12			14,000		
13	Multiply line 12, column (b) by line 7			13	2,800		
14	Add line 12, column (a) and line 13					14	2,800
15	Subtract line 14 from line 8. If zero or less, enter -0-					15	600
16	Excess mortgage interest (see instructions)	16					
17	Insurance	17			1,200		
18	Repairs and maintenance	18					
19	Utilities	19			1,800		
20	Other expenses (see instructions)	20					
21	Add lines 16 through 20	21			3,000		
22	Multiply line 21, column (b) by line 7			22	600		
23	Carryover of operating expenses from 2005 Form 8829, line 41			23			
24	Add line 21 in column (a), line 22, and line 23					24	600
25	Allowable operating expenses. Enter the **smaller** of line 15 or line 24					25	600
26	Limit on excess casualty losses and depreciation. Subtract line 25 from line 15					26	- 0 -
27	Excess casualty losses (see instructions)			27			
28	Depreciation of your home from Part III below			28	1,200		
29	Carryover of excess casualty losses and depreciation from 2005 Form 8829, line 42			29			
30	Add lines 27 through 29					30	1,200
31	Allowable excess casualty losses and depreciation. Enter the **smaller** of line 26 or line 30					31	- 0 -
32	Add lines 14, 25, and 31					32	3,400
33	Casualty loss portion, if any, from lines 14 and 31. Carry amount to **Form 4684**, Section B					33	
34	Allowable expenses for business use of your home. Subtract line 33 from line 32. Enter here and on Schedule C, line 30. If your home was used for more than one business, see instructions ▶					34	3,400

Part III Depreciation of Your Home

No.	Description	Line	Amount
35	Enter the **smaller** of your home's adjusted basis or its fair market value (see instructions)	35	238,975
36	Value of land included on line 35	36	50,000
37	Basis of building. Subtract line 36 from line 35	37	188,975
38	Business basis of building. Multiply line 37 by line 7	38	37,795
39	Depreciation percentage (see instructions)	39	3.175 %
40	Depreciation allowable (see instructions). Multiply line 38 by line 39. Enter here and on line 28 above	40	1,200

Part IV Carryover of Unallowed Expenses to 2007

No.	Description	Line	Amount
41	Operating expenses. Subtract line 25 from line 24. If less than zero, enter -0-	41	- 0 -
42	Excess casualty losses and depreciation. Subtract line 31 from line 30. If less than zero, enter -0-	42	1,200

For Paperwork Reduction Act Notice, see page 4 of separate instructions. Cat. No. 13232M Form **8829** (2006)

40.16 Home Office for Sideline Business

You may have an occupation and also run a sideline business from an office in your home. The home office expenses are deductible on Form 8829 if the office is a principal place of operating the sideline business or a place to meet with clients, customers, or patients. *See* the deduction tests at *40.12* and the income limit computation at *40.15*. Managing rental property may qualify as a business.

EXAMPLE

A doctor was employed full time by a hospital. He also owned six rental properties that he personally managed. He sought new tenants, supplied furnishings, and cleaned and prepared the units for tenants. He used one bedroom in his two-bedroom home exclusively as an office to manage the properties. The room was furnished with a desk, bookcase, filing cabinet, calculators, and answering service; furnishings and other materials for preparing rental units for tenants were stored there. According to the Tax Court, the doctor's efforts in managing the rental properties constituted a business; he could deduct expenses allocable to the home office.

Planning Reminder

Substantiating the Sideline Business

In claiming home office expenses of a sideline business, it is important to be ready to prove that you are actually in business; *see 40.10*. In the case cited in the Example in *40.16*, the Tax Court held that the doctor's personal efforts in managing the six units for tenants were sufficiently systematic and continuous to put him in the rental real estate business. In some cases, the rental of even a single piece of real property may be a business if additional services are provided such as cleaning or maid service.

Managing your own securities portfolio. Investors managing their own securities portfolios may find it difficult to convince a court that investment management is a business activity. According to Congressional committee reports, a home office deduction should be denied to an investor who uses a home office to read financial periodicals and reports, clip bond coupons, and perform similar activities. In one case, the Claims Court allowed a deduction to Moller, who spent about 40 hours a week at a home office managing a substantial stock portfolio. The Claims Court held these activities amounted to a business. However, an appeals court reversed the decision. According to the appeals court, the test is whether or not a person is a trader. A trader is in a business; an investor is not. A trader buys and sells frequently to catch daily market swings. An investor buys securities for capital appreciation and income without regard to daily market developments. Therefore, to be a trader, one's activities must be directed to short-term trading, not the long-term holding of investments. Here, Moller was an investor; he was primarily interested in the long-term growth potential of stock. He did not earn his income from the short-term turnovers of stocks. He had no significant trading profits. His interest and dividend income was 98% of his income. *See 30.16* for trader expenses.

40.17 Depreciation of Office in Cooperative Apartment

If your home office meets the tests discussed in *40.12*, you may deduct depreciation on your stock interest in the cooperative. The basis for depreciation may be your share of the cooperative corporation's basis for the building or an amount computed from the price you paid for the stock. The method you use depends on whether you are the first or a later owner of the stock.

You are the first owner. In figuring your depreciation, you start with the cooperative's depreciable basis of the building. You then take your share of depreciation according to the percentage of stock interest you own. The cooperative can provide the details needed for the computation.

If space in the building is rented to commercial tenants who do not have stock interests in the corporation, the total allowable depreciation is reduced by the amount allocated to the space used by the commercial tenants.

You are a later owner of the cooperative's stock. When you buy stock from a prior owner, your depreciable basis is determined by the price of your stock and your share of the co-op's outstanding mortgage, reduced by amounts allocable to land and to commercial space.

Figuring Net Operating Losses for Refund of Prior Taxes

40.18 Net Operating Losses (NOLs)

A loss incurred in your profession or unincorporated business is deducted from other income reported on Form 1040. If the net loss from your business plus certain nonbusiness deductions *(40.19)* exceeds income for your tax year ending in 2006, the excess is a net operating loss (NOL) and may be first carried back two years, and *then* forward 20 years. However, a three-year carryback is allowed for a 2006 NOL attributable to casualty or theft losses, and for a qualified small business NOL attributable to a Presidentially declared disaster. A farming net operating loss may be carried back five years. Similarly, losses in the Gulf Opportunity Zone following Hurricane Katrina, which includes certain expenses incurred before January 1, 2008, have a five-year carryback. *See* the instructions to Form 1045 for further details. A loss carried back to a prior year reduces income of that year and entitles you to a refund. A loss applied to a later year reduces income for that year. You may elect to carry forward your 2006 loss for 20 years, foregoing the carryback; *see 40.22*.

The rules below apply not only to self-employed individuals, farmers, and professionals, but also to individuals whose casualty losses exceed income, stockholders in S corporations, and partners whose partnerships have suffered losses. Each partner claims his or her share of the partnership loss.

Carryover of loss from prior year to 2006. If you had a net operating loss in an earlier year that is being carried forward to 2006, the loss carryover is reported as a minus figure on Line 21 of Form 1040. You must attach a detailed statement showing how you figured the carryover.

Net operating losses from tax years beginning on or before August 5, 1997, expire after 15 carryforward years.

Change in marital status. If you incur a net operating loss while single but are married filing jointly in a carryback or carryforward year, the loss may be used only to offset your own income on the joint return.

If the net operating loss was claimed on a joint return and in the carryback or carryforward year you are not filing jointly with the same spouse, only your allocable share of the original loss may be claimed; *see* IRS Publication 536.

Passive activity limitation. Losses subject to passive activity rules of Chapter 10 are not deductible as net operating losses. However, losses of rental operations coming within the $25,000 allowance discussed at *10.2* may be treated as net operating loss if the loss exceeds passive and other income.

Filing Instruction

Adjustment for Capital Losses

A net nonbusiness capital loss may not be included in a net operating loss. If nonbusiness capital losses exceed nonbusiness capital gains, the excess is an adjustment that reduces your loss on Schedule A of Form 1045. In figuring your loss, you may take into account business capital losses only up to the total of business capital gains plus any nonbusiness capital gains remaining after the adjustment for nonbusiness deductions.

40.19 Your Net Operating Loss

A net operating loss is generally the excess of deductible business expenses over business income. The net operating loss may also include the following losses and deductions:

- Casualty and theft losses, even if the property was used for personal purposes; *see* Chapter 18.
- Expenses of moving to a new job location; *see* Chapter 12.
- Deductible job expenses such as travel expenses, work clothes, costs, and union dues; *see 19.3*.
- Your share of a partnership or S corporation operating loss.
- Loss on the sale of small business investment company (SBIC) stock.
- Loss incurred on Section 1244 stock.

An operating loss may *not* include:

- Net operating loss carryback or carryover from any year.
- Capital losses that exceed capital gain.
- Excess of nonbusiness deductions over nonbusiness income plus nonbusiness net capital gain.
- Deductions for personal exemptions.
- A self-employed person's contribution to a Keogh plan.
- An IRA deduction.

Income from other sources may eliminate or reduce your net operating loss.

EXAMPLE

You are self-employed and incur a business loss of $10,000. Your spouse earns a salary of $10,000. When you file a joint return, your business loss will be eliminated by your spouse's salary. Similarly, if you also had salary from another position, the salary would reduce your business loss.

40.20 Form 1045

You compute your net operating loss deduction on Schedule A of Form 1045. You start with adjusted gross income and personal deductions shown on your tax return. As these figures include items not allowed for net operating loss purposes, you follow the line-by-line steps of Schedule A (Form 1045) to eliminate them. That is, you reduce the loss by the nonallowed items such as deductions for personal exemptions, net capital loss, and nonbusiness deductions exceeding nonbusiness income. The Example at the end of this section illustrates the steps in the schedule.

Adjustment for nonbusiness deductions. Nonbusiness deductions that exceed nonbusiness income may not be included in a net operating loss deduction. Nonbusiness deductions include deductions for IRA and Keogh plans and itemized deductions such as charitable contributions, interest expense, state taxes, and medical expenses. Do not include in this non-allowed group deductible casualty and theft losses, which for net operating loss purposes are treated as business losses. If you do not claim itemized deductions in the year of the loss, you must treat the standard deduction as a nonbusiness deduction.

Nonbusiness income is income that is *not* from a trade or business—such as dividends, interest, and annuity income. The excess of nonbusiness capital gains over nonbusiness capital losses is also treated as part of nonbusiness income that offsets nonbusiness deductions.

EXAMPLE

Income from dividends and interest is $6,000 and nonbusiness deductions are $6,500. The excess deduction of $500 is an adjustment that reduces your loss on Form 1045.

At-risk loss limitations. The loss used to figure your net operating loss deduction is subject to the at-risk rules discussed at *10.17*. If part of your investment is in nonrecourse loans or is otherwise not at risk, you must compute your deductible loss on Form 6198, which you attach to Form 1040. The deductible loss from Form 6198 is reflected in the income and deduction figures you enter on the Form 1045 schedule to compute your net operating loss deduction.

EXAMPLE

You are single and in 2006 you have a salary of $3,000, interest of $1,200, a net business loss of $10,000 (income of $50,000 and expenses of $60,000), itemized Schedule A deductions of $5,900, and a net nonbusiness capital gain of $1,000. After the required addbacks and adjustments are made, your net operating loss is $7,000. The following computation approximates the steps of the computation on Schedule A, Form 1045.

Salary		$3,000
Interest		1,200
Capital gain income		1,000
Business loss		($10,000)
Adjusted gross income		($4,800)
Add: Exemption and itemized deductions		(9,200)
		($14,000)
Adjustments:		
Exemption	$3,300	
Excess nonbusiness deduction*	3,700	7,000
Net operating loss		($7,000)

**The excess nonbusiness expenses deduction was figured as follows:*

Itemized deductions		$5,900
Net capital gain income	$1,000	
Interest income	1,200	2,200
Excess		$3,700

Planning Reminder

Advantage of Relinquishing the Carryback

You will generally make the election to relinquish the carryback if you expect greater tax savings by carrying the loss forward. You might also make the election if you are concerned you might be audited for earlier years if you carry back a loss for a refund. You make the election by attaching a statement to this effect to your return for the year of the loss, which must be filed by the due date plus extensions. The IRS refuses to allow a late election and received court approval for its position.

40.21 How To Carry Back Your Net Operating Loss

As discussed in *40.18*, the carryback period for a 2006 net operating loss (NOL) is generally two years. When you carry back the loss, you recompute your tax for the earlier year on Form 1045. After recomputing the tax on Form 1045, your refund is the difference between the tax originally paid and the lower tax figured after taking the net operating loss deduction. *See* the instructions to Form 1045 and also IRS Publication 536 for details of the recomputation calculation.

Use Form 1045 as a "quick refund" claim. The IRS will usually allow or reject your claim within 90 days from the time you file Form 1045. Do not attach Form 1045 to your 2006 Form 1040. File Form 1045 separately, together with a copy of your return. You may file Form 1045 within

Caution

Domestic Production Activities Deduction and NOLs

The domestic production activities deduction *(40.23)* cannot create or increase an NOL carryback or carryforward (with very limited exceptions).

12 months after the end of your tax year. If the IRS allows the refund, it may still determine later that the refund was excessive and assess additional tax.

Although using Form 1045 is the quickest way to obtain the refund, you may instead file an amended return on Form 1040X to claim the refund. You have three years after the due date (including extensions) of your 2006 tax return to file Form 1040X.

40.22 Election To Carry Forward Losses

Instead of carrying back your 2006 net operating loss under the rules in *40.21*, you may elect to forego the carryback. Instead, you just carry forward losses. The carryforward period remains 20 years under the election. The election is irrevocable.

If you are carrying forward a net operating loss from an earlier year to 2006, report the loss carryover as a minus figure on Line 21 of Form 1040 and attach a statement explaining how the carryover was computed.

Domestic Production Activities Deduction

40.23 Overview of the Domestic Production Activities Deduction

To encourage manufacturing and other production activities in the United States, a special deduction (also referred to as the "manufacturer's deduction"). The deduction is a fixed percentage of income from qualified production activities or adjusted gross income, whichever is lower.

The percentage for 2006 is 3%. This percentage increases to 6% in 2007 and to 9% starting in 2010.

Reporting the deduction. The deduction is figured on Form 8903. It is entered on Line 35 of Form 1040.

40.24 Qualified Production Activities

The law takes a broad view of the type of activities that can qualify for the domestic production activities deduction. These include not only traditional manufacturing, but also:

- Selling, leasing, or licensing items manufactured, produced, grown, or extracted in the U.S.
- Selling, leasing, or licensing films produced in the U.S.
- Construction in the U.S. Construction includes both erection and substantial renovation of residential and commercial buildings.
- Engineering and architectural services relating to a construction project performed in the U.S.
- Software developed in the U.S., regardless of whether it is to be purchased off the shelf or downloaded from the Internet. The term "software" includes video games. But, with some minor exceptions, the term does not include fees for online use of software, fees for customer support, and fees for playing computer games online.

Safe harbor. The deduction is limited to activities in whole or "significant part" in the U.S. Under a safe harbor, a taxpayer is treated as having manufactured, produced, grown, or extracted property in "significant part" within the U.S. if direct labor and overhead costs incurred within the U.S. account for at least 20% of the total cost of the property. But even if you cannot meet this safe harbor, you may rely on the facts and circumstances to demonstrate that a significant part of the activities are in the U.S.

The following activities are specifically *not* qualified production activities:

- Cosmetic activities related to construction, such as painting
- Leasing or licensing to a related party
- The sale of food or beverages prepared at a retail establishment. However, if a business both manufactures food and sells it at a restaurant or take-out store, income and expenses can be allocated so that those related to manufacture and wholesale distribution qualify for the deduction. Thus, in the so-called "Starbucks" situation, roasting and packaging coffee beans could qualify, but selling the beans or brewed coffee at their stores would not.

40.25 Figuring the Deduction

To figure the domestic production activities deduction, start with domestic production gross receipts. If there are gross receipts from domestic and foreign production, you must make an allocation of gross receipts based on any reasonable method to determine qualified production activities income (QPAI).

Reduce this amount by all of the following (based on your books and records if possible, or on any reasonable method):

- The cost of goods sold that is allocable to domestic gross receipts
- Other deductions, expenses, and losses that are directly allocable to domestic gross receipts
- An appropriate share of other deductions, expenses and losses that are not directly allocable to domestic gross receipts or another class of income

Limitations. The deduction for 3% of qualified production activities income cannot exceed adjusted gross income for sole proprietors and owners of partnerships, limited liability companies, or S corporations (a taxable income limitation applies for C corporations).

The deduction also cannot exceed 50% of W-2 wages paid during the year to employees. W-2 wages include both taxable compensation and elective deferrals (e.g., employee contributions to 401(k) plans). It appears that *all* wages of a business, not just those related to domestic production, are taken into account for purposes of the 50%-of-W-2-wages limitation. There are three methods provided for determining W-2 income. One method looks to the lesser of the amounts in Box 1 or Box 5 of Form W-2, while the other methods are more complex; *see* the instructions to Form 8903.

Partnerships and S corporations. The deduction is applied at the owner, not the entity, level. This means that the business must allocate gross receipts, cost of goods sold, and related expenses from qualified production activities to the owners, who then claim the deduction on their personal returns.

A special allocation rule applies for purposes of the 50%-of-W-2-wages limitation. A partner or shareholder is treated as having been allocated W-2 wages from the business entity equal to the lesser of (1) his or her regular allocable share of wages, or (2) two times (double) the deductible percentage of his or her allocable qualified production activities income (QPAI), which for 2006 is 6% of allocable QPAI (2 × 3%).

Caution

Wage Limitation

For S corporations, only wages allocable to a shareholder (and not the shareholder's personal wages) are taken into account for the limitation on the domestic production activities deduction. For both partnerships and S corporations in tax years beginning after May 17, 2006, wages for the W-2 limit include only amounts paid to determine qualified production activity income.

Business Tax Credits

40.26 General Business Credit

The *general business credit* includes the following credits:

- The work opportunity credit on Form 5884;*
- The welfare-to-work credit on Form 8861;*
- The investment credit on Form 3468, consisting of the rehabilitation property credit *(see 31.8)*, the energy credit, and the reforestation credit;
- The alcohol fuels credit on Form 6478;
- The research credit on Form 6765;*
- The low-income housing credit on Form 8586 *(see 31.8)*;
- The enhanced oil recovery credit on Form 8830;
- The disabled access credit on Form 8826;
- The renewable electricity production credit on Form 8835;
- The credit for small employer pension plan startup costs on Form 8881;
- The credit for employer-provided child-care facilities and services on Form 8882;
- The Indian employment credit on Form 8845;*
- The orphan drug credit on Form 8820;
- The credit for employer-paid Social Security and Medicare taxes on certain tips received by employees of food and beverage establishments on Form 8846;
- The credit for contributions to certain community development corporations on Form 8847;
- The new markets credit on Form 8874;
- The railroad track maintenance credit on Form 8900;
- The biodiesel fuels credit on Form 8864;
- The low sulfuride diesel fuel production on Form 8896;
- The qualified marginal well oil and gas production credit;

Planning Reminder

Small Employer Credit for Retirement Plan Startup Costs

Employers with 100 or fewer employees that do not have a qualified retirement plan generally may claim a tax credit on Form 8881 for administrative costs of setting up a pension plan, profit-sharing plan, 401(k) plan, SEP, or SIMPLE plan. *At least one non-highly-compensated employee must be covered.* The maximum credit is $500, 50% of the first $1,000 of startup costs. The credit is allowed for costs incurred in the year in which the plan takes effect and in the next two years.

- The energy efficient home credit on Form 8908;
- The alternative motor vehicle fuel credit on Form 8910; and
- The alternative fuel vehicle refueling property credit on Form 8911.

**Note:* These credits expired at the end of 2005 and had not yet been extended to 2006 when this book went to press. However, an extension is likely. *See* the *e-Supplement* and Form 3800 for 2006.

Planning Reminder

Fuel-Related Credits

For a qualified business use, a refundable credit may be claimed for *gasoline or special fuels.* For example, a credit applies for fuel used in non-highway vehicles (other than motorboats), including generators, compressors, fork-lift trucks, and bulldozers. A credit may also be claimed for aviation fuel used for farming or commercial aviation. Different credit rates apply depending on the type of fuel. You must claim the credit on a timely filed income tax return, including extensions. You compute the credit on Form 4136, which you attach to Form 1040. For further details, *see* IRS Publication 378; farmers should *see* IRS Publication 225.

Computing the general business credit. You compute each credit separately. If you claim only one credit, that credit is considered your *general business credit* for 2006. The credit is subject to a limitation based on tax liability that is figured on the form used to compute that particular credit. You then enter the allowable credit as your general business credit on Form 1040.

If you claim more than one credit, each of the credits is first computed separately and then listed on Form 3800. The combined credit is subject to a limitation based on tax liability. To figure the limit, you must compute tentative alternative minimum tax (AMT) on Form 6251 even if the complete computation on Form 6251 shows that you do not have an actual AMT liability for the year. Your limit for the general business credit on Form 3800 is your regular tax liability (after tax credits other than the general business credit), *plus* actual AMT liability from Form 6251 (if any), *minus* whichever of the following is larger: either (1) tentative AMT from Form 6251 or (2) 25% of your regular income tax liability (after other credits) over $25,000.

Keep separate records of each of the component credits making up the general business credit. The credits are considered to be used up in a specific order; *see* the instructions to Form 3800.

If your full 2006 general business credit may not be claimed because of the tax liability limitation, you may be able to *carry back* the excess one year, starting with the earliest year. Check the Form 3800 instructions for restrictions on carrying back certain credits. After the carryback, any remaining credit may be *carried forward* 20 years until used up. The carrybacks and carryforwards are listed on Form 3800.

For credits arising in tax years beginning before 1998, the carryforward period is 15 years.

If you have business credits from a passive activity under the rules discussed in Chapter 10, you must figure the credits on Form 8582-CR; generally, the credits are limited to the tax liability from passive activities.

Chapter 41

Retirement Plans for Self-Employed

Self-employed persons and partners can take advantage of tax-sheltered Keogh retirement plans or simplified employee pension plans (SEPs).

Advantages flow from: (1) tax deductions allowed for contributions to the plan (a form of forced savings); (2) tax-free accumulations of income earned on assets held by the plan; and (3) in some cases, special averaging for lump-sum benefits paid from a Keogh plan on retirement.

If you have employees, you must consider the cost of covering them when setting up your plan.

If you do not have any other retirement plan and have no more than 100 employees, you may set up a salary-reduction SIMPLE plan.

Planning Reminder

Employees Who Are Self-Employed on the Side

If you are an employee-member of a company retirement plan, you may set up a Keogh plan if you carry on a self-employed enterprise or profession on the side. For example, you are employed by a company that has a qualified 401(k) plan to which you make salary deferrals. At the same time, you have a sideline consulting business. You may set up a Keogh plan based on your consultant earnings. Each plan is independent of the other. As an alternative to a Keogh plan, you may contribute to a simplified employee pension plan (SEP), as discussed in *41.3*, or a SIMPLE IRA, discussed in *41.9*.

Planning Reminder

One-Person 401(k) Plan

If you have no employees other than your spouse, you may want to consider a "one-person" 401(k) plan, which allows you to contribute more than a Keogh plan. For example, for 2006, elective deferrals of up to $15,000 could be made, or $20,000 if age 50 or older during the year. In addition to the deferrals, a contribution of up to 20% of net earnings (reduced by 50% of self-employment tax liability; *see 41.4*) can be made to your account, subject to the overall limit, which for 2006 was $44,000. Starting in 2006, you can add a Roth 401(k) option to your plan, allowing after-tax contributions to produce tax-free returns. The income limitation on eligibility to contribute to a Roth IRA does *not* apply to a Roth 401(k). *See* the *e-Supplement* for the 2007 overall limit.

41.1 Who May Set Up a Keogh Plan?

You may set up a self-employed retirement plan called a *Keogh plan* if you have *net earnings* (gross business or professional income less allowable business deductions) from your sole proprietorship or partnership for which the plan is established. If you are an inactive owner, such as a limited partner, you do not qualify to set up a Keogh plan—unless you receive guaranteed payments for services that are treated as earnings from self-employment.

Set-up deadline. To deduct contributions for a tax year, your Keogh plan must be adopted by the last day of that year (December 31 if you report on a calendar year basis). If it is, contributions can be made up to the due date of your return for that year, plus extensions.

Partnership plans. An individual partner or partners, although self-employed, may not set up a Keogh plan. The plan must be established by the partnership. Partnership deductions for contributions to an individual partner's account are reported on the partner's Schedule K-1 (Form 1065) and deducted by the partner as an adjustment to income on Line 28 of Form 1040.

Including employees in your plan. You must include in your plan all employees who have reached age 21 with at least one year of service. An employee may be required to complete two years of service before participating if your plan provides for full and immediate vesting after no more than two years. You generally are not required to cover seasonal or part-time employees who work less than 1,000 hours during a 12-month period.

A minimum coverage rule requires that a defined benefit plan must include at least 40% of all employees, or 50 employees if that is less.

Your plan may not exclude employees who are over a certain age.

A plan may not discriminate in favor of officers or other highly compensated personnel. Benefits must be for the employees and their beneficiaries, and their plan rights may not be subject to forfeiture. A plan may not allow any of its funds to be diverted for purposes other than pension benefits. Contributions made on your behalf may not exceed the ratio of contributions made on behalf of employees.

41.2 Choosing a Keogh Plan

There are two types of Keogh plans: defined-benefit plans and defined-contribution plans, and different rules apply to each. A defined-benefit plan provides in advance for a specific retirement benefit funded by quarterly contributions based on an IRS formula and actuarial assumptions. A defined-contribution plan does not fix a specific retirement benefit, but rather sets the amount of annual contributions so that the amount of retirement benefits depends on contributions and income earned on those contributions. If contributions are geared to profits, the plan is a profit-sharing plan. A plan that requires fixed contributions regardless of profits is a money-purchase plan. If you have a profit-sharing plan, a 401(k) plan arrangement can be included to allow you (and other participants) to make elective deferral contributions of before-tax compensation to the plan.

A defined-benefit plan may prove costly if you have older employees who also must be provided with proportionate defined benefits. Furthermore, a defined-benefit plan requires you to contribute to their accounts even if you do not have profits. For 2006, the benefit limit was the lesser of (a) 100% of the participant's average compensation for the three consecutive years of highest compensation as an active participant or (b) $175,000. This dollar limit is reduced if benefits begin before age 62 and increased if benefits begin after age 65. The $175,000 limit is subject to cost-of-living increases; *see* the *e-Supplement* for the 2007 limit.

For defined contribution plans, the 2006 limit on annual contributions and other additions (excluding earnings) was the lesser of 100% of compensation or $44,000. For years after 2006, the $44,000 limit may be adjusted for inflation; *see* the *e-Supplement*.

41.3 Choosing a SEP

Under a SEP (simplified employee pension plan), you may contribute to a special type of IRA more than is allowed under the regular IRA rules. Contributions do not have to be made every year. When you do make contributions, they must be based on a written allocation formula and must not discriminate in favor of yourself, other owners with more than a 5% interest, or highly compensated employees. Coverage requirements for employees are at *8.15*. A salary-reduction arrangement for employees may be provided under a qualifying SEP established before 1997 or under a SIMPLE IRA plan established after 1996; *see 8.17*.

The deadline for both setting up and contributing to a SEP is the due date for your return, *including extensions*. Thus, if you have not set up a Keogh plan by the end of the taxable year *(41.1)*, you may still make a deductible retirement contribution for the year by contributing to a SEP by the due date of your return.

41.4 Deductible Keogh or SEP Contributions

The deductible limit for a Keogh plan depends on whether you have a defined-contribution plan (profit-sharing or money-purchase pension plan) or a defined-benefit plan. A SEP is treated as a profit-sharing plan subject to the defined-contribution plan deduction limits explained below.

If you have a defined-benefit plan, you generally may deduct contributions needed to produce the accrued benefits provided for by the plan, including any unfunded current liability. This is a complicated calculation requiring actuarial computations that call for the services of a pension expert.

Deductible contribution for 2006 to a defined-contribution Keogh Plan or a SEP. Before figuring the deductible contribution you can make for 2006 to a profit-sharing Keogh or SEP account, or to a money-purchase pension plan, you must first figure your self-employment tax liability on Schedule SE and the 50% deduction for self-employment tax to be claimed on Line 27 of Form 1040. In computing your deductible plan contribution, your net profit from Line 31 of Schedule C, Line 3 of Schedule C-EZ, or Line 36 of Schedule F is *reduced* by the deduction for 50% of self-employment tax; *see* the Example below.

As a self-employed person, you are *not* allowed to figure the deductible contribution for yourself by applying the contribution rate stated in your plan. The rate must be reduced, as required by law, to reflect the reduction of net earnings by the deductible contribution itself. If your plan rate is a whole number, the reduced percentage is shown in the Rate Table for Self-Employed on Page 649. If the plan rate is fractional, the reduced percentage is figured using the Fractional Rate Worksheet for Self-Employed on page 649.

Figuring your maximum deductible contribution for 2006. After figuring your net earnings and reducing that amount by 50% of your self-employment tax liability, you multiply the balance by the reduced rate from the Rate Table or Fractional Rate Worksheet for Self-Employed on page 649. This is generally your maximum deductible contribution to a profit-sharing Keogh plan or SEP. However, the maximum deductible contribution cannot exceed the annual limit on additions to a defined contribution plan. The annual limit for 2006 is the lesser of (1) $44,000, or (2) $220,000 (maximum compensation that can be taken into account) multiplied by the stated plan contribution rate, not the reduced rate. *See* the Deduction Worksheet for Self-Employed on the next page, which takes you through the steps of figuring your deductible contribution.

If elective deferrals were made during the year, extra steps are required to compute the maximum deductible contribution; *see* Step 9 of the the Deduction Worksheet for Self-Employed shown below.

EXAMPLE

You are a sole proprietor with no employees and have a profit-sharing plan that provides for a 25% contribution rate. Your net self-employment earnings for 2006 from Line 31 of Schedule C are $147,000. On Schedule SE, you figure your self-employment tax liability of $15,618, and you claim a 50% deduction for self-employment taxes of $7,809 ($^1/_2$of $15,618 self-employment tax from Schedule SE) on Line 27 of Form 1040. By completing the Deduction Worksheet for Self-Employed below, you figure your maximum deductible profit-sharing contribution for 2006 is $27,838:

Caution

Deadline for Setting Up Keogh Plan or SEP

You must formally set up a Keogh plan in writing on or before the end of the taxable year in which you want the plan to be effective. For example, if you want to make a contribution for 2006, your plan must be set up on or before December 31, 2006, if you report on a calendar year basis. If a profit-sharing Keogh plan is established by the end of 2006, you have up until the due date for filing your 2006 return, plus the extension, to make a deductible contribution within the limits discussed in this section.

If you miss the deadline for setting up a Keogh plan, you may contribute to a simplified employee pension plan (SEP) set up by the filing deadline for Form 1040, including extensions. *See 41.4*.

Deduction Worksheet for Self-Employed

Step 1 Enter your net profit from line 31, Schedule C (Form 1040); line 3, Schedule C-EZ (Form 1040); line 36, Schedule F (Form 1040); or line 14*, Schedule K-1 (Form 1065) . . . . *General partners should reduce this amount by the same additional expenses subtracted from line 14 to determine the amount on line 1 or 2 of Schedule SE	**147,000**
Step 2 Enter your deduction for self-employment tax from line 27, Form 1040	**7,809**
Step 3 Net earnings from self-employment. Subtract step 2 from step 1	**139,191**
Step 4 Enter your rate from the *Rate Table for Self-Employed* or *Fractional Rate Worksheet for Self-Employed*.	**.20**
Step 5 Multiply step 3 by step 4	**27,838**
Step 6 Multiply $220,000 by your plan contribution rate (not the reduced rate)	**55,000**
Step 7 Enter the **smaller** of step 5 or step 6	**27,838**
Step 8 Contribution dollar limit . . . . • **If you made any elective deferrals, go to step 9.** • **Otherwise, skip steps 9 through 18 and enter the smaller of step 7 or step 8 on step 19.**	$44,000
Step 9 Enter your elective deferrals made during 2006. Do not enter more than $15,000	
Step 10 Subtract step 9 from step 8	
Step 11 Subtract step 9 from step 3	
Step 12 Enter one-half of step 11	
Step 13 Enter the **smallest** of step 7, 10, or 12	
Step 14 Subtract step 13 from step 3	
Step 15 Enter the **smaller** of step 9 or step 14 . . . . • **If you made catch-up contributions, go to step 16.** • **Otherwise, skip steps 16 through 18 and go to step 19.**	
Step 16 Subtract step 15 from step 14	
Step 17 Enter your catch-up contributions, if any. Do not enter more than $5,000	
Step 18 Enter the **smaller** of step 16 or step 17	
Step 19 Add steps 13, 15, and 18. This is your ***maximum deductible contribution***	27,838
Step 20 Enter your total contributions for 2006 . . .	
Step 21 Enter the smaller of step 19 or step 20. This is your ***deduction*** . . . . **Next:** Enter your deduction on line 28, Form 1040.	

Table 41-1 Rate Table for Self-Employed

If plan rate is—	*Self-employed person's reduced rate is—*
1 %	.009901
2	.019608
3	.029126
4	.038462
5	.047619
6	.056604
7	.065421
8	.074074
9	.082569
10	.090909
11	.099099
12	.107143
13	.115044
14	.122807
15	.130435
16	.137931
17	.145299
18	.152542
19	.159664
20	.166667
21	.173554
22	.180328
23	.186992
24	.193548
25*	.200000*

* *The maximum deductible percentage for contributions (other than elective deferrals) to your own profit-sharing Keogh, money-purchase Keogh, or SEP is 20% and for your employees, 25%.*

Fractional Rate Worksheet for Self-Employed

If the plan rate is fractional and thus not listed in the table above, figure your deductible percentage this way:

1. Write the plan rate as a decimal. For example, if the plan rate is 10.5%, write .105 as the decimal amount. ________
2. Add 1 to the decimal rate. For example, if the rate is .105, the result is 1.105. ________
3. Divide Step 1 by Step 2. This gives you the deductible percentage. If the plan rate is .105, the deductible percentage is .0950 (.105 ÷ 1.105). ________

Contributions for your employees. The deduction complications that apply to your own contributions do not apply to contributions for employees. You make contributions for your employees at the rate specified in your plan, based upon their compensation, subject to the annual limit discussed above. Thus, if your plan contribution rate is 25%, you would contribute 25% of your employees' pay to the plan, even though your own contribution rate is reduced to 20% under the Rate Table for Self Employed shown above. You deduct contributions for employees when figuring your net earnings from self-employment on Schedule C or Schedule F before figuring your own deductible contribution using the steps shown in the Example above.

Contributions allowed after age 70½. You may continue to make contributions for yourself to a Keogh plan or SEP as long as you have self-employment income. However, you must begin to receive required minimum distributions from a SEP by April 1 of the year following the year in which you reach age 70½; *see 8.15*. This age 70½ required distribution beginning date also applies to a Keogh plan if you are a more-than-5% owner of the business; *see 7.13*.

Excess contributions. Contributions to a plan exceeding the deduction ceiling may be carried over and deducted in later years subject to the ceiling for those years. However, if contributions exceed the deductible amount, you are generally subject to a 10% penalty on nondeductible contributions that are not returned by the end of your tax year. The penalty is computed on Form 5330, which must be filed with the IRS by the end of the seventh month following the end of the tax year.

41.5 How To Claim the Keogh or SEP Deduction

Contributions made to your Keogh or SEP account as a self-employed person are deducted as an adjustment to gross income on Line 28 of Form 1040. A deduction for a contribution made for your benefit may not be part of a net operating loss.

Contributions for your employees are entered as deductions on Schedule C (or Schedule F) for purposes of computing profit or loss from your business. Trustees' fees not provided for by contributions are deductible in addition to the maximum contribution deduction.

Deductible Keogh plan contributions may generally be made at any time up to the due date of your return, including any extension of time. However, the plan itself must be set up before the close of the taxable year for which the deduction is sought. If you miss the December 31 deadline for setting up a Keogh plan, you have at least up to April 16, 2007, to set up a SEP for 2006. If you have a filing extension, you have until the extended due date to set up a SEP and make your contribution.

Planning Reminder

Small Employer Credit for Retirement Plan Startup Costs

Employers with 100 or fewer employees that do not have a qualified retirement plan generally may claim a tax credit on Form 8881 for administrative costs of setting up a pension plan, profit-sharing plan, 401(k) plan, SEP, or SIMPLE plan. *At least one non-highly-compensated employee must be covered.* The maximum credit is $500, 50% of the first $1,000 of startup costs. The credit is allowed for costs incurred in the year in which the plan takes effect and in the next two years.

41.6 How To Qualify a Keogh Plan or SEP Plan

You may set up a Keogh plan and contribute to it without advance approval. But since advance approval is advisable, you may, in a determination letter, ask the IRS to review your plan. Approval requirements depend on whether you set up your own administered plan or join a master plan administered by a bank, insurance company, mutual fund, or a prototype plan sponsored by a trade or professional association. If you start your own individually designed plan, you pay the IRS a fee and request a determination letter; *see* IRS Publication 560.

If you join a master or prototype plan, the sponsoring organization applies to the IRS for approval of its plan. You should then be given a copy of the approved plan and copies of any subsequent amendments.

To set up a SEP with a bank, broker, or other financial institution, you do not need IRS approval. If you do not maintain any other qualified retirement plan and other tests are met, a model SEP may be adopted using Form 5305-SEP.

41.7 Annual Keogh Plan Return

Partial relief from one burdensome IRS paperwork requirement may be available if your pension or profit-sharing Keogh plan covers only yourself, or you and your spouse, or you and your business partners and the spouses of the partners. Such plans are treated as one-participant plans by the IRS.

If a one-participant Keogh plan meets minimum coverage requirements, does not cover a business that leases employees, and is not part of a controlled group or affiliated service group, an annual information return for the plan may be filed on Form 5500-EZ instead of the more extensive Form 5500.

Under an exception for small one-participant plans, Form 5500-EZ does not have to be filed at all for the plan year beginning in 2006 if the plan does not have an accumulated funding deficiency and had total assets of $100,000 or less at the end of every plan year beginning on or after January 1, 1994. The exception applies if you have two or more one-participant plans that together have not exceeded the $100,000 asset threshold at the end of all post-1993 plan years. All one-participant plans must file a Form 5500-EZ for their final plan year even if the plan assets have always been below $100,000.

The filing deadline for Form 5500-EZ or Form 5500 is the last day of the seventh month after the end of the plan year unless an extension is obtained; *see* the form instructions. Forms 5500

Caution

Prohibited Transactions

As an owner-employee (owning more than 10% of the business), your dealings with the Keogh trust are subject to restrictions. You are generally subject to penalties if you buy property from or sell property to the trust; or charge any fees for services you render to the trust. These restrictions also apply to any member of your immediate family and any corporation in which you own more than half the voting stock, either directly or indirectly.

and 5500-EZ are not filed with the IRS; *see* the form instructions for the mailing address and the electronic filing alternative.

New law for plan years starting after 2006. Under the Pension Protection Act of 2006, one-participant plans will not have to file any return for plan years beginning after 2006 if the total value of the plan assets at the end of the plan year is $250,000 or less.

41.8 How Keogh Plan Distributions Are Taxed

Distributions from a Keogh plan generally may not be received without penalty before age 59$^{1}/_{2}$ unless you are disabled or meet the other exceptions listed at *7.15*. If you are a more-than-5% owner you must begin to receive minimum required distributions by April 1 of the year following the year in which you reach age 70$^{1}/_{2}$; penalties may apply if an insufficient distribution is received *(see 7.13)*.

A lump-sum and other eligible distributions *(7.7)* may be rolled over tax free to another employer plan or IRA. For participants born before January 2, 1936, 10-year averaging may be available; *see 7.2* for details. Pension distributions from a Keogh are taxed under the annuity rules discussed in *7.25*, but for purposes of figuring your cost investment, include only nondeductible voluntary contributions; deductible contributions made on your behalf are not part of your investment.

If you receive amounts in excess of the benefits provided for you under the plan formula and you own more than a 5% interest in the employer, the excess benefit is subject to a 10% penalty. The penalty also applies if you were a more-than-5% owner at any time during the five plan years preceding the plan year that ends within the year of an excess distribution.

Other rules discussed at *7.1* to *7.16* apply to Keogh plans as well as qualified corporate plans.

After the death of a Keogh plan owner, distributions to beneficiaries may be spread over the periods discussed at *7.14* provided the plan covers more than one person. However, an extended payment period may not be available when a one-person Keogh plan owner dies and the beneficiary is not his or her surviving spouse. This is because the plan may not be maintained following the death of the sole owner. The plan assets must be distributed to a non-spouse beneficiary by the end of the calendar year following the year of the owner's death and for any distribution received before 2007, the beneficiary must pay the tax on the full amount at that time. But for distributions made after 2006, non-spouse beneficiaries are permitted to make rollovers to IRAs, enabling them to spread distributions over their life expectancy *(see 7.8)*.

SEP distributions. Distributions from a SEP are subject to the IRA rules at *7.8*.

41.9 SIMPLE IRA Plans

If you do not maintain any other retirement plan and have 100 or fewer employees, you may set up a salary-reduction type of plan for yourself and your employees. The SIMPLE IRA contribution rules are discussed at *8.17*. A SIMPLE plan may also be made as part of a 401(k) plan; *see 7.17*.

Under a SIMPLE IRA for 2006, you may contribute to your own account $10,000 of net earnings plus an additional $2,500 if age 50 or over by the end of the year. You may also make a "matching" contribution of up to 3% of your net earnings.

If you have employees, they generally could make elective salary-reduction contributions for 2006 up to $10,000 (plus $2,500 if age 50 or over). You must make a 3% matching contribution unless you choose to make a 2% non-elective contribution.

See 8.17 and *8.18* for further details on SIMPLE IRAs.

Chapter 42

Claiming Depreciation Deductions

There are three methods of claiming expense deductions for your purchases in 2006 of equipment, fixtures, autos, and trucks used in your business:

- First-year expensing (Section 179 deduction), which allows a deduction of up to $108,000 in 2006.
- Regular depreciation, which allows a prorated deduction over a period of years. Most business equipment is depreciable under MACRS (modified accelerated cost recovery system) over a six-year period. MACRS applies to new and used property. The objective of MACRS is to provide rapid depreciation and to eliminate disputes over useful life, salvage value, and depreciation methods. Useful life and depreciation methods are fixed by law; salvage value is treated as zero. If you do not want to use MACRS accelerated rates, you may elect the straight-line method.

Capital investments in buildings are depreciable using the straight-line method; residential buildings are depreciated over 27.5 years; nonresidential real property placed in service after May 12, 1993, is depreciated over 39 years; *see 42.13*. Specific annual rates for each class of property are provided by IRS tables.

Land is not depreciable.

42.1 What Property May Be Depreciated?

Depreciation deductions may be claimed only for property used in your business or other income-producing activity. If the primary purpose of the property is to produce income but it fails to yield any income, the property may still be depreciated.

Depreciation may not be claimed on property held for personal purposes such as a personal residence or pleasure car. If property, such as a car, is used both for business and pleasure, only the business portion may be depreciated.

EXAMPLES

1. An anesthesiologist suspended his practice indefinitely because of malpractice premium rate increases. He continued to maintain his professional competence by taking courses and keeping up his equipment. The IRS ruled that he could not take depreciation on his equipment. Since he was no longer practicing, the depreciation did not relate to a current trade or business.
2. An electrician spent $1,325 on a trailer to carry his tools and protective clothing. Based on a useful life of three years less salvage value of $25, annual depreciation deductions came to $433. However, the IRS claimed that he could not claim depreciation during the months he was unemployed and the trailer was not used. The Tax Court disagreed. Depreciation is allowed as long as the asset is held for use in a trade or business, even though the asset is idle or its use is temporarily suspended due to business conditions.

Caution

Corrections to Prior Year Returns

If you did not deduct the correct amount of depreciation for a prior year, you may be able to make a correction by filing an amended return. However, if you did not deduct the correct amount of depreciation for two or more consecutive years, you must request an accounting method change; *see* IRS Publication 946 for details. *See also 5.20* for adjustments to basis for unclaimed depreciation taken in prior years.

Nondepreciable assets. Not all assets used in your business or for the production of income may be depreciable. Land is not depreciable, but the cost of landscaping business property may be depreciated if the landscaping is so closely associated with a building that it would have to be destroyed if the building were replaced. Qualifying trees and bushes are depreciable over 15 years.

Property held primarily for sale to customers or property includible in inventory is not depreciable, regardless of its useful life.

Amortization for business intangibles. The cost of goodwill, going concern value, and other intangibles including covenants not to compete, information bases, customer lists, franchises, licenses, and trademarks is amortizable over a 15-year period.

The amortization rule generally applies to property acquired after August 10, 1993. *See 42.18* for further details.

Residences. For depreciation of rented residences, *see 9.5*. For depreciation of a home office, *see 40.13*. For depreciation of a sublet cooperative apartment or one used in business, *see 40.17*.

Farm property. Farmland is not depreciable; farm machinery and buildings are. Livestock acquired for work, breeding, or dairy purposes and not included in inventory may also be depreciated. For a detailed explanation of the highly technical rules for depreciating farm property and livestock, *see* IRS Publication 225, Farmer's Tax Guide.

Dispute over importance of useful life. According to the Tax Court, under ACRS (1981–86) and current MACRS law, useful life is irrelevant for claiming depreciation if you can show that an asset is subject to exhaustion, wear and tear, or obsolescence. Thus, in the case of antique musical instruments played by professional musicians, depreciation is allowable because of wear and tear, even though the instruments have an indeterminable useful life. Two federal appeals courts have agreed, allowing professional violinists to deduct ACRS depreciation for their instruments.

In a case involving exotic cars that were not used for transportation but for exhibition, MACRS depreciation was allowed because the owner showed that they were subject to obsolescence. The autos were purchased solely for exhibition. The three state-of-the-art autos were a 1987 Lotus Pantera costing $63,000, a Lotus Espirit costing $48,000, and a Ferrari Testarossa costing $290,453. Over a four-year period, the owner deducted depreciation of over $298,000 while reporting gross income from exhibition fees of $96,630. The IRS disallowed the depreciation because the cars had no determinable useful life. The Tax Court allowed the depreciation because such cars are subject to obsolescence in the car-show business when new models appear with newer designs and high-tech features. One witness testified this could occur in some cases within a year.

The Tax Court warned that such exotic cars should not be confused with museum pieces. If they had been museum pieces, such as antique cars, no depreciation would have been allowed. In the case of art objects and antiques used as business assets, the useful life requirement remains relevant because such assets are not subject to exhaustion, wear or tear, or obsolescence.

The IRS may continue to dispute and litigate cases in which depreciation is claimed on assets with indeterminable useful lives. For example, in a private ruling, the IRS did not allow a developer to depreciate street improvements that had been turned over to a city. The improvements were an intangible asset that improved the developer's access to its real estate projects, but this asset had an unlimited life. There was no determinable useful life because the city had agreed to maintain and replace the improvements as necessary, and there was no evidence that the city would ever assess the developer for replacement costs.

Basis for depreciation. Generally, the basis of the property on which you figure depreciation is its adjusted basis, which usually is its cost. To determine basis when property is acquired other than by purchase, *see 5.16* through *5.20.*

If you convert property from personal to business use, the basis for depreciation purposes is the lower of its adjusted basis or its fair market value.

EXAMPLE

In 2004, you buy a computer for $2,400 for personal use. In 2006, when it is worth $800, you convert the computer to business use. The basis for depreciation is $800, the fair market value of the computer, which is lower than its adjusted basis of $2,400.

42.2 Claiming Depreciation on Your Tax Return

If you report business or professional self-employed income, use Form 4562 for assets placed in service during 2006 and enter the total deduction on Line 13, Schedule C. For claiming depreciation on "listed property" such as cars, computers, and cellular phones, you use Form 4562, regardless of the year placed in service. Listed property is explained at *42.10.* If your only depreciation deduction is for pre-2006 assets, none of which is listed property, you do not need to use Form 4562; figure the deduction on your own worksheet, and enter it on Line 13, Schedule C.

If you are an employee claiming auto expenses, you must use Form 2106 to claim depreciation on an automobile used for business purposes.

If you claim a home office deduction, you must use Form 8829 to claim depreciation on the portion of your home used for business.

If you report rental income on Schedule E, you must use Form 4562 for claiming depreciation on buildings placed in service in 2006. For buildings placed in service before 2006, enter the depreciation deduction directly on Schedule E. If you have a rental loss on Schedule E, your deduction for depreciation and other expenses may have to be included on Form 8582 to figure net passive activity income or loss; *see* Chapter 10.

42.3 First-Year Expensing Deduction

Law Alert

Increased Expensing Limit Through 2009

The expensing limit for 2006 of $108,000 will be adjusted for inflation in 2007 through 2009. The 2007 limit has not yet been announced. After 2009, the limit is scheduled to fall to $25,000.

For qualifying business equipment purchased and placed in service in 2006, you may elect to deduct up to $108,000 of the cost. For equipment placed in service by a business in an "enterprise zone" and for qualified "New York Liberty Zone property," the deduction may be as high as $143,000. For equipment placed in service in the Gulf Opportunity Zone, the limit for 2006 is $208,000. For an automobile placed in service in 2006, the maximum expensing deduction is $2,960 and for certain SUVs the expensing limit is $25,000; *see 43.4.* The portion of cost not eligible for first-year expensing may be recovered by depreciation under the regular MACRS rules *(42.4–42.5).* The first-year expensing deduction is technically called the "Section 179 deduction."

You may *not* elect first-year expensing for property purchased before 2006, even if 2006 is the first year you use it for business. For example, if you buy a computer in 2004 for personal use and convert it to business use in 2006, no expensing is allowed.

The election is limited to tangible personal property bought in 2006 for business use, such as machinery, office equipment, a computer, car, or truck acquired from nonrelated parties. It also applies to off-the-shelf software; *see 42.19.* The deduction is not allowed for buildings, structural components of buildings, or furniture and refrigerators used in operating apartment buildings. The deduction also is not allowed for property held for the production of income, or equipment previously used for personal purposes, such as an automobile bought for pleasure but later used for business.

Electing first-year expensing. You make the election simply by reporting on Form 4562 the assets for which the election applies. For 2003 through 2009, you are permitted to make an election or revoke an election (or change the amount of an election or the assets for which the election applies) on an amended return. You do not need IRS consent. A revocation, once made, is irrevocable.

Partial business use. If you use the equipment for both business and personal use, business use must exceed 50% in the year the equipment is first placed into service to claim a first-year expensing deduction. The expensing deduction may be claimed for the cost allocated to business use up to the $108,000 limit; the 2006 limit is $2,960 for cars placed in service during 2006 *(43.4)*.

To elect first-year expensing for "listed property" such as a computer or car *(42.10)*, business use in the first year you use it must exceed 50%. If it does, you show the amount eligible for expensing in the section for "Listed Property" on Form 4562 and then transfer the amount to the part of Form 4562 where the expensing election is claimed.

Figuring the deduction. The maximum expensing deduction in 2006 is $108,000 of the cost of qualifying property and $2,960 for a car *(43.4)*. For business use of less than 100% (but more than 50%), the expensing deduction is limited to the business portion of the cost. As discussed below, the $108,000 limit may have to be reduced because your taxable income is lower than $108,000, eligible purchases exceed $430,000, or you are married filing separately.

If you qualify for the full $108,000 limit, you do not have to claim the entire amount. If in 2006 you place in service more than one item of property, you may allocate the $108,000 deduction between the items. If you placed in service only one item of qualifying property that cost less than $108,000, your deduction is limited to that cost.

If you acquire property in a trade-in, the cost eligible for expensing is limited to the cash you paid. You may not include the adjusted basis of the property traded in, although your basis for the new property includes that amount.

Effect on regular depreciation. If the cost basis of the property exceeds the first-year expensing limit, you compute depreciation on the cost of the property less the amount of the first-year deduction.

EXAMPLE

In 2006, you placed in service a $99,000 machine and $20,000 of office furniture. You elect to deduct as a first-year expense $99,000 for the machine and $9,000 of the furniture, a total of $108,000, the maximum first-year deduction. The $99,000 deduction has completely recovered the cost of the machine. The cost of the furniture is reduced by $9,000, giving a depreciable basis of $11,000 ($20,000 – $9,000).

$108,000 limit reduced if taxable income is lower. Your expensing deduction may not exceed net income from all your active businesses; *see* the Caution on this page.

$108,000 limit reduced if qualifying purchases exceed $430,000. If the total cost of qualifying property placed in service during 2006 is over $430,000, the $108,000 expensing limit is reduced dollar for dollar by the cost of qualifying property exceeding $430,000. For example, if you place in service machinery costing $436,000, the $108,000 limit is reduced by $6,000. The reduced limit of $102,000 is shown on Form 4562 on the line labeled "Dollar limitation for tax year." If the total cost is $538,000 or more, no first-year expensing deduction is allowed. Special rules apply to property in an enterprise zone or the New York Liberty Zone. The $430,000 phaseout threshold may be adjusted for inflation in 2007.

$108,000 limit reduced if married filing separately. If you and your spouse file separate returns, the expensing limit for both of you is $108,000. Unless you agree to a different allocation, you are each allowed only a $54,000 expensing limit. The $430,000 cost threshold also applies to both of you as a unit. For example, if you place in service qualifying property costing $210,000 and your spouse places $225,000 of property in service, the total cost of $435,000 reduces the $108,000 limit by $5,000 to $103,000. The reduced limit for each of you on separate returns is $51,500.

Caution

Losses and Low Income May Limit Deduction

The expensing deduction may not exceed the net taxable income from all businesses that you actively conduct. Net income from active businesses is figured without regard to expensing, the deduction for 50% of self-employment liability, or any net operating loss carryback or carryforward. You may include wage or salary income as active business income and if you are married filing jointly, also include your spouse's net taxable income.

If you have an overall net loss from all actively conducted businesses, you may not claim an expensing deduction for 2006. If net income is less than the cost of qualifying assets, expensing is limited to the income. However, the cost over the income limit is carried forward to 2007 on Form 4562 provided you complete the expensing section of Form 4562 for 2006. You do not get a carryover unless the deduction is claimed on the return for the first year the property is placed in service.

Planning Reminder

Higher Phaseout Threshold for GO Zone Property

For Gulf Opportunity Zone property, the $430,000 phaseout threshold is increased by $600,000, to $1,030,000 in 2006.

Partners and S corporation stockholders. For property bought by a partnership or an S corporation, the $108,000 limit and taxable income limit applies to the business, as well as the owners as individual taxpayers. The partnership or S corporation determines its expensing deduction subject to the limits and allocates the deduction, if any, among the partners or shareholders. The allocated deduction may not exceed the net taxable income of the partnership or S corporation from actively conducted businesses.

An individual partner's expensing deduction may not exceed $108,000, regardless of how many partnership interests he or she has. However, the partner must reduce the basis of each partnership interest by the full allocable share of each partnership's expensing deduction, even if that amount is not deductible because of the $108,000 limit.

Disqualified acquisitions from related parties. Property does not qualify for the expense election if:

1. It is acquired from a spouse, ancestor, or lineal descendant, or from non–family-related parties subject to the loss disallowance rule, discussed in *5.6*. For purposes of the expensing election, a corporation is controlled by you and thus subject to the loss disallowance rule discussed in *5.6* if 50% or more of the stock is owned by you, your spouse, your ancestors, or your descendants.
2. The property is acquired by a member of the same controlled group (using a 50% control test).
3. The basis of the property is determined in whole or in part (a) by reference to the adjusted basis of the property of the person from whom you acquired it or (b) under the stepped-up basis rules for inherited property.

Planning Reminder

Year-End Purchases

Equipment placed in service on the last day of the 2006 taxable year may qualify for the entire $108,000 first-year expensing deduction. You do not have to prorate the $108,000 limit for the amount of time you held the property.

Recapture of expensing deduction. Recapture of the first-year expensing deduction may occur on a disposition of the asset or if business use falls to 50% or less. If business use falls to 50% or less after the year the property is placed in service but before the end of the depreciable recovery period *(42.4, 42.10)*, you must "recapture" the benefit from the first-year expensing deduction. The amount recaptured is the excess of the expensing deduction over the amount of depreciation that would have been claimed (through the year of recapture) without expensing; *see 42.10*. Recaptured amounts are reported as ordinary income on Form 4797.

When you sell or dispose of the property, the first-year expensing deduction is treated as depreciation for purposes of the recapture rules *(44.3)* that treat gain as ordinary income to the extent of depreciation claimed.

42.4 MACRS Recovery Periods

Depreciable assets other than buildings fall within a three-, five-, seven-, 10-, 15-, or 20-year recovery period under the general depreciation system (GDS).

Straight-line recovery for buildings is claimed over a period of 27.5 years for residential rental property or 39 years for nonresidential real property, as discussed at *42.13*.

Note: The actual write-off period of depreciation for an asset is one year longer than the class life because of the convention rules explained in *42.5-42.7*.

Planning Reminder

Recovery Periods

The depreciation recovery periods for different types of assets are generally fixed by law according to the rules on this page.

Three-year property. This class includes property with a class life of four years or less, other than cars and light-duty trucks, which are in the five-year class.

This class includes: special handling devices for the manufacture of food and beverages; special tools and devices for the manufacture of rubber products; special tools for the manufacture of finished plastic products, fabricated metal products, or motor vehicles; and breeding hogs. By law, racehorses more than two years old when placed in service and other horses more than 12 years old when placed in service are also in the three-year class.

Five-year property. This class includes property with a class life of more than four years and less than 10 years such as computers *(42.10)*, typewriters, copiers, duplicating equipment, heavy general-purpose trucks, trailers, cargo containers, and trailer-mounted containers. Also included by law in the five-year class are cars, light-duty trucks (actual unloaded weight less than 13,000 pounds), taxis, buses, computer-based telephone central office switching equipment, computer-related peripheral equipment, semiconductor manufacturing equipment, and property used in research and experimentation. It also includes qualified New York Liberty Zone leasehold improvements to a nonresidential building located in the New York Liberty Zone (in southern Manhattan) placed in service after September 10, 2001, and before January 1, 2007; *see* the *e-Supplement* for an expected extension beyond 2006.

These leasehold improvements eligible for a five-year recovery period must be depreciated using the straight-line method.

Seven-year property. This class includes any property with a class life of 10 years or more but less than 16 years. This is also a catch-all category for assets with no class life that have not been assigned by law to another class. Included in the seven-year class are: office furniture and fixtures, such as desks, safes, and files; cellular phones; fax machines; refrigerators; dishwashers; and machines used to produce jewelry, musical instruments, toys, and sporting goods.

Ten-year property. This includes property with a class life of 16 years or more and less than 20 years, such as vessels, barges, tugs, and water transportation equipment, and assets used in petroleum refining or in the manufacture of tobacco products and certain food products. The 10-year class also includes single-purpose agricultural and horticultural structures, and trees or vines bearing fruit or nuts.

Fifteen-year property. This includes land improvements such as fences, sidewalks, docks, shrubbery, roads, and bridges. It also includes other property with a class life of 20 years or more but less than 25 years, such as municipal sewage plants and telephone distribution plants. Gas station convenience stores are in the 15-year class if the property is no more than 1,400 square feet, or at least 50% of the floor space is devoted to selling petroleum products, or at least 50% of revenues are from petroleum sales. The owner of the gas station property does not have to be the operator of businesses on the property.

Twenty-year property. This class includes property with a class life of 25 years or more, such as farm buildings and municipal sewers, except that residential and nonresidential real estate is excluded; *see 42.13*.

42.5 MACRS Rates

The MACRS rate under the general depreciation system depends on the recovery period *(42.4)* for the property and whether the half-year or mid-quarter convention applies. The 200% declining balance rate applies to three-year property, five-year property, and seven-year property. *See 42.8* for the 150% declining balance rate election. These rates are adjusted for the convention rules explained below. When the 200% declining balance rate provides a lower annual deduction than the straight-line rate, the 200% declining balance rate is replaced by the straight-line rate. The rates in the tables at the end of this section incorporate the applicable convention and the change from the 200% declining balance rate to a straight-line recovery. *See 42.9* for MACRS straight-line rates.

Conventions. Under the half-year convention, all property acquired during the year, regardless of when acquired during the year, is treated as acquired in the middle of the year. As a result, only one-half of the full first-year depreciation is deductible and in the year after the last class life year, the balance of the depreciation is written off. Furthermore, in the year property is sold, only half of the full depreciation for that year is deductible; *see 42.6*.

The half-year convention applies unless the total cost bases of depreciable assets placed in service during the last three months of the taxable year exceed 40% of the total bases of all property placed in service during the entire year. If this 40% test applies, you must use a mid-quarter convention to figure your annual depreciation deduction, as explained at *42.7*.

Buildings are depreciated using a mid-month convention; *see 42.13*.

Depreciation tables. The following table provides year-by-year rates for property in the three, five-, and seven-year classes. The rates incorporate the adjustment for the half-year or mid-quarter convention and the switch from the 200% declining balance rate to the straight-line method. Use the rate shown in the table under the convention for your asset. The rate is applied to original basis, minus any first-year expensing deduction *(42.3)* and bonus depreciation you claimed for eligible property placed in service before 2006. After applying the rate from the table to the basis, you claim the deduction on Form 4562, Part III, Section B, labeled "General Depreciation System" (GDS).

You use the tables for the entire recovery period unless you claim a deductible casualty loss that reduces your basis in the property. For the year of the casualty loss and later years, depreciation must be based on the adjusted basis of the property at the end of the year. The tables may no longer be used; *see* IRS Publication 946 for further details.

1040 *Filing Instruction*

Basis Reduction for Bonus Depreciation

If you were eligible for 30% first-year bonus depreciation for property placed in service after September 10, 2001, and before May 6, 2003, or eligible for 50% bonus depreciation (30% if so elected) for property placed in service after May 5, 2003, and before 2005, or claimed 50% bonus depreciation on Gulf Opportunity Zone property placed in service after August 26, 2005, and before January 1, 2008 (January 1, 2009, for nonresidential real property and residential rental property), you must reduce basis for MACRS purposes by the applicable deduction (30% or 50% of adjusted basis) unless you elected on your tax return to "opt out" of bonus depreciation for that class of property.

Table 42-1 MACRS Depreciation Rates

Year	Half-Year Convention	Mid-Quarter Convention 1st (Quarter)	2nd (Quarter)	3rd (Quarter)	4th (Quarter)
		3-Year Property			
1	33.33%	58.33%	41.67%	25.00%	8.33%
2	44.45	27.78	38.89	50.00	61.11
3	14.81	12.35	14.14	16.67	20.37
4	7.41	1.54	5.30	8.33	10.19
		5-Year Property			
1	20.00%	35.00%	25.00%	15.00%	5.00%
2	32.00	26.00	30.00	34.00	38.00
3	19.20	15.60	18.00	20.40	22.80
4	11.52	11.01	11.37	12.24	13.68
5	11.52	11.01	11.37	11.30	10.94
6	5.76	1.38	4.26	7.06	9.58
		7-Year Property			
1	14.29%	25.00%	17.85%	10.71%	3.57%
2	24.49	21.43	23.47	25.51	27.55
3	17.49	15.31	16.76	18.22	19.68
4	12.49	10.93	11.97	13.02	14.06
5	8.93	8.75	8.87	9.30	10.04
6	8.92	8.74	8.87	8.85	8.73
7	8.93	8.75	8.87	8.86	8.73
8	4.46	1.09	3.33	5.53	7.64

EXAMPLE

During June 2006, you place in business service a machine costing $20,000. It is your only acquisition in 2006. (Assume you do not elect to expense the cost. The machine is five-year property and is subject to the half-year convention. The depreciation rate for the first year is 20% (*see* the table above for five-year property). Your 2006 depreciation deduction is $4,000 ($20,000 × 20%). If you hold the machine for the entire six-year recovery period, your total deduction for all years will equal your $20,000 cost.

Summary of Deductions

Year	*Deduction*
1 (2006)	$4,000
2 (2007)	6,400
3 (2008)	3,840
4 (2009)	2,304
5 (2010)	2,304
6 (2011)	1,152
Total	$20,000

42.6 Half-Year Convention for MACRS

The half-year convention treats all business equipment placed in service during a tax year as placed in service in the midpoint of that tax year. The same rule applies in the year in which the property is disposed of. The effect of this rule is as follows: A half-year of depreciation is allowed in the first year property is placed in service, regardless of when the property is placed in service during the tax year. For each of the remaining years of the recovery period, a full year of depreciation is claimed. If you hold the property for the entire recovery period, a half-year of depreciation is claimed for the year following the end of the recovery period. If you dispose of the property before the end of the recovery period, a half-year of depreciation is allowable for the year of disposition.

See the Table of MACRS Depreciation Rates in *42.5* for year-by-year rates under the half-year convention. Apply the rate from the table to the original basis, minus any first-year expensing *(42.3)* deduction and bonus depreciation claimed. The Example in *42.5* shows the year-by-year deduction computation for five-year property under the half-year convention.

If you dispose of property before the end of its recovery period shown in *42.5*, your deduction for the year of disposition is one-half of the deduction that would be allowed for the full year using the rate shown in the table. For example, if you sell the machine in the Example in *42.5* in year three, the deduction is $1,920 ($^1/_2$ of $3,840).

Planning Reminder

Half-Year Convention

The half-year convention applies unless the total cost basis of depreciable assets placed in service during the last three months of the year exceeds 40% of the total basis of all property placed in service during the year.

Under the half-year convention, all assets placed in service during the year are treated as placed in service at the midpoint of the year.

42.7 Last Quarter Placements—Mid-Quarter Convention

A mid-quarter convention generally applies if the total cost basis of business equipment placed in service during the last three months of the tax year exceeds 40% of the total basis of all the property placed in service during the year. In applying the 40% rule, you do not count residential rental property, nonresidential realty, and assets that were placed in service and disposed of during the same year.

Under the mid-quarter convention, the first-year depreciation allowance for all property (other than nonresidential real property and residential rental property) placed in service during the year is based on the number of quarters that the asset was in service. Property placed in service at any time during a quarter is treated as having been placed in service in the middle of the quarter. The mid-quarter convention also applies to sales and disposals of property. The disposal is treated as occurring in the midpoint of the quarter.

EXAMPLE

During August 2006, you place in service office furniture costing $1,000, and in October, a computer costing $5,000. You are on the calendar year. The total basis of all property placed in service in 2006 is $6,000. As the $5,000 basis of the computer placed in service in the last quarter exceeds 40% of the total basis of all property placed in service during 2006, you must use the mid-quarter convention for the furniture and the computer. The office furniture, which is seven-year property, and the computer, which is five-year property, are depreciated using MACRS and a mid-quarter convention.

You first multiply the $1,000 basis of the furniture by 10.71%—the seven-year property mid-quarter convention rate for the third quarter (*see* the table in *42.5*). The depreciation deduction is $107. You then multiply the $5,000 basis of the computer by 5%—the five-year property mid-quarter convention rate for the fourth quarter (*see* the table in *42.5*). The deduction is $250. Total depreciation is $357.

If you dispose of property before the end of its recovery period shown in *42.5*, your deduction for the year is figured by multiplying a full year of depreciation by the percentage listed in the following chart for the quarter in which you disposed of the property.

Quarter	*Percentage*
First	12.5%
Second	37.5%
Third	62.5%
Fourth	87.5%

EXAMPLE

On November 1, 2003, you placed in service a machine costing $10,000 with a five-year recovery period. You used the mid-quarter convention because it was the only item placed in service during the year. In May 2006, you sell the machine.

To determine depreciation for 2006, first figure the deduction for the full year (*see* the chart in *42.5*). This is $1,368 (13.68% (rate for fourth year, fourth quarter) of $10,000). Since May, the month of disposition, is in the second quarter of the year, you multiply $1,368 by 37.5% to figure your depreciation deduction for 2006 of $513.

42.8 150% Rate Election

Instead of using the 200% declining balance rate for property in the three-, five-, seven-, and 10-year classes, you may elect a 150% declining balance rate. You may prefer the 150% rate when you are subject to the alternative minimum tax (AMT). For AMT purposes, you must use the 150% rate and adjust your taxable income if the 200% rate was used for regular tax purposes; *see 23.2.* If for regular tax purposes you elect to apply the 150% rate, use the same recovery period *(see 42.4)* you would have used if you had claimed the 200% declining balance rate. Thus, the recovery period is five years for cars and computers and seven years for office furniture and fixtures. If the half-year convention applies, the first-year rate for the five-year class is 15%, and 10.71% for the seven-year class; *see* the table below. Apply the rate from the table to your original basis, minus any first-year expensing deduction and bonus depreciation claimed. If you are subject to the mid-quarter convention, *see* IRS Publication 946 for the tables showing mid-quarter convention rates.

The election to use the 150% rate must be made for all property within a given class placed in service in the same year. The election is irrevocable.

For property placed in service before 1999, the 150% rate is applied over the ADS *(42.9)* recovery periods, which in some cases are different from the GDS recovery periods.

Table 42-2 Half-Year Convention—150% Rate

	Recovery Period	
Year—	*5-Year—*	*7-Year—*
1	15.00%	10.71%
2	25.50	19.13
3	17.85	15.03
4	16.66	12.25
5	16.66	12.25
6	8.33	12.25
7		12.25
8		6.13

Filing Tip

Should You Elect Straight-Line Recovery?

Accelerated rates of MACRS merely give you an opportunity to advance the time of taking your deduction. This may be a decided advantage where the higher deductions in the first few years will provide you with cash for working capital or for investments in other income-producing sources. That is, by accelerating the deductions, you defer the payment of taxes that would be due if you claimed smaller depreciation deductions, using more conservative straight-line rates. The tax deferral lasts until the rapid method provides lower depreciation deductions than would the more conservative method. You are generally more likely to benefit from accelerated MACRS in an ongoing business.

If you are starting a new business in which you expect losses or low income at the start, accelerated MACRS may waste depreciation deductions that could be used in later years when your income increases. Therefore, before deciding to use accelerated MACRS rates, consider your income prospects.

42.9 Straight-Line Depreciation

You may not want an accelerated rate and may prefer to write off depreciation at an even pace. There are two straight-line methods. You may make an irrevocable election to use the straight-line method over the regular MACRS recovery period *(42.4)* under the general depreciation system (GDS). Alternatively, you may elect straight-line recovery over the designated recovery period for the class life under the alternative depreciation system (ADS). For some assets, such as cars, the GDS and ADS recovery periods are the same (five years for a car). In most cases, the ADS recovery period is longer than the GDS recovery period. For example, the recovery period for office furniture and fixtures is seven years under GDS and 10 years under ADS; for New York Liberty Zone leasehold improvement property, it is five years under GDS and nine years under ADS.

Half-year and quarter-year conventions apply to both straight-line methods; *see 42.6* and *42.7.* A mid-month convention applies under the straight-line rule for buildings; *see 42.13.*

Straight-line over regular recovery period (GDS). You make this election on Form 4562, Part III, Section B, labeled "General Depreciation System" (GDS). To elect this method for one asset, you must also use it for all other assets in the same class that are placed in service during the year. The straight-line election is irrevocable.

Straight-line under the alternative depreciation system (ADS). Under the alternative depreciation system (ADS), the straight-line recovery period is generally the same as the "class life" of the asset as determined by the IRS; the ADS recovery periods are shown in IRS Publication 946. The ADS recovery period for cars, light trucks, and computers is five years, the same as under the GDS. For business office furniture and fixtures, the ADS straight-line recovery period is 10 years. The ADS recovery period for personal property with no class life is 12 years. For nonresidential real and residential rental property, you may elect ADS straight-line recovery over 40 years. *See* IRS Publication 946 for other ADS class lives.

Except for real estate, the ADS election applies to all property within the same class placed in service during the taxable year. For real estate, the election to use the alternative depreciation method may be made on a property-by-property basis. The election is irrevocable. The deduction is claimed on Form 4562, Part III, Section C, labeled "Alternative Depreciation System" (ADS).

Straight-line rate table. The table below shows straight-line rates for five-year, seven-year, and 10-year property under the half-year convention. As discussed earlier, the recovery period depends on whether the GDS or ADS straight-line method is used. If you are subject to the mid-quarter convention *(42.7)*, *see* IRS Publication 946 for tables showing the applicable rates.

Table 42-3 Half-Year Convention—Straight-Line Rate

	Recovery Period		
Year—	*5-Year—*	*7-Year—*	*10-Year—*
1	10.00%	7.14%	5.00%
2	20.00	14.29	10.00
3	20.00	14.29	10.00
4	20.00	14.28	10.00
5	20.00	14.29	10.00
6	10.00	14.28	10.00
7		14.29	10.00
8		7.14	10.00
9			10.00
10			10.00
11			5.00

AMT depreciation. There is no AMT adjustment for depreciation if for regular tax purposes straight-line depreciation is claimed on tangible personal property placed in service after 1998. Similarly, for real estate placed in service after 1998, the straight-line depreciation deduction claimed for regular tax purposes does not have to be refigured for AMT. If for regular tax purposes straight-line depreciation is claimed for tangible personal property placed in service before 1999, then for AMT purposes straight-line depreciation is figured over the property's class life under the alternative depreciation system (ADS). For real property placed in service before 1999, regular tax straight-line depreciation is refigured for AMT purposes using the straight-line method over 40 years.

Mandatory straight-line depreciation. You are required to use the alternative depreciation system for automobiles *(43.3)* and certain computers *(42.10)* used 50% or less for business.

Alternative MACRS depreciation must also be used for:

- Figuring earnings and profits;
- Tangible property which, during the taxable year, is used predominantly outside the United States;
- Tax-exempt use property;
- Tax-exempt bond financed property; *and*
- Imported property covered by an executive order.

42.10 Computers and Other Listed Property

"Listed property" is a term applied to certain equipment that may be used for personal and business purposes. For such property, the law allows first-year expensing *(42.3)* or accelerated MACRS *(42.5)* deductions only if business use exceeds 50%. For business use of 50% or less, you must use ADS straight-line depreciation; *see 42.9*. Deductions for listed property are claimed on Part V of Form 4562. If the more-than-50%-business-use test is met in the first year and first-year expensing or accelerated MACRS is claimed, but business use of listed property falls to 50% or less during the ADS straight-line recovery period *(42.9)*, you must "recapture" first-year expensing and accelerated MACRS deductions; *see* Example 2 below.

What is "listed property"? Listed property includes passenger autos and other transportation vehicles (*see 43.4* for exceptions), cellular phones, computers and peripheral equipment, boats, airplanes, and any photographic, sound, or video recording equipment that could be used for entertainment or recreational purposes. However, exceptions remove some items from the listed property category for many businesses. Listed property does not include (1) any computer or peripheral equipment that you own or lease that is used exclusively at a regular business establishment, and (2) photographic, phonographic, communications, or video equipment used exclusively and regularly in your business or regular business establishment. A home office that meets the rules in *40.12* is considered a regular business establishment.

EXAMPLES

1. You buy a computer in 2006 and use it exclusively in your regular business office. The computer is not listed property. You may claim either first-year expensing *(42.3)* or accelerated MACRS depreciation *(42.5)* for your investment on Form 4562. If business use falls to 50% or less after 2006, the only deduction subject to recapture is the first-year deduction; *see 42.3.*
2. You have no regular business establishment and use a computer bought in 2006 as a freelance consultant. The computer is listed property and you may claim MACRS and/or first-year expensing only if you use the computer more than 50% for business. If business use does not exceed 50%, you may only claim ADS straight-line depreciation *(42.9)*. Your deductions are claimed in the section for "Listed Property" on Form 4562.

Caution

Depreciation Restrictions for a Computer

If you use a home computer for business but not in a qualified home office *(40.12)*, it must be used more than 50% of the time for business to claim a first-year expensing deduction. If used 50% or less for business, straight-line depreciation over the ADS recovery period is required.

Deductions subject to recapture. If business use exceeds 50% in the first year but in a later year drops to 50% or less, MACRS and any first-year expensing deduction are subject to "recapture." In the year in which business use drops to 50% or less, you recapture the excess of (1) the MACRS and first-year expensing deductions claimed in prior years over (2) the deductions that would have been allowed using ADS straight-line depreciation *(42.9)*. For the rest of the recovery period, you continue to use the alternative straight-line rate.

Recapture is figured on Form 4797. The recapture computation follows the steps shown in *43.10* for recapture of excess depreciation on an automobile.

Planning Reminder

Computer Software

Software purchased "off the shelf" and used for business or investment purposes qualifies for first-year expensing in 2003–2009. If not expensed, it is depreciable over a three-year period provided it has a useful life exceeding one year. If the useful life does not exceed one year, the cost is immediately deductible. Also *see 42.19.*

Investor's use of a computer. For an investor who uses a home computer for managing an investment portfolio, the computer is treated as listed property. Unless the computer is also used for business, and the computer time spent on business work exceeds 50% of the total, only straight-line depreciation may be claimed; neither first-year expensing nor accelerated MACRS is allowed. Although the investment use is disregarded for purposes of the more-than-50%-business-use test, the investment use is combined with the business use for purposes of determining the percentage of depreciable cost. Depreciable investment use must relate to managing investments that produce taxable income. *See* the Examples below.

EXAMPLES

1. In 2006, Jane Adams buys a computer; she uses it 10% of the time for personal purposes, 50% of the time to manage her stock investments and 40% in a part-time research business. The more-than-50%-business-use test is not met for claiming first-year expensing or accelerated MACRS deductions. She must use ADS straight-line depreciation over five years *(42.9)*; her depreciable basis is 90% of cost.
2. Assume that Jane used the computer 60% of the time for business and 30% for investment. As business use exceeds 50%, she may claim first-year expensing under the rules discussed in *42.3.* If she instead claims accelerated MACRS, the MACRS rate is applied to 90% of her cost.

Leasing a computer or cellular phone. You may deduct the portion of your lease payments attributable to business use. However, if business use is 50% or less for any year, you must report as income an amount based on the fair market value of the unit, the percentage of business plus investment use, and percentages from two IRS tables shown in Publication 946.

42.11 Assets in Service Before 1987

Assets placed in service before 1987 were depreciated under a different recovery system called ACRS. Most of the assets have already been fully depreciated, although some assets, such as certain real estate placed in service before 1987, continue to be governed by these rules. For ACRS rates for real estate, *see 42.16.*

42.12 Straight-Line Recovery for Assets in Service Before 1987

You may still be able to claim straight-line deductions for five-year ACRS property if a recovery period of 25 years was elected. For 10-year property, an election could have been made for straight-line depreciation over 25 or 35 years.

If you made the straight-line election, the straight-line rate to be used on your 2006 return is as follows:

Recovery Period—	*Rate—*
25 years	4.000%
35 years	2.857%

Because of the half-year convention, only 50% of the above percentages was allowed in the year the property was placed in service. If the property is held for the entire elected recovery period, another half-year of depreciation is allowed for the year following the end of the recovery period. If property is disposed of prior to the end of the recovery period, no cost recovery is allowable in the year of disposition. *See* IRS Publication 534 for further details.

42.13 MACRS for Real Estate Placed in Service After 1986

The recovery period for residential rental property placed in service after December 31, 1986, is 27.5 years. The recovery period for nonresidential real property is either 39 years or 31.5 years, depending on when the property was placed in service.

The method of recovery for nonresidential or residential property is the straight-line method using a mid-month convention. See the next page for rate tables for each class of property.

For nonresidential real property placed in service after December 31, 1986, but before May 13, 1993, the depreciation recovery period is 31.5 years.

For nonresidential real property placed in service after May 12, 1993, the recovery period is 39 years. Under a transition rule, the 31.5-year recovery period rather than the 39-year recovery period applies to a building placed in service before 1994 if before May 13, 1993, you had entered into a binding, written contract to buy or build it, or if, before that date, you had begun construction. The transition rule also applies if you obtained the contract or property from someone else who satisfied the pre–May 13, 1993, contract or construction requirement, provided he or she never put the building in service and you did so before 1994.

Residential rental property subject to the 27.5 year recovery period is defined as a rental building or structure for which 80% or more of the gross rental income for the tax year is rental income from dwelling units. If you occupy any part of the building, the gross rental income includes the fair rental value of the part you occupy.

A dwelling unit is a house or an apartment used to provide living accommodations in a building or structure, but not a unit in a hotel, motel, inn, or other establishment where more than one-half of the units are used on a transient basis.

Mid-month convention. Under a mid-month convention, all residential rental property and nonresidential real property placed in service or disposed of during any month is treated as placed in service or disposed of at the midpoint of that month. You may determine the first-year deduction for your property by applying the percentage from Table 42-4 on the following page to the original depreciable basis. In later years, use the same column of the table to figure your deduction. If the property is disposed of before the end of the recovery period, the deduction for the year of disposition is figured by prorating the full-year deduction for the months the property was in service, treating the month of dispostion as one-half of a month of use.

EXAMPLES

1. In February 2006, you buy an apartment building for $100,000 and place it in service. You use the calendar year. Table 42-4 below gives a first-year depreciation rate of 3.182% for 27.5-year residential rental property placed in service during February. Applying this rate, you get a deduction of $3,182.

   For 2007, the rate will be 3.636%, for a deduction of $3,636.
2. Assume that you sell the apartment building in Example 1 on March 7, 2008. A full year of depreciation for 2008 is $3,636 (3.636% × $100,000). You are treated as using the property for 2.5 months in 2008, so your deduction is $757.50 ($3,636 ÷ 12 × 2.5).

Filing Tip

Additions and Improvements

The MACRS class for an addition or improvement is generally determined by the MACRS class of the property to which the addition or improvement is made. For example, if you put an addition on a rental home that you are depreciating over 27.5 years, the addition is depreciated as 27.5-year residential rental property. The period for figuring depreciation begins on the date that the addition or improvement is placed in service, or, if later, the date that the property to which the addition or improvement was made is placed in service.

See the Law Alert below for the special 15-year recovery rule allowed for qualified leasehold or restaurant improvements.

Law Alert

15-Year Recovery for Qualified Leasehold or Restaurant Improvements

Qualifying improvements made after October 22, 2004, and before 2006 to the interior of a nonresidential building are depreciable over 15 years using the straight-line method if the improvement was placed in service more than three years after the building was first placed in service. A similar 15-year recovery period is allowed for improvements to restaurant property placed in service after October 22, 2004, and before 2006 if it was made more than three years after the building was placed in service. However, when this book went to press, Congress had not yet extended the 15-year writeoff to eligible improvements after 2005. *See* the *e-Supplement* and the Form 4562 instructions for an update.

Additions or improvements to property. The depreciation deduction for any additions to, or improvement of, any property is figured in the same way as the deduction for the property would be figured if the property had been placed in service at the same time as the addition or improvement.

Table 42-4 MACRS Real Estate Depreciation

Residential Rental Property (27.5 years; *see 42.13*)

Use the column for the month of taxable year placed in service.

Month	*1*	*2*	*3*	*4*	*5*	*6*	*7*	*8*	*9*	*10*	*11*	*12*
Year												
1	3.485%	3.182%	2.879%	2.576%	2.273%	1.970%	1.667%	1.364%	1.061%	0.758%	0.455%	0.152%
2–9	3.636	3.636	3.636	3.636	3.636	3.636	3.636	3.636	3.636	3.636	3.636	3.636
10	3.637	3.637	3.637	3.637	3.637	3.637	3.636	3.636	3.636	3.636	3.636	3.636
11	3.636	3.636	3.636	3.636	3.636	3.636	3.637	3.637	3.637	3.637	3.637	3.637
12	3.637	3.637	3.637	3.637	3.637	3.637	3.636	3.636	3.636	3.636	3.636	3.636
13	3.636	3.636	3.636	3.636	3.636	3.636	3.637	3.637	3.637	3.637	3.637	3.637
14	3.637	3.637	3.637	3.637	3.637	3.637	3.636	3.636	3.636	3.636	3.636	3.636
15	3.636	3.636	3.636	3.636	3.636	3.636	3.637	3.637	3.637	3.637	3.637	3.637
16	3.637	3.637	3.637	3.637	3.637	3.637	3.636	3.636	3.636	3.636	3.636	3.636
17	3.636	3.636	3.636	3.636	3.636	3.636	3.637	3.637	3.637	3.637	3.637	3.637
18	3.637	3.637	3.637	3.637	3.637	3.637	3.636	3.636	3.636	3.636	3.636	3.636
19	3.636	3.636	3.636	3.636	3.636	3.636	3.637	3.637	3.637	3.637	3.637	3.637
20	3.637	3.637	3.637	3.637	3.637	3.637	3.636	3.636	3.636	3.636	3.636	3.636
21	3.636	3.636	3.636	3.636	3.636	3.636	3.637	3.637	3.637	3.637	3.637	3.637

Nonresidential Real Property (31.5 years—placed in service before May 13, 1993; *see 42.13*)

Use the column for the month of taxable year placed in service

Month	*1*	*2*	*3*	*4*	*5*	*6*	*7*	*8*	*9*	*10*	*11*	*12*
Year												
12	3.175	3.174	3.175	3.174	3.175	3.174	3.175	3.174	3.175	3.174	3.175	3.174
13	3.174	3.175	3.174	3.175	3.174	3.175	3.174	3.175	3.174	3.175	3.174	3.175
14	3.175	3.174	3.175	3.174	3.175	3.174	3.175	3.174	3.175	3.174	3.175	3.174
15	3.174	3.175	3.174	3.175	3.174	3.175	3.174	3.175	3.174	3.175	3.174	3.175
16	3.175	3.174	3.175	3.174	3.175	3.174	3.175	3.174	3.175	3.174	3.175	3.174
17	3.174	3.175	3.174	3.175	3.174	3.175	3.174	3.175	3.174	3.175	3.174	3.175
18	3.175	3.174	3.175	3.174	3.175	3.174	3.175	3.174	3.175	3.174	3.175	3.174
19	3.174	3.175	3.174	3.175	3.174	3.175	3.174	3.175	3.174	3.175	3.174	3.175
20	3.175	3.174	3.175	3.174	3.175	3.174	3.175	3.174	3.175	3.174	3.175	3.174
21	3.174	3.175	3.174	3.175	3.174	3.175	3.174	3.175	3.174	3.175	3.174	3.175

Nonresidential Real Property (39 years—placed in service on or after May 13, 1993; *see 42.13*)

Use the column for the month of taxable year placed in service.

Month	1	2	3	4	5	6	7	8	9	10	11	12
Year												
1	2.461%	2.247%	2.033%	1.819%	1.605%	1.391%	1.177%	0.963%	0.749%	0.535%	0.321%	0.107%
2–39	2.564	2.564	2.564	2.564	2.564	2.564	2.564	2.564	2.564	2.564	2.564	2.564
40	0.107	0.321	0.535	0.749	0.963	1.177	1.391	1.605	1.819	2.033	2.247	2.461

42.14 Demolishing a Building

When you buy improved property, the purchase price is allocated between the land and the building; only the building may be depreciated. The land may not; *see 42.1*. If you later demolish the building, you may not deduct the cost of the demolition or the undepreciated basis of the building as a loss in the year of demolition. Expenses or losses in connection with the demolition of any structure, including certified historic structures, are not deductible. They must be capitalized and added to the basis of the land on which the structure is located.

Major rehabilitation. Where you are considering a major rehabilitation of a building that involves some demolition of the building, IRS guidelines may allow you to deduct the costs of demolition and a removal of part of the structure. Under the IRS rules, the costs of structural modification may avoid capitalization if 75% or more of the existing external walls are retained as internal or external walls and 75% or more of the existing internal framework is also retained. For certified historic structures, the modification must also be part of a certified rehabilitation.

42.15 Leasehold Improvements

Improvements. Leasehold improvements are depreciated under MACRS real estate rates listed at *42.13*, except for qualified New York Liberty Zone leasehold improvements to nonresidential buildings, which are depreciable over five years *(42.4)* under the straight-line method. Also *see* the Law Alert on page 663 for the 15-year recovery rule for qualified leasehold improvements. You ignore the term of the lease. If the lease term is shorter than the MACRS life and you do not retain the improvements at the end of the term, the remaining undepreciated basis is a deductible loss.

Pre-1987 improvements. For leasehold improvements placed in service before 1987, the cost of improvements is deductible over the *shorter* of the following periods:

1. The useful life of the improvement if the improvement was before 1981, or the ACRS recovery period if after 1980 but before 1987, *or*
2. The remaining term of the lease.

If (1) is the shorter period, the cost of the improvement is depreciated. If (2) is the shorter period, the cost is amortized ratably.

In determining the shorter period, you must add optional lease renewals to the remaining lease term under (2) if, at the completion of the improvement, the remaining term of the original lease (excluding unexercised renewal options) is less than 60% of the useful life (or ACRS recovery period) of the improvement. Renewals do not have to be taken into account under the 60% test if the lessee can show that it is more probable that the lease would not be renewed than that it would be renewed.

If the lessee and lessor are related, the term of the lease is treated as being equal to the remaining useful life (or recovery period) of the improvement. Related parties include spouses, children, grandchildren, parents, grandparents, brothers, sisters, and certain controlled corporations, partnerships, and trusts.

Planning Reminder

Demolition and Cleanup Costs in the GO Zone

A deduction of up to 50% of demolition and site cleanup costs can be claimed for property in the Gulf Opportunity Zone incurred after August 28, 2005, and before January 1, 2008.

Planning Reminder

Abandonment of Leasehold Improvements

Upon the termination of a lease, the adjusted basis of a lessee's leasehold improvements that are abandoned may be claimed as a loss. For dispositions after June 12, 1996, a lessor may follow the rule applied to lessees if the improvements are irrevocably disposed of or abandoned at the termination of the lease. The lessor may recognize loss for the remaining adjusted basis of the improvements.

42.16 Depreciating Real Estate Placed in Service After 1980 and Before 1987

The ACRS recovery period of almost all buildings placed in service before 1987 has already ended. Some pre-1987 buildings are still being depreciated over a 35-year or 45-year period if the straight-line election discussed in the next paragraph was made.

Election to use straight-line depreciation. For 15-year, 18-year, or 19-year real property, you may have elected to use the straight-line method over 35 or 45 years. An election of the straight-line method for real property had to be made on a property-by-property basis, by the return due date, plus extensions, for the year the property was placed in service.

Rate of recovery. The rate of recovery is listed in Treasury tables that are available in IRS Publication 534.

Substantial improvements. Substantial improvements made after 1986 to an ACRS building are depreciable under MACRS *(42.13)*, not ACRS.

Recapture. *See 44.1* for recapture rules on the sale of ACRS property.

42.17 When MACRS Is Not Allowed

If you place in service personal property that you previously used or that was previously owned by a related taxpayer before 1987, you may not be able to apply MACRS rules. This anti-churning restriction is designed to discourage asset transfers between related persons to take advantage of MACRS deductions that exceed the deductions allowed before 1987 under ACRS. The anti-churning restriction does not apply to personal property if, for the first full taxable year of service, the deduction allowable under ACRS would be greater than the deduction allowable under MACRS.

The anti-churning rule also does not bar MACRS rules for real estate acquired after 1986, unless you lease back the real estate to a related party who owned it before 1987.

Special rules also apply to the transfer of property in certain tax-free corporate or partnership transactions where the property was used before 1987. If you receive property in a tax-free exchange, you may have to use the method used by the transferor in computing the ACRS deduction for that part of basis that does not exceed what was the transferor's basis in the property. To the extent that basis exceeds the transferor's, the MACRS rules may apply; for example, when you paid boot in addition to transferring property.

Where property is disposed of and reacquired, the depreciation deduction is computed as if the disposition had not occurred.

42.18 Amortizing Goodwill and Other Intangibles (Section 197)

The costs of intangibles coming within Section 197 are amortized over a 15-year period. The 15-year period applies regardless of the actual useful life of "Section 197 intangibles" acquired after August 10, 1993 (or after July 25, 1991, if elected), and held in connection with a business or income-producing activity.

Generally, the amount subject to amortization is cost. Annual amortization is reported on Form 4562. The 15-year period starts with the month the intangible was acquired.

A "Section 197 intangible" is: (1) goodwill; (2) going-concern value; (3) workforce in place; (4) information base; (5) know-how, but *see* exceptions below; (6) any customer-based intangible; (7) any supplier-based intangible; (8) any license, permit, or other right granted by a governmental unit or agency; (9) any covenant not to compete made in the acquisition of a business; and (10) any franchise, trademark, or trade name.

Goodwill. Goodwill is the value of a business attributable to the expectancy of continued customer patronage, due to the name or reputation of a business or any other factor.

Franchises, trademarks, and trade names. A franchise (excluding sports franchises), trademark, or trade name is a Section 197 intangible. Amounts, whether fixed or contingent, paid on the transfer of a trademark, trade name, or franchise are chargeable to capital account and must be ratably amortized over a 15-year period. The renewal of a franchise, trademark, or trade name is treated as an acquisition of the franchise, trademark, or trade name. Renewal costs are amortized over 15 years beginning in the month of renewal.

Know-how. A patent, copyright, formula, process, design, pattern, format, or similar item may be a Section 197 intangible. However, the following interests are not Section 197 intangibles unless acquired as part of the acquisition of a business: patents, copyrights, and interests in films, sound recordings, videotapes, books, or other similar property.

Customer-based intangibles. Customer-based intangibles include the portion of an acquired trade or business attributable to a customer base, circulation base, undeveloped market or market growth, insurance in force, investment management contracts, or other relationships with customers that involve the future provision of goods or services.

Supplier-based intangibles. The portion of the purchase price of an acquired business attributable to a favorable relationship with persons who provide distribution services, such as favorable shelf or display space at a retail outlet, the existence of a favorable credit rating, or the existence of favorable supply contracts, are Section 197 intangibles.

Going-concern value. This is the additional value that attaches to property because it is an integral part of a going concern. This includes the value attributable to the ability of a trade or business to continue to operate and generate sales without interruption in spite of a change in ownership.

Workforce in place. The portion of the purchase price of an acquired business attributable to a highly skilled workforce is amortizable over 15 years. Similarly, the cost of acquiring an existing employment contract is amortizable over 15 years.

Information base. This includes the cost of acquiring customer lists; subscription lists; insurance expirations; patient or client files; lists of newspaper, magazine, radio, or television advertisers; business books and records; and operating systems. The intangible value of technical manuals, training manuals or programs, data files, and accounting or inventory control systems is also a Section 197 intangible.

Self-created intangibles. A Section 197 intangible created by a taxpayer is generally not amortizable, unless created in connection with a transaction that involves the acquisition of assets of a business. However, this deduction bar for self-created intangibles does not apply to the following: (1) any license, permit, or other right granted by a governmental unit or agency; (2) a covenant not to compete entered into on the acquisition of a business; or (3) any franchise, trademark, or trade name. For example, the 15-year amortization period may apply to the capitalized costs of registering or developing a trademark or trade name.

A person who contracts for or renews a contract for the use of a Section 197 intangible may not be considered to have created that intangible. For example, a licensee who contracts for the use of know-how may amortize capitalized costs over 15 years.

The following intangible assets are not Section 197 intangibles. (1) interests in a corporation, partnership, trust, or estate; (2) interests under certain financial contracts; (3) interests in land; (4) certain computer software *(see 42.19)*; (5) certain separately acquired rights and interests; (6) interests under existing leases of tangible property; (7) interests under existing indebtedness; (8) sports franchises; (9) certain residential mortgage servicing rights; and (10) certain corporate transaction costs.

Loss limitations. A person who disposes of an amortizable Section 197 intangible at a loss and at the same time retains other Section 197 intangibles acquired in the same transaction may not deduct the loss. The disallowed loss is added to the basis of the retained Section 197 intangibles. The same rule applies if a Section 197 intangible is abandoned or becomes worthless and other Section 197 intangibles acquired in the same transaction are kept. The basis of the remaining intangibles is increased by the disallowed loss.

You may not treat a covenant not to compete as worthless any earlier than the disposition or worthlessness of the entire interest in a business.

Anti-churning rule. No deduction is allowed for goodwill, going-concern value, or any other Section 197 intangibles acquired by a taxpayer after August 10, 1993, if:

1. The taxpayer or a related person held or used the intangible at any time on or after July 25, 1991, and on or before August 10, 1993;
2. The taxpayer acquired the intangible from a person who held it at any time on or after July 25, 1991, and on or before August 10, 1993, and, as part of the transaction, the user of the intangible does not change; or
3. The taxpayer grants the right to use the intangible to a person or a related person who held or used the intangible at any time on or after July 25, 1991, and on or before August 10, 1993.

See IRS Publication 535 for the definition of "related persons" and exceptions to the anti-churning rule.

Dispositions. An amortizable Section 197 intangible is not a capital asset. It is treated as depreciable property, and if held for more than one year, it will generally qualify as a Section 1231 asset; *see 44.1*. Amortization claimed on a Section 197 intangible is subject to recapture under Section 1245 and gain on its sale to certain related persons is subject to ordinary income treatment under Section 1239.

Planning Reminder

Covenants Not To Compete

A covenant not to compete is a Section 197 intangible if paid for in connection with the acquisition of a business. Excessive compensation or rental paid to a former owner of a business for continuing to perform services or provide the use of property is considered an amount paid for a covenant not to compete if the services or property benefits the trade or business. But an amount paid under a covenant not to compete that actually represents additional consideration for corporate stock is not a Section 197 intangible and must be added to the basis of the acquired stock.

42.19 Deducting the Cost of Computer Software

The cost of software installed in a computer that you buy and use in your business is not deducted separately, unless the software cost is separately stated. In most cases, the cost of software bundled with a computer is not separately stated. The cost of the computer including such software is depreciable under the rules in *42.10*.

If you buy software for business use, such as a database or spreadsheet program, the treatment of the cost depends on your use of the program. If you use it for a year or less, such as an annual tax program, you may deduct the cost as a business expense for that year. If the useful life in your business exceeds a year, and the software meets the three tests in the Planning Reminder on this page, it is considered off-the-shelf software eligible for first-year expensing if bought in 2003–2009; *see 42.3.* Alternatively, you may depreciate the cost over 36 months.

Software acquired in the acquisition of a business is eligible for first-year expensing *(42.3)* or depreciable over 36 months if it meets the three tests listed in the Planning Reminder on this page; otherwise, 15-year amortization applies.

Planning Reminder

Computer Software Not Subject to Amortization

Computer software is *not* a Section 197 intangible *(42.18)* if it: (1) is readily available to the general public; (2) is not subject to an exclusive license; and (3) has not been substantially changed. If these three tests are met, software purchased in 2003–2009 is eligible for first-year expensing *(42.3)*, or it may be depreciated over 36 months; *see 42.19.* Computer software falling outside of this exception is considered a Section 197 intangible subject to 15-year amortization if it is acquired in the acquisition of a business.

42.20 Amortizing Song Rights

Expenses paid or incurred with respect to musical compositions and rights to musical compositions placed in service in 2006–2010 can be amortized over five years. This would include, for example, advances made by song publishers to composers. If elected, the five-year amortization period begins with the month in which the compositions or rights are placed in service.

Chapter 43

Deducting Car and Truck Expenses

The costs of buying and operating a car, truck, or van for business are deductible under rules hedged with restrictions. Depreciation deductions for most cars, trucks, and vans are subject to annual ceilings. For most cars placed in service in 2006, the ceiling on first-year depreciation is $2,960, and the limit for most light trucks and vans is $3,260. The $2,960 or $3,260 limit is reduced for personal use. If a vehicle placed in service in 2006 is used 50% or less for business, depreciation must be based on the straight-line method and the maximum deduction of $2,960 or $3,260 is reduced by personal use. *See 43.4* for details on the limits.

To avoid accounting for actual vehicle expenses and depreciation, you may claim an IRS mileage allowance. For 2006, the allowance is 44.5 cents per mile. Keep a record of business trip mileage.

If you are self-employed, you deduct your vehicle expenses on Schedule C or Schedule C-EZ if eligible; *see 40.6.* Use Form 4562 to compute depreciation if you claim actual operating costs instead of the IRS mileage allowance. If you are an employee, use Form 2106 to claim unreimbursed vehicle expenses, which are deductible only to the extent that together with other miscellaneous itemized deductions they exceed 2% of your adjusted gross income.

If you bought a hybrid vehicle in 2006 for business and/or personal use, you may be eligible for a new tax credit. The former $2,000 deduction for buying a hybrid vehicle no longer applies. See *25.21* for credit details.

Also see:

43.1 Standard Mileage Rate

If you start to use your car for business in 2006, you have a choice of either deducting the actual operating costs of your car during business trips or deducting a flat IRS allowance. For 2006, the rate is 44.5 cents per mile. The mileage allowance also applies to business trips in a van or pickup or panel truck as if it were a car.

If you placed a car, van, pick-up, or panel truck in service before 2006 and have always used the IRS mileage allowance, you may apply the 44.5-cents-per-mile rate to your 2006 business mileage or deduct your actual operating costs plus straight-line depreciation over the remaining estimated useful life of the vehicle (assuming the vehicle is not considered fully depreciated).

The rate may not be used to deduct the costs of a vehicle used for nonbusiness income-producing activities such as looking after investment property.

Allowance must be elected for the first year. The choice of the allowance must be made in the first year you place the vehicle in service for business travel. If you do not use the allowance in the year you first use the vehicle for business, you may not use the allowance for that vehicle in any other year. Thus, if you bought a car for business in 2005 and on your 2005 return you deducted actual operating costs plus depreciation, you may not use the mileage allowance on your 2006 return or in any later year.

Planning Reminder

First-Year Election Affects Later Years

In deciding whether to elect the allowance in the first year, consider not only whether you will get a bigger first-year deduction using the allowance, or deducting actual operating costs plus depreciation, but also project your mileage, operating expenses, and depreciation expenses over the years you expect to use the vehicle. If in the first year you elect to deduct actual costs, including MACRS or straight-line MACRS depreciation, you may not use the IRS auto allowance for *that vehicle* in a later year. On the other hand, claiming the IRS allowance in the first year you put a vehicle in service forfeits your privilege to use MACRS and first-year expensing. If you switch from the allowance to deducting actual expenses in later years, you may claim straight-line depreciation over the remaining estimated useful life of the vehicle if the vehicle is not considered fully depreciated.

Allowance takes the place of fixed operating costs plus depreciation. If you claim the allowance, you cannot deduct your actual outlays for expenses such as gasoline (including state and local taxes), oil, repairs, license tags, or insurance, nor can you deduct depreciation or lease payments. Parking fees and tolls during business trips are deductible in addition to the mileage allowance. The IRS will not disallow a deduction based on the allowance even though it exceeds your actual vehicle costs. If you use more than one automobile in your business travel and elect the allowance, total the business mileage traveled in both cars.

EXAMPLES

1. You buy a car in 2006 and drive it on business trips. You keep a record of your business mileage. You traveled 20,000 miles on business in 2006. You may deduct $8,900 (20,000 × 44.5 cents). In addition, you may deduct your expenses for tolls and parking.
2. You use one car primarily for business and occasionally your spouse's car for business trips. In 2006, you drove your car on business trips 10,000 miles and your spouse's car 2,000 miles. Total business mileage is 12,000 miles for purposes of the 44.5-cents-per-mile allowance.

Records. You may decide to use the allowance if you do not keep accurate records of operating costs. However, you must keep a record of your business trips, dates, customers or clients visited, business purpose of the trips, your total mileage during the year, and the number of miles traveled on business. An IRS agent may attempt to verify mileage by asking for repair bills near the beginning and end of the year if the bills note mileage readings.

Mileage allowance for leased vehicle. The IRS mileage allowance is also available for leased cars, vans, and pick-up or panel trucks, but it must be used for the entire lease period or not at all. For example, if in 2006 you leased a car for business purposes and you claim the 44.5-cents-per-mile allowance, you will also have to use it for the remainder of the lease period, including renewals.

Interest on a vehicle loan and taxes. *See 43.2* for deduction rules.

Mileage allowance disallowed. You may not claim the 44.5-cents-a-mile allowance if:

- You have depreciated your vehicle using the ACRS or MACRS method, including straight-line MACRS, or you claimed first-year expensing or first-year bonus depreciation.
- You use in your business five or more vehicles simultaneously, such as in a fleet operation.
- You use your vehicle for hire—that is, you use it as a taxicab, carrying passengers for a fare.

Employer reimbursements. If your employer reimburses your vehicle costs at a rate lower than the IRS allowance, you may use the IRS rate to deduct the excess over your employer's reimbursement; *see* Example 3 at *20.33*.

IRS allowance includes depreciation. When you use the IRS mileage allowance, you may not claim a separate depreciation deduction. The IRS mileage allowance includes an estimate for depreciation. For purposes of figuring gain or loss on a disposition, you must reduce the basis of the vehicle by the following depreciation amounts: 12 cents per mile for 1994–1999, 14 cents per mile for 2000, 15 cents per mile for 2001 and 2002, 16 cents per mile for 2003 and 2004, and 17 cents per mile in 2005 and 2006.

Depreciation when switching from allowance to actual costs. If you use the IRS mileage allowance in the first year, you may switch to the actual-cost method in a later year, but depreciation must be based on the straight-line method over the remaining estimated useful life. However, no depreciation may be claimed if basis has been reduced to zero under the annual cents-per-mile reduction rule in the preceding paragraph.

Table 43-1 Deducting Car and Truck Expenses

Item—	*Tax Rule—*
IRS mileage allowance	You may avoid the trouble of keeping a record of actual vehicle expenses and calculating depreciation by electing the IRS mileage allowance for a car, van, or pick-up or panel truck. However, to claim the allowance, you must be ready to prove business use of the vehicle and keep a record of your mileage. The allowance may give you a larger deduction than your actual outlays plus depreciation. You must elect the allowance in the first year you use the vehicle for business. If you do not, you may not use the allowance for that vehicle in any other year If your actual operating costs plus depreciation exceed the allowance for the first year you place the vehicle in business service, you may claim your actual operating expenses and depreciation, but doing so will forfeit your right to elect the allowance for that vehicle in any later year.
Depreciation	If you claim actual operating expenses, such as gasoline, repairs, and insurance costs, you may also claim depreciation. There is a cap on the annual depreciation deduction. For a car placed in service in 2006, the 2006 depreciation limit is $2,960, and for a light truck or van the limit is $3,260. These limits must be reduced for personal use; *see 43.4.* Electing first-year expensing does not increase the $2,960/$3,260 limit (as reduced by personal use). The total of the first-year expensing and regular depreciation cannot exceed the applicable limit; *see 43.4.* Electing first-year expensing or regular depreciation for a car or truck placed in service in 2006 prevents you from using the IRS mileage allowance *(43.1)* for that car in later years. For a cars and trucks placed in business service in 2006 that are used 50% or less for business, you must use straight-line depreciation subject to the $2,960 or $3,260 ceiling; *see 43.6.* If business use is initially over 50% but declines to 50% or less in a later year, prior year depreciation deductions, including first-year expensing, must be recaptured as income to the extent they exceeded straight-line deductions; *see 43.10.* For a vehicle placed in service before 2006, *see* Tables 43-2 and 43-3 on page 675 for the maximum depreciation you can claim for 2006.
Vehicle used for business and personal driving	You may deduct only the amount allocated to business mileage. For example, total mileage is 20,000 in 2006 and your business mileage is 15,000. You may claim only 75% of your deductible costs (15,000 ÷ 20,000).
Tax return reporting	If you are an *employee*, you claim actual vehicle expenses or the IRS allowance on Form 2106. Form 2106 requires you to list mileage for business, commuting, and other personal trips. If your vehicle costs are not reimbursed by your employer, you must deduct them as miscellaneous deductions subject to the 2% AGI floor on Schedule A. If you are *self-employed*, you deduct business costs on Schedule C and use Form 4562 to compute depreciation if you claim actual operating costs. Costs deducted on Schedule C are not limited by the 2% adjusted gross income (AGI) floor.

43.2 Expense Allocations

If you do not claim the IRS mileage allowance, you may deduct car, truck, or van expenses on business trips such as the cost of gas and oil (including state and local taxes), repairs, parking, and tolls.

If you use your vehicle exclusively for business, all of your operating expenses are deductible. However, if you are an employee, the deduction is limited by the 2% adjusted gross income (AGI) floor; *see 19.1.*

Apportioning vehicle expenses between business and personal use. For a vehicle used for business and personal purposes, deduct only the depreciation and expenses allocated to your business use of the vehicle. Depreciation is discussed at *43.3*, *43.4*, and *43.5*.

The business portion of vehicle expenses is determined by the percentage of mileage driven on business trips during the year.

EXAMPLE

In 2006, you drove your car 15,000 miles. Of this, 12,000 miles was on business trips. The percentage of business use is 80%:

$$\frac{\text{Business Mileage}}{\text{Total Mileage}} = \frac{12{,}000}{15{,}000} = 80\%$$

Your actual car expenses (gas, oil, repairs, etc.) for the year were $1,000, of which $800 ($1,000 × 80%) is deductible. If you are an employee, the $800 is only deductible as a miscellaneous itemized deduction subject to the 2% AGI floor; *see 19.1.*

Interest on vehicle loan. If you are an *employee*, all of the interest is considered personal interest and is not deductible even if you use the vehicle 100% of the time for your job. If you are *self-employed*, the allocated business percentage of the interest is fully deductible on Schedule C; the personal percentage is not deductible.

Taxes paid on your car. The business portion of sales taxes paid on your vehicle is not deductible whether you are an employee or self-employed; the tax is added to the basis of the vehicle for depreciation purposes; *see 43.3.* The non-business portion of sales tax paid in 2006 is deductible on Schedule A only if Congress passes legislation extending to 2006 the pre-2006 election to deduct state and local sales taxes in lieu of state and local income taxes; *see 16.3.*

State and local personal property taxes are deductible as itemized deductions on Schedule A if you are an employee. If you are self-employed, deduct the business portion of the personal property taxes on Schedule C and the personal percentage on Schedule A if you itemize.

Leased vehicle. If you lease a car, truck, or van for business use and do not claim the IRS mileage allowance *(43.1)*, you deduct the lease payments plus other costs of operating the vehicle. If the vehicle is also used for personal driving, the lease payments must be allocated between business and personal mileage. *See also 43.12* for rules requiring the reporting of extra income attributable to the lease.

43.3 Depreciation Restrictions on Cars, Trucks, and Vans

The law contains restrictions on so-called "listed property" that limit and, in some cases, deny depreciation deductions for a business car, truck, or van. Employees may be unable to claim any deduction at all under an employer convenience test. Employees meeting that test and self-employed individuals must determine if they can use accelerated MACRS rates or must use straight-line rates. Finally, regardless of which depreciation method is used, the annual deduction may not exceed a ceiling set by law for passenger cars and certain light trucks and vans; *see 43.4* for details on the annual ceilings.

Caution

Recapture of MACRS Deductions

If you meet the more-than-50% test in the year the car or other vehicle is placed in service, which entitles you to claim first-year expensing or accelerated MACRS, but business use falls to 50% or less in a later year, the recapture rules discussed at *43.10* apply.

Employee must satisfy employer convenience test. If you are an employee and use your own vehicle for work, you must be ready to prove that you use it for the *convenience of your employer* who requires you to use it in your job. If you do not meet this employer convenience test, you may not claim depreciation or first-year expensing. A letter from your employer stating you need the vehicle for business will not meet this test.

The facts and circumstances of your use of the vehicle may show that it is a condition of employment. For example, an inspector for a construction company uses his automobile to visit construction sites over a scattered area. The company reimburses him for his expenses. According to the IRS, the inspector's use of the car is for the convenience of the company and is a condition of the job. However, if a company car were available to the inspector, the use of his own car would not meet the condition of employment and convenience of the employer tests.

More-than-50%-business-use test for claiming expensing or accelerated MACRS depreciation. Automobiles and other vehicles used to transport persons or goods are considered "listed property" *(42.10)*, whether you are an employee or are self-employed, but there are exceptions for ambulances, hearses, and trucks or vans that are qualified non-personal-use vehicles *(see 43.4)*. Unless the vehicle is excepted from the listed property rules, you may claim first-year expensing or accelerated MACRS *(43.5)* for a vehicle placed in service during 2006 only if you use it in 2006 more than 50% of the time for business. The annual ceiling, if applicable *(43.4)*, applies to the total of first-year expensing and MACRS depreciation.

If business use is *50% or less* in the year the vehicle is placed in service, first-year expensing and accelerated MACRS are barred; depreciation must be claimed over a six-year period under the straight-line method. Technically, the recovery period is five years but the period is extended to six years because, in the first year, a convention rule limits the deductible percentage. *See* the straight-line rate tables at *43.6*. The straight-line method must also be used in future years, even if business use in those years exceeds 50%.

If a vehicle is used for both business and investment purposes, only business use is considered in determining whether you meet the more-than-50%-business-use test and therefore qualify for MACRS. However, investment use is added to business use in determining your actual deduction.

EXAMPLE

Brown buys an automobile for $30,000 and places it in service in 2006. He uses it 40% for business and 20% for investment activity. Because he does not use his car more than 50% in his business, he may not claim first-year expensing or accelerated MACRS. He figures depreciation using the straight-line method as shown in *43.6*. The business use allocation rate for depreciation is 60% (40% for business use plus 20% investment use).

Do your employees use the vehicle? In certain cases, an employer who provides a vehicle to employees as part of their compensation may be unable to count the employee's use as qualified business use, thereby preventing the employer from meeting the more-than-50%-business-use test for claiming MACRS. An employer is allowed to treat the employee's use as qualified business use only if: (1) the employee is not a relative and does not own more than 5% of the business and (2) the employer treats the fair market value of the employee's personal use of the vehicle as wage income and withholds tax on that amount. If such income is reported, all of the employee's use, including personal use, may be counted by an employer as qualified business use.

If an employee owning more than a 5% interest is allowed use of a company-owned vehicle as part of his or her compensation, the employer may not count that use as qualified business use, even if the personal use is reported as income. The same strict rule applies if the vehicle is provided to a person who is related to the employer.

43.4 Annual Ceilings on Depreciation

Annual ceilings limit the amount of depreciation you may deduct for passenger cars and certain light trucks and vans. The ceilings apply both to self-employed individuals and employees. As a result of the ceilings, the actual write-off period for your car may be several years longer than the minimum recovery period of six years; *see 43.5*.

Passenger cars. The 2006 depreciation deduction ceiling for a car placed in service in 2006 is $2,960. The $2,960 limit must be reduced for personal use. For example, if business use is 80% and personal use 20%, the limit is $2,368 (80% × $2,960). The limit applies whether you elect first-year expensing or claim MACRS accelerated or straight-line depreciation.

For purposes of the annual depreciation ceilings, a car is any four-wheeled vehicle that is manufactured primarily for use on public thoroughfares and that is weight-rated by the manufacturer at 6,000 pounds or less when unloaded (without passengers or cargo). However, these vehicles are excluded from the car category and are thus exempt from the annual depreciation limits: (1) an ambulance, hearse, or combination ambulance-hearse used directly in a business, and (2) a vehicle such as a taxi cab used directly in the business of transporting persons or property for compensation or hire.

Year-by-year limits for cars placed in service in 2006 and prior years can be found in Table 43-2 on page 675.

EXAMPLE

Theodore bought a new car on March 4, 2006, for $20,000 and for the rest of the year used it 75% for business.

Theodore does not claim a Section 179 deduction (first-year expensing) for the car. His depreciable unadjusted basis is $15,000 ($20,000 × 75%). The MACRS deduction *(43.5)* using the 200% declining balance method and the half-year convention is $3,000 ($15,000 × .20). However, Theodore's depreciation deduction is limited to $2,220 ($2,960 limit for a car placed in service in 2006 × 75% business use).

Even if Theodore had claimed first-year expensing, the deduction could not exceed the $2,220 limit.

Filing Tip

Claiming First-Year Expensing or Depreciation for Your Car

First-year expensing or depreciation (under the 200% or 150% declining balance method, or the straight-line method) is claimed on Form 4562 and then entered on Schedule C of Form 1040 if you are self employed. If you are an employee, use Form 2106 to calculate your deduction, which along with your other unreimbursed job expenses is subject to the 2% AGI floor *(19.3)* for miscellaneous itemized deductions on Schedule A of Form 1040.

Electric cars. Electric cars have higher dollar limits than gas-propelled passenger cars. Electric cars are vehicles propelled primarily by electricity and built by an original equipment manufacturer. Hybrid cars *(see 25.21)* are not treated as electric cars even though they are powered partially by electricity. For electric cars placed in service in 2006, the depreciation limit is $8,980. The limits for coming years will be $14,400 in 2007, $8,650 in 2008, and $5,225 in succeeding years. Each limit must be reduced for personal use.

Light trucks, vans, and SUVs. A light truck, van, minivan, or SUV (sport utility vehicle) built on a truck chassis that is weight-rated by the manufacturer at 6,000 pounds or less when fully loaded (gross vehicle weight rating) is generally subject to annual depreciation ceilings.

However, the depreciation limits do not apply to trucks and vans that are qualified non-personal-use vehicles. These include moving vans, flatbed trucks, and delivery trucks with seating only for the driver (or driver seat plus folding jump seat). Also included are specially modified trucks and vans that are unlikely to be used more than a minimal amount for personal purposes. An example would be a van that has been painted to display advertising or the company's name and which has permanent shelving for carrying merchandise or equipment.

Where an exception does not apply, the deduction limits for light trucks, vans, and SUVs are slightly higher than those for cars; this has been true since 2003. For trucks and vans placed in service in 2006, the 2006 limit is $3,260. The $3,260 limit must be reduced for personal use. Table 43-3 on page 675 shows the year-by-year limits for trucks and vans.

Heavy trucks, vans, and SUVs. Trucks, vans, and SUVs built on a truck chassis that are weight-rated by the manufacturer at more than 6,000 pounds gross vehicle weight are not subject to the annual depreciation ceilings. However, first-year expensing *(42.3)* for the vehicle may be limited to $25,000 rather than the general expensing limit, which for 2006 is $108,000. The vehicle must be used more than 50% for business to qualify for first-year expensing. If first-year expensing is not or cannot be elected *(42.3)*, a full depreciation deduction using the MACRS rate shown in *43.5* is allowed with no dollar limit.

The $25,000 limit on first-year expensing applies to SUVs rated at more than 6,000 pounds but not more than 14,000 pounds gross vehicle weight. For purposes of the $25,000 expensing limit, an SUV means any four-wheeled vehicle primarily designed or which can be used to carry passengers over public thoroughfares. Trucks and vans as well as SUVs can be covered by this definition, but the law allows certain exceptions. Exceptions are allowed for vehicles with seating for more than nine passengers behind the driver, for pickup trucks with an interior cargo bed at least six feet long that is an open area or is enclosed by a cap and not readily accessible to passengers, and cargo vans without rear seating and with no body sections protruding more than 30 inches ahead of the windshield. For these excepted vehicles, the $25,000 limit on first-year expensing does not apply.

Table 43-2 Maximum Depreciation Deduction for Cars (Must Be Reduced for Personal Use)

Date Placed In Service	1st Year	2nd Year	3rd Year	4th and Later Years
2006	$ 2,960	$ 4,800	$ 2,850	$ 1,775
2005	2,960	4,700	2,850	1,675
2004	10,610[1]	4,800	2,850	1,675
5/06/2003 – 12/31/2003	10,710[2]	4,900	2,950	1,775
1/01/2003 – 5/05/2003	7,660[3]	4,900	2,950	1,775
2002	7,660[3]	4,900	2,950	1,775
2001	7,660[4]	4,900	2,950	1,775
2000	3,060	4,900	2,950	1,775
1999	3,060	5,000	2,950	1,775

[1] $2,960 if the car does not qualify for the special allowance or if you elect not to claim any allowance.

[2] 7,660 if you acquire the car before 5/06/2003. $3,060 if the car does not qualify for the special allowance or if you elect not to claim any special depreciation allowance.

[3] $3,060 if the car does not qualify for the special allowance or if you elect not to claim the special depreciation allowance.

[4] $3,060 if you acquired the car before 9/11/2001, the car does not qualify for the special allowance, or you elect not to claim the special depreciation allowance.

Table 43-3 Maximum Depreciation Deduction for Trucks and Vans (Must Be Reduced for Personal Use)

Date Placed In Service	1st Year	2nd Year	3rd Year	4th and Later Years
2006	$ 3,260	$ 5,200	$ 3,150	$ 1,875
2005	3,260	5,200	3,150	1,875
2004	10,910[1]	5,300	3,150	1,875
2003	11,010[2, 3]	5,400	3,250	1,975

Before 2003: Use the Maximum Depreciation Deduction for Cars table shown above.

[1] $3,260 if the truck or van does not qualify for the special allowance or if you elect not to claim any allowance.

[2] If the special depreciation allowance does not apply or if you make the election not to claim the special depreciation allowance, the first year limit is $3,360.

[3] If the truck or van is acquired before 5/06/03, the truck or van is qualified property, and you claim the special depreciation allowance for the truck or van, the maximum deduction is $7,960.

43.5 MACRS Rates for Cars, Trucks, and Vans

Business autos, trucks, and vans are technically in a five-year MACRS class *(42.4)*, but because of the half-year or mid-quarter convention and the annual deduction ceilings *(43.3)*, the minimum depreciation period is six years.

Accelerated MACRS rate allowed only if business use in the first year exceeds 50%. To use accelerated MACRS rates, you must meet the more-than-50%-business-use test *(see 43.3)* in the year the vehicle is placed in business service. Generally, the accelerated MACRS rate is based on the 200% declining balance method, but a 150% declining balance rate may be elected, which may be advantageous when you are subject to the alternative minimum tax *(23.2)*.

If you meet the more-than-50%-business-use test, figure your first-year deduction using the rate from either Table 43-4 (half-year convention) or Table 43-5 (mid-quarter convention) on pages 677–678. The MACRS rates from the appropriate table will be used for each year of the recovery period unless business use for a year falls to 50% or less. However, the deduction figured under the MACRS table may be claimed only to the extent that it does not exceed the annual depreciation ceiling discussed in *43.4* and shown in Table 43-2 or Table 43-3; *see* the Bill Johnston Example on page 678. *See* page 676 for details on using the MACRS tables.

If you do *not* meet the more-than-50%-business-use test in the year the vehicle is placed in service, you must compute your depreciation deductions using the straight-line rates shown in *43.6*, subject to the annual limit; *see 43.4* and Table 43-2 or Table 43-3.

Deduction for year of disposition. If you dispose of your vehicle before the end of the six-year MACRS recovery period, a partial-year deduction is allowed for the year of disposition under the half-year or mid-quarter convention; *see 43.7.*

Use of vehicle after end of recovery period. If you continue to use the vehicle for business after the end of the recovery period, and the annual deduction ceilings prevented you from deducting your full unadjusted basis during the recovery period, you generally may deduct depreciation in the succeeding years up to the annual ceiling; *see 43.8.*

Business use falls to 50% or less after the first year. What if business use exceeds 50% in the year the vehicle is placed in service but in a later year within the recovery period business use drops to 50% or lower? In that case, the right to use accelerated MACRS (200% or 150% declining balance method) terminates. You must use the straight-line method and recapture the benefit of the accelerated deductions claimed for the prior years; *see 43.10* for the recapture rule.

Straight-line election for vehicle if business use exceeds 50%. If business use of your vehicle exceeds 50%, you may elect to write off your cost under the straight-line method instead of using the regular MACRS 200% declining balance method. The straight-line rates are shown in *43.6.* The straight-line deduction is limited by the annual ceilings shown on page 675. By electing straight-line depreciation, you avoid the recapture of excess MACRS deductions if business use drops to 50% or less in a later year; *see 43.10.* If the election is made, you must also use the straight-line method for all other five-year property placed in service during the same year as the vehicle.

Filing Tip

Capital Improvements

A capital improvement to a business vehicle is depreciable under MACRS in the year the improvement is made. The MACRS deductions for the improvement and the vehicle are considered as a unit for purposes of applying the limits on the annual MACRS depreciation deduction.

Electing 150% declining balance method. Depreciation rates under the half-year and mid-quarter conventions are generally based on the 200% declining balance method. You may instead make an irrevocable election to apply the 150% declining balance method. The 150% method may be advantageous when you are subject to the alternative minimum tax. For alternative minimum tax (AMT) purposes *(23.2)*, vehicle depreciation is based on the 150% declining balance method unless you use the straight-line method for regular tax purposes. If you are subject to AMT and use the 150% declining balance method instead of the 200% declining balance method for regular tax purposes, you do not have to report an AMT adjustment on Form 6251.

An election to use the 150% declining balance method is irrevocable and must be applied to all depreciable assets placed in service in the same year, except for nonresidential real and residential rental property.

MACRS Tables Applying the Half-Year Convention or Mid-Quarter Convention if Business Use Exceeds 50%

For the year you place the vehicle in service and the year (within the recovery period) you dispose of the property, you may not claim a full year's worth of depreciation. The deduction is limited by either the half-year convention or the mid-quarter convention, depending on the month in which the vehicle was placed in service and the other business assets, if any, placed in service during that year.

The applicable convention determines the rate table you will use to figure your depreciation deduction for the entire six-year recovery period, assuming that your business use each year exceeds 50%. The half-year and mid-quarter convention tables shown below reflect the 200% or 150% declining balance method, with a switch to the straight-line method when that method provides a larger deduction; the switch to straight line is built into the tables.

Rate applied to unadjusted basis. For each year in the recovery period, the rate from the applicable table is applied against the business use percentage of your unadjusted basis for the vehicle. Investment use may be added to the business use percentage, but keep in mind that the MACRS table below may be used only if business use by itself exceeds 50%; *see 43.3.*

Unadjusted basis is your cost minus any first-year expensing deduction as well as any special first-year bonus depreciation for a vehicle placed into service after September 10, 2001, and before January 1, 2005. The basis reduction for bonus depreciation applies if you were eligible for the special allowance (vehicle purchased new and used over 50% for business) even if you did not claim it, unless on your return you "elected out" of the special allowance for the vehicle and all other five-year property placed in service during the same year. The deduction figured under the table rate may be claimed to the extent that it does not exceed the annual depreciation ceiling *(43.4)*; *see* the Bill Johnston Example on page 678.

Basis for vehicle converted from personal to business use. The basis for depreciation is the lower of the market value of the vehicle at the time of conversion or its adjusted basis, which is your original cost plus any substantial improvements and minus any deductible casualty losses or diesel fuel tax credit claimed for the vehicle. In most cases, the value of the vehicle will be lower than adjusted basis, and thus the value will be your depreciable basis. For a vehicle converted to business use in 2006, the MACRS rate is applied to basis allocated to business travel. Unless you have mileage records for the entire year, you should base your business-use percentage on driving after the conversion. For example, in April 2006, you started to use your car for business and in the last nine months of the year you drove 10,000 miles, 8,000 of which were for business. This business percentage of 80% is multiplied by the fraction $^{9}/_{12}$ (months used for business divided by 12) to give you a business-use percentage for the year of 60% ($^{9}/_{12}$ of 80%).

Determining whether the half-year convention or mid-quarter convention applies. If you bought a vehicle for use in your business in 2006, and it was the only business equipment placed in service during the year, then the half-year convention applies, unless you bought the vehicle in the last quarter of 2006 (October, November, or December). Under the half-year convention, the vehicle is treated as if it were placed in service in the middle of the year. Use the table below to determine your deduction under the half-year convention.

If the only business equipment bought in 2006 was a vehicle bought in the last quarter (October, November, or December), the mid-quarter convention applies. Under the table for mid-quarter convention rates on page 678, a 5% rate applies for fourth-quarter property under the 200% declining balance method, subject to the deduction ceiling in 2006; *see 43.4.*

If you bought other business equipment in addition to the vehicle, you must consider the total cost basis of property placed in service during the last quarter of 2006. If the total bases of such acquisitions (other than realty) exceed 40% of the total bases of all property placed in service during the year, then a mid-quarter rate applies to *all* of the property (other than realty). The mid-quarter rate for each asset then depends on the quarter the asset was placed in service. If the 40% test is not met, then the half-year convention applies to all the property acquisitions. As shown in the mid-quarter convention table on page 678, mid-quarter rates for each year of the recovery period depend on the quarter the property is placed in service.

Deduction from table cannot exceed annual ceiling. If the deduction figured under the half-year or mid-quarter convention MACRS table (Table 43-4 or 43-5) exceeds the annual deduction ceiling discussed in *43.4*, your deduction is limited to the annual ceiling, reduced by the percentage of your personal use. Keep in mind that if you were eligible for the special first-year depreciation allowance (bonus depreciation) for a vehicle placed in service after September 10, 2001, and before January 1, 2005, basis for MACRS purposes is reduced by the special allowance unless you elected on your return not to claim it.

Caution

Basis Reduction for First-Year Bonus Depreciation

If you were eligible for the special first-year depreciation allowance for a vehicle placed in service after September 10, 2001, and before January 1, 2005, you must reduce depreciable basis by the amount of the available allowance even if you did not claim it, unless you specifically elected not to claim the allowance on a statement attached to your return.

Table 43-4 MACRS Deduction: Half-Year Convention

Year—	*200% Rate*	*150% Rate*
1	20.00%	15.00%
2	32.00	25.50
3	19.20	17.85
4	11.52	16.66
5	11.52	16.66
6	5.76	8.33

EXAMPLE

On May 1, 2003, Bill Johnston placed in service a new car he used 100% for business. The car cost $20,000. He did not claim first-year expensing and "elected out" of the special first-year depreciation allowance. Here is Bill's depreciation schedule using the 200% declining balance rate, assuming the car is kept for the period shown below and is used 100% for business trips:

Year	*Deduction from rate table*	*Annual ceiling (43.4)*	*Allowable deduction*
2003	$4,000 (20% × $20,000)	$ 3,060	$ 3,060
2004	6,400 (32% × $20,000)	4,900	4,900
2005	3,840 (19.20% × $20,000)	2,950	2,950
2006	2,304 (11.52% × $20,000)	1,775	1,775
2007	2,304 (11.52% × $20,000)	1,775	1,775
2008*	1,152 (5.76% × $20,000)	1,775	1,152
2009		1,775	1,775
2010		1,775	1,775
2011		838	838

* Note that for the first five years (2003–2008), the allowable deduction is limited to the annual ceiling but in year six (2008), the deduction is based on the MACRS rate table because $1,152 (5.76% × $20,000) is less than the $1,775 annual ceiling.

Table 43-5 MACRS Deduction: Mid-Quarter Convention

	Placed in service in—							
Year—	*First Quarter*		*Second Quarter*		*Third Quarter*		*Fourth Quarter*	
	200% Rate	*150% Rate*	*200% Rate*	*150% Rate*	*200% Rate*	*150% Rate*	*200% Rate*	*150% Rate*
1	35.00%	26.25%	25.00%	18.75%	15.00%	11.25%	5.00%	3.75%
2	26.00	22.13	30.00	24.38	34.00	26.63	38.00	28.88
3	15.60	16.52	18.00	17.06	20.40	18.64	22.80	20.21
4	11.01	16.52	11.37	16.76	12.24	16.56	13.68	16.40
5	11.01	16.52	11.37	16.76	11.30	16.57	10.94	16.41
6	1.38	2.06	4.26	6.29	7.06	10.35	9.58	14.35

43.6 Straight-Line Method

You may not use first-year expensing (Section 179 deduction) or accelerated MACRS *(43.5)* if your business use of your car, truck, or van is 50% or less in the year you place it in service. Mandatory straight-line recovery rates for business use of 50% or less using the half-year or mid-quarter convention are shown below. These straight-line rates are also used if your business use exceeds 50% and you elect straight-line recovery instead of the regular MACRS method. *See 43.5* for determining whether the half-year or mid-quarter convention applies.

For each year of the six-year recovery period, apply the straight-line rate from the applicable table against your unadjusted basis, which is the business part of your cost minus any first-year expensing deduction or special depreciation allowance *(43.5)*. The deduction from the table is allowed only to the extent that it does not exceed the annual deduction ceiling *(43.4)*.

If business use initially exceeds 50% and accelerated MACRS is claimed but business use drops to 50% or less before the end of the six-year recovery period, a recapture rule applies a straight-line computation retroactively; *see 43.10*.

Table 43-6 Straight-Line Half-Year Convention*

Straight-line year—	*Half-year convention rate—*
1	10%
2	20
3	20
4	20
5	20
6	10

**The deduction may not exceed the annual deduction ceiling;* see 43.4.

EXAMPLE

In April 2006, you place in service an automobile which cost $24,000. You used it 40% for business. The depreciable basis is $9,600 (40% of $24,000). The depreciation deduction in 2006 is $960 (10% of $9,600) if the half-year convention applies. It is less than the annual deduction ceiling of $1,184 (40% of the $2,960 first-year ceiling for 2006; *see 43.4*).

Table 43-7 Straight-Line Mid-Quarter Convention*

	Placed in service in—			
Year	*First Quarter*	*Second Quarter*	*Third Quarter*	*Fourth Quarter*
1	17.50%	12.50%	7.50%	2.50%
2	20.00	20.00	20.00	20.00
3	20.00	20.00	20.00	20.00
4	20.00	20.00	20.00	20.00
5	20.00	20.00	20.00	20.00
6	2.50	7.50	12.50	17.50

**The deduction may not exceed the annual deduction ceiling;* see 43.4.

EXAMPLE

In 2006, you place in service a car costing $15,000 used 40% for business. Assume the mid-quarter convention applies. Depending on the applicable quarter, the deduction is listed below, figured on a basis of $6,000 ($15,000 × 40%). The first-year ceiling at 40% business use is $1,184 ($2,960 × 40%). The ceiling does not apply because the mid-quarter rates provide a lower deduction.

Quarter	*Deduction*
1	$1,050 ($6,000 × 17.5%)
2	750 ($6,000 × 12.5%)
3	450 ($6,000 × 7.5%)
4	150 ($6,000 × 2.5%)

43.7 Depreciation for Year Vehicle Is Disposed Of

If you dispose of your car, truck, or van before the end of the six-year recovery period, you are allowed a partial depreciation deduction for the year of disposition. The deduction depends on the depreciation method and convention being used.

If you were depreciating the vehicle under the half-year convention *(43.5)*, you may claim for the year of disposition 50% of the deduction that would be allowed for the full year under the 200% or 150% declining balance method, or the straight-line method.

If you were depreciating the vehicle under the mid-quarter convention *(43.5)*, your deduction for the year of disposition depends on the month of disposition. You deduct 87.5% of the full-year mid-quarter convention deduction *(43.5)* if the disposition occurred in October–December. If the disposition is in July–September, 62.5% of the full year's deduction is allowed. Your deduction is 37.5% of the full-year deduction if the disposition is in April–June, or 12.5% of the full-year deduction if the disposition is in January–March.

EXAMPLE

In December 2002, you bought a car costing $20,000 that you used exclusively for business until you sold it in April 2006. You "elected out" of the special depreciation allowance and depreciated the car under the mid-quarter convention.

For 2006, the year of disposition, the full-year deduction would be $1,775. The $1,775 annual ceiling (fifth-year ceiling for cars placed in service in 2002) is less than the $2,188 deduction (10.94% × $20,000) allowed under the fourth quarter 200% rate mid-quarter convention table *(43.5)*. Since the car was disposed of in April, you may deduct 37.5% of $1,775, or $666, on your 2006 return.

43.8 Depreciation After Recovery Period Ends

If your business use of a car, truck, or van during the recovery period is 100% and your deductions are limited by the annual ceilings *(43.4)*, any remaining basis that was not deducted because of the ceilings may be depreciated in the years after the end of the recovery period.

If the vehicle was used less than 100% for business, any unrecovered basis may be deductible, but to determine unrecovered basis, original basis must be reduced by the depreciation that would have been allowed had the vehicle been used 100% for business.

EXAMPLE

In January 2000 you bought a car costing $28,600 that you used 100% for business every year from 2000 through 2005. Your depreciation deductions for the six-year recovery period under the 200% declining balance method were limited because of the annual deduction ceilings (*see* the ceilings at *43.4*). For 2000 through 2004, you deducted the annual ceiling amounts. For 2005, your deduction was based on the MACRS half-year convention rate table *(43.5)* because this amount was less than the annual ceiling. Total depreciation deductions for 2000–2005 were $16,107, as shown below.

Year	*200% rate deduction*	*Annual ceiling*	*Allowable deduction*
2000	$5,720 (20% × $28,600)	$3,060	$3,060
2001	9,152 (32% × $28,600)	4,900	4,900
2002	5,491 (19.20% × $28,600)	2,950	2,950
2003	3,295 (11.52% × $28,600)	1,775	1,775
2004	3,295 (11.52% × $28,600)	1,775	1,775
2005	1,647 (5.76% × $28,600)	1,775	1,647

At the beginning of 2006, your unrecovered basis in the car is $12,493 (the original basis of $28,600 minus the $16,107 of depreciation deductions allowed from 2000 through 2005). If you continue to use the car 100% for business in 2006 and later years, you can deduct $1,775 in 2006 and also in later years until the $12,493 of unrecovered basis is used up. In years of partial business use, the deduction will be limited to $1,775 multiplied by the business-use percentage.

If you had *not* used the car for business 100% of the time in all prior years, your unrecovered basis would still be $12,493. That is because for purposes of figuring unrecovered basis, you must reduce original basis by the depreciation that would have been allowed based on 100% business use.

43.9 Trade-in of Business Vehicle

No gain or loss is recognized when you trade in your old car, truck, or van for a new one where you opt to treat the disposition as tax free (different rules apply if you do not make this election, as explained in IRS Publication 946). However, the trade-in affects the basis of the new vehicle for purposes of depreciation. The basis adjustment depends on whether the car you traded in was used solely or partially for business.

Old vehicle used entirely for business. The basis of the new vehicle acquired in the trade-in is the adjusted basis of the old vehicle (its cost reduced by depreciation deductions), plus any cash you had to pay.

EXAMPLE

You trade in your 2000 car used exclusively for business to acquire a new car this year that costs $20,000. The adjusted basis of the 2000 car is $3,000 and you pay $17,000 cash. Your basis in the new car is $20,000 ($3,000 adjusted basis of the trade-in car plus $17,000 cash).

If you claimed first-year expensing, or bonus depreciation, you must make additional adjustments to basis (*see* IRS Publication 463).

Old vehicle used partially for business. There is a special "trade-in adjustment" for cars, trucks, or vans used for both personal and business use. This adjustment reduces the basis of the new vehicle (but not below zero) by the amount of depreciation you would have claimed if you had used the old vehicle entirely for business. To figure the basis of the new vehicle, including the trade-in adjustment, start with the adjusted basis of the old vehicle (*see* above). Add any cash you pay to acquire the new vehicle. Then subtract the excess, if any, of the depreciation you could have claimed had you used the old vehicle entirely for business over your actual depreciation for the old vehicle (the trade-in adjustment). *See* the examples in IRS Publication 463.

Caution

Trade-in Adjustment

The trade-in adjustment is *not* used for determining gain or loss on the disposition of the new car when it is later sold. It is used solely for depreciation purposes.

43.10 Recapture of Deductions on Business Car, Truck, or Van

If you use your car, truck, or van more than 50% for business in the year you place it in service, you may use MACRS accelerated rates; *see 43.5*. If business use drops to 50% or less in the second, third, fourth, fifth, or sixth year, earlier MACRS deductions must be recaptured and reported as ordinary income. In the year in which business use drops to 50% or less, you must recapture excess depreciation for all prior years. Excess depreciation is the difference between: (1) the MACRS deductions allowed in previous years, including the first-year expensing deduction and bonus first-year depreciation allowance *(43.4)*, if any, and (2) the amount of depreciation that would have been allowed if you claimed straight-line depreciation based on a six-year recovery period. *See 43.6* for straight-line rates.

The recapture rules do not apply if you elected straight-line recovery instead of applying accelerated MACRS rates.

Recapture is reported on Form 4797, which must be attached to Form 1040. Under the listed property rules, the 50%-business-use test and recapture rule apply to cars, trucks, vans, boats, airplanes, motorcycles, and other vehicles used to transport persons or goods, but there are exceptions for ambulances, hearses, and other trucks and vans that are considered qualified non-personal-use vehicles as discussed at *43.4*.

Any recaptured amount increases the basis of the property. To compute depreciation for the year in which business use drops to 50% or less and for later years within the six-year straight-line recovery period, you apply the straight-line rates shown at *43.6*.

EXAMPLE

On June 25, 2002, you bought a car for $11,000 that you used exclusively for business in 2002, 2003, 2004, and 2005. You "elected out" of the special depreciation allowance. The half-year convention applied to your MACRS deductions *(43.5)*. The deductions figured under the half-year convention table ($2,200 for 2002, $3,520 for 2003, $2,112 for 2004, and $1,267 for 2005) applied as they were less than the annual ceilings for those years ($3,060, $4,900, $2,950, and $1,775, respectively). During 2006, you used the car 40% for business and 60% for personal purposes. As you did not meet the more-than-50%-business-use test in 2006, excess depreciation of $1,399 is recaptured and reported on Form 4797 for 2006:

Total MACRS depreciation claimed (2002–2005)		$9,099
Total straight-line depreciation *(43.6)* allowable:		
2002—10% of $11,000	$1,100	
2003—20% of $11,000	2,200	
2004—20% of $11,000	2,200	
2005—20% of $11,000	2,200	7,700
Excess depreciation recaptured		$1,399

Your 2006 depreciation deduction is $880 ($11,000 × 20% straight-line rate in fifth year × 40% business use).

The amount of recaptured depreciation increases the adjusted basis for purposes of computing gain or loss on a disposition of the automobile.

43.11 Keeping Records of Business Use

Keep a log or diary or similar record of the business use of a car. Record the purpose of the business trips and mileage covered for business travel. In the record book, also note the odometer reading for the beginning and end of the taxable year. You need this data to prove business use. If you do not keep written records of business mileage and your return is examined, you will have to convince an IRS agent of your business mileage through oral testimony. Without written evidence, you may be unable to convince an IRS agent that you use the car for business travel or that you meet the business-use tests for claiming MACRS. You may also be subject to general negligence penalties for claiming deductions that you cannot prove you incurred.

Mileage records are not required for vehicles that are unlikely to be used for personal purposes, such as delivery trucks with seating only for the driver.

Employees using company cars are not required to keep mileage records if (1) a written company policy allows them to use the car for commuting and no other personal driving other than personal errands while commuting home or (2) a written company policy bars all personal driving except for minor stops, such as for lunch, between business travel. Owners, directors, and officers of the company generally do not qualify for exception (1).

Caution

Leased Vehicle

If in 2006 you leased a car, truck, or van for at least 30 days and you deduct the lease charges as a business expense *(43.12)*, you generally must reduce the deduction by an "income inclusion amount" based on an IRS table. If you claim the standard mileage allowance *(43.1)*, the income inclusion rule does not apply. *See* IRS Publication 463 for details.

43.12 Leased Business Vehicles: Deductions and Income

If you lease rather than purchase a car, truck, or van for business use, you may deduct the lease charges as a business expense deduction if you use the vehicle exclusively for business. If you also use the vehicle for personal driving, you may deduct only the lease payments allocated to business travel. Also keep a record of business use; *see 43.11*.

Added income. If in 2006 you lease a vehicle for 30 days or more, you may have to report as income an amount based on an IRS table. This income rule applies if you deduct the business portion of your lease payments plus other operating costs; it does not apply if you claim the standard mileage allowance *(43.1)*. On Schedule C (if self-employed) or Form 2106 (if an employee), the income inclusion amount reduces your deduction for lease payments so that it equals the amount that would be deductible as depreciation if you had bought the vehicle outright. The income amount is reduced where you leased the vehicle for less than the entire year or business use is less than 100%.

The lease tables, which are in IRS Publication 463, show income amounts for each year of the lease. Publication 463 also has tables showing income amounts for vehicles leased before 2006.

Chapter 44

Sales of Business Property

On the sale of business assets, the tax treatment depends on the type of asset sold.

Inventory items: Profits are taxable as ordinary income; losses are fully deductible. Sales of merchandise are reported on Schedule C if you are self-employed or Schedule F if you are a farmer.

Depreciable property, such as buildings, machinery, and equipment: If you sell at a gain, the gain is taxable as ordinary income to the extent depreciation is recaptured under *44.1* and *44.2*. Any remaining gain may be treated as capital gain or ordinary income, depending on the Section 1231 computation at *44.8*. Losses may be deductible as ordinary losses; *see 44.8*. Sales are reported on Form 4797. Depreciable business equipment subject to recapture is described as a Section 1245 asset. Depreciable livestock is also a Section 1245 asset. Depreciable realty is generally described as a Section 1250 asset.

Land: If used in your business, capital gain or ordinary income may be realized under the rules of Section 1231; *see 44.8*. If land owned by your business is held for investment, gain or loss is subject to capital gain treatment. Schedule D is used to report the sale of capital assets.

See also:

44.1 Depreciation Recaptured as Ordinary Income on Sale of Personal Property

Caution

Dispositions Other than Sales

See 44.4 for how recapture rules affect gifts, charitable donations, and inheritances of depreciable property, and *44.5* for like-kind exchanges and involuntary conversions.

On Form 4797, you report gain or loss on the sale of depreciable property. Gain realized on the sale of depreciable *personal property* (Section 1245 property) is treated as ordinary income to the extent the gain is attributed to depreciation deductions that reduced basis. In other words, the depreciation deductions are "recaptured" as ordinary income. If gain exceeds the amount of depreciation subject to recapture, the excess may be capital gain under Section 1231; *see 44.8.*

Gain on the sale of real estate placed in service before 1987 may be subject to depreciation recapture as discussed in *44.2.*

Gain subject to recapture for Section 1245 property is limited to the lower of (1) the amount of gain on the sale (amount realized less adjusted basis) or (2) the depreciation allowed or allowable while you held the property. Generally, the depreciation deduction taken into account for each year is the amount allowed or allowable, whichever is greater. However, for purposes of figuring what portion of the gain is treated as ordinary income under the recapture rules (but not for purposes of figuring gain or loss), the depreciation taken into account for any year will be the amount actually "allowed" on your prior returns under a proper depreciation method, rather than the amount "allowable," if the allowed deduction is smaller and you can prove its amount.

The adjusted basis of personal property depreciable under ACRS, such as business equipment and machinery, is fixed as of the beginning of the year of disposition. However, property depreciated under MACRS is subject to the convention rules so that partial depreciation under the applicable convention is allowed in the year of sale; this year of sale depreciation reduces adjusted basis.

EXAMPLE

In March 2004, you bought and placed in service a light truck (five-year property) at a cost of $10,000. You used the truck 100% for business. You deducted depreciation under the half-year convention of $2,000 for 2004 and $3,200 for 2005; *see* the MACRS rates at *42.5.* In January 2006, you sold the truck for $6,000. For 2005, you are allowed an MACRS deduction of one-half of the full year deduction, or $960 (19.20% x $10,000 ÷ 2). Your adjusted basis is $3,840 ($10,000 cost – $6,160 total depreciation). Your gain on the sale is $2,160 ($6,000 proceeds – $3,840 adjusted basis). You must recapture the entire $2,160 gain as ordinary income, as it is less than the $6,160 depreciation.

44.2 Depreciation Recaptured as Ordinary Income on Sale of Real Estate

All or part of gain on the sale of depreciable real property may be attributable to depreciation deductions that reduced the basis of the property. On Form 4797, gain attributable to depreciation on Section 1250 realty placed in service before 1987 is subject to recapture as ordinary income unless straight-line depreciation was used. The amount of depreciation recapture depends on when the building was placed in service and whether it was residential or nonresidential; *see* below.

There is no ordinary income recapture for residential rental and nonresidential real property placed in service after 1986 because such properties are depreciated using the straight-line MACRS method *(42.13).* However, 30% or 50% bonus depreciation on qualifying New York Liberty Zone real property and 50% bonus depreciation on GO Zone property is subject to recapture on Form 4797.

To the extent depreciation is not subject to ordinary income recapture, the gain on the sale is subject to the Section 1231 netting rules discussed at *44.8.* If there is a net Section 1231 gain, the gain attributed to the depreciation is entered on the Unrecaptured Section 1250 Gain Worksheet in the Schedule D (Form 1040) instructions. The unrecaptured Section 1250 gain from that worksheet is subject to a top rate of 25% on the Schedule D Tax Worksheet included in the Schedule D instructions.

Recaptured depreciation. Ordinary income recapture may apply to Section 1250 realty placed in service before 1987. Section 1250 property includes buildings and structural components, *except* for elevators and escalators or other tangible property used as an integral part of manufacturing, production, or extraction, or of furnishing transportation, electrical energy, water, gas, sewage disposal services, or communications. Property may initially be Section 1250 property and then, on a change of use, become Section 1245 property *(44.1).* Such property may not be reconverted to Section 1250 property.

Depreciation claimed on realty during the years 1964 through 1969. Depreciation claimed during this period is not recaptured.

Depreciation claimed after 1969 for realty placed in service before 1981. For nonresidential realty, 100 percent of the depreciation claimed after 1969 in excess of straight-line recovery is subject to recapture but not in excess of the actual gain.

For residential rental property, there is no recapture of excess depreciation (over straight-line) claimed after 1969 and before 1976. Real property is considered residential rental property if 80% or more of gross income is from dwelling units. One hundred percent of the excess depreciation claimed after 1975 is subject to recapture. Part III of Form 4797 is used to compute the amount of depreciation recapture that is to be reported as ordinary income.

Depreciation claimed on realty placed in service after 1980 and before 1987. For real property placed in service after 1980 and before 1987 that was subject to ACRS, adjusted basis for computing gain or loss is the adjusted basis at the start of the year reduced by the ACRS deduction allowed for the number of months the realty is in service in the year of disposition; *see 42.16*. The recapture rules distinguish between residential and nonresidential property.

If the prescribed accelerated method is used to recover the cost of *nonresidential* property, all gain on the disposition of the realty is recaptured as ordinary income to the extent of recovery allowances previously taken. Thus, nonresidential realty will be treated in the same way as personal property *(44.1)* for purposes of recapture if the accelerated recovery allowance was claimed. If the straight-line method was elected, there is no recapture; all gain is subject to the netting rules of Section 1231 *(44.8)*.

If accelerated cost recovery is used for a *nonresidential* building and straight-line depreciation is used for a substantial improvement to that building that you are allowed to depreciate separately *(42.16)*, all gain on a disposition of the entire building is treated as ordinary income to the extent of the accelerated cost recovery claimed. Remaining gain is subject to the rules for Section 1231 assets *(44.8)*.

For *residential* real estate, 100% of the excess depreciation claimed is subject to recapture. That is, there is ordinary income recapture to the extent the depreciation allowed under the prescribed accelerated method exceeds the recovery that would have been allowable if the straight-line method over the ACRS recovery period had been used. If the straight-line method was elected, there is no recapture. All gain is subject to Section 1231 netting *(44.8)*.

For *low-income rental housing,* the percentage of excess depreciation (over straight-line) subject to recapture is 100% minus 1% for each full month the property was held over 100 months, so that there is no recapture of cost recovery deductions for property held at least 200 months (16 years and 8 months). If you dispose of low-income housing with separate improvements, or with units placed in service at different times, the amount of excess depreciation must be computed separately for each element. *See* IRS Publication 544 for details on the recapture rules for low-income housing.

44.3 Recapture of First-Year Expensing

On Form 4797, the first-year expensing deduction (Section 179 deduction; *see 42.3*) is treated as depreciation for purposes of recapture. When expensed property is sold or exchanged, gain is ordinary income to the extent of the first-year expense deduction plus ACRS or MACRS deductions and bonus depreciation *(42.20)*, if any; *see 44.1*. If the entire cost of the property was expensed, adjusted basis will generally be reduced to zero, gain on a sale or exchange will equal the sales price (less expenses), and the entire gain will be recaptured as ordinary income.

Expensing deductions are also subject to recapture if property placed in service after 1986 is not used more than 50% of the time for business in any year before the end of the recovery period. The amount recaptured is the excess of the first-year *expensing* deduction over the amount of depreciation that would have been claimed in prior years and in the recapture year without expensing.

Automobiles and other "listed property." If the more-than-50%-business-use test for a business automobile or other "listed property" such as certain computers *(see 42.10)* is not met in a year after the auto or other "listed property" is placed in service and before the end of the recovery period, any first-year expensing deduction is subject to recapture on Form 4797; *see* the Example at *43.10*.

Caution

Installment Sale

If you sell property on the installment basis, the first-year expensing deduction claimed for the property in a prior year is recaptured in the year of sale on Form 4797. An installment sale does not defer recapture of the first-year deduction; *see 44.6*.

44.4 Gifts and Inheritances of Depreciable Property

Gifts and charitable donations of depreciable property may be affected by the recapture rules. On the gift of depreciable property, the ordinary income potential of the depreciation carries over into the hands of the donee. When the donee later sells the property at a profit, he or she will realize ordinary income to the extent described in *44.1*. A person receiving a gift of low-income housing property includes in the holding period the period for which the donor held the property for purposes of applying the 200-month phaseout of recapture rule *(44.2)*.

On the donation of depreciable property, the amount of the contribution deduction is reduced by the amount that would be taxed as ordinary income had the donor sold the equipment at its fair market value.

The transfer of depreciable property to an heir through inheritance is not a taxable event for recapture purposes. The ordinary income potential does not carry over to the heir because his or her basis is usually fixed as of the date of the decedent's death.

Important: A gift of depreciable property subject to a mortgage may be taxed to the extent that the liability exceeds the basis of the property; *see 14.6* and *31.15*.

Caution

Tax-Free Exchanges

Ordinary income generally is not realized on a tax-free exchange or trade-in of the same type of property (unless some gain is taxed because the exchange is accompanied by "boot" *(6.3)* such as money). The ordinary income potential is assumed in the basis of the new property. However, where depreciable realty acquired before 1987 is exchanged for land, the amount of any depreciation recapture is immediately taxable in the year of the exchange.

44.5 Involuntary Conversions and Tax-Free Exchanges

Involuntary conversions. Gain may be taxed as ordinary income in either of the following two cases: (1) you do not buy qualified replacement property or (2) you buy a qualified replacement, but the cost of the replacement is less than the amount realized on the conversion; *see 18.23*. The amount taxable as ordinary income may not exceed the amount of gain that is normally taxed under involuntary conversion rules when the replacement cost is less than the amount realized on the conversion. Also, the amount of ordinary income is increased by the value of any nondepreciable property that is bought as qualified replacement property, such as the purchase of 80% or more of stock in a company that owns property similar to the converted property.

Distributions by a partnership to a partner. A distribution of depreciable property by a partnership to a partner does not result in ordinary income to the distributee at the time of the distribution. But the partner assumes the ordinary income potential of the depreciation deduction taken by the partnership on the property. When he or she later disposes of the property, ordinary income may be realized.

44.6 Installment Sale of Depreciable Property

All depreciation recapture income (including the first-year expensing deduction) is fully taxable in the year of sale, without regard to the time of payment. Recapture is figured on Form 4797. On Form 6252, the gain in excess of the recapture income is reported under the installment method *(5.21)*.

44.7 Sale of a Proprietorship

The sale of a sole proprietorship is not considered as the sale of a business unit but as sales of individual business assets. Each sale is reported separately on your tax return.

A purchase of a business involves the purchase of various individual business assets of the business. To force buyers and sellers to follow the same allocation rules, current law requires both the buyer and the seller to allocate the purchase price of a business among the transferred assets using a residual method formula. Allocations are based on the proportion of sales price to an asset's fair market value and they are made in a specific order set out on Form 8594.

Caution

Capital Gain or Ordinary Loss

Profitable sales and involuntary conversions of Section 1231 assets are generally treated as capital gain, except for profits on equipment *(44.1)* and real estate allocated to recaptured depreciation *(44.2)*, and losses are deducted as ordinary loss. However, the exact tax result depends on the net profit and loss realized for all sales of such property made during the tax year. Under the netting rules explained at *44.8*, the net result of these sales determines the tax treatment of each individual sale. In making the computation on Form 4797, you must also consider losses and gains from casualty, theft, and other involuntary conversions involving business and investment property held more than one year. Follow the Form 4797 instructions.

44.8 Property Used in a Business (Section 1231 Assets)

Form 4797 is used to report the sale or exchange of Section 1231 assets. The following properties used in a business are considered "Section 1231 assets":

- Depreciable assets such as buildings, machinery, and other equipment held more than one year. Depreciable rental property and royalty property fits in this category if held more than one year.
- Land (including growing crops and water rights underlying farmland) held more than one year.
- Timber, coal, or domestic iron ore subject to special capital gain treatment.
- Leaseholds held more than one year.
- An unharvested crop on farmlands, if the crop and land are sold, exchanged, or involuntarily converted at the same time and to the same person and the land has been held more than one year. Such property is not included here if you retain an option to reacquire the land.
- Cattle and horses held for draft, breeding, dairy, or sporting purposes for at least 24 months.
- Livestock (other than cattle and horses) held for draft, breeding, dairy, or sporting purposes for at least 12 months. Poultry is not treated as livestock for purposes of Section 1231.

Section 1231 netting. On Form 4797, you combine all losses and gains, except gains allocated to depreciation recapture, from:

- The sale of Section 1231 assets (from the list at the beginning of this section).
- The involuntary conversion of Section 1231 assets and capital assets held for more than one year for business or investment purposes. You include casualty and theft losses incurred on business or investment property held for more than one year. However, there is an exception if losses exceed gains from casualties or thefts in one taxable year.

Involuntary conversions of capital assets held for personal purposes are not subject to a Section 1231 computation but are subject to a separate computation; *see 18.25*.

Result of netting. A net gain on Section 1231 assets from Form 4797 is entered on Schedule D as a long-term capital gain unless the recapture rule (*see* the Caution on this page) for net ordinary losses applies. A net loss on Section 1231 assets is combined on Form 4797 with ordinary income from depreciation recapture *(44.1)* and with ordinary gains and losses from the sale of business property that does not qualify for Section 1231 netting.

Installment sale. Gain realized on the installment sale of business or income-producing property held for more than a year may be capital gain one year and ordinary income another year. Actual treatment in each year depends on the net result of all sales, including installment payments received in that year; also *see 44.6*.

Losses exceed gains from casualties or thefts. On Form 4684, you must compute the net financial result from all involuntary conversions arising from fire, storm, or other casualty or theft of assets used in your business and capital assets held for business or income-producing purposes and held more than one year. The purpose of the computation is to determine whether these involuntary conversions enter into the above Section 1231 computation. If the net result is a gain, all of the assets enter into the Section 1231 computation. If the net result is a loss, then these assets do not enter into the computation; the losses are deducted separately as casualty losses, and the gains reported separately as ordinary income. If you incur only losses, the losses similarly do not enter into the Section 1231 computation.

Caution

Recapture of Net Ordinary Losses

Net Section 1231 gain is not treated as capital gain but as ordinary income to the extent of net Section 1231 losses realized in the five most recent prior taxable years. Losses are recaptured in chronological order on Form 4797. Losses that have already been "recaptured" under this rule in prior years are not taken into account.

EXAMPLE

You suffer an uninsured fire loss of $2,000 on business equipment and gain of $1,000 on other insured investment property damaged by a storm. All of the property was held more than one year. Because loss exceeds gain, neither transaction enters into a Section 1231 computation. The gain is reported as ordinary income and the loss is deducted as an ordinary loss. The effect is a net $1,000 loss deduction. If the figures were reversed, that is, if the gain were $2,000 and the loss $1,000, both assets would enter into the Section 1231 computation. If only the fire loss occurred, the loss would be treated as a casualty loss and would not enter into the Section 1231 computation.

44.9 Sale of Property Used for Business and Personal Purposes

One sale will be reported as two separate sales for tax purposes when you sell a car or any other equipment used for business and personal purposes, or in some cases where a sold residence *(see 29.7)* was used partly as a residence and partly as a place of business or to produce rent income.

You allocate the sales price and the basis of the property between the business portion and the personal portion. The allocation is based on use. For example, with a car, the allocation is based on mileage used in business and personal driving.

EXAMPLE

Two partners bought an airplane for about $54,000. They used approximately 75% of its flying time for personal flights and 25% for business flights. After using the plane for eight years, they sold it for about $35,000. Depreciation taken on the business part of the plane amounted to $13,000. The partners figured they incurred a loss of $6,000 on the sale. The

IRS, allocating the proceeds and basis between business and personal use, claimed they realized a profit of $8,250 on the business part of the plane and a nondeductible loss of $14,250 on the personal part. The allocation was as follows:

	Partners' claim	IRS Position Business (25%)	IRS Position Personal (75%)
Original cost	$54,000	$13,500	$40,500
Depreciation	13,000	13,000	
Adjusted basis	41,000	500	40,500
Selling price	35,000	8,750	26,250
Gain (Nondeductible loss)	($6,000)	$8,250	($14,250)

The partners argued that the IRS could not split the sale into two separate sales. They sold only one airplane and therefore there was only one sale. A federal district court and appeals court disagreed and held that the IRS method of allocation is practical and fair.

44.10 Should You Trade in Business Equipment?

The purchase of new business equipment is often partially financed by trading in old equipment. For tax purposes, a trade-in may not be a good decision. If the market value of the equipment is below its adjusted basis, it may be preferable to sell the equipment to realize an immediate deductible loss. You may not deduct a loss on a trade-in. However, if you do trade, the potential deduction reflected in the cost basis of the old equipment is not forfeited. The undepreciated basis of the old property becomes part of the basis of the new property and may be depreciated. Therefore, in deciding whether to trade or sell where a loss may be realized, determine whether you will get a greater tax reduction by taking an immediate loss on a sale or by claiming larger depreciation deductions.

If the fair market value of the old equipment exceeds its adjusted basis, you have a potential gain. To defer tax on this gain, you may want to trade the equipment in for new equipment. Your decision to sell or trade will generally be based on a comparison between (1) tax imposed on an immediate sale and larger depreciation deductions taken on the cost basis of the new property, and (2) the tax consequences of a trade-in in which the tax is deferred but reduced depreciation deductions are taken on a lower cost basis of the property. In making this comparison, you will have to estimate your future income and tax rates. Also pay attention to the possibility that gain on a sale may be taxed as ordinary income under the depreciation recapture rules; *see 44.1*.

The tax consequences of a trade-in may not be avoided by first selling the used property to the dealer who sells you the new property. The IRS will disregard the sale made to the same dealer from whom you purchase the new equipment. The two transactions will be treated as one trade-in.

44.11 Corporate Liquidation

Liquidation of a corporation and distribution of its assets for your stock is generally subject to capital gain or loss treatment. For example, on a corporate liquidation, you receive property worth $10,000 from the corporation. Assume the basis of your shares, which you have held long term, is $6,000. You have realized a long-term gain of $4,000.

If you incur legal expenses in pressing payment of a claim, you treat the fee as a capital expense, according to the IRS. The Tax Court and an appeals court hold that the fee is deductible as an expense incurred to earn income; the deduction is subject to the 2% adjusted gross income (AGI) floor discussed at *19.1*.

If you recover a judgment against the liquidator of a corporation for misuse of corporate funds, the judgment is considered part of the amount you received on liquidation and gives you capital gain, not ordinary income.

If you paid a corporate debt after liquidation, the payment reduces the gain realized on the corporate liquidation in the earlier year; thus, in effect, it is a capital loss.

If the corporation distributes liquidating payments over a period of years, gain is not reported until the distributions exceed the adjusted basis of your stock.

Chapter 45

Figuring Self-Employment Tax

Self-employment tax provides funds for Social Security and Medicare benefits. The self-employment tax is calculated on Schedule SE. You are required to prepare Schedule SE if you have self-employment net earnings of $400 or more in 2006, but you will not incur the tax unless your net self-employment earnings exceed $433.13. The tax is added to your income tax liability. When preparing your estimated tax liability, you must also include an estimate of self-employment tax; *see* Chapter 27.

On Schedule SE, self-employment income is reduced by a deduction reflected in the decimal of .9235 listed on the form. You also deduct 50% of the self-employment tax on Line 27 of Form 1040.

For 2006, the self-employment tax of 15.3% consists of the following two rates: 12.4% for Social Security and 2.9% for Medicare. After multiplying the net earnings by .9235, the combined 15.3% rate applies to a taxable earnings base of $94,200 or less; the 2.9% rate applies to all taxable earnings exceeding $94,200.

You are required to pay self-employment tax on self-employment income even after you retire and receive Social Security benefits.

45.1 What Is Self-Employment Income?

On Schedule SE, you generally figure self-employment tax on the net profit from your business or profession whether you participate in its activities full or part time. Net profit is generally the amount shown on Line 31 of Schedule C (or Line 3 of Schedule C-EZ) if you are a sole proprietor. If you are a partner, net earnings subject to self-employment tax are taken from Box 14, Schedule K-1, of Form 1065. If you are a farmer, net farm profit is shown on Line 36, Schedule F.

If you have more than one self-employed operation, your net profit from all the operations is combined. A loss in one self-employed business will reduce the income from another business. You file separate Schedules C for each operation and one Schedule SE showing the combined income (less losses, if any).

For self-employment tax purposes, net earnings are not reduced by deductible contributions to your own SEP or Keogh plan *(41.4)*. Current law also bars you from reducing net earnings by the above-the-line deduction for health insurance *(12.2)*, although proposals have been made in Congress to allow the deduction for self-employment tax purposes.

Filing Tip

Real Estate Investor

The owner of one office building who holds it for investment (rather than for sale in the ordinary course of business) is not a real estate dealer, but a real estate investor. If the only tenant services provided are heat, light, water, and trash collection, report the rental income and expenses on Schedule E. The activity is not a Schedule C business subject to self-employment tax.

Married couples. Where you and your spouse *each* have self-employment income, each spouse must figure separate self-employment income on a separate schedule. Each pays the tax on the separate self-employment income. Both schedules are attached to the joint return.

If you live in a community property state, business income is not treated as community property for self-employment tax purposes. The spouse who is actually carrying on the business is subject to self-employment tax on the earnings.

Caution

Freelancer Fees

Fees you earn for freelance work as an independent contractor are business earnings reportable on Schedule C, and if you have a net profit, they are subject to self-employment tax on Schedule SE.

Exceptions. The following types of income or items are *not* included as self-employment income on Schedule SE:

1. Rent from real estate is generally not self-employment income. However, self-employment tax applies to the business income of a real estate dealer or income in a rental business where substantial services are rendered to the occupant, as in the leasing of—

- Rooms in a hotel or in a boarding house.
- Apartments, but only if extra services for the occupants' convenience, such as maid service or changing linens, are provided.
- Cabins or cabanas in tourist camps where you provide maid services, linens, utensils, and swimming, boating, fishing, and other facilities, for which you do not charge separately.
- Farmland in which the landlord materially participates in the actual production of the farm or in the management of production. For purposes of "material participation," the activities of a landlord's agent are not counted, only the landlord's actual participation.

2. Capital gains are not self-employment income. Self-employment income does *not* include gains from the sale of property unless it is inventory or held for sale to customers in the ordinary course of business. Thus, traders in securities *(30.16)* who buy and sell securities for their own account do not treat net gains or losses from the sales as self-employment income or loss. Dealers in commodities and options are subject to self-employment tax; *see* the chart in *45.6*.

Filing Tip

Trader in Securities

If you are a trader in securities *(30.16)*, gains or losses from your trading business are not subject to self-employment tax.

3. Dividends and interest. Generally, dividends and interest are not self-employment income. However, dividends earned by a dealer in securities and interest on accounts receivable are treated as self-employment income if the securities are not being held for investment. A dealer is one who buys stock as inventory to sell to customers.

Net operating loss deduction. A loss carryover from past years does not reduce business income for self-employment tax purposes. Similarly, the personal exemption may not be used to reduce self-employment income.

Statutory employees. Wages of a statutory employee, such as a full-time life insurance salesperson *(40.6)*, are not subject to self-employment tax, as Social Security and Medicare tax have been withheld.

Farmers. Cash or a payment in kind under the "Payment-in-Kind" program is considered earned income subject to self-employment tax.

Business interruption proceeds. The IRS and the Tax Court disagree over whether business interruption insurance proceeds must be reported as earnings subject to self-employment tax. The Tax Court held that insurance payments made to a grocer as compensation for lost earnings due to a fire were not subject to self-employment tax because the payment was not for actual services. The IRS refuses to follow the decision, holding that such payments represented income that would have been earned had business operations not been interrupted.

45.2 Partners Pay Self-Employment Tax

A general partner includes his or her share of partnership income or loss in net earnings from self-employment, including guaranteed payments. If your personal tax year is different from the partnership's tax year, you include your share of partnership income or loss for the partnership tax year ending within 2006.

A limited partner is not subject to self-employment tax on his or her share of partnership income except for guaranteed payments for services performed, which are subject to the tax.

If a general partner dies within the partnership's tax year, self-employment income includes his or her distributive share of the income earned by the partnership through the end of the month in which the death occurs. This is true even though his or her heirs or estate succeeds to the partnership rights. For this purpose, partnership income for the year is considered to be earned ratably each month.

Retirement payments from partnership. Retirement payments you receive from your partnership are *not* subject to self-employment tax if the following conditions are met:

1. The payments are made under a qualified written plan providing for periodic payments on retirement of partners with payments to continue until death.
2. You rendered no services in any business conducted by the partnership during the tax year of the partnership ending within or with your tax year.
3. By the end of the partnership's tax year, your share in the partnership's capital has been paid to you in full, and there is no obligation from the other partners to you other than with respect to the retirement payments under the plan.

Limited liability company (LLC) members. Are LLC members treated as general or limited partners for purposes of self-employment tax? The matter is not completely settled, but it appears that members owe self-employment tax when they perform services for their business, participate in management activities, and are not mere investors.

Worksheet—Short Schedule SE

Section A—Short Schedule SE. Caution. Read above to see if you can use Short Schedule SE.

Line	Description	Box	Amount
1	Net farm profit or (loss) from Schedule F, line 36, and farm partnerships, Schedule K-1 (Form 1065), box 14, code A	1	
2	Net profit or (loss) from Schedule C, line 31; Schedule C-EZ, line 3; Schedule K-1 (Form 1065), box 14, code A (other than farming); and Schedule K-1 (Form 1065-B), box 9, code J1. Ministers and members of religious orders, see page SE-1 for amounts to report on this line. See page SE-2 for other income to report	2	120,000
3	Combine lines 1 and 2	3	120,000
4	**Net earnings from self-employment.** Multiply line 3 by 92.35% (.9235). If less than $400, **do not** file this schedule; you do not owe self-employment tax ▶	4	110,820
5	**Self-employment tax.** If the amount on line 4 is: • $94,200 or less, multiply line 4 by 15.3% (.153). Enter the result here and on **Form 1040, line 58.** • More than $94,200, multiply line 4 by 2.9% (.029). Then, add $11,680.80 to the result. Enter the total here and on **Form 1040, line 58.**	5	14,895
6	**Deduction for one-half of self-employment tax.** Multiply line 5 by 50% (.5). Enter the result here and on **Form 1040, line 27** — 6: 7,448		

For Paperwork Reduction Act Notice, see Form 1040 instructions. Cat. No. 11358Z **Schedule SE (Form 1040) 2006**

Filing Tip

50% Deduction

After you figure your self-employment tax on Schedule SE, deduct one-half of it on Line 27 of Form 1040.

45.3 Schedule SE

Schedule SE has an introductory "road map" designed to lead you to either the short or long version of Schedule SE. Once you pass through the road map, the preparation of either the short or long schedule is not difficult. In both versions, you multiply your net earnings by a decimal of .9235. Only 92.35% of net earnings is subject to the self-employment tax. The .9235 adjustment is the equivalent of a 7.65% reduction to net earnings, which, along with the income tax deduction for 50% of self-employment tax on Line 27 of Form 1040, attempts to place self-employed individuals on the same level as employees subject to FICA taxes.

The .9235 adjustment is made on Line 4 of either the short or long Schedule SE. For example, if your net profit reported on Line 31 of Schedule C is $120,000, the amount subject to self-employment tax after the adjustment is $110,820; *see* the filled-in short Schedule SE worksheet on page 691, and *see* below for the long Schedule SE.

After the .9235 adjustment is made, net earnings are subject to the 12.4% and 2.9% rates, assuming the resulting net earnings are $400 or more. For 2006, the 12.4% Social Security rate applies to the first $94,200 of net earnings and the 2.9% Medicare rate applies to all of the net earnings.

45.4 How Wages Affect Self-Employment Tax

If you have both a net profit from self-employment and also wage and/or tip income subject to FICA taxes (Social Security and Medicare), the amount of such FICA earnings may affect your self-employment tax liability.

If your 2006 FICA wages or tips were $94,200 or over, your net self-employment profit is subject only to the 2.9% Medicare rate.

Worksheet—Long Schedule SE

Part I **Self-Employment Tax**

Note. If your only income subject to self-employment tax is **church employee income,** skip lines 1 through 4b. Enter -0- on line 4c and go to line 5a. Income from services you performed as a minister or a member of a religious order **is not** church employee income. See page SE-1.

A	If you are a minister, member of a religious order, or Christian Science practitioner **and** you filed Form 4361, but you had $400 or more of **other** net earnings from self-employment, check here and continue with Part I . . . ▶ ☐					
1	Net farm profit or (loss) from Schedule F, line 36, and farm partnerships, Schedule K-1 (Form 1065), box 14, code A. **Note.** Skip this line if you use the farm optional method (see page SE-4)			**1**		
2	Net profit or (loss) from Schedule C, line 31; Schedule C-EZ, line 3; Schedule K-1 (Form 1065), box 14, code A (other than farming); and Schedule K-1 (Form 1065-B), box 9, code J1. Ministers and members of religious orders, see page SE-1 for amounts to report on this line. See page SE-2 for other income to report. **Note.** Skip this line if you use the nonfarm optional method (see page SE-4)			**2**	70,000	
3	Combine lines 1 and 2			**3**	70,000	
4a	If line 3 is more than zero, multiply line 3 by 92.35% (.9235). Otherwise, enter amount from line 3			**4a**	64,645	
b	If you elect one or both of the optional methods, enter the total of lines 15 and 17 here			**4b**		
c	Combine lines 4a and 4b. If less than $400, **stop**; you do not owe self-employment tax. **Exception.** If less than $400 and you had **church employee income,** enter -0- and continue. ▶			**4c**	64,645	
5a	Enter your **church employee income** from Form W-2. See page SE-1 for definition of church employee income	**5a**				
b	Multiply line 5a by 92.35% (.9235). If less than $100, enter -0-			**5b**		
6	**Net earnings from self-employment.** Add lines 4c and 5b			**6**	64,645	
7	Maximum amount of combined wages and self-employment earnings subject to social security tax or the 6.2% portion of the 7.65% railroad retirement (tier 1) tax for 2006			**7**	94,200	00
8a	Total social security wages and tips (total of boxes 3 and 7 on Form(s) W-2) and railroad retirement (tier 1) compensation. If $94,200 or more, skip lines 8b through 10, and go to line 11	**8a**	35,100			
b	Unreported tips subject to social security tax (from Form 4137, line 9)	**8b**				
c	Add lines 8a and 8b			**8c**	35,100	
9	Subtract line 8c from line 7. If zero or less, enter -0- here and on line 10 and go to line 11 . ▶			**9**	59,100	
10	Multiply the **smaller** of line 6 or line 9 by 12.4% (.124)			**10**	7,328	
11	Multiply line 6 by 2.9% (.029)			**11**	1,875	
12	**Self-employment tax.** Add lines 10 and 11. Enter here and on **Form 1040, line 58**			**12**	9,203	
13	**Deduction for one-half of self-employment tax.** Multiply line 12 by 50% (.5). Enter the result here and on **Form 1040, line 27**	**13**	4,602			

Schedule SE (Form 1040) 2006

If the total of your 2006 FICA wages (and tips) plus net earnings was $94,200 or less, your entire net earnings are subject to the 12.4% Social Security rate and the 2.9% Medicare rate.

If the total of your 2006 FICA wages (and tips) plus net earnings was over the $94,200 limit for the 12.4% Social Security rate, your net self-employment earnings shown on Line 6 of long Schedule SE (after the .9235 adjustment) are subject to the 12.4% rate only to the extent of the excess of $94,200 over your FICA wages or tips. The 2.9% Medicare rate applies to the entire amount of net self-employment earnings. *See* the following Example and the filled-in long Schedule SE worksheet on page 692.

EXAMPLE

You earn a salary of $35,100 in 2006 and have a net profit from self-employment of $70,000. As shown on the long Schedule SE worksheet above, the 12.4% rate applies to the smaller of Line 6 or Line 9. Here, the smaller amount is $59,100 shown on Line 9, the excess of $94,200 over the $35,100 of wages. The 2.9% rate applies to the total net earnings of $64,645 ($70,000 × .9235 adjustment) shown on Line 6.

12.4% × $59,100	$7,328
2.9% × $64,645	+ 1,875
	9,203

Your self-employment tax liability is $9,203. One-half of that, or $4,602, is deductible on Line 27 of Form 1040.

Filing Tip

Optional Method

Electing the optional method to increase the base for Social Security coverage may also increase earned income for dependent care and earned income credit purposes.

45.5 Optional Method If 2006 Was a Low-Income or Loss Year

The law provides a small increased tax base for Social Security coverage if you have a low net profit or loss.

The increased tax base is called the optional method. One optional method is for nonfarm self-employment and another for farm income. You may not use the optional method to report an amount less than your actual net earnings from self-employment.

Nonfarm method. You may use the nonfarm optional method for 2006 if you meet all the following tests:

Test 1. Your net earnings (profit) from nonfarm self-employment on Line 31 of Schedule C, Line 3 of Schedule C-EZ, or Line 15a of Schedule K-1 (Form 1065) are less than $1,733 (.9235 × $1,733 = $1,600 maximum income subject to the optional method).

Test 2. Your net earnings from nonfarm self-employment are less than 72.189% of the total gross income you made from nonfarm self-employment.

Test 3. You had net earnings from self-employment of $400 or more in at least two of the following years: 2003, 2004, and 2005.

Test 4. You have not previously used this method for more than four years. There is a five-year lifetime limit for use of the nonfarm optional base. The years do not have to be consecutive.

Nonfarm income of $2,400 or less. If your gross income from all nonfarm trades or businesses is $2,400 or less and you meet the four tests just discussed, you may report two-thirds of the gross income from your nonfarm business as net earnings from self-employment.

EXAMPLES

1. Brown had net earnings from self-employment of $800 in 2004 and $900 in 2005 and so meets Test 3 above. In 2006, she has gross nonfarm self-employment income of $2,100 and net nonfarm self-employment earnings of $1,200. Net earnings from self-employment of $1,200 are less than $1,733 (Test 1 above) and also less than 72.189% of $2,100 gross income, or $1,516 (Test 2). Brown may figure self-employment tax on $1,400 ($^2/_3$ of $2,100).
2. Same facts as in Example 1, but Brown has a net self-employment loss of $700. She may elect to report $1,400 ($^2/_3$ of $2,100) as net earnings under the optional method.

3. Smith had gross nonfarm income of $1,000 and net nonfarm self-employment earnings of $800. He may not use the optional method because net earnings of $800 are not less than 72.189% of $1,000 gross income, or $722.
4. Jones has gross nonfarm income of $525 and net nonfarm self-employment earnings of $175. Jones may not use the optional method because two-thirds of his gross income, or $350, is less than the minimum income of $400 required to be subject to the self-employment tax.

Nonfarm income over $2,400. If your gross income from all nonfarm businesses exceeds $2,400, and you meet the four tests just discussed, you may report $1,600 as your net earnings from nonfarm self-employment.

EXAMPLES

1. White had net earnings from self-employment in 2003 of $8,500; in 2004, $10,500; and in 2005, $9,500. His 2006 gross nonfarm income is $12,000 and net nonfarm earnings are $1,200. Because his net earnings of $1,200 from self-employment are less than $1,733 and also less than 72.189% of his gross income, he may report $1,600 as his net earnings from self-employment.
2. Same facts as in Example 1, but assume net earnings for 2006 are $1,800. White may not use the optional method because his actual net earnings of $1,800 from self-employment are not less than $1,733. He reports $1,800 as net earnings using the regular method.
3. Assume White has a net loss of $700 in 2006. He may use the optional method to report $1,600 of net earnings from self-employment.

Optional farm method. If you have farming income (other than as a limited partner) you may use the farm optional method to figure your net earnings from farm self-employment.

Unlike the nonfarm optional method, the farm optional method does *not* have a two-year self-employment test (Test 3) or a requirement that actual net earnings be less than 72.189% of gross income (Test 2). There is also no limitation on the number of years you may use this method (Test 4).

If your gross income from farming is $2,400 or less, you may report two-thirds of your gross income as your net earnings from farm self-employment. If your gross income from farming exceeds $2,400 and your net earnings from farm self-employment are less than $1,733, you may report $1,600 as your net earnings from farm self-employment. If your gross income from farming exceeds $2,400 and your net earnings from farm self-employment are $1,733 or more, you may not use the optional method.

Farm income includes income from cultivating the soil or harvesting any agricultural commodities. It also includes income from the operation of a livestock, dairy, poultry, bee, fish, fruit, or truck farm, or plantation, ranch, nursery, range, orchard, or oyster bed, as well as income in the form of crop shares if you materially participate in production or management of production.

45.6 Self-Employment Tax Rules for Certain Positions

Table 45-1 Self-Employed or Employee?

If you are—	*Tax rule—*
Babysitter	Where you perform services in your own home and determine the nature and manner of the services to be performed, you are considered to have self-employment income. However, where services are performed in the parent's home according to instructions by the parents, you are an employee of the parents and do not have self-employment earnings.
Clergy	If you are an ordained minister, priest, or rabbi, a member of a religious order who has not taken a vow of poverty, or a Christian Science practitioner, you are subject to self-employment tax, unless you elect not to be covered on the grounds of conscientious or religious objection to Social Security benefits. An application for exemption from Social Security coverage must be filed on Form 4361 by the due date, including extensions, of your income tax return for the second taxable year for which you have net earnings from services of $400 or more. An exemption, once granted, is irrevocable. Self-employment tax does not apply to the rental value of any parsonage or parsonage allowance provided after retirement. Other retirement benefits from a church plan are also exempted.
Consultant	The IRS generally takes the position that income earned by a consultant is subject to self-employment tax. The IRS has also held that a retired executive hired as a consultant by his former firm received self-employment income, even though he was subject to an agreement prohibiting him from giving advice to competing companies. According to the IRS, consulting for one firm is a business; it makes no difference that you act as a consultant only with your former company. The IRS has also imposed self-employment tax on consulting fees, although no services were performed for them. The courts have generally approved the IRS position.
Dealer in commodities and options	Registered options dealers and commodities dealers are subject to self-employment tax on net gains from trading in Section 1256 contracts, which include regulated futures contracts, foreign currency contracts, dealer equity options, and non-equity options. Self-employment tax also applies to net gains from trading property related to such contracts, like stock used to hedge options.
Director	You are taxed as a self-employed person if you are not an employee of the company. Fees for attendance at meetings are self-employment income. If the fees are not received until after the year you provide the services, you treat the fees as self-employment earnings in the year they are received.
Employee of foreign government or international organization	If you are a U.S. citizen and you work in the United States for a foreign government or its wholly owned instrumentality, or an international organization, you pay self-employment tax if Social Security and Medicare taxes are not withheld from your pay.
Executor or guardian	If you are a professional fiduciary, you will always be treated as having self-employment income, regardless of the assets held by the estate. But if you serve as a nonprofessional executor or administrator for the estate of a deceased friend or relative, you will not be treated as having self-employment income unless all of the following tests are met: (1) the estate includes a business; (2) you actively participate in the operation of the business; and (3) all or part of your fee is related to your operation of the business. The IRS applied similar business tests to deny self-employment treatment for a guardian who was appointed by a court to care for a disabled cousin. The guardian negotiated sales of the cousin's property and invested the proceeds, but these activities were not extensive enough to be considered management of a business.
Former insurance salespersons	Termination payments by a former insurance salesperson may be exempt from self-employment tax. They must be received from an insurance company after the termination of a services agreement. No services may be performed for the company after the agreement ends and before the end of the tax year. The payments must be conditioned on the salesperson's entering into a covenant not to compete with the company for at least one year after termination. The amount of the payment must be primarily based on policies sold by (or credited to) the salesperson during the last year of the services agreement or on the period for which such policies remain in force after the termination.
Lecturer	You are not taxed as a self-employed person if you give only occasional lectures. If, however, you seek lecture engagements and get them with reasonable regularity, your lecture fees are treated as self-employment income.

Table 45-1 Self-Employed or Employee? (continued)

If you are—	*Tax rule—*
Nonresident alien	You do not pay Social Security tax on your self-employment income derived from a trade, business, or profession. This is so even though you pay income tax. Your exemption from self-employment tax is not influenced by the fact that your business in the United States is carried on by an agent, employee, or partnership of which you are a member. However, if you live in Puerto Rico, the Virgin Islands, American Samoa, the Commonwealth of the Northern Mariana Islands, or Guam, you are not considered a nonresident alien and are subject to self-employment tax.
Nurse	If you are a registered nurse or licensed practical nurse who is hired directly by clients for private nursing services, you are considered self-employed. You are an employee if hired directly by a hospital or a private physician and work for a salary following a strict routine during fixed hours, or if you provide primarily domestic services in the home of a client. Where registered or licensed practical nurses are assigned nursing jobs by an agency that pays them, the IRS, in several rulings, has treated such nurses as employees of the agency. Nurses' aides, domestics, and other unlicensed individuals who classify themselves as practical nurses are treated by the IRS as employees, regardless of whether they work for a medical institution, a private physician, or a private household.
Real estate agent or door-to-door salesperson	Licensed real estate agents are considered self-employed if they have a contract specifying that they are not to be treated as employees and if substantially all of their pay is related to sales rather than number of hours worked. The same rule also applies to door-to-door salespeople with similar contracts who work on a commission basis selling products in homes or other non-retail establishments.
Technical service contractor	Consulting engineers and computer technicians who receive assignments from technical service agencies are generally treated as employees and do not pay self-employment tax. The IRS distinguishes between (1) technicians who in three-party arrangements are assigned clients by a technical services agency and (2) those who directly enter into contracts with clients. Employee status covers only technicians in Group 1. Technical specialists who contract directly with clients may be classified as independent contractors by showing that they have been consistently treated as independent contractors by the client, and that other workers in similar positions have also been treated as independent contractors. Thus, they may treat their income as self-employment income. Firms that are treated as employers of technical specialists are responsible for withholding and payroll taxes.
Writer	Royalties from writing books are self-employment income to a writer. Royalties on books by a professor employed by a university may also be self-employment income despite employment as a professor.

PART 7

Filing Your Return and What Happens After You File

This part is designed to help you —

- Organize your tax data. Whether you plan to prepare your own tax return or have someone else prepare it, you must first gather and organize your tax information.
  In Chapter 46, you will find record-keeping guides for income items and expense deductions.
- Understand how the IRS reviews your return and initiates audit procedures, including information on how the IRS matches your return with reports of distributions to you from banks, corporations, and government agencies.
- Avoid penalties for underpaying your tax. You may avoid penalties for positions taken on your tax return by making certain disclosures, obtaining authoritative support for your position, or showing reasonable cause for a tax underpayment; *see 46.8.*
- Understand the factors that might lead to an audit. Your chances of being selected for an examination depend on your income, profession, deductions claimed, and even where you live; *see 48.1.*
- Prepare for an audit. Advance preparations and knowing your rights can help support your position; *see 48.4.*
- Dispute adverse IRS determinations. You can appeal within the IRS and go to court if you disagree with the IRS audit results. If you win, you may receive attorneys' fees and other expenses; *see 48.8.*
- File a timely refund claim if you have overpaid your tax; *see 47.2.*
- File an amended return if you omitted income or claimed excessive deductions on your original return; *see 47.8.*

Chapter 46

Filing Your Return

Whether you prepare your return yourself or retain a professional preparer, you must first collect and organize your tax records. You cannot prepare your return unless you get your personal tax data in order. Good records will help you figure your income and deductions and will serve as a written record to present to the IRS in the event that you are audited.

Review income statements from banks, employers, brokers, and governmental agencies on their respective Forms 1099. Check for miscalculations, additions, and omissions.

Survey Chapters 12–21 of this book for deductions you can claim directly from gross income and itemized deductions you can claim on Schedule A of Form 1040.

Reviewing your tax return from prior years will help refresh your memory as to how you handled income and expenses in prior years. This review will also remind you of deductions, carryover losses, and other items you might otherwise have overlooked that you might be eligible for. If your prior year returns were prepared by a professional, he or she can probably provide you with a copy of your returns if you do not have them. Otherwise, you may obtain copies of prior year tax returns by filing Form 4506 with the IRS and paying a fee.

In this chapter you will find a checklist of steps to take when preparing and checking your return. If you need an extension to file, *see 46.3.*

46.1 Keeping Tax Records

To maximize tax-savings opportunities, you must keep good records throughout the year. Good record-keeping makes it easier to prepare your return, reduces errors, and provides a defense to any challenge from the IRS.

- Make a habit of jotting down deductible items as they come along.
- Keep a calender or diary of expenses to record deductible items.
- Keep a file of bills. This can be an ordinary folder in which you arrange your bills and receipts alphabetically. This will remind you of deductible items and provide you with supporting evidence to present to the IRS if audited.
- Use your checkbook stubs as a record. If you own a business, you must keep a complete set of account books for it.

IRA records. If you have made nondeductible contributions to a traditional IRA, keep a record of both your nondeductible and deductible contributions. This will help you when you withdraw IRA money to figure the tax-free and taxed parts of the withdrawal *(see 8.9)*. Also keep records of contributions and conversions to Roth IRAs *(8.20–8.21)*. For these purposes, you should keep copies of Form 8606 and Form 5498; *see 8.8*.

Reinvested mutual-fund distributions. Keep annual statements that record the amount of mutual-fund distributions that you have reinvested in additional fund shares. The reinvested amounts are part of your cost basis in the fund. Unless your fund keeps track of basis for you, you need to know your basis when computing gain or loss on the redemption of fund shares; *see 32.10*.

Passive losses. If you have losses that are suspended and carried forward to future years under the passive loss restrictions *(10.13)*, keep the worksheets to Form 8582 as a record of the carry-forward losses.

Home mortgage interest. Keep your bank statements and cancelled checks. If a loan secured by a first or second home is used to make substantial home improvements, keep records of the improvement costs to support your home interest deduction; *see 15.5*.

How long should you keep your records? Your records should be kept for a minimum of three years after the year to which they are applicable, since the IRS generally has three years from the date your return is filed to audit your return. Some authorities advise keeping them for six years, since in some cases where income has not been reported, the IRS may go back as far as six years to question a tax return. In cases of suspected tax fraud, there is no time limitation at all.

Keep records of transactions relating to the *basis* of property for as long as they are important in figuring the basis of the original or replacement property. For example, records of the purchase of rental property or improvements thereto must be held as long as you own the property.

As mentioned above, if you have made any nondeductible IRA contributions, records of IRA contributions and distributions must be kept until all funds have been withdrawn. Similarly, you should save mutual-fund confirmations or other records showing reinvested dividends and cash purchases of shares; these are part of your cost basis and will reduce taxable gain when you sell shares in the fund.

IRS Alert

Getting a Copy of an Old Tax Return

You can obtain a copy of a prior year tax return from the IRS by filing Form 4506 and paying a $39 fee per return. Copies of Forms 1040, 1040A, and 1040EZ are generally available for seven years from filing before they are destroyed.

You can use Form 4506-T to order free of charge a transcript of tax return information that provides line entries from tax returns for the three prior years and data from Forms W-2 and 1099.

46.2 Getting Ready To File Your Return

You must collect your tax records before you can start the preparation of your return. Even if you employ a tax professional to prepare your return, organizing your tax data is essential. Once you have compiled all your return information and your records are complete, decide whether to use Form 1040EZ, 1040A, or 1040 with the aid of the checklist at the front of this book on page 7. After you have decided which return to file, review the form to familiarize yourself with its details.

You may use the forms in Part 9 to prepare your return. The *e-Supplement* will also contain forms suitable for filing, and you can obtain forms by phone from the IRS by calling (800) 829-3676. Check the IRS instructions for obtaining forms by fax. If you have access to the Internet, you may obtain forms from the IRS website at www.irs.gov.

Planning Reminder

Keep Copies

Photocopy your signed return and keep the copy along with copies of Form W-2 and other income statements, receipts, cancelled checks, and other items to substantiate your deductions.

Checking for possible errors. After you have completed your return, put it aside and postpone checking your completed return for several hours or even a day so that you can review it in a fresh state of mind. *See* below for common errors that might delay a refund or result in a tax deficiency and interest costs.

If mailing your return. If you are mailing your return to the IRS, first check it to ensure the following:

- Your arithmetic is correct.
- Your Social Security number, and that of your spouse if you are filing jointly, is recorded correctly on each form and schedule.
- You have filled in the proper boxes that state your filing status and exemption claims, and reported the Social Security number of each dependent; *see 21.11.*
- You have claimed the full standard deduction you are entitled to if you are age 65 or older, or blind; *see 13.4.*
- You have used the Tax Table, Tax Computation Worksheet, or special capital gain worksheet applicable to your tax status. If you do not have net capital gain or qualified dividends, use the Tax Table if your taxable income is less than $100,000, or the Tax Computation Worksheet if your taxable income is $100,000 or more. *See 22.4* if you have net capital gain or qualified dividends.
- You have put the refund due you or your tax payable on the correct line.
- If you owe tax and are paying by check, your check should be made out to the "United States Treasury" for the correct amount due and your Social Security number should be on the check. The IRS encourages, but does not require, that you send payment voucher Form 1040-V along with your Form 1040 payment.
- You have signed your return and, if you are filing a joint return, your spouse has also signed; *see 1.4.*
- You have attached the correct copy of your Form W-2 and all appropriate forms and schedules to your return.
- If you have elected to have your refund directly deposited into your personal account, verify that you have provided the IRS with the correct routing information on Line 74 of Form 1040, Line 45 of Form 1040A, or Line 12 of Form 1040EZ.
- You have correctly addressed the envelope and affixed proper postage.
- You use certified or registered mail or an IRS-specified private delivery service to prove that your return was postmarked on or before the filing date.

Planning Reminder

Get Timely Postmark for Last Minute Mailing

Last minute filers may use specified services from *DHL*, *Federal Express*, and *UPS* as well as the *U.S. Postal Service*. If using the U.S. Postal Service, send the return certified (or registered) mail and keep the postmark receipt. If you use a private delivery service, keep a copy of the mailing label or obtain a receipt to verify a timely postmark. If your return is postmarked before or at any time on the filing due date (April 16, 2007, for 2006 returns), it is considered timely filed under a "timely-mailing-is-timely-filing" rule, even if the IRS receives it after the due date.

The timely mailing rule also applies if you obtain a filing extension and are mailing your return on or before the extended due date.

A timely foreign postmark for a return filed from abroad will also be accepted by the IRS as proof of a timely filing.

46.3 Applying for an Extension

If you cannot file your return on time, apply by the due date of the return for an extension of time to file. Send the extension request on Form 4868 to the Internal Revenue Service office with which you file your return.

Automatic filing extension. You may get an extension without waiting for the IRS to act on your request. You receive an automatic six-month extension for your 2006 return if you file Form 4868 by April 16, 2007. The extension gives you until October 15, 2007, to file your return. A late *filing* penalty will not be imposed if you fail to submit a payment with Form 4868 provided you make a good faith estimate of your liability based upon available information at the time of filing. However, although the extension will be allowed without a payment, you will be subject to interest charges and possible penalties (discussed below) on 2006 taxes due after April 16, 2007.

You may file Form 4868 electronically and use a credit card (American Express, MasterCard, Visa, or Discover Card) to make a tax payment; Form 4868 does not have to be filed if you use a credit card. Payment is made through a service provider that handles the credit card transaction and charges you a fee. *See* the Form 4868 instructions for the phone numbers and web addresses of the service providers.

When you file your return within the extension period, you enter on the appropriate line of the return any tax payment that you sent with your extension request, and include the balance of the unpaid tax, if any.

While the extension is automatically obtained by a proper filing on Form 4868, the IRS may

Planning Reminder

You Can Get a Six-Month Filing Extension

You can get an automatic six-month extension to file your 2006 return by filing Form 4868 by April 16, 2007. The extension is for filing only and does not extend the time to pay your taxes for 2006.

terminate the extension by mailing you a notice at least 10 days prior to the termination date designated in the notice.

Interest and penalty for late payment. You have to pay interest on any 2006 tax not paid by April 16, 2007, even if you obtain a filing extension. In addition, if the tax paid with Form 4868, plus withholdings and estimated tax payments for 2006, is less than 90% of the amount due, you will be subject to a late-payment penalty (usually one-half of 1% of the unpaid tax per month)—unless you can show reasonable cause.

Abroad on April 16, 2007. You do not get an automatic extension for filing and paying your tax merely because you are out of the country on the filing due date. If you plan to be traveling abroad on April 16, 2007, and want to get a filing extension, you must submit a claim for the automatic six-month filing extension on Form 4868 or use a credit card (*see* above) to make a payment with an extension request.

The only exception is for U.S. citizens or residents who live and have their main place of business outside the U.S. or Puerto Rico, or military personnel stationed outside the U.S. or Puerto Rico, on April 16, 2007. If you qualify, you are allowed an automatic two-month extension, until June 15, 2007, to file your return and also pay any tax due. However, the IRS will charge interest from the original April 16 due date on any unpaid tax. If you cannot file within the two-month extension period, you can obtain an additional four-month extension by filing Form 4868 by June 15, 2007. This additional four-month extension is for filing only and not payment. In addition to interest, a late payment penalty may be imposed (*see* above) on any tax not paid by June 15, 2007.

If you are eligible for the two-month extension but expect to qualify for the foreign earned income exclusion *(36.3)* under the foreign residence or presence test after June 15, 2007, you can request on Form 2350 an extension until after the expected qualification date; *see 36.7.*

Installment arrangements. If you cannot pay the tax due for 2006 by the October 15, 2007, extension date, you should file your return and attach Form 9465 to request an installment arrangement; *see 46.4.*

46.4 Getting Your Refund

If you show an overpayment of tax on your 2006 return, you can have a refund check mailed to you or have the IRS directly deposit the refund into as many as three bank, brokerage, or mutual-fund accounts; *see* below. For a direct deposit you must provide the IRS with the correct routing information for your account. On Form 1040 and 1040A, you can apply all or part of your refund to your 2007 estimated tax; this is an irrevocable election.

File Form 8888 for split-direct-deposit refund option. If you want the IRS to directly deposit your refund into two or three accounts, File Form 8888 with your Form 1040, 1040A, or 1040EZ. You can have the refund directly deposited into a checking or savings account, or even to an IRA *(8.1)*, Coverdell education savings account *(33.11)*, or health savings account *(12.9)*. If you want the deposit to go into an IRA, you must establish the IRA before you request direct deposit. Make sure that you notify the IRA trustee if you want the deposit to count as an IRA contribution for 2006 (rather than for 2007 when the deposit is made).

Form 8888 is not needed to have a refund deposited into only one account. In that case, just give the IRS the appropriate routing and account numbers on the refund line of your return.

If you file Form 8379 (*see* below) for a refund as an injured spouse, you cannot use Form 8888.

Checking refund status by phone or online. You can call the IRS to check on the status of an expected refund. When you call the IRS automated phone service, you must provide the Social Security number shown on the return (or the first Social Security number if you filed a joint return), filing status, and the amount of the refund.

The IRS automated refund information phone number is 1-800-829-4477, or you may call the IRS at 1-800-829-1040.

You can also check refund status online at www.irs.gov. The information needed to access the system is identical to that required by the phone system. Online, you can learn if the IRS has received the return, if the refund was processed, and when the direct deposit was made or the date the check was sent.

Credit for federal telephone excise tax on 2006 returns. After five federal appeals courts held that the 3% federal excise tax was being improperly applied to long-distance telephone services, the IRS conceded the legal dispute and agreed to refund the taxes paid on long-distance and wireless services billed after February 28, 2003, and before August 1, 2006.

Individuals can obtain the refund on their 2006 Forms 1040, 1040A, or 1040EZ by claiming a standard IRS rate, or they can rely on phone records to get a refund of their actual tax payments. Individuals who are not otherwise required to file a 2006 return must file Form 1040 EZ-T to request the refund.

The IRS standard rate is based on the number of exemptions *(21.1)* claimed by the taxpayer on his or her 2006 return and not on the number of telephones in the household. The minimum standard rate of $30 for taxpayers claiming one exemption is increased by $10 for each additional exemption but only up to $60 for four or more exemptions. These amounts may not reflect the true taxes paid in a household with several cell phones in addition to a land line, so for such taxpayers, claiming a refund for actual taxes paid would be more beneficial, but only if they have 41 months of old phone bills to back up their claim. On the other hand, parents with newborns or other young children may benefit from the standard IRS amount because an additional $10 refund is allowed for each dependent (up to a rate of $60 for four or more exemptions).

Check the IRS instructions for conditions on claiming the standard rate and the requirements for claiming actual tax payments.

Planning Reminder

Interest Not Paid on Most Refunds

If your 2006 return is filed on or before the April 16, 2007, filing deadline, the IRS does not have to pay interest if the refund is issued before June 1, 2007, which is 46 days after the April 16 filing due date. If the return is filed after April 16, 2007, with or without an extension, no interest is due on refunds issued within 45 days after the actual filing date. If the overpayment is not refunded within 45 days, interest is paid from the date the tax was overpaid up to a date determined by the IRS that can be as much as 30 days before the date of the refund check.

Form 8379: Injured spouse may get refund that was withheld to pay spouse's debts. If you showed a refund due on a joint return filed with a spouse who owed child or spousal support, federal student loans, or state income tax, the Treasury Department's Financial Management Service (FMS) may have withheld payment of the refund to cover the obligations. If your spouse owed federal taxes, the refund may have been offset by the IRS. If you are not liable for the past-due payments, and your tax payments (withholdings or estimated tax installments) or refundable credits exceed your income reported on the joint return, you may file Form 8379 to get back your share of the refund.

46.5 Paying Taxes Due

If you owe tax on a return that you are mailing to the IRS, you may pay by check, money order, or credit card. Payments can also be made by direct debit from your account, either by phone or online using the IRS's Electronic Federal Tax Payment System (EFTPS).

If paying by check or money order, make it payable to the "United States Treasury." Write your Social Security number on the check or money order. The IRS encourages you to send Form 1040-V along with your payment, but the form is not required.

A credit card payment can be made by phone or over the Internet with a service provider that handles the transaction for the IRS. The service provider will impose a fee based on the amount you are paying. The tax form instruction booklet includes the toll-free number and website addresses of the service providers.

IRS online or phone option for making payments. The IRS's Electronic Federal Tax Payment System (EFTPS) accepts online tax payments from individual as well as business taxpayers. You may use EFTPS to pay the balance due on your individual tax return or to pay estimated tax installments.

Payments are made by direct debit from an account that you designate when you enroll with EFTPS. Individual tax payments may be scheduled up to 365 days in advance and business taxes up to 120 days in advance. You can enroll online at www.eftps.gov.

Payments via EFTPS can also be made by phone after you enroll with EFTPS and set up a direct debit arrangement. Call 1-800-945-8400 for enrollment information.

Payments by electronic filers. If you file electronically, you may pay taxes by authorizing a direct debit from your checking or savings account, or by using a credit card. Check with the companies that process credit card payments for the fee that will be imposed.

Installment arrangements. If you cannot pay the full amount due on your return when you file, you may request an installment arrangement. On Form 9465, you may request a monthly payment plan. The IRS may enter into an installment arrangement which provides for less than the full liability to be paid over the life of the agreement. The IRS will usually inform you within 30 days if your proposed payment plan is accepted. If it is, you will have to pay a processing fee. Even if the IRS agrees to an installment agreement, you will have to pay interest and possibly a late-payment penalty (*see* above) on the amount not paid by the due date.

If you owe $10,000 or less and certain conditions are met, the IRS must enter into an installment arrangement if you request one. You must show that full payment cannot be currently made, and that in the previous five years you filed income tax returns and paid the tax and did not enter into an installment arrangement during that period. If the current return is a joint return, your spouse must also meet these tests for the five-year period. You must agree to pay the tax liability within three years.

If you are using an installment agreement to pay the tax due on a timely filed return (including extensions), the late payment penalty is reduced by half from .5% to .25% per month.

46.6 Electronic Filing

Electronic filing involves the transmission of your tax return to the IRS from the computer of a tax preparer, tax preparation software program, or online tax preparation service. To file electronically, you must use an authorized service; you cannot electronically file directly with the IRS. You may be eligible for free tax preparation and electronic filing services from commercial tax software companies that have joined with the IRS to form the Free File Alliance. At the IRS website, www.irs.gov, the free services provided by the companies are described and links are provided to their websites. Each company sets its own eligibility criteria, which generally are based on adjusted gross income, but your age, state residency, or military status may also be factors.

Filing Tip

Free E-Filing

Go to www.irs.gov to find a description of the free tax preparation and electronic filing services offered by companies that have partnered with the IRS and determine whether you meet the eligibility criteria.

Electronic filing offers a faster refund—a check mailed within three weeks or a direct deposit to your bank account. You authorize a direct deposit to a financial institution that was designated in the electronic portion of your return. On the electronic portion of the return, you provide the savings or checking account number and the "routing transit number" of your bank. The routing transit number is the electronic mailing address of your bank that directs the refund to the correct account. The number is on your checks or other account statements. Before naming a bank, first ask if it accepts direct deposits and what its conditions are for receiving a deposit.

If you must pay a fee for electronic filing, you must decide whether the faster refund is worth the fee. Keep in mind that even without electronic filing, you may instruct the IRS to directly deposit your refund to an account that you designate on your return; *see 46.4.*

If you file electronically and owe taxes, you may be able to pay by credit card or by direct debit from your checking or savings account.

Refund anticipation loans. An electronic filing service may offer a refund anticipation loan to a taxpayer who wants to receive an expected refund even sooner than the three weeks or so offered by electronic filing. The loans are received from lenders affiliated with the electronic filing service. This service is strictly an agreement between you and the filing service; the IRS is not a party to the arrangement. Before agreeing to such a loan, consider the high additional cost and whether it is worthwhile in light of the short refund payment period.

46.7 Notify the IRS of Address Changes

If the IRS does not have your current address, payment of a refund due you may be delayed. If you owe taxes, the IRS may enforce a deficiency notice sent to the address on your most recently filed tax return, even if you never receive the IRS notice.

To avoid these problems, file Form 8822 with the IRS to provide notice of an address change. Alternatively, you may send a signed written statement to the IRS Service Center covering your old residence. The statement should state the new and old address, your full name, and your Social Security or employer identification number.

If you and your spouse separate after filing a joint return, you should each notify the IRS of your current address.

If after you move you receive an IRS correspondence that has been forwarded by the Post Office, you may correct the address shown on the letter and mail it back to the IRS. Your correction is considered notice of an address change.

46.8 Interest on Tax Underpayments

You may be charged interest by the IRS if you have underpaid the tax due. The interest rate, which equals the federal short-term rate plus 3%, is determined every quarter. Interest begins to accrue from the due date of the return. Interest is compounded daily except for estimated tax penalties. If you relied on IRS assistance in preparing a return, and taxes are owed because of a mathematical or clerical error, interest does not begin to accrue until 30 days from a formal demand by the IRS for the payment of additional taxes. *See* the Planning Reminder on page 695 for interest on refunds and *47.6* for interest on refund claims filed on amended returns.

IRS interest rates on taxes owed are as follows:

From—	*To—*	*Underpayment Rate—*
7/1/2006	12/31/2006	8%
10/1/2005	6/30/2006	7
4/1/2005	9/30/2005	6
10/1/2004	3/31/2005	5
7/1/2004	9/30/2004	4
4/1/2004	6/30/2004	5
10/1/2003	3/31/2004	4
1/1/2003	9/30/2003	5

46.9 Tax Penalties for Late Filing and Late Payment

Late filing. If your return is filed late without reasonable cause, the IRS may impose a penalty of 5% of the net tax due for each month the return is late, with a maximum penalty of 25%. If the return is more than 60 days late, the penalty will not be less than the smaller of $100 and 100% of the tax due. In one case, the IRS tried to impose the $100 minimum penalty on a taxpayer who did not owe any tax because her withholdings exceeded her liability. However, the Tax Court held that the minimum $100 penalty does not apply unless tax is underpaid. The IRS has agreed to follow the decision.

If failure to file is fraudulent, the monthly penalty is 15% of the net tax due, with a maximum penalty of 75%.

If you are subject to penalties for both late payment and late filing, the 0.5% penalty for late payment (but not the 1% penalty) offsets the penalty for late filing during the period that the penalties run concurrently.

Late payments. If you are late in paying your taxes, a monthly penalty of 0.5% ($^{1}/_{2}$ of 1%) is imposed on the net amount of tax due and not paid by the due date. The maximum penalty is 25% of the tax due. The penalty is in addition to the regular interest charge. This penalty does not apply to the estimated tax; *see 27.1.* The late payment penalty does not apply if you can show that the failure to pay is due to reasonable cause and not to willful neglect.

A special reasonable cause rule applies if you obtain a filing extension. If by the original due date you paid at least 90% of your total tax liability through withholdings, estimated tax installments, or payment with your extension request, reasonable cause is presumed and the penalty does not apply for the period covered by the extension.

Unless reasonable cause is shown, the 0.5% monthly penalty also applies for failure to pay a tax deficiency within 21 calendar days of the date of notice and demand for payment if the tax due is less than $100,000. If the tax is $100,000 or more, the penalty-free payment period is 10 business days.

The monthly penalty may be doubled to 1%, if, after repeated requests to pay and a notice of levy, you do not pay. The increased penalty applies starting in the month that begins after the earlier of the following IRS notices: (1) a notice that the IRS will levy upon your assets within 10 days unless payment is made or (2) a notice demanding immediate payment where the IRS believes collection of the tax is in jeopardy. If the tax is not paid after such a demand for immediate payment, the IRS may levy upon your assets without waiting 10 days.

Law Alert

Making a Deposit To Suspend Interest

So long as the IRS has not yet assessed an underpayment of income tax (or gift, estate, or generation-skipping tax), you can make a cash deposit in order to suspend the running of interest on a potential underpayment. If you are later found to owe tax and the IRS uses the deposit to pay it, you will not be charged interest. The running of interest is suspended on the date the IRS receives the deposit, not later when the liability is assessed or the deposit is actually applied to the liability. If the dispute is resolved in your favor, the deposit is returned to you and you are paid interest. You may also request the return of all or part of the deposit at any time before the IRS has used it to pay tax, unless the IRS determines that collection of tax is in jeopardy. You are paid interest on a returned deposit that was attributable to a disputable tax. Revenue Procedure 2005-18 has guidelines for making and recouping deposits.

Table 46-1 Income Record Keeper

Type of income	*Records Needed*	*Report on*
Wages and salaries	Form W-2. Your employer must send your 2006 Form W-2 by January 31, 2007. Attach Copy B to your federal return. Keep Copy C for your records. If you worked for more than one employer during 2006, attach all Copy B forms to your return.	Form 1040EZ, Line 1 Form 1040A, Line 7 Form 1040, Line 7
Tip income	Form 4070 or other record showing your monthly reports of cash tips of $20 or more. Form W-2. Also *see 26.8* for reporting FICA taxes on unreported tips.	Form 1040EZ, Line 1 Form 1040A, Line 7 Form 1040, Line 7
Interest income	Form 1099-INT Form 1099-OID Deposit slips of interest received on money you loaned to others	Form 1040EZ, Line 2 ($1,500 or less) Form 1040A, Line 8(a); Schedule 1, Part I (over $1,500) Form 1040, Line 8(a); Schedule B, Part I (over $1,500)
Dividend income	Form 1099-DIV Company statements of dividend payments, especially if stock dividends have been paid	Form 1040A, Line 9a for total ordinary dividends, Line 9b for qualified dividends eligible for long-term capital gain treatment; Schedule 1, Part II (ordinary dividends over $1,500) Form 1040, Line 9a for total ordinary dividends, Line 9b for qualified dividends eligible for long-term capital gain treatment; Schedule B, Part II (ordinary dividends over $1,500)
Taxable refund of state and local income tax	Form 1099-G	Form 1040, Line 10
Alimony received	Deposit slips of alimony received and ex-spouse's Social Security number Copy of divorce or separation decree or agreements	Form 1040, Line 11 if taxable
Business income or loss	Business accounting records, deposit slips Business checkbook, deposit slips, invoice receipts, cancelled checks, bank statements Form 1099-MISC	Form 1040, Line 12; Schedule C or C-EZ; Form 8582 if passive activity rules apply; *see* Chapter 10
Sale of stocks and bonds	Form 1099-B and broker confirmation statements	Schedule D Form 1040, Line 13
Sale of personal residence	Closing papers, records of purchase, improvements; *see 29.6.*	If taxable gain is realized, Schedule D
Sale of real estate	Closing statement, records of cost and improvements Records of depreciation	Form 4797 Schedule D Form 1040, Line 13
IRA distributions	Form 1099-R	Form 1040A, Line 11 Form 1040, Line 15
Pensions and annuities	Form 1099-R if you receive annuity payments or lump-sum distributions	Form 1040A, Line 12 Form 1040, Line 16
Commercial annuity income	Form 1099-R	Form 1040A, Line 12 Form 1040, Line 16
Rent income	Account records, checkbook, cancelled checks, and receipts	Schedule E Form 1040, Line 17 Form 8582 if passive activity rules apply

Table 46-1 Income Record Keeper (continued)

Type of income	*Records Needed*	*Report on*
Royalty income	Form 1099-MISC	Schedule E Form 1040, Line 17
Partnership income	Schedule K-1, Form 1065	Schedule E Form 1040, Line 17
Beneficiary of trust or estate	Schedule K-1, Form 1041	Schedule E Form 1040, Line 17
S corporation	Schedule K-1, Form 1120S	Schedule E Form 1040, Line 17
Unemployment compensation	Form 1099-G	Form 1040A, Line 13 Form 1040, Line 19
Social Security benefits	Form SSA-1099	Form 1040A, Line 14 Form 1040, Line 20
Gambling income	Form W-2G, diary or other record showing wins and losses, losing tickets	Form 1040, Line 21
Other income	Form 1099-MISC, records of amounts received, date received	Form 1040, Line 21
"Kiddie" tax on income of a child under age 14	Child's Forms 1099-INT, 1099-DIV, and 1099-OID	Form 1040A, Line 28 Form 1040, Line 44 Form 8615 if income is reported on child's return Form 8814 if parent elects to report child's income on Form 1040

Table 46-2 Deduction Record Keeper

Type of deduction	Records Needed	Report on
Exemptions for dependents	Records of support contribution for food, lodging, medical expenses, such as cancelled checks, diary entries. Birth certificates in case age of a child is questioned. School attendance record if student status is questioned. Form 8332 allowing noncustodial parent to claim the exemption. This form must also be attached to return by noncustodial parent claiming exemption; *see 21.7.* Forms 2120 if dependent's support is shared; *see 21.6.*	Form 1040A, Line 6(c) Form 1040, Line 6(c)
Educator expenses	Records of expenses/purchase and business use	See below*
IRA deductible contribution	Trustee's statements of contribution, copy of plan	Form 1040A, Line 17 Form 1040, Line 32
Student loan interest deduction	Bank statement showing interest paid	Form 1040A, Line 18 Form 1040, Line 33
Tuition and fees deduction	Student's name and taxpayer identification number, cancelled checks and statements of tuition and enrollment fees. For dependents, records of support contributions.	See below*
Health savings account deduction	Trustee's statements and Form 5498-SA, showing contributions	Form 1040, Line 25 Form 8889
Moving expenses	Cancelled checks or receipts for expenses incurred, diary or log	Form 1040, Line 26 Form 3903
One-half of self-employment tax	Schedule SE, Form 1040	Form 1040, Line 27
Self-employed health insurance premium	Cancelled check of payment, copy of contract, insurance statement	Form 1040, Line 29
Keogh, SEP, or SIMPLE contribution for yourself	Trustee statement, copy of plan	Form 1040, Line 28
Penalty on early withdrawal of savings	Form 1099-INT	Form 1040, Line 30
Alimony deduction	Cancelled checks, copy of divorce or separation decree, written separation agreement, ex-spouse's Social Security number	Form 1040, Line 31
Domestic production activities deduction	Business records, Forms W-2	Form 1040, Line 35 Form 8903
Employee expenses	Diary logs, receipts, copy of accounting to employer	Form 2106 Schedule A, Line 20
Home office expenses	Records of expenses, business use, and allocation	Form 8829 if self-employed; Schedule C, Line 30 Form 2106 if an employee; Schedule A, Line 20
Medical and dental expenses	Cancelled checks, statements, prescriptions; log of travel expenses and lodging costs	Form 1040 Schedule A, Lines 1–4

*When this book went to press, the "extenders" legislation extending this deduction to 2006 had not yet been enacted. An extension is expected. *See* "What's New for 2006" on page xxv. *Also see* the *e-Supplement* for a legislation update and information on the line number for reporting the deduction, assuming the legislation passes.

Table 46-2 Deduction Record Keeper (continued)

Type of deduction	Records Needed	Report on
Taxes—state and local income, personal property, real estate. See below for state and local general sales taxes.*	Form W-2 for withholding of income tax Cancelled checks Credit card receipts showing sales tax Bank statements of property taxes paid by bank (mortgages) Form 1099-DIV for foreign tax Form 1099-INT or tax receipt for foreign tax withheld at source	Form 1040 Schedule A, Lines 5–9 *See* below for state and local general sales taxes*
Mortgage interest	Bank statement showing interest paid Form 1098	Form 1040 Schedule A, Lines 10 and 11
Points	Copy of bank statements, canceled checks	Form 1040 Schedule A, Lines 10 and 12
Cash donations	Cancelled checks, receipt from charity	Form 1040; Schedule A, Line 15
Volunteer expenses for charitable organizations	Log of travel, cancelled checks showing purpose	Form 1040 Schedule A, Line 15
Property donation	Description of property, records of fair market value and cost. Receipt from organization. If at least $250, a written receipt from organization to substantiate donation. Cancelled check is not sufficient. If car is valued at over $500, a written acknowledgment showing gross proceeds if the organization sold the car. If in excess of $5,000, qualified appraisal report and statement from organization	Form 1040 Schedule A, Line 16
Casualty and theft losses	*See* "Proving a Casualty Loss" on page 369. For thefts, statements from witnesses, police records, or a newspaper account of the crime might help.	Form 1040 Schedule A, Line 19 Form 4684
Gambling losses	Losing tickets or receipts, diary showing daily wagers, wins, and losses	Form 1040 Schedule A, Line 27
Union dues	Wage statements showing withholding for dues or cancelled checks	Form 1040 Schedule A, Line 20
Unreimbursed travel and entertainment expenses	Diary log and receipts kept according to the rules of *20.26*	Form 2106 Form 1040; Schedule A, Line 20
Unreimbursed auto expenses if you are employed	Statement from employer requiring use of car Mileage log Receipts of expenses if actual costs are claimed Cost records of auto if depreciation is claimed	Form 2106 Form 1040 Schedule A, Line 20
Investment expenses	Cancelled checks	Form 1040; Schedule A, Line 22
Safe deposit box fee	Bank statements	Form 1040; Schedule A, Line 22
Tax preparation fees	Cancelled checks	Form 1040; Schedule A, Line 21

*When this book went to press, the "extenders" legislation extending this deduction to 2006 had not yet been enacted. An extension is expected. *See* "What's New for 2006" on page xxv. *Also see* the *e-Supplement* for a legislation update and information on the line number for reporting the deduction, assuming the legislation passes.

Table 46-3 Tax Credit Record Keeper

Type of credit	*Records Needed*	*Report on*
Earned income credit	Form W-2 if an employee, Schedule SE if self-employed, to show earnings	Form 1040 EZ, Line 8 Form 1040A, Line 41; Schedule EIC Form 1040, Line 66; Schedule EIC
Advance payment of earned income credit	Form W-2, Box 9	Form 1040A, Line 37 Form 1040, Line 61
Child and dependent care expenses	Cancelled checks for amounts paid to care for child	Form 1040A, Line 29; Schedule 2 Form 1040, Line 48; Form 2441
Credit for the elderly or the disabled	Physician's statement of condition	Form 1040A, Line 30; Schedule 3 Form 1040, Line 49; Schedule R
Child tax credit and additional child tax credit	Records of support contribution Birth certificates in case age of a child is questioned School attendance record if student status is questioned	Form 1040A, Line 33 and Line 42 Form 1040, Line 52 and Line 68 Form 8812
Education credits	Student's name and taxpayer identification number Cancelled checks and statements of tuition and enrollment fees For dependents, records for support contributions	Form 1040A, Line 31 Form 1040, Line 50 Form 8863
Adoption credit	Adopted child's name, date of birth, and taxpayer identification number Adoption papers showing the date the adoption became final	Form 1040A, Line 34 Form 1040, Line 53 Form 8839
Credit for federal telephone excise tax paid	None if you choose the safe harbor amount. If you claim the actual amount paid you will need to have proof of the amount assessed and proof of payment	Form 1040 EZ-T (for those not otherwise required to file a tax return) Form 1040 EZ Line 9, Form 1040A Line 42 Form 1040 Line 71 Form 8613
Residential energy credit	Certification—if provided by manufacturer—and proof of purchase	Form 1040 Line 52; Form 5695
Hybrid car credit	Certification from manufacturer	Form 1040 Line 55; Form 8910
Foreign tax credit	Form 1099-DIV; foreign tax returns or statements	Form 1116 Form 1040, Line 47
Prior alternative minimum tax credit	Copy of prior year's Form 6251 Form 8801	Form 1040, Line 55
Credit for federal taxes withheld	Form 1099 Form W-2 Form W-4V	Form 1040EZ, Line 7 Form 1040A, Line 39 Form 1040, Line 64
Credit for estimated tax payments	Cancelled checks and copy of Form 1040-ES	Form 1040A, Line 40 Form 1040, Line 65

Filing Refund Claims, and Amended Returns

File a refund claim on Form 1040X if you want to take advantage of a retroactive change in the law, if you have overpaid your tax because you failed to take allowable deductions or credits, or overstated your income. You may use Form 1040X to correct your return if you underreported your income or improperly claimed deductions.

File a refund claim on time. The time limits discussed at *47.2* must be strictly observed; otherwise, even if you file a valid refund claim, it will be denied because of late filing.

You do not have to file a refund claim if you have overpaid your tax due to excessive withholding of taxes on your wages or salary, or if you have overpaid your estimated tax. You get a refund on these overpayments by filing your tax return and requesting a refund for these amounts. You must file your return within three years from the time the tax was paid to get the refund; *see 47.2.*

For a refund of an overpayment of FICA taxes, *see 26.10* for how to claim a refund on your tax return. If you are not required to file a tax return, you file a refund claim on Form 843.

If you are entitled to a refund due to the earned income credit for certain low-income working families, you must file your tax return to get your refund, even though your income and filing status would not otherwise require that a return be filed. *See* Chapter 25.

47.1 Who Should File a Refund Claim

You may file a refund claim on Form 1040X if you have overpaid your tax on your original return because you failed to take allowable deductions or credits, or overstated your income. You may also file for a refund if you wish to take advantage of a retroactive change in the law. You do not have to file a refund claim if you have overpaid your tax due to excessive withholding of taxes on your wages or salary, or if you have overpaid your estimated tax. You will receive a refund on those overpayments by filing your tax return and requesting a refund at that time; *see 46.4.*

47.2 When To File a Refund Claim

You may file a refund claim on Form 1040X within three years from the time your return was filed, or within two years from the time you paid your tax, whichever is later. However, a refund claim on a late-filed return may be barred under a three-year "look back" rule; *see* below. A return filed before its due date is treated as having been filed on the due date. The filing deadlines are suspended while you are financially disabled; *see* the Planning Reminder on this page.

A refund claim based on a bad debt or worthless securities may be made within seven years of the due date of the return for the year in which the debt or security became worthless.

The time for filing refund claims based on carrybacks of net operating losses or general business credits is within three years of the due date (including extensions) of the return for the year the loss or credit arose.

A refund claim based on your share of a joint return refund withheld by the IRS to pay your spouse's debts *(46.4)* may be made within six years of the date you received the IRS notice that the refund had been withheld.

If you filed an agreement giving the IRS an extended period of time in which to assess a tax against you, you are allowed an additional period in which to file a claim for refund. The claim, up to certain amounts, may be filed through the extension period and for six months afterwards.

Caution

Time Limits Must Be Observed

Failure to file a timely refund claim is fatal, regardless of its merits. Even if you expect that your claim will have to be pursued in court, you must still file a timely refund claim with the IRS. Mailing a refund claim so that it is postmarked by the due date (including extensions) qualifies as a timely filing if you use the U.S. Postal Service. The timely mailing rule also applies to refund claims that are timely deposited with private delivery services that have been designated by the IRS.

Refund claim for withholdings and estimated tax on late-filed original return. A refund for withheld income taxes or estimated tax installments can be lost if you delay filing your original return too long. The Supreme Court agrees with the IRS that the withholdings and estimated tax are considered to be paid on the original due date of the return. To obtain a refund of these taxes, you must file the return within three years of the due date, or within three years plus any extension period if a filing extension is obtained. If the return is filed after the end of this three-year (plus extension) "look-back" period, the withholdings and estimated taxes cannot be refunded. For example, if taxes were withheld from your 2003 wages and you are due a refund but have not yet filed your 2003 return, you must do so by April 16, 2007, to obtain a refund of the withholdings. If you had obtained an extension until August 16, 2004, to file your 2003 return, the deadline for filing the refund claim would be August 16, 2007. Where such a refund is claimed on an original return mailed and postmarked (U.S. Postal Service) on or slightly before the last day of the "three years plus extension" period, the IRS at one time argued that the timely mailing/timely filing rule did not apply. But following a contrary appeals decision, the IRS now allows a refund in this situation. The IRS treats refund claims included on delinquent original returns as filed on the date of mailing for purposes of applying the "three years plus extension" look-back rule.

Planning Reminder

Disability Suspends Limitation

In filing a refund claim during any period in which a person is unable to manage his or her financial affairs due to a physical or mental impairment that has lasted or is expected to last for at least one year or to result in death, the law suspends the limitation period. The suspension does not apply during a period in which a guardian is authorized to handle the individual's financial affairs.

Armed Forces service members and veterans. In determining the time limits within which a refund claim may be filed, you disregard intervening periods of service in a combat zone or hazardous duty area, plus periods of continuous hospitalization outside the United States as a result of combat zone injury, and the next 180 days thereafter.

47.3 Joint Refund Claims

If a joint return was filed for a year in which a refund is due, both spouses are entitled to recover jointly and both must file a joint refund claim. Where separate returns were filed, each spouse is a separate taxpayer and may not file a claim to recover a refund based on the other spouse's return, except if that spouse becomes the fiduciary when one spouse becomes incompetent or dies. To claim a refund on behalf of a deceased spouse, you should complete Form 1310. If you are divorced and incur a net operating loss or credit that may be carried back to a year in which you were married, you may file a refund claim with your signature alone and the refund check will be made out only to you; *see 40.18.*

47.4 Stating the Reasons for Refund Claims

The most important part of a refund claim is a statement of the "reasons" for the refund. A general claim simply noting an overpayment, without supporting facts and grounds, is not sufficient. If a claim is denied by the IRS, it may become the basis of a court suit. If you have not stated all the grounds, you may not be allowed to argue them in court. You must make a claim showing:

- All the facts that support the claim. Attach all supporting documents and tax forms supporting your claim.
- All the grounds for the claim. If you are uncertain about the exact legal grounds, alternate and even inconsistent grounds may be given. For example: "The loss was incurred from an embezzlement; if not, from a bad debt." To protect against understating the amount of the claim, you might preface the claim with this phrase: "The following or such greater amounts as may be legally refunded."

47.5 Quick Refund Claims

Form 1045 may be used for filing refunds due to carrybacks from net operating losses, and the general business credit. Form 1045 also may be used for a quick refund based on a repayment exceeding $3,000 of income reported in an earlier year. Form 1045 must be filed within 12 months after the loss year. The IRS must act on the claim within 90 days. Payment of quick refund claims is not a final settlement of your return; the IRS may still audit and then disallow the refund claim. Note that the filing of a quick refund, if rejected, may not be the basis of a suit for refund; a regular refund claim must be filed.

Tax-shelter claims. If you file a quick refund claim on Form 1045 and the IRS determines it is likely that you claimed excessive tax-shelter benefits, the IRS will offset the quick refund claim by a deficiency attributable to the tax-shelter items. You will receive the balance and receive a notice of the tax-shelter deficiency.

47.6 Interest Paid on Refund Claims

If a refund claim is filed within the time limits in *47.2* and the IRS pays the refund within 45 days, interest is paid from the date of overpayment to the date the claim was filed. If the refund is not made within the 45-day period, interest is paid from the date of overpayment to a date set by the IRS that is not more than 30 days before the date of the refund check.

The IRS does not have to pay interest on overpayments resulting from net operating loss carrybacks or business credit carrybacks if a refund is paid within 45 days of the filing of the refund claim. If a refund claim based on a loss or credit carryback is filed and subsequently a quick refund claim is filed on Form 1045 for the same refund, the 45-day period starts to run on the date Form 1045 is filed.

Interest rates applied to overpayments are as follows:

Amounts outstanding between—	*Overpayment rate is—*
7/1/2006 – 12/31/2006	8%
10/1/2005 – 6/30/2006	7
4/1/2005 – 9/30/2005	6
10/1/2004 – 3/31/2005	5
7/1/2004 – 9/30/2004	4
4/1/2004 – 6/30/2004	5
10/1/2003 – 3/31/2004	4
1/1/2003 – 9/30/2003	5

47.7 Refunds Withheld To Cover Debts

The IRS may withhold all or part of your refund if you owe federal taxes. The Treasury Department's Financial Management Service may withhold all or part of your refund if you owe child or spousal support or federal non-tax debts such as student loans or state income taxes. If you file a joint return with a spouse who owes child support or federal debts, you may be able to obtain your share of a refund due on the joint return by filing Form 8379; for further details, *see 46.4.*

Caution

Refund Offset for Overdue State Taxes

If you owe state income taxes, the state can refer the debt to the Treasury Department's Financial Management Service (FMS). The FMS will offset your federal tax refund by the state tax if your address on the return is within the state seeking the offset. The state must give you written notice that the debt is being referred to the FMS and provide an opportunity for disputing the liability.

47.8 Amended Returns Showing Additional Tax

If, after filing your 2006 return, you find that you did not report some income or claimed excessive deductions, you should file an amended return on Form 1040X to limit interest charges and possible tax penalties. You may also file an amended return to change the status of your return from a separate return to a joint return with your spouse. It is important to note that you may not switch from a joint return to a separate return after the due date of the return. An amended return may also be filed if you want to change from itemized deductions to the standard deduction method, or vice versa.

If you filed early and then file an amended return by the filing due date (including any extensions) that shows additional tax due, you will not be charged interest or penalties based on the original return; the amended return is considered a substitute for the original.

You must pay the additional tax due as shown on Form 1040X. Even if you expect a refund on your original return, the IRS will not reduce the refund check to cover the additional tax. You must pay it and you will receive the original refund separately.

Chapter 48

If the IRS Examines Your Return

Because the IRS is unable to examine every return, it follows a policy of examining returns which, upon preliminary inspection, indicate the largest possible source of potential tax deficiency.

Returns are rated for audit according to a mathematical formula called the discriminant function system (DIF). Various weights are assigned to separate items on each tax return, thus permitting the ranking of returns for the greatest potential error.

This chapter discusses what may trigger an audit and how you can handle an audit if your return is selected for examination.

48.1 Odds of Being Audited

Caution

Audits on the Rise

The IRS has been ramping up the number of audits, with a focus on high-income taxpayers, Schedule C filers, S corporations, partnerships, abusive tax shelters, and corporations.

The odds are low that your return will be picked for an audit. However, the number has been increasing, particularly with respect to high-income taxpayers.

Audit odds vary depending on your income, profession, type of return, type of transactions reported, and where you live. Individual returns are classified by all income items on the return without regard to losses. Professional or business income reported on Schedule C and farm income reported on Schedule F is classified by total gross receipts, and corporate returns are classified by total assets.

Your return may command special IRS scrutiny because of your profession, the type of transactions reported, or the deductions claimed. The chances of being audited are greater under the following circumstances:

- Your information reported on the tax return does not match information received from third-party documentation, such as Forms 1099 and W-2.
- Your itemized deductions exceed IRS targets.
- You claim tax-shelter losses.
- You report complex investment or business transactions without clear explanations.
- You receive cash payments in your work that the IRS thinks are easy to conceal, such as cash fees received by doctors or tips received by cab drivers and waiters.
- Business expenses are large in relation to income.
- Cash contributions to charity are large in relation to income.
- You are a shareholder of a closely held corporation whose return has been examined.
- A prior audit resulted in a tax deficiency.
- An informer gives the IRS grounds to believe that you are omitting income from your return.

Itemized deductions. If your itemized deductions exceed target ranges set by the IRS, the chances of being audited increase. The IRS does not publicize its audit criteria for excessive deductions, but it does release statistics showing the average amount of deductions claimed according to reported income. Here are IRS figures based on deductions claimed on 2004 returns filed through September 2005.

Table 48-1 Average Itemized Deductions for 2004

AGI (thousands)	*Medical*	*Taxes*	*Interest*	*Charitable*
15 to <30	$ 6,229	$ 2,761	$ 6,664	$ 1,969
30 to <50	5,324	3,592	6,933	2,132
50 to <100	6,125	5,808	8,310	2,663
100 to <200	9,811	10,528	10,949	4,130
200+	31,332	38,143	19,721	19,014

Taxpayer Bill of Rights. As a taxpayer, you have the right to be treated fairly, professionally, promptly, and courteously by the IRS and its employees. Because of many complaints of abuse in the past, Congress has passed several statutes, collectively referred to as the Taxpayer Bill of Rights, to protect taxpayers from mistreatment by IRS personnel.

One aim of the Taxpayer Bill of Rights is to have the IRS inform you of the effect of the tax action it is taking and how you can proceed and protect your rights. *See* IRS Publication 1, *Your Rights as a Taxpayer*. Thus, when the IRS starts an action against you, you should ask for an explanation of the procedural rules affecting your case, if these are not already included in the documents sent to you. For example, before the IRS may enforce a tax lien by seizing property by levy, the IRS must provide you with a notice of your right to a hearing before an appeals officer, an explanation of the levy procedures, the availability of administrative appeals and the appeals procedures, the alternatives to the proposed levy such as an installment agreement, and the rules for obtaining the release of a lien. *See* IRS Publication 556, *Examination of Returns, Appeal Rights, and Claims for Refund*; IRS Publication 594, *The IRS Collection Process;* and IRS Publication 5, *Your Appeal Rights and How to Prepare a Protest if You Don't Agree*.

Planning Reminder

Taxpayer Rights Web Page

For IRS publications outlining taxpayer rights, notices, examinations of tax returns, appeal rights, and collection procedures, go to the "Individuals" page of the IRS website, www.irs.gov, and click on the link for "Taxpayer Rights." From there, you can link to the "Taxpayer Advocate" page. The Taxpayer Advocate Service may help you resolve a problem that could not be settled through normal IRS channels.

Taxpayer Advocate. An important part of the Taxpayer Bill of Rights is the Taxpayer Advocate Service. The function of the Taxpayer Advocate is to assist taxpayers in resolving problems with the IRS, identify areas in which taxpayers have problems dealing with the IRS, propose changes in administrative practices of the IRS, and identify potential legislative changes that may mitigate the problems. From the Taxpayer Advocate, you can receive assistance if you have unsuccessfully tried to resolve your problem with the IRS and have not had your calls or letters returned. You will be assigned a personal advocate who is in the best position to try to resolve your problem. If you face a significant hardship because of an impending IRS action or lack of IRS response to your problem, you may apply to the Taxpayer Advocate for a Taxpayer Assistance order on Form 911. Contact the Taxpayer Advocate Service by calling 1-877-777-4778, or you may write to the Advocate at the IRS office that last contacted you. Publication 1546, *The Taxpayer Advocate Service of the IRS*, has a state-by-state list of addresses and phone numbers for Advocate offices. The Taxpayer Advocate page at the IRS website has comprehensive information concerning the Taxpayer Advocate Service; go to www.irs.gov.

48.2 When the IRS Can Assess Additional Taxes

Three-year statute of limitations. The IRS has three years after the date on which your return is filed to assess additional taxes. When you file a return before the due date, however, the three-year period starts from the due date, generally April 15.

Where the due date of a return falls on a Saturday, Sunday, or legal holiday, the due date is postponed to the next business day.

Caution

No Limitation Period for Fraud

There is no limitation on when tax may be assessed where a false or fraudulent return is filed with intent to evade tax, or where no return is filed.

EXAMPLES

1. You filed your 2006 return on February 5, 2007. The last day on which the IRS can make an assessment on your 2006 return is April 15, 2010.
2. You filed your 2004 return on May 23, 2005. The IRS has until May 23, 2008, to assess a deficiency.

Amended returns. If you file an amended return shortly before the three-year limitations period is about to expire and the return shows that you owe additional tax, the IRS has 60 days from the date it receives the return to assess the additional tax, even though the regular limitations period would expire before the 60-day period.

Six-year statute. When you fail to report an item of gross income which is more than 25% of the gross income reported on your return, the IRS has six years after the return is filed to assess additional taxes. An item that is adequately disclosed is not considered an omission.

IRS request for audit extension. If the IRS cannot complete an audit within three years, it may request that you sign Form 872 to extend the time for assessing the tax. However, where an individual was "scared" into signing such an agreement, it was held invalid. *See* the following Example.

EXAMPLE

Robertson, a plumber, won $30,000 in a sweepstakes. An IRS agent asked him to sign an extension agreement. Robertson never had any prior dealings with the IRS, he did not know that his return was under examination, and he was not in touch with the lawyer who prepared the return on which his sweepstakes winnings were averaged.

Robertson wanted to see his lawyer before signing Form 872, but the agent pressed hard for the signature, phoning him and his wife at home and at work 20 times in a week. The agent did not tell him the amount of additional tax that might be involved, or explain that if he refused to sign he would have an opportunity before the IRS and the courts to contest any additional tax. Instead, the agent's comments gave him the impression that his home could be confiscated if he refused to sign. Robertson signed and the IRS later increased his tax.

Robertson argued that the agreement was not valid. He signed under duress. The Tax Court agreed. He convinced the court that he really believed he could lose his house and property if he did not comply. No adequate explanation of the real consequences of refusal to sign was made, although Robertson asked. Since he signed Form 872 under duress, the IRS could not increase his tax after the three-year period.

48.3 Audit Overview

When you file, the IRS checks your return for computational accuracy and clerical errors, such as a missing signature or missing or inaccurate Social Security numbers. To check whether you have omitted income from your return, the IRS will match your return against the Forms W-2 and Forms 1099 it receives from employers, brokers, payers of interest and dividends, and others who have filed information returns reporting payments to you.

If an error is found, or you have not submitted required attachments, you will probably be advised by mail of the corrections and of additional tax due, or you may be asked to provide additional information to substantiate tax deductions or credits. If you disagree with an IRS assessment of additional tax, you may request an interview or submit additional information. If you file early for 2006, are advised of an error, and the correction is made before April 16, 2007, interest is not charged.

If your refund is selected for a more thorough review, you will be notified by mail. This may not happen for a year or two; *see 48.2.*

Filing Tip

Authorize Someone To Discuss Return Processing Problems

Generally, a person authorized to practice before the IRS may discuss your tax return issues with the IRS only if you sign a power of attorney on Form 2848. However, just above the signature section of your 2006 Form 1040, 1040A, or 1040EZ, you may consent to contacts between the IRS and your designee to resolve return processing issues such as mathematical errors, missing return information, or questions about refunds or payments. The designee can be a friend or relative and need not be a tax professional. A power of attorney will still be needed to handle an audit, underreported income issues, appeals within the IRS, and collection notices.

Types of audits. An examination may be held by correspondence, at a local IRS office, or at the taxpayer's place of business, office, or home. An examination at an IRS office is called a desk or office examination; an examination at a place of business or home is called a field examination. When you are contacted by the IRS, you should receive an explanation of the examination process.

In a correspondence audit, the IRS sends you a letter asking for additional information about an item on your return. For example, the IRS may ask you to document a claimed deduction for charitable contributions or medical expenses. If the IRS is not satisfied with your response, you may be called in for an office audit. The IRS also notifies you by letter of mathematical or clerical errors you have made on your return, or if you have failed to report income, such as interest or dividends, that are shown by payers on information returns and matched to taxpayer returns by IRS computers.

The complexity of the transactions reported on a return generally determines whether a return will be reviewed at an office or field examination.

Most audits of individual returns, except for the self-employed, are conducted at IRS offices. An office audit usually covers only a few specific issues which the IRS specifies in its notice to you. For example, the examining agent may only be interested in seeing proof for travel expense deductions or educational expenses.

Field audits generally involve business returns; they are more extensive and time-consuming than office audits and are handled by more experienced IRS agents. For self-employed individuals, most examinations are field audits at their place of business. It is advisable to have a tax professional go over the potential weak spots in your return and represent you at the examination.

48.4 Preparing for the Audit

After an office audit is scheduled, the first thing to do is look over your return. Refresh your memory. Examine the items the IRS questioned in its notice of audit, and organize your records accordingly. Also check the rest of your return and gather proof for items you are unsure of. At this point, you should take a broad view of your return to anticipate problems you may encounter. Before the actual examination begins, consider possible settlement terms. Assume that the agent will assess additional tax, but establish the range you will consider reasonable. You can always change your mind, but giving some thought beforehand to possible settlement terms will help you later when settlements are actually discussed.

Planning Reminder

Audit Scheduling

Make sure that the examination is scheduled far enough in advance for you to get ready. Do not let the IRS hurry you into an examination until you are prepared. In some localities, particularly rural areas, the IRS may give short notice in scheduling a field audit. An agent may even appear at your home or place of business and try to begin the audit immediately. Resist this pressure and reschedule the meeting at your convenience.

You may authorize an attorney, CPA, enrolled agent, or other individual recognized to practice before the IRS to represent you at the examination without your being there. To do so, give your representative authorization on Form 2848. An attorney or other representative authorized on Form 2848 can perform any acts that you could, including entering into a binding settlement agreement.

If you attend the audit, take only the records related to the items questioned in the IRS notice. Do not volunteer extra records; if the agent sees them, it might suggest new areas for investigation.

If you are concerned that there may be a problem of fraud, see a qualified attorney before you come into contact with an IRS official. The attorney can put your actions in perspective and help protect your legal rights. Besides, what you tell an attorney is privileged information; he or she cannot divulge or be forced to divulge data you have provided, other than data used to prepare your tax return.

A field audit of your business return is likely to involve a comprehensive examination and requires careful preparation. Together with your tax adviser, go over your return for potential areas of weakness. For example, the agent is likely to question deductions you have claimed for business travel. If you are an incorporated professional, the corporation's deductions for expenses of company-owned cars or planes will probably be reviewed. The agent may suspect that a portion of these business deductions are actually nondeductible personal travel costs; be prepared to substantiate the business portion of your total mileage and operating expenses.

Under the Taxpayer Bill of Rights *(48.1),* the IRS is generally required to hold an office audit at the office located nearest to your home. The IRS generally may not conduct a field audit at the site of a small business if the audit would essentially require the shutting down of the business, unless a direct visit is necessary to determine inventory or verify assets.

48.5 Handling the Audit

If you have authorized someone to represent you at the examination, your representative may appear at the examination without you. If the IRS wants to question you, it must issue you an administrative summons. If you are present and questioned, you may stop the examination to consult with counsel, unless the examination is pursuant to an administrative summons.

Audits conducted at an IRS office may conclude quickly because they usually involve only a few specific issues. In some cases, the audit may take less than an hour. The key to handling the audit is advance preparation. When you arrive at the IRS office, be prepared to produce your records quickly. Records should be organized by topic so that you do not waste time leafing through pages for a receipt or other document.

If the agent decides to question an item not mentioned in the notice of audit, refuse politely but firmly to answer the questions. Tell the agent that you must first review your records. If the agent insists on pursuing the matter, another meeting will have to be scheduled. The agent might decide it is not worth the time and drop the issue.

Common sense rules of courtesy should be your guide in your contacts with the agent. Avoid personality clashes; they can only interfere with a speedy and fair resolution of the examination. However, be firm in your approach and, if the agent appears to be unreasonable in his or her approach, make it clear that—if necessary—you will go all the way to court to win your point. A vacillating approach may weaken your position in reaching a settlement.

If the IRS has scheduled a field audit, ask that the examination be held at your representative's office. If you have not retained professional help and the examination takes place on your business premises, do not allow the agent free run of the area: Provide the agent with a comfortable work area for examining your records. If possible, the workplace should be isolated so that the agent can concentrate on the examination without being distracted by office operations that might spark questions. Tell your employees not to answer questions about your business or engage in small talk with the agent. As with an office audit, help speed along the field examination by having prepared your records so that requested information can be quickly produced.

Recording the examination. You have the right to make an audio recording of any interview with an IRS official. Video recordings are not permitted. No later than 10 calendar days before the interview, give written notice to the agent conducting the interview that you will make a recording. Later requests are at the discretion of the IRS. You must pay for all recording expenses and supply the equipment. The IRS may also make a recording of the interview, upon giving notice of at least 10 calendar days. However, IRS notice is not necessary if you have already submitted a request to make a recording. You have the right to obtain a transcript, at your own expense, of any recording made by the IRS. Generally, a request for a copy must be received by the IRS agent within 30 calendar days after the recording, although later requests may be honored.

48.6 Tax Penalties for Inaccurate Returns

A 20% penalty generally applies to the portion of any tax underpayment attributable to any of the following: (1) negligence or disregard of IRS rules and regulations; (2) substantial understatement of tax liability; (3) overvaluation of property; or (4) undervaluation of property on a gift tax or estate tax return. These penalties may be avoided by showing good faith and reasonable cause for the underpayment; a stricter version of this exception applies to charitable contribution overvaluations as discussed later in this section. There is no stacking of penalties. Only one 20% penalty can be imposed on a portion of an underpayment, even if that portion is attributable to more than one of the above types of prohibited conduct.

There are also penalties on taxpayers who fail to disclose participation in "reportable" transactions, and on taxpayers who understate tax liability on reportable transactions with a significant tax avoidance purpose; *see* the Caution on this page.

Caution

Penalties Relating to Reportable Transactions

Effective for returns and statements due after, and filed after, October 22, 2004, a $10,000 penalty may be imposed on individuals who fail to adequately disclose a "reportable" transaction on Form 8886; the penalty is $50,000 for taxpayers that are not natural persons. If the reportable transaction is also a "listed" transaction, the penalty amounts increase to $100,000 and $200,000, respectively. *See* the Form 8886 instructions for definitions of "reportable" and "listed" transactions. These penalties apply whether or not there is an understatement of tax liability due to the transaction. They apply in addition to the other penalties discussed in *48.6.*

Penalties are also imposed for understating tax liability attributable to reportable transactions with a significant tax avoidance purpose, effective for taxable years ending after October 22, 2004. The penalty is generally 20% of the understatement if the transaction was adequately disclosed on Form 8886. There is an exception for reasonable cause, but to qualify, stringent requirements must be met; *see* Code Section 6664(d). If the transaction was not adequately disclosed, the penalty increases to 30% of the understatement and there is no reasonable cause exception.

Negligence or disregard of IRS rules or regulations. The 20% penalty applies to the portion of the underpayment attributable to negligence. Negligence is defined as failing to make a reasonable attempt to comply with the law. Failure to report income shown on an information return, such as interest or dividends, is considered strong evidence of negligence.

The 20% penalty may also apply if you take a position on a return which is contrary to IRS revenue rulings, notices, or regulations. This penalty for disregarding IRS rules or regulations may be avoided if you have a reasonable basis for your position and you disclose that position on Form 8275 or on Form 8275-R in the case of a good faith position contrary to a regulation. Thus, disclosure will not avoid a penalty for a position that does not have a reasonable basis.

Substantial understatement of tax. If you understate tax liability on a return by the greater of $5,000 or 10% of the proper tax, you may be subject to a penalty equal to 20% of the underpayment attributable to the understatement.

The penalty may be avoided if you have a reasonable basis for your position and you disclose the position to the IRS on Form 8275, or on Form 8275-R in the case of a position that is contrary to an IRS regulation.

The penalty also may be avoided if you can show that your position was supported by "substantial authority" such as statutes, court decisions, final, temporary, or proposed IRS regulations, IRS revenue rulings and procedures, and press releases or notices published by the IRS in the weekly Internal Revenue Bulletin. You may also rely on IRS private letter rulings and technical advice memoranda, as well as IRS actions on decisions and general counsel memoranda. However, according to the IRS, such rulings and internal IRS memoranda that are more than 10 years old should be accorded very little weight. Congressional committee reports and the tax law explanations prepared by Congress's Joint Committee on Taxation, known as the "Blue Book," may be relied on as authority for your position.

However, if an understatement of tax is due to tax-shelter items, having substantial authority for your position is not enough to avoid the penalty; you must also reasonably believe that your position was "more likely than not" correct. Disclosure does not avoid a penalty for tax-shelter items.

Overvaluing property value or basis. The thresholds for the 20% and 40% penalties for overvaluing charitable contributions of property have been lowered; *see 14.16.* The same penalty thresholds and rates apply where the basis of depreciable property has been inflated.

Undervaluation on gift or estate tax return. If the value of property reported on a gift tax or estate tax return filed after August 17, 2006, is 65% or less of the correct value, and the resulting tax underpayment from the undervaluation exceeds $5,000, the penalty is 20% of the underpayment. The penalty doubles to 40% of the underpayment if the claimed value of the property is 40% or less of the correct value. For returns filed on or before August 17, 2006, the 20% penalty applied if the claimed value was 50% or less of the correct amount and the 40% penalty applied if the claimed value was 25% or less of the correct amount.

Fraud penalty. A 75% penalty applies to the portion of any tax underpayment due to fraud. If the IRS establishes that any part of an underpayment is due to fraud, the entire underpayment will be attributed to fraud, unless you prove otherwise.

Interest on penalties. A higher interest cost is imposed on individuals subject to the following penalties: failure to file a timely return, negligence or fraud, overvaluation of property, undervaluation of gift or estate tax property, *or* substantial understatement of tax liability. Interest starts to run from the due date of the return (including extensions) until the date the penalty is paid. For other penalties, interest is imposed only if the penalty is not paid within 21 calendar days of an IRS demand for payment if the penalty is less than $100,000. The interest-free period is 10 business days after the IRS demand for payment if the penalty is $100,000 or more.

Caution

Too Good to Be True

If you claim a deduction, credit, or exclusion on your return that would seem to a reasonable person to be "too good to be true" under the circumstances, the IRS is likely to consider you negligent unless you show you made an attempt to verify the correctness of the position.

Acting on wrong IRS advice. A penalty will not be imposed if you reasonably rely on erroneous advice provided in writing by IRS officials in response to your specific written request. It is necessary for you to show that you provided accurate information when asking for advice.

48.7 Agreeing to the Audit Changes

After the audit, the agent will discuss proposed changes either with you or your representative.

If you agree with the agent's proposed changes, you will be asked to sign a Form 870, which, when signed, permits an immediate assessment of a deficiency plus penalties and interest, if due. The Form 870 is called "Waiver of Restrictions on Assessment and Collection of Deficiency in Tax and Acceptance of Overassessment."

If you believe that you have done as well or better than expected regarding the proposed deficiency, you can bring the case to a close by signing the Form 870, but the agent's supervisor must also approve the assessment.

By signing the form, you limit the amount of interest charges added to the deficiency. A signed Form 870 does not prevent the IRS from reopening the case to assess an additional deficiency. If on review the deficiency is increased, you will receive a revised Form 870. You can refuse to sign the form. The signed first form has the effect of stopping the interest on the original deficiency. As a matter of practice, however, waivers of acceptances ordinarily result in closing of the case.

It is possible, although unlikely, that upon examining your return, the agent will determine that you are due a refund. In this situation, a signed Form 870 is considered a valid refund claim. You should file a protective refund claim even if you sign the Form 870 acknowledging the overpayment. Generally, the agent will process the refund, but if he or she fails to do so or the review staff puts it aside for some reason and the limitations period expires, the refund will be lost. The refund claim will protect you from such a mishap.

The payment of tax before the deficiency notice (90-day letter) is mailed is, in effect, a waiver of the restrictions on assessment and collection. If the payment satisfies your entire tax liability for that year, you cannot appeal to the Tax Court. You must sue for a refund in either federal district court or the Court of Federal Claims.

Caution

Waiving Your Right To Appeal

Before deciding whether to sign the Form 870, consider that, by signing, you are giving up your right of appeal to both the IRS Office of Appeals and the Tax Court. However, you may still file a refund suit in a federal district court or in the Court of Federal Claims unless you have agreed not to do so on the Form 870.

48.8 Disputing the Audit Changes

If you disagree with the agent and the examination takes place in an IRS office, you may ask for an immediate meeting with a supervisor to argue your side of the dispute. If an agreement is not reached at this meeting or the audit is at your office or home, the agent prepares a report of the proposed adjustments. You will receive a 30-day letter in which you are given the opportunity to request a conference. You may decide not to ask for a conference and await a formal notice of deficiency (90-day letter).

Appeals conference. If your examination was conducted as an office audit or by correspondence, or the disputed amount does not exceed $25,000, you do not have to prepare a written protest for a conference with the IRS Appeals Office. The written protest is a detailed presentation of your reasons for disagreeing with the agent's report. Even where a formal written protest is not required, you must provide a brief written statement indicating your reasons for disagreeing with the agent when you request an appeals conference. *See* IRS Publication 5, "Appeal Rights and Preparation of Protests for Unagreed Cases."

At the conference you may appear for yourself or be represented by an attorney or other agent, and you may bring witnesses. The conference is held in an informal manner and you are given ample opportunity to present your case.

If you cannot reach a settlement, you will receive a Notice of Deficiency, commonly called a 90-day letter. In it, you are notified that at the end of 90 days from the date it was mailed, the government will assess the additional tax.

Caution

Notice of Deficiency

If you do not respond to the 30-day letter, or if you later do not reach an agreement with an appeals officer, the IRS will send you a 90-day letter, also called a "notice of deficiency." The IRS is required to specify on the notice the 90th day by which you must file your petition with the Tax Court.

Interest abatement. An IRS delay in completing an audit increases the interest that you have to pay when a deficiency notice is eventually issued. You may ask the IRS on Form 843 for an abatement of interest charges that are attributable to unreasonable errors or delays by IRS employees in performing a ministerial or managerial act.

A ministerial act is defined as a procedural or mechanical act that does not involve the exercise of an IRS employee's discretion or judgment, such as the transfer of a taxpayer's case to a different IRS office after the transfer is approved by a group manager. A managerial act refers to the exercise of discretion or judgment by an IRS employee in managing personnel. Misplacing the taxpayer's case file is also a managerial act. General IRS administrative decisions, such as prioritizing the order of processing returns, or decisions on applying the tax law, that result in delay, are not ministerial or management acts for which interest abatement is available.

Caution

Penalty for Frivolous Tax Court Action

If you bring a frivolous case to the Tax Court or unreasonably fail to pursue IRS administrative remedies, the Tax Court may impose a penalty of up to $25,000. Furthermore, if you appeal a Tax Court decision and the federal appeals court finds that the appeal was frivolous, the court may impose a penalty.

Law Alert

Upfront Payment for OIC

A new law requires taxpayers to make an upfront payment when they submit an offer-in-compromise to the IRS on or after July 16, 2006. For a lump-sum offer, the taxpayer must include 20% of the offer with the application; the same requirement applies for offers to pay in five or fewer installments. For periodic payment offers, the first proposed installment must accompany the offer. The IRS can allow exceptions for low-income taxpayers or for offers based on doubt as to liability. Any upfront payment is in addition to the user fee that generally must accompany the submission, but the fee will be credited toward the outstanding tax liability.

Going to court. When you receive a 90-day letter, if you are still convinced that your position is correct, you may take your case to one of three courts. You may within 90 days file a petition with the Tax Court without having to pay the tax. The Tax Court has a small tax case procedure for deficiencies of $50,000 or less. Such cases are handled expeditiously and informally. Cases may be heard by appointed special trial judges. A small claim case may be discontinued at any time before a decision, but the decision when made is final. No appeal may be taken by you or the IRS.

Instead of petitioning the Tax Court, you may pay the additional tax, file a refund claim for it, and—after the refund claim is denied—sue for a refund in a federal district court or the U.S. Court of Federal Claims.

Generally, the decision to litigate should be considered by an experienced tax practitioner.

48.9 Offer in Compromise

If you are unable to pay a tax debt in full, you may be able to make an offer in compromise (OIC), but it should be considered a last resort. An OIC is an agreement between a taxpayer and the IRS in which the IRS accepts less than full payment of the outstanding tax liabilities as settlement of the tax debt. However, the IRS says that it resolves less than 1% of all outstanding tax debts through the OIC program.

Grounds for an Offer in Compromise. The IRS has authority to settle or "compromise" for one of the following reasons: Doubt as to liability, doubt as to collectibility, and effective tax administration. Doubt as to liability means that doubt exists concerning the correctness of the IRS's tax assessment. Doubt as to collectibility means that you may never be able to pay the full amount of tax owed. Even where there is no doubt that you owe the tax and you could manage full repayment, you can apply for an OIC on "effective tax administration" grounds if there are exceptional circumstances under which collection of the full tax would cause you economic hardship or would be unfair and inequitable.

Applying for an Offer in Compromise on Form 656. You must submit an OIC on Form 656. The IRS will consider the OIC only after other payment options have been exhausted, including an installment agreement. You must make an upfront payment when you submit the OIC; *see* the Law Alert on this page. The Form 656 booklet includes an explanation of the OIC program and instructions for completing the form. The package also includes financial disclosure statements that must be attached to support an OIC based on doubt as to collectibility or effective tax administration. Wage earners and self-employed individuals must use Form 433-A, while partnerships and corporations use Form 433-B. In some cases, the IRS may request Form 433-A from corporate officers or individual partners. The Form 656 package is available online at www.irs.gov or can be obtained by calling 1-800-829-3676.

An OIC submitted on or after July 16, 2006, will be deemed accepted if the IRS does not reject it within two years of the submission date. If your offer is rejected, you will be given an opportunity to appeal the decision and to amend the offer.

Application fee. A $150 application fee must be paid with Form 656 unless the OIC is based solely on doubt as to liability or you certify on Form 656-A that your total monthly income is at or below federal poverty guidelines. The OIC Application Fee Worksheet in the Form 656 package is used to determine eligibility for the fee exception. A fee submitted with an offer on or after July 16, 2006, is applied against the underlying tax, interest, and penalties.

Compliance conditions. If the IRS accepts an OIC, you must pay the agreed-to amount in accordance with the acceptance agreement and must timely file and pay all required taxes for a period of five years from the acceptance date, or until the accepted amount is paid in full, whichever is longer. You may also be asked as part of the agreement to pay a percentage of your future earnings to the IRS. A failure to comply with the agreement causes default of the OIC and the reinstatement of the original liability.

48.10 Recovering Costs of a Tax Dispute

In a tax dispute, you may believe that the IRS has taken an unreasonable position, forcing you to incur legal fees and other expenses to win your case. Here are highlights of the rules for recovering costs from the IRS in a case that commenced after July 30, 1996.

Generally, you may recover all or part of—

1. Reasonable administrative costs of proceedings within the IRS, and
2. Reasonable litigation costs in a court proceeding.

A judgment for reasonable litigation costs will *not* be awarded in any court proceeding if you did not exhaust all IRS administrative remedies. A refusal by the taxpayer to agree to an extension of time for a tax assessment is not a bar to an award, but unreasonably delaying the proceedings is.

You may *not* recover costs if your net worth at the time the action begins exceeds $2 million. The $2 million net worth limit applies separately to each spouse in determining whether a married couple filing jointly is entitled to recover legal fees. No recovery is allowed to sole proprietors, partnerships, and corporations if their net worth exceeds $7 million or they have more than 500 employees.

To receive an award, you must "substantially prevail" as to the key issues in the case or the amount of tax involved. If you do, you will be entitled to a recovery unless the IRS proves that it was "substantially justified" in maintaining the position that it did. You may be treated as the prevailing party if a court determines that your liability is equal to or less than an amount that you offered in settlement. The offer must be considered a qualified offer made during a period that begins on the date of the first letter of proposed deficiency allowing for an IRS administrative appeal and ends 30 days before the date first set for trial.

The Tax Court and other courts have interpreted "substantially justified" to be a reasonableness standard. The IRS is presumed not to be "substantially justified" if it does not follow its own published regulations, revenue rulings, procedures, notices, announcements, or a private ruling issued to the taxpayer. The IRS may try to rebut the presumption. For costs incurred after January 18, 1999, a court may also consider whether an IRS position has been rejected by federal courts of appeal of other circuits in determining whether the IRS position was substantially justified.

Reasonable administrative costs include IRS fees and expenses of attorney fees, witnesses, and experts. The IRS determines the amount of such an award, which may include costs incurred from the date the IRS sent its first letter of a proposed deficiency allowing you to ask for an administrative appeal. For an award of administrative costs, you must file an application with the IRS before the 91st day after the date on which the IRS mailed you its final decision. To appeal a denial of your application, you must petition the Tax Court within 90 days from the date the IRS mailed the denial.

Reasonable litigation costs include reasonable court costs, fees of witnesses and experts, and attorneys' fees. Fees of witnesses may not exceed the rate paid by the U.S. government. For attorneys' fees incurred in 2003, 2004, and 2005, the limit is $150 per hour, and for 2006 the limit is $160 per hour. The $160 hourly limit may be increased for 2007 by an inflation adjustment. The court may also increase the award for attorneys' fees to account for special factors, such as the difficulty of the issues and the availability of local tax expertise. However, an attorney's general expertise in tax law or experience in tax litigation is not in itself a special factor warranting a higher fee award.

You may *not* recover attorneys' fees if you represent yourself *(pro se)*. However, you are still entitled to recover fees for witnesses and experts. If you represent a prevailing taxpayer on a *pro bono* basis or for a nominal fee (after January 18, 1999) a court may award you or your employer reasonable attorneys' fees.

Planning Reminder

Recovering Attorneys' Fees

Attorneys' fees include the fees paid by a taxpayer for the services of anyone who is authorized to practice before the Tax Court or IRS.

48.11 Suing the IRS for Unauthorized Collection

If an IRS employee or officer recklessly, intentionally, or negligently disregards the law or IRS regulations when taking a collection action, you may sue the IRS in federal district court for actual economic damages resulting from the IRS employee's misconduct, plus certain costs of bringing the action. The lawsuit must be filed within two years of the date your right to sue accrued.

Caution

Penalty for Frivolous Action

If you bring an action in federal district court for unauthorized collection activities that the court considers to be frivolous, it may impose a penalty of up to $10,000.

Planning Reminder

IRS Failure To Release Lien

A suit for damages may also be brought in federal district court against the IRS if IRS employees improperly fail to release a lien on your property. Before you sue, you must file an administrative claim for damages. The lawsuit must be filed within two years after your claim arose. You may sue for actual economic damages plus costs of the action; the types of damages that may be recovered are similar to those discussed for suing the IRS for unauthorized collection actions.

For negligent IRS collection activities, you may sue for damages of up to $100,000, and for reckless or intentional misconduct, the maximum damage award is $1 million. Administrative remedies must be exhausted to obtain an award.

According to IRS regulations, actual economic damages that may be recovered are monetary losses you suffer as a direct result of the IRS's action. For example, a business may lose loyal customers and suffer an actual cash loss if the IRS's action damages the business's reputation. Other actual expenses could include the cost of renting a house or a car if the IRS puts a lien on or seizes your property, or loss of income due to the garnishment of your paycheck. Damages from the IRS for loss of reputation, inconvenience, or emotional distress are allowed only to the extent that they result in such actual monetary loss.

The IRS defines "costs of action" that you may recover as (1) fees of the clerk and marshall; (2) fees of the court reporter; (3) fees and disbursements for printing and witnesses; (4) copying fees; (5) docket fees; and (6) compensation for court-appointed experts and interpreters.

Litigation costs and administrative proceeding costs are not treated as "costs of the action." However, if the IRS denies your administrative claim for damages and you successfully sue in federal district court, you are considered a "prevailing party" and may recover attorneys' fees, related litigation expenses, and administrative costs before the IRS as discussed at 48.10.

Sample 2006 Tax Forms and Tables

In the following pages, you will find sample tax forms for 2006 that are based on advance proofs from the IRS. You can use them as worksheets. The final version of the tax forms may vary. Final IRS forms are available in the download section of our website: www.jklasser.com. Forms can also be downloaded from the IRS website: www.irs.gov.

Use the Tax Table starting on page 759 to look up your tax liability if your taxable income is less than $100,000. If your taxable income is $100,000 or more, use the Tax Computation Worksheet on page 771.

If you have net capital gain or qualified dividends, do not use the Tax Table or the Tax Computation Worksheet. Depending on the nature of your capital gain income, figure your regular tax liability on the Qualified Dividends and Capital Gains Tax Worksheet, or the Schedule D Tax Worksheet; *see 22.4.*

Note: All forms in this section are based on IRS advance proofs that are subject to change. Use the IRS final version for filing your tax return. Final forms suitable for filing are available in the download section of our website: www.jklasser.com. You can also download forms at the IRS website: www.irs.gov.

Form **1040** Department of the Treasury—Internal Revenue Service
U.S. Individual Income Tax Return **2006** (99) IRS Use Only—Do not write or staple in this space.

For the year Jan. 1–Dec. 31, 2006, or other tax year beginning , 2006, ending , 20 OMB No. 1545-0074

Label

(See instructions on page 16.)

Use the IRS label. Otherwise, please print or type.

LABEL HERE

Your first name and initial	Last name	**Your social security number**
If a joint return, spouse's first name and initial	Last name	**Spouse's social security number**
Home address (number and street). If you have a P.O. box, see page 16.	Apt. no.	▲ You **must** enter your SSN(s) above. ▲
City, town or post office, state, and ZIP code. If you have a foreign address, see page 16.		Checking a box below will not change your tax or refund.

Presidential Election Campaign ▶ Check here if you, or your spouse if filing jointly, want $3 to go to this fund (see page 16) ▶ ☐ **You** ☐ **Spouse**

Filing Status

Check only one box.

1 ☐ Single
2 ☐ Married filing jointly (even if only one had income)
3 ☐ Married filing separately. Enter spouse's SSN above and full name here. ▶
4 ☐ Head of household (with qualifying person). (See page 17.) If the qualifying person is a child but not your dependent, enter this child's name here. ▶
5 ☐ Qualifying widow(er) with dependent child (see page 17)

Exemptions

6a ☐ **Yourself.** If someone can claim you as a dependent, **do not** check box 6a . . . .
b ☐ **Spouse** . . . . . .

Boxes checked on 6a and 6b ____

c **Dependents:**

(1) First name	Last name	(2) Dependent's social security number	(3) Dependent's relationship to you	(4) ✓ if qualifying child for child tax credit (see page 19)
				☐
				☐
				☐
				☐

If more than four dependents, see page 19.

No. of children on 6c who:
- **lived with you** ____
- **did not live with you due to divorce or separation (see page 20)** ____

Dependents on 6c not entered above ____

d Total number of exemptions claimed . . . . **Add numbers on lines above** ▶ ☐

Income

Attach Form(s) W-2 here. Also attach Forms W-2G and 1099-R if tax was withheld.

If you did not get a W-2, see page 22.

Enclose, but do not attach, any payment. Also, please use **Form 1040-V.**

7	Wages, salaries, tips, etc. Attach Form(s) W-2		7
8a	**Taxable** interest. Attach Schedule B if required		8a
b	**Tax-exempt** interest. **Do not** include on line 8a	8b	
9a	Ordinary dividends. Attach Schedule B if required		9a
b	Qualified dividends (see page 23)	9b	
10	Taxable refunds, credits, or offsets of state and local income taxes (see page 23)		10
11	Alimony received		11
12	Business income or (loss). Attach Schedule C or C-EZ		12
13	Capital gain or (loss). Attach Schedule D if required. If not required, check here ▶ ☐		13
14	Other gains or (losses). Attach Form 4797		14
15a	IRA distributions	15a	b Taxable amount (see page 25) 15b
16a	Pensions and annuities	16a	b Taxable amount (see page 25) 16b
17	Rental real estate, royalties, partnerships, S corporations, trusts, etc. Attach Schedule E		17
18	Farm income or (loss). Attach Schedule F		18
19	Unemployment compensation		19
20a	Social security benefits	20a	b Taxable amount (see page 27) 20b
21	Other income. List type and amount (see page 29)		21
22	Add the amounts in the far right column for lines 7 through 21. This is your **total income** ▶		22

Adjusted Gross Income

23	Archer MSA deduction. Attach Form 8853	23	
24	Certain business expenses of reservists, performing artists, and fee-basis government officials. Attach Form 2106 or 2106-EZ	24	
25	Health savings account deduction. Attach Form 8889	25	
26	Moving expenses. Attach Form 3903	26	
27	One-half of self-employment tax. Attach Schedule SE	27	
28	Self-employed SEP, SIMPLE, and qualified plans	28	
29	Self-employed health insurance deduction (see page 30)	29	
30	Penalty on early withdrawal of savings	30	
31a	Alimony paid b Recipient's SSN ▶	31a	
32	IRA deduction (see page 31)	32	
33	Student loan interest deduction (see page 33)	33	
34	Jury duty pay you gave to your employer	34	
35	Domestic production activities deduction. Attach Form 8903	35	
36	Add lines 23 through 31a and 32 through 35		36
37	Subtract line 36 from line 22. This is your **adjusted gross income** ▶		37

For Disclosure, Privacy Act, and Paperwork Reduction Act Notice, see page 78. Cat. No. 11320B Form **1040** (2006)

Tax and Credits

38	Amount from line 37 (adjusted gross income)			38
39a	Check if: ☐ **You** were born before January 2, 1942, ☐ Blind. ☐ **Spouse** was born before January 2, 1942, ☐ Blind. **Total boxes checked ▶ 39a**			
b	If your spouse itemizes on a separate return or you were a dual-status alien, see page 35 and check here ▶**39b** ☐			
40	**Itemized deductions** (from Schedule A) **or** your **standard deduction** (see left margin)			40
41	Subtract line 40 from line 38			41
42	If line 38 is over $112,875, or you provided housing to a person displaced by Hurricane Katrina, see page 37. Otherwise, multiply $3,300 by the total number of exemptions claimed on line 6d			42
43	**Taxable income.** Subtract line 42 from line 41. If line 42 is more than line 41, enter -0-			43
44	**Tax** (see page 37). Check if any tax is from: **a** ☐ Form(s) 8814 **b** ☐ Form 4972			44
45	**Alternative minimum tax** (see page 39). Attach Form 6251			45
46	Add lines 44 and 45 ▶			46
47	Foreign tax credit. Attach Form 1116 if required	47		
48	Credit for child and dependent care expenses. Attach Form 2441	48		
49	Credit for the elderly or the disabled. Attach Schedule R	49		
50	Education credits. Attach Form 8863	50		
51	Retirement savings contributions credit. Attach Form 8880	51		
52	Residential energy credits. Attach Form 5695	52		
53	Child tax credit (see page XX). Attach Form 8901 if required	53		
54	Credits from: **a** ☐ Form 8396 **b** ☐ Form 8839 **c** ☐ Form 8859	54		
55	Other credits: **a** ☐ Form 3800 **b** ☐ Form 8801 **c** ☐ Form____	55		
56	Add lines 47 through 55. These are your **total credits**			56
57	Subtract line 56 from line 46. If line 56 is more than line 46, enter -0- ▶			57

Standard Deduction for—

- People who checked any box on line 39a or 39b **or** who can be claimed as a dependent, see page 36.
- All others:

Single or Married filing separately, $5,150

Married filing jointly or Qualifying widow(er), $10,300

Head of household, $7,550

Other Taxes

58	Self-employment tax. Attach Schedule SE	58
59	Social security and Medicare tax on tip income not reported to employer. Attach Form 4137	59
60	Additional tax on IRAs, other qualified retirement plans, etc. Attach Form 5329 if required	60
61	Advance earned income credit payments from Form(s) W-2, box 9	61
62	Household employment taxes. Attach Schedule H	62
63	Add lines 57 through 62. This is your **total tax** ▶	63

Payments

64	Federal income tax withheld from Forms W-2 and 1099	64		
65	2006 estimated tax payments and amount applied from 2005 return	65		
66a	**Earned income credit (EIC)**	66a		
b	Nontaxable combat pay election ▶ 66b			
67	Excess social security and tier 1 RRTA tax withheld (see page 59)	67		
68	Additional child tax credit. Attach Form 8812	68		
69	Amount paid with request for extension to file (see page 59)	69		
70	Payments from: **a** ☐ Form 2439 **b** ☐ Form 4136 **c** ☐ Form 8885	70		
71	Credit for federal telephone excise tax paid. Attach Form 8913 if required	71		
72	Add lines 64, 65, 66a, and 67 through 71. These are your **total payments** ▶			72

If you have a qualifying child, attach Schedule EIC.

Refund

Direct deposit? See page 59 and fill in 74b, 74c, and 74d, or Form 8888.

73	If line 72 is more than line 63, subtract line 63 from line 72. This is the amount you **overpaid**		73
74a	Amount of line 73 you want **refunded to you.** If Form 8888 is attached, check here ▶ ☐		74a
▶ b	Routing number ▶ **c** Type: ☐ Checking ☐ Savings		
▶ d	Account number		
75	Amount of line 73 you want **applied to your 2007 estimated tax** ▶	75	

Amount You Owe

76	**Amount you owe.** Subtract line 72 from line 63. For details on how to pay, see page 60 ▶		76
77	Estimated tax penalty (see page 60)	77	

Third Party Designee

Do you want to allow another person to discuss this return with the IRS (see page 61)? ☐ **Yes.** Complete the following. ☐ **No**

Designee's name ▶ Phone no. ▶ ( ) Personal identification number (PIN) ▶

Sign Here

Joint return? See page 17. Keep a copy for your records.

Under penalties of perjury, I declare that I have examined this return and accompanying schedules and statements, and to the best of my knowledge and belief, they are true, correct, and complete. Declaration of preparer (other than taxpayer) is based on all information of which preparer has any knowledge.

Your signature	Date	Your occupation	Daytime phone number ( )
Spouse's signature. If a joint return, **both** must sign.	Date	Spouse's occupation	

Paid Preparer's Use Only

Preparer's signature	Date	Check if self-employed ☐	Preparer's SSN or PTIN
Firm's name (or yours if self-employed), address, and ZIP code		EIN	
		Phone no. ( )	

Form **1040** (2006)

SCHEDULES A&B (Form 1040)	Schedule A—Itemized Deductions	OMB No. 1545-0074
Department of the Treasury Internal Revenue Service (99)	(Schedule B is on back) ▶ Attach to Form 1040. ▶ See Instructions for Schedules A&B (Form 1040).	2006 Attachment Sequence No. 07

Name(s) shown on Form 1040 | Your social security number

Medical and Dental Expenses		**Caution.** Do not include expenses reimbursed or paid by others.		
	1	Medical and dental expenses (see page A-2)	1	
	2	Enter amount from Form 1040, line 38 [2]		
	3	Multiply line 2 by 7.5% (.075)	3	
	4	Subtract line 3 from line 1. If line 3 is more than line 1, enter -0-		4
Taxes You Paid (See page A-2.)	5	State and local income taxes	5	
	6	Real estate taxes (see page A-5)	6	
	7	Personal property taxes	7	
	8	Other taxes. List type and amount ▶	8	
	9	Add lines 5 through 8		9
Interest You Paid (See page A-5.)	10	Home mortgage interest and points reported to you on Form 1098	10	
	11	Home mortgage interest not reported to you on Form 1098. If paid to the person from whom you bought the home, see page A-6 and show that person's name, identifying no., and address ▶	11	
Note. Personal interest is not deductible.	12	Points not reported to you on Form 1098. See page A-6 for special rules	12	
	13	Investment interest. Attach Form 4952 if required. (See page A-6.)	13	
	14	Add lines 10 through 13		14
Gifts to Charity If you made a gift and got a benefit for it, see page A-7.	15	Gifts by cash or check. If you made any gift of $250 or more, see page A-7	15	
	16	Other than by cash or check. If any gift of $250 or more, see page A-7. You **must** attach Form 8283 if over $500	16	
	17	Carryover from prior year	17	
	18	Add lines 15 through 17		18
Casualty and Theft Losses	19	Casualty or theft loss(es). Attach Form 4684. (See page A-8.)		19
Job Expenses and Certain Miscellaneous Deductions (See page A-8.)	20	Unreimbursed employee expenses—job travel, union dues, job education, etc. Attach Form 2106 or 2106-EZ if required. (See page A-8.) ▶	20	
	21	Tax preparation fees	21	
	22	Other expenses—investment, safe deposit box, etc. List type and amount ▶	22	
	23	Add lines 20 through 22	23	
	24	Enter amount from Form 1040, line 38 [24]		
	25	Multiply line 24 by 2% (.02)	25	
	26	Subtract line 25 from line 23. If line 25 is more than line 23, enter -0-		26
Other Miscellaneous Deductions	27	Other—from list on page A-9. List type and amount ▶		27
Total Itemized Deductions	28	Is Form 1040, line 38, over $150,500 (over $75,250 if married filing separately)? ☐ **No.** Your deduction is not limited. Add the amounts in the far right column for lines 4 through 27. Also, enter this amount on Form 1040, line 40. ☐ **Yes.** Your deduction may be limited. See page A-9 for the amount to enter. ▶		28
	29	If you elect to itemize deductions even though they are less than your standard deduction, check here ▶ ☐		

For Paperwork Reduction Act Notice, see Form 1040 instructions. Cat. No. 11330X **Schedule A (Form 1040) 2006**

Name(s) shown on Form 1040. Do not enter name and social security number if shown on other side. | **Your social security number**

Schedule B—Interest and Ordinary Dividends

Attachment Sequence No. **08**

Part I Interest

(See page B-1 and the instructions for Form 1040, line 8a.)

Note. If you received a Form 1099-INT, Form 1099-OID, or substitute statement from a brokerage firm, list the firm's name as the payer and enter the total interest shown on that form.

			Amount
1	List name of payer. If any interest is from a seller-financed mortgage and the buyer used the property as a personal residence, see page B-1 and list this interest first. Also, show that buyer's social security number and address ▶	1	
2	Add the amounts on line 1	2	
3	Excludable interest on series EE and I U.S. savings bonds issued after 1989. Attach Form 8815	3	
4	Subtract line 3 from line 2. Enter the result here and on Form 1040, line 8a ▶	4	

Note. If line 4 is over $1,500, you must complete Part III.

Part II Ordinary Dividends

(See page B-1 and the instructions for Form 1040, line 9a.)

Note. If you received a Form 1099-DIV or substitute statement from a brokerage firm, list the firm's name as the payer and enter the ordinary dividends shown on that form.

			Amount
5	List name of payer ▶	5	
6	Add the amounts on line 5. Enter the total here and on Form 1040, line 9a ▶	6	

Note. If line 6 is over $1,500, you must complete Part III.

Part III Foreign Accounts and Trusts

(See page B-2.)

		Yes	No
	You must complete this part if you **(a)** had over $1,500 of taxable interest or ordinary dividends; or **(b)** had a foreign account; or **(c)** received a distribution from, or were a grantor of, or a transferor to, a foreign trust.		
7a	At any time during 2006, did you have an interest in or a signature or other authority over a financial account in a foreign country, such as a bank account, securities account, or other financial account? See page B-2 for exceptions and filing requirements for Form TD F 90-22.1	☐	☐
b	If "Yes," enter the name of the foreign country ▶		
8	During 2006, did you receive a distribution from, or were you the grantor of, or transferor to, a foreign trust? If "Yes," you may have to file Form 3520. See page B-2	☐	☐

For Paperwork Reduction Act Notice, see Form 1040 instructions. **Schedule B (Form 1040) 2006**

SCHEDULE C (Form 1040)

Department of the Treasury
Internal Revenue Service (99)

Profit or Loss From Business

(Sole Proprietorship)

► **Partnerships, joint ventures, etc., must file Form 1065 or 1065-B.**

► **Attach to Form 1040, 1040NR, or 1041.** ► **See Instructions for Schedule C (Form 1040).**

OMB No. 1545-0074

2006

Attachment Sequence No. **09**

Name of proprietor	**Social security number (SSN)**
A Principal business or profession, including product or service (see page C-2 of the instructions)	**B Enter code from pages C-8, 9, & 10** ►
C Business name. If no separate business name, leave blank.	**D Employer ID number (EIN), if any**

E Business address (including suite or room no.) ► ....
City, town or post office, state, and ZIP code

F Accounting method: **(1)** ☐ Cash **(2)** ☐ Accrual **(3)** ☐ Other (specify) ► ....

G Did you "materially participate" in the operation of this business during 2006? If "No," see page C-2 for limit on losses ☐ **Yes** ☐ **No**

H If you started or acquired this business during 2006, check here ► ☐

Part I Income

1	Gross receipts or sales. **Caution.** If this income was reported to you on Form W-2 and the "Statutory employee" box on that form was checked, see page C-3 and check here ► ☐	**1**	
2	Returns and allowances	**2**	
3	Subtract line 2 from line 1	**3**	
4	Cost of goods sold (from line 42 on page 2)	**4**	
5	**Gross profit.** Subtract line 4 from line 3	**5**	
6	Other income, including federal and state gasoline or fuel tax credit or refund (see page C-3)	**6**	
7	**Gross income.** Add lines 5 and 6 ►	**7**	

Part II **Expenses.** Enter expenses for business use of your home **only** on line 30.

8	Advertising	**8**		**18**	Office expense	**18**	
9	Car and truck expenses (see page C-4)	**9**		**19**	Pension and profit-sharing plans	**19**	
10	Commissions and fees	**10**		**20**	Rent or lease (see page C-5):		
11	Contract labor (see page C-4)	**11**		**a**	Vehicles, machinery, and equipment	**20a**	
12	Depletion	**12**		**b**	Other business property	**20b**	
13	Depreciation and section 179 expense deduction (not included in Part III) (see page C-4)	**13**		**21**	Repairs and maintenance	**21**	
				22	Supplies (not included in Part III)	**22**	
				23	Taxes and licenses	**23**	
				24	Travel, meals, and entertainment:		
				a	Travel	**24a**	
14	Employee benefit programs (other than on line 19)	**14**		**b**	Deductible meals and entertainment (see page C-5)	**24b**	
15	Insurance (other than health)	**15**		**25**	Utilities	**25**	
16	Interest:			**26**	Wages (less employment credits)	**26**	
a	Mortgage (paid to banks, etc.)	**16a**		**27**	Other expenses (from line 48 on page 2)	**27**	
b	Other	**16b**					
17	Legal and professional services	**17**					

28	**Total expenses** before expenses for business use of home. Add lines 8 through 27 in columns ►	**28**	
29	Tentative profit (loss). Subtract line 28 from line 7	**29**	
30	Expenses for business use of your home. Attach **Form 8829**	**30**	
31	**Net profit or (loss).** Subtract line 30 from line 29. • If a profit, enter on **Form 1040, line 12,** and **also** on **Schedule SE, line 2** or **Form 1040NR, line 13** (statutory employees, see page C-6). Estates and trusts, enter on Form 1041, line 3. • If a loss, you **must** go to line 32.	**31**	

32 If you have a loss, check the box that describes your investment in this activity (see page C-6).
- If you checked 32a, enter the loss on **Form 1040, line 12,** and **also** on **Schedule SE, line 2** or **Form 1040NR, line 13** (statutory employees, see page C-6). Estates and trusts, enter on Form 1041, line 3.
- If you checked 32b, you **must** attach **Form 6198.** Your loss may be limited.

32a ☐ All investment is at risk.
32b ☐ Some investment is not at risk.

For Paperwork Reduction Act Notice, see page C-7 of the instructions. Cat. No. 11334P **Schedule C (Form 1040) 2006**

Part III **Cost of Goods Sold** (see page C-7)

33 Method(s) used to value closing inventory: a ☐ Cost b ☐ Lower of cost or market c ☐ Other (attach explanation)

34 Was there any change in determining quantities, costs, or valuations between opening and closing inventory? If "Yes," attach explanation . . . ☐ **Yes** ☐ **No**

35 Inventory at beginning of year. If different from last year's closing inventory, attach explanation	35	
36 Purchases less cost of items withdrawn for personal use	36	
37 Cost of labor. Do not include any amounts paid to yourself	37	
38 Materials and supplies	38	
39 Other costs	39	
40 Add lines 35 through 39	40	
41 Inventory at end of year	41	
42 **Cost of goods sold.** Subtract line 41 from line 40. Enter the result here and on page 1, line 4	42	

Part IV **Information on Your Vehicle.** Complete this part **only** if you are claiming car or truck expenses on line 9 and are not required to file Form 4562 for this business. See the instructions for line 13 on page C-4 to find out if you must file Form 4562.

43 When did you place your vehicle in service for business purposes? (month, day, year) ▶ ______ / ______ / ______

44 Of the total number of miles you drove your vehicle during 2006, enter the number of miles you used your vehicle for:

a Business ______________ b Commuting (see instructions) ______________ c Other ______________

45 Do you (or your spouse) have another vehicle available for personal use? . . . ☐ **Yes** ☐ **No**

46 Was your vehicle available for personal use during off-duty hours? . . . ☐ **Yes** ☐ **No**

47a Do you have evidence to support your deduction? . . . ☐ **Yes** ☐ **No**

b If "Yes," is the evidence written? . . . ☐ **Yes** ☐ **No**

Part V **Other Expenses.** List below business expenses not included on lines 8–26 or line 30.

48 **Total other expenses.** Enter here and on page 1, line 27 . . . 48	

Schedule C (Form 1040) 2006

SCHEDULE C-EZ (Form 1040)

Department of the Treasury
Internal Revenue Service

Net Profit From Business

(Sole Proprietorship)

▶ Partnerships, joint ventures, etc., must file Form 1065 or 1065-B.
▶ Attach to Form 1040, 1040NR, or 1041. ▶ See instructions on back.

OMB No. 1545-0074

2006

Attachment Sequence No. **09A**

Name of proprietor | **Social security number (SSN)**

Part I General Information

You May Use Schedule C-EZ Instead of Schedule C Only If You:

- Had business expenses of $5,000 or less.
- Use the cash method of accounting.
- Did not have an inventory at any time during the year.
- Did not have a net loss from your business.
- Had only one business as either a sole proprietor or statutory employee.

And You:

- Had no employees during the year.
- Are not required to file **Form 4562,** Depreciation and Amortization, for this business. See the instructions for Schedule C, line 13, on page C-4 to find out if you must file.
- Do not deduct expenses for business use of your home.
- Do not have prior year unallowed passive activity losses from this business.

A Principal business or profession, including product or service

B Enter code from pages C-8, 9, & 10 ▶

C Business name. If no separate business name, leave blank.

D Employer ID number (EIN), if any

E Business address (including suite or room no.). Address not required if same as on Form 1040, page 1.

City, town or post office, state, and ZIP code

Part II Figure Your Net Profit

1 **Gross receipts. Caution.** If this income was reported to you on Form W-2 and the "Statutory employee" box on that form was checked, see **Statutory Employees** in the instructions for Schedule C, line 1, on page C-3 and check here . . . . ▶ ☐ **1**

2 **Total expenses** (see instructions). If more than $5,000, you **must** use Schedule C **2**

3 **Net profit.** Subtract line 2 from line 1. If less than zero, you **must** use Schedule C. Enter on **Form 1040, line 12,** and on **Schedule SE, line 2,** or **Form 1040NR, line 13.** (Statutory employees **do not** report this amount on Schedule SE, line 2. Estates and trusts, enter on Form 1041, line 3.) **3**

Part III Information on Your Vehicle. Complete this part only if you are claiming car or truck expenses on line 2.

4 When did you place your vehicle in service for business purposes? (month, day, year) ▶ ..../........../..........

5 Of the total number of miles you drove your vehicle during 2006, enter the number of miles you used your vehicle for:

a Business .... **b** Commuting (see instructions) .... **c** Other ....

6 Do you (or your spouse) have another vehicle available for personal use? . . . . ☐ **Yes** ☐ **No**

7 Was your vehicle available for personal use during off-duty hours? . . . . ☐ **Yes** ☐ **No**

8a Do you have evidence to support your deduction? . . . . ☐ **Yes** ☐ **No**

b If "Yes," is the evidence written? . . . . ☐ **Yes** ☐ **No**

For Paperwork Reduction Act Notice, see page 2. Cat. No. 14374D **Schedule C-EZ (Form 1040) 2006**

SCHEDULE D (Form 1040)

Department of the Treasury Internal Revenue Service (99)

Capital Gains and Losses

▶ Attach to Form 1040 or Form 1040NR. ▶ See Instructions for Schedule D (Form 1040).

▶ Use Schedule D-1 to list additional transactions for lines 1 and 8.

OMB No. 1545-0074

2006

Attachment Sequence No. 12

Name(s) shown on Form 1040 | Your social security number

Part I Short-Term Capital Gains and Losses—Assets Held One Year or Less

	(a) Description of property (Example: 100 sh. XYZ Co.)	(b) Date acquired (Mo., day, yr.)	(c) Date sold (Mo., day, yr.)	(d) Sales price (see page D-6 of the instructions)	(e) Cost or other basis (see page D-7 of the instructions)	(f) Gain or (loss) Subtract (e) from (d)
1						

2 Enter your short-term totals, if any, from Schedule D-1, line 2 2

3 **Total short-term sales price amounts.** Add lines 1 and 2 in column (d) 3

4 Short-term gain from Form 6252 and short-term gain or (loss) from Forms 4684, 6781, and 8824 4

5 Net short-term gain or (loss) from partnerships, S corporations, estates, and trusts from Schedule(s) K-1 5

6 Short-term capital loss carryover. Enter the amount, if any, from line 10 of your **Capital Loss Carryover Worksheet** on page D-7 of the instructions . . . . 6 ( )

7 **Net short-term capital gain or (loss).** Combine lines 1 through 6 in column (f) 7

Part II Long-Term Capital Gains and Losses—Assets Held More Than One Year

	(a) Description of property (Example: 100 sh. XYZ Co.)	(b) Date acquired (Mo., day, yr.)	(c) Date sold (Mo., day, yr.)	(d) Sales price (see page D-6 of the instructions)	(e) Cost or other basis (see page D-7 of the instructions)	(f) Gain or (loss) Subtract (e) from (d)
8						

9 Enter your long-term totals, if any, from Schedule D-1, line 9 9

10 **Total long-term sales price amounts.** Add lines 8 and 9 in column (d) 10

11 Gain from Form 4797, Part I; long-term gain from Forms 2439 and 6252; and long-term gain or (loss) from Forms 4684, 6781, and 8824 11

12 Net long-term gain or (loss) from partnerships, S corporations, estates, and trusts from Schedule(s) K-1 12

13 Capital gain distributions. See page D-1 of the instructions 13

14 Long-term capital loss carryover. Enter the amount, if any, from line 15 of your **Capital Loss Carryover Worksheet** on page D-7 of the instructions . . . . 14 ( )

15 **Net long-term capital gain or (loss).** Combine lines 8 through 14 in column (f). Then go to Part III on the back 15

For Paperwork Reduction Act Notice, see Form 1040 instructions. Cat. No. 11338H **Schedule D (Form 1040) 2006**

Part III **Summary**

16	Combine lines 7 and 15 and enter the result. If line 16 is a loss, skip lines 17 through 20, and go to line 21. If a gain, enter the gain on Form 1040, line 13, or Form 1040NR, line 14. Then go to line 17 below	16	
17	Are lines 15 and 16 **both** gains? ☐ **Yes.** Go to line 18. ☐ **No.** Skip lines 18 through 21, and go to line 22.		
18	Enter the amount, if any, from line 7 of the **28% Rate Gain Worksheet** on page D-8 of the instructions . . . . ▶	18	
19	Enter the amount, if any, from line 18 of the **Unrecaptured Section 1250 Gain Worksheet** on page D-9 of the instructions . . . . ▶	19	
20	Are lines 18 and 19 **both** zero or blank? ☐ **Yes.** Complete Form 1040 through line 43, or Form 1040NR through line 40. Then complete the **Qualified Dividends and Capital Gain Tax Worksheet** on page 38 of the Instructions for Form 1040 (or in the Instructions for Form 1040NR). **Do not** complete lines 21 and 22 below. ☐ **No.** Complete Form 1040 through line 43, or Form 1040NR through line 40. Then complete the **Schedule D Tax Worksheet** on page D-10 of the instructions. **Do not** complete lines 21 and 22 below.		
21	If line 16 is a loss, enter here and on Form 1040, line 13, or Form 1040NR, line 14, the **smaller** of: • The loss on line 16 or • ($3,000), or if married filing separately, ($1,500) } . . . . **Note.** When figuring which amount is smaller, treat both amounts as positive numbers.	21	( )
22	Do you have qualified dividends on Form 1040, line 9b, or Form 1040NR, line 10b? ☐ **Yes.** Complete Form 1040 through line 43, or Form 1040NR through line 40. Then complete the **Qualified Dividends and Capital Gain Tax Worksheet** on page 38 of the Instructions for Form 1040 (or in the Instructions for Form 1040NR). ☐ **No.** Complete the rest of Form 1040 or Form 1040NR.		

SCHEDULE E (Form 1040)

Department of the Treasury Internal Revenue Service (99)

Supplemental Income and Loss

(From rental real estate, royalties, partnerships, S corporations, estates, trusts, REMICs, etc.)

▶ Attach to Form 1040, 1040NR, or Form 1041. ▶ See Instructions for Schedule E (Form 1040).

OMB No. 1545-0074

2006

Attachment Sequence No. 13

Name(s) shown on return | Your social security number

Part I **Income or Loss From Rental Real Estate and Royalties** **Note.** If you are in the business of renting personal property, use **Schedule C** or **C-EZ** (see page E-3). Report farm rental income or loss from **Form 4835** on page 2, line 40.

1	List the type and location of each **rental real estate property:**	2 For each rental real estate property listed on line 1, did you or your family use it during the tax year for personal purposes for more than the greater of: • 14 days **or** • 10% of the total days rented at fair rental value? (See page E-3.)		Yes	No
A			A		
B			B		
C			C		

Income:		Properties A	Properties B	Properties C		Totals (Add columns A, B, and C.)
3 Rents received	3				3	
4 Royalties received	4				4	
Expenses:						
5 Advertising	5					
6 Auto and travel (see page E-4)	6					
7 Cleaning and maintenance	7					
8 Commissions	8					
9 Insurance	9					
10 Legal and other professional fees	10					
11 Management fees	11					
12 Mortgage interest paid to banks, etc. (see page E-4)	12				12	
13 Other interest	13					
14 Repairs	14					
15 Supplies	15					
16 Taxes	16					
17 Utilities	17					
18 Other (list) ▶	18					
19 Add lines 5 through 18	19				19	
20 Depreciation expense or depletion (see page E-4)	20				20	
21 Total expenses. Add lines 19 and 20	21					
22 Income or (loss) from rental real estate or royalty properties. Subtract line 21 from line 3 (rents) or line 4 (royalties). If the result is a (loss), see page E-5 to find out if you must file **Form 6198**	22					
23 Deductible rental real estate loss. **Caution.** Your rental real estate loss on line 22 may be limited. See page E-5 to find out if you must file **Form 8582.** Real estate professionals must complete line 43 on page 2	23	( )	( )	( )		
24 **Income.** Add positive amounts shown on line 22. **Do not** include any losses					24	
25 **Losses.** Add royalty losses from line 22 and rental real estate losses from line 23. Enter total losses here					25	( )
26 **Total rental real estate and royalty income or (loss).** Combine lines 24 and 25. Enter the result here. If Parts II, III, IV, and line 40 on page 2 do not apply to you, also enter this amount on Form 1040, line 17, or Form 1040NR, line 18. Otherwise, include this amount in the total on line 41 on page 2					26	

For Paperwork Reduction Act Notice, see page E-7 of the instructions. Cat. No. 11344L **Schedule E (Form 1040) 2006**

Name(s) shown on return. Do not enter name and social security number if shown on other side. | **Your social security number**

Caution. The IRS compares amounts reported on your tax return with amounts shown on Schedule(s) K-1.

Part II Income or Loss From Partnerships and S Corporations

Note. If you report a loss from an at-risk activity for which **any** amount is **not** at risk, you **must** check the box in column **(e)** on line 28 and attach **Form 6198.** See page E-1.

27 Are you reporting any loss not allowed in a prior year due to the at-risk or basis limitations, a prior year unallowed loss from a passive activity (if that loss was not reported on Form 8582), or unreimbursed partnership expenses? ☐ **Yes** ☐ **No**
If you answered "Yes," see page E-6 before completing this section.

28	(a) Name	(b) Enter P for partnership; S for S corporation	(c) Check if foreign partnership	(d) Employer identification number	(e) Check if any amount is not at risk
A			☐		☐
B			☐		☐
C			☐		☐
D			☐		☐

	Passive Income and Loss		Nonpassive Income and Loss		
	(f) Passive loss allowed (attach **Form 8582** if required)	(g) Passive income from **Schedule K–1**	(h) Nonpassive loss from **Schedule K–1**	(i) Section 179 expense deduction from **Form 4562**	(j) Nonpassive income from **Schedule K–1**
A					
B					
C					
D					
29a Totals					
b Totals					

30 Add columns (g) and (j) of line 29a 30

31 Add columns (f), (h), and (i) of line 29b . . . . . 31 ( )

32 **Total partnership and S corporation income or (loss).** Combine lines 30 and 31. Enter the result here and include in the total on line 41 below 32

Part III Income or Loss From Estates and Trusts

33	(a) Name	(b) Employer identification number
A		
B		

	Passive Income and Loss		Nonpassive Income and Loss	
	(c) Passive deduction or loss allowed (attach **Form 8582** if required)	(d) Passive income from **Schedule K–1**	(e) Deduction or loss from **Schedule K–1**	(f) Other income from **Schedule K–1**
A				
B				
34a Totals				
b Totals				

35 Add columns (d) and (f) of line 34a 35

36 Add columns (c) and (e) of line 34b . . . . . 36 ( )

37 **Total estate and trust income or (loss).** Combine lines 35 and 36. Enter the result here and include in the total on line 41 below 37

Part IV Income or Loss From Real Estate Mortgage Investment Conduits (REMICs)—Residual Holder

38 (a) Name	(b) Employer identification number	(c) Excess inclusion from **Schedules Q,** line 2c (see page E-6)	(d) Taxable income (net loss) from **Schedules Q,** line 1b	(e) Income from **Schedules Q,** line 3b

39 Combine columns (d) and (e) only. Enter the result here and include in the total on line 41 below 39

Part V Summary

40 Net farm rental income or (loss) from **Form 4835.** Also, complete line 42 below 40

41 **Total income or (loss).** Combine lines 26, 32, 37, 39, and 40. Enter the result here and on Form 1040, line 17, or Form 1040NR, line 18 ▶ 41

42 **Reconciliation of farming and fishing income.** Enter your **gross** farming and fishing income reported on Form 4835, line 7; Schedule K-1 (Form 1065), box 14, code B; Schedule K-1 (Form 1120S), box 17, code T; and Schedule K-1 (Form 1041), line 14, code F (see page E-7) 42

43 **Reconciliation for real estate professionals.** If you were a real estate professional (see page E-1), enter the net income or (loss) you reported anywhere on Form 1040 or Form 1040NR from all rental real estate activities in which you materially participated under the passive activity loss rules . 43

Schedule E (Form 1040) 2006

SCHEDULE SE (Form 1040)

Department of the Treasury Internal Revenue Service (99)

Self-Employment Tax

▶ Attach to Form 1040. ▶ See Instructions for Schedule SE (Form 1040).

OMB No. 1545-0074

2006

Attachment Sequence No. 17

Name of person with **self-employment** income (as shown on Form 1040)	Social security number of person with **self-employment** income ▶	

Who Must File Schedule SE

You must file Schedule SE if:

- You had net earnings from self-employment from **other than** church employee income (line 4 of Short Schedule SE or line 4c of Long Schedule SE) of $400 or more, **or**
- You had church employee income of $108.28 or more. Income from services you performed as a minister or a member of a religious order **is not** church employee income (see page SE-1).

Note. Even if you had a loss or a small amount of income from self-employment, it may be to your benefit to file Schedule SE and use either "optional method" in Part II of Long Schedule SE (see page SE-3).

Exception. If your only self-employment income was from earnings as a minister, member of a religious order, or Christian Science practitioner **and** you filed Form 4361 and received IRS approval not to be taxed on those earnings, **do not** file Schedule SE. Instead, write "Exempt–Form 4361" on Form 1040, line 58.

May I Use Short Schedule SE or Must I Use Long Schedule SE?

Note. Use this flowchart **only if** you must file Schedule SE. If unsure, see Who Must File Schedule SE, above.

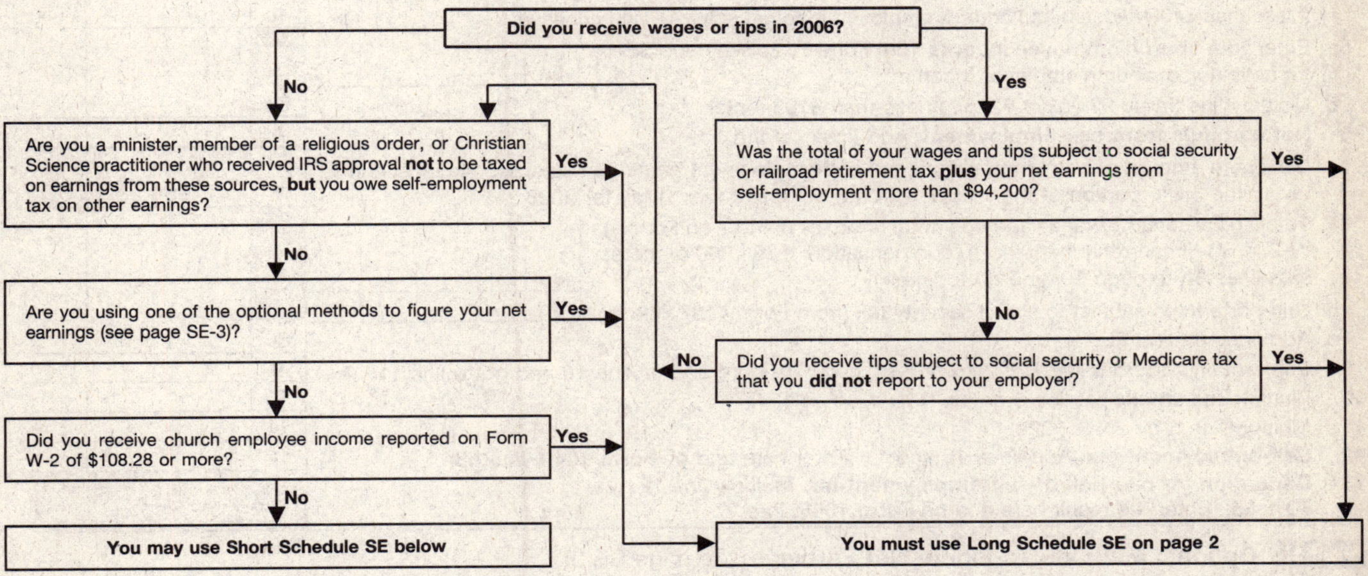

Section A—Short Schedule SE. Caution. Read above to see if you can use Short Schedule SE.

1	Net farm profit or (loss) from Schedule F, line 36, and farm partnerships, Schedule K-1 (Form 1065), box 14, code A	1	
2	Net profit or (loss) from Schedule C, line 31; Schedule C-EZ, line 3; Schedule K-1 (Form 1065), box 14, code A (other than farming); and Schedule K-1 (Form 1065-B), box 9, code J1. Ministers and members of religious orders, see page SE-1 for amounts to report on this line. See page SE-2 for other income to report	2	
3	Combine lines 1 and 2	3	
4	**Net earnings from self-employment.** Multiply line 3 by 92.35% (.9235). If less than $400, **do not** file this schedule; you do not owe self-employment tax . . . . ▶	4	
5	**Self-employment tax.** If the amount on line 4 is: • $94,200 or less, multiply line 4 by 15.3% (.153). Enter the result here and on **Form 1040, line 58.** • More than $94,200, multiply line 4 by 2.9% (.029). Then, add $11,680.80 to the result. Enter the total here and on **Form 1040, line 58.** . . .	5	
6	**Deduction for one-half of self-employment tax.** Multiply line 5 by 50% (.5). Enter the result here and on **Form 1040, line 27** . . .	6			

For Paperwork Reduction Act Notice, see Form 1040 instructions. Cat. No. 11358Z **Schedule SE (Form 1040) 2006**

Name of person with **self-employment** income (as shown on Form 1040)	Social security number of person with **self-employment** income ▶	

Section B—Long Schedule SE

Part I Self-Employment Tax

Note. If your only income subject to self-employment tax is **church employee income,** skip lines 1 through 4b. Enter -0- on line 4c and go to line 5a. Income from services you performed as a minister or a member of a religious order **is not** church employee income. See page SE-1.

A If you are a minister, member of a religious order, or Christian Science practitioner **and** you filed Form 4361, but you had $400 or more of **other** net earnings from self-employment, check here and continue with Part I . . . . ▶ ☐

Line	Description			Line	Amount	
1	Net farm profit or (loss) from Schedule F, line 36, and farm partnerships, Schedule K-1 (Form 1065), box 14, code A. **Note.** Skip this line if you use the farm optional method (see page SE-4)			1		
2	Net profit or (loss) from Schedule C, line 31; Schedule C-EZ, line 3; Schedule K-1 (Form 1065), box 14, code A (other than farming); and Schedule K-1 (Form 1065-B), box 9, code J1. Ministers and members of religious orders, see page SE-1 for amounts to report on this line. See page SE-2 for other income to report. **Note.** Skip this line if you use the nonfarm optional method (see page SE-4)			2		
3	Combine lines 1 and 2			3		
4a	If line 3 is more than zero, multiply line 3 by 92.35% (.9235). Otherwise, enter amount from line 3			4a		
b	If you elect one or both of the optional methods, enter the total of lines 15 and 17 here . . .			4b		
c	Combine lines 4a and 4b. If less than $400, **stop**; you do not owe self-employment tax. **Exception.** If less than $400 and you had **church employee income,** enter -0- and continue. . . . . . ▶			4c		
5a	Enter your **church employee income** from Form W-2. See page SE-1 for definition of church employee income	5a				
b	Multiply line 5a by 92.35% (.9235). If less than $100, enter -0-			5b		
6	**Net earnings from self-employment.** Add lines 4c and 5b			6		
7	Maximum amount of combined wages and self-employment earnings subject to social security tax or the 6.2% portion of the 7.65% railroad retirement (tier 1) tax for 2006			7	94,200	00
8a	Total social security wages and tips (total of boxes 3 and 7 on Form(s) W-2) and railroad retirement (tier 1) compensation. If $94,200 or more, skip lines 8b through 10, and go to line 11	8a				
b	Unreported tips subject to social security tax (from Form 4137, line 9)	8b				
c	Add lines 8a and 8b			8c		
9	Subtract line 8c from line 7. If zero or less, enter -0- here and on line 10 and go to line 11 . ▶			9		
10	Multiply the **smaller** of line 6 or line 9 by 12.4% (.124)			10		
11	Multiply line 6 by 2.9% (.029)			11		
12	**Self-employment tax.** Add lines 10 and 11. Enter here and on **Form 1040, line 58**			12		
13	**Deduction for one-half of self-employment tax.** Multiply line 12 by 50% (.5). Enter the result here and on **Form 1040, line 27**	13				

Part II Optional Methods To Figure Net Earnings (see page SE-3)

Farm Optional Method. You may use this method **only** if **(a)** your gross farm income[1] was not more than $2,400, **or (b)** your net farm profits[2] were less than $1,733.

Line	Description	Line	Amount	
14	Maximum income for optional methods	14	1,600	00
15	Enter the **smaller** of: two-thirds (⅔) of gross farm income[1] (not less than zero) **or** $1,600. Also include this amount on line 4b above	15		

Nonfarm Optional Method. You may use this method **only** if **(a)** your net nonfarm profits[3] were less than $1,733 and also less than 72.189% of your gross nonfarm income,[4] **and (b)** you had net earnings from self-employment of at least $400 in 2 of the prior 3 years.

Caution. You may use this method no more than five times.

Line	Description	Line	Amount	
16	Subtract line 15 from line 14	16		
17	Enter the **smaller** of: two-thirds (⅔) of gross nonfarm income[4] (not less than zero) **or** the amount on line 16. Also include this amount on line 4b above	17		

[1] From Sch. F, line 11, and Sch. K-1 (Form 1065), box 14, code B.

[2] From Sch. F, line 36, and Sch. K-1 (Form 1065), box 14, code A.

[3] From Sch. C, line 31; Sch. C-EZ, line 3; Sch. K-1 (Form 1065), box 14, code A; and Sch. K-1 (Form 1065-B), box 9, code J1.

[4] From Sch. C, line 7; Sch. C-EZ, line 1; Sch. K-1 (Form 1065), box 14, code C; and Sch. K-1 (Form 1065-B), box 9, code J2.

Form **1040X** (Rev. November 2006)

Department of the Treasury—Internal Revenue Service

Amended U.S. Individual Income Tax Return

▶ See separate instructions.

OMB No. 1545-0074

This return is for calendar year ▶ , or fiscal year ended ▶ ,

Please print or type

Your first name and initial	Last name	Your social security number
If a joint return, spouse's first name and initial	Last name	Spouse's social security number
Home address (no. and street) or P.O. box if mail is not delivered to your home	Apt. no.	Phone number ( )
City, town or post office, state, and ZIP code. If you have a foreign address, see page 2 of the instructions.		

A If the address shown above is different from that shown on your last return filed with the IRS, would you like us to change it in our records? . . . ▶ ☐ Yes ☐ No

B Filing status. Be sure to complete this line. **Note.** You cannot change from joint to separate returns after the due date.

On original return ▶ ☐ Single ☐ Married filing jointly ☐ Married filing separately ☐ Head of household ☐ Qualifying widow(er)

On this return ▶ ☐ Single ☐ Married filing jointly ☐ Married filing separately ☐ Head of household* ☐ Qualifying widow(er)

* If the qualifying person is a child but not your dependent, see page 2 of the instructions.

Use Part II on the back to explain any changes		A. Original amount or as previously adjusted (see page 3)	B. Net change—amount of increase or (decrease)—explain in Part II	C. Correct amount
Income and Deductions (see instructions)				
1 Adjusted gross income (see page 3)	1			
2 Itemized deductions or standard deduction (see page 3)	2			
3 Subtract line 2 from line 1	3			
4 Exemptions. If changing, fill in Parts I and II on the back (see page 3)	4			
5 Taxable income. Subtract line 4 from line 3	5			
Tax Liability				
6 Tax (see page 4). Method used in col. C ______	6			
7 Credits (see page 4)	7			
8 Subtract line 7 from line 6. Enter the result but not less than zero	8			
9 Other taxes (see page 4)	9			
10 Total tax. Add lines 8 and 9	10			
Payments				
11 Federal income tax withheld and excess social security and tier 1 RRTA tax withheld. If changing, see page 4	11			
12 Estimated tax payments, including amount applied from prior year's return	12			
13 Earned income credit (EIC)	13			
14 Additional child tax credit from Form 8812	14			
15 Credits from Form 2439, Form 4136, or Form 8885	15			
16 Amount paid with request for extension of time to file (see page 4)			16	
17 Amount of tax paid with original return plus additional tax paid after it was filed			17	
18 Total payments. Add lines 11 through 17 in column C			18	

Refund or Amount You Owe

19 Overpayment, if any, as shown on original return or as previously adjusted by the IRS	19	
20 Subtract line 19 from line 18 (see page 5)	20	
21 **Amount you owe.** If line 10, column C, is more than line 20, enter the difference and see page 5	21	
22 If line 10, column C, is less than line 20, enter the difference	22	
23 Amount of line 22 you want **refunded to you**	23	
24 Amount of line 22 you want **applied to your** estimated tax 24		

Sign Here

Joint return? See page 2. Keep a copy for your records.

Under penalties of perjury, I declare that I have filed an original return and that I have examined this amended return, including accompanying schedules and statements, and to the best of my knowledge and belief, this amended return is true, correct, and complete. Declaration of preparer (other than taxpayer) is based on all information of which the preparer has any knowledge.

▶ Your signature Date ▶ Spouse's signature. If a joint return, **both** must sign. Date

Paid Preparer's Use Only

Preparer's signature ▶	Date	Check if self-employed ☐	Preparer's SSN or PTIN
Firm's name (or yours if self-employed), address, and ZIP code ▶		EIN	
		Phone no. ( )	

For Paperwork Reduction Act Notice, see page 6 of instructions. Cat. No. 11360L Form **1040X** (Rev. 11-2006)

Part I **Exemptions.** See Form 1040 or 1040A instructions.

Complete this part **only** if you are:

- Increasing or decreasing the number of exemptions claimed on line 6d of the return you are amending, or
- Increasing or decreasing the exemption amount for housing individuals displaced by Hurricane Katrina.

		Line	A. Original number of exemptions reported or as previously adjusted	B. Net change	C. Correct number of exemptions
25	Yourself and spouse . . . . **Caution.** If someone can claim you as a dependent, you cannot claim an exemption for yourself.	25			
26	Your dependent children who lived with you	26			
27	Your dependent children who did not live with you due to divorce or separation	27			
28	Other dependents	28			
29	Total number of exemptions. Add lines 25 through 28	29			
30	Multiply the number of exemptions claimed on line 29 by the amount listed below for the tax year you are amending. Enter the result here and on line 4.	30			
31	If you are claiming an exemption amount for housing individuals displaced by Hurricane Katrina, enter the amount from Form 8914, line 2 for 2005 or line 6 for 2006 (see instructions for line 4)	31			
32	Add lines 30 and 31. Enter the result here and on line 4	32			

Tax year	Exemption amount	But see the instructions for line 4 on page 3 if the amount on line 1 is over:
2006	$3,300	$112,875
2005	3,200	109,475
2004	3,100	107,025
2003	3,050	104,625

33 Dependents (children and other) not claimed on original (or adjusted) return:

(a) First name	Last name	(b) Dependent's social security number	(c) Dependent's relationship to you	(d) ✓ if qualifying child for child tax credit (see page 5)
				☐
				☐
				☐
				☐
				☐
				☐

No. of children on 33 who:

- lived with you . . ▶ ☐
- **did not** live with you due to divorce or separation (see page 5) . . ▶ ☐

Dependents on 33 not entered above ▶ ☐

Part II **Explanation of Changes**

Enter the line number from the front of the form for each item you are changing and give the reason for each change. Attach only the supporting forms and schedules for the items changed. If you do not attach the required information, your Form 1040X may be returned. Be sure to include your name and social security number on any attachments.

If the change relates to a net operating loss carryback or a general business credit carryback, attach the schedule or form that shows the year in which the loss or credit occurred. See page 2 of the instructions. Also, check here. . . . . . ▶ ☐

Part III **Presidential Election Campaign Fund.** Checking below will not increase your tax or reduce your refund.

If you did not previously want $3 to go to the fund but now want to, check here . . . . ▶ ☐

If a joint return and your spouse did not previously want $3 to go to the fund but now wants to, check here . . . . ▶ ☐

Form **1040X** (Rev. 11-2006)

Form **2441**

Department of the Treasury
Internal Revenue Service (99)

Child and Dependent Care Expenses

▶ Attach to Form 1040 or Form 1040NR.

▶ See separate instructions.

OMB No. 1545-0074

2006

Attachment Sequence No. **21**

Name(s) shown on Form 1040 | Your social security number

Before you begin: You need to understand the following terms. See **Definitions** on page 1 of the instructions.

- **Dependent Care Benefits**
- **Qualifying Person(s)**
- **Qualified Expenses**

Part I **Persons or Organizations Who Provided the Care—**You **must** complete this part.
(If you need more space, use the bottom of page 2.)

1 (a) Care provider's name	(b) Address (number, street, apt. no., city, state, and ZIP code)	(c) Identifying number (SSN or EIN)	(d) Amount paid (see instructions)

Did you receive **dependent care benefits?**
- **No** ⟶ Complete only Part II below.
- **Yes** ⟶ Complete Part III on the back next.

Caution. If the care was provided in your home, you may owe employment taxes. See the instructions for Form 1040, line 62, or Form 1040NR, line 57.

Part II **Credit for Child and Dependent Care Expenses**

2 Information about your **qualifying person(s).** If you have more than two qualifying persons, see the instructions.

(a) Qualifying person's name — First	Last	(b) Qualifying person's social security number	(c) **Qualified expenses** you incurred and paid in 2006 for the person listed in column (a)

3 Add the amounts in column (c) of line 2. **Do not** enter more than $3,000 for one qualifying person or $6,000 for two or more persons. If you completed Part III, enter the amount from line 33 . . . . . **3**

4 Enter your **earned income.** See instructions **4**

5 If married filing jointly, enter your spouse's earned income (if your spouse was a student or was disabled, see the instructions); **all others,** enter the amount from line 4 . . . **5**

6 Enter the **smallest** of line 3, 4, or 5 . . . . . **6**

7 Enter the amount from Form 1040, line 38, or Form 1040NR, line 36 . . . . . **7**

8 Enter on line 8 the decimal amount shown below that applies to the amount on line 7

If line 7 is: Over	But not over	Decimal amount is	If line 7 is: Over	But not over	Decimal amount is
$0	15,000	.35	$29,000	31,000	.27
15,000	17,000	.34	31,000	33,000	.26
17,000	19,000	.33	33,000	35,000	.25
19,000	21,000	.32	35,000	37,000	.24
21,000	23,000	.31	37,000	39,000	.23
23,000	25,000	.30	39,000	41,000	.22
25,000	27,000	.29	41,000	43,000	.21
27,000	29,000	.28	43,000	No limit	.20

8 X .

9 Multiply line 6 by the decimal amount on line 8. If you paid 2005 expenses in 2006, see the instructions **9**

10 Enter the amount from Form 1040, line 46, minus any amount on Form 1040, line 47, or Form 1040NR, line 43, minus any amount on Form 1040NR, line 44 . . . . . **10**

11 **Credit for child and dependent care expenses.** Enter the **smaller** of line 9 or line 10 here and on Form 1040, line 48, or Form 1040NR, line 45 . . . . . **11**

For Paperwork Reduction Act Notice, see page 4 of the instructions. Cat. No. 11862M Form **2441** (2006)

Part III Dependent Care Benefits

12 Enter the total amount of **dependent care benefits** you received in 2006. Amounts you received as an employee should be shown in box 10 of your Form(s) W-2. **Do not** include amounts reported as wages in box 1 of Form(s) W-2. If you were self-employed or a partner, include amounts you received under a dependent care assistance program from your sole proprietorship or partnership **12**

13 Enter the amount, if any, you carried over from 2005 and used in 2006 during the grace period. See instructions **13**

14 Enter the amount, if any, you forfeited or carried forward to 2007. See instructions . . **14** ( )

15 Combine lines 12 through 14. See instructions **15**

16 Enter the total amount of **qualified expenses** incurred in 2006 for the care of the **qualifying person(s)** . . **16**

17 Enter the **smaller** of line 15 or 16 . . . . . **17**

18 Enter your **earned income.** See instructions . . . **18**

19 Enter the amount shown below that applies to you.

- If married filing jointly, enter your spouse's earned income (if your spouse was a student or was disabled, see the instructions for line 5).
- If married filing separately, see the instructions for the amount to enter.
- All others, enter the amount from line 18.

. . . **19**

20 Enter the **smallest** of line 17, 18, or 19 . . . . . **20**

21 Enter the amount from line 12 that you received from your sole proprietorship or partnership. If you did not receive any such amounts, enter -0- **21**

22 Subtract line 21 from line 15 . . . . . **22**

23 Enter $5,000 ($2,500 if married filing separately **and** you were required to enter your spouse's earned income on line 19) **23**

24 **Deductible benefits.** Enter the **smallest** of line 20, 21, or 23. Also, include this amount on the appropriate line(s) of your return. See instructions **24**

25 Enter the **smaller** of line 20 or 23 . . . . . **25**

26 Enter the amount from line 24 . . . . . **26**

27 **Excluded benefits.** Subtract line 26 from line 25. If zero or less, enter -0- **27**

28 **Taxable benefits.** Subtract line 27 from line 22. If zero or less, enter -0-. Also, include this amount on Form 1040, line 7, or Form 1040NR, line 8. On the dotted line next to Form 1040, line 7, or Form 1040NR, line 8, enter "DCB". **28**

To claim the child and dependent care credit, complete lines 29–33 below.

29 Enter $3,000 ($6,000 if two or more qualifying persons) **29**

30 Add lines 24 and 27 . . . . . **30**

31 Subtract line 30 from line 29. If zero or less, **stop.** You cannot take the credit. **Exception.** If you paid 2005 expenses in 2006, see the instructions for line 9 . . . . **31**

32 Complete line 2 on the front of this form. **Do not** include in column (c) any benefits shown on line 30 above. Then, add the amounts in column (c) and enter the total here **32**

33 Enter the **smaller** of line 31 or 32. Also, enter this amount on line 3 on the front of this form and complete lines 4–11 . . . . . **33**

Form **4562**

Department of the Treasury
Internal Revenue Service

Depreciation and Amortization
(Including Information on Listed Property)

▶ See separate instructions. ▶ Attach to your tax return.

OMB No. 1545-0172

2006

Attachment Sequence No. 67

Name(s) shown on return	Business or activity to which this form relates	Identifying number

Part I **Election To Expense Certain Property Under Section 179**

Note: *If you have any listed property, complete Part V before you complete Part I.*

1	Maximum amount. See the instructions for a higher limit for certain businesses	1	$108,000
2	Total cost of section 179 property placed in service (see instructions)	2	
3	Threshold cost of section 179 property before reduction in limitation	3	$430,000
4	Reduction in limitation. Subtract line 3 from line 2. If zero or less, enter -0-	4	
5	Dollar limitation for tax year. Subtract line 4 from line 1. If zero or less, enter -0-. If married filing separately, see instructions	5	

	(a) Description of property	(b) Cost (business use only)	(c) Elected cost
6			
7	Listed property. Enter the amount from line 29	7	

8	Total elected cost of section 179 property. Add amounts in column (c), lines 6 and 7	8	
9	Tentative deduction. Enter the **smaller** of line 5 or line 8	9	
10	Carryover of disallowed deduction from line 13 of your 2005 Form 4562	10	
11	Business income limitation. Enter the smaller of business income (not less than zero) or line 5 (see instructions)	11	
12	Section 179 expense deduction. Add lines 9 and 10, but do not enter more than line 11	12	
13	Carryover of disallowed deduction to 2007. Add lines 9 and 10, less line 12 ▶ 13		

Note: *Do not use Part II or Part III below for listed property. Instead, use Part V.*

Part II **Special Depreciation Allowance and Other Depreciation (Do not** include listed property.) (See instructions.)

14	Special allowance for qualified New York Liberty or Gulf Opportunity Zone property (other than listed property) placed in service during the tax year (see instructions)	14	
15	Property subject to section 168(f)(1) election	15	
16	Other depreciation (including ACRS)	16	

Part III **MACRS Depreciation (Do not** include listed property.) (See instructions.)

Section A

17	MACRS deductions for assets placed in service in tax years beginning before 2006	17	
18	If you are electing to group any assets placed in service during the tax year into one or more general asset accounts, check here ▶ ☐		

Section B—Assets Placed in Service During 2006 Tax Year Using the General Depreciation System

(a) Classification of property	(b) Month and year placed in service	(c) Basis for depreciation (business/investment use only—see instructions)	(d) Recovery period	(e) Convention	(f) Method	(g) Depreciation deduction
19a 3-year property						
b 5-year property						
c 7-year property						
d 10-year property						
e 15-year property						
f 20-year property						
g 25-year property			25 yrs.		S/L	
h Residential rental property			27.5 yrs.	MM	S/L	
			27.5 yrs.	MM	S/L	
i Nonresidential real property			39 yrs.	MM	S/L	
				MM	S/L	

Section C—Assets Placed in Service During 2006 Tax Year Using the Alternative Depreciation System

20a Class life					S/L	
b 12-year			12 yrs.		S/L	
c 40-year			40 yrs.	MM	S/L	

Part IV **Summary** (see instructions)

21	Listed property. Enter amount from line 28	21	
22	**Total.** Add amounts from line 12, lines 14 through 17, lines 19 and 20 in column (g), and line 21. Enter here and on the appropriate lines of your return. Partnerships and S corporations—see instr.	22	
23	For assets shown above and placed in service during the current year, enter the portion of the basis attributable to section 263A costs . . 23		

For Paperwork Reduction Act Notice, see separate instructions. Cat. No. 12906N Form **4562** (2006)

Part V **Listed Property** (Include automobiles, certain other vehicles, cellular telephones, certain computers, and property used for entertainment, recreation, or amusement.)

Note: *For any vehicle for which you are using the standard mileage rate or deducting lease expense, complete* ***only*** *24a, 24b, columns (a) through (c) of Section A, all of Section B, and Section C if applicable.*

Section A—Depreciation and Other Information (Caution: *See the instructions for limits for passenger automobiles.***)**

24a Do you have evidence to support the business/investment use claimed? ☐ **Yes** ☐ **No** | **24b** If "Yes," is the evidence written? ☐ **Yes** ☐ **No**

(a) Type of property (list vehicles first)	(b) Date placed in service	(c) Business/ investment use percentage	(d) Cost or other basis	(e) Basis for depreciation (business/investment use only)	(f) Recovery period	(g) Method/ Convention	(h) Depreciation deduction	(i) Elected section 179 cost
25 Special allowance for qualified New York Liberty or Gulf Opportunity Zone property placed in service during the tax year and used more than 50% in a qualified business use (see instructions)						**25**		
26 Property used more than 50% in a qualified business use:								
		%						
		%						
		%						
27 Property used 50% or less in a qualified business use:								
		%				S/L –		
		%				S/L –		
		%				S/L –		
28 Add amounts in column (h), lines 25 through 27. Enter here and on line 21, page 1. .						**28**		
29 Add amounts in column (i), line 26. Enter here and on line 7, page 1.							**29**	

Section B—Information on Use of Vehicles

Complete this section for vehicles used by a sole proprietor, partner, or other "more than 5% owner," or related person.
If you provided vehicles to your employees, first answer the questions in Section C to see if you meet an exception to completing this section for those vehicles.

	(a) Vehicle 1		(b) Vehicle 2		(c) Vehicle 3		(d) Vehicle 4		(e) Vehicle 5		(f) Vehicle 6	
30 Total business/investment miles driven during the year (**do not** include commuting miles)												
31 Total commuting miles driven during the year												
32 Total other personal (noncommuting) miles driven												
33 Total miles driven during the year. Add lines 30 through 32												
	Yes	**No**	**Yes**	**No**	**Yes**	**No**	**Yes**	**No**	**Yes**	**No**	**Yes**	**No**
34 Was the vehicle available for personal use during off-duty hours?												
35 Was the vehicle used primarily by a more than 5% owner or related person?												
36 Is another vehicle available for personal use?												

Section C—Questions for Employers Who Provide Vehicles for Use by Their Employees

Answer these questions to determine if you meet an exception to completing Section B for vehicles used by employees who **are not** more than 5% owners or related persons (see instructions).

	Yes	**No**
37 Do you maintain a written policy statement that prohibits all personal use of vehicles, including commuting, by your employees?		
38 Do you maintain a written policy statement that prohibits personal use of vehicles, except commuting, by your employees? See the instructions for vehicles used by corporate officers, directors, or 1% or more owners		
39 Do you treat all use of vehicles by employees as personal use?		
40 Do you provide more than five vehicles to your employees, obtain information from your employees about the use of the vehicles, and retain the information received?		
41 Do you meet the requirements concerning qualified automobile demonstration use? (See instructions.)		
Note: *If your answer to 37, 38, 39, 40, or 41 is "Yes," do not complete Section B for the covered vehicles.*		

Part VI **Amortization**

(a) Description of costs	(b) Date amortization begins	(c) Amortizable amount	(d) Code section	(e) Amortization period or percentage	(f) Amortization for this year
42 Amortization of costs that begins during your 2006 tax year (see instructions):					
43 Amortization of costs that began before your 2006 tax year.				**43**	
44 **Total.** Add amounts in column (f). See the instructions for where to report				**44**	

Form **4562** (2006)

Form **4684**

Department of the Treasury
Internal Revenue Service

Casualties and Thefts

▶ See separate instructions.
▶ Attach to your tax return.
▶ Use a separate Form 4684 for each casualty or theft.

OMB No. 1545-0177

2006

Attachment Sequence No. **26**

Name(s) shown on tax return | **Identifying number**

SECTION A—Personal Use Property (Use this section to report casualties and thefts of property **not** used in a trade or business or for income-producing purposes.)

1 Description of properties (show type, location, and date acquired for each property). Use a separate line for each property lost or damaged from the same casualty or theft.

Property **A** ____________________

Property **B** ____________________

Property **C** ____________________

Property **D** ____________________

		Properties			
		A	**B**	**C**	**D**
2 Cost or other basis of each property	2				
3 Insurance or other reimbursement (whether or not you filed a claim) (see instructions)	3				
Note: *If line 2 is* ***more*** *than line 3, skip line 4.* **4** Gain from casualty or theft. If line 3 is **more** than line 2, enter the difference here and skip lines 5 through 9 for that column. See instructions if line 3 includes insurance or other reimbursement you did not claim, or you received payment for your loss in a later tax year.	4				
5 Fair market value **before** casualty or theft	5				
6 Fair market value **after** casualty or theft	6				
7 Subtract line 6 from line 5	7				
8 Enter the **smaller** of line 2 or line 7	8				
9 Subtract line 3 from line 8. If zero or less, enter -0-	9				

10 Casualty or theft loss. Add the amounts on line 9 in columns A through D **10**

11 Enter the **smaller** of line 10 or $100. But if the loss arose in the Hurricane Katrina disaster area after August 24, 2005; Hurricane Rita disaster area after September 22, 2005; or Hurricane Wilma disaster area after October 22, 2005, and was caused by that particular hurricane, enter -0- **11**

12 Subtract line 11 from line 10 . . . . **12**

Caution: *Use only one Form 4684 for lines 13 through 21.*

13 Add the amounts on line 12 of all Forms 4684 . . . . **13**

14 Add the amounts on line 4 of all Forms 4684 . . . . **14**

15
- If line 14 is **more** than line 13, enter the difference here and on Schedule D. **Do not** complete the rest of this section (see instructions).
- If line 14 is **less** than line 13, enter -0- here and go to line 16.
- If line 14 is **equal** to line 13, enter -0- here. **Do not** complete the rest of this section.

. . . . **15**

16 If line 14 is **less** than line 13, enter the difference **16**

17 Add the amounts on line 12 of all Forms 4684 on which you entered -0- on line 11. . . . . **17**

18 Is line 17 less than line 16?

☐ **No.** Stop. Enter the amount from line 16 on Schedule A (Form 1040), line 19. Estates and trusts, enter the amount from line 16 on the "Other deductions" line of your tax return.

☐ **Yes.** Subtract line 17 from line 16. **18**

19 Enter 10% of your adjusted gross income from Form 1040, line 38. Estates and trusts, see instructions . . **19**

20 Subtract line 19 from line 18. If zero or less, enter -0- **20**

21 Add lines 17 and 20. Also enter the result on Schedule A (Form 1040), line 19. Estates and trusts, enter the result on the "Other deductions" line of your tax return **21**

For Paperwork Reduction Act Notice, see page 4 of the instructions. Cat. No. 12997O Form **4684** (2006)

Name(s) shown on tax return. Do not enter name and identifying number if shown on other side. | Identifying number

SECTION B—Business and Income-Producing Property

Part I Casualty or Theft Gain or Loss (Use a separate Part I for each casualty or theft.)

22 Description of properties (show type, location, and date acquired for each property). Use a separate line for each property lost or damaged from the same casualty or theft.

Property **A** ________

Property **B** ________

Property **C** ________

Property **D** ________

			Properties		
		A	**B**	**C**	**D**
23 Cost or adjusted basis of each property	**23**				
24 Insurance or other reimbursement (whether or not you filed a claim). See the instructions for line 3. **Note:** *If line 23 is* ***more*** *than line 24, skip line 25.*	**24**				
25 Gain from casualty or theft. If line 24 is **more** than line 23, enter the difference here and on line 32 or line 37, column (c), except as provided in the instructions for line 36. Also, skip lines 26 through 30 for that column. See the instructions for line 4 if line 24 includes insurance or other reimbursement you did not claim, or you received payment for your loss in a later tax year.	**25**				
26 Fair market value **before** casualty or theft	**26**				
27 Fair market value **after** casualty or theft	**27**				
28 Subtract line 27 from line 26	**28**				
29 Enter the **smaller** of line 23 or line 28. **Note:** *If the property was totally destroyed by casualty or lost from theft, enter on line 29 the amount from line 23.*	**29**				
30 Subtract line 24 from line 29. If zero or less, enter -0-	**30**				

31 Casualty or theft loss. Add the amounts on line 30. Enter the total here and on line 32 **or** line 37 (see instructions). **31** ____

Part II Summary of Gains and Losses (from separate Parts I)

	(a) Identify casualty or theft		**(b)** Losses from casualties or thefts: *(i)* Trade, business, rental or royalty property	**(b)** *(ii)* Income-producing and employee property	**(c)** Gains from casualties or thefts includible in income
	Casualty or Theft of Property Held One Year or Less				
32			( )	( )	
			( )	( )	
33	Totals. Add the amounts on line 32	**33**	( )	( )	
34	Combine line 33, columns (b)(i) and (c). Enter the net gain or (loss) here and on Form 4797, line 14. If Form 4797 is not otherwise required, see instructions			**34**	
35	Enter the amount from line 33, column (b)(ii) here. Individuals, enter the amount from income-producing property on Schedule A (Form 1040), line 27, and enter the amount from property used as an employee on Schedule A (Form 1040), line 22. Estates and trusts, partnerships, and S corporations, see instructions			**35**	
	Casualty or Theft of Property Held More Than One Year				
36	Casualty or theft gains from Form 4797, line 32			**36**	
37			( )	( )	
			( )	( )	
38	Total losses. Add amounts on line 37, columns (b)(i) and (b)(ii)	**38**	( )	( )	
39	Total gains. Add lines 36 and 37, column (c)			**39**	
40	Add amounts on line 38, columns (b)(i) and (b)(ii)			**40**	
41	If the loss on line 40 is **more** than the gain on line 39:				
a	Combine line 38, column (b)(i) and line 39, and enter the net gain or (loss) here. Partnerships (except electing large partnerships) and S corporations, see the note below. All others, enter this amount on Form 4797, line 14. If Form 4797 is not otherwise required, see instructions			**41a**	
b	Enter the amount from line 38, column (b)(ii) here. Individuals, enter the amount from income-producing property on Schedule A (Form 1040), line 27, and enter the amount from property used as an employee on Schedule A (Form 1040), line 22. Estates and trusts, enter on the "Other deductions" line of your tax return. Partnerships (except electing large partnerships) and S corporations, see the note below. Electing large partnerships, enter on Form 1065-B, Part II, line 11.			**41b**	
42	If the loss on line 40 is **less** than or **equal** to the gain on line 39, combine lines 39 and 40 and enter here. Partnerships (except electing large partnerships), see the note below. All others, enter this amount on Form 4797, line 3			**42**	

Note: *Partnerships, enter the amount from line 41a, 41b, or line 42 on Form 1065, Schedule K, line 11. S corporations, enter the amount from line 41a or 41b on Form 1120S, Schedule K, line 10.*

Form **4684** (2006)

Form **5695**

Department of the Treasury
Internal Revenue Service

Residential Energy Credits

▶ See instructions.
▶ Attach to Form 1040 or Form 1040NR.

OMB No. 1545-0074

2006

Attachment Sequence No. **158**

Name(s) shown on return | Your social security number

Part I **Nonbusiness Energy Property Credit** (See instructions before completing this part.)

1	Were the energy efficiency improvements or residential energy property costs made to your main home located in the United States? (see instructions) . . . ▶		☐ Yes ☐ No
	Caution: *If you checked the "No" box, you cannot claim the nonbusiness energy property credit. Do not complete Part I.*		
2	Energy efficiency improvements (see instructions).		
a	Insulation material or system primarily designed to reduce heat loss or gain in your home . . .	**2a**	
b	Exterior windows (including skylights). Do not enter more than $2,000	**2b**	
c	Exterior doors . . .	**2c**	
d	Metal roof with appropriate pigmented coatings that meet the Energy Star program requirements primarily designed to reduce heat gain in your home . . .	**2d**	
3	Add lines 2a through 2d . . .		**3**
4	Multiply line 3 by 10% (.10) . . .		**4**
5	Residential energy property costs (see instructions).		
a	Energy-efficient building property. Do not enter more than $300 . .	**5a**	
b	Qualified natural gas, propane, or oil furnace or hot water boiler. Do not enter more than $150 . . .	**5b**	
c	Advanced main circulating fan used in a natural gas, propane, or oil furnace. Do not enter more than $50 . . .	**5c**	
6	Add lines 5a through 5c . . .		**6**
7	Add lines 4 and 6 . . .		**7**
8	Enter the smaller of line 7 or $500 . . .		**8**
9	Enter the amount from Form 1040, line 46, or Form 1040NR, line 43	**9**	
10	Enter the total, if any, of your credits from Form 1040, lines 47 through 51, or Form 1040NR, lines 44 through 46 . . .	**10**	
11	Subtract line 10 from line 9. If zero or less, **stop**. You cannot take a nonbusiness energy property credit . . .		**11**
12	**Nonbusiness energy credit.** Enter the smaller of line 8 or line 11 . . .		**12**

For Paperwork Reduction Act Notice, see instructions. Cat. No. 13540P Form **5695** (2006)

Before you begin: Figure the amount of any of the following credits that you are claiming.

- Child tax credit
- Mortgage interest credit
- Adoption credit
- District of Columbia first-time homebuyer credit

Part II **Residential Energy Efficient Property Credit** (See instructions before completing this part.)

13	Qualified photovoltaic property costs	13			
14	Multiply line 13 by 30% (.30)	14			
15	Maximum credit amount	15	2,000		
16	Enter the smaller of line 14 or line 15			16	
17	Qualified solar water heating property costs	17			
18	Multiply line 17 by 30% (.30)	18			
19	Maximum credit amount	19	2,000		
20	Enter the smaller of line 18 or line 19			20	
21	Qualified fuel cell property costs	21			
22	Multiply line 21 by 30% (.30)	22			
23	Kilowatt capacity of property on line 21 above ▶ ____________ X $1,000	23			
24	Enter the smaller of line 22 or line 23			24	
25	Add lines 16, 20, and 24			25	
26	Enter the amount from Form 1040, line 46, or Form 1040NR, line 43	26			
27	**1040 filers:** Enter the total, if any, of your credits from Form 1040, lines 47 through 51, 53, and 54, plus the amount, if any, from line 12 of this form. **1040NR filers:** Enter the total, if any, of your credits from Form 1040NR, lines 44 through 46, 48, and 49, plus the amount, if any, from line 12 of this form.	27			
28	Subtract line 27 from line 26. If zero or less, enter -0- here and on line 29			28	
29	**Residential energy efficient property credit.** Enter the smaller of line 25 or line 28			29	
30	Credit carryforward to 2007. If line 29 is less than line 25, subtract line 29 from line 25	30			

Part III **Current Year Residential Energy Credits**

31	Add lines 12 and 29. Enter here and on Form 1040, line 52, or Form 1040NR, line 47	31	

Form **5695** (2006)

Form **6251**

Department of the Treasury
Internal Revenue Service (99)

Alternative Minimum Tax—Individuals

▶ See separate instructions.

▶ Attach to Form 1040 or Form 1040NR.

OMB No. 1545-0074

2006

Attachment Sequence No. **32**

Name(s) shown on Form 1040 | **Your social security number**

Part I Alternative Minimum Taxable Income (See instructions for how to complete each line.)

1	If filing Schedule A (Form 1040), enter the amount from Form 1040, line 41 (minus any amount on Form 8914, line 6), and go to line 2. Otherwise, enter the amount from Form 1040, line 38 (minus any amount on Form 8914, line 6), and go to line 7. (If less than zero, enter as a negative amount.)	1	
2	Medical and dental. Enter the **smaller** of Schedule A (Form 1040), line 4, **or** 2½ % of Form 1040, line 38	2	
3	Taxes from Schedule A (Form 1040), line 9	3	
4	Enter the home mortgage interest adjustment, if any, from line 6 of the worksheet on page 2 of the instructions	4	
5	Miscellaneous deductions from Schedule A (Form 1040), line 26	5	
6	If Form 1040, line 38, is over $150,500 (over $75,250 if married filing separately), enter the amount from line 11 of the **Itemized Deductions Worksheet** on page A-6 of the Instructions for Schedule A (Form 1040)	6	( )
7	Tax refund from Form 1040, line 10 or line 21	7	( )
8	Investment interest expense (difference between regular tax and AMT)	8	
9	Depletion (difference between regular tax and AMT)	9	
10	Net operating loss deduction from Form 1040, line 21. Enter as a positive amount	10	
11	Interest from specified private activity bonds exempt from the regular tax	11	
12	Qualified small business stock (7% of gain excluded under section 1202)	12	
13	Exercise of incentive stock options (excess of AMT income over regular tax income)	13	
14	Estates and trusts (amount from Schedule K-1 (Form 1041), box 12, code A)	14	
15	Electing large partnerships (amount from Schedule K-1 (Form 1065-B), box 6)	15	
16	Disposition of property (difference between AMT and regular tax gain or loss)	16	
17	Depreciation on assets placed in service after 1986 (difference between regular tax and AMT)	17	
18	Passive activities (difference between AMT and regular tax income or loss)	18	
19	Loss limitations (difference between AMT and regular tax income or loss)	19	
20	Circulation costs (difference between regular tax and AMT)	20	
21	Long-term contracts (difference between AMT and regular tax income)	21	
22	Mining costs (difference between regular tax and AMT)	22	
23	Research and experimental costs (difference between regular tax and AMT)	23	
24	Income from certain installment sales before January 1, 1987	24	( )
25	Intangible drilling costs preference	25	
26	Other adjustments, including income-based related adjustments	26	
27	Alternative tax net operating loss deduction	27	( )
28	**Alternative minimum taxable income.** Combine lines 1 through 27. (If married filing separately and line 28 is more than $200,100, see page 7 of the instructions.)	28	

Part II Alternative Minimum Tax

29 Exemption. (If this form is for a child under age 18, see page 7 of the instructions.)

IF your filing status is . . .	AND line 28 is not over . . .	THEN enter on line 29 . . .
Single or head of household	$112,500	$42,500
Married filing jointly or qualifying widow(er)	150,000	62,550
Married filing separately	75,000	31,275

If line 28 is **over** the amount shown above for your filing status, see page 7 of the instructions. — **29**

30	Subtract line 29 from line 28. If more than zero **or** you are filing Form 2555 or 2555-EZ, go to line 31. If zero or less and you are not filing Form 2555 or 2555-EZ, enter -0- on lines 33 and 35 and skip the rest of Part II	30	
31	• If you are filing Form 2555 or 2555-EZ, see page 8 of the instructions for the amount to enter. • If you reported capital gain distributions directly on Form 1040, line 13; you reported qualified dividends on Form 1040, line 9b; **or** you had a gain on both lines 15 and 16 of Schedule D (Form 1040) (as refigured for the AMT, if necessary), complete Part III on the back and enter the amount from line 55 here. • **All others:** If line 30 is $175,000 or less ($87,500 or less if married filing separately), multiply line 30 by 26% (.26). Otherwise, multiply line 30 by 28% (.28) and subtract $3,500 ($1,750 if married filing separately) from the result.	31	
32	Alternative minimum tax foreign tax credit (see page 7 of the instructions)	32	
33	Tentative minimum tax. Subtract line 32 from line 31	33	
34	Tax from Form 1040, line 44 (minus any tax from Form 4972 and any foreign tax credit from Form 1040, line 47). If you used Schedule J to figure your tax, the amount for line 44 of Form 1040 must be refigured without using Schedule J (see page 9 of the instructions)	34	
35	**Alternative minimum tax.** Subtract line 34 from line 33. If zero or less, enter -0-. Enter here and on Form 1040, line 45	35	

For Paperwork Reduction Act Notice, see page 9 of the instructions. Cat. No. 13600G Form **6251** (2006)

Part III Tax Computation Using Maximum Capital Gains Rates

36 Enter the amount from Form 6251, line 30 36

37 Enter the amount from line 6 of the Qualified Dividends and Capital Gain Tax Worksheet in the instructions for Form 1040, line 44, or the amount from line 13 of the Schedule D Tax Worksheet on page D-9 of the instructions for Schedule D (Form 1040), whichever applies (as refigured for the AMT, if necessary) (see page 9 of the instructions) 37

38 Enter the amount from Schedule D (Form 1040), line 19 (as refigured for the AMT, if necessary) (see page 9 of the instructions) 38

39 If you did not complete a Schedule D Tax Worksheet for the regular tax or the AMT, enter the amount from line 37. Otherwise, add lines 37 and 38, and enter the **smaller** of that result or the amount from line 10 of the Schedule D Tax Worksheet (as refigured for the AMT, if necessary) 39

40 Enter the **smaller** of line 36 or line 39 40

41 Subtract line 40 from line 36 41

42 If line 41 is $175,000 or less ($87,500 or less if married filing separately), multiply line 41 by 26% (.26). Otherwise, multiply line 41 by 28% (.28) and subtract $3,500 ($1,750 if married filing separately) from the result . . . . . ▶ 42

43 Enter:
- $61,300 if married filing jointly or qualifying widow(er),
- $30,650 if single or married filing separately, or
- $41,050 if head of household.

} 43

44 Enter the amount from line 7 of the Qualified Dividends and Capital Gain Tax Worksheet in the instructions for Form 1040, line 44, or the amount from line 14 of the Schedule D Tax Worksheet on page D-9 of the instructions for Schedule D (Form 1040), whichever applies (as figured for the regular tax). If you did not complete either worksheet for the regular tax, enter -0- . . . 44

45 Subtract line 44 from line 43. If zero or less, enter -0- 45

46 Enter the **smaller** of line 36 or line 37 46

47 Enter the **smaller** of line 45 or line 46 47

48 Multiply line 47 by 5% (.05) . . . . . ▶ 48

49 Subtract line 47 from line 46 49

50 Multiply line 49 by 15% (.15) . . . . . ▶ 50

If line 38 is zero or blank, skip lines 51 and 52 and go to line 53. Otherwise, go to line 51.

51 Subtract line 46 from line 40 51

52 Multiply line 51 by 25% (.25) . . . . . ▶ 52

53 Add lines 42, 48, 50, and 52 53

54 If line 36 is $175,000 or less ($87,500 or less if married filing separately), multiply line 36 by 26% (.26). Otherwise, multiply line 36 by 28% (.28) and subtract $3,500 ($1,750 if married filing separately) from the result 54

55 Enter the **smaller** of line 53 or line 54 here and on line 31 55

Form **8829**

Department of the Treasury
Internal Revenue Service (99)

Expenses for Business Use of Your Home

▶ **File only with Schedule C (Form 1040). Use a separate Form 8829 for each home you used for business during the year.**

▶ **See separate instructions.**

OMB No. 1545-0074

2006

Attachment Sequence No. **66**

Name(s) of proprietor(s) | **Your social security number**

Part I Part of Your Home Used for Business

1	Area used regularly and exclusively for business, regularly for daycare, or for storage of inventory or product samples (see instructions)	1	
2	Total area of home	2	
3	Divide line 1 by line 2. Enter the result as a percentage	3	%
	• **For daycare facilities not used exclusively for business, also complete lines 4–6.**		
	• **All others, skip lines 4–6 and enter the amount from line 3 on line 7.**		
4	Multiply days used for daycare during year by hours used per day — 4: hr.		
5	Total hours available for use during the year (365 days × 24 hours) (see instructions) — 5: 8,760 hr.		
6	Divide line 4 by line 5. Enter the result as a decimal amount — 6: .		
7	Business percentage. For daycare facilities not used exclusively for business, multiply line 6 by line 3 (enter the result as a percentage). All others, enter the amount from line 3 ▶	7	%

Part II Figure Your Allowable Deduction

			(a) Direct expenses	(b) Indirect expenses		
8	Enter the amount from Schedule C, line 29, **plus** any net gain or (loss) derived from the business use of your home and shown on Schedule D or Form 4797. If more than one place of business, see instructions				8	
	See instructions for columns (a) and (b) before completing lines 9–20.					
9	Casualty losses (see instructions)	9				
10	Deductible mortgage interest (see instructions)	10				
11	Real estate taxes (see instructions)	11				
12	Add lines 9, 10, and 11	12				
13	Multiply line 12, column (b) by line 7		13			
14	Add line 12, column (a) and line 13				14	
15	Subtract line 14 from line 8. If zero or less, enter -0-				15	
16	Excess mortgage interest (see instructions)	16				
17	Insurance	17				
18	Repairs and maintenance	18				
19	Utilities	19				
20	Other expenses (see instructions)	20				
21	Add lines 16 through 20	21				
22	Multiply line 21, column (b) by line 7		22			
23	Carryover of operating expenses from 2005 Form 8829, line 41		23			
24	Add line 21 in column (a), line 22, and line 23				24	
25	Allowable operating expenses. Enter the **smaller** of line 15 or line 24				25	
26	Limit on excess casualty losses and depreciation. Subtract line 25 from line 15				26	
27	Excess casualty losses (see instructions)		27			
28	Depreciation of your home from Part III below		28			
29	Carryover of excess casualty losses and depreciation from 2005 Form 8829, line 42		29			
30	Add lines 27 through 29				30	
31	Allowable excess casualty losses and depreciation. Enter the **smaller** of line 26 or line 30				31	
32	Add lines 14, 25, and 31				32	
33	Casualty loss portion, if any, from lines 14 and 31. Carry amount to **Form 4684,** Section B				33	
34	Allowable expenses for business use of your home. Subtract line 33 from line 32. Enter here and on Schedule C, line 30. If your home was used for more than one business, see instructions ▶				34	

Part III Depreciation of Your Home

35	Enter the **smaller** of your home's adjusted basis or its fair market value (see instructions)	35	
36	Value of land included on line 35	36	
37	Basis of building. Subtract line 36 from line 35	37	
38	Business basis of building. Multiply line 37 by line 7	38	
39	Depreciation percentage (see instructions)	39	%
40	Depreciation allowable (see instructions). Multiply line 38 by line 39. Enter here and on line 28 above	40	

Part IV Carryover of Unallowed Expenses to 2007

41	Operating expenses. Subtract line 25 from line 24. If less than zero, enter -0-	41	
42	Excess casualty losses and depreciation. Subtract line 31 from line 30. If less than zero, enter -0-	42	

For Paperwork Reduction Act Notice, see page 4 of separate instructions. Cat. No. 13232M Form **8829** (2006)

Form **8863**

Department of the Treasury
Internal Revenue Service (99)

Education Credits (Hope and Lifetime Learning Credits)

▶ See instructions.
▶ Attach to Form 1040 or Form 1040A.

OMB No. 1545-0074
2006
Attachment Sequence No. 50

Name(s) shown on return | Your social security number

Caution: *You* ***cannot*** *take the Hope credit and the lifetime learning credit for the* ***same student*** *in the same year.*

Part I — Hope Credit. Caution: *You* ***cannot*** *take the Hope credit for more than* ***2*** *tax years for the* ***same student.***

1	**(a)** Student's name (as shown on page 1 of your tax return) First name / Last name	**(b)** Student's social security number (as shown on page 1 of your tax return)	**(c)** Qualified expenses (see instructions). **Do not** enter more than $2,200* for each student.	**(d)** Enter the **smaller** of the amount in column (c) or $1,100**	**(e)** Add column (c) and column (d)	**(f)** Enter one-half of the amount in column (e)

* For each student who attended an eligible educational institution in the Gulf Opportunity Zone, **do not** enter more than $4,400.
** For each student who attended an eligible educational institution in the Gulf Opportunity Zone, enter the **smaller** of the amount in column (c) or $2,200.

2 **Tentative Hope credit.** Add the amounts on line 1, column (f). If you are taking the lifetime learning credit for another student, go to Part II; otherwise, go to Part III . . . . ▶ **2**

Part II — Lifetime Learning Credit

3	**(a)** Student's name (as shown on page 1 of your tax return) First name / Last name	**(b)** Student's social security number (as shown on page 1 of your tax return)	**(c)** Qualified expenses (see instructions)

4 Add the amounts on line 3, column (c), and enter the total **4**

5a Enter the **smaller** of line 4 or $10,000 . . . . **5a**

b For students who attended an eligible educational institution in the Gulf Opportunity Zone, enter the smaller of $10,000 or their qualified expenses included on line 4 (see special rules on page 3) **5b**

c Subtract line 5b from line 5a **5c**

6a Multiply line 5b by 40% (.40) **6a**

b Multiply line 5c by 20% (.20) **6b**

c **Tentative lifetime learning credit.** Add lines 6a and 6b and go to Part III **6c**

Part III — Allowable Education Credits

7 Tentative education credits. Add lines 2 and 6c **7**

8 Enter: $110,000 if married filing jointly; $55,000 if single, head of household, or qualifying widow(er) **8**

9 Enter the amount from Form 1040, line 38*, or Form 1040A, line 22 . . **9**

10 Subtract line 9 from line 8. If zero or less, **stop;** you cannot take any education credits **10**

11 Enter: $20,000 if married filing jointly; $10,000 if single, head of household, or qualifying widow(er) **11**

12 If line 10 is equal to or more than line 11, enter the amount from line 7 on line 13 and go to line 14. If line 10 is less than line 11, divide line 10 by line 11. Enter the result as a decimal (rounded to at least three places) . . . . **12** × .

13 Multiply line 7 by line 12 . . . . ▶ **13**

14 Enter the amount from Form 1040, line 46, or Form 1040A, line 28 . . . . **14**

15 Enter the total, if any, of your credits from Form 1040, lines 47 through 49, or Form 1040A, lines 29 and 30 . . . . **15**

16 Subtract line 15 from line 14. If zero or less, **stop;** you cannot take any education credits **16**

17 **Education credits.** Enter the **smaller** of line 13 or line 16 here and on Form 1040, line 50, or Form 1040A, line 31 . . . . **17**

* If you are filing Form 2555, 2555-EZ, or 4563, or you are excluding income from Puerto Rico, see Pub. 970 for the amount to enter.

For Paperwork Reduction Act Notice, see page 4. Cat. No. 25379M Form **8863** (2006)

Form **8910**

Department of the Treasury
Internal Revenue Service

Alternative Motor Vehicle Credit

▶ **Attach to your tax return.**

OMB No. 1545-1998

2006

Attachment Sequence No. **152**

Name(s) shown on return	**Identifying number**

Part I Tentative Credit

Use a separate column for each vehicle. If you need more columns, use additional Forms 8910 and include the totals on lines 8 and 12.		(a)	(b)	(c)
1 Year, make, and model of vehicle	1			
2 Enter date vehicle was placed in service (MM/DD/YYYY)	2	/ /	/ /	/ /
3 Maximum credit allowable (see instructions)	3			
4 Phaseout percentage (see instructions)	4	%	%	%
5 **Tentative credit.** Multiply line 3 by line 4	5			

Part II Credit for Business/Investment Use Part of Vehicle

		(a)	(b)	(c)
6 Business/investment use percentage (see instructions)	6	%	%	%
7 Multiply line 5 by line 6	7			

8 Add columns (a) through (c) on line 7	8	
9 Alternative motor vehicle credit from partnerships and S corporations	9	
10 **Business/investment use part of credit.** Add lines 8 and 9. Partnerships and S corporations, report this amount on Schedule K; all others, report this amount on Form 3800, line 1v	10	

Part III Credit for Personal Use Part of Vehicle

		(a)	(b)	(c)
11 Subtract line 7 from line 5	11			

12 Add columns (a) through (c) on line 11			12	
13 Regular tax before credits: • Individuals. Enter the amount from Form 1040, line 44 (or Form 1040NR, line 41) • Other filers. Enter the regular tax before credits from your return			13	
14 Credits that reduce regular tax before the alternative motor vehicle credit:				
a Foreign tax credit	14a			
b Credits from Form 1040, lines 48 through 54 (or Form 1040NR, lines 45 through 49)	14b			
c Qualified electric vehicle credit (Form 8834, line 20)	14c			
d Add lines 14a through 14c			14d	
15 Net regular tax. Subtract line 14d from line 13. If zero or less, stop here; **do not** file this form unless you are claiming a credit on line 10			15	
16 Tentative minimum tax (see instructions): • Individuals. Enter the amount from Form 6251, line 33 • Other filers. Enter the tentative minimum tax from your alternative minimum tax form or schedule			16	
17 Subtract line 16 from line 15. If zero or less, stop here; **do not** file this form unless you are claiming a credit on line 10			17	
18 **Personal use part of credit.** Enter the **smaller** of line 12 or 17 here and on Form 1040, line 55; Form 1040NR, line 50; or the appropriate line of your return. If line 17 is smaller than line 12, see instructions			18	

For Paperwork Reduction Act Notice, see instructions. Cat. No. 37720F Form **8910** (2006)

2006 Tax Table

CAUTION *See the instructions for line 44 that begin on page 37 to see if you must use the Tax Table below to figure your tax.*

Example. Mr. and Mrs. Brown are filing a joint return. Their taxable income on Form 1040, line 43, is $25,300. First, they find the $25,300–25,350 taxable income line. Next, they find the column for married filing jointly and read down the column. The amount shown where the taxable income line and filing status column meet is $3,044. This is the tax amount they should enter on Form 1040, line 44.

Sample Table

At least	But less than	Single	Married filing jointly *	Married filing separately	Head of a household
		Your tax is—			
25,200	**25,250**	3,406	3,029	3,406	3,246
25,250	**25,300**	3,414	3,036	3,414	3,254
25,300	**25,350**	3,421	(3,044)	3,421	3,261
25,350	**25,400**	3,429	3,051	3,429	3,269

If line 43 (taxable income) is—		And you are—			
At least	But less than	Single	Married filing jointly *	Married filing separately	Head of a household
		Your tax is—			
0	**5**	0	0	0	0
5	**15**	1	1	1	1
15	**25**	2	2	2	2
25	**50**	4	4	4	4
50	**75**	6	6	6	6
75	**100**	9	9	9	9
100	**125**	11	11	11	11
125	**150**	14	14	14	14
150	**175**	16	16	16	16
175	**200**	19	19	19	19
200	**225**	21	21	21	21
225	**250**	24	24	24	24
250	**275**	26	26	26	26
275	**300**	29	29	29	29
300	**325**	31	31	31	31
325	**350**	34	34	34	34
350	**375**	36	36	36	36
375	**400**	39	39	39	39
400	**425**	41	41	41	41
425	**450**	44	44	44	44
450	**475**	46	46	46	46
475	**500**	49	49	49	49
500	**525**	51	51	51	51
525	**550**	54	54	54	54
550	**575**	56	56	56	56
575	**600**	59	59	59	59
600	**625**	61	61	61	61
625	**650**	64	64	64	64
650	**675**	66	66	66	66
675	**700**	69	69	69	69
700	**725**	71	71	71	71
725	**750**	74	74	74	74
750	**775**	76	76	76	76
775	**800**	79	79	79	79
800	**825**	81	81	81	81
825	**850**	84	84	84	84
850	**875**	86	86	86	86
875	**900**	89	89	89	89
900	**925**	91	91	91	91
925	**950**	94	94	94	94
950	**975**	96	96	96	96
975	**1,000**	99	99	99	99
1,000					
1,000	**1,025**	101	101	101	101
1,025	**1,050**	104	104	104	104
1,050	**1,075**	106	106	106	106
1,075	**1,100**	109	109	109	109
1,100	**1,125**	111	111	111	111
1,125	**1,150**	114	114	114	114
1,150	**1,175**	116	116	116	116
1,175	**1,200**	119	119	119	119
1,200	**1,225**	121	121	121	121
1,225	**1,250**	124	124	124	124
1,250	**1,275**	126	126	126	126
1,275	**1,300**	129	129	129	129

If line 43 (taxable income) is—		And you are—			
At least	But less than	Single	Married filing jointly *	Married filing separately	Head of a household
		Your tax is—			
1,300	**1,325**	131	131	131	131
1,325	**1,350**	134	134	134	134
1,350	**1,375**	136	136	136	136
1,375	**1,400**	139	139	139	139
1,400	**1,425**	141	141	141	141
1,425	**1,450**	144	144	144	144
1,450	**1,475**	146	146	146	146
1,475	**1,500**	149	149	149	149
1,500	**1,525**	151	151	151	151
1,525	**1,550**	154	154	154	154
1,550	**1,575**	156	156	156	156
1,575	**1,600**	159	159	159	159
1,600	**1,625**	161	161	161	161
1,625	**1,650**	164	164	164	164
1,650	**1,675**	166	166	166	166
1,675	**1,700**	169	169	169	169
1,700	**1,725**	171	171	171	171
1,725	**1,750**	174	174	174	174
1,750	**1,775**	176	176	176	176
1,775	**1,800**	179	179	179	179
1,800	**1,825**	181	181	181	181
1,825	**1,850**	184	184	184	184
1,850	**1,875**	186	186	186	186
1,875	**1,900**	189	189	189	189
1,900	**1,925**	191	191	191	191
1,925	**1,950**	194	194	194	194
1,950	**1,975**	196	196	196	196
1,975	**2,000**	199	199	199	199
2,000					
2,000	**2,025**	201	201	201	201
2,025	**2,050**	204	204	204	204
2,050	**2,075**	206	206	206	206
2,075	**2,100**	209	209	209	209
2,100	**2,125**	211	211	211	211
2,125	**2,150**	214	214	214	214
2,150	**2,175**	216	216	216	216
2,175	**2,200**	219	219	219	219
2,200	**2,225**	221	221	221	221
2,225	**2,250**	224	224	224	224
2,250	**2,275**	226	226	226	226
2,275	**2,300**	229	229	229	229
2,300	**2,325**	231	231	231	231
2,325	**2,350**	234	234	234	234
2,350	**2,375**	236	236	236	236
2,375	**2,400**	239	239	239	239
2,400	**2,425**	241	241	241	241
2,425	**2,450**	244	244	244	244
2,450	**2,475**	246	246	246	246
2,475	**2,500**	249	249	249	249
2,500	**2,525**	251	251	251	251
2,525	**2,550**	254	254	254	254
2,550	**2,575**	256	256	256	256
2,575	**2,600**	259	259	259	259
2,600	**2,625**	261	261	261	261
2,625	**2,650**	264	264	264	264
2,650	**2,675**	266	266	266	266
2,675	**2,700**	269	269	269	269

If line 43 (taxable income) is—		And you are—			
At least	But less than	Single	Married filing jointly *	Married filing separately	Head of a household
		Your tax is—			
2,700	**2,725**	271	271	271	271
2,725	**2,750**	274	274	274	274
2,750	**2,775**	276	276	276	276
2,775	**2,800**	279	279	279	279
2,800	**2,825**	281	281	281	281
2,825	**2,850**	284	284	284	284
2,850	**2,875**	286	286	286	286
2,875	**2,900**	289	289	289	289
2,900	**2,925**	291	291	291	291
2,925	**2,950**	294	294	294	294
2,950	**2,975**	296	296	296	296
2,975	**3,000**	299	299	299	299
3,000					
3,000	**3,050**	303	303	303	303
3,050	**3,100**	308	308	308	308
3,100	**3,150**	313	313	313	313
3,150	**3,200**	318	318	318	318
3,200	**3,250**	323	323	323	323
3,250	**3,300**	328	328	328	328
3,300	**3,350**	333	333	333	333
3,350	**3,400**	338	338	338	338
3,400	**3,450**	343	343	343	343
3,450	**3,500**	348	348	348	348
3,500	**3,550**	353	353	353	353
3,550	**3,600**	358	358	358	358
3,600	**3,650**	363	363	363	363
3,650	**3,700**	368	368	368	368
3,700	**3,750**	373	373	373	373
3,750	**3,800**	378	378	378	378
3,800	**3,850**	383	383	383	383
3,850	**3,900**	388	388	388	388
3,900	**3,950**	393	393	393	393
3,950	**4,000**	398	398	398	398
4,000					
4,000	**4,050**	403	403	403	403
4,050	**4,100**	408	408	408	408
4,100	**4,150**	413	413	413	413
4,150	**4,200**	418	418	418	418
4,200	**4,250**	423	423	423	423
4,250	**4,300**	428	428	428	428
4,300	**4,350**	433	433	433	433
4,350	**4,400**	438	438	438	438
4,400	**4,450**	443	443	443	443
4,450	**4,500**	448	448	448	448
4,500	**4,550**	453	453	453	453
4,550	**4,600**	458	458	458	458
4,600	**4,650**	463	463	463	463
4,650	**4,700**	468	468	468	468
4,700	**4,750**	473	473	473	473
4,750	**4,800**	478	478	478	478
4,800	**4,850**	483	483	483	483
4,850	**4,900**	488	488	488	488
4,900	**4,950**	493	493	493	493
4,950	**5,000**	498	498	498	498

* This column must also be used by a qualifying widow(er)

If line 43 (taxable income) is—		And you are—			
At least	But less than	Single	Married filing jointly *	Married filing separately	Head of a household
		Your tax is—			
5,000					
5,000	5,050	503	503	503	503
5,050	5,100	508	508	508	508
5,100	5,150	513	513	513	513
5,150	5,200	518	518	518	518
5,200	5,250	523	523	523	523
5,250	5,300	528	528	528	528
5,300	5,350	533	533	533	533
5,350	5,400	538	538	538	538
5,400	5,450	543	543	543	543
5,450	5,500	548	548	548	548
5,500	5,550	553	553	553	553
5,550	5,600	558	558	558	558
5,600	5,650	563	563	563	563
5,650	5,700	568	568	568	568
5,700	5,750	573	573	573	573
5,750	5,800	578	578	578	578
5,800	5,850	583	583	583	583
5,850	5,900	588	588	588	588
5,900	5,950	593	593	593	593
5,950	6,000	598	598	598	598
6,000					
6,000	6,050	603	603	603	603
6,050	6,100	608	608	608	608
6,100	6,150	613	613	613	613
6,150	6,200	618	618	618	618
6,200	6,250	623	623	623	623
6,250	6,300	628	628	628	628
6,300	6,350	633	633	633	633
6,350	6,400	638	638	638	638
6,400	6,450	643	643	643	643
6,450	6,500	648	648	648	648
6,500	6,550	653	653	653	653
6,550	6,600	658	658	658	658
6,600	6,650	663	663	663	663
6,650	6,700	668	668	668	668
6,700	6,750	673	673	673	673
6,750	6,800	678	678	678	678
6,800	6,850	683	683	683	683
6,850	6,900	688	688	688	688
6,900	6,950	693	693	693	693
6,950	7,000	698	698	698	698
7,000					
7,000	7,050	703	703	703	703
7,050	7,100	708	708	708	708
7,100	7,150	713	713	713	713
7,150	7,200	718	718	718	718
7,200	7,250	723	723	723	723
7,250	7,300	728	728	728	728
7,300	7,350	733	733	733	733
7,350	7,400	738	738	738	738
7,400	7,450	743	743	743	743
7,450	7,500	748	748	748	748
7,500	7,550	753	753	753	753
7,550	7,600	759	758	759	758
7,600	7,650	766	763	766	763
7,650	7,700	774	768	774	768
7,700	7,750	781	773	781	773
7,750	7,800	789	778	789	778
7,800	7,850	796	783	796	783
7,850	7,900	804	788	804	788
7,900	7,950	811	793	811	793
7,950	8,000	819	798	819	798

If line 43 (taxable income) is—		And you are—			
At least	But less than	Single	Married filing jointly *	Married filing separately	Head of a household
		Your tax is—			
8,000					
8,000	8,050	826	803	826	803
8,050	8,100	834	808	834	808
8,100	8,150	841	813	841	813
8,150	8,200	849	818	849	818
8,200	8,250	856	823	856	823
8,250	8,300	864	828	864	828
8,300	8,350	871	833	871	833
8,350	8,400	879	838	879	838
8,400	8,450	886	843	886	843
8,450	8,500	894	848	894	848
8,500	8,550	901	853	901	853
8,550	8,600	909	858	909	858
8,600	8,650	916	863	916	863
8,650	8,700	924	868	924	868
8,700	8,750	931	873	931	873
8,750	8,800	939	878	939	878
8,800	8,850	946	883	946	883
8,850	8,900	954	888	954	888
8,900	8,950	961	893	961	893
8,950	9,000	969	898	969	898
9,000					
9,000	9,050	976	903	976	903
9,050	9,100	984	908	984	908
9,100	9,150	991	913	991	913
9,150	9,200	999	918	999	918
9,200	9,250	1,006	923	1,006	923
9,250	9,300	1,014	928	1,014	928
9,300	9,350	1,021	933	1,021	933
9,350	9,400	1,029	938	1,029	938
9,400	9,450	1,036	943	1,036	943
9,450	9,500	1,044	948	1,044	948
9,500	9,550	1,051	953	1,051	953
9,550	9,600	1,059	958	1,059	958
9,600	9,650	1,066	963	1,066	963
9,650	9,700	1,074	968	1,074	968
9,700	9,750	1,081	973	1,081	973
9,750	9,800	1,089	978	1,089	978
9,800	9,850	1,096	983	1,096	983
9,850	9,900	1,104	988	1,104	988
9,900	9,950	1,111	993	1,111	993
9,950	10,000	1,119	998	1,119	998
10,000					
10,000	10,050	1,126	1,003	1,126	1,003
10,050	10,100	1,134	1,008	1,134	1,008
10,100	10,150	1,141	1,013	1,141	1,013
10,150	10,200	1,149	1,018	1,149	1,018
10,200	10,250	1,156	1,023	1,156	1,023
10,250	10,300	1,164	1,028	1,164	1,028
10,300	10,350	1,171	1,033	1,171	1,033
10,350	10,400	1,179	1,038	1,179	1,038
10,400	10,450	1,186	1,043	1,186	1,043
10,450	10,500	1,194	1,048	1,194	1,048
10,500	10,550	1,201	1,053	1,201	1,053
10,550	10,600	1,209	1,058	1,209	1,058
10,600	10,650	1,216	1,063	1,216	1,063
10,650	10,700	1,224	1,068	1,224	1,068
10,700	10,750	1,231	1,073	1,231	1,073
10,750	10,800	1,239	1,078	1,239	1,079
10,800	10,850	1,246	1,083	1,246	1,086
10,850	10,900	1,254	1,088	1,254	1,094
10,900	10,950	1,261	1,093	1,261	1,101
10,950	11,000	1,269	1,098	1,269	1,109

If line 43 (taxable income) is—		And you are—			
At least	But less than	Single	Married filing jointly *	Married filing separately	Head of a household
		Your tax is—			
11,000					
11,000	11,050	1,276	1,103	1,276	1,116
11,050	11,100	1,284	1,108	1,284	1,124
11,100	11,150	1,291	1,113	1,291	1,131
11,150	11,200	1,299	1,118	1,299	1,139
11,200	11,250	1,306	1,123	1,306	1,146
11,250	11,300	1,314	1,128	1,314	1,154
11,300	11,350	1,321	1,133	1,321	1,161
11,350	11,400	1,329	1,138	1,329	1,169
11,400	11,450	1,336	1,143	1,336	1,176
11,450	11,500	1,344	1,148	1,344	1,184
11,500	11,550	1,351	1,153	1,351	1,191
11,550	11,600	1,359	1,158	1,359	1,199
11,600	11,650	1,366	1,163	1,366	1,206
11,650	11,700	1,374	1,168	1,374	1,214
11,700	11,750	1,381	1,173	1,381	1,221
11,750	11,800	1,389	1,178	1,389	1,229
11,800	11,850	1,396	1,183	1,396	1,236
11,850	11,900	1,404	1,188	1,404	1,244
11,900	11,950	1,411	1,193	1,411	1,251
11,950	12,000	1,419	1,198	1,419	1,259
12,000					
12,000	12,050	1,426	1,203	1,426	1,266
12,050	12,100	1,434	1,208	1,434	1,274
12,100	12,150	1,441	1,213	1,441	1,281
12,150	12,200	1,449	1,218	1,449	1,289
12,200	12,250	1,456	1,223	1,456	1,296
12,250	12,300	1,464	1,228	1,464	1,304
12,300	12,350	1,471	1,233	1,471	1,311
12,350	12,400	1,479	1,238	1,479	1,319
12,400	12,450	1,486	1,243	1,486	1,326
12,450	12,500	1,494	1,248	1,494	1,334
12,500	12,550	1,501	1,253	1,501	1,341
12,550	12,600	1,509	1,258	1,509	1,349
12,600	12,650	1,516	1,263	1,516	1,356
12,650	12,700	1,524	1,268	1,524	1,364
12,700	12,750	1,531	1,273	1,531	1,371
12,750	12,800	1,539	1,278	1,539	1,379
12,800	12,850	1,546	1,283	1,546	1,386
12,850	12,900	1,554	1,288	1,554	1,394
12,900	12,950	1,561	1,293	1,561	1,401
12,950	13,000	1,569	1,298	1,569	1,409
13,000					
13,000	13,050	1,576	1,303	1,576	1,416
13,050	13,100	1,584	1,308	1,584	1,424
13,100	13,150	1,591	1,313	1,591	1,431
13,150	13,200	1,599	1,318	1,599	1,439
13,200	13,250	1,606	1,323	1,606	1,446
13,250	13,300	1,614	1,328	1,614	1,454
13,300	13,350	1,621	1,333	1,621	1,461
13,350	13,400	1,629	1,338	1,629	1,469
13,400	13,450	1,636	1,343	1,636	1,476
13,450	13,500	1,644	1,348	1,644	1,484
13,500	13,550	1,651	1,353	1,651	1,491
13,550	13,600	1,659	1,358	1,659	1,499
13,600	13,650	1,666	1,363	1,666	1,506
13,650	13,700	1,674	1,368	1,674	1,514
13,700	13,750	1,681	1,373	1,681	1,521
13,750	13,800	1,689	1,378	1,689	1,529
13,800	13,850	1,696	1,383	1,696	1,536
13,850	13,900	1,704	1,388	1,704	1,544
13,900	13,950	1,711	1,393	1,711	1,551
13,950	14,000	1,719	1,398	1,719	1,559

* This column must also be used by a qualifying widow(er)

If line 43 (taxable income) is— At least	But less than	Single	Married filing jointly *	Married filing separately	Head of a household
		Your tax is—			
14,000					
14,000	14,050	1,726	1,403	1,726	1,566
14,050	14,100	1,734	1,408	1,734	1,574
14,100	14,150	1,741	1,413	1,741	1,581
14,150	14,200	1,749	1,418	1,749	1,589
14,200	14,250	1,756	1,423	1,756	1,596
14,250	14,300	1,764	1,428	1,764	1,604
14,300	14,350	1,771	1,433	1,771	1,611
14,350	14,400	1,779	1,438	1,779	1,619
14,400	14,450	1,786	1,443	1,786	1,626
14,450	14,500	1,794	1,448	1,794	1,634
14,500	14,550	1,801	1,453	1,801	1,641
14,550	14,600	1,809	1,458	1,809	1,649
14,600	14,650	1,816	1,463	1,816	1,656
14,650	14,700	1,824	1,468	1,824	1,664
14,700	14,750	1,831	1,473	1,831	1,671
14,750	14,800	1,839	1,478	1,839	1,679
14,800	14,850	1,846	1,483	1,846	1,686
14,850	14,900	1,854	1,488	1,854	1,694
14,900	14,950	1,861	1,493	1,861	1,701
14,950	15,000	1,869	1,498	1,869	1,709
15,000					
15,000	15,050	1,876	1,503	1,876	1,716
15,050	15,100	1,884	1,508	1,884	1,724
15,100	15,150	1,891	1,514	1,891	1,731
15,150	15,200	1,899	1,521	1,899	1,739
15,200	15,250	1,906	1,529	1,906	1,746
15,250	15,300	1,914	1,536	1,914	1,754
15,300	15,350	1,921	1,544	1,921	1,761
15,350	15,400	1,929	1,551	1,929	1,769
15,400	15,450	1,936	1,559	1,936	1,776
15,450	15,500	1,944	1,566	1,944	1,784
15,500	15,550	1,951	1,574	1,951	1,791
15,550	15,600	1,959	1,581	1,959	1,799
15,600	15,650	1,966	1,589	1,966	1,806
15,650	15,700	1,974	1,596	1,974	1,814
15,700	15,750	1,981	1,604	1,981	1,821
15,750	15,800	1,989	1,611	1,989	1,829
15,800	15,850	1,996	1,619	1,996	1,836
15,850	15,900	2,004	1,626	2,004	1,844
15,900	15,950	2,011	1,634	2,011	1,851
15,950	16,000	2,019	1,641	2,019	1,859
16,000					
16,000	16,050	2,026	1,649	2,026	1,866
16,050	16,100	2,034	1,656	2,034	1,874
16,100	16,150	2,041	1,664	2,041	1,881
16,150	16,200	2,049	1,671	2,049	1,889
16,200	16,250	2,056	1,679	2,056	1,896
16,250	16,300	2,064	1,686	2,064	1,904
16,300	16,350	2,071	1,694	2,071	1,911
16,350	16,400	2,079	1,701	2,079	1,919
16,400	16,450	2,086	1,709	2,086	1,926
16,450	16,500	2,094	1,716	2,094	1,934
16,500	16,550	2,101	1,724	2,101	1,941
16,550	16,600	2,109	1,731	2,109	1,949
16,600	16,650	2,116	1,739	2,116	1,956
16,650	16,700	2,124	1,746	2,124	1,964
16,700	16,750	2,131	1,754	2,131	1,971
16,750	16,800	2,139	1,761	2,139	1,979
16,800	16,850	2,146	1,769	2,146	1,986
16,850	16,900	2,154	1,776	2,154	1,994
16,900	16,950	2,161	1,784	2,161	2,001
16,950	17,000	2,169	1,791	2,169	2,009

If line 43 (taxable income) is— At least	But less than	Single	Married filing jointly *	Married filing separately	Head of a household
		Your tax is—			
17,000					
17,000	17,050	2,176	1,799	2,176	2,016
17,050	17,100	2,184	1,806	2,184	2,024
17,100	17,150	2,191	1,814	2,191	2,031
17,150	17,200	2,199	1,821	2,199	2,039
17,200	17,250	2,206	1,829	2,206	2,046
17,250	17,300	2,214	1,836	2,214	2,054
17,300	17,350	2,221	1,844	2,221	2,061
17,350	17,400	2,229	1,851	2,229	2,069
17,400	17,450	2,236	1,859	2,236	2,076
17,450	17,500	2,244	1,866	2,244	2,084
17,500	17,550	2,251	1,874	2,251	2,091
17,550	17,600	2,259	1,881	2,259	2,099
17,600	17,650	2,266	1,889	2,266	2,106
17,650	17,700	2,274	1,896	2,274	2,114
17,700	17,750	2,281	1,904	2,281	2,121
17,750	17,800	2,289	1,911	2,289	2,129
17,800	17,850	2,296	1,919	2,296	2,136
17,850	17,900	2,304	1,926	2,304	2,144
17,900	17,950	2,311	1,934	2,311	2,151
17,950	18,000	2,319	1,941	2,319	2,159
18,000					
18,000	18,050	2,326	1,949	2,326	2,166
18,050	18,100	2,334	1,956	2,334	2,174
18,100	18,150	2,341	1,964	2,341	2,181
18,150	18,200	2,349	1,971	2,349	2,189
18,200	18,250	2,356	1,979	2,356	2,196
18,250	18,300	2,364	1,986	2,364	2,204
18,300	18,350	2,371	1,994	2,371	2,211
18,350	18,400	2,379	2,001	2,379	2,219
18,400	18,450	2,386	2,009	2,386	2,226
18,450	18,500	2,394	2,016	2,394	2,234
18,500	18,550	2,401	2,024	2,401	2,241
18,550	18,600	2,409	2,031	2,409	2,249
18,600	18,650	2,416	2,039	2,416	2,256
18,650	18,700	2,424	2,046	2,424	2,264
18,700	18,750	2,431	2,054	2,431	2,271
18,750	18,800	2,439	2,061	2,439	2,279
18,800	18,850	2,446	2,069	2,446	2,286
18,850	18,900	2,454	2,076	2,454	2,294
18,900	18,950	2,461	2,084	2,461	2,301
18,950	19,000	2,469	2,091	2,469	2,309
19,000					
19,000	19,050	2,476	2,099	2,476	2,316
19,050	19,100	2,484	2,106	2,484	2,324
19,100	19,150	2,491	2,114	2,491	2,331
19,150	19,200	2,499	2,121	2,499	2,339
19,200	19,250	2,506	2,129	2,506	2,346
19,250	19,300	2,514	2,136	2,514	2,354
19,300	19,350	2,521	2,144	2,521	2,361
19,350	19,400	2,529	2,151	2,529	2,369
19,400	19,450	2,536	2,159	2,536	2,376
19,450	19,500	2,544	2,166	2,544	2,384
19,500	19,550	2,551	2,174	2,551	2,391
19,550	19,600	2,559	2,181	2,559	2,399
19,600	19,650	2,566	2,189	2,566	2,406
19,650	19,700	2,574	2,196	2,574	2,414
19,700	19,750	2,581	2,204	2,581	2,421
19,750	19,800	2,589	2,211	2,589	2,429
19,800	19,850	2,596	2,219	2,596	2,436
19,850	19,900	2,604	2,226	2,604	2,444
19,900	19,950	2,611	2,234	2,611	2,451
19,950	20,000	2,619	2,241	2,619	2,459

If line 43 (taxable income) is— At least	But less than	Single	Married filing jointly *	Married filing separately	Head of a household
		Your tax is—			
20,000					
20,000	20,050	2,626	2,249	2,626	2,466
20,050	20,100	2,634	2,256	2,634	2,474
20,100	20,150	2,641	2,264	2,641	2,481
20,150	20,200	2,649	2,271	2,649	2,489
20,200	20,250	2,656	2,279	2,656	2,496
20,250	20,300	2,664	2,286	2,664	2,504
20,300	20,350	2,671	2,294	2,671	2,511
20,350	20,400	2,679	2,301	2,679	2,519
20,400	20,450	2,686	2,309	2,686	2,526
20,450	20,500	2,694	2,316	2,694	2,534
20,500	20,550	2,701	2,324	2,701	2,541
20,550	20,600	2,709	2,331	2,709	2,549
20,600	20,650	2,716	2,339	2,716	2,556
20,650	20,700	2,724	2,346	2,724	2,564
20,700	20,750	2,731	2,354	2,731	2,571
20,750	20,800	2,739	2,361	2,739	2,579
20,800	20,850	2,746	2,369	2,746	2,586
20,850	20,900	2,754	2,376	2,754	2,594
20,900	20,950	2,761	2,384	2,761	2,601
20,950	21,000	2,769	2,391	2,769	2,609
21,000					
21,000	21,050	2,776	2,399	2,776	2,616
21,050	21,100	2,784	2,406	2,784	2,624
21,100	21,150	2,791	2,414	2,791	2,631
21,150	21,200	2,799	2,421	2,799	2,639
21,200	21,250	2,806	2,429	2,806	2,646
21,250	21,300	2,814	2,436	2,814	2,654
21,300	21,350	2,821	2,444	2,821	2,661
21,350	21,400	2,829	2,451	2,829	2,669
21,400	21,450	2,836	2,459	2,836	2,676
21,450	21,500	2,844	2,466	2,844	2,684
21,500	21,550	2,851	2,474	2,851	2,691
21,550	21,600	2,859	2,481	2,859	2,699
21,600	21,650	2,866	2,489	2,866	2,706
21,650	21,700	2,874	2,496	2,874	2,714
21,700	21,750	2,881	2,504	2,881	2,721
21,750	21,800	2,889	2,511	2,889	2,729
21,800	21,850	2,896	2,519	2,896	2,736
21,850	21,900	2,904	2,526	2,904	2,744
21,900	21,950	2,911	2,534	2,911	2,751
21,950	22,000	2,919	2,541	2,919	2,759
22,000					
22,000	22,050	2,926	2,549	2,926	2,766
22,050	22,100	2,934	2,556	2,934	2,774
22,100	22,150	2,941	2,564	2,941	2,781
22,150	22,200	2,949	2,571	2,949	2,789
22,200	22,250	2,956	2,579	2,956	2,796
22,250	22,300	2,964	2,586	2,964	2,804
22,300	22,350	2,971	2,594	2,971	2,811
22,350	22,400	2,979	2,601	2,979	2,819
22,400	22,450	2,986	2,609	2,986	2,826
22,450	22,500	2,994	2,616	2,994	2,834
22,500	22,550	3,001	2,624	3,001	2,841
22,550	22,600	3,009	2,631	3,009	2,849
22,600	22,650	3,016	2,639	3,016	2,856
22,650	22,700	3,024	2,646	3,024	2,864
22,700	22,750	3,031	2,654	3,031	2,871
22,750	22,800	3,039	2,661	3,039	2,879
22,800	22,850	3,046	2,669	3,046	2,886
22,850	22,900	3,054	2,676	3,054	2,894
22,900	22,950	3,061	2,684	3,061	2,901
22,950	23,000	3,069	2,691	3,069	2,909

* This column must also be used by a qualifying widow(er)

If line 43 (taxable income) is—		And you are—			
At least	But less than	Single	Married filing jointly *	Married filing separately	Head of a household
		Your tax is—			
23,000					
23,000	**23,050**	3,076	2,699	3,076	2,916
23,050	**23,100**	3,084	2,706	3,084	2,924
23,100	**23,150**	3,091	2,714	3,091	2,931
23,150	**23,200**	3,099	2,721	3,099	2,939
23,200	**23,250**	3,106	2,729	3,106	2,946
23,250	**23,300**	3,114	2,736	3,114	2,954
23,300	**23,350**	3,121	2,744	3,121	2,961
23,350	**23,400**	3,129	2,751	3,129	2,969
23,400	**23,450**	3,136	2,759	3,136	2,976
23,450	**23,500**	3,144	2,766	3,144	2,984
23,500	**23,550**	3,151	2,774	3,151	2,991
23,550	**23,600**	3,159	2,781	3,159	2,999
23,600	**23,650**	3,166	2,789	3,166	3,006
23,650	**23,700**	3,174	2,796	3,174	3,014
23,700	**23,750**	3,181	2,804	3,181	3,021
23,750	**23,800**	3,189	2,811	3,189	3,029
23,800	**23,850**	3,196	2,819	3,196	3,036
23,850	**23,900**	3,204	2,826	3,204	3,044
23,900	**23,950**	3,211	2,834	3,211	3,051
23,950	**24,000**	3,219	2,841	3,219	3,059
24,000					
24,000	**24,050**	3,226	2,849	3,226	3,066
24,050	**24,100**	3,234	2,856	3,234	3,074
24,100	**24,150**	3,241	2,864	3,241	3,081
24,150	**24,200**	3,249	2,871	3,249	3,089
24,200	**24,250**	3,256	2,879	3,256	3,096
24,250	**24,300**	3,264	2,886	3,264	3,104
24,300	**24,350**	3,271	2,894	3,271	3,111
24,350	**24,400**	3,279	2,901	3,279	3,119
24,400	**24,450**	3,286	2,909	3,286	3,126
24,450	**24,500**	3,294	2,916	3,294	3,134
24,500	**24,550**	3,301	2,924	3,301	3,141
24,550	**24,600**	3,309	2,931	3,309	3,149
24,600	**24,650**	3,316	2,939	3,316	3,156
24,650	**24,700**	3,324	2,946	3,324	3,164
24,700	**24,750**	3,331	2,954	3,331	3,171
24,750	**24,800**	3,339	2,961	3,339	3,179
24,800	**24,850**	3,346	2,969	3,346	3,186
24,850	**24,900**	3,354	2,976	3,354	3,194
24,900	**24,950**	3,361	2,984	3,361	3,201
24,950	**25,000**	3,369	2,991	3,369	3,209
25,000					
25,000	**25,050**	3,376	2,999	3,376	3,216
25,050	**25,100**	3,384	3,006	3,384	3,224
25,100	**25,150**	3,391	3,014	3,391	3,231
25,150	**25,200**	3,399	3,021	3,399	3,239
25,200	**25,250**	3,406	3,029	3,406	3,246
25,250	**25,300**	3,414	3,036	3,414	3,254
25,300	**25,350**	3,421	3,044	3,421	3,261
25,350	**25,400**	3,429	3,051	3,429	3,269
25,400	**25,450**	3,436	3,059	3,436	3,276
25,450	**25,500**	3,444	3,066	3,444	3,284
25,500	**25,550**	3,451	3,074	3,451	3,291
25,550	**25,600**	3,459	3,081	3,459	3,299
25,600	**25,650**	3,466	3,089	3,466	3,306
25,650	**25,700**	3,474	3,096	3,474	3,314
25,700	**25,750**	3,481	3,104	3,481	3,321
25,750	**25,800**	3,489	3,111	3,489	3,329
25,800	**25,850**	3,496	3,119	3,496	3,336
25,850	**25,900**	3,504	3,126	3,504	3,344
25,900	**25,950**	3,511	3,134	3,511	3,351
25,950	**26,000**	3,519	3,141	3,519	3,359

If line 43 (taxable income) is—		And you are—			
At least	But less than	Single	Married filing jointly *	Married filing separately	Head of a household
		Your tax is—			
26,000					
26,000	**26,050**	3,526	3,149	3,526	3,366
26,050	**26,100**	3,534	3,156	3,534	3,374
26,100	**26,150**	3,541	3,164	3,541	3,381
26,150	**26,200**	3,549	3,171	3,549	3,389
26,200	**26,250**	3,556	3,179	3,556	3,396
26,250	**26,300**	3,564	3,186	3,564	3,404
26,300	**26,350**	3,571	3,194	3,571	3,411
26,350	**26,400**	3,579	3,201	3,579	3,419
26,400	**26,450**	3,586	3,209	3,586	3,426
26,450	**26,500**	3,594	3,216	3,594	3,434
26,500	**26,550**	3,601	3,224	3,601	3,441
26,550	**26,600**	3,609	3,231	3,609	3,449
26,600	**26,650**	3,616	3,239	3,616	3,456
26,650	**26,700**	3,624	3,246	3,624	3,464
26,700	**26,750**	3,631	3,254	3,631	3,471
26,750	**26,800**	3,639	3,261	3,639	3,479
26,800	**26,850**	3,646	3,269	3,646	3,486
26,850	**26,900**	3,654	3,276	3,654	3,494
26,900	**26,950**	3,661	3,284	3,661	3,501
26,950	**27,000**	3,669	3,291	3,669	3,509
27,000					
27,000	**27,050**	3,676	3,299	3,676	3,516
27,050	**27,100**	3,684	3,306	3,684	3,524
27,100	**27,150**	3,691	3,314	3,691	3,531
27,150	**27,200**	3,699	3,321	3,699	3,539
27,200	**27,250**	3,706	3,329	3,706	3,546
27,250	**27,300**	3,714	3,336	3,714	3,554
27,300	**27,350**	3,721	3,344	3,721	3,561
27,350	**27,400**	3,729	3,351	3,729	3,569
27,400	**27,450**	3,736	3,359	3,736	3,576
27,450	**27,500**	3,744	3,366	3,744	3,584
27,500	**27,550**	3,751	3,374	3,751	3,591
27,550	**27,600**	3,759	3,381	3,759	3,599
27,600	**27,650**	3,766	3,389	3,766	3,606
27,650	**27,700**	3,774	3,396	3,774	3,614
27,700	**27,750**	3,781	3,404	3,781	3,621
27,750	**27,800**	3,789	3,411	3,789	3,629
27,800	**27,850**	3,796	3,419	3,796	3,636
27,850	**27,900**	3,804	3,426	3,804	3,644
27,900	**27,950**	3,811	3,434	3,811	3,651
27,950	**28,000**	3,819	3,441	3,819	3,659
28,000					
28,000	**28,050**	3,826	3,449	3,826	3,666
28,050	**28,100**	3,834	3,456	3,834	3,674
28,100	**28,150**	3,841	3,464	3,841	3,681
28,150	**28,200**	3,849	3,471	3,849	3,689
28,200	**28,250**	3,856	3,479	3,856	3,696
28,250	**28,300**	3,864	3,486	3,864	3,704
28,300	**28,350**	3,871	3,494	3,871	3,711
28,350	**28,400**	3,879	3,501	3,879	3,719
28,400	**28,450**	3,886	3,509	3,886	3,726
28,450	**28,500**	3,894	3,516	3,894	3,734
28,500	**28,550**	3,901	3,524	3,901	3,741
28,550	**28,600**	3,909	3,531	3,909	3,749
28,600	**28,650**	3,916	3,539	3,916	3,756
28,650	**28,700**	3,924	3,546	3,924	3,764
28,700	**28,750**	3,931	3,554	3,931	3,771
28,750	**28,800**	3,939	3,561	3,939	3,779
28,800	**28,850**	3,946	3,569	3,946	3,786
28,850	**28,900**	3,954	3,576	3,954	3,794
28,900	**28,950**	3,961	3,584	3,961	3,801
28,950	**29,000**	3,969	3,591	3,969	3,809

If line 43 (taxable income) is—		And you are—			
At least	But less than	Single	Married filing jointly *	Married filing separately	Head of a household
		Your tax is—			
29,000					
29,000	**29,050**	3,976	3,599	3,976	3,816
29,050	**29,100**	3,984	3,606	3,984	3,824
29,100	**29,150**	3,991	3,614	3,991	3,831
29,150	**29,200**	3,999	3,621	3,999	3,839
29,200	**29,250**	4,006	3,629	4,006	3,846
29,250	**29,300**	4,014	3,636	4,014	3,854
29,300	**29,350**	4,021	3,644	4,021	3,861
29,350	**29,400**	4,029	3,651	4,029	3,869
29,400	**29,450**	4,036	3,659	4,036	3,876
29,450	**29,500**	4,044	3,666	4,044	3,884
29,500	**29,550**	4,051	3,674	4,051	3,891
29,550	**29,600**	4,059	3,681	4,059	3,899
29,600	**29,650**	4,066	3,689	4,066	3,906
29,650	**29,700**	4,074	3,696	4,074	3,914
29,700	**29,750**	4,081	3,704	4,081	3,921
29,750	**29,800**	4,089	3,711	4,089	3,929
29,800	**29,850**	4,096	3,719	4,096	3,936
29,850	**29,900**	4,104	3,726	4,104	3,944
29,900	**29,950**	4,111	3,734	4,111	3,951
29,950	**30,000**	4,119	3,741	4,119	3,959
30,000					
30,000	**30,050**	4,126	3,749	4,126	3,966
30,050	**30,100**	4,134	3,756	4,134	3,974
30,100	**30,150**	4,141	3,764	4,141	3,981
30,150	**30,200**	4,149	3,771	4,149	3,989
30,200	**30,250**	4,156	3,779	4,156	3,996
30,250	**30,300**	4,164	3,786	4,164	4,004
30,300	**30,350**	4,171	3,794	4,171	4,011
30,350	**30,400**	4,179	3,801	4,179	4,019
30,400	**30,450**	4,186	3,809	4,186	4,026
30,450	**30,500**	4,194	3,816	4,194	4,034
30,500	**30,550**	4,201	3,824	4,201	4,041
30,550	**30,600**	4,209	3,831	4,209	4,049
30,600	**30,650**	4,216	3,839	4,216	4,056
30,650	**30,700**	4,226	3,846	4,226	4,064
30,700	**30,750**	4,239	3,854	4,239	4,071
30,750	**30,800**	4,251	3,861	4,251	4,079
30,800	**30,850**	4,264	3,869	4,264	4,086
30,850	**30,900**	4,276	3,876	4,276	4,094
30,900	**30,950**	4,289	3,884	4,289	4,101
30,950	**31,000**	4,301	3,891	4,301	4,109
31,000					
31,000	**31,050**	4,314	3,899	4,314	4,116
31,050	**31,100**	4,326	3,906	4,326	4,124
31,100	**31,150**	4,339	3,914	4,339	4,131
31,150	**31,200**	4,351	3,921	4,351	4,139
31,200	**31,250**	4,364	3,929	4,364	4,146
31,250	**31,300**	4,376	3,936	4,376	4,154
31,300	**31,350**	4,389	3,944	4,389	4,161
31,350	**31,400**	4,401	3,951	4,401	4,169
31,400	**31,450**	4,414	3,959	4,414	4,176
31,450	**31,500**	4,426	3,966	4,426	4,184
31,500	**31,550**	4,439	3,974	4,439	4,191
31,550	**31,600**	4,451	3,981	4,451	4,199
31,600	**31,650**	4,464	3,989	4,464	4,206
31,650	**31,700**	4,476	3,996	4,476	4,214
31,700	**31,750**	4,489	4,004	4,489	4,221
31,750	**31,800**	4,501	4,011	4,501	4,229
31,800	**31,850**	4,514	4,019	4,514	4,236
31,850	**31,900**	4,526	4,026	4,526	4,244
31,900	**31,950**	4,539	4,034	4,539	4,251
31,950	**32,000**	4,551	4,041	4,551	4,259

* This column must also be used by a qualifying widow(er)

If line 43 (taxable income) is—		And you are—			
At least	But less than	Single	Married filing jointly *	Married filing separately	Head of a household
		Your tax is—			
32,000					
32,000	32,050	4,564	4,049	4,564	4,266
32,050	32,100	4,576	4,056	4,576	4,274
32,100	32,150	4,589	4,064	4,589	4,281
32,150	32,200	4,601	4,071	4,601	4,289
32,200	32,250	4,614	4,079	4,614	4,296
32,250	32,300	4,626	4,086	4,626	4,304
32,300	32,350	4,639	4,094	4,639	4,311
32,350	32,400	4,651	4,101	4,651	4,319
32,400	32,450	4,664	4,109	4,664	4,326
32,450	32,500	4,676	4,116	4,676	4,334
32,500	32,550	4,689	4,124	4,689	4,341
32,550	32,600	4,701	4,131	4,701	4,349
32,600	32,650	4,714	4,139	4,714	4,356
32,650	32,700	4,726	4,146	4,726	4,364
32,700	32,750	4,739	4,154	4,739	4,371
32,750	32,800	4,751	4,161	4,751	4,379
32,800	32,850	4,764	4,169	4,764	4,386
32,850	32,900	4,776	4,176	4,776	4,394
32,900	32,950	4,789	4,184	4,789	4,401
32,950	33,000	4,801	4,191	4,801	4,409
33,000					
33,000	33,050	4,814	4,199	4,814	4,416
33,050	33,100	4,826	4,206	4,826	4,424
33,100	33,150	4,839	4,214	4,839	4,431
33,150	33,200	4,851	4,221	4,851	4,439
33,200	33,250	4,864	4,229	4,864	4,446
33,250	33,300	4,876	4,236	4,876	4,454
33,300	33,350	4,889	4,244	4,889	4,461
33,350	33,400	4,901	4,251	4,901	4,469
33,400	33,450	4,914	4,259	4,914	4,476
33,450	33,500	4,926	4,266	4,926	4,484
33,500	33,550	4,939	4,274	4,939	4,491
33,550	33,600	4,951	4,281	4,951	4,499
33,600	33,650	4,964	4,289	4,964	4,506
33,650	33,700	4,976	4,296	4,976	4,514
33,700	33,750	4,989	4,304	4,989	4,521
33,750	33,800	5,001	4,311	5,001	4,529
33,800	33,850	5,014	4,319	5,014	4,536
33,850	33,900	5,026	4,326	5,026	4,544
33,900	33,950	5,039	4,334	5,039	4,551
33,950	34,000	5,051	4,341	5,051	4,559
34,000					
34,000	34,050	5,064	4,349	5,064	4,566
34,050	34,100	5,076	4,356	5,076	4,574
34,100	34,150	5,089	4,364	5,089	4,581
34,150	34,200	5,101	4,371	5,101	4,589
34,200	34,250	5,114	4,379	5,114	4,596
34,250	34,300	5,126	4,386	5,126	4,604
34,300	34,350	5,139	4,394	5,139	4,611
34,350	34,400	5,151	4,401	5,151	4,619
34,400	34,450	5,164	4,409	5,164	4,626
34,450	34,500	5,176	4,416	5,176	4,634
34,500	34,550	5,189	4,424	5,189	4,641
34,550	34,600	5,201	4,431	5,201	4,649
34,600	34,650	5,214	4,439	5,214	4,656
34,650	34,700	5,226	4,446	5,226	4,664
34,700	34,750	5,239	4,454	5,239	4,671
34,750	34,800	5,251	4,461	5,251	4,679
34,800	34,850	5,264	4,469	5,264	4,686
34,850	34,900	5,276	4,476	5,276	4,694
34,900	34,950	5,289	4,484	5,289	4,701
34,950	35,000	5,301	4,491	5,301	4,709

If line 43 (taxable income) is—		And you are—			
At least	But less than	Single	Married filing jointly *	Married filing separately	Head of a household
		Your tax is—			
35,000					
35,000	35,050	5,314	4,499	5,314	4,716
35,050	35,100	5,326	4,506	5,326	4,724
35,100	35,150	5,339	4,514	5,339	4,731
35,150	35,200	5,351	4,521	5,351	4,739
35,200	35,250	5,364	4,529	5,364	4,746
35,250	35,300	5,376	4,536	5,376	4,754
35,300	35,350	5,389	4,544	5,389	4,761
35,350	35,400	5,401	4,551	5,401	4,769
35,400	35,450	5,414	4,559	5,414	4,776
35,450	35,500	5,426	4,566	5,426	4,784
35,500	35,550	5,439	4,574	5,439	4,791
35,550	35,600	5,451	4,581	5,451	4,799
35,600	35,650	5,464	4,589	5,464	4,806
35,650	35,700	5,476	4,596	5,476	4,814
35,700	35,750	5,489	4,604	5,489	4,821
35,750	35,800	5,501	4,611	5,501	4,829
35,800	35,850	5,514	4,619	5,514	4,836
35,850	35,900	5,526	4,626	5,526	4,844
35,900	35,950	5,539	4,634	5,539	4,851
35,950	36,000	5,551	4,641	5,551	4,859
36,000					
36,000	36,050	5,564	4,649	5,564	4,866
36,050	36,100	5,576	4,656	5,576	4,874
36,100	36,150	5,589	4,664	5,589	4,881
36,150	36,200	5,601	4,671	5,601	4,889
36,200	36,250	5,614	4,679	5,614	4,896
36,250	36,300	5,626	4,686	5,626	4,904
36,300	36,350	5,639	4,694	5,639	4,911
36,350	36,400	5,651	4,701	5,651	4,919
36,400	36,450	5,664	4,709	5,664	4,926
36,450	36,500	5,676	4,716	5,676	4,934
36,500	36,550	5,689	4,724	5,689	4,941
36,550	36,600	5,701	4,731	5,701	4,949
36,600	36,650	5,714	4,739	5,714	4,956
36,650	36,700	5,726	4,746	5,726	4,964
36,700	36,750	5,739	4,754	5,739	4,971
36,750	36,800	5,751	4,761	5,751	4,979
36,800	36,850	5,764	4,769	5,764	4,986
36,850	36,900	5,776	4,776	5,776	4,994
36,900	36,950	5,789	4,784	5,789	5,001
36,950	37,000	5,801	4,791	5,801	5,009
37,000					
37,000	37,050	5,814	4,799	5,814	5,016
37,050	37,100	5,826	4,806	5,826	5,024
37,100	37,150	5,839	4,814	5,839	5,031
37,150	37,200	5,851	4,821	5,851	5,039
37,200	37,250	5,864	4,829	5,864	5,046
37,250	37,300	5,876	4,836	5,876	5,054
37,300	37,350	5,889	4,844	5,889	5,061
37,350	37,400	5,901	4,851	5,901	5,069
37,400	37,450	5,914	4,859	5,914	5,076
37,450	37,500	5,926	4,866	5,926	5,084
37,500	37,550	5,939	4,874	5,939	5,091
37,550	37,600	5,951	4,881	5,951	5,099
37,600	37,650	5,964	4,889	5,964	5,106
37,650	37,700	5,976	4,896	5,976	5,114
37,700	37,750	5,989	4,904	5,989	5,121
37,750	37,800	6,001	4,911	6,001	5,129
37,800	37,850	6,014	4,919	6,014	5,136
37,850	37,900	6,026	4,926	6,026	5,144
37,900	37,950	6,039	4,934	6,039	5,151
37,950	38,000	6,051	4,941	6,051	5,159

If line 43 (taxable income) is—		And you are—			
At least	But less than	Single	Married filing jointly *	Married filing separately	Head of a household
		Your tax is—			
38,000					
38,000	38,050	6,064	4,949	6,064	5,166
38,050	38,100	6,076	4,956	6,076	5,174
38,100	38,150	6,089	4,964	6,089	5,181
38,150	38,200	6,101	4,971	6,101	5,189
38,200	38,250	6,114	4,979	6,114	5,196
38,250	38,300	6,126	4,986	6,126	5,204
38,300	38,350	6,139	4,994	6,139	5,211
38,350	38,400	6,151	5,001	6,151	5,219
38,400	38,450	6,164	5,009	6,164	5,226
38,450	38,500	6,176	5,016	6,176	5,234
38,500	38,550	6,189	5,024	6,189	5,241
38,550	38,600	6,201	5,031	6,201	5,249
38,600	38,650	6,214	5,039	6,214	5,256
38,650	38,700	6,226	5,046	6,226	5,264
38,700	38,750	6,239	5,054	6,239	5,271
38,750	38,800	6,251	5,061	6,251	5,279
38,800	38,850	6,264	5,069	6,264	5,286
38,850	38,900	6,276	5,076	6,276	5,294
38,900	38,950	6,289	5,084	6,289	5,301
38,950	39,000	6,301	5,091	6,301	5,309
39,000					
39,000	39,050	6,314	5,099	6,314	5,316
39,050	39,100	6,326	5,106	6,326	5,324
39,100	39,150	6,339	5,114	6,339	5,331
39,150	39,200	6,351	5,121	6,351	5,339
39,200	39,250	6,364	5,129	6,364	5,346
39,250	39,300	6,376	5,136	6,376	5,354
39,300	39,350	6,389	5,144	6,389	5,361
39,350	39,400	6,401	5,151	6,401	5,369
39,400	39,450	6,414	5,159	6,414	5,376
39,450	39,500	6,426	5,166	6,426	5,384
39,500	39,550	6,439	5,174	6,439	5,391
39,550	39,600	6,451	5,181	6,451	5,399
39,600	39,650	6,464	5,189	6,464	5,406
39,650	39,700	6,476	5,196	6,476	5,414
39,700	39,750	6,489	5,204	6,489	5,421
39,750	39,800	6,501	5,211	6,501	5,429
39,800	39,850	6,514	5,219	6,514	5,436
39,850	39,900	6,526	5,226	6,526	5,444
39,900	39,950	6,539	5,234	6,539	5,451
39,950	40,000	6,551	5,241	6,551	5,459
40,000					
40,000	40,050	6,564	5,249	6,564	5,466
40,050	40,100	6,576	5,256	6,576	5,474
40,100	40,150	6,589	5,264	6,589	5,481
40,150	40,200	6,601	5,271	6,601	5,489
40,200	40,250	6,614	5,279	6,614	5,496
40,250	40,300	6,626	5,286	6,626	5,504
40,300	40,350	6,639	5,294	6,639	5,511
40,350	40,400	6,651	5,301	6,651	5,519
40,400	40,450	6,664	5,309	6,664	5,526
40,450	40,500	6,676	5,316	6,676	5,534
40,500	40,550	6,689	5,324	6,689	5,541
40,550	40,600	6,701	5,331	6,701	5,549
40,600	40,650	6,714	5,339	6,714	5,556
40,650	40,700	6,726	5,346	6,726	5,564
40,700	40,750	6,739	5,354	6,739	5,571
40,750	40,800	6,751	5,361	6,751	5,579
40,800	40,850	6,764	5,369	6,764	5,586
40,850	40,900	6,776	5,376	6,776	5,594
40,900	40,950	6,789	5,384	6,789	5,601
40,950	41,000	6,801	5,391	6,801	5,609

* This column must also be used by a qualifying widow(er)

If line 43 (taxable income) is—		And you are—			
At least	But less than	Single	Married filing jointly *	Married filing separately	Head of a household
		Your tax is—			
41,000					
41,000	**41,050**	6,814	5,399	6,814	5,616
41,050	**41,100**	6,826	5,406	6,826	5,626
41,100	**41,150**	6,839	5,414	6,839	5,639
41,150	**41,200**	6,851	5,421	6,851	5,651
41,200	**41,250**	6,864	5,429	6,864	5,664
41,250	**41,300**	6,876	5,436	6,876	5,676
41,300	**41,350**	6,889	5,444	6,889	5,689
41,350	**41,400**	6,901	5,451	6,901	5,701
41,400	**41,450**	6,914	5,459	6,914	5,714
41,450	**41,500**	6,926	5,466	6,926	5,726
41,500	**41,550**	6,939	5,474	6,939	5,739
41,550	**41,600**	6,951	5,481	6,951	5,751
41,600	**41,650**	6,964	5,489	6,964	5,764
41,650	**41,700**	6,976	5,496	6,976	5,776
41,700	**41,750**	6,989	5,504	6,989	5,789
41,750	**41,800**	7,001	5,511	7,001	5,801
41,800	**41,850**	7,014	5,519	7,014	5,814
41,850	**41,900**	7,026	5,526	7,026	5,826
41,900	**41,950**	7,039	5,534	7,039	5,839
41,950	**42,000**	7,051	5,541	7,051	5,851
42,000					
42,000	**42,050**	7,064	5,549	7,064	5,864
42,050	**42,100**	7,076	5,556	7,076	5,876
42,100	**42,150**	7,089	5,564	7,089	5,889
42,150	**42,200**	7,101	5,571	7,101	5,901
42,200	**42,250**	7,114	5,579	7,114	5,914
42,250	**42,300**	7,126	5,586	7,126	5,926
42,300	**42,350**	7,139	5,594	7,139	5,939
42,350	**42,400**	7,151	5,601	7,151	5,951
42,400	**42,450**	7,164	5,609	7,164	5,964
42,450	**42,500**	7,176	5,616	7,176	5,976
42,500	**42,550**	7,189	5,624	7,189	5,989
42,550	**42,600**	7,201	5,631	7,201	6,001
42,600	**42,650**	7,214	5,639	7,214	6,014
42,650	**42,700**	7,226	5,646	7,226	6,026
42,700	**42,750**	7,239	5,654	7,239	6,039
42,750	**42,800**	7,251	5,661	7,251	6,051
42,800	**42,850**	7,264	5,669	7,264	6,064
42,850	**42,900**	7,276	5,676	7,276	6,076
42,900	**42,950**	7,289	5,684	7,289	6,089
42,950	**43,000**	7,301	5,691	7,301	6,101
43,000					
43,000	**43,050**	7,314	5,699	7,314	6,114
43,050	**43,100**	7,326	5,706	7,326	6,126
43,100	**43,150**	7,339	5,714	7,339	6,139
43,150	**43,200**	7,351	5,721	7,351	6,151
43,200	**43,250**	7,364	5,729	7,364	6,164
43,250	**43,300**	7,376	5,736	7,376	6,176
43,300	**43,350**	7,389	5,744	7,389	6,189
43,350	**43,400**	7,401	5,751	7,401	6,201
43,400	**43,450**	7,414	5,759	7,414	6,214
43,450	**43,500**	7,426	5,766	7,426	6,226
43,500	**43,550**	7,439	5,774	7,439	6,239
43,550	**43,600**	7,451	5,781	7,451	6,251
43,600	**43,650**	7,464	5,789	7,464	6,264
43,650	**43,700**	7,476	5,796	7,476	6,276
43,700	**43,750**	7,489	5,804	7,489	6,289
43,750	**43,800**	7,501	5,811	7,501	6,301
43,800	**43,850**	7,514	5,819	7,514	6,314
43,850	**43,900**	7,526	5,826	7,526	6,326
43,900	**43,950**	7,539	5,834	7,539	6,339
43,950	**44,000**	7,551	5,841	7,551	6,351
44,000					
44,000	**44,050**	7,564	5,849	7,564	6,364
44,050	**44,100**	7,576	5,856	7,576	6,376
44,100	**44,150**	7,589	5,864	7,589	6,389
44,150	**44,200**	7,601	5,871	7,601	6,401
44,200	**44,250**	7,614	5,879	7,614	6,414
44,250	**44,300**	7,626	5,886	7,626	6,426
44,300	**44,350**	7,639	5,894	7,639	6,439
44,350	**44,400**	7,651	5,901	7,651	6,451
44,400	**44,450**	7,664	5,909	7,664	6,464
44,450	**44,500**	7,676	5,916	7,676	6,476
44,500	**44,550**	7,689	5,924	7,689	6,489
44,550	**44,600**	7,701	5,931	7,701	6,501
44,600	**44,650**	7,714	5,939	7,714	6,514
44,650	**44,700**	7,726	5,946	7,726	6,526
44,700	**44,750**	7,739	5,954	7,739	6,539
44,750	**44,800**	7,751	5,961	7,751	6,551
44,800	**44,850**	7,764	5,969	7,764	6,564
44,850	**44,900**	7,776	5,976	7,776	6,576
44,900	**44,950**	7,789	5,984	7,789	6,589
44,950	**45,000**	7,801	5,991	7,801	6,601
45,000					
45,000	**45,050**	7,814	5,999	7,814	6,614
45,050	**45,100**	7,826	6,006	7,826	6,626
45,100	**45,150**	7,839	6,014	7,839	6,639
45,150	**45,200**	7,851	6,021	7,851	6,651
45,200	**45,250**	7,864	6,029	7,864	6,664
45,250	**45,300**	7,876	6,036	7,876	6,676
45,300	**45,350**	7,889	6,044	7,889	6,689
45,350	**45,400**	7,901	6,051	7,901	6,701
45,400	**45,450**	7,914	6,059	7,914	6,714
45,450	**45,500**	7,926	6,066	7,926	6,726
45,500	**45,550**	7,939	6,074	7,939	6,739
45,550	**45,600**	7,951	6,081	7,951	6,751
45,600	**45,650**	7,964	6,089	7,964	6,764
45,650	**45,700**	7,976	6,096	7,976	6,776
45,700	**45,750**	7,989	6,104	7,989	6,789
45,750	**45,800**	8,001	6,111	8,001	6,801
45,800	**45,850**	8,014	6,119	8,014	6,814
45,850	**45,900**	8,026	6,126	8,026	6,826
45,900	**45,950**	8,039	6,134	8,039	6,839
45,950	**46,000**	8,051	6,141	8,051	6,851
46,000					
46,000	**46,050**	8,064	6,149	8,064	6,864
46,050	**46,100**	8,076	6,156	8,076	6,876
46,100	**46,150**	8,089	6,164	8,089	6,889
46,150	**46,200**	8,101	6,171	8,101	6,901
46,200	**46,250**	8,114	6,179	8,114	6,914
46,250	**46,300**	8,126	6,186	8,126	6,926
46,300	**46,350**	8,139	6,194	8,139	6,939
46,350	**46,400**	8,151	6,201	8,151	6,951
46,400	**46,450**	8,164	6,209	8,164	6,964
46,450	**46,500**	8,176	6,216	8,176	6,976
46,500	**46,550**	8,189	6,224	8,189	6,989
46,550	**46,600**	8,201	6,231	8,201	7,001
46,600	**46,650**	8,214	6,239	8,214	7,014
46,650	**46,700**	8,226	6,246	8,226	7,026
46,700	**46,750**	8,239	6,254	8,239	7,039
46,750	**46,800**	8,251	6,261	8,251	7,051
46,800	**46,850**	8,264	6,269	8,264	7,064
46,850	**46,900**	8,276	6,276	8,276	7,076
46,900	**46,950**	8,289	6,284	8,289	7,089
46,950	**47,000**	8,301	6,291	8,301	7,101
47,000					
47,000	**47,050**	8,314	6,299	8,314	7,114
47,050	**47,100**	8,326	6,306	8,326	7,126
47,100	**47,150**	8,339	6,314	8,339	7,139
47,150	**47,200**	8,351	6,321	8,351	7,151
47,200	**47,250**	8,364	6,329	8,364	7,164
47,250	**47,300**	8,376	6,336	8,376	7,176
47,300	**47,350**	8,389	6,344	8,389	7,189
47,350	**47,400**	8,401	6,351	8,401	7,201
47,400	**47,450**	8,414	6,359	8,414	7,214
47,450	**47,500**	8,426	6,366	8,426	7,226
47,500	**47,550**	8,439	6,374	8,439	7,239
47,550	**47,600**	8,451	6,381	8,451	7,251
47,600	**47,650**	8,464	6,389	8,464	7,264
47,650	**47,700**	8,476	6,396	8,476	7,276
47,700	**47,750**	8,489	6,404	8,489	7,289
47,750	**47,800**	8,501	6,411	8,501	7,301
47,800	**47,850**	8,514	6,419	8,514	7,314
47,850	**47,900**	8,526	6,426	8,526	7,326
47,900	**47,950**	8,539	6,434	8,539	7,339
47,950	**48,000**	8,551	6,441	8,551	7,351
48,000					
48,000	**48,050**	8,564	6,449	8,564	7,364
48,050	**48,100**	8,576	6,456	8,576	7,376
48,100	**48,150**	8,589	6,464	8,589	7,389
48,150	**48,200**	8,601	6,471	8,601	7,401
48,200	**48,250**	8,614	6,479	8,614	7,414
48,250	**48,300**	8,626	6,486	8,626	7,426
48,300	**48,350**	8,639	6,494	8,639	7,439
48,350	**48,400**	8,651	6,501	8,651	7,451
48,400	**48,450**	8,664	6,509	8,664	7,464
48,450	**48,500**	8,676	6,516	8,676	7,476
48,500	**48,550**	8,689	6,524	8,689	7,489
48,550	**48,600**	8,701	6,531	8,701	7,501
48,600	**48,650**	8,714	6,539	8,714	7,514
48,650	**48,700**	8,726	6,546	8,726	7,526
48,700	**48,750**	8,739	6,554	8,739	7,539
48,750	**48,800**	8,751	6,561	8,751	7,551
48,800	**48,850**	8,764	6,569	8,764	7,564
48,850	**48,900**	8,776	6,576	8,776	7,576
48,900	**48,950**	8,789	6,584	8,789	7,589
48,950	**49,000**	8,801	6,591	8,801	7,601
49,000					
49,000	**49,050**	8,814	6,599	8,814	7,614
49,050	**49,100**	8,826	6,606	8,826	7,626
49,100	**49,150**	8,839	6,614	8,839	7,639
49,150	**49,200**	8,851	6,621	8,851	7,651
49,200	**49,250**	8,864	6,629	8,864	7,664
49,250	**49,300**	8,876	6,636	8,876	7,676
49,300	**49,350**	8,889	6,644	8,889	7,689
49,350	**49,400**	8,901	6,651	8,901	7,701
49,400	**49,450**	8,914	6,659	8,914	7,714
49,450	**49,500**	8,926	6,666	8,926	7,726
49,500	**49,550**	8,939	6,674	8,939	7,739
49,550	**49,600**	8,951	6,681	8,951	7,751
49,600	**49,650**	8,964	6,689	8,964	7,764
49,650	**49,700**	8,976	6,696	8,976	7,776
49,700	**49,750**	8,989	6,704	8,989	7,789
49,750	**49,800**	9,001	6,711	9,001	7,801
49,800	**49,850**	9,014	6,719	9,014	7,814
49,850	**49,900**	9,026	6,726	9,026	7,826
49,900	**49,950**	9,039	6,734	9,039	7,839
49,950	**50,000**	9,051	6,741	9,051	7,851

* This column must also be used by a qualifying widow(er)

If line 43 (taxable income) is—		And you are—			
At least	But less than	Single	Married filing jointly *	Married filing separately	Head of a household
		Your tax is—			
50,000					
50,000	**50,050**	9,064	6,749	9,064	7,864
50,050	**50,100**	9,076	6,756	9,076	7,876
50,100	**50,150**	9,089	6,764	9,089	7,889
50,150	**50,200**	9,101	6,771	9,101	7,901
50,200	**50,250**	9,114	6,779	9,114	7,914
50,250	**50,300**	9,126	6,786	9,126	7,926
50,300	**50,350**	9,139	6,794	9,139	7,939
50,350	**50,400**	9,151	6,801	9,151	7,951
50,400	**50,450**	9,164	6,809	9,164	7,964
50,450	**50,500**	9,176	6,816	9,176	7,976
50,500	**50,550**	9,189	6,824	9,189	7,989
50,550	**50,600**	9,201	6,831	9,201	8,001
50,600	**50,650**	9,214	6,839	9,214	8,014
50,650	**50,700**	9,226	6,846	9,226	8,026
50,700	**50,750**	9,239	6,854	9,239	8,039
50,750	**50,800**	9,251	6,861	9,251	8,051
50,800	**50,850**	9,264	6,869	9,264	8,064
50,850	**50,900**	9,276	6,876	9,276	8,076
50,900	**50,950**	9,289	6,884	9,289	8,089
50,950	**51,000**	9,301	6,891	9,301	8,101
51,000					
51,000	**51,050**	9,314	6,899	9,314	8,114
51,050	**51,100**	9,326	6,906	9,326	8,126
51,100	**51,150**	9,339	6,914	9,339	8,139
51,150	**51,200**	9,351	6,921	9,351	8,151
51,200	**51,250**	9,364	6,929	9,364	8,164
51,250	**51,300**	9,376	6,936	9,376	8,176
51,300	**51,350**	9,389	6,944	9,389	8,189
51,350	**51,400**	9,401	6,951	9,401	8,201
51,400	**51,450**	9,414	6,959	9,414	8,214
51,450	**51,500**	9,426	6,966	9,426	8,226
51,500	**51,550**	9,439	6,974	9,439	8,239
51,550	**51,600**	9,451	6,981	9,451	8,251
51,600	**51,650**	9,464	6,989	9,464	8,264
51,650	**51,700**	9,476	6,996	9,476	8,276
51,700	**51,750**	9,489	7,004	9,489	8,289
51,750	**51,800**	9,501	7,011	9,501	8,301
51,800	**51,850**	9,514	7,019	9,514	8,314
51,850	**51,900**	9,526	7,026	9,526	8,326
51,900	**51,950**	9,539	7,034	9,539	8,339
51,950	**52,000**	9,551	7,041	9,551	8,351
52,000					
52,000	**52,050**	9,564	7,049	9,564	8,364
52,050	**52,100**	9,576	7,056	9,576	8,376
52,100	**52,150**	9,589	7,064	9,589	8,389
52,150	**52,200**	9,601	7,071	9,601	8,401
52,200	**52,250**	9,614	7,079	9,614	8,414
52,250	**52,300**	9,626	7,086	9,626	8,426
52,300	**52,350**	9,639	7,094	9,639	8,439
52,350	**52,400**	9,651	7,101	9,651	8,451
52,400	**52,450**	9,664	7,109	9,664	8,464
52,450	**52,500**	9,676	7,116	9,676	8,476
52,500	**52,550**	9,689	7,124	9,689	8,489
52,550	**52,600**	9,701	7,131	9,701	8,501
52,600	**52,650**	9,714	7,139	9,714	8,514
52,650	**52,700**	9,726	7,146	9,726	8,526
52,700	**52,750**	9,739	7,154	9,739	8,539
52,750	**52,800**	9,751	7,161	9,751	8,551
52,800	**52,850**	9,764	7,169	9,764	8,564
52,850	**52,900**	9,776	7,176	9,776	8,576
52,900	**52,950**	9,789	7,184	9,789	8,589
52,950	**53,000**	9,801	7,191	9,801	8,601

If line 43 (taxable income) is—		And you are—			
At least	But less than	Single	Married filing jointly *	Married filing separately	Head of a household
		Your tax is—			
53,000					
53,000	**53,050**	9,814	7,199	9,814	8,614
53,050	**53,100**	9,826	7,206	9,826	8,626
53,100	**53,150**	9,839	7,214	9,839	8,639
53,150	**53,200**	9,851	7,221	9,851	8,651
53,200	**53,250**	9,864	7,229	9,864	8,664
53,250	**53,300**	9,876	7,236	9,876	8,676
53,300	**53,350**	9,889	7,244	9,889	8,689
53,350	**53,400**	9,901	7,251	9,901	8,701
53,400	**53,450**	9,914	7,259	9,914	8,714
53,450	**53,500**	9,926	7,266	9,926	8,726
53,500	**53,550**	9,939	7,274	9,939	8,739
53,550	**53,600**	9,951	7,281	9,951	8,751
53,600	**53,650**	9,964	7,289	9,964	8,764
53,650	**53,700**	9,976	7,296	9,976	8,776
53,700	**53,750**	9,989	7,304	9,989	8,789
53,750	**53,800**	10,001	7,311	10,001	8,801
53,800	**53,850**	10,014	7,319	10,014	8,814
53,850	**53,900**	10,026	7,326	10,026	8,826
53,900	**53,950**	10,039	7,334	10,039	8,839
53,950	**54,000**	10,051	7,341	10,051	8,851
54,000					
54,000	**54,050**	10,064	7,349	10,064	8,864
54,050	**54,100**	10,076	7,356	10,076	8,876
54,100	**54,150**	10,089	7,364	10,089	8,889
54,150	**54,200**	10,101	7,371	10,101	8,901
54,200	**54,250**	10,114	7,379	10,114	8,914
54,250	**54,300**	10,126	7,386	10,126	8,926
54,300	**54,350**	10,139	7,394	10,139	8,939
54,350	**54,400**	10,151	7,401	10,151	8,951
54,400	**54,450**	10,164	7,409	10,164	8,964
54,450	**54,500**	10,176	7,416	10,176	8,976
54,500	**54,550**	10,189	7,424	10,189	8,989
54,550	**54,600**	10,201	7,431	10,201	9,001
54,600	**54,650**	10,214	7,439	10,214	9,014
54,650	**54,700**	10,226	7,446	10,226	9,026
54,700	**54,750**	10,239	7,454	10,239	9,039
54,750	**54,800**	10,251	7,461	10,251	9,051
54,800	**54,850**	10,264	7,469	10,264	9,064
54,850	**54,900**	10,276	7,476	10,276	9,076
54,900	**54,950**	10,289	7,484	10,289	9,089
54,950	**55,000**	10,301	7,491	10,301	9,101
55,000					
55,000	**55,050**	10,314	7,499	10,314	9,114
55,050	**55,100**	10,326	7,506	10,326	9,126
55,100	**55,150**	10,339	7,514	10,339	9,139
55,150	**55,200**	10,351	7,521	10,351	9,151
55,200	**55,250**	10,364	7,529	10,364	9,164
55,250	**55,300**	10,376	7,536	10,376	9,176
55,300	**55,350**	10,389	7,544	10,389	9,189
55,350	**55,400**	10,401	7,551	10,401	9,201
55,400	**55,450**	10,414	7,559	10,414	9,214
55,450	**55,500**	10,426	7,566	10,426	9,226
55,500	**55,550**	10,439	7,574	10,439	9,239
55,550	**55,600**	10,451	7,581	10,451	9,251
55,600	**55,650**	10,464	7,589	10,464	9,264
55,650	**55,700**	10,476	7,596	10,476	9,276
55,700	**55,750**	10,489	7,604	10,489	9,289
55,750	**55,800**	10,501	7,611	10,501	9,301
55,800	**55,850**	10,514	7,619	10,514	9,314
55,850	**55,900**	10,526	7,626	10,526	9,326
55,900	**55,950**	10,539	7,634	10,539	9,339
55,950	**56,000**	10,551	7,641	10,551	9,351

If line 43 (taxable income) is—		And you are—			
At least	But less than	Single	Married filing jointly *	Married filing separately	Head of a household
		Your tax is—			
56,000					
56,000	**56,050**	10,564	7,649	10,564	9,364
56,050	**56,100**	10,576	7,656	10,576	9,376
56,100	**56,150**	10,589	7,664	10,589	9,389
56,150	**56,200**	10,601	7,671	10,601	9,401
56,200	**56,250**	10,614	7,679	10,614	9,414
56,250	**56,300**	10,626	7,686	10,626	9,426
56,300	**56,350**	10,639	7,694	10,639	9,439
56,350	**56,400**	10,651	7,701	10,651	9,451
56,400	**56,450**	10,664	7,709	10,664	9,464
56,450	**56,500**	10,676	7,716	10,676	9,476
56,500	**56,550**	10,689	7,724	10,689	9,489
56,550	**56,600**	10,701	7,731	10,701	9,501
56,600	**56,650**	10,714	7,739	10,714	9,514
56,650	**56,700**	10,726	7,746	10,726	9,526
56,700	**56,750**	10,739	7,754	10,739	9,539
56,750	**56,800**	10,751	7,761	10,751	9,551
56,800	**56,850**	10,764	7,769	10,764	9,564
56,850	**56,900**	10,776	7,776	10,776	9,576
56,900	**56,950**	10,789	7,784	10,789	9,589
56,950	**57,000**	10,801	7,791	10,801	9,601
57,000					
57,000	**57,050**	10,814	7,799	10,814	9,614
57,050	**57,100**	10,826	7,806	10,826	9,626
57,100	**57,150**	10,839	7,814	10,839	9,639
57,150	**57,200**	10,851	7,821	10,851	9,651
57,200	**57,250**	10,864	7,829	10,864	9,664
57,250	**57,300**	10,876	7,836	10,876	9,676
57,300	**57,350**	10,889	7,844	10,889	9,689
57,350	**57,400**	10,901	7,851	10,901	9,701
57,400	**57,450**	10,914	7,859	10,914	9,714
57,450	**57,500**	10,926	7,866	10,926	9,726
57,500	**57,550**	10,939	7,874	10,939	9,739
57,550	**57,600**	10,951	7,881	10,951	9,751
57,600	**57,650**	10,964	7,889	10,964	9,764
57,650	**57,700**	10,976	7,896	10,976	9,776
57,700	**57,750**	10,989	7,904	10,989	9,789
57,750	**57,800**	11,001	7,911	11,001	9,801
57,800	**57,850**	11,014	7,919	11,014	9,814
57,850	**57,900**	11,026	7,926	11,026	9,826
57,900	**57,950**	11,039	7,934	11,039	9,839
57,950	**58,000**	11,051	7,941	11,051	9,851
58,000					
58,000	**58,050**	11,064	7,949	11,064	9,864
58,050	**58,100**	11,076	7,956	11,076	9,876
58,100	**58,150**	11,089	7,964	11,089	9,889
58,150	**58,200**	11,101	7,971	11,101	9,901
58,200	**58,250**	11,114	7,979	11,114	9,914
58,250	**58,300**	11,126	7,986	11,126	9,926
58,300	**58,350**	11,139	7,994	11,139	9,939
58,350	**58,400**	11,151	8,001	11,151	9,951
58,400	**58,450**	11,164	8,009	11,164	9,964
58,450	**58,500**	11,176	8,016	11,176	9,976
58,500	**58,550**	11,189	8,024	11,189	9,989
58,550	**58,600**	11,201	8,031	11,201	10,001
58,600	**58,650**	11,214	8,039	11,214	10,014
58,650	**58,700**	11,226	8,046	11,226	10,026
58,700	**58,750**	11,239	8,054	11,239	10,039
58,750	**58,800**	11,251	8,061	11,251	10,051
58,800	**58,850**	11,264	8,069	11,264	10,064
58,850	**58,900**	11,276	8,076	11,276	10,076
58,900	**58,950**	11,289	8,084	11,289	10,089
58,950	**59,000**	11,301	8,091	11,301	10,101

* This column must also be used by a qualifying widow(er)

If line 43 (taxable income) is—		And you are—			
At least	But less than	Single	Married filing jointly *	Married filing separately	Head of a household
		Your tax is—			
59,000					
59,000	**59,050**	11,314	8,099	11,314	10,114
59,050	**59,100**	11,326	8,106	11,326	10,126
59,100	**59,150**	11,339	8,114	11,339	10,139
59,150	**59,200**	11,351	8,121	11,351	10,151
59,200	**59,250**	11,364	8,129	11,364	10,164
59,250	**59,300**	11,376	8,136	11,376	10,176
59,300	**59,350**	11,389	8,144	11,389	10,189
59,350	**59,400**	11,401	8,151	11,401	10,201
59,400	**59,450**	11,414	8,159	11,414	10,214
59,450	**59,500**	11,426	8,166	11,426	10,226
59,500	**59,550**	11,439	8,174	11,439	10,239
59,550	**59,600**	11,451	8,181	11,451	10,251
59,600	**59,650**	11,464	8,189	11,464	10,264
59,650	**59,700**	11,476	8,196	11,476	10,276
59,700	**59,750**	11,489	8,204	11,489	10,289
59,750	**59,800**	11,501	8,211	11,501	10,301
59,800	**59,850**	11,514	8,219	11,514	10,314
59,850	**59,900**	11,526	8,226	11,526	10,326
59,900	**59,950**	11,539	8,234	11,539	10,339
59,950	**60,000**	11,551	8,241	11,551	10,351
60,000					
60,000	**60,050**	11,564	8,249	11,564	10,364
60,050	**60,100**	11,576	8,256	11,576	10,376
60,100	**60,150**	11,589	8,264	11,589	10,389
60,150	**60,200**	11,601	8,271	11,601	10,401
60,200	**60,250**	11,614	8,279	11,614	10,414
60,250	**60,300**	11,626	8,286	11,626	10,426
60,300	**60,350**	11,639	8,294	11,639	10,439
60,350	**60,400**	11,651	8,301	11,651	10,451
60,400	**60,450**	11,664	8,309	11,664	10,464
60,450	**60,500**	11,676	8,316	11,676	10,476
60,500	**60,550**	11,689	8,324	11,689	10,489
60,550	**60,600**	11,701	8,331	11,701	10,501
60,600	**60,650**	11,714	8,339	11,714	10,514
60,650	**60,700**	11,726	8,346	11,726	10,526
60,700	**60,750**	11,739	8,354	11,739	10,539
60,750	**60,800**	11,751	8,361	11,751	10,551
60,800	**60,850**	11,764	8,369	11,764	10,564
60,850	**60,900**	11,776	8,376	11,776	10,576
60,900	**60,950**	11,789	8,384	11,789	10,589
60,950	**61,000**	11,801	8,391	11,801	10,601
61,000					
61,000	**61,050**	11,814	8,399	11,814	10,614
61,050	**61,100**	11,826	8,406	11,826	10,626
61,100	**61,150**	11,839	8,414	11,839	10,639
61,150	**61,200**	11,851	8,421	11,851	10,651
61,200	**61,250**	11,864	8,429	11,864	10,664
61,250	**61,300**	11,876	8,436	11,876	10,676
61,300	**61,350**	11,889	8,446	11,889	10,689
61,350	**61,400**	11,901	8,459	11,901	10,701
61,400	**61,450**	11,914	8,471	11,914	10,714
61,450	**61,500**	11,926	8,484	11,926	10,726
61,500	**61,550**	11,939	8,496	11,939	10,739
61,550	**61,600**	11,951	8,509	11,951	10,751
61,600	**61,650**	11,964	8,521	11,964	10,764
61,650	**61,700**	11,976	8,534	11,976	10,776
61,700	**61,750**	11,989	8,546	11,989	10,789
61,750	**61,800**	12,001	8,559	12,001	10,801
61,800	**61,850**	12,014	8,571	12,014	10,814
61,850	**61,900**	12,026	8,584	12,027	10,826
61,900	**61,950**	12,039	8,596	12,041	10,839
61,950	**62,000**	12,051	8,609	12,055	10,851

If line 43 (taxable income) is—		And you are—			
At least	But less than	Single	Married filing jointly *	Married filing separately	Head of a household
		Your tax is—			
62,000					
62,000	**62,050**	12,064	8,621	12,069	10,864
62,050	**62,100**	12,076	8,634	12,083	10,876
62,100	**62,150**	12,089	8,646	12,097	10,889
62,150	**62,200**	12,101	8,659	12,111	10,901
62,200	**62,250**	12,114	8,671	12,125	10,914
62,250	**62,300**	12,126	8,684	12,139	10,926
62,300	**62,350**	12,139	8,696	12,153	10,939
62,350	**62,400**	12,151	8,709	12,167	10,951
62,400	**62,450**	12,164	8,721	12,181	10,964
62,450	**62,500**	12,176	8,734	12,195	10,976
62,500	**62,550**	12,189	8,746	12,209	10,989
62,550	**62,600**	12,201	8,759	12,223	11,001
62,600	**62,650**	12,214	8,771	12,237	11,014
62,650	**62,700**	12,226	8,784	12,251	11,026
62,700	**62,750**	12,239	8,796	12,265	11,039
62,750	**62,800**	12,251	8,809	12,279	11,051
62,800	**62,850**	12,264	8,821	12,293	11,064
62,850	**62,900**	12,276	8,834	12,307	11,076
62,900	**62,950**	12,289	8,846	12,321	11,089
62,950	**63,000**	12,301	8,859	12,335	11,101
63,000					
63,000	**63,050**	12,314	8,871	12,349	11,114
63,050	**63,100**	12,326	8,884	12,363	11,126
63,100	**63,150**	12,339	8,896	12,377	11,139
63,150	**63,200**	12,351	8,909	12,391	11,151
63,200	**63,250**	12,364	8,921	12,405	11,164
63,250	**63,300**	12,376	8,934	12,419	11,176
63,300	**63,350**	12,389	8,946	12,433	11,189
63,350	**63,400**	12,401	8,959	12,447	11,201
63,400	**63,450**	12,414	8,971	12,461	11,214
63,450	**63,500**	12,426	8,984	12,475	11,226
63,500	**63,550**	12,439	8,996	12,489	11,239
63,550	**63,600**	12,451	9,009	12,503	11,251
63,600	**63,650**	12,464	9,021	12,517	11,264
63,650	**63,700**	12,476	9,034	12,531	11,276
63,700	**63,750**	12,489	9,046	12,545	11,289
63,750	**63,800**	12,501	9,059	12,559	11,301
63,800	**63,850**	12,514	9,071	12,573	11,314
63,850	**63,900**	12,526	9,084	12,587	11,326
63,900	**63,950**	12,539	9,096	12,601	11,339
63,950	**64,000**	12,551	9,109	12,615	11,351
64,000					
64,000	**64,050**	12,564	9,121	12,629	11,364
64,050	**64,100**	12,576	9,134	12,643	11,376
64,100	**64,150**	12,589	9,146	12,657	11,389
64,150	**64,200**	12,601	9,159	12,671	11,401
64,200	**64,250**	12,614	9,171	12,685	11,414
64,250	**64,300**	12,626	9,184	12,699	11,426
64,300	**64,350**	12,639	9,196	12,713	11,439
64,350	**64,400**	12,651	9,209	12,727	11,451
64,400	**64,450**	12,664	9,221	12,741	11,464
64,450	**64,500**	12,676	9,234	12,755	11,476
64,500	**64,550**	12,689	9,246	12,769	11,489
64,550	**64,600**	12,701	9,259	12,783	11,501
64,600	**64,650**	12,714	9,271	12,797	11,514
64,650	**64,700**	12,726	9,284	12,811	11,526
64,700	**64,750**	12,739	9,296	12,825	11,539
64,750	**64,800**	12,751	9,309	12,839	11,551
64,800	**64,850**	12,764	9,321	12,853	11,564
64,850	**64,900**	12,776	9,334	12,867	11,576
64,900	**64,950**	12,789	9,346	12,881	11,589
64,950	**65,000**	12,801	9,359	12,895	11,601

If line 43 (taxable income) is—		And you are—			
At least	But less than	Single	Married filing jointly *	Married filing separately	Head of a household
		Your tax is—			
65,000					
65,000	**65,050**	12,814	9,371	12,909	11,614
65,050	**65,100**	12,826	9,384	12,923	11,626
65,100	**65,150**	12,839	9,396	12,937	11,639
65,150	**65,200**	12,851	9,409	12,951	11,651
65,200	**65,250**	12,864	9,421	12,965	11,664
65,250	**65,300**	12,876	9,434	12,979	11,676
65,300	**65,350**	12,889	9,446	12,993	11,689
65,350	**65,400**	12,901	9,459	13,007	11,701
65,400	**65,450**	12,914	9,471	13,021	11,714
65,450	**65,500**	12,926	9,484	13,035	11,726
65,500	**65,550**	12,939	9,496	13,049	11,739
65,550	**65,600**	12,951	9,509	13,063	11,751
65,600	**65,650**	12,964	9,521	13,077	11,764
65,650	**65,700**	12,976	9,534	13,091	11,776
65,700	**65,750**	12,989	9,546	13,105	11,789
65,750	**65,800**	13,001	9,559	13,119	11,801
65,800	**65,850**	13,014	9,571	13,133	11,814
65,850	**65,900**	13,026	9,584	13,147	11,826
65,900	**65,950**	13,039	9,596	13,161	11,839
65,950	**66,000**	13,051	9,609	13,175	11,851
66,000					
66,000	**66,050**	13,064	9,621	13,189	11,864
66,050	**66,100**	13,076	9,634	13,203	11,876
66,100	**66,150**	13,089	9,646	13,217	11,889
66,150	**66,200**	13,101	9,659	13,231	11,901
66,200	**66,250**	13,114	9,671	13,245	11,914
66,250	**66,300**	13,126	9,684	13,259	11,926
66,300	**66,350**	13,139	9,696	13,273	11,939
66,350	**66,400**	13,151	9,709	13,287	11,951
66,400	**66,450**	13,164	9,721	13,301	11,964
66,450	**66,500**	13,176	9,734	13,315	11,976
66,500	**66,550**	13,189	9,746	13,329	11,989
66,550	**66,600**	13,201	9,759	13,343	12,001
66,600	**66,650**	13,214	9,771	13,357	12,014
66,650	**66,700**	13,226	9,784	13,371	12,026
66,700	**66,750**	13,239	9,796	13,385	12,039
66,750	**66,800**	13,251	9,809	13,399	12,051
66,800	**66,850**	13,264	9,821	13,413	12,064
66,850	**66,900**	13,276	9,834	13,427	12,076
66,900	**66,950**	13,289	9,846	13,441	12,089
66,950	**67,000**	13,301	9,859	13,455	12,101
67,000					
67,000	**67,050**	13,314	9,871	13,469	12,114
67,050	**67,100**	13,326	9,884	13,483	12,126
67,100	**67,150**	13,339	9,896	13,497	12,139
67,150	**67,200**	13,351	9,909	13,511	12,151
67,200	**67,250**	13,364	9,921	13,525	12,164
67,250	**67,300**	13,376	9,934	13,539	12,176
67,300	**67,350**	13,389	9,946	13,553	12,189
67,350	**67,400**	13,401	9,959	13,567	12,201
67,400	**67,450**	13,414	9,971	13,581	12,214
67,450	**67,500**	13,426	9,984	13,595	12,226
67,500	**67,550**	13,439	9,996	13,609	12,239
67,550	**67,600**	13,451	10,009	13,623	12,251
67,600	**67,650**	13,464	10,021	13,637	12,264
67,650	**67,700**	13,476	10,034	13,651	12,276
67,700	**67,750**	13,489	10,046	13,665	12,289
67,750	**67,800**	13,501	10,059	13,679	12,301
67,800	**67,850**	13,514	10,071	13,693	12,314
67,850	**67,900**	13,526	10,084	13,707	12,326
67,900	**67,950**	13,539	10,096	13,721	12,339
67,950	**68,000**	13,551	10,109	13,735	12,351

* This column must also be used by a qualifying widow(er)

If line 43 (taxable income) is—		And you are—			
At least	But less than	Single	Married filing jointly *	Married filing sepa-rately	Head of a house-hold
		Your tax is—			
68,000					
68,000	68,050	13,564	10,121	13,749	12,364
68,050	68,100	13,576	10,134	13,763	12,376
68,100	68,150	13,589	10,146	13,777	12,389
68,150	68,200	13,601	10,159	13,791	12,401
68,200	68,250	13,614	10,171	13,805	12,414
68,250	68,300	13,626	10,184	13,819	12,426
68,300	68,350	13,639	10,196	13,833	12,439
68,350	68,400	13,651	10,209	13,847	12,451
68,400	68,450	13,664	10,221	13,861	12,464
68,450	68,500	13,676	10,234	13,875	12,476
68,500	68,550	13,689	10,246	13,889	12,489
68,550	68,600	13,701	10,259	13,903	12,501
68,600	68,650	13,714	10,271	13,917	12,514
68,650	68,700	13,726	10,284	13,931	12,526
68,700	68,750	13,739	10,296	13,945	12,539
68,750	68,800	13,751	10,309	13,959	12,551
68,800	68,850	13,764	10,321	13,973	12,564
68,850	68,900	13,776	10,334	13,987	12,576
68,900	68,950	13,789	10,346	14,001	12,589
68,950	69,000	13,801	10,359	14,015	12,601
69,000					
69,000	69,050	13,814	10,371	14,029	12,614
69,050	69,100	13,826	10,384	14,043	12,626
69,100	69,150	13,839	10,396	14,057	12,639
69,150	69,200	13,851	10,409	14,071	12,651
69,200	69,250	13,864	10,421	14,085	12,664
69,250	69,300	13,876	10,434	14,099	12,676
69,300	69,350	13,889	10,446	14,113	12,689
69,350	69,400	13,901	10,459	14,127	12,701
69,400	69,450	13,914	10,471	14,141	12,714
69,450	69,500	13,926	10,484	14,155	12,726
69,500	69,550	13,939	10,496	14,169	12,739
69,550	69,600	13,951	10,509	14,183	12,751
69,600	69,650	13,964	10,521	14,197	12,764
69,650	69,700	13,976	10,534	14,211	12,776
69,700	69,750	13,989	10,546	14,225	12,789
69,750	69,800	14,001	10,559	14,239	12,801
69,800	69,850	14,014	10,571	14,253	12,814
69,850	69,900	14,026	10,584	14,267	12,826
69,900	69,950	14,039	10,596	14,281	12,839
69,950	70,000	14,051	10,609	14,295	12,851
70,000					
70,000	70,050	14,064	10,621	14,309	12,864
70,050	70,100	14,076	10,634	14,323	12,876
70,100	70,150	14,089	10,646	14,337	12,889
70,150	70,200	14,101	10,659	14,351	12,901
70,200	70,250	14,114	10,671	14,365	12,914
70,250	70,300	14,126	10,684	14,379	12,926
70,300	70,350	14,139	10,696	14,393	12,939
70,350	70,400	14,151	10,709	14,407	12,951
70,400	70,450	14,164	10,721	14,421	12,964
70,450	70,500	14,176	10,734	14,435	12,976
70,500	70,550	14,189	10,746	14,449	12,989
70,550	70,600	14,201	10,759	14,463	13,001
70,600	70,650	14,214	10,771	14,477	13,014
70,650	70,700	14,226	10,784	14,491	13,026
70,700	70,750	14,239	10,796	14,505	13,039
70,750	70,800	14,251	10,809	14,519	13,051
70,800	70,850	14,264	10,821	14,533	13,064
70,850	70,900	14,276	10,834	14,547	13,076
70,900	70,950	14,289	10,846	14,561	13,089
70,950	71,000	14,301	10,859	14,575	13,101

If line 43 (taxable income) is—		And you are—			
At least	But less than	Single	Married filing jointly *	Married filing sepa-rately	Head of a house-hold
		Your tax is—			
71,000					
71,000	71,050	14,314	10,871	14,589	13,114
71,050	71,100	14,326	10,884	14,603	13,126
71,100	71,150	14,339	10,896	14,617	13,139
71,150	71,200	14,351	10,909	14,631	13,151
71,200	71,250	14,364	10,921	14,645	13,164
71,250	71,300	14,376	10,934	14,659	13,176
71,300	71,350	14,389	10,946	14,673	13,189
71,350	71,400	14,401	10,959	14,687	13,201
71,400	71,450	14,414	10,971	14,701	13,214
71,450	71,500	14,426	10,984	14,715	13,226
71,500	71,550	14,439	10,996	14,729	13,239
71,550	71,600	14,451	11,009	14,743	13,251
71,600	71,650	14,464	11,021	14,757	13,264
71,650	71,700	14,476	11,034	14,771	13,276
71,700	71,750	14,489	11,046	14,785	13,289
71,750	71,800	14,501	11,059	14,799	13,301
71,800	71,850	14,514	11,071	14,813	13,314
71,850	71,900	14,526	11,084	14,827	13,326
71,900	71,950	14,539	11,096	14,841	13,339
71,950	72,000	14,551	11,109	14,855	13,351
72,000					
72,000	72,050	14,564	11,121	14,869	13,364
72,050	72,100	14,576	11,134	14,883	13,376
72,100	72,150	14,589	11,146	14,897	13,389
72,150	72,200	14,601	11,159	14,911	13,401
72,200	72,250	14,614	11,171	14,925	13,414
72,250	72,300	14,626	11,184	14,939	13,426
72,300	72,350	14,639	11,196	14,953	13,439
72,350	72,400	14,651	11,209	14,967	13,451
72,400	72,450	14,664	11,221	14,981	13,464
72,450	72,500	14,676	11,234	14,995	13,476
72,500	72,550	14,689	11,246	15,009	13,489
72,550	72,600	14,701	11,259	15,023	13,501
72,600	72,650	14,714	11,271	15,037	13,514
72,650	72,700	14,726	11,284	15,051	13,526
72,700	72,750	14,739	11,296	15,065	13,539
72,750	72,800	14,751	11,309	15,079	13,551
72,800	72,850	14,764	11,321	15,093	13,564
72,850	72,900	14,776	11,334	15,107	13,576
72,900	72,950	14,789	11,346	15,121	13,589
72,950	73,000	14,801	11,359	15,135	13,601
73,000					
73,000	73,050	14,814	11,371	15,149	13,614
73,050	73,100	14,826	11,384	15,163	13,626
73,100	73,150	14,839	11,396	15,177	13,639
73,150	73,200	14,851	11,409	15,191	13,651
73,200	73,250	14,864	11,421	15,205	13,664
73,250	73,300	14,876	11,434	15,219	13,676
73,300	73,350	14,889	11,446	15,233	13,689
73,350	73,400	14,901	11,459	15,247	13,701
73,400	73,450	14,914	11,471	15,261	13,714
73,450	73,500	14,926	11,484	15,275	13,726
73,500	73,550	14,939	11,496	15,289	13,739
73,550	73,600	14,951	11,509	15,303	13,751
73,600	73,650	14,964	11,521	15,317	13,764
73,650	73,700	14,976	11,534	15,331	13,776
73,700	73,750	14,989	11,546	15,345	13,789
73,750	73,800	15,001	11,559	15,359	13,801
73,800	73,850	15,014	11,571	15,373	13,814
73,850	73,900	15,026	11,584	15,387	13,826
73,900	73,950	15,039	11,596	15,401	13,839
73,950	74,000	15,051	11,609	15,415	13,851

If line 43 (taxable income) is—		And you are—			
At least	But less than	Single	Married filing jointly *	Married filing sepa-rately	Head of a house-hold
		Your tax is—			
74,000					
74,000	74,050	15,064	11,621	15,429	13,864
74,050	74,100	15,076	11,634	15,443	13,876
74,100	74,150	15,089	11,646	15,457	13,889
74,150	74,200	15,101	11,659	15,471	13,901
74,200	74,250	15,115	11,671	15,485	13,914
74,250	74,300	15,129	11,684	15,499	13,926
74,300	74,350	15,143	11,696	15,513	13,939
74,350	74,400	15,157	11,709	15,527	13,951
74,400	74,450	15,171	11,721	15,541	13,964
74,450	74,500	15,185	11,734	15,555	13,976
74,500	74,550	15,199	11,746	15,569	13,989
74,550	74,600	15,213	11,759	15,583	14,001
74,600	74,650	15,227	11,771	15,597	14,014
74,650	74,700	15,241	11,784	15,611	14,026
74,700	74,750	15,255	11,796	15,625	14,039
74,750	74,800	15,269	11,809	15,639	14,051
74,800	74,850	15,283	11,821	15,653	14,064
74,850	74,900	15,297	11,834	15,667	14,076
74,900	74,950	15,311	11,846	15,681	14,089
74,950	75,000	15,325	11,859	15,695	14,101
75,000					
75,000	75,050	15,339	11,871	15,709	14,114
75,050	75,100	15,353	11,884	15,723	14,126
75,100	75,150	15,367	11,896	15,737	14,139
75,150	75,200	15,381	11,909	15,751	14,151
75,200	75,250	15,395	11,921	15,765	14,164
75,250	75,300	15,409	11,934	15,779	14,176
75,300	75,350	15,423	11,946	15,793	14,189
75,350	75,400	15,437	11,959	15,807	14,201
75,400	75,450	15,451	11,971	15,821	14,214
75,450	75,500	15,465	11,984	15,835	14,226
75,500	75,550	15,479	11,996	15,849	14,239
75,550	75,600	15,493	12,009	15,863	14,251
75,600	75,650	15,507	12,021	15,877	14,264
75,650	75,700	15,521	12,034	15,891	14,276
75,700	75,750	15,535	12,046	15,905	14,289
75,750	75,800	15,549	12,059	15,919	14,301
75,800	75,850	15,563	12,071	15,933	14,314
75,850	75,900	15,577	12,084	15,947	14,326
75,900	75,950	15,591	12,096	15,961	14,339
75,950	76,000	15,605	12,109	15,975	14,351
76,000					
76,000	76,050	15,619	12,121	15,989	14,364
76,050	76,100	15,633	12,134	16,003	14,376
76,100	76,150	15,647	12,146	16,017	14,389
76,150	76,200	15,661	12,159	16,031	14,401
76,200	76,250	15,675	12,171	16,045	14,414
76,250	76,300	15,689	12,184	16,059	14,426
76,300	76,350	15,703	12,196	16,073	14,439
76,350	76,400	15,717	12,209	16,087	14,451
76,400	76,450	15,731	12,221	16,101	14,464
76,450	76,500	15,745	12,234	16,115	14,476
76,500	76,550	15,759	12,246	16,129	14,489
76,550	76,600	15,773	12,259	16,143	14,501
76,600	76,650	15,787	12,271	16,157	14,514
76,650	76,700	15,801	12,284	16,171	14,526
76,700	76,750	15,815	12,296	16,185	14,539
76,750	76,800	15,829	12,309	16,199	14,551
76,800	76,850	15,843	12,321	16,213	14,564
76,850	76,900	15,857	12,334	16,227	14,576
76,900	76,950	15,871	12,346	16,241	14,589
76,950	77,000	15,885	12,359	16,255	14,601

* This column must also be used by a qualifying widow(er)

2006 Tax Table–*Continued*

If line 43 (taxable income) is—		And you are—			
At least	But less than	Single	Married filing jointly *	Married filing separately	Head of a household
		Your tax is—			
77,000					
77,000	**77,050**	15,899	12,371	16,269	14,614
77,050	**77,100**	15,913	12,384	16,283	14,626
77,100	**77,150**	15,927	12,396	16,297	14,639
77,150	**77,200**	15,941	12,409	16,311	14,651
77,200	**77,250**	15,955	12,421	16,325	14,664
77,250	**77,300**	15,969	12,434	16,339	14,676
77,300	**77,350**	15,983	12,446	16,353	14,689
77,350	**77,400**	15,997	12,459	16,367	14,701
77,400	**77,450**	16,011	12,471	16,381	14,714
77,450	**77,500**	16,025	12,484	16,395	14,726
77,500	**77,550**	16,039	12,496	16,409	14,739
77,550	**77,600**	16,053	12,509	16,423	14,751
77,600	**77,650**	16,067	12,521	16,437	14,764
77,650	**77,700**	16,081	12,534	16,451	14,776
77,700	**77,750**	16,095	12,546	16,465	14,789
77,750	**77,800**	16,109	12,559	16,479	14,801
77,800	**77,850**	16,123	12,571	16,493	14,814
77,850	**77,900**	16,137	12,584	16,507	14,826
77,900	**77,950**	16,151	12,596	16,521	14,839
77,950	**78,000**	16,165	12,609	16,535	14,851
78,000					
78,000	**78,050**	16,179	12,621	16,549	14,864
78,050	**78,100**	16,193	12,634	16,563	14,876
78,100	**78,150**	16,207	12,646	16,577	14,889
78,150	**78,200**	16,221	12,659	16,591	14,901
78,200	**78,250**	16,235	12,671	16,605	14,914
78,250	**78,300**	16,249	12,684	16,619	14,926
78,300	**78,350**	16,263	12,696	16,633	14,939
78,350	**78,400**	16,277	12,709	16,647	14,951
78,400	**78,450**	16,291	12,721	16,661	14,964
78,450	**78,500**	16,305	12,734	16,675	14,976
78,500	**78,550**	16,319	12,746	16,689	14,989
78,550	**78,600**	16,333	12,759	16,703	15,001
78,600	**78,650**	16,347	12,771	16,717	15,014
78,650	**78,700**	16,361	12,784	16,731	15,026
78,700	**78,750**	16,375	12,796	16,745	15,039
78,750	**78,800**	16,389	12,809	16,759	15,051
78,800	**78,850**	16,403	12,821	16,773	15,064
78,850	**78,900**	16,417	12,834	16,787	15,076
78,900	**78,950**	16,431	12,846	16,801	15,089
78,950	**79,000**	16,445	12,859	16,815	15,101
79,000					
79,000	**79,050**	16,459	12,871	16,829	15,114
79,050	**79,100**	16,473	12,884	16,843	15,126
79,100	**79,150**	16,487	12,896	16,857	15,139
79,150	**79,200**	16,501	12,909	16,871	15,151
79,200	**79,250**	16,515	12,921	16,885	15,164
79,250	**79,300**	16,529	12,934	16,899	15,176
79,300	**79,350**	16,543	12,946	16,913	15,189
79,350	**79,400**	16,557	12,959	16,927	15,201
79,400	**79,450**	16,571	12,971	16,941	15,214
79,450	**79,500**	16,585	12,984	16,955	15,226
79,500	**79,550**	16,599	12,996	16,969	15,239
79,550	**79,600**	16,613	13,009	16,983	15,251
79,600	**79,650**	16,627	13,021	16,997	15,264
79,650	**79,700**	16,641	13,034	17,011	15,276
79,700	**79,750**	16,655	13,046	17,025	15,289
79,750	**79,800**	16,669	13,059	17,039	15,301
79,800	**79,850**	16,683	13,071	17,053	15,314
79,850	**79,900**	16,697	13,084	17,067	15,326
79,900	**79,950**	16,711	13,096	17,081	15,339
79,950	**80,000**	16,725	13,109	17,095	15,351
80,000					
80,000	**80,050**	16,739	13,121	17,109	15,364
80,050	**80,100**	16,753	13,134	17,123	15,376
80,100	**80,150**	16,767	13,146	17,137	15,389
80,150	**80,200**	16,781	13,159	17,151	15,401
80,200	**80,250**	16,795	13,171	17,165	15,414
80,250	**80,300**	16,809	13,184	17,179	15,426
80,300	**80,350**	16,823	13,196	17,193	15,439
80,350	**80,400**	16,837	13,209	17,207	15,451
80,400	**80,450**	16,851	13,221	17,221	15,464
80,450	**80,500**	16,865	13,234	17,235	15,476
80,500	**80,550**	16,879	13,246	17,249	15,489
80,550	**80,600**	16,893	13,259	17,263	15,501
80,600	**80,650**	16,907	13,271	17,277	15,514
80,650	**80,700**	16,921	13,284	17,291	15,526
80,700	**80,750**	16,935	13,296	17,305	15,539
80,750	**80,800**	16,949	13,309	17,319	15,551
80,800	**80,850**	16,963	13,321	17,333	15,564
80,850	**80,900**	16,977	13,334	17,347	15,576
80,900	**80,950**	16,991	13,346	17,361	15,589
80,950	**81,000**	17,005	13,359	17,375	15,601
81,000					
81,000	**81,050**	17,019	13,371	17,389	15,614
81,050	**81,100**	17,033	13,384	17,403	15,626
81,100	**81,150**	17,047	13,396	17,417	15,639
81,150	**81,200**	17,061	13,409	17,431	15,651
81,200	**81,250**	17,075	13,421	17,445	15,664
81,250	**81,300**	17,089	13,434	17,459	15,676
81,300	**81,350**	17,103	13,446	17,473	15,689
81,350	**81,400**	17,117	13,459	17,487	15,701
81,400	**81,450**	17,131	13,471	17,501	15,714
81,450	**81,500**	17,145	13,484	17,515	15,726
81,500	**81,550**	17,159	13,496	17,529	15,739
81,550	**81,600**	17,173	13,509	17,543	15,751
81,600	**81,650**	17,187	13,521	17,557	15,764
81,650	**81,700**	17,201	13,534	17,571	15,776
81,700	**81,750**	17,215	13,546	17,585	15,789
81,750	**81,800**	17,229	13,559	17,599	15,801
81,800	**81,850**	17,243	13,571	17,613	15,814
81,850	**81,900**	17,257	13,584	17,627	15,826
81,900	**81,950**	17,271	13,596	17,641	15,839
81,950	**82,000**	17,285	13,609	17,655	15,851
82,000					
82,000	**82,050**	17,299	13,621	17,669	15,864
82,050	**82,100**	17,313	13,634	17,683	15,876
82,100	**82,150**	17,327	13,646	17,697	15,889
82,150	**82,200**	17,341	13,659	17,711	15,901
82,200	**82,250**	17,355	13,671	17,725	15,914
82,250	**82,300**	17,369	13,684	17,739	15,926
82,300	**82,350**	17,383	13,696	17,753	15,939
82,350	**82,400**	17,397	13,709	17,767	15,951
82,400	**82,450**	17,411	13,721	17,781	15,964
82,450	**82,500**	17,425	13,734	17,795	15,976
82,500	**82,550**	17,439	13,746	17,809	15,989
82,550	**82,600**	17,453	13,759	17,823	16,001
82,600	**82,650**	17,467	13,771	17,837	16,014
82,650	**82,700**	17,481	13,784	17,851	16,026
82,700	**82,750**	17,495	13,796	17,865	16,039
82,750	**82,800**	17,509	13,809	17,879	16,051
82,800	**82,850**	17,523	13,821	17,893	16,064
82,850	**82,900**	17,537	13,834	17,907	16,076
82,900	**82,950**	17,551	13,846	17,921	16,089
82,950	**83,000**	17,565	13,859	17,935	16,101
83,000					
83,000	**83,050**	17,579	13,871	17,949	16,114
83,050	**83,100**	17,593	13,884	17,963	16,126
83,100	**83,150**	17,607	13,896	17,977	16,139
83,150	**83,200**	17,621	13,909	17,991	16,151
83,200	**83,250**	17,635	13,921	18,005	16,164
83,250	**83,300**	17,649	13,934	18,019	16,176
83,300	**83,350**	17,663	13,946	18,033	16,189
83,350	**83,400**	17,677	13,959	18,047	16,201
83,400	**83,450**	17,691	13,971	18,061	16,214
83,450	**83,500**	17,705	13,984	18,075	16,226
83,500	**83,550**	17,719	13,996	18,089	16,239
83,550	**83,600**	17,733	14,009	18,103	16,251
83,600	**83,650**	17,747	14,021	18,117	16,264
83,650	**83,700**	17,761	14,034	18,131	16,276
83,700	**83,750**	17,775	14,046	18,145	16,289
83,750	**83,800**	17,789	14,059	18,159	16,301
83,800	**83,850**	17,803	14,071	18,173	16,314
83,850	**83,900**	17,817	14,084	18,187	16,326
83,900	**83,950**	17,831	14,096	18,201	16,339
83,950	**84,000**	17,845	14,109	18,215	16,351
84,000					
84,000	**84,050**	17,859	14,121	18,229	16,364
84,050	**84,100**	17,873	14,134	18,243	16,376
84,100	**84,150**	17,887	14,146	18,257	16,389
84,150	**84,200**	17,901	14,159	18,271	16,401
84,200	**84,250**	17,915	14,171	18,285	16,414
84,250	**84,300**	17,929	14,184	18,299	16,426
84,300	**84,350**	17,943	14,196	18,313	16,439
84,350	**84,400**	17,957	14,209	18,327	16,451
84,400	**84,450**	17,971	14,221	18,341	16,464
84,450	**84,500**	17,985	14,234	18,355	16,476
84,500	**84,550**	17,999	14,246	18,369	16,489
84,550	**84,600**	18,013	14,259	18,383	16,501
84,600	**84,650**	18,027	14,271	18,397	16,514
84,650	**84,700**	18,041	14,284	18,411	16,526
84,700	**84,750**	18,055	14,296	18,425	16,539
84,750	**84,800**	18,069	14,309	18,439	16,551
84,800	**84,850**	18,083	14,321	18,453	16,564
84,850	**84,900**	18,097	14,334	18,467	16,576
84,900	**84,950**	18,111	14,346	18,481	16,589
84,950	**85,000**	18,125	14,359	18,495	16,601
85,000					
85,000	**85,050**	18,139	14,371	18,509	16,614
85,050	**85,100**	18,153	14,384	18,523	16,626
85,100	**85,150**	18,167	14,396	18,537	16,639
85,150	**85,200**	18,181	14,409	18,551	16,651
85,200	**85,250**	18,195	14,421	18,565	16,664
85,250	**85,300**	18,209	14,434	18,579	16,676
85,300	**85,350**	18,223	14,446	18,593	16,689
85,350	**85,400**	18,237	14,459	18,607	16,701
85,400	**85,450**	18,251	14,471	18,621	16,714
85,450	**85,500**	18,265	14,484	18,635	16,726
85,500	**85,550**	18,279	14,496	18,649	16,739
85,550	**85,600**	18,293	14,509	18,663	16,751
85,600	**85,650**	18,307	14,521	18,677	16,764
85,650	**85,700**	18,321	14,534	18,691	16,776
85,700	**85,750**	18,335	14,546	18,705	16,789
85,750	**85,800**	18,349	14,559	18,719	16,801
85,800	**85,850**	18,363	14,571	18,733	16,814
85,850	**85,900**	18,377	14,584	18,747	16,826
85,900	**85,950**	18,391	14,596	18,761	16,839
85,950	**86,000**	18,405	14,609	18,775	16,851

* This column must also be used by a qualifying widow(er)

If line 43 (taxable income) is—		And you are—			
At least	But less than	Single	Married filing jointly *	Married filing separately	Head of a household
		Your tax is—			
86,000					
86,000	**86,050**	18,419	14,621	18,789	16,864
86,050	**86,100**	18,433	14,634	18,803	16,876
86,100	**86,150**	18,447	14,646	18,817	16,889
86,150	**86,200**	18,461	14,659	18,831	16,901
86,200	**86,250**	18,475	14,671	18,845	16,914
86,250	**86,300**	18,489	14,684	18,859	16,926
86,300	**86,350**	18,503	14,696	18,873	16,939
86,350	**86,400**	18,517	14,709	18,887	16,951
86,400	**86,450**	18,531	14,721	18,901	16,964
86,450	**86,500**	18,545	14,734	18,915	16,976
86,500	**86,550**	18,559	14,746	18,929	16,989
86,550	**86,600**	18,573	14,759	18,943	17,001
86,600	**86,650**	18,587	14,771	18,957	17,014
86,650	**86,700**	18,601	14,784	18,971	17,026
86,700	**86,750**	18,615	14,796	18,985	17,039
86,750	**86,800**	18,629	14,809	18,999	17,051
86,800	**86,850**	18,643	14,821	19,013	17,064
86,850	**86,900**	18,657	14,834	19,027	17,076
86,900	**86,950**	18,671	14,846	19,041	17,089
86,950	**87,000**	18,685	14,859	19,055	17,101
87,000					
87,000	**87,050**	18,699	14,871	19,069	17,114
87,050	**87,100**	18,713	14,884	19,083	17,126
87,100	**87,150**	18,727	14,896	19,097	17,139
87,150	**87,200**	18,741	14,909	19,111	17,151
87,200	**87,250**	18,755	14,921	19,125	17,164
87,250	**87,300**	18,769	14,934	19,139	17,176
87,300	**87,350**	18,783	14,946	19,153	17,189
87,350	**87,400**	18,797	14,959	19,167	17,201
87,400	**87,450**	18,811	14,971	19,181	17,214
87,450	**87,500**	18,825	14,984	19,195	17,226
87,500	**87,550**	18,839	14,996	19,209	17,239
87,550	**87,600**	18,853	15,009	19,223	17,251
87,600	**87,650**	18,867	15,021	19,237	17,264
87,650	**87,700**	18,881	15,034	19,251	17,276
87,700	**87,750**	18,895	15,046	19,265	17,289
87,750	**87,800**	18,909	15,059	19,279	17,301
87,800	**87,850**	18,923	15,071	19,293	17,314
87,850	**87,900**	18,937	15,084	19,307	17,326
87,900	**87,950**	18,951	15,096	19,321	17,339
87,950	**88,000**	18,965	15,109	19,335	17,351
88,000					
88,000	**88,050**	18,979	15,121	19,349	17,364
88,050	**88,100**	18,993	15,134	19,363	17,376
88,100	**88,150**	19,007	15,146	19,377	17,389
88,150	**88,200**	19,021	15,159	19,391	17,401
88,200	**88,250**	19,035	15,171	19,405	17,414
88,250	**88,300**	19,049	15,184	19,419	17,426
88,300	**88,350**	19,063	15,196	19,433	17,439
88,350	**88,400**	19,077	15,209	19,447	17,451
88,400	**88,450**	19,091	15,221	19,461	17,464
88,450	**88,500**	19,105	15,234	19,475	17,476
88,500	**88,550**	19,119	15,246	19,489	17,489
88,550	**88,600**	19,133	15,259	19,503	17,501
88,600	**88,650**	19,147	15,271	19,517	17,514
88,650	**88,700**	19,161	15,284	19,531	17,526
88,700	**88,750**	19,175	15,296	19,545	17,539
88,750	**88,800**	19,189	15,309	19,559	17,551
88,800	**88,850**	19,203	15,321	19,573	17,564
88,850	**88,900**	19,217	15,334	19,587	17,576
88,900	**88,950**	19,231	15,346	19,601	17,589
88,950	**89,000**	19,245	15,359	19,615	17,601

If line 43 (taxable income) is—		And you are—			
At least	But less than	Single	Married filing jointly *	Married filing separately	Head of a household
		Your tax is—			
89,000					
89,000	**89,050**	19,259	15,371	19,629	17,614
89,050	**89,100**	19,273	15,384	19,643	17,626
89,100	**89,150**	19,287	15,396	19,657	17,639
89,150	**89,200**	19,301	15,409	19,671	17,651
89,200	**89,250**	19,315	15,421	19,685	17,664
89,250	**89,300**	19,329	15,434	19,699	17,676
89,300	**89,350**	19,343	15,446	19,713	17,689
89,350	**89,400**	19,357	15,459	19,727	17,701
89,400	**89,450**	19,371	15,471	19,741	17,714
89,450	**89,500**	19,385	15,484	19,755	17,726
89,500	**89,550**	19,399	15,496	19,769	17,739
89,550	**89,600**	19,413	15,509	19,783	17,751
89,600	**89,650**	19,427	15,521	19,797	17,764
89,650	**89,700**	19,441	15,534	19,811	17,776
89,700	**89,750**	19,455	15,546	19,825	17,789
89,750	**89,800**	19,469	15,559	19,839	17,801
89,800	**89,850**	19,483	15,571	19,853	17,814
89,850	**89,900**	19,497	15,584	19,867	17,826
89,900	**89,950**	19,511	15,596	19,881	17,839
89,950	**90,000**	19,525	15,609	19,895	17,851
90,000					
90,000	**90,050**	19,539	15,621	19,909	17,864
90,050	**90,100**	19,553	15,634	19,923	17,876
90,100	**90,150**	19,567	15,646	19,937	17,889
90,150	**90,200**	19,581	15,659	19,951	17,901
90,200	**90,250**	19,595	15,671	19,965	17,914
90,250	**90,300**	19,609	15,684	19,979	17,926
90,300	**90,350**	19,623	15,696	19,993	17,939
90,350	**90,400**	19,637	15,709	20,007	17,951
90,400	**90,450**	19,651	15,721	20,021	17,964
90,450	**90,500**	19,665	15,734	20,035	17,976
90,500	**90,550**	19,679	15,746	20,049	17,989
90,550	**90,600**	19,693	15,759	20,063	18,001
90,600	**90,650**	19,707	15,771	20,077	18,014
90,650	**90,700**	19,721	15,784	20,091	18,026
90,700	**90,750**	19,735	15,796	20,105	18,039
90,750	**90,800**	19,749	15,809	20,119	18,051
90,800	**90,850**	19,763	15,821	20,133	18,064
90,850	**90,900**	19,777	15,834	20,147	18,076
90,900	**90,950**	19,791	15,846	20,161	18,089
90,950	**91,000**	19,805	15,859	20,175	18,101
91,000					
91,000	**91,050**	19,819	15,871	20,189	18,114
91,050	**91,100**	19,833	15,884	20,203	18,126
91,100	**91,150**	19,847	15,896	20,217	18,139
91,150	**91,200**	19,861	15,909	20,231	18,151
91,200	**91,250**	19,875	15,921	20,245	18,164
91,250	**91,300**	19,889	15,934	20,259	18,176
91,300	**91,350**	19,903	15,946	20,273	18,189
91,350	**91,400**	19,917	15,959	20,287	18,201
91,400	**91,450**	19,931	15,971	20,301	18,214
91,450	**91,500**	19,945	15,984	20,315	18,226
91,500	**91,550**	19,959	15,996	20,329	18,239
91,550	**91,600**	19,973	16,009	20,343	18,251
91,600	**91,650**	19,987	16,021	20,357	18,264
91,650	**91,700**	20,001	16,034	20,371	18,276
91,700	**91,750**	20,015	16,046	20,385	18,289
91,750	**91,800**	20,029	16,059	20,399	18,301
91,800	**91,850**	20,043	16,071	20,413	18,314
91,850	**91,900**	20,057	16,084	20,427	18,326
91,900	**91,950**	20,071	16,096	20,441	18,339
91,950	**92,000**	20,085	16,109	20,455	18,351

If line 43 (taxable income) is—		And you are—			
At least	But less than	Single	Married filing jointly *	Married filing separately	Head of a household
		Your tax is—			
92,000					
92,000	**92,050**	20,099	16,121	20,469	18,364
92,050	**92,100**	20,113	16,134	20,483	18,376
92,100	**92,150**	20,127	16,146	20,497	18,389
92,150	**92,200**	20,141	16,159	20,511	18,401
92,200	**92,250**	20,155	16,171	20,525	18,414
92,250	**92,300**	20,169	16,184	20,539	18,426
92,300	**92,350**	20,183	16,196	20,553	18,439
92,350	**92,400**	20,197	16,209	20,567	18,451
92,400	**92,450**	20,211	16,221	20,581	18,464
92,450	**92,500**	20,225	16,234	20,595	18,476
92,500	**92,550**	20,239	16,246	20,609	18,489
92,550	**92,600**	20,253	16,259	20,623	18,501
92,600	**92,650**	20,267	16,271	20,637	18,514
92,650	**92,700**	20,281	16,284	20,651	18,526
92,700	**92,750**	20,295	16,296	20,665	18,539
92,750	**92,800**	20,309	16,309	20,679	18,551
92,800	**92,850**	20,323	16,321	20,693	18,564
92,850	**92,900**	20,337	16,334	20,707	18,576
92,900	**92,950**	20,351	16,346	20,721	18,589
92,950	**93,000**	20,365	16,359	20,735	18,601
93,000					
93,000	**93,050**	20,379	16,371	20,749	18,614
93,050	**93,100**	20,393	16,384	20,763	18,626
93,100	**93,150**	20,407	16,396	20,777	18,639
93,150	**93,200**	20,421	16,409	20,791	18,651
93,200	**93,250**	20,435	16,421	20,805	18,664
93,250	**93,300**	20,449	16,434	20,819	18,676
93,300	**93,350**	20,463	16,446	20,833	18,689
93,350	**93,400**	20,477	16,459	20,847	18,701
93,400	**93,450**	20,491	16,471	20,861	18,714
93,450	**93,500**	20,505	16,484	20,875	18,726
93,500	**93,550**	20,519	16,496	20,889	18,739
93,550	**93,600**	20,533	16,509	20,903	18,751
93,600	**93,650**	20,547	16,521	20,917	18,764
93,650	**93,700**	20,561	16,534	20,931	18,776
93,700	**93,750**	20,575	16,546	20,945	18,789
93,750	**93,800**	20,589	16,559	20,959	18,801
93,800	**93,850**	20,603	16,571	20,973	18,814
93,850	**93,900**	20,617	16,584	20,987	18,826
93,900	**93,950**	20,631	16,596	21,001	18,839
93,950	**94,000**	20,645	16,609	21,015	18,851
94,000					
94,000	**94,050**	20,659	16,621	21,029	18,864
94,050	**94,100**	20,673	16,634	21,043	18,876
94,100	**94,150**	20,687	16,646	21,057	18,889
94,150	**94,200**	20,701	16,659	21,071	18,901
94,200	**94,250**	20,715	16,671	21,085	18,914
94,250	**94,300**	20,729	16,684	21,102	18,926
94,300	**94,350**	20,743	16,696	21,118	18,939
94,350	**94,400**	20,757	16,709	21,135	18,951
94,400	**94,450**	20,771	16,721	21,151	18,964
94,450	**94,500**	20,785	16,734	21,168	18,976
94,500	**94,550**	20,799	16,746	21,184	18,989
94,550	**94,600**	20,813	16,759	21,201	19,001
94,600	**94,650**	20,827	16,771	21,217	19,014
94,650	**94,700**	20,841	16,784	21,234	19,026
94,700	**94,750**	20,855	16,796	21,250	19,039
94,750	**94,800**	20,869	16,809	21,267	19,051
94,800	**94,850**	20,883	16,821	21,283	19,064
94,850	**94,900**	20,897	16,834	21,300	19,076
94,900	**94,950**	20,911	16,846	21,316	19,089
94,950	**95,000**	20,925	16,859	21,333	19,101

* This column must also be used by a qualifying widow(er)

2006 Tax Table–*Continued*

If line 43 (taxable income) is—		And you are—			
At least	But less than	Single	Married filing jointly *	Married filing sepa-rately	Head of a house-hold
		Your tax is—			
95,000					
95,000	**95,050**	20,939	16,871	21,349	19,114
95,050	**95,100**	20,953	16,884	21,366	19,126
95,100	**95,150**	20,967	16,896	21,382	19,139
95,150	**95,200**	20,981	16,909	21,399	19,151
95,200	**95,250**	20,995	16,921	21,415	19,164
95,250	**95,300**	21,009	16,934	21,432	19,176
95,300	**95,350**	21,023	16,946	21,448	19,189
95,350	**95,400**	21,037	16,959	21,465	19,201
95,400	**95,450**	21,051	16,971	21,481	19,214
95,450	**95,500**	21,065	16,984	21,498	19,226
95,500	**95,550**	21,079	16,996	21,514	19,239
95,550	**95,600**	21,093	17,009	21,531	19,251
95,600	**95,650**	21,107	17,021	21,547	19,264
95,650	**95,700**	21,121	17,034	21,564	19,276
95,700	**95,750**	21,135	17,046	21,580	19,289
95,750	**95,800**	21,149	17,059	21,597	19,301
95,800	**95,850**	21,163	17,071	21,613	19,314
95,850	**95,900**	21,177	17,084	21,630	19,326
95,900	**95,950**	21,191	17,096	21,646	19,339
95,950	**96,000**	21,205	17,109	21,663	19,351
96,000					
96,000	**96,050**	21,219	17,121	21,679	19,364
96,050	**96,100**	21,233	17,134	21,696	19,376
96,100	**96,150**	21,247	17,146	21,712	19,389
96,150	**96,200**	21,261	17,159	21,729	19,401
96,200	**96,250**	21,275	17,171	21,745	19,414
96,250	**96,300**	21,289	17,184	21,762	19,426
96,300	**96,350**	21,303	17,196	21,778	19,439
96,350	**96,400**	21,317	17,209	21,795	19,451
96,400	**96,450**	21,331	17,221	21,811	19,464
96,450	**96,500**	21,345	17,234	21,828	19,476
96,500	**96,550**	21,359	17,246	21,844	19,489
96,550	**96,600**	21,373	17,259	21,861	19,501
96,600	**96,650**	21,387	17,271	21,877	19,514
96,650	**96,700**	21,401	17,284	21,894	19,526
96,700	**96,750**	21,415	17,296	21,910	19,539
96,750	**96,800**	21,429	17,309	21,927	19,551
96,800	**96,850**	21,443	17,321	21,943	19,564
96,850	**96,900**	21,457	17,334	21,960	19,576
96,900	**96,950**	21,471	17,346	21,976	19,589
96,950	**97,000**	21,485	17,359	21,993	19,601
97,000					
97,000	**97,050**	21,499	17,371	22,009	19,614
97,050	**97,100**	21,513	17,384	22,026	19,626
97,100	**97,150**	21,527	17,396	22,042	19,639
97,150	**97,200**	21,541	17,409	22,059	19,651
97,200	**97,250**	21,555	17,421	22,075	19,664
97,250	**97,300**	21,569	17,434	22,092	19,676
97,300	**97,350**	21,583	17,446	22,108	19,689
97,350	**97,400**	21,597	17,459	22,125	19,701
97,400	**97,450**	21,611	17,471	22,141	19,714
97,450	**97,500**	21,625	17,484	22,158	19,726
97,500	**97,550**	21,639	17,496	22,174	19,739
97,550	**97,600**	21,653	17,509	22,191	19,751
97,600	**97,650**	21,667	17,521	22,207	19,764
97,650	**97,700**	21,681	17,534	22,224	19,776
97,700	**97,750**	21,695	17,546	22,240	19,789
97,750	**97,800**	21,709	17,559	22,257	19,801
97,800	**97,850**	21,723	17,571	22,273	19,814
97,850	**97,900**	21,737	17,584	22,290	19,826
97,900	**97,950**	21,751	17,596	22,306	19,839
97,950	**98,000**	21,765	17,609	22,323	19,851
98,000					
98,000	**98,050**	21,779	17,621	22,339	19,864
98,050	**98,100**	21,793	17,634	22,356	19,876
98,100	**98,150**	21,807	17,646	22,372	19,889
98,150	**98,200**	21,821	17,659	22,389	19,901
98,200	**98,250**	21,835	17,671	22,405	19,914
98,250	**98,300**	21,849	17,684	22,422	19,926
98,300	**98,350**	21,863	17,696	22,438	19,939
98,350	**98,400**	21,877	17,709	22,455	19,951
98,400	**98,450**	21,891	17,721	22,471	19,964
98,450	**98,500**	21,905	17,734	22,488	19,976
98,500	**98,550**	21,919	17,746	22,504	19,989
98,550	**98,600**	21,933	17,759	22,521	20,001
98,600	**98,650**	21,947	17,771	22,537	20,014
98,650	**98,700**	21,961	17,784	22,554	20,026
98,700	**98,750**	21,975	17,796	22,570	20,039
98,750	**98,800**	21,989	17,809	22,587	20,051
98,800	**98,850**	22,003	17,821	22,603	20,064
98,850	**98,900**	22,017	17,834	22,620	20,076
98,900	**98,950**	22,031	17,846	22,636	20,089
98,950	**99,000**	22,045	17,859	22,653	20,101
99,000					
99,000	**99,050**	22,059	17,871	22,669	20,114
99,050	**99,100**	22,073	17,884	22,686	20,126
99,100	**99,150**	22,087	17,896	22,702	20,139
99,150	**99,200**	22,101	17,909	22,719	20,151
99,200	**99,250**	22,115	17,921	22,735	20,164
99,250	**99,300**	22,129	17,934	22,752	20,176
99,300	**99,350**	22,143	17,946	22,768	20,189
99,350	**99,400**	22,157	17,959	22,785	20,201
99,400	**99,450**	22,171	17,971	22,801	20,214
99,450	**99,500**	22,185	17,984	22,818	20,226
99,500	**99,550**	22,199	17,996	22,834	20,239
99,550	**99,600**	22,213	18,009	22,851	20,251
99,600	**99,650**	22,227	18,021	22,867	20,264
99,650	**99,700**	22,241	18,034	22,884	20,276
99,700	**99,750**	22,255	18,046	22,900	20,289
99,750	**99,800**	22,269	18,059	22,917	20,301
99,800	**99,850**	22,283	18,071	22,933	20,314
99,850	**99,900**	22,297	18,084	22,950	20,326
99,900	**99,950**	22,311	18,096	22,966	20,339
99,950	**100,000**	22,325	18,109	22,983	20,351

$100,000 or over — use the Tax Computation Worksheet on page 771

* This column must also be used by a qualifying widow(er)

2006 Tax Computation Worksheet—Line 44

CAUTION *See the instructions for line 44 that begin on page 36 to see if you must use the worksheet below to figure your tax.*

Note. If you are required to use this worksheet to figure the tax on an amount from another form or worksheet, such as the Qualified Dividends and Capital Gain Tax Worksheet, the Schedule D Tax Worksheet, Schedule J, Form 8615, or the Foreign Earned Income Tax Worksheet, enter the amount from that form or worksheet in column (a) of the row that applies to the amount you are looking up. Enter the result on the appropriate line of the form or worksheet that you are completing.

Section A — Use if your filing status is **Single.** Complete the row below that applies to you.

Taxable income. If line 43 is —	**(a)** Enter the amount from line 43	**(b)** Multiplication amount	**(c)** Multiply (a) by (b)	**(d)** Subtraction amount	**Tax.** Subtract (d) from (c). Enter the result here and on Form 1040, line 44
At least $100,000 but not over $154,800	$	× 28% (.28)	$	$ 5,668.50	$
Over $154,800 but not over $336,550	$	× 33% (.33)	$	$ 13,408.50	$
Over $336,550	$	× 35% (.35)	$	$ 20,139.50	$

Section B — Use if your filing status is **Married filing jointly** or **Qualifying widow(er).** Complete the row below that applies to you.

Taxable income. If line 43 is —	**(a)** Enter the amount from line 43	**(b)** Multiplication amount	**(c)** Multiply (a) by (b)	**(d)** Subtraction amount	**Tax.** Subtract (d) from (c). Enter the result here and on Form 1040, line 44
At least $100,000 but not over $123,700	$	× 25% (.25)	$	$ 6,885.00	$
Over $123,700 but not over $188,450	$	× 28% (.28)	$	$ 10,596.00	$
Over $188,450 but not over $336,550	$	× 33% (.33)	$	$ 20,018.50	$
Over $336,550	$	× 35% (.35)	$	$ 26,749.50	$

Section C — Use if your filing status is **Married filing separately.** Complete the row below that applies to you.

Taxable income. If line 43 is —	**(a)** Enter the amount from line 43	**(b)** Multiplication amount	**(c)** Multiply (a) by (b)	**(d)** Subtraction amount	**Tax.** Subtract (d) from (c). Enter the result here and on Form 1040, line 44
At least $100,000 but not over $168,275	$	× 33% (.33)	$	$ 10,009.25	$
Over $168,275	$	× 35% (.35)	$	$ 13,374.75	$

Section D — Use if your filing status is **Head of household.** Complete the row below that applies to you.

Taxable income. If line 43 is —	**(a)** Enter the amount from line 43	**(b)** Multiplication amount	**(c)** Multiply (a) by (b)	**(d)** Subtraction amount	**Tax.** Subtract (d) from (c). Enter the result here and on Form 1040, line 44
At least $100,000 but not over $106,000	$	× 25% (.25)	$	$ 4,642.50	$
Over $106,000 but not over $171,650	$	× 28% (.28)	$	$ 7,822.50	$
Over $171,650 but not over $336,550	$	× 33% (.33)	$	$ 16,405.00	$
Over $336,550	$	× 35% (.35)	$	$ 23,136.00	$

2006 Earned Income Credit (EIC) Table

Caution. This is **not** a tax table.

1. To find your credit, read down the "At least - But less than" columns and find the line that includes the amount you were told to look up from your EIC Worksheet.

2. Then, go to the column that includes your filing status and the number of qualifying children you have. Enter the credit from that column on your EIC Worksheet.

Example. If your filing status is single, you have one qualifying child, and the amount you are looking up from your EIC Worksheet is $2,455, you would enter $842.

If the amount you are looking up from the worksheet is—		And your filing status is— Single, head of household, or qualifying widow(er) and you have—		
At least	But less than	No children	One child	Two children
		Your credit is—		
2,400	2,450	186	825	970
2,450	2,500	189	842	990

If the amount you are looking up from the worksheet is–		And your filing status is– Single, head of household, or qualifying widow(er) and you have–			Married filing jointly and you have–		
At least	But less than	No children	One child	Two children	No children	One child	Two children
		Your credit is–			Your credit is–		
$1	**$50**	$2	$9	$10	$2	$9	$10
50	**100**	6	26	30	6	26	30
100	**150**	10	43	50	10	43	50
150	**200**	13	60	70	13	60	70
200	**250**	17	77	90	17	77	90
250	**300**	21	94	110	21	94	110
300	**350**	25	111	130	25	111	130
350	**400**	29	128	150	29	128	150
400	**450**	33	145	170	33	145	170
450	**500**	36	162	190	36	162	190
500	**550**	40	179	210	40	179	210
550	**600**	44	196	230	44	196	230
600	**650**	48	213	250	48	213	250
650	**700**	52	230	270	52	230	270
700	**750**	55	247	290	55	247	290
750	**800**	59	264	310	59	264	310
800	**850**	63	281	330	63	281	330
850	**900**	67	298	350	67	298	350
900	**950**	71	315	370	71	315	370
950	**1,000**	75	332	390	75	332	390
1,000	**1,050**	78	349	410	78	349	410
1,050	**1,100**	82	366	430	82	366	430
1,100	**1,150**	86	383	450	86	383	450
1,150	**1,200**	90	400	470	90	400	470
1,200	**1,250**	94	417	490	94	417	490
1,250	**1,300**	98	434	510	98	434	510
1,300	**1,350**	101	451	530	101	451	530
1,350	**1,400**	105	468	550	105	468	550
1,400	**1,450**	109	485	570	109	485	570
1,450	**1,500**	113	502	590	113	502	590
1,500	**1,550**	117	519	610	117	519	610
1,550	**1,600**	120	536	630	120	536	630
1,600	**1,650**	124	553	650	124	553	650
1,650	**1,700**	128	570	670	128	570	670
1,700	**1,750**	132	587	690	132	587	690
1,750	**1,800**	136	604	710	136	604	710
1,800	**1,850**	140	621	730	140	621	730
1,850	**1,900**	143	638	750	143	638	750
1,900	**1,950**	147	655	770	147	655	770
1,950	**2,000**	151	672	790	151	672	790
2,000	**2,050**	155	689	810	155	689	810
2,050	**2,100**	159	706	830	159	706	830
2,100	**2,150**	163	723	850	163	723	850
2,150	**2,200**	166	740	870	166	740	870
2,200	**2,250**	170	757	890	170	757	890
2,250	**2,300**	174	774	910	174	774	910
2,300	**2,350**	178	791	930	178	791	930
2,350	**2,400**	182	808	950	182	808	950
2,400	**2,450**	186	825	970	186	825	970
2,450	**2,500**	189	842	990	189	842	990

If the amount you are looking up from the worksheet is–		And your filing status is– Single, head of household, or qualifying widow(er) and you have–			Married filing jointly and you have–		
At least	But less than	No children	One child	Two children	No children	One child	Two children
		Your credit is–			Your credit is–		
2,500	**2,550**	193	859	1,010	193	859	1,010
2,550	**2,600**	197	876	1,030	197	876	1,030
2,600	**2,650**	201	893	1,050	201	893	1,050
2,650	**2,700**	205	910	1,070	205	910	1,070
2,700	**2,750**	208	927	1,090	208	927	1,090
2,750	**2,800**	212	944	1,110	212	944	1,110
2,800	**2,850**	216	961	1,130	216	961	1,130
2,850	**2,900**	220	978	1,150	220	978	1,150
2,900	**2,950**	224	995	1,170	224	995	1,170
2,950	**3,000**	228	1,012	1,190	228	1,012	1,190
3,000	**3,050**	231	1,029	1,210	231	1,029	1,210
3,050	**3,100**	235	1,046	1,230	235	1,046	1,230
3,100	**3,150**	239	1,063	1,250	239	1,063	1,250
3,150	**3,200**	243	1,080	1,270	243	1,080	1,270
3,200	**3,250**	247	1,097	1,290	247	1,097	1,290
3,250	**3,300**	251	1,114	1,310	251	1,114	1,310
3,300	**3,350**	254	1,131	1,330	254	1,131	1,330
3,350	**3,400**	258	1,148	1,350	258	1,148	1,350
3,400	**3,450**	262	1,165	1,370	262	1,165	1,370
3,450	**3,500**	266	1,182	1,390	266	1,182	1,390
3,500	**3,550**	270	1,199	1,410	270	1,199	1,410
3,550	**3,600**	273	1,216	1,430	273	1,216	1,430
3,600	**3,650**	277	1,233	1,450	277	1,233	1,450
3,650	**3,700**	281	1,250	1,470	281	1,250	1,470
3,700	**3,750**	285	1,267	1,490	285	1,267	1,490
3,750	**3,800**	289	1,284	1,510	289	1,284	1,510
3,800	**3,850**	293	1,301	1,530	293	1,301	1,530
3,850	**3,900**	296	1,318	1,550	296	1,318	1,550
3,900	**3,950**	300	1,335	1,570	300	1,335	1,570
3,950	**4,000**	304	1,352	1,590	304	1,352	1,590
4,000	**4,050**	308	1,369	1,610	308	1,369	1,610
4,050	**4,100**	312	1,386	1,630	312	1,386	1,630
4,100	**4,150**	316	1,403	1,650	316	1,403	1,650
4,150	**4,200**	319	1,420	1,670	319	1,420	1,670
4,200	**4,250**	323	1,437	1,690	323	1,437	1,690
4,250	**4,300**	327	1,454	1,710	327	1,454	1,710
4,300	**4,350**	331	1,471	1,730	331	1,471	1,730
4,350	**4,400**	335	1,488	1,750	335	1,488	1,750
4,400	**4,450**	339	1,505	1,770	339	1,505	1,770
4,450	**4,500**	342	1,522	1,790	342	1,522	1,790
4,500	**4,550**	346	1,539	1,810	346	1,539	1,810
4,550	**4,600**	350	1,556	1,830	350	1,556	1,830
4,600	**4,650**	354	1,573	1,850	354	1,573	1,850
4,650	**4,700**	358	1,590	1,870	358	1,590	1,870
4,700	**4,750**	361	1,607	1,890	361	1,607	1,890
4,750	**4,800**	365	1,624	1,910	365	1,624	1,910
4,800	**4,850**	369	1,641	1,930	369	1,641	1,930
4,850	**4,900**	373	1,658	1,950	373	1,658	1,950
4,900	**4,950**	377	1,675	1,970	377	1,675	1,970
4,950	**5,000**	381	1,692	1,990	381	1,692	1,990

2006 Earned Income Credit (EIC) Table–*Continued*

(Caution. This is **not** a tax table.)

If the amount you are looking up from the worksheet is–		And your filing status is– Single, head of household, or qualifying widow(er) and you have–			Married filing jointly and you have–		
		No children	One child	Two children	No children	One child	Two children
At least	But less than	Your credit is–			Your credit is–		
5,000	**5,050**	384	1,709	2,010	384	1,709	2,010
5,050	**5,100**	388	1,726	2,030	388	1,726	2,030
5,100	**5,150**	392	1,743	2,050	392	1,743	2,050
5,150	**5,200**	396	1,760	2,070	396	1,760	2,070
5,200	**5,250**	400	1,777	2,090	400	1,777	2,090
5,250	**5,300**	404	1,794	2,110	404	1,794	2,110
5,300	**5,350**	407	1,811	2,130	407	1,811	2,130
5,350	**5,400**	412	1,828	2,150	412	1,828	2,150
5,400	**5,450**	412	1,845	2,170	412	1,845	2,170
5,450	**5,500**	412	1,862	2,190	412	1,862	2,190
5,500	**5,550**	412	1,879	2,210	412	1,879	2,210
5,550	**5,600**	412	1,896	2,230	412	1,896	2,230
5,600	**5,650**	412	1,913	2,250	412	1,913	2,250
5,650	**5,700**	412	1,930	2,270	412	1,930	2,270
5,700	**5,750**	412	1,947	2,290	412	1,947	2,290
5,750	**5,800**	412	1,964	2,310	412	1,964	2,310
5,800	**5,850**	412	1,981	2,330	412	1,981	2,330
5,850	**5,900**	412	1,998	2,350	412	1,998	2,350
5,900	**5,950**	412	2,015	2,370	412	2,015	2,370
5,950	**6,000**	412	2,032	2,390	412	2,032	2,390
6,000	**6,050**	412	2,049	2,410	412	2,049	2,410
6,050	**6,100**	412	2,066	2,430	412	2,066	2,430
6,100	**6,150**	412	2,083	2,450	412	2,083	2,450
6,150	**6,200**	412	2,100	2,470	412	2,100	2,470
6,200	**6,250**	412	2,117	2,490	412	2,117	2,490
6,250	**6,300**	412	2,134	2,510	412	2,134	2,510
6,300	**6,350**	412	2,151	2,530	412	2,151	2,530
6,350	**6,400**	412	2,168	2,550	412	2,168	2,550
6,400	**6,450**	412	2,185	2,570	412	2,185	2,570
6,450	**6,500**	412	2,202	2,590	412	2,202	2,590
6,500	**6,550**	412	2,219	2,610	412	2,219	2,610
6,550	**6,600**	412	2,236	2,630	412	2,236	2,630
6,600	**6,650**	412	2,253	2,650	412	2,253	2,650
6,650	**6,700**	412	2,270	2,670	412	2,270	2,670
6,700	**6,750**	412	2,287	2,690	412	2,287	2,690
6,750	**6,800**	409	2,304	2,710	412	2,304	2,710
6,800	**6,850**	405	2,321	2,730	412	2,321	2,730
6,850	**6,900**	401	2,338	2,750	412	2,338	2,750
6,900	**6,950**	397	2,355	2,770	412	2,355	2,770
6,950	**7,000**	394	2,372	2,790	412	2,372	2,790
7,000	**7,050**	390	2,389	2,810	412	2,389	2,810
7,050	**7,100**	386	2,406	2,830	412	2,406	2,830
7,100	**7,150**	382	2,423	2,850	412	2,423	2,850
7,150	**7,200**	378	2,440	2,870	412	2,440	2,870
7,200	**7,250**	374	2,457	2,890	412	2,457	2,890
7,250	**7,300**	371	2,474	2,910	412	2,474	2,910
7,300	**7,350**	367	2,491	2,930	412	2,491	2,930
7,350	**7,400**	363	2,508	2,950	412	2,508	2,950
7,400	**7,450**	359	2,525	2,970	412	2,525	2,970
7,450	**7,500**	355	2,542	2,990	412	2,542	2,990
7,500	**7,550**	352	2,559	3,010	412	2,559	3,010
7,550	**7,600**	348	2,576	3,030	412	2,576	3,030
7,600	**7,650**	344	2,593	3,050	412	2,593	3,050
7,650	**7,700**	340	2,610	3,070	412	2,610	3,070
7,700	**7,750**	336	2,627	3,090	412	2,627	3,090
7,750	**7,800**	332	2,644	3,110	412	2,644	3,110
7,800	**7,850**	329	2,661	3,130	412	2,661	3,130
7,850	**7,900**	325	2,678	3,150	412	2,678	3,150
7,900	**7,950**	321	2,695	3,170	412	2,695	3,170
7,950	**8,000**	317	2,712	3,190	412	2,712	3,190

If the amount you are looking up from the worksheet is–		And your filing status is– Single, head of household, or qualifying widow(er) and you have–			Married filing jointly and you have–		
		No children	One child	Two children	No children	One child	Two children
At least	But less than	Your credit is–			Your credit is–		
8,000	**8,050**	313	2,729	3,210	412	2,729	3,210
8,050	**8,100**	309	2,747	3,230	412	2,747	3,230
8,100	**8,150**	306	2,747	3,250	412	2,747	3,250
8,150	**8,200**	302	2,747	3,270	412	2,747	3,270
8,200	**8,250**	298	2,747	3,290	412	2,747	3,290
8,250	**8,300**	294	2,747	3,310	412	2,747	3,310
8,300	**8,350**	290	2,747	3,330	412	2,747	3,330
8,350	**8,400**	286	2,747	3,350	412	2,747	3,350
8,400	**8,450**	283	2,747	3,370	412	2,747	3,370
8,450	**8,500**	279	2,747	3,390	412	2,747	3,390
8,500	**8,550**	275	2,747	3,410	412	2,747	3,410
8,550	**8,600**	271	2,747	3,430	412	2,747	3,430
8,600	**8,650**	267	2,747	3,450	412	2,747	3,450
8,650	**8,700**	264	2,747	3,470	412	2,747	3,470
8,700	**8,750**	260	2,747	3,490	412	2,747	3,490
8,750	**8,800**	256	2,747	3,510	409	2,747	3,510
8,800	**8,850**	252	2,747	3,530	405	2,747	3,530
8,850	**8,900**	248	2,747	3,550	401	2,747	3,550
8,900	**8,950**	244	2,747	3,570	397	2,747	3,570
8,950	**9,000**	241	2,747	3,590	394	2,747	3,590
9,000	**9,050**	237	2,747	3,610	390	2,747	3,610
9,050	**9,100**	233	2,747	3,630	386	2,747	3,630
9,100	**9,150**	229	2,747	3,650	382	2,747	3,650
9,150	**9,200**	225	2,747	3,670	378	2,747	3,670
9,200	**9,250**	221	2,747	3,690	374	2,747	3,690
9,250	**9,300**	218	2,747	3,710	371	2,747	3,710
9,300	**9,350**	214	2,747	3,730	367	2,747	3,730
9,350	**9,400**	210	2,747	3,750	363	2,747	3,750
9,400	**9,450**	206	2,747	3,770	359	2,747	3,770
9,450	**9,500**	202	2,747	3,790	355	2,747	3,790
9,500	**9,550**	199	2,747	3,810	352	2,747	3,810
9,550	**9,600**	195	2,747	3,830	348	2,747	3,830
9,600	**9,650**	191	2,747	3,850	344	2,747	3,850
9,650	**9,700**	187	2,747	3,870	340	2,747	3,870
9,700	**9,750**	183	2,747	3,890	336	2,747	3,890
9,750	**9,800**	179	2,747	3,910	332	2,747	3,910
9,800	**9,850**	176	2,747	3,930	329	2,747	3,930
9,850	**9,900**	172	2,747	3,950	325	2,747	3,950
9,900	**9,950**	168	2,747	3,970	321	2,747	3,970
9,950	**10,000**	164	2,747	3,990	317	2,747	3,990
10,000	**10,050**	160	2,747	4,010	313	2,747	4,010
10,050	**10,100**	156	2,747	4,030	309	2,747	4,030
10,100	**10,150**	153	2,747	4,050	306	2,747	4,050
10,150	**10,200**	149	2,747	4,070	302	2,747	4,070
10,200	**10,250**	145	2,747	4,090	298	2,747	4,090
10,250	**10,300**	141	2,747	4,110	294	2,747	4,110
10,300	**10,350**	137	2,747	4,130	290	2,747	4,130
10,350	**10,400**	133	2,747	4,150	286	2,747	4,150
10,400	**10,450**	130	2,747	4,170	283	2,747	4,170
10,450	**10,500**	126	2,747	4,190	279	2,747	4,190
10,500	**10,550**	122	2,747	4,210	275	2,747	4,210
10,550	**10,600**	118	2,747	4,230	271	2,747	4,230
10,600	**10,650**	114	2,747	4,250	267	2,747	4,250
10,650	**10,700**	111	2,747	4,270	264	2,747	4,270
10,700	**10,750**	107	2,747	4,290	260	2,747	4,290
10,750	**10,800**	103	2,747	4,310	256	2,747	4,310
10,800	**10,850**	99	2,747	4,330	252	2,747	4,330
10,850	**10,900**	95	2,747	4,350	248	2,747	4,350
10,900	**10,950**	91	2,747	4,370	244	2,747	4,370
10,950	**11,000**	88	2,747	4,390	241	2,747	4,390

2006 Earned Income Credit (EIC) Table–*Continued*

(**Caution.** This is **not** a tax table.)

If the amount you are looking up from the worksheet is–		And your filing status is–					
		Single, head of household, or qualifying widow(er) and you have–			Married filing jointly and you have–		
		No children	One child	Two children	No children	One child	Two children
At least	But less than	Your credit is–			Your credit is–		
11,000	11,050	84	2,747	4,410	237	2,747	4,410
11,050	11,100	80	2,747	4,430	233	2,747	4,430
11,100	11,150	76	2,747	4,450	229	2,747	4,450
11,150	11,200	72	2,747	4,470	225	2,747	4,470
11,200	11,250	68	2,747	4,490	221	2,747	4,490
11,250	11,300	65	2,747	4,510	218	2,747	4,510
11,300	11,350	61	2,747	4,536	214	2,747	4,536
11,350	11,400	57	2,747	4,536	210	2,747	4,536
11,400	11,450	53	2,747	4,536	206	2,747	4,536
11,450	11,500	49	2,747	4,536	202	2,747	4,536
11,500	11,550	46	2,747	4,536	199	2,747	4,536
11,550	11,600	42	2,747	4,536	195	2,747	4,536
11,600	11,650	38	2,747	4,536	191	2,747	4,536
11,650	11,700	34	2,747	4,536	187	2,747	4,536
11,700	11,750	30	2,747	4,536	183	2,747	4,536
11,750	11,800	26	2,747	4,536	179	2,747	4,536
11,800	11,850	23	2,747	4,536	176	2,747	4,536
11,850	11,900	19	2,747	4,536	172	2,747	4,536
11,900	11,950	15	2,747	4,536	168	2,747	4,536
11,950	12,000	11	2,747	4,536	164	2,747	4,536
12,000	12,050	7	2,747	4,536	160	2,747	4,536
12,050	12,100	3	2,747	4,536	156	2,747	4,536
12,100	12,150	*	2,747	4,536	153	2,747	4,536
12,150	12,200	0	2,747	4,536	149	2,747	4,536
12,200	12,250	0	2,747	4,536	145	2,747	4,536
12,250	12,300	0	2,747	4,536	141	2,747	4,536
12,300	12,350	0	2,747	4,536	137	2,747	4,536
12,350	12,400	0	2,747	4,536	133	2,747	4,536
12,400	12,450	0	2,747	4,536	130	2,747	4,536
12,450	12,500	0	2,747	4,536	126	2,747	4,536
12,500	12,550	0	2,747	4,536	122	2,747	4,536
12,550	12,600	0	2,747	4,536	118	2,747	4,536
12,600	12,650	0	2,747	4,536	114	2,747	4,536
12,650	12,700	0	2,747	4,536	111	2,747	4,536
12,700	12,750	0	2,747	4,536	107	2,747	4,536
12,750	12,800	0	2,747	4,536	103	2,747	4,536
12,800	12,850	0	2,747	4,536	99	2,747	4,536
12,850	12,900	0	2,747	4,536	95	2,747	4,536
12,900	12,950	0	2,747	4,536	91	2,747	4,536
12,950	13,000	0	2,747	4,536	88	2,747	4,536
13,000	13,050	0	2,747	4,536	84	2,747	4,536
13,050	13,100	0	2,747	4,536	80	2,747	4,536
13,100	13,150	0	2,747	4,536	76	2,747	4,536
13,150	13,200	0	2,747	4,536	72	2,747	4,536
13,200	13,250	0	2,747	4,536	68	2,747	4,536
13,250	13,300	0	2,747	4,536	65	2,747	4,536
13,300	13,350	0	2,747	4,536	61	2,747	4,536
13,350	13,400	0	2,747	4,536	57	2,747	4,536
13,400	13,450	0	2,747	4,536	53	2,747	4,536
13,450	13,500	0	2,747	4,536	49	2,747	4,536
13,500	13,550	0	2,747	4,536	46	2,747	4,536
13,550	13,600	0	2,747	4,536	42	2,747	4,536
13,600	13,650	0	2,747	4,536	38	2,747	4,536
13,650	13,700	0	2,747	4,536	34	2,747	4,536
13,700	13,750	0	2,747	4,536	30	2,747	4,536
13,750	13,800	0	2,747	4,536	26	2,747	4,536
13,800	13,850	0	2,747	4,536	23	2,747	4,536
13,850	13,900	0	2,747	4,536	19	2,747	4,536
13,900	13,950	0	2,747	4,536	15	2,747	4,536
13,950	14,000	0	2,747	4,536	11	2,747	4,536
14,000	14,050	0	2,747	4,536	7	2,747	4,536
14,050	14,100	0	2,747	4,536	3	2,747	4,536
14,100	14,150	0	2,747	4,536	*	2,747	4,536
14,150	14,200	0	2,747	4,536	0	2,747	4,536
14,200	14,250	0	2,747	4,536	0	2,747	4,536
14,250	14,300	0	2,747	4,536	0	2,747	4,536
14,300	14,350	0	2,747	4,536	0	2,747	4,536
14,350	14,400	0	2,747	4,536	0	2,747	4,536
14,400	14,450	0	2,747	4,536	0	2,747	4,536
14,450	14,500	0	2,747	4,536	0	2,747	4,536
14,500	14,550	0	2,747	4,536	0	2,747	4,536
14,550	14,600	0	2,747	4,536	0	2,747	4,536
14,600	14,650	0	2,747	4,536	0	2,747	4,536
14,650	14,700	0	2,747	4,536	0	2,747	4,536
14,700	14,750	0	2,747	4,536	0	2,747	4,536
14,750	14,800	0	2,747	4,536	0	2,747	4,536
14,800	14,850	0	2,747	4,536	0	2,747	4,536
14,850	14,900	0	2,737	4,522	0	2,747	4,536
14,900	14,950	0	2,729	4,512	0	2,747	4,536
14,950	15,000	0	2,721	4,501	0	2,747	4,536
15,000	15,050	0	2,713	4,491	0	2,747	4,536
15,050	15,100	0	2,705	4,480	0	2,747	4,536
15,100	15,150	0	2,697	4,470	0	2,747	4,536
15,150	15,200	0	2,689	4,459	0	2,747	4,536
15,200	15,250	0	2,681	4,449	0	2,747	4,536
15,250	15,300	0	2,673	4,438	0	2,747	4,536
15,300	15,350	0	2,665	4,428	0	2,747	4,536
15,350	15,400	0	2,657	4,417	0	2,747	4,536
15,400	15,450	0	2,649	4,406	0	2,747	4,536
15,450	15,500	0	2,641	4,396	0	2,747	4,536
15,500	15,550	0	2,633	4,385	0	2,747	4,536
15,550	15,600	0	2,625	4,375	0	2,747	4,536
15,600	15,650	0	2,617	4,364	0	2,747	4,536
15,650	15,700	0	2,609	4,354	0	2,747	4,536
15,700	15,750	0	2,601	4,343	0	2,747	4,536
15,750	15,800	0	2,593	4,333	0	2,747	4,536
15,800	15,850	0	2,585	4,322	0	2,747	4,536
15,850	15,900	0	2,577	4,312	0	2,747	4,536
15,900	15,950	0	2,569	4,301	0	2,747	4,536
15,950	16,000	0	2,561	4,291	0	2,747	4,536

*If the amount you are looking up from the worksheet is at least $12,100 ($14,100 if married filing jointly) but less than $12,120 ($14,120 if married filing jointly), your credit is $1. Otherwise, you cannot take the credit.

2006 Earned Income Credit (EIC) Table–*Continued*

(**Caution.** This is **not** a tax table.)

If the amount you are looking up from the worksheet is–		And your filing status is– Single, head of household, or qualifying widow(er) and you have–			Married filing jointly and you have–		
		No children	One child	Two children	No children	One child	Two children
At least	But less than	Your credit is–			Your credit is–		
16,000	**16,050**	0	2,553	4,280	0	2,747	4,536
16,050	**16,100**	0	2,545	4,270	0	2,747	4,536
16,100	**16,150**	0	2,537	4,259	0	2,747	4,536
16,150	**16,200**	0	2,529	4,249	0	2,747	4,536
16,200	**16,250**	0	2,521	4,238	0	2,747	4,536
16,250	**16,300**	0	2,513	4,227	0	2,747	4,536
16,300	**16,350**	0	2,505	4,217	0	2,747	4,536
16,350	**16,400**	0	2,497	4,206	0	2,747	4,536
16,400	**16,450**	0	2,489	4,196	0	2,747	4,536
16,450	**16,500**	0	2,481	4,185	0	2,747	4,536
16,500	**16,550**	0	2,473	4,175	0	2,747	4,536
16,550	**16,600**	0	2,465	4,164	0	2,747	4,536
16,600	**16,650**	0	2,457	4,154	0	2,747	4,536
16,650	**16,700**	0	2,449	4,143	0	2,747	4,536
16,700	**16,750**	0	2,441	4,133	0	2,747	4,536
16,750	**16,800**	0	2,433	4,122	0	2,747	4,536
16,800	**16,850**	0	2,425	4,112	0	2,747	4,536
16,850	**16,900**	0	2,417	4,101	0	2,737	4,522
16,900	**16,950**	0	2,409	4,091	0	2,729	4,512
16,950	**17,000**	0	2,401	4,080	0	2,721	4,501
17,000	**17,050**	0	2,393	4,070	0	2,713	4,491
17,050	**17,100**	0	2,385	4,059	0	2,705	4,480
17,100	**17,150**	0	2,377	4,048	0	2,697	4,470
17,150	**17,200**	0	2,369	4,038	0	2,689	4,459
17,200	**17,250**	0	2,361	4,027	0	2,681	4,449
17,250	**17,300**	0	2,353	4,017	0	2,673	4,438
17,300	**17,350**	0	2,345	4,006	0	2,665	4,428
17,350	**17,400**	0	2,337	3,996	0	2,657	4,417
17,400	**17,450**	0	2,329	3,985	0	2,649	4,406
17,450	**17,500**	0	2,321	3,975	0	2,641	4,396
17,500	**17,550**	0	2,313	3,964	0	2,633	4,385
17,550	**17,600**	0	2,305	3,954	0	2,625	4,375
17,600	**17,650**	0	2,297	3,943	0	2,617	4,364
17,650	**17,700**	0	2,289	3,933	0	2,609	4,354
17,700	**17,750**	0	2,281	3,922	0	2,601	4,343
17,750	**17,800**	0	2,273	3,912	0	2,593	4,333
17,800	**17,850**	0	2,265	3,901	0	2,585	4,322
17,850	**17,900**	0	2,257	3,891	0	2,577	4,312
17,900	**17,950**	0	2,249	3,880	0	2,569	4,301
17,950	**18,000**	0	2,241	3,869	0	2,561	4,291
18,000	**18,050**	0	2,233	3,859	0	2,553	4,280
18,050	**18,100**	0	2,225	3,848	0	2,545	4,270
18,100	**18,150**	0	2,217	3,838	0	2,537	4,259
18,150	**18,200**	0	2,209	3,827	0	2,529	4,249
18,200	**18,250**	0	2,201	3,817	0	2,521	4,238
18,250	**18,300**	0	2,193	3,806	0	2,513	4,227
18,300	**18,350**	0	2,186	3,796	0	2,505	4,217
18,350	**18,400**	0	2,178	3,785	0	2,497	4,206
18,400	**18,450**	0	2,170	3,775	0	2,489	4,196
18,450	**18,500**	0	2,162	3,764	0	2,481	4,185
18,500	**18,550**	0	2,154	3,754	0	2,473	4,175
18,550	**18,600**	0	2,146	3,743	0	2,465	4,164
18,600	**18,650**	0	2,138	3,733	0	2,457	4,154
18,650	**18,700**	0	2,130	3,722	0	2,449	4,143
18,700	**18,750**	0	2,122	3,712	0	2,441	4,133
18,750	**18,800**	0	2,114	3,701	0	2,433	4,122
18,800	**18,850**	0	2,106	3,690	0	2,425	4,112
18,850	**18,900**	0	2,098	3,680	0	2,417	4,101
18,900	**18,950**	0	2,090	3,669	0	2,409	4,091
18,950	**19,000**	0	2,082	3,659	0	2,401	4,080
19,000	**19,050**	0	2,074	3,648	0	2,393	4,070
19,050	**19,100**	0	2,066	3,638	0	2,385	4,059
19,100	**19,150**	0	2,058	3,627	0	2,377	4,048
19,150	**19,200**	0	2,050	3,617	0	2,369	4,038
19,200	**19,250**	0	2,042	3,606	0	2,361	4,027
19,250	**19,300**	0	2,034	3,596	0	2,353	4,017
19,300	**19,350**	0	2,026	3,585	0	2,345	4,006
19,350	**19,400**	0	2,018	3,575	0	2,337	3,996
19,400	**19,450**	0	2,010	3,564	0	2,329	3,985
19,450	**19,500**	0	2,002	3,554	0	2,321	3,975
19,500	**19,550**	0	1,994	3,543	0	2,313	3,964
19,550	**19,600**	0	1,986	3,532	0	2,305	3,954
19,600	**19,650**	0	1,978	3,522	0	2,297	3,943
19,650	**19,700**	0	1,970	3,511	0	2,289	3,933
19,700	**19,750**	0	1,962	3,501	0	2,281	3,922
19,750	**19,800**	0	1,954	3,490	0	2,273	3,912
19,800	**19,850**	0	1,946	3,480	0	2,265	3,901
19,850	**19,900**	0	1,938	3,469	0	2,257	3,891
19,900	**19,950**	0	1,930	3,459	0	2,249	3,880
19,950	**20,000**	0	1,922	3,448	0	2,241	3,869
20,000	**20,050**	0	1,914	3,438	0	2,233	3,859
20,050	**20,100**	0	1,906	3,427	0	2,225	3,848
20,100	**20,150**	0	1,898	3,417	0	2,217	3,838
20,150	**20,200**	0	1,890	3,406	0	2,209	3,827
20,200	**20,250**	0	1,882	3,396	0	2,201	3,817
20,250	**20,300**	0	1,874	3,385	0	2,193	3,806
20,300	**20,350**	0	1,866	3,375	0	2,186	3,796
20,350	**20,400**	0	1,858	3,364	0	2,178	3,785
20,400	**20,450**	0	1,850	3,353	0	2,170	3,775
20,450	**20,500**	0	1,842	3,343	0	2,162	3,764
20,500	**20,550**	0	1,834	3,332	0	2,154	3,754
20,550	**20,600**	0	1,826	3,322	0	2,146	3,743
20,600	**20,650**	0	1,818	3,311	0	2,138	3,733
20,650	**20,700**	0	1,810	3,301	0	2,130	3,722
20,700	**20,750**	0	1,802	3,290	0	2,122	3,712
20,750	**20,800**	0	1,794	3,280	0	2,114	3,701
20,800	**20,850**	0	1,786	3,269	0	2,106	3,690
20,850	**20,900**	0	1,778	3,259	0	2,098	3,680
20,900	**20,950**	0	1,770	3,248	0	2,090	3,669
20,950	**21,000**	0	1,762	3,238	0	2,082	3,659
21,000	**21,050**	0	1,754	3,227	0	2,074	3,648
21,050	**21,100**	0	1,746	3,217	0	2,066	3,638
21,100	**21,150**	0	1,738	3,206	0	2,058	3,627
21,150	**21,200**	0	1,730	3,196	0	2,050	3,617
21,200	**21,250**	0	1,722	3,185	0	2,042	3,606
21,250	**21,300**	0	1,714	3,174	0	2,034	3,596
21,300	**21,350**	0	1,706	3,164	0	2,026	3,585
21,350	**21,400**	0	1,698	3,153	0	2,018	3,575
21,400	**21,450**	0	1,690	3,143	0	2,010	3,564
21,450	**21,500**	0	1,682	3,132	0	2,002	3,554
21,500	**21,550**	0	1,674	3,122	0	1,994	3,543
21,550	**21,600**	0	1,666	3,111	0	1,986	3,532
21,600	**21,650**	0	1,658	3,101	0	1,978	3,522
21,650	**21,700**	0	1,650	3,090	0	1,970	3,511
21,700	**21,750**	0	1,642	3,080	0	1,962	3,501
21,750	**21,800**	0	1,634	3,069	0	1,954	3,490
21,800	**21,850**	0	1,626	3,059	0	1,946	3,480
21,850	**21,900**	0	1,618	3,048	0	1,938	3,469
21,900	**21,950**	0	1,610	3,038	0	1,930	3,459
21,950	**22,000**	0	1,602	3,027	0	1,922	3,448

2006 Earned Income Credit (EIC) Table—*Continued*

(Caution. This is **not** a tax table.)

If the amount you are looking up from the worksheet is—		And your filing status is— Single, head of household, or qualifying widow(er) and you have—			Married filing jointly and you have—		
At least	But less than	No children	One child	Two children	No children	One child	Two children
		Your credit is—			Your credit is—		
22,000	22,050	0	1,594	3,017	0	1,914	3,438
22,050	22,100	0	1,586	3,006	0	1,906	3,427
22,100	22,150	0	1,578	2,995	0	1,898	3,417
22,150	22,200	0	1,570	2,985	0	1,890	3,406
22,200	22,250	0	1,562	2,974	0	1,882	3,396
22,250	22,300	0	1,554	2,964	0	1,874	3,385
22,300	22,350	0	1,546	2,953	0	1,866	3,375
22,350	22,400	0	1,538	2,943	0	1,858	3,364
22,400	22,450	0	1,530	2,932	0	1,850	3,353
22,450	22,500	0	1,522	2,922	0	1,842	3,343
22,500	22,550	0	1,514	2,911	0	1,834	3,332
22,550	22,600	0	1,506	2,901	0	1,826	3,322
22,600	22,650	0	1,498	2,890	0	1,818	3,311
22,650	22,700	0	1,490	2,880	0	1,810	3,301
22,700	22,750	0	1,482	2,869	0	1,802	3,290
22,750	22,800	0	1,474	2,859	0	1,794	3,280
22,800	22,850	0	1,466	2,848	0	1,786	3,269
22,850	22,900	0	1,458	2,838	0	1,778	3,259
22,900	22,950	0	1,450	2,827	0	1,770	3,248
22,950	23,000	0	1,442	2,816	0	1,762	3,238
23,000	23,050	0	1,434	2,806	0	1,754	3,227
23,050	23,100	0	1,426	2,795	0	1,746	3,217
23,100	23,150	0	1,418	2,785	0	1,738	3,206
23,150	23,200	0	1,410	2,774	0	1,730	3,196
23,200	23,250	0	1,402	2,764	0	1,722	3,185
23,250	23,300	0	1,394	2,753	0	1,714	3,174
23,300	23,350	0	1,387	2,743	0	1,706	3,164
23,350	23,400	0	1,379	2,732	0	1,698	3,153
23,400	23,450	0	1,371	2,722	0	1,690	3,143
23,450	23,500	0	1,363	2,711	0	1,682	3,132
23,500	23,550	0	1,355	2,701	0	1,674	3,122
23,550	23,600	0	1,347	2,690	0	1,666	3,111
23,600	23,650	0	1,339	2,680	0	1,658	3,101
23,650	23,700	0	1,331	2,669	0	1,650	3,090
23,700	23,750	0	1,323	2,659	0	1,642	3,080
23,750	23,800	0	1,315	2,648	0	1,634	3,069
23,800	23,850	0	1,307	2,637	0	1,626	3,059
23,850	23,900	0	1,299	2,627	0	1,618	3,048
23,900	23,950	0	1,291	2,616	0	1,610	3,038
23,950	24,000	0	1,283	2,606	0	1,602	3,027
24,000	24,050	0	1,275	2,595	0	1,594	3,017
24,050	24,100	0	1,267	2,585	0	1,586	3,006
24,100	24,150	0	1,259	2,574	0	1,578	2,995
24,150	24,200	0	1,251	2,564	0	1,570	2,985
24,200	24,250	0	1,243	2,553	0	1,562	2,974
24,250	24,300	0	1,235	2,543	0	1,554	2,964
24,300	24,350	0	1,227	2,532	0	1,546	2,953
24,350	24,400	0	1,219	2,522	0	1,538	2,943
24,400	24,450	0	1,211	2,511	0	1,530	2,932
24,450	24,500	0	1,203	2,501	0	1,522	2,922
24,500	24,550	0	1,195	2,490	0	1,514	2,911
24,550	24,600	0	1,187	2,479	0	1,506	2,901
24,600	24,650	0	1,179	2,469	0	1,498	2,890
24,650	24,700	0	1,171	2,458	0	1,490	2,880
24,700	24,750	0	1,163	2,448	0	1,482	2,869
24,750	24,800	0	1,155	2,437	0	1,474	2,859
24,800	24,850	0	1,147	2,427	0	1,466	2,848
24,850	24,900	0	1,139	2,416	0	1,458	2,838
24,900	24,950	0	1,131	2,406	0	1,450	2,827
24,950	25,000	0	1,123	2,395	0	1,442	2,816

If the amount you are looking up from the worksheet is—		And your filing status is— Single, head of household, or qualifying widow(er) and you have—			Married filing jointly and you have—		
At least	But less than	No children	One child	Two children	No children	One child	Two children
		Your credit is—			Your credit is—		
25,000	25,050	0	1,115	2,385	0	1,434	2,806
25,050	25,100	0	1,107	2,374	0	1,426	2,795
25,100	25,150	0	1,099	2,364	0	1,418	2,785
25,150	25,200	0	1,091	2,353	0	1,410	2,774
25,200	25,250	0	1,083	2,343	0	1,402	2,764
25,250	25,300	0	1,075	2,332	0	1,394	2,753
25,300	25,350	0	1,067	2,322	0	1,387	2,743
25,350	25,400	0	1,059	2,311	0	1,379	2,732
25,400	25,450	0	1,051	2,300	0	1,371	2,722
25,450	25,500	0	1,043	2,290	0	1,363	2,711
25,500	25,550	0	1,035	2,279	0	1,355	2,701
25,550	25,600	0	1,027	2,269	0	1,347	2,690
25,600	25,650	0	1,019	2,258	0	1,339	2,680
25,650	25,700	0	1,011	2,248	0	1,331	2,669
25,700	25,750	0	1,003	2,237	0	1,323	2,659
25,750	25,800	0	995	2,227	0	1,315	2,648
25,800	25,850	0	987	2,216	0	1,307	2,637
25,850	25,900	0	979	2,206	0	1,299	2,627
25,900	25,950	0	971	2,195	0	1,291	2,616
25,950	26,000	0	963	2,185	0	1,283	2,606
26,000	26,050	0	955	2,174	0	1,275	2,595
26,050	26,100	0	947	2,164	0	1,267	2,585
26,100	26,150	0	939	2,153	0	1,259	2,574
26,150	26,200	0	931	2,143	0	1,251	2,564
26,200	26,250	0	923	2,132	0	1,243	2,553
26,250	26,300	0	915	2,121	0	1,235	2,543
26,300	26,350	0	907	2,111	0	1,227	2,532
26,350	26,400	0	899	2,100	0	1,219	2,522
26,400	26,450	0	891	2,090	0	1,211	2,511
26,450	26,500	0	883	2,079	0	1,203	2,501
26,500	26,550	0	875	2,069	0	1,195	2,490
26,550	26,600	0	867	2,058	0	1,187	2,479
26,600	26,650	0	859	2,048	0	1,179	2,469
26,650	26,700	0	851	2,037	0	1,171	2,458
26,700	26,750	0	843	2,027	0	1,163	2,448
26,750	26,800	0	835	2,016	0	1,155	2,437
26,800	26,850	0	827	2,006	0	1,147	2,427
26,850	26,900	0	819	1,995	0	1,139	2,416
26,900	26,950	0	811	1,985	0	1,131	2,406
26,950	27,000	0	803	1,974	0	1,123	2,395
27,000	27,050	0	795	1,964	0	1,115	2,385
27,050	27,100	0	787	1,953	0	1,107	2,374
27,100	27,150	0	779	1,942	0	1,099	2,364
27,150	27,200	0	771	1,932	0	1,091	2,353
27,200	27,250	0	763	1,921	0	1,083	2,343
27,250	27,300	0	755	1,911	0	1,075	2,332
27,300	27,350	0	747	1,900	0	1,067	2,322
27,350	27,400	0	739	1,890	0	1,059	2,311
27,400	27,450	0	731	1,879	0	1,051	2,300
27,450	27,500	0	723	1,869	0	1,043	2,290
27,500	27,550	0	715	1,858	0	1,035	2,279
27,550	27,600	0	707	1,848	0	1,027	2,269
27,600	27,650	0	699	1,837	0	1,019	2,258
27,650	27,700	0	691	1,827	0	1,011	2,248
27,700	27,750	0	683	1,816	0	1,003	2,237
27,750	27,800	0	675	1,806	0	995	2,227
27,800	27,850	0	667	1,795	0	987	2,216
27,850	27,900	0	659	1,785	0	979	2,206
27,900	27,950	0	651	1,774	0	971	2,195
27,950	28,000	0	643	1,763	0	963	2,185

2006 Earned Income Credit (EIC) Table–*Continued* (**Caution.** This is **not** a tax table.)

If the amount you are looking up from the worksheet is–		And your filing status is–					
		Single, head of household, or qualifying widow(er) and you have–			Married filing jointly and you have–		
		No children	One child	Two children	No children	One child	Two children
At least	But less than	Your credit is–			Your credit is–		
28,000	**28,050**	0	635	1,753	0	955	2,174
28,050	**28,100**	0	627	1,742	0	947	2,164
28,100	**28,150**	0	619	1,732	0	939	2,153
28,150	**28,200**	0	611	1,721	0	931	2,143
28,200	**28,250**	0	603	1,711	0	923	2,132
28,250	**28,300**	0	595	1,700	0	915	2,121
28,300	**28,350**	0	588	1,690	0	907	2,111
28,350	**28,400**	0	580	1,679	0	899	2,100
28,400	**28,450**	0	572	1,669	0	891	2,090
28,450	**28,500**	0	564	1,658	0	883	2,079
28,500	**28,550**	0	556	1,648	0	875	2,069
28,550	**28,600**	0	548	1,637	0	867	2,058
28,600	**28,650**	0	540	1,627	0	859	2,048
28,650	**28,700**	0	532	1,616	0	851	2,037
28,700	**28,750**	0	524	1,606	0	843	2,027
28,750	**28,800**	0	516	1,595	0	835	2,016
28,800	**28,850**	0	508	1,584	0	827	2,006
28,850	**28,900**	0	500	1,574	0	819	1,995
28,900	**28,950**	0	492	1,563	0	811	1,985
28,950	**29,000**	0	484	1,553	0	803	1,974
29,000	**29,050**	0	476	1,542	0	795	1,964
29,050	**29,100**	0	468	1,532	0	787	1,953
29,100	**29,150**	0	460	1,521	0	779	1,942
29,150	**29,200**	0	452	1,511	0	771	1,932
29,200	**29,250**	0	444	1,500	0	763	1,921
29,250	**29,300**	0	436	1,490	0	755	1,911
29,300	**29,350**	0	428	1,479	0	747	1,900
29,350	**29,400**	0	420	1,469	0	739	1,890
29,400	**29,450**	0	412	1,458	0	731	1,879
29,450	**29,500**	0	404	1,448	0	723	1,869
29,500	**29,550**	0	396	1,437	0	715	1,858
29,550	**29,600**	0	388	1,426	0	707	1,848
29,600	**29,650**	0	380	1,416	0	699	1,837
29,650	**29,700**	0	372	1,405	0	691	1,827
29,700	**29,750**	0	364	1,395	0	683	1,816
29,750	**29,800**	0	356	1,384	0	675	1,806
29,800	**29,850**	0	348	1,374	0	667	1,795
29,850	**29,900**	0	340	1,363	0	659	1,785
29,900	**29,950**	0	332	1,353	0	651	1,774
29,950	**30,000**	0	324	1,342	0	643	1,763
30,000	**30,050**	0	316	1,332	0	635	1,753
30,050	**30,100**	0	308	1,321	0	627	1,742
30,100	**30,150**	0	300	1,311	0	619	1,732
30,150	**30,200**	0	292	1,300	0	611	1,721
30,200	**30,250**	0	284	1,290	0	603	1,711
30,250	**30,300**	0	276	1,279	0	595	1,700
30,300	**30,350**	0	268	1,269	0	588	1,690
30,350	**30,400**	0	260	1,258	0	580	1,679
30,400	**30,450**	0	252	1,247	0	572	1,669
30,450	**30,500**	0	244	1,237	0	564	1,658
30,500	**30,550**	0	236	1,226	0	556	1,648
30,550	**30,600**	0	228	1,216	0	548	1,637
30,600	**30,650**	0	220	1,205	0	540	1,627
30,650	**30,700**	0	212	1,195	0	532	1,616
30,700	**30,750**	0	204	1,184	0	524	1,606
30,750	**30,800**	0	196	1,174	0	516	1,595
30,800	**30,850**	0	188	1,163	0	508	1,584
30,850	**30,900**	0	180	1,153	0	500	1,574
30,900	**30,950**	0	172	1,142	0	492	1,563
30,950	**31,000**	0	164	1,132	0	484	1,553

If the amount you are looking up from the worksheet is–		And your filing status is–					
		Single, head of household, or qualifying widow(er) and you have–			Married filing jointly and you have–		
		No children	One child	Two children	No children	One child	Two children
At least	But less than	Your credit is–			Your credit is–		
31,000	**31,050**	0	156	1,121	0	476	1,542
31,050	**31,100**	0	148	1,111	0	468	1,532
31,100	**31,150**	0	140	1,100	0	460	1,521
31,150	**31,200**	0	132	1,090	0	452	1,511
31,200	**31,250**	0	124	1,079	0	444	1,500
31,250	**31,300**	0	116	1,068	0	436	1,490
31,300	**31,350**	0	108	1,058	0	428	1,479
31,350	**31,400**	0	100	1,047	0	420	1,469
31,400	**31,450**	0	92	1,037	0	412	1,458
31,450	**31,500**	0	84	1,026	0	404	1,448
31,500	**31,550**	0	76	1,016	0	396	1,437
31,550	**31,600**	0	68	1,005	0	388	1,426
31,600	**31,650**	0	60	995	0	380	1,416
31,650	**31,700**	0	52	984	0	372	1,405
31,700	**31,750**	0	44	974	0	364	1,395
31,750	**31,800**	0	36	963	0	356	1,384
31,800	**31,850**	0	28	953	0	348	1,374
31,850	**31,900**	0	20	942	0	340	1,363
31,900	**31,950**	0	12	932	0	332	1,353
31,950	**32,000**	0	4	921	0	324	1,342
32,000	**32,050**	0	0	911	0	316	1,332
32,050	**32,100**	0	0	900	0	308	1,321
32,100	**32,150**	0	0	889	0	300	1,311
32,150	**32,200**	0	0	879	0	292	1,300
32,200	**32,250**	0	0	868	0	284	1,290
32,250	**32,300**	0	0	858	0	276	1,279
32,300	**32,350**	0	0	847	0	268	1,269
32,350	**32,400**	0	0	837	0	260	1,258
32,400	**32,450**	0	0	826	0	252	1,247
32,450	**32,500**	0	0	816	0	244	1,237
32,500	**32,550**	0	0	805	0	236	1,226
32,550	**32,600**	0	0	795	0	228	1,216
32,600	**32,650**	0	0	784	0	220	1,205
32,650	**32,700**	0	0	774	0	212	1,195
32,700	**32,750**	0	0	763	0	204	1,184
32,750	**32,800**	0	0	753	0	196	1,174
32,800	**32,850**	0	0	742	0	188	1,163
32,850	**32,900**	0	0	732	0	180	1,153
32,900	**32,950**	0	0	721	0	172	1,142
32,950	**33,000**	0	0	710	0	164	1,132
33,000	**33,050**	0	0	700	0	156	1,121
33,050	**33,100**	0	0	689	0	148	1,111
33,100	**33,150**	0	0	679	0	140	1,100
33,150	**33,200**	0	0	668	0	132	1,090
33,200	**33,250**	0	0	658	0	124	1,079
33,250	**33,300**	0	0	647	0	116	1,068
33,300	**33,350**	0	0	637	0	108	1,058
33,350	**33,400**	0	0	626	0	100	1,047
33,400	**33,450**	0	0	616	0	92	1,037
33,450	**33,500**	0	0	605	0	84	1,026
33,500	**33,550**	0	0	595	0	76	1,016
33,550	**33,600**	0	0	584	0	68	1,005
33,600	**33,650**	0	0	574	0	60	995
33,650	**33,700**	0	0	563	0	52	984
33,700	**33,750**	0	0	553	0	44	974
33,750	**33,800**	0	0	542	0	36	963
33,800	**33,850**	0	0	531	0	28	953
33,850	**33,900**	0	0	521	0	20	942
33,900	**33,950**	0	0	510	0	12	932
33,950	**34,000**	0	0	500	0	4	921

2006 Earned Income Credit (EIC) Table—*Continued*

(Caution. This is **not** a tax table.)

If the amount you are looking up from the worksheet is—		And your filing status is— Single, head of household, or qualifying widow(er) and you have—			Married filing jointly and you have—		
At least	But less than	No children	One child	Two children	No children	One child	Two children
		Your credit is—			Your credit is—		
34,000	**34,050**	0	0	489	0	0	911
34,050	**34,100**	0	0	479	0	0	900
34,100	**34,150**	0	0	468	0	0	889
34,150	**34,200**	0	0	458	0	0	879
34,200	**34,250**	0	0	447	0	0	868
34,250	**34,300**	0	0	437	0	0	858
34,300	**34,350**	0	0	426	0	0	847
34,350	**34,400**	0	0	416	0	0	837
34,400	**34,450**	0	0	405	0	0	826
34,450	**34,500**	0	0	395	0	0	816
34,500	**34,550**	0	0	384	0	0	805
34,550	**34,600**	0	0	373	0	0	795
34,600	**34,650**	0	0	363	0	0	784
34,650	**34,700**	0	0	352	0	0	774
34,700	**34,750**	0	0	342	0	0	763
34,750	**34,800**	0	0	331	0	0	753
34,800	**34,850**	0	0	321	0	0	742
34,850	**34,900**	0	0	310	0	0	732
34,900	**34,950**	0	0	300	0	0	721
34,950	**35,000**	0	0	289	0	0	710
35,000	**35,050**	0	0	279	0	0	700
35,050	**35,100**	0	0	268	0	0	689
35,100	**35,150**	0	0	258	0	0	679
35,150	**35,200**	0	0	247	0	0	668
35,200	**35,250**	0	0	237	0	0	658
35,250	**35,300**	0	0	226	0	0	647
35,300	**35,350**	0	0	216	0	0	637
35,350	**35,400**	0	0	205	0	0	626
35,400	**35,450**	0	0	194	0	0	616
35,450	**35,500**	0	0	184	0	0	605
35,500	**35,550**	0	0	173	0	0	595
35,550	**35,600**	0	0	163	0	0	584
35,600	**35,650**	0	0	152	0	0	574
35,650	**35,700**	0	0	142	0	0	563
35,700	**35,750**	0	0	131	0	0	553
35,750	**35,800**	0	0	121	0	0	542
35,800	**35,850**	0	0	110	0	0	531
35,850	**35,900**	0	0	100	0	0	521
35,900	**35,950**	0	0	89	0	0	510
35,950	**36,000**	0	0	79	0	0	500
36,000	**36,050**	0	0	68	0	0	489
36,050	**36,100**	0	0	58	0	0	479
36,100	**36,150**	0	0	47	0	0	468
36,150	**36,200**	0	0	37	0	0	458
36,200	**36,250**	0	0	26	0	0	447
36,250	**36,300**	0	0	15	0	0	437
36,300	**36,350**	0	0	**	0	0	426
36,350	**36,400**	0	0	0	0	0	416
36,400	**36,450**	0	0	0	0	0	405
36,450	**36,500**	0	0	0	0	0	395
36,500	**36,550**	0	0	0	0	0	384
36,550	**36,600**	0	0	0	0	0	373
36,600	**36,650**	0	0	0	0	0	363
36,650	**36,700**	0	0	0	0	0	352
36,700	**36,750**	0	0	0	0	0	342
36,750	**36,800**	0	0	0	0	0	331
36,800	**36,850**	0	0	0	0	0	321
36,850	**36,900**	0	0	0	0	0	310
36,900	**36,950**	0	0	0	0	0	300
36,950	**37,000**	0	0	0	0	0	289
37,000	**37,050**	0	0	0	0	0	279
37,050	**37,100**	0	0	0	0	0	268
37,100	**37,150**	0	0	0	0	0	258
37,150	**37,200**	0	0	0	0	0	247
37,200	**37,250**	0	0	0	0	0	237
37,250	**37,300**	0	0	0	0	0	226
37,300	**37,350**	0	0	0	0	0	216
37,350	**37,400**	0	0	0	0	0	205
37,400	**37,450**	0	0	0	0	0	194
37,450	**37,500**	0	0	0	0	0	184
37,500	**37,550**	0	0	0	0	0	173
37,550	**37,600**	0	0	0	0	0	163
37,600	**37,650**	0	0	0	0	0	152
37,650	**37,700**	0	0	0	0	0	142
37,700	**37,750**	0	0	0	0	0	131
37,750	**37,800**	0	0	0	0	0	121
37,800	**37,850**	0	0	0	0	0	110
37,850	**37,900**	0	0	0	0	0	100
37,900	**37,950**	0	0	0	0	0	89
37,950	**38,000**	0	0	0	0	0	79
38,000	**38,050**	0	0	0	0	0	68
38,050	**38,100**	0	0	0	0	0	58
38,100	**38,150**	0	0	0	0	0	47
38,150	**38,200**	0	0	0	0	0	37
38,200	**38,250**	0	0	0	0	0	26
38,250	**38,300**	0	0	0	0	0	15
38,300	**38,348**	0	0	0	0	0	5
38,348	**or more**	0	0	0	0	0	0

**If the amount you are looking up from the worksheet is at least $36,300 but less than $36,348, your credit is $5. Otherwise, you cannot take the credit.

A

Accelerated cost recovery system (ACRS). A statutory method of depreciation allowing accelerated rates for most types of property used in business and income-producing activities during the years 1981 through 1986. It has been superseded by the modified accelerated cost recovery system (MACRS) for assets placed in service after 1986; *see 42.4* and *42.11.*

Accelerated depreciation. Depreciation methods that allow faster write-offs than straight-line rates in the earlier periods of the useful life of an asset. For example, in the first few years of recovery, MACRS allows a 200% double declining balance write-off, twice the straight-line rate; *see 42.5–42.8.*

Accountable reimbursement plan. An employer reimbursement or allowance arrangement that requires you to adequately substantiate business expenses to your employer, and to return any excess reimbursement; *see 20.31.*

Accrual method of accounting. A business method of accounting requiring income to be reported when earned and expenses to be deducted when incurred. However, deductions generally may not be claimed until economic performance has occurred; *see 40.3.*

Acquisition debt. Debt used to buy, build, or construct a principal residence or second home and that generally qualifies for a full interest expense deduction; *see 15.2.*

Active participation. Test for determining deductibility of IRA deductions. Active participants in employer retirement plans are subject to IRA deduction phase-out rules if adjusted gross income exceeds certain thresholds; *see 8.4.*

Adjusted basis. A statutory term describing the cost used to determine your profit or loss from a sale or exchange of property. It is generally your original cost, increased by capital improvements, and decreased by depreciation, depletion, and other capital write-offs; *see 5.20.*

Adjusted gross income (AGI). Gross income less allowable adjustments, such as IRA, alimony, and Keogh deductions. AGI determines whether various tax benefits are phased out, such as personal exemptions, itemized deductions, and the rental loss allowance; *see 12.1* and modified adjusted gross income (MAGI).

Alimony. Payments made to a separated or divorced spouse as required by a decree or agreement. Qualifying payments are deductible by the payor and taxable to the payee; *see* Chapter 37.

Alternative minimum tax (AMT). A tax triggered if certain tax benefits reduce your regular income tax below the tax computed on Form 6251 for AMT purposes; *see* Chapter 23.

Amended return. On Form 1040X, you may file an amended return within a three-year period to claim a refund or correct a mistake made on an original or previously amended return; *see Chapter 47.*

Amortizable bond premium. The additional amount paid over the face amount of an obligation that may be deducted under the rules in *4.17.*

Amortization of intangibles. Writing off an investment in intangible assets over the projected life of the assets; *see 42.18.*

Amount realized. A statutory term used to figure your profit or loss on a sale or exchange. Generally, it is sales proceeds plus mortgages assumed or taken subject to, less transaction expenses, such as commissions and legal costs; *see 5.14.*

Amount recognized. The amount of gain reportable and subject to tax. On certain tax-free exchanges of property, gain is not recognized in the year it is realized; *see 6.1.*

Annualized rate. A rate for a period of less than a year computed as though for a full year.

Annuity. An annual payment of money by a company or individual to a person called the annuitant. Payment is for a fixed period or the life of the annuitant. Tax consequences depend on the type of contract and funding; *see 7.23–7.29.*

Applicable federal rate. Interest rate fixed by the Treasury for determining imputed interest; *see 4.30–4.32.*

Appreciation in value. Increase in value of property due to market conditions. When you sell appreciated property, you pay tax on the appreciation since the date of purchase. When you donate appreciated property held long term, you may generally deduct the appreciated value; *see 14.6.*

Archer Medical Savings Account (MSA). A type of medical plan combining high deductible medical insurance protection with an IRA-type savings account fund to pay unreimbursed medical expenses; *see 12.12.*

Assessment. The IRS action of fixing tax liability that sets in motion collection procedures, such as charging interest, imposing penalties, and, if necessary, seizing property; *see 48.2.*

Assignment. The legal transfer of property, rights, or interest to another person called an assignee. You cannot avoid tax on income by assigning the income to another person.

At-risk rules. Rules limiting loss deductions to cash investments and personal liability notes. An exception for real estate treats certain nonrecourse commercial loans as amounts "at risk"; *see 10.18.*

Audit. An IRS examination of your tax return, generally limited to a three-year period after you file; *see* Chapter 48.

Away from home. A tax requirement for deducting travel expenses on a business trip. Sleeping arrangements are required for at least one night before returning home; *see 20.3* and *20.5–20.6.*

B

Balloon. A final payment on a loan in one lump sum.

Basis. Generally, the amount paid for property. You need to know your basis to figure gain or loss on a sale; *see 5.16.*

Boot. Generally, the receipt of cash or its equivalent accompanying an exchange of property. In a tax-free exchange, boot is subject to immediate tax; *see 6.3.*

C

Cancellation of debt. Release of a debt without consideration by a creditor. Cancellations of debt are generally taxable; *see 11.8.*

Capital. The excess of assets over liabilities.

Capital asset. Property subject to capital gain or loss treatment. Almost all assets you own are considered capital assets except for certain business assets or works you created; *see 5.2.*

Capital expenses. Costs that are not currently deductible and that are added to the basis of property. A capital expense generally increases the value of property. When added to depreciable property, the cost is deductible over the life of the asset.

Capital gain or loss. The difference between amount realized and adjusted basis on the sale or exchange of capital assets. Long-term capital gains are taxed favorably, as explained in Chapter 5. Capital losses are deducted first against capital gains, and then again up to $3,000 of other income; *see 5.1–5.5.*

Capital gain distribution. A mutual-fund distribution allocated to gains realized on the sale of fund portfolio assets. You report the distribution as long-term capital gain even if you held the fund shares short term; *see 32.4–32.5.*

Capital loss carryover. A capital loss that is not deductible because it exceeds the annual $3,000 capital loss ceiling. A carryover loss may be deducted from capital gains of later years plus up to $3,000 of ordinary income; *see 5.4.*

Capitalization. Adding a cost or expense to the basis of the property.

Carryback. A tax technique for receiving a refund of back taxes by applying a deduction or credit from a current tax year to a prior tax year. For example, a business net operating loss may be carried back for two years.

Carryforward. A tax technique of applying a loss or credit from a current year to a later year. For example, a business net operating loss may be carried forward 20 years instead of being carried back; *see 40.18.*

Cash method of accounting. Reporting income when actually or constructively received and deducting expenses when paid. Certain businesses may not use the cash method; *see 40.3.*

Casualty loss. Loss from an unforeseen and sudden event that is deductible, subject to a 10% income floor and $100 reduction for personal losses; *see 18.1.*

Child and dependent care credit. A credit of up to 30% based on certain care expenses incurred to allow you to work; *see 25.4.*

Community income. Income earned by persons domiciled in community property states and treated as belonging equally to husband and wife; *see 1.6.*

Condemnation. The seizure of property by a public authority for a public purpose. Tax on gain realized on many conversions may be deferred; *see 18.19–18.20.*

Constructive receipt. A tax rule that taxes income that is not received by you but that you may draw upon; *see 2.2.*

Consumer interest. Interest incurred on personal debt and consumer credit. Consumer interest is not deductible.

Convention. Rule for determining MACRS depreciation in the year property is placed in service. Either a half-year convention or mid-quarter convention applies; *see 42.5–42.7.*

Coverdell Education Savings Account. A special account set up to fund education expenses of a student; *see 33.11–33.12.*

Credit. A tax credit directly reduces tax liability, as opposed to a deduction that reduces income subject to tax.

D

Declining balance method. A rapid depreciation method determined by a constant percentage based on useful life and applied to the adjusted basis of the property; *see 42.5* and *42.8.*

Deductions. Items directly reducing income. Personal deductions such as for mortgage interest, state and local taxes, and charitable contributions are allowed only if deductions are itemized on Schedule A, but deductions such as for alimony, capital losses, moving expenses to a new job location, business losses, student loan interest, and IRA and Keogh deductions are deducted from gross income even if itemized deductions are not claimed; *see* Chapter 12.

Deferred compensation. A portion of earnings withheld by an employer or put into a retirement plan for distribution to the employee at a later date. If certain legal requirements are met, the deferred amount is not taxable until actually paid, for example, after retirement; *see 2.7.*

Deficiency. The excess of the tax assessed by the IRS over the amount reported on your return; *see 48.8.*

Defined benefit plan. A retirement plan that pays fixed benefits based on actuarial projections; *see 41.2.*

Defined contribution plan. A retirement plan that pays benefits based on contributions to individual accounts, plus accumulated earnings. Contributions are generally based on a percentage of salary or earned income; *see 41.2.*

Dependent. A relative or household member for whom an exemption may be claimed; *see* Chapter 21.

Depletion. Deduction claimed for the use of mineral resources; *see 9.15.*

Depreciable property. A business or income-producing asset with a useful life exceeding one year; *see 42.1.*

Depreciation. Writing off the cost of depreciable property over a period of years, usually its class life or recovery period specified in the tax law; *see 42.4.*

Depreciation recapture. An amount of gain on the sale of certain depreciable property that is treated as ordinary income in the case of personal property. Recapture is computed on Form 4797; *see 44.1.* For recapture on the sale of realty, *see 44.2.*

Disaster losses. Casualty losses such as from a storm, in areas declared by the President to warrant federal assistance. An election may be made to deduct the loss in the year before the loss or the year of the loss; *see 18.3.*

Dividend. A distribution made by a corporation to its shareholders generally of company earnings or surplus. Most dividends are taxable but exceptions are explained in Chapter 4.

E

Earned income. Compensation for performing personal services. You must have earned income for a deductible IRA, *see 8.2,* or to claim the earned income credit, *see 25.10.*

Earned income credit. A credit allowed to taxpayers with earned income or adjusted gross income (AGI) below certain thresholds; *see 25.10.*

Education IRA. *See* Coverdell Education Savings Account and *33.11–33.12.*

Electronic Federal Tax Payment System (EFTPS). An online and phone tax payment system available 24 hours a day. For enrollment information, call 1-800-555-4477, or go to www.eftps.gov.

Estimated tax. Advance payment of current tax liability based either on wage withholdings or installment payments of your estimated tax liability. To avoid penalties, you generally must pay to the IRS either 90% of your final tax liability, or either 100% or 110% of the prior year's tax liability, depending on your adjusted gross income; *see* Chapter 27.

Exemption. A fixed deduction allowed to every taxpayer, except those who may be claimed as a dependent by another person. Extra exemption deductions are allowed for a spouse on a joint return and for each qualifying dependent. A deduction of $3,300 is allowed for each exemption claimed on 2006 returns, but the deduction is phased out for certain high income individuals; *see* Chapter 21.

F

Fair market value. What a willing buyer would pay to a willing seller when neither is under any compulsion to buy or sell.

Fiduciary. A person or corporation such as a trustee, executor, or guardian who manages property for another person.

First-year expensing (or Section 179 deduction). A deduction of the cost of business equipment in the year placed in service; *see 42.3* for limitations.

Fiscal year. A 12-month period ending on the last day of any month other than December. Partnerships, S corporations, and personal service corporations are limited in their choice of fiscal years and face special restrictions.

Flexible spending arrangement. A salary reduction plan that allows employees to pay for enhanced medical coverage or dependent care expenses on a tax-free basis; *see 3.15.*

Foreign earned income exclusion. In 2006, up to $82,400 of foreign earned income is exempt from tax if a foreign residence or physical presence test is met; *see 36.1–36.2.*

Foreign tax credit. A credit for income taxes paid to a foreign country or U.S. possession; *see 36.14.*

401(k) plan. A deferred pay plan, authorized by Section 401(k) of the Internal Revenue Code, under which a percentage of an employee's salary is withheld and placed in a savings account or the company's profit-sharing plan. Income accumulates on the deferred amount until withdrawn by the employee at age $59^1/_2$ or when the employee retires or leaves the company; *see 7.17.*

G

Gift tax. Gifts in excess of an $12,000-per-donee annual exclusion are subject to gift tax, but the tax may be offset by a gift tax credit; *see 39.2.*

Grantor trust rules. Tax rules that tax the grantor of a trust on the trust income; *see 39.6.*

Gross income. The total amount of income received from all sources before exclusions and deductions.

Gross receipts. Total business receipts reported on Schedule C or Schedule C-EZ before deducting adjustments for returns and allowances and cost of goods sold; *see 40.6.*

Group-term life insurance. Employees are not taxed on up to $50,000 of group-term coverage; *see 3.4.*

H

Head of household. Generally, an unmarried person who maintains a household for dependents and is allowed to compute his or her tax based on head of household rates, which are more favorable than single person rates; *see 1.12.*

Health reimbursement arrangement (HRA). Employer established account that provides tax-free reimbursements to employees for deductibles and other expenses that could be taken as itemized deductions; *see 3.3.*

Health savings account. For calendar year 2006, taxpayers covered by an HDHP may contribute up to the lesser of the annual deductible or $2,700 ($5,450 for family coverage); *see 3.2* and *12.10.*

High deductible health plan (HDHP). For 2006, a high deductible health plan is a health plan with an annual deductible that is not less than $1,050 for self-only coverage or $2,100 for family coverage, and with annual out-of-pocket expenses that do not exceed $5,250 or $10,500, respectively.

Hobby loss. Hobby expenses are deductible only up to income from the activity; loss deductions are not allowed; *see 40.10.*

Holding period. The length of time that an asset is owned and that generally determines long- or short-term capital gain treatment; *see 5.3* and *5.9–5.12.*

Home equity debt. Debt secured by a principal residence or second home to the extent of the excess of fair market value over acquisition debt. An interest deduction is generally allowed for home equity debt up to $100,000 ($50,000 if married filing separately); *see 15.3.*

I

Imputed interest. Interest deemed earned on seller-financed sales or low-interest loans, where the parties' stated interest rate is below the applicable IRS federal rate; *see 4.31* and *4.32.*

Incentive stock option. Option meeting tax law tests that defers tax on the option transaction until the obtained stock is sold; *see 2.16.*

Inclusion amount for leased cars. Based on an IRS table, an amount that reduces a business deduction taken for payments on an auto leased for a minimum of 30 days; *see 43.12.*

Income in respect of a decedent. Income earned by a person before death but taxable to an estate or heir who receives it; *see 1.14* and *11.16.*

Independent contractor. One who controls his or her own work and reports as a self-employed person; *see* Chapters 40 and 45.

Individual retirement account (IRA). A retirement account to which up to $4,000 (or $5,000 if you are 50 or over) may be contributed for 2006, but deductions for the contribution are restricted if you are covered by a company retirement plan. Earnings accumulate tax free; *see* Chapter 8.

Installment sale. A sale of property that allows for tax deferment if at least one payment is received after the end of the tax year in which the sale occurs. The installment method does not apply to year-end sales of publicly traded securities. Dealers may not use the installment method. Investors with very large installment balances could face a special tax; *see 5.21.*

Intangible assets. Intangible assets that come within Section 197, such as goodwill, are amortizable over a 15-year period; *see 42.18.*

Inter vivos or lifetime trust. A trust created during the lifetime of the person who created the trust. If irrevocable, income on the trust principal is generally shifted to the trust beneficiaries; *see 39.6.*

Investment in the contract. The total cost investment in an annuity. When annuity payments are made, the portion allocable to the cost investment is tax free; *see 7.23* and *7.28.*

Investment interest. Interest on debt used to carry investments, but not including interest expense from a passive activity. Deductions are limited to net investment income; *see 15.10.*

Involuntary conversion. Forced disposition of property due to condemnation, theft, or casualty. Tax on gain from involuntary conversions may be deferred if replacement property is purchased; *see 18.19.*

Itemized deductions. Items, such as interest, state and local income and sales taxes, charitable contributions, and medical deductions, claimed on Schedule A of Form 1040. Itemized deductions are subtracted from adjusted gross income to arrive at taxable income; *see* Chapter 13. The amount of itemized deductions is also subject to a reduction when adjusted gross income exceeds certain limits; *see 13.7.*

J

Joint return. A return filed by a married couple reporting their combined income and deductions. Joint return status provides tax savings to many couples; *see 1.4.*

Joint tenants. Ownership of property by two persons. When one dies, the decedent's interest passes to the survivor; *see 5.18.*

K

Keogh plan. Retirement plan set up by a self-employed person, providing tax-deductible contributions, tax-free income accumulations until withdrawal, and favorable averaging for qualifying lump-sum distributions; *see* Chapter 41.

Kiddie tax. The tax on the investment income in excess of $1,700 (may change after 2006) of a child under age 18, based on the parents' marginal tax rate and computed on Form 8615; *see 24.3.*

L

Legally separated. A husband and wife who are required to live apart from each other by the terms of a decree of separate maintenance. Payments under the decree are deductible by the payor and taxable to the payee as alimony; *see 37.2.*

Like-kind exchange. An exchange of similar assets used in a business or held for investment on which gain may be deferred; *see 6.1.*

Lump-sum distribution. Payments within one tax year of the entire amount due to a participant in a qualified retirement plan. Qualifying lump sums may be directly rolled over tax free, or, in some cases, are eligible for current tax under a favorable averaging method; *see 7.2.*

M

Marital deduction. An estate tax and gift tax deduction for assets passing to a spouse. It allows estate and gift transfers completely free of tax; *see 39.12.*

Market discount. The difference between face value of a bond and lower market price, attributable to rising interest rates. On a sale, gain on the bond is generally taxed as ordinary income to the extent of the discount; *see 4.20.*

Material participation tests. Rules for determining whether a person is active in a business activity for passive activity rule purposes. Unless the tests are met, passive loss limits apply; *see 10.6.*

Miscellaneous itemized deductions. Generally, itemized deductions for job and investment expenses subject to a 2% of adjusted gross income floor; *see* Chapter 19.

Modified ACRS (MACRS). Depreciation methods applied to assets placed in service after 1986.

Modified adjusted gross income (MAGI). This is generally adjusted gross income increased by certain items such as tax-free foreign earned income. MAGI usually is used to determine phaseouts of certain deductions and credits.

Mortgage interest. Fully deductible interest on up to two residences if acquisition debt secured by a home is $1 million or less, and home equity debt is $100,000 or less; *see 15.1.*

N

Net operating loss. A business loss that exceeds current income may be carried back against income of prior years and carried forward as a deduction from future income until eliminated. The carryback and carryforward periods are discussed in *40.18–40.22.*

Nonperiodic distributions. A 20% withholding rule applies to nonperiodic distributions, such as lump-sum distributions, paid directly to employees from an employer plan; *see 7.8* and *26.10.*

Nonrecourse financing. Debt on which a person is not personally liable. In case of nonpayment, the creditor must foreclose on property securing the debt. At-risk rules generally bar losses where there is nonrecourse financing, but an exception applies to certain nonrecourse financing for real estate; *see 10.18.*

O

Ordinary and necessary. A statutory requirement for the deductibility of a business expense.

Ordinary income. Income other than capital gains.

Ordinary loss. A loss other than a capital loss.

Original issue discount (OID). The difference between the face value of a bond and its original issue price. OID is reported on an annual basis as interest income; *see 4.19.*

P

Partnership. An unincorporated business or income-producing entity organized by two or more persons. A partnership is not subject to tax but passes through to the partners all income, deductions, and credits, according to the terms of the partnership agreement; *see 11.9–11.13.*

Passive activity loss rules. Rules that limit the deduction of losses from passive activities to income from other passive activities. Passive activities include investment rental operations or businesses in which you do not materially participate; *see 10.1.*

Patronage dividend. A taxable distribution made by a cooperative to its members or patrons.

Percentage depletion. A deduction method that applies a fixed percentage to the gross income generated by mineral property; *see 9.15.*

Personal interest. Tax term for interest on personal loans and consumer purchases. Such interest is not deductible.

Placed in service. The time when a depreciable asset is ready to be used. The date fixes the beginning of the depreciation period.

Points. Charges to the homeowner at the time of the loan. A point is equal to 1 percent. Depending on the type of loan, points may be currently deductible or amortized over the life of the loan; *see 15.8.*

Premature distributions. Withdrawals before age 59½ from qualified retirement plans are subject to penalties unless specific exceptions are met; *see 7.15 and 8.12.*

Principal residence. On a sale of a principal residence, you may avoid tax under the rules explained in Chapter 29.

Private letter ruling A written determination issued to a taxpayer by the IRS that interprets and applies the tax laws to the taxpayer's specific set of facts. A letter ruling advises the taxpayer regarding the tax treatment that can be expected from the IRS in the circumstances specified by the ruling. It may not be used or cited as precedent by another taxpayer.

Probate estate. Property held in a decedent's name passing by will; *see 39.7.*

Profit-sharing plan. A defined contribution plan under which the amount contributed to the employees' accounts is based on a percentage of the employer's profits; *see 8.5* and *41.2.*

Provisional income. If your provisional income exceeds a base amount, part of your Social Security benefits may be subject to tax. To figure provisional income, *see 34.3.*

Q

Qualified charitable organization. A nonprofit philanthropic organization that is approved by the U.S. Treasury to receive charitable contribution deductions; *see 14.1.*

Qualified dividends. Dividends received after 2002 and before January 1, 2011, that are taxed at the long-term capital gain rate; *see 4.2.*

Qualified domestic relations order (QDRO). A specialized domestic relations court order that conforms to IRS regulations and provides instructions to pension plan administrators and IRA custodians as to how to pay benefits to a divorced spouse; *see 7.12* and *8.11.*

Qualified plan. A retirement plan that meets tax law tests and allows for tax deferment and tax-free accumulation of income until benefits are withdrawn. Pension, profit-sharing, stock bonus, employee stock ownership, and Keogh plans and IRAs may be qualified plans; *see* Chapters 7, 8, and 41.

Qualified tuition program (QTP). A state-sponsored college savings plan or prepayment plan, or a prepayment plan established by a private college; *see 33.5.*

Qualifying widow or widower. A filing status entitling the taxpayer with dependents to use joint tax rates for up to two tax years after the death of a spouse; *see 1.11.*

R

Real estate investment trust (REIT). An entity that invests primarily in real estate and mortgages and passes through income to investors; *see 31.1.*

Real estate professional. An individual who, because of his or her real estate activity, qualifies to deduct rental losses from nonpassive income; *see 10.3.*

Real property. Land and the buildings on land. Buildings are depreciable; *see 42.13* and *42.16.*

Recognized gain or loss. The amount of gain or loss to be reported on a tax return. Gain may not be recognized on certain exchanges of property; *see 6.1.*

Recovery property. Tangible depreciable property placed in service after 1980 and before 1987 and depreciable under ACRS; *see 42.11* and *42.16.*

Refundable tax credit. A credit that entitles you to a refund even if you owe no tax for the year.

Required Minimum Distributions (RMDs). Distributions that must be taken annually to avoid a 50% IRS penalty by a traditional IRA account holder starting with the year age 70½ is reached. For qualified plan participants the starting date may be delayed for employees working beyond age 70½. Minimum distribution rules also apply to beneficiaries of qualified plans, traditional IRAs, and Roth IRAs. *See 7.13–7.14, 8.13–8.14,* and *8.24.*

Residence interest. Term for deductible mortgage interest on a principal residence and a second home; *see 15.1–15.2.*

Residential rental property. Real property in which 80% or more of the gross income is from dwelling units. Under MACRS, depreciation is claimed over 27.5 years under the straight-line method; *see 42.13.*

Retirement savers credit. Eligible taxpayers may claim a tax credit for 10%, 20%, or 50% of up to $2,000 of retirement plan contributions; *see 25.16.*

Return of capital. A distribution of your investment that is not subject to tax unless the distribution exceeds your investment; *see 4.11.*

Revenue ruling. A revenue ruling is the Commissioner's "official interpretation of the interpretation of the law" and generally is binding on revenue agents and other IRS officials. Taxpayers generally may rely on published revenue rulings in determining the tax treatment of their own transactions that arise out of similar facts and circumstances.

Revocable trust. A trust that may be changed or terminated by its creator or another person. Such trusts do not provide an income tax savings to the creator; *see 39.6.*

Rollover. A tax-free reinvestment of a distribution from a qualified retirement plan into an IRA or other qualified plan within 60 days; *see 7.3, 7.8,* and *8.10.*

Roth IRA. A nondeductible contributory IRA that allows for tax-free accumulation of income. Qualifying distributions are completely tax free. *See 8.19–8.24.*

S

Salvage value. The estimated value of an asset at the end of its useful life. Salvage value is ignored by ACRS and MACRS rules.

S corporation. A corporation that elects S

status in order to receive tax treatment similar to that of a partnership; *see* Chapter 11.

Section 179 deduction (or First-year expensing). A deduction allowed for investments in depreciable business equipment in the year the property is placed in service; *see 42.3* for limitations.

Section 457 plan. Deferred compensation plan set up by a state or local government, or tax-exempt organization, which allows tax-free deferrals of salary; *see 7.22.*

Section 1231 property. Depreciable property used in a trade or business and held for more than a year. All Section 1231 gains and losses are netted; a net gain is treated as capital gain, a net loss as an ordinary loss; *see 44.8.*

Self-employed person. An individual who operates a business or profession as a proprietor or independent contractor and reports self-employment income on Schedule C; *see* Chapters 40 and 45.

Self-employment tax. Tax paid by self-employed persons to finance Social Security coverage. In 2006, there are two rates. A 12.4% rate applies to a taxable earnings base of $94,200 or less and a 2.9% rate applies to all net earnings; *see* Chapter 45.

Separate return. Return filed by a married person who does not file a joint return. Filing separately may save taxes where each spouse has separate deductions, but certain tax benefits require a joint return; *see 1.3.*

Short sale. Sale of borrowed securities made to freeze a paper profit or to gain from a declining market; *see 30.5.*

Short tax year. A tax year of less than 12 months. May occur with the startup of a business or change in accounting method.

Short-term capital gain or loss. Gain or loss on the sale or exchange of a capital asset held one year or less; *see 5.1, 5.2,* and *5.10.*

Simplified employee plan (SEP). IRA-type plan set up by an employer, rather than the employee. Salary-reduction contributions may be allowed to plans of small employers set up before 1997; *see 8.15–8.16.*

Standard deduction. A fixed deduction allowed to taxpayers who do not itemize deductions. The amount depends on filing status, age, and blindness; *see 13.1.*

Standard mileage rate. A fixed rate allowed by the IRS for business auto expenses in place of deducting actual expenses; *see 43.1.*

Statutory employees. Certain employees, such as full-time life insurance salespersons, who may report income and deductions on Schedule C, rather than on Schedule A as miscellaneous itemized deductions; *see 40.6.*

Stock dividend. A distribution of additional shares of a corporation's stock to its shareholders; *see 4.6.*

Stock option. A right to buy stock at a fixed price.

Straddle. Taking an offsetting investment position to reduce the risk of loss in a similar investment; *see 30.9.*

Straight-line method. A method of depreciating the cost of a depreciable asset on a pro rata basis over its cost recovery period; *see 42.9, 42.12.*

T

Tangible personal property. Movable property, such as desks, computers, machinery, and autos, depreciable over a five-year or seven-year period; *see 42.4.*

Taxable income. Net income after claiming all deductions from gross income and adjusted gross income, such as IRA deductions, itemized deductions, or the standard deduction, and personal exemptions; *see 22.1.*

Tax attributes. When debts are cancelled in bankruptcy cases, the cancelled amount is excluded from gross income. Tax attributes are certain losses, credits, and property basis that must be reduced to the extent of the exclusion; *see 11.8.*

Tax deferral. Shifting income to a later year, such as where you defer taxable interest to the following year by purchasing a T-bill or savings certificate maturing after the end of the current year; *see* Chapter 4. Investments in qualified retirement plans provide tax deferral (*see* Chapters 7, 8, and 41).

Tax home. The area of your principal place of business or employment. You must be away from your tax home on a business trip to deduct travel expenses; *see 20.6–20.9.*

Tax identification number. For an individual, his or her Social Security number; for businesses, fiduciaries, and other non-individual taxpayers, the employer identification number.

Tax preference items. Items that may subject a taxpayer to the alternative minimum tax (AMT); *see 23.3.*

Tax-sheltered annuity. A type of retirement annuity offered to employees of charitable organizations and educational systems, generally funded by employee salary-reduction contributions; *see 7.20.*

Tax year. A period (generally 12 months) for reporting income and expenses; *see 40.4.*

Tenancy by the entireties. A joint tenancy in real property in the name of both husband and wife. On the death of one tenant, the survivor receives entire interest.

Tenants in common. Two or more persons who have undivided ownership rights in property. Upon death of a tenant, his or her share passes to his or her estate, rather than to the surviving tenants.

Testamentary trust. A trust established under a will.

Trust. An arrangement under which one person transfers legal ownership of assets to another person or corporation (the trustee) for the benefit of one or more third persons (beneficiaries).

U

Unrecaptured Section 1250 gain. Long-term gain realized on the sale of depreciable realty attributed to depreciation deductions and subject to a 25% capital gain rate; *see 5.3 and 44.2.*

Useful life. For property not depreciated under ACRS or MACRS, the estimate of time in which a depreciable asset will be used.

W

Wash sales. Sales on which losses are disallowed because you recover your market position within a 61-day period; *see 30.6.*

Withholding. An amount taken from income as a prepayment of an individual's tax liability for the year. In the case of wages, the employer withholds part of every wage payment. Backup withholding from dividend or interest income is required if you do not provide the payer with a correct taxpayer identification number. Withholding on pensions and IRAs is automatic unless you elect to waive withholding; *see* Chapter 26.

INDEX

NOTE: **References are to section numbers in Parts 1–8, followed by page numbers in boldface.**

A

NOTE: **References are to section numbers in Parts 1–8, followed by page numbers in boldface.**

Note: **References are to section numbers in Parts 1–8, followed by page numbers in boldface.**

***NOTE:* References are to section numbers in Parts 1–8, followed by page numbers in boldface.**

D

***NOTE:* References are to section numbers in Parts 1–8, followed by page numbers in boldface.**

***NOTE:* References are to section numbers in Parts 1–8, followed by page numbers in boldface.**

***NOTE:* References are to section numbers in Parts 1–8, followed by page numbers in boldface.**

Note: **References are to section numbers in Parts 1–8, followed by page numbers in boldface.**

G

***NOTE:* References are to section numbers in Parts 1–8, followed by page numbers in boldface.**

H

Note: **References are to section numbers in Parts 1–8, followed by page numbers in boldface.**

I

NOTE: **References are to section numbers in Parts 1–8, followed by page numbers in boldface.**

NOTE: References are to section numbers in Parts 1–8, followed by page numbers in boldface.

NOTE: **References are to section numbers in Parts 1–8, followed by page numbers in boldface.**

M

NOTE: **References are to section numbers in Parts 1–8, followed by page numbers in boldface.**

Note: **References are to section numbers in Parts 1–8, followed by page numbers in boldface.**

N

O

***NOTE:* References are to section numbers in Parts 1–8, followed by page numbers in boldface.**

***Note:* References are to section numbers in Parts 1–8, followed by page numbers in boldface.**

***NOTE:* References are to section numbers in Parts 1–8, followed by page numbers in boldface.**

Note: **References are to section numbers in Parts 1–8, followed by page numbers in boldface.**

NOTE: **References are to section numbers in Parts 1–8, followed by page numbers in boldface.**

S

***NOTE:* References are to section numbers in Parts 1–8, followed by page numbers in boldface.**

***NOTE:* References are to section numbers in Parts 1–8, followed by page numbers in boldface.**

T

Note: **References are to section numbers in Parts 1–8, followed by page numbers in boldface.**

***NOTE:* References are to section numbers in Parts 1–8, followed by page numbers in boldface.**

Note: **References are to section numbers in Parts 1–8, followed by page numbers in boldface.**

V

W

Y

Z